Kingston upon Hull
126 127
Grimsby
117 118 119
Skegness
Boston
103 104 10
Kin Lyn
Peterborough
89 90
Thetford
Cambri
75 76
Bedford
59 60 61
Chelmsford
LONDON
44 45 46
Mai
Sevenoaks
31 32 33
Brighton
19
Hastings
20 21
135

To help you navigate safely and easily, see the AA's France and Europe atlases... theAA.com/shop

Atlas contents

Scale 1:250,000 or 3.95 miles to 1 inch

Map pages south inside front cover

Route planner II–VII

Mileage chart VIII

Atlas Symbols 1

Road maps 1:250,000 scale 2–237

Western Isles 1:700,000 scale 232–233
Orkney Islands 1:636,000 scale 234
Shetland Islands 1:636,000 scale 235
Channel Islands 1:150,000 scale 236
Isle of Man 1:317,000 scale 237

Restricted junctions 238–239

Index to place names 240–320

County, administrative area map 240–241
Place name index 242–320

Ireland endpaper

Map pages north inside back cover

15th edition June 2016

Cartography:

All cartography in this atlas edited, designed and produced by the Mapping Services Department of AA Publishing (A05392).

Publisher's notes:
Published by AA Publishing (a trading name of AA Media Limited, whose registered office is Fanum House, Basing View, Basingstoke, Hampshire RG21 4EA, UK. Registered number 06112600).

ISBN: 978 0 7495 7776 6 (flexibound)

A CIP catalogue record for this book is available from The British Library.

Disclaimer:
The contents of this atlas are believed to be correct at the time of the latest revision, it will not contain any subsequent amended, new or temporary information including diversions and traffic control or enforcement systems. The publishers cannot be held responsible or liable for any loss or damage occasioned to any person acting or refraining from action as a result of any use or reliance on material in this atlas, nor for any errors, omissions or changes in such material. This does not affect your statutory rights.

The publishers would welcome information to correct any errors or omissions and to keep this atlas up to date. Please write to the Atlas Editor, AA Publishing, The Automobile Association, Fanum House, Basing View, Basingstoke, Hampshire RG21 4EA, UK.
E-mail: *roadatlasfeedback@theaa.com*

Acknowledgements:
AA Publishing would like to thank the following for their assistance in producing this atlas:

Information on fixed speed camera locations provided by and © 2016 RoadPilot Ltd. Crematoria database provided by Cremation Society of Great Britain. Cadw, English Heritage, Forestry Commission, Historic Scotland, Johnsons, National Trust and National Trust for Scotland, RSPB, The Wildlife Trust, Scottish Natural Heritage, Natural England, The Countryside Council for Wales.

Printer:
1010 Printing International Ltd.

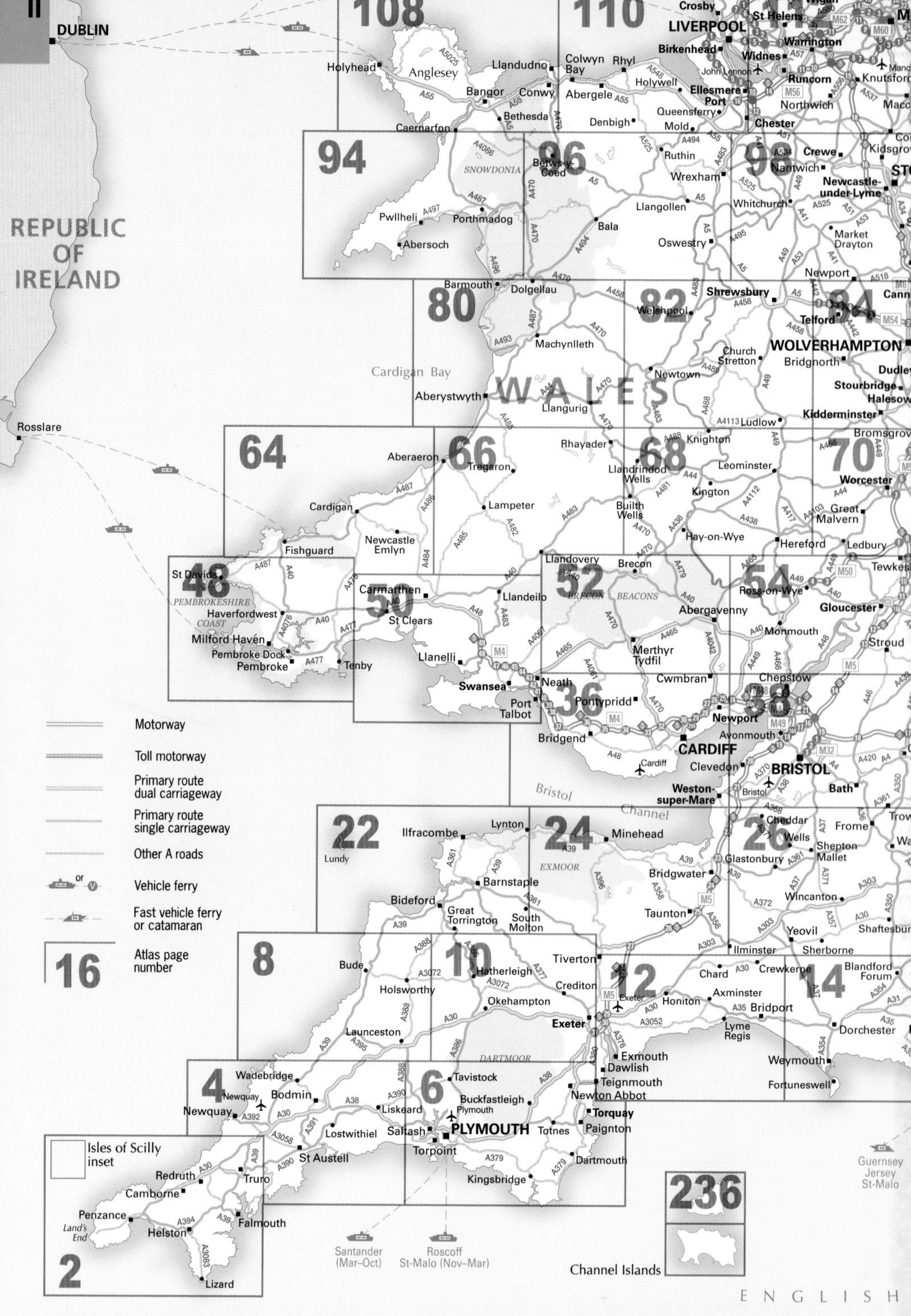
DUBLIN
REPUBLIC OF IRELAND
Rosslare
108
110
Holyhead
Anglesey
Llandudno
Colwyn Bay
Rhyl
Bangor
Conwy
Abergele
Holywell
Caernarfon
Bethesda
Denbigh
Formby
Crosby
LIVERPOOL
Birkenhead
St Helens
Wigan
Warrington
Widnes
John Lennon
Runcorn
Knutsford
Ellesmere Port
Northwich
Queensferry
Mold
Chester
94
96
98
SNOWDONIA
Betws-y-Coed
Ruthin
Wrexham
Crewe
Nantwich
Newcastle-under-Lyme
Kidsgrove
Pwllheli
Porthmadog
Abersoch
Llangollen
Bala
Whitchurch
Oswestry
Market Drayton
Newport
Barmouth
Dolgellau
80
82
84
Welshpool
Shrewsbury
Telford
Machynlleth
WOLVERHAMPTON
Church Stretton
Bridgnorth
Dudley
Cardigan Bay
Newtown
Aberystwyth
WALES
Llangurig
Stourbridge
Halesowen
Kidderminster
Ludlow
Bromsgrove
64
66
68
70
Aberaeron
Tregaron
Rhayader
Knighton
Llandrindod Wells
Leominster
Worcester
Kington
Cardigan
Lampeter
Builth Wells
Great Malvern
Newcastle Emlyn
Hay-on-Wye
Hereford
Ledbury
Fishguard
Llandovery
Brecon
Tewkesbury
48
50
52
54
St Davids
PEMBROKESHIRE COAST
Carmarthen
Llandeilo
BRECON BEACONS
Ross-on-Wye
Gloucester
Haverfordwest
St Clears
Abergavenny
Milford Haven
Monmouth
Stroud
Pembroke Dock
Pembroke
Tenby
Llanelli
Merthyr Tydfil
Cwmbran
Chepstow
Swansea
Neath
36
58
Port Talbot
Pontypridd
Newport
Avonmouth
Bridgend
CARDIFF
Cardiff
Clevedon
BRISTOL
Bristol
Bath
Weston-super-Mare
Bristol Channel
22
24
26
Lundy
Ilfracombe
Lynton
Minehead
EXMOOR
Cheddar
Wells
Frome
Shepton Mallet
Glastonbury
Barnstaple
Bridgwater
Bideford
Great Torrington
South Molton
Taunton
Wincanton
Yeovil
Shaftesbury
Sherborne
8
10
12
14
Bude
Hatherleigh
Tiverton
Ilminster
Chard
Crewkerne
Blandford Forum
Holsworthy
Crediton
Exeter
Honiton
Axminster
Bridport
Okehampton
Lyme Regis
Dorchester
Launceston
DARTMOOR
Exmouth
Weymouth
Dawlish
Teignmouth
Fortuneswell
4
6
Wadebridge
Tavistock
Newquay
Bodmin
Liskeard
Buckfastleigh
Newton Abbot
Torquay
Plymouth
PLYMOUTH
Paignton
Lostwithiel
Saltash
Totnes
Torpoint
St Austell
Dartmouth
Kingsbridge
Redruth
Truro
Camborne
Penzance
Land's End
Helston
Falmouth
Lizard
2
Isles of Scilly inset
Santander (Mar–Oct)
Roscoff St-Malo (Nov–Mar)
236
Channel Islands
Guernsey Jersey St-Malo
ENGLISH
Motorway
Toll motorway
Primary route dual carriageway
Primary route single carriageway
Other A roads
or
Vehicle ferry
Fast vehicle ferry or catamaran
16
Atlas page number

Route planner

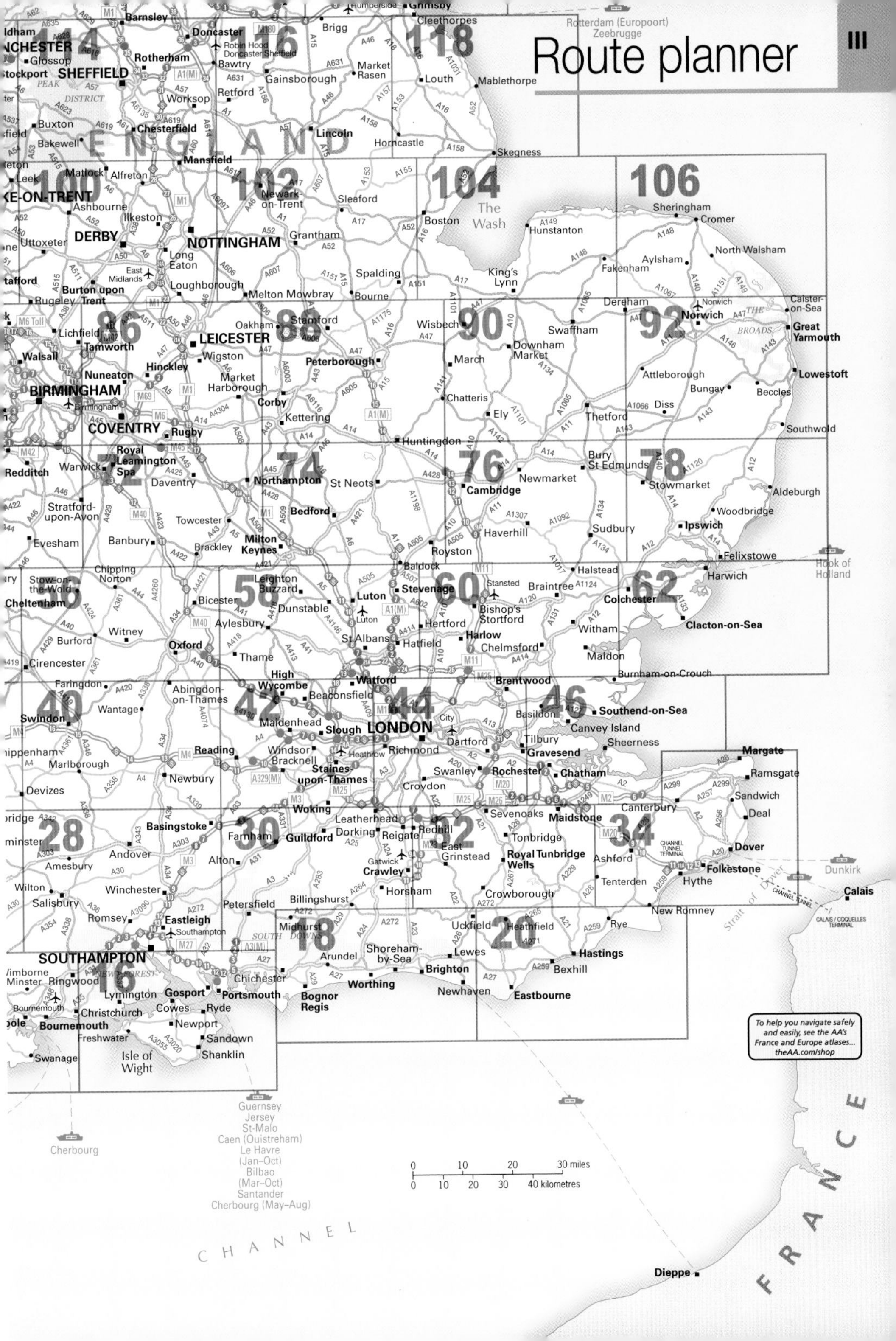

To help you navigate safely and easily, see the AA's France and Europe atlases... theAA.com/shop

0 10 20 30 miles
0 10 20 30 40 kilometres

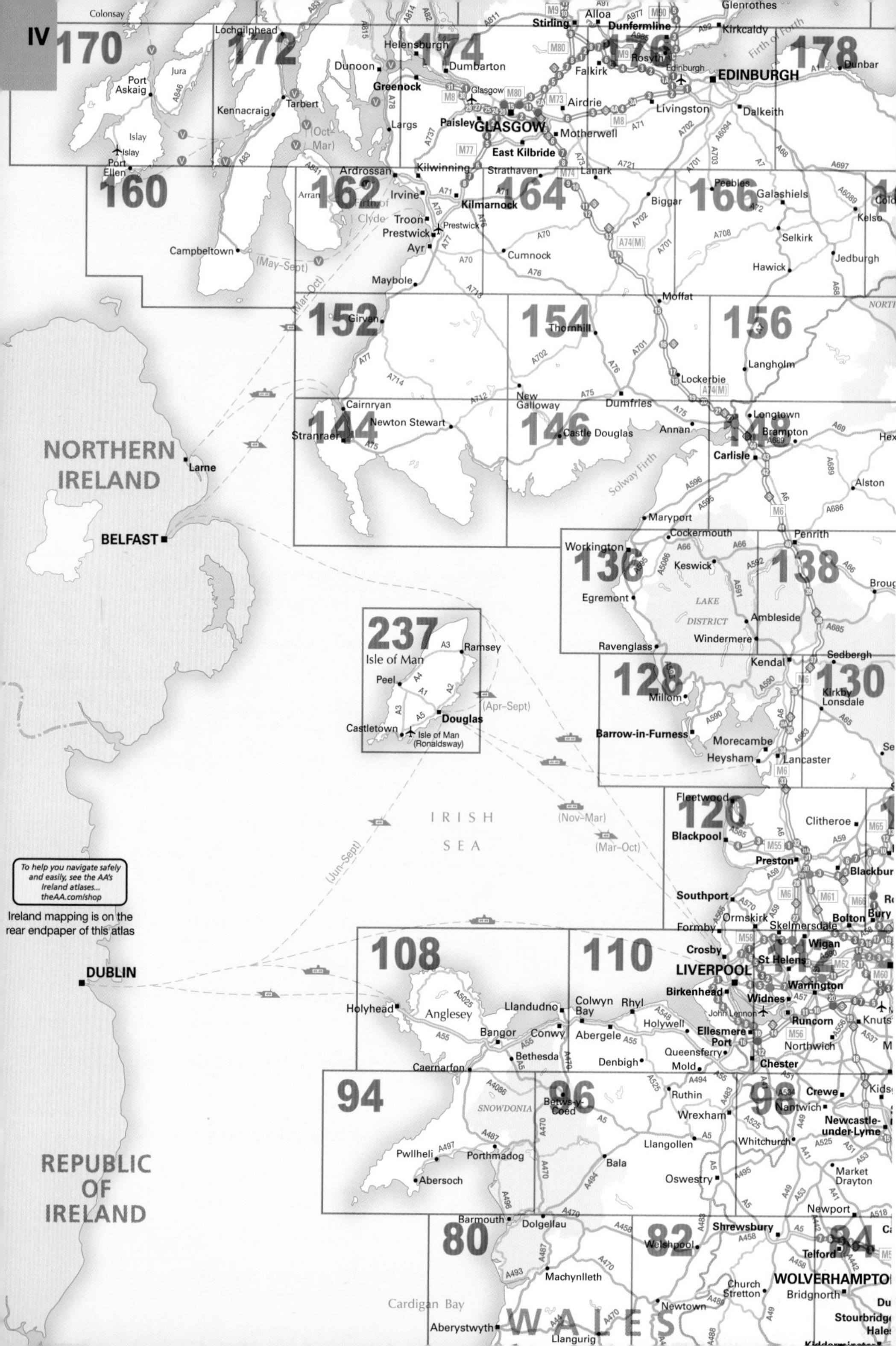
170
172
174
176
178
160
162
164
166
152
154
156
144
146
148
136
138
237
128
130
120
108
110
112
94
96
98
80
82
84
Colonsay
Lochgilphead
Helensburgh
Stirling
Alloa
Dunfermline
Glenrothes
Kirkcaldy
Firth of Forth
Dunbar
Port Askaig
Jura
Dunoon
Dumbarton
Greenock
Glasgow
Falkirk
Rosyth
Edinburgh
EDINBURGH
Tarbert
Kennacraig
Islay
Port Ellen
Largs
Paisley
GLASGOW
Airdrie
Livingston
Dalkeith
Motherwell
East Kilbride
(Oct–Mar)
Ardrossan
Kilwinning
Strathaven
Lanark
Peebles
Galashiels
Kelso
Arran
Irvine
Firth of Clyde
Kilmarnock
Biggar
Troon
Prestwick
Ayr
Selkirk
Jedburgh
Hawick
Campbeltown
(May–Sept)
Cumnock
Maybole
Moffat
(Mar–Oct)
Girvan
Thornhill
Langholm
Lockerbie
Cairnryan
New Galloway
Dumfries
Longtown
Brampton
Stranraer
Newton Stewart
Castle Douglas
Annan
Carlisle
NORTHERN IRELAND
Larne
Solway Firth
Alston
BELFAST
Maryport
Cockermouth
Penrith
Workington
Keswick
Egremont
LAKE DISTRICT
Ambleside
Windermere
Ravenglass
Kendal
Sedbergh
Isle of Man
Ramsey
Peel
Douglas
Castletown
Isle of Man (Ronaldsway)
(Apr–Sept)
Millom
Kirkby Lonsdale
Barrow-in-Furness
Morecambe
Heysham
Lancaster
Fleetwood
Clitheroe
Blackpool
IRISH SEA
(Nov–Mar)
(Mar–Oct)
(Jun–Sept)
Preston
Blackburn
To help you navigate safely and easily, see the AA's Ireland atlases... theAA.com/shop
Ireland mapping is on the rear endpaper of this atlas
Southport
Ormskirk
Skelmersdale
Bolton
Bury
Formby
Wigan
Crosby
St Helens
DUBLIN
LIVERPOOL
Birkenhead
Widnes
Warrington
Holyhead
Anglesey
Llandudno
Colwyn Bay
Rhyl
Holywell
John Lennon
Runcorn
Knutsford
Bangor
Conwy
Abergele
Ellesmere Port
Northwich
Bethesda
Denbigh
Queensferry
Mold
Chester
Caernarfon
SNOWDONIA
Betws-y-Coed
Ruthin
Crewe
Nantwich
Wrexham
Newcastle-under-Lyme
Llangollen
Whitchurch
Pwllheli
Porthmadog
Bala
Oswestry
Market Drayton
REPUBLIC OF IRELAND
Abersoch
Newport
Barmouth
Dolgellau
Shrewsbury
Welshpool
Telford
Machynlleth
WOLVERHAMPTON
Church Stretton
Bridgnorth
Cardigan Bay
Newtown
Stourbridge
Aberystwyth
WALES
Llangurig

EMERGENCY DIVERSION ROUTES

In an emergency it may be necessary to close a section of motorway or other main road to traffic, so a temporary sign may advise drivers to follow a diversion route. To help drivers navigate the route, black symbols on yellow patches may be permanently displayed on existing direction signs, including motorway signs. Symbols may also be used on separate signs with yellow backgrounds.

For further information see *theaa.com/motoring_advice/general-advice/emergency-diversion-routes.html*

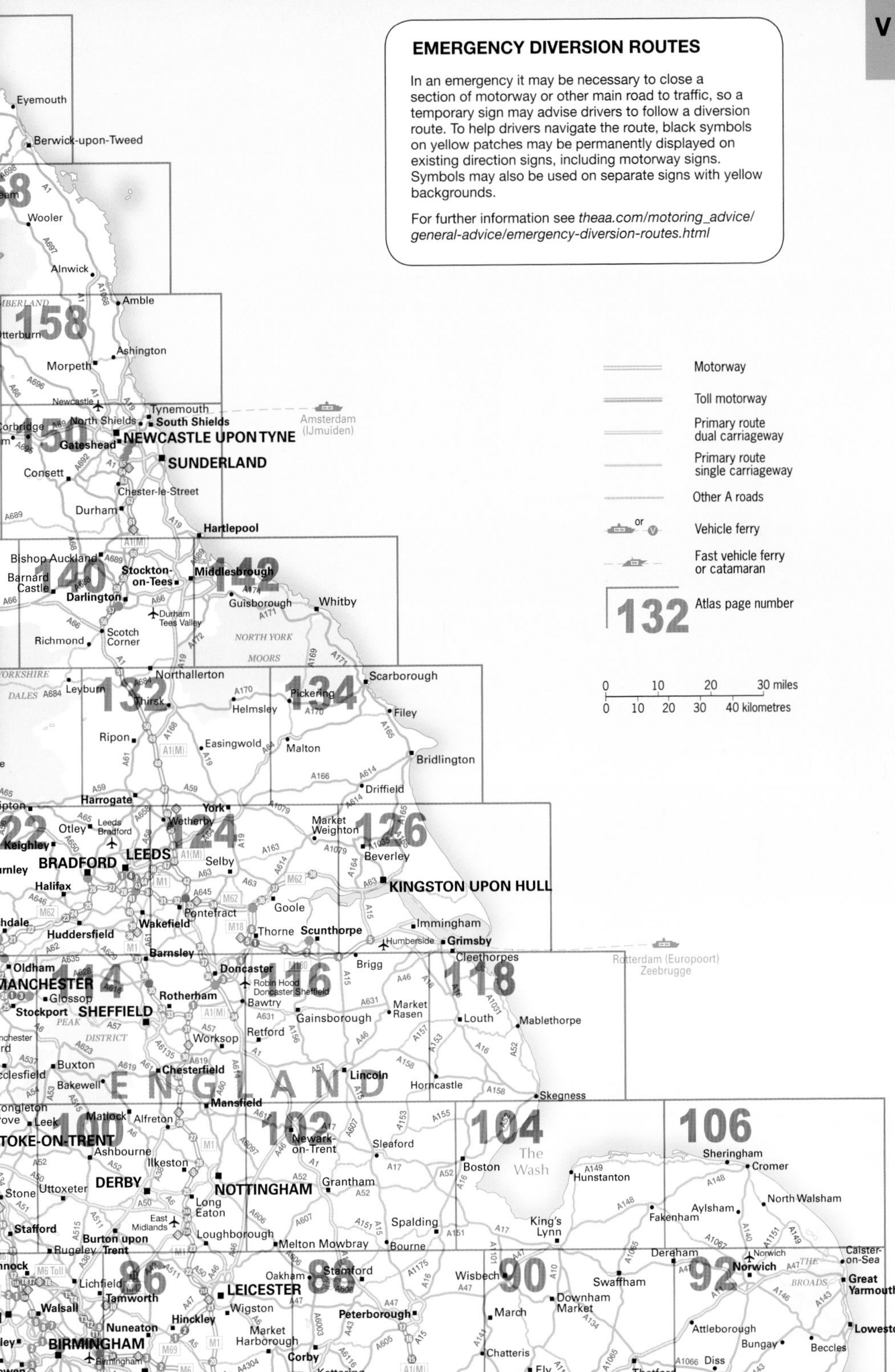

FERRY OPERATORS

Hebrides and west coast Scotland
calmac.co.uk
skyeferry.co.uk
western-ferries.co.uk

Orkney and Shetland
northlinkferries.co.uk
pentlandferries.co.uk
orkneyferries.co.uk
shetland.gov.uk/ferries

Isle of Man
steam-packet.com

Ireland
irishferries.com
poferries.com
stenaline.co.uk

North Sea (Scandinavia and Benelux)
dfdsseaways.co.uk
poferries.com

Isle of Wight
wightlink.co.uk
redfunnel.co.uk

Channel Islands
condorferries.co.uk

France and Belgium
brittany-ferries.co.uk
condorferries.co.uk
eurotunnel.com
dfdsseaways.co.uk
poferries.com

Northern Spain
brittany-ferries.co.uk

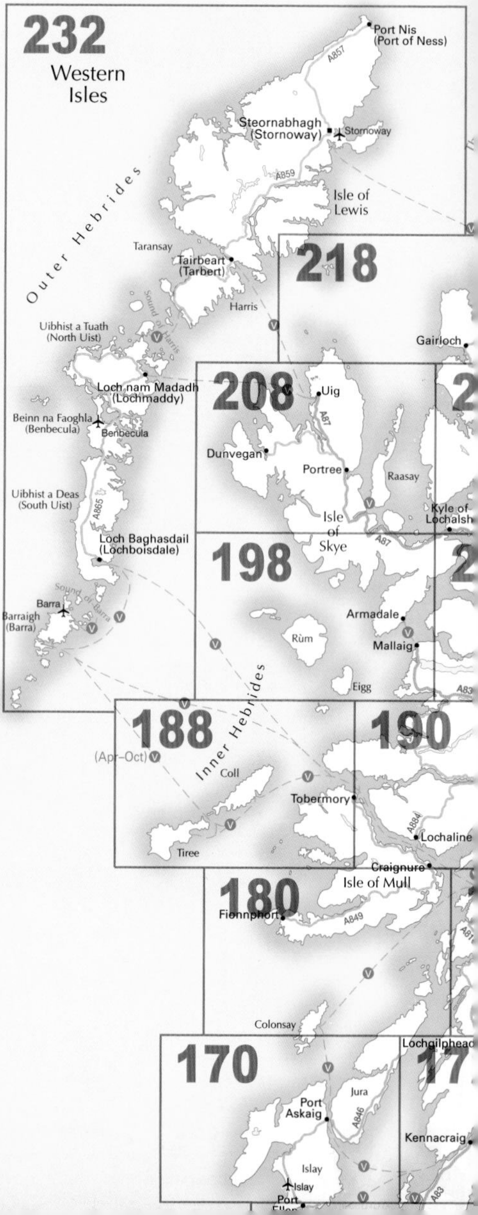

232
Western Isles
Port Nis (Port of Ness)
Steornabhagh (Stornoway)
Stornoway
Isle of Lewis
Outer Hebrides
Taransay
Tairbeart (Tarbert)
Harris
Sound of Harris
Uibhist a Tuath (North Uist)
Loch nam Madadh (Lochmaddy)
Beinn na Faoghla (Benbecula)
Benbecula
Uibhist a Deas (South Uist)
Loch Baghasdail (Lochboisdale)
Barra
Barraigh (Barra)
Sound of Barra
218
Gairloch
208
Uig
Dunvegan
Portree
Raasay
Kyle of Lochalsh
Isle of Skye
198
Armadale
Mallaig
Rùm
Eigg
Inner Hebrides
188
(Apr–Oct)
Coll
Tiree
Tobermory
190
Lochaline
Craignure
Isle of Mull
180
Fionnphort
Colonsay
170
Lochgilphead
Jura
Port Askaig
Islay
Port Ellen
Kennacraig

Motorway
Toll motorway
Primary route dual carriageway
Primary route single carriageway
Other A roads
Vehicle ferry (or V)
Fast vehicle ferry or catamaran
192 Atlas page number

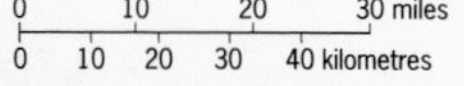

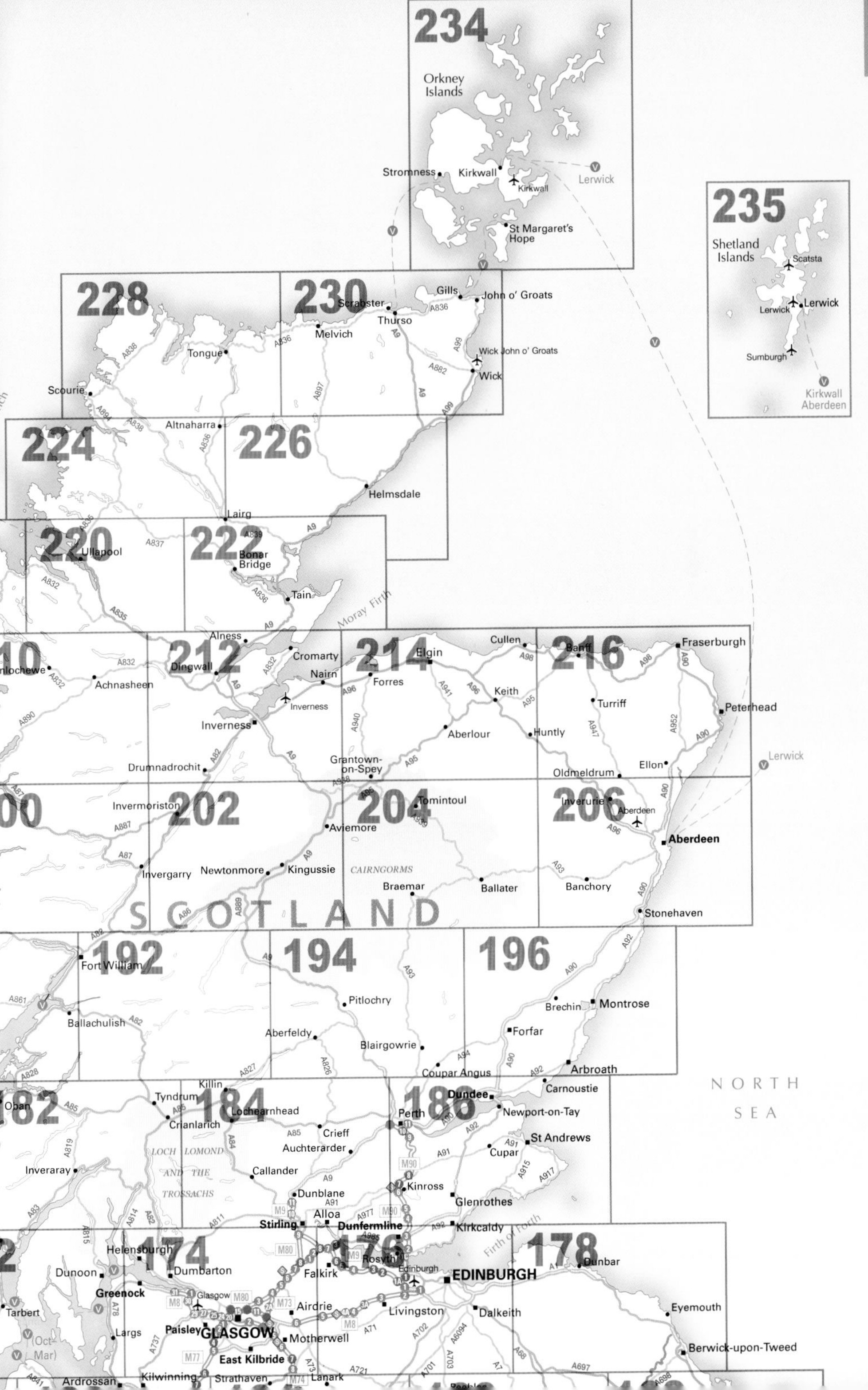

234
Orkney Islands
Stromness
Kirkwall
Kirkwall
Lerwick
St Margaret's Hope
235
Shetland Islands
Scatsta
Lerwick
Lerwick
Sumburgh
Kirkwall Aberdeen
228
230
Scrabster
Thurso
Gills
John o' Groats
Melvich
Tongue
Scourie
Wick John o' Groats
Wick
A838
A836
A9
A99
A882
A897
A894
224
226
Altnaharra
Helmsdale
Lairg
220
222
Ullapool
Bonar Bridge
Tain
Moray Firth
A835
A832
A837
A839
10
212
214
216
Kinlochewe
Achnasheen
Alness
Dingwall
Cromarty
Nairn
Elgin
Cullen
Banff
Fraserburgh
Forres
Keith
Turriff
Peterhead
Inverness
Inverness
Aberlour
Huntly
Drumnadrochit
Grantown-on-Spey
Oldmeldrum
Ellon
Lerwick
00
202
204
206
Invermoriston
Tomintoul
Inverurie
Aberdeen
Aviemore
Aberdeen
Invergarry
Newtonmore
Kingussie
CAIRNGORMS
Braemar
Ballater
Banchory
Stonehaven
SCOTLAND
192
194
196
Fort William
Pitlochry
Brechin
Montrose
Ballachulish
Aberfeldy
Forfar
Blairgowrie
Coupar Angus
Arbroath
Carnoustie
NORTH SEA
182
184
186
Oban
Tyndrum
Killin
Crianlarich
Lochearnhead
Dundee
Perth
Newport-on-Tay
Crieff
St Andrews
Auchterarder
Cupar
LOCH LOMOND AND THE TROSSACHS
Inveraray
Callander
Kinross
Dunblane
Glenrothes
Stirling
Alloa
Dunfermline
Kirkcaldy
Firth of Forth
174
176
178
Helensburgh
Dumbarton
Dunoon
Falkirk
Rosyth
Edinburgh
EDINBURGH
Dunbar
Greenock
Glasgow
Airdrie
Livingston
Dalkeith
Eyemouth
Tarbert
Largs
Paisley
GLASGOW
Motherwell
(Oct–Mar)
East Kilbride
Berwick-upon-Tweed
Ardrossan
Kilwinning
Strathaven
Lanark
M8
M9
M73
M74
M77
M80
M90

Mileage chart

The mileage chart shows distances in miles between two towns along AA-recommended routes. Using motorways and other main roads this is normally the fastest route, though not necessarily the shortest.

The journey times, shown in hours and minutes, are average off-peak driving times along AA-recommended routes. These times should be used as a guide only and do not allow for unforeseen traffic delays, rest breaks or fuel stops.

For example, the 378 miles (608 km) journey between Glasgow and Norwich should take approximately 7 hours 28 minutes.

Journey times

	Aberystwyth	Barnstaple	Birmingham	Brighton	Bristol	Cambridge	Cardiff	Carlisle	Carmarthen	Dorchester	Dover	Edinburgh	Exeter	Fort William	Glasgow	Gloucester	Guildford	Hereford	Holyhead	Hull	Inverness	Kendal	Leeds	Lincoln	Liverpool	Maidstone	Manchester	Middlesbrough	Newcastle	Northampton	Norwich	Nottingham	Oxford	Penzance	Perth	Peterborough	Plymouth	Portsmouth	Preston	Salisbury	Sheffield	Shrewsbury	Southampton	Stoke-on-Trent	Stranraer	Taunton	Wick	York	LONDON
Aberdeen	906	1052	750	1051	913	907	936	426	1020	1047	1108	236	1027	357	301	836	1007	850	843	735	240	517	655	753	636	1029	632	545	510	840	1007	757	907	1246	151	837	1114	1039	558	1009	721	747	1024	703	505	950	513	643	955
Aberystwyth		436	249	538	301	431	229	444	115	432	612	647	412	901	624	251	443	158	234	436	959	359	345	430	244	533	304	456	527	340	554	339	354	631	720	419	459	455	317	412	350	154	439	252	713	335	1231	410	455
Barnstaple			326	423	200	501	234	629	335	206	513	832	115	1047	810	227	339	303	636	547	1144	544	529	507	456	434	448	628	700	409	624	422	319	233	906	452	145	324	503	232	500	403	307	400	858	109	1417	543	403
Birmingham				310	147	154	210	327	311	321	334	530	301	745	507	110	226	125	334	233	842	242	216	157	153	255	146	315	346	102	316	108	126	520	604	142	348	258	200	243	146	101	243	058	556	224	1115	229	217
Brighton					301	213	336	628	436	232	154	831	351	1045	808	301	102	348	635	451	1143	543	436	353	454	116	447	535	606	223	320	329	200	610	905	248	438	109	501	151	406	402	127	359	857	319	1416	449	128
Bristol						315	059	451	159	144	337	654	134	908	631	048	206	124	457	408	1005	405	351	328	317	258	310	450	521	224	439	243	134	353	727	313	221	217	324	128	321	224	202	221	720	057	1238	404	218
Cambridge							347	448	448	345	210	637	438	906	628	247	200	302	516	248	1003	422	242	149	336	131	319	335	407	112	135	144	201	657	721	044	525	252	342	254	221	243	244	240	717	401	1236	250	129
Cardiff								514	116	230	413	717	210	931	654	117	241	117	455	431	1029	429	414	351	340	334	333	513	544	257	511	307	210	429	751	337	257	253	347	210	345	239	237	245	743	133	1302	428	254
Carlisle									558	625	649	207	605	422	145	414	545	429	421	316	519	056	237	334	214	610	210	200	125	418	549	338	445	824	241	418	652	618	136	547	300	326	602	241	233	528	752	225	533
Carmarthen										330	513	756	310	1011	734	217	341	200	349	531	1108	508	454	451	359	434	414	605	637	357	611	407	310	529	830	436	357	353	427	310	444	249	337	344	822	233	1341	520	354
Dorchester											345	828	123	1042	805	222	208	258	631	542	1139	539	525	454	451	306	444	624	655	315	503	417	222	342	901	356	210	135	458	102	455	358	118	355	854	104	1412	538	242
Dover												838	445	1106	829	337	145	424	656	449	1204	604	442	350	515	046	508	536	607	241	318	345	236	704	922	245	532	238	522	254	422	423	244	420	918	411	1436	450	145
Edinburgh													807	311	057	616	747	630	623	505	332	257	426	523	416	759	412	315	240	620	738	527	647	1026	049	607	854	819	338	749	455	527	804	442	301	730	605	414	735
Exeter														1022	745	202	311	238	611	522	1119	519	504	442	431	406	423	603	635	344	559	357	254	225	841	427	057	254	438	203	435	338	237	335	833	044	1352	518	338
Fort William															242	831	1002	845	838	733	140	512	653	751	631	1027	627	615	541	835	1005	754	902	1241	234	835	1109	1034	552	1004	716	742	1019	657	441	945	413	641	950
Glasgow																554	725	609	601	456	353	235	417	514	354	750	350	340	305	558	728	518	625	1004	115	558	832	757	316	727	440	506	742	421	207	708	625	404	713
Gloucester																	208	053	420	331	928	328	314	251	240	258	232	413	444	155	410	206	110	421	650	236	249	219	247	147	244	147	204	144	643	125	1201	327	217
Guildford																		254	551	410	1059	459	352	314	410	106	403	451	523	139	310	245	116	530	821	210	358	058	418	120	323	318	106	315	813	238	1332	406	052
Hereford																			353	345	943	343	328	305	254	345	247	427	458	211	425	221	156	457	704	251	325	306	301	233	258	122	250	159	657	201	1215	341	303
Holyhead																				412	935	335	321	426	221	617	241	432	503	424	638	351	451	830	657	457	658	623	254	553	327	239	608	247	649	534	1208	347	539
Hull																					831	249	109	105	217	410	148	200	234	239	332	143	326	740	549	219	608	458	209	447	115	312	443	229	545	444	1103	058	349
Inverness																						609	751	848	728	1124	724	642	607	932	1102	852	959	1338	243	932	1206	1131	650	1101	814	840	1116	755	556	1042	237	738	1047
Kendal																							158	308	129	526	125	149	205	333	522	300	400	739	332	352	607	532	050	502	214	240	517	155	324	443	843	209	448
Leeds																								129	124	405	054	124	155	223	343	127	310	722	510	213	550	442	116	431	048	224	427	139	506	426	1024	040	338
Lincoln																									236	311	205	221	253	151	227	057	238	701	607	117	529	407	228	359	108	242	355	200	603	405	1122	136	250
Liverpool																										437	046	237	308	244	450	211	311	650	450	317	518	444	047	413	142	137	428	107	443	354	1001	152	359
Maidstone																											429	457	528	201	239	306	157	625	843	206	453	159	443	215	343	343	205	341	839	332	1357	411	106
Manchester																												208	239	236	419	146	304	642	446	249	510	436	045	405	106	144	420	059	439	346	957	122	352
Middlesbrough																													048	321	436	225	408	822	359	306	650	540	226	529	153	338	525	253	429	526	914	109	436
Newcastle																														351	506	256	438	853	324	336	721	611	244	559	223	408	555	323	354	557	839	142	506
Northampton																															234	114	058	604	653	100	432	231	250	219	152	150	215	147	646	308	1204	235	123
Norwich																																253	324	820	823	154	648	400	444	413	324	406	403	355	820	524	1338	352	245
Nottingham																																	201	615	611	115	443	333	218	322	056	151	318	108	607	319	1125	139	229
Oxford																																		514	721	152	342	136	318	125	238	218	120	215	714	217	1232	321	115
Penzance																																			1100	646	148	514	657	423	654	557	457	554	1053	303	1611	737	558
Perth																																				652	928	853	412	823	535	601	838	517	318	804	516	458	809
Peterborough																																					514	303	313	306	152	232	255	214	648	350	1206	221	146
Plymouth																																						341	525	250	522	425	324	422	920	131	1439	605	425
Portsmouth																																							450	054	410	350	030	347	846	222	1404	453	145
Preston																																								420	134	159	435	114	405	401	923	144	406
Salisbury																																									359	320	037	317	816	130	1334	442	150
Sheffield																																										224	356	124	529	357	1047	107	307
Shrewsbury																																											335	102	554	301	1112	251	306
Southampton																																												332	830	205	1349	437	140
Stoke-on-Trent																																													509	258	1028	206	302
Stranraer																																														757	829	453	802
Taunton																																															1315	441	301
Wick																																																1011	1320
York																																																	352

Distances in miles (one mile equals 1.6093 km)

	Aberdeen	Aberystwyth	Barnstaple	Birmingham	Brighton	Bristol	Cambridge	Cardiff	Carlisle	Carmarthen	Dorchester	Dover	Edinburgh	Exeter	Fort William	Glasgow	Gloucester	Guildford	Hereford	Holyhead	Hull	Inverness	Kendal	Leeds	Lincoln	Liverpool	Maidstone	Manchester	Middlesbrough	Newcastle	Northampton	Norwich	Nottingham	Oxford	Penzance	Perth	Peterborough	Plymouth	Portsmouth	Preston	Salisbury	Sheffield	Shrewsbury	Southampton	Stoke-on-Trent	Stranraer	Taunton	Wick	York
Aberystwyth	472
Barnstaple	608	214
Birmingham	436	124	180
Brighton	613	288	210	171
Bristol	518	130	100	90	169
Cambridge	463	215	267	97	120	170
Cardiff	537	111	128	109	202	44	203
Carlisle	236	236	371	199	376	281	256	300
Carmarthen	520	48	190	172	264	107	266	68	284
Dorchester	600	206	94	172	119	62	184	120	364	182
Dover	587	326	272	208	82	205	124	239	381	301	200
Edinburgh	126	336	471	299	476	381	333	400	100	386	463	458
Exeter	593	198	44	165	178	84	259	113	356	175	57	248	455
Fort William	156	435	570	398	576	480	456	499	199	485	562	580	137	554
Glasgow	150	332	467	295	472	377	353	396	96	382	459	477	47	451	102
Gloucester	484	113	126	56	155	36	150	63	248	125	118	192	346	110	445	343
Guildford	571	224	175	128	44	106	96	139	335	201	97	97	433	150	532	430	99
Hereford	487	79	144	59	189	54	153	59	250	85	136	225	349	129	448	346	34	133
Holyhead	464	102	339	167	345	249	259	202	228	150	331	369	326	323	425	323	215	302	156
Hull	376	227	320	139	258	230	138	250	170	311	312	262	247	304	367	266	196	239	198	218
Inverness	106	496	631	459	637	541	517	561	260	546	623	641	157	616	66	176	507	595	510	488	430
Kendal	283	189	324	153	330	234	251	254	47	240	316	354	145	309	245	143	200	288	203	181	164	307
Leeds	329	173	301	120	262	211	146	230	123	224	293	271	200	285	321	219	177	220	179	165	59	383	110
Lincoln	388	199	275	98	216	185	95	205	182	267	246	220	258	260	379	277	151	173	154	204	44	441	176	74
Liverpool	362	110	272	101	278	182	193	202	126	158	264	302	224	257	324	222	148	236	151	102	128	386	79	74	139
Maidstone	545	284	234	166	50	167	82	200	339	262	161	41	416	209	537	435	153	58	186	327	220	599	313	231	178	261
Manchester	357	134	261	89	266	171	160	190	120	184	253	290	219	245	318	216	136	224	139	125	97	380	74	44	85	34	248
Middlesbrough	276	244	357	176	318	267	197	286	95	294	349	322	146	341	283	190	232	276	235	235	89	308	84	64	122	145	280	114
Newcastle	235	275	388	207	349	298	229	317	60	325	380	353	106	372	242	153	264	307	266	266	142	267	102	95	154	176	311	145	39
Northampton	486	174	212	56	133	115	56	162	249	224	159	155	348	196	447	345	79	90	111	217	152	509	203	136	94	151	113	139	189	220
Norwich	488	278	329	160	168	233	63	266	282	328	241	172	359	313	480	378	212	160	215	321	147	542	276	174	103	240	130	185	223	254	118
Nottingham	395	162	232	51	193	142	86	161	189	223	224	210	266	216	387	285	107	151	110	178	93	449	164	77	39	112	168	71	130	161	64	119
Oxford	510	160	170	68	109	73	82	107	274	169	115	146	373	154	472	370	48	67	81	242	190	534	228	174	132	176	107	164	227	258	44	146	102
Penzance	702	308	108	274	287	193	368	222	466	284	167	357	564	109	663	562	220	259	238	434	415	726	419	403	370	367	318	356	451	482	326	433	326	265
Perth	86	388	523	351	529	433	378	453	152	438	515	503	42	507	102	64	399	486	401	379	291	114	199	245	303	278	461	275	192	150	400	404	310	426	617
Peterborough	435	204	263	86	158	173	37	193	229	255	204	162	306	248	427	325	139	115	142	225	110	489	223	121	51	159	120	132	170	201	45	78	58	86	357	351
Plymouth	633	239	62	205	218	124	299	153	397	215	98	288	495	44	594	493	151	190	169	365	346	657	350	334	301	298	249	287	382	413	257	364	257	196	78	544	288
Portsmouth	596	244	162	154	53	125	137	158	360	220	73	141	458	132	558	456	118	45	152	328	276	620	314	260	215	262	102	250	313	344	130	204	188	85	241	508	157	172
Preston	326	146	281	110	287	191	209	211	89	197	273	311	188	266	287	185	157	245	160	138	122	349	43	69	134	36	269	35	103	139	159	235	121	184	375	237	180	306	270
Salisbury	549	184	118	121	90	52	145	98	313	160	39	160	411	93	511	409	72	62	105	281	261	573	267	244	202	215	121	203	298	329	115	212	173	70	203	461	165	134	44	223
Sheffield	397	166	272	91	233	182	122	201	161	263	264	247	236	256	359	257	148	191	150	157	66	421	115	38	47	79	205	39	100	131	104	148	45	142	366	309	93	297	228	73	212
Shrewsbury	417	75	220	48	226	130	140	111	181	110	212	250	279	205	379	277	96	184	52	105	162	441	135	119	124	65	208	71	190	221	98	203	87	123	314	329	129	245	209	92	161	88
Southampton	578	225	142	135	66	106	136	140	342	201	53	152	440	111	539	437	100	49	133	309	258	601	295	241	199	243	113	232	294	325	111	204	169	67	221	489	157	152	20	252	23	209	191
Stoke-on-Trent	392	112	220	48	226	130	140	150	156	211	212	250	254	205	353	251	96	184	99	123	129	415	109	93	91	57	208	46	164	195	98	172	54	123	314	303	99	245	209	66	161	50	38	191
Stranraer	235	342	477	305	482	387	363	406	106	392	469	487	132	461	181	86	352	440	355	333	276	261	153	229	288	232	445	229	201	163	354	388	295	380	571	149	333	502	466	195	418	267	287	447	261
Taunton	560	165	50	132	160	51	226	80	323	142	45	224	422	34	521	419	77	126	96	291	272	583	277	261	228	225	185	213	309	340	183	291	184	123	144	471	215	75	114	234	70	224	172	94	172	429
Wick	207	597	732	560	738	642	618	662	361	647	724	742	258	716	166	277	608	695	610	588	531	104	408	484	543	487	700	484	409	367	609	644	550	635	826	215	589	757	721	451	673	523	542	702	516	362	684
York	323	201	314	133	275	224	154	243	116	251	306	279	193	298	314	212	189	233	192	192	38	376	91	24	79	102	237	71	51	89	146	180	87	184	408	239	125	339	269	96	254	57	146	251	120	223	265	477
LONDON	550	239	216	121	54	120	59	153	314	215	125	78	413	200	512	410	102	31	136	282	186	574	268	201	143	216	39	204	254	285	68	118	129	56	310	462	86	241	75	225	85	169	163	77	161	420	167	675	211

Atlas symbols

M4 Motorway with number

Toll T4 Toll Toll motorway with toll station

3 Restricted motorway junctions

S Fleet Motorway service area

Motorway and junction under construction

A3 Primary route single/dual carriageway

11 Primary route junction with and without number

3 Restricted primary route junctions

S Primary route service area

BATH Primary route destination

A1123 Other A road single/dual carriageway

B2070 B road single/dual carriageway

Minor road, more than 4 metres wide, less than 4 metres wide

Roundabout

Interchange/junction

Narrow primary/other A/B road with passing places (Scotland)

Road under construction/ approved

Road tunnel

Toll Road toll, steep gradient (arrows point downhill)

5 Distance in miles between symbols

Railway line, in tunnel

Railway station and level crossing

Tourist railway

628 637 Lecht Summit Height in metres, mountain pass

30 Safety camera site (fixed location) with speed limit in mph

40 Section of road with two or more fixed safety cameras, with speed limit in mph

50 50 Average speed (SPECS™) camera system with speed limit in mph

V Fixed safety camera site with variable speed limit

or V Vehicle ferry

Fast vehicle ferry or catamaran

H F Airport, heliport, international freight terminal

H 24-hour Accident & Emergency hospital

C Crematorium

P+R Park and Ride (at least 6 days per week)

City, town, village or other built-up area

National boundary, county or administrative boundary

Scenic route

Tourist Information Centre (all year/seasonal)

Visitor or heritage centre

Picnic site

Caravan site (AA inspected)

Camping site (AA inspected)

Caravan & camping site (AA inspected)

Abbey, cathedral or priory

Ruined abbey, cathedral or priory

Castle

Historic house or building

Museum or art gallery

Industrial interest

Aqueduct or viaduct

Garden, arboretum

Vineyard

Country park

Agricultural showground

Theme park

Farm or animal centre

Zoological or wildlife collection

Bird collection, aquarium

RSPB RSPB site

National Nature Reserve (England, Scotland, Wales)

Local nature reserve

Wildlife Trust reserve

Forest drive

National trail

Viewpoint

Hill-fort

Prehistoric monument, Roman antiquity

1066 Battle site with year

Steam railway centre

Cave

Windmill, monument

Golf course (AA listed)

County cricket ground

Rugby Union national stadium

International athletics stadium

Horse racing, show jumping

Air show venue, motor-racing circuit

Ski slope (natural, artificial)

National Trust property (England & Wales, Scotland)

English Heritage site

Historic Scotland site

Cadw (Welsh heritage) site

Major shopping centre, other place of interest

Attraction within urban area

World Heritage Site (UNESCO)

National Park and National Scenic Area (Scotland)

Forest Park

Heritage coast

Isles of Scilly
White Island
ST MARTIN'S
St Martin's Head
King Charles's
BRYHER
Old Grimsby
Cromwell's
Old Blockhouse
Higher Town
Isles of Scilly Heritage Coast
New Grimsby
Lizard Point
Great Ganilly
Eastern Isles
Tresco Abbey
TRESCO
Crow Bar
Innisidgen Tomb
Great Arthur
Crow Sound
Samson
Bant's Carn Burial
Harry's Walls
ST MARY'S
North West Channel
Higher & Lower Moors
Deep Point
Hugh Town
Porth Hellick Downs Tombs
Garrison Walls
Isles of Scilly (St Mary's)
Old Town
Peninnis Head
Annet
St Mary's Sound
Broad Sound
Gugh
Middle Town
ST AGNES
Horse Point
Smith Sound
Western Rocks
0 1 2 3 miles
0 1 2 3 4 5 kilometres
Godrevy
Carn Naun Point
The Island or St Ives Head
St Ives Bay
St Ives
Zennor Head
Gurnards Head
Wayside
Halsetown
Carbis Bay
South West Coast Path
Zennor
Towednack
Hayle
Lelant
Pendeen Watch
Lighthouse
Carn Galver Mine
Men-An-Tol
Mulfra Quoit
Chysauster Ancient Village
Penwith Heritage Coast
Morvah
Canonstown
St Erth
Geevor Tin Mine
Levant Mine and Beam Engine
Pendeen
New Mill
R Hayle
Lanyon Quoit
Crowlas
St Just Mining District
Trengwainton Garden
Ludgvan
Botallack
Gulval
Relubbus
St Just
Madron
Longrock
St Hilary
Cape Cornwall
Newbridge
Heamoor
Chyandour
Marazion
Ballowall Barrow
Goldsithney
Penzance
Perranuthnoe
Kelynack
Carn Euny Ancient Village
Sancreed
St Michael's Mount
Drift
Newlyn
Whitesand Bay
Land's End
Kerris
Paul
Crows-an-Wra
Cudden Point
Sennen Cove
Mousehole
St Buryan
MOUNT'S BAY
LAND'S END
Sennen
The Merry Maidens
Trevescan
Lamorna
Trethewey
Porthcurno
Treen
Lamorna Cove
Telegraph
Merthen Point
Porthgwarra
St Levan
Minack Open Air Theatre
Cribba Head
Gwennap Head
0 1 2 3 4 miles
0 1 2 3 4 5 kilometres

G
H
4
J
Ligger or Perran Bay
K
St Newlyn East
L
Lappa Valley
M
Summercourt
Rose
Perranporth
Cligga Point
Bolingey
Goonhavern
Fiddlers Green
Mitchell
Scarcewater
St Agnes Heritage Coast
Trevellas Downs
ST AGNES HEAD
St Agnes
Penhallow
Perranzabuloe
Zelah
St Allen
Trispen
Ladock
Wheal Coates
Mithian
Barkla Shop
Callestick
St Erme
Goonvrea
St Agnes Mining District
Goonbell
Probus
Porthtowan
Mount Hawke
Shortlanesend
Idless
South West Coast Path
Mawla
Tresillian
Portreath
Cambrose
Wheal Peevor
Blackwater
Threemilestone
Kenwyn
Truro
Godrevy-Portreath Heritage Coast
Illogan
Chacewater
Higher Town
St Clement
Navax Point
Tehidy
Scorrier
Mount Ambrose
Gwennap Mining District
Kea
Malpas
St Michael Penkevil
Ruan Lanihorne
South Tehidy
St Day
Twelveheads
Playing Place
Lamorran
Reskadinnick
East Pool Mine
Redruth
Tuckingmill
Pool
Carn Brea
Carharrack
Bissoe
Carnon Downs
Trelissick Garden
Philleigh
Kehelland
Camborne
Carnkie
Gwennap
Devoran
Penponds
Lanner
Perranwell
Connor Downs
Four Lanes
Perranarworthal
Kennall Vale
Devoran & Perran
Feock
Angarrack
Barripper
Troon
Penhalvean
Ponsanooth
Trewithian
Carnhell Green
Gwinear
Realwa
St Erth Praze
Stithians
Mylor Bridge
St Just-in-Roseland
Gerrans Bay
Nare Head
Portscatho
Praze-an-Beeble
Carnkie
Longdowns
Mylor
Gerrans
Carrick Roads
Leedstown
Crowan
Porkellis
Rame
Mabe Burnthouse
Penryn
Flushing
Greeb Point
Godolphin House
Wendron Mining District
Castle
St Mawes
Argal & College Water Park
Budock Water
Pendennis Castle
Bohortha
Godolphin Cross
Trenear
Poldark Mine
Treverva
Falmouth
Prospidnick
Wendron
Pendennis Point
Trescowe
Seworgan
Penjerrick
South West Coast Path
ZONE POINT
Crowntown
Helston Heritage Railway
Carleen
Falmouth Bay
Coverack Bridges
Brill
Sithney
Ashton
Breage
Constantine
Mawnan Smith
Helston
Trebah
Carwinion
ROSEMULLION HEAD
Praa Sands
Porth Navas
Gweek
Glendurgan Garden
Helford Passage
Durgan
Mawnan
Trewavas Mining District
Seal Sanctuary
Helford River
Trewavas Head
Flambards
Helford
St Anthony
Porthleven
Mawgan
Manaccan
Nare Point
St Martin
Garras
Halliggye Fogou
Porthallow
Gunwalloe
White Cross
Porthoustock
Manacle Point
Cury
St Keverne
The Lizard
Poldhu Point
Marconi Memorial
GOONHILLY DOWNS
Lowland Point
Mullion Cove
Mullion
Mullion Island
Coverack
Ruan Major
Predannack Head
Kuggar
South West Coast Path
Black Head
Ruan Minor
Vellan Head
Cadgwith
The Lizard
The Lizard Heritage Coast
Devil's Frying Pan
Lizard Head
Kynance Cove
Church Cove
Lizard
Bass Point
Lizard Lighthouse & Heritage Centre
LIZARD POINT
1
2
3
4
5
6
7
8
A30
A3075
A3076
A39
A390
A393
A394
A3083
A3078
A3301
B3285
B3284
B3277
B3300
B3298
B3297
B3303
B3280
B3302
B3304
B3296
B3293
B3294
B3275
B3289

4
Padstow Bay
Padstow
Wadebridge
Newquay
Watergate Bay
Ligger or Perran Bay
St Austell
Truro
Redruth
Falmouth
Penryn
St Mawes
Veryan Bay
Gerrans Bay
TREVOSE HEAD
ST AGNES HEAD
DODMAN POINT
Trevose Head Heritage Coast
St Agnes Heritage Coast
The Roseland Heritage Coast
South West Coast Path
0 1 2 3 4 miles
0 1 2 3 4 5 kilometres

BODMIN MOOR
Bodmin
Liskeard
Looe
Fowey
Callington
Lostwithiel
Polperro
Polruan
Dobwalls
St Neot
St Cleer
Minions
Jamaica Inn
Bolventor
Altarnun
Camelford
St Breward
Blisland
Cardinham
Warleggan
Lanreath
Pelynt
Duloe
St Keyne
Menheniot
Seaton
Downderry
Portwrinkle
Sheviock
St Austell Bay
Mevagissey
Gribbin Head
Due to open Winter 16/17
Gribbin Head - Polperro Heritage Coast

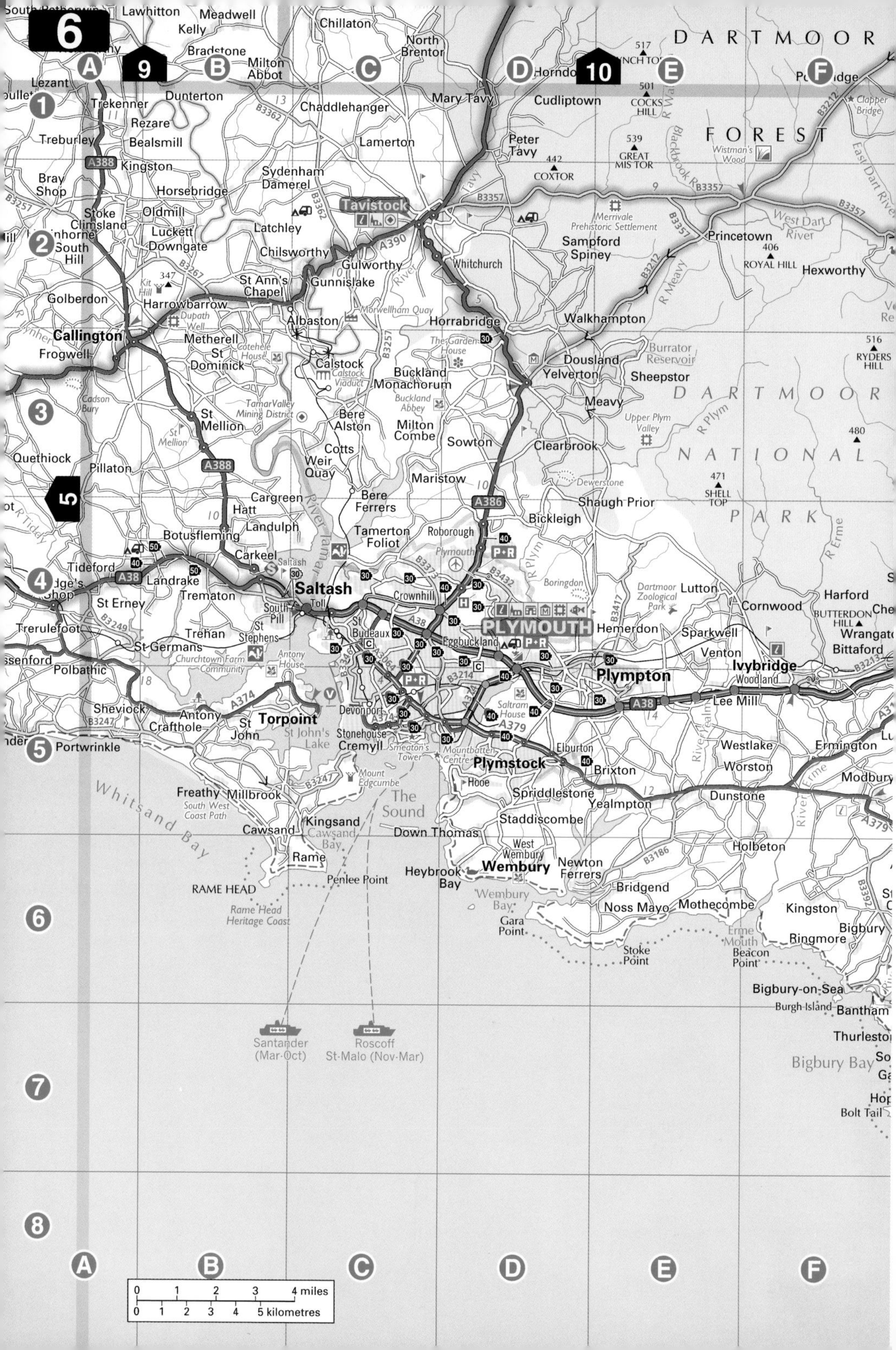

6
9
10
5
A
B
C
D
E
F
1
2
3
4
5
6
7
8
Lawhitton
Meadwell
Kelly
Chillaton
Bradstone
Milton Abbot
North Brentor
DARTMOOR
517
501
COCKS HILL
Lezant
Trekenner
Dunterton
Chaddlehanger
Mary Tavy
Cudliptown
Rezare
Treburley
Bealsmill
Lamerton
Peter Tavy
539
GREAT MIS TOR
FOREST
Wistman's Wood
Clapper Bridge
442
COXTOR
A388
Kingston
Bray Shop
Sydenham Damerel
Horsebridge
Tavistock
B3257
B3362
B3357
Stoke Climsland
Oldmill
Merrivale Prehistoric Settlement
West Dart River
South Hill
Luckett
Downgate
Latchley
Chilsworthy
A390
Sampford Spiney
Princetown
406
ROYAL HILL
Hexworthy
Gulworthy
Whitchurch
347
Kit Hill
Golberdon
St Ann's Chapel
Gunnislake
B3267
Harrowbarrow
Albaston
Morwellham Quay
Horrabridge
Walkhampton
B3212
R Meavy
Dupath Well
Callington
Metherell
St Dominick
Cotehele House
Calstock
Calstock Viaduct
B3257
The Garden House
Burrator Reservoir
516
RYDERS HILL
Frogwell
Buckland Monachorum
Dousland
Yelverton
Sheepstor
Cadson Bury
Tamar Valley Mining District
Buckland Abbey
Bere Alston
Meavy
St Mellion
Milton Combe
Upper Plym Valley
R Plym
NATIONAL
480
Quethiock
Cotts
Sowton
Clearbrook
Weir Quay
A388
Pillaton
Maristow
Dewerstone
471
SHELL TOP
Cargreen
Bere Ferrers
A386
Shaugh Prior
Hatt
Landulph
River Tamar
Bickleigh
PARK
R Erme
R Tiddy
Botusfleming
Tamerton Foliot
Roborough
Plymouth
Carkeel
Tideford
Saltash
B3373
B3432
Boringdon
Dartmoor Zoological Park
Lutton
Harford
A38
Landrake
Crownhill
Cornwood
BUTTERDON HILL
Wrangaton
St Erney
Trematon
South Pill
Toll
PLYMOUTH
B3417
Hemerdon
Sparkwell
Bittaford
Trerulefoot
B3249
St Budeaux
Eggbuckland
Venton
Trehan
St Stephens
St Germans
Antony House
Plympton
Ivybridge
Polbathic
Churchtown Farm Community
B3396
A3064
B3214
Woodland
B3213
Lee Mill
Sheviock
A374
Torpoint
Devonport
Saltram House
A374
A379
Antony
St John
St John's Lake
Crafthole
B3247
Stonehouse
Cremyll
Smeaton's Tower
Mountbatten Centre
Elburton
Plymstock
Brixton
Westlake
Ermington
Portwrinkle
Worston
River Yealm
River Erme
Modbury
Mount Edgcumbe
Hooe
Whitsand Bay
Freathy
Millbrook
B3247
The Sound
Spriddlestone
Yealmpton
Dunstone
South West Coast Path
Kingsand
Staddiscombe
Cawsand
Cawsand Bay
Down Thomas
A379
Rame
West Wembury
Holbeton
Heybrook Bay
Wembury
Newton Ferrers
B3186
RAME HEAD
Penlee Point
Bridgend
Rame Head Heritage Coast
Wembury Bay
Noss Mayo
Mothecombe
Kingston
B3392
Gara Point
Bigbury
Ringmore
Erme Mouth
Stoke Point
Beacon Point
Bigbury-on-Sea
Burgh Island
Bantham
Thurlestone
Santander (Mar-Oct)
Roscoff
St-Malo (Nov-Mar)
Bigbury Bay
Bolt Tail
0
1
2
3
4 miles
0
1
2
3
4
5 kilometres

Bovey Tracey
Newton Abbot
Kingsteignton
Teignmouth
Dawlish
Ashburton
Buckfastleigh
Kingskerswell
TORQUAY
Paignton
Tor Bay
Babbacombe Bay
Totnes
Brixham
Dartmouth
Kingsbridge
Salcombe
Start Bay
South Devon Heritage Coast
Manaton
Lustleigh
Hennock
Chudleigh
Harcombe
Ashcombe
Ideford
Luton
Widecombe in the Moor
Haytor Vale
Ilsington
Liverton
Coldeast
Sandygate
Preston
Teigngrace
Bishopsteignton
Holcombe
Shaldon
Ringmore
Combeinteignhead
Stokeinteignhead
Lower Gabwell
Higher Gabwell
Maidencombe
Daccombe
Coffinswell
Abbotskerswell
Denbury
East Ogwell
West Ogwell
Ipplepen
Torbryan
Broadhempstead
Staverton
Dartington
Compton
Marldon
Cockington
Shiphay
Westerland
Blagdon
Collaton St Mary
Goodrington
Galmpton
Churston Ferrers
Dittisham
Cornworthy
Tuckenhay
Ashprington
Harberton
Harbertonford
Halwell
Moreleigh
Blackawton
Kingswear
Stoke Fleming
Blackpool
Strete
Slapton
Stokenham
Torcross
Beesands
Kellaton
Chivelstone
East Prawle
Start Point
Bolt Head
Prawle Point
Malborough
Loddiswell
Aveton Gifford
Churchstow
Frogmore
Chillington
Ugborough
South Brent
Holne
Poundsgate
Dunstone
Ponsworthy
Southcott
Deancombe
Dean Prior
Harbourneford
Rattery
Tigley
Avonwick
Diptford
Berry Head
Sharkham Point
Scabbacombe Head
Hopes Nose
A38
A380
A381
A385
A379
A3022
A3122
A383
A384

A
B
C
D
E
F
1
2
3
4
5
6
7
8
Higher Sharpno
Lower Sharpno
Bude
Bay
Dizzard Point
St
Gennys
Crackington Haven
Cambeak
Sweets
Coxford
Wainhouse
Corner
B3263
A39
Marshgate
Witchcraft
Pentire Point - Widemouth
Heritage Coast
Boscastle
Tresparrett
Trevalga
Lesnewth
Otterham
Castle
TINTAGEL HEAD
B3263
Trethevey
B3266
Tintagel
Bossiney
B3262
Old Post Office
Davidstow
Penhallic Point
Trewarmett
Treknow
B3314
Tremail
B3266
South West Coast Path
Delabole
Pengelly
Westdowns
Camelford
Crowdy
Reservoir
Port Isaac
Bay
Rumps
Point
Kelland
Head
Varley
Head
Lanteglos
Trewalder
Port Quin
Bay
Helstone
Pentire Point
Port
Quin
Port
Isaac
Port Gaverne
B3314
B3267
Padstow Bay
St Teath
419
BROWN
WILLY
Hayle Bay
Bee Centre
Long
Cross
B3267
Treveighan
Trelights
Pendoggett
Stepper Point
Polzeath
Michaelstow
B3314
St Endellion
A39
BODMIN
Trevose Heritage Coast
St Minver
Churchtown
TREVOSE HEAD
Mother Ivey's Bay
St
Tudy
Jamaica Inn
Dinas
Head
Trequite
St Breward
De Lank River
Constantine
Trevone
St Kew
St Kew
Highway
0 1 2 3 4 miles
0 1 2 3 4 5 kilometres

4

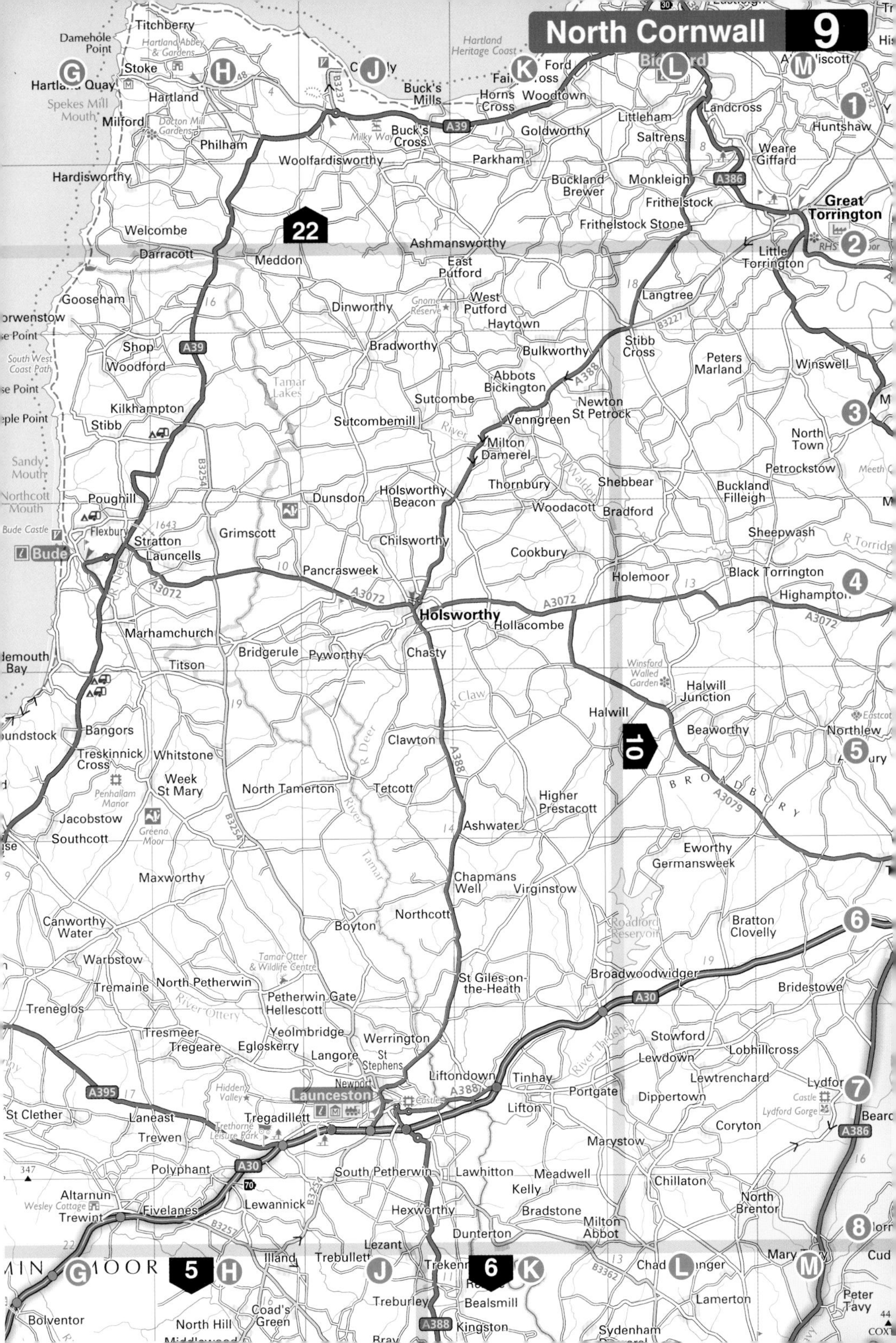

Titchberry
Damehole Point
Hartland Abbey & Gardens
Stoke
Hartland Quay
Hartland
Spekes Mill Mouth
Milford
Docton Mill Gardens
Philham
Hardisworthy
Welcombe
Darracott
Gooseham
Morwenstow
Shop
Woodford
South West Coast Path
Kilkhampton
Stibb
Sandy Mouth
Northcott Mouth
Poughill
Bude Castle
Flexbury
Bude
Stratton
Launcells
Marhamchurch
Widemouth Bay
Titson
Bangors
Treskinnick Cross
Whitstone
Week St Mary
Penhallam Manor
Jacobstow
Greena Moor
Southcott
Maxworthy
Canworthy Water
Warbstow
Tremaine
North Petherwin
Treneglos
Tresmeer
Tregeare
Egloskerry
St Clether
Laneast
Trewen
Polyphant
Altarnun
Wesley Cottage
Trewint
Fivelanes
Bolventor
North Hill
Hartland Heritage Coast
Clovelly
Buck's Mills
Buck's Cross
Milky Way
Horns Cross
Fairy Cross
Ford
Woodtown
Bideford
Woolfardisworthy
Parkham
Goldworthy
Littleham
Landcross
Saltrens
Alverdiscott
Huntshaw
Weare Giffard
Buckland Brewer
Monkleigh
Frithelstock
Frithelstock Stone
Great Torrington
RHS Rosemoor
Little Torrington
Ashmansworthy
Meddon
East Putford
West Putford
Dinworthy
Gnome Reserve
Haytown
Bradworthy
Bulkworthy
Langtree
Stibb Cross
Peters Marland
Winswell
Tamar Lakes
Abbots Bickington
Sutcombe
Sutcombemill
Venngreen
Newton St Petrock
Milton Damerel
River Waldon
North Town
Petrockstow
Thornbury
Shebbear
Buckland Filleigh
Holsworthy Beacon
Dunsdon
Woodacott
Bradford
Grimscott
Chilsworthy
Cookbury
Sheepwash
R Torridge
Pancrasweek
Holemoor
Black Torrington
Highampton
Holsworthy
Hollacombe
Bridgerule
Pyworthy
Chasty
Winsford Walled Garden
Halwill Junction
Halwill
Beaworthy
Northlew
R Claw
Clawton
R Deer
North Tamerton
Tetcott
Higher Prestacott
BROADBURY
Ashwater
River Tamar
Eworthy
Germansweek
Chapmans Well
Virginstow
Northcott
Boyton
Roadford Reservoir
Bratton Clovelly
Tamar Otter & Wildlife Centre
St Giles-on-the-Heath
Broadwoodwidger
Bridestowe
Petherwin Gate
Hellescott
River Ottery
Yeolmbridge
Werrington
Langore
St Stephens
River Thrushel
Stowford
Lewdown
Lobhillcross
Newport
Launceston
Castle
Liftondown
Tinhay
Portgate
Lewtrenchard
Lydford
Castle
Lydford Gorge
Hidden Valley
Tregadillett
Trethorne Leisure Park
Lifton
Dippertown
Coryton
Marystow
South Petherwin
Lawhitton
Meadwell
Kelly
Chillaton
Lewannick
Hexworthy
Bradstone
North Brentor
Dunterton
Milton Abbot
Lezant
Illand
Trebullett
Trekenner
Chadlanger
Mary Tavy
Treburley
Bealsmill
Kingston
Lamerton
Peter Tavy
Coad's Green
Sydenham
Bray
BODMIN MOOR
A39
B3237
A386
B3227
A388
B3254
A3072
A3079
A30
A395
B3257
B3362
22
10
5
6

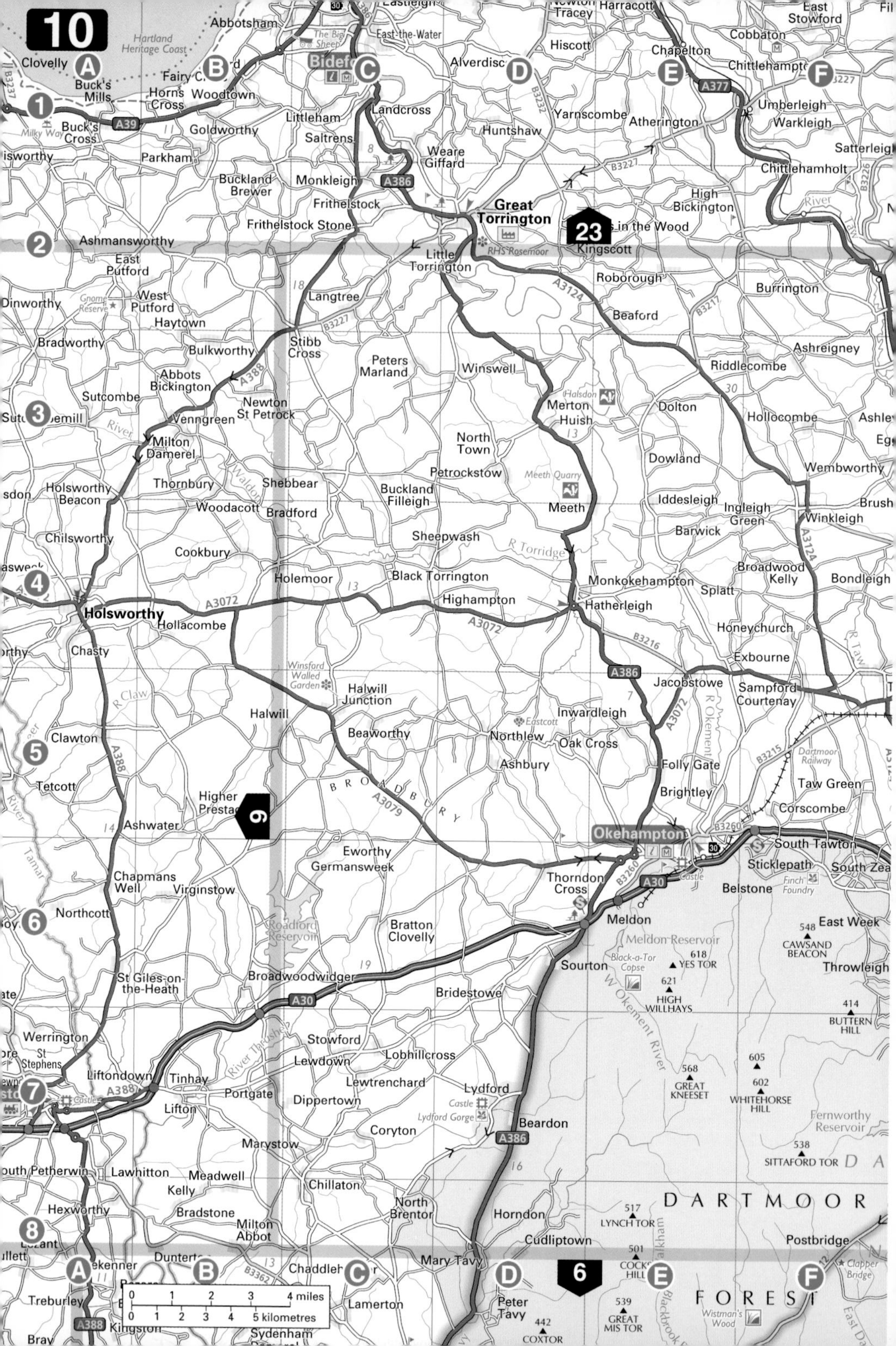

10
Clovelly
Hartland Heritage Coast
Abbotsham
Buck's Mills
Fairy Cross
Horns Cross
Woodtown
Buck's Cross
Milky Way
A39
B3237
Goldworthy
Parkham
Littleham
Landcross
Saltrens
Monkleigh
Buckland Brewer
Frithelstock
Frithelstock Stone
Bideford
The Big Sheep
East-the-Water
Eastleigh
Alverdiscott
Weare Giffard
Huntshaw
A386
B3232
Newton Tracey
Harracott
Hiscott
Yarnscombe
Chapelton
Atherington
A377
Cobbaton
East Stowford
Chittlehampton
Umberleigh
Warkleigh
Satterleigh
Chittlehamholt
B3227
B3226
High Bickington
Great Torrington
RHS Rosemoor
Little Torrington
Kingscott
23
Roborough
Burrington
Beaford
A3124
B3217
Ashreigney
Riddlecombe
Ashmansworthy
East Putford
West Putford
Gnome Reserve
Dinworthy
Bradworthy
Haytown
Langtree
Stibb Cross
Bulkworthy
Abbots Bickington
A388
Peters Marland
Winswell
Sutcombe
Newton St Petrock
Venngreen
Milton Damerel
Halsdon
Merton
Huish
Dolton
Hollocombe
North Town
Dowland
Wembworthy
Thornbury
Shebbear
Holsworthy Beacon
Woodacott
Bradford
Buckland Filleigh
Petrockstow
Meeth Quarry
Meeth
Iddesleigh
Ingleigh Green
Barwick
Winkleigh
Chilsworthy
Cookbury
Sheepwash
R Torridge
Broadwood Kelly
Bondleigh
Holemoor
Black Torrington
Monkokehampton
Splatt
Holsworthy
Hollacombe
A3072
Highampton
Hatherleigh
Honeychurch
Chasty
B3216
Exbourne
Winsford Walled Garden
Halwill Junction
Halwill
A386
Jacobstowe
Sampford Courtenay
R Claw
Beaworthy
Eastcott
Inwardleigh
Clawton
Northlew
Oak Cross
R Okement
Ashbury
Folly Gate
Dartmoor Railway
B3215
Tetcott
BROADBURY
A3079
Taw Green
Higher Prestacott
Brightley
Corscombe
9
Ashwater
Okehampton
B3260
South Tawton
Sticklepath
South Zeal
Eworthy
Germansweek
Thorndon Cross
Castle
Belstone
Finch Foundry
Chapmans Well
Virginstow
A30
Northcott
Roadford Reservoir
Bratton Clovelly
Meldon
Meldon Reservoir
548 CAWSAND BEACON
East Week
Black-a-Tor Copse
618 YES TOR
Sourton
621 HIGH WILLHAYS
Throwleigh
St Giles-on-the-Heath
Broadwoodwidger
Bridestowe
W Okement River
414 BUTTERN HILL
Werrington
River Thrushel
Stowford
Lobhillcross
568 GREAT KNEESET
605
602 WHITEHORSE HILL
St Stephens
Liftondown
Tinhay
Lewdown
Lewtrencharde
Lydford
Castle
Lydford Gorge
A388
Lifton
Portgate
Dippertown
Beardon
Fernworthy Reservoir
Coryton
Marystow
538 SITTAFORD TOR
South Petherwin
Lawhitton
Meadwell
Kelly
Chillaton
North Brentor
DARTMOOR
Hexworthy
Bradstone
Horndon
517 LYNCH TOR
Milton Abbot
Cudliptown
Postbridge
Lezant
Dunterton
Mary Tavy
501 COCKS HILL
Clapper Bridge
Chaddlehanger
6
B3362
Treburley
Peter Tavy
Lamerton
539 GREAT MIS TOR
FOREST
Wistman's Wood
Kingston
A388
Sydenham
442 COXTOR
Bray
0 1 2 3 4 miles
0 1 2 3 4 5 kilometres

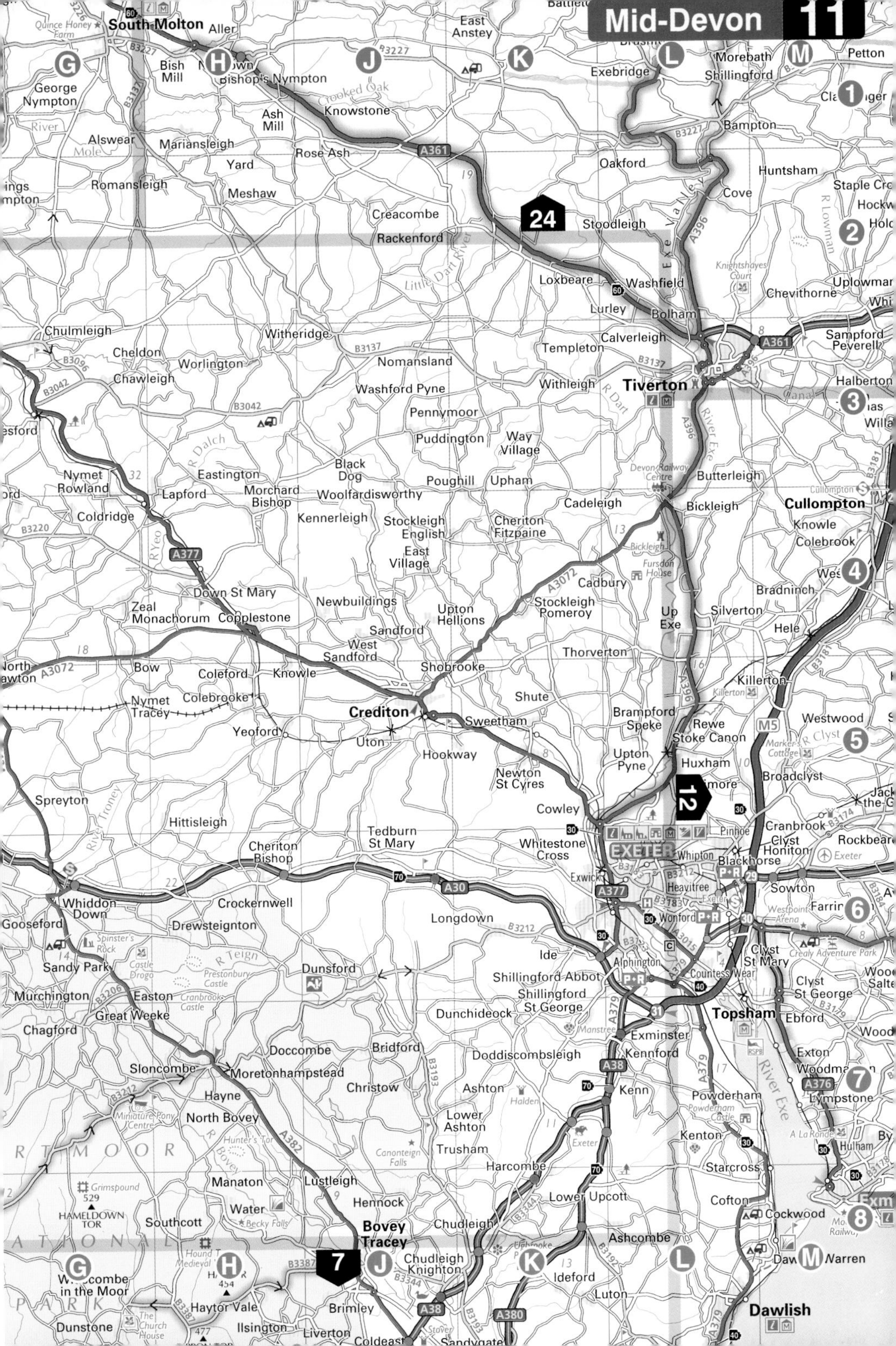
South Molton
Quince Honey Farm
George Nympton
Bish Mill
Bishop's Nympton
Aller
East Anstey
Crooked Oak
Knowstone
Ash Mill
Alswear
Mariansleigh
River Mole
Rose Ash
A361
Yard
Romansleigh
Meshaw
Creacombe
Rackenford
Little Dart River
Exebridge
Morebath
Petton
Shillingford
Bampton
B3227
Oakford
Huntsham
Cove
Staple Cross
Stoodleigh
Exe Valley
A396
R Lowman
Knightshayes Court
Loxbeare
Washfield
Uplowman
Chevithorne
Lurley
Bolham
Chulmleigh
Witheridge
Calverleigh
Sampford Peverell
Templeton
B3137
Cheldon
Worlington
Nomansland
Chawleigh
B3096
B3042
Washford Pyne
Withleigh
R Dart
Tiverton
Halberton
Pennymoor
River Exe
Puddington
Way Village
R Dalch
Nymet Rowland
Eastington
Black Dog
Poughill
Upham
Devon Railway Centre
Butterleigh
Lapford
Morchard Bishop
Woolfardisworthy
Cadeleigh
Bickleigh
Cullompton
Coldridge
Kennerleigh
Stockleigh English
Cheriton Fitzpaine
Knowle
B3220
Colebrook
R Yeo
A377
East Village
Fursdon House
Cadbury
A3072
Down St Mary
Newbuildings
Stockleigh Pomeroy
Bradninch
Zeal Monachorum
Copplestone
Upton Hellions
Up Exe
Silverton
Sandford
Hele
West Sandford
Thorverton
North Tawton
Bow
Coleford
Knowle
Shobrooke
Killerton
Nymet Tracey
Colebrooke
Shute
Crediton
Brampford Speke
Westwood
Sweetham
Rewe
M5
Yeoford
Uton
Hookway
Stoke Canon
R Clyst
Marker's Cottage
Upton Pyne
Huxham
Newton St Cyres
Broadclyst
Spreyton
River Troney
Cowley
Hittisleigh
Tedburn St Mary
Cranbrook
Pinhoe
Cheriton Bishop
Whitestone Cross
EXETER
Whipton
Clyst Honiton
Blackhorse
Rockbeare
Exeter
Exwick
Heavitree
Sowton
Whiddon Down
A30
Crockernwell
Wonford
Farringdon
Gooseford
Drewsteignton
Longdown
B3212
Westpoint Arena
Spinster's Rock
Castle Drogo
R Teign
Ide
Alphington
Clyst St Mary
Crealy Adventure Park
Sandy Park
Prestonbury Castle
Dunsford
Countess Wear
A3015
A379
Shillingford Abbot
Woodbury Salterton
Murchington
Easton
Cranbrook Castle
Shillingford St George
Clyst St George
B3206
Great Weeke
Dunchideock
Topsham
Ebford
Chagford
Manstree
Exminster
Doccombe
Bridford
Doddiscombsleigh
Kennford
RSPB
River Exe
Exton
Sloncombe
Moretonhampstead
Christow
A38
Kenn
Woodmanton
A376
Hayne
Ashton
Halden
Powderham
Lympstone
Miniature Pony Centre
North Bovey
Lower Ashton
Powderham Castle
A la Ronde
A382
R Bovey
Hunter's Tor
Kenton
Hulham
DARTMOOR NATIONAL PARK
Canonteign Falls
Trusham
Exeter
Grimspound
Manaton
Lustleigh
Harcombe
Starcross
529
HAMELDON TOR
Hennock
Lower Upcott
Cofton
Water
Becky Falls
Southcott
Bovey Tracey
Chudleigh
Cockwood
B3344
Ashcombe
Hound Tor Medieval Village
Ugbrooke
Dawlish Warren
B3387
Widecombe in the Moor
454
Chudleigh Knighton
Ideford
B3192
Haytor Vale
Luton
Dunstone
The Church House
477
Ilsington
Brimley
A380
Dawlish
Liverton
Coldeast
Stover
Sandygate

12
A
B
C
D
E
F
1
2
3
4
5
6
7
8
25
11
7
Templeton
Calverleigh
Withleigh
Sampford Peverell
Appledore
Woodgate
Prescott
Culmstock
Hemyock
Stapley
Bolham Water
Churchinford
Craddock
Tiverton
Halberton
Ash Thomas
Willand
Coldharbour Mill
Ashill
Way Village
Upham
Diggerland
Blackborough
Bradfield
Kentisbeare
Smeatharpe
Sheldon
Devon Railway Centre
Butterleigh
Cadeleigh
Cullompton
Bickleigh
Cheriton Fitzpaine
Knowle
Colebrook
Dunkeswell
Upottery
Luppitt
Rawridge
Dulford
Kerswell
Fursdon House
Cadbury
Stockleigh Pomeroy
Westcott
Wolford Chapel
Broadhembury
Beacon
Upton Hellions
Bradninch
Norman's Green
Colliton
Hembury Castle
Up Exe
Silverton
Langford
Upton
Combe Raleigh
Hele
Plymtree
Luton
Thorverton
Payhembury
Awliscombe
Buckerell
Weston
Killerton
Clyst Hydon
Shute
Talaton
Feniton
Offwell
Brampford Speke
Rewe
Stoke Canon
Westwood
Clyst St Lawrence
Newtown
Fenny Bridges
Honiton
Gittisham
Marker's Cottage
R Clyst
Escot
Alfington
Newton St Cyres
Upton Pyne
Huxham
Poltimore
Broadclyst
Whimple
Fairmile
Taleford
Ottery St Mary
Church Green
Cowley
Jack-in-the-Green
Hand and Pen
Cadhay House
Cranbrook
Pinhoe
Whitestone Cross
EXETER
Whipton
Clyst Honiton
Rockbeare
Allercombe
Exeter
West Hill
Fluxton
Southleigh
Exwick
Blackhorse
Heavitree
Sowton
Marsh Green
Wiggaton
Blackbury Camp
Aylesbeare
Tipton St John
Coombe
Wonford
Westpoint Arena
Farringdon
Perkins Village
Venn Ottery
Sidbury
Ide
Crealy Adventure Park
Southerton
Harpford
Bowd
Sidford
Harcombe
Shillingford Abbot
Alphington
Countess Wear
Clyst St Mary
Woodbury Salterton
Clyst St George
Newton Poppleford
Woolbrook
The Donkey Sanctuary
The Old Bakery
Shillingford St George
Topsham
Ebford
Colaton Raleigh
Salcombe Regis
Street
Weston
Exminster
Manstree
Woodbury
South West Coast Path
Sidmouth
Kennford
Exton
Woodmanton
Yettington
Bicton Park
Pinn
Otterton
Ashton
Kenn
Powderham
Powderham Castle
Lympstone
East Budleigh
Bystock
Otterton Mill
Jurassic Coast (Dorset & East Devon Coast)
Halden
Lower Ashton
River Exe
Kenton
A La Ronde
Dalditch
Ladram Bay
Hulham
Bystock
Knowle
Kersbrook
Harcombe
Starcross
Littleham
Budleigh Salterton
Lower Upcott
Cofton
Exmouth
Cockwood
Model Railway
World of Country Life
Ashcombe
Ugbrooke Park
Dawlish Warren
Ideford
Luton
Dawlish
Bishopsteignton
Coombe
Holcombe
Teignmouth
Coombe Cellars
R Teign
Ringmore
Shaldon
Netherton
Combeinteignhead
Stokeinteignhead
Middle Rocombe
Lower Gabwell
Higher Gabwell
Decoy
Abbotskerswell
Coffinswell
Maidencombe
Kingskerswell
Daccombe
Barton
Coombe
Pafford
Babbacombe Bay
St Marychurch
Babbacombe
Ellacombe
TORQUAY
Compton Castle
Compton
Cockington
Marldon
Hollicombe
Rockend
Hopes Nose
Bolham R
Madford River
River Culm
R Dart
River Exe
River Otter
Canal
A361
A396
A3072
A373
A30
A375
A3052
A377
A38
A376
A379
A380
A381
A3015
M5
B3181
B3174
B3177
B3180
B3184
B3179
B3178
B3176
B3212
B3183
B3192
B3193
B3344
0 1 2 3 4 miles
0 1 2 3 4 5 kilometres

Horton
Buckland St Mary
Birch Wood
Donyatt
Ilminster
Dowlish Wake
Ludney
St George
Merriott
Hardington Mandeville
East Coker
Beetham
Combe St Nicholas
Chardleigh Green
Knowle St Giles
Cudworth
Chillington
Higher Chillington
Crewkerne
Haselbury Plucknett
North Perrott
Hardington Marsh
Pendomer
Closworth
Northay
Wadeford
Whitestaunton
Howley
Higher Wambrook
Chaffcombe
Purtington
Roundham
Hewish
Cricket St Thomas
Woolminstone
Misterton
South Perrott
Halstock
BIRTS HILL
Yarcombe
Wambrook
Chard
Forton
Whatley
Wayford
Clapton
Winsham
Burridge
Tatworth
Netherhay
Seaborough
Mosterton
River Axe
Corscombe
Chedington
Drimpton
Stockland
STOCKLAND HILL
Furley
Chardstock
Chard Junction
Forde Abbey
Laymore
Membury
Alston
Tytherleigh
Hewood
Blackdown
Holditch
Thorncombe
Burstock
Broadwindsor
Benville
Cotleigh
Ham
Churchill
Pilsdon Pen
Stoke Abbott
Beaminster
Higher Wraxhall
Dalwood
Wilmington
Loughwood Meeting House
Smallridge
Birdsmoorgate
Hawkchurch
Bettiscombe
Pilsdon
Mapperton
Hooke
Weycroft
Axminster
Marshwood
Netherbury
Melplash
North Poorton
Waytown
South Poorton
Shute
Kilmington
Monkton Wyld
Marshwood Vale
Broadoak
Salway Ash
West Milton
Powerstock
Wootton Fitzpaine
Whitchurch Canonicorum
Nettlecombe
Shute Barton
Whitford
Musbury
Maidenhayne
Harcombe Bottom
Catherston Leweston
Ryall
North Chideock
Pymore
Bradpole
Loders
Colyton
Symondsbury
Uploders
Uplyme
Charmouth
Morcombelake
Allington
St Andrews Well
Colyford
Chideock
Bridport
Walditch
GOLDEN CAP
Seatown
Eype
Watton
Bothenhampton
Seaton
Axmouth
Rousdon
Lyme Regis
Seaton Tramway
Shipton Gorge
Chilcombe
West Bay
Litton Cheney
Beer
Pecorama
Jurassic Coast (Dorset & East Devon Coast)
Burton Bradstock
Puncknowle
Swyre
Abbotsbury Castle
West Bexington
LYME BAY
South West Coast Path
A303
A30
A358
A356
A3066
A35
A3052
B3162
B3167
B3165
B3164
B3163
B3261
B3174
25
26
14
G
H
J
K
L
M
1
2
3
4
5
6
7
8

14
Brympton
Barwick
Bradford Abbas
North Wootton
Allweston
Stourton Caundle
Bishop's Caundle
Lydlinch
Bagber
Sturminster Newton
Hammoon
Fontmell Parva
26
Thornford
Folke
A3030
Caundle Marsh
A357
Manor
Hardington Moor
East Coker
Stoford
Yetminster
Ryme Intrinseca
Beer Hackett
Knighton
Longburton
Holwell
Fifehead Neville
Sturminster Common
Fiddleford
Okeford
Hambledon Hill
Pendomer
Hardington Marsh
Closworth
Hamlet
Leigh
A352
Crouch Hill
King's Stag
Kingston
Okeford Fitzpaine
Shillingstone
Fifehead St Quintin
Belchalwell
Hazelbury Bryan
A37
182
BIRTS HILL
Halstock
Melbury Osmond
Chetnole
Stockwood
Glanvilles Wootton
Middlemarsh
B3146
Pulham
Wonston
Droop
Ibberton
Durweston
Turnworth
B3143
Hermitage
Woolland
Bulbarrow Hill
Blandford
East Chelborough
Melbury Bubb
Lyon's Gate
Dultish
Mappowder
Winterborne Houghton
Batcombe
Minterne Magna
Minterne House
Buckland Newton
Evershot
Holywell
Henley
Higher Ansty
Lower Ansty
Melcombe Bingham
Hilton
Winterborne Clenston
A356
Benville
Uphall
B3163
Rampisham
Frome St Quintin
Alton Pancras
Cerne Giant
Plush
Milton Abbey
Milton Abbas
Lower Wraxhall
Higher Wraxhall
Hooke
Mapperton
Cerne Abbas
Cerne Abbey
Cattistock
Sydling St Nicholas
Piddletrenthide
Cheselbourne
North Poorton
Chilfrome
Nether Cerne
White Lackington
PUDDLETOWN DOWN
Bingham
Dewlish
A354
Winterborne Kingston
Toller Porcorum
Maiden Newton
Godmanstone
Piddlehinton
Milborne St Andrew
South Poorton
Powerstock
Toller Fratrum
Hog Cliff
R Cerne
Milton
13
Nettlecombe
West Compton Abbas
Wynford Eagle
Frampton
Higher Waterston
Athelhampton
Tolpuddle
Bere Regis
EGGARDON HILL
Southover
Grimstone
Charlton Down
B3142
Puddletown
A35
Loders
Uploders
Compton Valence
Stratton
YELLOWHAM HILL
Athelhampton
Burleston
Affpuddle
Spyway
Askerswell
Bradford Peverell
Charminster
Hardy's Cottage
Briantspuddle
Tincleton
Kingston Russell
Winterbourne Abbas
Dorchester
Higher Bockhampton
Pallington
B3390
Chilcombe
Barrows
Long Bredy
The Nine Stones
B3150
Stinsford
Woodsford
Clouds Hill
Litton Cheney
B3159
Poundbury
Kingston Maurward
West Stafford
River Frome
R. Bride
Winterbourne Steepleton
Martinstown
Winterborne Came
Moreton
B3157
Littlebredy
Maiden Castle
Whitcombe
West Knighton
Puncknowle
Valley of Stones
Crossways
Winfrith
Tank
Swyre
West Bexington
Abbotsbury Castle
Kingston Russell
Hardy Monument
Winterborne Monkton
Tadnoll
WHITE HILL
Portesham
Broadmayne
Warmwell
Wool
Abbotsbury
South West Coast Path
Abbey Remains
Bincombe
White Horse
Owermoigne
East Knighton
Jurassic Coast (Dorset & East Devon Coast)
St Catherine's Chapel
Swannery
Rodden
Poxwell
Osmington
A353
Winfrith Newburgh
Langton Herring
Buckland Ripers
Overcombe
Preston
Upton
West Chaldon
East Chaldon (Chaldon Herring)
Lulworth Castle
B3071
Jordan Hill
P+R
RSPB
Osmington Mills
CHALDON DOWN
Chesil Beach
The Fleet
Fleet
Chickerell
B3155
Weymouth Bay
Ringstead Bay
West Lulworth
Lulworth Cove
B3070
BINDON HILL
Water Gardens
Chesil Bank and The Fleet
Westham
Weymouth
Sea Life Tower
Durdle Door
Lulworth Cove
Worbarrow Bay
B3156
Nothe Fort
Wyke Regis
Sandsfoot
Portland Harbour
Chesil Beach
A354
Portland Castle
West Bay
Fortuneswell
Easton
PORTLAND
Portland
Portland Bill Lighthouse
PORTLAND BILL
A B C D E F
1 2 3 4 5 6 7 8
0 1 2 3 4 miles
0 1 2 3 4 5 kilometres

Waldron
New Town
Farnham
Gussage
St Andrew
Boveridge
Cranborne
Alderholt
Iwerne
Minster
Tarrant
27
28
Chettle
Gussage
St Michael
Edmondsham
North Gorley
South Gorley
Tarrant Hinton
Long
Crichel
Gussage
All Saints
Church and
Earthworks
Dorset Heavy Horse
Farm Park
Romford
Verwood
Ibsley
Ibsley Common
Rockford Common
Stourpaine
Pimperne
Tarrant
Launceston
Tarrant
Monkton
Moor
Crichel
Woodlands
Horton
Royal Signals
Manswood
Tarrant
Rawston
Witchampton
Mannington
Three
Legged
Cross
Moors
Valley
Ringwood
Poulner
Forum
Tarrant
Rushton
Hinton
Martell
Liberty's Owl, Raptor
& Reptile Centre
Charlton
Marshall
Charlton
on the Hill
Tarrant Keyneston
St
Leonards
Kingston
Great
Common
Tarrant
Crawford
Badbury Rings
Holt
West
Moors
Thornicombe
Honeybrook
Avon Heath
Spetisbury
Kingston Lacy
Colehill
Ferndown
FOXBURY
HILL
Sandford
Bisterne
Shapwick
Abbott
Street
Hillbutts
Sturminster
Marshall
Pamphill
Wimborne Minster
Leigh
Park
Hampreston
Knoll
Bournemouth
Avon
Ripley
Bransgore
Longham
Dudsbury
Winterborne
Zelston
Merley
West
Parley
Bournemouth
Aviation
Hurn
Sopley
Adventure
Wonderland
West
Morden
Morden
Corfe
Mullen
Bearwood
West Howe
Kinson
Cudnell
Ensbury
Red Hill
Throop
Lytchett
Matravers
East
Morden
Broadstone
East Howe
Moordown
Burton
Upton Heath
Canford
Heath
Wallisdown
Winton
16
Iford
Somerford
Christchurch
Morden
Bog
Organford
Upton
Lytchett
Minster
Newtown
Branksome
Pokesdown
Tuckton
Wick
Mudeford
Castle
Boscombe
Southbourne
Christchurch
Bay
Hengistbury
Head
HENGISTBURY
Hamworthy
Lower
Hamworthy
Parkstone
Lilliput
Westbourne
Branksome
Park
BOURNEMOUTH
POOLE
Canford
Cliffs
Sandford
Northport
Arne
Poole
Harbour
Brownsea
Island
Sandbanks
Binnegar
Wareham
POOLE BAY
East
Stoke
Stoborough
Ridge
Toll
West
Holme
East
Holme
Stoborough
Heath
Purbeck
Heritage Coast
Hartland
Moor
Studland
Beach
Studland
Bay
The
Blue Pool
ISLE
OF PURBECK
THE
FORELAND
East
Lulworth
Corfe
Castle
Studland
Purbeck Hills
Swanage Railway
Church
Knowle
Corfe
Castle
Harman's
Cross
Ulwell
Ballard Point
Cherbourg
Tyneham Village
Purbeck
Marine
Kingston
Swanage
Bay
Swanage
Kimmeridge
Kimmeridge
Bay
South West
Coast Path
Langton
Matravers
Guernsey
Jersey
St-Malo
Durlston
DURLSTON
HEAD
Jurassic Coast
(Dorset & East Devon Coast)
Chapman's
Pool
Worth
Matravers
Anvil
Point
ST ALDHELM'S OR
ST ALBAN'S HEAD
A31
A35
A338
A350
A351
A354
A341
A348
A347
A3049
A3060
A3073
B3078
B3081
B3072
B3082
B3075
B3074
B3068
B3061
B3065
B3369
B3351
B3069
B3070
B3347
G
H
J
K
L
M
1
2
3
4
5
6
7
8

28
15
Fritham
Brook Hill
Brook
Copythorne
Cadnam
Winsor
Calmore
Testwood
Totton
Millbrook
Shirley
Portswood
West End
Bitterne
Rufus Stone
Bartley
Netley Marsh
Eling
Southampton
Northam
Sholing
Woolston
North Gorley
South Gorley
Ibsley Common
Rockford Common
Furzey
Woodlands
Minstead
Ashurst
Longdown Activity Farm
Marchwood
Isle of Wight Ferry Terminal
Netley Abbey
Bursledon
New Forest
National Park
Emery Down
Lyndhurst
New Forest Wildlife Park
Dibden
Netley
Southampton Water
Bank
Beaulieu River
Langdown
Dibden Purlieu
Hythe
Royal Victoria
Hamble-le-Rice
Warsash
Liberty's Owl, Raptor & Reptile Centre
Burley Street
Rhinefield Ornamental Drive
Hardley
Holbury
Fawley
Kingston Great Common
Markway Hill
Burley
National Motor Museum
Blackfield
Calshot Castle
Activity
Calshot
Sandford
Bisterne
Brockenhurst
Beaulieu
North Solent
Langley
Thorney Hill
Bucklers Hard
Exbury
Stanswood Bay
Ripley
Bransgore
Sway
Boldre
East Boldre
Pilley
Norleywood
Spinners
South Baddesley
Needs Ore Point
The Solent
Cowes
Sammy Miller Motorcycle Museum
New Milton
Hordle
Ashley
East End
Lymington
Gurnard Bay
Gurnard
Burton
Walkford
Everton
Rew Street
Somerford
Highcliffe
Highcliffe Castle
Braxton
Hamstead Heritage Coast
Thorness Bay
Christchurch
Mudeford
Barton-on-Sea
Wick
Southbourne
Christchurch Bay
Keyhaven
Newtown Bay
Northwood
Porchfield
Newtown
Milford on Sea
Hengistbury Head
HENGISTBURY HEAD
Hurst Castle
Sconce Point
Yarmouth
Old Town Hall
Colemans
Yarmouth Castle
Colwell Bay
Norton Green
Thorley Street
Ningwood
Shalfleet
Carisbrooke
Totland
Totland Bay
Newbridge
Wellow
Freshwater
Afton
Needles Park
Dimbola
Alum Bay
Chessell Pottery Barns
Water Mill
Calbourne
Brighstone Down
Isle of Wight
Bowcombe
Carisbrooke Castle
Blackwater
The Needles
Needles Old Battery & New Battery
Compton Bay & Downs
Compton Bay
Hanover Point
Brook
Hulverstone
Manor Garden
Gatcombe
Chillerton
Tennyson Heritage Coast
Mottistone
Brighstone
Limerstone
Shorwell
Chilton Chine
Kingston
Brighstone Bay
Chale Green
St Catherine's Down
Atherfield Point
Chale
Whale Chine
Blackgang Chine
Niton
Rocken End
St Catherine's Point
0 1 2 3 4 miles
0 1 2 3 4 5 kilometres

Isle of Wight
17
29
30
18
G
H
J
K
L
M
1
2
3
4
5
6
7
8
Curdridge
Shedfield
Shirrell Heath
Soberton Heath
Hambledon
Catherington
Newtown
Wickham
Curbridge
Burridge
Whiteley
Swanwick
Worlds End
North Boarhunt
Anmore
Soake
Cowplain
WATERLOOVILLE
Southwick
Rowland's Castle
Forestside
Stoughton
Bow Hill
Walderton
Funtington
Woodend
West Stoke
Mid Lavant
East Ashling
West Ashling
Woodmancote
Westbourne
HAVANT
Stakes
Purbrook
Bedhampton
Boarhunt
Ports Down
Royal Armouries Fort Nelson
Titchfield Abbey
Catisfield
Wallington
Titchfield
FAREHAM
Portchester
Portchester Castle
Cosham
Drayton
Farlington
Langstone
Brockhampton
Emsworth
Hambrook
Southbourne
Broadbridge
Nutbourne
Chidham
Bosham
Fishbourne
Walton
Stubbington
Hill Head
Portsmouth Harbour
Bridgemary
Whale Island
Continental Ferry Terminal
Fort Brockhurst
Elson
Rowner
Hardway
Portsmouth Dockyard
North End
Hilsea
Northney
North Hayling
Stoke
HAYLING ISLAND
THORNEY ISLAND
West Thorney
Dell Quay
Apuldram
Donnington
Langstone Harbour
Chichester Harbour
West Itchenor
Birdham
Shipton Green
GOSPORT
Lee-on-the-Solent
Portsea
Fratton
Spinnaker Tower
Southsea
Isle of Wight Ferry Terminal
Alverstoke
Stokes Bay
Eastney
Fort Cumberland
West Town
South Hayling
Hayling Bay
Somerley
West Wittering
East Wittering
Earnley
Bracklesham
Bracklesham Bay
PORTSMOUTH
Gilkicker Point
Spitbank Fort
SPITHEAD
Osborne Bay
East Cowes
Osborne House
Whippingham
Wootton Bridge
Fishbourne
Ryde
Binstead
Seaview Wildlife Encounter
Puckpool Point
Nettlestone Point
Seaview
Brickfields Horse Country
Rosemary
Havenstreet
Little Whitefield
Isle of Wight Steam Railway
Nettlestone
St Helens
The Duver
Robin Hill
Newport
East Ashey
Bembridge
Bembridge Windmill
Lifeboat Station
FORELAND
Nunwell
Brading
Shipwreck Centre
Arreton
Newchurch
Alverstone
Bembridge Down
Whitecliff Bay
Bembridge & Culver Downs
Guernsey
Jersey
St-Malo
Bilbao (Mar-Oct)
Caen (Ouistreham)
Cherbourg (May-Aug)
Le Havre (Jan-Oct)
Santander
Merstone
Queen's Bower
Dinosaur Isle
Yaverland
Culver Cliff
Rookley
Winford
Lake
Sandown
Branstone
Sandown Bay
Apse Heath
Model Village
Sandford
Whiteley Bank
Godshill
Shanklin
Old Smithy & Gardens
Shanklin Chine
Luccombe Village
Luccombe Chine
Appuldurcombe House
Wroxall
Ventnor Downs
DUNNOSE
Whitwell
Ventnor
IOW Glass
Botanic Garden
St Lawrence
The Undercliffe
Binnel Bay
M27
M275
A27
A32
A3(M)
A3
A259
A2030
A3023
A288
A3054
A3055
A3056
A3020
A286
B3395
B3330
B3333
B3385
B3334
B3327
B2177
B2150
B2149
B2148
B2147
B2146
B2178
B2179
B2198
B2145
B2201
A3051
A334
A3021
SELSEY

A
B
C
D
E
F
1
2
3
4
5
6
7
8
Liphook
Linchmere
Kingsley Green
Hollycombe Steam
Fernhurst
Black Down 280
BLACKDOWN HILL
Lurgashall
Northchapel
Plaistow
Ifold
Five Oaks
Barns Green
Billingshurst
Milland
Woodmansgreen
Lickfold
Lurgashall
Ebernoe Common
Kirdford
Redford
Henley
Balls Cross
Wisborough Green
Fishers
SOUTH DOWNS NATIONAL PARK
Fyning
Chithurst
Iping
Woolbeding
Lodsworth
River
Upperton
Coneyhurst Common
Adversane
Petworth House
Trotton
Stedham
Easebourne
Petworth
Byworth
Broadford Bridge
Coolham
Nyewood
Midhurst
Tillington
Little Bognor
Codmore Hill
Harting
Minsted
Selham
Elsted
Cocking Causeway
West Lavington
South Ambersham
Stopham
Nutbourne
Didling
Fittleworth
Pulborough
Treyford
Bepton
249
LINCH DOWN
Cocking
Upper Norwood
Duncton
Coates
Marehill
West Chiltington
Thakeham
Heyshott
Graffham
Duncton Hill
Barlavington
Coldwaltham
Hardham
Abingworth
Ashington
South Downs Way
East Lavington
255
DUNCTON HILL
Sutton
Roman Villa
Greatham
Watersfield
Chilgrove
LEVIN DOWN 170
East Marden
Singleton
West Dean
Bignor
225
BIGNOR HILL
Rackham
Parham
Storrington
Upwaltham
Charlton
East Dean
Weald & Downland Open Air
Goodwood
Bury
Amberley
Amberley Museum
212
KITHURST HILL
Washington
Stoughton
Bow Hill
The Trundle
206
THE TRUNDLE
Houghton
North Stoke
South Stoke
South Downs Way
Walderton
Kingley Vale
Halnaker Hill
144
NORE HILL
167
HARROW HILL
West Stoke
Eartham
Offham
Burpham
East Lavant
Mid Lavant
Waterbeach
Denmans Garden
Slindon
Wepham
Findon
West Ashling
East Ashling
Goodwood
Strettington
Halnaker
Priory
Fontwell
Arundel
Arundel Wetland Centre
Warningcamp
Clapham
Cissbury Ring
Summersdale
Boxgrove
Fontwell Park
Binsted
Poling Corner
Patching
High Salvington
Broadbridge
Roman Palace
Tangmere
Norton
Nyton
Aldingbourne
Walberton
Westhampnett
Eastergate
Poling
HIGHDOWN HILL
Durrington
Salvington
Walton
Fishbourne
Chichester
Oving
Westergate
Woodgate
North End
Lyminster
Angmering
Broadwater
Bosham
Dell Quay
Apuldram
Merston
Barnham
Yapton
Ford
Wick
West Tarring
Runcton
Colworth
Shripney
Climping
Rustington
Ferring
Donnington
North Mundham
North Bersted
Bilsham
Littlehampton
East Preston
Goring-by-Sea
West Worthing
Hunston
Birdham
South Mundham
South Bersted
Flansham
Middleton-on-Sea
Street End
Sidlesham
Rose Green
Felpham
Somerley
Aldwick
Highleigh
Nyetimber
BOGNOR REGIS
Pagham Harbour
Pagham
Earnley
Bracklesham Bay
Church Norton
Selsey
SELSEY BILL
A272
A283
A286
A285
A29
A27
A259
A284
A280
A24
A264
A2032
A2031
B2070
B2133
B2139
B2138
B2141
B2146
B2178
B2132
B2233
B2187
B2140
B2201
B2166
B2132
B2179
B2198
B2145
17
30
0 1 2 3 4 miles
0 1 2 3 4 5 kilometres

Horsham
St Leonards Forest
Balcombe
Handcross
Nymans House
Staplefield
Ardingly Reservoir
Wakehurst Place
South of England
Ouse Valley
Highbrook
Ardingly
Horsted Keynes
Bluebell Railway
Danehill
Nutley
Fairwarp
Sweethaws
Mannings Heath
Southwater
Monk's Gate
Lower Beeding
Slaugham
Warninglid
Nuthurst
Copsale
Maplehurst
Crabtree
Cuckfield
Borde Hill
Lindfield
Haywards Heath
Ansty
Bolney
Bolney Wine Estate
Bolnore
Sheffield Park
Fletching
Maresfield
Splayne's Green
Five Ash Down
High Hurstwood
Buxted
Scayne's Hill
Piltdown
Newick
Uckfield
West Grinstead
Cowfold
Worlds End
Wivelsfield
North Chailey
Chailey
New Town
Framfield
Ridgewood
Partridge Green
Twineham
Hickstead
Sayers Common
Burgess Hill
Wivelsfield Green
Town Littleworth
South Chailey
East Sussex National
Lavender Line
Isfield
Little Horsted
Halland
Henfield
Blackstone
Albourne
Hurstpierpoint
Plumpton Green
Keymer
Ditchling
East Chiltington
Plumpton
Barcombe Cross
Barcombe
Upper Wellingham
Bentley Wildfowl & Motor Museum
Shortgate
Woodmancote
Hassocks
Clayton
Westmeston
Streat
College
Small Dole
Woods Mill
Pyecombe
Ditchling Beacon
Hamsey
Laughton
Ringmer
Upper Beeding
Edburton
Poynings
Pangdean
Mount Harry
Offham
South Downs National Park
Fulking
Devil's Dyke
Truleigh Hill
Saddlescombe
Stanmer
Lewes
Wallands Park
South Malling
Glynde Place
Glynde
Bramber
St Mary's House
Botolphs
Coombes
Lancing College Chapel
Patcham
Coldean
Withdean
Hollingbury
Falmer
Kingston near Lewes
Iford
Beddingham
Firle
Firle Place
Charleston
Firle Beacon
Mile Oak
Hangleton
West Blatchington
Portslade
Preston
Moulsecoomb
Castle Hill
South Downs Way
Newmarket Hill
Rodmell
Monk's House
Breaky Bottom
Southease
Tarring Neville
Berwick
Old Shoreham
Shoreham
Southwick
Woodingdean
Telscombe
South Heighton
Denton
Alfriston
Lancing
Shoreham-by-Sea
Portslade-by-Sea
HOVE
BRIGHTON
Kemp Town
Ovingdean
Piddinghoe
Paradise Park
Newhaven
Norton
Bishopstone
East Blatchington
Sutton
WORTHING
Rottingdean
Saltdean
Peacehaven
Newhaven Fort
Seaford Bay
Seaford
Seaford Head
Dieppe
31
32
20
G H J K L M
1 2 3 4 5 6 7 8

20
Tidebrook
Rotherfield
Ticehurst
Hawkhurst
Highgate
The Moor
Sweethaws
Fairwarp
Stonegate
Pashley Manor
River Limden
Merriments
Kent Ditch
Hurst Green
Witherenden Hill
Etchingham
Mayfield
River Rother
High Hurstwood
Five Ash Down
Pound Green
32
33
Five Ashes
Bodiam
Bodiam Castle
Burwash
Salehurst
Buxted
Hadlow Down
Wilderness Wood
Bateman's
Robertsbridge
Broad Oak
Burwash Common
Burwash Weald
Staplecross
Cross in Hand
Heathfield
Cade St
R Dudwell
Uckfield
Blackboys
Framfield
Brightling
Darwell Reservoir
Punnett's Town
New Town
Mountfield
Three Cups Corner
Wood's Corner
East Sussex National
Ridgewood
Waldron
Little London
Maynard's Green
Netherfield
Dallington
Whatlington
Lavender Line
Little Horsted
Rushlake Green
Warbleton
Sedlescombe
Vines Cross
Horam
Battle
Halland
East Hoathly
Gun Hill
Bodle Street Green
1066 Hastings
Wildfowl
Motor Museum
Shortgate
Chiddingly
Cowbeech
Whitesmith
Catsfield
Muddles Green
Crowhurst
Laughton
Herstmonceux
Hellingly
Ringmer
Windmill Hill
Ninfield
Henley's Down
Lower Dicker
The Truggery
Boreham Street
Horsebridge
Magham Down
19
Lunsford's Cross
Ripe
Upper Dicker
Knockhatch
Leap Cross
Hailsham
Herstmonceux Castle Gardens
Observatory Science Centre
Hooe
Glynde Place
Chalvington
Wartling
Sidley
St Leonards
Michelham Priory
Little Common
Pevensey Levels
Firle
Selmeston
Arlington
Cooden
Firle Place
Charleston
Bexhill
Firle Beacon
Alciston
Polegate
Tarring Neville
Berwick
Drusillas
Wilmington
Westham
Pevensey
South Heighton
Folkington
Wannock
Castle
Pevensey Bay
Alfriston
Lower Willingdon
Langney
The Long Man of Wilmington
Clergy House
Willingdon
Hampden Park
Norton
Litlington
Ratton Village
Sovereign Harbour
Jevington
Roselands
St Anthony's Hill
Bishopstone
East Blatchington
Lullington Heath
South Downs Way
Langney Point
Seaford Bay
Sutton
Westdean
Old Town
Seaford
Friston
Eastbourne
Seven Sisters
East Dean
Seaford Head
South Downs Way
Beachy Head Countryside Centre
Beachy Head
Sussex Heritage Coast
Dieppe
0 1 2 3 4 miles
0 1 2 3 4 5 kilometres

Rolvenden
Reading Street
Newchurch
Burmarsh
A2070
A259
Small Hythe
Chapel Down Winery
Smallhythe Place
B2080
Rolvenden Layne
Kent & East Sussex Railway
34
Snargate
St Mary in the Marsh
Martello
St Mary's Bay
Newenden
ISLE OF OXNEY
B2082
Aeronautical
Brenzett
Ivychurch
Great Dixter House & Gardens
Wittersham
The Stocks
Stone in Oxney
Romney Marsh
Romney Warren
Old Romney
Royal Military Canal
River Rother
Rother Levels
Brookland
Northiam
Iden
New Romney
B2071
B2088
A268
Rye Foreign
A259
Beckley
Clayhill
B2165
Houghton Green
WALLAND MARSH
Peasmarsh
Playden
Rye
Lydd
B2075
East Guldeford
Broad Oak
R. Tillingham
Cock Marling
B2089
Camber
Broadland Row
Udimore
Camber Castle
Rye Harbour
RSPB
Brede
River Brede
Winchelsea
Broad Street
Icklesham
The Old Lighthouse
DUNGENESS
Rye Bay
A28
Three Oaks
Guestling Thorn
A259
Pett
Guestling Green
Cliff End
Helen's
Ore
Fairlight
HASTINGS
G
H
J
K
L
M
1
2
3
4
5
6
7
8

North West Point
Lundy Heritage Coast
LUNDY
142
Marine Reserve
Marisco
Surf Point
Shutter Point
Baggy Point
Croyde
BARNSTAPLE OR BIDEFORD BAY
Westward
HARTLAND POINT
Shipload Bay
Titchberry
Dameholе Point
Hartland Abbey & Gardens
Stoke
Hartland Quay
Hartland
B3248
Spekes Mill Mouth
Milford
Docton Mill Gardens
Philham
Clovelly
B3237
Buck's Mills
Hartland Heritage Coast
Abbotsham
Fairy Cross
Ford
Horns Cross
Woodtown
A39
Goldworthy
Milky Way
Buck's Cross
Woolfardisworthy
Parkham
Hardisworthy
Buckland Brewer
Welcombe
Frith
Ashmansworthy
Darracott
East Putford
Gooseham
Dinworthy
Gnome Reserve
West Putford
Haytown
Morwenstow
Higher Sharpnose Point
South West Coast Path
Shop
Bradworthy
Bulkworthy
Woodford
Tamar Lakes
Abbots Bickington
A388
Lower Sharpnose Point
Kilkhampton
Sutcombe
New St Pe
Steeple Point
Milton Damerel
Thornbury
Holsworthy
B3254
0 1 2 3 4 miles
0 1 2 3 4 5 kilometres

9

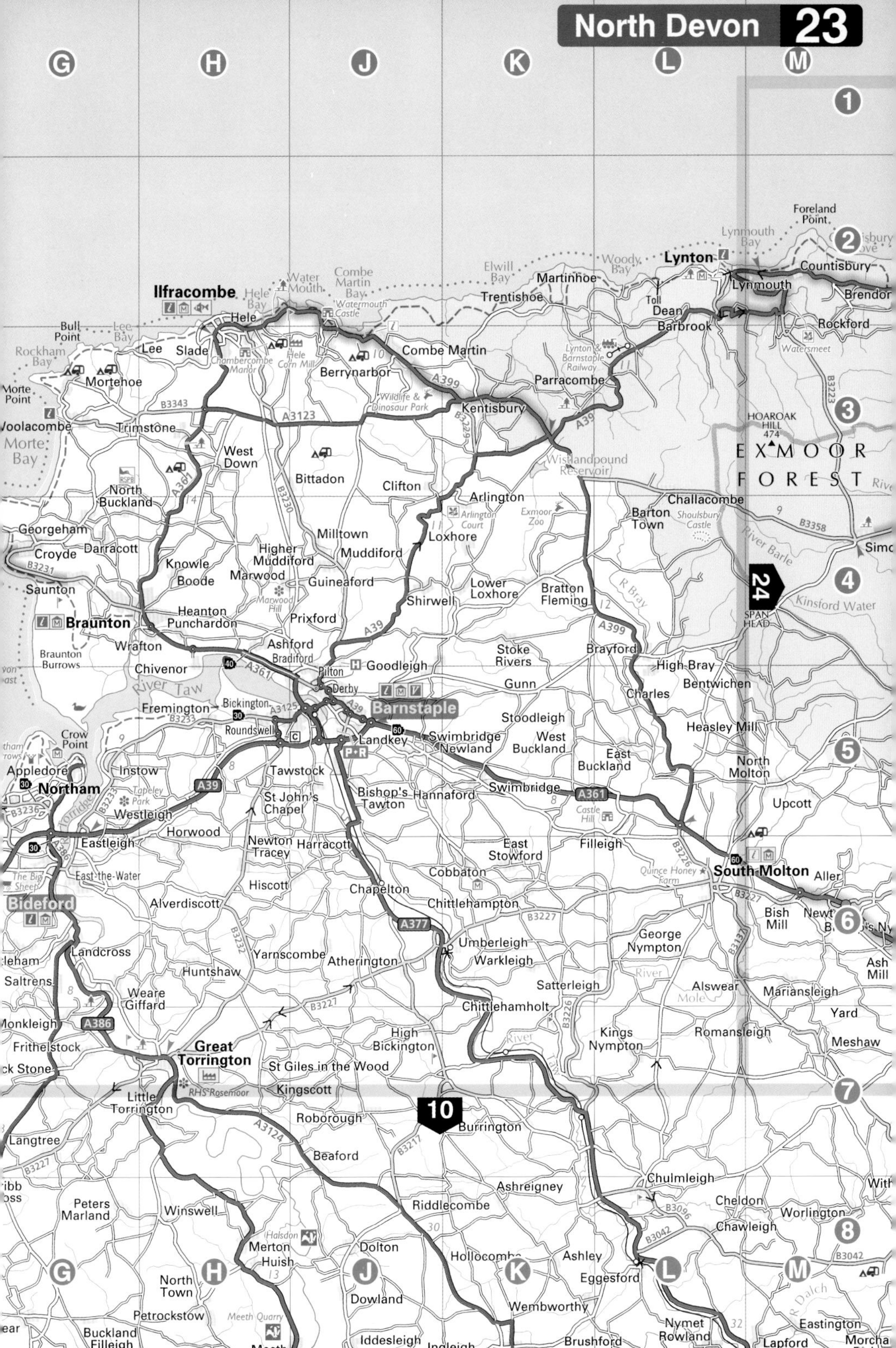
Ilfracombe
Lynton
Lynmouth
Countisbury
Combe Martin
Barnstaple
Braunton
Bideford
Northam
Appledore
South Molton
Great Torrington
Chulmleigh
Woolacombe
Mortehoe
Croyde
Georgeham
Saunton
Instow
Westleigh
Fremington
Bickington
Roundswell
Landkey
Swimbridge
Tawstock
Chittlehampton
Umberleigh
Atherington
Kings Nympton
Burrington
Beaford
Dolton
Eggesford
Winkleigh
Parracombe
Kentisbury
Arlington
Challacombe
Exmoor Forest
Hoaroak Hill 474
Rockford
Brendon
Barbrook
Martinhoe
Trentishoe
Berrynarbor
Bittadon
West Down
Shirwell
Goodleigh
Filleigh
North Molton
Heasley Mill
Alswear
Romansleigh
Meshaw
Chawleigh
Cheldon
Worlington
Ashreigney
Riddlecombe
Merton
Huish
North Town
Petrockstow
Peters Marland
Langtree
Little Torrington
Frithelstock
Monkleigh
Saltrens
Landcross
Weare Giffard
Huntshaw
Yarnscombe
Alverdiscott
Horwood
Eastleigh
Hiscott
Chapelton
Harracott
Newton Tracey
St John's Chapel
Bishop's Tawton
Hannaford
Cobbaton
East Stowford
Warkleigh
Chittlehamholt
Satterleigh
George Nympton
Bish Mill
Mariansleigh
High Bickington
St Giles in the Wood
Kingscott
Roborough
Iddesleigh
Dowland
Wembworthy
Ashley
Brushford
Nymet Rowland
Lapford
Eastington
RHS Rosemoor
Barnstaple
A39
A361
A377
A386
A399
A3123
A3124
A3125
B3343
B3230
B3231
B3233
B3227
B3226
B3358
B3223
B3217
B3096
B3042
B3137
Exmoor Zoo
Arlington Court
Wistlandpound Reservoir
Lynton & Barnstaple Railway
Watermouth Castle
Chambercombe Manor
Hele Corn Mill
Wildlife & Dinosaur Park
Marwood Hill
Shoulsbury Castle
Castle Hill
Quince Honey Farm
Halsdon
Meeth Quarry
Watersmeet
Tapeley Park
The Big Sheep
Braunton Burrows
River Taw
River Barle
Kinsford Water
River Mole
Morte Point
Morte Bay
Bull Point
Lee Bay
Rockham Bay
Hele Bay
Water Mouth
Combe Martin Bay
Elwill Bay
Woody Bay
Lynmouth Bay
Foreland Point
Crow Point
Span Head
10
24

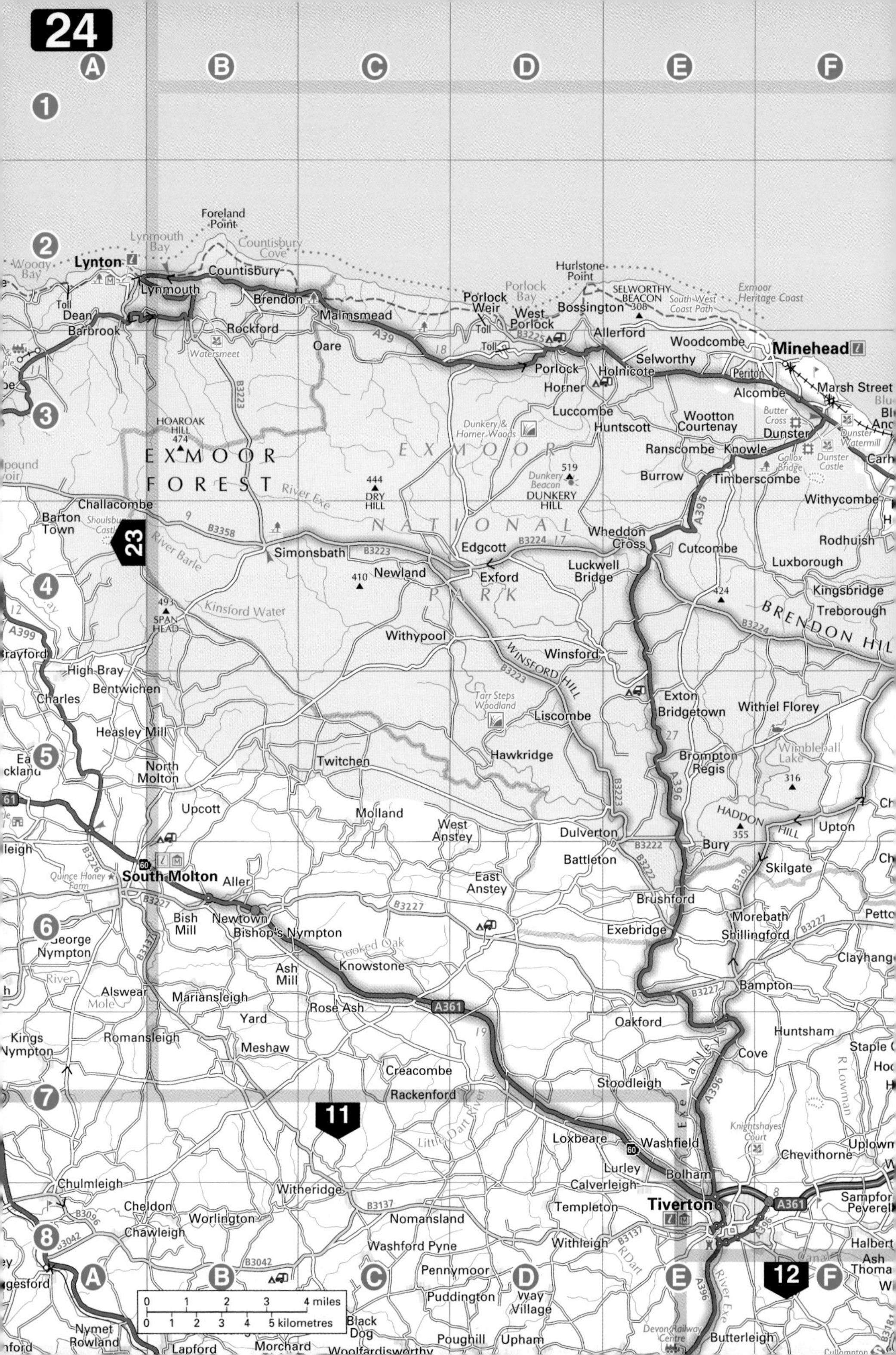
24
A
B
C
D
E
F
1
2
3
4
5
6
7
8
Foreland Point
Lynmouth Bay
Countisbury Cove
Woody Bay
Lynton
Lynmouth
Countisbury
Brendon
Malmsmead
Toll
Dean
Barbrook
Rockford
Watersmeet
Oare
A39
Porlock Bay
Porlock Weir
West Porlock
Hurlstone Point
Bossington
SELWORTHY BEACON 308
South West Coast Path
Exmoor Heritage Coast
Allerford
Woodcombe
Minehead
Selworthy
Porlock
Holnicote
Horner
Periton
Alcombe
Marsh Street
Luccombe
Huntscott
Wootton Courtenay
Butter Cross
Dunster
Dunster Watermill
Ranscombe
Knowle
Gallox Bridge
Dunster Castle
Burrow
Timberscombe
Withycombe
B3225
18
B3223
HOAROAK HILL 474
EXMOOR FOREST
EXMOOR
Dunkery & Horner Woods
Dunkery Beacon
519
DUNKERY HILL
444
DRY HILL
River Exe
NATIONAL PARK
Challacombe
Barton Town
Shoulsbury Castle
23
B3358
River Barle
Simonsbath
B3223
Edgcott
B3224
Wheddon Cross
Cutcombe
Rodhuish
Luxborough
Kingsbridge
Treborough
BRENDON HILL
410
Newland
Exford
Luckwell Bridge
424
A396
493
SPAN HEAD
Kinsford Water
Withypool
WINSFORD HILL
Winsford
A399
Brayford
High Bray
Bentwichen
Charles
Heasley Mill
Tarr Steps Woodland
Liscombe
Exton
Bridgetown
Withiel Florey
Hawkridge
Brompton Regis
Wimbleball Lake
316
Twitchen
North Molton
Upcott
Molland
West Anstey
Dulverton
HADDON HILL
355
Upton
Bury
B3222
Battleton
Skilgate
B3226
Quince Honey Farm
South Molton
Aller
East Anstey
Brushford
B3190
B3227
Bish Mill
Newtown
Bishop's Nympton
Exebridge
Morebath
Shillingford
George Nympton
Crooked Oak
Knowstone
Ash Mill
Clayhanger
River Mole
Alswear
Mariansleigh
Rose Ash
A361
Bampton
Yard
Oakford
Kings Nympton
Romansleigh
Meshaw
Huntsham
Cove
Staple
R Lowman
Creacombe
Stoodleigh
Exe Valley
Rackenford
11
Little Dart River
Knightshayes Court
Loxbeare
Washfield
Uplowman
Chevithorne
Lurley
Bolham
Chulmleigh
Witheridge
Calverleigh
Tiverton
Sampford Peverell
Cheldon
B3096
Chawleigh
Worlington
B3137
Nomansland
Templeton
Withleigh
B3042
Washford Pyne
Halberton
Ash Thomas
Pennymoor
R Dart
12
Puddington
Way Village
River Exe
Nymet Rowland
Lapford
Morchard
Black Dog
Woolfardisworthy
Poughill
Upham
Devon Railway Centre
Butterleigh
Cullompton
0 1 2 3 4 miles
0 1 2 3 4 5 kilometres

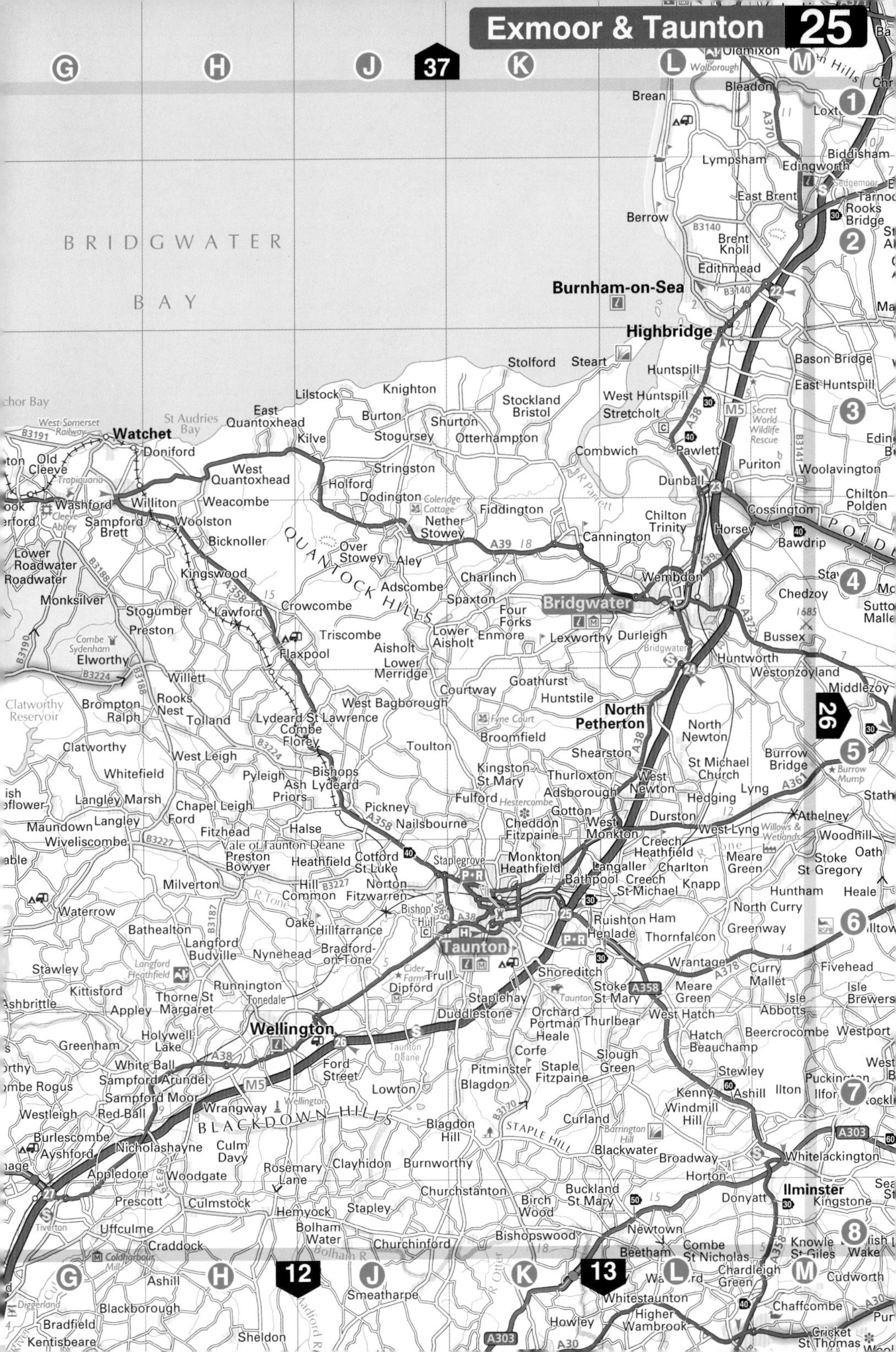

G
H
J
37
K
L
M
Oldmixon
Walborough
Bleadon
Brean
1
Loxton
A370
Lympsham
Edingworth
Biddisham
Sedgemoor
East Brent
Tarnock
Rooks Bridge
Berrow
B3140
Brent Knoll
2
Edithmead
BRIDGWATER
BAY
Burnham-on-Sea
22
Highbridge
Stolford
Steart
Huntspill
Bason Bridge
East Huntspill
Lilstock
Knighton
Stockland Bristol
West Huntspill
Stretcholt
M5
Secret World Wildlife Rescue
3
chor Bay
St Audries Bay
East Quantoxhead
Burton
Shurton
A38
West Somerset Railway
B3191
Watchet
Kilve
Stogursey
Otterhampton
Combwich
Pawlett
B3141
Doniford
Puriton
Woolavington
Old Cleeve
West Quantoxhead
Stringston
Holford
R Parrett
Dunball
23
Tropiquaria
Dodington
Coleridge Cottage
Chilton Polden
Washford
Williton
Weacombe
Fiddington
Chilton Trinity
Cossington
Cleeve Abbey
Sampford Brett
Woolston
Nether Stowey
Cannington
Horsey
POLDEN
Bawdrip
Lower Roadwater
Bicknoller
QUANTOCK HILLS
Over Stowey
A39
Aley
Roadwater
B3188
Kingswood
Charlinch
Wembdon
Stawell
4
Monksilver
A358
Adscombe
Spaxton
Bridgwater
Chedzoy
Sutton Mallet
Stogumber
Lawford
Crowcombe
Four Forks
A372
1685
Preston
Triscombe
Lower Aisholt
Enmore
Lexworthy
Durleigh
Bussex
B3190
Combe Sydenham
Aisholt
Bridgwater
Huntworth
Elworthy
Flaxpool
Lower Merridge
24
Westonzoyland
B3224
Willett
Goathurst
Middlezoy
Clatworthy Reservoir
Brompton Ralph
Rooks Nest
West Bagborough
Courtway
Huntstile
26
Tolland
Lydeard St Lawrence
Fyne Court
North Petherton
North Newton
Combe Florey
Broomfield
Clatworthy
West Leigh
Toulton
Shearston
Burrow Bridge
5
Whiteheld
Pyleigh
Bishops Lydeard
Kingston St Mary
Thurloxton
West Newton
St Michael Church
Burrow Mump
Ash Priors
Adsborough
Hedging
Lyng
A361
Langley Marsh
Chapel Leigh
Fulford
Hestercombe
Stathe
Pickney
Gotton
Durston
Athelney
Maundown
Langley
Ford
Nailsbourne
Cheddon Fitzpaine
West Monkton
West Lyng
Willows & Wetlands
Woodhill
Wiveliscombe
Fitzhead
Halse
Creech Heathfield
R Tone
B3227
Vale of Taunton Deane
Meare Green
Stoke St Gregory
Oath
Preston Bowyer
Heathfield
Cotford St Luke
Monkton Heathfield
Langaller
Charlton
Staplegrove
Bathpool
Creech St Michael
Knapp
Milverton
Hill Common
Norton Fitzwarren
Huntham
Heale
Waterrow
R Tone
Bishop's Hull
Ruishton
Ham
North Curry
B3187
Oake
25
Bathealton
Hillfarrance
Henlade
Thornfalcon
Greenway
6
Langford Budville
Bradford-on-Tone
Taunton
Nynehead
Wrantage
A378
Fivehead
Stawley
Langford Heathfield
Cider Farm
Trull
Shoreditch
Curry Mallet
Isle Brewers
Kittisford
Runnington
Dipford
Stoke St Mary
A358
Meare Green
Ashbrittle
Thorne St Margaret
Tonedale
Staplehay
Taunton
Isle Abbotts
Appley
Orchard Portman
West Hatch
Wellington
Duddlestone
Thurlbear
Holywell Lake
Heale
Hatch Beauchamp
Beercrocombe
Westport
Greenham
26
Taunton Deane
Corfe
Slough Green
White Ball
A38
Ford Street
Pitminster
Staple Fitzpaine
Stewley
Sampford Arundel
M5
Lowton
Blagdon
Puckington
Sampford Moor
Wellington
Kenny
Ashill
Ilton
Ilford
7
Westleigh
Red Ball
Wrangway
BLACKDOWN HILLS
B3170
Windmill Hill
Burlescombe
Blagdon Hill
STAPLE HILL
Curland
Barrington Hill
A303
Ayshford
Nicholashayne
Culm Davy
Blackwater
Whitelackington
Appledore
Woodgate
Rosemary Lane
Clayhidon
Burnworthy
Broadway
Horton
27
Prescott
Culmstock
Churchstanton
Birch Wood
Buckland St Mary
Donyatt
Ilminster
Kingstone
Tiverton
Uffculme
Hemyock
Stapley
Newtown
Bolham Water
Churchinford
Bishopswood
Knowle St Giles
Wake
8
Craddock
Combe St Nicholas
Coldharbour Mill
Bolham R
Beetham
Chardleigh Green
A358
G
H
12
J
K
13
L
M
Ashill
Wadeford
Cudworth
R Otter
Smeatharpe
Whitestaunton
Diggerland
Blackborough
Higher Wambrook
Chaffcombe
Bradfield
Howley
Madford R
Kentisbeare
Sheldon
A303
A30
Cricket St Thomas

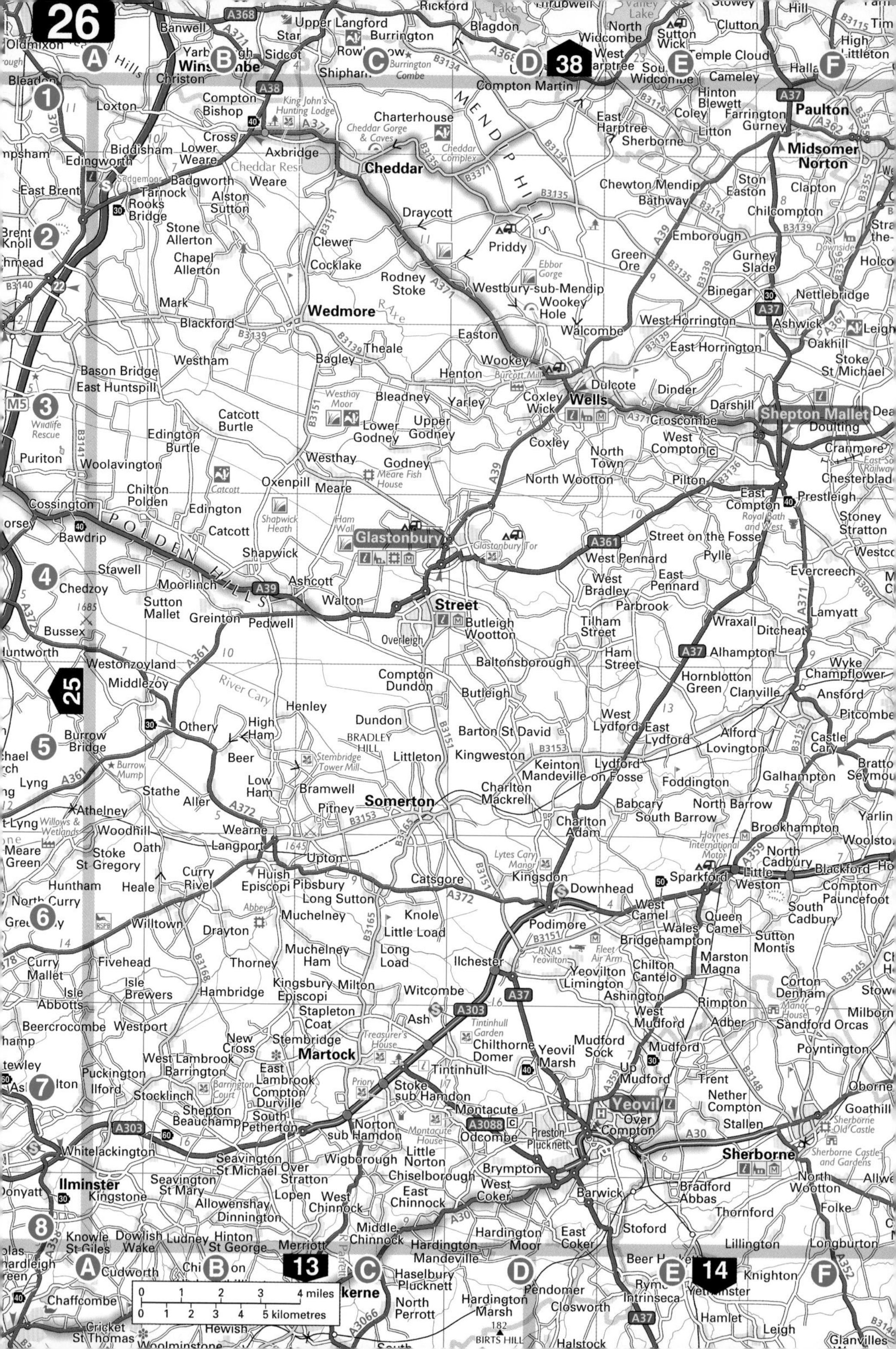
26
Oldmixon
A
Hills
Banwell
A368
Yarborough
B
Winscombe
Christon
Sidcot
Star
Upper Langford
Burrington
Rowberrow
C
Burrington Combe
Shipham
Rickford
Blagdon
B3134
A368
D
38
North Widcombe
West Harptree
Sutton Wick
Clutton
Temple Cloud
E
South Widcombe
Cameley
Hinton Blewett
High Littleton
F
Hallatrow
B3115
A37
Paulton
Bleadon
1
Loxton
Compton Bishop
A38
King John's Hunting Lodge
Charterhouse
Compton Martin
MENDIP HILLS
East Harptree
Coley
Litton
Farrington Gurney
A362
Midsomer Norton
Cheddar Gorge & Caves
Cheddar Complex
Cross
Biddisham
Lower Weare
Axbridge
Cheddar Resr
Cheddar
A371
B3135
B3371
B3134
Sherborne
Edingworth
East Brent
Sedgemoor
Tarnock
Badgworth
Weare
Rooks Bridge
Alston Sutton
Chewton Mendip
Ston Easton
Clapton
Bathway
Brent Knoll
2
Stone Allerton
Chapel Allerton
Clewer
Cocklake
Draycott
Priddy
B3135
B3151
Emborough
Chilcompton
B3139
Green Ore
Gurney Slade
Downside
Ebbor Gorge
Rodney Stoke
Westbury-sub-Mendip
Wookey Hole
Binegar
Nettlebridge
B3140
22
Mark
Blackford
Wedmore
Walcombe
West Horrington
East Horrington
Ashwick
Oakhill
A367
Stoke St Michael
Theale
Bagley
Easton
B3139
Westham
Bason Bridge
East Huntspill
Wookey
Henton
Burcott Mill
Dulcote
Dinder
Westhay Moor
Bleadney
Yarley
Coxley Wick
Wells
Darshill
Shepton Mallet
Doulting
M5
3
Wildlife Rescue
Catcott Burtle
Edington Burtle
Lower Godney
Upper Godney
Croscombe
West Compton
Cranmore
East Somerset Railway
Puriton
Woolavington
Westhay
Godney
Coxley
North Town
Chesterblade
Meare Fish House
Oxenpill
Meare
A39
North Wootton
Pilton
B3136
Catcott
Chilton Polden
Edington
Cossington
Shapwick Heath
Ham Wall
East Compton
Prestleigh
Royal Bath and West
Stoney Stratton
Bawdrip
Catcott
POLDEN HILLS
Glastonbury
Glastonbury Tor
A361
Street on the Fosse
Shapwick
West Pennard
Pylle
4
Stawell
Chedzoy
Moorlinch
A39
Ashcott
West Bradley
East Pennard
Evercreech
Sutton Mallet
Greinton
Walton
Pedwell
Street
Parbrook
1685
Bussex
Butleigh Wootton
Overleigh
Tilham Street
Wraxall
Lamyatt
Ditcheat
A371
Huntworth
Westonzoyland
A361
Ham Street
A37
Alhampton
Baltonsborough
25
Middlezoy
River Cary
Compton Dundon
Hornblotton Green
Wyke Champflower
Clanville
Butleigh
Ansford
Henley
West Lydford
Pitcombe
Burrow Bridge
5
Othery
High Ham
Dundon
Barton St David
East Lydford
Alford
B3152
Castle Cary
Bradley Hill
Stembridge Tower Mill
Littleton
Kingweston
B3153
Lovington
Burrow Mump
Beer
Keinton Mandeville
Lydford-on-Fosse
Galhampton
Lyng
A361
Stathe
Aller
Low Ham
Bramwell
Charlton Mackrell
Foddington
Somerton
Athelney
Willows & Wetlands
A372
Pitney
Babcary
North Barrow
Woodhill
Wearne
B3153
South Barrow
Charlton Adam
Brookhampton
Meare Green
Stoke St Gregory
Oath
Langport
1645
Haynes International Motor
North Cadbury
Upton
Lytes Cary Manor
Kingsdon
Sparkford
A359
Little Weston
Blackford
Huntham
Heale
Curry Rivel
Huish Episcopi
Pibsbury
Catsgore
A372
B3151
Downhead
Compton Pauncefoot
North Curry
Long Sutton
Knole
West Camel
South Cadbury
Greenway
6
Willtown
Abbey
Muchelney
Podimore
Queen Camel
Drayton
B3165
Little Load
Wales
RSPB
B3151
Bridgehampton
Sutton Montis
Curry Mallet
Fivehead
Thorney
Muchelney Ham
Long Load
RNAS Yeovilton
Fleet Air Arm
Ilchester
Marston Magna
Isle Brewers
Hambridge
B3168
Kingsbury Episcopi
Milton
Yeovilton
Limington
Chilton Cantelo
Corton Denham
B3145
Isle Abbotts
Witcombe
A37
Ashington
Rimpton
Beercrocombe
Westport
Stapleton Coat
A303
Ash
Tintinhull Garden
West Mudford
Adber
Manor House
Sandford Orcas
Milborne
New Cross
Stembridge
Treasurer's House
Chilthorne Domer
Mudford Sock
Mudford
West Lambrook
Barrington
Martock
Yeovil Marsh
Poyntington
Puckington
Ilford
East Lambrook
Tintinhull
Up Mudford
Trent
B3148
Oborne
7
Barrington Court
Stocklinch
Compton Durville
Priory
Stoke sub Hamdon
Montacute
Yeovil
Nether Compton
Goathill
Shepton Beauchamp
South Petherton
Norton sub Hamdon
A3088
Odcombe
Preston Plucknett
Over Compton
Stallen
Sherborne Old Castle
A303
Montacute House
A30
Whitelackington
Seavington St Michael
Over Stratton
Wigborough
Little Norton
Brympton
Sherborne
Sherborne Castle and Gardens
Ilminster
Seavington St Mary
Chiselborough
West Coker
North Wootton
Donyatt
Kingstone
Allowenshay
Lopen
West Chinnock
East Chinnock
Barwick
Bradford Abbas
Dinnington
A30
Thornford
Folke
8
Knowle St Giles
Dowlish Wake
Ludney
Hinton St George
Merriott
Middle Chinnock
Hardington Moor
East Coker
Stoford
Lillington
Longburton
A358
Hardington Mandeville
A352
A
Cudworth
B
Chillington
13
C
Haselbury Plucknett
D
Pendomer
Beer Hackett
E
Ryme Intrinseca
14
Yetminster
Knighton
F
Chaffcombe
North Perrott
Hardington Marsh
Closworth
Cricket St Thomas
Hewish
A3066
182
BIRTS HILL
A37
Hamlet
Leigh
Glanvilles
Woolminstone
Halstock
0 1 2 3 4 miles
0 1 2 3 4 5 kilometres

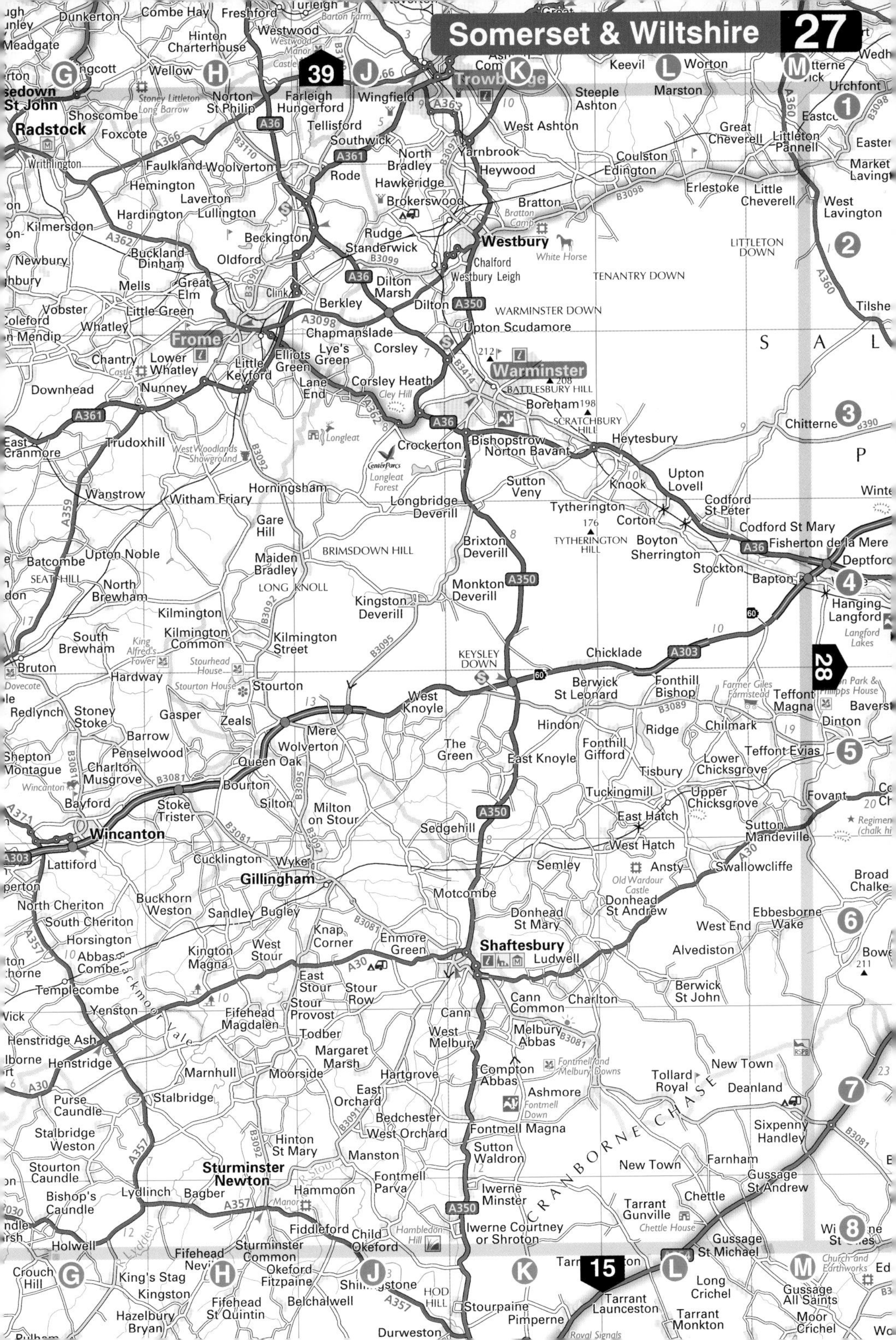

Radstock
Frome
Trowbridge
Westbury
Warminster
Wincanton
Gillingham
Shaftesbury
Sturminster Newton
Mere
Longleat
Stourhead House
CRANBORNE CHASE
Blackmore Vale
39
28
15

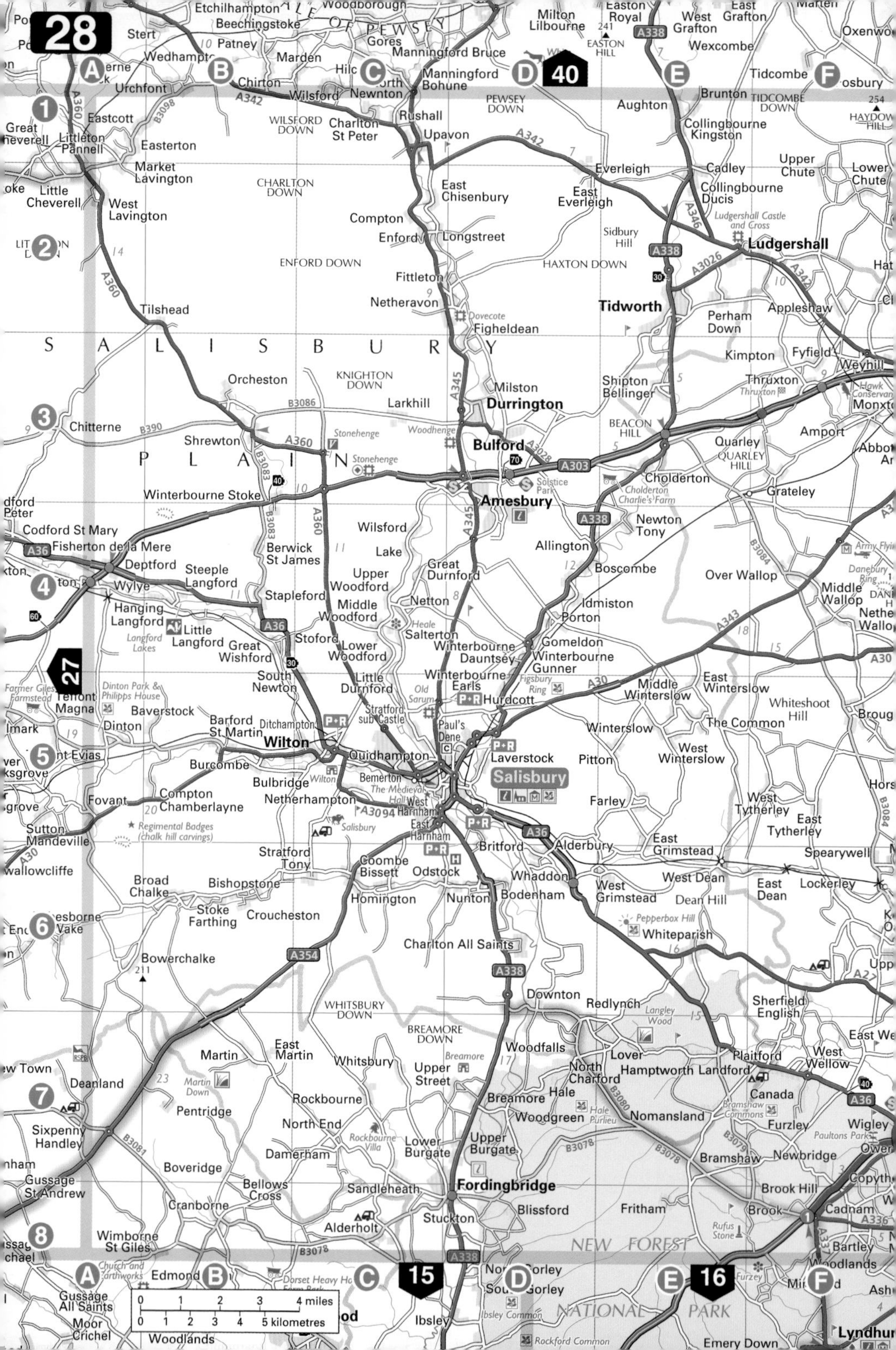
28
Etchilhampton
VALE OF PEWSEY
Woodborough
Beechingstoke
Stert
Patney
Marden
Gores
Manningford Bruce
Milton Lilbourne
Easton Royal
241
EASTON HILL
West Grafton
East Grafton
Oxenwood
A338
Wexcombe
Wedhampton
Urchfont
Chirton
Wilsford
Hilcott
North Newnton
Manningford Bohune
40
Tidcombe
Brunton
TIDCOMBE DOWN
254
HAYDOWN HILL
A360
A342
B3098
Eastcott
WILSFORD DOWN
Charlton St Peter
Rushall
Upavon
PEWSEY DOWN
Aughton
Collingbourne Kingston
Great Cheverell
Littleton Pannell
Easterton
Market Lavington
Everleigh
Cadley
Upper Chute
Lower Chute
Little Cheverell
West Lavington
CHARLTON DOWN
East Chisenbury
East Everleigh
Collingbourne Ducis
Compton
Enford
Longstreet
Sidbury Hill
A346
Ludgershall Castle and Cross
Ludgershall
ENFORD DOWN
HAXTON DOWN
A3026
Fittleton
Netheravon
Tidworth
Perham Down
Appleshaw
Tilshead
Dovecote
Figheldean
SALISBURY
Kimpton
Fyfield
Weyhill
Orcheston
KNIGHTON DOWN
A345
Milston
Shipton Bellinger
Thruxton
Hawk Conservancy
Larkhill
Durrington
Monxton
B3086
BEACON HILL
Quarley
Amport
Chitterne
B390
Stonehenge
Woodhenge
QUARLEY HILL
Shrewton
Bulford
A3028
A303
PLAIN
Stonehenge
Solstice Park
Cholderton
Cholderton Charlie's Farm
Grateley
B3083
Winterbourne Stoke
Amesbury
Codford St Peter
Codford St Mary
Wilsford
Newton Tony
A36
Fisherton de la Mere
Berwick St James
Lake
Great Durnford
Allington
B3084
Deptford
Steeple Langford
Boscombe
Over Wallop
Danebury Ring
Wylye
Upper Woodford
Stapleford
Middle Woodford
Netton
Idmiston
Middle Wallop
Nether Wallop
Hanging Langford
Little Langford
Porton
Heale
Salterton
Langford Lakes
Stoford
Lower Woodford
Gomeldon
A343
Great Wishford
Winterbourne Dauntsey
Winterbourne Gunner
South Newton
Little Durnford
Winterbourne Earls
Figsbury Ring
27
A30
Farmer Giles Farmstead
Teffont Magna
Dinton Park & Philipps House
Old Sarum
Hurdcott
Middle Winterslow
East Winterslow
Whiteshoot Hill
Baverstock
Barford St Martin
Ditchampton
Stratford sub Castle
Paul's Dene
Winterslow
The Common
Dinton
Wilton
Quidhampton
Laverstock
Pitton
West Winterslow
Burcombe
Bulbridge
Bemerton
Salisbury
Fovant
Compton Chamberlayne
Netherhampton
The Medieval Hall
West Harnham
Farley
West Tytherley
East Tytherley
A3094
Sutton Mandeville
Regimental Badges (chalk hill carvings)
East Harnham
Britford
Alderbury
East Grimstead
Spearywell
Stratford Tony
Coombe Bissett
Odstock
Swallowcliffe
Broad Chalke
Bishopstone
Whaddon
West Dean
East Dean
Lockerley
West Grimstead
Dean Hill
Homington
Nunton
Bodenham
Ebbesborne Wake
Stoke Farthing
Croucheston
Pepperbox Hill
Whiteparish
Charlton All Saints
Bowerchalke
211
A354
A338
Downton
Redlynch
Sherfield English
WHITSBURY DOWN
Langley Wood
BREAMORE DOWN
East Wellow
West Wellow
East Martin
Martin
Whitsbury
Breamore
Woodfalls
Lover
Plaitford
Upper Street
North Charford
Hamptworth
Landford
New Town
Deanland
Martin Down
Canada
Hale
A27
Breamore
Rockbourne
Pentridge
Woodgreen
Hale Purlieu
Nomansland
Bramshaw Commons
Furzley
Wigley
Sixpenny Handley
North End
Rockbourne Villa
Paultons Park
B3081
Damerham
Lower Burgate
Upper Burgate
B3078
B3079
B3080
Bramshaw
Newbridge
Boveridge
Ower
Gussage St Andrew
Bellows Cross
Sandleheath
Fordingbridge
Copythorne
Brook Hill
Cranborne
Blissford
Fritham
Cadnam
Stuckton
Alderholt
Brook
A336
A337
Wimborne St Giles
Rufus Stone
NEW FOREST
Bartley
Church and Earthworks
Edmondsham
Dorset Heavy Horse Farm Park
15
North Gorley
Woodlands
16
Minstead
Gussage All Saints
South Gorley
NATIONAL PARK
Furzey
Ashurst
Moor Crichel
Ibsley
Ibsley Common
Lyndhurst
Woodlands
Rockford Common
Emery Down
0 1 2 3 4 miles
0 1 2 3 4 5 kilometres
A B C D E F
1 2 3 4 5 6 7 8

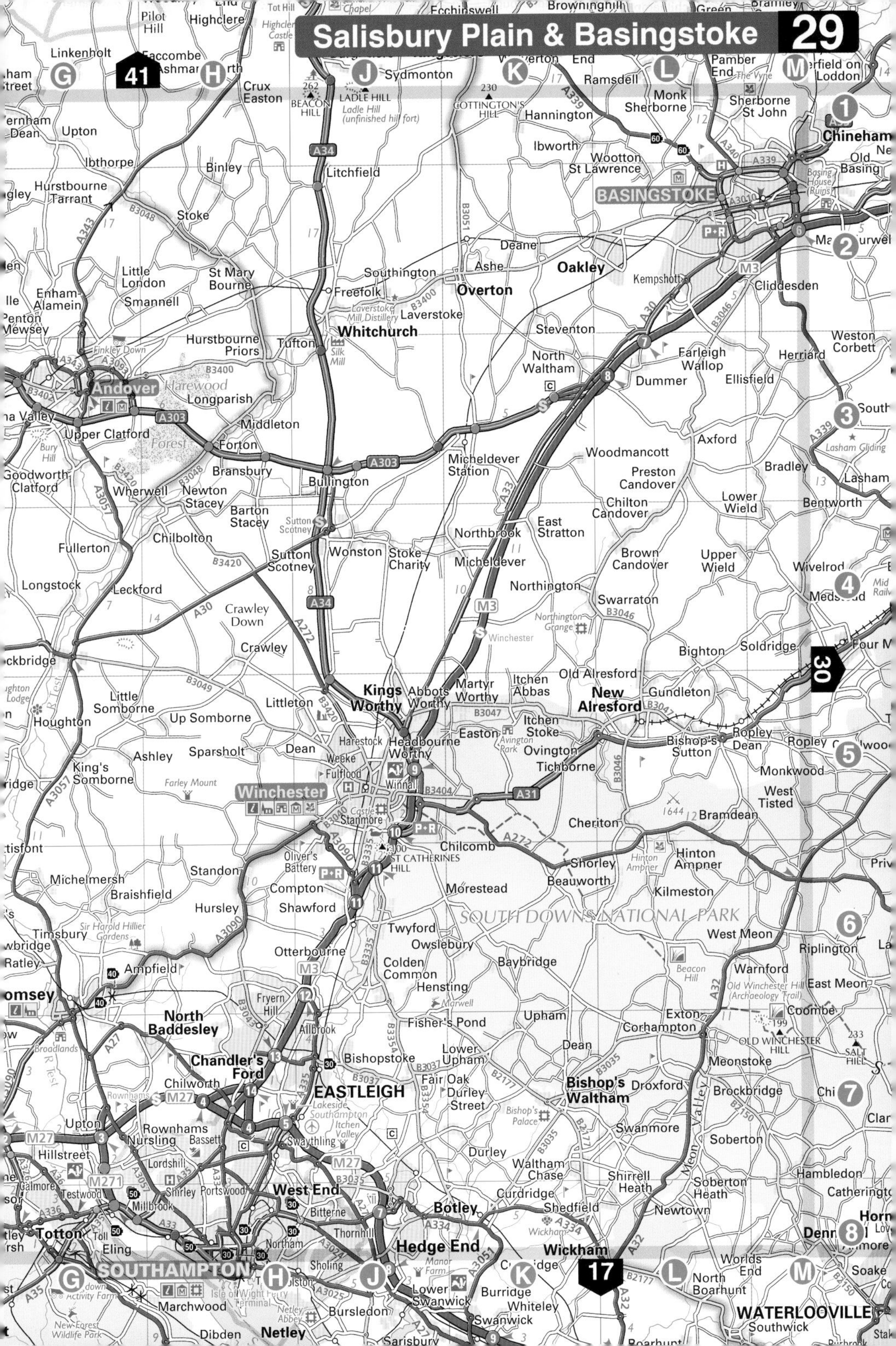

Salisbury Plain & Basingstoke
29
41
30
17
Pilot Hill
Highclere
Highclere Castle
Tot Hill
Ecchinswell
Linkenholt
Faccombe
Ashmansworth
Crux Easton
BEACON HILL
LADLE HILL
Ladle Hill (unfinished hill fort)
Sydmonton
COTTINGTON'S HILL
Hannington
Ramsdell
Monk Sherborne
Sherborne St John
Pamber End
The Vyne
Chineham
Old Basing
Basing House (Ruins)
Upton
Ibthorpe
Binley
Litchfield
Ibworth
Wootton St Lawrence
BASINGSTOKE
Hurstbourne Tarrant
Stoke
Deane
Ashe
Oakley
Kempshott
Cliddesden
Little London
St Mary Bourne
Southington
Freefolk
Overton
Laverstoke
Laverstoke Mill Distillery
Enham-Alamein
Smannell
Whitchurch
Silk Mill
Steventon
Weston Corbett
Hurstbourne Priors
Tufton
Farleigh Wallop
Herriard
Finkley Down
North Waltham
Dummer
Ellisfield
Andover
Harewood Forest
Longparish
Middleton
Upper Clatford
Forton
Axford
Bury Hill
Woodmancott
Lasham Gliding
Goodworth Clatford
Bransbury
Micheldever Station
Preston Candover
Bradley
Lasham
Wherwell
Newton Stacey
Bullington
Chilton Candover
Lower Wield
Bentworth
Barton Stacey
Sutton Scotney
Fullerton
Chilbolton
Northbrook
East Stratton
Wonston
Stoke Charity
Brown Candover
Upper Wield
Micheldever
Wivelrod
Longstock
Leckford
Northington
Medstead
Crawley Down
Swarraton
Crawley
Northington Grange
Winchester
Bighton
Soldridge
Four Marks
Stockbridge
Houghton Lodge
Little Somborne
Littleton
Kings Worthy
Abbots Worthy
Martyr Worthy
Itchen Abbas
Old Alresford
New Alresford
Gundleton
Houghton
Up Somborne
Easton
Avington Park
Itchen Stoke
Ropley Dean
Ropley
Ashley
Sparsholt
Dean
Harestock
Headbourne Worthy
Ovington
Bishop's Sutton
King's Somborne
Weeke
Fulflood
Tichborne
Monkwood
Farley Mount
Winnall
West Tisted
Winchester
Castle
Stanmore
Cheriton
Bramdean
Chilcomb
ST CATHERINES HILL
Oliver's Battery
Standon
Shorley
Hinton Ampner
Michelmersh
Compton
Beauworth
Kilmeston
Braishfield
Morestead
Hursley
Shawford
SOUTH DOWNS NATIONAL PARK
Sir Harold Hillier Gardens
Twyford
West Meon
Timsbury
Owslebury
Ripplington
Otterbourne
Colden Common
Baybridge
Warnford
Beacon Hill
Ampfield
Hensting
Old Winchester Hill (Archaeology Trail)
East Meon
Romsey
Fryern Hill
Marwell
Upham
Exton
Coombe
North Baddesley
Allbrook
Fisher's Pond
Corhampton
OLD WINCHESTER HILL
SALT HILL
Broadlands
Chandler's Ford
Bishopstoke
Lower Upham
Dean
Meonstoke
Chilworth
EASTLEIGH
Fair Oak
Bishop's Waltham
Droxford
Brockbridge
Durley Street
Bishop's Palace
Upton
Rownhams
Lakeside
Southampton Itchen Valley
Swanmore
Nursling
Bassett
Swaythling
Soberton
Hillstreet
Lordshill
Durley
Waltham Chase
Shirrell Heath
Hambledon
Calmore
Testwood
Shirley
Portswood
West End
Soberton Heath
Catherington
Millbrook
Curdridge
Bitterne
Botley
Shedfield
Newtown
Totton
Toll
Eling
Thornhill
Northam
Hedge End
Wickham
Denmead
SOUTHAMPTON
Sholing
Manor Farm
Curdridge
Worlds End
Soake
Longdown Activity Farm
Isle of Wight Ferry Terminal
Lower Swanwick
Burridge
North Boarhunt
Marchwood
Netley Abbey
Bursledon
Whiteley
WATERLOOVILLE
New Forest Wildlife Park
Dibden
Netley
Sarisbury
Swanwick
Southwick
Meon Valley
R Test
A34
A303
A343
A3057
A30
A272
A33
A31
A3090
A27
A335
A36
A35
A32
A339
A340
A3010
A334
A3051
A3024
A3025
M3
M27
M271
B3048
B3400
B3051
B3046
B3420
B3049
B3047
B3404
B3040
B3335
B3043
B3354
B3037
B3035
B2177
B2150

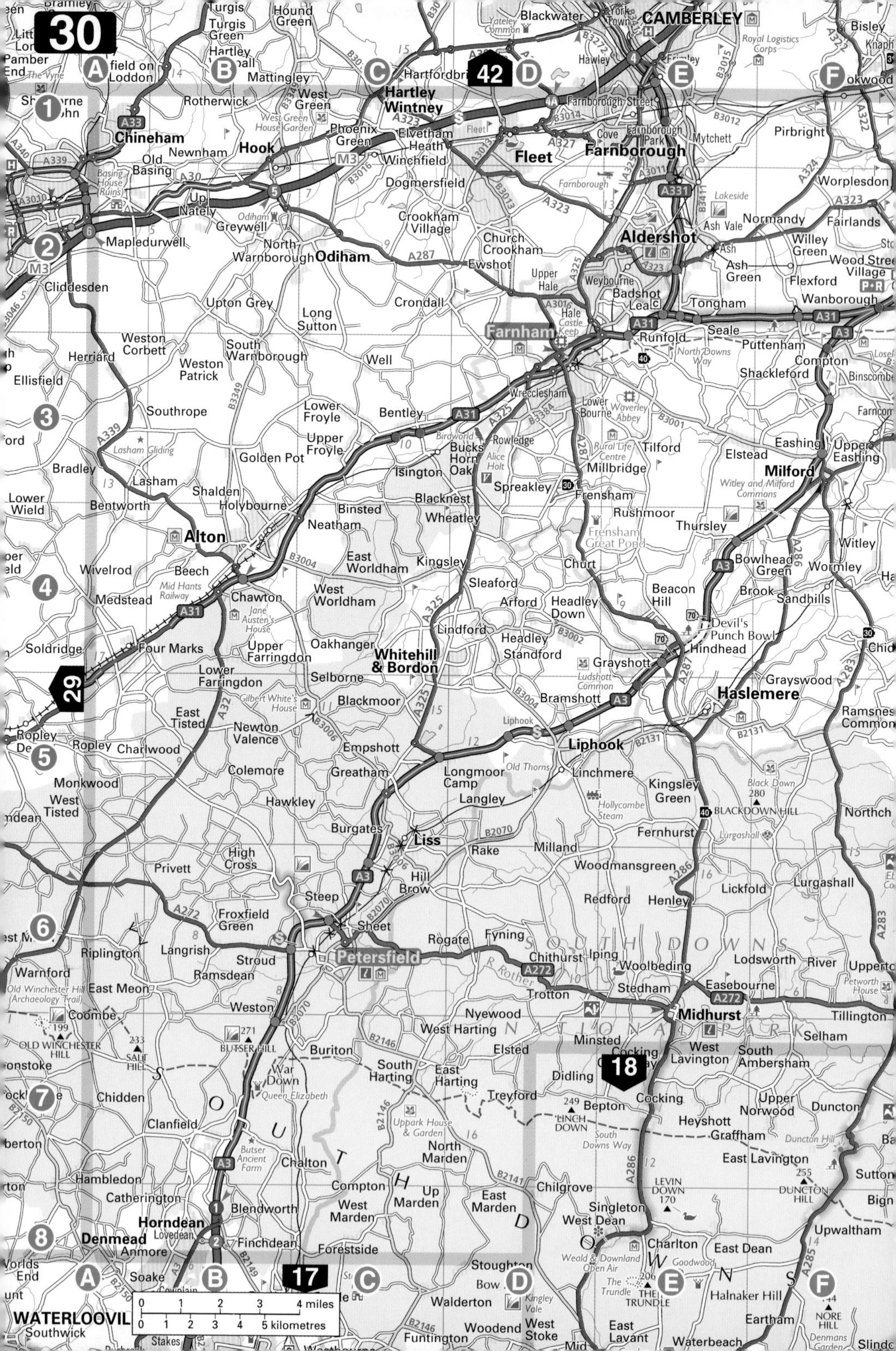
30
A
B
C
D
E
F
42
Turgis Green
Hound Green
Blackwater
York Town
CAMBERLEY
Bisley
Pamber End
The Vyne
Sherborne St John
Stratfield on Loddon
Hartley Wespall
Mattingley
Hartfordbridge
Yateley Common
Hawley
Frimley
Royal Logistics Corps
Pirbright
Rotherwick
West Green
Hartley Wintney
Farnborough Street
Mytchett
Chineham
West Green House Garden
Phoenix Green
Elvetham Heath
Cove
Farnborough Park
Old Basing
Newnham
Hook
Winchfield
Fleet
Farnborough
Basing House (Ruins)
Dogmersfield
Worplesdon
Up Nately
Greywell
Odiham
Crookham Village
Church Crookham
Lakeside
Ash Vale
Normandy
Fairlands
Mapledurwell
North Warnborough
Odiham
Ewshot
Aldershot
Ash
Willey Green
Ash Green
Wood Street Village
Cliddesden
Upper Hale
Weybourne
Flexford
Upton Grey
Long Sutton
Crondall
Badshot Lea
Tongham
Wanborough
Hale
Castle Keep
Farnham
Runfold
Seale
Puttenham
Weston Corbett
South Warnborough
Herriard
Weston Patrick
Well
North Downs Way
Compton
Ellisfield
Shackleford
Wrecclesham
Lower Bourne
Waverley Abbey
Southrope
Lower Froyle
Bentley
Upper Froyle
Birdworld
Bucks Horn Oak
Rowledge
Rural Life Centre
Tilford
Eashing
Upper Eashing
Lasham Gliding
Golden Pot
Alice Holt
Elstead
Bradley
Isington
Millbridge
Milford
Lasham
Spreakley
Witley and Milford Commons
Shalden
Binsted
Blacknest
Frensham
Lower Wield
Bentworth
Holybourne
Neatham
Wheatley
Rushmoor
Thursley
Alton
Frensham Great Pond
Witley
Wivelrod
Beech
East Worldham
Kingsley
Churt
Bowlhead Green
Wormley
Mid Hants Railway
West Worldham
Sleaford
Medstead
Chawton
Arford
Headley Down
Beacon Hill
Brook
Sandhills
Jane Austen's House
Lindford
Devil's Punch Bowl
Soldridge
Four Marks
Upper Farringdon
Oakhanger
Whitehill & Bordon
Headley
Standford
Hindhead
Lower Farringdon
Selborne
Grayshott
Ludshott Common
Grayswood
29
Gilbert White's House
Blackmoor
Bramshott
Haslemere
East Tisted
Liphook
Ramsnest Common
Ropley Dean
Ropley
Newton Valence
Charlwood
Empshott
Liphook
Monkwood
Colemore
Greatham
Longmoor Camp
Old Thorns
Linchmere
Kingsley Green
West Tisted
Black Down
Hawkley
Langley
Hollycombe Steam
BLACKDOWN HILL
Northchapel
Burgates
Liss
Fernhurst
Lurgashall
Rake
Milland
High Cross
Privett
Hill Brow
Woodmansgreen
Lurgashall
Steep
Redford
Henley
Lickfold
Froxfield Green
Sheet
Rogate
Fyning
SOUTH DOWNS
Ripplington
Langrish
Stroud
Petersfield
Chithurst
Iping
Woolbeding
Lodsworth
River
Upperton
Warnford
Ramsdean
Trotton
R. Rother
Stedham
Easebourne
Petworth House
Old Winchester Hill (Archaeology Trail)
East Meon
Weston
Midhurst
Tillington
Coombe
Nyewood
NATIONAL PARK
Selham
OLD WINCHESTER HILL
SALT HILL
BUTSER HILL
West Harting
Minsted
Buriton
Elsted
Cocking Causeway
West Lavington
South Ambersham
War Down
South Harting
East Harting
18
Didling
Queen Elizabeth
Chidden
Treyford
Bepton
Cocking
Upper Norwood
Duncton
LINCH DOWN
Heyshott
Clanfield
Uppark House & Garden
South Downs Way
Graffham
Duncton Hill
Butser Ancient Farm
Chalton
North Marden
East Lavington
Hambledon
Compton
LEVIN DOWN
DUNCTON HILL
Sutton
Catherington
West Marden
Up Marden
East Marden
Chilgrove
Singleton
Blendworth
Horndean
West Dean
Upwaltham
Denmead
Lovedean
Finchdean
Forestside
Charlton
East Dean
Anmore
Weald & Downland Open Air
Goodwood
17
Stoughton
Bow Hill
Soake
The Trundle
THE TRUNDLE
Halnaker Hill
Walderton
Kingley Vale
WATERLOOVILLE
Southwick
Woodend
West Stoke
East Lavant
Eartham
NORE HILL
Denmans Garden
Funtington
Waterbeach
0 1 2 3 4 miles
0 1 2 3 4 5 kilometres

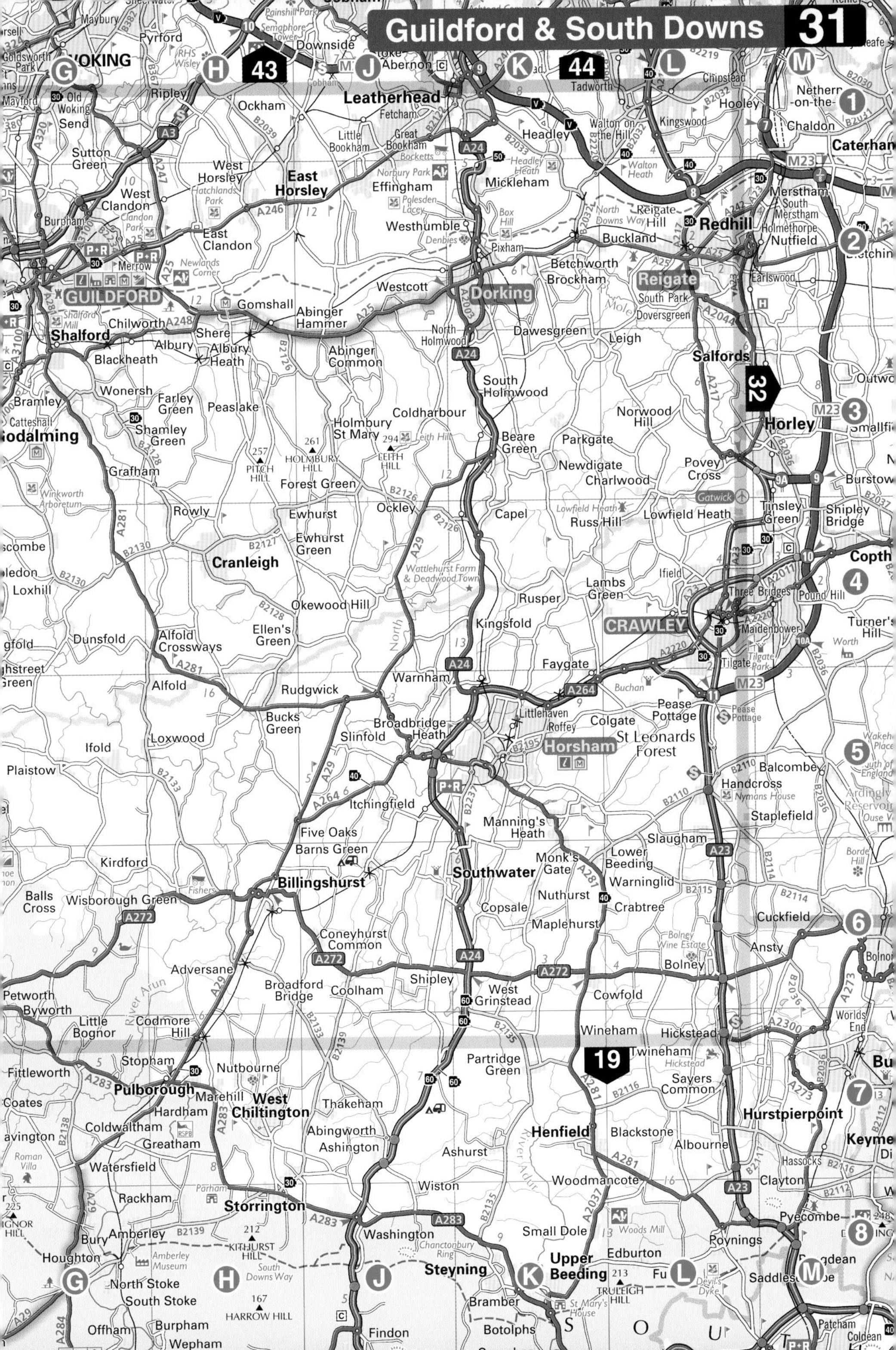

Guildford & South Downs
31
43
44
32
19
WOKING
Pyrford
Ripley
Send
Old Woking
Sutton Green
Ockham
Downside
Stoke Abernon
Cobham
Leatherhead
Fetcham
Little Bookham
Great Bookham
Tadworth
Walton on the Hill
Kingswood
Chipstead
Hooley
Netherne-on-the-Hill
Chaldon
Caterham
Headley
Mickleham
West Horsley
East Horsley
West Clandon
East Clandon
Burpham
Merrow
Effingham
Polesden Lacey
Westhumble
Box Hill
Pixham
Buckland
Reigate Hill
Redhill
Merstham
South Merstham
Nutfield
Earlswood
Betchworth
Brockham
Reigate
South Park
Doversgreen
GUILDFORD
Gomshall
Abinger Hammer
Westcott
Dorking
North Holmwood
Dawesgreen
Leigh
Salfords
Shalford
Chilworth
Albury
Shere
Albury Heath
Blackheath
Abinger Common
South Holmwood
Bramley
Wonersh
Farley Green
Peaslake
Shamley Green
Catteshall
Godalming
Coldharbour
Holmbury St Mary
Leith Hill
Beare Green
Parkgate
Norwood Hill
Horley
Newdigate
Charlwood
Povey Cross
Grafham
Pitch Hill
Holmbury Hill
Forest Green
Winkworth Arboretum
Ockley
Capel
Lowfield Heath
Russ Hill
Gatwick
Tinsley Green
Burstow
Shipley Bridge
Rowly
Ewhurst
Ewhurst Green
Cranleigh
Loxhill
Dunsfold
Okewood Hill
Wattlehurst Farm & Deadwood Town
Rusper
Lambs Green
Ifield
Three Bridges
Pound Hill
CRAWLEY
Maidenbower
Turner's Hill
Worth
Alfold Crossways
Ellen's Green
Kingsfold
Faygate
Tilgate
Tilgate Park
Alfold
Rudgwick
Warnham
Buchan
Pease Pottage
Loxwood
Bucks Green
Broadbridge Heath
Slinfold
Littlehaven
Roffey
Colgate
Horsham
St Leonards Forest
Ifold
Plaistow
Itchingfield
Balcombe
Handcross
Nymans House
Staplefield
Ardingly Reservoir
Five Oaks
Barns Green
Manning's Heath
Slaugham
Kirdford
Billingshurst
Southwater
Monk's Gate
Lower Beeding
Warninglid
Balls Cross
Wisborough Green
Fishers
Nuthurst
Crabtree
Copsale
Maplehurst
Cuckfield
Coneyhurst Common
Bolney Wine Estate
Ansty
Bolney
Adversane
Shipley
Broadford Bridge
Coolham
West Grinstead
Cowfold
Petworth
Byworth
Little Bognor
Codmore Hill
Wineham
Hickstead
Worlds End
Fittleworth
Stopham
Nutbourne
Partridge Green
Twineham
Sayers Common
Pulborough
Marehill
West Chiltington
Thakeham
Hurstpierpoint
Coates
Hardham
Coldwaltham
Abingworth
Ashington
Henfield
Blackstone
Albourne
Greatham
Watersfield
Ashurst
Woodmancote
Hassocks
Clayton
Roman Villa
Rackham
Parham
Wiston
Storrington
Washington
Pyecombe
Small Dole
Woods Mill
Poynings
Amberley
Bury
Kithurst Hill
Chanctonbury Ring
Edburton
Houghton
Amberley Museum
South Downs Way
Steyning
Upper Beeding
Truleigh Hill
Devil's Dyke
Saddlescombe
North Stoke
South Stoke
Harrow Hill
Bramber
St Mary's House
Offham
Burpham
Wepham
Findon
Botolphs
Patcham
Coldean

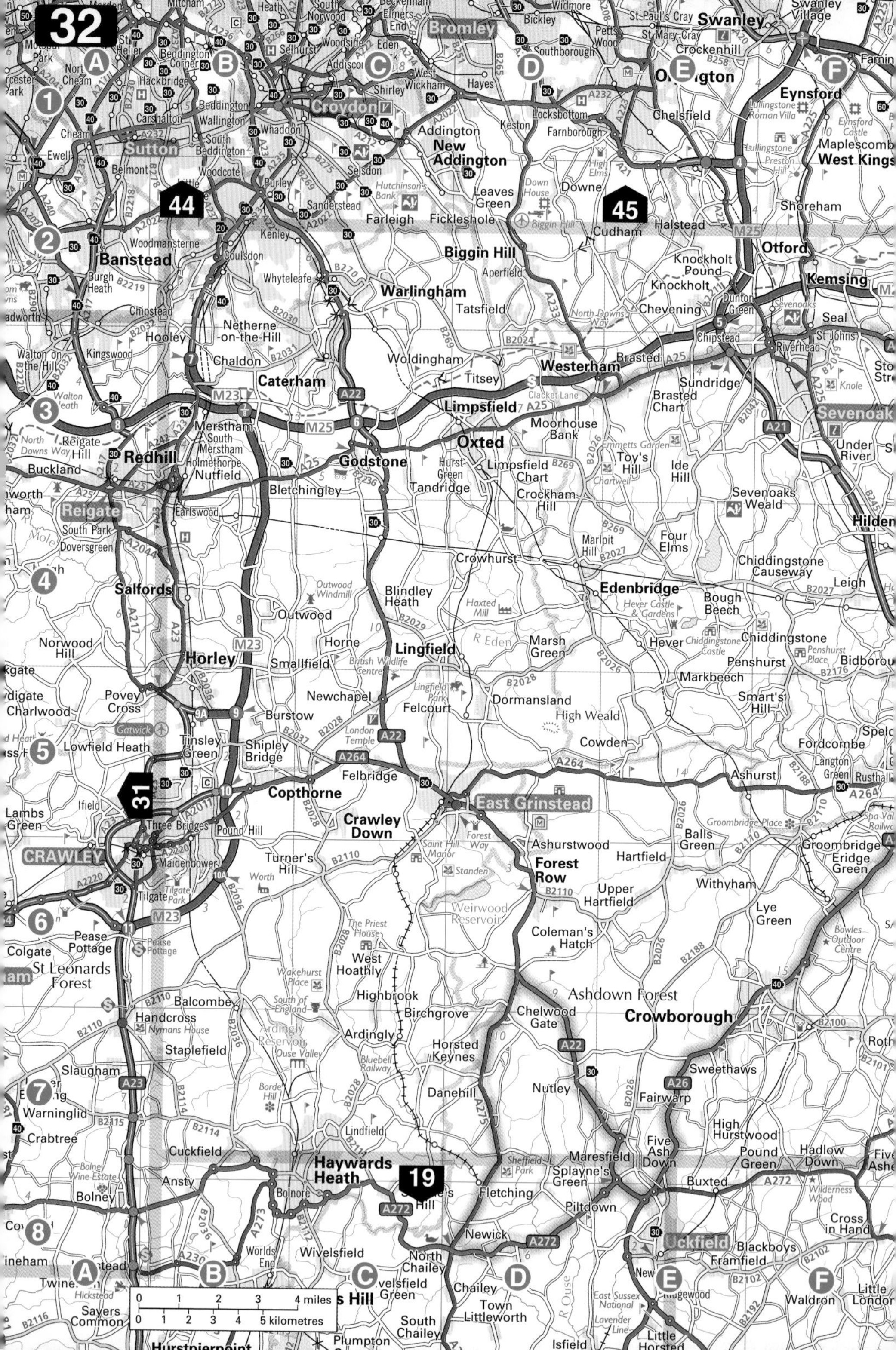
32
Mitcham
Morden
Motspur Park
North Cheam
Worcester Park
Cheam
Ewell
Sutton
Belmont
St Helier
Beddington Corner
Hackbridge
Carshalton
Beddington
Wallington
South Beddington
Woodcote
Heath
South Norwood
Norwood
Selhurst
Woodside
Addiscombe
Croydon
Shirley
West Wickham
Elmers End
Eden Park
Beckenham
Bromley
Hayes
Bickley
Widmore
Petts Wood
Southborough
St Paul's Cray
St Mary Cray
Swanley
Swanley Village
Crockenhill
Orpington
Eynsford
Lullingstone Roman Villa
Eynsford Castle
Lullingstone
Maplescombe
West Kingsdown
Farningham
Chelsfield
Locksbottom
Farnborough
Keston
Addington
New Addington
Whaddon
Selsdon
Purley
Sanderstead
Hutchinson's Bank
Farleigh
Fickleshole
Leaves Green
Down House
Downe
High Elms
Biggin Hill
Cudham
Halstead
Shoreham
Preston Hill
Otford
Knockholt Pound
Knockholt
Kemsing
Dunton Green
Chevening
Chipstead
Riverhead
Sevenoaks
Seal
St Johns
Knole
Sevenoaks
Under River
Sevenoaks Weald
Hildenborough
44
45
Banstead
Woodmansterne
Coulsdon
Kenley
Whyteleafe
Warlingham
Aperfield
Tatsfield
Burgh Heath
Chipstead
Hooley
Netherne-on-the-Hill
Kingswood
Walton on the Hill
Walton Heath
Chaldon
Caterham
Woldingham
Titsey
Westerham
Brasted
Sundridge
Brasted Chart
North Downs Way
Clacket Lane
Limpsfield
Oxted
Moorhouse Bank
Merstham
South Merstham
Reigate Hill
Redhill
Holmethorpe
Nutfield
Godstone
Bletchingley
Hurst Green
Tandridge
Limpsfield Chart
Crockham Hill
Emmetts Garden
Toy's Hill
Chartwell
Ide Hill
Buckland
Reigate
South Park
Doversgreen
Earlswood
Salfords
Outwood
Outwood Windmill
Blindley Heath
Crowhurst
Marlpit Hill
Four Elms
Edenbridge
Hever Castle & Gardens
Bough Beech
Chiddingstone Causeway
Leigh
Haxted Mill
R Eden
Hever
Chiddingstone Castle
Chiddingstone
Penshurst Place
Penshurst
Bidborough
Norwood Hill
Horne
Lingfield
Marsh Green
Horley
Smallfield
British Wildlife Centre
Newchapel
Lingfield Park
Felcourt
Dormansland
High Weald
Markbeech
Smart's Hill
Charlwood
Povey Cross
Burstow
Gatwick
Lowfield Heath
Tinsley Green
Shipley Bridge
London Temple
Felbridge
Cowden
Fordcombe
Langton Green
Rusthall
Speldhurst
Ashurst
Ifield
Lambs Green
31
Three Bridges
Pound Hill
Copthorne
Crawley Down
East Grinstead
Ashurstwood
Forest Row
Hartfield
Balls Green
Groombridge Place
Groombridge
Eridge Green
Withyham
CRAWLEY
Maidenbower
Turner's Hill
Saint Hill Manor
Forest Way
Standen
Weirwood Reservoir
Upper Hartfield
Coleman's Hatch
Lye Green
Bowles Outdoor Centre
Worth
Tilgate
Tilgate Park
Pease Pottage
Colgate
St Leonards Forest
The Priest House
West Hoathly
Wakehurst Place
Highbrook
Ashdown Forest
Crowborough
Balcombe
Handcross
Nymans House
South of England
Birchgrove
Chelwood Gate
Ardingly
Ardingly Reservoir
Ouse Valley
Staplefield
Slaugham
Bluebell Railway
Horsted Keynes
Sweethaws
Warninglid
Crabtree
Borde Hill
Danehill
Nutley
Fairwarp
High Hurstwood
Cuckfield
Lindfield
Five Ash Down
Pound Green
Hadlow Down
Bolney Wine Estate
Ansty
Bolney
Haywards Heath
19
Sheffield Park
Maresfield
Splayne's Green
Fletching
Buxted
Wilderness Wood
Bolnore
Piltdown
Newick
Cross in Hand
Blackboys
Uckfield
Framfield
Worlds End
Wivelsfield
North Chailey
Chailey
Twineham
Hickstead
Sayers Common
Wivelsfield Green
Town Littleworth
South Chailey
Plumpton
Hurstpierpoint
East Sussex National
Lavender Line
R Ouse
Isfield
Little Horsted
Ridgewood
Waldron
Little London
0 1 2 3 4 miles
0 1 2 3 4 5 kilometres
M25
M23
A22
A25
A264
A272
A23
A26
A21
A2022
A217
A232
A233
B2110
B2026
B2028
B2036

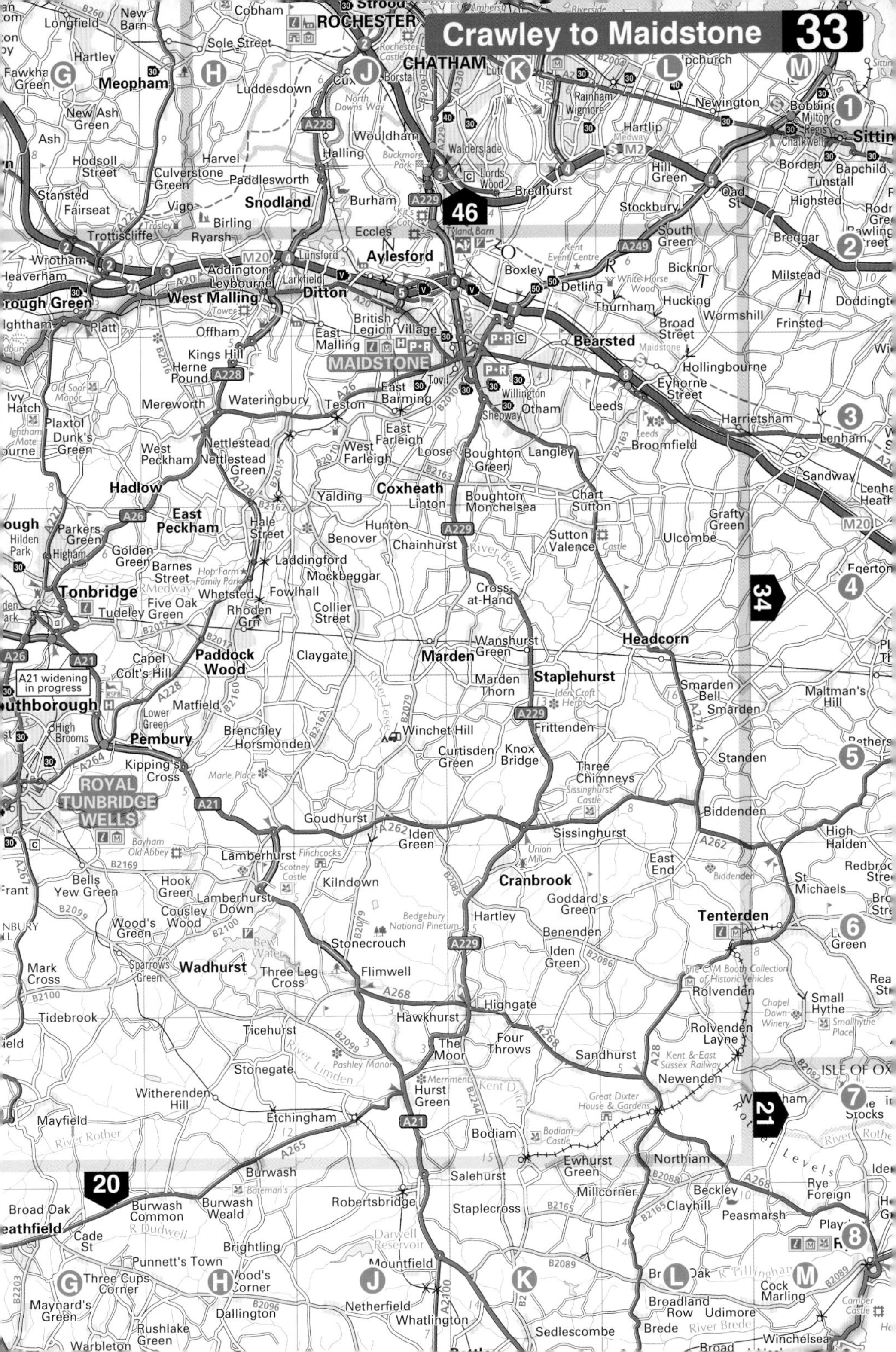
ROCHESTER
CHATHAM
MAIDSTONE
ROYAL TUNBRIDGE WELLS
Tonbridge
Aylesford
Snodland
West Malling
Bearsted
Headcorn
Staplehurst
Marden
Paddock Wood
Pembury
Cranbrook
Tenterden
Hawkhurst
Wadhurst
Goudhurst
Lamberhurst
Coxheath
Hadlow
East Peckham
Meopham
Ditton
Southborough
Heathfield
A21 widening in progress
46
34
21
20

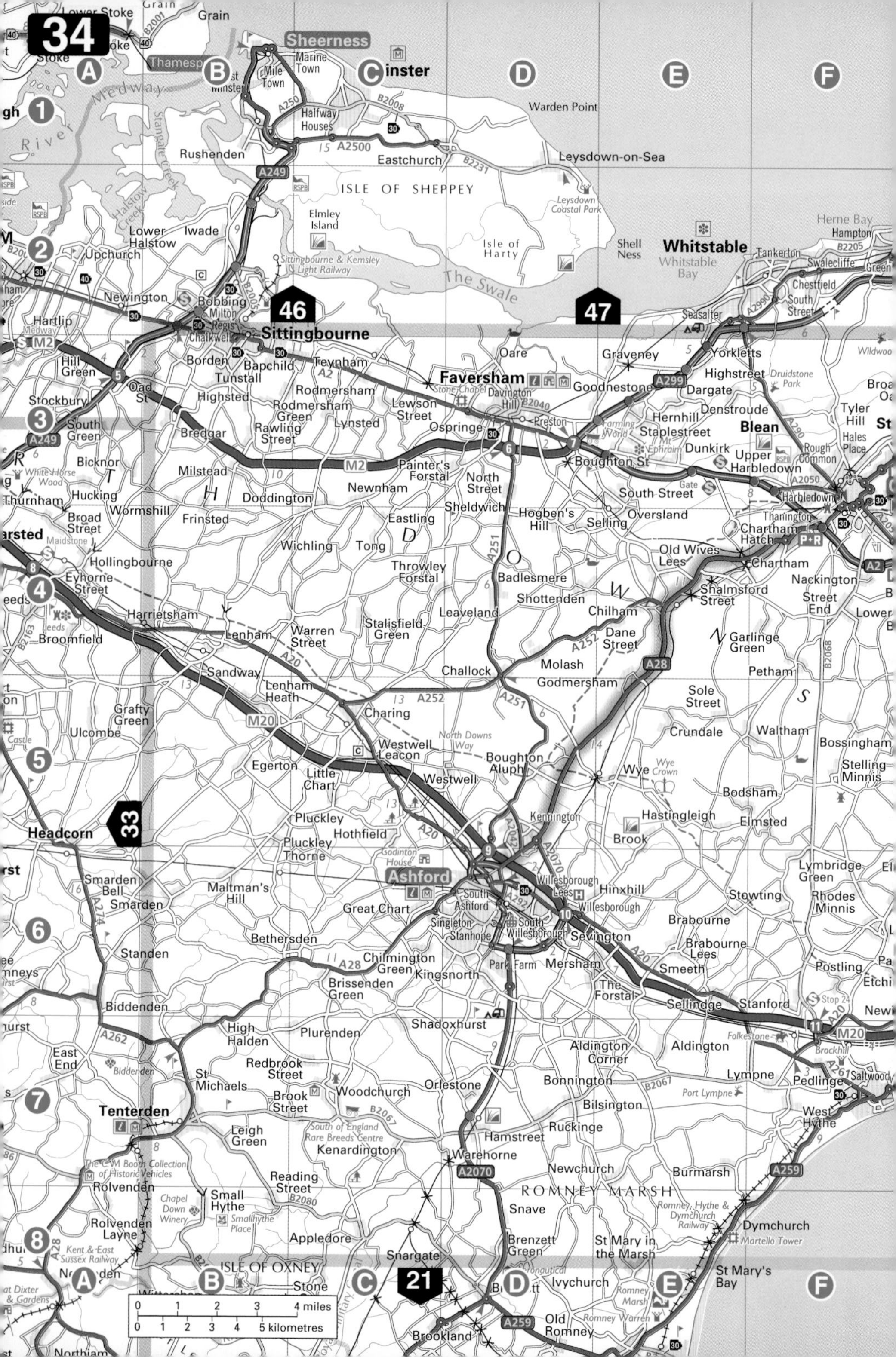

34
Lower Stoke
Grain
Stoke
Thamesport
Sheerness
Marine Town
Mile Town
Minster
A
B
C
D
E
F
1
River Medway
Stangate Creek
Halfway Houses
A250
B2008
A2500
Warden Point
Rushenden
Eastchurch
B2231
Leysdown-on-Sea
A249
ISLE OF SHEPPEY
Leysdown Coastal Park
Elmley Island
Isle of Harty
Halstow Creek
Lower Halstow
Iwade
Herne Bay
Hampton
2
Upchurch
Sittingbourne & Kemsley Light Railway
Shell Ness
Whitstable
Whitstable Bay
Tankerton
B2205
Swalecliffe
Chestfield
South Street
The Swale
Newington
Bobbing
Milton Regis
46
47
Hartlip
Chalkwell
Sittingbourne
Seasalter
A2990
M2
Hill Green
Borden
Bapchild
Teynham
A2
Oare
Graveney
Yorkletts
Wildwood
Oad St
Tunstall
Highsted
Rodmersham
Rodmersham Green
Faversham
Stone Chapel
Davington Hill
B2040
Goodnestone
A299
Highstreet
Dargate
Druidstone Park
Stockbury
Lewson Street
Lynsted
Hernhill
Denstroude
Tyler Hill
3
South Green
Bredgar
Rawling Street
Ospringe
Preston
Farming World
Staplestreet
Mt Ephraim
Dunkirk
Blean
Hales Place
A249
Bicknor
Milstead
Painter's Forstal
North Street
Boughton St
Upper Harbledown
Rough Common
White Horse Wood
Hucking
Newnham
Gate
South Street
A2050
Harbledown
Thurnham
Broad Street
Wormshill
Doddington
Sheldwich
Hogben's Hill
Selling
Oversland
Thanington
Frinsted
Eastling
Chartham Hatch
P+R
Bearsted
Maidstone
Wichling
Tong
A251
Old Wives Lees
Chartham
Hollingbourne
Throwley Forstal
Badlesmere
A2
8
Eyhorne Street
Shottenden
Shalmsford Street
Nackington
4
Leeds
Harrietsham
Leaveland
Chilham
Street End
Lower
B2163
Broomfield
Lenham
Warren Street
Stalisfield Green
Dane Street
A252
Garlinge Green
A20
Molash
A28
Petham
Challock
Godmersham
Sandway
Lenham Heath
A252
Charing
A251
Sole Street
B2068
Grafty Green
M20
Crundale
Waltham
Ulcombe
Castle
North Downs Way
Bossingham
Westwell Leacon
Boughton Aluph
Wye
Wye Crown
Stelling Minnis
5
Egerton
Little Chart
Westwell
Bodsham
Pluckley
Kennington
Hastingleigh
Headcorn
33
Hothfield
A2042
A2070
Brook
Elmsted
Pluckley Thorne
Godinton House
Lymbridge Green
Smarden Bell
Maltman's Hill
Ashford
Willesborough Lees
Hinxhill
Stowting
Rhodes Minnis
Smarden
A274
South Ashford
A292
Willesborough
Great Chart
Singleton
Stanhope
South Willesborough
Sevington
Brabourne
6
Bethersden
Brabourne Lees
Standen
Chilmington Green
Park Farm
Mersham
Smeeth
Postling
A28
Kingsnorth
A20
Brissenden Green
The Forstal
Sellindge
Stanford
Stop 24
Biddenden
Shadoxhurst
High Halden
Plurenden
Folkestone
M20
A262
Aldington Corner
Aldington
Brockhill
East End
Biddenden
Redbrook Street
St Michaels
Orlestone
Bonnington
B2067
Lympne
Pedlinge
Saltwood
A261
Port Lympne
7
Brook Street
Woodchurch
B2067
Bilsington
West Hythe
Tenterden
South of England Rare Breeds Centre
Hamstreet
Ruckinge
Leigh Green
Kenardington
Warehorne
The C.M Booth Collection of Historic Vehicles
Reading Street
Newchurch
Burmarsh
A259
A2070
Rolvenden
Chapel Down Winery
Small Hythe
Smallhythe Place
B2080
ROMNEY MARSH
Snave
Romney, Hythe & Dymchurch Railway
Dymchurch
Rolvenden Layne
Appledore
Brenzett Green
St Mary in the Marsh
Martello Tower
8
Kent & East Sussex Railway
A28
Snargate
ISLE OF OXNEY
St Mary's Bay
21
Stone
Ivychurch
Romney Marsh
Great Dixter House & Gardens
A259
Old Romney
Romney Warren
Brookland
Northiam
0
1
2
3
4 miles
5 kilometres

G
H
J
K
L
M
1
2
3
4
5
6
7
8
Foreness Point
MARGATE
Cliftonville
Kingsgate
NORTH FORELAND
Lighthouse
Westgate on Sea
Westbrook
Northdown
Reading Street
Minnis Bay
Herne Bay
Reculver Towers & Roman Fort
Reculver
Bishopstone
Beltinge
Birchington
Garlinge
Hornby
Westwood
St Peter's
Broadstairs
ISLE OF THANET
Lydden
Acol
RAF Manston
Dumpton
Hereson
Broomfield
St Nicholas at Wade
Herne
Boyden Gate
Sarre
Manston
Monkton
St Lawrence
Ramsgate
Chislet
Durlock
Minster
Pegwell
Viking Ship 'Hugin'
St Augustine's Cross
Hoath
Upstreet
West Stourmouth
R Stour
Pegwell Bay
Hersden
East Stourmouth
Westmarsh
Richborough Roman Fort
Westbere
Stodmarsh
Preston
Elmstone
Cop Street
Sandwich Bay
Hoaden
Town Hall
Fordwich
Wickhambreaux
Littlebourne
Wingham
Seaton
Ash
Sandwich
Royal St Georges
Canterbury
Ickham
Durlock
Wingham
Marshborough
Stone Cross
Toll
Howletts
Bramling
Woodnesborough
Bekesbourne
Staple
Statenborough
Worth
Goodnestone
Eastry
Patrixbourne
Ham
Hacklinge
Adisham
Ratling
Chillenden
Finglesham
Fowlmead
Sholden
The Downs
Aylesham
Nonington
Betteshanger
Northbourne
Deal
North Downs Way
Kingston
Tilmanstone
Great Mongeham
Upper Deal
Womenswold
Elvington
Barham
Plant Centre
Ripple
Walmer
Castle
Lower Eythorne
Barfrestone
Eythorne
Sutton
Derringstone
Woolage Green
East Kent Railway
East Studdal
Ringwould
Shepherdswell
Ashley
Sutton Downs
Kingsdown
North Downs Way
West Langdon
Martin
Denton
Lydden Hill
Coldred
Wootton
Lydden
Whitfield
East Langdon
St Margaret's at Cliffe
Selsted
Guston
St Margaret's Bay
Ewell Minnis
Kearsney
West Cliffe
The Pines
SOUTH FORELAND
Swingfield Minnis
Swingfield Street
River
Lighthouse
South Foreland Heritage Coast
World of Butterflies
Buckland
Castle
The White Cliffs of Dover
Densole
Alkham
St Radigunds
South Alkham
Maxton
Dunkirk
Calais
Hawkinge
Upper Standen
Drellingore
West Hougham
DOVER
Lower Standen
Channel Tunnel Terminal
Battle of Britain
Capel-le-Ferne
Peene
Samphire Hoe
Dover - Folkestone Heritage Coast
Channel Tunnel (Rail)
Cheriton
Morehall
East Wear Bay
FOLKESTONE
Sandgate
Seabrook
Hythe
STRAIT OF DOVER
A299
A28
A253
A256
A257
A258
A2
A20
A260
A259
A291
A255
B2051
B2052
B2050
B2190
B2046
B2011

Craig Llangiwg
Cilybebyll
Gellinudd
Crynant
Blaengwrach
Hirwaun
Penywaun
Llwydcoed
Aber-nant
Cwmdare
Trecynon
Aberdare
(Aberdâr)
Alltwen
Mynydd March Hywel
Vale of Neath
River Neath
River Dulais
383
RESOLVEN MOUNTAIN
Resolven
Melin Cwrt Waterfalls
600
CRAIG-Y-LLYN
Mynydd Ystradffernol
Aberaman
Cwmaman
Abercwmboi
Cilfrew
Clyne
493
MOEL-YR HYRDDAD
Blaenrhondda
Glais
Bryn-côch
Cadoxton
Juxta-Neath
Aberdulais
Tin Works and Waterfall
Birchgrove
Llansamlet
Tonna
Cefn Mawr
Glyncorrwg
Treherbert
Rhondda Valley
Maerdy
478
Neath
(Castell-nedd)
Cefn Morfydd
Afan Forest Park
Blaengwynfi
Treorchy
Ferndale
Winsh-wen
Abercregan
Cymer
Abergwynfi
Cwmparc
Pentre
Ystrad
Cimla
Tonmawr
Duffryn
Cynonville
Efail-fach
Pont-rhyd-y-fen
Afan Forest Park
Croeserw
Caerau
556
MYNYDD CAERAU
571
WERFA
Tylorstown
Pentre-chwyth
Crymlyn Bog
Briton Ferry
FOEL MYNYDDAU
371
371
MOEL TRAWSNANT
Clydach Vale
Llwynypia
Trealaw
Nant-y-moel
Pwll-y-glaw
Baglan
Blaengarw
Swansea Bay
Bryn
Cwmafan
Pontycymer
Mynydd Llangeinwyr
Cricklepit Mill
Tonypandy
Penygraig
Maesteg
Glanllynfi
Aberavon
Port Talbot
Mynydd Margam
Cwmfelin
Ogmore Vale
Gilfach Goch
Taibach
Llangynwyd
Lewistown
Stones Museum
321
MOEL TON-MAWR
Llangeinor
Betws
Margam
Blackmill
Coytrahen
Bryngarw
Brynmenyn
Mynydd Maendy
Tondu
Heol-y-Cyw
Brynna Woods
Afon Kenfig
Cefn Cribwr
Aberkenfig
Sarn Park
Pant-ffrwyth
Brynna
Llanharan
Pyle
(Y-Pil)
Mawdlam
North Cornelly
Bridgend
(Pen-y-Bont-ar-Ogwr)
Castle
Coity
Pencoed
Llanilid
Llanharry
Brynsadler
Kenfig
South Cornelly
Laleston
Coychurch
Rest Bay
Nottage
NEWTON DOWN
Tythegston
Merthyr Mawr
Candleston
Ogmore Castle
Treoes
Llangan
Ystradowen
Trerhyngyll
Porthcawl
Newton
Porthcawl Point
Ogmore
Ewenny
Corntown
Penllyn
Maendy
St Bride's Major
Colwinston
Pentre Meyrick
St Quentin's Castle
Aberthin
Ogmore-by-Sea
Llysworney
Cowbridge
Southerndown
Llandow
Llanblethian
Llandough
St Hilary
Old Beaupre Castle
Wick
Sigingstone
St Mary Church
Broughton
Flemingston
Monknash
Llanmaes
Marcross
St Donats
Llantwit Major
(Llanilltud Fawr)
St Athan
Nash Point
Gileston
Glamorgan Heritage Coast
Cwm Colhuw
Limpert Bay
Aberthaw
Breaksea Point
51
52
0 1 2 3 4 miles
0 1 2 3 4 5 kilometres

(Merthyr Tudful)
Pentrebach
Abercanaid
Pennar
Troedyrhiw
Tirphil
New Tredegar
Manmoel
Abertillery
(Abertyleri)
Monkswood
Usk
(Brynbuga)
Mynydd Merthyr
Deri
Bedlinog
Brithdir
Markham
Pen-y-fan Pond
Llanhilleth
Pontypool
(Pont-y-Pŵl)
Llandegfedd Reservoir
Aberfan
Cwmfelin
Bedwellty
Argoed
Llanbadoc
Merthyr Vale
Bargoed
(Bargod)
Griffithstown
New Inn
Llanllowell
Ash
Gilfach
Llancaiach Fawr
Oakdale
Crumlin
Coed-y-paen
Treharris
Pengam
Penmaen
Mynydd Maen
Llangybi
Trelewis
Gelligaer
Blackwood
Newbridge
Pontllanfraith
Greenmeadow Community Farm
Pontnewydd
Croesyceiliog
Llandegveth
Ynysboeth
Nelson
Pentwynmawr
Forge Hammer
Hengoed
Maesycwmmer
Abercarn
Cwmbran
(Cwmbrân)
Tredunnock
Abercynon
Ynysybwl
Ystrad Mynach
Mynydd Lan
Cwmcarn
Cwmcarn Forest Drive
Llantarnam
Llanfrechfa
Ynysddu
Pontywaun
Ponthir
Llanhennock
Rhondda Heritage Park
Cilfynydd
Mynydd Eglwysilan
Senghenydd
Crosskeys
Caerleon
Cwmfelinfach
Risca
Henllys
Trehafod
Wattsville
Malpas
Celtic Manor
Llanbradach
Machen
Bettws
Pontypridd
Abertridwr
Bedwas
Castle
Maindee
Christchurch
Trefforest
Lower Machen
Cefn
Rhymney
Rogerstone
Groes-Wen
Pen-y-coedcae
Llantwit Fardre
Caerphilly
(Caerffili)
Draethen
Bassaleg
Rhiwderyn
Liswerry
Llanwern
Rudry
Transporter Bridge
NEWPORT
(CASNEWYDD-AR-WYSG)
Church Village
Beddau
Tyn-y-nant
Michaelstone-y-Fedw
Tredegar House
Efail Isaf
Parc Cefn Onn
Llantrisant
Castell Coch
Lisvane
Nash
Goldcliff
Taff's Well
Cardiff Gate
Solutia
Castleton
Creigiau
Pentyrch
Tongwynlais
Rhiwbina
Llanishen
Llanedeyrn
Marshfield
St Brides Wentlooge
Groes-faen
St Mellons
Miskin
Radyr
Whitchurch
Birchgrove
Llanrumney
Cardiff West
Rumney
CARDIFF
Peterstone Wentlooge
Taff
Llandaff
Pengam
Roath
Clawdd-coch
St Fagans
Fairwater
National History
St Brides-super-Ely
Pendoylan
River Ely
Ely
Canton
Splottlands
Peterston-super-Ely
St George's
Caerau
CARDIFF
(CAERDYDD)
St Nicholas
SEVERN ESTUARY
Michaelston-le-Pit
Wales Millennium Centre
Bonvilston
Tinkinswood
Llandough
Llantrithyd
St Lythans
Wenvoe
Penarth Head
Burial Chamber
St Andrew's Major
Cogan
Penarth
Dinas Powys
Lower Penarth
Cosmeston Lakes & Medieval Village
Moulton
Penmark
Welsh Hawking Centre
Cadoxton
Lavernock
Woodspring Bay
Lavernock Point
Sully
Barry
(Y Barri)
Sand Point
Wick St Lawrence
Cardiff
Sully Island
Porthkerry
Barry Island
Rhoose
Cold Knap Point
Flat Holm
Sand Bay
Kewstoke
St Georges
Worle
Milton
Toll
Ashcombe
Steep Holm
WESTON-SUPER-MARE
Locking
Hutton
Brean Down
Uphill
Tropical Bird Garden
Oldmixon
Bleadon
Walborough
Brean
Loxton
Lympsham
Edingworth
Biddisham
Sedgemoor
Clevedon
A470
A4054
A4059
A472
A4049
A467
A4042
A4051
A469
A468
A4232
A48
A48(M)
A4119
A4160
A4055
A4226
A4231
A4050
A4161
A370
A371
A4046
A4048
B4251
B4591
B4236
B4596
B4562
B4239
B4273
B4595
B4263
B4600
B4623
B4262
B4267
B4487
B4254
B4255
B4511
B4471
B4598
B3440
B4261
M4
53
38
25
G
H
J
K
L
M
1
2
3
4
5
6
7
8

38
Llandenny
Wye Valley
Llanishen
Llansoy
Forest Park
St Briavels
Bream
Allaston
Lydney
Sharpness
Llandogo
Offa's Dyke Path
Hewelsfield
Aylburton
Brockweir
Tintern Parva
Tintern Abbey
Woolaston Common
Alvington
Gwernesney
Pentre
Wolvesnewton
Usk
(Brynbuga)
Usk Rural Life
Llangwm
Springdale Farm
Llanbadoc
Llanllowell
Kilgwrrwg Common
Devauden
Chapel Hill
54
Netherend
Woolaston
Berkeley
Coed-y-paen
Newchurch
Stroat
Llangybi
Gaerllwyd
Itton Common
St Arvans
Llantrisant
Woodcroft
A48
Tidenham
Tutshill
Sedbury
Itton
Mynydd-bach
Tredunnock
A449
Llanfrechfa
Llanhennock
Llanvair Discoed
Shirenewton
Mounton
Port Wall
Chepstow
(Cas-gwent)
River Severn
Oldbury-on-Severn
Rockhampton
Lower Morton
Hill
Parc Seymour
Pwllmeyric
Bulwarks Camp
Caerleon
Runston Chapel
Llanvaches
Newton Green
Cowhill
Kington
Milbury Heath
Penhow
Caerwent
Mathern
M48
Severn Bridge
Littleton-on-Severn
Thornbury
Llanbeder
Celtic Manor
Llandevaud
St Pierre
Caldicot
(Cil-y-coed)
Severn View
Elberton
Roman Town
Llanmartin
Bishton
Magor
Llanfihangel Rogiet
Portskewett
Aust
Alveston
Christchurch
Rogiet
Ifton
M4
Toll
Ingst
A403
Olveston
Liswerry
Llanwern
Llandevenny
Sudbrook
Redwick
Tockington
Rudgeway
NEWPORT
(CASNEWYDD-AR-WYSG)
A4810
Transporter Bridge
Magor Marsh
Undy
Second Severn Crossing
Severn Beach
Pilning
Almondsbury
Nash
Goldcliff
Whitson
Redwick
Latteridge
Iron Acton
Easter Compton
Compton Greenfield
Frampton Cotterell
SEVERN ESTUARY
Wild Place
Patchway
Bradley Stoke
Great Stoke
Winterbourne
Cribbs Causeway
Hallen
M49
Filton
Stoke Gifford
A403
Battery Point
Avonmouth
Kings Weston
Blaise Hamlet
Shirehampton
Westbury-on-Trym
Horfield
Frenchay
Downend
37
Portishead
P+R
A4
BRISTOL
M32
Mangotsfield
A369
Portbury
Gordano
Redland
Fishponds
Soundwell
Weston-in-Gordano
Clapton-in-Gordano
Easton-in-Gordano
Abbots Leigh
Eastville
Walton-in-Gordano
Clifton
Warmley
Noah's Ark
Lower Failand
Failand
Leigh Woods
Kingswood
Hanham
Walton Park
Clevedon Court
M5
Cadbury Camp
Tyntesfield
Ashton Court
Oldland
Clevedon
Tickenham
Wraxall
Bedminster
Nailsea
Long Ashton
Brislington
Knowle
Flax Bourton
Bedminster Down
R Kenn
Kenn
West End
Chelvey
Farleigh
Backwell
Bishopsworth
Stockwood
Keynsham
Woodspring Bay
Kingston Seymour
West Town
Barrow Gurney
A38
Withywood
Queen Charlton
Wick St Lawrence
Claverham
Brockley
Dundry
East Dundry
Whitchurch
Maes Knoll
Lulsgate Bottom
Upper Town
Maiden Head
Chewton Keynsham
Yatton
Cleeve
Felton
Norton Malreward
West Hewish
Congresbury
R Yeo
Winford
Norton Hawkfield
Kewstoke
St Georges
Worle
Puxton
Chew Magna
Belluton
Publow
Compton Dando
Wrington
Redhill
Regil
Stanton Drew
Stone Circle
Pensford
Hunstrete
Butcombe
Stock
Blackmoor
Cowslip Green
Chew Stoke
Stanton Wick
Chelwood
Havyat
A370
Locking
Hutton
Stonebridge
Sandford
Churchill
Lower Langford
Rickford
Blagdon Lake
Nempnett Thrubwell
Chew Valley Lake
Bishop Sutton
Stowey
Clutton Hill
A368
Banwell
Upper Langford
Star
Burrington
Blagdon
North Widcombe
Sutton Wick
Clutton
Farmborough
Timsbury
Oldmixon
Bleadon Hills
Yarborough
Sidcot
Rowberrow
Burrington Combe
Ubley
West Harptree
Temple Cloud
High Littleton
Winscombe
Christon
Shipham
Compton Martin
South Widcombe
Cameley
Hallatrow
Bleadon
King John's Hunting Lodge
26
Hinton Blewett
Farrington Gurney
Paulton
Loxton
Charterhouse
East Harptree
Litton
Midsomer Norton
Sherborne
Cheddar Gorge & Caves
Cheddar Complex
Edingworth
Cheddar Reservoir
Cheddar
Sedgemoor
Badgworth
Weare
Chewton Mendip
Ston Easton
0 1 2 3 4 miles
0 1 2 3 4 5 kilometres

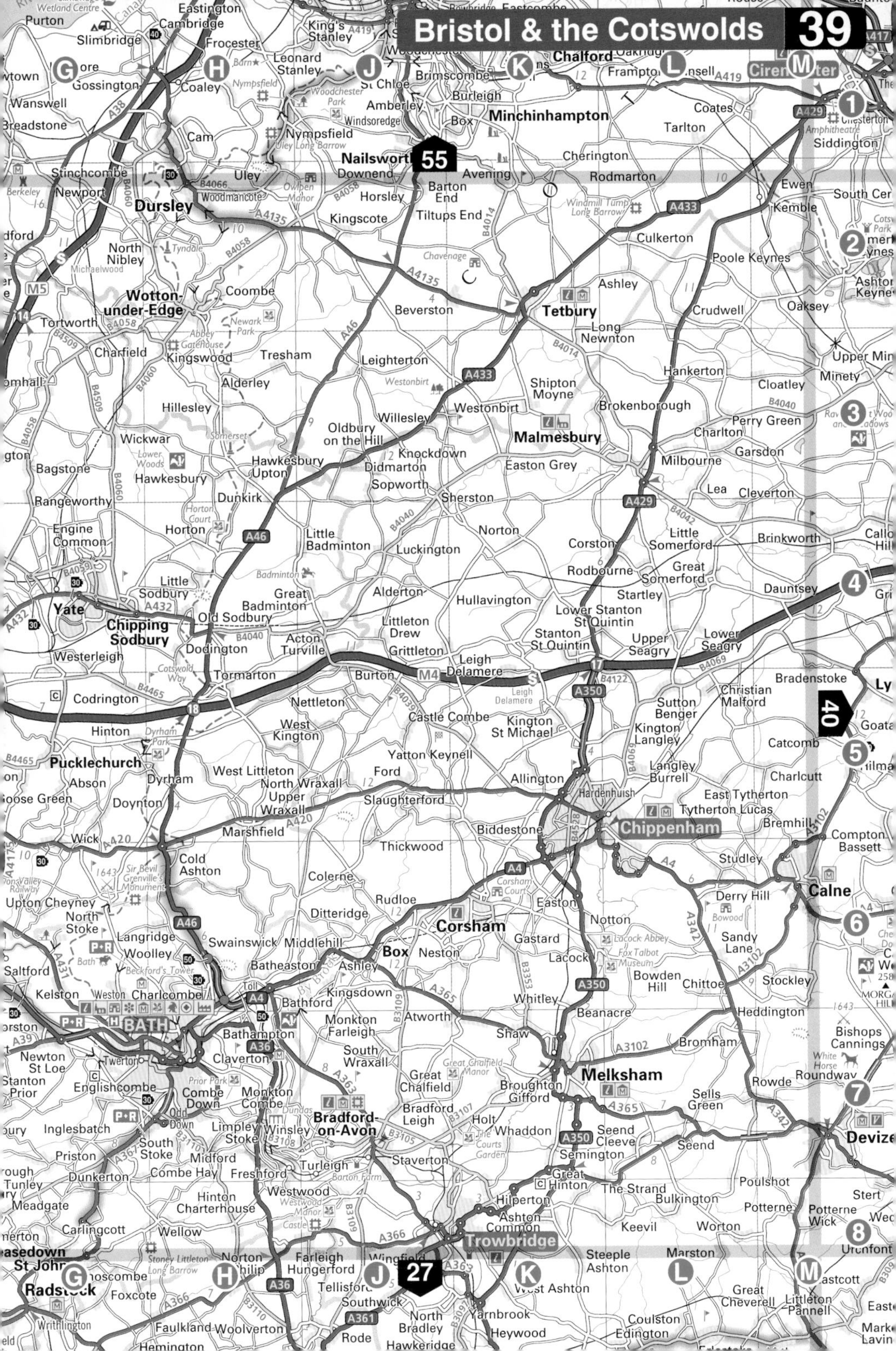

Purton
Slimbridge
Eastington
Cambridge
Frocester
King's Stanley
Leonard Stanley
Chalford
Frampton Mansell
Cirencester
Gore
Gossington
Coaley
Nympsfield
St Chloe
Brimscombe
Woodchester Park
Amberley
Burleigh
Minchinhampton
Coates
Wanswell
Breadstone
Windsoredge
Box
Tarlton
Chesterton
Amphitheatre
Siddington
Cam
Nympsfield
Uley Long Barrow
Nailsworth
55
Cherington
Stinchcombe
Uley
Downend
Avening
Rodmarton
Ewen
Berkeley
Newport
Dursley
B4066
Woodmancote
Owlpen Manor
B4058
Horsley
Barton End
South Cerney
Windmill Tump Long Barrow
A433
Kemble
A4135
Kingscote
Tiltups End
B4014
North Nibley
Tyndale
B4058
Culkerton
Cotswold Water Park
Michaelwood
Chavenage
Poole Keynes
Ashley
Ashton Keynes
M5
Wotton-under-Edge
Coombe
A4135
Tetbury
Crudwell
Oakey
Tortworth
B4058
Newark Park
Beverston
Long Newnton
Abbey Gatehouse
A46
B4014
Upper Minety
B4509
Charfield
Kingswood
Tresham
Leighterton
Hankerton
Minety
A433
Westonbirt
Shipton Moyne
Cloatley
Alderley
B4060
B4040
Hillesley
Willesley
Westonbirt
Brokenborough
Perry Green
B4058
Oldbury on the Hill
Malmesbury
Charlton
Ravensroost Wood and Meadows
Wickwar
Somerset
Knockdown
Garsdon
Lower Woods
Hawkesbury Upton
Didmarton
Easton Grey
Milbourne
Bagstone
Hawkesbury
Sopworth
Lea
Cleverton
Dunkirk
Sherston
Rangeworthy
B4060
Horton Court
A429
B4042
Engine Common
Horton
A46
Little Badminton
B4040
Norton
Little Somerford
Brinkworth
Luckington
Corston
Callow Hill
B4059
Badminton
Great Somerford
Rodbourne
Little Sodbury
Alderton
Startley
Dauntsey
Yate
A432
Great Badminton
Hullavington
Lower Stanton St Quintin
A432
Chipping Sodbury
Old Sodbury
Littleton Drew
B4040
Stanton St Quintin
Lower Seagry
Westerleigh
Dodington
Acton Turville
Grittleton
Upper Seagry
Cotswold Way
Leigh Delamere
B4069
Tormarton
Burton
M4
17
B4122
Bradenstoke
Codrington
B4465
Leigh Delamere
A350
Christian Malford
Nettleton
Sutton Benger
18
B4039
Castle Combe
Kington St Michael
Hinton
Dyrham Park
West Kington
Kington Langley
Catcombe
Goatacre
40
B4465
Pucklechurch
Yatton Keynell
B4069
Langley Burrell
Hilmarton
Abson
Dyrham
West Littleton
Ford
Allington
Charlcutt
Goose Green
North Wraxall
Upper Wraxall
Hardenhuish
East Tytherton
Doynton
Slaughterford
Tytherton Lucas
A420
Marshfield
Biddestone
B4528
Chippenham
Bremhill
Wick
A420
A3102
Compton Bassett
A4175
Thickwood
Cold Ashton
A4
Studley
Avon Valley Railway
Sir Bevil Grenville's Monument
Colerne
Corsham Court
Calne
Upton Cheyney
Rudloe
Derry Hill
North Stoke
Ditteridge
Easton
Bowood
A46
Corsham
Notton
A342
Langridge
Swainswick
Middlehill
Gastard
Sandy Lane
Woolley
Box
Neston
Lacock Abbey
Fox Talbot Museum
A431
Bath
Beckford's Tower
Batheaston
Ashley
Lacock
A3102
Saltford
By Brook
B3353
Bowden Hill
Chittoe
Stockley
Kelston
Weston
Charlcombe
Toll
Kingsdown
A350
Bathford
A365
Whitley
BATH
Monkton Farleigh
Atworth
Beanacre
Heddington
A39
Bathampton
B3109
Shaw
Bishops Cannings
A36
Newton St Loe
Twerton
Claverton
South Wraxall
A3102
Bromham
White Horse
Stanton Prior
Englishcombe
Prior Park
A363
Great Chalfield Manor
Great Chalfield
Melksham
Roundway
Combe Down
Monkton Combe
Broughton Gifford
Rowde
Odd Down
Dundas
Bradford-on-Avon
Bradford Leigh
Holt
Sells Green
Inglesbatch
Limpley Stoke
Winsley
B3107
Whaddon
A365
B3108
B3105
The Courts Garden
Seend Cleeve
Devizes
South Stoke
A367
Midford
A350
Seend
Priston
B3110
Turleigh
Staverton
Semington
Combe Hay
Freshford
Barton Farm
Great Hinton
Dunkerton
Westwood
Westwood Manor
The Strand
Poulshot
Tunley
Hinton Charterhouse
Hilperton
Bulkington
Stert
Meadgate
Farleigh Hungerford Castle
B3109
Ashton Common
Potterne
Potterne Wick
Carlingcott
Wellow
A366
Keevil
Worton
Trowbridge
Stoney Littleton Long Barrow
Norton St Philip
Farleigh Hungerford
Wingfield
Steeple Ashton
Marston
Urchfont
Midsomer Norton
27
A363
Radstock
Foxcote
A366
A36
Tellisford
West Ashton
Great Cheverell
Littleton Pannell
Eastcott
A361
Southwick
North Bradley
Yarnbrook
Writhlington
B3110
B3097
Faulkland
Woolverton
Coulston
Edington
Rode
Hawkeridge
Heywood
Hemington

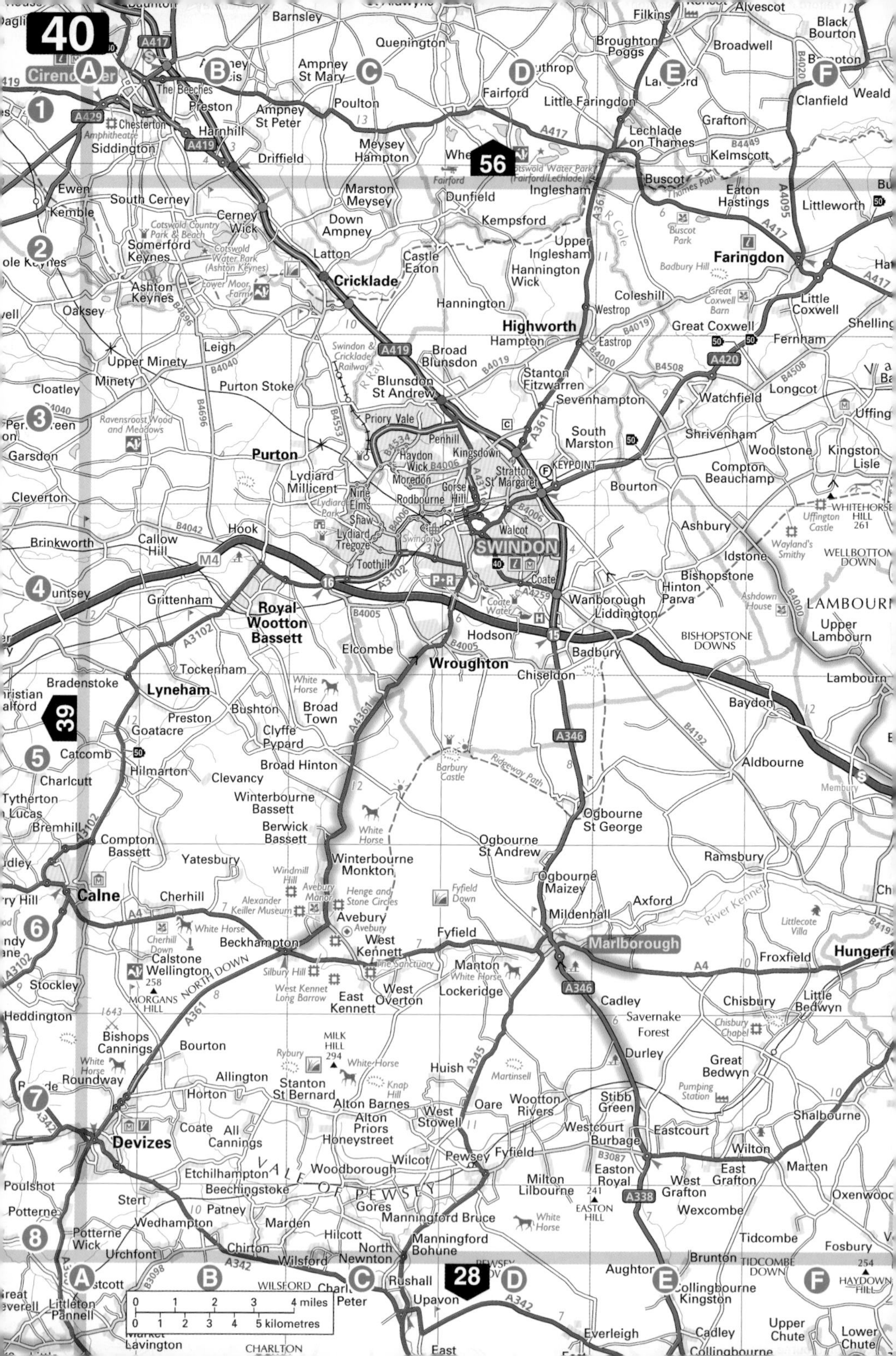
Barnsley
Quenington
Filkins
Alvescot
Black Bourton
Broughton Poggs
Broadwell
Ampney St Mary
Cirencester
The Beeches
Preston
Ampney St Peter
Poulton
Fairford
Little Faringdon
Clanfield
Weald
Chesterton
Amphitheatre
Siddington
Harnhill
Driffield
Meysey Hampton
Lechlade on Thames
Grafton
Kelmscott
Cotswold Water Park (Fairford/Lechlade)
Inglesham
Buscot
Eaton Hastings
Littleworth
Thames Path
Ewen
Kemble
South Cerney
Marston Meysey
Dunfield
Kempsford
Buscot Park
Cerney Wick
Down Ampney
Cotswold Country Park & Beach
Somerford Keynes
Cotswold Water Park (Ashton Keynes)
Upper Inglesham
Faringdon
Latton
Castle Eaton
Hannington Wick
Badbury Hill
Ashton Keynes
Lower Moor Farm
Cricklade
Coleshill
Great Coxwell Barn
Little Coxwell
Oaksey
Hannington
Westrop
Highworth
Great Coxwell
Shellingford
Swindon & Cricklade Railway
Broad Blunsdon
Hampton
Eastrop
Fernham
Leigh
Upper Minety
Minety
Purton Stoke
Blunsdon St Andrew
Stanton Fitzwarren
Sevenhampton
Watchfield
Longcot
Cloatley
Ravensroost Wood and Meadows
Priory Vale
Uffington
Penhill
South Marston
Shrivenham
Garsdon
Purton
Haydon Wick
Kingsdown
Woolstone
Kingston Lisle
Moredon
Stratton St Margaret
KEYPOINT
Compton Beauchamp
Lydiard Millicent
Nine Elms
Rodbourne
Gorse Hill
Bourton
Cleverton
Lydiard Park
Shaw
WHITEHORSE HILL 261
Uffington Castle
Brinkworth
Callow Hill
Hook
Lydiard Tregoze
Walcot
SWINDON
Ashbury
Wayland's Smithy
Toothill
Idstone
WELLBOTTOM DOWN
Coate
Bishopstone
Hinton Parva
Ashdown House
LAMBOURN
Grittenham
Royal Wootton Bassett
Coate Water
Wanborough
Liddington
Upper Lambourn
Hodson
BISHOPSTONE DOWNS
Elcombe
Wroughton
Badbury
Tockenham
Chiseldon
Lambourn
Bradenstoke
White Horse
Lyneham
Broad Town
Baydon
Preston
Bushton
Goatacre
Clyffe Pypard
Catcomb
Aldbourne
Barbury Castle
Ridgeway Path
Broad Hinton
Charlcutt
Hilmarton
Clevancy
Tytherton Lucas
Winterbourne Bassett
Membury
Ogbourne St George
Bremhill
Berwick Bassett
Compton Bassett
Ogbourne St Andrew
Yatesbury
Winterbourne Monkton
Ramsbury
Windmill Hill
Ogbourne Maizey
Calne
Avebury Manor
Henge and Stone Circles
Fyfield Down
Cherhill
Alexander Keiller Museum
Avebury
Mildenhall
Axford
River Kennet
Littlecote Villa
Beckhampton
West Kennett
Fyfield
Marlborough
Cherhill Down
Calstone Wellington
Silbury Hill
The Sanctuary
Manton
Froxfield
Hungerford
Stockley
NORTH DOWN
West Kennet Long Barrow
East Kennett
West Overton
Lockeridge
Cadley
Chisbury
Little Bedwyn
MORGANS HILL
Heddington
Savernake Forest
Chisbury Chapel
Bishops Cannings
MILK HILL 294
Bourton
Rybury
Durley
Great Bedwyn
Roundway
Allington
Huish
Martinsell
Knap Hill
Horton
Stanton St Bernard
Alton Barnes
Oare
Wootton Rivers
Stibb Green
Pumping Station
Alton Priors
West Stowell
Shalbourne
Coate
All Cannings
Honeystreet
Westcourt
Burbage
Eastcourt
Devizes
Wilcot
Pewsey
Fyfield
Wilton
Marten
Poulshot
Etchilhampton
Woodborough
VALE OF PEWSEY
Milton Lilbourne
Easton Royal
East Grafton
Beechingstoke
EASTON HILL 241
West Grafton
Oxenwood
Stert
Gores
Potterne
Patney
Manningford Bruce
Wexcombe
Wedhampton
Marden
Potterne Wick
Hilcott
Tidcombe
Fosbury
Urchfont
Chirton
North Newnton
Manningford Bohune
Wilsford
Brunton
TIDCOMBE DOWN
HAYDOWN HILL 254
WILSFORD
Charlton
Rushall
Aughton
Collingbourne Kingston
Littleton Pannell
Upavon
Everleigh
Cadley
Upper Chute
Lower Chute
Market Lavington
CHARLTON
Collingbourne
0 1 2 3 4 miles
0 1 2 3 4 5 kilometres
56
39
28

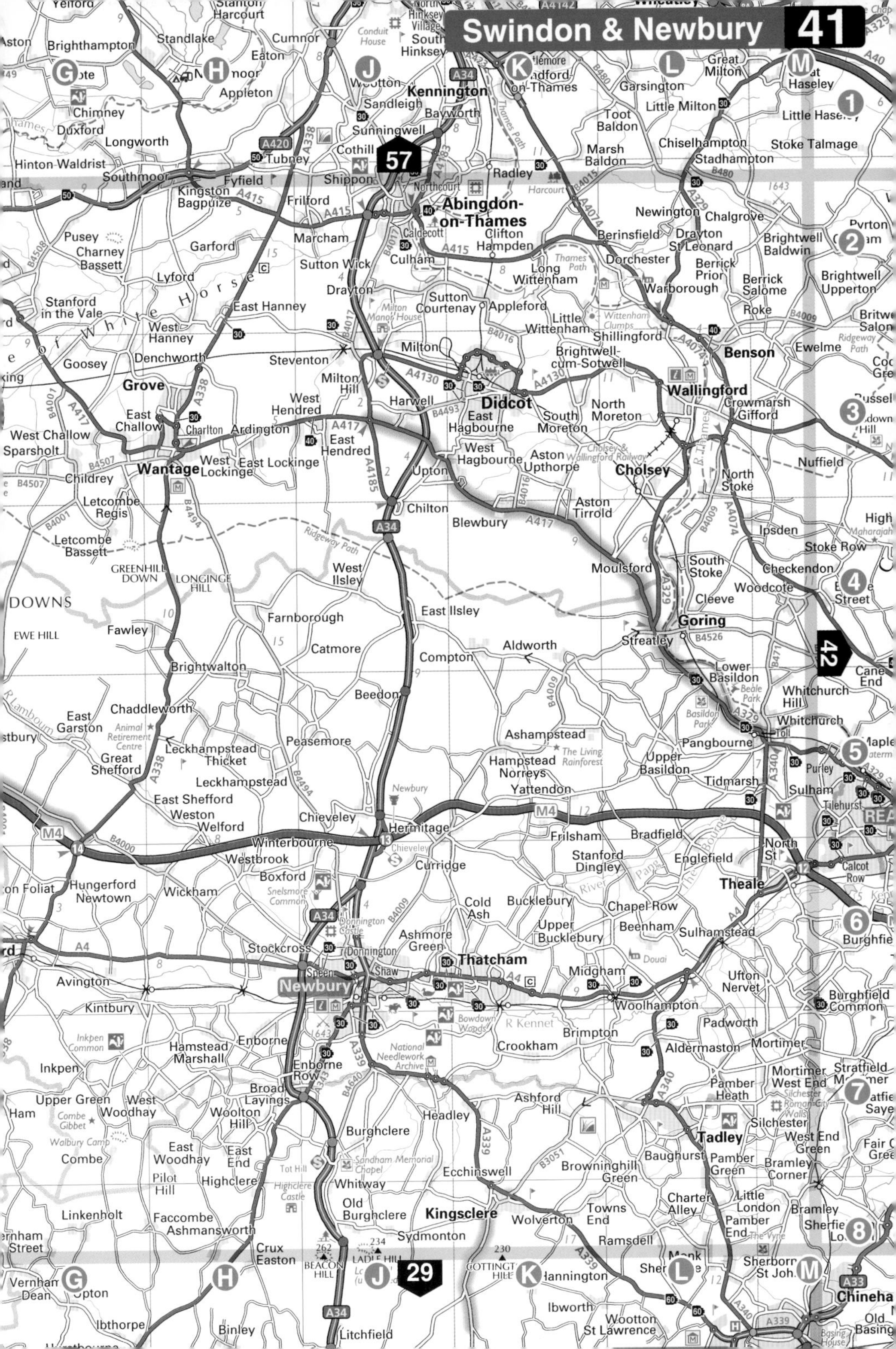

Rycote Chapel
Moreton
Towersey
Longwick
Monks Risborough
Dunsmore
The Lee
Lee Clump
Bellingdon
Asheridge
Chartridge
Whiteleaf
Cross (hill carving)
Pitch Green
Princes Risborough
Great Hampden
Haseley
Tetsworth
Emmington
Sydenham
Hent
Bledlow
Saunderton
Loosley Row
Lacey Green
Prestwood
Great Missenden
Ballinger Common
South Heath
Hyde Heath
Chesham Bois
Little Haseley
Postcombe
Chinnor
Chinnor & Princes Risborough Railway
Crowell
Lodge Hill
Stoke Talmage
Kingston Blount
Aston Rowant
Radnage
Walter's Ash
Hughenden Valley
Little Kingshill
Great Kingshill
Little Missenden
Amersham
Amersham Old Town
South Weston
Lewknor
Pyrton
Cuxham
Shirburn
Stokenchurch
The City
Bledlow Ridge
Beacon's Bottom
Bradenham
Naphill
Hughenden Manor
Cryers Hill
Holmer Green
Penn Street
Widmer End
Hazlemere
Downley
Hell-Fire Caves
Winchmore Hill
Coleshill
Berrick Salome
Brightwell Upperton
Watlington
Roke
Britwell Salome
Ridgeway Path
Ibstone
Cadmore End
West Wycombe Park
High Wycombe
Cressex
Wycombe Marsh
Booker
Chalfont St Giles
Bekonscot Model Village
Benson
Ewelme
Turville
Lane End
Loudwater
Beaconsfield
Cookley Green
Fingest
Skirmett
Frieth
Flackwell Heath
Russell's Water
Pishill
Stonor House & Gardens
Marlow Bottom
Wooburn Green
Gangsdown Hill
Park Corner
Stonor
Nuffield Place
Warburg
Nettlebed
Rockwell End
Marlow
Bourne End
Little Marlow
Wooburn
Hedgerley
Nuffield
Crocker End
Fawley
Hambleden
Odds Farm Park
Egypt
Hedsor
Cookham
Mill End
Highmoor
Maharajah's Well
Bix
Lower Assendon
Remenham
Bisham
Medmenham
Cliveden
Burnham Beeches
Cookham Rise
Ipsden
Stoke Row
Highmoor Cross
Greys Court
Aston
River & Rowing
Remenham Hill
Hurley
Cookham Dean
Checkendon
Greys Green
Rotherfield Greys
Henley-on-Thames
Maidenhead
Taplow
Farnham Royal
Burnham
Exlade Street
Rotherfield Peppard
Cockpole Green
Burchett's Green
Warren Row
North Town
Sonning Common
Knowl Hill
Cippenham
Slough
The Herb Farm
Lower Shiplake
Wargrave
Littlewick Green
Bray
Braywick
Dorney
Eton Wick
Chalvey
Cane End
Kidmore End
Woodlands Park
Dorney Court
Whitchurch
Tokers Green
Dunsden Green
Binfield Heath
Shiplake
White Waltham
Holyport
Eton
Hare Hatch
Waltham St Lawrence
Ruscombe
Thames Path
Mapledurham
Watermill
Play Hatch
Charvil
Fifield
Dedworth
Purley
Sonning
Caversham
Twyford
Paley Street
Windsor
Sulham
Tilehurst
Reading
Woodley
Whistley Green
Shurlock Row
Legoland
Hurst
Maiden's Green
Cranbourne
Great Park
North Street
Calcot Row
Dinton Pastures
Binfield
Warfield
Newell Green
Winkfield
Winkfield Row
Woodside
Guards Polo Club
Savill Garden
Whitley
Earley
Winnersh
Kennet & Avon
Burghfield
Sindlesham
North Ascot
Bullbrook
Ascot
Virginia Water
Three Mile Cross
Shinfield
Wokingham
Arborfield
Great Hollands
Bracknell
Sunninghill
Sunningdale
Burghfield Common
Spencers Wood
Arborfield Cross
Barkham
Gardeners Green
Tower Hill
Mortimer
Swallowfield
Farley Hill
California
Look Out Discovery Centre
Swinley Forest
Windlesham
Mortimer West End
Stratfield Mortimer
Beech Hill
Wellingtonia Avenue
Silchester Roman City Walls
Stratfield Saye
Riseley
Wellington
Finchampstead
Crowthorne
Wildmoor Heath
Bagshot
Lightwater
Silchester
West End Green
Eversley
Eversley Cross
Owlsmoor
Sandhurst
West End
Bramley Corner
Fair Oak Green
Stratfield Turgis
Heckfield
Hound Green
Yateley
College Town
York Town
Camberley
Turgis Green
Hartley Wespall
Blackwater
Yateley Common
Royal Logistics Corps
Bisley
Knaphill
Little London
Bramley
Sherfield on Loddon
Mattingley
Hartfordbridge
Hawley
Frimley
Sherborne St John
Rotherwick
West Green
Hartley Wintney
Farnborough Street
Brookwood
Chineham
Elvetham Heath
Fleet
Cove
Farnborough Park
Farnborough
Mytchett
Pirbright
Basing
Basing House
Winchfield
Dogmersfield
Worplesdon
0 1 2 3 4 miles
0 1 2 3 4 5 kilometres

58
41
30

Bovingdon
Kings Langley
Chesham
Chipperfield
Abbots Langley
Radlett
Shenley
South Mimms
Potters Bar
Goff's Oak
Ley Hill
Flaunden
Belsize
Sarratt
Ridge
Botany Bay
Latimer
Aldenham
Green Street
Chenies
Chandler's Cross
WATFORD
Letchmore Heath
Hadley Wood
Chorleywood
Little Chalfont
Borehamwood
Monken Hadley
Cockfosters
Rickmansworth
Croxley Green
Bushey
Barnet
Arkley
New Barnet
Elstree
East Barnet
Oxhey
Merry Hill
Bushey Heath
Totteridge
Winchmore Hill
Chiltern Open Air
Batchworth
London Gateway
Highwood Hill
Southgate
Mill Hill
Friern Barnet
Chalfont Common
Eastbury
Stanmore
Edgware
Chalfont St Peter
Northwood
Hatch End
Harrow Weald
Church End
Finchley
Muswell Hill
Wood Green
Harefield
Pinner Green
Wealdstone
Hendon
Tottenham
Denham Green
Pinner
Kingsbury
Gerrards Cross
Eastcote
Harrow
Kenton
Hornsey
Crouch End
Denham
Ruislip
Harrow on the Hill
Brent Cross
Golders Green
Highgate
Neasden
Hampstead
Holloway
Highbury
Sudbury
Wembley
Cricklewood
Ickenham
Fulmer
New Denham
Uxbridge
Willesden
Kentish Town
North Hillingdon
Northolt
Perivale
Alperton
Harlesden
Kilburn
St John's Wood
Camden Town
Islington
Iver Heath
Hayes End
Yeading
Greenford
Park Royal
Cowley
Wood End
Ealing
Marylebone
Holborn
Paddington
George Green
Iver
Yiewsley
Hayes
Acton
Shepherd's Bush
Southall
Norwood Green
Hammersmith
Kensington
Westminster
Southwark
West Drayton
Upton
Langley
Harlington
Cranford
Heston
Chiswick
Chelsea
Lambeth
Brentford
Kew
Osterley
Colnbrook
Poyle
Barnes
Fulham
Battersea
Brixton
Horton
Heathrow
Hounslow
Isleworth
Mortlake
East Sheen
Clapham
Old Windsor
Stanwell
West Bedfont
Hatton
Richmond
Roehampton
Putney
Wandsworth
Herne Hill
Wraysbury
East Bedfont
Twickenham
Petersham
Earlsfield
Balham
Tulse Hill
Hythe End
Feltham
Ham
Tooting Bec
Streatham
Ashford
Lower Feltham
West Norwood
Egham
Felthamhill
Teddington
Kingston upon Thames
Wimbledon
Tooting
Englefield Green
Thorpe Lea
Staines-upon-Thames
Hanworth
Merton
Hampton
Sunbury-on-Thames
Hampton Wick
Norbiton
Raynes Park
Morden
Mitcham
Norbury
Thorpe
Virginia Water
Littleton
Upper Halliford
West Molesey
East Molesey
Surbiton
New Malden
St Helier
Thames Ditton
Lower Halliford
Long Ditton
Motspur Park
Beddington Corner
Lyne
Chertsey
Shepperton
Walton-on-Thames
Tolworth
Worcester Park
North Cheam
Hackbridge
Hinchley Wood
Oatlands Park
Beddington
Wallington
Addlestone
Weybridge
Esher
Hook
Cheam
Ottershaw
Hersham
Claygate
Chessington
Ewell
Carshalton
Sutton
South Beddington
Chobham
New Haw
Woodham
Belmont
Woodcote
Little Woodcote
Purley
Byfleet
West Byfleet
Fairmile
Epsom
Sheerwater
Cobham
Oxshott
Kenley
Banstead
Woodmansterne
Maybury
Coulsdon
Pyrford
Downside
Whyteleafe
WOKING
Stoke D'Abernon
Burgh Heath
Old Woking
Ashtead
Chipstead
Leatherhead
Tadworth
Ripley
Ockham
Hooley
Chaldon
Kingswood
Walton on the Hill
Headley
Little Bookham
Great Bookham
Caterham
Sutton Green
West Horsley
East Horsley
Effingham
Mickleham
59
44
31

Langley
How Wood
Chipperfield
Abbots Langley
Bricket Wood
De Havilland Aircraft Heritage Centre
A1(M)
Northaw
South Mimms
Potters Bar
Radlett
Ridge
Belsize
Sarratt
Latimer
Flaunden
Amersham on the Hill
Amersham Common
Chenies
Little Chalfont
Chorleywood
Chorleywood West
Rickmansworth
Chandler's Cross
WATFORD
Studio Tour
Aldenham
Green Street
Letchmore Heath
Borehamwood
Bushey
Bushey Heath
Oxhey
Merry Hill
Elstree
London Gateway
Barnet
Arkley
Totteridge Fields
Totteridge
Highwood Hill
Mill Hill
Hadley Wood
Monken Hadley
Cockfosters
New Barnet
East Barnet
Southgate
Friern Barnet
Botany Bay
Winchmore
Chiltern Open Air
Croxley Green
Batchworth
Chalfont St Giles
Seer Green
Chalfont Common
Chalfont St Peter
Eastbury
Stanmore
Edgware
Harrow Weald
Wealdstone
Northwood
Hatch End
Pinner Green
Pinner
Eastcote
Harefield
Ruislip Woods
Bayhurst Wood
Grand Union Canal
Denham Green
Gerrards Cross
Denham
Ruislip
Harrow
Harrow on the Hill
Kenton
Kingsbury
Brent Resr
Fryent
Hendon
RAF Hendon
Church End
Finchley
Muswell Hill
Hornsey
Crouch End
Highgate
Golders Green
Brent Cross
Neasden
Cricklewood
Kenwood House
Hampstead
Fenton House
Wood Green
Farnham Common
Fulmer
Ickenham
New Denham
Uxbridge
Black Park
Iver Heath
Stoke Poges
North Hillingdon
Gutteridge Wood
Hayes End
Yeading
Northolt
Sudbury
Wembley
Wembley Complex
Alperton
Perivale
Greenford
Park Royal
Willesden
Harlesden
Kilburn
St John's Wood
Lord's
Camden Town
Kentish Town
Marylebone
Holborn
Paddington
Cowley
George Green
Iver
Yiewsley
Wood End
Hayes
Lake Farm
Stockley Park
West Drayton
Minet
Southall
Norwood Green
Hanwell
Ealing
Acton
Shepherd's Bush
Kensington Palace
Kensington
Westminster
Hammersmith
Olympia
Chiswick
Chelsea
Lambeth
Upton
Langley
Harlington
Heston
Cranford
Datchet
Colnbrook
Poyle
Heathrow
Osterley
Brentford
Kew
Syon
Kew Palace
Chiswick House
London Wetland Centre
Barnes
Mortlake
Fulham
Carlyle's House
Battersea
Clapham
Brixton
Frogmore House
Horton
Old Windsor
Hounslow
Hatton
Stanwell
West Bedfont
Isleworth
Twickenham
Richmond
East Sheen
Putney
Roehampton
Wandsworth
Wraysbury
Hythe End
Runnymede
East Bedfont
Bedfont Lakes
Feltham
Marble Hill
Petersham
Ham House
Richmond Park
Earlsfield
Balham
Tooting Bec
Tulse Hill
Egham
Englefield Green
Savill Garden
Ashford
Lower Feltham
Ham
Teddington
Streatham
Thorpe Lea
Thorpe
Staines-upon-Thames
Queen Mary Resr
Feltham Hill
Hanworth
Kempton Park
Kingston upon Thames
Wimbledon
Tooting
Merton
Valley Gardens
Sunbury-on-Thames
Hampton
Hampton Wick
Norbiton
Raynes Park
Morden
Mitcham
Norbury
Thornton Heath
Virginia Water
Thorpe Park
Littleton
Upper Halliford
Lower Halliford
West Molesey
East Molesey
Hampton Court Palace
Surbiton
New Malden
Motspur Park
St Helier
Beddington Corner
Lyne
Chertsey
Shepperton
Walton-on-Thames
Thames Ditton
Long Ditton
Tolworth
Worcester Park
North Cheam
Hackbridge
Great Cockrow
Thames Path
Oatlands Park
Sandown Park
Hinchley Wood
Addlestone
Weybridge
Hersham
Esher
Hook
Cheam
Carshalton
Sutton
Beddington
Wallington
South Beddington
Chobham Common
Ottershaw
Burrowhill
Chobham
New Haw
Claremont Landscape Garden
Claygate
Chessington
Ewell
Belmont
Woodham
West Byfleet
Byfleet
Sheerwater
Chessington World of Adventures
Little Woodcote
Woodcote
Purley
Fairmile
Cobham
Oxshott
Epsom
Ashtead Common
Woodmansterne
Coulsdon
Maybury
Horsell
Pyrford
Painshill Park
Semaphore Tower
Downside
Epsom Downs
Banstead
Goldsworth Park
WOKING
St Johns
Mayford
Old Woking
Send
RHS Wisley
Ripley
Stoke D'Abernon
Leatherhead
Ashtead
Tadworth
Burgh Heath
Chipstead
Hooley
Netherne-on-the-Hill
Ockham
Fetcham
Headley
Walton on the Hill
Kingswood
Chaldon
Sutton Green
West
Little Bookham
Great Bookham
Bocketts
Headley Heath
Mickleham
Norbury Park
Effingham
Polesden Lacey
Westhumble
Box Hill
North Downs Way
Reigate Hill
Redhill
Merstham
South Merstham
Burpham
Stoughton
East
Clandon Park
59
43
31
0 1 2 3 4 miles
0 1 2 3 4 5 kilometres

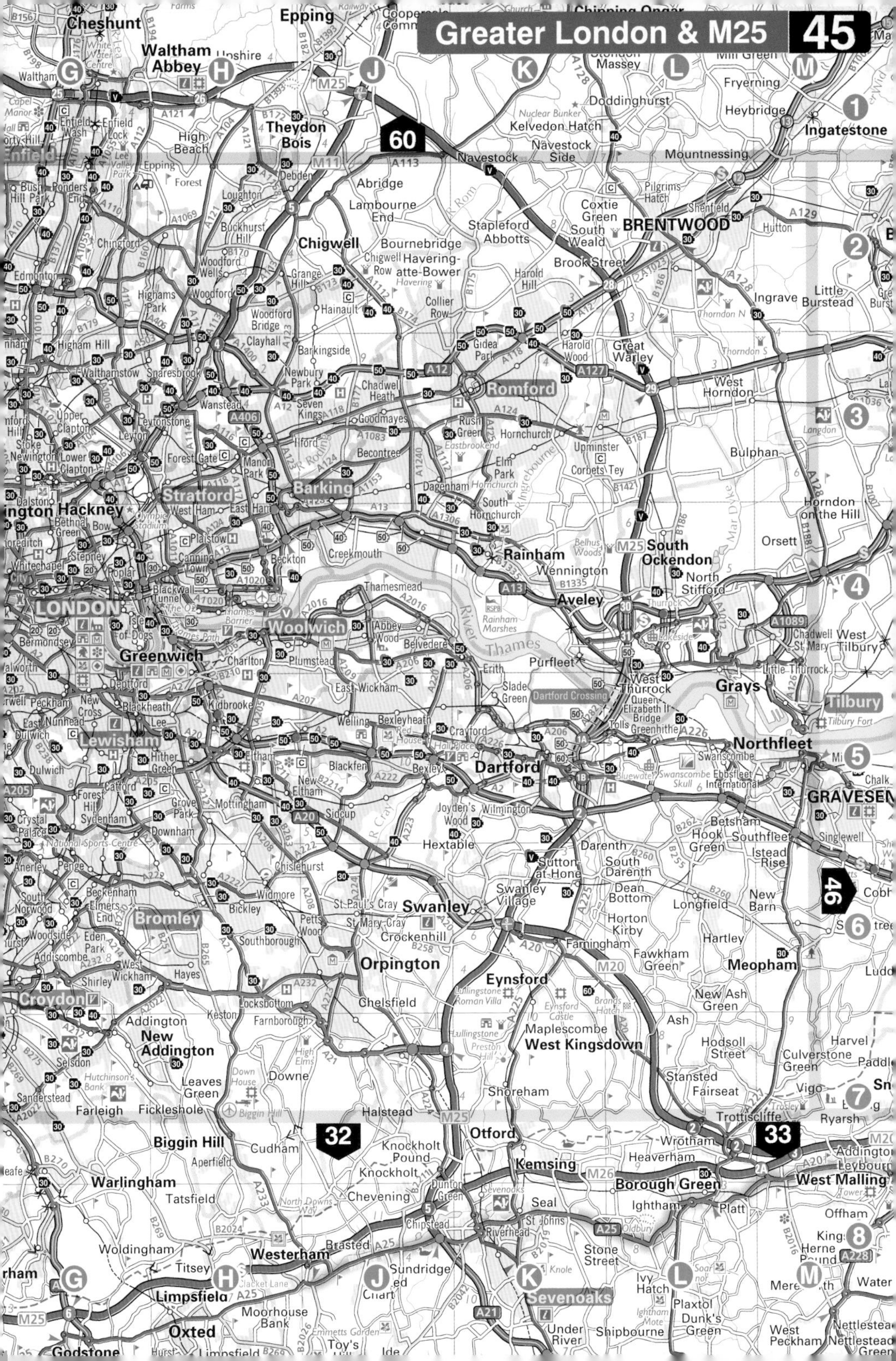

Cheshunt
Epping
Chipping Ongar
Waltham Abbey
Upshire
Theydon Bois
Navestock
Navestock Side
Kelvedon Hatch
Doddinghurst
Stondon Massey
Mill Green
Fryerning
Heybridge
Ingatestone
Mountnessing
Enfield
High Beach
Debden
Abridge
Loughton
Lambourne End
Chigwell
Buckhurst Hill
Chingford
Woodford
Stapleford Abbotts
Pilgrims Hatch
Coxtie Green
South Weald
BRENTWOOD
Shenfield
Hutton
Brook Street
Havering-atte-Bower
Harold Hill
Collier Row
Ingrave
Little Burstead
Hainault
Woodford Bridge
Clayhall
Barkingside
Gidea Park
Harold Wood
Great Warley
Edmonton
Higham Hill
Highams Park
Walthamstow
Snaresbrook
Wanstead
Newbury Park
Chadwell Heath
Romford
West Horndon
Seven Kings
Goodmayes
Rush Green
Hornchurch
Upminster
Langdon
Upper Clapton
Leytonstone
Leyton
Ilford
Becontree
Elm Park
Corbets Tey
Bulphan
Stoke Newington
Lower Clapton
Forest Gate
Manor Park
Dagenham
Stratford
Barking
South Hornchurch
Hackney
West Ham
East Ham
Horndon on the Hill
Bethnal Green
Bow
Plaistow
Beckton
Creekmouth
Rainham
Belhus Woods
South Ockendon
Orsett
Shoreditch
Stepney
Whitechapel
Poplar
Canning Town
Wennington
North Stifford
Blackwall Tunnel
Thamesmead
Aveley
LONDON
Isle of Dogs
Woolwich
Abbey Wood
Rainham Marshes
River Thames
Chadwell St Mary
West Tilbury
Bermondsey
Greenwich
Charlton
Belvedere
Purfleet
Lakeside
Plumstead
Erith
West Thurrock
Grays
Little Thurrock
Walworth
Deptford
East Wickham
Slade Green
Dartford Crossing
Tilbury
Tilbury Fort
Peckham
New Cross
Blackheath
Kidbrooke
Queen Elizabeth II Bridge
Welling
Bexleyheath
Crayford
Greenhithe
Northfleet
East Dulwich
Lewisham
Lee
Eltham
Hall Place
Swanscombe
Ebbsfleet International
Dulwich
Hither Green
Blackfen
Bexley
Dartford
Bluewater
GRAVESEND
Forest Hill
Catford
New Eltham
Chalk
Crystal Palace
Sydenham
Grove Park
Mottingham
Sidcup
Joyden's Wood
Wilmington
Betsham
Southfleet
Hook Green
Singlewell
Downham
Hextable
Darenth
South Darenth
Istead Rise
Anerley
Penge
Chislehurst
Sutton-at-Hone
Swanley Village
Dean Bottom
New Barn
Cobham
South Norwood
Beckenham
Elmers End
Widmore
St Paul's Cray
Swanley
Longfield
Bromley
Bickley
Petts Wood
St Mary Cray
Horton Kirby
Crockenhill
Farningham
Hartley
Woodside
Eden Park
Southborough
Fawkham Green
Meopham
Addiscombe
West Wickham
Hayes
Orpington
Eynsford
Shirley
Lullingstone Roman Villa
Eynsford Castle
Brands Hatch
New Ash Green
Croydon
Locksbottom
Chelsfield
Addington
Keston
Farnborough
Maplescombe
West Kingsdown
Ash
New Addington
Hodsoll Street
Harvel
Culverstone Green
Selsdon
Downe
Shoreham
Stansted
Fairseat
Vigo
Sanderstead
Leaves Green
Farleigh
Fickleshole
Biggin Hill
Halstead
Trottiscliffe
Ryarsh
Otford
Wrotham
Biggin Hill
Cudham
Knockholt Pound
Knockholt
Heaverham
Kemsing
Addington
Leybourne
Aperfield
Dunton Green
Borough Green
West Malling
Warlingham
Tatsfield
Chevening
Sevenoaks
Seal
Ightham
Platt
Offham
Chipstead
Riverhead
St Johns
Kings Hill
Woldingham
Westerham
Brasted
Sundridge
Stone Street
Knole
Oldbury
Herne Pound
Titsey
Clacket Lane
Mereworth
Limpsfield
Ide Hill
Sevenoaks
Ivy Hatch
Plaxtol
Dunk's Green
Moorhouse Bank
Oxted
Emmetts Garden
Under River
Shipbourne
West Peckham
Nettlestead
Nettlestead Green
Godstone
Limpsfield Chart
Toy's Hill
River Rom
River Roding
River Cray
River Thames
Mar Dyke
Thorndon N
Thorndon S
Nuclear Bunker
Olympic Stadium
Thames Barrier
Thames Path
The O2
City
National Sports Centre
Hutchinson's Bank
Down House
North Downs Way
Lullingstone
Preston Hill
High Elms
Swanscombe Skull
Red House
Trosley
Ightham Mote
60
32
33
46
M25
M11
M20
M26
A12
A13
A127
A406
A20
A21
A25
A228
A1089
G
H
J
K
L
M
1
2
3
4
5
6
7
8

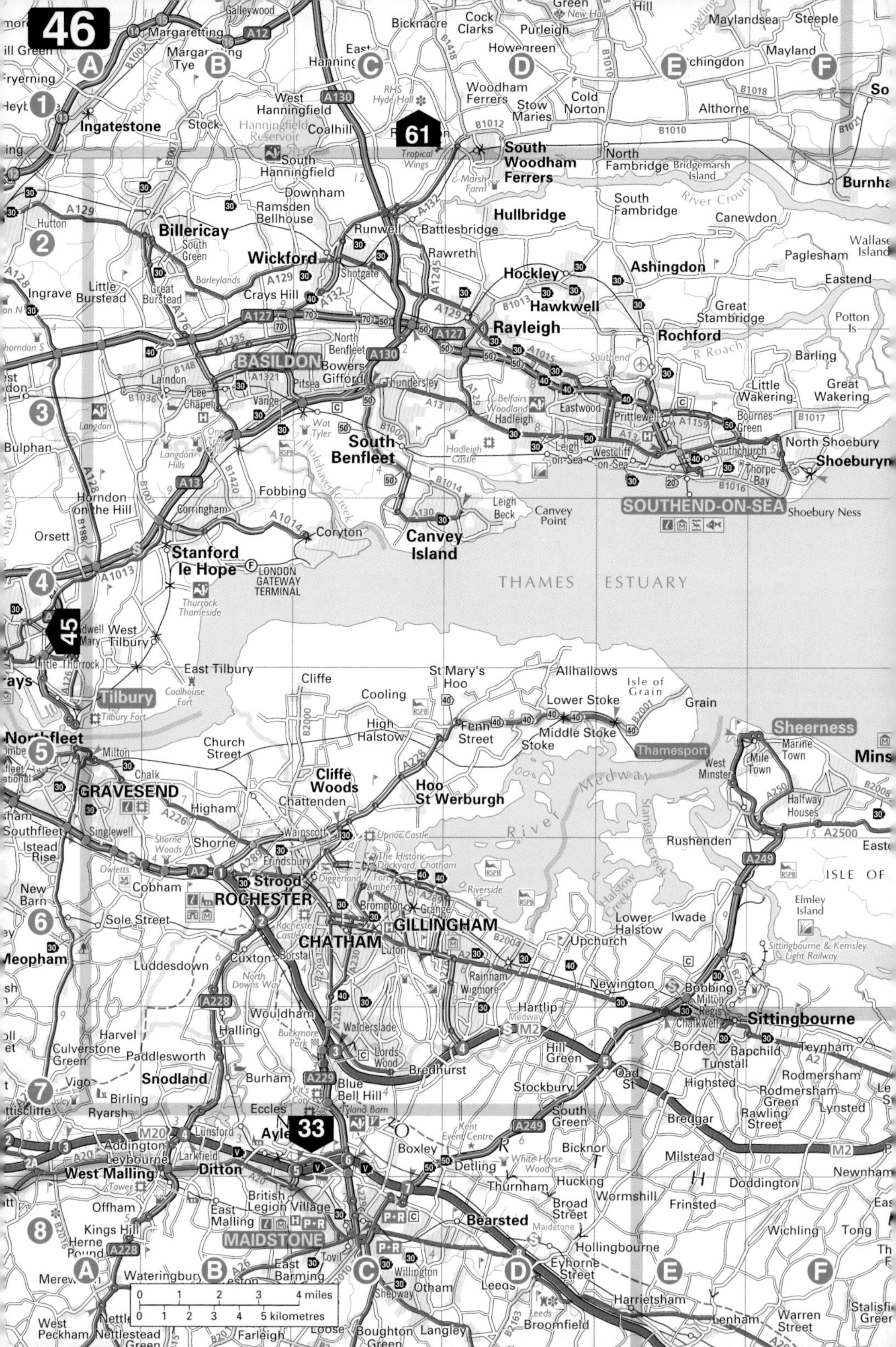
Margaretting
Margaretting Tye
Galleywood
Ingatestone
Stock
Hanningfield Reservoir
West Hanningfield
East Hanningfield
RHS Hyde Hall
Bicknacre
Cock Clarks
Purleigh
Howegreen
Woodham Ferrers
Stow Maries
Cold Norton
Maylandsea
Steeple
Mayland
Latchingdon
Althorne
61
Tropical Wings
South Woodham Ferrers
North Fambridge
Bridgemarsh Island
Burnham
Marsh Farm
River Crouch
South Hanningfield
Downham
Ramsden Bellhouse
Hutton
Billericay
South Green
Wickford
Runwell
Battlesbridge
Hullbridge
South Fambridge
Canewdon
Rawreth
Hockley
Ashingdon
Paglesham
Wallasea Island
Eastend
Shotgate
Barleylands
Little Burstead
Great Burstead
Ingrave
Crays Hill
Hawkwell
Great Stambridge
Potton Is
Rayleigh
Rochford
R Roach
Barling
Basildon
North Benfleet
Bowers Gifford
Thundersley
Laindon
Lee Chapel
Pitsea
Vange
Langdon
Belfairs Woodland
Hadleigh
Eastwood
Prittlewell
Little Wakering
Great Wakering
Bournes Green
Wat Tyler
One Tree Hill
Langdon Hills
South Benfleet
Hadleigh Castle
Leigh-on-Sea
Westcliff-on-Sea
Southchurch
North Shoebury
Shoeburyness
Thorpe Bay
Bulphan
Horndon on the Hill
Fobbing
Corringham
Southend-on-Sea
Shoebury Ness
Leigh Beck
Canvey Point
Canvey Island
Orsett
Coryton
Stanford le Hope
London Gateway Terminal
Thames Estuary
Thurrock Thameside
West Tilbury
East Tilbury
Little Thurrock
45
Tilbury
Tilbury Fort
Coalhouse Fort
Cliffe
Cooling
St Mary's Hoo
Allhallows
Isle of Grain
Lower Stoke
Grain
High Halstow
Fenn Street
Middle Stoke
Stoke
Thamesport
Sheerness
Marine Town
Mile Town
West Minster
Northfleet
Milton
Chalk
Church Street
Cliffe Woods
Hoo St Werburgh
Gravesend
Higham
Chattenden
River Medway
Halfway Houses
Southfleet
Singlewell
Shorne
Shorne Woods
Wainscott
Upnor Castle
Rushenden
Istead Rise
Frindsbury
The Historic Dockyard, Chatham
Isle of Sheppey
Cobham
Owletts
Strood
Rochester
Diggerland
Fort Amherst
Riverside
Brompton
Grange
New Barn
Sole Street
Rochester Castle
Chatham
Gillingham
Lower Halstow
Iwade
Elmley Island
Meopham
Luddesdown
Cuxton
Borstal
Luton
Upchurch
Sittingbourne & Kemsley Light Railway
North Downs Way
Rainham
Wigmore
Newington
Bobbing
Milton Regis
Wouldham
Hartlip
Chalkwell
Sittingbourne
Harvel
Halling
Buckmore Park
Walderslade
Culverstone Green
Paddlesworth
Lords Wood
Hill Green
Borden
Bapchild
Teynham
Tunstall
Snodland
Burham
Bredhurst
Oad Street
Highsted
Rodmersham
Rodmersham Green
Vigo
Birling
Blue Bell Hill
Kit's Coty
Stockbury
Lynsted
Trottiscliffe
Ryarsh
Eccles
Tyland Barn
South Green
Bredgar
Rawling Street
Lunsford
Aylesford
33
Kent Event Centre
Addington
Leybourne
Larkfield
Boxley
Bicknor
Milstead
West Malling
Ditton
Detling
White Horse Wood
Newnham
Tower
Thurnham
Hucking
Wormshill
Doddington
Offham
East Malling
British Legion Village
Broad Street
Frinsted
Kings Hill
Bearsted
Hollingbourne
Wichling
Tong
Herne Pound
Maidstone
Tovil
Eyhorne Street
East Barming
Willington
Wateringbury
Otham
Leeds
Shepway
Harrietsham
Lenham
Warren Street
West Peckham
Nettlestead
Nettlestead Green
Farleigh
Loose
Boughton Green
Langley
Leeds Castle
Broomfield
0 1 2 3 4 miles
0 1 2 3 4 5 kilometres

Dengie
Holliwell Point
Foulness Point
Courtsend
Churchend
FOULNESS ISLAND
Warden Point
Leysdown-on-Sea
Leysdown Coastal Park
Isle of Harty
Shell Ness
The Swale
Whitstable
Whitstable Bay
Herne Bay
Hampton
Tankerton
Swalecliffe
Chestfield
Greenhill
South Street
Seasalter
Bishopstone
Reculver
Reculver Towers & Roman Fort
Beltinge
Broomfield
Herne
Minnis Bay
Westgate on Sea
Birchington
Acol
St Nicholas at Wade
Boyden Gate
Sarre
Monkton
Durlock
Chislet
Hoath
Upstreet
West Stourmouth
Minster
East Stourmouth
Westmarsh
Oare
Faversham
Davington Hill
Goodnestone
Yorkletts
Highstreet
Druidstone Park
Dargate
Denstroude
Hernhill
Staplestreet
Mt Ephraim
Dunkirk
Blean
Rough Common
Upper Harbledown
Harbledown
Thanington
Chartham Hatch
Chartham
Broad Oak
Tyler Hill
Hales Place
Sturry
Wildwood
Hersden
Westbere
Stodmarsh
Fordwich
Town Hall
Wickhambreaux
Littlebourne
Canterbury
Howletts
Preston
Elmstone
Cop Street
Hoaden
Wingham
Seaton
Ickham
Ash
Durlock
Marshborough
Stone Cross
Woodnesborough
Statenborough
Staple
Bramling
Bekesbourne
Patrixbourne
Bridge
Adisham
Goodnestone
Eastry
Chillenden
Nonington
Aylesham
Lower Hardres
Bishopsbourne
North Downs Way
Betteshanger
Ospringe
Preston
Boughton St
Farming World
South Street
Oversland
Selling
North Street
Sheldwich
Hogben's Hill
Badlesmere
Shottenden
Chilham
Leaveland
Old Wives Lees
Shalmsford Street
Petham
Street End
Garlinge Green
Dane Street
A299
A28
A253
A257
A2050
A290
A291
A2990
A251
A252
A2
B2205
B2231
B2040
B2046
B2190
62
34
35

Pen Brush
Trefasser
Llanw
Pembrokeshire Coast Path
Manorowen
St Nicholas
Ynys Daullyn
Granston
Carreg Sampson
64
Jordanston
Porthgain
Trefin
Mathry
A487
B4331
Abereiddy
Llanrhian
Llangloffan Fen
Berea
Croes-goch
Letterston
Treglemais
ST DAVID'S HEAD
Treleddyd-fawr
B4330
Rhodiad-y-brenin
Caer Farchell
River Solva
Llandeloy
Whitesands Bay
B4583
Bishop's Palace
Whitchurch
Treffgarne Owen
St Davids (Tyddewi)
Hayscastle
Hayscastle Cross
RAMSEY ISLAND
RSPB
Ramsey Sound
Solva
Treffga
Penycwn
178
DUDWELL MT
Leweston
St David's Peninsula Heritage Coast
Newgale
Roch
Wolfsdale
PEMBROKESHIRE COAST NATIONAL PARK
Simpson Cross
Camrose
Rickets Head
Keeston
Nolton Haven
Nolton
St Brides Bay
St Brides Bay Heritage Coast
Druidston
Haroldston West
Portfield Gate
B4341
Broad Haven
Broadway
B4327
Dreen Hill
A4076
Little Haven
Walton West
Pembrokeshire Coast Path
Talbenny
Tiers Cross
Freys
Walwyn's Castle
Johns
SKOMER ISLAND
Wooltack Point
Marloes
A477
St Ishmael's
Herbrandston
Steynton
Broad Sound
Hubberston
Waterston
Marloes and Dale Heritage Coast
Dale
Hakin
B4325
Westdale Bay
Great Castle Head
Llanstadwell
SKOKHOLM ISLAND
Dale Point
Milford Haven (Aberdaugleddau)
Milford Haven
Pembroke Dock (Doc Penfro
Angle
Angle Bay
St Ann's Head
Rhoscrowther
B4320
Rosslare
Hund
Freshwater West
Castlemartin Brook
B4319
Castlemartin
Twyn
Warren
Merrion
Linney Head
PEMBROKESHIRE COAST NATIONAL PARK
Boshe
Pembrokeshire Coast Path
0 1 2 3 4 miles
0 1 2 3 4 5 kilometres

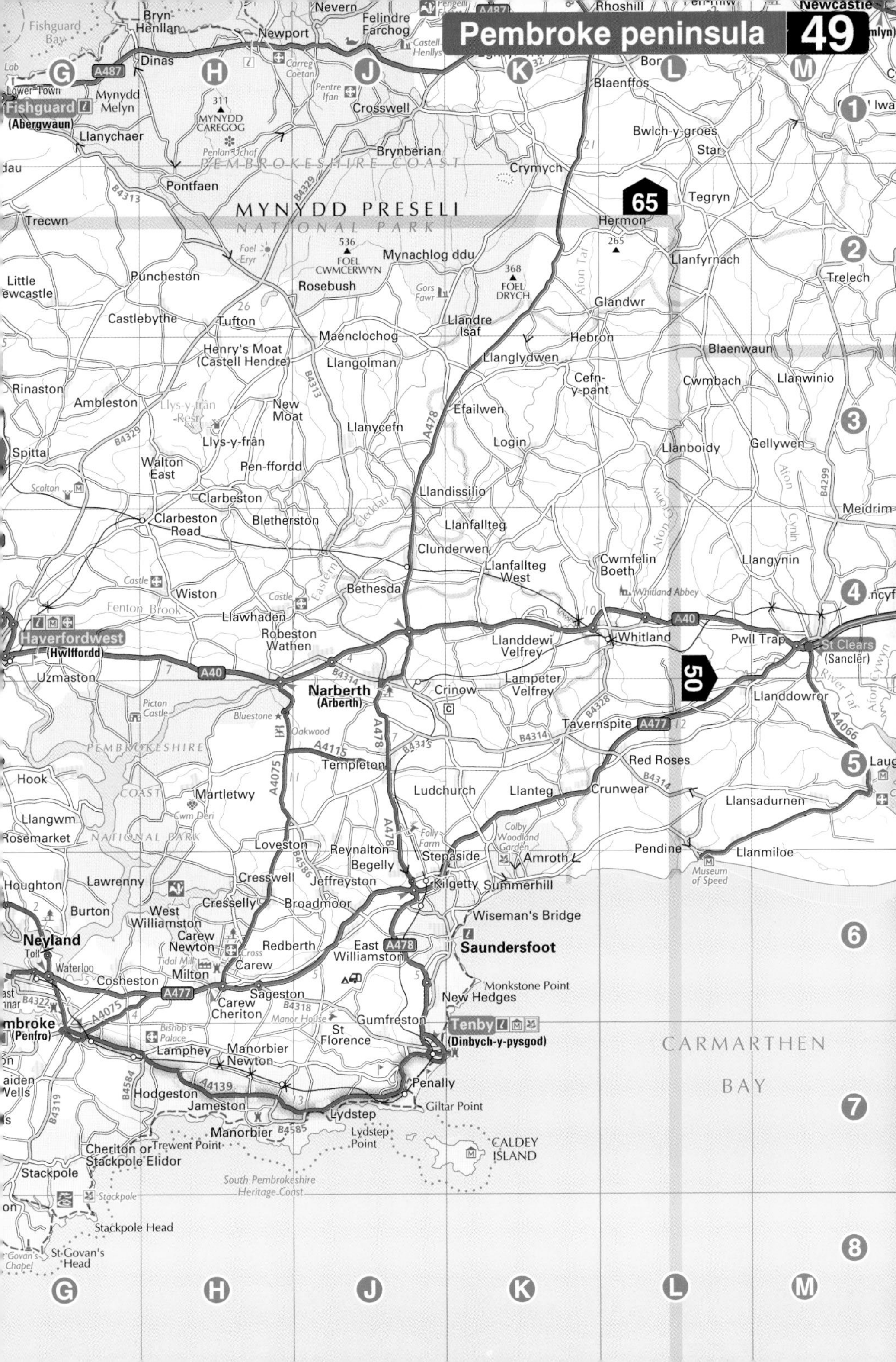
Fishguard Bay
Fishguard
(Abergwaun)
Lower Town
Bryn-Henllan
Dinas
Newport
Nevern
Felindre Farchog
Castell Henllys
Rhoshill
Blaenffos
Newcastle
Carreg Coetan
Pentre Ifan
Crosswell
Mynydd Melyn
Llanychaer
311
MYNYDD CAREGOG
Penlan Uchaf
Brynberian
PEMBROKESHIRE COAST
Pontfaen
Crymych
MYNYDD PRESELI
NATIONAL PARK
Bwlch-y-groes
Star
Tegryn
65
Hermon
265
Llanfyrnach
Trelech
Trecwn
Foel Eryr
536
FOEL CWMCERWYN
Mynachlog ddu
368
FOEL DRYCH
Gors Fawr
Puncheston
Rosebush
Little Newcastle
Afon Taf
Glandwr
Castlebythe
Tufton
Llandre Isaf
Maenclochog
Hebron
Henry's Moat (Castell Hendre)
Llangolman
Llanglydwen
Blaenwaun
Cwmbach
Llanwinio
Cefn-y-pant
Rinaston
Ambleston
Llys-y-frân Resr
New Moat
Efailwen
Llanycefn
Login
Llanboidy
Gellywen
Llys-y-frân
Spittal
Walton East
Pen-fforddd
Scolton
Llandissilio
Clarbeston
Meidrim
Clarbeston Road
Bletherston
Llanfallteg
Clunderwen
Cwmfelin Boeth
Llangynin
Llanfallteg West
Castle
Wiston
Bethesda
Whitland Abbey
Fenton Brook
Llawhaden
Haverfordwest
(Hwlffordd)
Robeston Wathen
Llanddewi Velfrey
Whitland
Pwll Trap
St Clears
(Sanclêr)
50
Uzmaston
Narberth
(Arberth)
Crinow
Lampeter Velfrey
Llanddowror
Picton Castle
Bluestone
Oakwood
Tavernspite
PEMBROKESHIRE
Templeton
Red Roses
Hook
COAST
Martletwy
Ludchurch
Llanteg
Crunwear
Llansadurnen
Llangwm
Cwm Deri
Rosemarket
NATIONAL PARK
Folly Farm
Colby Woodland Garden
Loveston
Reynalton
Begelly
Stepaside
Amroth
Pendine
Llanmiloe
Museum of Speed
Houghton
Lawrenny
Cresswell
Jeffreyston
Kilgetty
Summerhill
Burton
Cresselly
Broadmoor
West Williamston
Wiseman's Bridge
Neyland
Toll
Carew Newton
Cross
Carew
Redberth
East Williamston
Saundersfoot
Tidal Mill
Waterloo
Milton
Cosheston
Monkstone Point
Sageston
Carew Cheriton
New Hedges
Pembroke
(Penfro)
Bishop's Palace
Manor House
St Florence
Gumfreston
Tenby
(Dinbych-y-pysgod)
CARMARTHEN BAY
Lamphey
Manorbier Newton
Penally
Hodgeston
Jameston
Giltar Point
Lydstep
Manorbier
Lydstep Point
CALDEY ISLAND
Cheriton or Stackpole Elidor
Trewent Point
Stackpole
South Pembrokeshire Heritage Coast
Stackpole Head
St Govan's Chapel
St Govan's Head
A487
A40
A478
A477
A4075
A4115
A4139
B4313
B4329
B4314
B4328
B4315
B4318
B4586
B4584
B4585
B4319
B4322
B4299
A4066
G
H
J
K
L
M
1
2
3
4
5
6
7
8

50
65
49
Trelech
Llanpumsaint
Glandwr
Hebron
Blaenwaun
Cynwyl Elfed
Rhydargaeau
Pontar
Blaen-y-Coed
Cwmbach
Llanwinio
Talog
Cefn-y-pant
Efailwen
Login
Llanboidy
Gellywen
Abernant
Bronwydd
Felingwm
Gwili Railway
River Gwili
Meidrim
Carmarthen
(Caerfyrddin)
Abergwili
Nantgar
Llangunnor
Tre-gynwr
Johnstown
Llanllwch
United Counties
Cwmfelin Boeth
Llanfallteg West
Llangynin
Bancyfelin
Whitland Abbey
Whitland
Llanddewi Velfrey
Pwll Trap
St Clears
(Sanclêr)
Cwmffrwd
Croesyceiliog
Llanddarog
Lampeter Velfrey
Llanddowror
River Taf
Afon Cywyn
Llangynog
Idole
Bancycapel
Llangendeirne
Tavernspite
Red Roses
Llanybri
Pontantwn
Crwbin
Bancffosfelen
Laugharne
Llansteffan
Llandyfaelog
Pontyberem
Llanteg
Crunwear
Llansadurnen
Castle
Ferryside
Meinciau
River Towy
Four Roads
Colby Woodland Garden
Amroth
Pendine
Llanmiloe
Museum of Speed
Wharley Point
Ginst Point
Llansaint
Pontyates
Mynyddgarreg
Summerhill
R Gwendraeth
Kidwelly
(Cydweli)
Carway
Five Roads
Ffos Las
Wiseman's Bridge
Saundersfoot
Trimsaran
Pen-y-Mynydd
Monkstone Point
Pembrey
Ffrwd Farm Mire
(Dinbych-y-pysgod)
Archddu
Burry Port
(Porth Tywyn)
Pwll
CARMARTHEN
BAY
CALDEY ISLAND
Burry Inlet
Whiteford Burrows
Broughton Bay
Llanmadoc
Burry Holms
Llangennith
Cheriton
Burry Green
Oldwalls
Rhossili Bay
Rhossili Downs
Reynoldston
Llanddewi
Rhossili
Knelston
Visitor Centre
Middleton
WORMS HEAD
Gower Coast
Paviland
Port Eynon
Horton
Overton
Culver Hole
Port Eynon Point
A40
A48
A484
A477
A4066
A4118
B4298
B4299
B4300
B4301
B4306
B4309
B4312
B4314
B4317
B4308
B4311
B4328
B4247
0 1 2 3 4 miles
0 1 2 3 4 5 kilometres

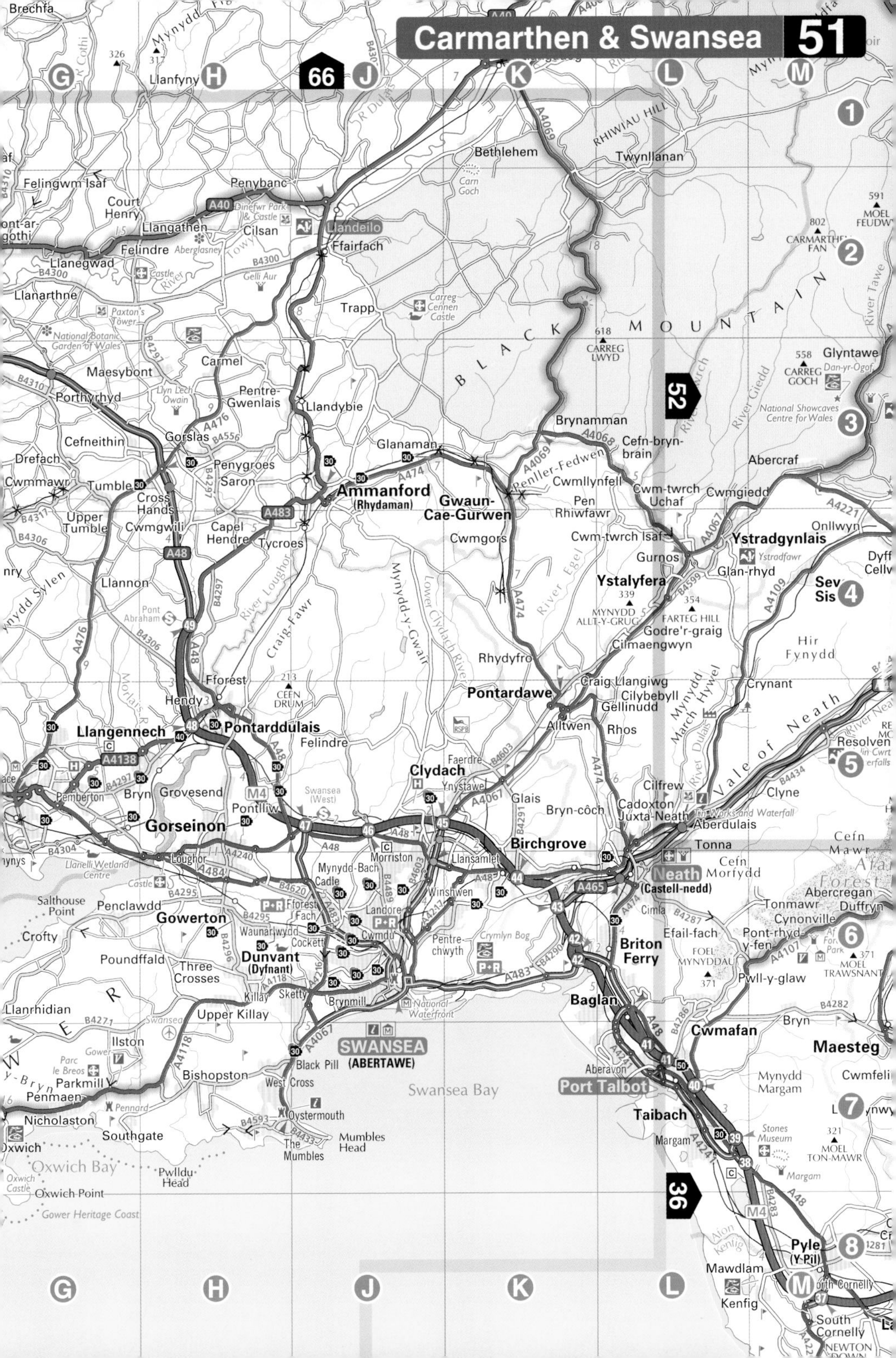
Llandeilo
Ammanford
(Rhydaman)
Gwaun-Cae-Gurwen
Ystradgynlais
Ystalyfera
Pontardawe
Pontarddulais
Llangennech
Gorseinon
Clydach
Birchgrove
Neath
(Castell-nedd)
Briton Ferry
Baglan
Port Talbot
Taibach
Cwmafan
Maesteg
Pyle
(Y-Pil)
Gowerton
Dunvant
(Dyfnant)
SWANSEA
(ABERTAWE)
Swansea Bay
Oxwich Bay
Gower Heritage Coast
BLACK MOUNTAIN
Vale of Neath
66
52
36

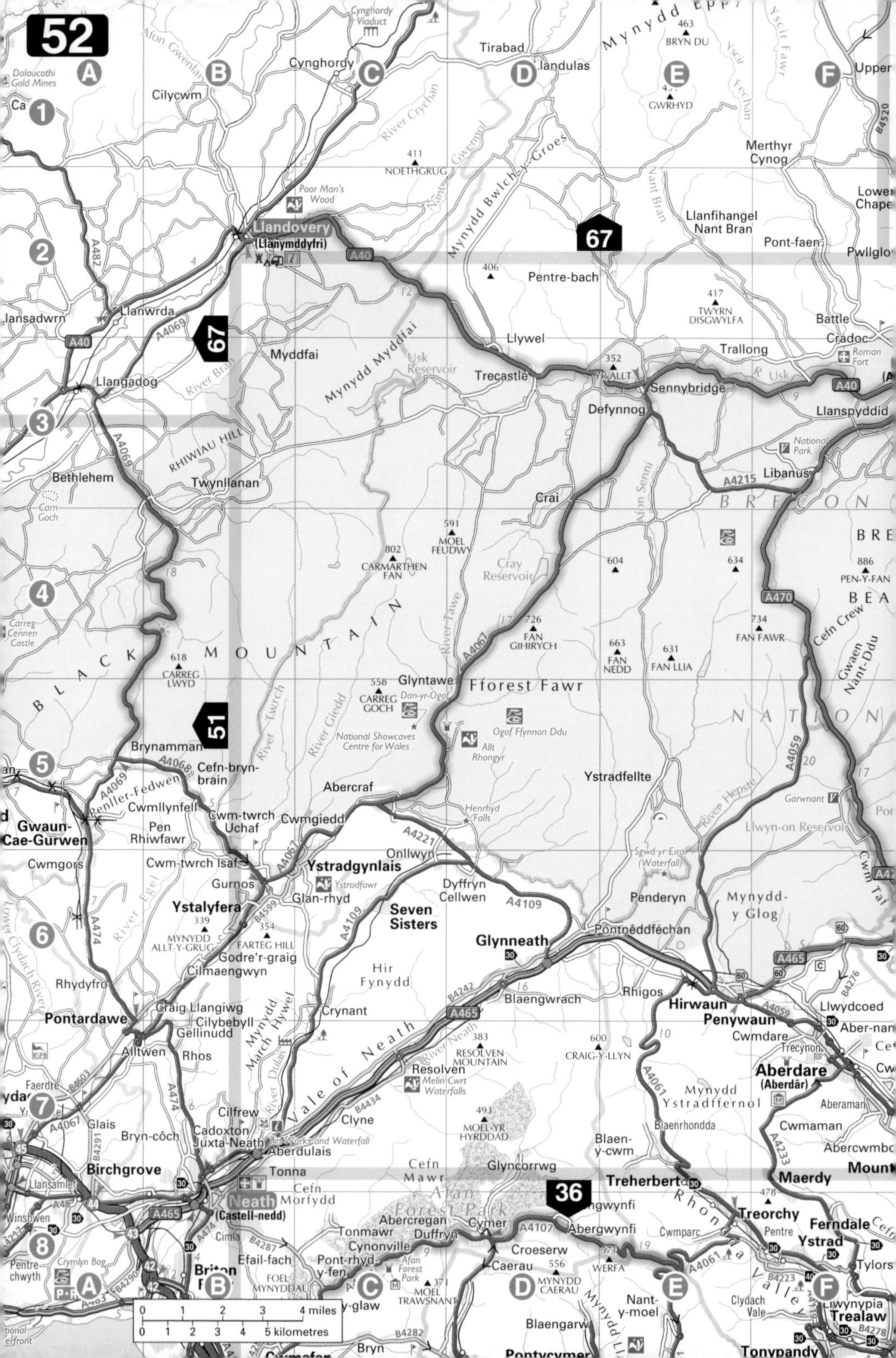

Dolaucothi Gold Mines
Cilycwm
Cynghordy
Cynghordy Viaduct
Tirabad
Llandulas
Mynydd Epynt
463 BRYN DU
GWRHYD
Upper
Merthyr Cynog
411 NOETHGRUG
Poor Man's Wood
Mynydd Bwlch-y-Groes
Llanfihangel Nant Bran
Pont-faen
Pwllglo
Lower Chape
Llandovery (Llanymddyfri)
67
406
Pentre-bach
417 TWYRN DISGWYLFA
Battle
Cradoc
Roman Fort
Llansadwrn
Llanwrda
A40
A4069
Myddfai
Mynydd Myddfai
Usk Reservoir
Llywel
Trallong
352 YR ALLT
Trecastle
Sennybridge
Llangadog
Defynnog
Llanspyddid
Bethlehem
Carn Goch
RHIWIAU HILL
Twynllanan
A4215
Libanus
National Park
Crai
BRECON
591 MOEL FEUDWY
802 CARMARTHEN FAN
Cray Reservoir
604
634
886 PEN-Y-FAN
A470
Carreg Cennen Castle
BLACK MOUNTAIN
618 CARREG LWYD
726 FAN GIHIRYCH
663 FAN NEDD
631 FAN LLIA
734 FAN FAWR
Cefn Crew
Gwaen Nant-Ddu
558 CARREG GOCH
Glyntawe
Dan-yr-Ogof
Fforest Fawr
Ogof Ffynnon Ddu
National Showcaves Centre for Wales
Allt Rhongyr
NATIONAL
51
Brynamman
Cefn-bryn-brain
A4068
Abercraf
Ystradfellte
A4059
Garwnant
Penller-Fedwen
Cwmllynfell
Cwm-twrch Uchaf
Cwmgiedd
Henrhyd Falls
Llwyn-on Reservoir
Gwaun-Cae-Gurwen
Pen Rhiwfawr
A4221
Onllwyn
Cwmgors
Cwm-twrch Isaf
Ystradgynlais
Ystradfawr
Dyffryn Cellwen
Sgwd-yr-Eira (Waterfall)
Gurnos
Glan-rhyd
A4109
Penderyn
Mynydd-y Glog
Ystalyfera
Seven Sisters
339 MYNYDD ALLT-Y-GRUG
354 FARTEG HILL
Glynneath
Pontneddfechan
Lower Clydach River
Godre'r-graig
Cilmaengwyn
Hir Fynydd
A465
Rhydyfro
Blaengwrach
Rhigos
Hirwaun
Llwydcoed
Penywaun
Pontardawe
Craig Llangiwg
Cilybebyll
Gellinudd
Crynant
Mynydd March Hywel
Cwmdare
Aber-nant
Alltwen
Rhos
Vale of Neath
383 RESOLVEN MOUNTAIN
600 CRAIG-Y-LLYN
Trecynon
Aberdare (Aberdâr)
Resolven
Melin Court Waterfalls
A4061
Mynydd Ystradffernol
Aberaman
Faerdre
Glais
Cilfrew
Clyne
493 MOEL-Y-HYRDDAD
Blaenrhondda
Cwmaman
Bryn-côch
Cadoxton Juxta-Neath
Aberdulais
Aberdulais Tin Works and Waterfall
Blaen-y-cwm
Abercwmbo
Birchgrove
Tonna
Cefn Mawr
Glyncorrwg
Treherbert
Maerdy
Mount
Llansamlet
36
Neath (Castell-nedd)
Cefn Morfydd
Afan Forest Park
Blaengwynfi
478
Treorchy
Ferndale
Winsh-wen
A465
Abercregan
Cymer
Abergwynfi
Cwmparc
Pentre
Ystrad
Tonmawr
Duffryn
Cimla
Cynonville
A4107
Croeserw
Rhondda Valley
Pentre-chwyth
Crymlyn Bog
Efail-fach
Pont-rhyd-y-fen
Afan Forest Park
Caerau
556 MYNYDD CAERAU
371 WERFA
Tylorstown
Briton Ferry
FOEL MYNYDDAU
371 MOEL TRAWSNANT
Clydach Vale
Llwynypia
Trealaw
Nant-y-moel
Blaengarw
Bryn
Pontycymer
Tonypandy
0 1 2 3 4 miles
0 1 2 3 4 5 kilometres

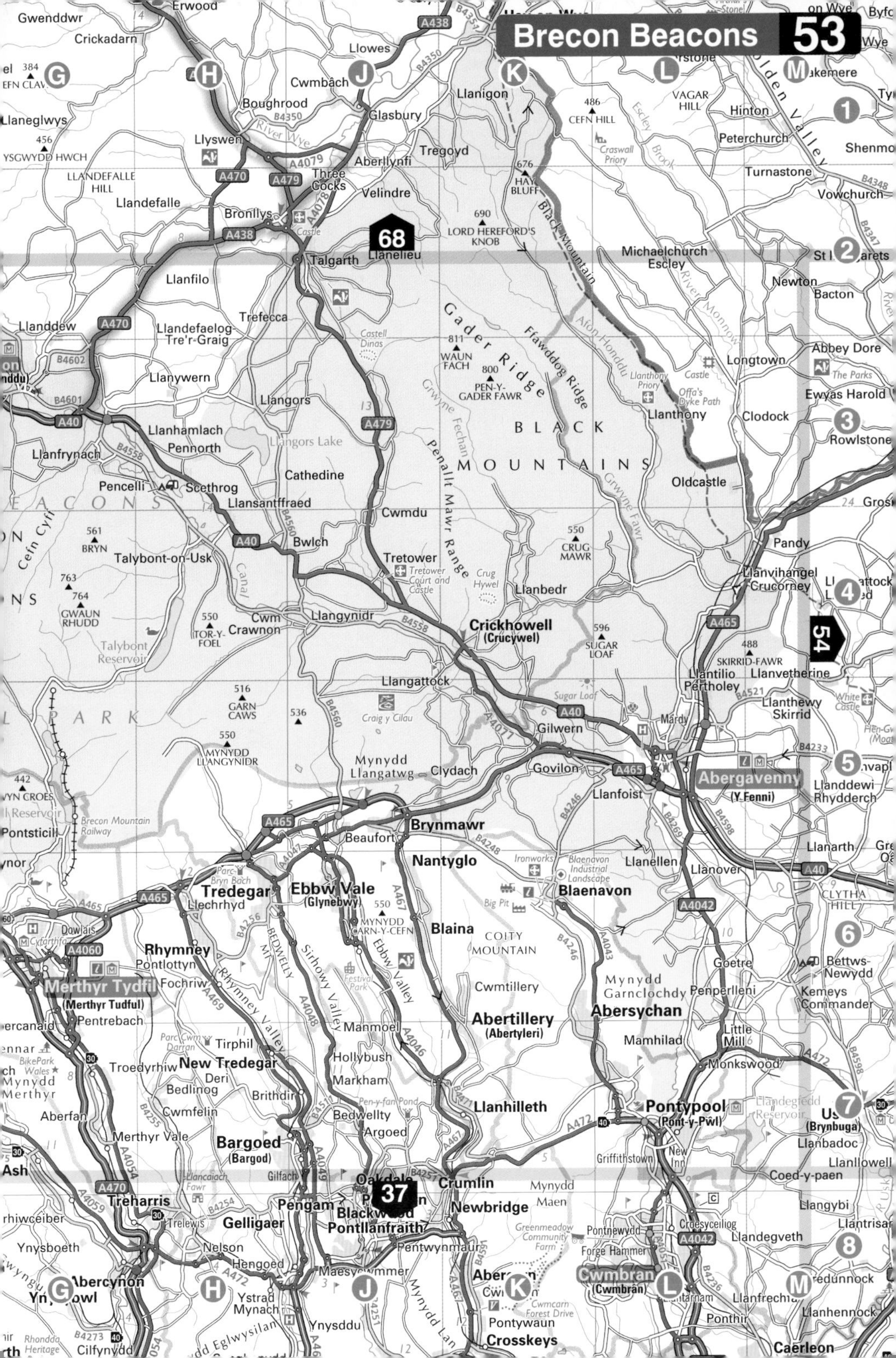
Erwood
Gwenddwr
Crickadarn
Llowes
Cwmbâch
Boughrood
Glasbury
Llanigon
Llaneglwys
Llyswen
River Wye
Tregoyd
Aberllynfi
Three Cocks
Velindre
Llandefalle Hill
Llandefalle
Bronllys
Castle
68
Talgarth
Llanelieu
Llanfilo
Trefecca
Llanddew
Llandefaelog-Tre'r-Graig
Llanywern
Llangors
Llanhamlach
Pennorth
Llangors Lake
Llanfrynach
Pencelli
Scethrog
Cathedine
Llansantffraed
Cwmdu
Bwlch
Talybont-on-Usk
Tretower
Tretower Court and Castle
Cwm Crawnon
Llangynidr
Talybont Reservoir
Crickhowell
(Crucywel)
Llangattock
Craig y Cilau
Gilwern
Govilon
Mynydd Llangatwg
Clydach
Llanfoist
Brynmawr
Beaufort
Nantyglo
Tredegar
Ebbw Vale
(Glynebwy)
Blaina
Blaenavon
Big Pit
Ironworks
Blaenavon Industrial Landscape
Coity Mountain
Cwmtillery
Abertillery
(Abertyleri)
Mynydd Garnclochdy
Abersychan
Mamhilad
Llanhilleth
Pontypool
(Pont-y-Pŵl)
Griffithstown
New Inn
Pontnewydd
Forge Hammer
Cwmbran
(Cwmbrân)
Croesyceiliog
Llandegveth
Crumlin
Newbridge
Mynydd Maen
Greenmeadow Community Farm
Cwmcarn Forest Drive
Pontywaun
Crosskeys
Oakdale
37
Blackwood
Pengam
Pontllanfraith
Pentwynmawr
Gelligaer
Bargoed
(Bargod)
Gilfach
Llancaiach Fawr
Treharris
Trelewis
Nelson
Hengoed
Ystrad Mynach
Ynysddu
Abercynon
Ynysboeth
Cilfynydd
Merthyr Tydfil
(Merthyr Tudful)
Pentrebach
Troedyrhiw
Aberfan
Merthyr Vale
Dowlais
Cyfarthfa
Rhymney
Pontlottyn
Fochriw
Rhymney Valley
Sirhowy Valley
Ebbw Valley
Llechryhd
Parc Bryn Bach
Tirphil
New Tredegar
Deri
Bedlinog
Cwmfelin
Brithdir
Manmoel
Hollybush
Markham
Bedwellty
Argoed
Pen-y-fan Pond
Festival Park
Parc Cwm Darran
BikePark Wales
Pontsticill
Brecon Mountain Railway
Hay Bluff
Lord Hereford's Knob
Waun Fach
Pen-y-Gader Fawr
Gader Ridge
Ffawddog Ridge
Black Mountain
Black Mountains
Penallt Mawr Range
Crug Mawr
Crug Hywel
Llanbedr
Sugar Loaf
Castell Dinas
Craswall Priory
Cefn Hill
Vagar Hill
Hinton
Peterchurch
Turnastone
Vowchurch
Golden Valley
Michaelchurch Escley
Escley Brook
River Monnow
Newton
Bacton
Longtown
Abbey Dore
The Parks
Ewyas Harold
Llanthony Priory
Llanthony
Offa's Dyke Path
Clodock
Rowlstone
Oldcastle
Pandy
Llanvihangel Crucorney
Skirrid-Fawr
Llantilio Pertholey
Llanvetherine
Llanthewy Skirrid
White Castle
Mardy
Abergavenny
(Y Fenni)
Llanddewi Rhydderch
Llanellen
Llanover
Llanarth
Clytha Hill
Goetre
Penperlleni
Bettws-Newydd
Kemeys Commander
Little Mill
Monkswood
Llandegfedd Reservoir
Usk
(Brynbuga)
Llanbadoc
Llanllowell
Coed-y-paen
Llangybi
Llantrisant
Tredunnock
Llanfrechfa
Llanhennock
Ponthir
Caerleon
54
A438
A470
A479
A4079
A40
A465
A4042
A467
A4046
A4048
A469
A4060
A4054
A4059
A472
B4350
B4558
B4560
B4602
B4601
B4246
B4248
B4269
B4598
B4521
B4233
B4348
B4347
B4254
B4255
B4256
B4251
B4273

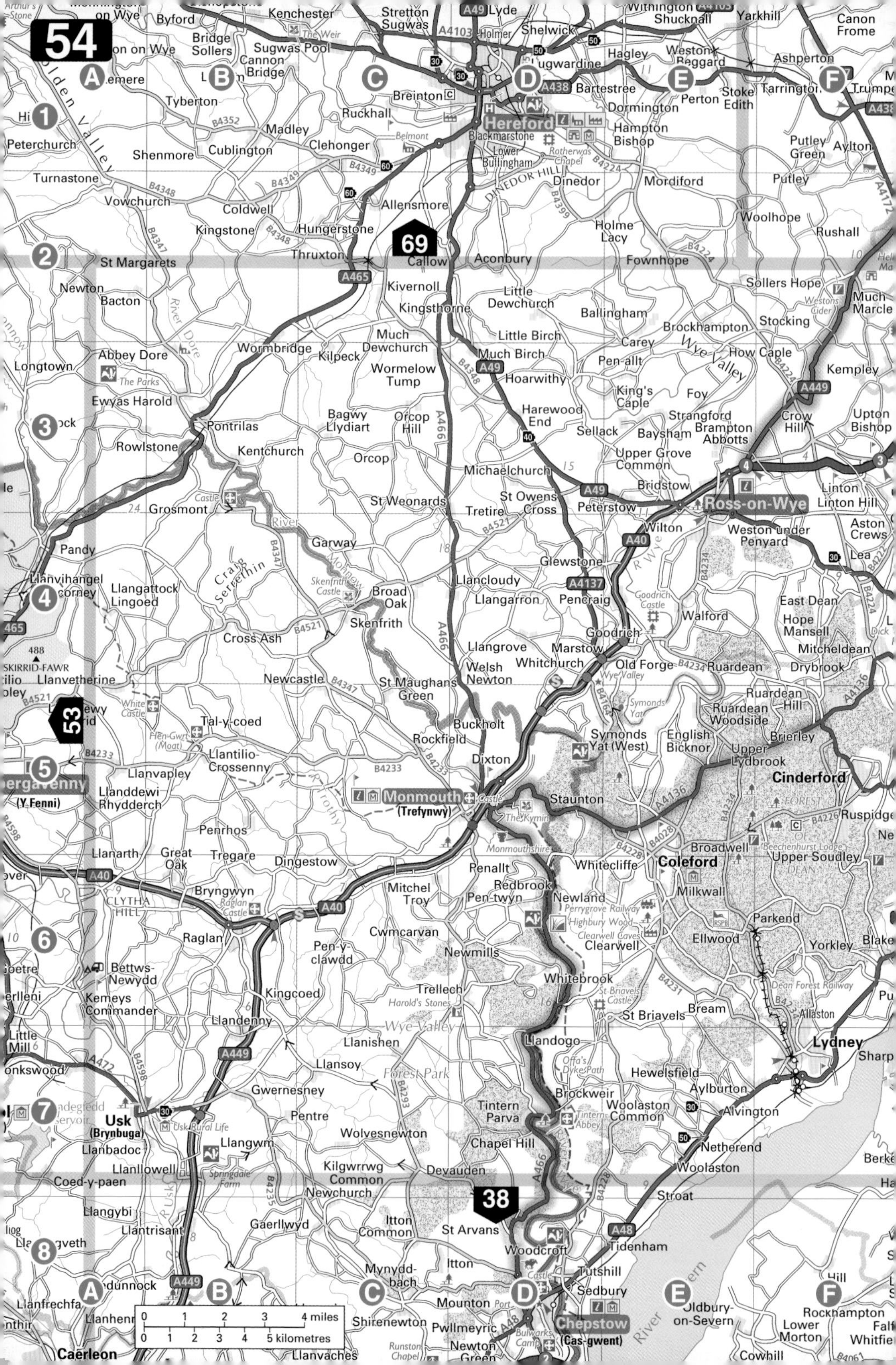

54
Byford
Kenchester
Stretton Sugwas
Lyde
Withington
Shucknall
Yarkhill
Canon Frome
Bridge Sollers
Sugwas Pool
The Weir
Holmer
Shelwick
Cannon Bridge
Lugwardine
Hagley
Weston Beggard
Ashperton
Tyberton
Breinton
Bartestree
Perton
Stoke Edith
Tarrington
Trumpet
Peterchurch
Ruckhall
Hereford
Dormington
Madley
Belmont
Blackmarstone
Hampton Bishop
Shenmore
Cublington
Clehonger
Lower Bullingham
Rotherwas Chapel
Putley Green
Aylton
Turnastone
DINEDOR HILL
Dinedor
Mordiford
Putley
Vowchurch
Coldwell
Allensmore
Woolhope
Kingstone
Hungerstone
Holme Lacy
Rushall
69
Thruxton
St Margarets
Callow
Aconbury
Fownhope
Newton
Kivernoll
Little Dewchurch
Sollers Hope
Bacton
Kingsthorne
Ballingham
Much Marcle
Westons Cider
River Dore
Little Birch
Carey
Brockhampton
Stocking
Abbey Dore
Wormbridge
Kilpeck
Much Dewchurch
Much Birch
Wye Valley
How Caple
Longtown
The Parks
Wormelow Tump
Pen-allt
Kempley
Hoarwithy
King's Caple
Foy
Ewyas Harold
Harewood End
Strangford
Crow Hill
Upton Bishop
Bagwy Llydiart
Orcop Hill
Brampton Abbotts
Pontrilas
Sellack
Baysham
Rowlstone
Kentchurch
Orcop
Upper Grove Common
Michaelchurch
Bridstow
Castle
St Owens Cross
Linton
Grosmont
St Weonards
Tretire
Peterstow
Ross-on-Wye
Linton Hill
Wilton
Aston Crews
Weston under Penyard
Pandy
River
Garway
Lea
Craig Serrerthin
Glewstone
Llanvihangel Crucorney
Skenfrith Castle
Broad Oak
Llancloudy
Llangattock Lingoed
Llangarron
Pencraig
Goodrich Castle
East Dean
Skenfrith
Walford
Hope Mansell
Cross Ash
Goodrich
Llangrove
Marstow
Mitcheldean
488
SKIRRID-FAWR
Llanvetherine
Whitchurch
Old Forge
Welsh Newton
Ruardean
Drybrook
Newcastle
St Maughans Green
Wye Valley
Symonds Yat
Ruardean Hill
White Castle
Ruardean Woodside
53
Tal-y-coed
Buckholt
Symonds Yat (West)
English Bicknor
Brierley
Hen Gwrt (Moat)
Llantilio-Crossenny
Rockfield
Upper Lydbrook
Cinderford
Llanvapley
Dixton
Llanddewi Rhydderch
Monmouth
(Trefynwy)
Castle
Staunton
The Kymin
Ruspidge
(Y Fenni)
Penrhos
FOREST OF DEAN
Beechenhurst Lodge
Monmouthshire
Broadwell
Upper Soudley
Llanarth
Great Oak
Tregare
Dingestow
Penallt
Whitecliffe
Coleford
Redbrook
Bryngwyn
Mitchel Troy
Pen-twyn
Newland
Milkwall
CLYTHA HILL
Raglan Castle
Perrygrove Railway
Highbury Wood
Parkend
Raglan
Cwmcarvan
Clearwell Caves
Clearwell
Ellwood
Yorkley
Blakeney
Pen-y-clawdd
Newmills
Bettws-Newydd
Whitebrook
Dean Forest Railway
Kemeys Commander
Kingcoed
Trellech
St Briavels Castle
Harold's Stones
St Briavels
Bream
Allaston
Llandenny
Wye Valley
Llandogo
Lydney
Little Mill
Llanishen
Offa's Dyke Path
Sharpness
Llansoy
Forest Park
Hewelsfield
Aylburton
Gwernesney
Brockweir
Usk
(Brynbuga)
Usk Rural Life
Tintern Parva
Tintern Abbey
Woolaston Common
Alvington
Pentre
Llanbadoc
Llangwm
Wolvesnewton
Chapel Hill
Netherend
Llanllowell
Springdale Farm
Kilgwrrwg Common
Devauden
Woolaston
Coed-y-paen
Newchurch
38
Stroat
Llangybi
Gaerllwyd
Itton Common
St Arvans
Llantrisant
Tidenham
Woodcroft
Tutshill
Itton
Mynydd-bach
Castle
Sedbury
Llanhennock
Shirenewton
Mounton
Port
Chepstow
(Cas-gwent)
River Severn
Oldbury-on-Severn
Rockhampton
Lower Morton
Llanfrechfa
Pwllmeyric
Bulwarks Camp
Caerleon
Runston Chapel
Newton Green
Llanvaches
Cowhill
0 1 2 3 4 miles
0 1 2 3 4 5 kilometres
A49
A4103
A438
A465
B4352
B4349
B4348
B4347
B4399
B4224
A466
A4137
A40
B4521
B4234
B4228
B4028
A4136
B4226
B4233
A449
A472
B4598
B4235
B4293
B4231
A48
B4228

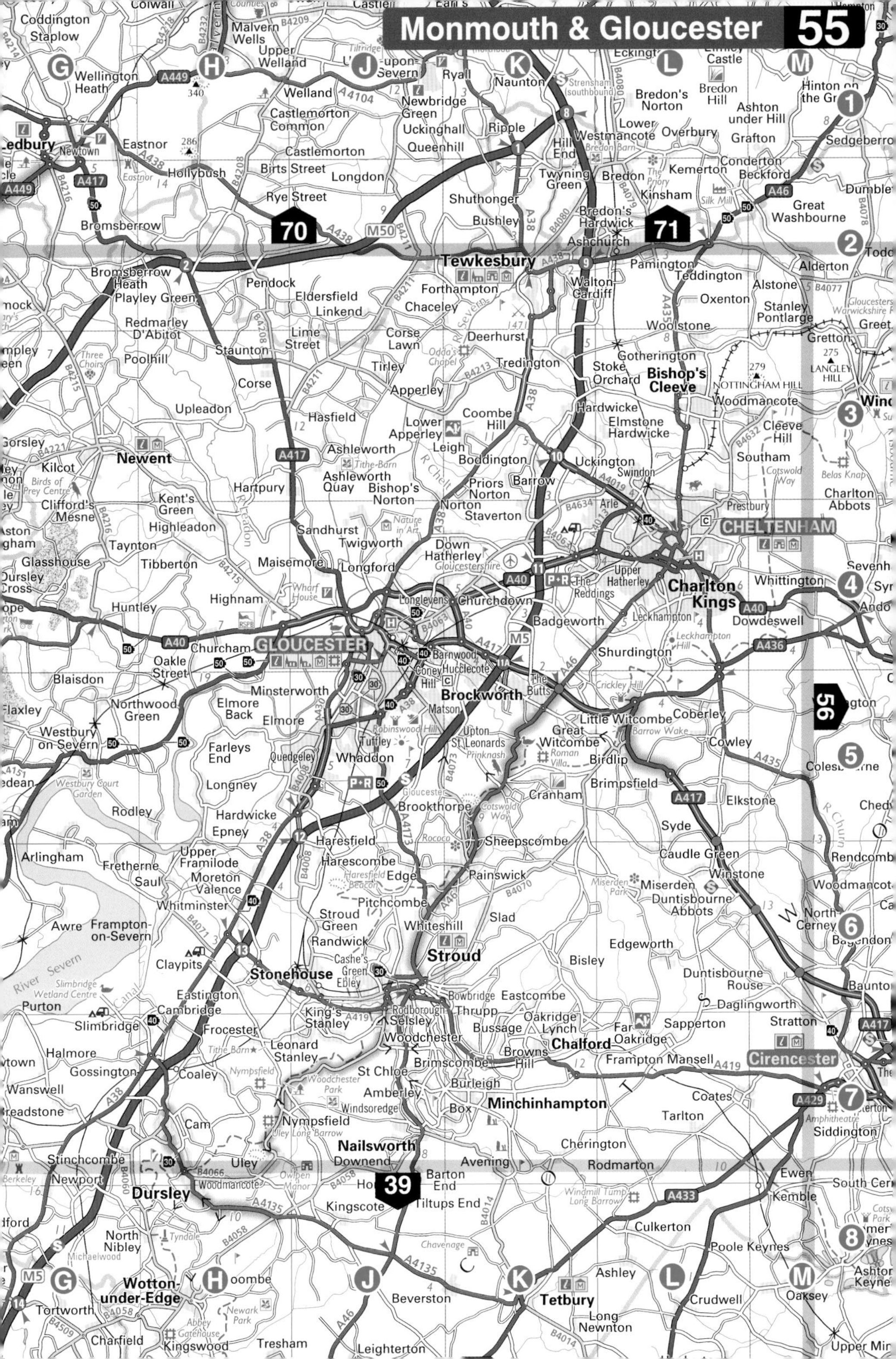
Coddington
Staplow
Malvern Wells
Upper Welland
Wellington Heath
Welland
Castlemorton Common
Castlemorton
Newbridge Green
Ryall
Naunton
Ripple
Uckinghall
Queenhill
Ledbury
Eastnor
Hollybush
Birts Street
Longdon
Rye Street
Bromsberrow
Shuthonger
Bushley
Twyning Green
Bredon
Kemerton
Kinsham
Bredon's Norton
Bredon Hill
Overbury
Ashton under Hill
Grafton
Conderton
Beckford
Great Washbourne
Hinton on the Green
Sedgeberrow
Westmancote
Bredon's Hardwick
Ashchurch
Tewkesbury
Pamington
Teddington
Alderton
Alstone
Walton Cardiff
Bromsberrow Heath
Playley Green
Pendock
Eldersfield
Linkend
Forthampton
Chaceley
Redmarley D'Abitot
Staunton
Lime Street
Corse Lawn
Deerhurst
Oxenton
Stanley Pontlarge
Woolstone
Gretton
Gotherington
Poolhill
Corse
Tirley
Tredington
Stoke Orchard
Bishop's Cleeve
Woodmancote
Upleadon
Apperley
Hasfield
Coombe Hill
Lower Apperley
Leigh
Hardwicke
Elmstone Hardwicke
Cleeve Hill
Newent
Ashleworth
Ashleworth Quay
Boddington
Uckington
Southam
Kilcot
Gorsley
Hartpury
Bishop's Norton
Priors Norton
Barrow
Swindon
Clifford's Mesne
Kent's Green
Highleadon
Norton
Staverton
Arle
Prestbury
Charlton Abbots
Taynton
Sandhurst
Twigworth
CHELTENHAM
Glasshouse
Tibberton
Maisemore
Longford
Down Hatherley
Upper Hatherley
Charlton Kings
Whittington
Highnam
Huntley
Longlevens
Churchdown
The Reddings
Badgeworth
Leckhampton
Dowdeswell
GLOUCESTER
Churcham
Oakle Street
Barnwood
Hucclecote
Coney Hill
Shurdington
Blaisdon
Minsterworth
Elmore Back
Elmore
Brockworth
The Butts
Matson
Northwood Green
Flaxley
Westbury on Severn
Farleys End
Quedgeley
Tuffley
Whaddon
Upton St Leonards
Little Witcombe
Great Witcombe
Coberley
Cowley
Birdlip
Brimpsfield
Longney
Rodley
Hardwicke
Epney
Brookthorpe
Cranham
Elkstone
Syde
Arlingham
Fretherne
Saul
Upper Framilode
Moreton Valence
Haresfield
Harescombe
Edge
Sheepscombe
Painswick
Caudle Green
Winstone
Miserden
Duntisbourne Abbots
Rendcomb
Woodmancote
North Cerney
Whitminster
Pitchcombe
Stroud Green
Randwick
Whiteshill
Slad
Stroud
Awre
Frampton-on-Severn
Claypits
Stonehouse
Bisley
Edgeworth
Duntisbourne Rouse
Daglingworth
Eastington
Cambridge
Slimbridge
Purton
King's Stanley
Selsley
Bowbridge
Thrupp
Eastcombe
Oakridge Lynch
Bussage
Chalford
Far Oakridge
Sapperton
Stratton
Cirencester
Frocester
Leonard Stanley
Woodchester
Brimscombe
Browns Hill
Frampton Mansell
Halmore
Gossington
Coaley
St Chloe
Amberley
Burleigh
Minchinhampton
Coates
Tarlton
Wanswell
Nympsfield
Box
Cam
Siddington
Stinchcombe
Newport
Uley
Nailsworth
Downend
Avening
Cherington
Rodmarton
Ewen
Dursley
Barton End
Tiltups End
Kingscote
Kemble
Culkerton
North Nibley
Poole Keynes
Ashley
Wotton-under-Edge
Tortworth
Beverston
Tetbury
Crudwell
Oaksey
Long Newton
Charfield
Kingswood
Tresham
Leighterton
Upper Minety
70
71
39
56

Hampton
Badsey
Vale of Evesham
Wickhamford
Aston-sub-Edge
Weston sub Edge
Willersey
Hidcote Manor Garden
Hidcote Boyce
Ilmington
Darlingscott
Honington
Shipston-on-Stour
Ebrington
Charingworth
Hinton on the Green
Saintbury
Broadway
Chipping Campden
Stretton on Fosse
Willington
Burmington
Sutton-under-Brailes
Ashton under Hill
Childswickham
Aston Somerville
Tidmington
Grafton
Sedgeberrow
Cotswold Way
Broad Campden
Paxford
Cherington
Stourton
Conderton
Beckford
Wormington
Todenham
Dumbleton
Buckland
Draycott
Great Washbourne
Laverton
Broadway Tower
Blockley
Aston Magna
Little Wolford
Whichford
Stanton
Snowshill
Snowshill Manor
Cotswold Lavender
Batsford
Great Wolford
Alderton
Toddington
Long Compton
Cotswold Falconry Centre
Alstone
Stanway
Bourton-on-the-Hill
Barton-on-the-Heath
Stanley Pontlarge
Gloucestershire Warwickshire Railway
Didbrook
Bourton Downs
Sezincote House
Moreton-in-Marsh
Greet
Hailes Abbey
Cutsdean
Little Rollright
Rollright Stones
Gretton
Chastleton
Little Compton
LANGLEY HILL
Ford
Longborough
NOTTINGHAM HILL
Farmcote
Condicote
Evenlode
Salford
Over Norton
Woodmancote
Winchcombe
Temple Guiting
Donnington
Chastleton House
Sudeley
Broadwell
Adlestrop
Cleeve Hill
R Isbourne
Upper Swell
Stow-on-the-Wold
Cornwell
Kineton
Lower Swell
Southam
Belas Knap
Barton
Daylesford
Oddington
Maugersbury
Guiting Power
Kingham
Churchill
Charlton Abbots
Prestbury
Naunton
Upper Slaughter
CHELTENHAM
Hawling
Wyck Rissington
Icomb
Bledington
Brockhampton
Lower Slaughter
Sarsden
Whittington
Sevenhampton
Aylworth
Bourton-on-the-Water
Miniatures
Foscot
Foxholes
Chadlington
Salperton
Westcote
Nether Westcote
Syreford
Model Village
Lyneham
Andoversford
Notgrove
Chilson
Dowdeswell
Shipton
Cold Aston
Motor & Toy
Clapton-on-the-Hill
Little Rissington
Upper Rissington
Idbury
Fifield
Hazleton
Ascott-under-Wychwood
Milton-under-Wychwood
Turkdean
Compton Abdale
Great Rissington
Shipton-under-Wychwood
Withington
Hampnett
HABBER GALLOWS HILL
R Windrush
Farmington
Fulbrook Hill
Yanworth
Northleach
Sherborne
Great Barrington
Colesbourne
Chedworth Roman Villa
World of Mechanical Music
Windrush
Taynton
Fulbrook
Eastington
Little Barrington
Asthall Leigh
Elkstone
Swinbrook
Chedworth
Burford
Minster Lovell
Fossebridge
Coln St Dennis
Asthall
R Churn
Rendcomb
Calcot
Westwell
Coln Rogers
Aldsworth
Cotswold Wildlife Park
Winstone
Woodmancote
Holwell
Winson
Shilton
Calmsden
North Cerney
Ablington
R Leach
Curbridge
Brize Norton
Bagendon
Bibury
Carterton
Duntisbourne Rouse
Coln St Aldwyns
Hatherop
Eastleach Turville
Eastleach Martin
Kencot
Alvescot
Baunton
Daglingworth
Barnsley
Filkins
Black Bourton
Stratton
Quenington
Broughton Poggs
Broadwell
Cirencester
Ampney Crucis
Ampney St Mary
Southrop
Bampton
The Beeches
Langford
Preston
Fairford
Little Faringdon
Clanfield
Chesterton
Amphitheatre
Ampney St Peter
Poulton
Grafton
Harnhill
Meysey Hampton
Lechlade on Thames
Siddington
Driffield
Whelford
Kelmscott
Cotswold Water Park (Fairford/Lechlade)
Fairford
Buscot
Thames Path
Ewen
South Cerney
Marston Meysey
Down Ampney
Inglesham
Eaton Hastings
Littleworth
Kemble
Cerney Wick
Kempsford
Cotswold Country Park & Beach
Cotswold Water Park (Ashton Keynes)
Upper Inglesham
R Cole
Buscot Park
Somerford Keynes
Latton
Castle Eaton
Hannington Wick
Faringdon
Badbury Hill
Ashton Keynes
Moor Farm
Cricklade
Great Coxwell Barn
Coleshill
Oaksey
Hannington
Westrop
Little Coxwell
Highworth
Great Coxwell
Shellingford
Upper Minety
Hampton
Eastrop
Fernham
Swindon & Cricklade Railway
Broad Blunsdon
0 1 2 3 4 miles
0 1 2 3 4 5 kilometres
A44
A46
A429
A424
A436
A40
A361
A417
A419
A4095
A420
A3400
B4035
B4632
B4081
B4479
B4077
B4078
B4068
B4450
B4425
B4020
B4477
B4449
B4019
B4000
B4040
B4508

71
72
55
40

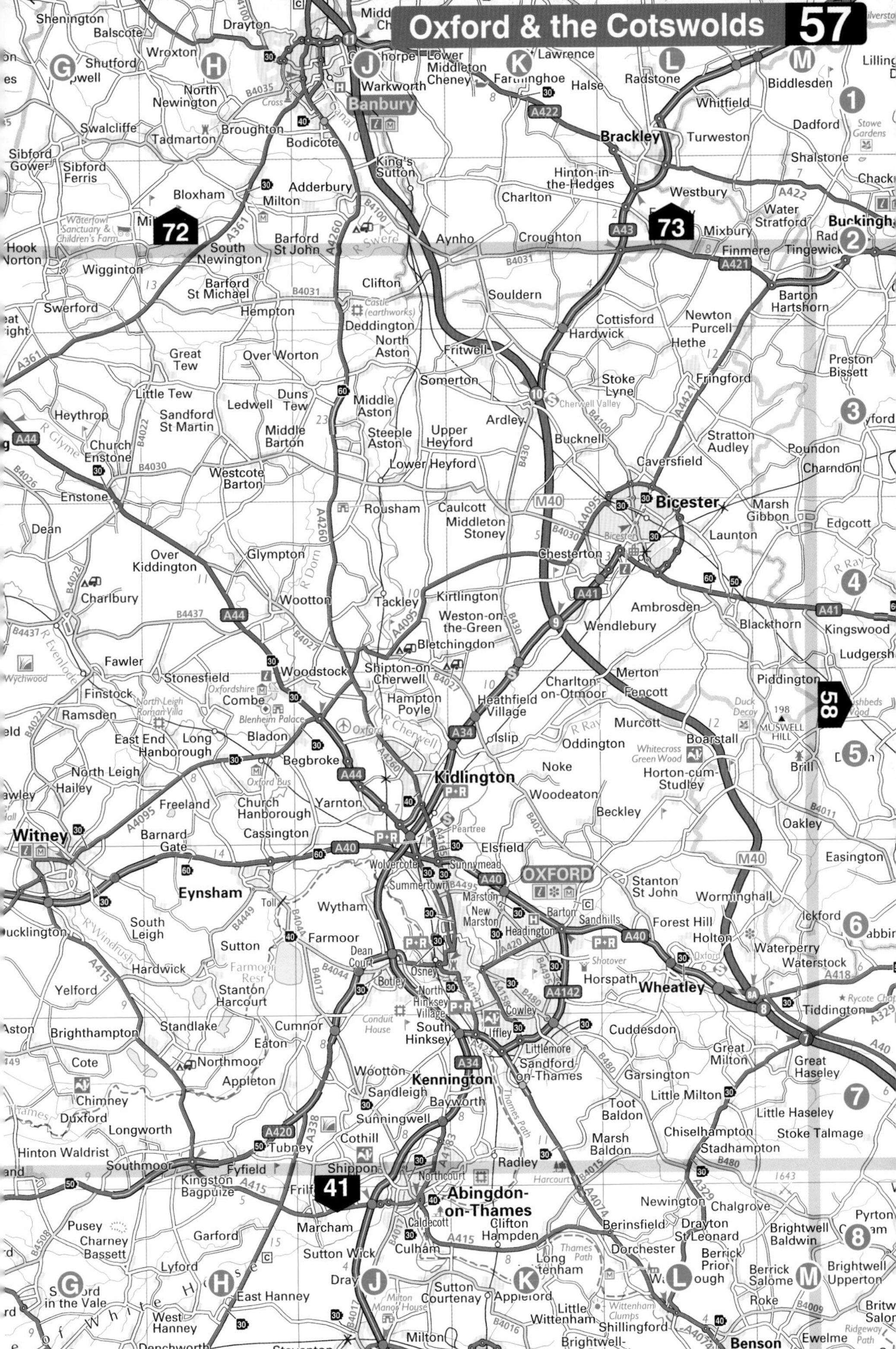
Shenington
Balscote
Drayton
Wroxton
Shutford
North Newington
Warkworth
Banbury
Lower Middleton Cheney
Farthinghoe
Lawrence
Halse
Radstone
Biddlesden
Whitfield
Broughton
Swalcliffe
Tadmarton
Bodicote
Sibford Gower
Sibford Ferris
Bloxham
Adderbury
Milton
King's Sutton
Brackley
Turweston
Dadford
Stowe Gardens
Shalstone
Hinton-in-the-Hedges
Charlton
Westbury
Water Stratford
Buckingham
Waterfowl Sanctuary & Children's Farm
Hook Norton
South Newington
Barford St John
Aynho
Croughton
Mixbury
Finmere
Tingewick
Wigginton
Barford St Michael
Clifton
Souldern
Barton Hartshorn
Swerford
Hempton
Castle (earthworks)
Deddington
North Aston
Cottisford
Hardwick
Newton Purcell
Hethe
Great Tew
Over Worton
Fritwell
Preston Bissett
Little Tew
Duns Tew
Ledwell
Middle Aston
Somerton
Stoke Lyne
Fringford
Heythrop
Sandford St Martin
Middle Barton
Steeple Aston
Upper Heyford
Ardley
Cherwell Valley
Bucknell
Stratton Audley
Poundon
Church Enstone
Westcote Barton
Lower Heyford
Caversfield
Charndon
Enstone
Rousham
Caulcott
Middleton Stoney
Bicester
Marsh Gibbon
Dean
Launton
Edgcott
Over Kiddington
Glympton
Chesterton
Charlbury
Wootton
Tackley
Kirtlington
Ambrosden
Weston-on-the-Green
Wendlebury
Blackthorn
Kingswood
Ludgershall
Fawler
Bletchingdon
Wychwood
Stonesfield
Woodstock
Shipton-on-Cherwell
Merton
Piddington
Finstock
Oxfordshire
Combe
North Leigh Roman Villa
Hampton Poyle
Heathfield Village
Charlton-on-Otmoor
Fencott
Duck Decoy
Muswell Hill
Ramsden
Blenheim Palace
Oxford
Murcott
East End
Long Hanborough
Bladon
Islip
Oddington
Boarstall
Whitecross Green Wood
Brill
North Leigh
Begbroke
Kidlington
Noke
Horton-cum-Studley
Hailey
Oxford Bus
Freeland
Church Hanborough
Yarnton
Woodeaton
Beckley
Oakley
Witney
Barnard Gate
Cassington
Peartree
Elsfield
Easington
Wolvercote
Sunnymead
Eynsham
Summertown
OXFORD
Stanton St John
Worminghall
Toll
Wytham
Marston
New Marston
Barton
Sandhills
Forest Hill
Ickford
South Leigh
Headington
Holton
Ducklington
Farmoor
Sutton
Dean Court
Shotover
Waterperry
Waterstock
Hardwick
Farmoor Resr
Botley
Osney
Horspath
Wheatley
Yelford
Stanton Harcourt
North Hinksey Village
Cowley
Rycote Chapel
Tiddington
Conduit House
Iffley
Standlake
Cumnor
South Hinksey
Littlemore
Cuddesdon
Brighthampton
Eaton
Great Milton
Great Haseley
Cote
Northmoor
Sandford-on-Thames
Garsington
Wootton
Kennington
Appleton
Sandleigh
Little Milton
Chimney
Bayworth
Toot Baldon
Thames Path
Little Haseley
Duxford
Sunningwell
Longworth
Chiselhampton
Stoke Talmage
Hinton Waldrist
Tubney
Cothill
Marsh Baldon
Stadhampton
Southmoor
Fyfield
Shippon
Radley
Kingston Bagpuize
Northcourt
Harcourt Arboretum
Abingdon-on-Thames
Newington
Chalgrove
Marcham
Caldecott
Clifton Hampden
Berinsfield
Drayton St Leonard
Brightwell Baldwin
Pyrton
Pusey
Charney Bassett
Garford
Culham
Dorchester
Berrick Prior
Sutton Wick
Lyford
Long Wittenham
Berrick Salome
Brightwell Upperton
Stanford in the Vale
East Hanney
Drayton
Sutton Courtenay
Appleford
Milton Manor House
Roke
Little Wittenham
Wittenham Clumps
Shillingford
West Hanney
Milton
Brightwell-
Benson
Ewelme
Britwell Salome
Ridgeway Path
Denchworth
Steventon
Vale of White Horse

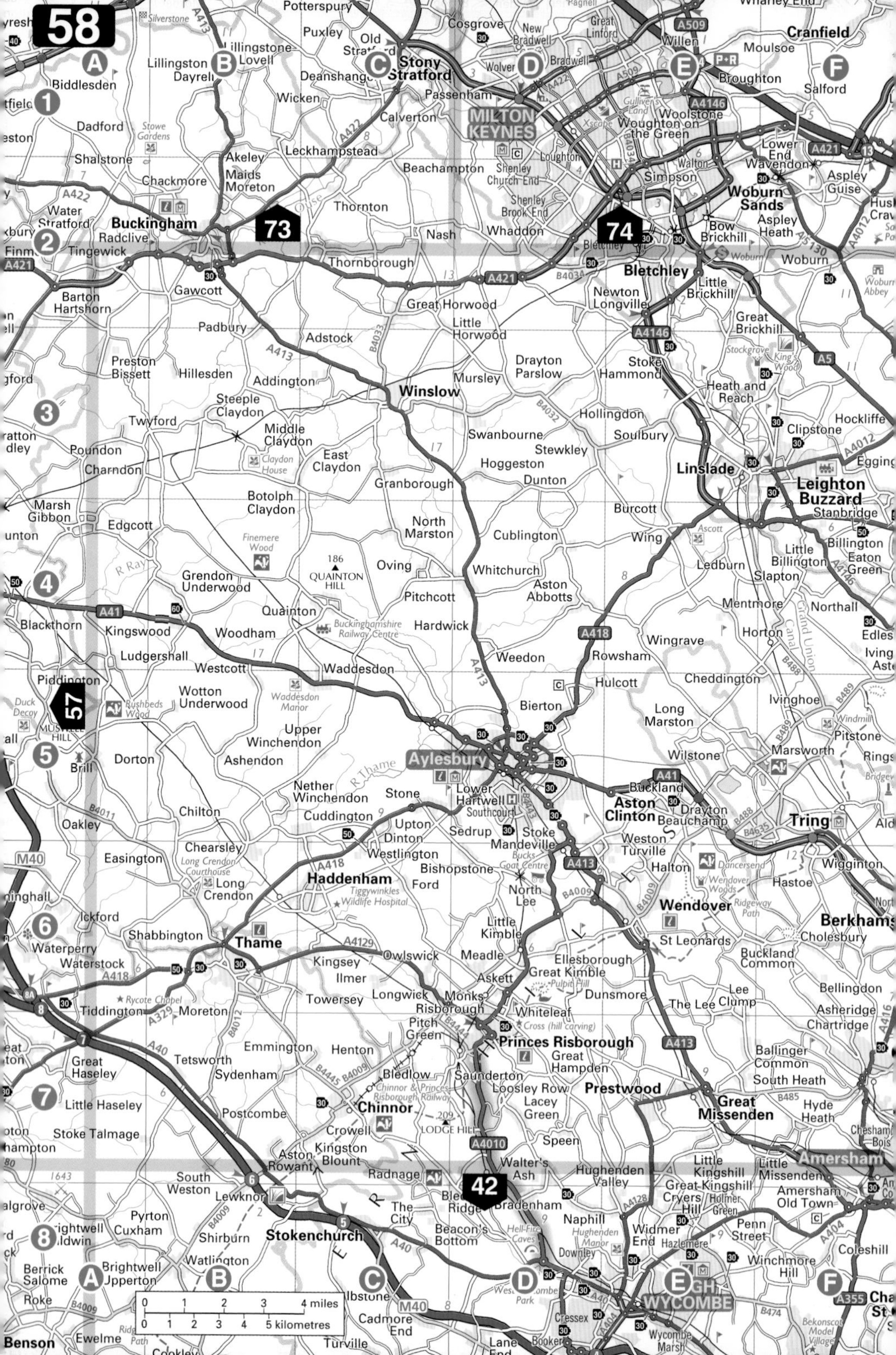
58
A
B
C
D
E
F
1
2
3
4
5
6
7
8
Silverstone
Potterspury
Cosgrove
Pagnell
Great Linford
Wharley End
Cranfield
A509
Lillingstone Lovell
Lillingston Dayrell
Puxley
Old Stratford
Stony Stratford
New Bradwell
Bradwell
Wolverton
Willen
P+R
Moulsoe
Broughton
Salford
Biddlesden
Deanshanger
Passenham
Wicken
MILTON KEYNES
Gulliver's Land
Xscape
Woughton on the Green
Woolstone
A4146
Dadford
Stowe Gardens
Calverton
A422
Leckhampstead
Shalstone
Akeley
Maids Moreton
Beachampton
Shenley Church End
Loughton
Walton
Lower End
Wavendon
A421
Aspley Guise
Chackmore
Simpson
Woburn Sands
Water Stratford
Buckingham
Radclive
Tingewick
73
Thornton
Ouse
Nash
Shenley Brook End
Whaddon
74
Bletchley
Bow Brickhill
Aspley Heath
A5130
A4012
Woburn
Woburn Abbey
Thornborough
B4034
Little Brickhill
Barton Hartshorn
Gawcott
Great Horwood
Newton Longville
Padbury
Little Horwood
Great Brickhill
Stockgrove
King's Wood
Adstock
B4033
A413
Preston Bissett
Hillesden
Addington
Drayton Parslow
Stoke Hammond
Mursley
Winslow
Heath and Reach
A5
Steeple Claydon
B4032
Hollingdon
Twyford
Middle Claydon
Swanbourne
Soulbury
Clipstone
Hockliffe
Poundon
Claydon House
East Claydon
Stewkley
Charndon
Hoggeston
Linslade
Leighton Buzzard
Granborough
Dunton
Marsh Gibbon
Botolph Claydon
Burcott
Stanbridge
Edgcott
North Marston
Cublington
Wing
Ascott
Billington
Finemere Wood
186
QUAINTON HILL
Eaton Green
Little Billington
R Ray
Oving
Ledburn
Grendon Underwood
Whitchurch
Slapton
A4146
Aston Abbotts
Pitchcott
Mentmore
Northall
A41
Quainton
Blackthorn
Kingswood
Woodham
Buckinghamshire Railway Centre
Hardwick
A418
Horton
Wingrave
Grand Union Canal
Ludgershall
Westcott
Weedon
Rowsham
Waddesdon
Hulcott
Cheddington
B488
B489
Piddington
57
Wotton Underwood
Waddesdon Manor
Bierton
Ivinghoe
Duck Decoy
Rushbeds Wood
Long Marston
Windmill
Pitstone
Muswell Hill
Upper Winchendon
Aylesbury
Marsworth
Brill
Dorton
Ashendon
R Thame
Wilstone
Bridgewater
Nether Winchendon
Stone
Lower Hartwell
Buckland
Aston Clinton
Drayton Beauchamp
B4011
Chilton
Cuddington
Southcourt
B4443
Tring
Oakley
Upton
Dinton
Sedrup
Stoke Mandeville
Weston Turville
B4635
Wigginton
M40
Chearsley
Westlington
Bucks Goat Centre
Halton
Easington
Long Crendon Courthouse
Haddenham
Bishopstone
Dancersend
Wendover Woods
Hastoe
Long Crendon
Tiggywinkles Wildlife Hospital
Ford
North Lee
B4009
Wendover
Ridgeway Path
Berkhamsted
Ickford
Little Kimble
St Leonards
Cholesbury
Shabbington
Thame
A4129
Waterperry
Owlswick
Meadle
Ellesborough
Buckland Common
Waterstock
Kingsey
Great Kimble
Pulpit Hill
Ilmer
Askett
Bellingdon
8A
Rycote Chapel
Towersey
Longwick
Monks Risborough
Dunsmore
The Lee
Lee Clump
Tiddington
A329
Moreton
Whiteleaf
Cross (hill carving)
Asheridge
Chartridge
Pitch Green
Princes Risborough
B4012
B4444
A40
Great Haseley
Tetsworth
Emmington
Henton
Great Hampden
Ballinger Common
Sydenham
B4445
Bledlow
Saunderton
Loosley Row
Prestwood
South Heath
Little Haseley
Chinnor & Princes Risborough Railway
Lacey Green
Great Missenden
B485
Hyde Heath
Postcombe
Chinnor
209
LODGE HILL
Stoke Talmage
Crowell
Speen
A4010
Chesham Bois
Aston Rowant
Kingston Blount
Little Kingshill
Little Missenden
Amersham
1643
South Weston
Radnage
Walter's Ash
Hughenden Valley
Great Kingshill
Amersham Old Town
Lewknor
42
Cryers Hill
Holmer Green
Pyrton
Bledlow Ridge
Bradenham
A4128
Cuxham
The City
Naphill
Hughenden Manor
Penn Street
Brightwell Baldwin
Shirburn
Stokenchurch
Beacon's Bottom
Hell-Fire Caves
Widmer End
Hazlemere
Watlington
Downley
Winchmore Hill
Coleshill
A404
Berrick Salome
Brightwell Upperton
West Wycombe Park
HIGH WYCOMBE
A355
Roke
Stonor
Ibstone
B474
Bekonscot Model Village
Cadmore End
Cressex
Benson
Ewelme
Ridgeway Path
Turville
Lane End
Booker
Wycombe Marsh
Cookley
0 1 2 3 4 miles
0 1 2 3 4 5 kilometres

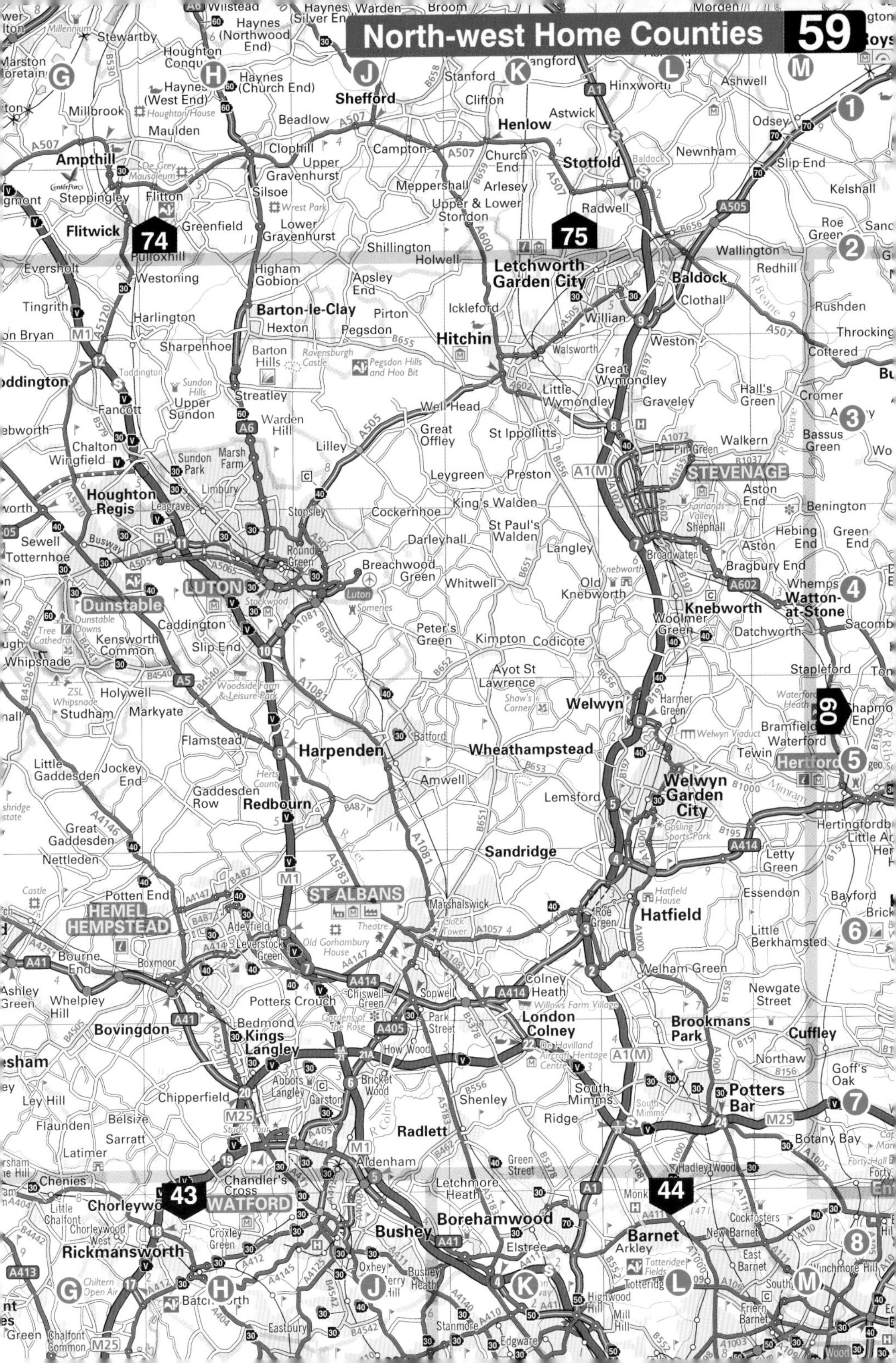
North-west Home Counties
59
Wilstead
Haynes (Silver End)
Warden
Broom
Morden
Stewartby
Millennium
Haynes (Northwood End)
Marston Moretaine
Houghton Conquest
Haynes (Church End)
Haynes (West End)
Shefford
Stanford
Langford
Hinxworth
Ashwell
Millbrook
Houghton House
Beadlow
Clifton
Astwick
Odsey
Maulden
Henlow
Newnham
Ampthill
Clophill
Campton
Church End
Stotfold
Baldock
Slip End
De Grey Mausoleum
Upper Gravenhurst
Meppershall
Arlesey
Kelshall
Steppingley
Flitton
Silsoe
Wrest Park
Upper & Lower Stondon
Radwell
Flitwick
Greenfield
Lower Gravenhurst
Roe Green
Pulloxhill
Shillington
Holwell
Letchworth Garden City
Wallington
Eversholt
Westoning
Higham Gobion
Apsley End
Baldock
Redhill
Tingrith
Harlington
Barton-le-Clay
Pirton
Ickleford
Willian
Clothall
Rushden
Hexton
Pegsdon
Hitchin
Weston
Throcking
Cottered
Sharpenhoe
Barton Hills
Ravensburgh Castle
Pegsdon Hills and Hoo Bit
Walsworth
Great Wymondley
Toddington
Sundon Hills
Little Wymondley
Graveley
Hall's Green
Cromer
Upper Sundon
Streatley
Well Head
Fancott
Warden Hill
Great Offley
St Ippollitts
Walkern
Bassus Green
Chalton
Lilley
Pin Green
Wingfield
Sundon Park
Marsh Farm
Leygreen
Preston
STEVENAGE
Aston End
Limbury
Houghton Regis
Leagrave
Stopsley
Cockernhoe
King's Walden
Fairlands Valley
Benington
Shephall
Sewell
Totternhoe
Busway
Round Green
Darleyhall
St Paul's Walden
Langley
Hebing End
Green End
Aston
Broadwater
Breachwood Green
Bragbury End
LUTON
Stockwood
Luton
Someries
Whitwell
Old Knebworth
Knebworth
Whemps
Watton-at-Stone
Dunstable
Caddington
Dunstable Downs
Tree Cathedral
Kensworth Common
Slip End
Peter's Green
Kimpton
Codicote
Woolmer Green
Datchworth
Sacombe
Whipsnade
Ayot St Lawrence
Stapleford
Woodside Farm & Leisure Park
Shaw's Corner
Welwyn
Harmer Green
Waterford Heath
ZSL Whipsnade
Holywell
Studham
Markyate
Welwyn Viaduct
Bramfield
Batford
Waterford
Flamstead
Harpenden
Wheathampstead
Tewin
Hertford
Little Gaddesden
Jockey End
Herts County
Amwell
Welwyn Garden City
Gaddesden Row
Redbourn
Lemsford
Hertingfordbury
Great Gaddesden
Gosling Sports Park
Letty Green
Nettleden
Sandridge
Castle
Potten End
ST ALBANS
Marshalswick
Hatfield House
Essendon
Bayford
HEMEL HEMPSTEAD
Adeyfield
Theatre
Clock Tower
Roe Green
Hatfield
Leverstock Green
Old Gorhambury House
Little Berkhamsted
Bourne End
Boxmoor
Welham Green
Ashley Green
Whelpley Hill
Chiswell Green
Sopwell
Colney Heath
Newgate Street
Potters Crouch
Willows Farm Village
Bovingdon
Bedmond
Gardens of the Rose
Park Street
London Colney
Brookmans Park
Cuffley
Kings Langley
How Wood
De Havilland Aircraft Heritage Centre
Northaw
Chesham
Abbots Langley
Bricket Wood
Goff's Oak
Ley Hill
Chipperfield
Garston
Shenley
South Mimms
Potters Bar
Flaunden
Belsize
Ridge
Sarratt
Studio Tour
Radlett
Botany Bay
Latimer
Aldenham
Green Street
Hadley Wood
Forty Hill
Chenies
Chandler's Cross
Letchmore Heath
Little Chalfont
Chorleywood
WATFORD
Monken Hadley
Cockfosters
Chorleywood West
Croxley Green
Borehamwood
Bushey
New Barnet
Rickmansworth
Elstree
Barnet
Arkley
East Barnet
Winchmore Hill
Chiltern Open Air
Batchworth
Oxhey
Bushey Heath
Totteridge Fields
Totteridge
Southgate
Highwood Hill
Chalfont Common
Eastbury
Stanmore
Edgware
Mill Hill
Friern Barnet
Wood Green
43
44
60
74
75

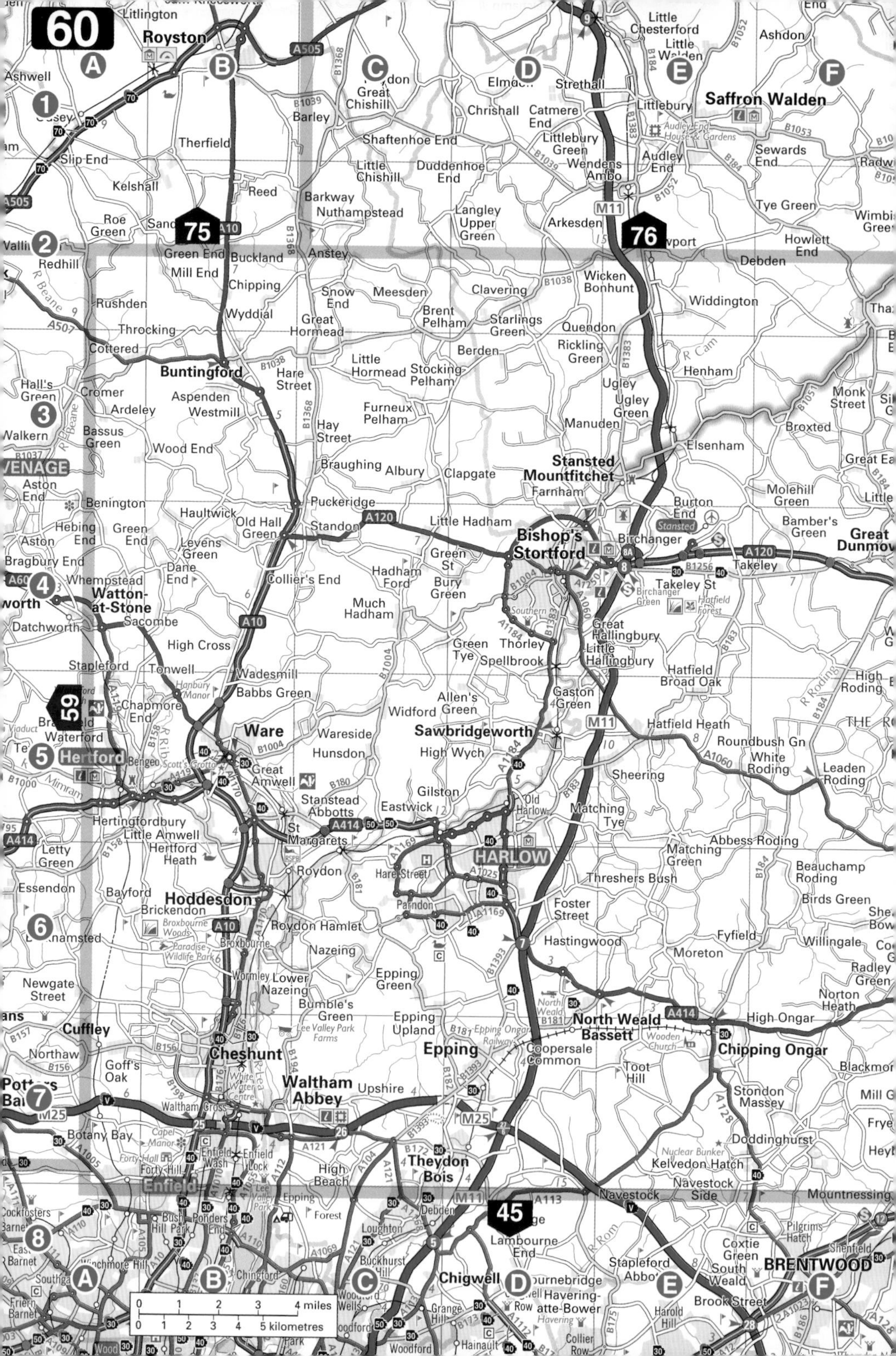

60
Litlington
Royston
Ashwell
Bassingbourn
A505
Therfield
Slip End
Kelshall
Reed
Roe Green
Sandon
75
Wallington
Redhill
Green End
Buckland
Mill End
Chipping
Rushden
Wyddial
Throcking
A507
R Beane
Cottered
Buntingford
Hall's Green
Cromer
Ardeley
Aspenden
Westmill
Walkern
Bassus Green
Wood End
B1037
STEVENAGE
Aston End
Benington
Haultwick
Aston
Hebing End
Green End
Old Hall Green
Levens Green
Bragbury End
Dane End
Whempstead
Watton-at-Stone
Datchworth
Sacombe
High Cross
Stapleford
Tonwell
Wadesmill
59
Hanbury Manor
Babbs Green
Chapmore End
Waterford
Ware
Hertford
Bengeo
Scott's Grotto
Great Amwell
Hertingfordbury
Little Amwell
Hertford Heath
Letty Green
Essendon
Bayford
Brickendon
Hoddesdon
Broxbourne Woods
Paradise Wildlife Park
Broxbourne
Wormley
Lower Nazeing
Newgate Street
Cuffley
Northaw
Goff's Oak
Cheshunt
Potters Bar
M25
Waltham Cross
White Water Centre
Botany Bay
Capel Manor
Forty Hall
Forty Hill
Enfield Wash
Enfield Lock
Enfield
Lee Valley Park
Cockfosters
Barnet
East Barnet
Winchmore Hill
Bush Hill Park
Ponders End
Southgate
Friern Barnet
Chingford
Barkway
Nuthampstead
Little Chishill
Great Chishill
Heydon
Barley
Shaftenhoe End
Duddenhoe End
Elmdon
Chrishall
Catmere End
Strethall
Little Chesterford
Little Walden
Ashdon
Saffron Walden
Littlebury
Littlebury Green
Audley End House & Gardens
Audley End
Wendens Ambo
Sewards End
Langley Upper Green
Arkesden
Tye Green
M11
76
Newport
Howlett End
Debden
Anstey
Snow End
Meesden
Great Hormead
Brent Pelham
Clavering
Wicken Bonhunt
Widdington
Starlings Green
Quendon
Berden
Rickling Green
Little Hormead
Stocking Pelham
Hare Street
Henham
R Cam
Ugley
Ugley Green
Monk Street
Furneux Pelham
Hay Street
Manuden
Broxted
Elsenham
Braughing
Albury
Clapgate
Stansted Mountfitchet
Farnham
Molehill Green
Puckeridge
Standon
A120
Little Hadham
Burton End
Stansted
Bamber's Green
Bishop's Stortford
Birchanger
Great Dunmow
Green St
Hadham Ford
Takeley
Takeley St
Bury Green
Collier's End
Birchanger Green
Hatfield Forest
Much Hadham
Southern
Great Hallingbury
Little Hallingbury
Green Tye
Thorley
Spellbrook
Hatfield Broad Oak
High Roding
Gaston Green
Allen's Green
Widford
Hatfield Heath
Sawbridgeworth
Wareside
Hunsdon
High Wych
Roundbush Gn
White Roding
Leaden Roding
A1060
Sheering
Gilston
Eastwick
Old Harlow
Matching Tye
Stanstead Abbotts
St Margarets
A414
HARLOW
Abbess Roding
Matching Green
Roydon
Hare Street
Threshers Bush
Beauchamp Roding
Parndon
Foster Street
Birds Green
Roydon Hamlet
Nazeing
Hastingwood
Fyfield
Moreton
Willingale
Epping Green
Radley Green
Norton Heath
Bumble's Green
Lee Valley Park Farms
Epping Upland
North Weald
North Weald Bassett
High Ongar
Epping Ongar Railway
Wooden Church
Epping
Coopersale Common
Chipping Ongar
Toot Hill
Blackmore
Waltham Abbey
Upshire
Stondon Massey
Doddinghurst
Nuclear Bunker
Kelvedon Hatch
High Beach
Theydon Bois
Navestock Side
Navestock
Mountnessing
Epping Forest
Debden
Loughton
A113
45
Lambourne End
Pilgrims Hatch
Coxtie Green
Shenfield
BRENTWOOD
Buckhurst Hill
Chigwell
Abridge
Stapleford Abbotts
South Weald
Woodford Wells
Grange Hill
Havering-atte-Bower
Harold Hill
Brook Street
Woodford
Hainault
Collier Row
R Rom
A B C D E F
1 2 3 4 5 6 7 8
0 1 2 3 4 miles
0 1 2 3 4 5 kilometres

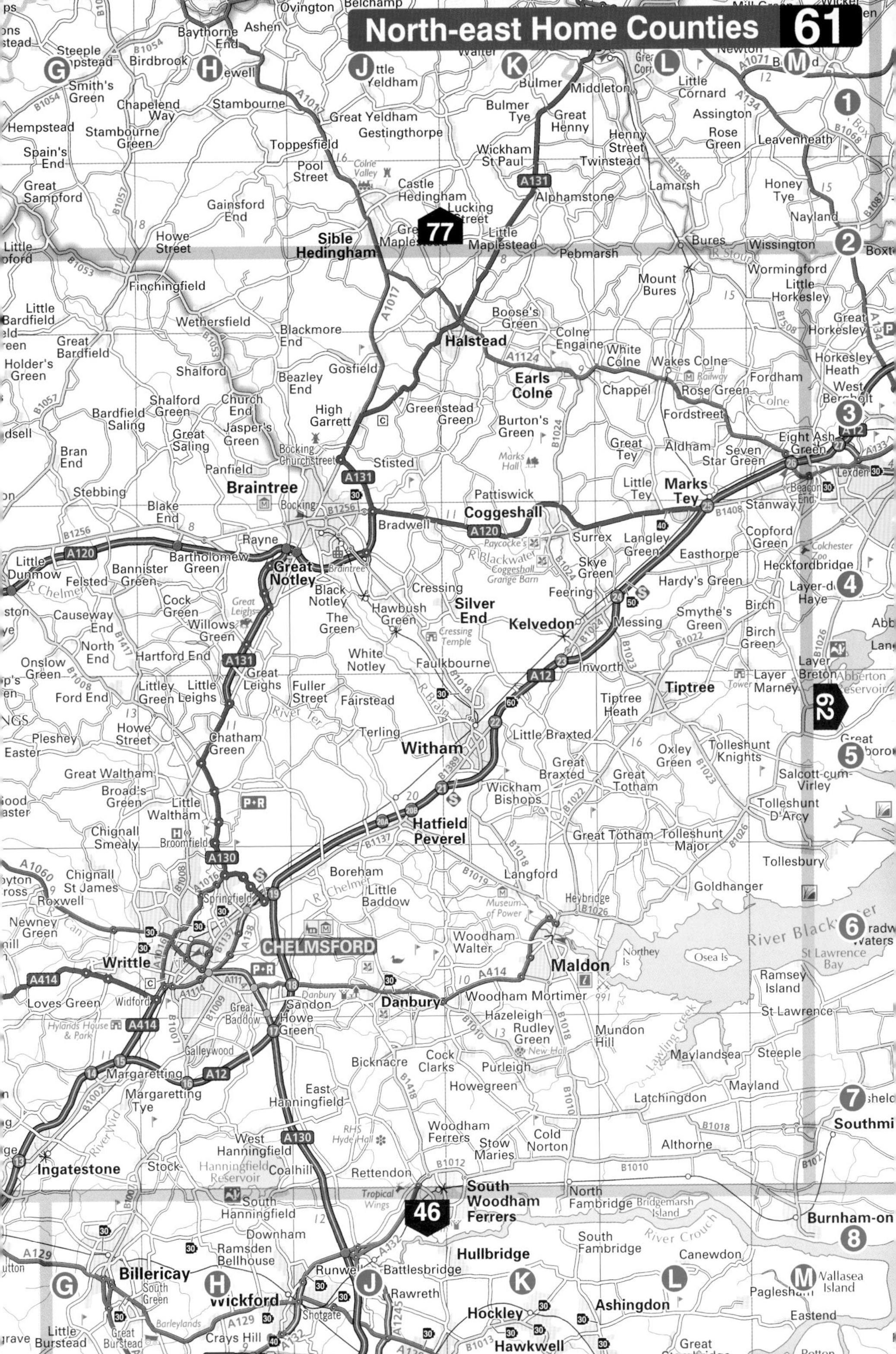

Ovington
Belchamp
Ashen
Baythorne End
Steeple Bumpstead
Birdbrook
Smith's Green
Chapelend Way
Stambourne
Hempstead
Stambourne Green
Great Yeldham
Gestingthorpe
Toppesfield
Spain's End
Great Sampford
Pool Street
Colne Valley
Castle Hedingham
Gainsford End
Howe Street
Sible Hedingham
Lucking Street
Little Maplestead
77
Little Sampford
Finchingfield
Little Bardfield
Wethersfield
Blackmore End
Great Bardfield
Holder's Green
Shalford
Beazley End
Gosfield
Halstead
Shalford Green
Church End
Bardfield Saling
Jasper's Green
Great Saling
High Garrett
Greenstead Green
Bran End
Panfield
Bocking Churchstreet
Stisted
Stebbing
Braintree
Bocking
Blake End
Bradwell
Rayne
Little Dunmow
Bartholomew Green
Bannister Green
Felsted
Great Notley
Black Notley
Cock Green
Causeway End
Willows Green
The Green
Hawbush Green
Cressing
Silver End
Cressing Temple
North End
Onslow Green
Hartford End
White Notley
Faulkbourne
Littley Green
Little Leighs
Great Leighs
Fuller Street
Fairstead
Ford End
Pleshey
Howe Street
Chatham Green
River Ter
Terling
Witham
Great Waltham
Broad's Green
Little Waltham
Chignall Smealy
Broomfield
Chignall St James
Roxwell
Springfield
Newney Green
Writtle
CHELMSFORD
Loves Green
Widford
Hylands House & Park
Great Baddow
Galleywood
Margaretting
Margaretting Tye
Ingatestone
Stock
West Hanningfield
Hanningfield Reservoir
Coalhill
South Hanningfield
Downham
Ramsden Bellhouse
Billericay
South Green
Little Burstead
Great Burstead
Barleylands
Wickford
Crays Hill
Shotgate
Runwell
Battlesbridge
Rawreth
Hullbridge
Hockley
Hawkwell
Ashingdon
Canewdon
Paglesham
Eastend
Wallasea Island
Great Stambridge
Bulmer
Bulmer Tye
Middleton
Great Henny
Henny Street
Wickham St Paul
Twinstead
Alphamstone
Lamarsh
Pebmarsh
Little Cornard
Assington
Rose Green
Leavenheath
Honey Tye
Nayland
Bures
Wissington
Boxted
Mount Bures
Wormingford
Little Horkesley
Great Horkesley
Boose's Green
Colne Engaine
White Colne
Wakes Colne
Earls Colne
Chappel
Horkesley Heath
Fordham
West Bergholt
Rose Green
Fordstreet
Burton's Green
Marks Hall
Great Tey
Aldham
Eight Ash Green
Seven Star Green
Lexden
Little Tey
Marks Tey
Beacon End
Stanway
Pattiswick
Coggeshall
Paycocke's
Coggeshall Grange Barn
R Blackwater
Surrex
Langley Green
Copford Green
Easthorpe
Colchester Zoo
Heckfordbridge
Skye Green
Feering
Hardy's Green
Layer-de-la-Haye
Kelvedon
Messing
Smythe's Green
Birch
Birch Green
Inworth
Layer Breton
Layer Marney
Abberton Reservoir
Tiptree
Tiptree Heath
62
Little Braxted
Great Braxted
Oxley Green
Tolleshunt Knights
Great Totham
Salcott-cum-Virley
Wickham Bishops
Tolleshunt D'Arcy
Hatfield Peverel
Great Totham
Tolleshunt Major
Tollesbury
Boreham
Little Baddow
Langford
Goldhanger
Heybridge
Museum of Power
Woodham Walter
River Blackwater
Northey Is
Osea Is
St Lawrence Bay
Maldon
Ramsey Island
Danbury
Sandon
Howe Green
Woodham Mortimer
St Lawrence
Hazeleigh
Rudley Green
New Hall
Mundon Hill
Bicknacre
Cock Clarks
Purleigh
Maylandsea
Steeple
Lawling Creek
East Hanningfield
Howegreen
Mayland
Latchingdon
Woodham Ferrers
RHS Hyde Hall
Stow Maries
Cold Norton
Althorne
Southminster
Retendon
Tropical Wings
South Woodham Ferrers
46
North Fambridge
Bridgemarsh Island
Burnham-on-Crouch
South Fambridge
River Crouch

Hadleigh
Layham
Raydon
Shelley
Polstead
Leavenheath
Stoke-by-Nayland
Higham
Thorington Street
Stratford St Mary
Holton St Mary
Capel St Mary
Great Wenham
Chattisham
Copdock
Washbrook
Wherstead
Freston
Woolverstone
Nacton
Levington
Bucklesham
Trimley St Martin
River Orwell
Tattingstone White Horse
Tattingstone
Holbrook
Alton Water
Chelmondiston
Shotley
Erwarton
Harkstead
Shotley Street
Shotley Gate
Stutton
Bentley
East Bergholt
Flatford Mill & Bridge Cottage
Cattawade
Mistley Towers
Mistley
River Stour
Holbrook Bay
Wrabness
International Ferry Terminal
Manningtree
Lawford
Dedham
New Mistley
Bradfield
Ramsey
Upper Dovercourt
Dovercourt
Harwich
Bradfield Heath
Wix
Horsleycross Street
Little Bromley
Ardleigh
Ardleigh Heath
Langham
Boxted
Boxted Cross
Wissington
Wormingford
Little Horkesley
Great Horkesley
Horkesley Heath
West Bergholt
Fordham
Eight Ash Green
Seven Star Green
Stanway
Lexden
Hythe
High Woods
Parson's Heath
COLCHESTER
Colchester Zoo
Copford Green
Heckfordbridge
Layer-de-la-Haye
Birch
Birch Green
Layer Breton
Layer Marney
Abberton
Abberton Reservoir
Langenhoe
Peldon
Rowhedge
Fingringhoe
Wivenhoe
High Park Corner
Alresford
Elmstead Market
Frating Green
Frating
Beth Chatto
Great Bromley
Great Bentley
Little Bentley
Hare Green
Tendring Heath
Tendring Green
Tendring
Goose Green
Stones Green
Great Oakley
Little Oakley
Pennyhole Bay
Horsey Island
Naze Tower
Beaumont
Thorpe Green
Thorpe-le-Soken
Kirby-le-Soken
Kirby Cross
Weeley
Weeley Heath
Frinton-on-Sea
Aingers Green
Thorrington
Little Clacton
Cook's Green
Great Holland
Great Clacton
Holland-on-Sea
CLACTON-ON-SEA
St Osyth
Rush Green
Jaywick
Colne Point
Brightlingsea
Hurst Green
Cudmore Grove
MERSEA ISLAND
East Mersea
West Mersea
Great Wigborough
Salcott-cum-Virley
Tolleshunt D'Arcy
Tollesbury
Shinglehead Point
Sales Point
River Blackwater
Bradwell Waterside
Bradwell-on-Sea
St Lawrence Bay
Ramsey Island
St Lawrence
Tillingham
Steeple
Dengie
Asheldham
Southminster
Burnham-on-Crouch
Holliwell Point
Foulness Point
Wallasea Island
Paglesham
Courtsend
Eastend
FOULNESS ISLAND
77
78
61
47
0 1 2 3 4 miles
0 1 2 3 4 5 kilometres

vbourne
Hemley
River Deben
Alderton
B1083
Hollesley
Bay
G
H
J
K
L
M
ton
Bawdsey
Falkenham
Trimley
St Mary
Walton
Old
Felixstowe
Felixstowe
79
A154
Landguard Fort
Landguard
Point
Hook of Holland
aze
on-
ze
ea
1
2
3
4
5
6
7
8
G
H
J
K
L
M

A
B
C
D
E
F
1
2
3
4
5
6
7
8
Pembrokeshire Coast Path
St Dogmaels Moylgrove Heritage Coast
Moylegrove
Rosslare
Trwyn-y-bwa
STRUMBLE HEAD
Dinas Head Heritage Coast
DINAS HEAD
Newport Bay
Carregwastad Head
Pen Brush
Fishguard Bay
Bryn-Henllan
Nevern
Felindre Farchog
Llanwnda
Newport
Trefasser
Pwll Deri
Dinas
Goodwick (Wdig)
Ocean Lab
A487
Carreg Coetan
Pembrokeshire Coast Path
Lower Town
Mynydd Melyn
Pentre Ifan
Manorowen
Fishguard (Abergwaun)
311
MYNYDD CAREGOG
Crosswell
St Nicholas
Llanychaer
Penlan Uchaf
Brynber
Ynys Daullyn
Granston
Scleddau
PEMBROKESHIRE CO
Carreg Sampson
Abercastle
A4219
Pontfaen
A40
B4313
B4329
Porthgain
Llangloffan
Jordanston
MYNYDD PRES
Trefin
Mathry
Trecwn
NATIONAL PAR
Abereiddy
16
48
49
Foel Eryr
536
Mynac
Llanrhian
A487
B4331
Llangloffan Fen
FOEL CWMCERWYN
Berea
Puncheston
Croes-goch
Little Newcastle
Rosebush
Letterston
26
Treglemais
Castlebythe
Tufton
B4330
15
River Solva
Llandeloy
Maenclochog
Henry's Moat (Castell Hendre)
Whitchurch
Wolf's Castle
Rinaston
B4313
Hayscastle Cross
Ambleston
Llys-y-frân Resr
New Moat
Solva
Treffgarne
B4329
Llys-y-frân
Llanycefn
0 1 2 3 4 miles
0 1 2 3 4 5 kilometres

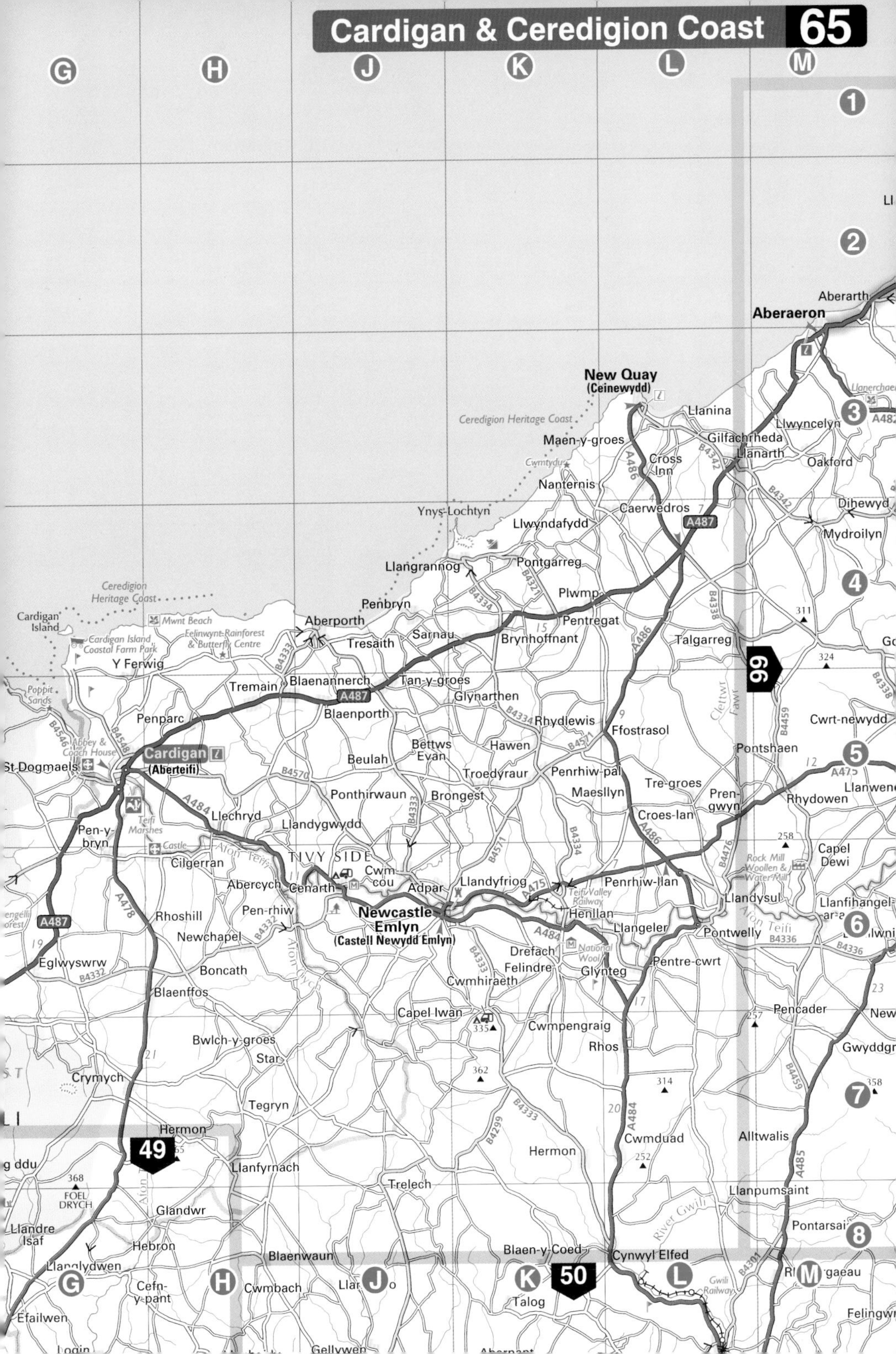

Cardigan
(Aberteifi)
Newcastle Emlyn
(Castell Newydd Emlyn)
New Quay
(Ceinewydd)
Aberaeron
Aberporth
Llangrannog
Ceredigion Heritage Coast
Cardigan Island
Mwnt Beach
Cardigan Island Coastal Farm Park
Felinwynt Rainforest & Butterfly Centre
Poppit Sands
St Dogmaels
Abbey & Coach House
Teifi Marshes
Castle
Cilgerran
TIVY SIDE
Teifi Valley Railway
National Wool
Rock Mill Woollen & Water Mill
Ynys-Lochtyn
Cwmtydu
Llandysul
Gwili Railway
Cynwyl Elfed
Crymych
Hermon
Llanfyrnach
Ffostrasol
Llanarth
Llanina
A487
A484
A486
A475
A478
A485

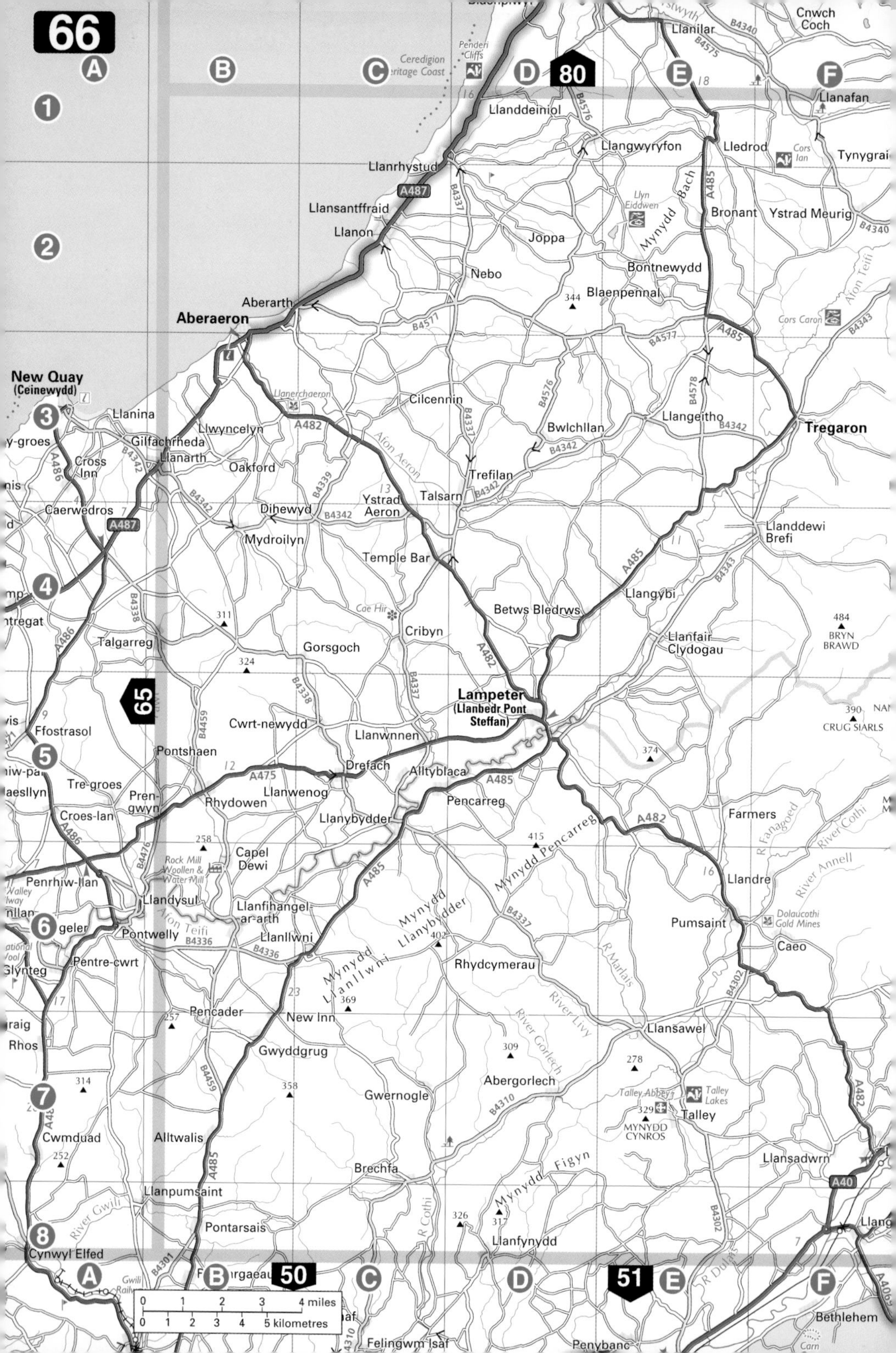
66
A
B
C
D
E
F
1
2
3
4
5
6
7
8
80
65
50
51
Ceredigion Heritage Coast
Penderi Cliffs
Llanilar
Cnwch Coch
Llanafan
Llanddeiniol
Llangwyryfon
Lledrod
Cors Ian
Tynygraig
Llanrhystud
Llansantffraid
Llanon
Llyn Eiddwen
Mynydd Bach
Bronant
Ystrad Meurig
Joppa
Nebo
Bontnewydd
Blaenpennal
Aberarth
Aberaeron
Cors Caron
Afon Teifi
New Quay
(Ceinewydd)
Llanina
Llanerchaeron
Cilcennin
Llangeitho
Tregaron
Llwyncelyn
Gilfachrheda
Llanarth
Cross Inn
Oakford
Bwlchllan
Afon Aeron
Trefilan
Talsarn
Caerwedros
Dihewyd
Ystrad Aeron
Mydroilyn
Temple Bar
Llanddewi Brefi
Llangybi
Cae Hir
Cribyn
Betws Bledrws
Talgarreg
Gorsgoch
Llanfair Clydogau
BRYN BRAWD
Lampeter
(Llanbedr Pont Steffan)
Cwrt-newydd
Llanwnnen
CRUG SIARLS
Ffostrasol
Pontshaen
Drefach
Alltyblaca
Tre-groes
Llanwenog
Pren-gwyn
Rhydowen
Pencarreg
Croes-lan
Llanybydder
Farmers
Capel Dewi
Rock Mill Woollen & Water Mill
Mynydd Pencarreg
River Cothi
River Annell
Penrhiw-llan
Llandysul
Llanfihangel-ar-arth
Llandre
Mynydd Llanybydder
Pumsaint
Dolaucothi Gold Mines
Pontwelly
Llanllwni
Caeo
Pentre-cwrt
Rhydcymerau
R Marlais
Mynydd Llanllwni
River Livy
River Gorlech
Pencader
New Inn
Llansawel
Rhos
Gwyddgrug
Abergorlech
Talley Abbey
Talley Lakes
Talley
MYNYDD CYNROS
Gwernogle
Cwmduad
Alltwalis
Llansadwrn
Brechfa
Mynydd Figyn
Llanpumsaint
River Gwili
Pontarsais
Llanfynydd
Cynwyl Elfed
R Cothi
R Dulais
Bethlehem
Felingwm Isaf
Penybanc
0 1 2 3 4 miles
0 1 2 3 4 5 kilometres
A487
A482
A485
A486
A475
A40
B4340
B4575
B4576
B4337
B4577
B4578
B4342
B4343
B4339
B4338
B4459
B4476
B4336
B4310
B4302
B4301

Lampeter & Southern Cambrians
67
81
52
68
Cwmystwyth
Pontrhydygroes
Ysbyty Ystwyth
Ffair Rhos
Pontrhydfendigaid
Abbey
DIBYN DU
Claerwen Reservoir
Craig-Goch Resr
Pen-y-Garreg Resr
Garreg-Ddu Resr
Elan Valley
Elan Village
Caban Coch Resr
Rhayader
(Rhaeadr Gwy)
Llansantffraed-Cwmdeuddwr
Gilfach Farm
St Harmon
Nantmel
Llanwrthwl
Llanyre
Llandrind
Howey
Newbridge-on-Wye
Llanafan-Fawr
Cwmbach Llechrhyd
Royal Welsh
Llanelwedd
Cilmery
Prince Llewelyn
Builth Wells
(Llanfair-ym-Muallt)
CARNEDDAU
PEN-MAEN-WERN
DRYGARN FAWR
CEFN CNWC
River Towi
Esgair Cerrig
Abergwesyn Common
Afon Irfon
PEN CARREG-DÂN
CEFN COCH
Vicarage Meadows
Abergwesyn
CEFN CRUG
PEN-Y-GURNOS
CEFN FANNOG
River Doethie
Llyn Brianne
MYNYDD TRAWSNANT
River Brun
Beulah
Garth
CARCWM
Llanwrtyd Wells
Llangammarch Wells
Cefngorwydd
BANC-Y-CELYN
DRUM DDU
Rhandirmwyn
Cynghordy Viaduct
Cynghordy
Cilycwm
Mynydd Eppynt
BRYN DU
Tirabad
Llandulas
Upper Chapel
CEFN CLAWDD
Gwenddwr
Crickad
Llaneglwys
GWRHYD
YSGWYDD HWCH
River Crychan
Merthyr Cynog
Lower Chapel
NOETHGRUG
Poor Man's Wood
Mynydd Bwlch-y-Groes
Nant Bran
Llanfihangel Nant Bran
Pont-faen
Pwllgloyw
Llandovery
(Llanymddyfri)
TWYRN DISGWYLFA
Battle
Llanddew
Cradoc
Roman Fort
Brecon
(Aberhonddu)
Llywel
Trallong
Myddfai
Mynydd Myddfai
Usk Reservoir
Trecastle
YR ALLT
Sennybridge
R Usk
Defynnog
Llanspyddid
Llanfrynach
Twynllanan
Crai
Libanus
BRECON BEACO
A483
A470
A44
A4081
A40
A4069
A4215
B4343
B4518
B4358
B4520
B4519
B4567
B4602

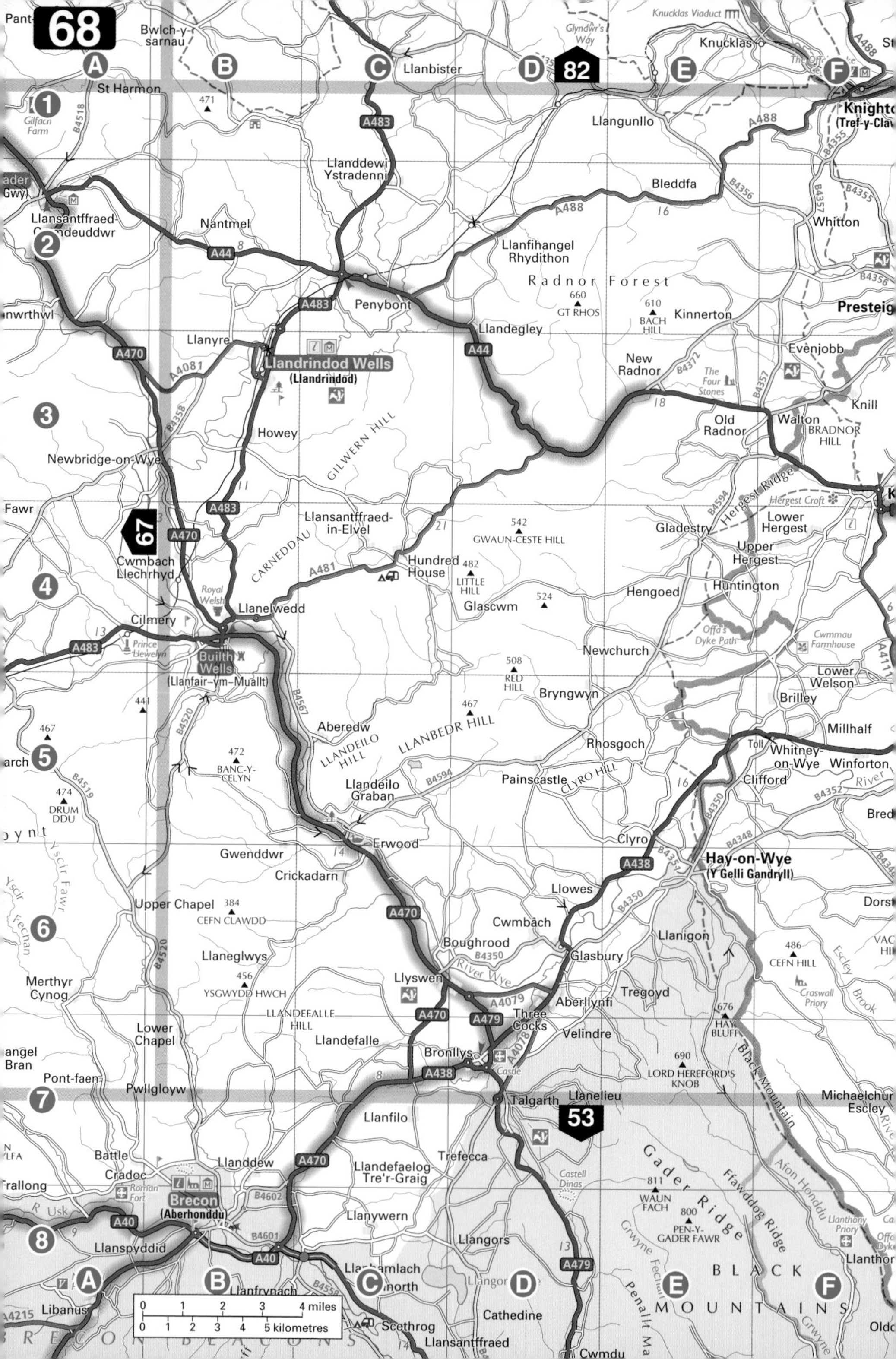
A
B
C
D
E
F
1
2
3
4
5
6
7
8
82
67
53
Bwlch-y-sarnau
Llanbister
Knucklas Viaduct
Glyndŵr's Way
Knucklas
Knighton
(Tref-y-Clawdd)
St Harmon
Gilfach Farm
Llangunllo
Llanddewi Ystradenni
Bleddfa
Llansantffraed-Cwmdeuddwr
Nantmel
Whitton
Llanfihangel Rhydithon
Radnor Forest
Penybont
GT RHOS
BACH HILL
Kinnerton
Presteigne
Llandegley
Llanyre
Llandrindod Wells
(Llandrindod)
Evenjobb
New Radnor
The Four Stones
Knill
Old Radnor
Walton
BRADNOR HILL
Howey
GILWERN HILL
Newbridge-on-Wye
Hergest Ridge
Hergest Croft
Llansantffraed-in-Elvel
GWAUN-CESTE HILL
Gladestry
Lower Hergest
Upper Hergest
Cwmbach Llechrhyd
CARNEDDAU
Hundred House
LITTLE HILL
Huntington
Hengoed
Royal Welsh
Llanelwedd
Glascwm
Cilmery
Prince Llewelyn
Builth Wells
(Llanfair-ym-Muallt)
Offa's Dyke Path
Cwmmau Farmhouse
Newchurch
RED HILL
Lower Welson
Bryngwyn
Brilley
Aberedw
LLANDEILO HILL
LLANBEDR HILL
Millhalf
Rhosgoch
Toll
Whitney-on-Wye
Winforton
BANC-Y-CELYN
Painscastle
CLYRO HILL
Clifford
DRUM DDU
Llandeilo Graban
River Wye
Yscir Fawr
Erwood
Clyro
Hay-on-Wye
(Y Gelli Gandryll)
Gwenddwr
Crickadarn
Yscir Fechan
Llowes
Upper Chapel
CEFN CLAWDD
Cwmbâch
Llanigon
CEFN HILL
Boughrood
Glasbury
Escley Brook
Llaneglwys
Merthyr Cynog
YSGWYDD HWCH
Llyswen
Tregoyd
Craswall Priory
LLANDEFALLE HILL
Three Cocks
Aberllynfi
HAY BLUFF
Lower Chapel
Llandefalle
Velindre
Bronllys
Castle
LORD HEREFORD'S KNOB
Black Mountain
Pont-faen
Pwllgloyw
Talgarth
Llanelieu
Michaelchurch Escley
Llanfilo
Battle
Trefecca
Gader Ridge
Ffawddog Ridge
Afon Honddu
Cradoc
Llanddew
Llandefaelog-Tre'r-Graig
Castell Dinas
Roman Fort
Brecon
(Aberhonddu)
WAUN FACH
PEN-Y-GADER FAWR
R Usk
Llanywern
Llanthony Priory
Llanspyddid
Llangors
Grwyne Fechan
Llanhamlach
Llangorse Lake
BLACK MOUNTAINS
Llanfrynach
Penallt Ma
Libanus
Cathedine
0 1 2 3 4 miles
0 1 2 3 4 5 kilometres
Scethrog
Llansantffraed
Cwmdu
BRECON BEACONS

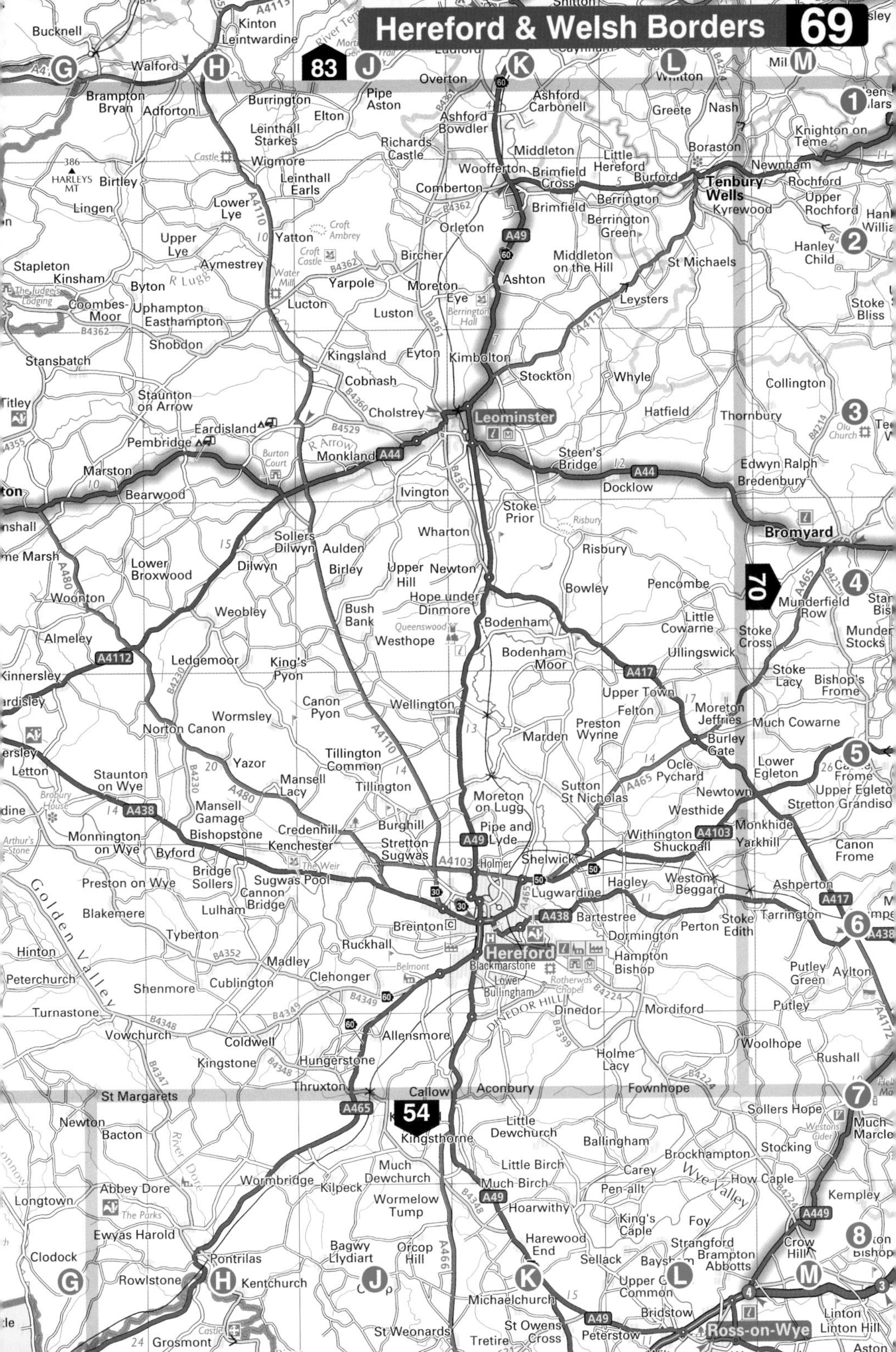

83
54
70
Bucknell
Kinton
Leintwardine
Walford
Brampton Bryan
Adforton
Burrington
Pipe Aston
Elton
Overton
Ashford Bowdler
Ashford Carbonell
Greete
Nash
Knighton on Teme
Leinthall Starkes
Richards Castle
Middleton
Little Hereford
Boraston
Newnham
Wigmore
Woofferton
Brimfield Cross
Burford
Tenbury Wells
Rochford
Upper Rochford
Kyrewood
HARLEYS MT
Birtley
Leinthall Earls
Comberton
Berrington
Lingen
Lower Lye
Brimfield
Berrington Green
Orleton
Croft Ambrey
Hanley Child
Upper Lye
Yatton
Croft Castle
Bircher
Middleton on the Hill
St Michaels
Stapleton
Kinsham
Aymestrey
Water Mill
Yarpole
Ashton
Byton
R Lugg
Moreton
Eye
Berrington Hall
Leysters
The Judge's Lodging
Coombes-Moor
Uphampton
Easthampton
Lucton
Luston
Stoke Bliss
Shobdon
Stansbatch
Kingsland
Eyton
Kimbolton
Cobnash
Stockton
Whyle
Collington
Titley
Staunton on Arrow
Cholstrey
Leominster
Hatfield
Thornbury
Old Church
Eardisland
Pembridge
Burton Court
R Arrow
Monkland
Steen's Bridge
Edwyn Ralph
Bredenbury
Marston
Docklow
Bearwood
Ivington
Stoke Prior
Risbury
Bromyard
Sollers Dilwyn
Aulden
Wharton
Dilwyn
Lower Broxwood
Birley
Upper Hill
Newton
Bowley
Pencombe
Woonton
Weobley
Hope under Dinmore
Bush Bank
Queenswood
Bodenham
Little Cowarne
Munderfield Row
Stoke Cross
Munderfield Stocks
Almeley
Westhope
Bodenham Moor
Ullingswick
Kinnersley
Ledgemoor
King's Pyon
Stoke Lacy
Bishop's Frome
Canon Pyon
Wellington
Upper Town
Felton
Moreton Jeffries
Much Cowarne
Wormsley
Norton Canon
Marden
Preston Wynne
Burley Gate
Letton
Yazor
Tillington Common
Ocle Pychard
Lower Egleton
Castle Frome
Staunton on Wye
Mansell Lacy
Tillington
Sutton St Nicholas
Moreton on Lugg
Newtown
Upper Egleton
Stretton Grandison
Brobury House
Mansell Gamage
Westhide
Monnington on Wye
Bishopstone
Credenhill
Burghill
Pipe and Lyde
Withington
Monkhide
Canon Frome
Arthur's Stone
Byford
Kenchester
Stretton Sugwas
Shucknall
Yarkhill
Golden Valley
Bridge Sollers
The Weir
Holmer
Shelwick
Preston on Wye
Sugwas Pool
Cannon Bridge
Lugwardine
Hagley
Weston Beggard
Ashperton
Blakemere
Lulham
Bartestree
Tarrington
Tyberton
Breinton
Dormington
Perton
Stoke Edith
Hinton
Ruckhall
Hereford
Hampton Bishop
Madley
Belmont
Blackmarstone
Putley Green
Aylton
Peterchurch
Clehonger
Lower Bullingham
Rotherwas Chapel
Shenmore
Cublington
DINEDOR HILL
Dinedor
Mordiford
Putley
Turnastone
Vowchurch
Allensmore
Woolhope
Coldwell
Kingstone
Hungerstone
Holme Lacy
Rushall
Thruxton
Callow
Aconbury
Fownhope
St Margarets
Newton
Bacton
Kingsthorne
Little Dewchurch
Sollers Hope
Westons Cider
Much Marcle
Ballingham
Stocking
River Dore
Much Dewchurch
Little Birch
Brockhampton
Carey
Abbey Dore
Wormbridge
Kilpeck
Much Birch
Wye Valley
How Caple
Longtown
The Parks
Wormelow Tump
Pen-allt
Kempley
Hoarwithy
King's Caple
Foy
Ewyas Harold
Bagwy Llydiart
Orcop Hill
Harewood End
Strangford
Brampton Abbotts
Crow Hill
Clodock
Pontrilas
Sellack
Rowlstone
Kentchurch
Upper Grove Common
Michaelchurch
Bridstow
Linton
Linton Hill
Ross-on-Wye
Grosmont
St Weonards
St Owens Cross
Tretire
Peterstow
Aston
A49
A44
A4110
A4112
A417
A465
A438
A480
A4103
A466
A449
A4214
B4361
B4362
B4360
B4529
B4230
B4352
B4349
B4348
B4347
B4399
B4224

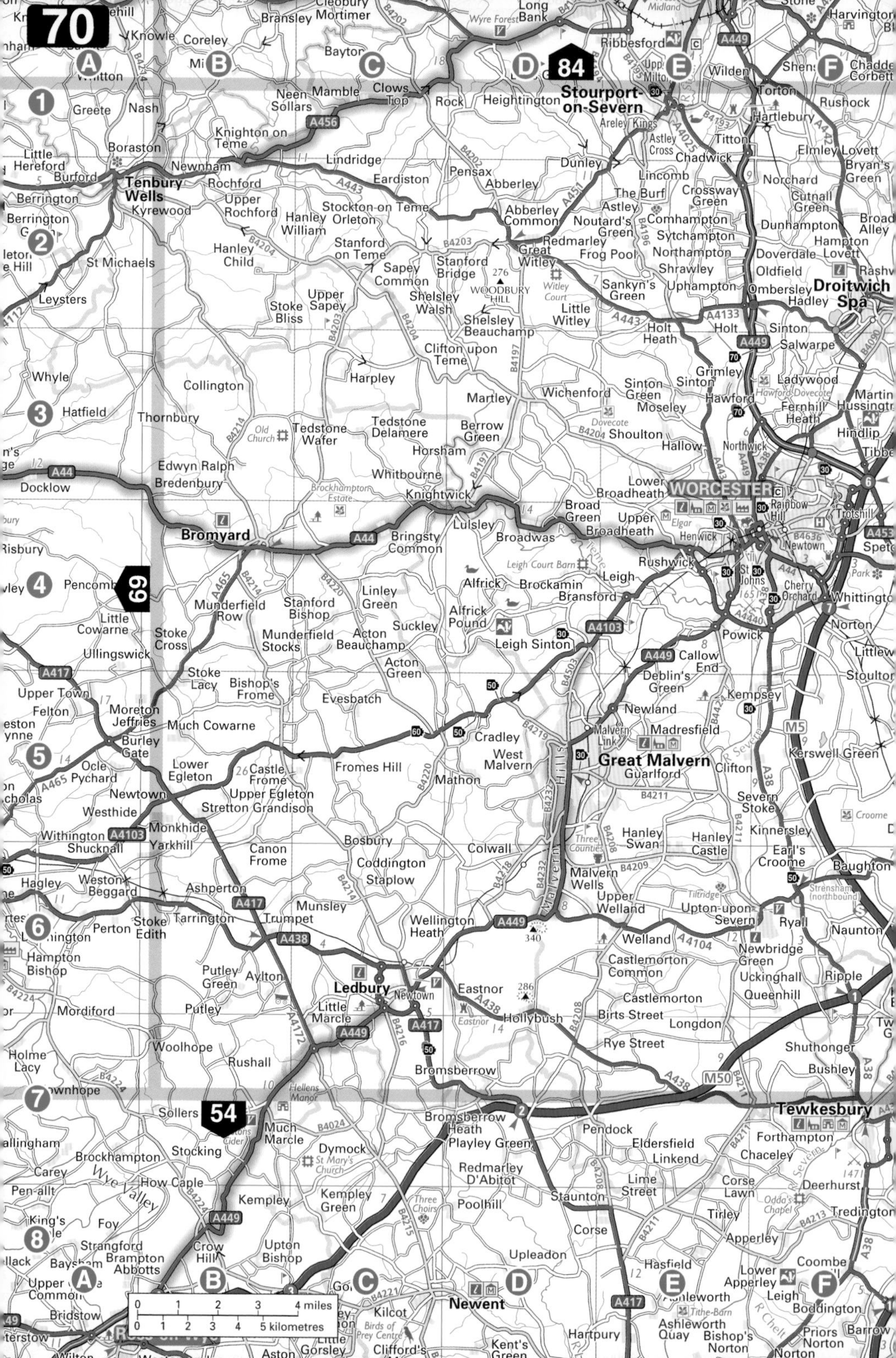

84
69
54
Cleobury Mortimer
Bransley
Long Bank
Wyre Forest
Ribbesford
Stourport-on-Severn
Knowle
Coreley
Baytor
Whitton
Neen Sollars
Mamble
Clows Top
Rock
Heightington
Areley Kings
Astley Cross
Greete
Nash
Knighton on Teme
Little Hereford
Boraston
Burford
Tenbury Wells
Newnham
Lindridge
Pensax
Dunley
Chadwick
Berrington
Kyrewood
Rochford
Upper Rochford
Eardiston
Abberley
Lincomb
The Burf
Hanley William
Stockton-on Teme
Orleton
Abberley Common
Astley
Noutard's Green
Comhampton
Crossway Green
Sytchampton
Northampton
Hanley Child
Stanford on Teme
Stanford Bridge
Great Witley
Redmarley
Frog Pool
St Michaels
Sapey Common
Woodbury Hill
Witley Court
Shrawley
Leysters
Upper Sapey
Stoke Bliss
Shelsley Walsh
Shelsley Beauchamp
Little Witley
Sankyn's Green
Uphampton
Ombersley
Holt Heath
Holt
Clifton upon Teme
Harpley
Whyle
Collington
Sinton Green
Grimley
Sinton
Hawford
Hawford Dovecote
Moseley
Wichenford
Martley
Hatfield
Thornbury
Old Church
Tedstone Wafer
Tedstone Delamere
Berrow Green
Dovecote
Shoulton
Hallow
Northwick
Horsham
Edwyn Ralph
Bredenbury
Whitbourne
Docklow
Brockhampton Estate
Knightwick
Lower Broadheath
Broad Green
Upper Broadheath
Worcester
Rainbow Hill
Trotshill
Bromyard
Bringsty Common
Lulsley
Broadwas
Elgar
Henwick
Newtown
Leigh Court Barn
Rushwick
St Johns
Risbury
Pencombe
Munderfield Row
Stanford Bishop
Linley Green
Alfrick
Brockamin
Leigh
Bransford
Cherry Orchard
Whittington
Little Cowarne
Stoke Cross
Munderfield Stocks
Acton Beauchamp
Suckley
Alfrick Pound
Leigh Sinton
Powick
Norton
Ullingswick
Acton Green
Callow End
Stoke Lacy
Bishop's Frome
Evesbatch
Deblin's Green
Upper Town
Felton
Moreton Jeffries
Much Cowarne
Kempsey
Newland
Madresfield
Malvern Link
Burley Gate
Cradley
West Malvern
Great Malvern
Guarlford
Clifton
Kerswell Green
Ocle Pychard
Lower Egleton
Castle Frome
Fromes Hill
Mathon
Newtown
Upper Egleton
Stretton Grandison
Westhide
Severn Stoke
Croome
Monkhide
Withington
Shucknall
Yarkhill
Canon Frome
Bosbury
Colwall
Three Counties
Hanley Swan
Hanley Castle
Kinnersley
Earl's Croome
Coddington
Staplow
Weston Beggard
Hagley
Ashperton
Malvern Wells
Upper Welland
Baughton
Strensham (northbound)
Tiltridge
Upton-upon-Severn
Ryall
Perton
Stoke Edith
Tarrington
Trumpet
Munsley
Wellington Heath
Welland
Naunton
Hampton Bishop
Putley Green
Aylton
Ledbury
Castlemorton Common
Newbridge Green
Uckinghall
Ripple
Queenhill
Mordiford
Putley
Little Marcle
Eastnor
Hollybush
Castlemorton
Birts Street
Longdon
Holme Lacy
Woolhope
Rushall
Rye Street
Shuthonger
Bromsberrow
Bushley
Fownhope
Hellens Manor
Sollers
Much Marcle
Bromsberrow Heath
Pendock
Tewkesbury
Forthampton
Fallingham
Brockhampton
Stocking
Dymock
St Mary's Church
Playley Green
Eldersfield
Linkend
Chaceley
Redmarley D'Abitot
Carey
Wye Valley
How Caple
Kempley
Kempley Green
Three Choirs
Poolhill
Staunton
Lime Street
Corse Lawn
Deerhurst
Pen-allt
Foy
Tirley
Odda's Chapel
Tredington
King's
Strangford
Brampton Abbotts
Crow Hill
Upton Bishop
Corse
Apperley
Upleadon
Hasfield
Lower Apperley
Coombe Hill
Baysham
Newent
Leigh
Ashleworth
Boddington
Upper Common
Bridstow
Kilcot
Birds of Prey Centre
Tithe Barn
Ashleworth Quay
Prior's Norton
Barrow
Hartpury
Bishop's Norton
Norton
Aston
Gorsley
Little Gorsley
Clifford's
Kent's Green
Wilton
Ross-on-Wye
Stone
Harvington
Shenstone
Chaddesley Corbett
Wilden
Upper Milton
Torton
Rushock
Hartlebury
Titton
Elmley Lovett
Bryan's Green
Norchard
Cutnall Green
Dunhampton
Broad Alley
Hampton Lovett
Doverdale
Oldfield
Droitwich Spa
Hadley
Salwarpe
Ladywood
Fernhill Heath
Martin Hussingtree
Hindlip
Tibberton
Spetchley
Littleworth
Stoulton
Midland
A449
A456
A443
A451
A44
A465
A4103
A417
A438
A4104
A4133
A4440
A4172
A4025
M5
M50
A38
B4202
B4214
B4203
B4204
B4197
B4196
B4220
B4219
B4218
B4232
B4208
B4209
B4211
B4224
B4024
B4215
B4216
B4221
B4213
B4090
B4636
B4503
B4424
B4193
B4194
B4195
276
340
286
0 1 2 3 4 miles
0 1 2 3 4 5 kilometres

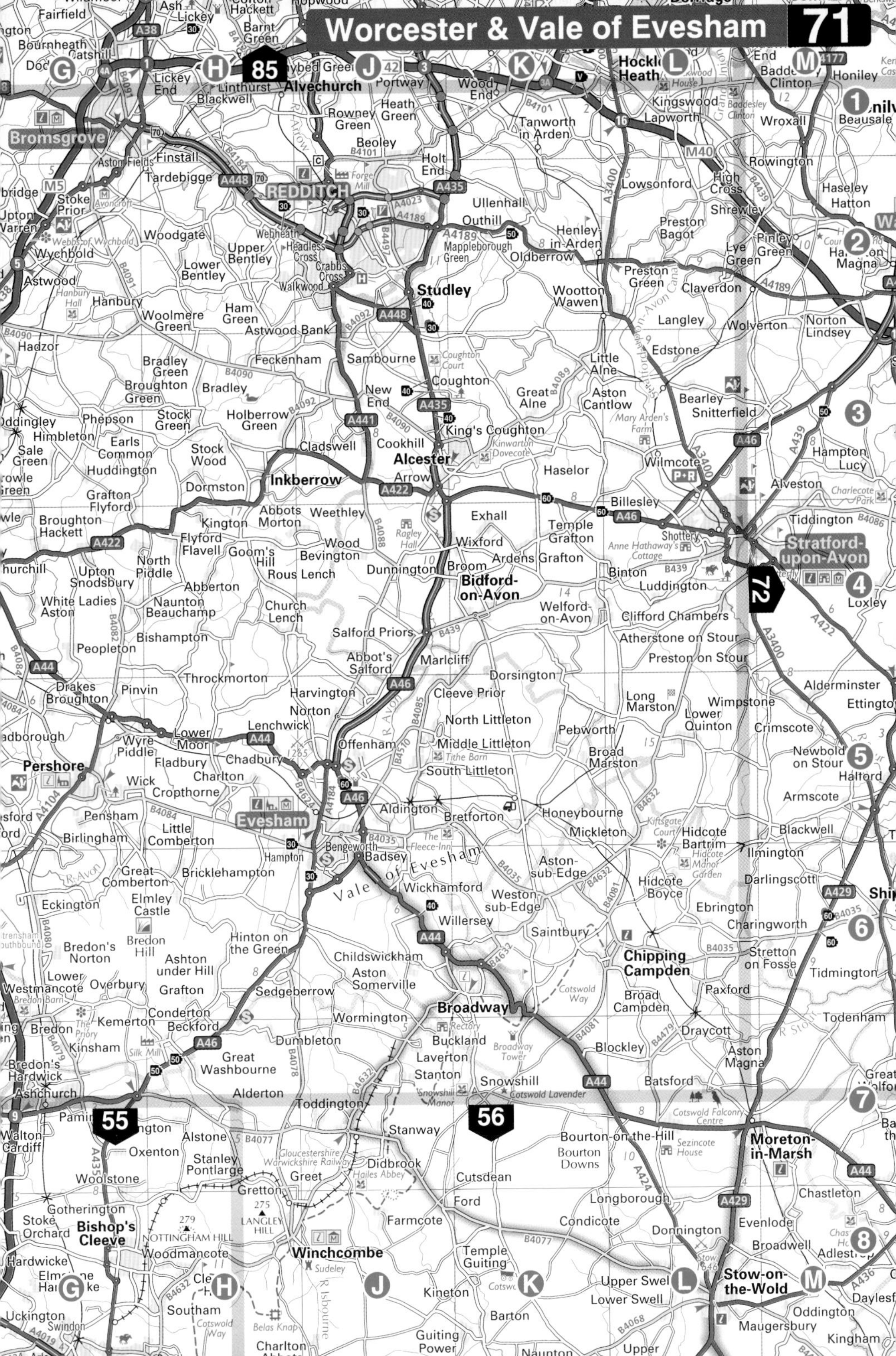

Fairfield
Bournheath
Catshill
Lickey
Barnt Green
Lickey End
Linthurst
Alvechurch
Blackwell
Portway
Rowney Green
Heath Green
Wood End
Tanworth in Arden
Hockley Heath
Kingswood
Lapworth
Baddesley Clinton
Honiley
Wroxall
Beausale
Bromsgrove
Finstall
Aston Fields
Tardebigge
Beoley
Holt End
Forge Mill
REDDITCH
Rowington
Lowsonford
High Cross
Haseley
Hatton
Stoke Prior
Avoncroft
Webheath
Headless Cross
Crabbs Cross
Walkwood
Ullenhall
Outhill
Mappleborough Green
Henley-in-Arden
Oldberrow
Preston Bagot
Shrewley
Pinley Green
Lye Green
Hampton Magna
Woodgate
Upper Bentley
Lower Bentley
Wychbold
Webbs of Wychbold
Astwood
Hanbury Hall
Hanbury
Woolmere Green
Ham Green
Astwood Bank
Studley
Wootton Wawen
Preston Green
Claverdon
Langley
Wolverton
Norton Lindsey
Hadzor
Feckenham
Sambourne
Coughton Court
Coughton
Little Alne
Edstone
Bradley Green
Broughton Green
Bradley
New End
Great Alne
Aston Cantlow
Bearley
Snitterfield
Mary Arden's Farm
Oddingley
Himbleton
Phepson
Stock Green
Holberrow Green
King's Coughton
Kinwarton Dovecote
Cookhill
Cladswell
Alcester
Arrow
Haselor
Wilmcote
Hampton Lucy
Alveston
Charlecote Park
Sale Green
Earls Common
Huddington
Stock Wood
Inkberrow
Dormston
Grafton Flyford
Abbots Morton
Weethley
Ragley Hall
Exhall
Billesley
Temple Grafton
Shottery
Anne Hathaway's Cottage
Tiddington
Stratford-upon-Avon
Broughton Hackett
Kington
Flyford Flavell
Goom's Hill
Wood Bevington
Wixford
Ardens Grafton
Binton
Luddington
Churchill
Upton Snodsbury
North Piddle
Rous Lench
Dunnington
Broom
Bidford-on-Avon
Welford-on-Avon
Loxley
White Ladies Aston
Naunton Beauchamp
Abberton
Church Lench
Clifford Chambers
Atherstone on Stour
Preston on Stour
Bishampton
Peopleton
Salford Priors
Abbot's Salford
Marlcliff
Throckmorton
Dorsington
Alderminster
Ettington
Drakes Broughton
Pinvin
Harvington
Cleeve Prior
Long Marston
Wimpstone
Lower Quinton
Norton
North Littleton
Crimscote
Pershore
Wyre Piddle
Lower Moor
Lenchwick
Offenham
Middle Littleton
Tithe Barn
South Littleton
Pebworth
Broad Marston
Newbold on Stour
Halford
Fladbury
Chadbury
Charlton
Cropthorne
Wick
Armscote
Pensham
Little Comberton
Evesham
Aldington
Bretforton
Honeybourne
Mickleton
Kiftsgate Court
Hidcote Bartrim
Hidcote Manor Garden
Blackwell
Birlingham
Hampton
Bengeworth
Badsey
The Fleece Inn
Ilmington
Great Comberton
Bricklehampton
Vale of Evesham
Aston-sub-Edge
Hidcote Boyce
Darlingscott
Eckington
Elmley Castle
Wickhamford
Weston-sub-Edge
Ebrington
Willersey
Saintbury
Charingworth
Bredon Hill
Bredon's Norton
Hinton on the Green
Ashton under Hill
Childswickham
Chipping Campden
Stretton on Fosse
Tidmington
Lower Westmancote
Overbury
Grafton
Aston Somerville
Sedgeberrow
Cotswold Way
Broad Campden
Paxford
Bredon Barn
Bredon
Kemerton
Conderton
Beckford
Wormington
Broadway
Rectory
Todenham
Kinsham
The Priory
Silk Mill
Dumbleton
Buckland
Broadway Tower
Blockley
Draycott
Aston Magna
Bredon's Hardwick
Great Washbourne
Laverton
Stanton
Snowshill
Snowshill Manor
Cotswold Lavender
Batsford
Ashchurch
Alderton
Toddington
Cotswold Falconry Centre
Walton Cardiff
Alstone
Oxenton
Stanway
Bourton-on-the-Hill
Bourton Downs
Sezincote House
Moreton-in-Marsh
Woolstone
Stanley Pontlarge
Gloucestershire Warwickshire Railway
Didbrook
Hailes Abbey
Greet
Cutsdean
Gretton
Gotherington
Langley Hill
Nottingham Hill
Ford
Longborough
Chastleton
Stoke Orchard
Bishop's Cleeve
Farmcote
Condicote
Evenlode
Woodmancote
Winchcombe
Sudeley
Temple Guiting
Donnington
Broadwell
Adlestrop
Hardwicke
Cleeve Hill
Southam
Kineton
Upper Swell
Lower Swell
Stow-on-the-Wold
Daylesford
Uckington
Swindon
Belas Knap
Barton
Oddington
Maugersbury
Charlton
Guiting Power
Kingham
R Isbourne
R Avon
R Arrow
Stratford-upon-Avon Canal
Grand Union Canal
M5
M40
A38
A448
A435
A441
A422
A46
A44
A3400
A4189
A439
A429
A424
A4104
A4184
A436
A4019
B4091
B4090
B4092
B4101
B4088
B4089
B4082
B4084
B4035
B4632
B4081
B4479
B4077
B4078
B4080
B4079
B4068
B4439
B4086
B4085
B4510
B4624
B4101
B4497
B4184
85
72
55
56

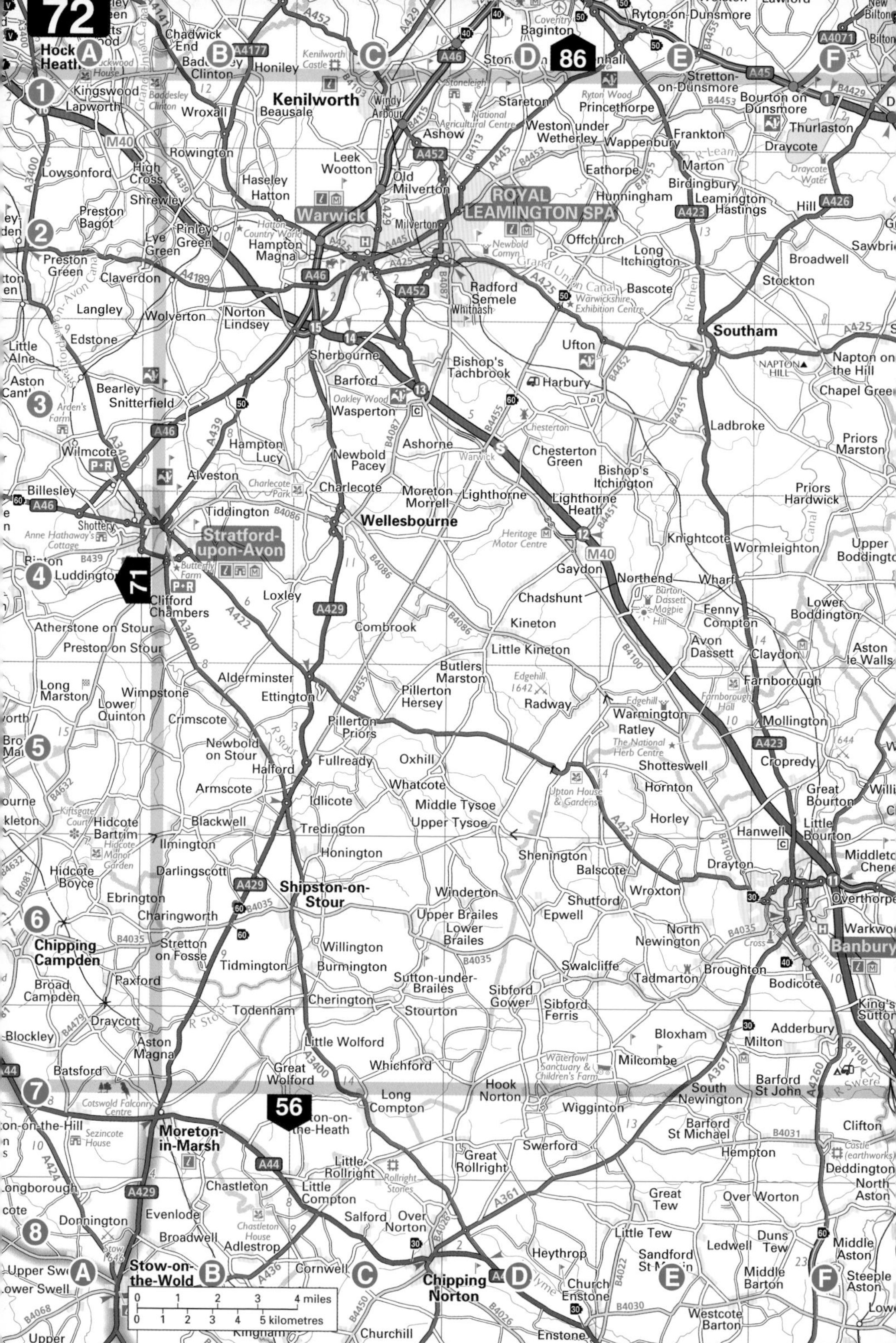

Hockley Heath
Chadwick End
Baddesley Clinton
Honiley
Kenilworth Castle
Kenilworth
Coventry
Baginton
Stoneleigh
Ryton-on-Dunsmore
Wolston
Lawford
New Bilton
Bilton
Stretton-on-Dunsmore
Bourton on Dunsmore
Thurlaston
Draycote
Draycote Water
86
Kingswood
Lapworth
Wroxall
Beausale
Windy Arbour
Ashow
Stareton
National Agricultural Centre
Ryton Wood
Princethorpe
Weston under Wetherley
Wappenbury
Frankton
Lowsonford
Rowington
High Cross
Shrewley
Haseley
Hatton
Leek Wootton
Old Milverton
Warwick
Milverton
ROYAL LEAMINGTON SPA
Eathorpe
Hunningham
Marton
Birdingbury
Leamington Hastings
Hill
Preston Bagot
Pinley Green
Lye Green
Hatton Country World
Hampton Magna
Newbold Comyn
Offchurch
Long Itchington
Broadwell
Sawbridge
Preston Green
Claverdon
Langley
Wolverton
Norton Lindsey
Radford Semele
Whitnash
Bascote
Grand Union Canal
Warwickshire Exhibition Centre
Stockton
Edstone
Little Alne
Sherbourne
Ufton
Southam
Napton on the Hill
Napton Hill
Aston Cantlow
Bearley
Snitterfield
Arden's Farm
Barford
Oakley Wood
Wasperton
Bishop's Tachbrook
Harbury
Chapel Green
Ladbroke
Wilmcote
Hampton Lucy
Ashorne
Chesterton
Chesterton Green
Priors Marston
Billesley
Alveston
Newbold Pacey
Charlecote Park
Charlecote
Moreton Morrell
Lighthorne
Bishop's Itchington
Priors Hardwick
Shottery
Anne Hathaway's Cottage
Tiddington
Wellesbourne
Lighthorne Heath
Heritage Motor Centre
Knightcote
Wormleighton
Upper Boddington
Stratford-upon-Avon
Binton
Luddington
Butterfly Farm
71
Clifford Chambers
Loxley
Gaydon
Northend
Wharf
Chadshunt
Burton Dassett
Magpie Hill
Fenny Compton
Lower Boddington
Atherstone on Stour
Preston on Stour
Combrook
Kineton
Little Kineton
Avon Dassett
Claydon
Aston le Walls
Alderminster
Butlers Marston
Edgehill 1642
Farnborough
Farnborough Hall
Long Marston
Wimpstone
Lower Quinton
Ettington
Pillerton Hersey
Radway
Edgehill
Warmington
Ratley
Mollington
Crimscote
Pillerton Priors
The National Herb Centre
Cropredy
Newbold on Stour
Fullready
Oxhill
Shotteswell
Halford
Armscote
Idlicote
Whatcote
Middle Tysoe
Upper Tysoe
Upton House & Gardens
Hornton
Horley
Great Bourton
Little Bourton
Kiftsgate Court
Hidcote Bartrim
Hidcote Manor Garden
Blackwell
Tredington
Ilmington
Darlingscott
Honington
Shenington
Balscote
Hanwell
Drayton
Hidcote Boyce
Ebrington
Charingworth
Shipston-on-Stour
Winderton
Shutford
Wroxton
Epwell
Upper Brailes
Lower Brailes
North Newington
Overthorpe
Warkworth
Banbury
Chipping Campden
Stretton on Fosse
Tidmington
Willington
Burmington
Swalcliffe
Tadmarton
Broughton
Bodicote
Broad Campden
Paxford
Sutton-under-Brailes
Sibford Gower
Sibford Ferris
Cherington
Stourton
Todenham
Draycott
Blockley
Aston Magna
Little Wolford
Bloxham
Adderbury
Milton
King's Sutton
Batsford
Great Wolford
Whichford
Waterfowl Sanctuary & Children's Farm
Milcombe
Hook Norton
Barford St John
Cotswold Falconry Centre
Long Compton
56
Barton-on-the-Heath
Moreton-in-Marsh
Sezincote House
Wigginton
South Newington
Barford St Michael
Clifton
Swerford
Great Rollright
Little Rollright
Rollright Stones
Hempton
Castle (earthworks)
Deddington
North Aston
Longborough
Chastleton
Little Compton
Evenlode
Great Tew
Over Worton
Donnington
Chastleton House
Broadwell
Adlestrop
Salford
Over Norton
Little Tew
Duns Tew
Middle Aston
Ledwell
Sandford St Martin
Heythrop
Middle Barton
Steeple Aston
Upper Swell
Lower Swell
Stow-on-the-Wold
Cornwell
Chipping Norton
Church Enstone
Westcote Barton
Enstone
Churchill
Kingham
Upper Slaughter
0 1 2 3 4 miles
0 1 2 3 4 5 kilometres

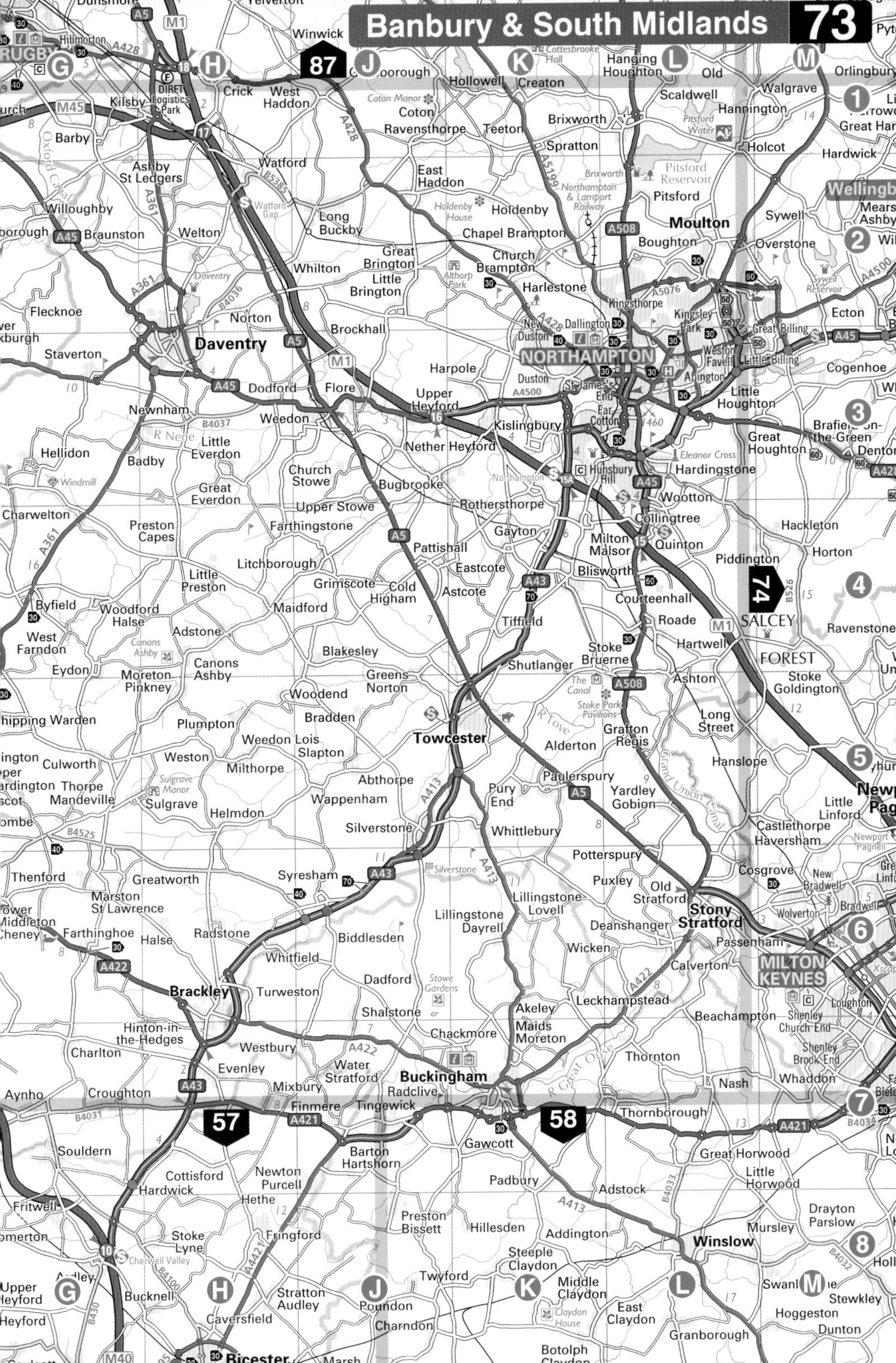
Dunsmore
Yelvertoft
Winwick
87
Cottesbrooke Hall
Hanging Houghton
Old
Orlingbury
Rugby
Hillmorton
Crick
West Haddon
Guilsborough
Hollowell
Creaton
Scaldwell
Walgrave
DIRFT Logistics Park
Kilsby
Coton Manor
Coton
Brixworth
Hannington
Great Harrowden
Barby
Ravensthorpe
Teeton
Spratton
Pitsford Water
Holcot
Hardwick
Oxford Canal
Ashby St Ledgers
Watford
Watford Gap
East Haddon
Brixworth
Northampton & Lamport Railway
Pitsford Reservoir
Pitsford
Wellingborough
Willoughby
Long Buckby
Holdenby House
Holdenby
Moulton
Sywell
Mears Ashby
Braunston
Welton
Chapel Brampton
Boughton
Overstone
Great Brington
Whilton
Church Brampton
Little Brington
Althorp Park
Harlestone
Daventry
Kingsthorpe
Kingsley Park
Sywell Reservoir
Flecknoe
Norton
Brockhall
New Duston
Dallington
Great Billing
Ecton
Staverton
Daventry
Northampton
Weston Favell
Little Billing
Cogenhoe
Harpole
Duston
St James's End
Abington
Dodford
Flore
Upper Heyford
Little Houghton
Newnham
Weedon
Kislingbury
Far Cotton
Brafield-on-the-Green
R Nene
Little Everdon
Nether Heyford
Great Houghton
Denton
Hellidon
Badby
Eleanor Cross
Hardingstone
Windmill
Church Stowe
Northampton
Hunsbury Hill
Great Everdon
Bugbrooke
Wootton
Charwelton
Upper Stowe
Rothersthorpe
Collingtree
Preston Capes
Farthingstone
Gayton
Quinton
Hackleton
Pattishall
Milton Malsor
Piddington
Horton
Litchborough
Eastcote
Blisworth
74
Little Preston
Grimscote
Cold Higham
Astcote
Courteenhall
Byfield
Woodford Halse
Maidford
Tiffield
Roade
Salcey
West Farndon
Adstone
Canons Ashby
Hartwell
Forest
Ravenstone
Blakesley
Stoke Bruerne
Eydon
Moreton Pinkney
Canons Ashby
Greens Norton
Shutlanger
Ashton
Stoke Goldington
Woodend
The Canal
Stoke Park Pavilions
Chipping Warden
Bradden
Long Street
Plumpton
Towcester
R Tove
Grafton Regis
Weedon Lois
Slapton
Alderton
Weston
Hanslope
Culworth
Milthorpe
Sulgrave Manor
Paulerspury
Yardley Gobion
Thorpe Mandeville
Sulgrave
Abthorpe
Pury End
Grand Union Canal
Newport Pagnell
Little Linford
Wappenham
Helmdon
Silverstone
Whittlebury
Castlethorpe
Haversham
Potterspury
Thenford
Greatworth
Syresham
Silverstone
Puxley
Old Stratford
Cosgrove
New Bradwell
Great Linford
Marston St Lawrence
Lillingstone Lovell
Stony Stratford
Bradwell
Lower Middleton Cheney
Lillingstone Dayrell
Deanshanger
Wolverton
Farthinghoe
Halse
Radstone
Biddlesden
Wicken
Passenham
Whitfield
Dadford
Calverton
Milton Keynes
Stowe Gardens
Brackley
Turweston
Leckhampstead
Loughton
Akeley
Shalstone
Beachampton
Shenley Church End
Hinton-in-the-Hedges
Maids Moreton
Chackmore
Westbury
Shenley Brook End
Charlton
Evenley
Water Stratford
Thornton
R Great Ouse
Buckingham
Whaddon
Aynho
Croughton
Mixbury
Radclive
Nash
Finmere
Tingewick
Thornborough
57
58
Souldern
Barton Hartshorn
Gawcott
Great Horwood
Newton Purcell
Cottisford
Hardwick
Padbury
Little Horwood
Adstock
Hethe
Fritwell
Preston Bissett
Drayton Parslow
Hillesden
Mursley
Somerton
Stoke Lyne
Fringford
Addington
Winslow
Cherwell Valley
Steeple Claydon
Ardley
Twyford
Middle Claydon
Swanbourne
Stewkley
Upper Heyford
Bucknell
Stratton Audley
Poundon
Claydon House
East Claydon
Hoggeston
Heyford
Caversfield
Charndon
Granborough
Dunton
Botolph Claydon
Bicester
Marsh Gibbon

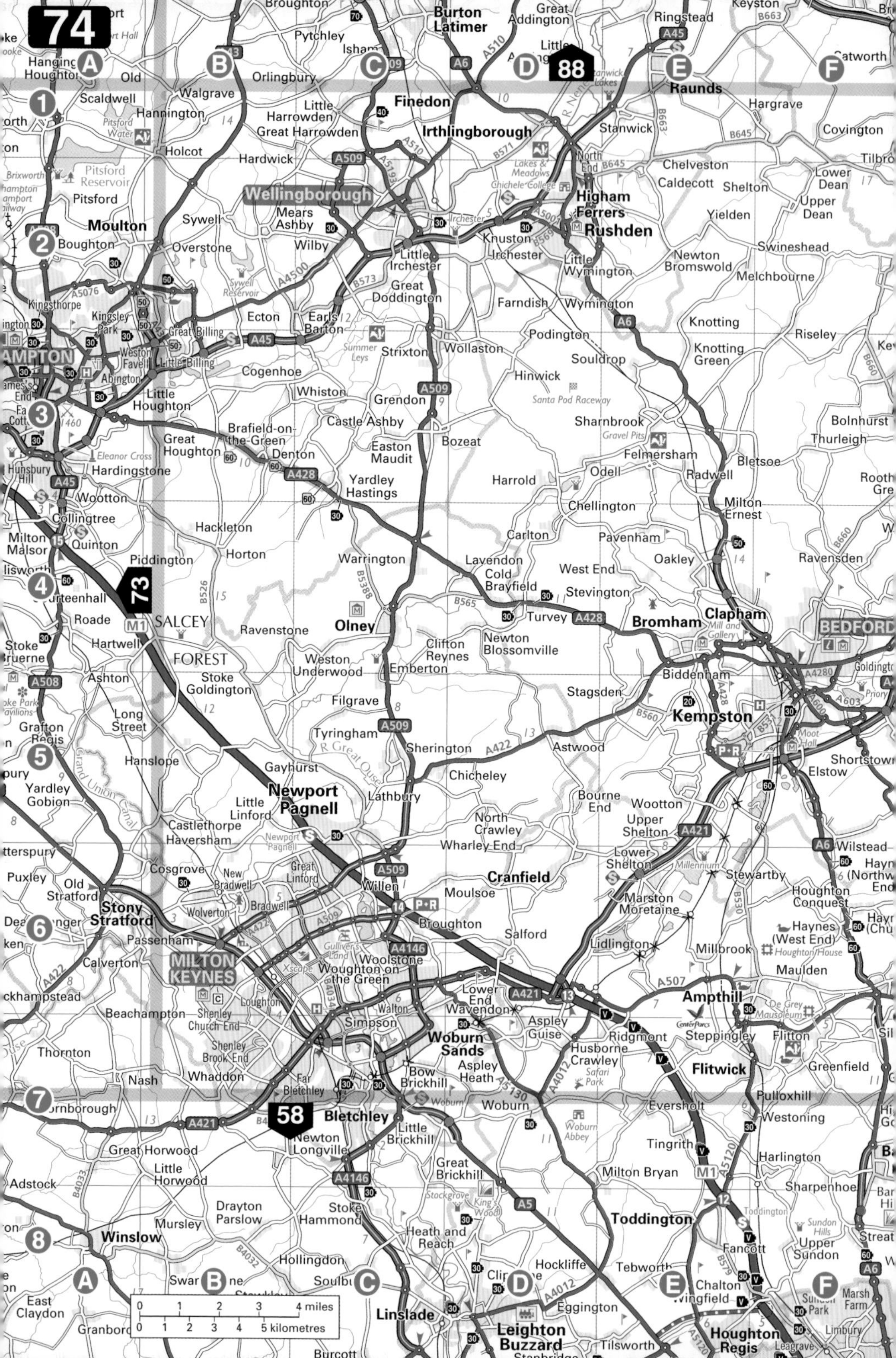
Broughton
Burton Latimer
Great Addington
Keyston
Ringstead
Pytchley
Isham
Little Addington
88
Hanging Houghton
Old
Orlingbury
Walgrave
Raunds
Catworth
Scaldwell
Hannington
Finedon
Little Harrowden
Great Harrowden
Irthlingborough
Stanwick
Hargrave
Covington
Pitsford Water
Holcot
Hardwick
Lakes & Meadows
North End
Chelveston
Caldecott
Shelton
Lower Dean
Upper Dean
Tilbrook
Brixworth
Pitsford Reservoir
Wellingborough
Chichele College
Higham Ferrers
Rushden
Pitsford
Moulton
Sywell
Mears Ashby
Irchester
Knuston
Yielden
Boughton
Overstone
Wilby
Little Irchester
Little Wymington
Newton Bromswold
Swineshead
Melchbourne
Sywell Reservoir
Great Doddington
Farndish
Wymington
Kingsthorpe
Kingsley Park
Ecton
Earls Barton
Great Billing
Weston Favell
Little Billing
Abington
Summer Leys
Strixton
Wollaston
Podington
Knotting
Riseley
Knotting Green
Souldrop
Hinwick
Santa Pod Raceway
Cogenhoe
Whiston
Grendon
Castle Ashby
Little Houghton
Brafield-on-the-Green
Great Houghton
Denton
Easton Maudit
Bozeat
Sharnbrook
Gravel Pits
Felmersham
Bolnhurst
Thurleigh
Eleanor Cross
Hardingstone
Hunsbury Hill
Yardley Hastings
Harrold
Odell
Radwell
Bletsoe
Wootton
Collingtree
Quinton
Milton Malsor
Hackleton
Horton
Piddington
Chellington
Milton Ernest
Carlton
Pavenham
Oakley
Ravensden
Warrington
Lavendon
Cold Brayfield
West End
Stevington
Roade
SALCEY FOREST
Ravenstone
Olney
Turvey
Bromham
Clapham
Mill and Gallery
BEDFORD
Hartwell
Stoke Bruerne
Weston Underwood
Emberton
Clifton Reynes
Newton Blossomville
Biddenham
Goldington
Ashton
Stoke Goldington
Filgrave
Stagsden
Kempston
Priory
Long Street
Grafton Regis
Tyringham
R Great Ouse
Sherington
Astwood
Moot Hall
Hanslope
Gayhurst
Chicheley
Elstow
Shortstown
Yardley Gobion
Grand Union Canal
Little Linford
Newport Pagnell
Lathbury
Bourne End
Wootton
Upper Shelton
Castlethorpe
Haversham
North Crawley
Wharley End
Lower Shelton
Millennium
Wilstead
Puxley
Old Stratford
Stony Stratford
Cosgrove
New Bradwell
Great Linford
Willen
Cranfield
Moulsoe
Marston Moretaine
Stewartby
Houghton Conquest
Wolverton
Bradwell
Broughton
Salford
Lidlington
Millbrook
Haynes (West End)
Houghton House
Passenham
Calverton
MILTON KEYNES
Gulliver's Land
Xscape
Woolstone
Woughton on the Green
Lower End
Wavendon
Aspley Guise
Ridgmont
Ampthill
De Grey Mausoleum
Maulden
Beachampton
Shenley Church End
Loughton
Walton
Simpson
Woburn Sands
Husborne Crawley
Center Parcs
Steppingley
Flitton
Thornton
Shenley Brook End
Whaddon
Nash
Far Bletchley
Bow Brickhill
Aspley Heath
Safari Park
Flitwick
Greenfield
Bletchley
Woburn
Eversholt
Pulloxhill
Westoning
Great Horwood
Little Horwood
Newton Longville
Little Brickhill
Woburn Abbey
Tingrith
Harlington
Adstock
Great Brickhill
Stockgrove
King's Wood
Milton Bryan
Sharpenhoe
Drayton Parslow
Mursley
Winslow
Stoke Hammond
Heath and Reach
Toddington
Fancott
Sundon Hills
Upper Sundon
Hollingdon
Hockliffe
Tebworth
Chalton
Wingfield
Sundon Park
Marsh Farm
East Claydon
Granborough
Linslade
Eggington
Leighton Buzzard
Tilsworth
Houghton Regis
Limbury
Leagrave
Burcott
73
58
0 1 2 3 4 miles
0 1 2 3 4 5 kilometres
M1
A5
A6
A45
A421
A422
A428
A509
A4146
A5130
A4012
A507
A508
A500
A5076
A4500
A510
A5193
A603
A600
A4280
B663
B645
B571
B573
B5388
B565
B526
B560
B530
B4033
B4032
B579
A5120
B660
A B C D E F
1 2 3 4 5 6 7 8

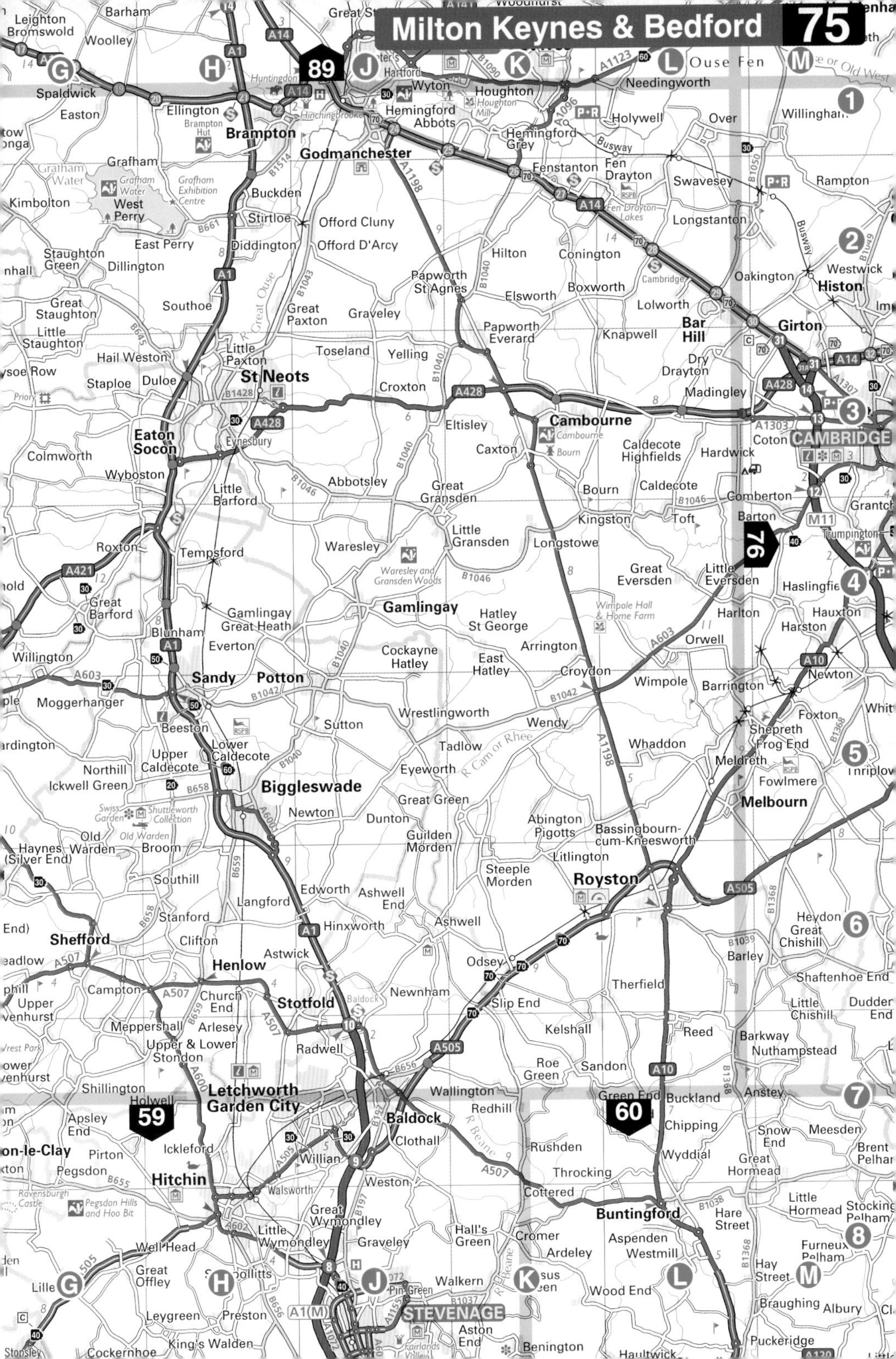
Leighton Bromswold
Barham
Woolley
Spaldwick
Easton
Ellington
Brampton Hut
Brampton
Huntingdon
Hinchingbrooke
Hartford
Wyton
Houghton
Houghton Mill
Hemingford Abbots
Godmanchester
Ouse Fen
Needingworth
Holywell
Over
Willingham
Hemingford Grey
Busway
Fenstanton
Fen Drayton
Fen Drayton Lakes
Swavesey
Rampton
Longstanton
Grafham
Grafham Water
Grafham Exhibition Centre
Kimbolton
West Perry
Buckden
Stirtloe
Offord Cluny
Offord D'Arcy
East Perry
Diddington
Staughton Green
Dillington
Hilton
Conington
Westwick
Oakington
Histon
Cambridge
Papworth St Agnes
Elsworth
Boxworth
Lolworth
Girton
Southoe
Great Staughton
Little Staughton
Great Paxton
Graveley
Papworth Everard
Knapwell
Bar Hill
Dry Drayton
Madingley
Little Paxton
Hail Weston
Toseland
Yelling
St Neots
Staploe
Duloe
Priory
Croxton
Eltisley
Cambourne
Eaton Socon
Eynesbury
Colmworth
Wyboston
Caxton
Bourn
Caldecote Highfields
Hardwick
Coton
CAMBRIDGE
Little Barford
Abbotsley
Great Gransden
Caldecote
Comberton
Grantchester
Kingston
Toft
Barton
Trumpington
Roxton
Tempsford
Waresley
Little Gransden
Longstowe
Great Eversden
Little Eversden
Haslingfield
Waresley and Gransden Woods
Great Barford
Gamlingay Great Heath
Gamlingay
Hatley St George
Wimpole Hall & Home Farm
Harlton
Hauxton
Harston
Blunham
Everton
Cockayne Hatley
East Hatley
Arrington
Orwell
Willington
Moggerhanger
Sandy
Potton
Croydon
Wimpole
Barrington
Newton
Beeston
Sutton
Wrestlingworth
Wendy
Foxton
Shepreth
Frog End
Tadlow
Whaddon
Meldreth
Fowlmere
Thriplow
Northill
Upper Caldecote
Lower Caldecote
Ickwell Green
Eyeworth
R Cam or Rhee
Biggleswade
Melbourn
Swiss Garden
Shuttleworth Collection
Newton
Great Green
Dunton
Guilden Morden
Abington Pigotts
Bassingbourn-cum-Kneesworth
Old Warden
Haynes (Silver End)
Broom
Litlington
Steeple Morden
Royston
Southill
Langford
Edworth
Ashwell End
Stanford
Hinxworth
Ashwell
Heydon
Great Chishill
Shefford
Clifton
Astwick
Barley
Henlow
Odsey
Shaftenhoe End
Campton
Church End
Stotfold
Baldock
Newnham
Therfield
Upper Stondon
Meppershall
Arlesey
Slip End
Little Chishill
Dudden End
Upper & Lower Stondon
Radwell
Kelshall
Reed
Barkway
Nuthampstead
Roe Green
Sandon
Shillington
Letchworth Garden City
Wallington
Green End
Buckland
Anstey
Holwell
Apsley End
Redhill
Baldock
Clothall
R Beane
Chipping
Snow End
Meesden
Brent Pelham
Pirton
Ickleford
Rushden
Wyddial
Great Hormead
Pegsdon
Willian
Throcking
Hitchin
Weston
Walsworth
Cottered
Buntingford
Little Hormead
Hare Street
Stocking Pelham
Ravensburgh Castle
Pegsdon Hills and Hoo Bit
Great Wymondley
Hall's Green
Cromer
Aspenden
Westmill
Furneux Pelham
Well Head
Little Wymondley
Graveley
Ardeley
Great Offley
Hay Street
Walkern
Lilley
Wood End
Pin Green
STEVENAGE
Braughing
Albury
Leygreen
Preston
Aston End
Puckeridge
King's Walden
Cockernhoe
Benington
Stopsley
Fairlands Valley
A1
A14
A428
A421
A603
A1198
A505
A507
A10
A1(M)
M11
A600
A6001
A602
A1123
A1096
A1303
A1307
B1040
B1043
B1046
B1042
B1514
B1428
B661
B645
B658
B659
B656
B655
B1368
B1039
B1038
B1037
B1050
B1049
B1090
B197
59
60
76
89

Earith
A1123
Haddenham
Wilburton
Thetford
Stretham
Aldreth
A
Ouse Fen
B
Ouse or Old West River
C
D
90
Mere
Soham
E
Isleham
Priory Church
F
West Row
Worlington
Needingworth
1
P+R
Holywell
Over
Willingham
A1123
Wicken Fen
Wicken
New River
Downfield
Fordham
Freckenham
Busway
Fen Drayton
Swavesey
B1050
Rampton
Chittering
R Cam
Chippenham
RSPB
A14
Fen Drayton Lakes
Longstanton
Denny Abbey
B1102
Snailwell
2
Busway
Cottenham
Burwell
Cambridge
B1049
Waterbeach
Reach
B1103
Exning
Boxworth
Oakington
Westwick
Landbeach
B1102
A142
Histon
A10
Swaffham Prior
Lolworth
Impington
A1304
Bar Hill
Girton
Milton
Lode
Newmarket
Knapwell
P+R
Anglesey Abbey
A14
National Stud
Dry Drayton
A14
Milton
Horningsea
Swaffham Bulbeck
Stow-cum-Quy
Bottisham
A1303
Cheveley
A428
A1307
A1309
Chesterton
Madingley
P+R
Fen Ditton
A1303
B1061
3
A1303
A1303
A14
Stetchworth
Woodditton
Coton
CAMBRIDGE
Romsey
Cambridge
Teversham
Little Wilbraham
A11
A1304
Caldecote Highfields
Hardwick
Six Mile Bottom
Dullingham
Ditton Green
Little Ditton
Great Wilbraham
Bourn
Caldecote
Comberton
A1134
Westley Waterless
B1046
Grantchester
Kingston
Toft
Barton
Cherry Hinton
Fulbourn
Burrough Green
75
M11
Trumpington
P+R
Brinkley
Wandlebury
Great Eversden
Little Eversden
Haslingfield
A1301
P+R
Great Shelford
A1307
Weston Colville
West Wratting
Great Bradley
4
Carlton
Wimpole Hall & Home Farm
Harlton
Hauxton
A11
Weston Green
Stapleford
Orwell
Harston
Little Shelford
R Granta
Balsham
Carlton Green
Little Thurlow
A603
Fourwentways
Babraham
A10
Little Abington
West Wickham
Wimpole
Newton
Barrington
Sawston
A505
Great Abington
Chilford Hall
Hildersham
Streetly End
Withersfield
Foxton
Whittlesford
Duxford Chapel
Pampisford
Shepreth
Frog End
B1368
Horseheath
Whaddon
A11
Linton
A1307
5
Meldreth
A1301
Mill Green
Thriplow
Duxford
Zoological Gardens
Fowlmere
IWM Duxford
Hinxton
Bartlow
Melbourn
Hadstock
Shudy Camps
Ickleton
Great Chesterford
Steventon End
Castle Camps
Bassingbourn-cum-Kneesworth
Royston
Little Chesterford
Ashdon
Helions Bumpstead
B1052
Little Walden
B1368
A505
B1184
Steeple Bumpstead
Elmdon
Heydon
Strethall
Great Chishill
6
Littlebury
Saffron Walden
Smith's Green
B1039
Barley
Chrishall
Catmere End
B1383
Audley End House & Gardens
B1053
B1054
Hempstead
Therfield
Shaftenhoe End
Littlebury Green
B1054
Sewards End
Little Chishill
Duddenhoe End
B1039
Wendens Ambo
Audley End
B184
Radwinter
Spain's End
B1053
Reed
B1052
Barkway
Nuthampstead
Langley Upper Green
Arkesden
M11
Tye Green
Great Sampford
Sandon
A10
Wimbish Green
B1368
Newport
Howlett End
B1051
Buckland
Anstey
Debden
7
Little Sampford
Mill End
60
Chipping
Snow End
Meesden
Clavering
B1038
Wicken Bonhunt
B1053
Brent Pelham
Widdington
Wyddial
Great Hormead
Starlings Green
Quendon
Thaxted
Little Bardfield
Rickling Green
Bardfield End Green
Great Bardfield
R Cam
Berden
Buntingford
B1038
Hare Street
Little Hormead
Stocking Pelham
B1383
Henham
Holder's Green
8
Westmill
Ugley
Ugley Green
Monk Street
Sibley's Green
B1057
B1051
B1368
Furneux Pelham
Hay Street
Manuden
Broxted
Lindsell
A
B
C
D
Elsenham
E
F
Wood End
Bran End
Stansted Mountfitchet
Great Easton
B184
4 miles
5 kilometres
Farnham
Molehill Green
Little Easton
Stebbing
Puckeridge
Burton End
Haultwick

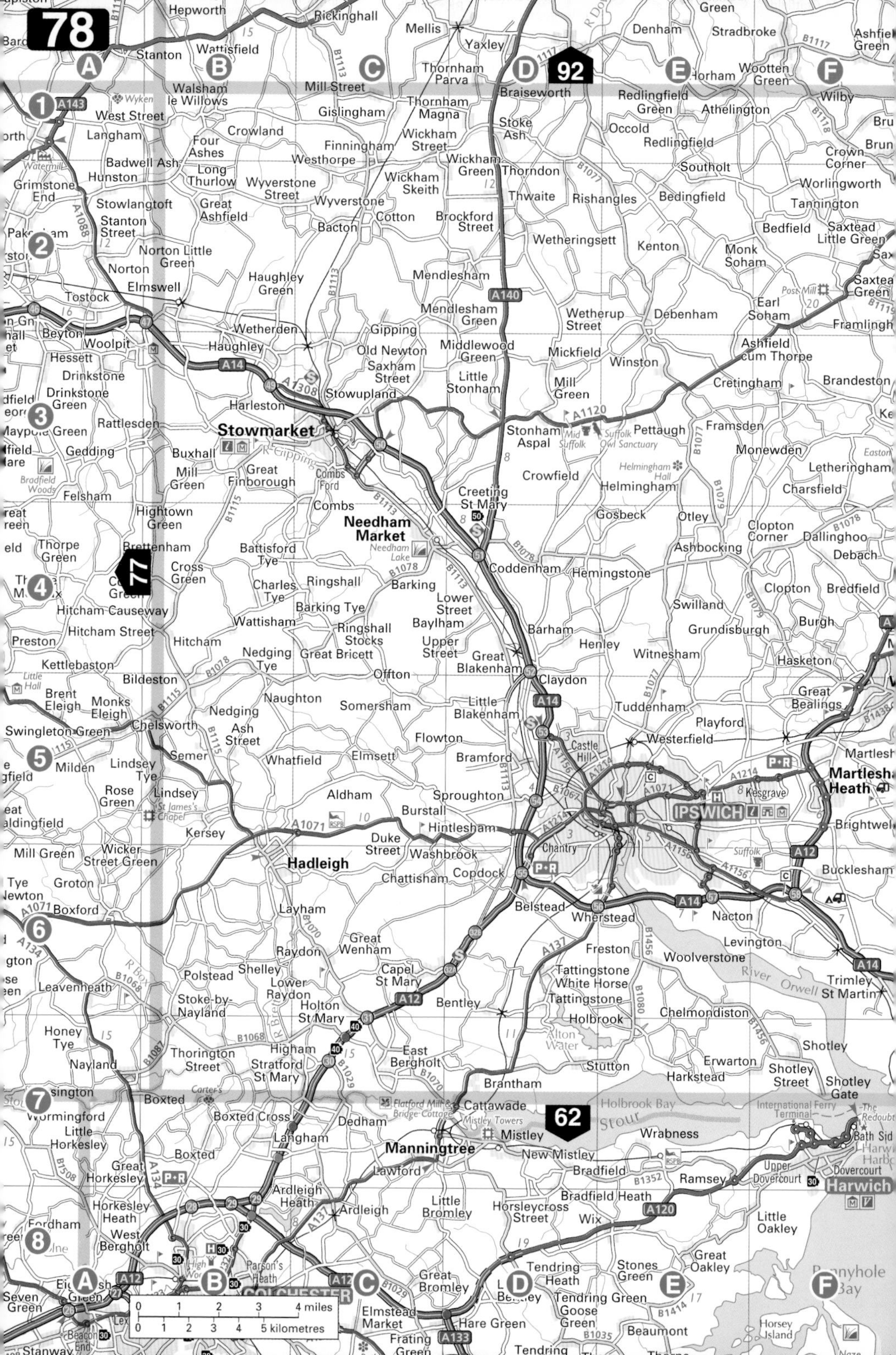

Hepworth
Rickinghall
Mellis
Yaxley
Denham
Stradbroke
Green
Stanton
Wattisfield
Thornham Parva
92
Horham
Wootten Green
Ashfield Green
Mill Street
Braiseworth
Redlingfield Green
Athelington
Wilby
Walsham le Willows
Wyken
West Street
Gislingham
Thornham Magna
Stoke Ash
Occold
Redlingfield
Langham
Crowland
Wickham Street
Finningham
Crown Corner
Four Ashes
Westhorpe
Wickham Green
Thorndon
Southolt
Watermill
Badwell Ash
Long Thurlow
Worlingworth
Grimstone End
Hunston
Wyverstone Street
Wickham Skeith
Thwaite
Rishangles
Bedingfield
Tannington
Stowlangtoft
Great Ashfield
Wyverstone
Cotton
Brockford Street
Bedfield
Saxtead Little Green
Stanton Street
Bacton
Wetheringsett
Kenton
Monk Soham
Norton Little Green
Norton
Haughley Green
Mendlesham
Elmswell
Post Mill
Saxtead Green
Tostock
Mendlesham Green
Wetherup Street
Debenham
Earl Soham
Beyton
Wetherden
Gipping
Framlingham
Woolpit
Haughley
Old Newton
Middlewood Green
Mickfield
Ashfield cum Thorpe
Hessett
Winston
Drinkstone
Saxham Street
Little Stonham
Mill Green
Cretingham
Brandeston
Drinkstone Green
Stowupland
Harleston
Rattlesden
Stowmarket
Stonham Aspal
Pettaugh
Framsden
Mid Suffolk
Suffolk Owl Sanctuary
Gedding
Buxhall
R Gipping
Monewden
Easton
Letheringham
Bradfield Woods
Mill Green
Great Finborough
Combs Ford
Helmingham Hall
Helmingham
Crowfield
Charsfield
Felsham
Combs
Creeting St Mary
Hightown Green
Needham Market
Gosbeck
Otley
Clopton Corner
Dallinghoo
Thorpe Green
Brettenham
Battisford Tye
Needham Lake
Ashbocking
Debach
77
Cross Green
Charles Tye
Ringshall
Barking
Coddenham
Hemingstone
Clopton
Bredfield
Hitcham Causeway
Barking Tye
Lower Street
Swilland
Hitcham Street
Wattisham
Ringshall Stocks
Baylham
Barham
Grundisburgh
Burgh
Preston
Hitcham
Nedging Tye
Great Bricett
Upper Street
Great Blakenham
Henley
Witnesham
Hasketon
Kettlebaston
Offton
Claydon
Little Hall
Bildeston
Brent Eleigh
Monks Eleigh
Naughton
Somersham
Little Blakenham
Tuddenham
Great Bealings
Nedging
Swingleton Green
Chelsworth
Ash Street
Flowton
Castle Hill
Westerfield
Playford
Milden
Semer
Whatfield
Elmsett
Bramford
Martlesham
Lindsey Tye
Martlesham Heath
Rose Green
Lindsey
Aldham
Sproughton
Kesgrave
St James's Chapel
Burstall
IPSWICH
Kersey
RSPB
Hintlesham
Brightwell
Mill Green
Wicker Street Green
Duke Street
Chantry
Hadleigh
Washbrook
Suffolk
Bucklesham
Groton
Chattisham
Copdock
Tye Newton
Boxford
Belstead
Wherstead
Nacton
Layham
Great Wenham
Freston
Levington
Raydon
Woolverstone
Leavenheath
Shelley
Capel St Mary
Tattingstone White Horse
River Orwell
Trimley St Martin
R Box
Polstead
Lower Raydon
Tattingstone
Stoke-by-Nayland
Holton St Mary
Bentley
Holbrook
Chelmondiston
Honey Tye
Alton Water
Shotley
Higham
Nayland
Thorington Street
Stratford St Mary
East Bergholt
Stutton
Erwarton
Shotley Street
Harkstead
Brantham
Shotley Gate
Boxted
Carter's
Flatford Mill & Bridge Cottage
Cattawade
Holbrook Bay
International Ferry Terminal
The Redoubt
Wormingford
Boxted Cross
Mistley Towers
62
Stour
Little Horkesley
Dedham
Mistley
Wrabness
Bath Side
Langham
Manningtree
New Mistley
Boxted
Harwich Harbour
Great Horkesley
Lawford
Bradfield
Ramsey
Upper Dovercourt
Dovercourt
Harwich
Ardleigh Heath
Bradfield Heath
Horkesley Heath
Ardleigh
Little Bromley
Horsleycross Street
Wix
Little Oakley
Fordham
West Bergholt
Parson's Heath
Great Oakley
Tendring Heath
Stones Green
Great Bromley
Hamford Water
COLCHESTER
Seven Green
Tendring Green
Elmstead Market
Goose Green
Hare Green
Beaumont
Horsey Island
Beacon End
Stanway
Frating Green
Tendring
A143
A1088
A14
A1308
A140
A1120
A1077
B1115
B1113
B1078
B1079
A1071
A1214
A1156
A12
A137
A134
B1068
B1070
B1029
B1080
B1456
B1352
A120
B1414
A133
B1035
B1117
B1118
B1119
B1438
B1087
B1508
B1115
0 1 2 3 4 miles
0 1 2 3 4 5 kilometres

Cratfield
Huntingfield
Walpole
Blackheath
Blythburgh
Thorington
Walberswick
Bramfield
93
Laxfield
Heveningham
Ubbeston Green
Street
Darsham
Dunwich Forest
Suffolk Coast
Westleton Heath
Dunwich
Sibton
Peasenhall
Yoxford
Westleton
Middleton
Minsmere
Dunwich Heath
Badingham
Middleton Moor
Bruisyard
Theberton
Eastbridge
Bruisyard Street
Rendham
Cransford
Kelsale
Leiston Abbey
Shawsgate
Carlton
Saxmundham
Swefling
North Green
Great Glemham
Benhall Street
Benhall Green
Knodishall
Sternfield
Leiston
Aldringham
Thorpe Ness
Stratford St Andrew
Friday Street
Farnham
Snape
Parham
Hacheston
Friston
Knodishall Common
Thorpeness
Easton
Marlesford
Little Glemham
Snape Street
Snape Maltings
Aldeburgh
Blaxhall
Campsea Ash
Tunstall
Aldeburgh Bay
Rendlesham
Ufford
Chillesford
Sudbourne
River Alde
Eyke
Bromeswell
Butley
Castle
Orford
Orford Ness
Capel St Andrew
Sutton
Boyton
Orfordness-Havergate
Waldringfield
Shottisham
Hollesley
River Ore
Suffolk Heritage Coast
North Weir Point
Hemley
Hollesley Bay
River Deben
Alderton
Bawdsey
Falkenham
Trimley St Mary
Old Felixstowe
Walton
Felixstowe
Landguard Fort
Landguard Point
Hook of Holland
A12
A144
A1120
A1094
A1152
A154
B1117
B1387
B1125
B1122
B1120
B1119
B1121
B1353
B1069
B1078
B1084
B1083
B1438
B1116
G H J K L M
1 2 3 4 5 6 7 8

95
66
CARDIGAN BAY
Barmouth Bay
Barmouth
Barmouth Bridge
Afon Mawddach
Penmaenpool
Llanelltyd
Toll
A496
A493
Fairbourne Steam Railway
Fairbourne
SNOWDONIA NATIONAL PARK
CADER
621
Tal-y-llyn
Llwyngwril
Llangelynin
Afon Dysynni
Castell y Bere
Abergynolwyn
667
Rhoslefain
Llanegryn
Bryncrug
B4405
Talyllyn Railway
Dolgoch Falls
633
TAREN HENDRE
Aber Dysynni
Tywyn
Pennal
Dovey
Aberdovey
Aberdyfi
Afon Dyfi (River Dovey)
Ynys-hir
Glandyfi
Dyfi Furnace
A487
B4353
Cwm Clettwr
Tre Taliesin
Borth
Tal-y-bont
Ceredigion Heritage Coast
Llandre
Rhyd-y-pennau
Bont-goch/ Elerch
B4572
Bow Street
Salem
Clarach Bay
Penrhyn-coch
Pen-bont Rhydybeddau
A4159
Cliff Railway & Camera Obscura
Capel-Dewi
Waunfawr
Aberystwyth
Llanbadarn Fawr
Capel Bangor
Goginan
Rheidol power station
Capel Seion
Coed Penglanowen
A4120
Llanfarian
Llanfihangel-y-Creuddyn
A485
Blaenplwyf
Afon Ystwyth
Cnwch Coch
Llanilar
B4340
B4575
Penderi Cliffs
Llanddeiniol
Llanafan
B4576
Llangwyryfon
Lledrod
Cors Ian
Tynygraig
Llanrhystud
0 1 2 3 4 miles
0 1 2 3 4 5 kilometres

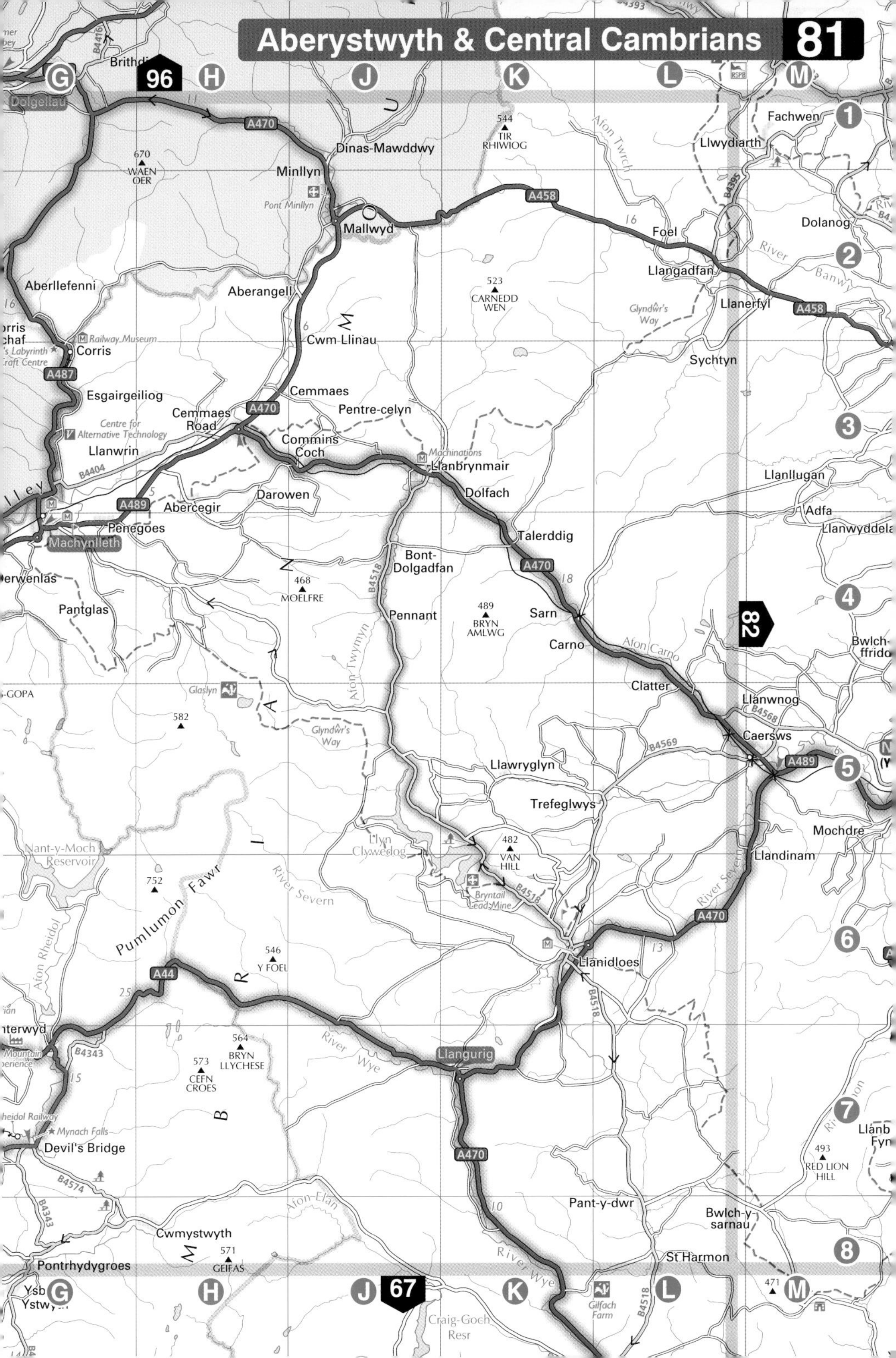
96
82
67
Dolgellau
Brithdir
A470
Dinas-Mawddwy
670
WAEN
OER
544
TIR
RHIWIOG
Minllyn
Pont Minllyn
Mallwyd
A458
Foel
Llangadfan
Llanerfyl
Fachwen
Llwydiarth
Dolanog
River Banwy
Afon Twrch
B4395
RSPB
Aberllefenni
Aberangell
523
CARNEDD
WEN
Glyndŵr's
Way
Corris
Railway Museum
A487
Cwm Llinau
Sychtyn
Esgairgeiliog
Cemmaes
Cemmaes
Road
Pentre-celyn
Centre for
Alternative Technology
Llanwrin
B4404
Commins
Coch
Machinations
Llanbrynmair
Dolfach
Llanllugan
Adfa
Llanwyddelan
A489
Abercegir
Darowen
Penegoes
Machynlleth
Talerddig
Bont-
Dolgadfan
468
MOELFRE
B4518
Pennant
489
BRYN
AMLWG
Sarn
Carno
Afon Carno
Pantglas
Afon Twymyn
Bwlch-
ffridd
Clatter
Llanwnog
B4568
Caersws
B4569
Glaslyn
582
Glyndŵr's
Way
Llawryglyn
Trefeglwys
Mochdre
Llandinam
Nant-y-Moch
Reservoir
Llyn
Clywedog
482
VAN
HILL
Bryntail
Lead Mine
River Severn
752
Pumlumon Fawr
Afon Rheidol
546
Y FOEL
Llanidloes
13
A44
B4343
564
BRYN
LLYCHESE
573
CEFN
CROES
River Wye
Llangurig
Mynach Falls
Devil's Bridge
B4574
493
RED LION
HILL
Pant-y-dwr
Bwlch-y-
sarnau
Cwmystwyth
571
GEIFAS
Afon Elan
St Harmon
Pontrhydygroes
Gilfach
Farm
Craig-Goch
Resr
471
C
A
M
B
R
I
A
N
M
O
U
N
T
A
I
N
S

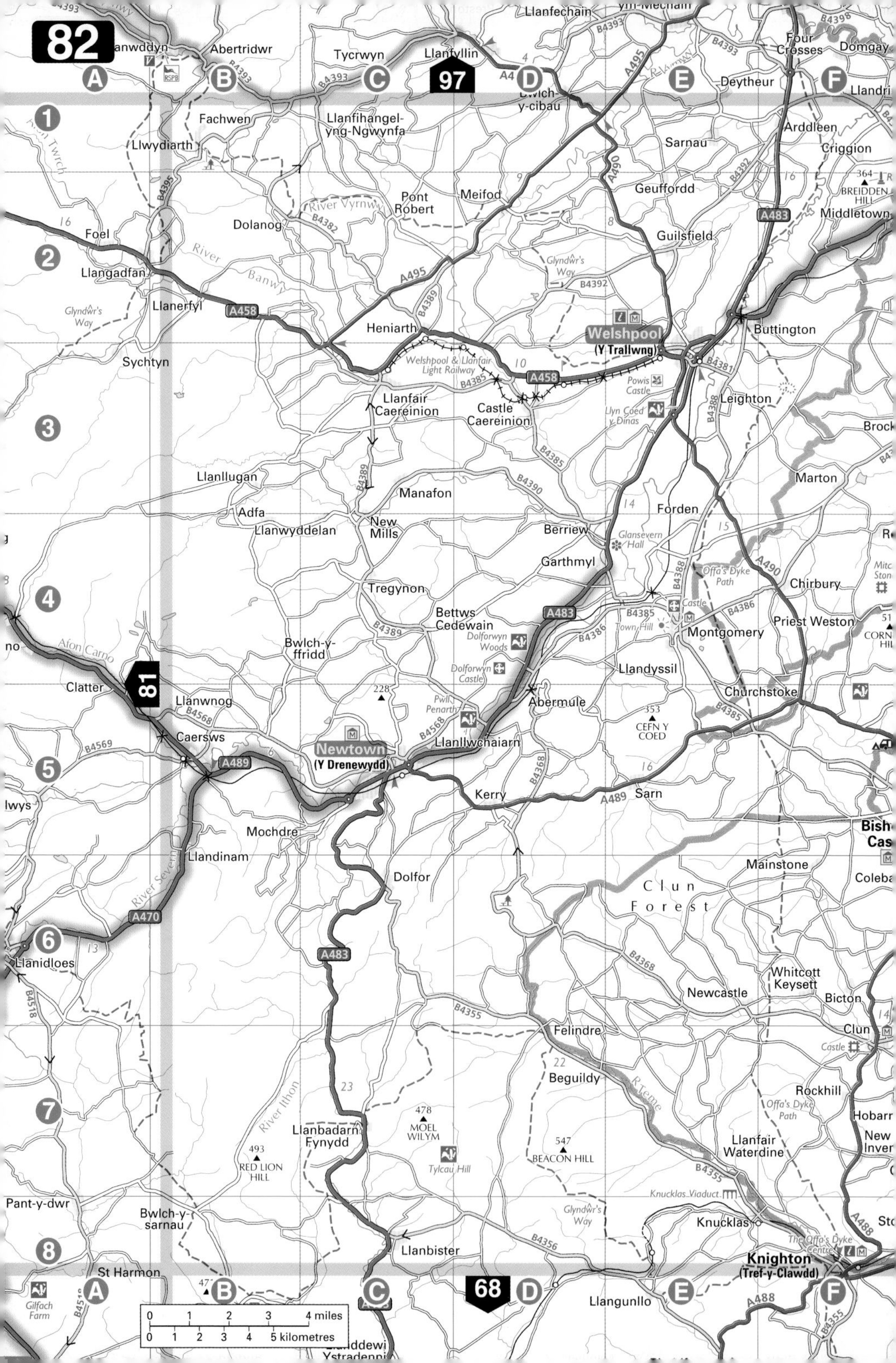

Abertridwr
Tycrwyn
Llanfyllin
97
Llanfechain
Four Crosses
Domgay
Deytheur
Bwlch-y-cibau
Fachwen
Llanfihangel-yng-Ngwynfa
Llwydiarth
Arddleen
Criggion
Sarnau
364
BREIDDEN HILL
Geufforddd
Meifod
Pont Robert
Dolanog
River Vyrnwy
Middletown
Foel
Guilsfield
Llangadfan
River Banwy
Glyndŵr's Way
Llanerfyl
A458
A495
A490
A483
B4393
B4395
B4382
B4389
B4392
Heniarth
Welshpool
(Y Trallwng)
Buttington
Sychtyn
Welshpool & Llanfair Light Railway
B4385
B4381
B4388
Powis Castle
Llanfair Caereinion
Castle Caereinion
Leighton
Llyn Coed y Dinas
Brock
Llanllugan
Manafon
B4390
Marton
Adfa
Forden
Llanwyddelan
New Mills
Berriew
Glansevern Hall
Garthmyl
Offa's Dyke Path
Tregynon
Chirbury
Bettws Cedewain
B4386
Castle
Town Hill
Montgomery
Priest Weston
Dolforwyn Woods
Afon Carno
Bwlch-y-ffridd
Dolforwyn Castle
Llandyssil
Clatter
81
228
Pwll Penarth
Abermule
Churchstoke
Llanwnog
353
CEFN Y COED
B4568
Caersws
B4569
Newtown
(Y Drenewydd)
Llanllwchaiarn
A489
Kerry
Sarn
B4368
Mochdre
Llandinam
River Severn
Dolfor
Mainstone
Clun Forest
A470
Llanidloes
B4518
B4355
Whitcott Keysett
Newcastle
Bicton
Clun
Felindre
Castle
Beguildy
R.Teme
Rockhill
River Ithon
478
MOEL WILYM
Llanbadarn Fynydd
Tylcau Hill
493
RED LION HILL
547
BEACON HILL
Llanfair Waterdine
Knucklas Viaduct
Pant-y-dwr
Bwlch-y-sarnau
Knucklas
A488
The Offa's Dyke Centre
Llanbister
B4356
Knighton
(Tref-y-Clawdd)
St Harmon
68
Llangunllo
Gilfach Farm
0 1 2 3 4 miles
0 1 2 3 4 5 kilometres

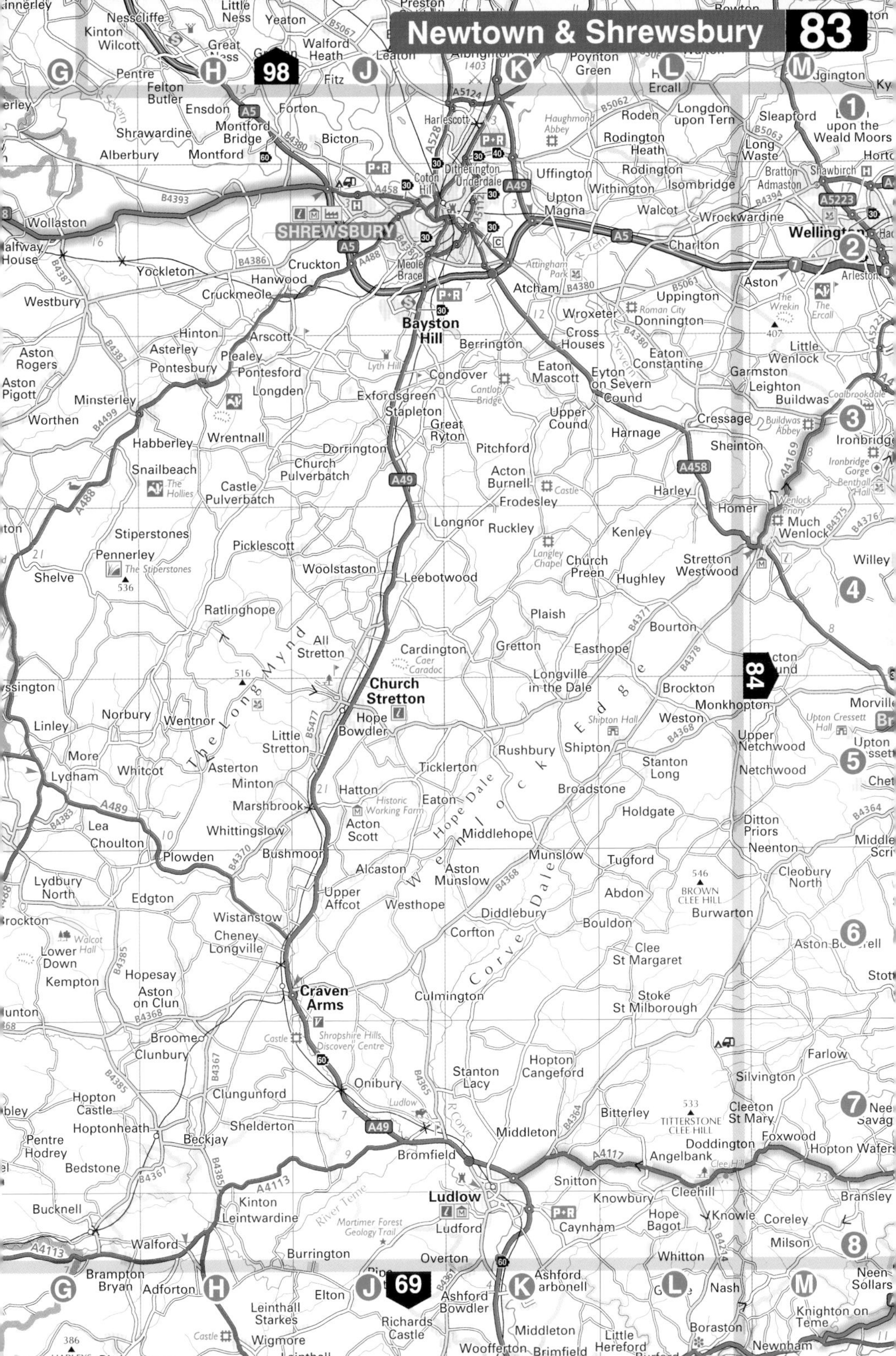

Newtown & Shrewsbury
83
98
84
69
SHREWSBURY
Wellington
Bayston Hill
Church Stretton
Craven Arms
Ludlow
Nesscliffe
Kinton
Wilcott
Little Ness
Great Ness
Yeaton
Walford Heath
Preston
Leaton
Albrighton
Poynton Green
High Ercall
Pentre
Felton Butler
Fitz
Forton
Ensdon
Montford Bridge
Montford
Shrawardine
Alberbury
Bicton
Harlescott
Ditherington
Underdale
Coton Hill
Haughmond Abbey
Roden
Longdon upon Tern
Sleapford
Rodington Heath
Rodington
Uffington
Withington
Isombridge
Upton Magna
Walcot
Wrockwardine
Long Waste
Bratton
Admaston
Shawbirch
Charlton
Wollaston
Halfway House
Yockleton
Cruckton
Hanwood
Cruckmeole
Westbury
Meole Brace
Atcham
Attingham Park
Aston
Arleston
Uppington
Wroxeter
Roman City
Donnington
The Wrekin
The Ercall
Hinton
Arscott
Asterley
Aston Rogers
Aston Pigott
Pontesbury
Plealey
Pontesford
Lyth Hill
Berrington
Cross Houses
Eaton Constantine
Little Wenlock
Condover
Cantlop Bridge
Eaton Mascott
Eyton on Severn
Cound
Garmston
Leighton
Buildwas
Coalbrookdale
Minsterley
Worthen
Longden
Exfordsgreen
Stapleton
Great Ryton
Upper Cound
Harnage
Cressage
Buildwas Abbey
Sheinton
Ironbridge
Ironbridge Gorge
Benthall Hall
Habberley
Wrentnall
Dorrington
Pitchford
Church Pulverbatch
Acton Burnell
Castle
Snailbeach
The Hollies
Castle Pulverbatch
Frodesley
Harley
Homer
Wenlock Priory
Much Wenlock
Longnor
Ruckley
Kenley
Stiperstones
Pennerley
The Stiperstones
Picklescott
Langley Chapel
Church Preen
Stretton Westwood
Willey
Shelve
Woolstaston
Leebotwood
Hughley
Ratlinghope
Plaish
Bourton
The Long Mynd
All Stretton
Cardington
Caer Caradoc
Gretton
Easthope
Acton Round
Longville in the Dale
Brockton
Monkhopton
Morville
Norbury
Wentnor
Hope Bowdler
Shipton Hall
Weston
Upton Cressett Hall
Linley
Little Stretton
Rushbury
Shipton
Upper Netchwood
Netchwood
More
Lydham
Whitcot
Asterton
Minton
Ticklerton
Stanton Long
Broadstone
Hatton
Eaton
Historic Working Farm
Wenlock Edge
Hope Dale
Marshbrook
Holdgate
Lea
Choulton
Whittingslow
Acton Scott
Middlehope
Ditton Priors
Neenton
Plowden
Bushmoor
Alcaston
Aston Munslow
Munslow
Tugford
Brown Clee Hill
Cleobury North
Lydbury North
Edgton
Upper Affcot
Westhope
Abdon
Burwarton
Brockton
Wistanstow
Diddlebury
Bouldon
Walcot Hall
Lower Down
Cheney Longville
Corfton
Corve Dale
Clee St Margaret
Aston Botterell
Kempton
Hopesay
Aston on Clun
Culmington
Stoke St Milborough
Broome
Clunbury
Shropshire Hills Discovery Centre
Farlow
Stanton Lacy
Hopton Cangeford
Silvington
Clungunford
Onibury
Hopton Castle
Hoptonheath
Shelderton
Bitterley
Titterstone Clee Hill
Cleeton St Mary
Pentre Hodrey
Beckjay
Middleton
Doddington
Foxwood
Hopton Wafers
Bedstone
Bromfield
Angelbank
Clee Hill
Snitton
Knowbury
Cleehill
Bransley
Bucknell
Kinton
Leintwardine
River Teme
Mortimer Forest Geology Trail
Ludford
Caynham
Hope Bagot
Knowle
Coreley
Walford
Burrington
Overton
Whitton
Milson
Brampton Bryan
Adforton
Elton
Ashford Bowdler
Ashford Carbonell
Nash
Neen Sollars
Leinthall Starkes
Richards Castle
Middleton
Little Hereford
Boraston
Knighton on Teme
Wigmore
Woofferton
Brimfield
Newnham
A5
A49
A458
A488
A489
A4113
A4117
A4169
A5112
A5124
A5223
A528
B4380
B4386
B4387
B4393
B4499
B4370
B4371
B4378
B4368
B4364
B4365
B4367
B4385
B4383
B4361
B4214
B5061
B5062
B5063
B4394
B4375
B4376
B5477

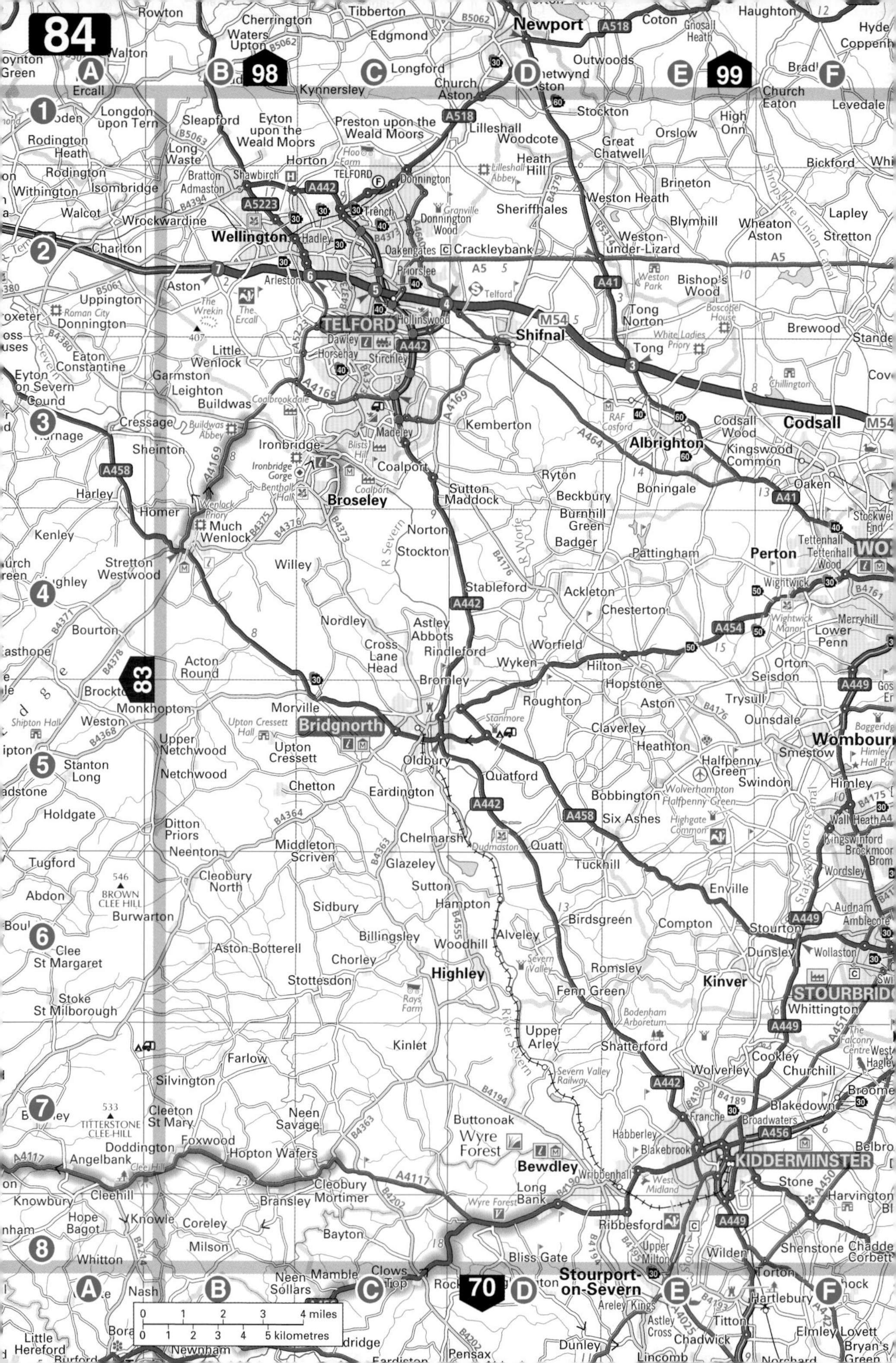
98
99
83
70
A
B
C
D
E
F
1
2
3
4
5
6
7
8
Rowton
Cherrington
Tibberton
Waters Upton
Edgmond
Newport
Coton
Gnosall Heath
Haughton
Hyde
Coppenhall
Walton
Ercall
Longford
Kynnersley
Church Aston
Outwoods
Chetwynd Aston
Bradley
Church Eaton
Levedale
Longdon upon Tern
Sleapford
Eyton upon the Weald Moors
Preston upon the Weald Moors
Lilleshall
Woodcote
Stockton
Great Chatwell
Orslow
High Onn
Rodington Heath
Rodington
Long Waste
Horton
Heath Hill
Lilleshall Abbey
Bickford
Withington
Isombridge
Bratton
Admaston
Shawbirch
TELFORD
Donnington
Brineton
Weston Heath
Blymhill
Wheaton Aston
Lapley
Stretton
Walcot
Wrockwardine
Wellington
Hadley
Trench
Granville
Donnington Wood
Sheriffhales
Weston-under-Lizard
Charlton
Oakengates
Crackleybank
Priorslee
Aston
Arleston
The Wrekin
The Ercall
Uppington
Roman City
Donnington
Telford
Weston Park
Bishop's Wood
Hollinswood
Shifnal
Tong Norton
Boscobel House
Brewood
Eaton Constantine
Little Wenlock
Dawley
Horsehay
Stirchley
White Ladies Priory
Tong
Chillington
Eyton on Severn
Cound
Garmston
Leighton
Buildwas
Coalbrookdale
Cressage
Buildwas Abbey
Kemberton
RAF Cosford
Albrighton
Codsall Wood
Codsall
Harnage
Sheinton
Ironbridge
Madeley
Ironbridge Gorge
Blists Hill
Coalport
Benthall Hall
Broseley
Ryton
Kingswood Common
Oaken
Harley
Sutton Maddock
Beckbury
Boningale
Homer
Wenlock Priory
Much Wenlock
Burnhill Green
Stockwell End
Kenley
Norton
Badger
Tettenhall
Tettenhall Wood
Stockton
Pattingham
Perton
Stretton Westwood
Willey
Hughley
Stableford
Ackleton
Wightwick
Chesterton
Bourton
Nordley
Astley Abbots
Wightwick Manor
Merryhill
Lower Penn
Easthope
Cross Lane Head
Rindleford
Worfield
Wyken
Hilton
Orton
Acton Round
Bromley
Hopstone
Seisdon
Brockton
Morville
Roughton
Aston
Trysull
Shipton Hall
Weston
Monkhopton
Upton Cressett Hall
Bridgnorth
Stanmore
Claverley
Ounsdale
Baggeridge
Wombourne
Shipton
Upper Netchwood
Upton Cressett
Oldbury
Heathton
Smestow
Himley Hall Park
Stanton Long
Netchwood
Quatford
Halfpenny Green
Swindon
Himley
Bradstone
Chetton
Eardington
Bobbington
Wolverhampton Halfpenny Green
Holdgate
Ditton Priors
Six Ashes
Highgate Common
Wall Heath
Kingswinford
Brockmoor
Neenton
Middleton Scriven
Chelmarsh
Dudmaston
Quatt
Tugford
Cleobury North
Glazeley
Tuckhill
Wordsley
546
BROWN CLEE HILL
Abdon
Sutton
Enville
Sidbury
Hampton
Audnam
Amblecote
Burwarton
Birdsgreen
Compton
Stourton
Clee St Margaret
Billingsley
Aston Botterell
Woodhill
Alveley
Dunsley
Wollaston
Chorley
Severn Valley
Romsley
Highley
Stottesdon
Kinver
STOURBRIDGE
Fenn Green
Stoke St Milborough
Rays Farm
Bodenham Arboretum
Whittington
Upper Arley
The Falconry Centre
Kinlet
Shatterford
Farlow
Cookley
Churchill
Hagley
Wolverley
Silvington
Severn Valley Railway
Broome
533
TITTERSTONE CLEE HILL
Cleeton St Mary
Neen Savage
Buttonoak
Franche
Blakedown
Broadwaters
Doddington
Foxwood
Wyre Forest
Habberley
Blakebrook
Belbroughton
Angelbank
Clee Hill
Hopton Wafers
Bewdley
KIDDERMINSTER
Wribbenhall
West Midland
Cleobury Mortimer
Long Bank
Stone
Knowbury
Cleehill
Bransley
Wyre Forest
Harvington
Hope Bagot
Knowle
Coreley
Ribbesford
Milson
Bayton
Upper Milton
Wilden
Shenstone
Chaddesley Corbett
Whitton
Bliss Gate
Torton
Nash
Neen Sollars
Mamble
Clows Top
Rock
Stourport-on-Severn
Hartlebury
Areley Kings
Astley Cross
Titton
Chadwick
Elmley Lovett
Bryan's Green
Little Hereford
Newnham
Dunley
Lincomb
Pensax
Burford
0 1 2 3 4 miles
0 1 2 3 4 5 kilometres
M54
A5
A41
A442
A518
A5223
A4169
A458
A454
A449
A456
A451
A4117
A464
B5062
B5063
B4394
B5061
B4380
B4373
B4375
B4376
B4371
B4378
B4368
B4364
B4363
B4555
B4176
B4194
B4190
B4202
B4189
B4193
B4195
B4214
B4379
B5314
B4161
B4175
Shropshire Union Canal
Staffs & Worcs Canal
R Severn
River Severn
R Worfe
Stour

Rugeley
Cannock Chase
Penkridge
Hednesford
Cannock
Lichfield
Burntwood
Brownhills
Tamworth
Walsall
Aldridge
Royal Sutton Coldfield
Wednesbury
West Bromwich
Dudley
Smethwick
Birmingham
Halesowen
Solihull
Coleshill
Knowle
Dorridge
Bromsgrove
Alvechurch
Kingsbury
Fazeley
100
98
71

86
100
85
72
Swadlincote
Ashby-de-la-Zouch
Shepshed
Coalville
Whitwick
Ibstock
Measham
Donisthorpe
TAMWORTH
Fazeley
Polesworth
Dordon
Baddesley Ensor
Atherstone
Kingsbury
Coleshill
Hartshill
NUNEATON
Hinckley
Barwell
Earl Shilton
Desford
Bedworth
COVENTRY
Knowle
Dorridge
Balsall Common
Kenilworth
0 1 2 3 4 miles
0 1 2 3 4 5 kilometres

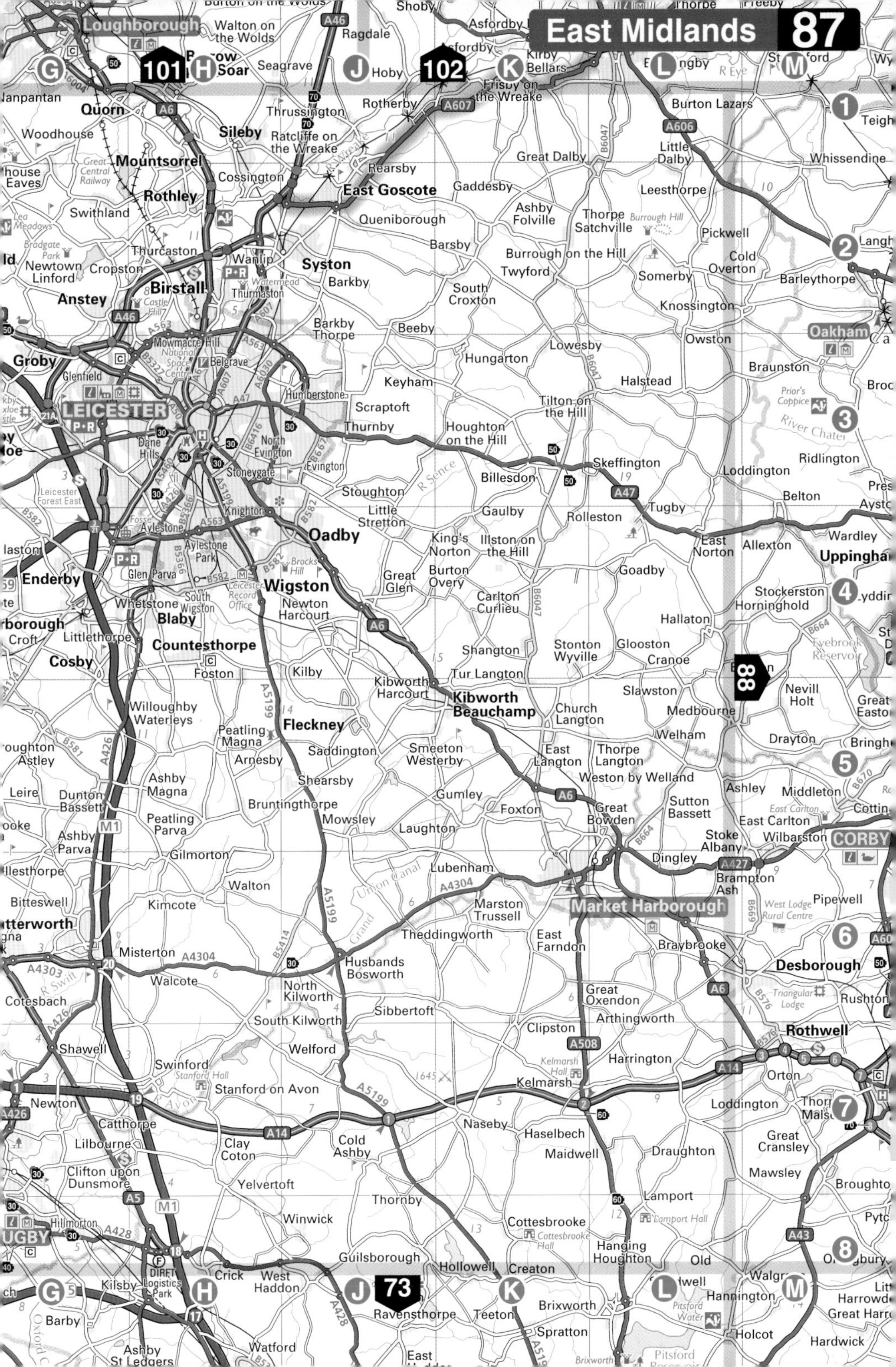
Loughborough
Walton on the Wolds
Shoby
Ragdale
Asfordby
Kirby Bellars
Burrow on the Hill
Seagrave
Hoby
Frisby on the Wreake
Burton Lazars
Teigh
Quorn
Thrussington
Rotherby
Woodhouse
Sileby
Ratcliffe on the Wreake
Little Dalby
Whissendine
Great Dalby
Mountsorrel
Great Central Railway
Cossington
Rearsby
Leesthorpe
Rothley
East Goscote
Gaddesby
Swithland
Queniborough
Ashby Folville
Thorpe Satchville
Burrough Hill
Pickwell
Bradgate Park
Thurcaston
Wanlip
Barsby
Burrough on the Hill
Cold Overton
Newtown Linford
Cropston
Syston
Twyford
Somerby
Barleythorpe
Birstall
Watermead
Thurmaston
Barkby
South Croxton
Anstey
Castle Hill
Knossington
Barkby Thorpe
Beeby
Oakham
Groby
Mowmacre Hill
National Space Centre
Belgrave
Lowesby
Owston
Glenfield
Hungarton
Braunston
Keyham
Halstead
Humberstone
Prior's Coppice
LEICESTER
Scraptoft
Tilton on the Hill
River Chater
Thurnby
Houghton on the Hill
Dane Hills
North Evington
Evington
Stoneygate
Skeffington
Ridlington
Billesdon
Loddington
R. Sence
Stoughton
Leicester Forest East
Belton
Knighton
Little Stretton
Gaulby
Tugby
Rolleston
Aylestone
Oadby
King's Norton
Illston on the Hill
East Norton
Allexton
Wardley
Aylestone Park
Brocks Hill
Uppingham
Glen Parva
Enderby
Great Glen
Burton Overy
Goadby
Wigston
Leicester Record Office
Whetstone
South Wigston
Newton Harcourt
Carlton Curlieu
Stockerston
Horninghold
Blaby
Hallaton
Littlethorpe
Countesthorpe
Shangton
Stonton Wyville
Glooston
Cranoe
Eyebrook Reservoir
Cosby
Foston
Kilby
Tur Langton
Kibworth Harcourt
Kibworth Beauchamp
Slawston
Nevill Holt
Willoughby Waterleys
Church Langton
Medbourne
Great Easton
Fleckney
Peatling Magna
Saddington
Smeeton Westerby
Welham
Drayton
Broughton Astley
Arnesby
East Langton
Thorpe Langton
Shearsby
Weston by Welland
Ashby Magna
Gumley
Ashley
Middleton
Leire
Dunton Bassett
Bruntingthorpe
Foxton
Great Bowden
Sutton Bassett
East Carlton
Cottingham
Peatling Parva
Mowsley
Laughton
Ashby Parva
Stoke Albany
Wilbarston
CORBY
Gilmorton
Dingley
Lubenham
Union Canal
Brampton Ash
Walton
Kimcote
Bitteswell
Marston Trussell
Market Harborough
West Lodge Rural Centre
Pipewell
Lutterworth
Theddingworth
East Farndon
Misterton
Braybrooke
Husbands Bosworth
Desborough
Walcote
Grand
R. Swift
North Kilworth
Great Oxendon
Triangular Lodge
Rushton
Cotesbach
Sibbertoft
Arthingworth
South Kilworth
Clipston
Rothwell
Shawell
Welford
Harrington
Swinford
Kelmarsh Hall
Stanford Hall
Orton
Stanford on Avon
Kelmarsh
Newton
R. Avon
Loddington
Naseby
Catthorpe
Haselbech
Great Cransley
Cold Ashby
Lilbourne
Clay Coton
Maidwell
Draughton
Clifton upon Dunsmore
Mawsley
Yelvertoft
Lamport
Thornby
Lamport Hall
Hillmorton
Winwick
Cottesbrooke
Cottesbrooke Hall
RUGBY
Hanging Houghton
Guilsborough
Crick
West Haddon
Hollowell
Creaton
Old
Walgrave
Kilsby
DIRFT Logistics Park
Hannington
Little Harrowden
Great Harrowden
Pitsford Water
Barby
Ravensthorpe
Teeton
Brixworth
Spratton
Holcot
Oxford Canal
Ashby St Ledgers
Watford
East Haddon
Pitsford Reservoir
Hardwick
A46
A6
A607
A606
A47
A563
A5199
A426
A4304
A427
A14
A508
A5
A428
A43
A4303
M1
B6047
B664
B582
B576
B669
B670
B5414
B581
G
H
J
K
L
M
1
2
3
4
5
6
7
8
101
102
88
73

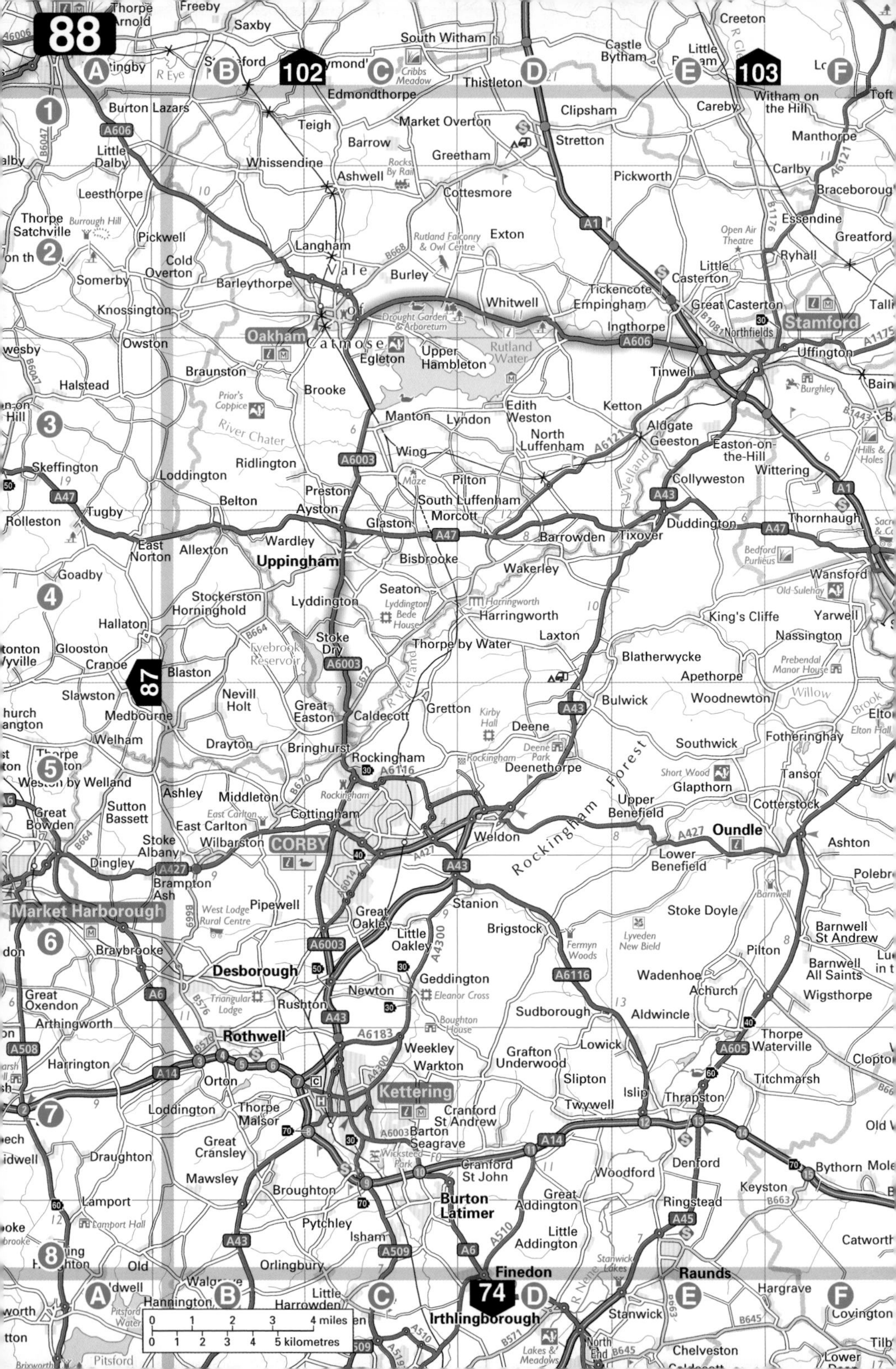

88
102
103
87
74
A
B
C
D
E
F
1
2
3
4
5
6
7
8
Thorpe Arnold
Freeby
Saxby
South Witham
Creeton
Castle Bytham
Little
R Eye
Cribbs Meadow
Thistleton
Witham on the Hill
Toft
Edmondthorpe
Burton Lazars
Clipsham
Careby
Teigh
Market Overton
Stretton
Manthorpe
Barrow
Greetham
Little Dalby
Whissendine
Rocks By Rail
Carlby
Ashwell
Pickworth
Leesthorpe
Cottesmore
Braceborough
Thorpe Satchville
Burrough Hill
Essendine
Pickwell
Exton
A1
Open Air Theatre
Greatford
Rutland Falconry & Owl Centre
Langham
Cold Overton
Ryhall
Somerby
Vale
Burley
Little Casterton
Barleythorpe
Tickencote
Whitwell
Empingham
Great Casterton
Knossington
Drought Garden & Arboretum
Oakham
Catmose
Stamford
Owston
Ingthorpe
Northfields
Upper Hambleton
Rutland Water
Egleton
A606
Uffington
Braunston
Tinwell
Halstead
Burghley
Brooke
Prior's Coppice
Edith Weston
Ketton
Manton
Lyndon
River Chater
North Luffenham
Aldgate
Geeston
Easton-on-the-Hill
Hills & Holes
Skeffington
Ridlington
Wing
Wittering
Loddington
A6003
Maze
Pilton
Collyweston
A47
Preston
South Luffenham
Welland
A43
Tugby
Belton
Morcott
Ayston
Glaston
Duddington
Thornhaugh
Rolleston
Barrowden
Tixover
Wardley
Bedford Purlieus
East Norton
Allexton
Uppingham
Bisbrooke
Wakerley
Wansford
Goadby
Old Sulehay
Stockerston
Seaton
Harringworth
Horninghold
Lyddington
Lyddington Bede House
King's Cliffe
Yarwell
Hallaton
Laxton
Nassington
Stoke Dry
B664
Eyebrook Reservoir
Thorpe by Water
Blatherwycke
Glooston
Prebendal Manor House
Cranoe
Apethorpe
Blaston
B672
Slawston
Nevill Holt
Woodnewton
Willow Brook
Great Easton
Bulwick
Caldecott
Gretton
Medbourne
Kirby Hall
Elton Hall
Deene
Welham
Drayton
Southwick
Fotheringhay
Bringhurst
Deene Park
Thorpe
Rockingham
Deenethorpe
Weston by Welland
Rockingham Forest
Short Wood
Tansor
A6116
Glapthorn
Ashley
Middleton
B670
Sutton Bassett
Upper Benefield
Cotterstock
Great Bowden
East Carlton
Cottingham
Oundle
Weldon
A427
East Carlton
Ashton
Stoke Albany
Wilbarston
CORBY
Lower Benefield
Dingley
Polebrook
Brampton Ash
Stanion
Market Harborough
Pipewell
Stoke Doyle
West Lodge Rural Centre
Great Oakley
Barnwell
Brigstock
Barnwell St Andrew
Little Oakley
Lyveden New Bield
Braybrooke
Fermyn Woods
Pilton
A4300
Barnwell All Saints
Desborough
Geddington
Wadenhoe
A6
Great Oxendon
Newton
Eleanor Cross
Achurch
Wigsthorpe
Triangular Lodge
Rushton
Sudborough
Arthingworth
Aldwincle
Boughton House
Rothwell
A6183
Thorpe Waterville
A508
Weekley
Grafton Underwood
Lowick
Harrington
A605
Clopton
Warkton
A14
Orton
Slipton
Titchmarsh
Kettering
Islip
Thrapston
Loddington
Thorpe Malsor
Cranford St Andrew
Twywell
Barton Seagrave
Old Weston
Great Cransley
Draughton
Wicksteed Park
Cranford St John
Denford
Woodford
Bythorn
Mawsley
Broughton
Great Addington
Lamport
Burton Latimer
Ringstead
Keyston
Lamport Hall
Pytchley
Little Addington
B663
Isham
A509
A510
A45
Catworth
Old
Orlingbury
Finedon
Stanwick Lakes
Raunds
Hargrave
Walgrave
Little Harrowden
R Nene
Hannington
Stanwick
Covington
Pitsford Water
Irthlingborough
B645
Pitsford
B571
Lakes & Meadows
North End
Chelveston
Lower
0 1 2 3 4 miles
0 1 2 3 4 5 kilometres

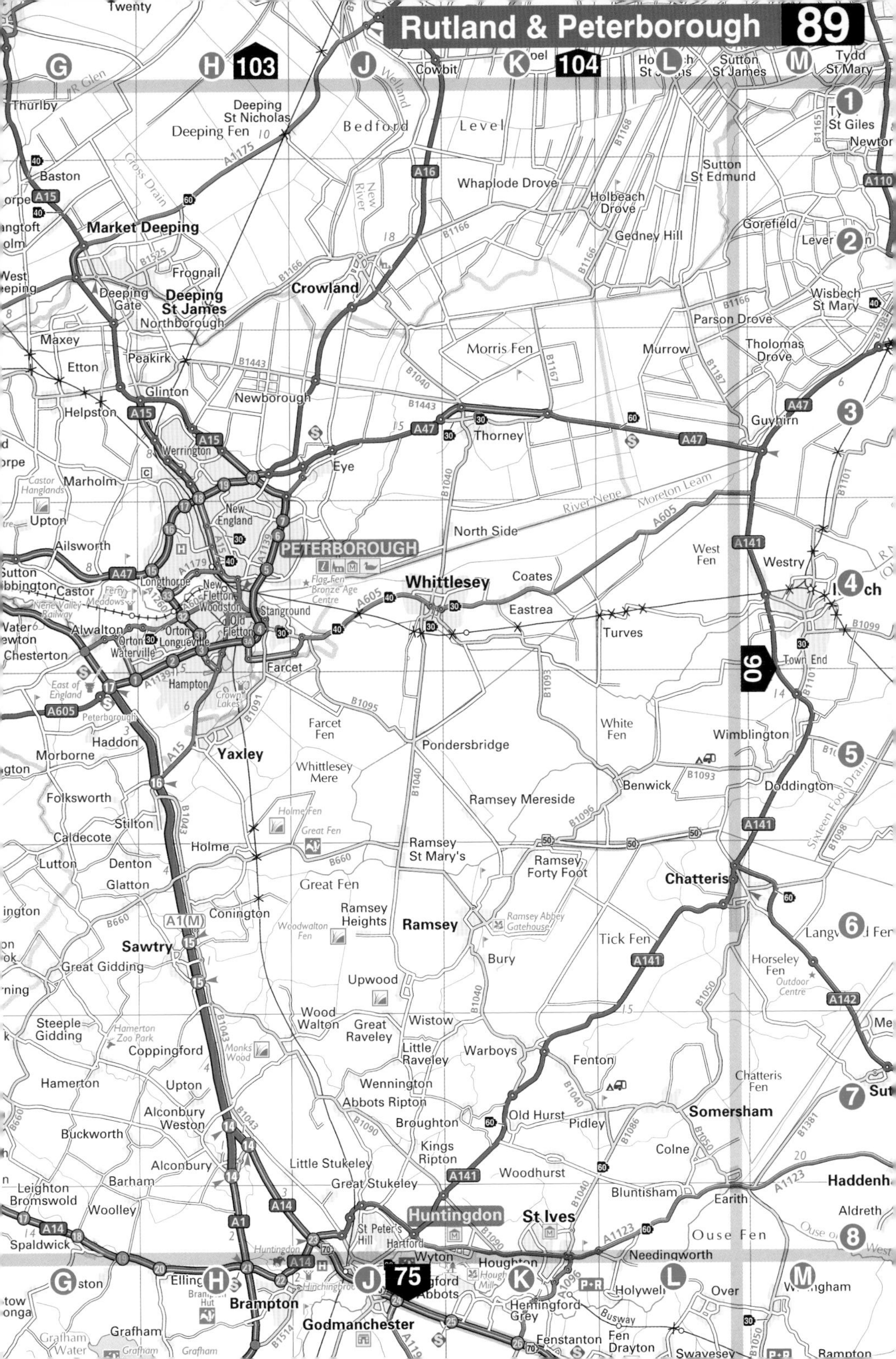
Thurlby
Deeping St Nicholas
Deeping Fen
Bedford Level
Cowbit
Baston
Whaplode Drove
Holbeach Drove
Sutton St Edmund
Market Deeping
Gedney Hill
Gorefield
Crowland
Deeping Gate
Deeping St James
Frognall
Northborough
Wisbech St Mary
Parson Drove
Maxey
Etton
Peakirk
Morris Fen
Murrow
Tholomas Drove
Glinton
Newborough
Helpston
Guyhirn
Thorney
Werrington
Eye
Marholm
Castor Hanglands
New England
Upton
North Side
Ailsworth
PETERBOROUGH
Whittlesey
Coates
West Fen
Westry
Castor
Longthorpe
New Fletton
Woodston
Stanground
Eastrea
Turves
Alwalton
Orton Longueville
Old Fletton
Chesterton
Orton Waterville
Farcet
Town End
Hampton
Yaxley
Farcet Fen
White Fen
Wimblington
Haddon
Morborne
Pondersbridge
Whittlesey Mere
Benwick
Doddington
Folksworth
Ramsey Mereside
Stilton
Caldecote
Holme
Ramsey St Mary's
Lutton
Denton
Ramsey Forty Foot
Glatton
Great Fen
Chatteris
Conington
Ramsey Heights
Ramsey
Sawtry
Tick Fen
Great Gidding
Bury
Horseley Fen
Upwood
Steeple Gidding
Wood Walton
Great Raveley
Wistow
Coppingford
Little Raveley
Warboys
Fenton
Hamerton
Upton
Wennington
Chatteris Fen
Abbots Ripton
Alconbury Weston
Old Hurst
Pidley
Somersham
Buckworth
Broughton
Kings Ripton
Colne
Alconbury
Little Stukeley
Woodhurst
Barham
Great Stukeley
Bluntisham
Earith
Leighton Bromswold
Woolley
Huntingdon
St Ives
Aldreth
Spaldwick
St Peter's Hill
Hartford
Ouse Fen
Wyton
Houghton
Needingworth
Brampton
Hemingford Grey
Holywell
Over
Godmanchester
Fenstanton
Fen Drayton
Swavesey
Rampton
Grafham
Grafham Water

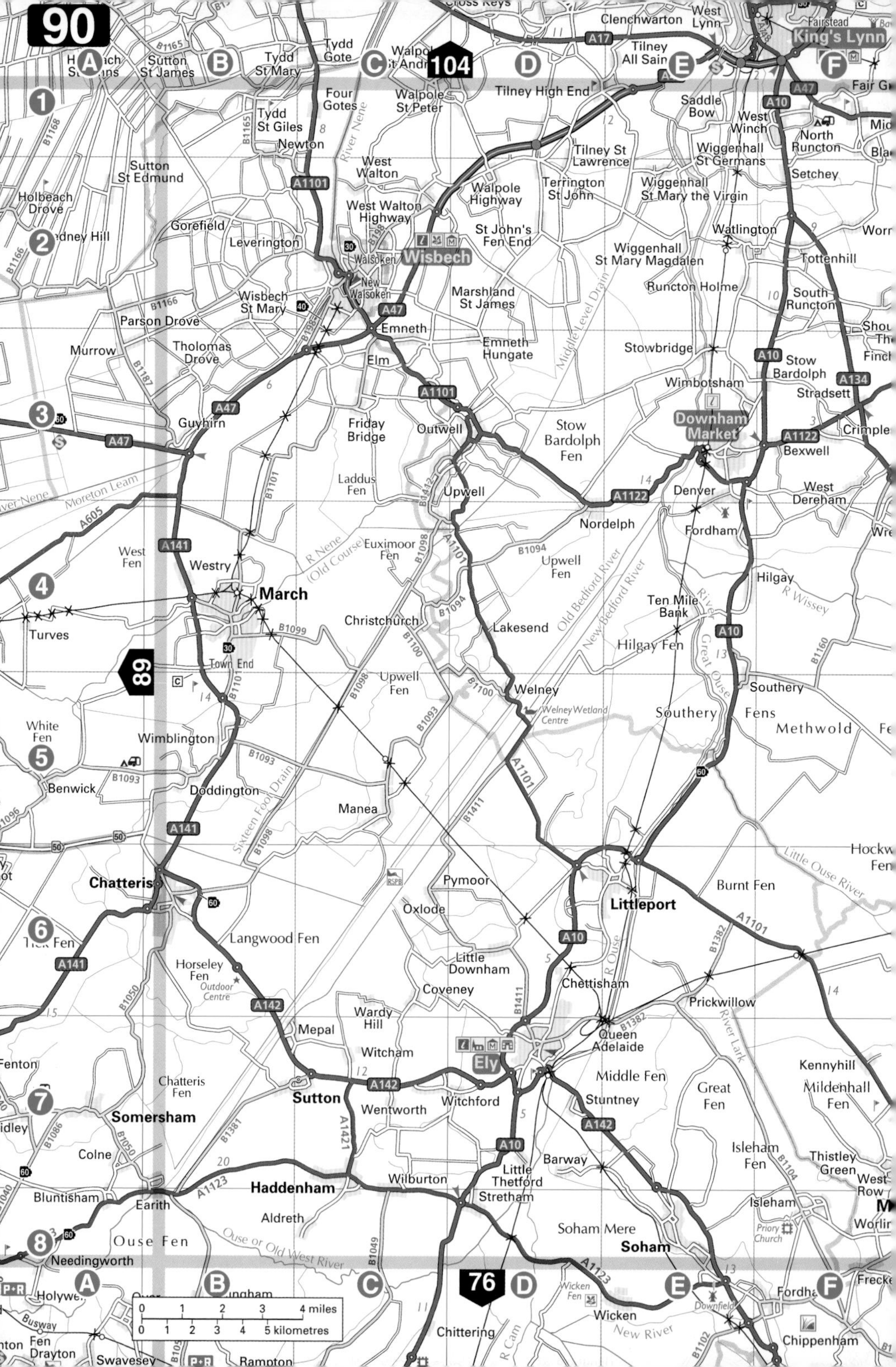
90
Sutton St James
Tydd St Mary
Tydd Gote
Clenchwarton
West Lynn
Fairstead
King's Lynn
104
Four Gotes
Walpole St Peter
Tilney High End
Tydd St Giles
Newton
River Nene
Saddle Bow
West Winch
North Runcton
Sutton St Edmund
West Walton
Tilney St Lawrence
Wiggenhall St Germans
Setchey
Holbeach Drove
Walpole Highway
Terrington St John
Wiggenhall St Mary the Virgin
West Walton Highway
Gorefield
Leverington
St John's Fen End
Watlington
Walsoken
Wisbech
New Walsoken
Wiggenhall St Mary Magdalen
Tottenhill
Runcton Holme
South Runcton
Parson Drove
Wisbech St Mary
Marshland St James
Emneth
Murrow
Tholomas Drove
Elm
Emneth Hungate
Middle Level Drain
Stowbridge
Stow Bardolph
Wimbotsham
Stradsett
Guyhirn
Friday Bridge
Outwell
Stow Bardolph Fen
Downham Market
Bexwell
Crimple
River Nene
Moreton Leam
Laddus Fen
Upwell
Denver
West Dereham
Nordelph
Fordham
West Fen
Westry
R Nene (Old Course)
Euximoor Fen
Upwell Fen
Old Bedford River
New Bedford River
Hilgay
R Wissey
March
Ten Mile Bank
Turves
Christchurch
Lakesend
Hilgay Fen
River Great Ouse
Town End
89
Upwell Fen
Welney
Welney Wetland Centre
Southery
Southery
Fens
Methwold
White Fen
Wimblington
Benwick
Doddington
Manea
Sixteen Foot Drain
Hockwold Fen
Chatteris
Pymoor
Littleport
Burnt Fen
Little Ouse River
Oxlode
Langwood Fen
Little Downham
Chettisham
R Ouse
Horseley Fen
Outdoor Centre
Coveney
Prickwillow
River Lark
Wardy Hill
Mepal
Queen Adelaide
Witcham
Ely
Kennyhill
Middle Fen
Chatteris Fen
Great Fen
Mildenhall Fen
Sutton
Witchford
Stuntney
Somersham
Wentworth
Colne
Barway
Isleham Fen
Thistley Green
Little Thetford
Bluntisham
Earith
Haddenham
Wilburton
Stretham
Isleham
Aldreth
Soham Mere
Priory Church
Ouse Fen
Ouse or Old West River
Soham
Needingworth
76
Wicken Fen
Downfield
Chippenham
Wicken
New River
Chittering
R Cam
Fen Drayton
Swavesey
Rampton
Busway
0 1 2 3 4 miles
0 1 2 3 4 5 kilometres

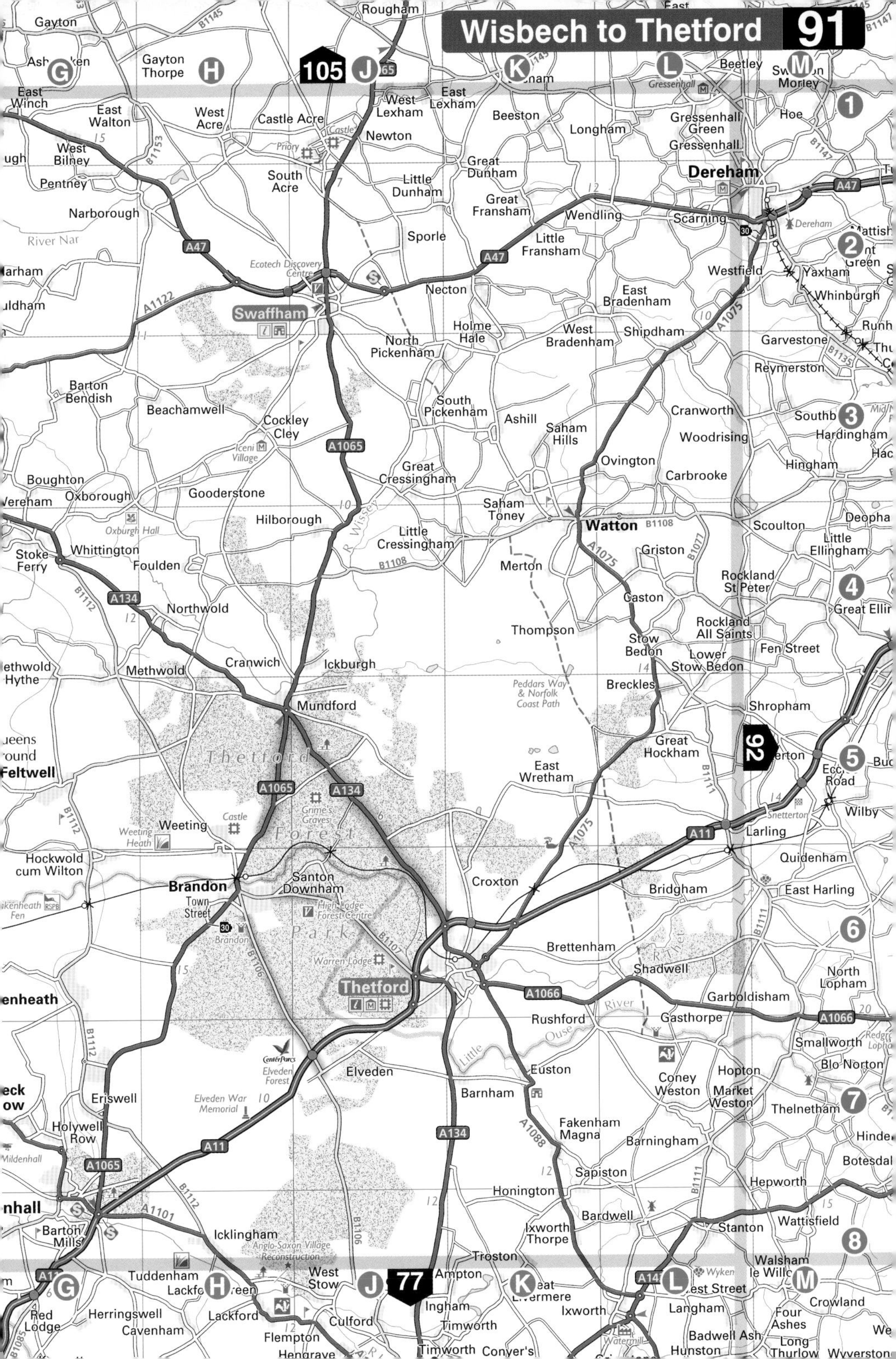
105
92
77
Rougham
Gayton
Gayton Thorpe
East Winch
East Walton
West Acre
Castle Acre
West Lexham
East Lexham
Beeston
Longham
Gressenhall Green
Gressenhall
Beetley
Morley
Hoe
West Bilney
Pentney
Narborough
River Nar
Priory
Castle
Newton
South Acre
Little Dunham
Great Dunham
Great Fransham
Dereham
Wendling
Scarning
Little Fransham
Sporle
Ecotech Discovery Centre
Swaffham
Necton
East Bradenham
Westfield
Yaxham
Whinburgh
Holme Hale
West Bradenham
Shipdham
Garvestone
Reymerston
North Pickenham
South Pickenham
Barton Bendish
Beachamwell
Cockley Cley
Ashill
Saham Hills
Cranworth
Woodrising
Hardingham
Hingham
Iceni Village
Great Cressingham
Ovington
Carbrooke
Boughton
Oxborough
Gooderstone
Saham Toney
Watton
Scoulton
Hilborough
Oxburgh Hall
Little Cressingham
Griston
Little Ellingham
Stoke Ferry
Whittington
Foulden
Merton
Rockland St Peter
Northwold
Caston
Thompson
Rockland All Saints
Stow Bedon
Lower Stow Bedon
Fen Street
Methwold Hythe
Methwold
Cranwich
Ickburgh
Breckles
Peddars Way & Norfolk Coast Path
Mundford
Shropham
Feltwell
Thetford Forest Park
Great Hockham
East Wretham
Eccles Road
Wilby
Weeting
Weeting Heath
Castle
Grime's Graves
Snetterton
Larling
Hockwold cum Wilton
Quidenham
Brandon
Santon Downham
Croxton
Bridgham
East Harling
Town Street
High Lodge Forest Centre
Brettenham
Warren Lodge
Shadwell
North Lopham
Thetford
Garboldisham
Rushford
Gasthorpe
River Little Ouse
Smallworth
Blo Norton
CenterParcs Elveden Forest
Elveden
Euston
Hopton
Coney Weston
Market Weston
Thelnetham
Eriswell
Elveden War Memorial
Barnham
Fakenham Magna
Barningham
Holywell Row
Mildenhall
Botesdale
Sapiston
Honington
Hepworth
Bardwell
Wattisfield
Barton Mills
Icklingham
Ixworth Thorpe
Stanton
Anglo-Saxon Village Reconstruction
Troston
Walsham le Willows
Tuddenham
West Stow
Ampton
Great Livermere
Wyken
Crowland
Red Lodge
Herringswell
Cavenham
Lackford
Culford
Ingham
Ixworth
Langham
Four Ashes
Flempton
Hengrave
Timworth
Conyer's
Badwell Ash
Hunston
Long Thurlow
Wyverstone
A47
A1122
A1065
A134
A1075
A11
A1066
A1088
A1101
B1145
B1153
B1147
B1135
B1108
B1077
B1112
B1111
B1106
B1107

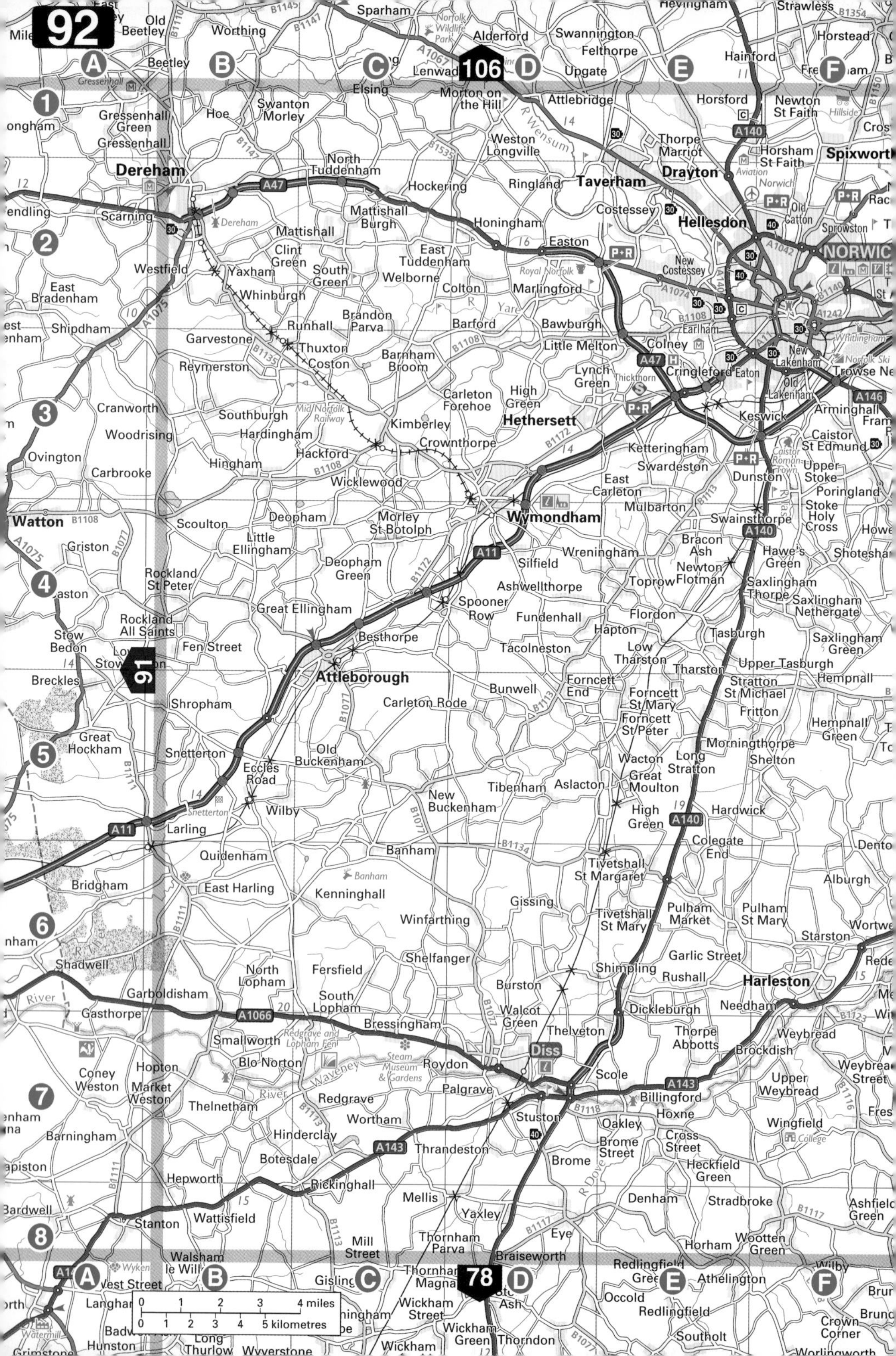

92
Old Beetley
Worthing
Sparham
Norfolk Wildlife Park
Alderford
Swannington
Felthorpe
Hevingham
Strawless
Horstead
Hainford
Beetley
Gressenhall
Lenwade
106
Upgate
Elsing
Morton on the Hill
Attlebridge
Horsford
Newton St Faith
Hillside
Swanton Morley
Hoe
Gressenhall Green
Gressenhall
Weston Longville
R Wensum
Thorpe Marriot
Horsham St Faith
Spixworth
Dereham
North Tuddenham
Hockering
Ringland
Taverham
Drayton
Aviation
Norwich
Mattishall Burgh
Scarning
Mattishall
Honingham
Costessey
Hellesdon
Old Catton
Sprowston
NORWICH
Clint Green
East Tuddenham
Easton
Westfield
Yaxham
South Green
Royal Norfolk
New Costessey
Welborne
Whinburgh
Colton
Marlingford
East Bradenham
Brandon Parva
Yare
Earlham
Shipdham
Runhall
Barford
Bawburgh
Garvestone
Thuxton
Little Melton
Colney
Reymerston
Coston
Barnham Broom
Lynch Green
Cringleford
Eaton
New Lakenham
Trowse Newton
Thickthorn
Old Lakenham
Whitlingham
Norfolk Ski
Carleton Forehoe
High Green
Cranworth
Southburgh
Hethersett
Keswick
Arminghall
Mid Norfolk Railway
Kimberley
Woodrising
Hardingham
Crownthorpe
Ketteringham
Caistor St Edmund
Ovington
Hackford
Hingham
Swardeston
Upper Stoke
Carbrooke
Wicklewood
East Carleton
Dunston
Caistor Roman Town
Poringland
Stoke Holy Cross
Mulbarton
Watton
Scoulton
Deopham
Morley St Botolph
Wymondham
Swainsthorpe
Howe
Griston
Little Ellingham
Bracon Ash
Wreningham
Shotesham
Hawe's Green
Deopham Green
Silfield
Newton Flotman
Caston
Rockland St Peter
Toprow
Saxlingham Thorpe
Ashwellthorpe
Saxlingham Nethergate
Spooner Row
Great Ellingham
Fundenhall
Flordon
Stow Bedon
Rockland All Saints
Hapton
Tasburgh
Saxlingham Green
Besthorpe
Fen Street
Low Tharston
Low Stow
Tacolneston
91
Tharston
Upper Tasburgh
Breckles
Attleborough
Stratton St Michael
Hempnall
Forncett End
Bunwell
Forncett St Mary
Shropham
Carleton Rode
Fritton
Forncett St Peter
Hempnall Green
Great Hockham
Snetterton
Old Buckenham
Morningthorpe
Eccles Road
Wacton
Long Stratton
Shelton
Great Moulton
Tibenham
Aslacton
New Buckenham
Wilby
Snetterton
High Green
Hardwick
Larling
Colegate End
Quidenham
Banham
Tivetshall St Margaret
Dento
Banham
Bridgham
East Harling
Kenninghall
Alburgh
Gissing
Winfarthing
Pulham Market
Tivetshall St Mary
Pulham St Mary
Wortwe
Starston
Shelfanger
Garlic Street
Shadwell
Shimpling
Rushall
Harleston
North Lopham
Fersfield
Burston
Garboldisham
Needham
South Lopham
Walcot Green
Dickleburgh
River
Gasthorpe
A1066
Bressingham
Smallworth
Redgrave and Lopham Fen
Thelveton
Thorpe Abbotts
Weybread
Brockdish
Steam Museum & Gardens
Diss
Coney Weston
Hopton
Blo Norton
Roydon
Scole
Weybread Street
Market Weston
Waveney
Palgrave
Upper Weybread
River
Billingford
Thelnetham
Redgrave
Stuston
Hoxne
Barningham
Wortham
Oakley
Wingfield
College
Hinderclay
Cross Street
Thrandeston
Brome Street
Botesdale
Brome
Heckfield Green
Hepworth
Rickinghall
R Dove
Denham
Stradbroke
Ashfield Green
Bardwell
Mellis
Yaxley
Stanton
Wattisfield
Eye
Thornham Parva
Mill Street
Horham
Wootten Green
Walsham le Willows
Braiseworth
Redlingfield Green
Wilby
West Street
Gislingham
Thornham Magna
78
Athelington
Occold
Langham
Wickham Street
Redlingfield
Crown Corner
Badwell
Hunston
Long Thurlow
Wyverstone
Wickham Green
Thorndon
Southolt
Worlingworth
Watermill
0 1 2 3 4 miles
0 1 2 3 4 5 kilometres

Norwich & The Broads
93
107
79
G
H
J
K
L
M
1
2
3
4
5
6
7
8
Wroxham Barns
Irstead
R Ant
Potter Heigham
Ludham
Martham
Hoveton
BeWILDerwood
A1062
Upper Street
Horning
Upper Street
Hemsby Hole
Hemsby
Ormesby Broad
Ormesby St Margaret
Scratby
Repps
Rollesby
Woodbastwick
Bure Marshes
Broadland Conservation Centre
Ranworth Broad
Thurne
Burgh St Margaret
Ormesby St Michael
California
Salhouse
Ranworth
Pilson Green
Clippesby
Billockby
Fairhaven
Caister-on-Sea
Little Plumstead
Panxworth
Cargate Green
South Walsham
R Bure
A1064
Thrigby
Filby
Mautby
Caister
A149
Upton
Thrigby Hall
West End
West Caister
Great Plumstead
Blofield Heath
North Burlingham
Acle
Stokesby
Runham
Witton
Stracey Arms Windpump
B1140
A47
Blofield
Lingwood
Damgate
Brundall
Beighton
Tunstall
THE BROADS
Postwick
Strumpshaw
South Burlingham
Moulton St Mary
Halvergate
River Yare
Elizabethan House
GREAT YARMOUTH
Southtown
RSPB
Buckenham
Burgh Castle
Bedon
Surlingham
Freethorpe
Bramerton
Hassingham
Wickhampton
Rockland St Mary
Cantley
Freethorpe Common
Berney Arms Windmill
Burgh Castle
Bradwell
Gorleston on Sea
East Port
Claxton
Limpenhoe
Belton
Ashby St Mary
Carleton St Peter
Langley Street
Pettitts Crafts & Animal Adventure Park
Yelverton
Hardley Street
Reedham
Thurton
Bergh Apton
Fritton
Fritton Lake
St Olave's Priory
Hopton on Sea
Chedgrave
Lound
Brooke
R Chet
Loddon
Norton Subcourse
Thurlton
A143
St Olaves
Herringfleet
A12
Mundham
Somerleyton Hall & Gardens
Blundeston
Corton
Hales
Seething
B1136
Kirstead Green
Raveningham
Haddiscoe
Somerleyton
B1074
B1375
B1385
Pleasurewood Hills
Thwaite St Mary
A146
Maypole Green
Toft Monks
Stockton
Oulton
A1117
Woodton
Kirby Cane
Wheatacre
Burgh St Peter
Lowestoft Ness
Hedenham
Ellingham
Aldeby
Oulton Broad
LOWESTOFT
B1332
Gillingham
Kirkley
Ditchingham
Broome
Geldeston
River Waveney
Shipmeadow
Worlingham
Pakefield
A1145
Bungay
B1062
Barnby
Earsham
Mettingham
Barsham
Beccles
North Cove
Gisleham
Carlton Colville
Ringsfield
Ilketshall St Andrew
Mutford
Rushmere
Kessingland
Aviation
Flixton
Ringsfield Corner
Winter Flora
Hulver Street
Black Street
Africa Alive!
Homersfield
Ilketshall St Margaret
A144
Henstead
Sotterley
St Margaret South Elmham
Redisham
B1127
Benacre
Benacre Ness
St Cross South Elmham
Shadingfield
A145
Wrentham
Stone Street
Stoven
Covehithe
Rumburgh
Brampton
South Cove
St James South Elmham
Spexhall
Westhall
Suffolk Heritage Coast
Wissett
Uggeshall
B1124
Wangford
B1126
Sole Bay
Linstead Parva
B1123
Chediston
Holton
Blyford
A1095
Lighthouse
Halesworth
Hen Reedbeds
Southwold
Cookley
Wenhaston
Blythburgh
Cratfield
Blackheath
Huntingfield
Walpole
B1117
B1387
Walberswick
Bramfield
Thorington
Laxfield
Heveningham
Dunwich Forest
Suffolk Coast
Ubbeston Green
Darsham
Westleton Heath
Dunwich
R Yox
Sibton
Peasenhall
A1120
Yoxford
Westleton

A B C D E F
1 2 3 4 5 6 7 8
Aberffraw Bay Heritage Coast
Malltrae
Llanddwyn
CAERNARFON
BAY
Lleyn Heritage Coast
Trefo
564
YR EIFL
Trwyn y Grolech
Porth Nefyn
Llithfae
Carreg Ddu
Morfa Nefyn
Pistyll
Nefyn
Edern
B4417
Bodfuan
Porth Ysgaden
Tudweiliog
LLEYN
A497
Llanno
Efailnew
Dinas
371
Carn Fadrun
B4415
Porth Colman
Bryn-mawr
Llaniestyn
Rhyd-y-clafdy
A499
Penrhos
Pen-y-graig
B4417
Llangwnnadl
Meyllteyrn
Llanbedrog
Sarn
Botwnnog
B4413
Bryncroes
Trwyn Llanbedrog
Porthoer
Rhoshirwaun
St Tudwal's Road
Plas yn Rhiw
Llangian
Abersoch
B4413
Y Rhiw
Llanengan
Aberdaron
Llanfaelrhys
Porth Neigwl or Hell's Mouth
Bwlchtocyn
Marchros
St Tudwal's Island East
Porth Ysgo
Aberdaron Bay
St Tudwal's Island West
Bardsey Sound
Porth Ceiriad
Lleyn Heritage Coast
St Mary's
Ynys Enlli
BARDSEY ISLAND
0 1 2 3 4 miles
0 1 2 3 4 5 kilometres

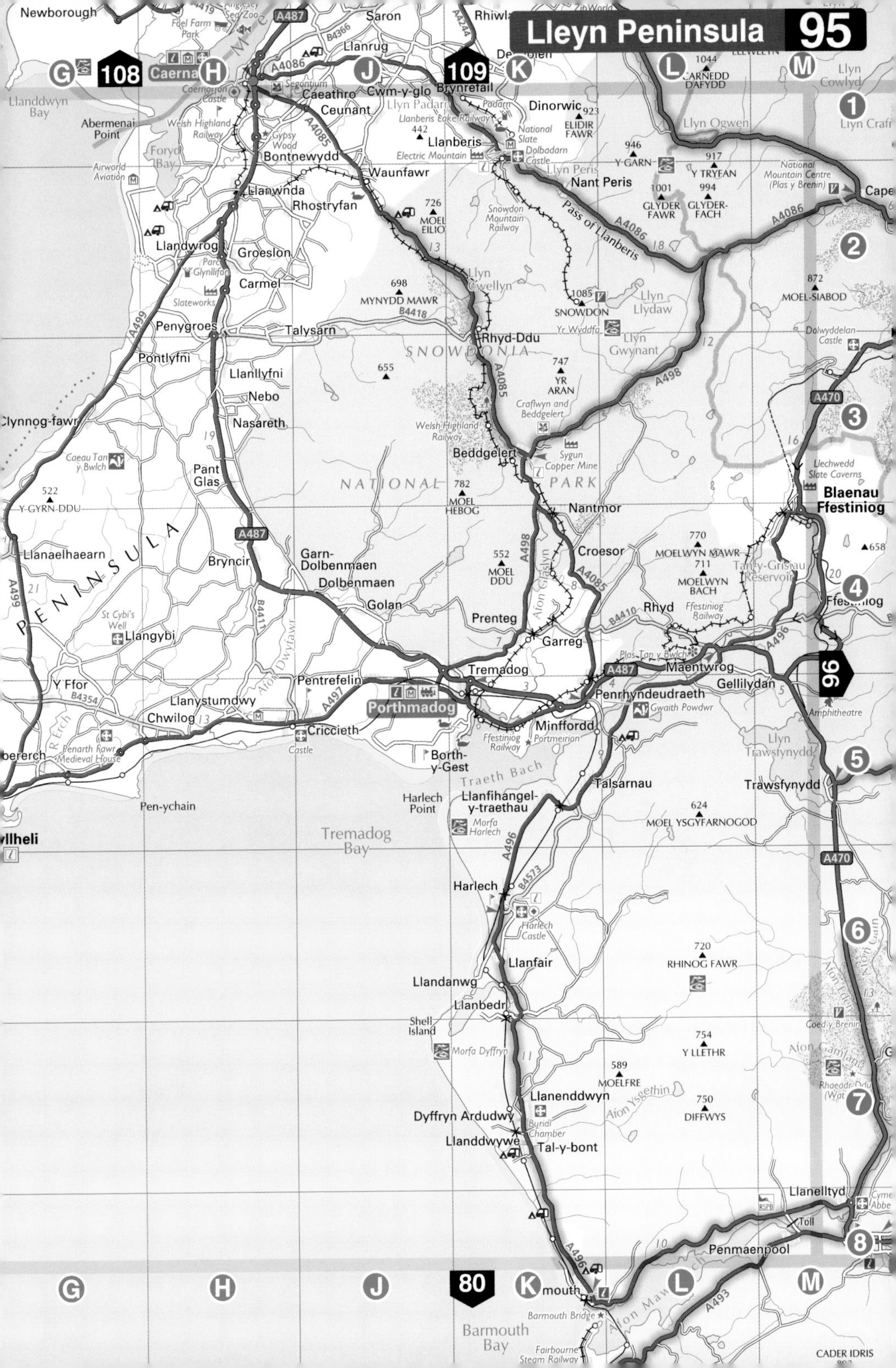
Newborough
Saron
Llanrug
Caernarfon Castle
Llanddwyn Bay
Abermenai Point
Foryd Bay
Airworld Aviation
Welsh Highland Railway
Gypsy Wood
Segontium
Caeathro
Cwm-y-glo
Ceunant
Brynrefail
Llyn Padarn
Llanberis Lake Railway
Dinorwic
923 ELIDIR FAWR
442
Llanberis
Electric Mountain
National Slate
Dolbadarn Castle
Bontnewydd
Waunfawr
Llanwnda
Rhostryfan
726 MOEL EILIO
Snowdon Mountain Railway
Pass of Llanberis
Nant Peris
Llyn Peris
946 Y GARN
917 Y TRYFAN
1001 GLYDER FAWR
994 GLYDER-FACH
1044 CARNEDD DAFYDD
Llyn Ogwen
Llyn Cowlyd
Llyn Crafnant
National Mountain Centre (Plas y Brenin)
872 MOEL-SIABOD
Llandwrog
Groeslon
Parc Glynllifon
Carmel
Slateworks
698 MYNYDD MAWR
Llyn Cwellyn
1085 SNOWDON
Llyn Llydaw
Yr Wyddfa
Llyn Gwynant
Penygroes
Talysarn
Pontlyfni
Rhyd-Ddu
SNOWDONIA
655
747 YR ARAN
Dolwyddelan Castle
Llanllyfni
Nebo
Nasareth
Clynnog-fawr
Craflwyn and Beddgelert
Welsh Highland Railway
Caeau Tan y Bwlch
Beddgelert
Sygun Copper Mine
Llechwedd Slate Caverns
Blaenau Ffestiniog
522 Y-GYRN-DDU
Pant Glas
NATIONAL PARK
782 MOEL HEBOG
Nantmor
770 MOELWYN MAWR
711 MOELWYN BACH
658
Tan-y-Grisiau Reservoir
Llanaelhaearn
Bryncir
Garn-Dolbenmaen
Dolbenmaen
552 MOEL DDU
Croesor
Afon Glaslyn
LLEYN PENINSULA
St Cybi's Well
Llangybi
Golan
Prenteg
Rhyd
Ffestiniog Railway
Ffestiniog
Garreg
Plas Tan y Bwlch
Maentwrog
Tremadog
Gellilydan
Y Ffor
Pentrefelin
Afon Dwyfawr
Porthmadog
Penrhyndeudraeth
Gwaith Powdwr
Amphitheatre
Llanystumdwy
Chwilog
Criccieth
Castle
Minffordd
Portmeirion
Ffestiniog Railway
Penarth Fawr Medieval House
Afon Erch
Abererch
Borth-y-Gest
Traeth Bach
Llyn Trawsfynydd
Trawsfynydd
Pen-ychain
Harlech Point
Llanfihangel-y-traethau
Talsarnau
624 MOEL YSGYFARNOGOD
Pwllheli
Morfa Harlech
Tremadog Bay
Harlech
Harlech Castle
720 RHINOG FAWR
Llanfair
Llandanwg
Llanbedr
Afon Eden
Coed y Brenin
Shell Island
Morfa Dyffryn
754 Y LLETHR
589 MOELFRE
Afon Ysgethin
Afon Gamlan
Rhaeadr Ddu (Waterfall)
Llanenddwyn
750 DIFFWYS
Dyffryn Ardudwy
Burial Chamber
Llanddwywe
Tal-y-bont
Llanelltyd
Cymer Abbey
RSPB
Toll
Penmaenpool
Barmouth
Barmouth Bridge
Afon Mawddach
Barmouth Bay
Fairbourne Steam Railway
CADER IDRIS
A487
A4086
A4085
A4244
B4366
A499
B4418
A498
A470
B4410
A496
A497
B4354
B4411
B4573
A493
108
109
96
80
G H J K L M
1 2 3 4 5 6 7 8

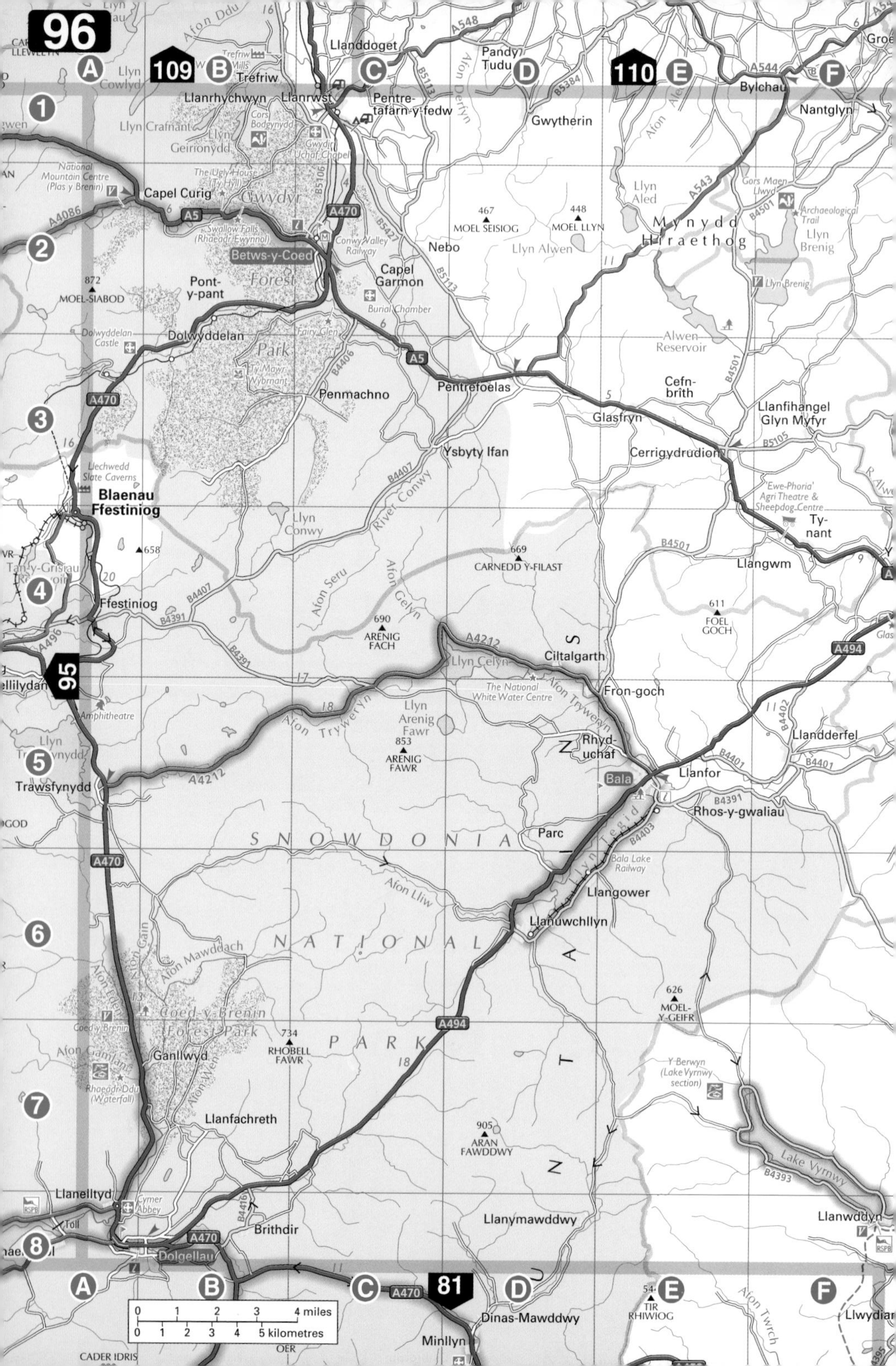

96
109
110
95
81
A
B
C
D
E
F
1
2
3
4
5
6
7
8
Trefriw
Llanddoget
Llanrwst
Pandy Tudu
Bylchau
Nantglyn
Llanrhychwyn
Pentre-tafarn-y-fedw
Gwytherin
Llyn Crafnant
Llyn Geirionydd
Cors Bodgynydd
Gwydir Uchaf Chapel
National Mountain Centre (Plas y Brenin)
Capel Curig
Gwydyr
The Ugly House (Ty Hyll)
Swallow Falls (Rhaeadr Ewynnol)
Betws-y-Coed
Conwy Valley Railway
Forest
Capel Garmon
Nebo
MOEL SEISIOG
MOEL LLYN
Llyn Alwen
Llyn Aled
Mynydd Hiraethog
Gors Maen Llwyd
Archaeological Trail
Llyn Brenig
Alwen Reservoir
MOEL-SIABOD
Pont-y-pant
Burial Chamber
Dolwyddelan Castle
Dolwyddelan
Fairy Glen
Park
Ty Mawr Wybrnant
Penmachno
Pentrefoelas
Cefn-brîth
Glasfryn
Llanfihangel Glyn Myfyr
Ysbyty Ifan
Cerrigydrudion
Llechwedd Slate Caverns
Blaenau Ffestiniog
'Ewe-Phoria' Agri Theatre & Sheepdog Centre
Ty-nant
Llyn Conwy
River Conwy
Tan-y-Grisiau Reservoir
CARNEDD Y-FILAST
Llangwm
Ffestiniog
Afon Seru
Afon Gelyn
ARENIG FACH
FOEL GOCH
Ciltalgarth
Llyn Celyn
The National White Water Centre
Fron-goch
Afon Tryweryn
Amphitheatre
Llyn Arenig Fawr
ARENIG FAWR
Rhyd-uchaf
Llandderfel
Llyn Trawsfynydd
Trawsfynydd
Llanfor
Bala
Rhos-y-gwaliau
SNOWDONIA
Parc
Llyn Tegid
Bala Lake Railway
Afon Lliw
Llangower
Llanuwchllyn
NATIONAL
Afon Gain
Afon Mawddach
Afon Eden
Coed-y-Brenin Forest Park
Coed y Brenin
MOEL-Y-GEIFR
Afon Gamlan
RHOBELL FAWR
PARK
Ganllwyd
Afon Wen
Rhaeadr Ddu (Waterfall)
Y Berwyn (Lake Vyrnwy section)
Llanfachreth
ARAN FAWDDWY
Lake Vyrnwy
Llanelltyd
Cymer Abbey
Toll
Brithdir
Llanymawddwy
Llanwddyn
Dolgellau
Dinas-Mawddwy
TIR RHIWIOG
Afon Twrch
Llwydiarth
Minllyn
CADER IDRIS
0 1 2 3 4 miles
0 1 2 3 4 5 kilometres
A5
A470
A4086
A548
A543
A544
B5106
B5113
B5384
B5427
B4406
B4407
B4391
B4501
B5105
A4212
A494
A496
B4402
B4401
B4403
B4416
B4393

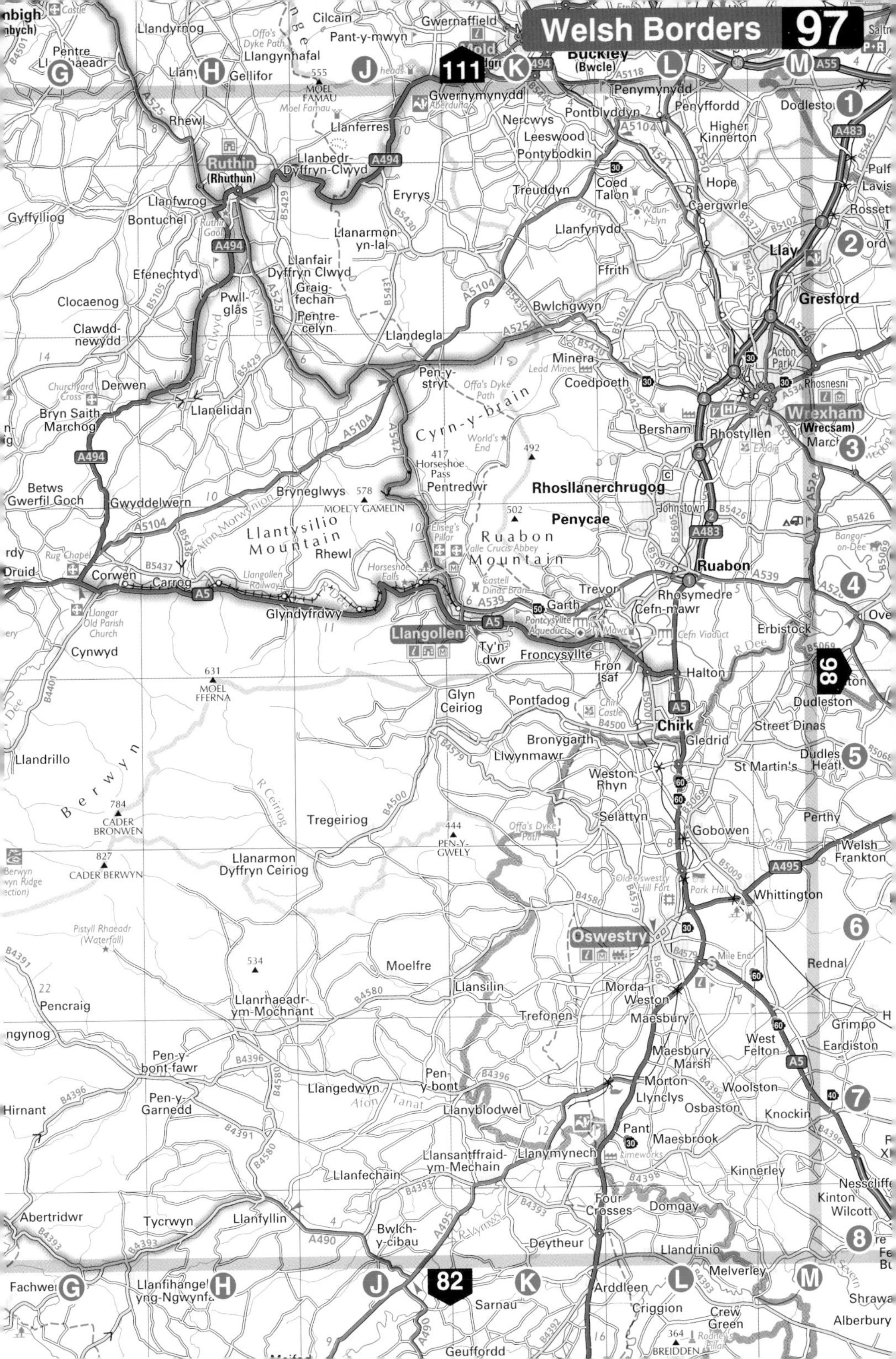
Ruthin
(Rhuthun)
Wrexham
(Wrecsam)
Llangollen
Oswestry
Mold
Buckley
(Bwcle)
Chirk
Ruabon
Gresford
Llay
Rhosllanerchrugog
Penycae
Corwen
Llantysilio Mountain
Ruabon Mountain
Cyrn-y-brain
Berwyn
Llanarmon Dyffryn Ceiriog
Llanrhaeadr-ym-Mochnant
Llansantffraid-ym-Mechain
Llanfyllin
Llanymynech
Four Crosses
Glyn Ceiriog
Froncysyllte
Trevor
Cefn-mawr
Llandegla
Bwlchgwyn
Minera
Coedpoeth
Bersham
Rhostyllen
Gobowen
Whittington
Weston Rhyn
Selattyn
St Martin's
Pontfadog
Llansilin
Trefonen
Morda
Maesbury
Knockin
Kinnerley
Nesscliffe
Llandrinio
Melverley
Arddleen
Sarnau
Meifod
Deytheur
Domgay
Llanfechain
Bwlch-y-cibau
Llangedwyn
Pen-y-bont
Llanyblodwel
Moelfre
Tregeiriog
Llandrillo
Cynwyd
Carrog
Glyndyfrdwy
Gwyddelwern
Bryneglwys
Pentredwr
Horseshoe Pass
Llanelidan
Derwen
Efenechtyd
Clocaenog
Llanfwrog
Bontuchel
Gyffylliog
Rhewl
Llanferres
Eryrys
Llanarmon-yn-Ial
Treuddyn
Leeswood
Nercwys
Pontblyddyn
Penyffordd
Higher Kinnerton
Hope
Caergwrle
Ffrith
Llanfynydd
Coed Talon
Pontybodkin
Penymynydd
Gwernymynydd
Gwernaffield
Cilcain
Pant-y-mwyn
Llandyrnog
Llangynhafal
Gellifor
Dodleston
Rossett
Marchwiel
Bangor-on-Dee
Overton
Erbistock
Halton
Dudleston
Dudleston Heath
Street Dinas
Gledrid
Perthy
Welsh Frankton
Rednal
Grimpo
West Felton
Eardiston
Woolston
Osbaston
Maesbrook
Morton
Llynclys
Pant
Kinton
Wilcott
Crew Green
Criggion
Alberbury
Shrawardine
Geuffordd
Llanfihangel-yng-Ngwynfa
Tycrwyn
Abertridwr
Pencraig
Hirnant
Pen-y-bont-fawr
Pen-y-Garnedd
Fachwen
Valle Crucis Abbey
Castell Dinas Bran
Pontcysyllte Aqueduct
Chirk Castle
Old Oswestry Hill Fort
Park Hall
Erddig
Moel Famau
Moel Fferna
Cader Bronwen
Cader Berwyn
Moel y Gamelin
Pen-y-Gwely
Breidden
Pistyll Rhaeadr (Waterfall)
Offa's Dyke Path
Llangollen Railway
Horseshoe Falls
A5
A483
A494
A525
A5104
A542
A539
A495
A490
A55
A541
A528
82
96
111

111
112
97
83
Handbridge
Saltney
Huntington
Eccleston
Saighton
Rowton
Duddon
Burton
Overton
Hargrave
Utkinton
Clotton
Eaton
Tarporley
Little Budworth
Oulton Park
Winsford
Dodleston
Huxley
Wettenhall
Church Minshull
Aldford
Pulford
Lavister
Rossett
Trevalyn
Marford
Gresford
Holt
Churton
Farndon
Milton Green
Handley
Tattenhall
Newton
Beeston
Castle
Cheshire Farm
Shropshire Union Canal
Tilstone Fearnall
Tiverton
Alpraham
Calveley
Bunbury
Haughton
Spurstow
Peckforton
Burwardsley
Harthill
Clutton
Barton
Watermill
Bulkeley
Wardle
Worleston
Burland
Faddiley
Acton
Nantwich
Crewe-by-Farndon
Acton Park
Rhosnesni
Wrexham
(Wrecsam)
Marchwiel
Erddig
R Clywedog
Tilston
Horton Green
Shocklach
Chorlton Lane
Ebnal
Malpas
Hampton Heath
No Man's Heath
Cholmondeley Castle
Chorley
Bickley
Norbury
Marbury
Wrenbury
Sound
Secret Bunker
Stapeley
Hatherton
Bangor-on-Dee
Worthenbury
Cuddington Heath
Threapwood
Tallarn Green
Higher Wych
Bell o' th' Hill
Wirswall
Aston
Newhall
Dodd's Green
Hankelow
Audlem
Overton
Erbistock
R Dee
Horseman's Green
Eglwys Cross
Grindley Brook
Whitchurch
Burleydam
Coxbank
Penley
Hanmer
Bronington
Redbrook
Broughall
Wilkesley
Ash Magna
Adderley
Knolton
Dudleston
Street Dinas
Dudleston Heath
Tilstock
Ightfield
Prees Heath
Calverhall
Prees Higher Heath
Ellesmere
Welshampton
Bettisfield
Canal
Whixall
Moreton Say
Longford
Perthy
Prees
Bletchley
Market Drayton
Welsh Frankton
Tetchill
Lyneal
Northwood
Colemere
Newtown
Edstaston
Fauls
Ternhill
Whittington
Hordley
English Frankton
Prees Green
Hawkstone
Wollerton
Weston-under-Redcastle
Marchamley
Hodnet
Hodnet Hall
Loppington
Wem
Aston
Rednal
Cockshutt
Noneley
Bury Walls
Stoke upon Tern
Bagley
Haughton
Grimpo
Lee Brockhurst
West Felton
Eardiston
Wykey
Burlton
Weston Lullingfields
Preston Brockhurst
Clive
High Hatton
Ollerton
Myddle
Grinshill
Stanton upon Hine Heath
Peplow
Child's Ercall
Knockin
Eyton
Moreton Corbet
Ellerdine Heath
Eaton upon Tern
Newtown
Harmer Hill
Ruyton-XI-Towns
Baschurch
Shawbury
Great Bolas
Nesscliffe
Little Ness
Preston Gubbals
Hadnall
Rowton
Cherrington
Kinton
Wilcott
Yeaton
Bomere Heath
Astley
Waters Upton
Great Ness
Grafton
Walford Heath
Leaton
Albrighton
Poynton Green
Walton
Pentre
Fitz
High Ercall
Crudgington
Felton Butler
Forton
Roden
Sleapford
Haughmond Abbey
Rodington Heath
Long Waste
Rodington
Uffington
Ditherington
Underdale
Coton
Bratton
Shawbirch
R Severn
R Perry
R Gowy
0 1 2 3 4 miles
0 1 2 3 4 5 kilometres
A55 A483 A41 A49 A51 A534 A525 A528 A539 A495 A5 A53 A442 A530 A529 A5124
B5445 B5102 B5130 B5069 B5426 B5068 B5063 B5476 B5065 B4397 B5067 B4396 B5062 B5063 B5395 B5341 B5074 B5425

Middlewich
Brereton Green
Arclid Green
Brookhouse Green
Astbury
Timbersbrook
Rushton Spencer
Meerbrook
Upper Hulme
The Roaches
Elworth
Sandbach
Ettiley Heath
Spen Green
Poolfold
Biddulph
Biddulph Moor
Rudyard
Abbey Green
Bradfield Green
Wheelock
Winterley
Mow Cop
Rode Heath
Alsager
Scholar Green
Brown Lees
Horton
Leek
Bradnop
Haslington
CREWE
Crewe Green
Packmoor
Kidsgrove
Brown Edge
Endon Bank
Longsdon
Talke
Talke Pits
Goldenhill
Great Chell
Ball Green
Norton in the Moors
Stockton Brook
Endon
Stanley
Shavington
Weston
Barthomley
Audley
Hough
Red Street
Bradeley
Baddeley Green
Baddeley Edge
Bagnall
Cheddleton
Chorlton
Wybunbury
Smallthorne
Milton
Crackley
Chesterton
Broad Meadow
Porthill
Cobridge
Wolstanton
Northwood
Wetley Rocks
Consall
Foxt
Walgherton
Betley
Blakenhall
NEWCASTLE-UNDER-LYME
May Bank
Etruria
Hanley
Bucknall
Cellarhead
Froghall
Wrinehill
Hunsterson
Checkley
Silverdale
Hartshill
Hulme
Kingsley
Keele
STOKE-ON-TRENT
Oakamoor
Dilhorne
Buerton
Madeley
Seabridge
Weston Coyney
Cheadle
Trent Vale
Caverswall
Onneley
Dresden
Meir
Butterton
Blurton
Woore
Pipe Gate
Aston
Hanford
Lightwood
Forsbrook
Dorrington
Whitmore
Acton
Hanchurch
Trentham
Mobberley
Knighton
Bearstone
Hill Chorlton
Shelton Under Harley
Draycott in the Moors
Cresswell
Blackbrook
Lower Tean
Norton in Hales
Maer
Beech
Barlaston
Fulford
Mucklestone
Chapel Chorlton
Ashley
Tittensor
Upper Leigh
Knenhall
Loggerheads
Cranberry
Swynnerton
Moddershall
Church Leigh
Podmore
Bowers
Standon
Oulton
Hilderstone
Stone
Dod's Leigh
Chatcull
Little Stoke
Garshall Green
Hales
Wetwood
Millmeece
Yarnfield
Fairoak
Coldmeece
Slindon
Milwich
Croxton
Little Sugnall
Sugnall
Fradswell
Chipnall
Norton Bridge
Aston-by-Stone
Cheswardine
Bishop's Offley
Pershall
Sandon
Lockleywood
Great Soudley
Copmere End
Eccleshall
Chebsey
Gayton
Sandon Bank
Stowe by Chartley
Little Soudley
Adbaston
Tunstall
Whitgreave
Salt
Knighton
Marston
Hopton
Weston
Ellenhall
Great Bridgeford
Hinstock
Shebdon
High Offley
Woodseaves
Seighford
Hixon
Weston Jones
Knightley
Holmcroft
STAFFORD
Sambrook
Ranton
Ranton Green
Coton Clanford
Aston
Ingestre
Norbury
Littleworth
Tixall
Derrington
Forebridge
Great Haywood
Little Haywood
Sutton
Long Compton
Colwich
Chetwynd
Shut Heath
Rickerscote
Milford
Forton
Gnosall
Coton
Haughton
Walton-on-the-Hill
Tibberton
Newport
Hyde Lea
Coppenhall
Acton Trussell
Brocton
Wolseley Bridge
Edgmond
Outwoods
Dunston
Bradley
CANNOCK CHASE
Longford
Chetwynd Aston
Church Aston
Church Eaton
Bednall
Preston upon the Weald Moors
Lilleshall
Woodcote
Great Chatwell
Orslow
High Onn
Levedale
Heath Hill
Bickford
Whiston
Penkridge
TELFORD
Donnington
Brineton
M6
A500
A34
A50
A53
A51
A52
A520
A521
A518
A519
A41
A449
113
84
85
100

115
87
102
G
H
J
K
L
M
1
2
3
4
5
6
7
8
North Wingfield
Clay Cross
Alton
Handley
Pilsley
Tibshelf
Stretton
Morton
Dunsill
Teversal
Skegby
New Houghton
MANSFIELD
Bilsthorpe
Sherwood Forest
SHERWOOD FOREST
Higham
Stonebroom
Newton
Sutton-in-Ashfield
Huthwaite
Brackenfield
Shirland
Blackwell
Rainworth
Farnsfield
White Post Farm
Wessington
Westhouses
South Normanton
Kirkby-in-Ashfield
Alfreton
South Wingfield
Bildworth
Edingley
Halam
Pinxton
Ravenshead
Blidworth Bottoms
Crich
Swanwick
Somercotes
Selston
Newstead Abbey
Papplewick Pumping Station
Pentrich
Pye Bridge
Fritchley
Ironville
Newstead
Halloughton
Linby
Papplewick
Oxton
Heage
Ripley
Underwood
Codnor
Calverton
Epperstone
Gonalston
Belper
Brinsley
Hucknall
Bestwood Village
Woodborough
Lowdham
Loscoe
Denby Potteries
Eastwood
Newthorpe
Arnold
Lambley
Kilburn
Denby
Heanor
Horsley
Woodhouse
Smalley
Awsworth
Kimberley
Burton Joyce
Milford
Holbrook
Horsley
Coxbench
Cotmanhay
Mapperley
Nuthall
Bulwell
Basford
Daybrook
Gedling
Shelford
Little Eaton
Cossall
Strelley
Bilborough
Whitemoor
Sherwood
Mapperley Park
Carlton
Ilkeston
NOTTINGHAM
Stoke Bardolph
West Hallam
Kirk Hallam
Little Hallam
Trowell
Morley
Stanley
Old Radford
Netherfield
Breadsall
Wollaton
Wollaton Hall
Lenton
Colwick
Holme Pierrepont
Darley Abbey
Oakwood
Adbolton
National Water Sports
DERBY
Dale
Stanton by Dale
Stapleford
Radcliffe on Trent
Chaddesden
Sandiacre
Wilford
Gamston
Spondon
Ockbrook
Beeston
Chilwell
West Bridgford
Risley
Borrowash
Rylands
Edwalton
Cotgrave
Breaston
Toton
Clifton
Tollerton
Clipston
Owthorpe
Crewton
Alvaston
Elvaston Castle
Barton in Fabis
Ruddington
Normanton on the Wolds
Allenton
Elvaston
Long Eaton
Plumtree
Rushcliffe
Bradmore
Keyworth
Sinfin
Stenson Fields
Shelton Lock
Thulston
Thrumpton
Chellaston
Shardlow
Derby South
Gotham
Great Central (Nottingham) Railway
Bunny
Stanton on the Wolds
Trent & Mersey Canal
Aston-upon-Trent
Ratcliffe on Soar
Barrow upon Trent
Swarkestone
Weston-upon-Trent
Hemington
Kingston on Soar
Widmerpool
Wysall
Stanton by Bridge
Castle Donington
Kegworth
West Leake
East Leake
Costock
Willoughby-on-the-Wolds
Donington Park
Grand Prix Collection
East Midlands
Melbourne
Sutton Bonington
West Thorpe
Diseworth
Long Whatton
Rempstone
Wilson
Isley Walton
Donington Park
Zouch
Normanton on Soar
Wymeswold
Ticknall
Calke Abbey
Breedon on the Hill
Tonge
Hathern
Stanford on Soar
Hoton
Calke
Cotes
Staunton Harold Church
Worthington
Burton on the Wolds
Belton
Lount
Shepshed
Loughborough
Walton on the Wolds
Ragdale
Smisby
Osgathorpe
Barrow upon Soar
Seagrave
Nanpantan
Ashby-de-la-Zouch
Charnwood
Thrussington
Swannington
Mount St Bernard
Woodhouse
Sileby
Ratcliffe on the Wreake
Packington
Whitwick
Forest
Beacon Hill
Mountsorrel
Woodhouse Eaves
Great Central Railway
Cossington
Rearsby
Ravenstone
M1
A38
A60
A61
A6
A52
A50
A42
A453
A46
A606
A614
A617
A610
A608
A609
A6097
A5111
A511
A512

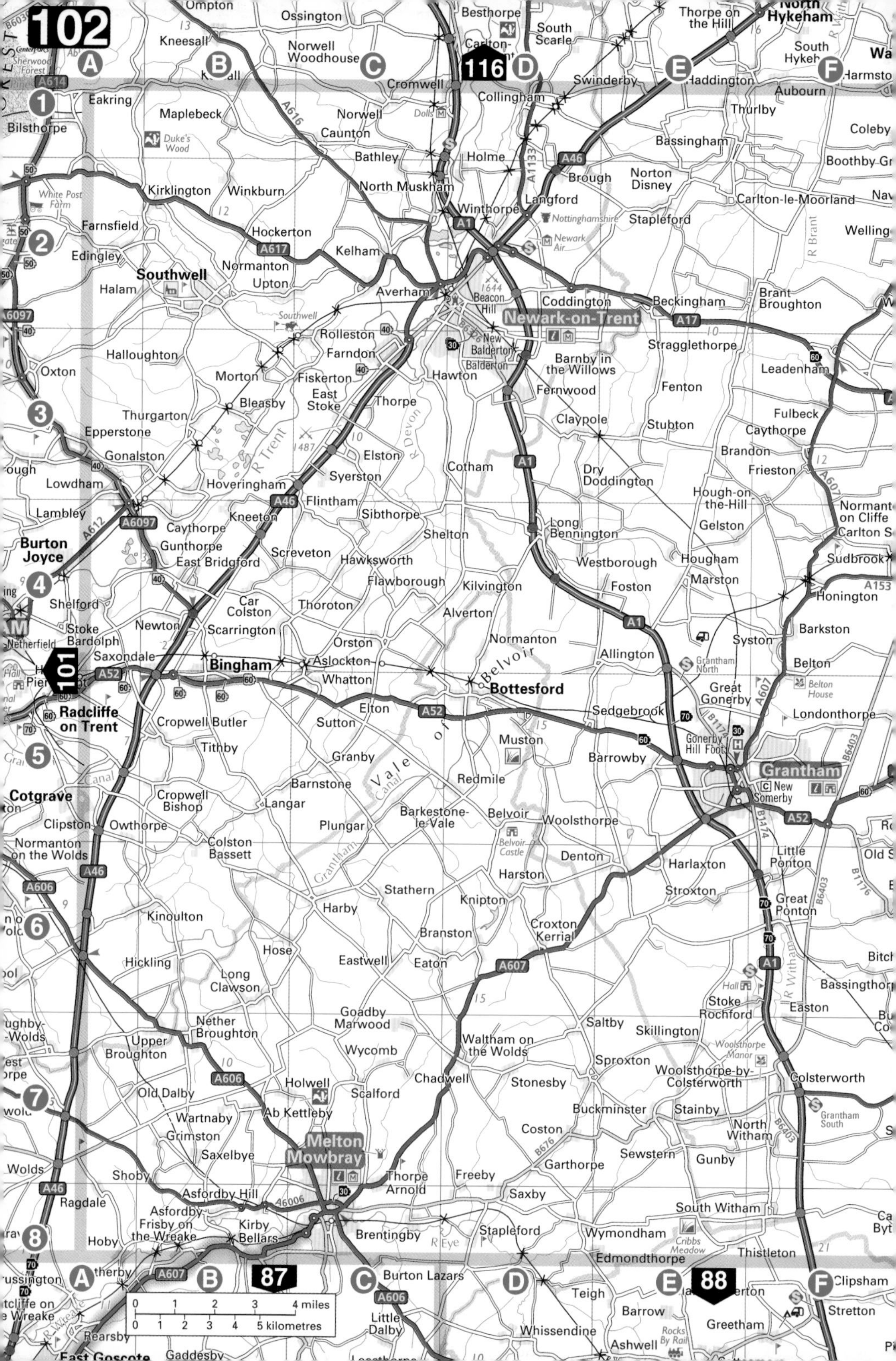

102
A
B
C
D
E
F
116
87
88
101
1
2
3
4
5
6
7
8
Ompton
Ossington
Besthorpe
South Scarle
Thorpe on the Hill
North Hykeham
Kneesall
Norwell Woodhouse
Carlton-on-Trent
South Hykeham
Sherwood Forest
Kersall
Cromwell
Swinderby
Haddington
Harmston
Eakring
Collingham
Aubourn
Maplebeck
Norwell
Dolls
Thurlby
Bilsthorpe
Caunton
Coleby
Duke's Wood
Bassingham
Bathley
Holme
Boothby Graffoe
Brough
Norton Disney
North Muskham
Kirklington
Winkburn
Langford
Carlton-le-Moorland
White Post Farm
Winthorpe
Stapleford
Nottinghamshire
Farnsfield
Hockerton
Newark Air
Welling
Edingley
Kelham
Normanton
Southwell
Upton
Halam
Averham
Beacon Hill
1644
Coddington
Beckingham
Brant Broughton
Newark-on-Trent
Southwell
Rolleston
New Balderton
Balderton
Stragglethorpe
Halloughton
Farndon
Leadenham
Oxton
Barnby in the Willows
Morton
Fiskerton
Hawton
Fernwood
Fenton
Bleasby
East Stoke
Thorpe
Fulbeck
Thurgarton
Claypole
Stubton
Caythorpe
Epperstone
1487
R Devon
Brandon
Elston
Gonalston
R Trent
Cotham
Dry Doddington
Frieston
Lowdham
Hoveringham
Syerston
Hough-on-the-Hill
Normanton on Cliffe
Flintham
Lambley
Kneeton
Sibthorpe
Gelston
Carlton Scroop
Caythorpe
Burton Joyce
Gunthorpe
Shelton
Long Bennington
Screveton
Hougham
Sudbrook
East Bridgford
Hawksworth
Westborough
Marston
Flawborough
Kilvington
Foston
Honington
Shelford
Car Colston
Thoroton
Stoke Bardolph
Alverton
Barkston
Newton
Scarrington
Netherfield
Orston
Normanton
Syston
Saxondale
Allington
Grantham North
Bingham
Aslockton
Belvoir
Belton
Whatton
Bottesford
Belton House
Radcliffe on Trent
Great Gonerby
Elton
Sedgebrook
Londonthorpe
Cropwell Butler
Sutton
Gonerby Hill Foot
Vale of Belvoir
Muston
Tithby
Barrowby
Granby
Grantham
Redmile
New Somerby
Barnstone
Canal
Cotgrave
Cropwell Bishop
Langar
Barkestone-le-Vale
Belvoir
Woolsthorpe
Clipston
Owthorpe
Plungar
Belvoir Castle
Little Ponton
Normanton on the Wolds
Colston Bassett
Denton
Harlaxton
Old Somerby
Grantham Canal
Harston
Stathern
Stroxton
Great Ponton
Harby
Knipton
Kinoulton
Croxton Kerrial
Branston
Hose
Bitchfield
Hickling
Eastwell
Eaton
Long Clawson
Bassingthorpe
R Witham
Stoke Rochford
Easton
Goadby Marwood
Nether Broughton
Saltby
Skillington
Upper Broughton
Waltham on the Wolds
Woolsthorpe Manor
Wycomb
Sproxton
Woolsthorpe-by-Colsterworth
Chadwell
Stonesby
Colsterworth
Holwell
Scalford
Old Dalby
Buckminster
Stainby
Grantham South
Ab Kettleby
Wartnaby
North Witham
Grimston
Coston
Melton Mowbray
Saxelbye
Sewstern
Gunby
Garthorpe
Wolds
Shoby
Thorpe Arnold
Freeby
Ragdale
Asfordby Hill
Saxby
Asfordby
South Witham
Frisby on the Wreake
Kirby Bellars
Hoby
Brentingby
Stapleford
Wymondham
R Eye
Cribbs Meadow
Thistleton
Edmondthorpe
Rotherby
Burton Lazars
Clipsham
Teigh
Market Overton
Barrow
Stretton
Little Dalby
Greetham
Whissendine
Rearsby
Rocks By Rail
Ashwell
East Goscote
Gaddesby
Cossington
Ratcliffe on the Wreake
R Wreake
A614
A616
A617
A1
A1133
A46
A17
A6097
A612
A52
A606
A607
A6006
B676
B6403
B1174
B1176
B6326
A153
0 1 2 3 4 miles
0 1 2 3 4 5 kilometres

117
118
104
89
Nocton
Metheringham
Blankney
Scopwick
Kirkby Green
Martin
Timberland
Timberland Delph
Thorpe Tilney
Rowston
Walcott
Ashby de la Launde
Digby
Billinghay
Bloxholm
Dorrington
North Kyme
Ruskington
Cranwell
Anwick
Leasingham
South Kyme
Evedon
North Rauceby
Holdingham
Sleaford
Kirkby la Thorpe
Ewerby
Howell
South Rauceby
Asgarby
Quarrington
Heckington
Ancaster
Wilsford
The Pearoom
Great Hale
Little Hale
Silk Willoughby
Burton Pedwardine
Kelby
Swarby
Helpringham
Culverthorpe
Aswarby
Scredington
Oasby
Heydour
Aisby
Aunsby
Osbournby
Spanby
Swaton
Dembleby
Newton
Threekingham
Haceby
Braceby
Walcot
Horbling
Sapperton
Pickworth
Billingborough
Folkingham
Humby
Laughton
Pointon
Aslackby
Lenton
Ingoldsby
Dowsby
Rippingale
Irnham
Kirkby Underwood
Dunsby
Corby Glen
Hacconby
Hanthorpe
Morton
Elsthorpe
Grimsthorpe
Dyke
Swinstead
Edenham
Bourne
Twenty
Creeton
R Glen
Little Bytham
Lound
Witham on the Hill
Toft
Manthorpe
Carlby
Thurlby
Baston
Deeping Fen
Kirkstead
Woodhall Spa
Kirkby on Bain
Wood Enderby
Revesby
East Kirkby
Mareham le Fen
Tumby
Tattershall Thorpe
Tattershall
Tattershall Castle
Tattershall College
Coningsby
Tumby Woodside
New Bolingbroke
Battle of Britain Memorial Flight
Hawthorn Hill
New York
Dogdyke
Scrub Hill
Chapel Hill
West Fen
Holland Fen
R Witham
Gipsey Bridge
Frithville
Sibsey Trader Windmill
Langrick
Anton's Gowt
Witham Way
East Heckington
Boston
Swineshead
Kirton
Bicker
Northorpe
Donington
Wigtoft
Sutterton
Algarkirk
Skeldyke
Burtoft
Quadring Eaudike
Quadring
Fosdyke
South Forty Foot Drain
Westhorpe
Gosberton
R Welland
Risegate
Surfleet
Moulton Seas End
Pinchbeck
Weston
Moulton
Springfields
Mill Green
Spalding
Fulney
Cowbit
Moulton Chapel
Bedford
Level
Whaplode Drove
A15
A17
A52
A151
A153
A155
A16
A1121
A152
A1175
A6121
B1178
B1202
B1188
B1189
B1191
B1192
B1183
B1184
B1395
B1429
B1209
B1517
B6403
B1394
B1397
B1391
B1181
B1177
B1176
B1356
B1180
B1193
B1173
B1172
B1357
B1165
G
H
J
K
L
M
1
2
3
4
5
6
7
8

104
Old Bolingbroke
Bolingbroke Castle
Toynton All Saints
Holegate
Great Steeping
Northcote
Bratoft
Burgh le Marsh
A158
Skegness
118
119
East Kirkby
Lincolnshire Aviation
Revesby
Mareham le Fen
Keal Cotes
Stickford
Little Steeping
Firsby
Croft
Fendike Corner
Thorpe St Peter
Wainfleet Haven
Wainfleet All Saints
Wainfleet St Mary
Gibraltar Point
Tumby Woodside
New Bolingbroke
Stickney
New Leake
Eastville
East Fen
Friskney
A16
A52
West Fen
Northlands
B1183
Leake Common Side
Sibsey Trader Windmill
Sibsey
Frithville
B1184
Fishtoft Drove
Wrangle
Old Leake
Hilldyke
Leverton
Anton's Gowt
Benington
Witham Way
Butterwick
Boston
A1121
Freiston
Fishtoft
Wyberton East
Scrane End
103
Kirton
Frampton
The Haven
RSPB
B1391
B1397
THE WASH
Skeldyke
Sutterton
Algarkirk
Fosdyke
Holbeach St Matthew
R Welland
Holbeach St Mark's
Holbeach Marsh
Gedney Drove End
B1359
B1357
A17
Moulton Seas End
Saracen's Head
Holbeach Bank
Holbeach Hurn
Gedney Dyke
Holbeach Clough
Fleet Hargate
Lutton
The Wash
Weston
B1515
A151
Moulton
Whaplode
Holbeach
Fleet
Gedney
Butterfly & Falconry Park
Great Ouse
Gedney Broadgate
Long Sutton
Sutton Bridge
B1165
B1168
Terrington St Clement
Walpole Cross Keys
B1390
Clenchwarton
West Lynn
Moulton Chapel
Holbeach St Johns
Sutton St James
Tydd St Mary
Tydd Gote
Walpole St Andrew
Tilney High End
Tilney All Saints
A47
Four Gotes
Walpole St Peter
89
90
Tydd St Giles
Newton
River Nene
Tilney St Lawrence
Wiggenhall St Germans
West Walton
Sutton St Edmund
Whaplode Drove
Level
0 1 2 3 4 miles
0 1 2 3 4 5 kilometres

Holkham Bay
North Norfolk Heritage Coast
Blakeney Poir
Brancaster Bay
Scolt Head Island
Peddars Way & Norfolk Coast Path
Holme Dunes
Holme next the Sea
Brancaster
Brancaster Staithe
Burnham Norton
Burnham Overy Staithe
Holkham
Wells-next-the-Sea
Old Hunstanton
Thornham
Titchwell
Branodunum Roman Fort
Burnham Deepdale
Burnham Market
Burnham Overy
Holkham Hall
Warham St Mary
Stif
Warham All Saints
Hunstanton
Ringstead
Burnham Thorpe
Wighton
Summerfield
North Creake
Creake Abbey
Wells & Walsingham Light Railway
The Shrine of Our Lady
Heacham
Norfolk Lavender
Peddars Way & Norfolk Coast Path
Docking
Stanhoe
Little Walsingham
Great Walsingham
Sedgeford
South Creake
North Barsham
Hindringham
Houghton St Giles
Snettisham
Park Farm
Fring
Bircham Newton
West Barsham
East Barsham
Great Snoring
Thursford
Ingoldisthorpe
Shernborne
Syderstone
R Stiffkey
Little Snoring
Great Bircham
Bircham Tofts
Wicken Green Village
Croxt
Dersingham
Sculthorpe
Kettlestone
Dersingham Bog
Anmer
Dunton
Shereford
Tattersett
Coxford
Fakenham
Volferton
Houghton Hall
Hempton
Sandringham
West Newton
West Rudham
New Houghton
Tatterford
Little Ryburgh
Babingley River
East Rudham
Toftrees
Flitcham
Great Ryburgh
Helhoughton
East Raynham
Colkirk
Harpley
Castle Rising
Hillington
Little Massingham
West Raynham
South Raynham
Gateley
Congham
Horningtoft
Castle
Roydon
Great Massingham
Weasenham St Peter
Whissonsett
Grimston
Wellingham
Brisley
Roydon Common
Weasenham All Saints
Tittleshall
North Elmham
Stanfield
Rougham
East Bilney
Gayton
Bawsey
Fairstead
King's Lynn
Old Beetley
Mileham
Ashwicken
Gayton Thorpe
Litcham
Fair Green
East Winch
East Lexham
Gressenhall
East Walton
West Lexham
Middleton
Newton
Gressenhall Green
North Runcton
Longham
Blackborough End
West Bilney
Great Dunham
Gressenhall
Setchey
Pentney
South Acre
Little
Dereha
A149
A148
A1065
A1067
A47
B1155
B1355
B1105
B1153
B1454
B1440
B1439
B1145
B1146
B1110
106
91
G
H
J
K
L
M
1
2
3
4
5
6
7
8

A
B
C
D
E
F
1
2
3
4
5
6
7
8
North Norfolk Heritage Coast
Blakeney Point
Blakeney Point
Morston Marshes
Guildhall
Cley Marshes
Wells-next-the Sea
Morston
Blakeney
Cley next the Sea
Muckleburgh Collection
Sheringham
West Runton
East Runton
Cromer
Overstrand
Sidestrand
Stiffkey
Cockthorpe
Wiveton
Salthouse
Weybourne
Sheringham Park
Kelling
Upper Sheringham
Beeston Regis
Norfolk Shire Horse Centre
St Mary
Warham All Saints
Langham
Glandford
A1082
A149
A148
Wighton
B1156
Saxlingham
North Norfolk Railway
Bodham
Aylmerton
Felbrigg
Felbrigg Hall
Northrepps
Binham
Binham Priory & Market Cross
Field Dalling
Letheringsett
R Glaven
Holt
West Beckham
East Beckham
Crossdale Street
Walsingham Railway
Shrine of Our Lady
105
Baconsthorpe Castle
Gresham
Sharrington
Holt
Bessingham
Sustead
Metton
B1436
Southrepps
Great Walsingham
Hindringham
Bale
Hempstead
B1110
Baconsthorpe
Roughton
Houghton St Giles
Brinton
Thornage
Hanworth
B1436
Thurgarton
Thorpe Market
Thursford
Hunworth
Plumstead
A140
East Barsham
Great Snoring
Stody
Edgefield Green
Matlask
Thursford
Gunthorpe
Briningham
Edgefield
Aldborough
Bradfield
B1354
Little Barningham
Barney
Wickmere
Antingham
Erpingham
Suffield
R Stiffkey
Little Snoring
Croxton
Melton Constable
Briston
B1354
B1149
Calthorpe
Mannington Gardens
Wolterton Park
North Walsham
Kettlestone
Fulmodeston
Swanton Novers
Saxthorpe
Itteringham
Banningham
R Bure
B1145
Pensthorpe Waterfowl Park
Hindolveston
Corpusty
Ingworth
Fakenham
B1146
Little Ryburgh
Stibbard
Thurning
Oulton
Blickling
Blickling Estate
Felmingham
Tuttington
Great Ryburgh
A1067
Wood Norton
Wood Dalling
Heydon
Oulton Street
Aylsham
Burgh next Aylsham
R Wensum
Guist
Guestwick
B1149
Foulsham
Salle
B1145
Bure Valley Railway
Swanton Abbott
Gateley
Twyford
Themelthorpe
Cawston
Marsham
Oxnead
Horningtoft
Lamas
Bintree
Foxley Wood
Reepham
Eastgate
Brampton
North Elmham Chapel
Foxley
B1145
Whitwell Street
Buxton Heath
Brisley
North Elmham
Billingford
Buxton
Brandiston
R Bure
Stratton Strawless
B1354
Bawdeswell
Hevingham
East Bilney
B1145
Sparham
Mileham
Old Beetley
Worthing
B1147
Norfolk Wildlife Park
Alderford
Swannington
Horstead
B1146
Felthorpe
A1067
Dinosaur
Hainford
Beetley
Swanton Morley
Lyng
Lenwade
Upgate
Frettenham
B1149
B1150
Gressenhall
Elsing
Morton on the Hill
Horsford
Newton St Faith
92
Gressenhall
Weston Longville
Thorpe Marriot
Horsham St Faith
Crostwick
0 1 2 3 4 miles
0 1 2 3 4 5 kilometres
R Wensum
B1535
Aviation
Spixworth
Dereham
Tuddenham
Taverham
Drayton

G
H
J
K
L
M
1
2
3
4
5
6
7
8
Trimingham
Mundesley
Stow Mill
Paston
B1159
B1145
Knapton
Bacton
Edingthorpe
Walcott
Happisburgh
Edingthorpe Green
Witton
Ridlington
Whimpwell Green
Meeting House Hill
Happisburgh Common
Hempstead
Honing
Lessingham
A149
Ingham Corner
Sea Palling
Briggate
East Ruston
B1159
Waxham
Worstead
Ingham
Stalham
Calthorpe Street
Dilham
Hickling
Smallburgh
A149
Barton Turf
Sutton
Hickling Green
Horsey
Wood Street
Tunstead
A1151
Barton Broad
Hickling Broad
Horsey Windpump
Neatishead
Catfield
Wroxham Barns
Irstead
R Ant
Potter Heigham
Winterton-on-Sea
Hoveton
Ludham
Martham
BeWILDerwood
Bastwick
Hemsby Hole
A1062
Hemsby
Upper Street
Repps
93
Horning
Scratby
Woodbastwick
Bure Marshes
Broadland Conservation Centre
Thurne
Burgh St Margaret
St Margaret
California
Ranworth Broad
Salhouse
Ranworth
Pilson Green
Clippesby
Ormesby St Michael
Billockby
Caister-on-
B1140
B1152
A1151

108
A
B
C
D
E
F
1
2
3
4
5
6
7
8
North Anglesey Heritage Coast
The Skerries
Wylfa Head
Cemaes Bay
Porth Wen
Bull Bay
Amlwch
Llaneilian
Cemlyn Bay
Hen Borth
Cemaes
Burwen
CARMEL HEAD
Tregele
A5025
Llanfairynghornwy
Llanfechell
Bodewryd
Penysarn
Neb
Swtan Folk
Holyhead Bay
Church Bay
Llanrhyddlad
Carreglefn
Rhosybol
Dublin
Dublin
Capel Parc
Llanfaethlu
Llyn Alaw
B5111
Porth Tywynmawr
Llanddeusant
Llynnon Mill
Afon Alaw
Elim
North Stack
Llanfwrog
Gogarth Bay
Breakwater
Llanerchymedd
Holyhead
(Caergybi)
Holyhead Mountain Hut Circles
B5112
Capel Coch
South Stack
Llanfachraeth
Llyn Llywenan
Holyhead Mountain Heritage Coast
Ellins Tower
Penrhos Feilw
Kingsland
Llanynghenedl
ANGLESEY
Presaddfed
Penrhyn Mawr
A5
Valley
B5109
Trefignath
A55
Bodedern
B5111
B5110
Trearddur Bay
B4545
Caergeiliog
B5112
Llanfihangel yn Nhowyn
Llynfaes
B5109
HOLY ISLAND
Four Mile Bridge
Bryngwran
Cefni Reservoir
Oriel Ynys Môn
Bodffordd
Llanfair-yn-Neubwll
Gwalchmai
Llang
Rhoscolyn
Rhoscolyn Head
Anglesey
A5
A5114
A4080
Ty Newydd
Cymyran Bay
A55
Pencarnisiog
Llanfaelog
Llangristiolus
Rhosneigr
Din Dryfol
Pentre Berw
A4080
Henblas
B4422
Gaerwen
Barclodiad y Gawres
Bethel
Porth Trecastell
Afon Cefni
B4419
Aberffraw
Llangadwaladr
Malltraeth
Llanddar
Anglesey Circuit
Bodowyr Burial Chamber
Llangaffo
A4080
B4421
B4419
Brynsie
Aberffraw Bay
Dwyran
Castell Bryn Gwyn
Aberffraw Bay Heritage Coast
Newborough
B4419
Foel Farm Park
Malltraeth Bay
Caernarfon
Llanddwyn Island
Caernarfon Castle
95
Highland Railway
Foryd Bay
Airworld Aviation
0 1 2 3 4 miles
0 1 2 3 4 5 kilometres

G
H
J
K
L
M
1
2
3
4
5
6
7
8
Lynas
Dulas Bay
Seawatch Centre
Moelfre
Llanallgo
Benllech
Red Wharf Bay
Red Wharf Bay
Great Orme Heritage Coast
GREAT ORMES HEAD
Toll
Great Orme Tramway
Little Ormes
Puffin Island
Penmon Priory
Toll
Black Point
Llandudno
Conwy Bay
Deganwy
Llanddona
Pentraeth
Llangoed
Talwrn
Gaol
Beaumaris Castle
Beaumaris
Llansadwrn
Courthouse
Llandegfan
Menai Bridge (Porthaethwy)
Bangor
Penrhyn
Llandygai
Llanfairpwllgwyngyll
Anglesey Column
Britannia Bridge
Bryn Celli Ddu
Plas Newydd
Y Felinheli
GreenWood Forest Park
Pentir
Rhyd-y-groes
Glasinfryn
Tal-y-bont
Llanllechid
Rachub
Tregarth
Bethesda
Seion
Bethel
Llanddeiniolen
Saron
Rhiwlas
ZipWorld
Llanrug
Deiniolen
Segontium
Caeathro
Cwm-y-glo
Brynrefail
Llyn Padarn
Llanberis Lake Railway
Llanberis
442
Electric Mountain
National Slate
Dolbadarn Castle
Waunfawr
Llyn Peris
Nant Peris
ELIDIR FAWR
923
946 Y GARN
917 Y TRYFAN
Llyn Ogwen
National Mountain Centre
Dwygyfylchi
Penmaenmawr
Llanfairfechan
Abergwyngregyn
Coedydd Aber
Afon Anafon
Aber Falls
580 MOEL WINION
757 Y DROSGL
942 FOEL-FRAS
Afon Caseg
Afon Dulyn
1062 CARNEDD LLEWELYN
1044 CARNEDD DAFYDD
SNOWDONIA NATIONAL PARK
610 TAL-Y-FAN
Conwy
Conwy Castle
Capelulo
Henryd
Rowen
Ty'n-y-Groes
Llanbedr-y-Cennin
Tal-y-Bont
Dolgarrog
Surf Snowdonia
Llyn Eigiau
Afon Ddu
Llyn Cowlyd
Trefriw Woollen Mills
Trefriw
Llyn Crafnant
Llyn Geirionydd
The Ugly House
Gwydir Uchaf Chapel
Llanrwst
R. Conwy
Vale of Conwy
Llandudno Junction
Llansanffraid Glan Conwy
Bodnant
Graig
Tal-y-Cafn
Eglwysbach
Llanddoget
Pentre-tafarn-y-fed
Llandrillo-yn-Rhos
Penrhyn Bay
RSPB
A55
A5
A470
A487
A4080
A4085
A4086
A4244
A4087
A545
A5025
A546
B5109
B5110
B5108
B5420
B4366
B4547
B4409
B5106
B5115
B5113
110
95
96

109
Little Ormes Head
Penrhyn Bay
Rhôs-on-Sea
Colwyn Bay
(Bae Colwyn)
Llandrillo-yn-Rhos
Old Colwyn
Abergele Roads
Kinmel Bay
Rhyl
Prestatyn
Gronant
Gwaenysgor
Llanasa
Meliden
Trelogan
Trelawnyd
Dyserth
Cwm
Rhuddlan
Miniature Railway
Towyn
Pensarn
Llanddulas
Abergele
Llysfaen
Rhyd-y-foel
Llandudno Junction
Llanelian-yn-Rhôs
Bryn-y-Maen
Llansanffraid Glan Conwy
Conwy Castle
Dolwen
Betws-yn-Rhos
Bodelwyddan
St George
Bodelwyddan Castle
St Asaph
Rhuallt
Offa's Dyke
Tremeirchion
Caerwys
Afon-wen
Bodfari
Trefnant
Llannefydd
Llanfair Talhaiarn
River Elwy
Llangernyw
Llansannan
Henllan
Denbigh
(Dinbych)
Denbigh Friary
Castle
River Clwyd
Vale of Clwyd
Llandyrnog
Groes
Pentre Llanrhaeadr
Llanynys
Bodnant
Graig
Tal-y-Cafn
Eglwysbach
Vale of Conwy
Llanddoget
Pandy Tudur
Afon Derfyn
Llanrwst
Pentre-tafarn-y-fedw
Gwytherin
Afon Aled
Bylchau
Gwydir Uchaf Chapel
Gors Maen
96
97
A55
A470
A547
A548
A525
A543
A544
A541
A5151
B5115
B5113
B5383
B5381
B5382
B5384
B5428
B5429
B5435
B4501
B5119
B5118
0 1 2 3 4 miles
0 1 2 3 4 5 kilometres

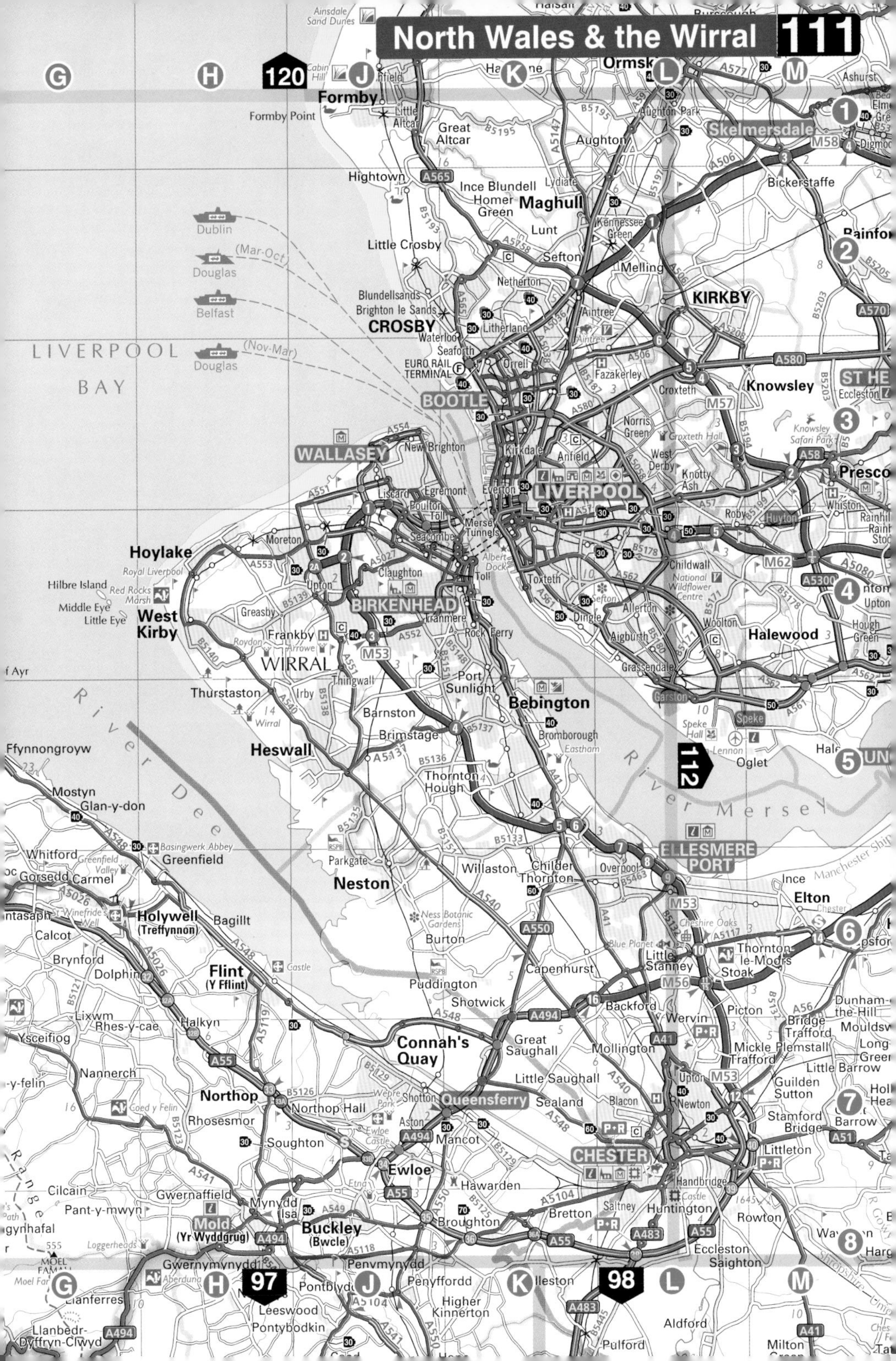

Ainsdale Sand Dunes
120
Cabin Hill
Formby
Formby Point
Little Altcar
Great Altcar
Ormskirk
Aughton Park
Aughton
Skelmersdale
M58
Bickerstaffe
Hightown
Ince Blundell
Homer Green
Maghull
Lydiate
Kennessee Green
Lunt
Little Crosby
Sefton
Melling
Netherton
KIRKBY
Blundellsands
Brighton le Sands
CROSBY
Waterloo
Litherland
Aintree
Seaforth
EURO RAIL TERMINAL
Orrell
Fazakerley
Knowsley
Croxteth
M57
BOOTLE
Dublin
Douglas
(Mar-Oct)
Belfast
(Nov-Mar)
LIVERPOOL BAY
WALLASEY
New Brighton
Norris Green
Croxteth Hall
Knowsley Safari Park
Kirkdale
Anfield
West Derby
Knotty Ash
Prescot
Liscard
Egremont
Everton
LIVERPOOL
Poulton
Roby
Huyton
Whiston
Rainhill
Moreton
Seacombe
Mersey Tunnels
Hoylake
Royal Liverpool
Claughton
Albert Dock
Childwall
M62
Hilbre Island
Red Rocks Marsh
Middle Eye
Little Eye
West Kirby
Greasby
Upton
BIRKENHEAD
Tranmere
Toxteth
National Wildflower Centre
Sefton
Dingle
Allerton
Woolton
Halewood
Hough Green
Frankby
Roydon
Arrowe
Rock Ferry
Aigburth
WIRRAL
Thingwall
M53
Port Sunlight
Grassendale
Garston
Thurstaston
Irby
Bebington
Barnston
Speke
Speke Hall
Wirral
Brimstage
Bromborough
Eastham
Oglet
Hale
Ffynnongroyw
Heswall
John Lennon
112
Thornton Hough
River Dee
River Mersey
Mostyn
Glan-y-don
Basingwerk Abbey
Greenfield
Whitford
Greenfield Valley
Parkgate
Neston
Willaston
Childer Thornton
Overpool
ELLESMERE PORT
Ince
Elton
Gorsedd
Carmel
Manchester Ship Canal
Holywell (Treffynnon)
St Winefride's Well
Bagillt
Ness Botanic Gardens
Cheshire Oaks
Calcot
Burton
Blue Planet
Little Stanney
Thornton-le-Moors
Brynford
Dolphin
Flint (Y Fflint)
Castle
Capenhurst
Stoak
Puddington
M56
Lixwm
Shotwick
Backford
Wervin
Picton
Dunham-on-the-Hill
Rhes-y-cae
Halkyn
Bridge Trafford
Mouldsworth
Ysceifiog
Connah's Quay
Great Saughall
Mollington
Mickle Trafford
Plemstall
Nannerch
Little Saughall
Upton
Little Barrow
Northop
Wepre Park
Shotton
Queensferry
Sealand
Blacon
Newton
Guilden Sutton
Northop Hall
Goed y Felin
Rhosesmor
Aston
Stamford Bridge
Barrow
Soughton
Ewloe Castle
Mancot
CHESTER
Littleton
Ewloe
Hawarden
Handbridge
Cilcain
Gwernaffield
Mynydd Isa
Bretton
Saltney
Huntington
Rowton
Pant-y-mwyn
Mold (Yr Wyddgrug)
Buckley (Bwcle)
Broughton
Loggerheads
MOEL FAMAU
Gwernymynydd
Penymynydd
Eccleston
Saighton
Moel Famau
Aberduna
97
Pontblyddyn
Penyffordd
Dodleston
98
Llanferres
Leeswood
Higher Kinnerton
Pontybodkin
Aldford
Llanbedr-Dyffryn-Clwyd
Pulford
Milton

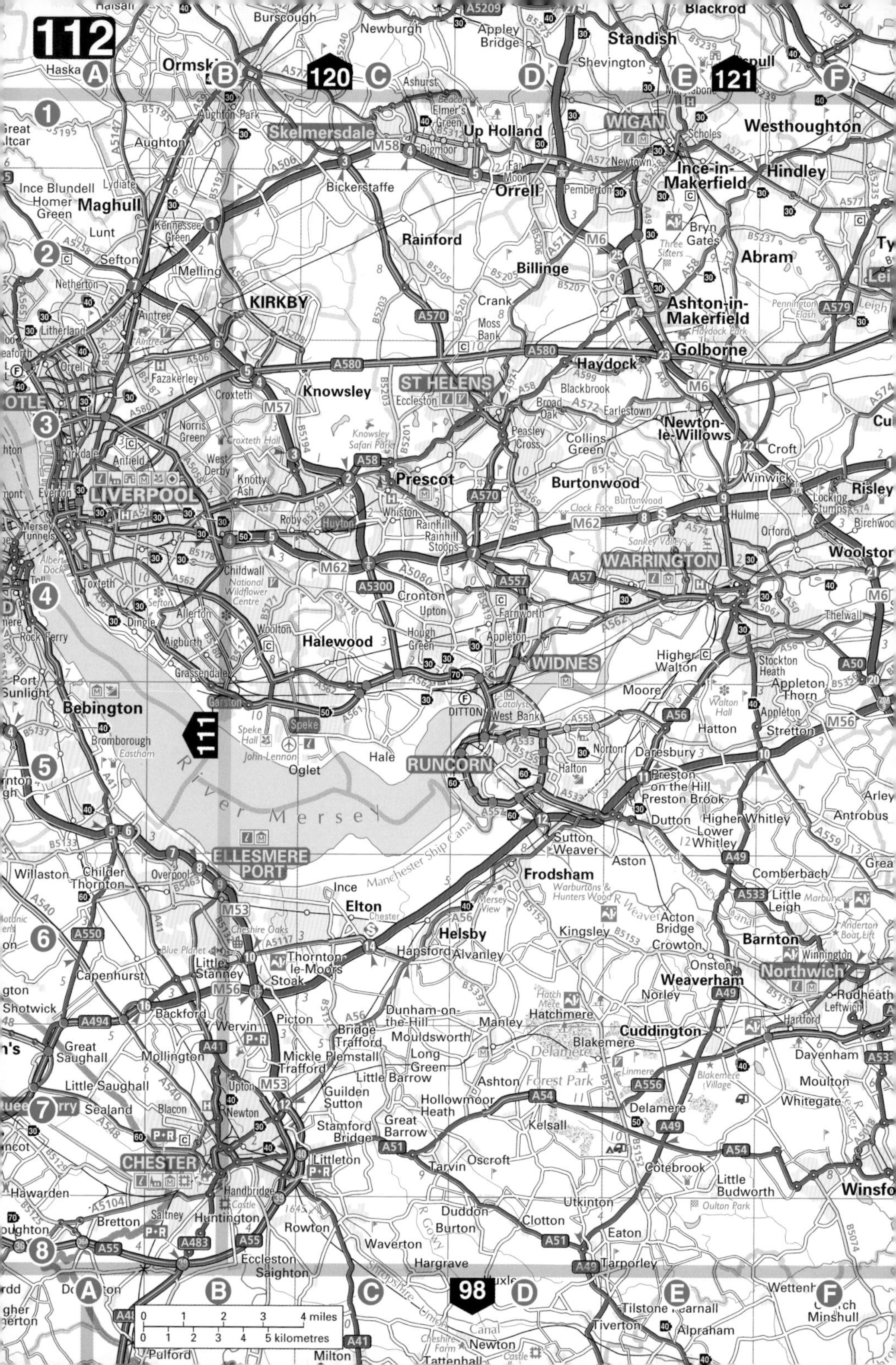

112
120
121
111
98
A
B
C
D
E
F
1
2
3
4
5
6
7
8
Ormskirk
Burscough
Newburgh
Appley Bridge
Standish
Shevington
Blackrod
WIGAN
Westhoughton
Skelmersdale
Up Holland
Orrell
Pemberton
Ince-in-Makerfield
Hindley
Aughton
Maghull
Lydiate
Ince Blundell
Lunt
Sefton
Bickerstaffe
Rainford
Billinge
Bryn Gates
Abram
Netherton
Melling
KIRKBY
Ashton-in-Makerfield
Golborne
Haydock
Crank
Moss Bank
Litherland
Aintree
Fazakerley
Knowsley
ST HELENS
Eccleston
Blackbrook
Earlestown
Newton-le-Willows
Croxteth
Norris Green
Anfield
Kirkdale
West Derby
Knotty Ash
Prescot
Whiston
Peasley Cross
Collins Green
Burtonwood
Croft
Winwick
Risley
LIVERPOOL
Everton
Roby
Huyton
Rainhill
Rainhill Stoops
Hulme
Woolston
Childwall
WARRINGTON
Toxteth
Dingle
Allerton
Woolton
Cronton
Upton
Farnworth
Appleton
Thelwall
Rock Ferry
Aigburth
Halewood
Hough Green
WIDNES
Higher Walton
Stockton Heath
Appleton Thorn
Port Sunlight
Bebington
Grassendale
Garston
Speke
Hale
DITTON
West Bank
Moore
Hatton
Stretton
Bromborough
Eastham
Oglet
RUNCORN
Norton
Halton
Daresbury
River Mersey
Preston on the Hill
Preston Brook
Dutton
Higher Whitley
Lower Whitley
Antrobus
Sutton Weaver
Aston
ELLESMERE PORT
Overpool
Willaston
Childer Thornton
Ince
Elton
Frodsham
Comberbach
Little Leigh
Helsby
Kingsley
Acton Bridge
Crowton
Barnton
Capenhurst
Little Stanney
Thornton-le-Moors
Stoak
Hapsford
Alvanley
Onston
Weaverham
Northwich
Shotwick
Backford
Wervin
Picton
Norley
Dunham-on-the-Hill
Bridge Trafford
Mouldsworth
Manley
Hatchmere
Cuddington
Great Saughall
Mollington
Mickle Trafford
Plemstall
Long Green
Blakemere
Delamere
Davenham
Moulton
Little Saughall
Upton
Guilden Sutton
Little Barrow
Ashton
Forest Park
Whitegate
Sealand
Blacon
Newton
Hollowmoor Heath
Stamford Bridge
Great Barrow
Kelsall
CHESTER
Littleton
Tarvin
Oscroft
Cotebrook
Little Budworth
Hawarden
Handbridge
Utkinton
Oulton Park
Bretton
Saltney
Huntington
Rowton
Duddon
Burton
Clotton
Eaton
Waverton
Eccleston
Saighton
Hargrave
Tarporley
Tilstone Fearnall
Tiverton
Alpraham
Pulford
Milton
Newton
Tattenhall
Manchester Ship Canal
Shropshire Union Canal
0 1 2 3 4 miles
0 1 2 3 4 5 kilometres

Merseyside & Manchester
113
122
114
99
Ainsworth
Halliwell
Breightmet
BOLTON
Royton
Diggle
Deane
Daubhill
Little Lever
Radcliffe
Whitefield
Dobcross
Farnworth
Chadderton
Uppermill
Kearsley
MIDDLETON
OLDHAM
Lees
Grasscroft
Greenfield
Walkden
Prestwich
Heaton Hall
Dove Stone Reservoir
Shakerley
Pendlebury
Blackley
Crumpsall
Moston
Failsworth
Mossley
Astley
Swinton
Sedgley Park
Cheetham Hill
Harpurhey
Broughton
Woodhouses
Daisy Nook
Charlestown
Newton Heath
Boothstown
Worsley
Strangeways
Miles Platting
Ashton-under-Lyne
Stalybridge
Canal
Weaste
MANCHESTER
Droylsden
Patricroft
Eccles
SALFORD
Guide Br
Dukinfield
Ardwick
Audenshaw
Trafford Centre
Trafford Park
Hulme
Gorton
Mottram in Longdendale
Hollingworth
Hadfield
Old Trafford
Rusholme
Irlam
Higher Irlam
Urmston
Denton
Hyde
Hattersley
Stretford
Lower Irlam
Flixton
Fallowfield
Levenshulme
Reddish
Broadbottom
Werneth Low
Chorlton-cum-Hardy
Withington
Burnage
Heaton Chapel
South Reddish
Charlesworth
Cadishead
Carrington
Didsbury
Romiley
Etherow
Chisworth
Manchester Ship Canal
Partington
Sale
Heaton Mersey
Heaton Norris
Bredbury
Compstall
Brooklands
Wythenshawe Hall
Northenden
STOCKPORT
Mill Brow
Toll
Sinderland Green
Broadheath
Timperley
Heatley
Dunham Town
Altrincham
Cheadle
Marple
Mellor
Rowarth
Thornsett
Dunham Woodhouses
Gatley
Cheadle Hulme
Hazel Grove
Dunham Massey
Little Bollington
Bowdon
Hale
Wythenshawe
Heald Green
New Mills
Birch Vale
Halebarns
Bramhall
High Lane
Disley
High Legh
Rostherne Mere
Ashley
Rostherne
Manchester
Runway Visitor Park
Poynton
Styal
Bucklow Hill
Handforth
Furness Vale
Hoo Green
Tatton Park
Quarry Bank Mill & Styal
Morley
Woodford
Lyme Park
Whaley Bridge
Morley Green
Wilmslow
Mere
Tatton Mere
Mobberley
Macclesfield Canal
411
SPONDS HILL
Cross Town
Mottram St Andrew
Taxal
Cockyard
Knolls Green
R Bollin
Pott Shrigley
Kettleshulme
Knutsford
Alderley Edge
Bollington
Dunge Valley
Fernilee
Tabley
Pickmere
Ollerton
Hare Hill
Higher Wincham
Watermill
Nether Alderley
Prestbury
Lostock Gralam
Chelford
Tytherington
Rainow
Goyt Valley
Plumley
Longmoss
Hurdsfield
SHINING TOR
559
Lower Peover
Over Peover
Monks Heath
Broken Cross
Macclesfield
Lostock Green
Swan Green
Capesthorne Hall
Tegg's Nose
Jodrell Bank
515
Forest Chapel
Lach Dennis
Danes Moss
551
AXE EDGE
Trentabank
Siddington
Warren
506
SHUTLINGSLOE
Goostrey
Lower Withington
Gawsworth
Twemlow Green
Wildboarclough
Byley
Cranage
Marton
Meadows
Holmes Chapel
Swettenham
North Rode
Flash
Allgreave
Sproston Green
Eaton
Wincle
Middlewich
Bosley
Danebridge
Hulme Walfield
R Dane
Brereton Green
Congleton
Key Green
Bradwall Green
Wimboldsley
THE CLOUD
Heaton
505
THE ROACHES
Arclid Green
Brookhouse Green
Timbersbrook
Rushton Spencer
373
GUN HILL
Elworth
Sandbach
Newtown
Meerbrook
Upper Hulme
Ettiley Heath
Rudyard Reservoir
Bradfield Green
Poolfold
Biddulph Grange Garden
Tittesworth Reservoir
Trent & Mersey
Little Moreton Hall
Rudyard Lake
Wheelock
Biddulph
Abbey

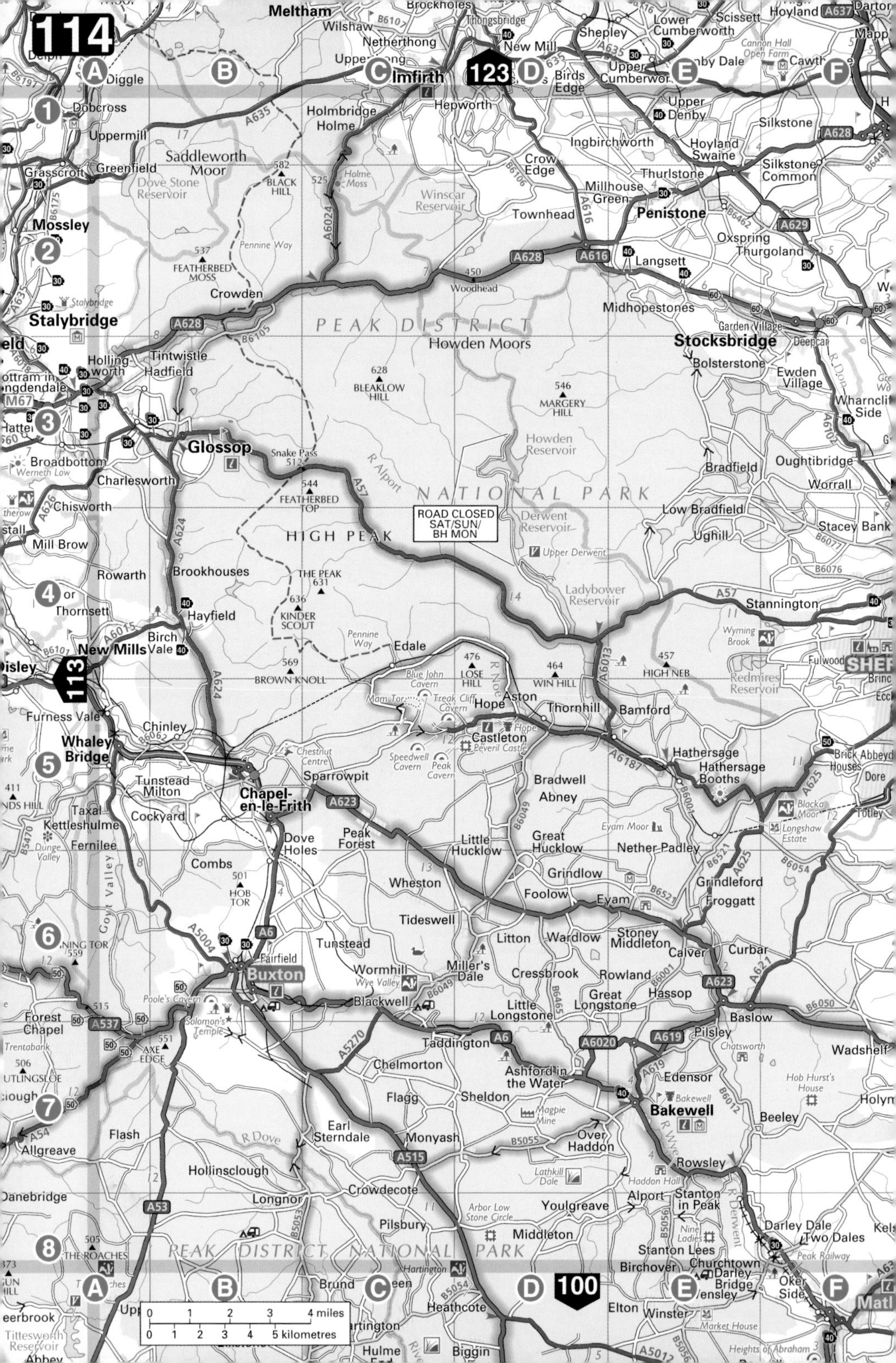

114
Meltham
Wilshaw
Netherthong
Upperthong
Brockholes
Thongsbridge
New Mill
Shepley
Lower Cumberworth
Scissett
Hoyland
Denby Dale
Cannon Hall Open Farm
Cawthorne
Delph
Diggle
Holmfirth
123
Birds Edge
Upper Cumberworth
Dobcross
Holmbridge
Holme
Hepworth
Upper Denby
Silkstone
Uppermill
Saddleworth Moor
Ingbirchworth
Hoyland Swaine
Grasscroft
Greenfield
582 BLACK HILL
Holme Moss
Crow Edge
Thurlstone
Silkstone Common
Dove Stone Reservoir
525
Winscar Reservoir
Millhouse Green
Mossley
Townhead
Penistone
Oxspring
Thurgoland
537 FEATHERBED MOSS
Pennine Way
Langsett
Stalybridge
Crowden
450 Woodhead
Midhopestones
PEAK DISTRICT
Howden Moors
Garden Village
Deepcar
Stocksbridge
Tintwistle
Hollingworth
Hadfield
628 BLEAKLOW HILL
546 MARGERY HILL
Bolsterstone
Ewden Village
Wharncliffe Side
Mottram in Longdendale
Hattersley
Glossop
Snake Pass 512
R Alport
Howden Reservoir
Bradfield
Oughtibridge
Broadbottom
Werneth Low
Charlesworth
544 FEATHERBED TOP
NATIONAL PARK
Worrall
Chisworth
ROAD CLOSED SAT/SUN/ BH MON
Derwent Reservoir
Low Bradfield
Ughill
Stacey Bank
Mill Brow
HIGH PEAK
Upper Derwent
Rowarth
Brookhouses
THE PEAK 631
Ladybower Reservoir
Stannington
Thornsett
Hayfield
636 KINDER SCOUT
Wyming Brook
New Mills
Birch Vale
Pennine Way
Edale
Disley
569 BROWN KNOLL
476 LOSE HILL
464 WIN HILL
457 HIGH NEB
Fulwood
Redmires Reservoir
113
Blue John Cavern
Mam Tor
Treak Cliff Cavern
Hope
Aston
Thornhill
Bamford
Furness Vale
Chinley
Castleton
Peveril Castle
Whaley Bridge
Chestnut Centre
Speedwell Cavern
Peak Cavern
Hathersage
Hathersage Booths
Brick Abbeydale Houses
Dore
Tunstead Milton
Sparrowpit
Bradwell
Abney
Blacka Moor
Totley
Chapel-en-le-Frith
411
Taxal
Cockyard
Eyam Moor
Longshaw Estate
Kettleshulme
Dove Holes
Peak Forest
Little Hucklow
Great Hucklow
Nether Padley
Dunge Valley
Fernilee
Goyt Valley
Combs
501 HOB TOR
Wheston
Grindlow
Grindleford
Foolow
Eyam
Froggatt
Tideswell
Stoney Middleton
Calver
Curbar
559
Tunstead
Litton
Wardlow
Fairfield
Buxton
Wormhill
Wye Valley
Miller's Dale
Cressbrook
Rowland
Hassop
Poole's Cavern
515
Blackwell
Little Longstone
Great Longstone
Baslow
Forest Chapel
Solomon's Temple
551 AXE EDGE
Taddington
Pilsley
Chatsworth
Wadshelf
Trentabank
506
Chelmorton
Ashford in the Water
Edensor
Hob Hurst's House
Flagg
Sheldon
Magpie Mine
Bakewell
Holymoorside
Beeley
Flash
Earl Sterndale
Monyash
Over Haddon
Allgreave
R Dove
Lathkill Dale
Rowsley
Hollinsclough
Haddon Hall
Danebridge
Longnor
Crowdecote
Alport
Stanton in Peak
R Derwent
R Wye
Arbor Low Stone Circle
Youlgreave
Pilsbury
Middleton
Nine Ladies
Darley Dale
Two Dales
Kelstedge
505 THE ROACHES
PEAK DISTRICT NATIONAL PARK
Hartington
Stanton Lees
Birchover
Churchtown
Darley Bridge
Wensley
Oker Side
Peak Railway
Brund
Sheen
100
Heathcote
Elton
Winster
Matlock
Meerbrook
Tittesworth Reservoir
Hartington
Market House
Hulme End
Biggin
Heights of Abraham
0 1 2 3 4 miles
0 1 2 3 4 5 kilometres

South Kirkby
Grimethorpe
124
Hooton Pagnell
Toll Bar
Dunsville
Cudworth
BARNSLEY
Monk Bretton Priory
Little Houghton
Great Houghton
Thurnscoe
Brodsworth Hall & Gardens
Pickburn
Arksey
Edenthorpe
Billingley
Hickleton
Scawthorpe
Bentley
Armthorpe
Darfield
Marr
Scawsby
Cusworth
Wheatley Hills
DONCASTER
Worsbrough Dale
Worsbrough Bridge
Broom Hill
Bolton upon Dearne
Goldthorpe
Cusworth Hall
Wombwell
Barnburgh
High Melton
Hexthorpe
Old Cantley
Worsbrough
Blacker Hill
Harlington
Adwick upon Dearne
Sprotbrough
Lakeside Village
Branton
Brampton
Mexborough
Warmsworth
DONCASTER RAILPORT
Auckley
Hoyland Nether
Wath upon Dearne
Cadeby
Balby
Bessacarr
Yorkshire
Tankersley
Elsecar Workshops
Castle
Denaby
New Edlington
Finningley
Robin Hood Doncaster Sheffield
Harley
Wentworth
Swinton
Conisbrough
Loversall
New Rossington
Rossington
Old Edlington
Nether Haugh
Chapeltown
Rawmarsh
Thrybergh
Hooton Roberts
Clifton
Wadworth
Thorpe Hesley
Scholes
Greasbrough
Ravenfield
Braithwell
Micklebring
Austerfield
Ecclesfield
Kimberworth
ROTHERHAM
Stainton
Tickhill
Spital Hill
Bawtry
Magna
Herringthorpe
Bramley
Maltby
Bircotes
Shiregreen
Wincobank
Meadowhall
Broom
Hooton Levitt
Harworth
Scaftworth
Tinsley
Wickersley
Styrrup
Scrooby
Grimesthorpe
Carbrook
Whiston
Slade Hooton
Stone
Owlerton
Brinsworth
Morthen
Thurcroft
Roche Abbey
Mattersey
Greenland
Attercliffe
Oldcotes
Treeton
Brookhouse
Laughton-en-le-Morthen
Firbeck
Catcliffe
Ulley
Brampton-en-le-Morthen
Blyth
Torworth
Langold
Handsworth
Aughton
Letwell
Dinnington
Sutton cum Lound
Arbourthorne
Richmond
Fence
Aston
North Anston
North Carlton
Hodsock
Woodhouse
Gildingwells
Intake
Hollins End
Hackenthorpe
Beighton
Todwick
Kiveton Park
South Anston
Woodsetts
South Carlton
Carlton in Lindrick
Wigthorpe
116
Highlane
Rother Valley
Wales
Ridgeway
R Ryton
Shireoaks
Mosborough
Killamarsh
Woodall
Harthill
Thorpe Salvin
Scofton
Ranby
Ford
Troway
Worksop
Eckington
Marsh Lane
Dronfield
Apperknowle
Spinkhill
Renishaw
West Handley
Middle Handley
Unstone
Barlborough
Whitwell
Hodthorpe
Revolution House
Mastin Moor
Harlesthorpe
Clumber Park
Whittington
Clowne
R Poulter
Barlow
Staveley
Creswell
Welbeck Abbey
Stanfree
Creswell Crags
Elmton
Bothamsall
Brimington
Shuttlewood
Holbeck
Linacres Reservoirs
Newbold
CHESTERFIELD
Whaley Thorns
Norton
Long Duckmanton
Old Brampton
New Brampton
Cuckney
Perlethorpe
Whaley
Meden Vale
Arkwright Town
Bolsover
Upper Langwith
Nether Langwith
R Meden
Langwith
Church Warsop
Budby
Sutton Scarsdale Hall
Hills Town
Scarcliffe
Langwith Junction
Sherwood Forest
Ollerton
Walton
Temple Normanton
Palterton
Market Warsop
New Ollerton
Heath
Shirebrook
Edwinstowe
Wingerworth
Grassmoor
Glapwell
Stony Houghton
Wellow
Stainsby Mill
Holmewood
Sherwood Forest Miniature Railway
New Houghton
Kings Clipstone
North Wingfield
Ault Hucknall
Rufford
Rufford Abbey
Mansfield Woodhouse
Sherwood Pines
Center Parcs Sherwood Forest
Alton
Pleasley
Hardwick Hall
Ashover
Hardstoft
Clay Cross
Eakring
Handley
Teversal
Pilsley
Dunsill
101
Stretton
Tibshelf
MANSFIELD
Morton
Bilsthorpe
Highoredish
Higham
Stonebroom
Newton
Sutton-in-Ashfield
Huthwaite
Brackenfield
Shirland
Blackwell
FOREST

M180
Burringham
Althorpe
Brumby
Wressle
Broughton
M181
Hatfield Woodhouse
Sandtoft
Ashby
Dunsville
Westgate
Belton
Beltoft
Yaddlethorpe
Bottesford
Carrhouse
West Butterwick
East Butterwick
M180
Scawby
M18
Epworth
Messingham
Sturton
Wroot
Old Rectory
Manton
Old Cantley
Branton
Low Burnham
Scotterthorpe
Susworth
Auckley
Blaxton
Owston Ferry
Scotter
Gainsthorpe Medieval Village
Westwoodside
B1396
Finningley
Haxey
East Lound
East Ferry
A159
Scotton
Kirton in Lindsey
Robin Hood Doncaster Sheffield
Rossington
Graiseland
Wildsworth
B1206
A638
R Idle
Gunthorpe
Laughton
Northorpe
A15
West Stockwith
Grayingham
Waddingham
Misson
Misterton
East Stockwith
Blyton
B1205
Blyborough
Austerfield
Bawtry
Walkerith
Pilham
Aisby
Willoughton
A631
Walkeringham
Morton
Corringham
Harwell
Chesterfield Canal
Gringley on the Hill
R Trent
Gainsborough
Hemswell
Scaftworth
Everton
A631
Hemswell Cliff
Scrooby
Drakeholes
Harpswell
A614
Wiseton
Beckingham
Springthorpe
Mattersey
Mattersey Abbey
Clayworth
Saundby
Heapham
Glentworth
Ranskill
Bole
Upton
Torworth
North Wheatley
Lea
R Till
Lound
B1403
Kexby
Fillingham
Sutton cum Lound
Hayton
South Wheatley
Knaith
A620
Sturton le Steeple
Willingham by Stow
B1241
Ingham
Barnby Moor
Idle Valley
Clarborough
North Leverton with Habblesthorpe
Fenton
A156
Gate Burton
Coates
Retford
Welham
Littleborough
Marton
Stow
Cammeringham
Babworth
Brattleby
Scofton
Ranby
South Leverton
Grove
A1500
Cottam
Brampton
Sturton by Stow
Scampton
Aisthorpe
A1
Ordsall
Treswell
Sundown Adventureland
Torksey
Bransby
B6420
Eaton
Nether Headon
Rampton
A57
A638
Stokeham
Laneham
Fenton
North Carlton
South Carlton
Headon
Gamston
Upton
East Drayton
A156
Saxilby
Clumber Park
Elkesley
Rockley
Askham
Dunham-on-Trent
Laughterton
Kettlethorpe
Fossdyke Navigation
Burton
West Drayton
Toll
Bothamsall
Markham Moor
A57
Ragnall
Newton on Trent
Milton
Darlton
North Clifton
Burton Waters
Sibthorpe
East Markham
Thorney
Skellingthorpe
Bevercotes
West Markham
Fledborough
Perlethorpe
Walesby
Tuxford
High Marnham
South Clifton
Harby
LINCOLN
A6075
Wigsley
Skegby
A46
B6387
Spalford
Doddington
Birchwood
Hartsholme
Kirton
Normanton on Trent
Low Marnham
Swanpool
Ollerton
Boughton
Egmanton
A1
A1133
B1190
New Ollerton
Weston
Grassthorpe
Swallow Beck
Whisby
Laxton
Sutton on Trent
Eagle
Road Transport
Bracebridge Low Fields
Wellow
Moorhouse
Girton
North Scarle
Ompton
Ossington
Besthorpe
Thorpe on the Hill
North Hykeham
Rufford
Kneesall
Norwell Woodhouse
South Scarle
South Hykeham
Rufford Abbey
Carlton-on-Trent
Center Parcs
Eakring
Kersall
Swinderby
Haddington
Harmston
Cromwell
Aubourn
Mapleb
Thurlby
Coleby
Bilsthorpe
Bassingham
Bathley
Holme
Boothby Gr
A46
Brough
Norton Disney
0 1 2 3 4 miles
0 1 2 3 4 5 kilometres
125
115
102

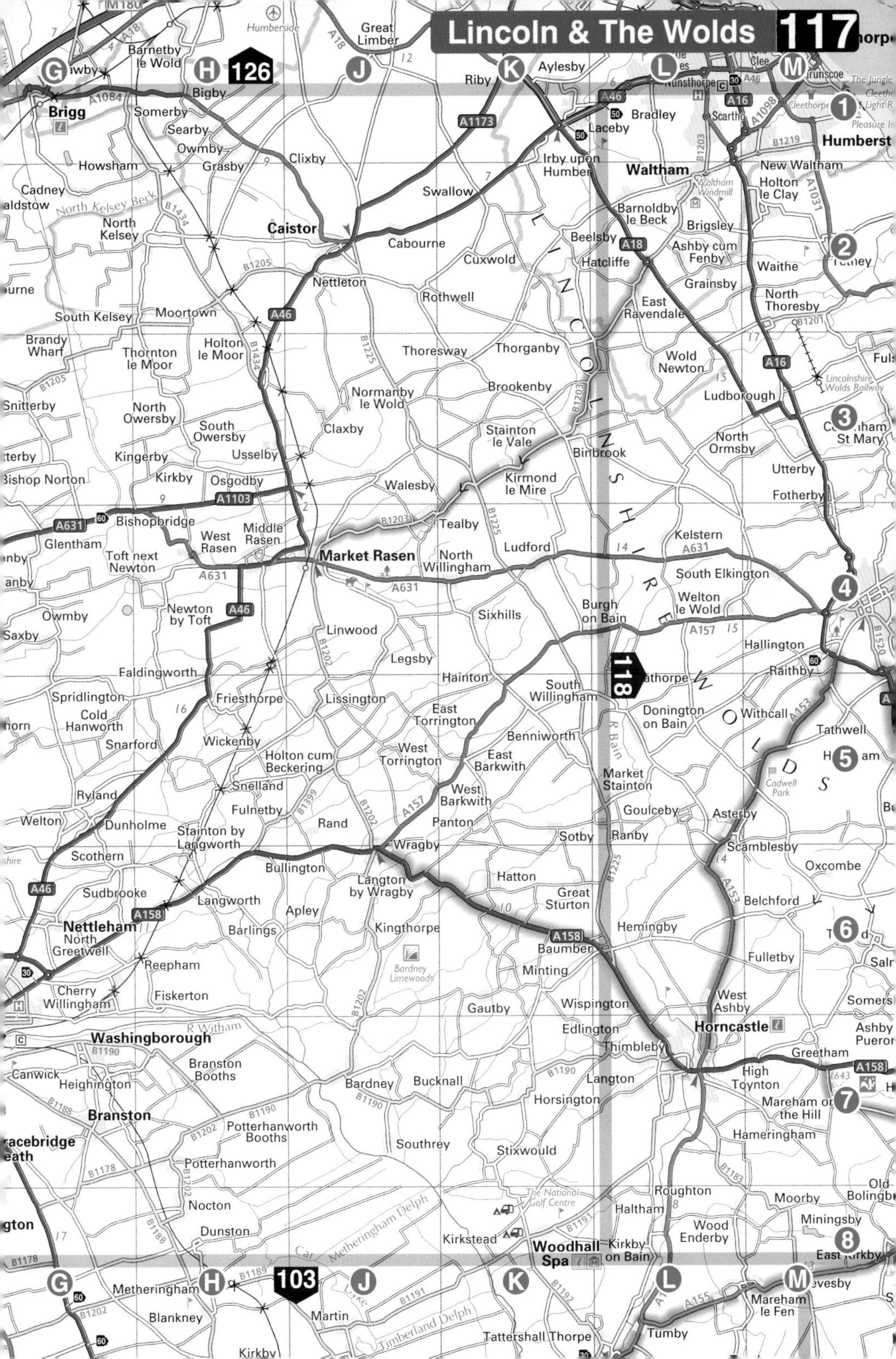
Humberside
Great Limber
Barnetby le Wold
126
Brigg
Bigby
Somerby
Searby
Owmby
Grasby
Clixby
Riby
Aylesby
Laceby
Bradley
Irby upon Humber
Waltham
Nunsthorpe
Scartho
Cleethorpes
Humberston
New Waltham
Holton le Clay
Howsham
Cadney
North Kelsey Beck
North Kelsey
Caistor
Cabourne
Swallow
Cuxwold
Beelsby
Barnoldby le Beck
Waltham Windmill
Brigsley
Ashby cum Fenby
Hatcliffe
Waithe
Nettleton
Rothwell
East Ravendale
Grainsby
North Thoresby
South Kelsey
Moortown
Brandy Wharf
Thornton le Moor
Holton le Moor
Thoresway
Thorganby
Wold Newton
Lincolnshire Wolds Railway
Snitterby
North Owersby
South Owersby
Normanby le Wold
Brookenby
Ludborough
Claxby
Stainton le Vale
North Ormsby
Kingerby
Usselby
Binbrook
Utterby
Bishop Norton
Kirkby
Osgodby
Walesby
Kirmond le Mire
Fotherby
Glentham
Bishopbridge
West Rasen
Middle Rasen
Tealby
Kelstern
Toft next Newton
Market Rasen
North Willingham
Ludford
South Elkington
Newton by Toft
Owmby
Saxby
Linwood
Sixhills
Burgh on Bain
Welton le Wold
Legsby
Hallington
Raithby
Faldingworth
Hainton
South Willingham
Spridlington
Friesthorpe
Lissington
East Torrington
118
Donington on Bain
Withcall
Cold Hanworth
Snarford
Wickenby
Benniworth
Tathwell
Holton cum Beckering
West Torrington
East Barkwith
Market Stainton
Cadwell Park
Ryland
Snelland
West Barkwith
Goulceby
Asterby
Welton
Dunholme
Fulnetby
Rand
Panton
Stainton by Langworth
Wragby
Sotby
Ranby
Scamblesby
Scothern
Bullington
Hatton
Oxcombe
Sudbrooke
Langton by Wragby
Great Sturton
Belchford
Langworth
Apley
Nettleham
North Greetwell
Barlings
Kingthorpe
Hemingby
Baumber
Fulletby
Reepham
Bardney Limewoods
Minting
Cherry Willingham
Fiskerton
Gautby
Wispington
West Ashby
Horncastle
R Witham
Washingborough
Edlington
Thimbleby
Greetham
Canwick
Heighington
Branston Booths
Bardney
Bucknall
Langton
High Toynton
Horsington
Mareham on the Hill
Branston
Potterhanworth Booths
Southrey
Hameringham
Stixwould
Potterhanworth
Nocton
The National Golf Centre
Roughton
Moorby
Haltham
Miningsby
Dunston
Metheringham Delph
Kirkstead
Woodhall Spa
Kirkby on Bain
Wood Enderby
East Kirkby
Metheringham
103
Martin
Blankney
Timberland Delph
Tattershall Thorpe
Tumby
Mareham le Fen
Kirkby
A46
A18
A16
A1173
A1103
A631
A157
A158
A153
A155
B1205
B1434
B1225
B1203
B1202
B1399
B1190
B1188
B1178
B1189
B1191
B1192
B1183
B1201
B1219
A1031
A1098
B1520

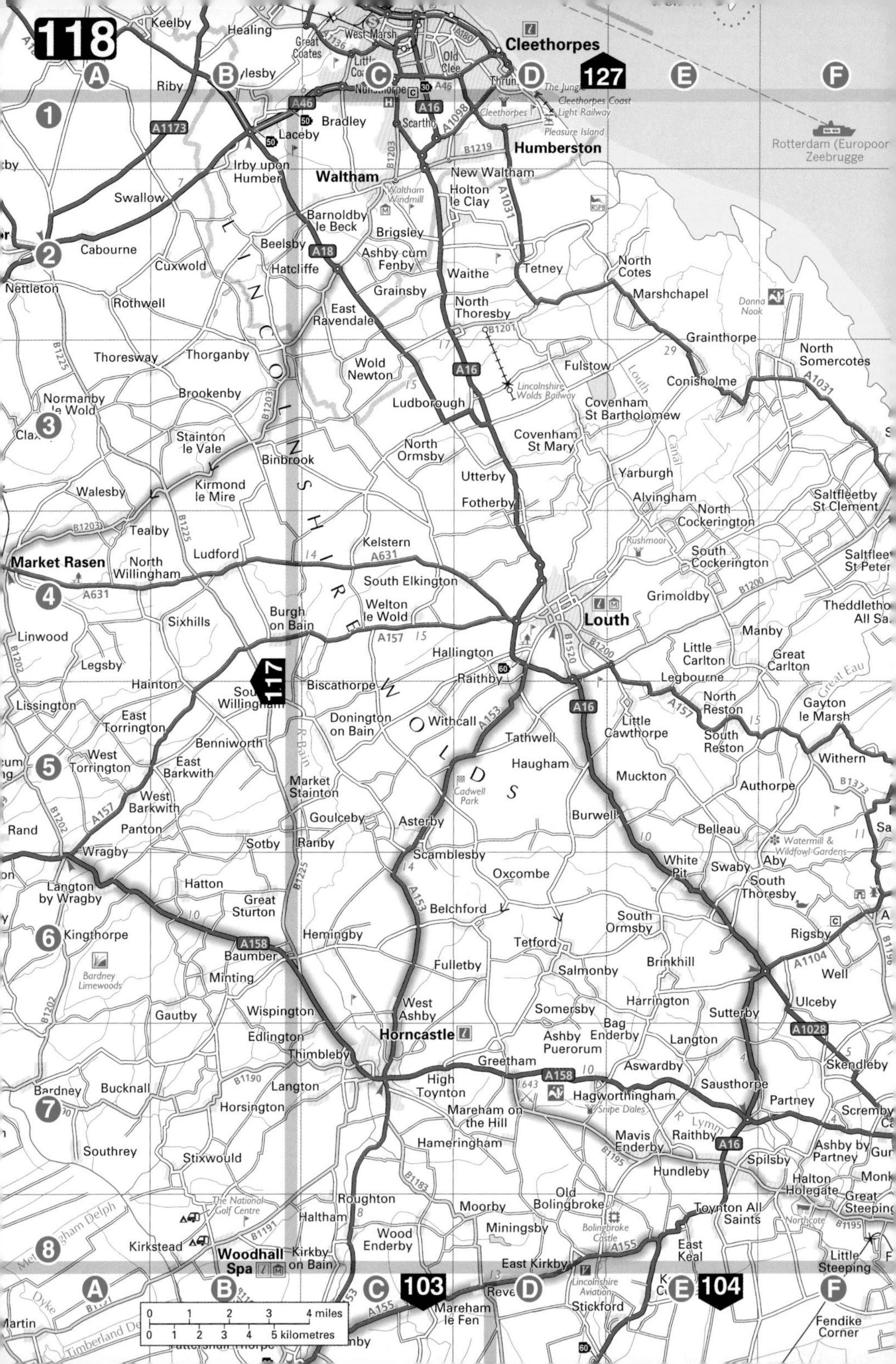
118
127
117
103
104
A
B
C
D
E
F
1
2
3
4
5
6
7
8
Keelby
Healing
Great Coates
West Marsh
Cleethorpes
Riby
Nunsthorpe
Bradley
Laceby
Scartho
The Jungle
Cleethorpes Coast Light Railway
Pleasure Island
Humberston
Rotterdam (Europoort)
Zeebrugge
Irby upon Humber
Waltham
Waltham Windmill
New Waltham
Holton le Clay
Swallow
Barnoldby le Beck
Brigsley
Beelsby
Ashby cum Fenby
Cabourne
Cuxwold
Hatcliffe
Waithe
Tetney
North Cotes
Nettleton
Rothwell
Grainsby
North Thoresby
Marshchapel
East Ravendale
Donna Nook
Grainthorpe
Thoresway
Thorganby
Wold Newton
Fulstow
North Somercotes
Normanby le Wold
Brookenby
Ludborough
Lincolnshire Wolds Railway
Conisholme
Covenham St Bartholomew
Stainton le Vale
Covenham St Mary
Binbrook
North Ormsby
Louth Canal
Kirmond le Mire
Utterby
Yarburgh
Walesby
Fotherby
Alvingham
Saltfleetby St Clement
North Cockerington
Tealby
Rushmoor
Market Rasen
North Willingham
Ludford
Kelstern
South Cockerington
Saltfleetby St Peter
South Elkington
Grimoldby
Sixhills
Burgh on Bain
Welton le Wold
Louth
Theddlethorpe All Saints
Linwood
Manby
Legsby
Hallington
Little Carlton
Great Carlton
Hainton
Raithby
Legbourne
Great Eau
South Willingham
Biscathorpe
North Reston
Gayton le Marsh
Lissington
East Torrington
Donington on Bain
Withcall
Little Cawthorpe
South Reston
Tathwell
West Torrington
Benniworth
East Barkwith
Haugham
Withern
Muckton
R Bain
Market Stainton
Cadwell Park
Authorpe
West Barkwith
Goulceby
Asterby
Burwell
Rand
Panton
Belleau
Watermill & Wildfowl Gardens
Wragby
Sotby
Ranby
Scamblesby
White Pit
Swaby
Aby
Langton by Wragby
Oxcombe
South Thoresby
Hatton
Great Sturton
Belchford
South Ormsby
Kingthorpe
Hemingby
Tetford
Rigsby
Bardney Limewoods
Baumber
Fulletby
Brinkhill
Minting
Salmonby
Well
Gautby
Wispington
West Ashby
Somersby
Harrington
Sutterby
Ulceby
Edlington
Horncastle
Bag Enderby
Ashby Puerorum
Langton
Thimbleby
Greetham
Aswardby
Skendleby
Bardney
Bucknall
Langton
High Toynton
Hagworthingham
Sausthorpe
Partney
Horsington
Mareham on the Hill
Snipe Dales
R Lymn
Scremby
Southrey
Hameringham
Mavis Enderby
Raithby
Ashby by Partney
Stixwould
Hundleby
Spilsby
Halton Holegate
Old Bolingbroke
Great Steeping
Roughton
The National Golf Centre
Moorby
Toynton All Saints
Northcote
Haltham
Miningsby
Bolingbroke Castle
Wood Enderby
East Keal
Little Steeping
Kirkstead
Woodhall Spa
Kirkby on Bain
East Kirkby
Lincolnshire Aviation
Stickford
Mareham le Fen
Fendike Corner
Martin
Timberland Delph
0 1 2 3 4 miles
0 1 2 3 4 5 kilometres

G
H
J
K
L
M
1
2
3
4
5
6
7
8
Theddlethorpe St Helen
A1031
Seal Sanctuary & Wildlife Centre
Mablethorpe
Trusthorpe
Sutton on Sea
Sandilands
A1104
A52
A1111
Markby
Huttoft
Thurlby
B1449
Anderby
Anderby Creek
Mumby
Chapel Point
Chapel St Leonards
Hogsthorpe
Sloothby
Habertoft
Addlethorpe
Fantasy Island
Ingoldmells
Ingoldmells Point
Lincolnshire Coast Light Railway
Orby
Burgh le Marsh
A158
Skegness
Croft
104
Thorpe St Peter
Wainfleet Haven
Wainfleet

A
B
C
D
E
129
F
1
2
3
4
5
6
7
8
Cockersand
Cockerham
COCKERHAM MO
Knott End-on-Sea
Pilling
Preesall
Fleetwood
Rossall Point
Winmarleigh
A588
A587
River Wyre
Stalmine
Eagland Hill
B5268
A585
Staynall
B5377
Cleveleys
Thornton
Hambleton
Out Rawcliffe
Moss Edge
B5412
Great Eccleston
Toll
Little Singleton
A586
Copp
A584
B5124
Warbreck
Poulton-le-Fylde
Singleton
Elswick
B5269
North Shore
Hoohill
B5266
Thistleton
BLACKPOOL
A585
Esprick
Wharles
Staining
Model Village
Great Marton
B5260
M55
Weeton
A583
Great Plumpton
Wesham
Treales
South Shore
B5262
Kirkham
A5230
Westby
A583
B5261
Blackpool
Wrea Green
Newton with Scales
Clifton
St Anne's
B5233
B5261
Lytham Hall
B5259
Kellamergh
A584
Freckleton
Warton
Royal Lytham & St Annes
Ansdell
Fairhaven
Lytham St Anne's
A584
Lytham
River Ribble
Discovery Centre
Hesketh Bank
West Lancs Light Rail
Becconsall
Banks
Tarleton
A565
SOUTHPORT
Mere Brow
New Pleasureland
P+R
A59
Leisure Lakes
B5246
Holmeswood
Rufford
Windmill Animal Farm
Birkdale
A5267
The Royal Birkdale
B5243
Martin Mere Wetland Centre
Scarisbrick
Shirdley Hill
Burscough Bridge
A570
Bescar
Rufford Canal
Ainsdale
A565
Heaton's Bridge
Ainsdale Sand Dunes
Halsall
Leeds & Liverpool Canal
B5242
Burscough
Barton
Cabin Hill
Freshfield
Haskayne
Ormskirk
A577
B5240
Formby
111
Little Altcar
Great Altcar
B5195
Aughton Park
A5147
Aughton
Skelmersdale
A506
Hightown
A565
Ince Blundell
Lydiate
Bickerstaffe
0 1 2 3 4 miles
0 1 2 3 4 5 kilometres

Forest of Bowland
Abbeystead
Dolphinholme
WHINS BROW
130
Slaidburn
HAWTHORNTHWAITE FELL
Newton-in-Bowland
Dunsop Bridge
Calder Fell
TOTRIDGE FELL
BRADFORD FELL
Holden
Bolton-by-Bowland
Scorton
Oakenclough
FAIRSNAPE FELL
PARLICK
Calder Vale
Whitewell
Sawley
Grindleton
West Bradford
Rimington
Downham
Bonds
Waddington
Chatburn
Horrocksford
Worston
Bashall Eaves
Chipping
Beacon Fell
Claughton
R Hodder
Clitheroe
PENDLE HILL
Barley
White Chapel
Inglewhite
Hesketh Lane
Longridge Fell
Pendleton
Bilsborrow
Knowle Green
Hurst Green
Cromwell's Bridge
Great Mitton
Barrow
Longridge
Wiswell
Sabden
Fence
Barton
Goosnargh
Whalley
Higham
Newsham
Old Langho
Chingle Hall
Broughton
Little Town
Ribchester
Copster Green
Billington
Read
Simonstone
Padiham
Gawthorpe Hall
Woodplumpton
Grimsargh
R Ribble
Langho
Higher Bartle
Habergham
Cottam
Sharoe Green
Balderstone
Great Harwood
Clayton-le-Moors
Hapton
Ingol
Cadley
Fulwood
Brockholes
Samlesbury Hall
Osbaldeston
Wilpshire
Ribbleton
Mellor Brook
Mellor
Rishton
122
PRESTON
Church
Dill Hall
BLACKBURN
Higher Walton
Walton-le-Dale
Higher Penwortham
Witton
Accrington
Oswaldtwistle
Baxenden
Hutton
Hoghton
Pleasington
Hoghton Tower
Bamber Bridge
Riley Green
Goodshaw Chapel
Feniscowles
New Longton
Farington
Belthorn
Reeds Holme
Brindle
Haslingden
Constable Lee
Tockholes
Abbey Village
Blackburn with Darwen
Waterside
Much Hoole
Higher Wheelton
Leyland
Cuerden Valley
Sunnyhurst
Clayton-le-Woods
Whittle-le-Woods
Withnell
Darwen
Hoddlesden
Helmshore
East Lancashire Railway
Brinscall
Textiles Museum
Buckshaw Village
Wheelton
Euxton
Chatterton
Edenfield
Stubbins
R Yarrow
Chorley
Ramsbottom
Shuttleworth
Eccleston
Edgworth
Charnock Richard
Cowling
Turton Tower
Turton Bottoms
Yarrow Valley
Belmont
Chapeltown
Nuttall
Egerton
WINTER HILL
Rivington
Summerseat
Coppull
Greenmount
Grimeford Village
Adlington
Horwich
Bromley Cross
Tottington
Mossy Lea
Eagley
Chesham
BURY
Smithills Hall
Astley Bridge
Parbold
Blackrod
Ainsworth
Appley Bridge
Halliwell
Breightmet
Standish
Aspull
BOLTON
Shevington
Haigh Hall
Marylebone
Moses Gate
Deane
Radcliffe
Daubhill
Whitefield
Holland
112
113
Little Lever
Westhoughton
Farnworth
Scholes
Newtown
Ince-in-Makerfield
Hindley
Kearsley
Orrell
Pemberton
Atherton
Walkden
Prestwich
M6
M65
M61
M60
A59
A6
A677
A666
A671
A680
A56
A675
A49
A5209
B6478
B6243
B6245
B6241
B6242
B6234
B6236
B6232
B6391
B6226
B6213
B6196
B6209
B6214
B5269

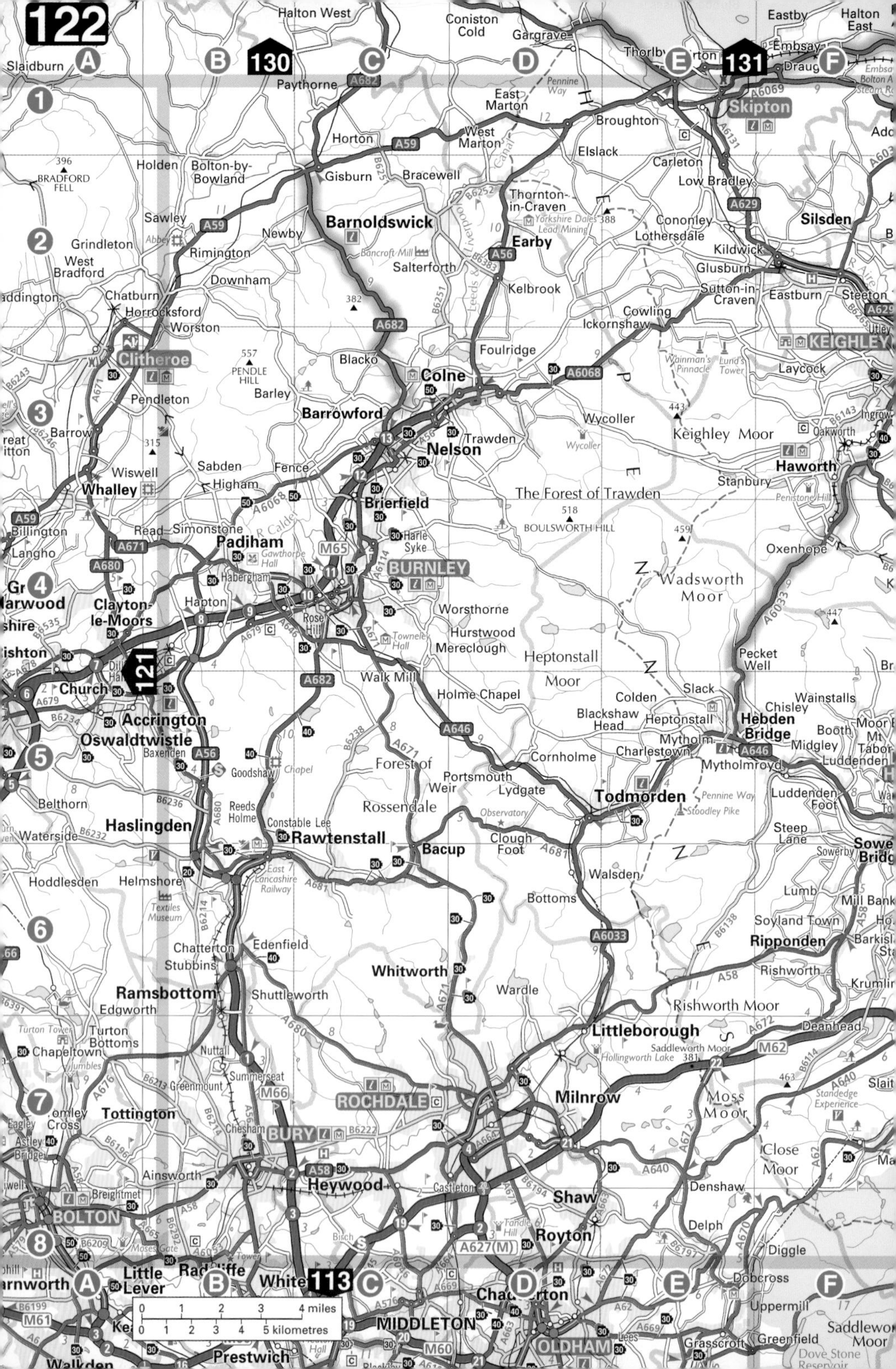

Halton West
Coniston Cold
Gargrave
Eastby
Halton East
Embsay
Slaidburn
130
Thorlby
131
Draug
Paythorne
A682
East Marton
Pennine Way
Skipton
A6069
Broughton
Horton
A59
West Marton
Elslack
Carleton
A6131
Holden
Bolton-by-Bowland
Gisburn
B6251
Bracewell
396
BRADFORD FELL
Thornton-in-Craven
Low Bradley
A629
Sawley
Yorkshire Dales Lead Mining
388
Cononley
Silsden
Barnoldswick
A59
Abbey
Newby
Lothersdale
Grindleton
Rimington
Bancroft Mill
Earby
A56
Kildwick
West Bradford
Salterforth
Glusburn
Downham
Kelbrook
Leeds & Liverpool Canal
Sutton-in-Craven
Eastburn
Steeton
Chatburn
382
Horrocksford
Worston
Cowling
Ickornshaw
A682
Clitheroe
557
PENDLE HILL
Blacko
Foulridge
A6068
Wainman's Pinnacle
Lund's Tower
KEIGHLEY
Laycock
Pendleton
Barley
Colne
Barrowford
443
Wycoller
Ingrow
Oakworth
Barrow
315
Trawden
Nelson
Keighley Moor
Haworth
Wiswell
Sabden
Fence
Whalley
Higham
Brierfield
The Forest of Trawden
Stanbury
Penistone Hill
518
BOULSWORTH HILL
A59
Billington
Read
Simonstone
A6068
R Calder
Padiham
Gawthorpe Hall
M65
Harle Syke
459
Langho
A671
A680
Oxenhope
Habergham
A6114
BURNLEY
Wadsworth Moor
Clayton-le-Moors
Hapton
Worsthorne
A6033
447
Rose Hill
A679
A646
Towneley Hall
Hurstwood
Mereclough
Heptonstall Moor
Pecket Well
Church
A682
Walk Mill
Holme Chapel
Colden
Slack
Wainstalls
Chisley
Accrington
A679
B6234
Blackshaw Head
Heptonstall
Hebden Bridge
Booth
Oswaldtwistle
A646
Mytholm
Charlestown
A646
Midgley
Baxenden
A56
Goodshaw
Chapel
Forest of Rossendale
Portsmouth
Weir
Cornholme
Lydgate
Mytholmroyd
Luddenden
Belthorn
B6236
Reeds Holme
Todmorden
Pennine Way
Stoodley Pike
Luddenden Foot
Haslingden
Constable Lee
Observatory
Waterside
B6232
Rawtenstall
Bacup
Clough Foot
A681
Steep Lane
Sowerby
Hoddlesden
Helmshore
East Lancashire Railway
A681
Walsden
Textiles Museum
Bottoms
Lumb
Mill Bank
B6214
Soyland Town
A6033
B6138
Ripponden
Chatterton
Edenfield
Stubbins
Whitworth
Rishworth
A58
Ramsbottom
Shuttleworth
Wardle
Edgworth
Rishworth Moor
Turton Tower
Turton Bottoms
A680
Littleborough
Deanhead
Chapeltown
Jumbles
Saddleworth Moor
Hollingworth Lake
381
M62
B6114
A672
463
B6213
Greenmount
Summerseat
Nuttall
M66
ROCHDALE
Milnrow
Moss Moor
Standedge Experience
A640
A676
Tottington
Chesham
A56
BURY
B6222
A664
B6196
Ainsworth
Close Moor
Heywood
A58
Castleton
B6194
Shaw
A640
A62
Denshaw
A672
Breightmet
BOLTON
A58
A665
Moses Gate
Tower
A6053
Birch
Fandle Hill
A627(M)
Royton
Delph
A670
B6209
A663
B6197
Diggle
Little Lever
Radcliffe
Whitefield
113
Chadderton
Farnworth
Dobcross
Uppermill
A669
A576
B6199
M61
Walkden
Kearsley
MIDDLETON
A663
A62
A669
Lees
Grasscroft
Greenfield
Saddleworth Moor
Dove Stone Reservoir
M60
Prestwich
OLDHAM
0 1 2 3 4 miles
0 1 2 3 4 5 kilometres

Blubberhouses
Kettlesing
Fewston Reservoir
Fewston
Swinsty Res
Bolton Priory
A59
409
G
H
J
K
L
M
132
Beamsley
Timble
Pannal Ash
Rossett Green
A61
Follifoot
A661
North Deighton
Ribston
Walshford
1
Langbar
B6451
255
A658
Pannal
Castle
Spofforth
Kirk Deighton
Nesfield
North Rigton
Kirkby Overblow
Middleton
Denton
Askwith
Clifton
Sicklinghall
Wetherby
Rombalds Moor
Farnley
Huby
Dunkeswick
Weston
Ilkley
Ben Rhydding
A65
Leathley
B6161
Weeton
Linton
Netherby
Chapel Hill
2
Burley in Wharfedale
Newall
A660
Otley
A659
Pool
Castley
Harewood
Collingham
403
Burley Wood Head
Chevin Forest Park
Arthington
Weardley
Harewood House
East Keswick
A6038
East Carlton
Bramhope
A61
Menston
Old Bramhope
Wike
Bardsey
East Rigton
East Riddlesden Hall
East Morton
Guiseley
Eccup Reservoir
A58
A650
B6265
A660
Bramham Park
Hawksworth
Park Gate
Leeds Bradford
Adel Dam
Scarcroft
Yeadon
Alwoodley
Cross Flatts
Baildon
Thorner
Bingley
Rawdon
P+R
Moortown
Shadwell
Sand Hills
3
Baildon Green
Charlestown
A6120
Moor Allerton
A64
Saltaire
Thackley
A65
Horsforth
Harden
B6429
Idle
Chapel Allerton
Tropical World
Roundhay
Aberford
A650
Weetwood
Cottingley
Moorhead
Shipley
Meanwood
Barwick in Elmet
Greengates
Kirkstall
Gledhow
Harehills
Scholes
Wilsden
Frizinghall
Wrose
Eccleshill
Headingley
Seacroft
Heaton
Bramley
Manston
Hare Croft
Manningham
Undercliffe
Woodhouse
LEEDS
Cross Gates
M1
Denholme
Allerton
Thornbury
Sheepscar
Halton
Garforth
Thornton
Laisterdyke
Fartown
Armley
Whitkirk
4
Great Horton
BRADFORD
Pudsey
Farnley
Osmondthorpe
Colton
B6145
Little Horton
Bowling
Wortley
Clayton
West Bowling
Tong
Beeston
Hunslet
Cross Green
Temple Newsam
Swillington
Kippax
Mountain
P+R
Queensbury
Wibsey
Gildersome
Churwell
M621
Great Preston
Ambler Thorn
Shibden Head
Buttershaw
Drighlington
White Rose
Middleton Railway
124
Odsal
Birkenshaw
Middleton
Rothwell
Bower's Row
Oakenshaw
M606
M621
Northowram
Hunsworth
Wyke
Morley
Carlton
Oulzewell Green
Oakwell Hall
A58
M62
Ardsley East
5
Shibden Hall
Hipperholme
Cleckheaton
Birstall
Lofthouse
Lofthouse Gate
Heckmondwike
Woodkirk
Carr Gate
WAKEFIELD EUROPORT
Hartshead Moor
Liversedge
Chidswell
Southowram
Clifton
Norristhorpe
Roberttown
Batley
Hanging Heaton
Kirkhamgate
Normanton
Brighouse
Hartshead
Dewsbury
Woodhouse
Ackton
Rastrick
Earlsheaton
Alverthorpe
Flanshaw
WAKEFIELD
Northorpe
A644
Savile Town
A638
Kirkthorpe
Warmfield
Elland
Ravensthorpe
Mirfield
Ossett
Lupset
Heath
New Sharlston
6
Netheroyd Hill
Sheepridge
Belle Vue
Sharlston
Broad Carr
Clough Head
Fartown
Upper Heaton
Upper Hopton
Thornhill
Horbury
Sandal Magna
Crofton
Nostell Priory
Lindley
HUDDERSFIELD
Whitley Lower
Edgerton
Kirkheaton
Middlestown
Calder Grove
New Crofton
Scapegoat Hill
Moldgreen
Hill Side
National Coal Mining Museum
Netherton
Crigglestone
Walton
Houses Hill
Grange Moor
A642
Overton
Golcar
Lower Houses
Greenside
Flockton Green
Hill Top
Newmillerdam
Almondbury
Lepton
West Bretton
Ryhill
Kinsley
Linthwaite
Newsome
Flockton
Midgley
Emley
Woolley Edge
Havercroft
Netherton
Blackmoorfoot
Highburton
Yorkshire Sculpture Park
M1
Notton
7
Hemsworth
Honley
Woolley
Helme
Farnley Tyas
Kirkburton
Kirklees Light Railway
Clayton West
Bretton
Staincross
Royston
Shafton
Shelley
Skelmanthorpe
Thurstonland
High Hoyland
Darton
Carlton
Meltham
Brockholes
A637
Wilshaw
Thongsbridge
Scissett
Lower Cumberworth
Shepley
Mapplewell
Netherthong
New Mill
Cannon Hall Open Farm
New Lodge
Cudworth
Upperthong
Upper Cumberworth
Denby Dale
Cawthorne
8
Holmfirth
Scholes
Birds Edge
BARNSLEY
Hepworth
114
Upper Denby
Higham
Little Houghton
Holmbridge
Silkstone
A628
Dodworth
Ingbirchworth
Hoyland Swaine
Darfield
Crow Edge
Thurlstone
Silkstone Common
Worsbrough
582

124
132
133
123
115
A
B
C
D
E
F
1
2
3
4
5
6
7
8
Starbeck
Goldsborough
Kirk Hammerton
Overton
Nether Poppleton
Upper Poppleton
New Earswick
East Huntington
Rawcliffe
Plumpton Rocks
Little Ribston
Cattal
Hunsingore
Tockwith
Hessay
Follifoot
North Deighton
Cowthorpe
Knapton
Pannal
Spofforth
Kirk Deighton
Bickerton
Long Marston
Rufforth
Acomb
Holgate
South Bank
YORK
Osbaldwick
Kirkby Overblow
Wetherby
Bilton
Hutton Wandesley
Nunthorpe
Heslington
Sicklinghall
Askham Bryan
Dringhouses
Fulford
Dunkeswick
Wetherby
Walton
Angram
Healaugh
Askham Richard
Bishopthorpe
Linton
Boston Spa
Thorp Arch
Bilbrough
Copmanthorpe
Netherby
Chapel Hill
Wighill
Catterton
Harewood
R Wharfe
Acaster Malbis
Naburn
Harewood House
Collingham
Newton Kyme
East Keswick
Clifford
Colton
Deighton
East Rigton
Tadcaster
Oxton
Wike
Bardsey
Bramham
Appleton Roebuck
Escrick
Eccup Reservoir
Bolton Percy
Bramham Park
Stutton
Kirkby Wharfe
Acaster Selby
Scarcroft
Thorner
Shadwell
Sand Hills
Towton
Ulleskelf
Stillingfleet
Moor Allerton
Ryther
Chapel Allerton
Tropical World
Roundhay
Aberford
Cawood
Kelfield
Gledhow
Harehills
R Cock
Barwick in Elmet
Saxton
Riccall
Scholes
Seacroft
Church Fenton
Barkston Ash
Wistow
Lotherton Hall
LEEDS
Manston
Cross Gates
R Ouse
Sheepscar
Little Fenton
Barlby
Halton
Whitkirk
Sherburn in Elmet
Osmondthorpe
Colton
Garforth
Micklefield
Cross Green
Temple Newsam
Thorpe Willoughby
Hunslet
Swillington
Kippax
South Milford
Steeton Hall Gatehouse
Monk Fryston
Hambleton
Brayton
Selby
Lumby
Middleton Railway
Middleton
Great Preston
Ledsham
Hillam
Gateforth
Burn
Rothwell
Bower's Row
Ledston
Fairburn
Burton Salmon
Birkin
Selby Canal
Carlton
Allerton Bywater
Chapel Haddlesey
Ouzlewell Green
Mickletown
Brotherton
West Haddlesey
Camblesforth
Ardsley
East Ardsley
Lofthouse
Lofthouse Gate
Diggerland
Castleford
Beal
Temple Hirst
Sutton
R Aire
Kellington
Hirst Courtney
Carr Gate
WAKEFIELD EUROPORT
Xscape
Knottingley
Hensall
Normanton
Woodhouse
Ackton
Ferrybridge
Eggborough
Snaith
Alverthorpe
Flanshaw
WAKEFIELD
Kirkthorpe
Warmfield
Pontefract
Gowdall
New Sharlston
Whitley
Heath
Featherstone
Darrington
Great Heck
Horbury
Belle Vue
Sharlston
High Ackworth
East Hardwick
Womersley
Pollington
Aire and Calder Navigation
Sandal Magna
Crofton
Nostell Priory
Low Ackworth
Brockadale
Balne
Calder Grove
Hessle
Wentbridge
Little Smeaton
Walden Stubbs
Crigglestone
Walton
New Crofton
Wragby
Ackworth Moor Top
R Went
Kirk Smeaton
Sykehouse
Hill Top
Fitzwilliam
Thorpe Audlin
Norton
Fenwick
Newmillerdam
Ryhill
Kinsley
Badsworth
Moss
Woolley Edge
Havercroft
Upton
Askern
Notton
South Hiendley
Hemsworth
North Elmsall
Campsall
Woolley
Skelbrooke
Haywood
Kirk Bramwith
Staincross
Royston
Shafton
South Elmsall
Burghwallis
Stainforth
Brierley
Moorthorpe
Owston
South Bramwith
Darton
Carlton
Hampole
Skellow
Thorpe in Balne
Barnby Dun
Mapplewell
New Lodge
South Kirkby
Grimethorpe
Carcroft
Cudworth
Clayton
Adwick le Street
Hooton Pagnell
Toll Bar
Kirk Sandall
Dunscroft
BARNSLEY
Monk Bretton
Woodlands
Little Houghton
Great Houghton
Thurnscoe
Brodsworth
Pickburn
Arksey
Edenthorpe
Scawthorpe
Hickleton
Bentley
Armthorpe
Dodworth
Billingley
Marr
Scawsby
Cusworth
Wheatley Hills
DONCASTER
Worsbrough
Bolton
Goldthorpe
0 1 2 3 4 miles
0 1 2 3 4 5 kilometres
A1(M)
A1
M1
M62
M621
A61
A64
A19
A59
A58
A63
A659
A658
A661
A168
A1237
A1036
A1079
A162
A642
A656
A639
A645
A628
A638
A636
A655
A6021
A6195
A635
A650
A1041
A1238
A18
A630
B6164
B1224
B1223
B1222
B1217
B6137
B6136
B6134
B6428
B6132
B6273
B6474
B6422
B1220
B6411
B6449
B6481

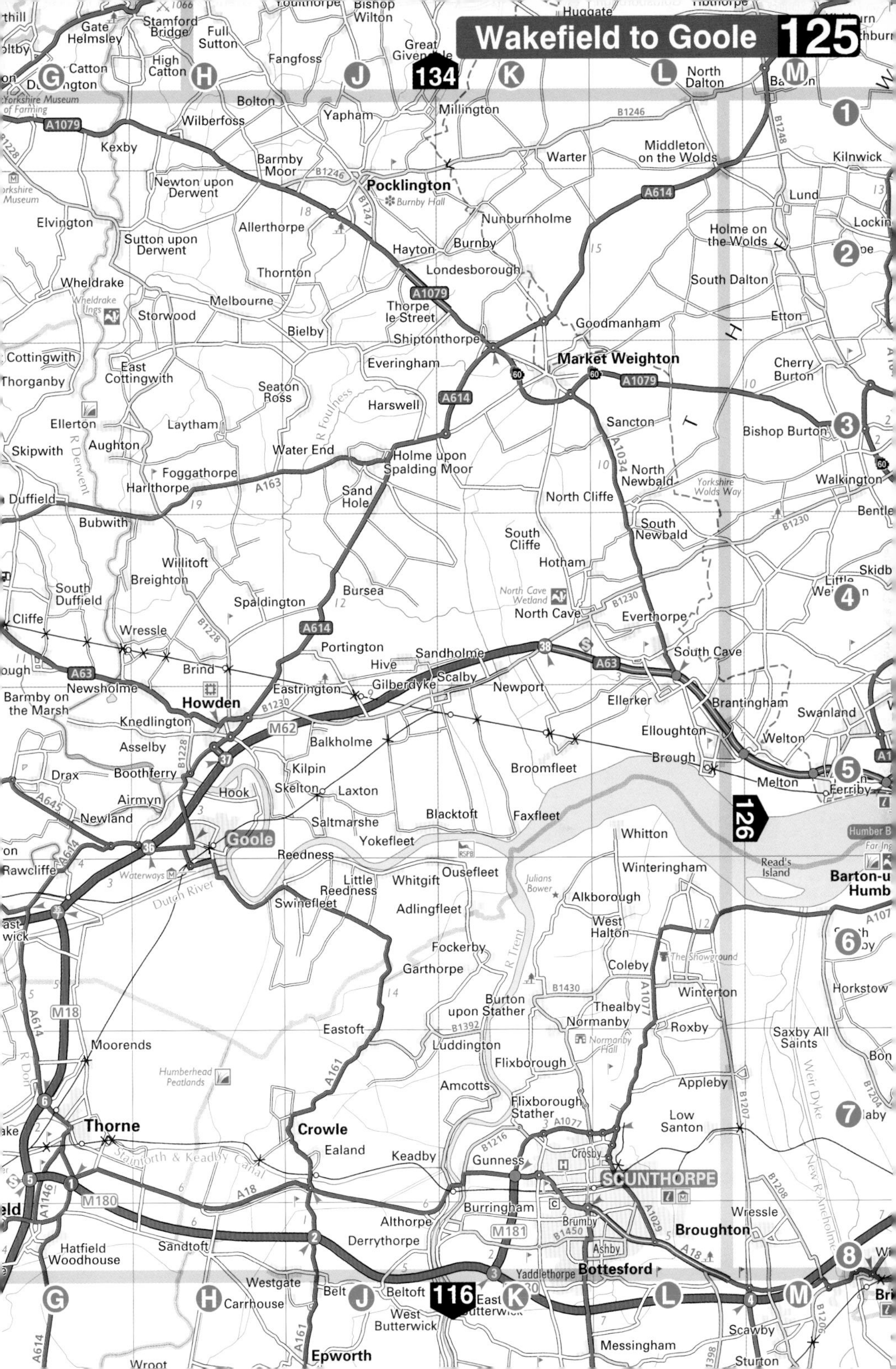
Wakefield to Goole
125
134
126
116
Gate Helmsley
Stamford Bridge
Full Sutton
High Catton
Catton
Fangfoss
Bishop Wilton
Great Givendale
Huggate
North Dalton
Bolton
Yapham
Millington
Wilberfoss
A1079
Kexby
Barmby Moor
B1246
Pocklington
Burnby Hall
Warter
Middleton on the Wolds
Kilnwick
A614
Lund
Newton upon Derwent
Elvington
Sutton upon Derwent
Allerthorpe
Nunburnholme
Burnby
Hayton
Holme on the Wolds
Londesborough
Thornton
South Dalton
Wheldrake
Wheldrake Ings
Melbourne
Storwood
Thorpe le Street
Bielby
Shiptonthorpe
Goodmanham
Etton
Cottingwith
Thorganby
East Cottingwith
Everingham
Market Weighton
Cherry Burton
Seaton Ross
Harswell
Ellerton
Laytham
Sancton
Bishop Burton
Aughton
Skipwith
Water End
Holme upon Spalding Moor
A1034
North Newbald
Yorkshire Wolds Way
Walkington
Foggathorpe
Harlthorpe
A163
Sand Hole
North Cliffe
Duffield
Bubwith
South Cliffe
South Newbald
B1230
Willitoft
Hotham
Breighton
South Duffield
Bursea
North Cave Wetland
Spaldington
North Cave
Everthorpe
Cliffe
A614
Wressle
B1228
Portington
Sandholme
Hive
South Cave
Brind
A63
Newsholme
Eastrington
Gilberdyke
Scalby
Newport
Barmby on the Marsh
Howden
Ellerker
Brantingham
Swanland
Knedlington
M62
Elloughton
Welton
Asselby
Balkholme
Brough
Drax
Boothferry
Kilpin
Broomfleet
Melton
Ferriby
Airmyn
Hook
Skelton
Laxton
A645
Newland
Saltmarshe
Blacktoft
Faxfleet
Goole
Yokefleet
Whitton
Reedness
Humber B
Rawcliffe
Waterways
Winteringham
Read's Island
Barton-u
Humb
Little Reedness
Whitgift
Ousefleet
Julians Bower
Alkborough
Dutch River
Swinefleet
Adlingfleet
West Halton
Fockerby
R Trent
Coleby
The Showground
Garthorpe
B1430
Winterton
Horkstow
M18
Burton upon Stather
Thealby
A1077
Normanby
Normanby Hall
Roxby
B1392
Saxby All Saints
Eastoft
Moorends
Luddington
Flixborough
Humberhead Peatlands
A161
Appleby
Amcotts
Weir Dyke
Flixborough Stather
Low Santon
B1207
Thorne
Crowle
B1216
Ealand
Keadby
Gunness
Crosby
Stainforth & Keadby Canal
SCUNTHORPE
M180
A18
Burringham
A1029
Wressle
B1208
Althorpe
Brumby
Broughton
New R Ancholme
Hatfield Woodhouse
Sandtoft
M181
Derrythorpe
B1450
Ashby
Yaddlethorpe
Bottesford
Westgate
Belt
Beltoft
Carrhouse
East Butterwick
West Butterwick
Scawby
Messingham
Epworth
Sturton
Wroot
A1146
B1204
B1206
B1248
B1398

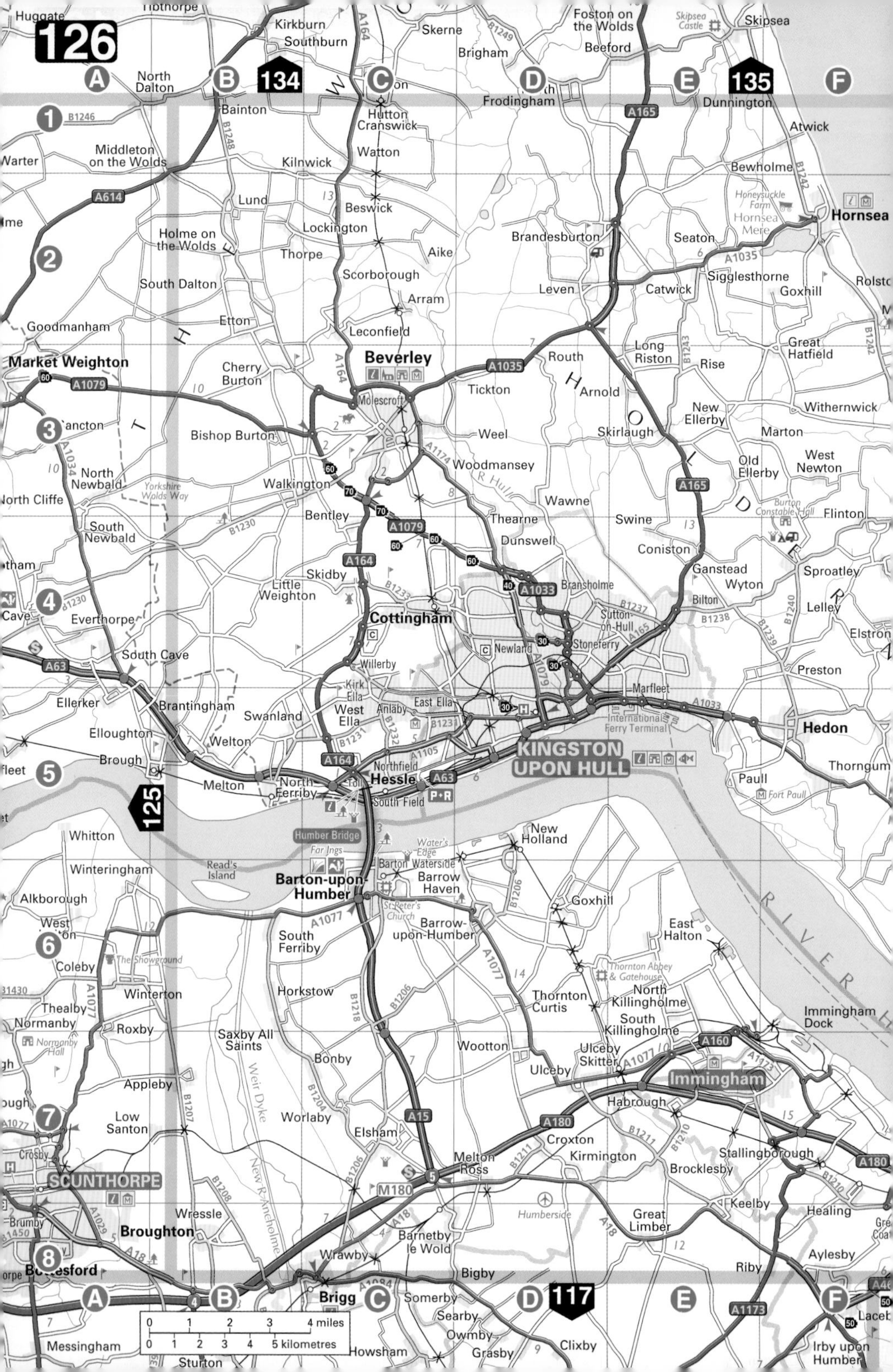
134
135
125
117
A
B
C
D
E
F
1
2
3
4
5
6
7
8
Huggate
Tibthorpe
Kirkburn
Southburn
Skerne
Brigham
Foston on the Wolds
Beeford
Skipsea Castle
Skipsea
North Dalton
Bainton
Hutton Cranswick
Frodingham
Dunnington
Atwick
Warter
Middleton on the Wolds
Kilnwick
Watton
Bewholme
Lund
Beswick
Lockington
Honeysuckle Farm
Hornsea Mere
Hornsea
Holme on the Wolds
Thorpe
Aike
Brandesburton
Seaton
Scorborough
Sigglesthorne
Goxhill
South Dalton
Arram
Leven
Catwick
Goodmanham
Etton
Leconfield
Long Riston
Great Hatfield
Market Weighton
Cherry Burton
Beverley
Routh
Rise
Tickton
Arnold
New Ellerby
Withernwick
Molescroft
Bishop Burton
Weel
Skirlaugh
Marton
West Newton
Woodmansey
Old Ellerby
North Newbald
Walkington
R Hull
Yorkshire Wolds Way
Wawne
North Cliffe
Bentley
Thearne
Swine
Burton Constable Hall
Flinton
South Newbald
Dunswell
Coniston
Skidby
Ganstead
Wyton
Sproatley
Bransholme
Bilton
Little Weighton
Lelley
Cave
Everthorpe
Cottingham
Sutton-on-Hull
Elstronwick
Newland
Stoneferry
South Cave
Willerby
Preston
Ellerker
Brantingham
Kirk Ella
Marfleet
Swanland
West Ella
Anlaby
East Ella
International Ferry Terminal
Hedon
Elloughton
Welton
Brough
Northfield
KINGSTON UPON HULL
Thorngumbald
Melton
North Ferriby
Hessle
South Field
Paull
Fort Paull
Whitton
Humber Bridge
Far Ings
Water's Edge
New Holland
Winteringham
Read's Island
Barton Waterside
Barton-upon-Humber
Barrow Haven
Alkborough
Goxhill
West Halton
St Peter's Church
Barrow-upon-Humber
South Ferriby
East Halton
RIVER HUMBER
Coleby
The Showground
Thornton Abbey & Gatehouse
Winterton
Horkstow
North Killingholme
Thornton Curtis
Thealby
South Killingholme
Immingham Dock
Normanby
Normanby Hall
Roxby
Saxby All Saints
Wootton
Ulceby Skitter
Bonby
Ulceby
Immingham
Appleby
Weir Dyke
Habrough
Low Santon
Worlaby
Elsham
Croxton
Kirmington
Stallingborough
Crosby
Melton Ross
Brocklesby
SCUNTHORPE
New R Ancholme
Humberside
Keelby
Healing
Wressle
Great Limber
Brumby
Broughton
Barnetby le Wold
Aylesby
Wrawby
Bottesford
Bigby
Riby
Brigg
Somerby
Searby
Laceby
Owmby
Messingham
Grasby
Clixby
Howsham
Irby upon Humber
Sturton
0 1 2 3 4 miles
0 1 2 3 4 5 kilometres

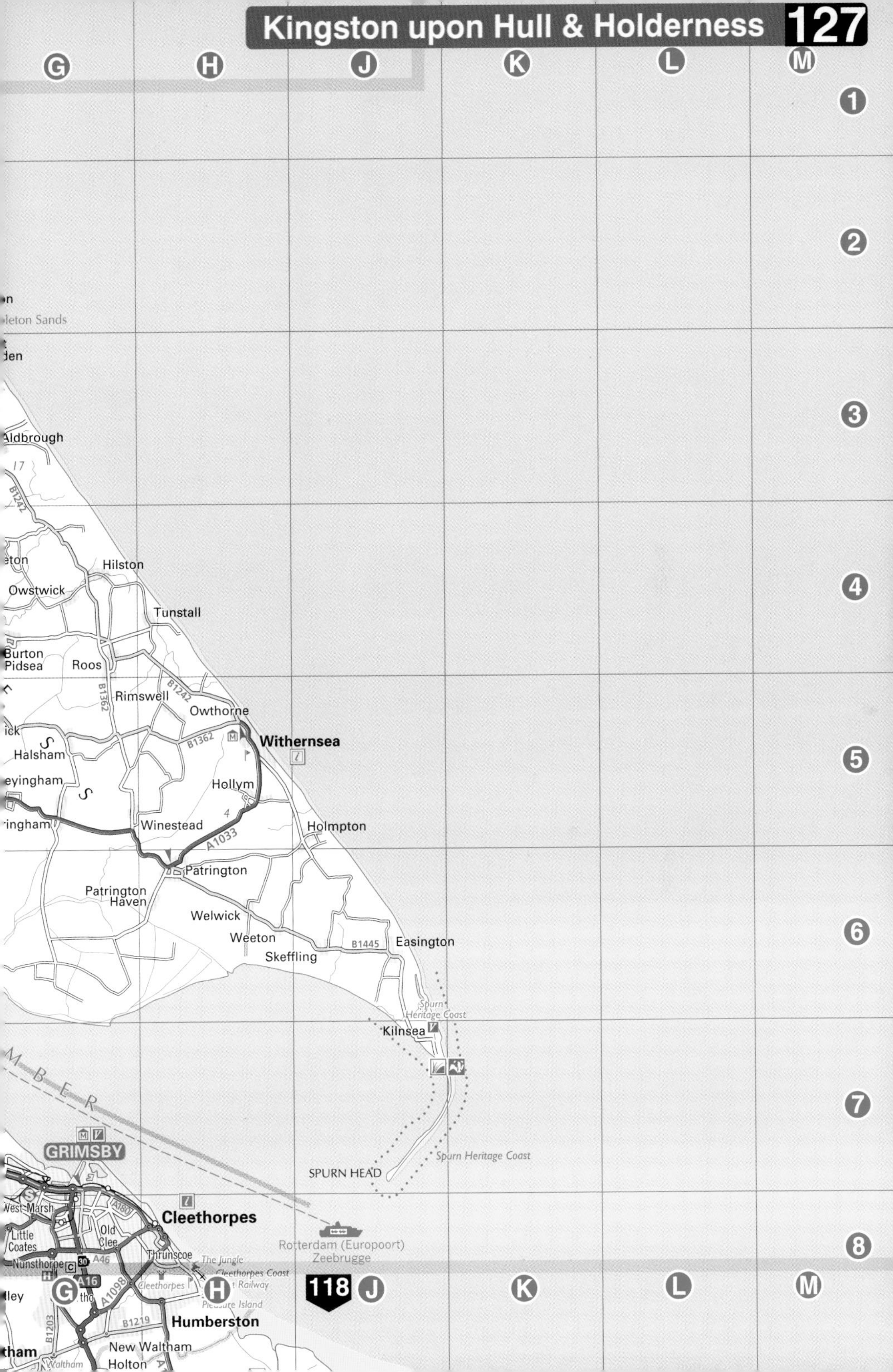
G
H
J
K
L
M
1
2
3
4
5
6
7
8
Aldbrough
B1242
Hilston
Owstwick
Tunstall
Burton Pidsea
Roos
B1362
Rimswell
B1242
Owthorne
B1362
Withernsea
Halsham
Hollym
Winestead
A1033
Holmpton
Patrington
Patrington Haven
Welwick
Weeton
Skeffling
B1445
Easington
Spurn Heritage Coast
Kilnsea
SPURN HEAD
Spurn Heritage Coast
GRIMSBY
A180
Cleethorpes
Old Clee
Little Coates
A46
Thrunscoe
The Jungle
Cleethorpes Coast Railway
Nunsthorpe
A16
A1098
Pleasure Island
B1219
Humberston
B1203
New Waltham
Holton
Waltham
Rotterdam (Europoort)
Zeebrugge

118

Hallsenna Moor
Drigg
Holmrook
Eskdale
652
HARTER FELL
Muncaster Mill
Ravenglass and Eskdale Railway
River Esk
Devoke Water
River Duddon
Seathwaite Tarn
Ravenglass
Roman Bath House
Muncaster
Hall Dunnerdale
Seathwaite
136
A595
137
Waberthwaite
573
WHITFELL
Ulpha
LAKE DISTRICT NATIONAL PARK
Broughton Mills
A593
Hycemoor
Selker Bay
Bootle
Swinside Stone Circle
Broughton-in-Furr
Lady Hall
Foxfield
600
BLACK COMBE
Grizeb
Gutterby Spa
Whitbeck
The Green
A5093
The Hill
Whicham
Silecroft
Kirkby-in-Fu
Beck Sid
Soutergate
Kirksanton
Millom
A595
RSPB
Haverigg
Haverigg Point
Ireleth
Askam in Furness
Penn
Lindal in Furness
South Lakes Safari Zoo
Sandscale Haws
North Walney
Little Urswick
Dalton-in-Furness
Newton
BARROW-IN-FURNESS
Stainton with Ad
Furness Abbey
Bow Bridge
Dendron
Leece
Vickerstown
Barrow Island
A590
A5087
ISLE OF WALNEY
Rampsid
Sheep Island
Piel Castle
Piel Island
Fouln
Piel Bar
Hilpsford Point
South Walney
0 1 2 3 4 miles
0 1 2 3 4 5 kilometres

Hawkshead Hill
Hawkshead
Outgate
Bowness-on-Windermere
Far Sawrey
Near Sawrey
Grizedale
Ings
Garth Row
Burneside
Grayrigg
Kendal
Firbank
Winster
Blackwell
Underbarrow
Crosthwaite
Satterthwaite
Furness Fells
Graythwaite Hall
Thwaite Head
High Nibthwaite
Brigsteer
Oxenholme
New Hutton
Killington Lake (southbound only)
Killington
Middleshaw
Natland
Old Hutton
Row
Stott Park Bobbin Mill
Gummers How
Rusland
Cross
Finsthwaite
Whitbarrow
Sizergh Castle
Oxen Park
Colton
Lowick Green
Fell Foot Park
Staveley
Newby Bridge
Lakeside and Haverthwaite Railway
Lakeland Motor Museum
Levens
Sedgwick
Stainton
Hincaster
Westmorland
Crooklands
Endmoor
Preston Patrick
Old Town
Gawthwaite
Spark Bridge
Bouth
Haverthwaite
Witherslack
Ayside
Levens Hall
Leasgill
Penny Bridge
Greenodd
High Newton
Heversham
Milnthorpe
Nook
Lupton
Arrad Foot
Barrow Monument
Meathop
River Kent
Whasset
Farleton
Kearstwick
Lindale
Brown Robin
Hampsfell
Storth
Beetham
Holme
Holme Park Fell
Priory Gatehouse
Cartmel
Arnside
Hale
Hutton Roof
High Biggins
Park Wood
Grange-over-Sands
Holker
Allithwaite
Arnside Knott
Lakeland Wildlife Oasis
Burton-in-Kendal
Swarthmoor
Cark
Conishead Priory
Whittington
Burton-in-Kendal (northbound only)
Great Urswick
Flookburgh
Silverdale
Yealand Redmayne
Leighton Hall
Bardsea
Priest Hutton
Jack Scout
Yealand Conyers
Humphrey Head
Heald Brow
Warton
Borwick
Arkholme
Baycliff
Old Rectory
Aldingham
MORECAMBE
BAY
Carnforth
Gressingham
Wennington
Over Kellet
Bolton-le-Sands
Hornby
Nether Kellet
Wray
Aughton
Claughton
Farleton
Hest Bank
Slyne
Caton Green
Morecambe
Bare
Halton
Brookhouse
Torrisholme
Caton
River Lune Millennium Park
Skerton
Crossgill
Sandylands
Lancaster
Lower Heysham
Higher Heysham
Heysham
Aldcliffe
Douglas
Scotforth
Ward's Stone
Overton
Jubilee Tower
Ellel
Sunderland
Glasson
River Lune
Galgate
Lancaster Canal
Cockersand
R Wyre
Abbeystead
Dolphinholme
Cockerham
Hawthorn Fell
Knott End-
Pilling
Cockerham Moss
Scorton
Calder Fell
R Roeburn
120
121
130
137
138
M6
A6
A591
A590
A592
A5074
A65
A684
A685
A683
A589
A588
A5105
A5092
A5084
A6070
B5284
B5285
B5278
B5277
B5282
B6254
B6384
B6385
B5273
B5274
B5272
B5281

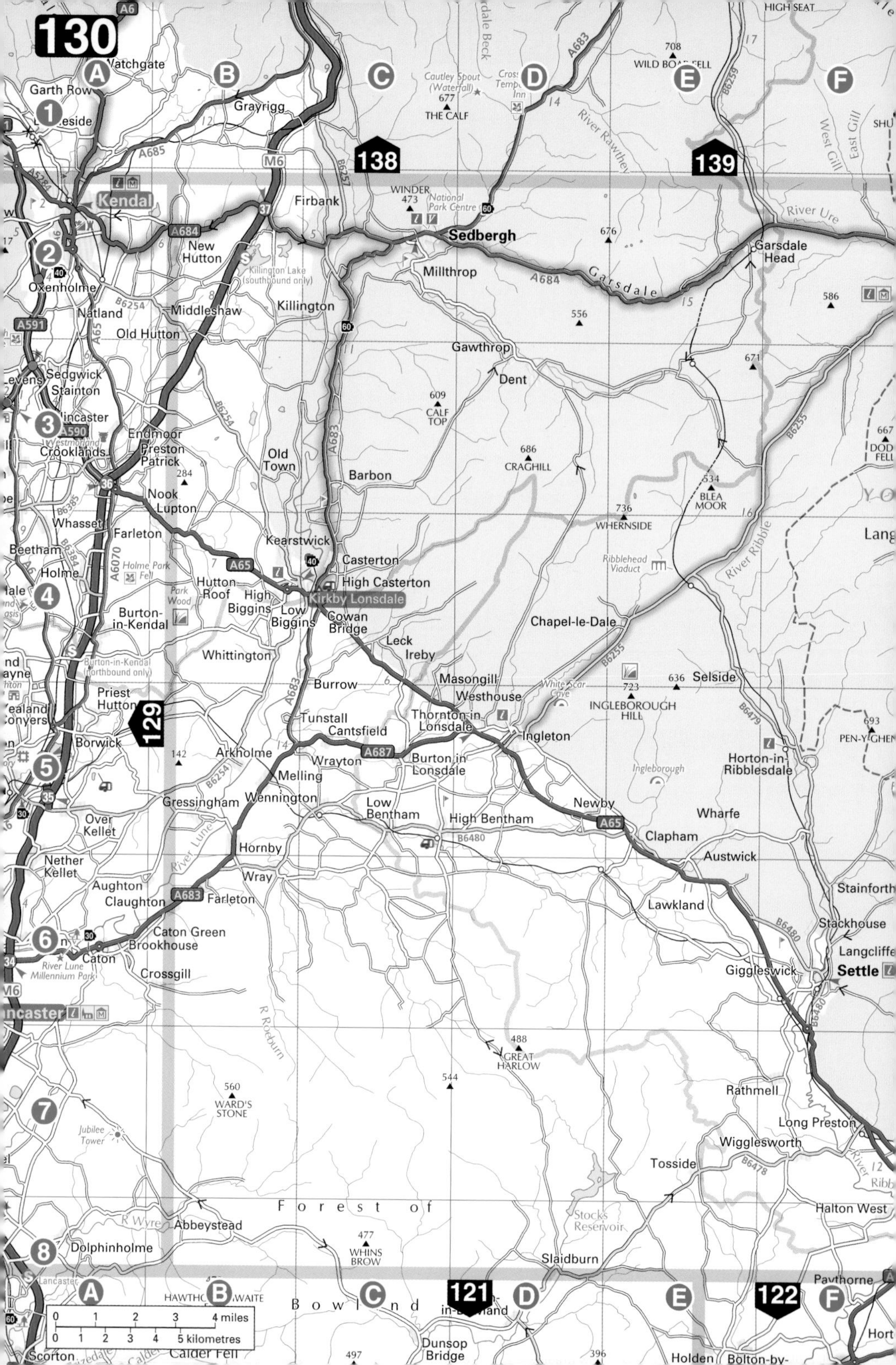

130
A6
Watchgate
Garth Row
Grayrigg
A685
M6
A5284
Kendal
A684
New Hutton
37
Killington Lake (southbound only)
Oxenholme
Natland
B6254
Middleshaw
Old Hutton
A591
A65
Sedgwick
Levens
Stainton
Endmoor
A590
Westmorland
Crooklands
Preston Patrick
284
36
Nook
Lupton
B6385
Whasset
Farleton
Beetham
B6384
Holme
A6070
Holme Park Fell
A65
Hutton Roof
Park Wood
High Biggins
Low Biggins
Burton-in-Kendal
Burton-in-Kendal (northbound only)
Whittington
Priest Hutton
129
Yealand Conyers
Borwick
142
Arkholme
B6254
Gressingham
Over Kellet
Nether Kellet
35
30
Hornby
Wray
River Lune
Aughton
Claughton
A683
Farleton
Caton Green
Brookhouse
Caton
River Lune Millennium Park
Crossgill
M6
34
Lancaster
R Roeburn
560
WARD'S STONE
Jubilee Tower
R Wyre
Abbeystead
Dolphinholme
Forest of
Bowland
477
WHINS BROW
Lancaster
HAWTHORNTHWAITE
Scorton
Calder Fell
0 1 2 3 4 miles
0 1 2 3 4 5 kilometres
121
Dunsop Bridge
497
396
Slaidburn
Stocks Reservoir
Tosside
Holden
Bolton-by-
122
Pavthorne
Halton West
B6478
Wigglesworth
Long Preston
River Ribble
12
Rathmell
488
GREAT HARLOW
544
Giggleswick
Settle
Langcliffe
Stackhouse
B6480
Stainforth
Lawkland
Austwick
Clapham
A65
Newby
Wharfe
Ingleborough
Horton-in-Ribblesdale
693
PEN-Y-GHENT
B6479
Selside
636
723
INGLEBOROUGH HILL
White Scar Cave
Ingleton
Thornton-in-Lonsdale
Westhouse
Masongill
Burton in Lonsdale
A687
Cantsfield
Tunstall
Wrayton
Melling
Wennington
Low Bentham
High Bentham
B6480
Burrow
A683
Leck
Ireby
Cowan Bridge
Kirkby Lonsdale
High Casterton
Casterton
40
Kearstwick
Old Town
Barbon
Chapel-le-Dale
B6255
Ribblehead Viaduct
736
WHERNSIDE
534
BLEA MOOR
River Ribble
686
CRAGHILL
609
CALF TOP
Dent
Gawthrop
556
671
B6255
667
DOD FELL
Lang
586
Garsdale Head
Garsdale
A684
River Ure
676
Sedbergh
Millthrop
Killington
60
A683
Firbank
B6257
WINDER
473
National Park Centre
138
139
677
THE CALF
Cautley Spout (Waterfall)
Cross Keys Temperance Inn
River Rawthey
dale Beck
A683
708
WILD BOAR FELL
B6259
HIGH SEAT
West Gill
East Gill
A B C D E F
1 2 3 4 5 6 7 8

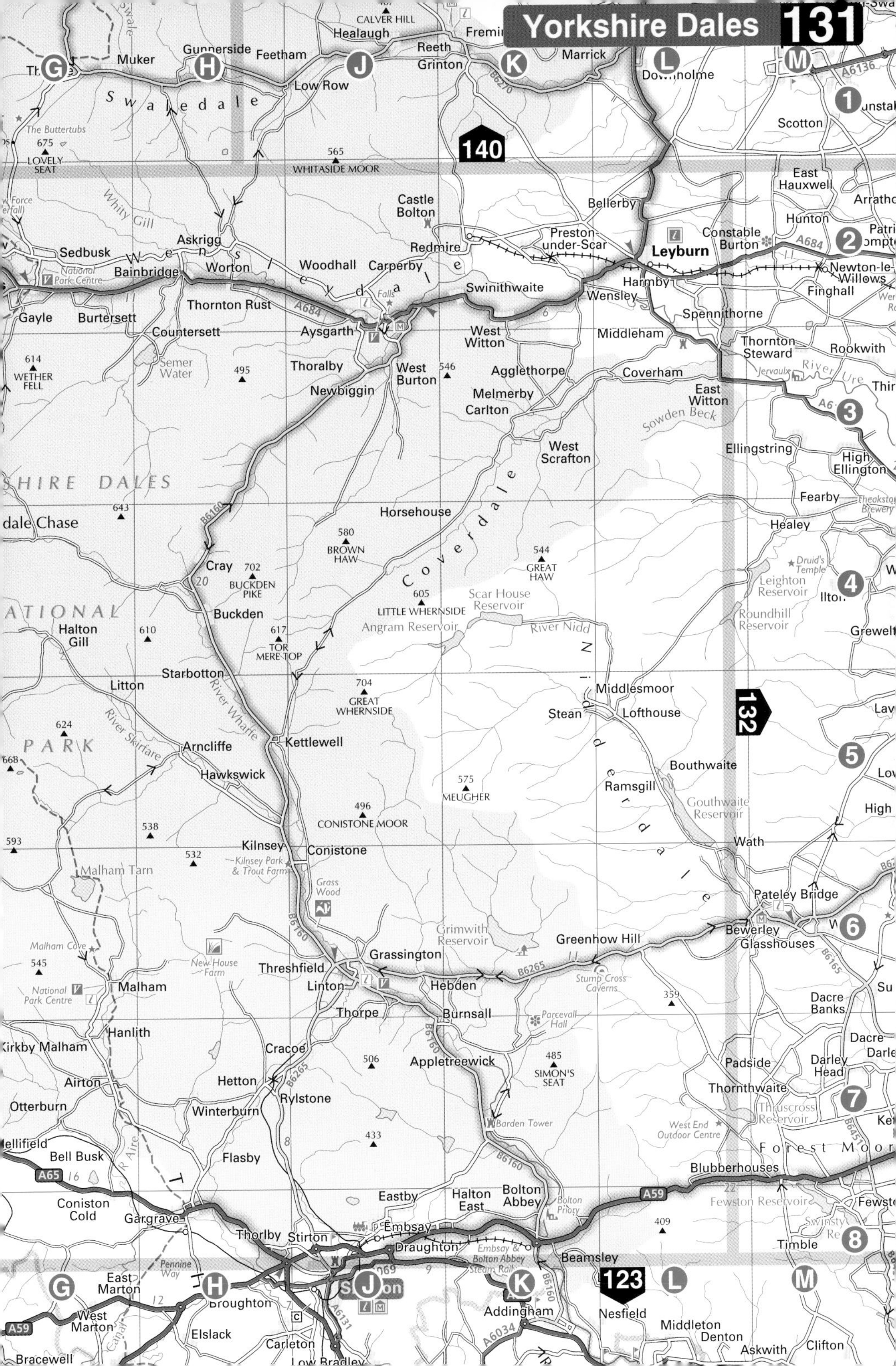

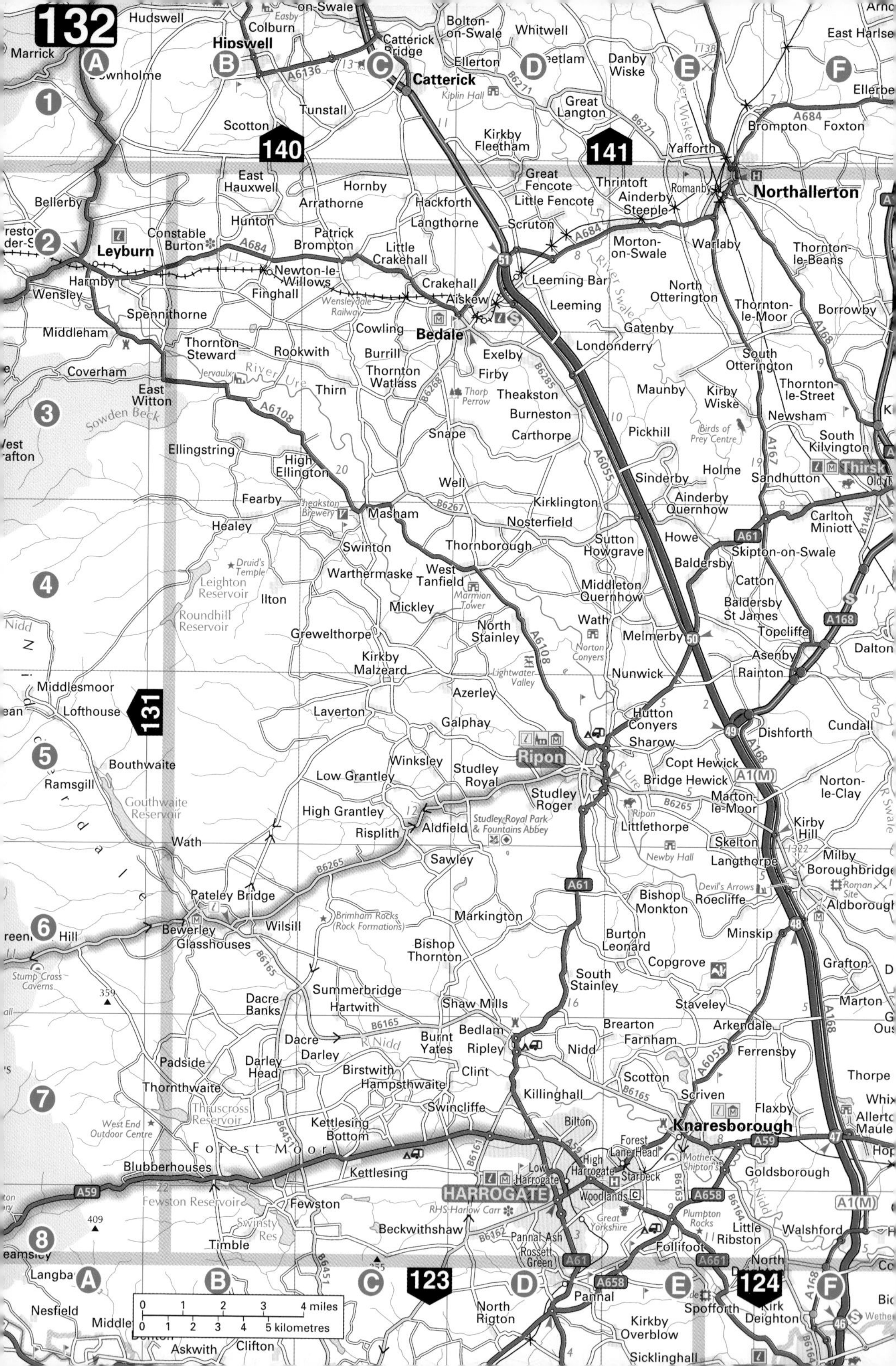

132
Hudswell
Marrick
Hipswell
Colburn
Easby
Richmond-on-Swale
Downholme
Catterick Bridge
Catterick
Bolton-on-Swale
Whitwell
Ellerton
Scorton
Streetlam
Danby Wiske
East Harlsey
Ellerbeck
A6136
B6271
Kiplin Hall
Scotton
Tunstall
Great Langton
Kirkby Fleetham
140
141
Yafforth
Brompton
A684
Foxton
East Hauxwell
Hornby
Great Fencote
Little Fencote
Thrintoft
Ainderby Steeple
Romanby
Northallerton
Bellerby
Hunton
Arrathorne
Hackforth
Langthorne
Scruton
Morton-on-Swale
Warlaby
Thornton-le-Beans
Constable Burton
Leyburn
Patrick Brompton
Little Crakehall
Harmby
Wensley
Newton-le-Willows
Finghall
Crakehall
Aiskew
Leeming Bar
Leeming
North Otterington
Thornton-le-Moor
Borrowby
River Swale
Wensleydale Railway
Spennithorne
Middleham
Cowling
Bedale
Gatenby
Londonderry
Thornton Steward
Rookwith
Burrill
Exelby
Firby
B6285
Coverham
Jervaulx
River Ure
Thornton Watlass
Thirn
South Otterington
Thornton-le-Street
East Witton
B6268
Thorp Perrow
Theakston
Maunby
Kirby Wiske
Newsham
Sowden Beck
A6108
Burneston
Snape
Carthorpe
Pickhill
Birds of Prey Centre
South Kilvington
West Scrafton
Ellingstring
A6055
A167
Thirsk
High Ellington
Sinderby
Holme
Sandhutton
Well
Ainderby Quernhow
Fearby
Theakston Brewery
Masham
B6267
Kirklington
Carlton Miniott
Healey
Nosterfield
Swinton
Thornborough
Sutton Howgrave
Howe
A61
Skipton-on-Swale
B1448
Druid's Temple
Warthermaske
West Tanfield
Baldersby
Catton
Leighton Reservoir
Ilton
Marmion Tower
Middleton Quernhow
Baldersby St James
Mickley
Roundhill Reservoir
Wath
Topcliffe
A168
North Stainley
Melmerby
Nidd
Grewelthorpe
Norton Conyers
Asenby
Dalton
Kirkby Malzeard
Lightwater Valley
Nunwick
Rainton
Middlesmoor
Azerley
Lofthouse
131
Laverton
Galphay
Hutton Conyers
Dishforth
Cundall
Sharow
Ripon
Winksley
Studley Royal
Copt Hewick
Bridge Hewick
Norton-le-Clay
Nidderdale
Bouthwaite
Low Grantley
R Ure
A1(M)
Ramsgill
Studley Roger
B6265
Marton-le-Moor
R Swale
Gouthwaite Reservoir
High Grantley
Studley Royal Park & Fountains Abbey
Kirby Hill
Aldfield
Littlethorpe
Risplith
Wath
Skelton
Sawley
Newby Hall
Langthorpe
Milby
Boroughbridge
Roman Site
Pateley Bridge
Devil's Arrows
Bishop Monkton
Roecliffe
Brimham Rocks (Rock Formations)
Markington
Aldborough
Bewerley
Greenhow Hill
Wilsill
Glasshouses
Burton Leonard
Minskip
Bishop Thornton
Copgrove
Grafton
Stump Cross Caverns
B6165
South Stainley
Marton
359
Summerbridge
Dacre Banks
Hartwith
Shaw Mills
Staveley
Bedlam
Brearton
Arkendale
Dacre
Burnt Yates
R Nidd
Farnham
Ripley
Nidd
Ferrensby
Darley
Darley Head
Padside
Birstwith
Clint
Hampsthwaite
Scotton
Thorpe
Thornthwaite
Killinghall
Scriven
Flaxby
Whixley
Thruscross Reservoir
Swincliffe
Bilton
Knaresborough
Allerton Mauleverer
West End Outdoor Centre
Kettlesing Bottom
A59
Forest Moor
Forest Lane Head
Hopperton
Blubberhouses
Kettlesing
Low Harrogate
High Harrogate
Starbeck
Mother Shipton's
Goldsborough
B6161
B6451
HARROGATE
Woodlands
A658
Fewston Reservoir
Fewston
RHS Harlow Carr
Great Yorkshire
Plumpton Rocks
B6163
B6164
R Nidd
Little Ribston
Walshford
409
Swinsty Res
Beckwithshaw
B6162
Pannal Ash
Follifoot
Timble
Rossett Green
A661
North Deighton
Weeton
Langbar
355
123
Pannal
Spofforth
124
Nesfield
Middleton
North Rigton
Kirkby Overblow
Kirk Deighton
Wetherby
Askwith
Clifton
Sicklinghall
0 1 2 3 4 miles
0 1 2 3 4 5 kilometres

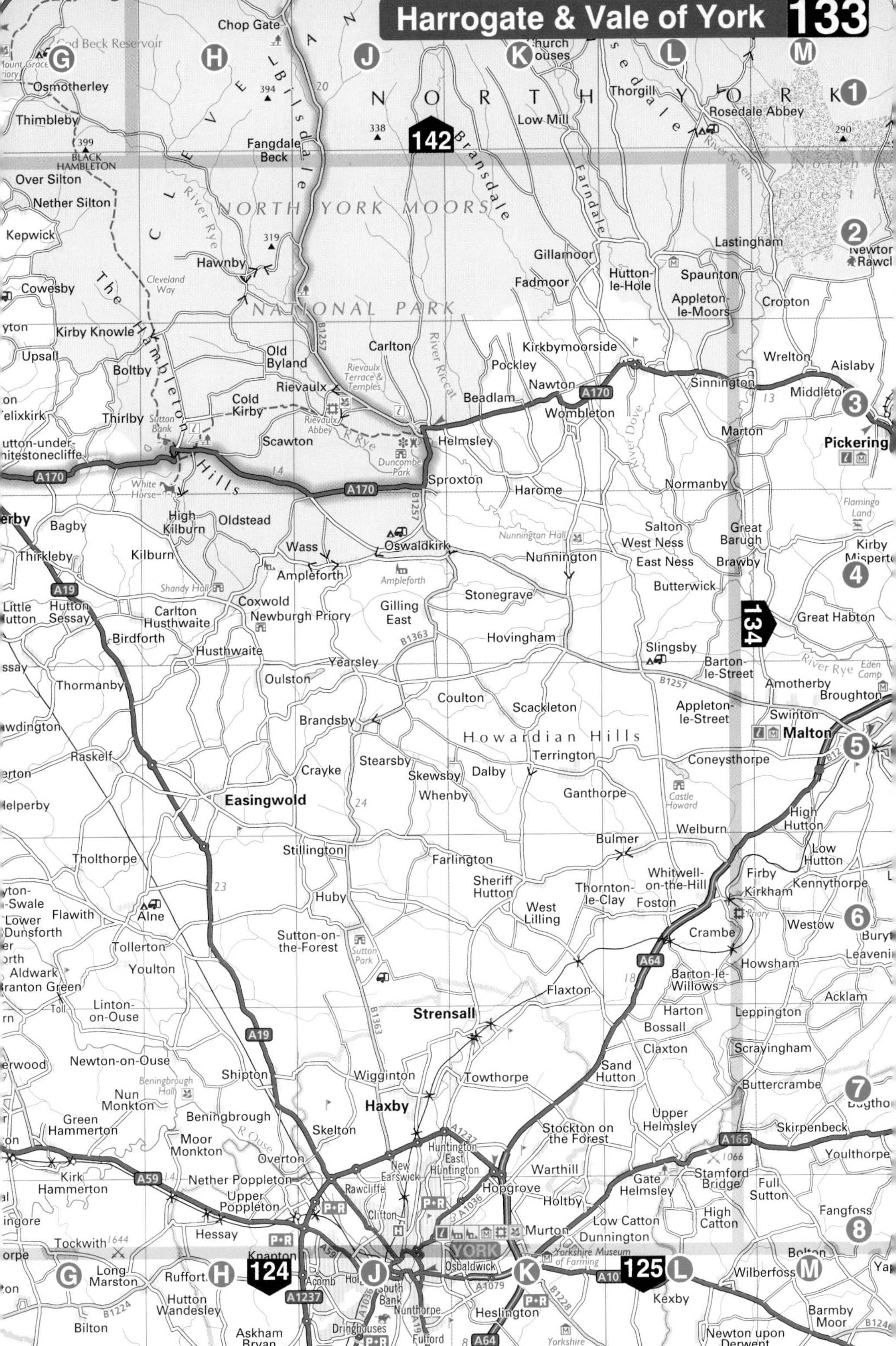
Chop Gate
Cod Beck Reservoir
Mount Grace Priory
Osmotherley
Thimbleby
BLACK HAMBLETON
Over Silton
Nether Silton
Kepwick
Cowesby
Kirby Knowle
Upsall
Boltby
Felixkirk
Thirlby
Sutton-under-Whitestonecliffe
Church Houses
Thorgill
Rosedale Abbey
Low Mill
Fangdale Beck
NORTH YORKSHIRE
NORTH YORK MOORS
NATIONAL PARK
CLEVELAND
Bilsdale
Bransdale
Farndale
Rosedale
River Seven
River Rye
North Yorkshire Forest Park
Lastingham
Newton Rawcliffe
Gillamoor
Hutton-le-Hole
Spaunton
Fadmoor
Appleton-le-Moors
Cropton
Hawnby
Cleveland Way
The Hambleton Hills
Kirkbymoorside
Pockley
Carlton
Old Byland
Rievaulx
Rievaulx Terrace & Temples
Rievaulx Abbey
Cold Kirby
Sutton Bank
Scawton
Beadlam
Nawton
Wombleton
Helmsley
Duncombe Park
River Riccal
River Dove
Sinnington
Wrelton
Aislaby
Middleton
Marton
Pickering
White Horse
Sproxton
Harome
Normanby
Flamingo Land
High Kilburn
Oldstead
Bagby
Thirkleby
Kilburn
Wass
Oswaldkirk
Ampleforth
Shandy Hall
Nunnington Hall
Nunnington
Salton
West Ness
East Ness
Great Barugh
Brawby
Kirby Misperton
Butterwick
Stonegrave
Little Hutton
Hutton Sessay
Carlton Husthwaite
Coxwold
Newburgh Priory
Gilling East
Great Habton
Birdforth
Husthwaite
Hovingham
Slingsby
Barton-le-Street
River Rye
Eden Camp
Yearsley
Oulston
Thormanby
Amotherby
Broughton
Coulton
Scackleton
Appleton-le-Street
Swinton
Malton
Brandsby
Howardian Hills
Raskelf
Crayke
Stearsby
Skewsby
Dalby
Terrington
Coneysthorpe
Whenby
Easingwold
Ganthorpe
Castle Howard
Helperby
High Hutton
Welburn
Bulmer
Stillington
Farlington
Low Hutton
Tholthorpe
Firby
Kirkham
Kennythorpe
Priory
Sheriff Hutton
Thornton-le-Clay
Whitwell-on-the-Hill
Foston
Huby
West Lilling
Flawith
Alne
Lower Dunsforth
Westow
Crambe
Sutton-on-the-Forest
Sutton Park
Tollerton
Howsham
Youlton
Aldwark
Barton-le-Willows
Leavening
Flaxton
Acklam
Linton-on-Ouse
Toll
Strensall
Harton
Leppington
Bossall
Claxton
Scrayingham
Newton-on-Ouse
Beningbrough Hall
Shipton
Wigginton
Towthorpe
Sand Hutton
Buttercrambe
Nun Monkton
Haxby
Green Hammerton
Beningbrough
Upper Helmsley
Skelton
Stockton on the Forest
Skirpenbeck
Moor Monkton
R Ouse
Huntington
East Huntington
Overton
New Earswick
Warthill
Gate Helmsley
Stamford Bridge
1066
Youlthorpe
Kirk Hammerton
Nether Poppleton
Upper Poppleton
Rawcliffe
Hopgrove
Holtby
Full Sutton
Clifton
Murton
Low Catton
High Catton
Fangfoss
Hessay
Dunnington
Tockwith
1644
YORK
Yorkshire Museum of Farming
Bolton
Knapton
Acomb
Osbaldwick
Wilberfoss
Long Marston
Rufforth
South Bank
Kexby
Hutton Wandesley
Nunthorpe
Heslington
Barmby Moor
Bilton
Dringhouses
Askham Bryan
Fulford
Yorkshire Air Museum
Newton upon Derwent
A170
A19
A64
A59
A1237
A1036
A1079
A166
B1257
B1363
B1224
B1228
142
134
124
125
P+R

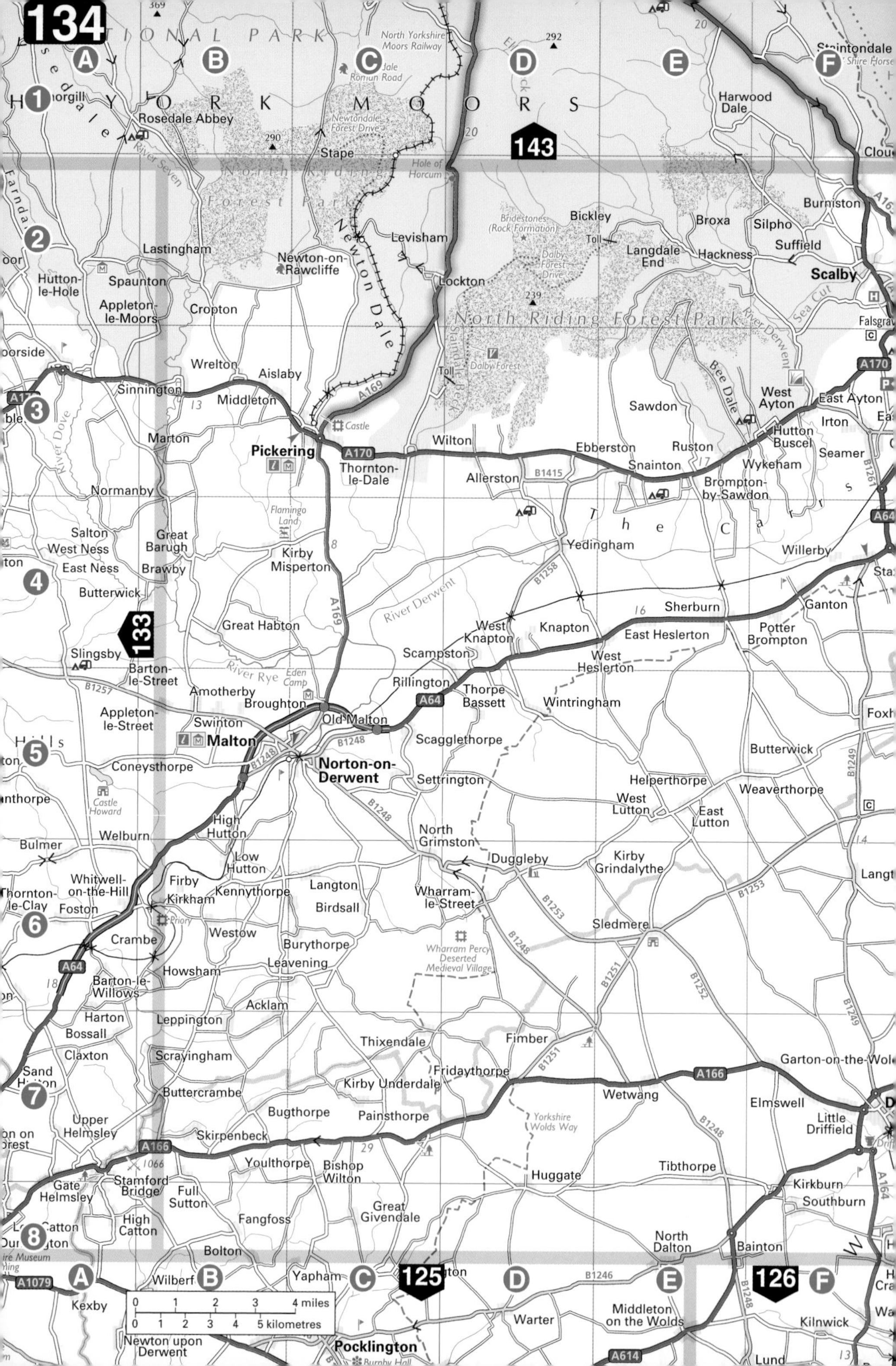

A
B
C
D
E
F
1
2
3
4
5
6
7
8
369
292
NORTH YORK MOORS NATIONAL PARK
North Yorkshire Moors Railway
Roman Road
Staintondale
Shire Horse
Harwood Dale
Rosedale Abbey
Rosedale
River Seven
Newtondale Forest Drive
290
Stape
143
Cloughton
Hole of Horcum
North Riding Forest Park
Farndale
Burniston
Bridestones (Rock Formation)
Bickley
Broxa
Silpho
Suffield
Toll
Levisham
Newton-on-Rawcliffe
Lastingham
Langdale End
Hackness
Scalby
Hutton-le-Hole
Spaunton
Newton Dale
Lockton
Dalby Forest Drive
239
Appleton-le-Moors
Cropton
Sea Cut
Falsgrave
River Derwent
Staindale Beck
Dalby Forest
A170
Wrelton
Aislaby
Bee Dale
Sinnington
Middleton
A169
Sawdon
West Ayton
East Ayton
River Dove
Castle
Hutton Buscel
Irton
Marton
Pickering
Wilton
Ebberston
Ruston
Seamer
Thornton-le-Dale
Allerston
B1415
Snainton
Wykeham
Brompton-by-Sawdon
B1261
Normanby
Flamingo Land
The Carrs
A64
Salton
Great Barugh
West Ness
East Ness
Brawby
Kirby Misperton
Yedingham
Willerby
B1258
Butterwick
River Derwent
Sherburn
Ganton
133
Great Habton
West Knapton
Knapton
East Heslerton
Potter Brompton
Slingsby
Scampston
West Heslerton
Barton-le-Street
River Rye
Eden Camp
Rillington
Thorpe Bassett
B1257
Amotherby
Broughton
Wintringham
Appleton-le-Street
Swinton
Old Malton
Foxholes
Hills
Malton
B1248
Scagglethorpe
Butterwick
Coneysthorpe
Norton-on-Derwent
Settrington
Helperthorpe
B1249
Ganthorpe
Castle Howard
West Lutton
Weaverthorpe
East Lutton
High Hutton
North Grimston
Welburn
Bulmer
Low Hutton
Duggleby
Kirby Grindalythe
Whitwell-on-the-Hill
Firby
Langtoft
Kirkham
Langton
Wharram-le-Street
Thornton-le-Clay
Foston
Kennythorpe
Birdsall
B1253
Priory
Sledmere
Westow
Crambe
Wharram Percy Deserted Medieval Village
Burythorpe
Leavening
B1251
B1252
Howsham
Barton-le-Willows
Acklam
Harton
Leppington
Bossall
Thixendale
Fimber
Claxton
Scrayingham
Fridaythorpe
Garton-on-the-Wolds
Sand Hutton
A166
Kirby Underdale
Buttercrambe
Wetwang
Elmswell
Bugthorpe
Painsthorpe
Yorkshire Wolds Way
Upper Helmsley
Little Driffield
Skirpenbeck
1066
Youlthorpe
Bishop Wilton
Huggate
Tibthorpe
Stamford Bridge
Gate Helmsley
Full Sutton
Kirkburn
Southburn
A164
High Catton
Fangfoss
Great Givendale
Low Catton
Dunnington
North Dalton
Bainton
Bolton
Yorkshire Museum of Farming
A1079
Wilberfoss
Yapham
125
B1246
126
Kexby
Middleton on the Wolds
Warter
Kilnwick
0 1 2 3 4 miles
0 1 2 3 4 5 kilometres
Newton upon Derwent
Pocklington
Burnby Hall
A614
Lund

G
H
J
K
L
M
1
2
3
4
5
6
7
8
Cloughton Wyke
Cromer Point
Cleveland Way
Castle
Scarborough
Oliver's Mount
A165
P+R
Osgodby
Cayton Bay
B1261
Cayton
The Wyke
Lebberston
Gristhorpe
A1039
Filey Brigg
Filey
R Hertford
Folkton
A1039
Muston
Flixton
Filey Bay
Hunmanby
Fordon
Reighton
Speeton
Flamborough Head Heritage Coast
Bempton Cliffs
RSPB
B1229
Thornwick Bay
Wold Newton
Buckton
Bempton
Burton Fleming
North Landing
B1229
Selwicks Bay
Grindale
A165
B1259
FLAMBOROUGH HEAD
Lighthouse
Thwing
B1255
Flamborough
Sewerby
Bondville Miniature Village
B1253
Boynton
Rudston
Monolith
Bridlington
BRIDLINGTON BAY
Bessingby
Hilderthorpe
Carnaby
Haisthorpe
Thornholme
Kilham
Burton Agnes
Norman Manor House
A165
Ruston Parva
Harpham
Lowthorpe
A614
Fraisthorpe
Nafferton
Gransmoor
Barmston
Great Kelk
Lissett
B1242
Wansford
Gembling
Ulrome
R Hull
Foston on the Wolds
Skipsea Castle
Skipsea
Skerne
B1249
Beeford
Brigham
North Frodingham
Dunnington
A165
126
Atwick
Bewholme
B1242

A
B
C
D
E
F
1
2
3
4
5
6
7
8
147
128
Crosscanonby
Crosby
Maryport
Gilcrux
Dearham
Tallentire
Bridekirk
Flimby
Broughton Moor
Standingstone
Dovenby
Great Broughton
Camerton
Papcastle
Seaton
Great Clifton
Brigham
Greysouthen
Stainburn
Little Clifton
Eaglesfield
Workington
Mossbay
Moss Bay
Westfield
Salterbeck
Deanscales
Harrington
Branthwaite
Dean
Ullock
Pardshaw
Distington
Common End
Gilgarran
Mockerkin
Lowca
Howgate
Low Moresby
Parton
Loweswater
Lamplugh
Asby
Arlecdon
Kirkland
Rowrah
Whitehaven
Hensingham
Frizington
High Leys
Saltom Bay
Sandwith
Mirehouse
Cleator Moor
Ennerdale Bridge
Ennerdale Water
Rottington
Cleator
St Bees Head
St Bees Head Heritage Coast
Bigrigg
St Bees
Egremont
LANK RIGG
533
572
615
Thornhill
Haile
Nethertown
Beckermet
Calder Bridge
Wellington
Sellafield Station
Gosforth
Seascale
Hallsenna Moor
Drigg
Holmrook
Santon Bridge
Muncaster Mill
Ravenglass
Roman Bath House
Muncaster
Waberthwaite
Hycemoor
Selker Bay
Bootle
River Ellen
River Ehen
River Calder
Worm Gill
River Bleng
River Esk
R Keekle
R Ehen
A594
A595
A66
A596
A597
A5086
B5306
B5295
B5294
B5345
B5343
0 1 2 3 4 miles
0 1 2 3 4 5 kilometres

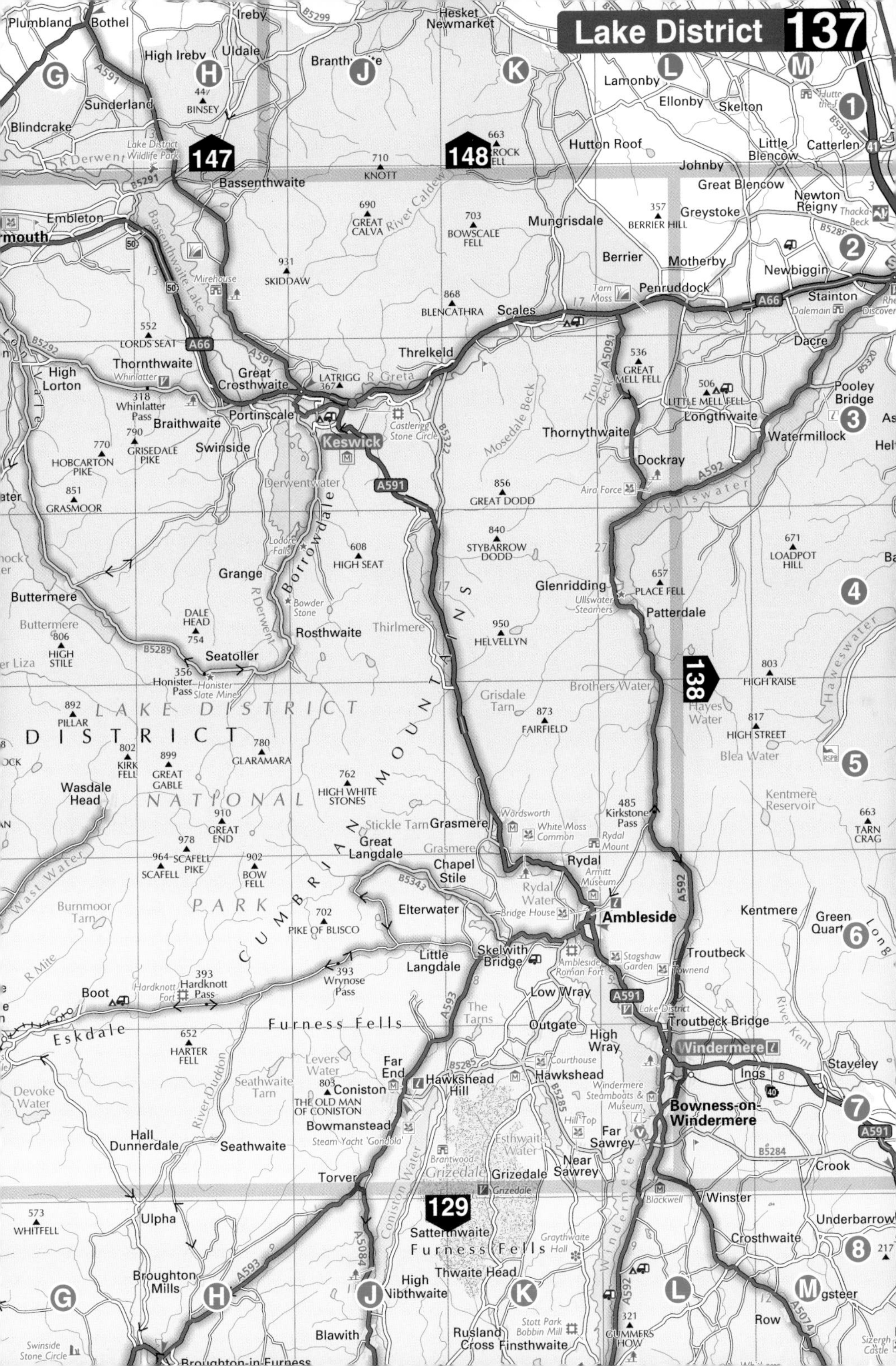
Plumbland
Bothel
Ireby
B5299
Hesket Newmarket
High Ireby
Uldale
Branthwaite
Lamonby
Ellonby
Skelton
Sunderland
447 BINSEY
Blindcrake
Lake District Wildlife Park
147
148
663
Hutton Roof
Little Blencow
Catterlen
R Derwent
710 KNOTT
Johnby
B5291
Bassenthwaite
Great Blencow
Newton Reigny
Embleton
690 GREAT CALVA
River Caldew
703 BOWSCALE FELL
Mungrisdale
357 BERRIER HILL
Greystoke
Thacka Beck
B5288
Bassenthwaite Lake
931 SKIDDAW
Berrier
Motherby
Newbiggin
Mirehouse
Tarn Moss
Penruddock
868 BLENCATHRA
Scales
A66
Stainton
Dalemain
552 LORDS SEAT
B5292
A591
Threlkeld
A5091
536 GREAT MELL FELL
Dacre
High Lorton
Thornthwaite
Whinlatter
Great Crosthwaite
LATRIGG 367
R Greta
B5320
318 Whinlatter Pass
Portinscale
506 LITTLE MELL FELL
Pooley Bridge
Braithwaite
Keswick
Castlerigg Stone Circle
Trout Beck
Longthwaite
790 GRISEDALE PIKE
770 HOBCARTON PIKE
Swinside
B5322
Mosedale Beck
Thornythwaite
Watermillock
Dockray
A592
Derwentwater
Aira Force
Ullswater
851 GRASMOOR
856 GREAT DODD
840 STYBARROW DODD
671 LOADPOT HILL
Lodore Falls
Borrowdale
608 HIGH SEAT
Grange
657 PLACE FELL
Glenridding
Ullswater Steamers
Patterdale
Buttermere
Bowder Stone
DALE HEAD 754
R Derwent
Rosthwaite
Thirlmere
950 HELVELLYN
Haweswater
806 HIGH STILE
B5289
Seatoller
356 Honister Pass
Honister Slate Mine
138
803 HIGH RAISE
Brothers Water
892 PILLAR
LAKE DISTRICT
Grisdale Tarn
873 FAIRFIELD
Hayes Water
817 HIGH STREET
DISTRICT
780 GLARAMARA
802 KIRK FELL
899 GREAT GABLE
Blea Water
Wasdale Head
NATIONAL
762 HIGH WHITE STONES
CUMBRIAN MOUNTAINS
485 Kirkstone Pass
Kentmere Reservoir
663 TARN CRAG
910 GREAT END
Stickle Tarn
Grasmere
Wordsworth
White Moss Common
Rydal Mount
978 SCAFELL PIKE
964 SCAFELL
902 BOW FELL
Great Langdale
Chapel Stile
Rydal
Armitt Museum
Wast Water
B5343
Rydal Water
Burnmoor Tarn
PARK
702 PIKE OF BLISCO
Elterwater
Bridge House
Ambleside
Kentmere
Green Quarter
R Mite
Little Langdale
Skelwith Bridge
Ambleside Roman Fort
Stagshaw Garden
Townend
Troutbeck
393 Hardknott Pass
Hardknott Fort
393 Wrynose Pass
Boot
A593
Low Wray
A591
Lake District
River Kent
The Tarns
Eskdale
Furness Fells
Outgate
High Wray
Troutbeck Bridge
652 HARTER FELL
Levers Water
Far End
B5285
Courthouse
Windermere
Staveley
Ings
Devoke Water
Seathwaite Tarn
803 THE OLD MAN OF CONISTON
Coniston
Hawkshead Hill
Hawkshead
Windermere Steamboats & Museum
Bowness-on-Windermere
River Duddon
Bowmanstead
Steam Yacht 'Gondola'
Hill Top
Far Sawrey
Hall Dunnerdale
Seathwaite
Brantwood
Esthwaite Water
Near Sawrey
B5284
Crook
Torver
Grizedale
Coniston Water
129
Blackwell
Winster
573 WHITFELL
Ulpha
A5084
Satterthwaite
Underbarrow
Furness Fells
Graythwaite Hall
Crosthwaite
Broughton Mills
A593
High Nibthwaite
Thwaite Head
A592
Windermere
321 GUMMERS HOW
Row
A5074
Blawith
Rusland
Stott Park Bobbin Mill
Cross Finsthwaite
Swinside Stone Circle
Broughton-in-Furness
Sizergh Castle

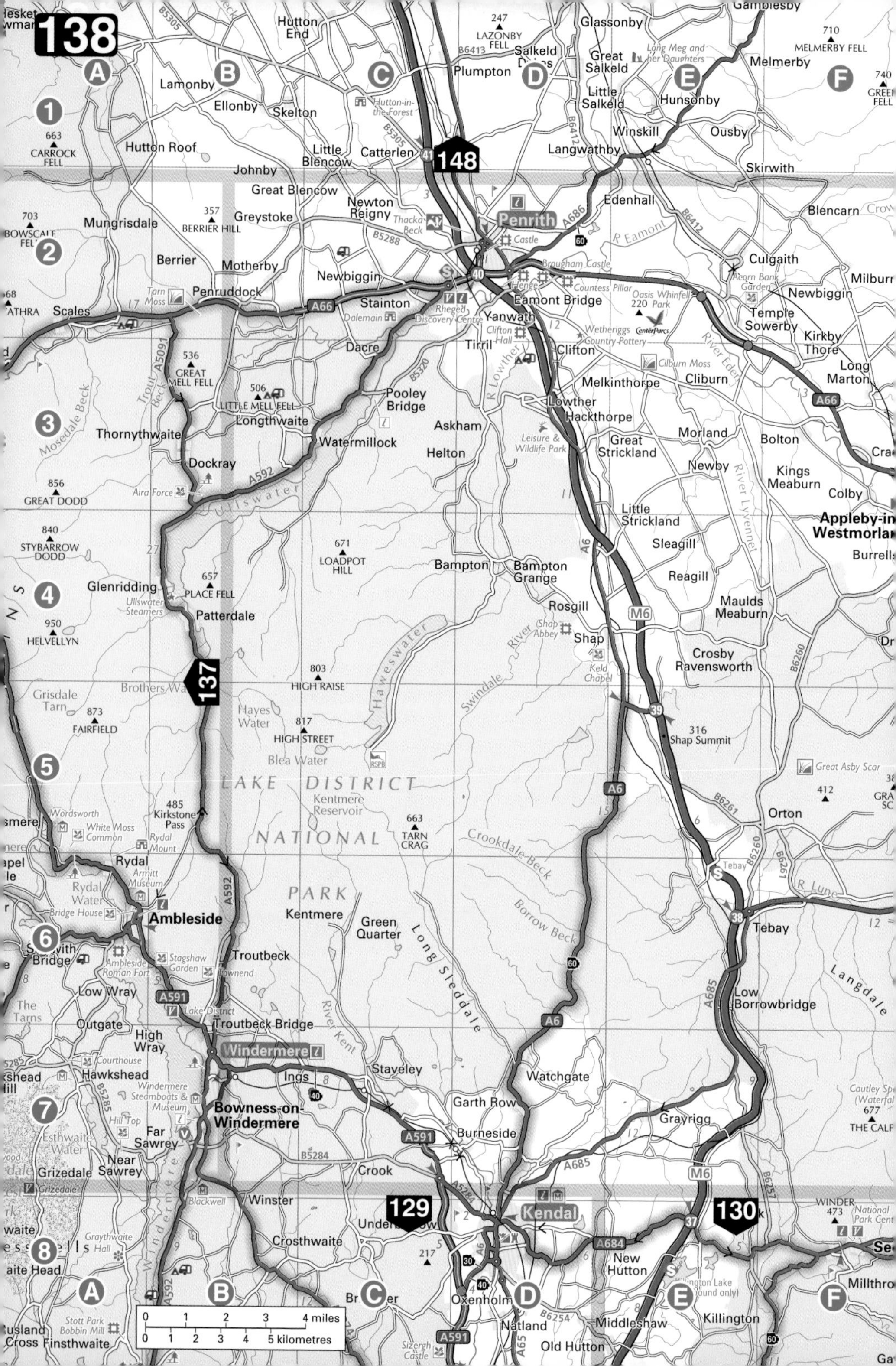
138
Hutton End
247 LAZONBY FELL
Glassonby
Gamblesby
710 MELMERBY FELL
Melmerby
Salkeld Dykes
Long Meg and her Daughters
Great Salkeld
Little Salkeld
Plumpton
Lamonby
Ellonby
Skelton
Hutton-in-the-Forest
Hunsonby
Winskill
Ousby
740 GREEN FELL
663 CARROCK FELL
Hutton Roof
Little Blencow
Catterlen
148
Langwathby
Skirwith
Johnby
Great Blencow
Newton Reigny
Edenhall
703 BOWSCALE FELL
Mungrisdale
357 BERRIER HILL
Greystoke
Thacka Beck
Penrith
Castle
R Eamont
Blencarn
Berrier
Motherby
Newbiggin
B5288
Brougham Castle
Culgaith
Acorn Bank Garden
Milburn
Newbiggin
Tarn Moss
Penruddock
Stainton
Henge
Countess Pillar
Eamont Bridge
Oasis Whinfell Park
220
CenterParcs
Temple Sowerby
ATHRA
Scales
A66
Dalemain
Rheged Discovery Centre
Yanwath
Clifton Hall
Tirril
Wetheriggs Country Pottery
Clifton
Cilburn Moss
River Eden
Kirkby Thore
Long Marton
536 GREAT MELL FELL
A5091
Trout Beck
Dacre
Pooley Bridge
B5320
R Lowther
Melkinthorpe
Cliburn
506 LITTLE MELL FELL
Longthwaite
Lowther
Hackthorpe
Mosedale Beck
Thornythwaite
Watermillock
Askham
Helton
Leisure & Wildlife Park
Great Strickland
Morland
Bolton
Dockray
A592
Newby
Kings Meaburn
Colby
856 GREAT DODD
Aira Force
Ullswater
River Lyvennet
Little Strickland
Appleby-in-Westmorland
840 STYBARROW DODD
671 LOADPOT HILL
Sleagill
Burrells
Bampton
Bampton Grange
Reagill
Glenridding
657 PLACE FELL
Ullswater Steamers
Patterdale
Rosgill
M6
Maulds Meaburn
950 HELVELLYN
Haweswater
Shap Abbey
Shap
Swindale River
Crosby Ravensworth
B6260
137
803 HIGH RAISE
Keld Chapel
Brothers Water
Grisdale Tarn
873 FAIRFIELD
Hayes Water
817 HIGH STREET
39
316 Shap Summit
Blea Water
RSPB
Great Asby Scar
LAKE DISTRICT NATIONAL PARK
Kentmere Reservoir
A6
412
Orton
485 Kirkstone Pass
B6261
Wordsworth
White Moss Common
Rydal Mount
663 TARN CRAG
Crookdale Beck
Tebay
Rydal
Rydal Water
Armitt Museum
Ambleside
R Lune
Bridge House
Kentmere
Green Quarter
Borrow Beck
38
Tebay
Skelwith Bridge
Ambleside Roman Fort
Stagshaw Garden
Townend
Troutbeck
Long Sleddale
Langdale
Low Wray
A591
A685
Low Borrowbridge
The Tarns
Outgate
Lake District
Troutbeck Bridge
River Kent
High Wray
Windermere
Courthouse
Hawkshead
Ings
Staveley
Watchgate
Cautley Spout (Waterfall)
Windermere Steamboats & Museum
B5285
Hill Top
Bowness-on-Windermere
Garth Row
677 THE CALF
Esthwaite Water
Far Sawrey
Burneside
Grayrigg
Near Sawrey
B5284
Crook
A685
M6
Grizedale
Grizedale
A5284
B6257
Blackwell
Winster
129
Kendal
130
WINDER 473
National Park Centre
Graythwaite Hall
Crosthwaite
Underbarrow
A684
37
New Hutton
217
Killington Lake (southbound only)
8
Oxenholme
Killington
Millthrop
Stott Park Bobbin Mill
B6254
Middleshaw
Rusland
Finsthwaite
Natland
A65
Old Hutton
A591
Sizergh Castle
0 1 2 3 4 miles
0 1 2 3 4 5 kilometres
A B C D E F
1 2 3 4 5 6 7 8

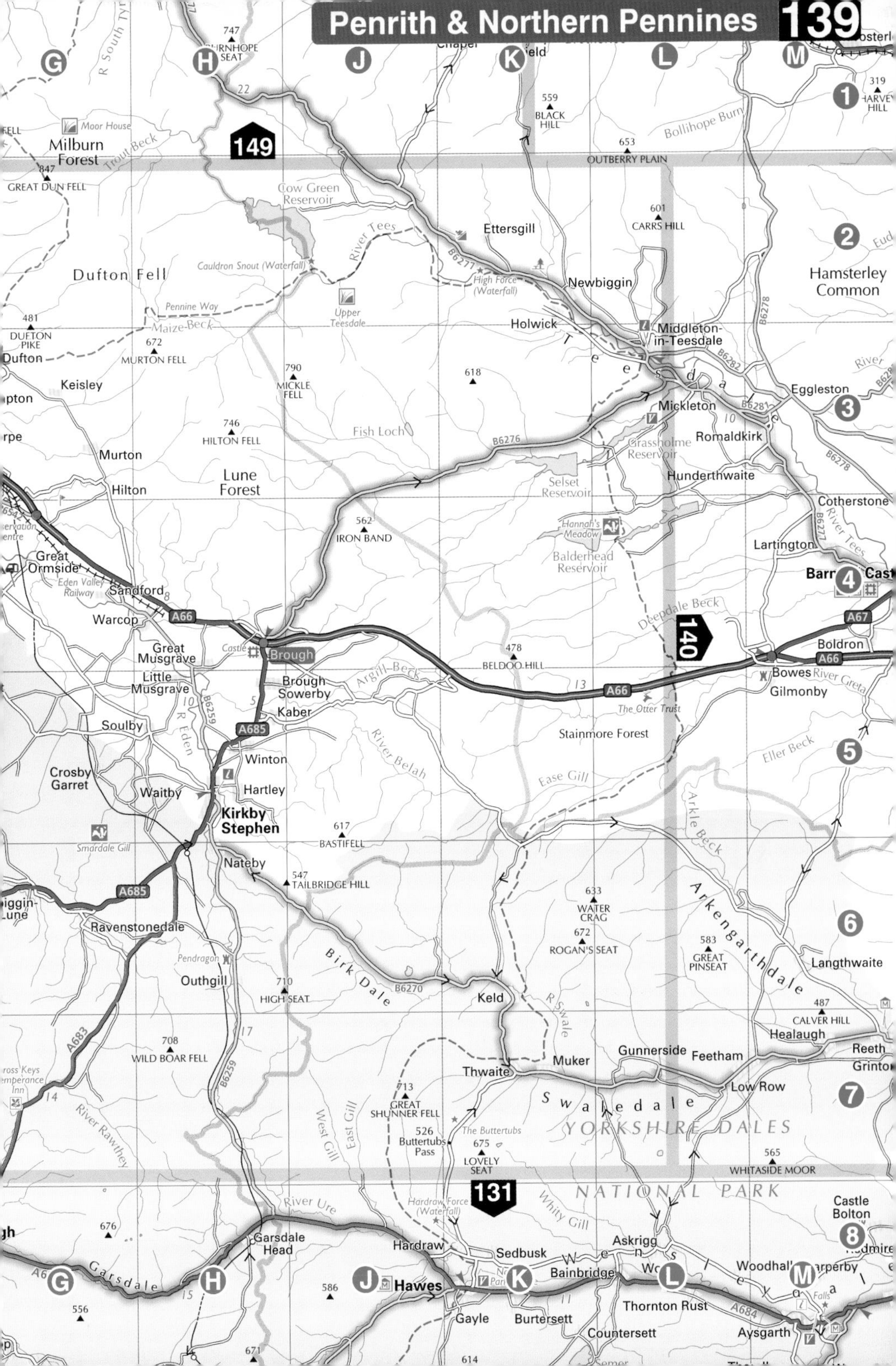
G
H
J
K
L
M
1
2
3
4
5
6
7
8
747
BURNHOPE SEAT
Chapel
Field
Mosterley
319
HARVEY HILL
R South Tyne
22
Moor House
Milburn Forest
Trout Beck
149
559
BLACK HILL
Bollihope Burn
653
OUTBERRY PLAIN
847
GREAT DUN FELL
Cow Green Reservoir
601
CARRS HILL
Ettersgill
Hamsterley Common
River Tees
Cauldron Snout (Waterfall)
B6277
High Force (Waterfall)
Newbiggin
Dufton Fell
Pennine Way
Upper Teesdale
Holwick
Middleton-in-Teesdale
B6278
481
DUFTON PIKE
Maize Beck
672
MURTON FELL
Dufton
790
MICKLE FELL
618
Teesdale
B6282
Eggleston
Keisley
Mickleton
B6281
10
746
HILTON FELL
Fish Loch
B6276
Grassholme Reservoir
Romaldkirk
Murton
Lune Forest
Selset Reservoir
Hunderthwaite
Hilton
Cotherstone
562
IRON BAND
Hannah's Meadow
River Tees
B6277
Great Ormside
Balderhead Reservoir
Lartington
Eden Valley Railway
Barnard Castle
Sandford
Deepdale Beck
A66
A67
Warcop
140
Boldron
Great Musgrave
Castle
Brough
478
BELDOO HILL
A66
Little Musgrave
Argill Beck
Bowes
River Greta
Brough Sowerby
Gilmonby
B6259
13
A66
Kaber
The Otter Trust
Soulby
R Eden
A685
Stainmore Forest
River Belah
Winton
Eller Beck
Crosby Garret
Hartley
Ease Gill
Waitby
Kirkby Stephen
617
BASTIFELL
Arkle Beck
Smardale Gill
Nateby
547
TAILBRIDGE HILL
A685
633
WATER CRAG
Arkengarthdale
Newbiggin-on-Lune
Ravenstonedale
672
ROGAN'S SEAT
583
GREAT PINSEAT
Pendragon
Langthwaite
Birk Dale
Outhgill
710
HIGH SEAT
B6270
Keld
R Swale
487
CALVER HILL
Healaugh
708
WILD BOAR FELL
17
Reeth
Grinton
Muker
Gunnerside
Feetham
A683
Cross Keys Temperance Inn
Thwaite
Low Row
B6259
713
GREAT SHUNNER FELL
Swaledale
14
YORKSHIRE DALES
West Gill
East Gill
526
Buttertubs Pass
The Buttertubs
675
LOVELY SEAT
565
WHITASIDE MOOR
River Rawthey
131
NATIONAL PARK
River Ure
Hardraw Force (Waterfall)
Whitfy Gill
Castle Bolton
676
Garsdale Head
Hardraw
Askrigg
Redmire
Garsdale
Sedbusk
Wensleydale
Bainbridge
Woodhall
Carperby
586
Hawes
15
11
Falls
556
Gayle
Burtersett
Thornton Rust
A684
Aysgarth
Countersett
671
614

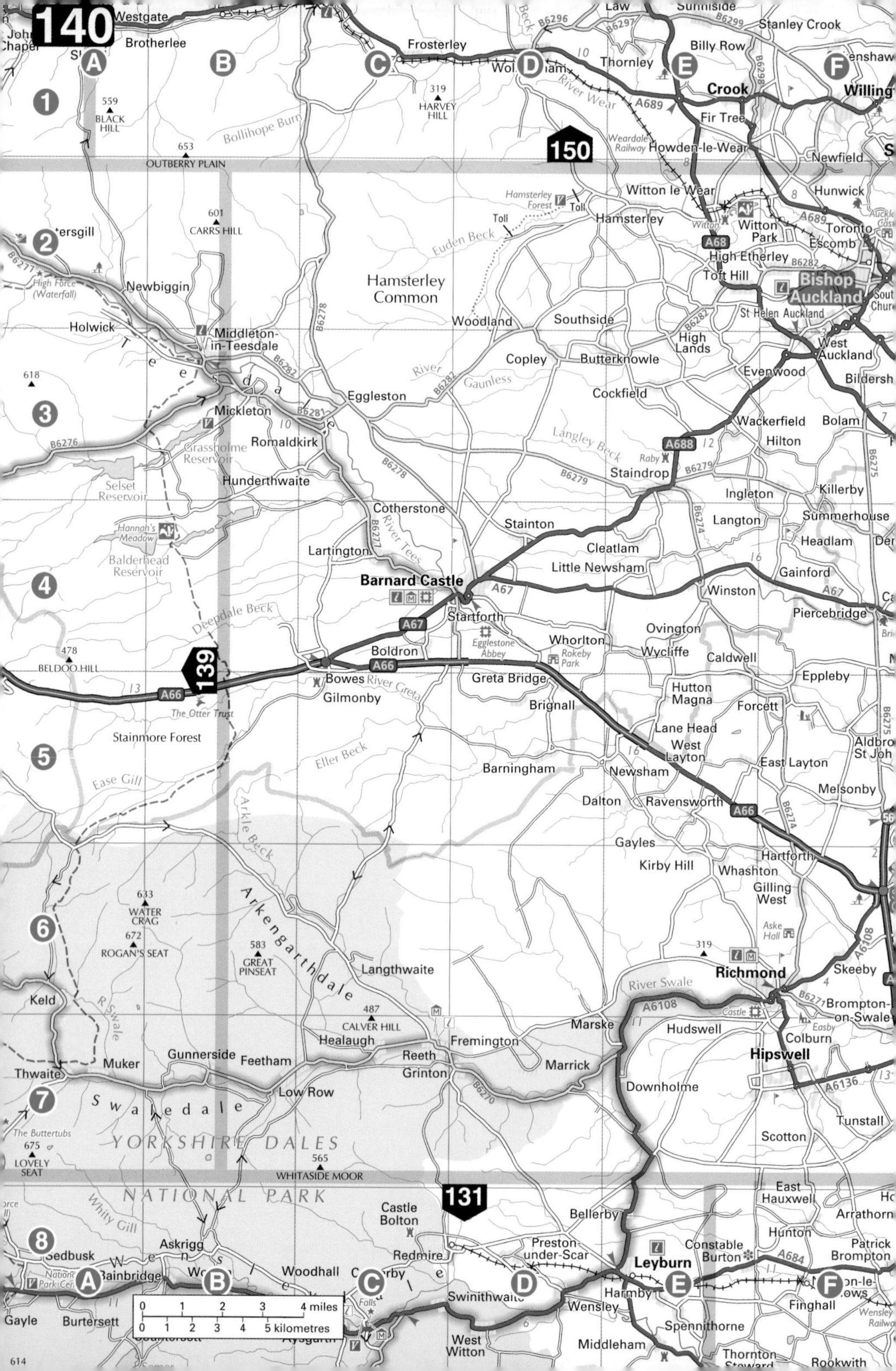

140
Westgate
Brotherlee
Frosterley
Wolsingham
Thornley
Billy Row
Stanley Crook
Crook
Fir Tree
Willington
Sunniside
Law
B6296
B6297
B6299
B6298
559 BLACK HILL
319 HARVEY HILL
Bollihope Burn
River Wear
A689
Weardale Railway
Howden-le-Wear
Newfield
150
653 OUTBERRY PLAIN
601 CARRS HILL
Hamsterley Forest
Toll
Hamsterley
Witton le Wear
Witton Park
Hunwick
Toronto
Escomb
A68
High Etherley
Toft Hill
Bishop Auckland
St Helen Auckland
West Auckland
Euden Beck
High Force (Waterfall)
B6277
Newbiggin
Holwick
Middleton-in-Teesdale
Teesdale
B6282
B6278
Hamsterley Common
Woodland
Southside
High Lands
Copley
Butterknowle
Evenwood
Cockfield
River Gaunless
Eggleston
B6281
618
Mickleton
B6276
Grassholme Reservoir
Romaldkirk
Selset Reservoir
Hunderthwaite
Langley Beck
Raby
Staindrop
B6279
A688
Wackerfield
Bolam
Hilton
Ingleton
Killerby
B6275
Cotherstone
River Tees
Hannah's Meadow
Balderhead Reservoir
Lartington
Stainton
Cleatlam
Little Newsham
Langton
Summerhouse
Headlam
Gainford
Winston
Piercebridge
A67
Barnard Castle
Startforth
Deepdale Beck
Egglestone Abbey
Whorlton
Rokeby Park
Ovington
Wycliffe
Caldwell
Eppleby
478 BELDOO HILL
139
A66
Boldron
Bowes
River Greta
Gilmonby
Greta Bridge
Brignall
The Otter Trust
Stainmore Forest
Hutton Magna
Forcett
Lane Head
West Layton
East Layton
Aldbrough St John
Eller Beck
Ease Gill
Barningham
Newsham
Dalton
Ravensworth
Melsonby
B6274
Arkle Beck
Gayles
Kirby Hill
Hartforth
Whashton
Gilling West
633 WATER CRAG
672 ROGAN'S SEAT
583 GREAT PINSEAT
Arkengarthdale
Langthwaite
Aske Hall
319
Richmond
Skeeby
A6108
River Swale
Keld
R Swale
487 CALVER HILL
Healaugh
Fremington
Marske
Hudswell
Castle
Easby
Brompton-on-Swale
Colburn
Hipswell
A6136
Thwaite
Muker
Gunnerside
Feetham
Reeth
Grinton
Marrick
Low Row
B6270
Downholme
Swaledale
Tunstall
The Buttertubs
YORKSHIRE DALES
675 LOVELY SEAT
565 WHITASIDE MOOR
Scotton
NATIONAL PARK
Whity Gill
131
Castle Bolton
Bellerby
East Hauxwell
Arrathorne
Hunton
Constable Burton
Patrick Brompton
Sedbusk
Askrigg
Redmire
Preston-under-Scar
Leyburn
A684
National Park Centre
Bainbridge
Woodhall
Carperby
Harmby
Finghall
Wensley
Swinithwaite
Spennithorne
Wensley Railway
Gayle
Burtersett
Falls
Aysgarth
West Witton
Middleham
Thornton Steward
Rookwith
0 1 2 3 4 miles
0 1 2 3 4 5 kilometres
614

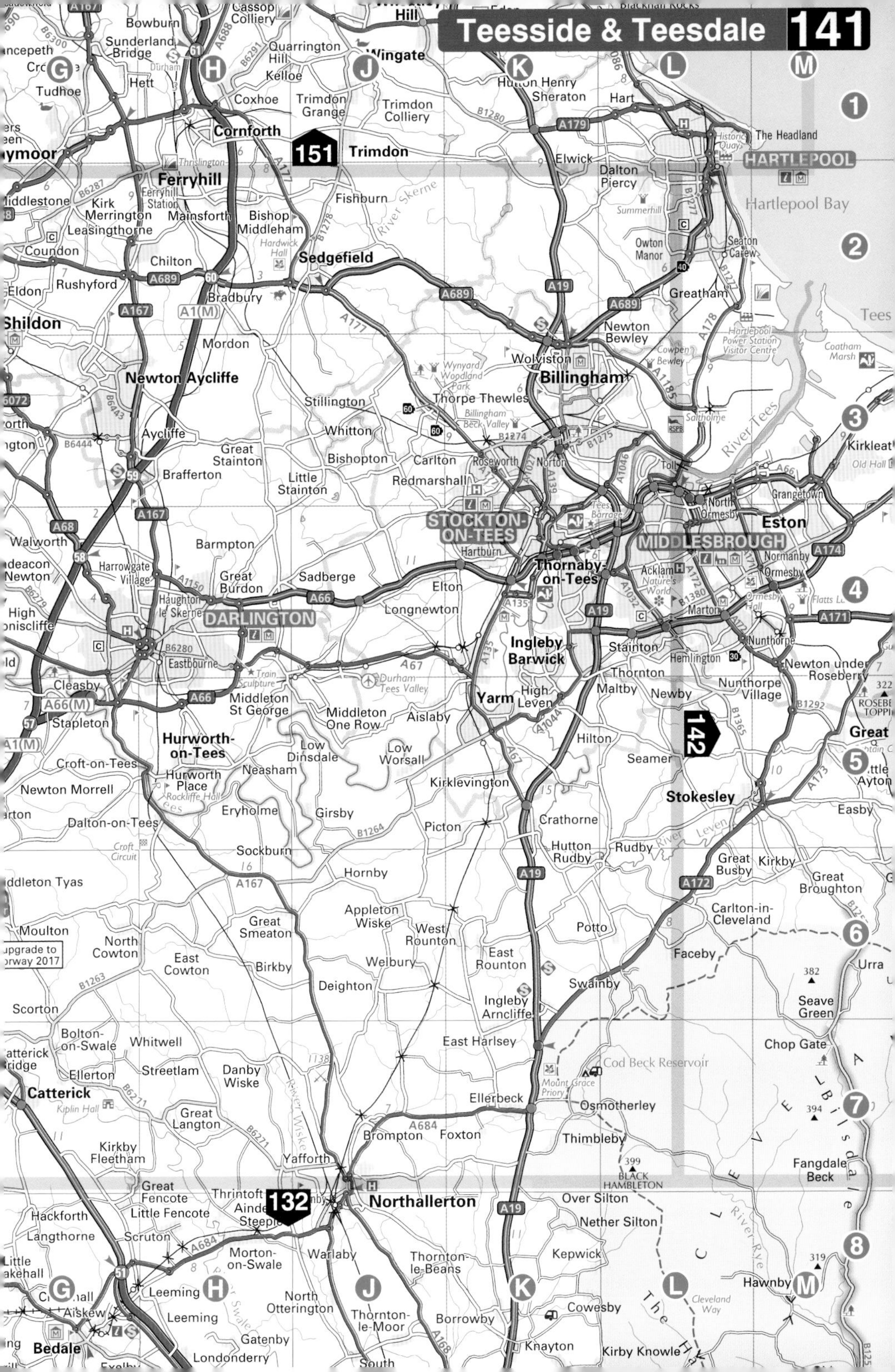

Teesside & Teesdale
141
HARTLEPOOL
Hartlepool Bay
MIDDLESBROUGH
STOCKTON-ON-TEES
DARLINGTON
Billingham
Ferryhill
Sedgefield
Trimdon
Newton Aycliffe
Shildon
Thornaby-on-Tees
Ingleby Barwick
Yarm
Eston
Stokesley
Northallerton
Catterick
Bedale
Hurworth-on-Tees
151
142
132
River Tees
Cod Beck Reservoir
Osmotherley

151
HARTLEPOOL
The Headland
Historic Quay
Hartlepool Bay
Hutton Henry
Sheraton
Hart
Elwick
Dalton Piercy
Summerhill
Owton Manor
Seaton Carew
Greatham
Newton Bewley
Tees Bay
Hartlepool Power Station Visitor Centre
Cowpen Bewley
Wolviston
Billingham
Saltholme
River Tees
Coatham Marsh
Redcar
Marske-by-the-Sea
Saltburn-by-the-Sea
Saltburn Smugglers
Kirkleatham
Old Hall
New Marske
Brotton
Skelton
Loftus
Kilton
Easington
Hummersea
Upleatham
Wilton
Dunsdale
Grangetown
Eston
North Ormesby
MIDDLESBROUGH
Normanby
Ormesby
Ormesby Hall
Flatts Lane
Norton
Roseworth
STOCKTON-ON-TEES
Hartburn
Thornaby-on-Tees
Acklam
Nature's World
Marton
Nunthorpe
Ingleby Barwick
Stainton
Hemlington
Thornton
Maltby
Newby
Nunthorpe Village
Newton under Roseberry
Roseberry Topping
Guisborough
Guisborough Forest
Hutton Lowcross
Cleveland Way
Boosbeck
Margrove Park
Lingdale
Kilton Thorpe
Woodhill
Stanghow
Liverton
Moorsholm
Scaling
Gerrick
Commondale
Yarm
High Leven
Hilton
Seamer
141
Great Ayton
Captain Cook Monument
Little Ayton
Stokesley
Easby
Kildale
Battersby
The Moors Centre
Danby
Castleton
Ainthorpe
Lealholm
River Esk
Glaisdale
Westerdale
Crathorne
Hutton Rudby
Rudby
River Leven
Great Busby
Kirkby
Great Broughton
Ingleby Greenhow
Carlton-in-Cleveland
Potto
Faceby
East Rounton
Swainby
Ingleby Arncliffe
Urra
Urra Moor
Seave Green
Chop Gate
Cod Beck Reservoir
Mount Grace Priory
Osmotherley
Thimbleby
Black Hambleton
Bilsdale
Fangdale Beck
Cleveland Hills
North York Moors National Park
Rosedale
Church Houses
Thorgill
Rosedale Abbey
Low Mill
River Seven
Bransdale
Farndale
133
Over Silton
Nether Silton
Kepwick
River Rye
Hawnby
Gillamoor
Fadmoor
Hutton-le-Hole
Spaunton
Lastingham
Appleton-le-Moors
Cropton
Knayton
Kirby Knowle
Cowesby
4 miles
5 kilometres

G
H
J
K
L
M
1
2
3
4
5
6
7
8
Staithes
Heritage Centre
Runswick Bay
Runswick
North Yorkshire and Cleveland Heritage Coast
Goldsborough
Overdale Wyke
Ellerby
B1266
A174
Lythe
Mickleby
Sandsend
Sandsend Wyke
East Barnby
West Barnby
Whitby
Abbey
Saltwick Bay
Dunsley
Ugthorpe
Newholm
Ruswarp
Stainsacre
B1410
A171
Aislaby
Briggswath
Sneaton
High Hawsker
Sleights
Ugglebarnby
B1447
Egton
Iburndale
Ness Point or North Cheek
The Green
Esk Dale
Grosmont
Robin Hood's Bay
A169
Fylingthorpe
Robin Hood's Bay
B1416
Old Peak or South Cheek
A171
Ravenscar
Goathland
20
North Yorkshire Moors Railway
292
Ellerbeck
Staintondale
Shire Horse Centre
Hayburn Wyke
Wheeldale Roman Road
MOORS
Harwood Dale
Newtondale Forest Drive
20
Cloughton
Cloughton Wyke
290
Stape
Hole of Horcum
134
Cromer Point
Burniston
A165
Bickley
Bridestones (Rock Formation)
Broxa
Silpho
Cleveland Way
Levisham
Toll
Suffield
Langdale End
Hackness
Dalby Forest Drive
Scalby
Castle
239
Sea Cut
North Riding Forest Park
Falsgrave
Scarborough

Belfast
Larne
Port
321
CARLOCK HILL
387
ALTIMEG
BENERAIRD
305
BENBRAKE HILL
A
B
C
D
E
F
1
2
3
4
5
6
7
8
Milleur Point
Glen App
Corsewall Point
Lady Bay
Southern Upland Way
Laggangairn Standing Stones
Barnhills
Portencalzie
Glenwhilly
152
B738
Kirkcolm
Cairnryan
Penwhirn Reservoir
Main Water of Luce
Cross Water of Luce
Loch Connell
A718
Ervie
B738
B798
Low Barbeth
271
ARTFIELD FELL
A77
Beoch Burn
Braid Fell
Low Salchrie
New Luce
Knocknain
Leswalt
Loch Ryan
B7043
Innermessan
A751
Black Loch
Castle of St John
THE RHINNS OF GALLOWAY
Castle Kennedy
White Loch
164
CRAIG FELL
Balgracie
Stranraer
Chlenry
Auchnotteroch
Aird
Castle Kennedy
A75
Portslogan
Broadsea Bay
Glenluce Abbey
Glenwhan
Dunragit
Glenluce
60
Lochans
Kildrochet House
Piltanton Burn
Whitecrook
Black Head
181
CAIRN PAT
B7084
Dunskey
B7077
Ringdoo Point
Milton
A747
A77
Portpatrick
A716
B7084
Stoneykirk
Stairhaven
North Milmain
Auchenmalg
Mull of Sinniness
B7042
Auchenmalg Bay
Sandhead
Cairngarroch
Kirkmadrine Stones
Money Head
High Ardwell
Ardwell
Ardwell Bay
Ardwell House
Chapel Rossan
Drumbreddon
Balgowan
LUCE BAY
Logan
Port Logan Bay
Port Logan
A716
B7065
Garrochtrie
Clanyard Bay
Kilstay
Laggantalluch Head
Kirkmaiden
Drummore
Barncorkrie
High Drummore
Killiness Point
Damnaglaur
Maryport
B7041
Cardryne
Cardrain
West Cairngaan
RSPB
MULL OF GALLOWAY
0 1 2 3 4 miles
0 1 2 3 4 5 kilometres

Drumlamford
Creebank
Bargrennan
Loch
G
H
J
K
L
M
716
LAMACHAN HILL
675
654
Loch
A712
1
325
CAIRN EDWARD
Loch Ochiltree
B7027
440
GARLICK HILL
Galloway Deer Range
Black Water of Dee
402
ROUND FELL
Knowe
River Bladnoch
153
471
FELL OF FLEET
184
URRALL FELL
G A L L O W A Y
Penkill Burn
Loch Grannoch
Loch Fleet
208
AUCHENCLOY HILL
2
Skerrow
Carseriggan
R Cree
Challoch
Minnigaff
710
CAIRNSMORE OF FLEET
Barfad
Newton Stewart
B7079
214
CULVENNAN FELL
Creebridge
Kirroughtree
Big Water of Fleet
Big Water of Fleet
Little Water of Fleet
Ronald
335
WHITE TOP OF CULREACH
Shennanton
A714
Palnure
15
B735
A75
3
B733
Craighlaw
A75
Kirkcowan
Baltersan
Upper Ruscoe
Carstramon Wood
Causeway End
R Bladnoch
Gem Rock
B796
146
B733
Fleet Valley
Creetown
lar Loch
Skyre Burn
Clugston
18
Gatehouse of Fleet
B7052
Torhouse Stone Circle
455
CAIRNHARROW
Anwoth
Kirkmabreck
Fell Loch
Cardoness Castle
THE
B733
Wigtown
4
Carsluith
Cairnholy Chambered Cairns
Bladnoch
B7005
Carsluith Castle
MACHARS
Kirwaugh
Girthon
Water of Malzie
Braehead
Loch
Ravenshall Point
Mossyard
Fleet Bay
Lennox Plunton
B7005
B7052
Kirkinner
Culshabbin
B7085
Orchardton Bay
Margrie
Chapel Finian (ruin)
Barrachan
Whauphill
Islands of Fleet
B7004
11
Culscadden
Little Airies
5
12
A746
Kirkandrews
A747
Elrig
13
Wigtown Bay
Druchtag Motte
Sorbie
B7085
B7052
Garlieston
Mochrum
Pouton
Borness
Drumtrodden Cup & Ring
Drumtrodden Standing Stones
Drummoddie
Broughton Mains
Cruggleton Bay
Ringdoo Point
Port William
B7004
B7063
Big Balcraig
6
'Wren's Egg' Standing Stones
B7021
Priory
Barsalloch Fort
Monreith
Whithorn Story
Barsalloch Point
Whithorn
Rispain Camp
Point of Leg
10
A747
A746
Portyerrock
St Ninian's Cave
B7004
Isle of Whithorn
Kidsdale
St Ninian's Chapel (ruin)
7
Cutcloy
BURROW HEAD
8
G
H
J
K
L
M

Galloway
Corsock
Shawhead
281
LARGLEAR HILL
Ironmacannie
325
CAIRN EDWARD
Eastlands
A75
Lochfoot
Crocketford
Auchenreoch Loch
Milton Loch
Lochrutton Loch
Knockvennie Smithy
154
A713
B794
Mossdale
Airds of Kells
208
AUCHENCLOY HILL
Loch Ken
Loch Roan
Walbutt
Kirkpatrick Durham
Springholm
Milton
Beeswing
Drumcoltran Tower
Old Bridge of Urr
Loch Skerrow
Woodhall Loch
A762
Crossmichael
Hardgate
Kirkgunzeon
334
LOTUS HILL
Clarebrand
B795
Haugh of Urr
Redcastle
Laurieston
Glenlochar
Townhead of Greenlaw
Hillowton
A745
335
WHITE TOP OF CULREACH
Threave Castle
Castle Douglas
Edingham
430
CUIL HILL
Glaisters Burn
Urr Water
Carstramon Wood
Loch Whinyeon
Longwood
Carlingwark Loch
Little Knox
Dalbeattie
367
BENGRAY
Threave Garden
Bridge of Dee
Rhonehouse
A710
B793
B796
Fleet Valley
Gelston
Craigley
B736
Barlochan
A711
Palnackie
Ringford
River Dee
Airieland
Barnbarroch
Fairgirth
Caulkerbush
Anworth
Gatehouse of Fleet
B727
Littleton
343
SCREEL HILL
390
BENGAIRN
Orchardton Tower
Kippford or Scaur
Mote of Mark
Drumburn
Sandyhills
Tongland
Colvend
Girthon
A75
Twynholm
Little Sypland
East Stewartry Coast
Rockcliffe
Portling
145
Compstonend
Galloway Wildlife Park
Whinnie Liggate
Castlehill Point
A755
Kirkchrist
MacLellan's Castle
Auchencairn
Auchencairn Bay
Margrie
Lennox Plunton
Gledpark
Kirkcudbright
Culnaightrie
Heston Island
Borgue
St Mary's Isle
Mutehill
Balcary
Balcary Point
Kirkandrews
Dundrennan
Rascarrel
Orroland
Kirkcudbright Bay
Dundrennan Abbey
Borness
Balmangan
Ringdoo Point
Ross
Balmae
Netherlaw
Abbey Head
Little Ross
A B C D E F
1 2 3 4 5 6 7 8
0 1 2 3 4 miles
0 1 2 3 4 5 kilometres

Lochside
Lincluden
Maxwell Town
Dumfries
Roucan
Collin
240 CARTHAT HILL
Roman Camp
Kettleholm
Greenlea
Racks
Dalton
Ecclefechan
Hoddom Cross
Thomas Carlyle's Birthplace
Eaglesfield
Merkland Cross
Kirtlebridge
Bonshaw Tower
Robgill Tower
Islesteps
Kingholm Quay
Mouswald
Carrutherstown
Hoddom Mains
Brydekirk
Kirkconnell Flow
Kelton
Conheath
Glencaple
Bankend
Clarencefield
Ruthwell Cross
Kelhead
Creca
Hollee
Annan
Kirkconnell
Nith Estuary
Ruthwell
Howes
Eastriggs
New Abbey
Corn Mill
Sweetheart Abbey
Ingleston
Bowhouse
Shearington
Caerlaverock Castle
Blackshaw
Caerlaverock Wetlands Centre
Savings Bank
Cummertrees
Powfoot
Dornock
Newbie
Torduff Point
Loch Kindar
569 CRIFFELL
Bowness-on-Solway
Port Carlisle
Glasson
Hadrian's Wall Path
Drumburgh
Drumburgh Moss
Bowness Common
Carse Bay
Kirkbean
Carsethorn
Cardurnock
Anthorn
Borron Point
Arbigland
Grune Point
SOLWAY FIRTH
Mainsriddle
Skinburness
Moricambe Bay
Kirkbride
Loaningfoot
Gill Foot Bay
Southerness
Southerness Point
Newton Arlosh
Wedholme Flow
Silloth
Seaville
Biglands
Abbey Town
Holm Cultram
Kelsick
Oulton
Lessonhall
Dundraw
Beckfoot
R Waver
Waverbridge
Wigton
Newtown
Blencogo
Waverton
Holme St Cuthbert
Bromfield
Mawbray
Dubmill Point
Langrigg
Westnewton
Bolton Low Houses
Allonby
Fletchertown
Allonby Bay
Hayton
Aspatria
Blennerhasset
Boltongate
Prospect
Oughterside
Torpenhow
Allerby
Crosscanonby
Crosby
Plumbland
Bothel
Ireby
Gilcrux
High Ireby
Uldale
Maryport
River Ellen
Dearham
447 BINSEY
Sunderland
Tallentire
Blindcrake
Flimby
Broughton Moor
Bridekirk
R Derwent
Lake District Wildlife Park
Standingstone
Dovenby
Bassenthwaite
Great Broughton
Papcastle
Embleton
Camerton
Seaton
Great Clifton
Cockermouth
Brigham
Bassenthwaite Lake
Greysouthen
Stainburn
Workington
Little Clifton
Eaglesfield
Mirehouse
931 SKIDDAW
Mossbay
Westfield
Moss Bay
Deanscales
552 LORDS SEAT
155
136
137
148

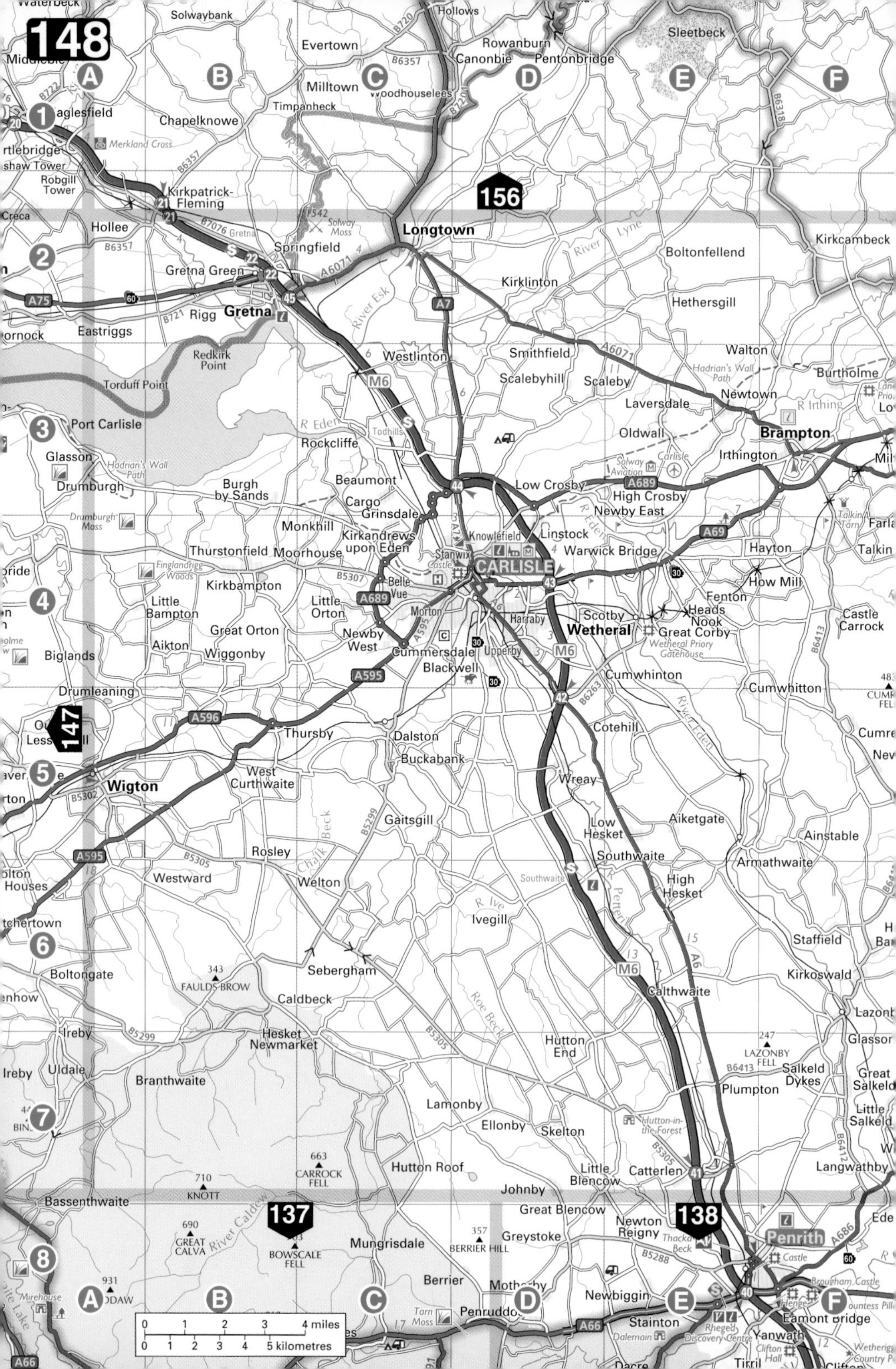

148
Solwaybank
Evertown
Hollows
Rowanburn
Canonbie
Pentonbridge
Sleetbeck
Milltown
Woodhouselees
Timpanheck
Chapelknowe
Merkland Cross
Robgill Tower
Kirkpatrick-Fleming
156
Longtown
Hollee
Springfield
Gretna Green
Gretna
Rigg
Eastriggs
Solway Moss
Boltonfellend
Kirkcambeck
Kirklinton
Hethersgill
Redkirk Point
Torduff Point
Westlinton
Smithfield
Walton
Scalebyhill
Scaleby
Laversdale
Newtown
Burtholme
Port Carlisle
Glasson
Drumburgh
Rockcliffe
Beaumont
Burgh by Sands
Oldwall
Brampton
Irthington
Low Crosby
High Crosby
Newby East
Cargo
Grinsdale
Monkhill
Kirkandrews upon Eden
Thurstonfield
Moorhouse
Knowlefield
Linstock
Stanwix
CARLISLE
Warwick Bridge
Hayton
Talkin
Kirkbampton
Belle Vue
How Mill
Fenton
Little Bampton
Little Orton
Morton
Scotby
Heads Nook
Great Orton
Newby West
Harraby
Wetheral
Great Corby
Wetheral Priory Gatehouse
Castle Carrock
Aikton
Wiggonby
Biglands
Cummersdale
Upperby
Blackwell
Cumwhinton
Cumwhitton
Drumleaning
147
Thursby
Dalston
Buckabank
Cotehill
Wigton
West Curthwaite
Wreay
Gaitsgill
Low Hesket
Aiketgate
Ainstable
Rosley
Southwaite
Armathwaite
Westward
Welton
High Hesket
Ivegill
Staffield
Boltongate
Sebergham
Caldbeck
Kirkoswald
FAULDS BROW
Calthwaite
Ireby
Hesket Newmarket
Hutton End
LAZONBY FELL
Uldale
Branthwaite
Salkeld Dykes
Plumpton
Great Salkeld
Lamonby
Ellonby
Skelton
Hutton-in-the-Forest
Little Salkeld
CARROCK FELL
Hutton Roof
Little Blencow
Catterlen
Langwathby
KNOTT
Johnby
Bassenthwaite
137
Great Blencow
Newton Reigny
138
GREAT CALVA
BOWSCALE FELL
Mungrisdale
BERRIER HILL
Greystoke
Penrith
Berrier
Newbiggin
Stainton
Eamont Bridge
Brougham Castle
Yanwath
Rheged Discovery Centre
Dalemain
Mirehouse
0 1 2 3 4 miles
0 1 2 3 4 5 kilometres

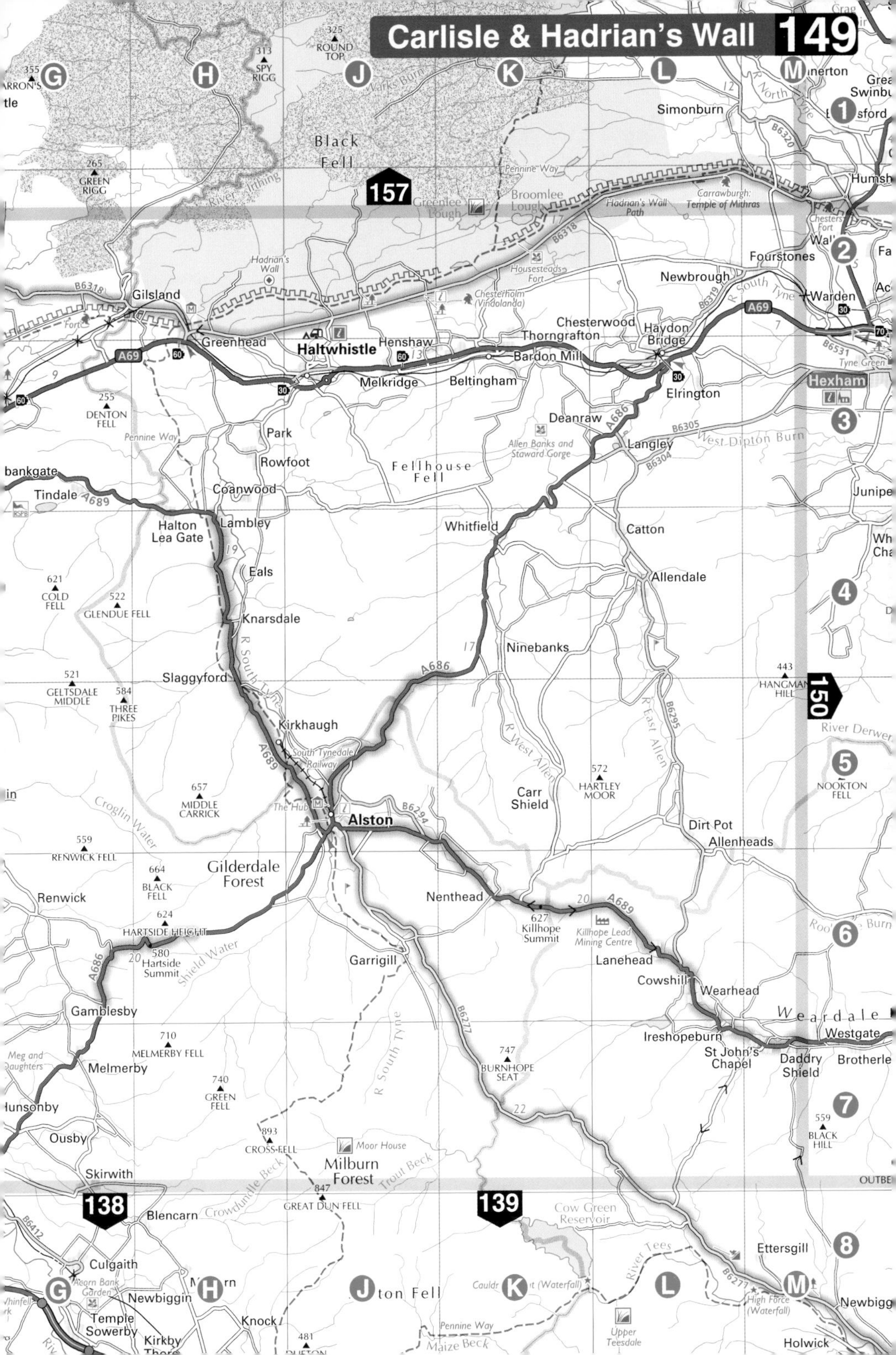

Simonburn
R North Tyne
B6320
Black Fell
157
Pennine Way
Greenlee Lough
Broomlee Lough
Hadrian's Wall Path
Carrawburgh: Temple of Mithras
Chesters Fort
Wall
Fourstones
Newbrough
Warden
Hexham
Tyne Green
B6531
A69
B6318
Housesteads Fort
Chesterholm (Vindolanda)
Hadrian's Wall
River Irthing
313 SPY RIGG
325 ROUND TOP
265 GREEN RIGG
Gilsland
Greenhead
Haltwhistle
Henshaw
Melkridge
Beltingham
Bardon Mill
Thorngrafton
Chesterwood
Haydon Bridge
Elrington
B6319
R South Tyne
255 DENTON FELL
Pennine Way
Park
Rowfoot
Coanwood
Deanraw
A686
Allen Banks and Staward Gorge
Langley
B6305
B6304
West Dipton Burn
Fellhouse Fell
Tindale
A689
RSPB
Halton Lea Gate
Lambley
Whitfield
Catton
Allendale
Eals
621 COLD FELL
522 GLENDUE FELL
Knarsdale
Ninebanks
Slaggyford
521 GELTSDALE MIDDLE
584 THREE PIKES
443 HANGMAN HILL
150
Kirkhaugh
South Tynedale Railway
R West Allen
R East Allen
B6295
River Derwent
657 MIDDLE CARRICK
Croglin Water
The Hub
Alston
B6294
Carr Shield
572 HARTLEY MOOR
NOOKTON FELL
Dirt Pot
Allenheads
559 RENWICK FELL
664 BLACK FELL
Gilderdale Forest
Renwick
Nenthead
627 Killhope Summit
Killhope Lead Mining Centre
624 HARTSIDE HEIGHT
580 Hartside Summit
Shield Water
Garrigill
Lanehead
Cowshill
Wearhead
Weardale
Gamblesby
B6277
Westgate
Ireshopeburn
St John's Chapel
Daddry Shield
710 MELMERBY FELL
Meg and Daughters
Melmerby
747 BURNHOPE SEAT
R South Tyne
740 GREEN FELL
559 BLACK HILL
Ousby
893 CROSS FELL
Moor House
Milburn Forest
Skirwith
Crowdundle Beck
Trout Beck
847 GREAT DUN FELL
138
139
Blencarn
Cow Green Reservoir
B6412
River Tees
Ettersgill
Culgaith
Acorn Bank Garden
Newbiggin
High Force (Waterfall)
Temple Sowerby
Knock
Pennine Way
Upper Teesdale
481
Maize Beck
Holwick

150
Swinburne
Bavington
Belsay Hall, Castle & Gardens
A696
Hallington Reservoir
Kirkheaton
Hallington
B6342
60
River Blyth
A
B
C
D
E
F
Colwell
Ryal
Milbourne
Berwick Hill
Great Swinburne
Ingoe
1
R. North Tyne
Barrasford
B6309
Heugh
Ponteland
Dinnington
B6320
A6079
A68
Chollerton
Bingfield
Fenwick
Stamfordham
Dalton
Darras Hall
Humshaugh
Great Whittington
Matfen
158
River Pont
Newcastle
Carrawburgh: Temple of Mithras
Hadrian's Wall
Chesters Fort
Walwick
Harlow Hill
Black Callerton
2
Fallowfield
B6318
Hadrian's Wall Path
Newbrough
Halton
Halton Shields
Rudchester
B6324
Aydon Castle
B6318
B6528
Throckley
Westerhope
R. South Tyne
Warden
Acomb
Sandhoe
B6321
Horsley
Heddon-on-the-Wall
A69
30
George Stephenson's Birthplace
Tyne Riverside
Newburn
70
Aydon
A69
B6531
Corbridge
Newton
B6530
Ovingham
Wylam
Claravale
Ryton
A6085
Tyne Green
Hexham
A695
Ovington
Crawcrook
B6317
Scotswood
Cherryburn
Dilston
Eltringham
A695
Prudhoe
Blaydon
B6306
B6307
R. Tyne
Riding Mill
Bywell
Mickley Square
Winlaton
3
West Dipton Burn
Broomhaugh
Stocksfield
Priestclose Wood
Greenside
Derwent Walk
High Mickley
Coalburns
Barlow
Painshawfield
B6315
Whickham
Juniper
New Ridley
Hedley on the Hill
High Spen
Highfield
Sunniside
Slaley
Chopwell
Gibside
Rowlands Gill
Whitley Chapel
Blackhall Mill
Derwentcote Steel Furnace
A68
Whittonstall
B6309
Hamsterley
Burnopfield
Causey Arch
Newlands
Hobson
Tanfield
4
357
DUKESFIELD FELL
B6310
B6306
Ebchester
Tantobie
Medomsley
Tanfield Lea
Derwent Reservoir
Shotley Bridge
Dipton
Stanley
443
149
B6278
Benfieldside
B6308
B6309
Bridgehill
Leadgate
A693
South Moor
Blackhill
Annfield Plain
Blanchland
Pow Hill
Consett
Iveston
River Derwent
Edmundbyers
A692
Templetown
Delves
B6278
Hunstanworth
Castleside
A6076
5
478
NOOKTON FELL
379
CROSS RIGG
Healeyfield
Rowley
Holmside
Burnhope
Lanchester
10
Allenheads
540
BOLT'S LAW
408
SKAYLOCK HILL
B6296
River Browney
A691
18
Diggerland
Esh
Cornsay
Satley
Cornsay Colliery
Quebec
Esh Winning
6
Rookhope Burn
Rookhope
B6278
516
COLLIER LAW
A68
Waskerley Beck
14
Hedleyhope Fell
B6301
Wearhead
Stanhope
East Hedleyhope
Weardale
Eastgate
A689
Tow Law
Westgate
B6296
Sunniside
B6297
B6299
Stanley Crook
St John's Chapel
Daddry Shield
Brotherlee
Frosterley
Billy Row
Oakenshaw
Wolsingham
Thornley
B6298
7
559
BLACK HILL
319
HARVEY HILL
River Wear
A689
Crook
Willington
Fir Tree
Bollihope Burn
Weardale Railway
Howden-le-Wear
653
OUTBERRY PLAIN
Newfield
140
Witton le Wear
Hunwick
Hamsterley Forest
601
CARRS HILL
Toll
Hamsterley
Witton
Witton Park
A689
Toronto
8
Ireshopeburn
Euden Beck
A68
Escomb
B6277
High Etherley
B6282
High Force (Waterfall)
Toft Hill
Hamsterley Common
Bishop Auckland
B6282
0
1
2
3
4 miles
0
1
2
3
4
5 kilometres
Holwick
Middleton
Woodland
Southside
St Helen Auckland

A
B
C
D
E
F
1
2
3
4
5
6
7
8
162
144
Culzean Bay
Culzean Castle & Country Park
Maidenhead Bay
Maidens
A719
Kirkoswald
Souter Johnnie's Cottage
Turnberry
Turnberry Bay
Dipple
Wallace
Kilgrammie
A77
B741
Water of Girvan
Ailsa Craig
340
RSPB
Old Dailly
B7035
Penkill
B734
Girvan
Dounepark
Woodland
Pinminnoch
297
GREY HILL
Pinmore
Balligmorrie
13
Lendalfoot
A714
Bennane Head
Colmonell
River Stinchar
Pinwherry
Muck Water
Duisk River
Heronsford
Water of Tig
Ballantrae
Barrhill
Belfast
Currarie Port
437
BENERAIRD
321
CARLOCK HILL
387
ALTIMEG HILL
Larne
Milleur Point
Glen App
305
BENBRAKE HILL
Southern Upland Way
Corsewall Point
Lady Bay
Laggangairn Standing Stones
Barnhills
Portencalzie
Glenwhilly
Main Water of Luce
Cross Water of Luce
B738
Kirkcolm
Cairnryan
Loch Connell
Ervie
A718
B798
271
ARTFIELD FELL
Low Barbeth
Beoch Burn
Braid Fell
Low Salchrie
New Luce
Knockna
Innermessan
Castle of St John
Black Loch
A751
0 1 2 3 4 miles
0 1 2 3 4 5 kilometres

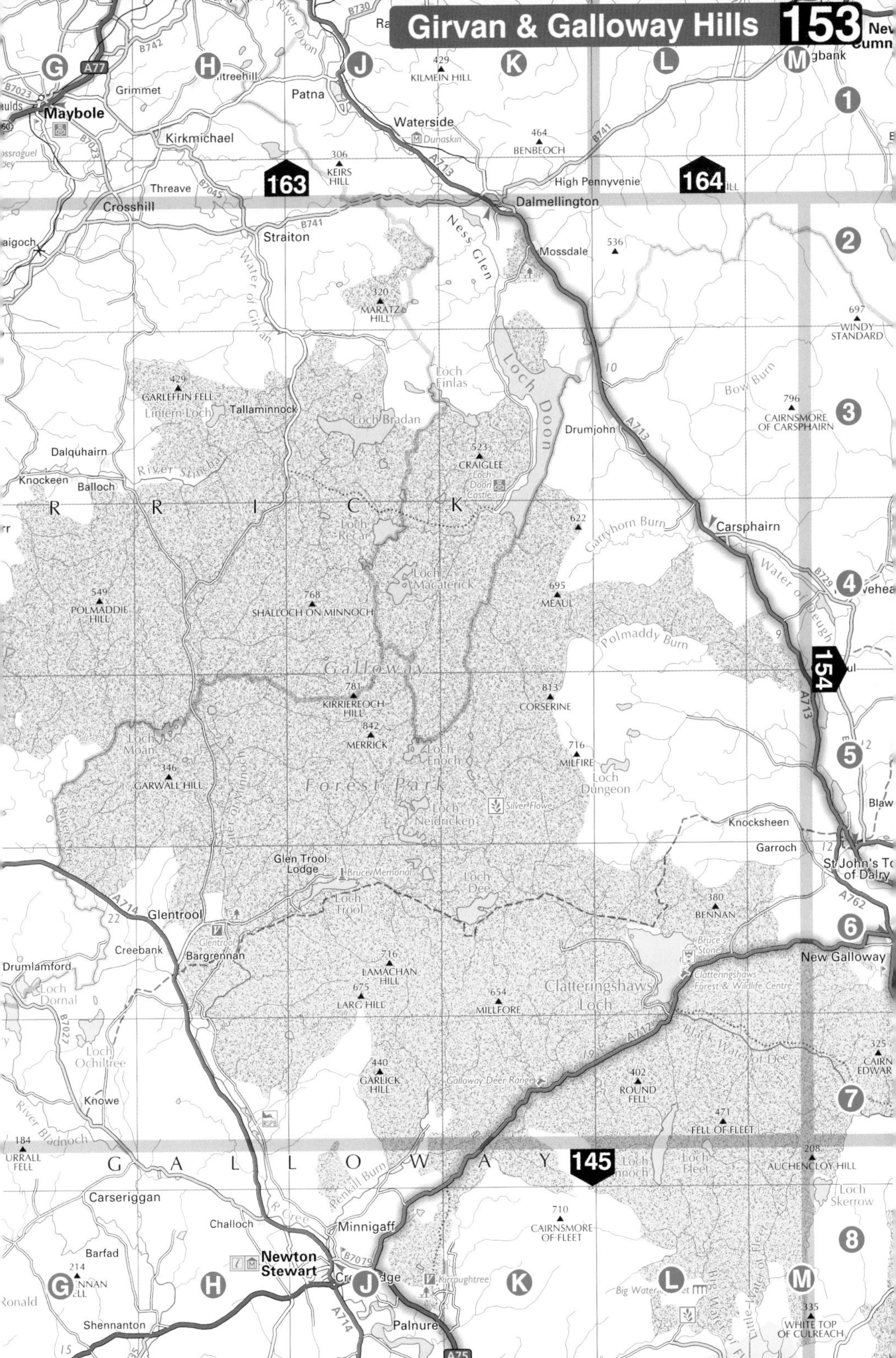

Maybole
Grimmet
Patna
Waterside
Dunaskin
429
KILMEIN HILL
464
BENBEOCH
Kirkmichael
306
KEIRS HILL
High Pennyvenie
163
164
Threave
Crosshill
Dalmellington
Straiton
Ness Glen
Mossdale
536
Water of Girvan
320
MARATZ HILL
697
WINDY STANDARD
Loch Finlas
Loch Doon
Bow Burn
796
CAIRNSMORE OF CARSPHAIRN
429
GARLEFFIN FELL
Linfern Loch
Tallaminnock
Loch Bradan
Drumjohn
Dalquhairn
River Stinchar
523
CRAIGLEE
Loch Doon Castle
Knockeen
Balloch
R R I C K
Loch Recar
622
Garryhorn Burn
Carsphairn
Water of Deugh
Loch Macaterick
695
MEAUL
549
POLMADDIE HILL
768
SHALLOCH ON MINNOCH
Polmaddy Burn
154
Galloway
781
KIRRIEREOCH HILL
813
CORSERINE
842
MERRICK
Loch Moan
Loch Enoch
716
MILFIRE
346
GARWALL HILL
Forest Park
Loch Dungeon
Silver Flowe
Loch Neldricken
Knocksheen
Garroch
Glen Trool Lodge
Bruce Memorial
Loch Dee
St John's Town of Dalry
Loch Trool
380
BENNAN
Glentrool
Creebank
Bargrennan
Bruce's Stone
New Galloway
Drumlamford
716
LAMACHAN HILL
Clatteringshaws Forest & Wildlife Centre
Loch Dornal
675
LARG HILL
654
MILLFORE
Clatteringshaws Loch
Black Water of Dee
Loch Ochiltree
325
440
GARLICK HILL
Galloway Deer Range
402
ROUND FELL
Knowe
471
FELL OF FLEET
River Bladnoch
184
URRALL FELL
208
AUCHENCLOY HILL
G A L L O W A Y
145
Loch Fleet
Loch Skerrow
Penkill Burn
Carseriggan
710
CAIRNSMORE OF FLEET
Challoch
Minnigaff
Barfad
Newton Stewart
Creebridge
Kirroughtree
Big Water of Fleet
214
Palnure
335
WHITE TOP OF CULREACH
Shennanton
A77
A713
A714
A712
A762
A75
B7023
B742
B730
B741
B7045
B729
B7027
B7079

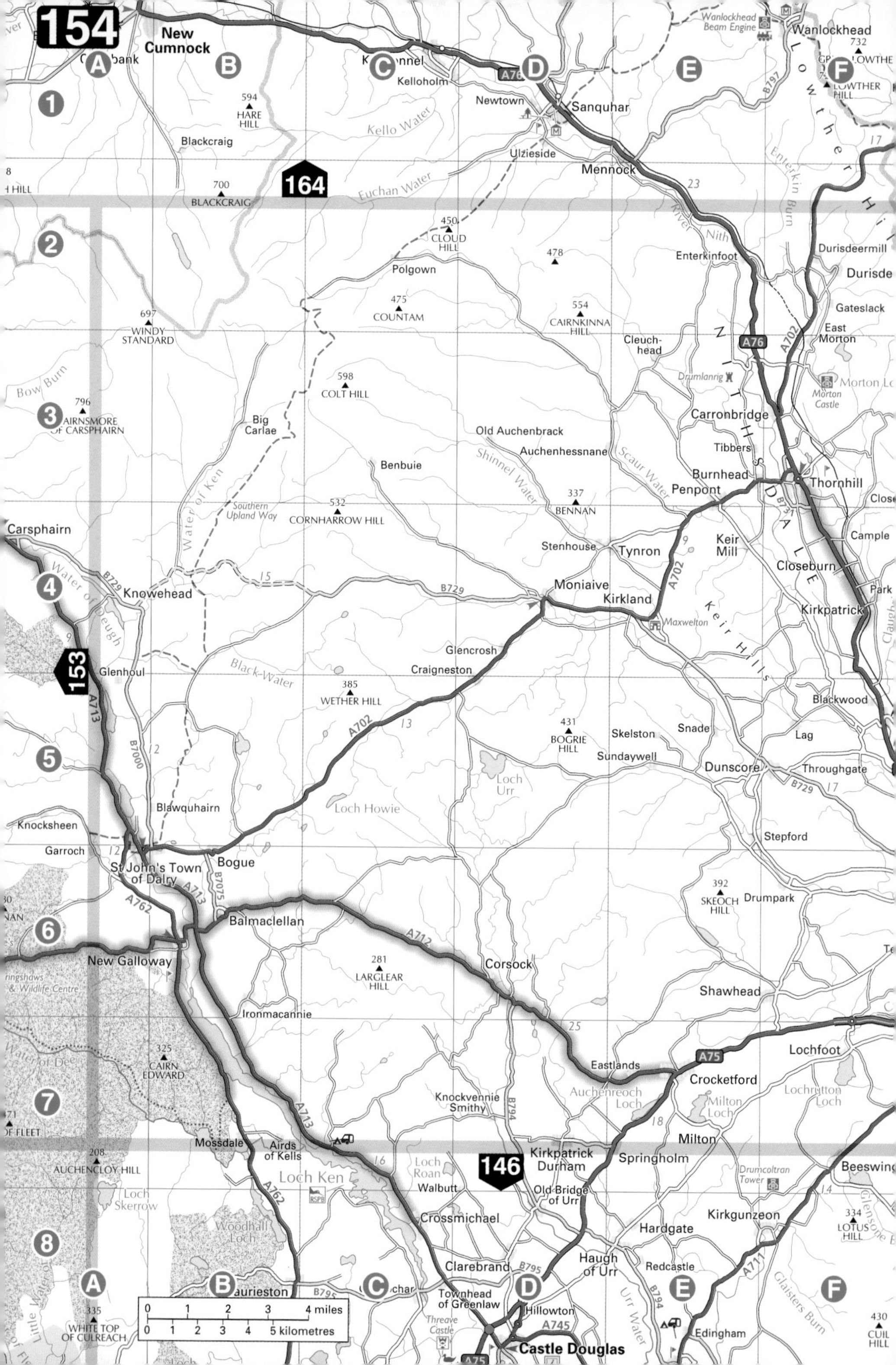

154
164
153
146
A
B
C
D
E
F
1
2
3
4
5
6
7
8
New Cumnock
Kelloholm
A76
Sanquhar
Newtown
Wanlockhead
Wanlockhead Beam Engine
732
LOWTHER HILL
Lowther Hills
B797
Kello Water
594
HARE HILL
Blackcraig
Ulzieside
Mennock
700
BLACKCRAIG
Euchan Water
Enterkin Burn
23
River Nith
17
450
CLOUD HILL
478
Enterkinfoot
Durisdeermill
Polgown
475
COUNTAM
554
CAIRNKINNA HILL
Gateslack
697
WINDY STANDARD
Cleuch-head
A702
East Morton
NITHSDALE
Drumlanrig
Morton Castle
Bow Burn
796
CAIRNSMORE OF CARSPHAIRN
598
COLT HILL
Big Carlae
Carronbridge
Old Auchenbrack
Auchenhessnane
Tibbers
Shinnel Water
Scaur Water
Benbuie
Burnhead
Penpont
Thornhill
Water of Ken
Southern Upland Way
532
CORNHARROW HILL
337
BENNAN
B731
Carsphairn
Stenhouse
Tynron
Keir Mill
Cample
Closeburn
Water of Deugh
B729
15
Knowehead
Moniaive
Kirkland
Park
Maxwelton
Keir Hills
Kirkpatrick
Glencrosh
Glenhoul
Black Water
Craigneston
A713
385
WETHER HILL
Blackwood
13
431
BOGRIE HILL
Skelston
Snade
Lag
B7000
12
Sundaywell
Dunscore
Throughgate
Loch Urr
Loch Howie
Blawquhairn
Knocksheen
Stepford
Garroch
St John's Town of Dalry
Bogue
B7075
392
SKEOCH HILL
Drumpark
A762
Balmaclellan
A712
New Galloway
281
LARGLEAR HILL
Corsock
Wildlife Centre
Shawhead
Ironmacannie
25
Water of Dee
325
CAIRN EDWARD
A75
Lochfoot
Eastlands
Crocketford
Auchenreoch Loch
Lochrutton Loch
Knockvennie Smithy
Milton Loch
B794
18
Milton
Mossdale
Airds of Kells
208
AUCHENCLOY HILL
Kirkpatrick Durham
Springholm
Beeswing
Loch Ken
16
Loch Roan
Walbutt
Drumcoltran Tower
RSPB
Loch Skerrow
Old Bridge of Urr
14
Woodhall Loch
Crossmichael
Kirkgunzeon
334
LOTUS HILL
Glensone Burn
Hardgate
Little Water of Fleet
Clarebrand
B795
Haugh of Urr
Redcastle
A711
Glaisters Burn
Laurieston
Townhead of Greenlaw
Urr Water
335
WHITE TOP OF CULREACH
Threave Castle
Hillowton
A745
Edingham
430
Castle Douglas
0 1 2 3 4 miles
0 1 2 3 4 5 kilometres

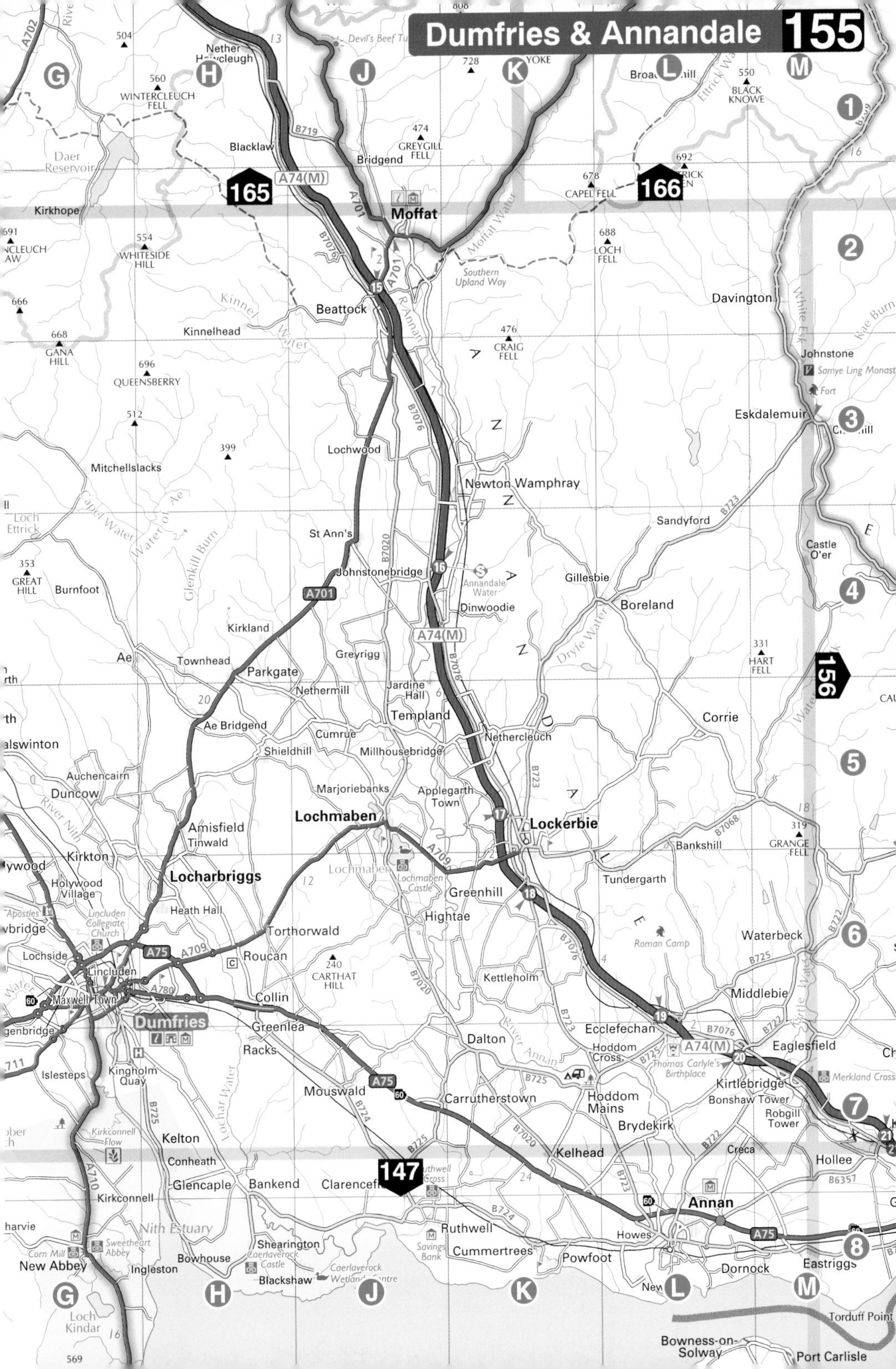
Moffat
Beattock
Lockerbie
Lochmaben
Locharbriggs
Dumfries
Annan
Kirkhope
Daer Reservoir
Blacklaw
Nether Howcleugh
Wintercleuch Fell
Whiteside Hill
Kinnelhead
Gana Hill
Queensberry
Mitchellslacks
Bridgend
Greygill Fell
Devil's Beef Tub
Yoke
Black Knowe
Capel Fell
Loch Fell
Southern Upland Way
Craig Fell
Davington
Johnstone
Samye Ling Monast
Fort
Eskdalemuir
Lochwood
Newton Wamphray
Sandyford
Castle O'er
St Ann's
Johnstonebridge
Annandale Water
Dinwoodie
Gillesbie
Boreland
Burnfoot
Great Hill
Kirkland
Greyrigg
Townhead
Parkgate
Ae
Hart Fell
Nethermill
Jardine Hall
Templand
Ae Bridgend
Corrie
Cumrue
Shieldhill
Millhousebridge
Nethercleuch
Auchencairn
Duncow
Marjoriebanks
Applegarth Town
Amisfield
Tinwald
Kirkton
Holywood Village
Bankshill
Grange Fell
Tundergarth
Lochmaben Castle
Greenhill
Hightae
Heath Hall
Torthorwald
Lincluden Collegiate Church
Lochside
Lincluden
Roucan
Carthat Hill
Roman Camp
Waterbeck
Kettleholm
Maxwell Town
Collin
Middlebie
Greenlea
Racks
Dalton
Ecclefechan
Hoddom Cross
Thomas Carlyle's Birthplace
Eaglesfield
Merkland Cross
Kirtlebridge
Bonshaw Tower
Robgill Tower
Islesteps
Kingholm Quay
Mouswald
Carrutherstown
Hoddom Mains
Brydekirk
Kirkconnell Flow
Kelton
Conheath
Kelhead
Creca
Hollee
Glencaple
Bankend
Clarencefield
Ruthwell Cross
Kirkconnell
Nith Estuary
Shearington
Ruthwell
Howes
Cummertrees
Powfoot
Sweetheart Abbey
Corn Mill
New Abbey
Ingleston
Bowhouse
Caerlaverock Castle
Blackshaw
Caerlaverock Wetland Centre
Savings Bank
Dornock
Eastriggs
Loch Kindar
Torduff Point
Bowness-on-Solway
Port Carlisle
A74(M)
A701
A75
A709
A710
B7076
B7020
B723
B725
B724
B722
B7068
B719
165
166
156
147

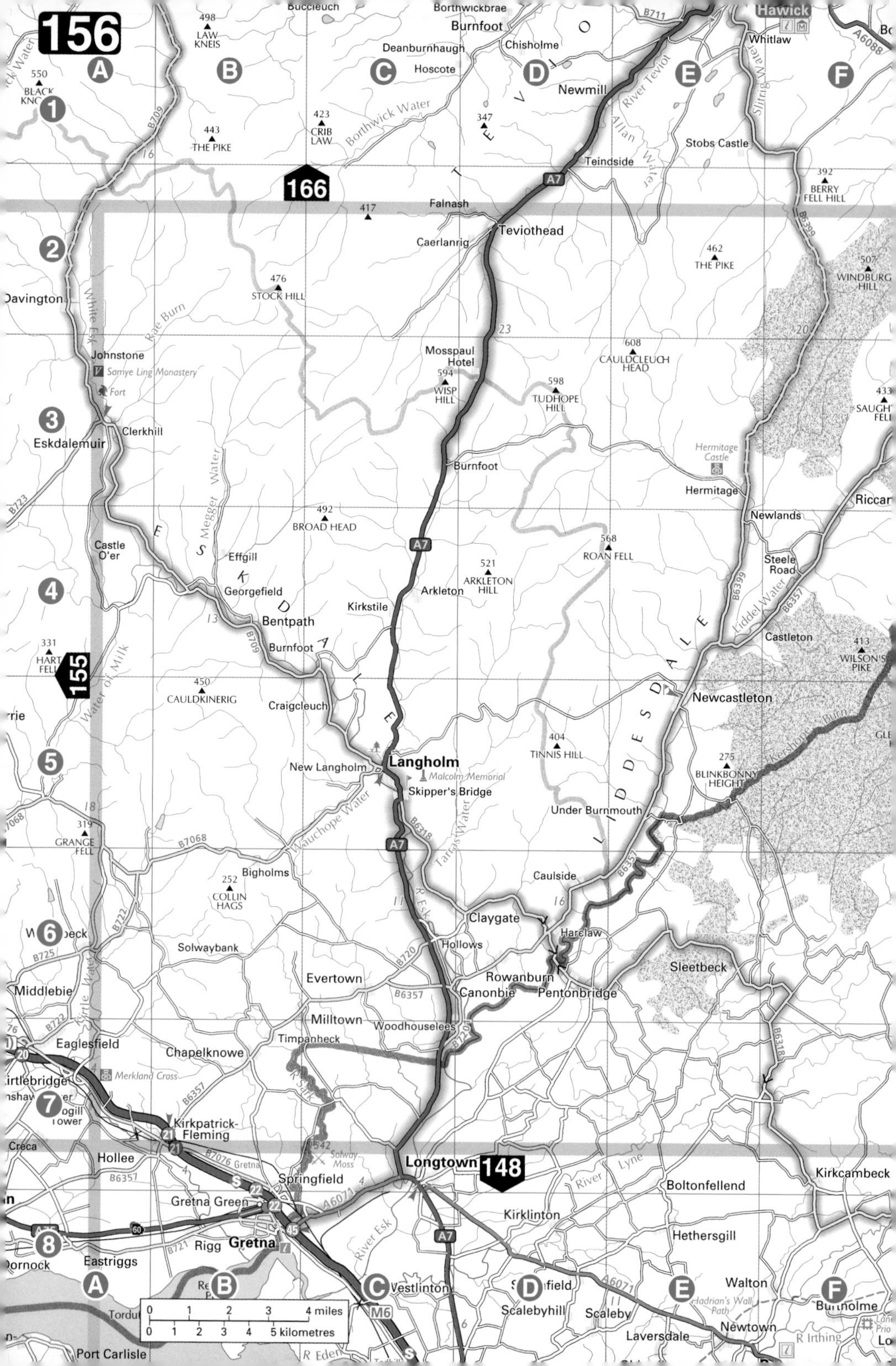
Hawick
Whitlaw
Burnfoot
Borthwickbrae
Buccleuch
Chisholme
Deanburnhaugh
Hoscote
Newmill
498
LAW KNEIS
550
BLACK KNO
443
THE PIKE
423
CRIB LAW
347
Borthwick Water
River Teviot
Allan Water
Slitrig Water
Stobs Castle
Teindside
B711
A6088
B709
A7
166
Falnash
417
Teviothead
Caerlanrig
392
BERRY FELL HILL
B6399
462
THE PIKE
507
WINDBURG HILL
476
STOCK HILL
Davington
White Esk
Rae Burn
Johnstone
Samye Ling Monastery
Fort
Clerkhill
Eskdalemuir
B723
Mosspaul Hotel
594
WISP HILL
598
TUDHOPE HILL
608
CAULDCLEUCH HEAD
433
SAUGHT FELL
Hermitage Castle
Hermitage
Burnfoot
Megget Water
492
BROAD HEAD
Newlands
Riccar
Castle O'er
Effgill
Georgefield
Bentpath
Kirkstile
Arkleton
521
ARKLETON HILL
568
ROAN FELL
Steele Road
Liddel Water
B6357
Castleton
413
WILSON'S PIKE
ESKDALE
LIDDESDALE
331
HART FELL
155
Water of Milk
Burnfoot
450
CAULDKINERIG
Craigcleuch
Newcastleton
rrie
404
TINNIS HILL
275
BLINKBONNY HEIGHT
Kershope Burn
Langholm
New Langholm
Malcolm Memorial
Skipper's Bridge
Under Burnmouth
Wauchope Water
Tarras Water
B6318
B7068
319
GRANGE FELL
Bigholms
252
COLLIN HAGS
Caulside
R Esk
B6357
B722
Claygate
Harelaw
Hollows
Solwaybank
B725
Middlebie
Kirtle Water
Evertown
B720
Rowanburn
Canonbie
Pentonbridge
Sleetbeck
Milltown
Woodhouselees
Timpanheck
Eaglesfield
Chapelknowe
Merkland Cross
Kirtlebridge
Bogill Tower
R Sark
Kirkpatrick-Fleming
B6318
Creca
Hollee
B7076 Gretna
B6357
1542 Solway Moss
Longtown
148
Springfield
A6071
River Lyne
Boltonfellend
Kirkcambeck
Gretna Green
Kirklinton
A75
Rigg
Gretna
B721
River Esk
Hethersgill
Dornock
Eastriggs
Walton
Westlinton
Smithfield
Hadrian's Wall Path
Burtholme
Tordu
Scalebyhill
Scaleby
Newtown
M6
Laversdale
R Irthing
Port Carlisle
R Eden
0 1 2 3 4 miles
0 1 2 3 4 5 kilometres

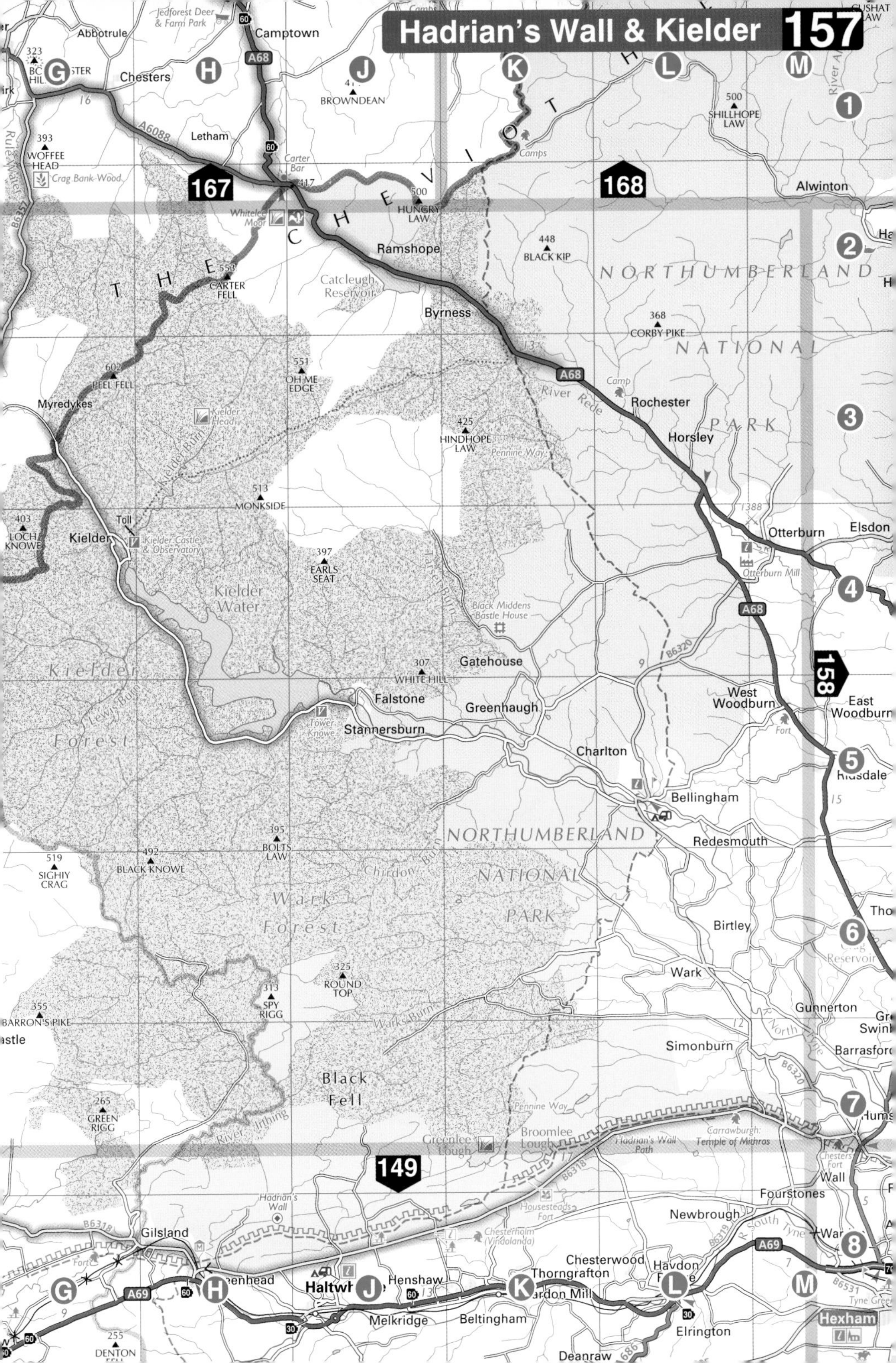
Jedforest Deer & Farm Park
Abbotrule
Camptown
Chesters
BROWNDEAN
Letham
WOFFEE HEAD
Crag Bank Wood
Carter Bar
167
168
Alwinton
SHILLHOPE LAW
Whitelee Moor
HUNGRY LAW
Ramshope
THE CHEVIOT
BLACK KIP
NORTHUMBERLAND
CARTER FELL
Catcleugh Reservoir
Byrness
CORBY PIKE
NATIONAL
PEEL FELL
OH ME EDGE
A68
River Rede
Rochester
Myredykes
Kielder Head
HINDHOPE LAW
Pennine Way
Horsley
PARK
Kielder Burn
MONKSIDE
Otterburn
Elsdon
LOCH KNOWE
Kielder
Toll
Kielder Castle & Observatory
EARLS SEAT
Otterburn Mill
Kielder Water
Tarset Burn
Black Middens Bastle House
B6320
158
WHITE HILL
Gatehouse
Kielder
Lewis Burn
Forest
Falstone
Greenhaugh
West Woodburn
East Woodburn
Tower Knowe
Stannersburn
Fort
Charlton
Ridsdale
Bellingham
Redesmouth
NORTHUMBERLAND
NATIONAL
PARK
BOLTS LAW
SIGHTY CRAG
BLACK KNOWE
Chirdon Burn
Wark
Forest
Birtley
Reservoir
Wark
ROUND TOP
SPY RIGG
BARRON'S PIKE
Warks Burn
Gunnerton
Simonburn
R North Tyne
Barrasford
Black Fell
GREEN RIGG
River Irthing
Pennine Way
Broomlee Lough
Greenlee Lough
Carrawburgh: Temple of Mithras
Hadrian's Wall Path
Chesters Fort
Wall
149
Hadrian's Wall
B6318
Housesteads Fort
Fourstones
Newbrough
Chesterholm (Vindolanda)
R South Tyne
B6319
Gilsland
Fort
A69
Chesterwood
Haydon
Thorngrafton
Henshaw
Haltwh
Bardon Mill
Melkridge
Beltingham
Elrington
Hexham
Tyne Green
B6531
DENTON FELL
Deanraw
686
G
H
J
K
L
M
1
2
3
4
5
6
7
8

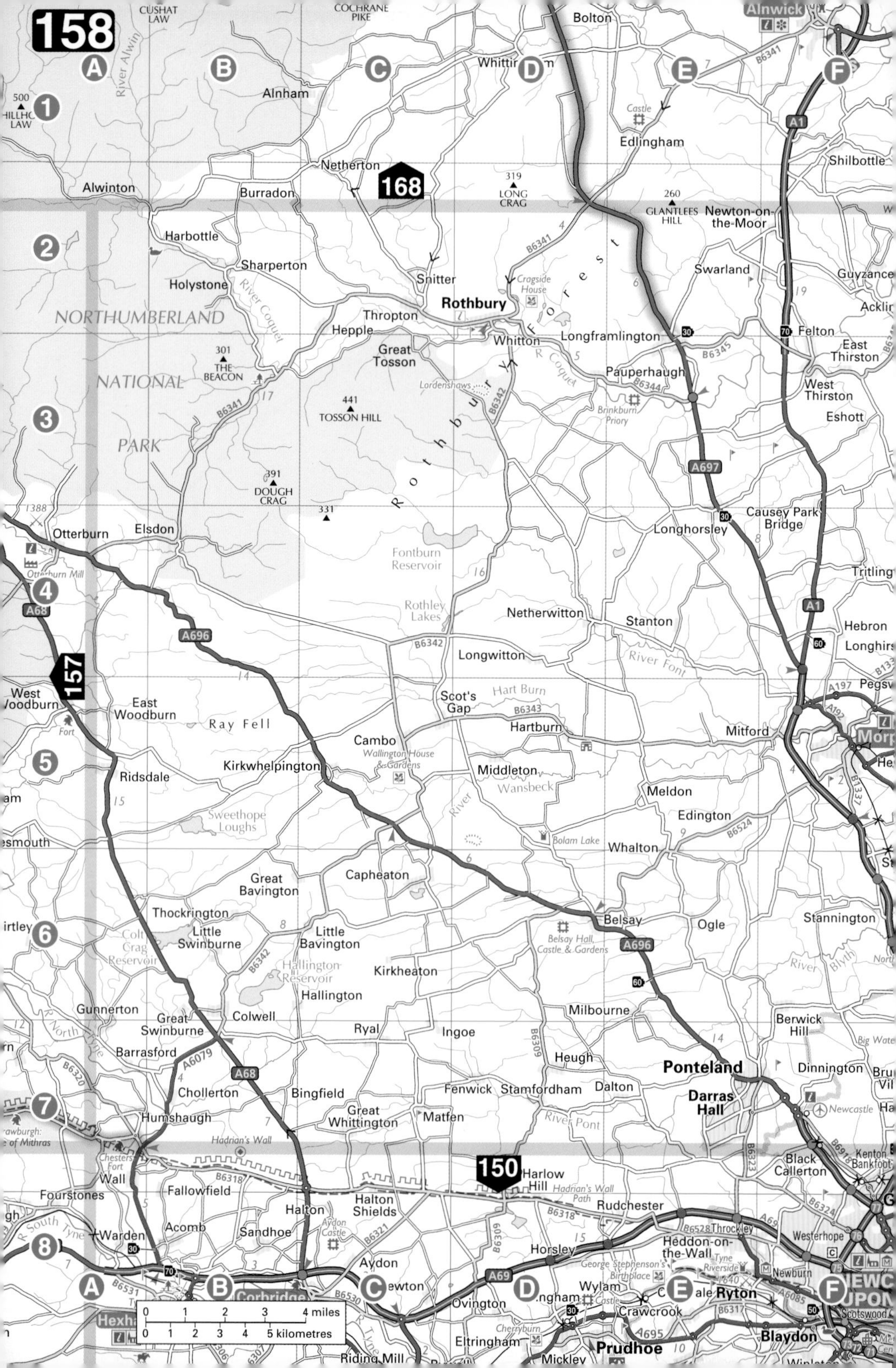
A
B
C
D
E
F
1
2
3
4
5
6
7
8
168
157
150
CUSHAT LAW
COCHRANE PIKE
Bolton
Alnwick
Whittingham
River Alwin
Alnham
500 HILLHOPE LAW
Castle
Edlingham
A1
Shilbottle
Netherton
Alwinton
Burradon
319 LONG CRAG
260 GLANTLEES HILL
Newton-on-the-Moor
Harbottle
B6341
Swarland
Guyzance
Sharperton
Snitter
Cragside House
Holystone
Rothbury
River Coquet
Acklington
NORTHUMBERLAND
NATIONAL
PARK
Thropton
Hepple
Whitton
Longframlington
Felton
Great Tosson
Rothbury Forest
R. Coquet
East Thirston
301 THE BEACON
Lordenshaws
Pauperhaugh
B6345
B6344
West Thirston
441 TOSSON HILL
Brinkburn Priory
B6342
Eshott
A697
391 DOUGH CRAG
331
1388
Causey Park Bridge
Otterburn
Elsdon
Longhorsley
Otterburn Mill
Fontburn Reservoir
Tritlington
A68
Rothley Lakes
Netherwitton
Stanton
Hebron
A696
B6342
Longwitton
River Font
Longhirst
B1337
Pegswood
West Woodburn
East Woodburn
Scot's Gap
Hart Burn
B6343
A197
A192
Fort
Ray Fell
Cambo
Hartburn
Mitford
Morpeth
Wallington House & Gardens
Ridsdale
Kirkwhelpington
Middleton
Wansbeck
Sweethope Loughs
River
Meldon
Edington
B6524
Bolam Lake
Whalton
Great Bavington
Capheaton
Thockrington
Belsay
Ogle
Stannington
Little Swinburne
Little Bavington
Colt Crag Reservoir
Hallington Reservoir
Belsay Hall, Castle & Gardens
River Blyth
Kirkheaton
Hallington
Gunnerton
Great Swinburne
Colwell
Milbourne
Berwick Hill
R. North Tyne
Ryal
Ingoe
B6309
Big Waters
Barrasford
A6079
Heugh
Dinnington
B6320
Ponteland
Chollerton
Bingfield
Fenwick
Stamfordham
Dalton
Darras Hall
Newcastle
Humshaugh
Great Whittington
Matfen
River Pont
Hadrian's Wall
Chesters Fort
Wall
Harlow Hill
Hadrian's Wall Path
B6323
Black Callerton
Kenton Bankfoot
B6918
B6318
Fallowfield
Fourstones
Halton
Halton Shields
Rudchester
B6324
Aydon Castle
B6321
B6528
Throckley
R. South Tyne
Warden
Acomb
Sandhoe
Heddon-on-the-Wall
Westerhope
B6309
Horsley
George Stephenson's Birthplace
Tyne Riverside
Newburn
Aydon
A69
A6085
B6531
Corbridge
B6530
Wylam
Ryton
Hexham
Ovington
Crawcrook
B6317
Scotswood
Cherryburn
A695
0 1 2 3 4 miles
0 1 2 3 4 5 kilometres
Eltringham
Prudhoe
Blaydon
Riding Mill
Mickley

Seaton Point
Lesbury
Alnmouth
Alnmouth Bay
A1068
169
Warkworth
Amble
Coquet Island
High Hauxley
Togston
Broomhill
Druridge Bay
Druridge Bay
Red Row
Widdrington
North Northumberland Heritage Coast
Cresswell
Widdrington Station
A1068
Ulgham
Ellington
Lynemouth
A189
Woodhorn
Beacon Point
Ashington
Hirst
Newbiggin-by-the-Sea
Bothal
Wansbeck Riverside
A196
Bedlington
Blyth
Cowpen
Newsham
A189
A192
A1061
New Hartley
Seaton Sluice
Cramlington
Seaton
Seaton Delaval
St Mary's Lighthouse
Dudley
Wide Open
Earsdon
Monkseaton
Whitley Bay
Cullercoats
Killingworth
Shiremoor
Tynemouth
Forest Hall
Tynemouth Priory & Castle
151
Amsterdam (IJmuiden)
Rising Sun
North Shields
Longbenton
South Gosforth
Willington
SOUTH SHIELDS
Jesmond
Wallsend
Int. Ferry Terminal
Heaton
Jarrow
Tyne Tunnel
Westoe
Marsden Bay
Walker
Hebburn
Marsden
Souter Lighthouse
Byker
Elswick
Felling
Monkton
Souter Point
West Boldon
Cleadon
Whitburn

BEINN SHOLUM
Eilean a' Chuirn
Rudha Mòr
171
Rudha na Gainmhich
165
MAOL BUIDHE
Port Ellen
A846
Ardbeg
Lagavulin
Laphroaig Distillery
Laphroaig
Kilnaughton Bay
THE OA
ISLAY
Port Ellen-Kennacraig
Texa
Lower Killeyan
Risabus
Kinnabus
Loch Kinnabus
American Monument
MULL OF OA
Rudha nan Leacan
Earadale
MULL OF KINTY
0 1 2 3 4 miles
0 1 2 3 4 5 kilometres

Rhunahaorine Point
Ardminish
Achamore
Rhunahaorine
CRUACH MHIC GOUGAIN
264
CNOC-AN SAMHLAI
172
Tayinloan
Sound of Gigha
Cara
Grogport
Barmollack
Pirnmill
Penrioch
Glen Catacol
North Ar
Loch Tanna
715
BEINN BHARRAIN
Glen Iorsa
Whitefarland
Imachar
Balliekine
Iorsa Water
354
CRUACH NAN GABHAR
A83
Muasdale
Carradale Water
39
B842
Carradale
Glenacardoch Point
Belloch
Barr Water
Bridgend
B879
Carradale House
Dippen
Glenbarr
MacAlister Clan
454
BEINN AN TUIRC
Torrisdale
Carradale Point
Carradale Bay
162
ARR
Auchagallon Stone Circle
Machrie
Machrie Bay
319
Cleongart
408
BORD MOR
Machrie Moor Stone Circles
Tormore
Moss Farm Road Stone Circle
Balmichae
Saddell
Bellochantuy Bay
Bellochantuy
Saddell Bay
Balmichae
Shiskine
Torbeg
396
SGREADAN HILL
Ugadale
Blackwaterfoot
Tangy Loch
Kilbrannan Sound
Drumadoon Bay
Kilpatrick
Kilpatrick Dun
Brown Head
Glen Lussa
Peninver
Ardnacross Bay
Kintyre
Kilkenzie
Corriecravie
Torr a' Chaisteal Fort
Sliddery
Kilmichael
Machrihanish Bay
Campbeltown
Campbeltown
Machrihanish
B842
6
B843
Campbeltown Loch
Island Davaar
Campbeltown-Ardrossan (May-Sept)
Drumlemble
Kilkerran
Kildalloig
352
BEINN GHUILEAN
Achinhoan
385
THE STATE
446
CNOC MOY
10
Conie Glen
Glen Kerran
Ru Stafnish
Dalsmeran
Glen Breakerie
Strone Glen
Cattadale
Polliwilline Bay
Macharioch
EINN NA LICE
428
Carskey
Southend
Dunaverty
Carskey Bay
Sanda Sound
Sheep Island
Borgadalemore Point
Sanda Island
G
H
J
K
L
M
1
2
3
4
5
6
7
8

162
173
161
152
Catacol
Glen Catacol
Glen Chalmadale
A841
Portencross
B7048
Farland Head
Seamil
Pirnmill
Penrioch
North Arran
834
CAISTEAL ABHAIL
Loch Tanna
Sannox
Corrie
715
BEINN BHARRAIN
Glen Iorsa
874
GOATFELL
792
BEINN NUIS
Glen Rosa
Merkland Point
Balliekine
Iorsa Water
Brodick Castle, Garden & Country Club
Brodick Bay
FIRTH OF CLYDE
ARRAN
Brodick
Strathwhillan
Auchagallon Stone Circle
Machrie Bay
Machrie
Corriegills
512
A'CHRUACH
B880
Machrie Moor Stone Circles
Tormore
Clauchlands Point
Moss Farm Road Stone Circle
Balmichael
503
BEINN BHREAC
Margnaheglish
Lamlash
Lamlash Bay
Balmichael
Holy Island
Torbeg
Shiskine
Cordon
Blackwaterfoot
Glen Scorrodale
(May-Sept, Sat only)
(May-Sept)
Drumadoon Bay
Kilpatrick
Auchencairn
Kingscross
Knockenkelly
Kilpatrick Dun
Carn Ban
Whiting Bay
Brown Head
Whiting Bay
Glen Ashdale
Kilmory Water
Largymore
Corriecravie
Torr a' Chaisteal Fort
Sliddery
Largybeg
Dippen
Dippen Head
Kilmory
Lagg
Torrylin Cairn
Bennan
Kildonan
Bennan Head
Pladda
Turnberry
Turnberry Bay
340
Ailsa Craig
RSPB
0 1 2 3 4 miles
0 1 2 3 4 5 kilometres

174
164
153
Dalry
Munnoch
West Kilbride
Blackshaw
Dalgarven
Kilwinning
Stevenston
Saltcoats
Ardeer
Irvine
Maritime
Fullarton
Eglinton
Irvine Bay
Gailes
Barassie
Troon
Royal Troon
Larne
(Mar-Oct)
Monkton
Prestwick
New Prestwick
Whitletts
Ayr Bay
Wallacetown
Ayr
Doonfoot
Heads of Ayr
Burns Cottage
Alloway
Robert Burns Birthplace
Fisherton
Dunure
Culroy
Drumshang
Croy Brae (Electric Brae)
Knoweside
Culzean Bay
Culzean Castle & Country Park
Pennyglen
Whitefaulds
Maybole
Crossraguel Abbey
Kirkoswald
Souter Johnnie's Cottage
Crosshill
Roan of Craigoch
Wallacetown
Kilgrammie
Dailly
Penkill
Burnhouse
Auchentiber
High Cross
Crossgates
Stewarton
Annick Water
Torranyard
Fergushill
Benslie
Cunninghamhead
Kilmaurs
Girdle Toll
Perceton
Springside
Knockentiber
Dreghorn
Crosshouse
Knockinlaw
Dean Castle
KILMARNOCK
Fenwick
Laigh Fenwick
Waterside
Moscow
Polbaith Burn
R. Irvine
Gatehead
Drybridge
Riccarton
Earlston
Shortlees
Dundonald
Castle
Hurlford
Crookedholm
Galston
Newmilns
Greenholm
Symington
Bogend
Craigie
Carnell
Crosshands
Loans
Helenton
Wallace Monument Tower
Middleyard
Auchmillan
Bachelors' Club
Mauchline
Tarbolton
Failford
Haugh
Catrine
Mossblown
St Quivox
Annbank
Ayr Gorge Woodland
Stair
Gadgirth
Trabboch
Trabbochburn
River Ayr
Lugar Water
Ochiltree
Auchinleck
Dumfries House
Joppa
Coylton
Drongan
Palmerston
Garrallan
Skares
Belmont
Barbieston
Martnaham Loch
Sinclairston
Hollybush
Minishant
Dalrymple
River Doon
Rankinston
Guiltreehill
Grimmet
Patna
KILMEIN HILL
Waterside
Dunaskin
Kirkmichael
BENBEOCH
KEIRS HILL
Threave
High Pennyvenie
Dalmellington
Straiton
Ness Glen
Mossdale
MARATZ HILL
Water of Girvan
Loch Finlas
GARLEFFIN FELL
Tallaminnock
Dalgig
Lochgoin Reservoir
CUNNINGHAME
Kilmarnock
A78
A71
A77
A76
A70
A719
A713
A759
A735
A737
A738
B7081
B730
B742
B743
B744
B741
B7023
B7034
B7045
B7035
B7036
B7037
B7046
B7038
B751
B769
B778
B780
B785
B705
B713

164
175
163
153
154
Waterside
Galston
Newmilns
Darvel
Greenholm
Priestland
Drumclog
Strathaven
Chapelton
Glassford
Stonehouse
Carnduff
Caldermill
Sandford
Blackwood
Kirkmuirhill
Lesmahagow
New Trows
Auchlochan
Stockbriggs
Coalburn
Dungavel
Draffan
Boghead
Whitelee Windfarm
Lochgoin
LAIRDS SEAT
Glen Water
Polbaith Burn
Avon Water
Kype Water
Logan Water
River Nethan
Spirit of Scotland
AUCHINGILLOCH
MILL RIG
DISTINKHORN
NUTBERRY HILL
PRIESTHILL HEIGHT
MID HILL
MIDDLEFIELD LAW
Douglas West
Glenbuck
Muirkirk
Kames
Carmacoup
Limmerhaugh
Sorn
Catrine
Haugh
Middleyard
Auchmillan
River Ayr
CAIRN TABLE
DRYRIGS HILL
WARDLAW HILL
Gass Water
Glenmuir Water
Cronberry
Lugar
Logan
Holmhead
Laigh Glenmuir
Auchinleck
Dumfries House
Cumnock
Palmerston
Garrallan
Skares
Roadside
Sinclairston
MOUNT STEWART
Spango Water
HALFMERK HILL
Fingland
COCKER HILL
Meikle Carco
Kirkland
CARSGAILOCH HILL
Mansfield
Dalgig
River Nith
Connel Park
Bankglen
Craigbank
New Cumnock
Kirkconnel
Kelloholm
Newtown
Sanquhar
HARE HILL
Blackcraig
Kello Water
Ulzieside
Mennock
High Pennyvenie
ENOCH HILL
BLACKCRAIG
Euchan Water
Dalmellington
Mossdale
CLOUD HILL
Polgown
COUNTAM
CAIRNKINNA HILL
COLT HILL
Cleuch-head
A71
A76
A70
A723
B743
B7086
B745
B7037
B713
B705
B7036
B7083
B744
B741
B7078
0 1 2 3 4 miles
0 1 2 3 4 5 kilometres

Roadmeetings
Kilncadzow
Carstairs
Carnwath
Dolphinton
Romannno Bridge
Blyth Bridge
Carstairs Junction
Kaimend
Newbigging
Walston
Netherurd
Kirkurd
Cartland
Hazelbank
Ravenstruther
Bankhead
R. Medwin
Elsrickle
Nemphlar
Lanark Moor
Pettinain
Libberton
Greenshields
Kirkfieldbank
Lanark
New Lanark
Hyndford Bridge
Grangehall
New Lanark Village
Falls of Clyde
Candy Mill
Broughton Heights
Shieldhill House Hotel
Hillhead
R Clyde
Covington
Skirling
Quothquan
Carmichael
Warrenhill
Cambuswallace
Drumalbin
Thankerton
Biggar
Stobo
Fallburn
Coulter Motte
Trahenna
Upper Tweed
Douglas Water
St John's Kirk
Wolfclyde
Causewayend
Broughton
Calzeat
Dawyck
Happendon
Rigside
Symington
Tinto
Coulter
Rachan Mill
Drumelzier
Uddington
Greenhill
River Clyde
Glenholm
Robert Law
Wiston
Cardon Hill
Pykestone Hill
Holms Water
Newton
Lamington
Douglas
Glencothe
Stanhope
Culter Fell
Roberton
Ladygill
Wandel Burn
Kingledoors Burn
Culter Reservoir
Crook Inn
Abington
Crawfordjohn
Balgray
Rome Hill
Tweedsmuir
Broad Law
Camps Reservoir
Glenbreck
River Tweed
Talla Reservoir
Lettershaw
Crawford
Bellfield
Talla Linnfoots
Midlock Water
Black Dod
Badlieu
Fruid Reservoir
Snar Water
Nether Whitecleuch
Wellgrain Dod
Elvanfoot
Harleburn Head
Beattock Summit
Clyde Law
Craiginaid
Lochcraig Head
Loch Skeen
Leadhills
Elvan Water
March
White Coomb
Grey Mare's Tail
Lead Mining
Tweed's Well
Tweedsmuir Hills
Hart Fell
Wanlockhead Beam Engine
Wanlockhead
Devil's Beef Tub
Saddle Yoke
Green Lowther
Nether Howcleugh
Lowther Hill
Nether Fingland
Wintercleuch Fell
Lowther Hills
Enterkin Burn
Blacklaw
Greygill Fell
Daer Reservoir
Bridgend
Moffat
Capel Fell
Kirkhope
Moffat Water
Nith
Enterkinfoot
Durisdeermill
Ballencleuch Law
Whiteside Hill
Loch Fell
Durisdeer
Southern Upland Way
Gateslack
Beattock
Kinnel Water
East Morton
Kinnelhead
Gana Hill
Craig Fell
Queensberry
Drumlanrig
Morton Loch
Morton Castle
R. Annan
Carronbridge

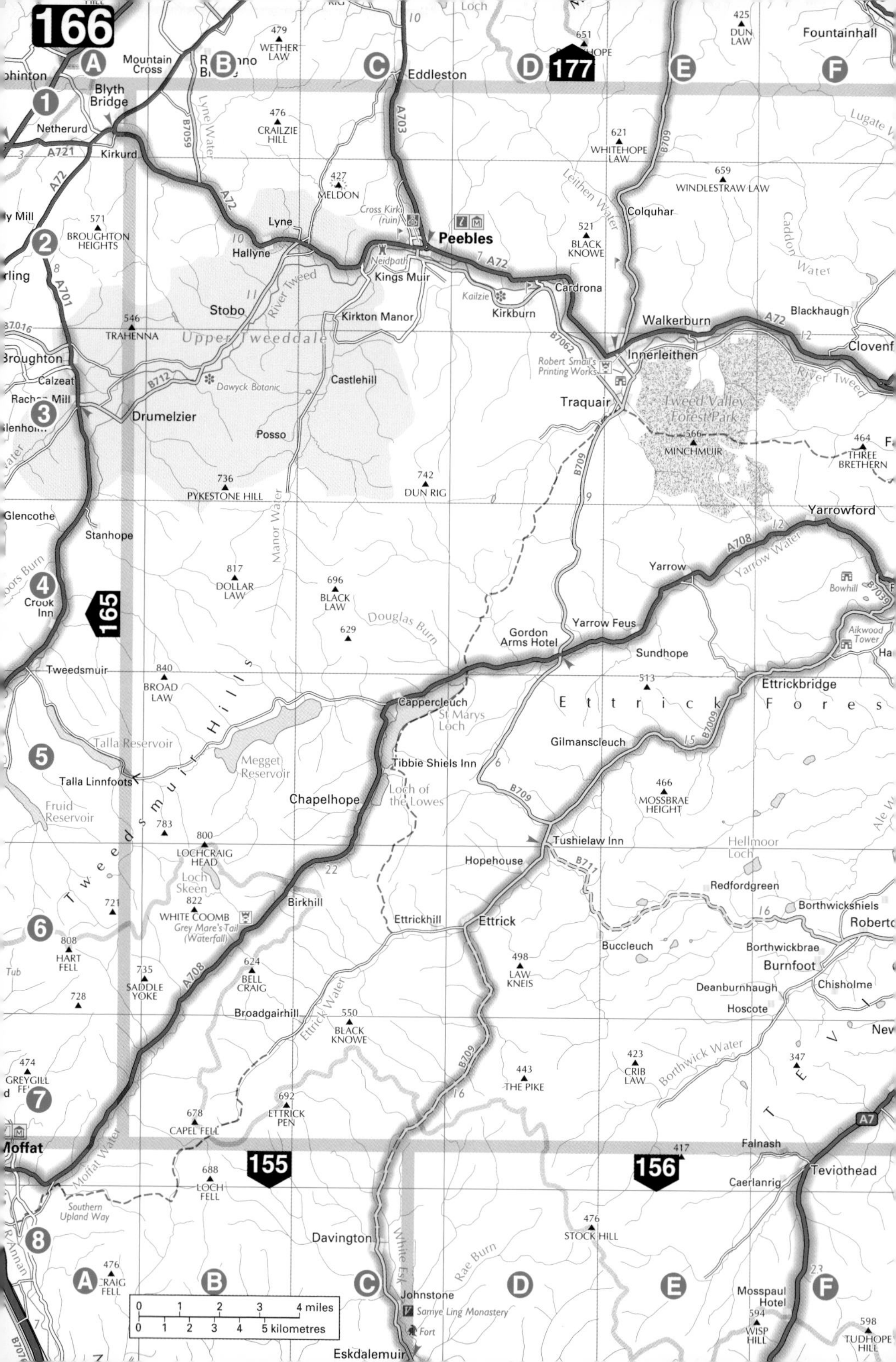
A
B
C
D
E
F
1
2
3
4
5
6
7
8
177
165
155
156
Mountain Cross
Eddleston
Blyth Bridge
Netherurd
Kirkurd
A721
A72
A701
A703
B7059
Lyne Water
479 WETHER LAW
476 CRAILZIE HILL
427 MELDON
651
425 DUN LAW
Fountainhall
621 WHITEHOPE LAW
659 WINDLESTRAW LAW
B709
Leithen Water
Colquhar
Lugate Water
Caddon Water
571 BROUGHTON HEIGHTS
Lyne
Hallyne
Cross Kirk (ruin)
Peebles
Neidpath
Kings Muir
521 BLACK KNOWE
Cardrona
Kailzie
Kirkburn
River Tweed
Stobo
Kirkton Manor
546 TRAHENNA
Upper Tweeddale
Broughton
Calzeat
B712
Dawyck Botanic
Castlehill
Drumelzier
Posso
Walkerburn
Blackhaugh
Clovenf
Innerleithen
Robert Smail's Printing Works
B7062
Traquair
Tweed Valley Forest Park
566 MINCHMUIR
464 THREE BRETHERN
736 PYKESTONE HILL
742 DUN RIG
Glencothe
Stanhope
Manor Water
Yarrowford
A708
Yarrow Water
Yarrow
Bowhill
B7039
817 DOLLAR LAW
696 BLACK LAW
629
Douglas Burn
Crook Inn
Gordon Arms Hotel
Yarrow Feus
Sundhope
Aikwood Tower
Tweedsmuir
840 BROAD LAW
Tweedsmuir Hills
Cappercleuch
St Marys Loch
513
Ettrick Forest
Ettrickbridge
B7009
Talla Reservoir
Megget Reservoir
Gilmanscleuch
Talla Linnfoots
Tibbie Shiels Inn
Fruid Reservoir
Chapelhope
Loch of the Lowes
B709
466 MOSSBRAE HEIGHT
783
800 LOCHCRAIG HEAD
Tushielaw Inn
Hopehouse
Hellmoor Loch
B711
Loch Skeen
822 WHITE COOMB
Grey Mare's Tail (Waterfall)
721
Birkhill
Redfordgreen
Borthwickshiels
808 HART FELL
Ettrickhill
Ettrick
Buccleuch
Borthwickbrae
Roberto
735 SADDLE YOKE
624 BELL CRAIG
498 LAW KNEIS
Burnfoot
Deanburnhaugh
Chisholme
728
Broadgairhill
Ettrick Water
550 BLACK KNOWE
Hoscote
474 GREYGILL FELL
443 THE PIKE
423 CRIB LAW
Borthwick Water
347
692 ETTRICK PEN
678 CAPEL FELL
Moffat
Moffat Water
A7
Falnash
417
Teviothead
688 LOCH FELL
Caerlanrig
Southern Upland Way
476 STOCK HILL
Davington
White Esk
Rae Burn
476 CRAIG FELL
R Annan
Johnstone
Samye Ling Monastery
Fort
Eskdalemuir
Mosspaul Hotel
594 WISP HILL
598 TUDHOPE HILL
0 1 2 3 4 miles
0 1 2 3 4 5 kilometres

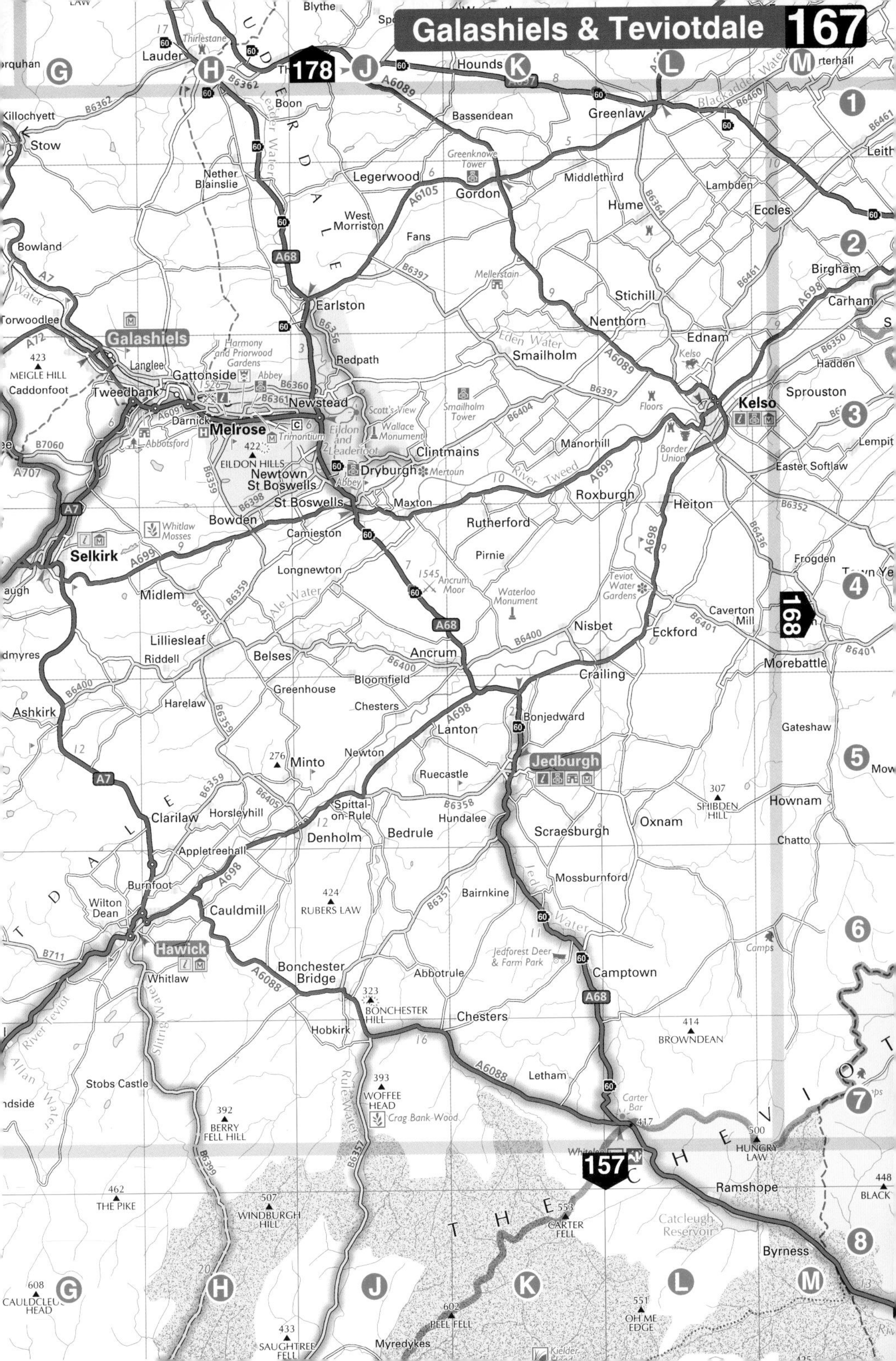

Galashiels & Teviotdale
167
178
168
157
Lauder
Thirlestane
Blythe
Hounds
Greenlaw
Boon
Bassendean
Killochyett
Stow
Nether Blainslie
Legerwood
Greenknowe Tower
Gordon
Middlethird
Lambden
Hume
Eccles
Leith
West Morriston
Fans
Bowland
Birgham
Carham
Mellerstain
Stichill
Earlston
Nenthorn
Ednam
Torwoodlee
Galashiels
Redpath
Eden Water
Smailholm
Kelso
Hadden
Sprouston
423
MEIGLE HILL
Caddonfoot
Langlee
Harmony and Priorwood Gardens
Gattonside
Abbey
Tweedbank
Newstead
Scott's View
Smailholm Tower
Floors
Darnick
Melrose
Trimontium
Eildon and Leaderfoot
Wallace Monument
Manorhill
Border Union
Abbotsford
422
EILDON HILLS
Clintmains
Easter Softlaw
Lempit
Newtown St Boswells
Dryburgh
Mertoun
River Tweed
Roxburgh
St Boswells
Maxton
Heiton
Bowden
Rutherford
Whitlaw Mosses
Camieston
Pirnie
Frogden
Selkirk
Longnewton
1545 Ancrum Moor
Teviot Water Gardens
Midlem
Ale Water
Waterloo Monument
Caverton Mill
Lilliesleaf
Nisbet
Eckford
Riddell
Belses
Ancrum
Morebattle
Crailing
Bloomfield
Greenhouse
Ashkirk
Harelaw
Chesters
Bonjedward
Lanton
Gateshaw
Newton
276
Minto
Jedburgh
Ruecastle
307
SHIBDEN HILL
Hownam
Clarilaw
Horsleyhill
Spittal-on-Rule
Hundalee
Denholm
Bedrule
Scraesburgh
Oxnam
Chatto
Appletreehall
Mossburnford
Burnfoot
424
RUBERS LAW
Bairnkine
Wilton Dean
Cauldmill
Jed Water
Camps
Hawick
Jedforest Deer & Farm Park
Camptown
Whitlaw
Bonchester Bridge
Abbotrule
323
BONCHESTER HILL
Chesters
River Teviot
Slitrig Water
Hobkirk
414
BROWNDEAN
Rule Water
Allan Water
Letham
Stobs Castle
393
WOFFEE HEAD
Carter Bar
392
BERRY FELL HILL
Crag Bank Wood
417
500
HUNGRY LAW
Ramshope
462
THE PIKE
507
WINDBURGH HILL
553
CARTER FELL
Catcleugh Reservoir
448
BLACK
Byrness
608
CAULDCLEUGH HEAD
602
PEEL FELL
551
OH ME EDGE
433
SAUGHTREE FELL
Myredykes
Kielder
THE CHEVIOT
LAUDERDALE
TEVIOTDALE
A7
A68
A6089
A6105
A699
A698
A6088
A72
A707
B6362
B6397
B6356
B6360
B6361
B6404
B6359
B6398
B6453
B6400
B6401
B6364
B6461
B6460
B6350
B6352
B6436
B6405
B6358
B6357
B6399
B7060
B711
B6091

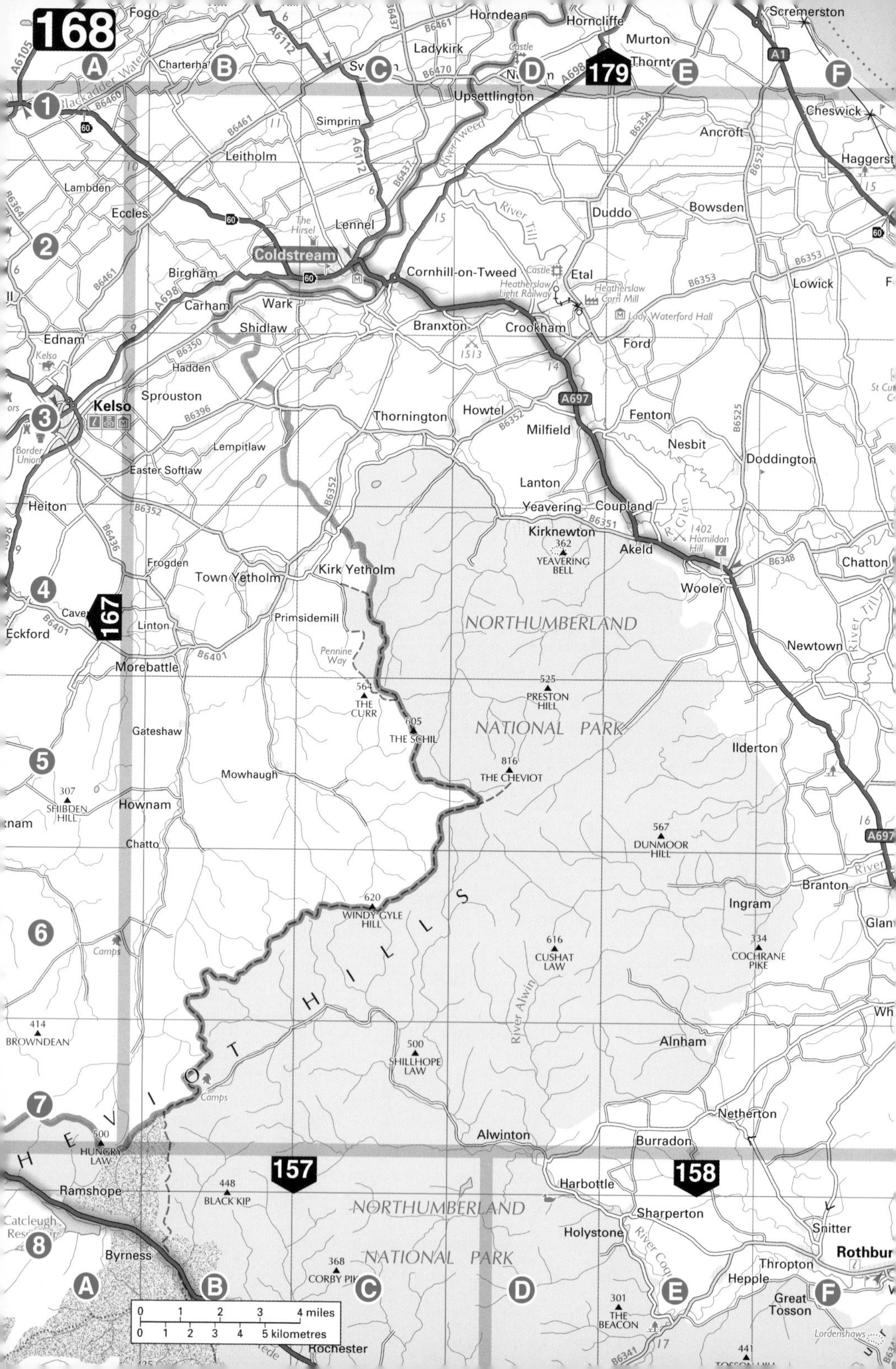
168
179
167
157
158
A
B
C
D
E
F
1
2
3
4
5
6
7
8
Fogo
Horndean
Horncliffe
Scremerston
Ladykirk
Murton
Castle
Charterhall
Upsettlington
Cheswick
Blackadder Water
Simprim
Ancroft
Haggerston
Leitholm
River Tweed
Lambden
Eccles
Duddo
Bowsden
River Till
The Hirsel
Lennel
Coldstream
Birgham
Cornhill-on-Tweed
Castle
Etal
Lowick
Heatherslaw Light Railway
Heatherslaw Corn Mill
Lady Waterford Hall
Carham
Wark
Ednam
Shidlaw
Branxton
Crookham
Ford
Kelso
1513
Hadden
Sprouston
Fenton
Thornington
Howtel
Milfield
Nesbit
Border Union
Lempitlaw
Doddington
Easter Softlaw
Lanton
Heiton
Yeavering
Coupland
Kirknewton
Akeld
R. Glen
1402 Homildon Hill
362 YEAVERING BELL
Chatton
Frogden
Town Yetholm
Kirk Yetholm
Wooler
Cavers
Linton
Primsidemill
NORTHUMBERLAND
Eckford
Newtown
River Till
Morebattle
Pennine Way
564 THE CURR
525 PRESTON HILL
605 THE SCHIL
NATIONAL PARK
Gateshaw
Ilderton
816 THE CHEVIOT
Mowhaugh
307 SHIBDEN HILL
Hownam
567 DUNMOOR HILL
Chatto
Branton
620 WINDY GYLE HILL
Ingram
Glanton
Camps
616 CUSHAT LAW
334 COCHRANE PIKE
C H E V I O T H I L L S
River Alwin
414 BROWNDEAN
Alnham
500 SHILLHOPE LAW
Camps
Netherton
500 HUNGRY LAW
Alwinton
Burradon
Ramshope
448 BLACK KIP
Harbottle
NORTHUMBERLAND
Catcleugh Reservoir
Sharperton
Holystone
Snitter
River Coquet
Rothbury
Byrness
NATIONAL PARK
368 CORBY PIKE
Thropton
Hepple
Great Tosson
301 THE BEACON
Rochester
Lordenshaws
441 TOSSON HILL
0 1 2 3 4 miles
0 1 2 3 4 5 kilometres
A6105
B6460
A6112
B6437
B6461
B6470
A698
A1
B6354
B6525
B6364
B6461
B6353
A697
B6350
B6396
B6352
B6351
B6436
B6348
B6401
B6341

CAUSEWAY FLOODED AT HIGH TIDE
HOLY ISLAND
Holy Island
Lindisfarne Castle
Lindisfarne Priory
Castle Point
Guile Point
Longstone Lighthouse
FARNE ISLANDS
Staple Sound
Inner Sound
North Northumberland Heritage Coast
Budle Bay
Bamburgh
Belford
Seahouses
North Sunderland
Lucker
Warenford
Beadnell
Swinhoe
Beadnell Bay
Chathill
Newstead
Tughall
Ellingham
Preston
Preston Pele Tower
Ros Castle
267 CATERAN HILL
Newton-by-the-Sea
Embleton & Newton Links
Christon Bank
Embleton
Embleton Bay
Dunstanburgh Castle
North Charlton
Fallodon
South Charlton
Old Bewick
Eglingham
Dunstan
Craster
Rock
Rennington
Stamford
Howick Hall
Howick
Cullernose Point
Beanley
Longhoughton
Denwick
Boulmer
River Aln
Alnwick
Bolton
Seaton Point
Lesbury
Alnmouth
Alnmouth Bay
Castle
Edlingham
Shilbottle
260 GLANTLEES HILL
Newton-on-the-Moor
Warkworth Castle & Hermitage
Warkworth
Amble
Coquet Island
159
Swarland
Gloster Hill
Guyzance
High Hauxley
Acklington
Togston
Felton
East Thirston
Broomhill
South Broomhill
West Thirston
Red Row
Pauperhaugh
Brinkburn
Druridge Bay
Eshott
A1
A1068
B1342
B1340
B1341
B6349
B6348
B6347
B6346
B6341
B1339
B6344
B1330

A
B
C
D
E
F
180
1
2
3
4
5
6
7
8
Dubh Eilea
ISLAY
Nave Island
Ardnave Point
Gortanta Point
Ton Mhòr
Kilnave
Sanaigmore
Loch Gruinart
Eilean Mòr
Loch Gòrr
Rudha Lamanais
Lecht Gruinart
RSPB
Saligo Bay
B8018
B8017
Gruinart
Gleann Mòr
Loch Gorm
Coul Point
Sunderland
B8018
Kilchoman
Machir Bay
A847
Loch Indaal
Bruichladdich
Kilchiaran Bay
Bowmore
RHINNS OF ISLAY
15
Port Charlotte
231
BEINN TART A'MHILL
River Lag
Lossit Bay
Nereabolls
Duich R
A846
Rudha na Faing
A847
Portnahaven
Port Wemyss
Orsay
Laggan Bay
Islay
RHINNS POINT
Rudha Mòr
Kintra
160
165
MAOL BU
0 1 2 3 4 miles
0 1 2 3 4 5 kilometres
Lower Killeyan
THE O
Risabus

Scalasaig
Machrins
Garvard
Rudha Bàn
Oronsay
ORONSAY
Eilean Ghurdmail
JURA
Colonsay-Port Askaig
Corpach Bay
466 BEINN BHREAC
Glen Grundale
Lussa River
Shian Bay
453 RAINBERG MÒR
Ardlussa
Lussa Point
Lussagiven
Loch Righ Mòr
A846
Rudh' ant-Sàilein
Loch Tarbert
Rudha' a' Mhàil
Rudha Bholsa
363 SGARBH BREAC
506 SCRINADLE
398 BEINN TARSUINN
Jura Forest
784 BEINN AN OIR
734
Paps of Jura
Loch a' Chnuic Bhric
Bunnahabhain
316 GUIR-BHEINN
Knockrome
Ardfernal
Jura
Sound of Islay
560 GLASS BHEINN
Port Askaig
Feolin Ferry
Finlaggan
Kiells
Loch Finlaggan
529 DUBHA BHEINN
Keils
Craighouse
Small Isles
Rudha na Gaillich
Ballygrant
Loch Ballygrant
Loch Lossit
342 BRAT BHEINN
Cabrach
266 BEINNE DUBH
Am Fraoch Eilean
Brosdale Island
Rudha na Tràille
ridgend
Gartachossan
429 SGÒRR NAM FAOILEANN
Kilennan Burn
471
McArthur's Head
490 BEINN BHEIGEIR
Port Askaig-Kennacraig
Rudha Liath
Ardtalla
454 BEINN URARAIDH
Loch Uraraidh
Claggain Bay
gedale
Kintour
Kildalton Cross
Ardmore Point
346 BEINN SHOLUM
Eilean a' Chuirn
Port Ellen-Kennacraig
Rudha na Gainn
Lagavulin
Laphroaig Distillery
Laphroaig
Texa
Kilnaughton Bay
Keills Cha
Loch Cille
Danr Islan
St Cormac's Chapel
Kilmory Knap Chapel
Kilmory Bay
Point of Knap
Sound of Jura
Kilberry Hea
Keppoch Poi
Kinerara
Tarbert
GIGHA
Rhunahaorine Point
Ardminish
Achamore
Tayinloan
Sound of Gigha
Cara
181
172
160
G H J K L M
1 2 3 4 5 6 7 8

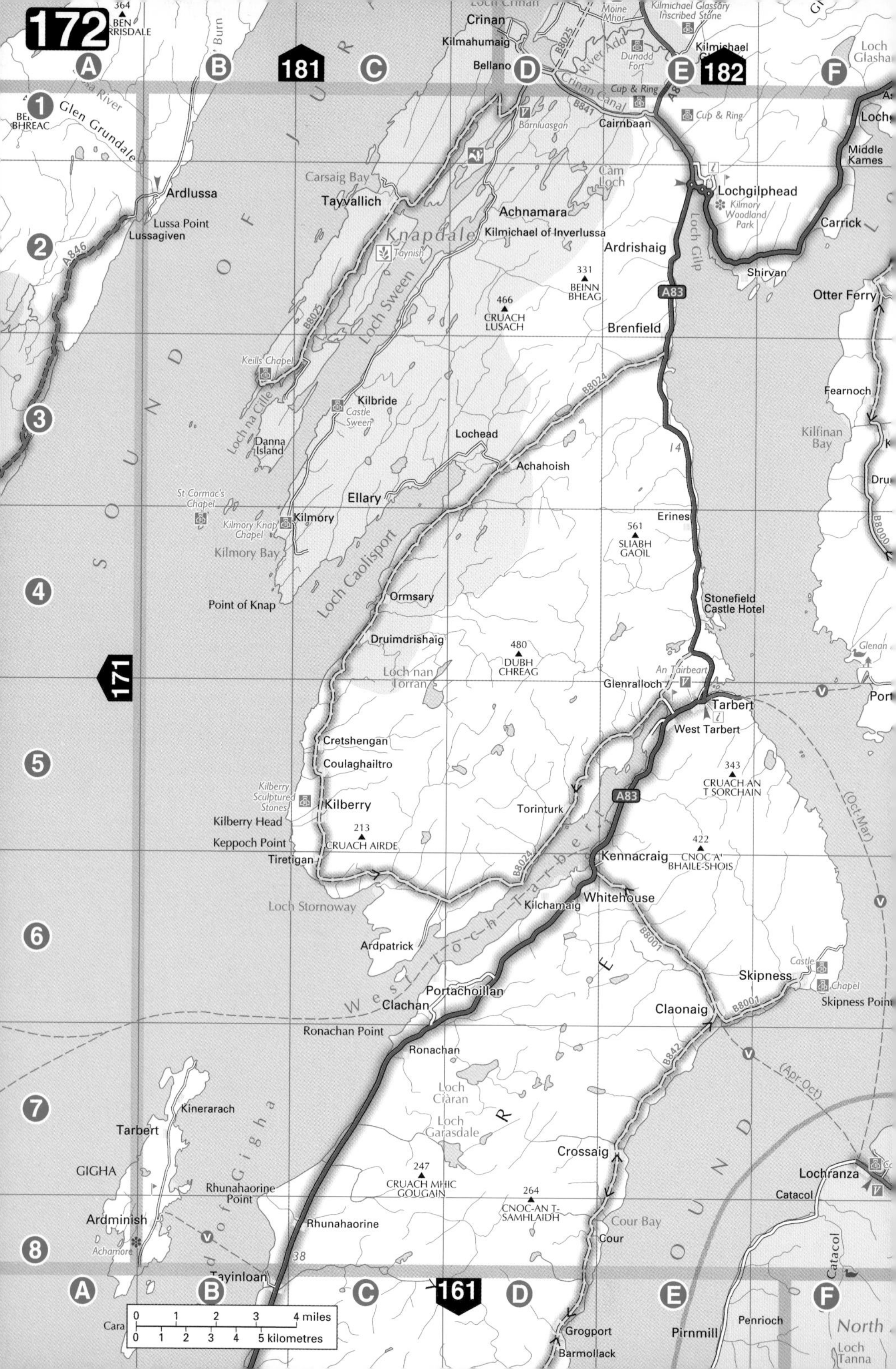
364
BEN
RRISDALE
Burn
181
Crinan
Kilmahumaig
Bellano
Moine
Mhor
B8025
River Add
Dunadd
Fort
Kilmichael Glassary
Inscribed Stone
Kilmichael
182
Loch
Glashan
A
B
C
D
E
F
1
Glen Grundale
BEN
BHREAC
Crinan Canal
Cup & Ring
Cup & Ring
B841
Barnluasgan
Cairnbaan
Lochgilphead
Kilmory
Woodland
Park
Middle
Kames
Carsaig Bay
Tayvallich
Càm
Loch
Ardlussa
Lussa Point
Lussagiven
Achnamara
Kilmichael of Inverlussa
Knapdale
Taynish
Carrick
2
A846
Ardrishaig
Loch Gilp
Shirvan
331
BEINN
BHEAG
466
CRUACH
LUSACH
A83
Otter Ferry
Loch Sween
B8025
Brenfield
Keills Chapel
Kilbride
Castle
Sween
B8024
Fearnoch
3
Loch na Cille
Danna
Island
Lochead
Achahoish
Kilfinan
Bay
St Cormac's
Chapel
Ellary
Kilmory Knap
Chapel
Kilmory
Kilmory Bay
Erines
561
SLIABH
GAOIL
B8000
4
Point of Knap
Loch Caolisport
Ormsary
Stonefield
Castle Hotel
Druimdrishaig
480
DUBH
CHREAG
171
Loch nan
Torran
An Tairbeart
Glenralloch
Tarbert
West Tarbert
Glenan
5
Cretshengan
Coulaghailtro
343
CRUACH AN
T SORCHAIN
Kilberry
Sculptured
Stones
Kilberry
Kilberry Head
213
CRUACH AIRDE
Keppoch Point
Tiretigan
Torinturk
A83
422
CNOC A'
BHAILE-SHOIS
Kennacraig
(Oct-Mar)
Loch Stornoway
B8024
Kilchamaig
Whitehouse
6
Ardpatrick
West Loch Tarbert
B8001
Castle
Chapel
Skipness
Skipness Point
Portachoillan
Clachan
Claonaig
B8001
Ronachan Point
Ronachan
B842
(Apr-Oct)
7
Kinerarach
Tarbert
Loch
Ciàran
Loch
Garasdale
Sound of Gigha
GIGHA
Crossaig
247
CRUACH MHIC
GOUGAIN
264
CNOC-AN T-
SAMHLAIDH
Lochranza
Catacol
Rhunahaorine
Point
Ardminish
Rhunahaorine
Cour Bay
Cour
8
Achamore
Tayinloan
161
Catacol
Cara
0 1 2 3 4 miles
0 1 2 3 4 5 kilometres
Grogport
Barmollack
Pirnmill
Penrioch
North
Loch
Tanna

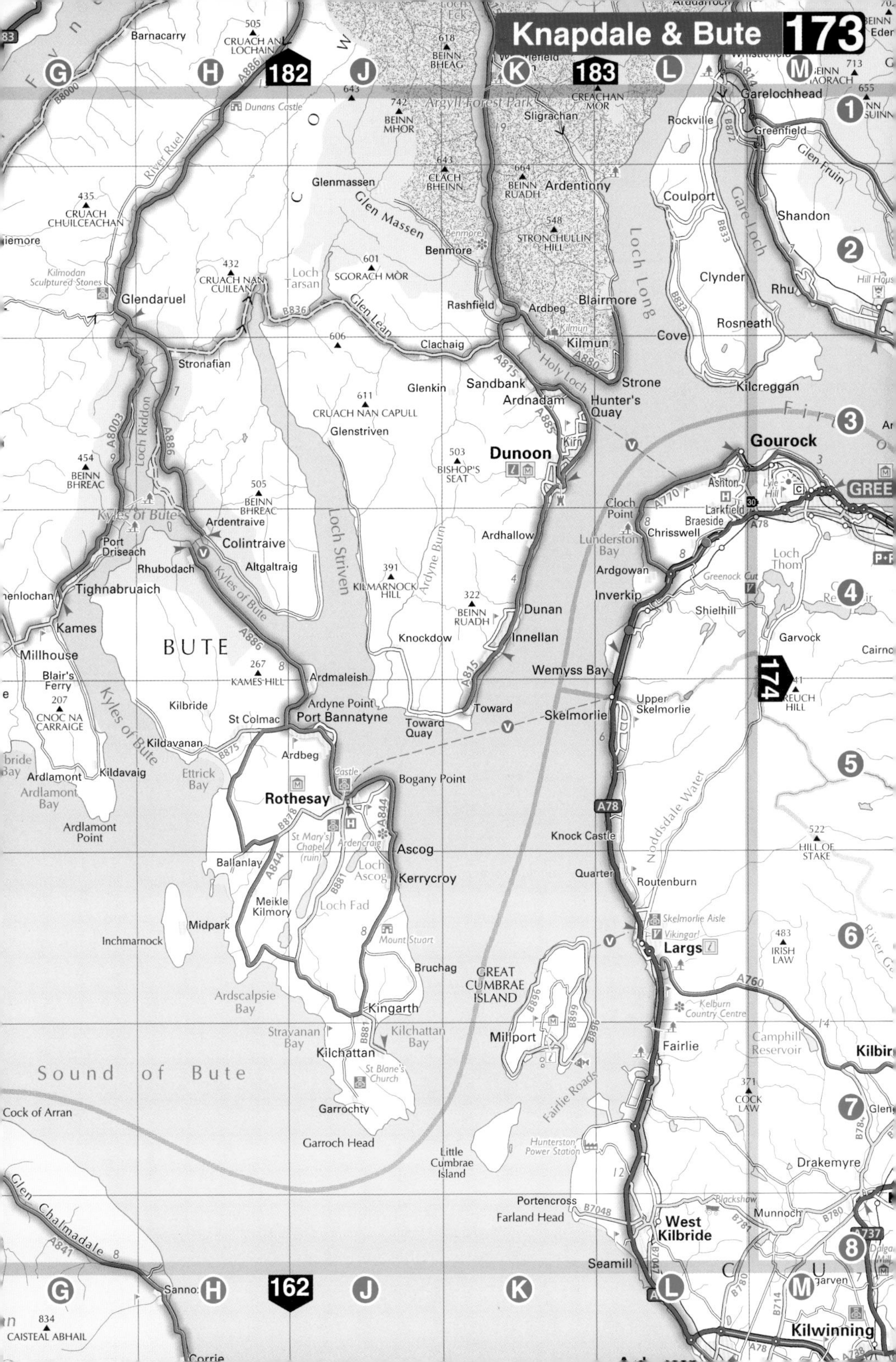
182
183
174
162
Dunoon
Rothesay
Gourock
Largs
West Kilbride
Kilwinning
BUTE
Sound of Bute
GREAT CUMBRAE ISLAND
Millport
Little Cumbrae Island
Loch Striven
Loch Long
Gare Loch
Holy Loch
Kyles of Bute
Argyll Forest Park
Glendaruel
Tighnabruaich
Colintraive
Port Bannatyne
Kilchattan
Kingarth
Garrochty
Garroch Head
Ardentinny
Kilmun
Strone
Sandbank
Hunter's Quay
Innellan
Toward
Wemyss Bay
Skelmorlie
Inverkip
Fairlie
Seamill
Portencross
Farland Head
Garelochhead
Rhu
Kilcreggan
Cove
Coulport
Clynder
Rosneath
Shandon
Benmore
Inchmarnock
Ettrick Bay
Kames
Millhouse
Ardlamont Point
Cock of Arran
Glen Chalmadale
Sannox
Corrie
CAISTEAL ABHAIL
Mount Stuart
Hunterston Power Station
Kelburn Country Centre

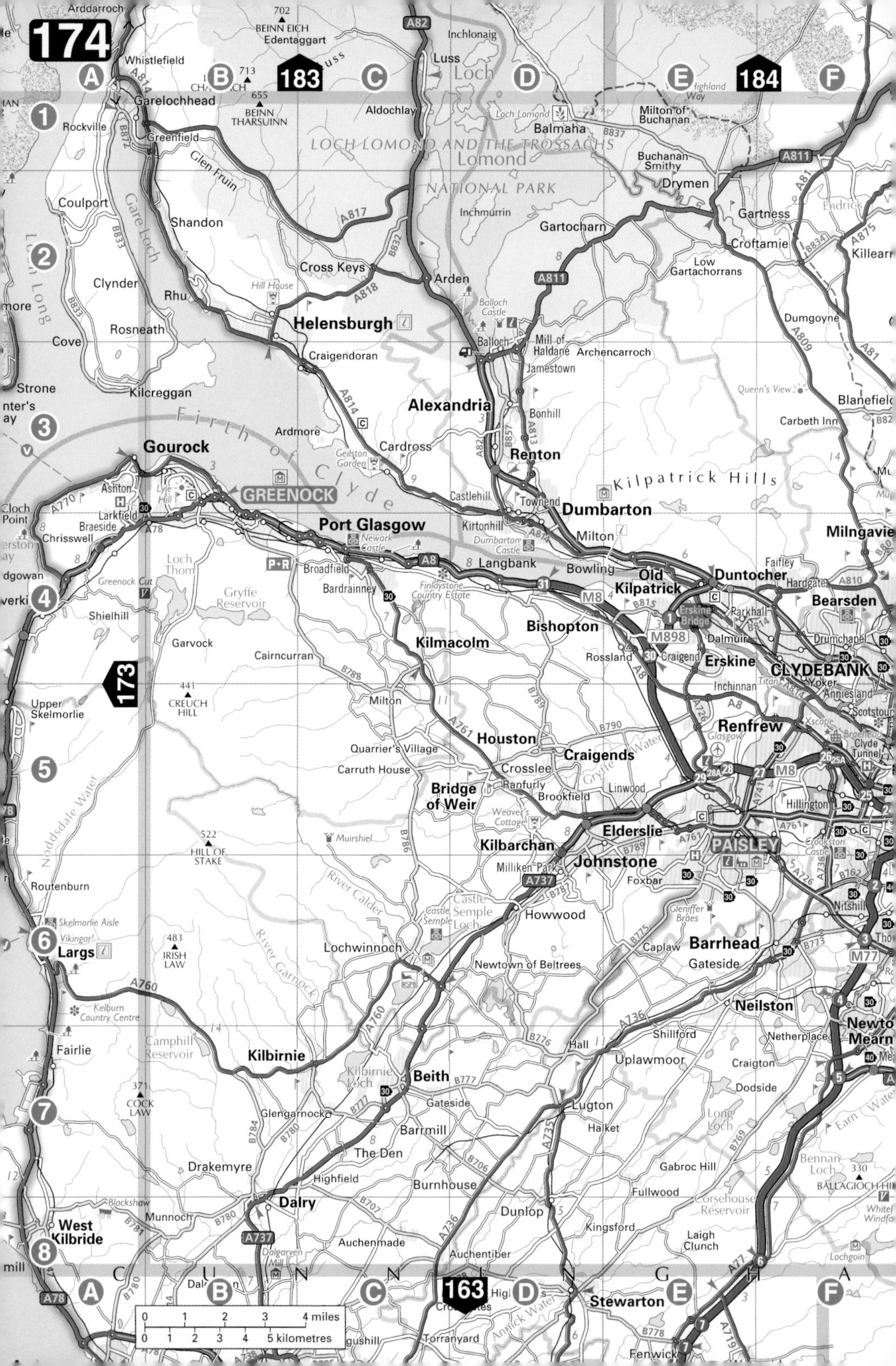
183
184
173
163
Arddarroch
Whistlefield
Garelochhead
Rockville
Greenfield
BEINN EICH
Edentaggart
BEINN THARSUINN
Luss
Inchlonaig
Loch Lomond
Aldochlay
Balmaha
Milton of Buchanan
LOCH LOMOND AND THE TROSSACHS
NATIONAL PARK
Buchanan Smithy
Drymen
Glen Fruin
Coulport
Shandon
Gare Loch
Loch Long
Inchmurrin
Gartocharn
Gartness
Croftamie
Killearn
Low Gartachorrans
Clynder
Cross Keys
Arden
Rhu
Hill House
Helensburgh
Balloch Castle
Dumgoyne
Rosneath
Cove
Craigendoran
Balloch
Mill of Haldane
Archencarroch
Jamestown
Strone
Kilcreggan
Queen's View
Blanefield
Alexandria
Bonhill
Carbeth Inn
Firth of Clyde
Ardmore
Gourock
Cardross
Geilston Garden
Renton
Kilpatrick Hills
Ashton
Lyle Hill
GREENOCK
Castlehill
Townend
Dumbarton
Cloch Point
Larkfield
Braeside
Chrisswell
Port Glasgow
Newark Castle
Kirtonhill
Milton
Milngavie
Dumbarton Castle
Loch Thom
Broadfield
Langbank
Bowling
Old Kilpatrick
Duntocher
Faifley
Hardgate
Greenock Cut
Gryffe Reservoir
Bardrainney
Finlaystone Country Estate
Erskine Bridge
Parkhall
Bearsden
Shielhill
Bishopton
Dalmuir
Drumchapel
Garvock
Cairncurran
Kilmacolm
Rossland
Craigend
Erskine
CLYDEBANK
Yoker
Inchinnan
Titan
Anniesland
Upper Skelmorlie
CREUCH HILL
Milton
Scotstoun
Houston
Renfrew
Glasgow
Xscape
Braehead
Clyde Tunnel
Quarrier's Village
Craigends
Gryffe Water
Carruth House
Crosslee
Bridge of Weir
Ranfurly
Brookfield
Linwood
Hillington
Weaver's Cottage
Elderslie
Noddsdale Water
Muirshiel
Kilbarchan
PAISLEY
Crookston Castle
HILL OF STAKE
Milliken Park
Johnstone
Foxbar
Routenburn
River Calder
Castle Semple Loch
Howwood
Nitshill
Gleniffer Braes
Skelmorlie Aisle
Vikingar!
Largs
IRISH LAW
River Garnock
Lochwinnoch
Caplaw
Barrhead
Gateside
Newtown of Beltrees
RSPB
Neilston
Kelburn Country Centre
Newton Mearns
Shillford
Netherplace
Fairlie
Camphill Reservoir
Kilbirnie
Hall
Uplawmoor
Craigton
Kilbirnie Loch
Beith
COCK LAW
Gateside
Lugton
Dodside
Glengarnock
Halket
Long Loch
Barrmill
Earn Water
The Den
Drakemyre
Highfield
Burnhouse
Gabroc Hill
Bennan Loch
BALLAGIOCH HILL
Fullwood
Corsehouse Reservoir
Blackshaw
Dalry
Munnoch
Dunlop
West Kilbride
Kingsford
Auchenmade
Laigh Clunch
Dalgarven Mill
Auchentiber
Lochgoin
Stewarton
Annick Water
Torranyard
Fenwick
A
B
C
D
E
F
1
2
3
4
5
6
7
8
A82
A814
A817
A818
A811
A809
A81
A875
B837
B834
B833
B872
B832
A813
B857
A770
A78
A8
M8
M898
B815
B814
A814
B788
B789
A761
B790
A726
A737
B787
B786
A760
B775
B773
M77
A736
B776
B777
B784
B780
B706
B769
B707
B781
A735
A77
B778
A719
0 1 2 3 4 miles
0 1 2 3 4 5 kilometres

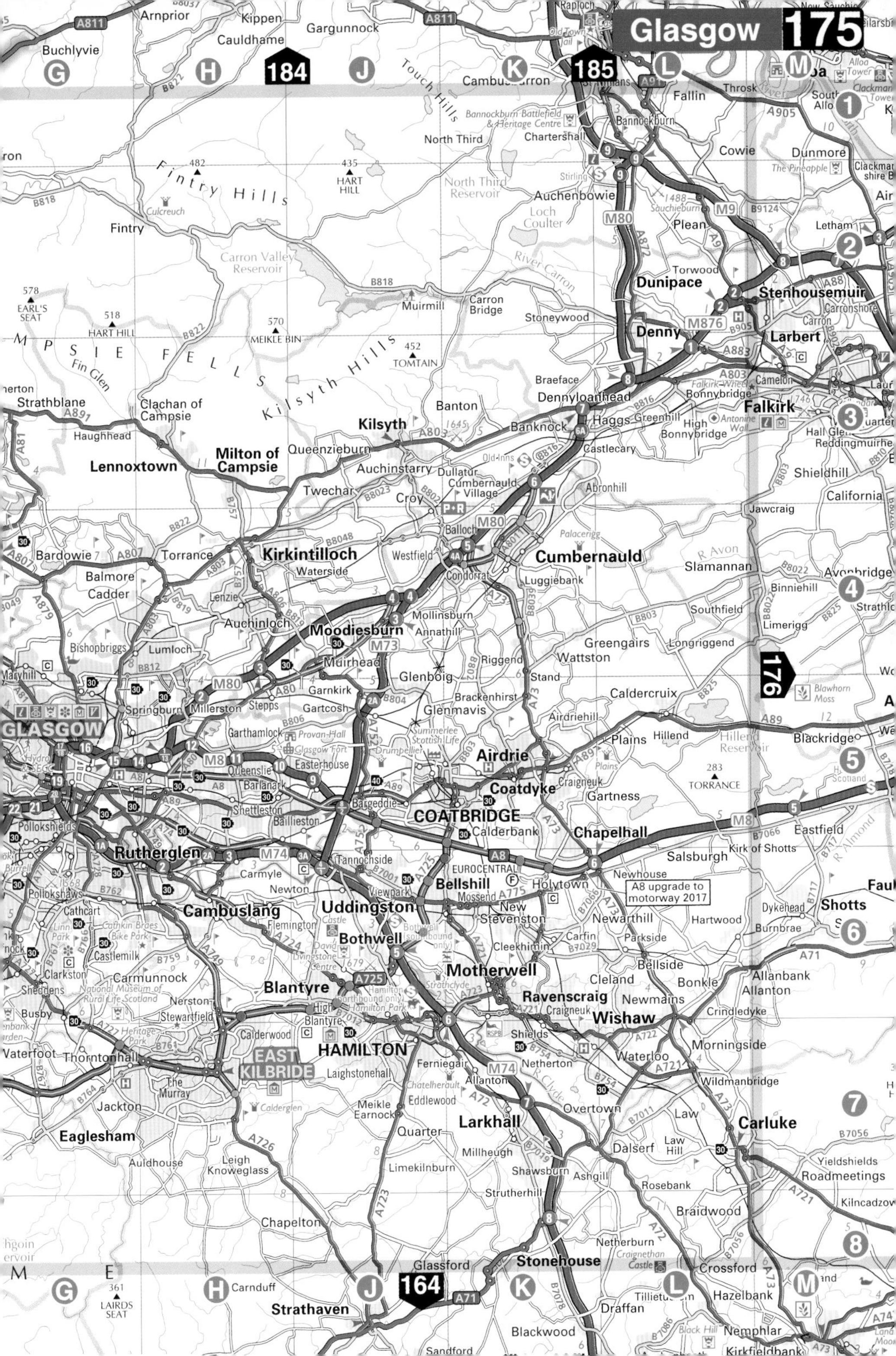

184
185
176
164
Buchlyvie
Arnprior
Kippen
Cauldhame
Gargunnock
Touch Hills
Cambusbarron
Fallin
Throsk
Bannockburn Battlefield & Heritage Centre
Bannockburn
Chartershall
North Third
Cowie
Dunmore
The Pineapple
Fintry Hills
HART HILL
Culcreuch
Fintry
North Third Reservoir
Auchenbowie
Loch Coulter
Plean
Letham
Carron Valley Reservoir
River Carron
Torwood
Dunipace
Stenhousemuir
EARL'S SEAT
HART HILL
MEIKLE BIN
Muirmill
Carron Bridge
Stoneywood
Denny
Carron
Larbert
Carronshore
CAMPSIE FELLS
Fin Glen
Kilsyth Hills
TOMTAIN
Braeface
Falkirk Wheel
Camelon
Strathblane
Clachan of Campsie
Banton
Dennyloanhead
Bonnybridge
Falkirk
Haughhead
Kilsyth
Banknock
Haggs
Greenhill
High Bonnybridge
Antonine Wall
Hall Glen
Reddingmuirhead
Lennoxtown
Milton of Campsie
Queenzieburn
Castlecary
Old Inns
Auchinstarry
Dullatur
Cumbernauld Village
Abronhill
Shieldhill
California
Twechar
Croy
Jawcraig
Balloch
Palacerigg
Bardowie
Torrance
Kirkintilloch
Westfield
Cumbernauld
R Avon
Slamannan
Avonbridge
Balmore
Cadder
Waterside
Condorrat
Luggiebank
Binniehill
Lenzie
Mollinsburn
Southfield
Limerigg
Auchinloch
Moodiesburn
Annathill
Bishopbriggs
Lumloch
Greengairs
Longriggend
Muirhead
Riggend
Wattston
Maryhill
Glenboig
Stand
Caldercruix
Blawhorn Moss
Garnkirk
Brackenhirst
Springburn
Millerston
Stepps
Gartcosh
Glenmavis
Airdriehill
GLASGOW
Garthamlock
Provan Hall
Summerlee Scottish Life
Plains
Hillend
Hillend Reservoir
Blackridge
Glasgow Fort
Drumpellier
Hydro
SECC
Queenslie
Easterhouse
Airdrie
TORRANCE
Barlanark
Coatdyke
Craigneuk
Gartness
Shettleston
Bargeddie
COATBRIDGE
Pollokshields
Baillieston
Calderbank
Chapelhall
Eastfield
Kirk of Shotts
Salsburgh
R Almond
Rutherglen
Tannochside
EUROCENTRAL
Carmyle
Newhouse
Bellshill
Holytown
Pollokshaws
Newton
Viewpark
Mossend
A8 upgrade to motorway 2017
Cathcart
Cambuslang
Uddingston
New Stevenston
Newarthill
Hartwood
Dykehead
Shotts
Linn Park
Cathkin Braes Bike Park
Flemington
Castle
Burnbrae
Bothwell
Castlemilk
David Livingstone Centre
Cleekhimin
Carfin
Parkside
Clarkston
Carmunnock
Motherwell
Bellside
Allanbank
Sheddens
National Museum of Rural Life Scotland
Blantyre
Strathclyde
Cleland
Bonkle
Allanton
Hamilton
Hamilton Park
Ravenscraig
Newmains
Nerston
Crindledyke
Busby
Stewartfield
High Blantyre
Craigneuk
Wishaw
Heritage Park
Calderwood
Shields
Waterfoot
Thorntonhall
EAST KILBRIDE
HAMILTON
Morningside
Laighstonehall
Netherton
Waterloo
Ferniegair
The Murray
Chatelherault
Allanton
Wildmanbridge
Jackton
Calderglen
Meikle Earnock
Eddlewood
R Clyde
Overtown
Law
Carluke
Eaglesham
Quarter
Larkhall
Dalserf
Law Hill
Millheugh
Auldhouse
Leigh Knoweglass
Limekilnburn
Shawsburn
Ashgill
Yieldshields
Roadmeetings
Rosebank
Strutherhill
Kilncadzow
Braidwood
Chapelton
Netherburn
Craignethan Castle
Glassford
Stonehouse
Crossford
Carnduff
LAIRDS SEAT
Tillietudlem
Hazelbank
Strathaven
Draffan
Black Hill
Blackwood
Nemphlar
Sandford
Kirkfieldbank

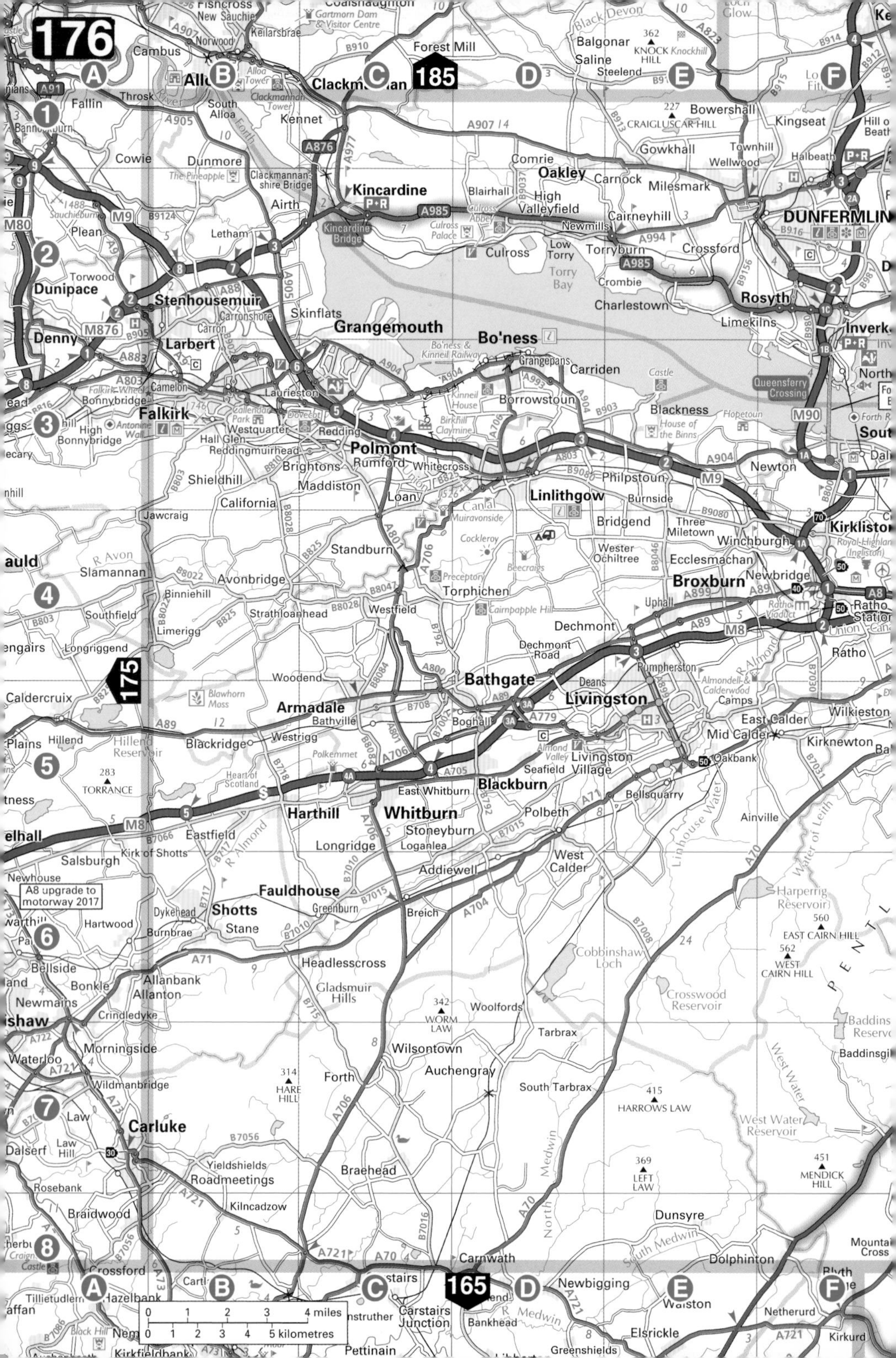

185
175
165
Alloa
Cambus
Clackmannan
Forest Mill
Balgonar
Saline
Steelend
KNOCK HILL
Fallin
Throsk
South Alloa
Kennet
Bowershall
CRAIGLUSCAR HILL
Kingseat
Cowie
Dunmore
Clackmannanshire Bridge
Comrie
Oakley
Carnock
Gowkhall
Townhill
Wellwood
Halbeath
Kincardine
Kincardine Bridge
Blairhall
High Valleyfield
Milesmark
Cairneyhill
Newmills
DUNFERMLINE
Airth
Plean
Letham
Culross
Culross Palace
Low Torry
Torryburn
Crossford
Torry Bay
Crombie
Charlestown
Rosyth
Limekilns
Torwood
Dunipace
Stenhousemuir
Carronshore
Carron
Skinflats
Grangemouth
Bo'ness
Denny
Larbert
Bo'ness & Kinneil Railway
Grangepans
Carriden
Queensferry Crossing
North
Camelon
Falkirk Wheel
Bonnybridge
Falkirk
Laurieston
Kinneil House
Borrowstoun
Blackness
Hopetoun
High Bonnybridge
Antonine Wall
Callendar Park
Westquarter
Dovecot
Redding
Birkhill Claymine
House of the Binns
Hall Glen
Reddingmuirhead
Polmont
Rumford
Whitecross
Philpstoun
Newton
Shieldhill
Brightons
Maddiston
Loan
Linlithgow
Burnside
Kirkliston
California
Jawcraig
Muiravonside
Bridgend
Three Miletown
Winchburgh
Cockleroy
Standburn
Wester Ochiltree
Ecclesmachan
Slamannan
Avonbridge
Beecraigs
Preceptory
Torphichen
Broxburn
Newbridge
Binniehill
Westfield
Cairnpapple Hill
Uphall
Ratho Station
Southfield
Strathloanhead
Limerigg
Dechmont
Longriggend
Dechmont Road
Ratho
Woodend
Bathgate
Pumpherston
Caldercruix
Blawhorn Moss
Armadale
Deans
Livingston
Almondell & Calderwood
Camps
Wilkieston
Hillend
Hillend Reservoir
Bathville
Westrigg
Blackridge
Boghall
East Calder
Mid Calder
Kirknewton
Oakbank
Polkemmet
Almond Valley
Livingston Village
Seafield
283 TORRANCE
Heart of Scotland
Blackburn
East Whitburn
Bellsquarry
Harthill
Whitburn
Polbeth
Ainville
Eastfield
Stoneyburn
Salsburgh
Kirk of Shotts
Longridge
Loganlea
West Calder
Addiewell
Newhouse
A8 upgrade to motorway 2017
Fauldhouse
Shotts
Dykehead
Greenburn
Breich
Harperrig Reservoir
Hartwood
Stane
Burnbrae
560 EAST CAIRN HILL
562 WEST CAIRN HILL
Cobbinshaw Loch
Bellside
Headlesscross
Bonkle
Allanbank
Allanton
Gladsmuir Hills
Crosswood Reservoir
Newmains
342 WORM LAW
Woolfords
Crindledyke
Baddinsgill Reservoir
Tarbrax
Morningside
Wilsontown
Waterloo
Auchengray
Wildmanbridge
314 HARE HILL
Forth
South Tarbrax
415 HARROWS LAW
Law
West Water
West Water Reservoir
Carluke
Dalserf
Law Hill
Yieldshields
Roadmeetings
Braehead
369 LEFT LAW
451 MENDICK HILL
Rosebank
Kilncadzow
Braidwood
Dunsyre
South Medwin
Carnwath
Mountain Cross
Crossford
Dolphinton
Craignethan Castle
Newbigging
Hazelbank
Tillietudlem
Carstairs Junction
Walston
Netherurd
Bankhead
Elsrickle
Kirkurd
Black Hill
Pettinain
Greenshields
Kirkfieldbank
0 1 2 3 4 miles
0 1 2 3 4 5 kilometres

Cardenden
Gallatown
Chapel
Kirkcaldy
Cowdenbeath
Auchtertool
Linktown
Donibristle
Balmule
Kinghorn
Aberdour
Pettycur
Pettycur Bay
Burntisland
Castle
St Bridget's Kirk
Silversands Bay
Dalgety Bay
Inchcolm Abbey
Inchkeith
FIRTH OF FORTH
Cramond Island
Eyebroughy
Dirleton
Gullane Bay
Gullane Point
Muirfield
Gullane
Aberlady Bay
Craigelaw Point
Aberlady
Luffness
Drem
Gosford Bay
Spittal
Ballencrieff
Athelstaneford
Cockenzie and Port Seton
Seton Collegiate Church
Preston Market Cross
Prestonpans
Heritage Museum
Longniddry
Seton Mains
Huntington
Elvingston
EDINBURGH
Britannia
Granton
Newhaven
Cramond
Lauriston Castle
Royal Botanic Garden
Barnton
Davidson's Mains
Warriston
Leith
St Triduana's Chapel
Blackhall
Dovecot
Castle
Dynamic Earth
ARTHUR'S SEAT 251
Portobello
Joppa
Musselburgh
Fisherrow
Tranent
Gladsmuir
Macmerry
Corstorphine
Duddingston
Newcraighall
Craigmillar
Craigmillar Castle
Craiglockhart
Morningside
Inveresk
Wallyford
New Winton
Samuelston
South Gyle
Elphinstone
Ormiston Market Cross
Ormiston
Boggs Holdings
Water of Leith
Blackford Hill
Royal Observatory
Newton
Whitecraig
Crossgatehall
Juniper Green
Colinton
Liberton
Gilmerton
Danderhall
Millerhill
Dalkeith Park
Pencaitland
Cousland
Currie
Bonaly
Malleny Garden
Kinleith
Malleny Mills
Hillend
Butterfly Farm
Eskbank
Dalkeith
East Saltoun
West Saltoun
493 ALLERMUIR HILL
Straiton
Lasswade
Newbattle
Mayfield
Boghall
Loanhead
Bonnyrigg
Gilchriston
Woodhouselee
Bilston
Chesterhill
Castlelaw Hill Fort
Polton
Newtongrange
Pathhead
Easter Howgate
Roslin
Dewarton
Vogrie
Red Moss of Balerno
Pentland Hills
Milton Bridge
Mining Museum
Newtonloan
Newlandrig
Humbie
448 HARE HILL
579 SCALD LAW
576 CARNETHY HILL
Rosewell
Arniston
Crichton
Fala Dam
Blegbie
Auchendinny
Crichton Castle
Fala
Silverburn
Penicuik
Gorebridge
Carrington
Soutra Summit 363
Pomathorn
North Middleton
R North Esk
Howgate
Temple
Mount Lothian
394 DUN LAW
Rosebery Reservoir
Gilston
380 TURF LAW
Carlops
Leadburn
Craigburn
Heriot
Gladhouse Reservoir
Oxton
Moorfoot Hills
Carfrae
Heriot Water
Linton
Waterheads
324 WHITE RIG
383 COLLIE LAW
Portmore Loch
425 DUN LAW
Fountainhall
479 WETHER LAW
651 BLACKHOPE SCAR
Torquhan
Romanno Bridge
Eddleston
Lauder
476 CRAILZIE HILL
621 WHITEHOPE LAW
Killochyett
Stow
659
427
Lyne Water
186
178
166

North Berwick
Haddington
Dunbar
Fidra
Craigleith
Bass Rock
Eyebroughy
Dirleton Castle & Gardens
Scottish Seabird
Tantallon Castle
Gullane Bay
Gullane Point
Dirleton
Muirfield
Gullane
Fenton Barns
Kingston
Cleghornie
Whitekirk
NORTH BERWICK LAW
St Baldred's Cradle
Tyne Mouth
Belhaven Bay
Belhaven
Aberlady Bay
Craigelaw Point
Aberlady
Luffness
Drem
Prora
East Fortune
Tyninghame
John Muir
Gosford Bay
Motor
Chesters Hill Fort
Museum of Flight
Preston Mill & Phantassie Doocot
Markle
Ballencrieff
Spittal
Athelstaneford
East Linton
West Barns
Broxburn
Barns Ness
East Barns
Chapel
Skateraw
Seton Collegiate Church
Longniddry
Seton Mains
Huntington
Elvingston
Hailes Castle
Traprain
Spott
Pitcox
Doonhill Homestead
Dry Burn
Tranent
Macmerry
Gladsmuir
St Martin's Kirk (ruin)
Lauderdale Aisle St Mary's Church
Traprain Law
Luggate Burn
Stenton
The Brunt
Innerwick
Crowhill
New Winton
Lennoxlove
Papple
Morham
Garvald
Nunraw Abbey
COCKLAW HILL
BRANSLY HILL
Oldhamstocks
Ormiston Market Cross
Ormiston
Boggs Holdings
Samuelston
Bolton
River Tyne
Pencaitland
Gifford
East Saltoun
West Saltoun
Danskine
LAMMERMUIR HILLS
Monynut Water
Bothwell Water
HEART LAW
Gilchriston
Long Newton
Longyester
SPARTLETON
St Agnes
Whiteadder Reservoir
athhead
Humbie
Fala Dam
Fala
Blegbie
LAMMER LAW
MEIKLE SAYS LAW
Cranshaws
Abbey St Bathans
Ellemford
Soutra Summit
CRIB LAW
SEENES LAW
MEIKLE LAW
HUNT LAW
Whitchester
DUN LAW
TURF LAW
Gilston
Soonhope Burn
Southern Upland Way
Longformacus
HOGS LAW
DIRRINGTON GREAT LAW
Wedderlie Burn
Oxton
Carfraemill
LAUDERDALE
COLLIE LAW
Blythe
Polwarth
Fountainhall
Spottiswoode
Westruther
Thornydykes
Lauder
Thirlestane
Houndslow
Torquhan
Killochyett
Lugate Water
Boon
Leader Water
Bassendean
Greenlaw
Legerwood
Greenknowe Tower
Middlethird
Nether Blainslie
Gavin
0 1 2 3 4 miles
0 1 2 3 4 5 kilometres

177

167

G
H
J
K
L
M
1
2
3
4
5
6
7
8
Reed Point
Cove
Pease Bay
Siccar Point
Fast Castle Head
Pease Dean
A1107
196
BROWN RIG
Coldingham Loch
ST ABB'S HEAD
St Abbs
Coldingham Bay
Grantshouse
Southern Upland Way
Butterdean
Coldingham
Houndwood
Heugh Head
Cairncross
Eyemouth
262
HORSELEY HILL
A1
Reston
Ayton
Burnmouth
B6438
Auchencrow
Marygold
Lintlaw
A6112
Preston
Lamberton
Chirnside
B6437
B6355
Marshall Meadows Bay
Cumledge
Edrom Church
Edrom
Chirnsidebridge
Foulden
North Northumberland Heritage Coast
1333
Manderston
Broadhaugh
Edington
Whiteadder Water
Foulden Tithe Barn
A6105
Berwick-upon-Tweed
Castle
Barracks & Main Guard
Duns
Allanton
Hutton
Paxton
Town Ramparts
Blackadder
B6460
B6461
Tweedmouth
Spittal
Whitsome
Hilton
Huds Head
Nisbet Hill
Sinclair's Hill
A1167
Scremerston
Horndean
Horncliffe
Murton
Ladykirk
Castle
Thornton
Swinton
B6470
Norham
A698
Cheswick
Upsettlington
168
CAUSEWAY FLOODED AT HIGH TIDE
Simprim
B6354
Ancroft
B6461
River Tweed
Leitholm
B6525
Haggerston

180
A
B
C
D
E
F
1
2
3
4
5
6
7
8
189
171
Bac Mòr or Dutchmans Cap
Staffa
Fingal's Cave
Little Colonsay
Loch na Keal,
Isle of Mull
Inch Kenneth
Inchkenneth Chapel
(ruin)
491
CREACH BHEINN
Fossil Tree
Burg
IONA
Iona Abbey
& Nunnery
Baile Mór
MacLean's Cross
Sound of Iona
Rudha nan Cearc
Kintra
Fionnphort
Aridhglas
St Columba
Exhibition
Centre
Loch na
Lathaich
A849
Bunessan
Loch Assapol
376
ROSS OF MULL
Uisken
Ardchiavaig
Erraid
Soa Island
Rudha Ardalanish
Torran Rocks
Eilean
Dubh
Balnahard
Kiloran Bay
COLONSAY
Kiloran
Kilchattan
B8087
Scalasaig
B8086
Machrins
Colonsay
B8085
Oronsay
Rudha
Bàn
Dubh Eilean
0 1 2 3 4 miles
0 1 2 3 4 5 kilometres

ISLE OF MULL
Craignure
Duart Bay
Duart Point
Torosay
Lochdonhead
Lochdon
Gorten
Loch Don
Grass Point
766
DUN DA GHAOITHE
BEINN MHEADHO
966
BEN MORE
704
CRUACHAN DEARG
Eorsa
BEINN A' GRAIG
Macquarie Mausoleum
190
A849
B8035
Glen More
Strathcoil
247
CARN BAN
Loch Spelve
Croggan
698
BEN CREACH
717
BEN BUIE
Loch Fuaran
Aird of Kinloch
Tiroran
Pennycross
Pennyghael
503
BEINN NA CROISE
Leidle Water
Lochbuie
Loch Uisg
337
MAOL BAN
Loch Buie
377
DRUIM FADA
376
BEINN CHREAGACH
Carsaig
Rudha Dubh
Malcolm's Point
FIRTH OF LORNE
Rudha Seanach
KERRERA
Colonsay-Oban
Insh Island
Clachan
Clachan-Seil
SEIL
Ellenabeich
Easdale
Balvicar
B844
B8003
Cuan
Seil Sound
182
Cullipool
Torsa
Degnish
Loch Melfort
Arduaine
Garbh Eileach
Eilean Dubh Mòr
GARVELLACHS
Monastery & Beehive Cells
Eileach an Naoimh
LUNGA
LUING
Sound of Luing
Toberonochy
Shuna Sound
SHUNA
Scarba, Lunga and the Garvellachs
Craobh Haven
Shuna Point
SCARBA
448
CRUACH SCARBA
Gulf of Corryvreckan
B8002
Aird
Loch Craignish
Craignish Point
Island Macaskin
295
CRUACH NA SEILCHEIG
Glengarrisdale Bay
Glendebadel Bay
364
BEN GARRISDALE
Lealt Burn
JURA
SOUND OF JURA
Loch Crinan
Crinan
Kilmahumaig
Bellanoch
B8025
Poltalloch
Corpach Bay
466
BEINN BHREAC
Glen Grundale
Lussa River
171
172
Barnluasgan
Carsaig Bay

182
A
B
C
D
E
F
1
2
3
4
5
6
7
8
191
181
172
173
Kilcheran
Kiel Crofts
Sea Life Sanctuary
BEINN MOLURGAINN
Benderloch
Ledaig
Ardmucknish Bay
Oban
Dunstaffnage Castle
Dunstaffnage Chapel (ruin)
North Connel
Connel
Black Crofts
Ardchattan Priory
Inveresragan
BEN MEEAN
Loch Etive
Achnacloich
Achaleven
Dunbeg
Ganavan Bay
Dunollie Castle
McCaig's Tower
A85
B845
Bonawe
Airds Bay
Bonawe Historic Iron Furnace
River Noe
Brochroy
Taynuilt
Ichrachan
1124
BEN CRUACHAN
Pass of Brander
River Awe
Glen Nant
Airdeny
Clenamacrie
Glen Lonan
River Lonan
Oban
(An t-Oban)
KERRERA
Sound of Kerrera
Gallanachbeg
Ariogan
Gallanachmore
Loch Nell
Lerags
Kilmore
515
BEINN GHLAS
Ardanaiseig
Ardanaiseig Hotel
Hayfield
Rudha Seanach
Ardentallen
Loch Feochan
A816
Loch Nant
Kilchrenan
Taychreggan Hotel
Cladich
Gorten
Kilninver
356
AN CREACHAN
482
BEINN DEARG
Loch Scamadale
Portsonachan Hotel
Clachan
Clachan-Seil
SEIL
Balvicar
B844
B8003
B840
Inverinan
Loch Tralaig
Lochavich
Loch Avich
Loch Awe
589
CRUACH MHOR
Glen Aray
A819
Cuan
Torsa
Melfort
Kilmelford
Barnline Stables
Dalavich
Falls of Blarghour
Degnish
Ardchonnel
Loch Melfort
Newyork
Portinnisherrich
Arduaine
Gleann Domhain
Glen Liever
Inveraray Castle
Inveraray
Inveraray Jail
Shuna Sound
SHUNA
Durran
Braevallich
525
BEINN BHREAC
Douglas Water
Craobh Haven
Shuna Point
Inverliever Lodge
Craigdhu
A83
Ardfern
Kintraw
Ford
Fincharn
Loch Leacann
En Mhic Chrion
Auchindrain
En Righ
B8002
458
CRUACH MHIC FHIONNLARDH
433
BEINN LAOIGH
Carnasserie Castle
Furnace
Loch Craignish
Aird
Loch Gaineamhach
Glebe Cairn
Kilmartin
Kilmartin House
Sandhole
Newton
Island Macaskin
Slockavullin
Temple Wood Stone Circles
The Nether Largie Cairns
Dunchraigaig Cairn
Loch Leathan
Crarae
Crarae Garden
480
CRUACH NAN CAPULL
Ri Cruin Cairn
Poltalloch
Minard
Castle Lachlan
Gleann Airidh
Loch Crinan
Moine Mhor
Tullochgorm
Kilmichael Glassary Inscribed Stone
Crinan
Kilmahumaig
Kilmichael Glassary
Loch Glashan
Barnacarry
505
CRUACH AN LOCHAIN
Bellanoch
Dunadd Fort
River Add
B8025
Crinan Canal
Cup & Ring
B841
B8000
A886
Loch Fyne
Asknish
643
Dunans Castle
Lochgair
Middle Kames
River Ruel
0 1 2 3 4 miles
0 1 2 3 4 5 kilometres

Bridge of Orchy
Tyndrum
Crianlarich
Dalmally
Stronmilchan
Inverlochy
Upper Kinchrackine
Kilchurn Castle
Inverherive Hotel
BEN LUI
BEN OSS
BEINN DUBHCHRAIG
BEN MORE
STOBINIAN
BEINN EUNAICH
BEINN DONACHAN
BEINN UDLAIDH
BEINN CHAORACH
BEINN CHEATHAICH
Glen Kinglass
Glen Strae
Glen Orchy
Glen Lochy
Glen Lochay
Strath Fillan
Glen Falloch
West Highland Way
Falls of Falloch
LOCH LOMOND AND THE TROSSACHS NATIONAL PARK
Inverarnan
Ardlui
BEINN A' CHROIN
STOB A' CHOIN
MEALL MÒR
BEINN BHUIDHE
CLACHAN HILL
Glenfyne Lodge
MAOL BREAC
Glen Fyne
Glen Shira
Lochan Shira
BEN VORLICH
Loch Sloy
Cairndow
Ardkinglas Woodland Garden
Loch Fyne
Glen Kinglas
Inveruglas
Inversnaid Hotel
Stronachlachar
Loch Katrine
Loch Arklet
BEN IME
BEINN AN LOCHAIN
Rest and be thankful
BEINN NARNAIN
THE COBBLER
Succoth
CRUACH TAIRBEIRT
Arrochar
Tarbet
Glen Croe
St Catherines
CRUACH NAN CAPULL
BEN DONICH
Argyll Forest Park
Ardgartan
CRUINN A' BHEINN
Queen Elizabeth Forest Park
BEN LOMOND
BEN REACH
Loch Chon
BEINN BHREAC
Kinlochard
Lochgoilhead
Corrow
Douglas Pier
Loch Goil
Loch Long
Glen Douglas
Inverbeg
Rowardennan
BEINN UIRD
BEN VRACKIE
Invernoaden
BEINN BHEULA
DOUNE HILL
Arddarroch
BEINN EICH
Edentaggart
Inchlonaig
Carrick Castle
Portincaple
Whistlefield
Whistlefield Inn
BEINN BHEAG
Loch Eck
Glen Luss
Luss
BEINN CHAORACH
BEINN THARSUINN
CREACHAN MOR
Garelochhead
Greenfield
Rockville
Sligrachan
Glen Fruin
Aldochlay
Balmaha
Milton of Buchanan
Buchanan Smithy
Drymen
Ardentinny
CLACH BHEINN
BEINN
Loch Lomond
Lomond
A82
A85
A83
A814
A815
A819
B8074
B8077
B839
B828
B829
B872
B837
192
184
173
174

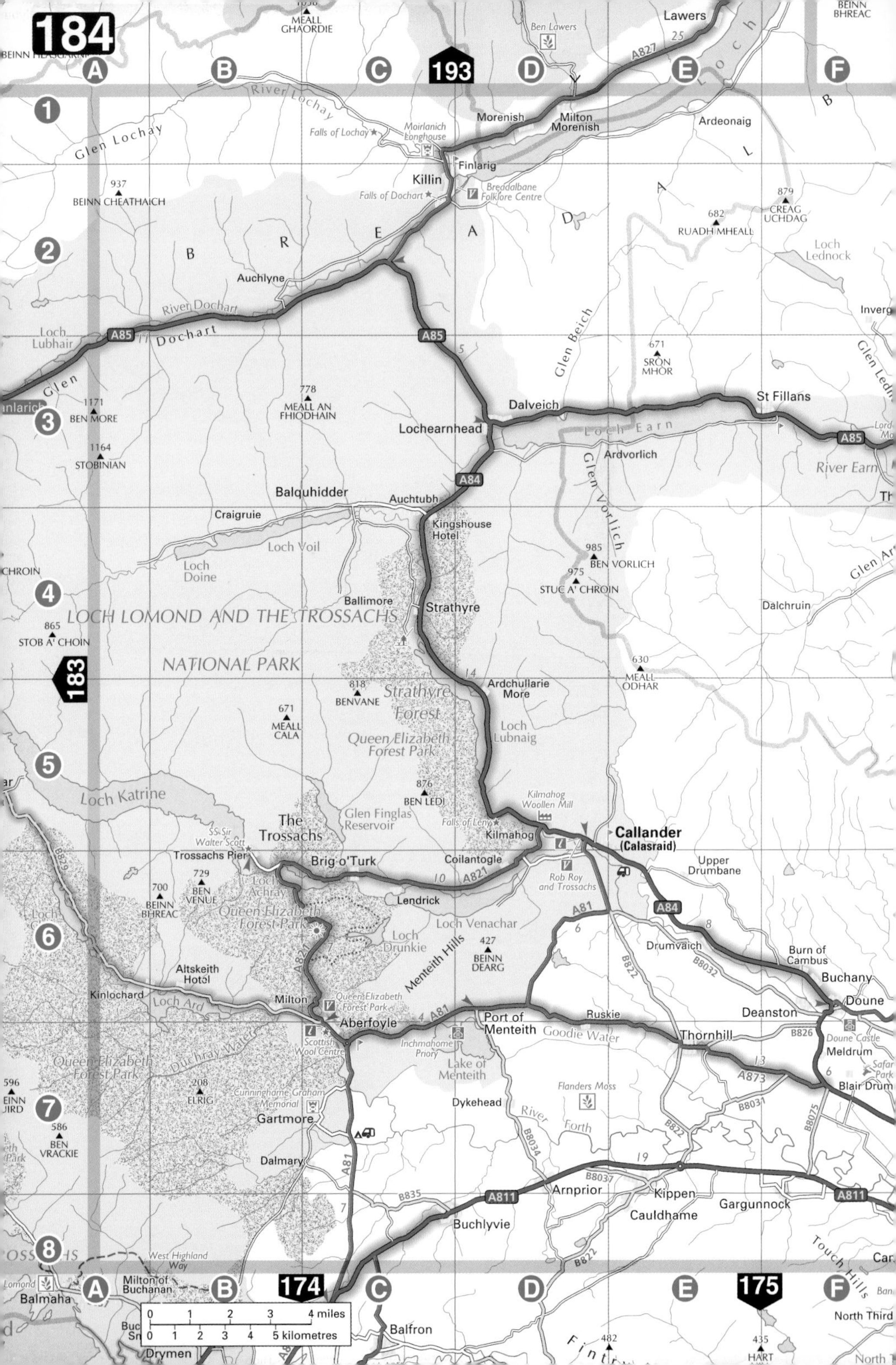

193
183
174
175
Lawers
MEALL GHAORDIE
Ben Lawers
A827
Loch
River Lochay
Glen Lochay
Morenish
Milton Morenish
Ardeonaig
Falls of Lochay
Moirlanich Longhouse
Finlarig
Killin
Falls of Dochart
Breadalbane Folklore Centre
937
BEINN CHEATHAICH
879
CREAG UCHDAG
682
RUADH MHEALL
Loch Lednock
B R E A D A L B A N E
Auchlyne
River Dochart
Loch Lubhair
A85
Dochart
Glen
Glen Beich
671
SRON MHOR
1171
BEN MORE
1164
STOBINIAN
778
MEALL AN FHIODHAIN
Dalveich
St Fillans
Lochearnhead
Loch Earn
Ardvorlich
River Earn
A84
Balquhidder
Auchtubh
Craigruie
Kingshouse Hotel
Loch Voil
Loch Doine
Glen Vorlich
985
BEN VORLICH
975
STUC A' CHROIN
Ballimore
Strathyre
Dalchruin
LOCH LOMOND AND THE TROSSACHS NATIONAL PARK
865
STOB A' CHOIN
630
MEALL ODHAR
818
BENVANE
Strathyre Forest
Ardchullarie More
671
MEALL CALA
Queen Elizabeth Forest Park
Loch Lubnaig
Loch Katrine
876
BEN LEDI
Kilmahog Woollen Mill
Glen Finglas Reservoir
The Trossachs
SS Sir Walter Scott
Falls of Leny
Kilmahog
Callander
(Calasraid)
Trossachs Pier
Brig o'Turk
Coilantogle
Upper Drumbane
Rob Roy and Trossachs
A821
B829
729
BEN VENUE
700
BEINN BHREAC
Loch Achray
Lendrick
Loch Venachar
A81
Loch Drunkie
427
BEINN DEARG
Menteith Hills
Drumvaich
B822
B8032
Burn of Cambus
Buchany
Altskeith Hotel
Kinlochard
Loch Ard
Milton
Queen Elizabeth Forest Park
Aberfoyle
Port of Menteith
Ruskie
Deanston
Doune
Doune Castle
Scottish Wool Centre
Inchmahome Priory
Goodie Water
Thornhill
B826
Meldrum
Duchray Water
Lake of Menteith
A873
Blair Drummond
596
586
BEN VRACKIE
208
ELRIG
Cunninghame Graham Memorial
Flanders Moss
Dykehead
River Forth
B8031
B8075
Gartmore
B8034
Dalmary
B8037
Arnprior
Kippen
Gargunnock
A811
B835
Cauldhame
Buchlyvie
West Highland Way
Touch Hills
B822
Milton of Buchanan
Balmaha
Balfron
Drymen
North Third
482
435
HART
0 1 2 3 4 miles
0 1 2 3 4 5 kilometres

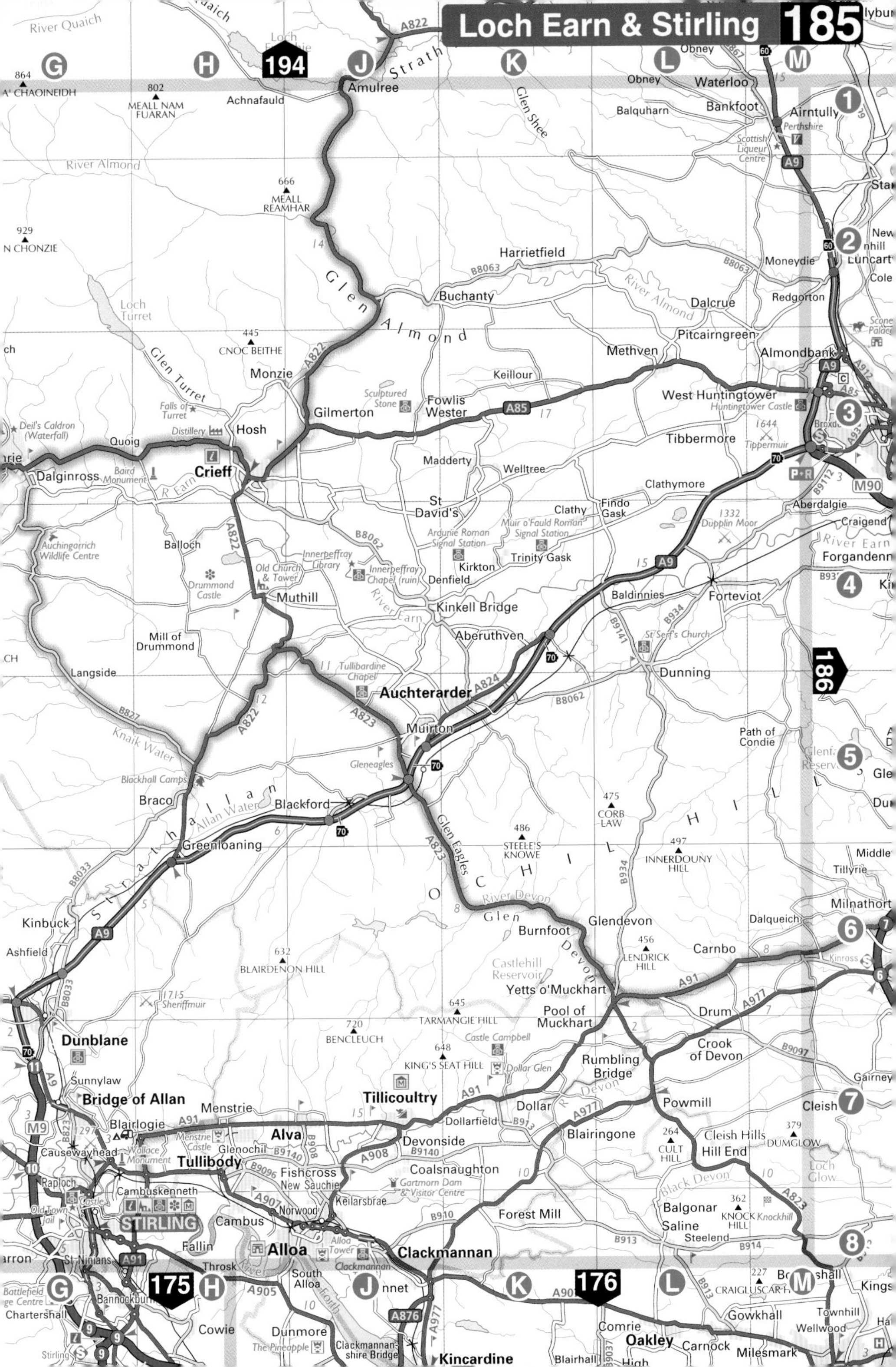

Amulree
Achnafauld
Obney
Waterloo
Bankfoot
Airntully
Balquharn
Glen Shee
Glen Almond
Harrietfield
Buchanty
Moneydie
Luncarty
Redgorton
Dalcrue
Pitcairngreen
Methven
Almondbank
Monzie
Gilmerton
Fowlis Wester
Keillour
West Huntingtower
Huntingtower Castle
Tibbermore
Hosh
Crieff
Quoig
Dalginross
Baird Monument
Madderty
Welltree
St David's
Clathy
Findo Gask
Clathymore
Aberdalgie
Craigend
Forgandenny
Dupplin Moor
Trinity Gask
Kirkton
Denfield
Balloch
Drummond Castle
Muthill
Kinkell Bridge
Aberuthven
Baldinnies
Forteviot
St Serf's Church
Dunning
Mill of Drummond
Langside
Auchterarder
Muirton
Gleneagles
Path of Condie
Braco
Blackford
Greenloaning
Blackhall Camps
Glen Eagles
Ochil Hills
Kinbuck
Ashfield
Dunblane
Sunnylaw
Bridge of Allan
Blairlogie
Causewayhead
Wallace Monument
Menstrie
Alva
Tillicoultry
Dollar
Dollarfield
Devonside
Tullibody
Glenochil
Fishcross
New Sauchie
Coalsnaughton
Cambuskenneth
Raploch
STIRLING
Cambus
Alloa
Clackmannan
Fallin
Throsk
St Ninians
Bannockburn
Chartershall
Cowie
South Alloa
Dunmore
Kincardine
Glendevon
Burnfoot
Carnbo
Yetts o'Muckhart
Pool of Muckhart
Drum
Crook of Devon
Rumbling Bridge
Powmill
Blairingone
Cleish
Cleish Hills
Hill End
Balgonar
Saline
Steelend
Forest Mill
Comrie
Oakley
Carnock
Gowkhall
Milesmark
Milnathort
Dalqueich
Kinross
Gairney
Townhill
Wellwood
Blairhall

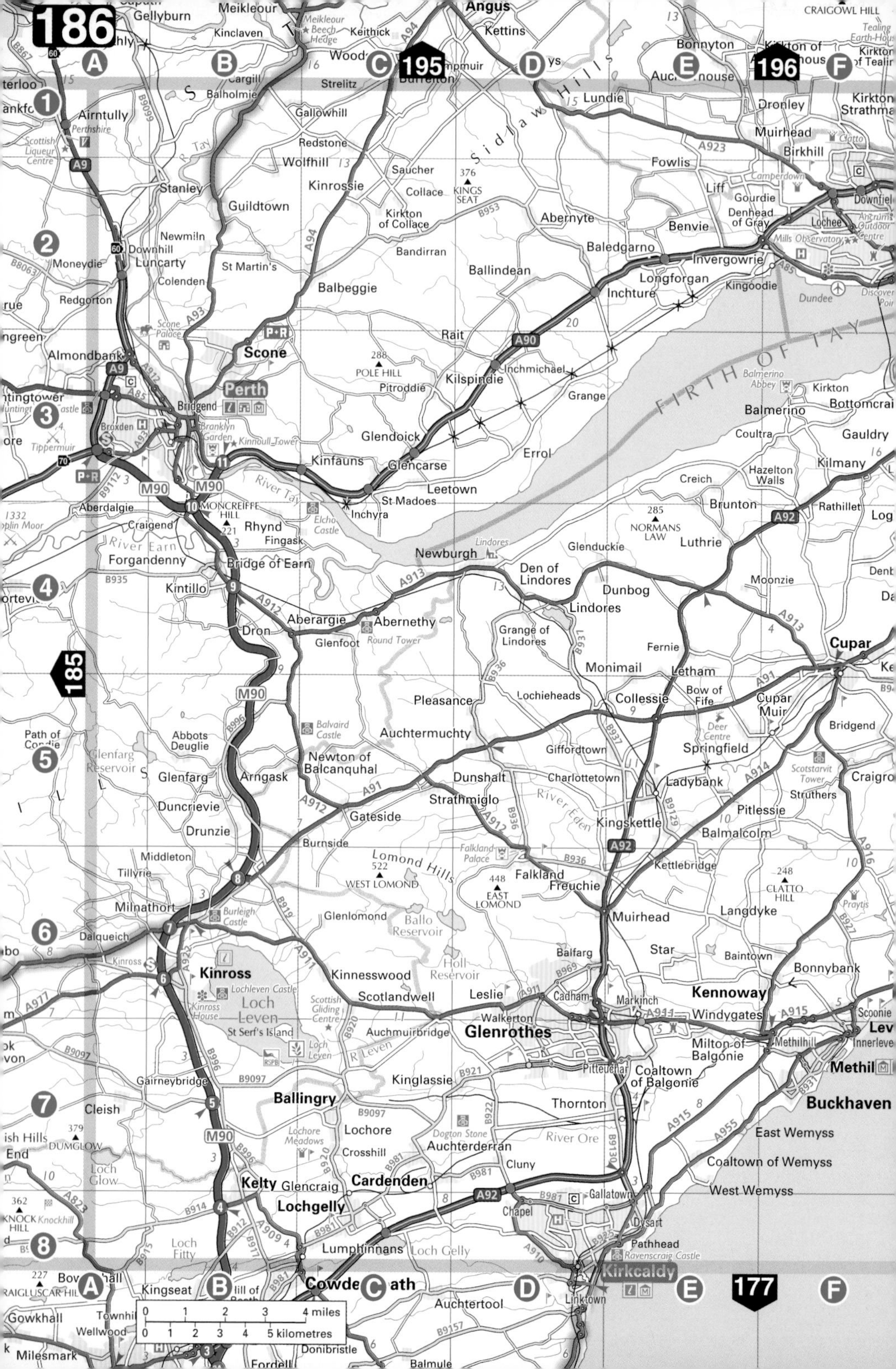

186
Gellyburn
Meikleour
Kinclaven
Meikleour Beech Hedge
Angus
Keithick
Kettins
Wood
Bonnyton
Kirkton of
CRAIGOWL HILL
Tealing Earth-House
195
196
Cargill
Balholmie
Strelitz
Burrelton
Lundie
Dronley
Airntully
Perthshire
Scottish Liqueur Centre
Gallowhill
Sidlaw Hills
Muirhead
Birkhill
Redstone
Wolfhill
Saucher
Fowlis
Liff
Camperdown
Kinrossie
Collace
376
KINGS SEAT
Stanley
Guildtown
Kirkton of Collace
Abernyte
Gourdie
Denhead of Gray
Downfield
Lochee
Newmiln
Benvie
Mills Observatory
Downhill
Luncarty
Moneydie
Bandirran
Baledgarno
Invergowrie
St Martin's
Ballindean
Colenden
Longforgan
Kingoodie
Redgorton
Balbeggie
Inchture
Dundee
Scone Palace
Rait
Almondbank
Scone
288
POLE HILL
Inchmichael
FIRTH OF TAY
Balmerino Abbey
Kirkton
Perth
Kilspindie
Pitroddie
Grange
Bottomcraig
Huntingtower Castle
Bridgend
Broxden
Branklyn Garden
Kinnoull Tower
Balmerino
Glendoick
Coultra
Gauldry
Tippermuir
Kinfauns
Errol
Kilmany
Glencarse
Creich
Hazelton Walls
River Tay
Leetown
Brunton
Rathillet
Aberdalgie
MONCREIFFE HILL
St Madoes
Inchyra
285
NORMANS LAW
Craigend
221
Rhynd
Elcho Castle
Luthrie
Fingask
River Earn
Lindores
Glenduckie
Forgandenny
Bridge of Earn
Newburgh
Den of Lindores
Kintillo
Dunbog
Moonzie
Lindores
Aberargie
Abernethy
Dron
Round Tower
Grange of Lindores
Glenfoot
Fernie
Cupar
185
Monimail
Letham
Bow of Fife
Lochieheads
Collessie
Cupar Muir
Pleasance
Path of Condie
Abbots Deuglie
Balvaird Castle
Auchtermuchty
Deer Centre
Bridgend
Glenfarg Reservoir
Giffordtown
Springfield
Newton of Balcanquhal
Glenfarg
Arngask
Dunshalt
Charlottetown
Ladybank
Scotstarvit Tower
Craigrothie
Strathmiglo
River Eden
Struthers
Duncrievie
Pitlessie
Gateside
Kingskettle
Balmalcolm
Drunzie
Burnside
Lomond Hills
Falkland Palace
Kettlebridge
Middleton
522
WEST LOMOND
448
EAST LOMOND
248
CLATTO HILL
Tillyrie
Falkland
Freuchie
Milnathort
Burleigh Castle
Glenlomond
Muirhead
Langdyke
Ballo Reservoir
Dalqueich
Balfarg
Star
Baintown
Kinross
Holl Reservoir
Bonnybank
Lochleven Castle
Kinnesswood
Kennoway
Kinross House
Loch Leven
Scotlandwell
Leslie
Cadham
Markinch
Windygates
Scoonie
Scottish Gliding Centre
Walkerton
St Serf's Island
Auchmuirbridge
Glenrothes
Methilhill
Innerleven
Milton of Balgonie
Loch Leven
R Leven
Pitteuchar
Methil
Coaltown of Balgonie
Gairneybridge
Kinglassie
Buckhaven
Ballingry
Thornton
Cleish
Lochore
Lochore Meadows
Dogton Stone
River Ore
379
DUMGLOW
East Wemyss
Crosshill
Auchterderran
Loch Glow
Cluny
Coaltown of Wemyss
Kelty
Glencraig
Cardenden
362
KNOCK HILL
Knockhill
Lochgelly
Chapel
Gallatown
West Wemyss
Dysart
Pathhead
Ravenscraig Castle
Loch Fitty
Lumphinnans
Loch Gelly
227
CRAIGLUSCAR HILL
Kingseat
Hill of Beath
Cowdenbeath
Kirkcaldy
Linktown
177
Auchtertool
Gowkhall
Townhill
Wellwood
Milesmark
Donibristle
Fordell
Balmule
0 1 2 3 4 miles
0 1 2 3 4 5 kilometres
A B C D E F
1 2 3 4 5 6 7 8

196
Petterden
Carrot Hill
Todhills
Monikie
Kirkton of Monikie
Wellbank
Newbigging
Burnside of Duntrune
Kellas
Murroes
Carlungie Earth House
Ardestie Earth-House
Upper Victoria
Barry Mill
Barry
East Haven
Panbride
West Haven
Carnoustie
Whitfield
Douglas and Angus
Baldovie
Claypotts Castle
Barnhill
Monifieth
Broughty Ferry
Broughty Castle
DUNDEE
BUDDON NESS
Tay Bridge
Tayport
Tentsmuir Point
Newport-on-Tay
Scottish National Golf Centre
Leuchars
RAF Leuchars
ST ANDREWS BAY
Balmullo
Guardbridge
River Eden
Kincaple
St Andrews
Castle
Strathkinness
Botanic Garden
Brownhills
Blebocraigs
Craigtoun
Boarhills
Denhead
Pitscottie
Cameron Reservoir
Kingsbarns
Baldinnie
Dunino
Peat Inn
Radernie
Balcomie Links
FIFE NESS
New Gilston
Kingsmuir
Lathones
Scotland's Secret Bunker
Crail
Woodside
Largoward
Lochty
Carnbee
Easter Pitkierie
Kellie Castle
Arncroach
Wester Pitkierie
Upper Largo
Kilrenny
Cellardyke
Colinsburgh
Newton of Balcormo
Fisheries
Anstruther
Drumeldrie
Lower Largo
Kilconquhar
Pittenweem
St Monans
Largo Bay
Earlsferry
Elie
Isle of May
A90
A92
A930
A914
A919
A91
A917
A915
B961
B962
B9128
B945
B939
B940
B941
B942
B9131
B9171
G
H
J
K
L
M
1
2
3
4
5
6
7
8

A
B
C
D
E
F
1
2
3
4
5
6
7
8
Arnabo
Grishipoll
Clabhach
Loch Cliad
Hogh Bay
Ballyhaugh
Ar
Bagh a Chaisteil
(Castlebay)
(Apr-Oct, Thursdays only)
Totronald
Coll
Feall Bay
Arileod
Acha
Uig
RSPB
Calgary Point
Crossapol Bay
Loch Breachacha
Rudha Fàsachd
Gunna
Rudha Port Bhiosd
Clachan Mor
Balephetrish Bay
Caoles
Rudha Dubh
B8069
Loch Bhasapoll
Haugh Bay
B8068
Ruaig
Ballevullin
Cornoigmore
Kenovay
Gott Bay
Kilkenneth
Tiree
Scarinish
Moss
B8065
Middleton
Heylipoll
Crossapoll
TIREE
Barrapoll
Hynish Bay
B8067
Balemartine
Loch a Phuill
Mannel
Rinn Thorbhais
Hynish
Balephuil Bay
0
1
2
3
4 miles
0
1
2
3
4
5 kilometres

198
190
180
MUCK
Eilean nan Each
Port Mor
Sanna Point
Sanna Bay
Portuairk
Achnaha
Kilmory
Ockle
Ockle Point
Branault
436
MEALL NAN CON
ARDNAMU
Ardnamurchan Point
Achosnich
B8007
Loch Mudle
342
BEINN NA SEILG
Kilchoan
Ormsaigmore
Mingary
527
BEN HIANT
Ardslignish
Bagh a Chaisteil (Castlebay)
Loch Baghasdail (Lochboisdale)
Eilean Mòr
Rudha Mòr
Rudha Sgor-innis
Bousd
Sorisdale
B8072
COLL
Eilean Ornsay
Coll - Oban
Ardmore Point
Auliston Point
Sorne Point
Glengorm Castle
Quinish Point
Tobermory
Calve Island
Caliach Point
292
'S AIRDE BEINN
Dervaig
Achnadrish House
B8073
A848
Calgary
Calgary Bay
444
SPEINNE MÒR
Loch Frisa
Treshnish Point
Ensay
342
CÀRN MÒR
ISLE OF MULL
Rudh' a' Chaoil
Burg
Glen Aros
Glenaros House
Fanmore
390
CNOC AN DÀ CHINN
Fladda
Ballygown
Loch Tuath
Eas Fors (Waterfall)
333
BEINN NAN CÀRN
Killiechronan
B8035
Lunga
TRESHNISH ISLES
Gometra
Oskamull
Gruline
ULVA
Macquarie Mausoleum
Loch na Keal, Isle of Mull
Loch na Keal
Eorsa
Bac Mòr or Dutchmans Cap
Bac Beag
Little Colonsay
591
BEINN A' GH
Staffa
Fingal's Cave
Inchkenneth Chapel (ruin)
Balnahard

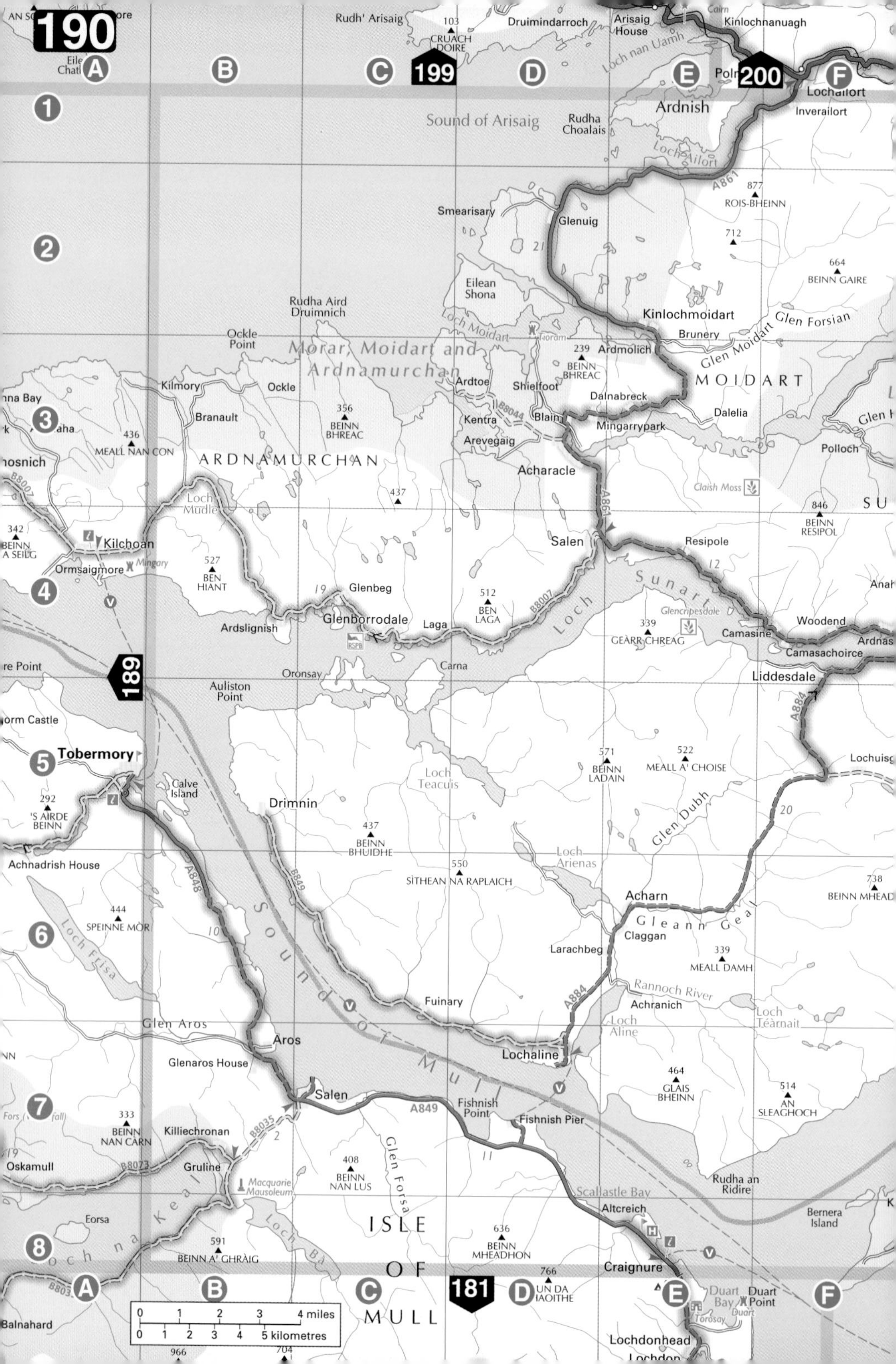
Rudh' Arisaig
103
CRUACH DOIRE
199
Druimindarroch
Arisaig House
Loch nan Uamh
Kinlochnanuagh
Polnish
200
Lochailort
Inverailort
Sound of Arisaig
Rudha Choalais
Ardnish
Loch Ailort
A861
877
ROIS-BHEINN
Smearisary
Glenuig
712
664
BEINN GAIRE
Eilean Shona
Rudha Aird Druimnich
Loch Moidart
Kinlochmoidart
Brunery
Glen Moidart
Glen Forsian
Ockle Point
Morar, Moidart and Ardnamurchan
239
BEINN BHREAC
Ardmolich
MOIDART
Kilmory
Ockle
Ardtoe
Shielfoot
Dalnabreck
Branault
356
BEINN BHREAC
B8044
Kentra
Blain
Mingarrypark
Dalelia
Arevegaig
Polloch
436
MEALL NAN CON
ARDNAMURCHAN
Acharacle
Claish Moss
B8007
Loch Mudle
437
846
BEINN RESIPOL
342
BEINN A SEILG
Kilchoan
Mingary
Ormsaigmore
527
BEN HIANT
Salen
Resipole
Glenbeg
512
BEN LAGA
Loch Sunart
Glenborrodale
Laga
RSPB
339
GEARR CHREAG
Glencripesdale
Ardslignish
Camasine
Woodend
Camasachoirce
189
Oronsay
Carna
Liddesdale
Auliston Point
A884
Tobermory
Calve Island
571
BEINN LADAIN
522
MEALL A' CHOISE
Lochuisge
Loch Teacuis
292
'S AIRDE BEINN
Drimnin
Glen Dubh
437
BEINN BHUIDHE
Loch Arienas
Achnadrish House
A848
B849
550
SÌTHEAN NA RAPLAICH
738
BEINN MHEADH
444
SPEINNE MÒR
Loch Frisa
Acharn
Gleann Geal
Claggan
Larachbeg
339
MEALL DAMH
Sound of Mull
Rannoch River
Achranich
Loch Téarnait
Loch Aline
Fuinary
Glen Aros
Aros
Lochaline
Glenaros House
464
GLAIS BHEINN
514
AN SLEAGHOCH
Salen
Fishnish Point
A849
Fishnish Pier
333
BEINN NAN CARN
Killiechronan
B8035
Glen Forsa
Oskamull
B8073
Gruline
408
BEINN NAN LUS
Macquarie Mausoleum
Rudha an Ridire
Scallastle Bay
Altcreich
Bernera Island
Eorsa
Loch na Keal
Loch Bà
ISLE OF MULL
636
BEINN MHEADHON
591
BEINN A' GHRÀIG
Craignure
766
DUN DA GHAOITHE
181
B8035
Duart Bay
Duart Point
Torosay
Balnahard
Lochdonhead
Lochdon
966
704
0 1 2 3 4 miles
0 1 2 3 4 5 kilometres

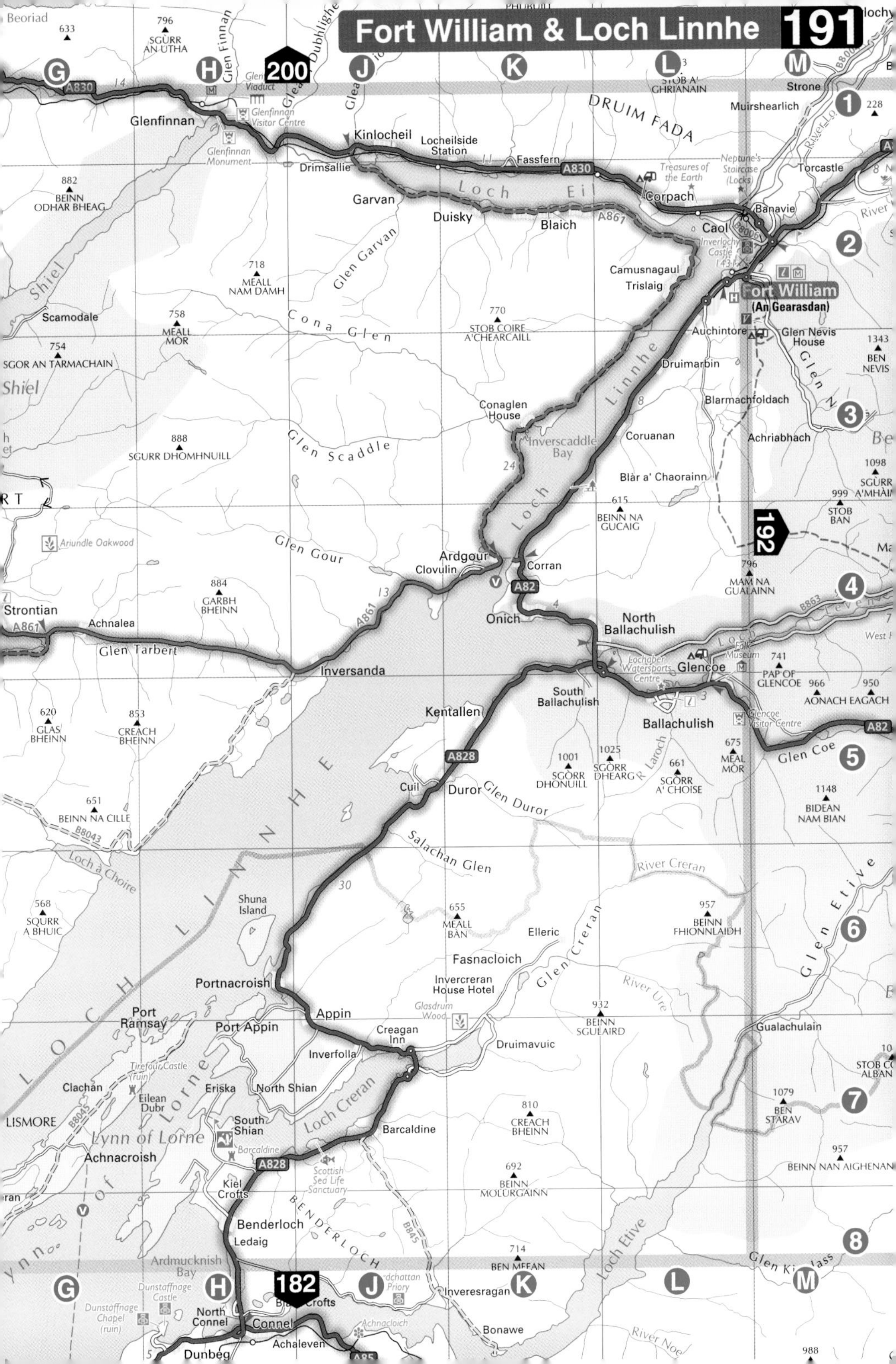
Beoriad
633
796
SGÙRR AN UTHA
Glen Finnan
200
Glenfinnan Viaduct
Glenfinnan Visitor Centre
Glenfinnan
Glenfinnan Monument
A830
Kinlocheil
Locheilside Station
Fassfern
Drimsallie
Garvan
Duisky
Blaich
DRUIM FADA
STOB A' GHRIANAIN
Strone
Muirshearlich
228
Treasures of the Earth
Neptune's Staircase (Locks)
Torcastle
Corpach
Banavie
Caol
Loch Eil
A861
B8006
Inverlochy Castle
Camusnagaul
Trislaig
Fort William
(An Gearasdan)
Auchintore
Glen Nevis House
1343
BEN NEVIS
Glen Nevis
Druimarbin
Blarmachfoldach
Achriabhach
Coruanan
Conaglen House
Inverscaddle Bay
Loch Linnhe
Blàr a' Chaorainn
615
BEINN NA GUCAIG
1098
SGÙRR A'MHÀIM
999
STOB BAN
192
796
MAM NA GUALAINN
882
BEINN ODHAR BHEAG
Shiel
Scamodale
718
MEALL NAM DAMH
Glen Garvan
758
MEALL MÒR
754
SGOR AN TARMACHAIN
Cona Glen
770
STOB COIRE A'CHEARCAILL
888
SGURR DHOMHNUILL
Glen Scaddle
Ariundle Oakwood
Glen Gour
Ardgour
Clovulin
Corran
A82
884
GARBH BHEINN
Strontian
A861
Achnalea
Glen Tarbert
Onich
North Ballachulish
B863
Loch Leven
Lochaber Watersports Centre
Folk Museum
Glencoe
741
PAP OF GLENCOE
966
950
AONACH EAGACH
Inversanda
South Ballachulish
Kentallen
Ballachulish
Glencoe Visitor Centre
A82
620
GLAS BHEINN
853
CREACH BHEINN
A828
1001
SGÒRR DHONUILL
1025
SGÒRR DHEARG
661
SGÒRR A' CHOISE
675
MEAL MÒR
Glen Coe
1148
BIDEAN NAM BIAN
651
BEINN NA CILLE
B8043
Cuil
Duror
Glen Duror
Loch a Choire
Salachan Glen
River Creran
Glen Etive
568
SGURR A BHUIC
Shuna Island
655
MEALL BÀN
Elleric
957
BEINN FHIONNLAIDH
Fasnacloich
Glen Creran
Invercreran House Hotel
River Ure
Portnacroish
Appin
Port Ramsay
Port Appin
Glasdrum Wood
932
BEINN SGULAIRD
Gualachulain
Creagan Inn
Druimavuic
Inverfolla
Tirefour Castle (ruin)
Clachan
Eilean Dubr
Eriska
North Shian
Loch Creran
1079
BEN STARAV
810
CREACH BHEINN
LISMORE
B8045
South Shian
Lynn of Lorne
Barcaldine
Achnacroish
Barcaldine
A828
Scottish Sea Life Sanctuary
692
BEINN MOLURGAINN
957
BEINN NAN AIGHENAN
Kiel Crofts
BENDERLOCH
B845
Benderloch
Ledaig
Loch Etive
Ardmucknish Bay
714
BEN MEAN
Glen Kinglass
182
Dunstaffnage Castle
Dunstaffnage Chapel (ruin)
Ardchattan Priory
Inveresragan
North Connel
Connel
Achnacloich
Achaleven
Bonawe
River Noe
Dunbeg
A85
988

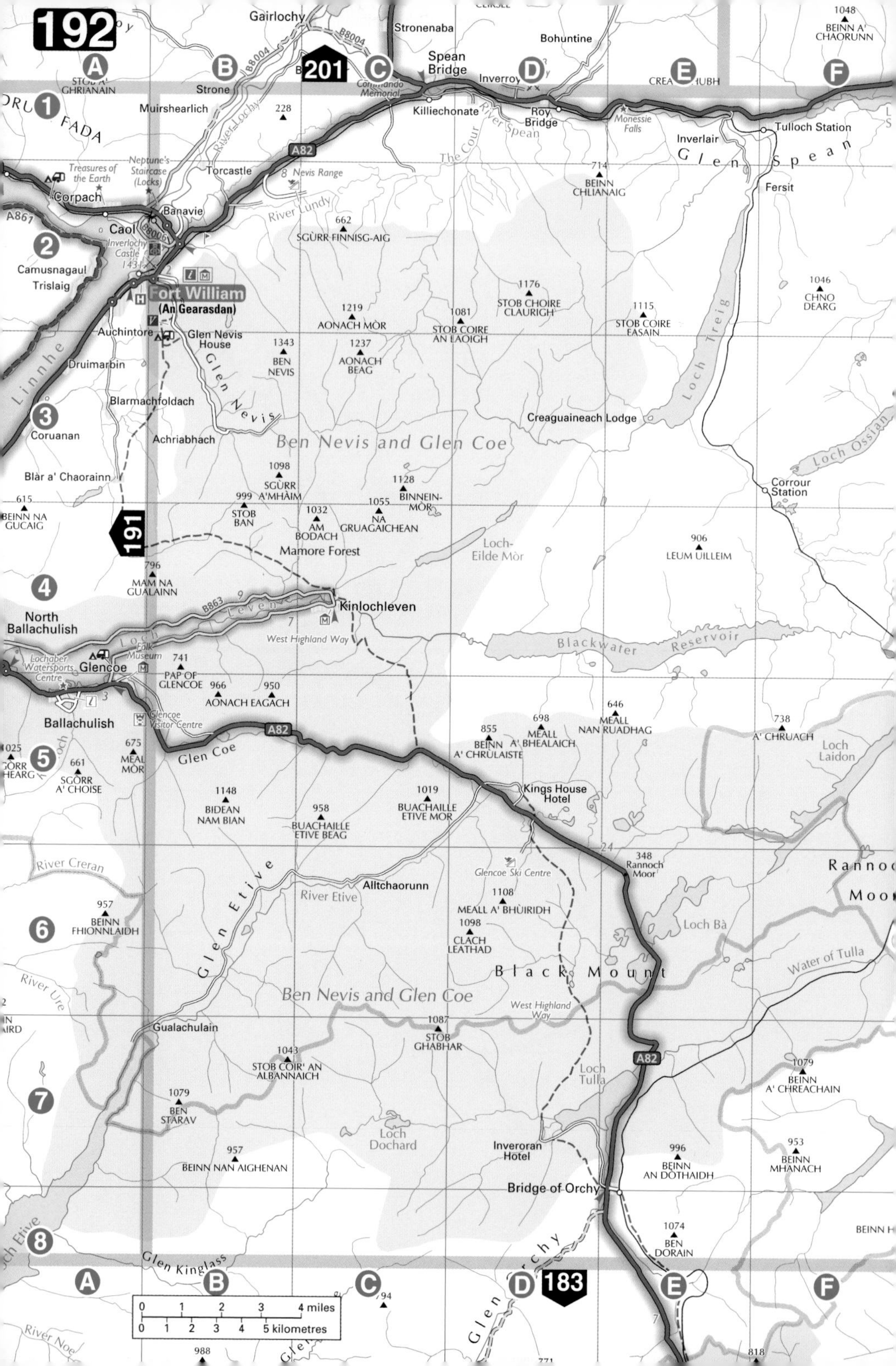

Gairlochy
Stronenaba
Bohuntine
Spean Bridge
Inverroy
Killiechonate
Roy Bridge
Monessie Falls
Tulloch Station
Inverlair
Glen Spean
Fersit
Strone
Muirshearlich
Commando Memorial
B8004
201
A82
Torcastle
Nevis Range
Neptune's Staircase (Locks)
Treasures of the Earth
Corpach
Banavie
Caol
Inverlochy Castle 1431
A861
B8006
Camusnagaul
Trislaig
Fort William
(An Gearasdan)
Auchintore
Glen Nevis House
Glen Nevis
Druimarbin
Blarmachfoldach
Coruanan
Achriabhach
Blàr a' Chaorainn
Loch Linnhe
River Lundy
The Cour
River Spean
662
SGÙRR FINNISG-AIG
1219
AONACH MÒR
1081
STOB COIRE AN LAOIGH
1176
STOB CHOIRE CLAURIGH
1115
STOB COIRE EASAIN
1046
CHNO DEARG
714
BEINN CHLIANAIG
1343
BEN NEVIS
1237
AONACH BEAG
Loch Treig
Creaguaineach Lodge
Loch Ossian
Corrour Station
Ben Nevis and Glen Coe
1098
SGÙRR A'MHÀIM
1128
BINNEIN-MÒR
999
STOB BAN
1032
AM BODACH
1055
NA GRUAGAICHEAN
615
BEINN NA GUCAIG
191
Mamore Forest
Loch Eilde Mòr
906
LEUM UILLEIM
796
MAM NA GUALAINN
Kinlochleven
B863
Loch Leven
North Ballachulish
West Highland Way
Blackwater Reservoir
Lochaber Watersports Centre
Folk Museum
Glencoe
741
PAP OF GLENCOE
966
AONACH EAGACH
950
Glencoe Visitor Centre
Ballachulish
Glen Coe
855
BEINN A' CHRÙLAISTE
698
MEALL A' BHEALAICH
646
MEALL NAN RUADHAG
738
A' CHRUACH
Loch Laidon
675
MEALL MÒR
661
SGORR A' CHOISE
1148
BIDEAN NAM BIAN
958
BUACHAILLE ETIVE BEAG
1019
BUACHAILLE ETIVE MOR
Kings House Hotel
348
Rannoch Moor
River Creran
Glen Etive
Alltchaorunn
River Etive
Glencoe Ski Centre
1108
MEALL A' BHÙIRIDH
1098
CLACH LEATHAD
957
BEINN FHIONNLAIDH
Loch Bà
Black Mount
Water of Tulla
River Ure
Ben Nevis and Glen Coe
West Highland Way
Gualachulain
1087
STOB GHABHAR
1043
STOB COIR' AN ALBANNAICH
Loch Tulla
1079
BEINN A' CHREACHAIN
1079
BEN STARAV
Loch Dochard
Inveroran Hotel
957
BEINN NAN AIGHENAN
996
BEINN AN DÒTHAIDH
953
BEINN MHANACH
Bridge of Orchy
1074
BEN DORAIN
Loch Etive
Glen Kinglass
Glen Orchy
183
River Noe
988
818
0 1 2 3 4 miles
0 1 2 3 4 5 kilometres

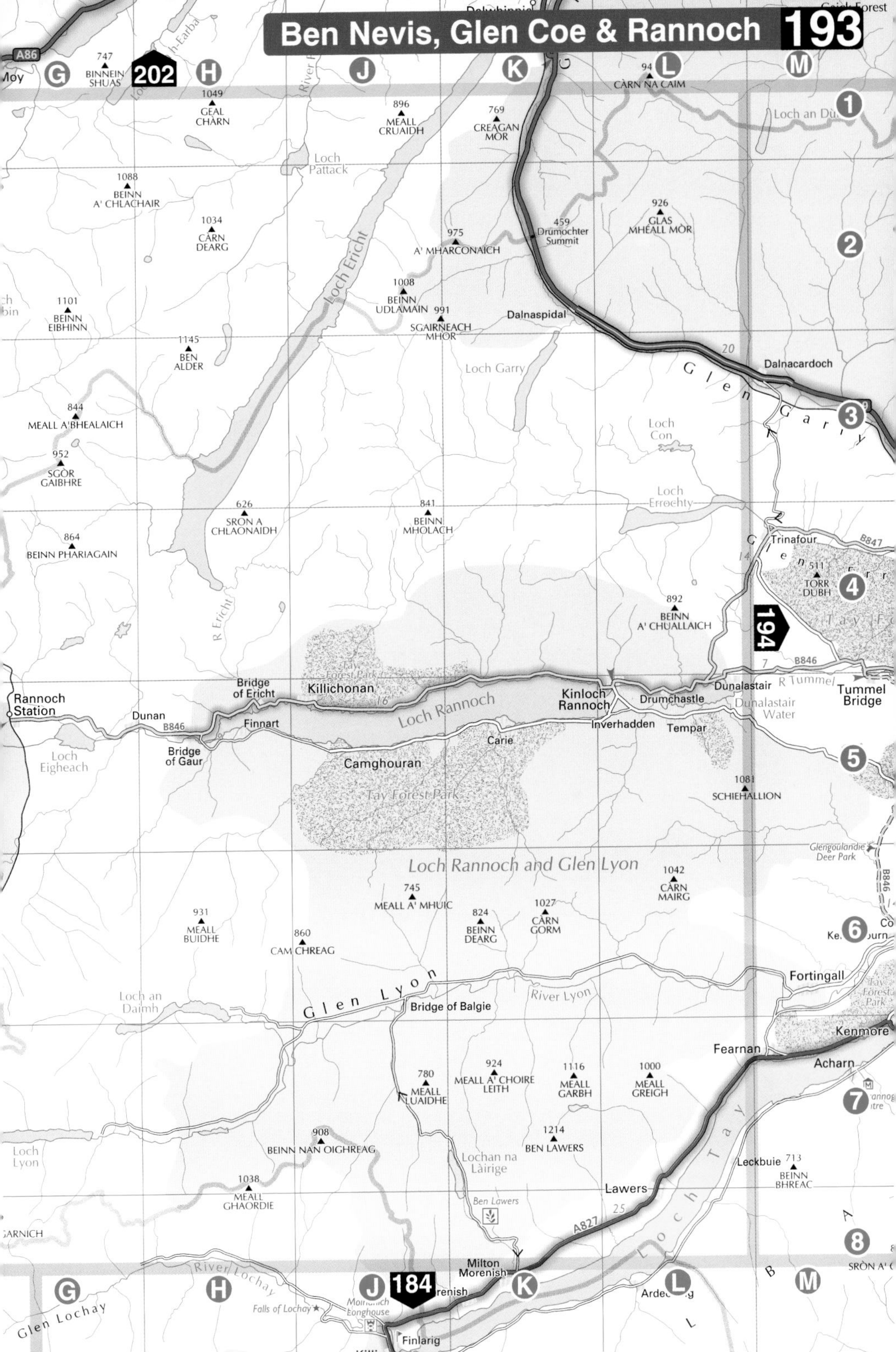

A86
Moy
747 BINNEIN SHUAS
202
1049 GEAL CHÀRN
896 MEALL CRUAIDH
769 CREAGAN MÒR
CÀRN NA CAIM
Loch an Dùin
Loch Pattack
1088 BEINN A' CHLACHAIR
1034 CÀRN DEARG
975 A' MHARCONAICH
459 Drumochter Summit
926 GLAS MHEALL MÒR
Loch Ericht
1008 BEINN UDLAMAIN
991 SGAIRNEACH MHOR
Dalnaspidal
1101 BEINN EIBHINN
1145 BEN ALDER
Loch Garry
Dalnacardoch
Glen Garry
844 MEALL A' BHEALAICH
952 SGÒR GAIBHRE
Loch Con
Loch Errochty
626 SRON A CHLAONAIDH
841 BEINN MHOLACH
864 BEINN PHARIAGAIN
Trinafour
B847
511 TORR DUBH
892 BEINN A' CHUALLAICH
194
R Ericht
Tay Forest Park
B846
Rannoch Station
Bridge of Ericht
Killichonan
Loch Rannoch
Kinloch Rannoch
Drumchastle
Dunalastair
R Tummel
Tummel Bridge
Dunan
B846
Finnart
Inverhadden
Tempar
Dunalastair Water
Bridge of Gaur
Carie
Loch Eigheach
Camghouran
Tay Forest Park
1081 SCHIEHALLION
Glengoulandie Deer Park
Loch Rannoch and Glen Lyon
1042 CÀRN MAIRG
745 MEALL A' MHUIC
931 MEALL BUIDHE
824 BEINN DEARG
1027 CÀRN GORM
860 CAM CHREAG
Fortingall
Loch an Daimh
Glen Lyon
Bridge of Balgie
River Lyon
Kenmore
Fearnan
Acharn
780 MEALL LUAIDHE
924 MEALL A' CHOIRE LEITH
1116 MEALL GARBH
1000 MEALL GREIGH
908 BEINN NAN OIGHREAG
1214 BEN LAWERS
Loch Lyon
Lochan na Làirige
Leckbuie
713 BEINN BHREAC
1038 MEALL GHAORDIE
Lawers
Ben Lawers
A827
Loch Tay
Milton Morenish
River Lochay
184
Glen Lochay
Falls of Lochay
Finlarig

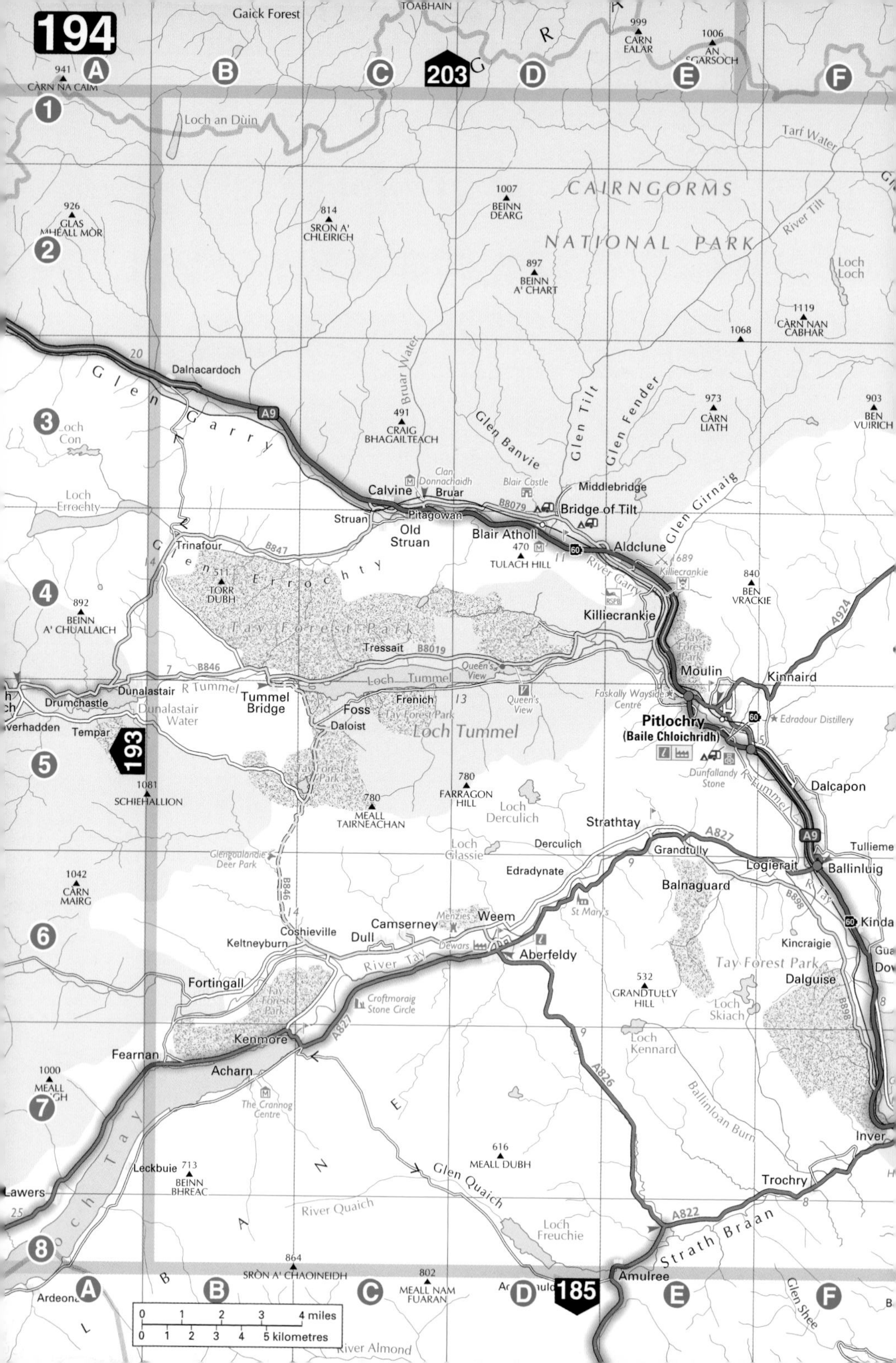
A
B
C
D
E
F
1
2
3
4
5
6
7
8
203
193
185
Gaick Forest
TOABHAIN
999
CARN EALAR
1006
AN SGARSOCH
941
CÀRN NA CAIM
Loch an Dùin
Tarf Water
CAIRNGORMS
NATIONAL PARK
926
GLAS MHEALL MÒR
814
SRON A' CHLEIRICH
1007
BEINN DEARG
River Tilt
Loch Loch
897
BEINN A' CHART
1119
CÀRN NAN CABHAR
1068
20
Glen Garry
Dalnacardoch
Bruar Water
A9
491
CRAIG BHAGAILTEACH
Glen Banvie
Glen Tilt
Glen Fender
973
CARN LIATH
903
BEN VUIRICH
Loch Con
Loch Errochty
Clan Donnachaidh
Blair Castle
Middlebridge
Calvine
Bruar
B8079
Bridge of Tilt
Glen Girnaig
Struan
Pitagowan
Old Struan
Blair Atholl
Trinafour
B847
470
TULACH HILL
60
Aldclune
689
Killiecrankie
River Garry
Glen Errochty
511
TORR DUBH
840
BEN VRACKIE
892
BEINN A' CHUALLAICH
Tay Forest Park
Killiecrankie
RSPB
A924
Tressait
B8019
B846
Queen's View
Moulin
Kinnaird
Dunalastair
R Tummel
Loch Tummel
Drumchastle
Tummel Bridge
Frenich
Foss
Faskally Wayside Centre
Pitlochry
(Baile Chloichridh)
Edradour Distillery
Dunalastair Water
Daloist
Loch Tummel
Tempar
Dunfallandy Stone
R Tummel
Dalcapon
1081
SCHIEHALLION
780
FARRAGON HILL
780
MEALL TAIRNEACHAN
Loch Derculich
Strathtay
A827
Glengoulandie Deer Park
Loch Glassie
Derculich
Grandtully
Tullieme
Logierait
Ballinluig
1042
CÀRN MAIRG
Edradynate
Balnaguard
R Tay
B898
B846
St Mary's
Camserney
Menzies
Weem
Coshieville
Keltneyburn
Dull
Dewars
Aberfeldy
Kincraigie
River Tay
Tay Forest Park
Dalguise
Fortingall
Croftmoraig Stone Circle
532
GRANDTULLY HILL
Loch Skiach
Kenmore
A827
Loch Kennard
Fearnan
Acharn
A826
1000
The Crannog Centre
Ballinloan Burn
Loch Tay
BREADALBANE
Inver
616
MEALL DUBH
713
BEINN BHREAC
Leckbuie
Glen Quaich
Lawers
Trochry
River Quaich
A822
Strath Braan
Loch Freuchie
864
SRÒN A' CHAOINEIDH
802
MEALL NAM FUARAN
Amulree
Glen Shee
Ardeonaig
0 1 2 3 4 miles
0 1 2 3 4 5 kilometres
River Almond

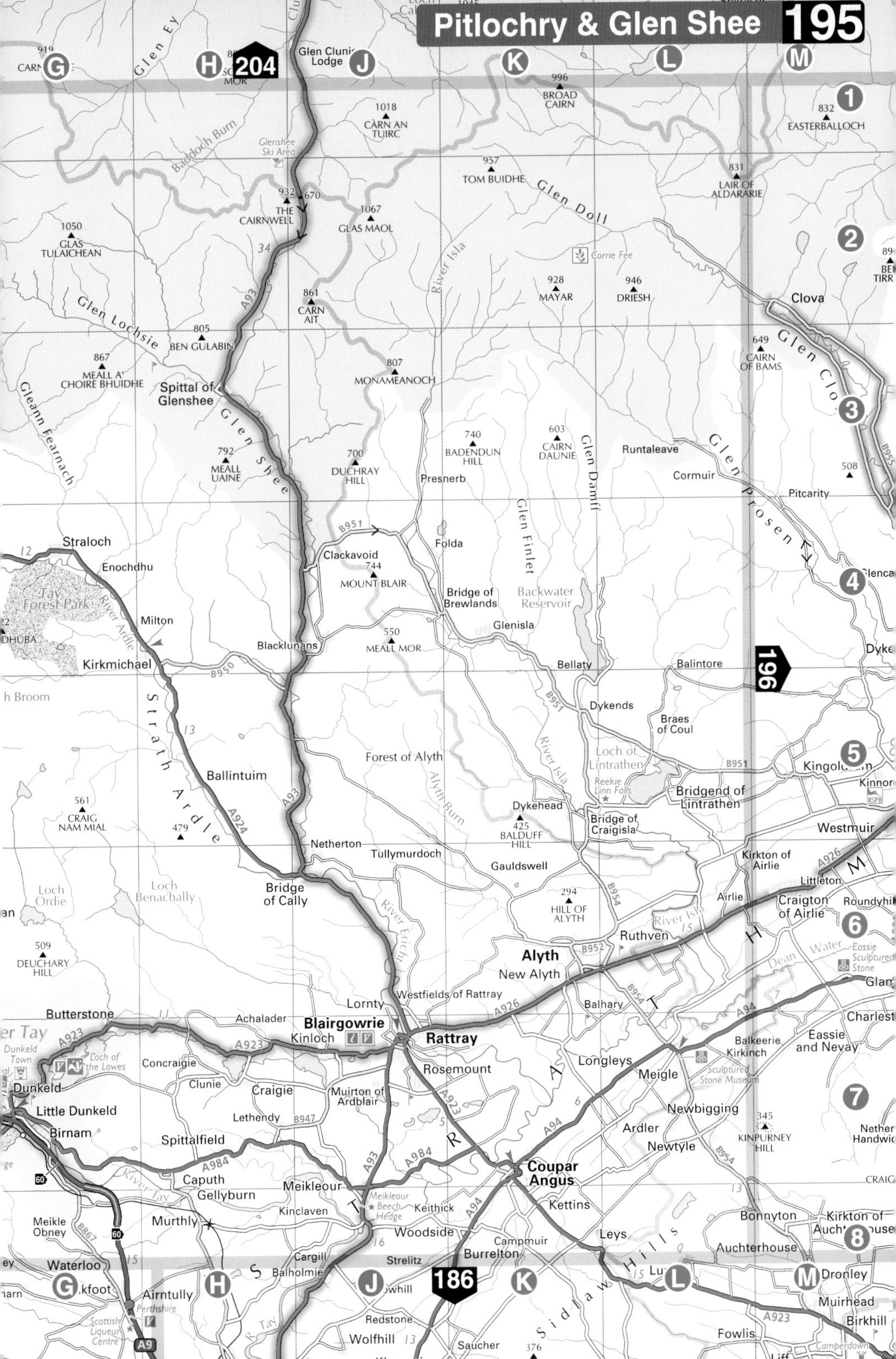
204
196
186
Glen Ey
Glen Clunie Lodge
BROAD CAIRN
EASTERBALLOCH
CARN AN TUIRC
Baddoch Burn
Glenshee Ski Area
TOM BUIDHE
Glen Doll
LAIR OF ALDARARIE
THE CAIRNWELL
GLAS MAOL
GLAS TULAICHEAN
Corrie Fee
River Isla
MAYAR
DRIESH
CARN AIT
Clova
Glen Lochsie
BEN GULABIN
MEALL A' CHOIRE BHUIDHE
CAIRN OF BAMS
Glen Clova
MONAMEANOCH
Spittal of Glenshee
Gleann Fearnach
Glen Shee
BADENDUN HILL
CAIRN DAUNIE
Glen Damff
Runtaleave
Glen Prosen
MEALL UAINE
DUCHRAY HILL
Presnerb
Cormuir
Pitcarity
Glen Finlet
Straloch
Folda
Clackavoid
MOUNT BLAIR
Enochdhu
Tay Forest Park
River Ardle
Bridge of Brewlands
Backwater Reservoir
Milton
Glenisla
Blacklunans
MEALL MOR
Kirkmichael
Bellaty
Balintore
Dykends
Braes of Coul
Strath Ardle
Forest of Alyth
Loch of Lintrathen
Ballintuim
Alyth Burn
Reekie Linn Falls
Bridgend of Lintrathen
Kinnordy
CRAIG NAM MIAL
Dykehead
BALDUFF HILL
Bridge of Craigisla
Westmuir
Netherton
Tullymurdoch
Gauldswell
Kirkton of Airlie
Loch Ordie
Loch Benachally
Bridge of Cally
Littleton
Craigton of Airlie
Roundyhill
Airlie
HILL OF ALYTH
River Ericht
Ruthven
River Isla
DEUCHARY HILL
Alyth
New Alyth
Dean Water
Eassie Sculptured Stone
Westfields of Rattray
Balhary
Butterstone
Lornty
Achalader
Blairgowrie
Kinloch
Rattray
Charleston
Eassie and Nevay
Balkeerie
Kirkinch
Loch of the Lowes
Dunkeld
Concraigie
Rosemount
Longleys
Meigle
Sculptured Stone Museum
Clunie
Craigie
Muirton of Ardblair
Little Dunkeld
Lethendy
Newbigging
Birnam
KINPURNEY HILL
Ardler
Spittalfield
Newtyle
Nether Handwick
Coupar Angus
River Tay
Caputh
Gellyburn
Meikleour
Meikleour Beech Hedge
Kettins
Meikle Obney
Murthly
Kinclaven
Keithick
Bonnyton
Kirkton of Auchterhouse
Woodside
Campmuir
Leys
Sidlaw Hills
Auchterhouse
Waterloo
Cargill
Burrelton
Strelitz
Balholmie
Dronley
Airntully
Perthshire
Scottish Liqueur Centre
Muirhead
Redstone
Fowlis
Birkhill
Wolfhill
Saucher
Camperdown

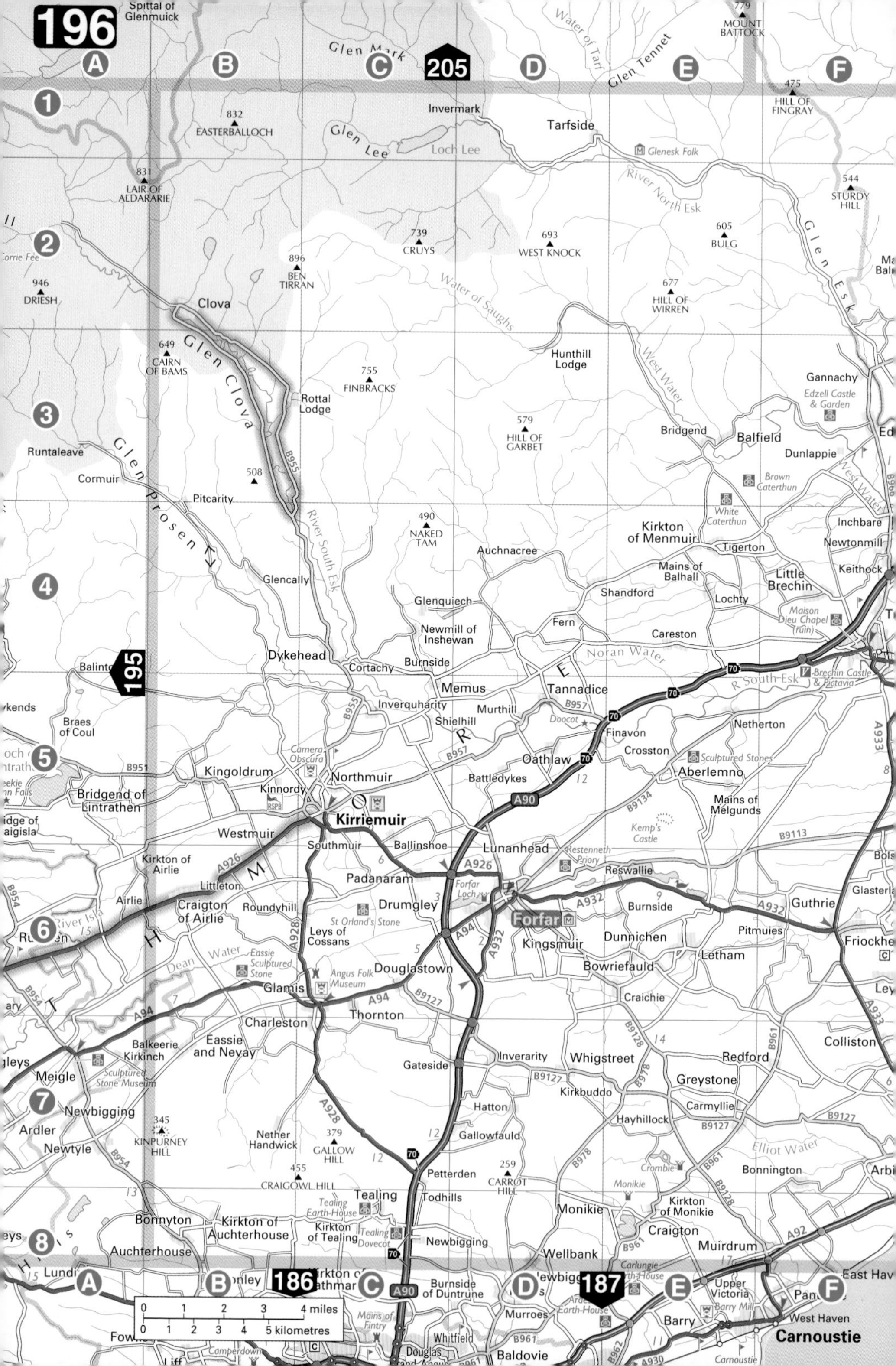
196
205
195
186
187
A
B
C
D
E
F
1
2
3
4
5
6
7
8
Spittal of Glenmuick
Glen Mark
Water of Tarf
779 MOUNT BATTOCK
Glen Tennet
475 HILL OF FINGRAY
832 EASTERBALLOCH
Invermark
Tarfside
Glen Lee
Loch Lee
Glenesk Folk
831 LAIR OF ALDARARIE
River North Esk
544 STURDY HILL
Glen Esk
739 CRUYS
693 WEST KNOCK
605 BULG
Corrie Fee
946 DRIESH
896 BEN TIRRAN
Water of Saughs
677 HILL OF WIRREN
Clova
649 CAIRN OF BAMS
Glen Clova
755 FINBRACKS
Hunthill Lodge
West Water
Gannachy
Edzell Castle & Garden
Rottal Lodge
579 HILL OF GARBET
Bridgend
Balfield
Dunlappie
Runtaleave
Glen Prosen
Cormuir
508
B955
Brown Caterthun
Pitcarity
River South Esk
490 NAKED TAM
White Caterthun
Kirkton of Menmuir
Inchbare
Newtonmill
Auchnacree
Tigerton
Mains of Balhall
Little Brechin
Keithock
Glencally
Shandford
Lochty
Glenquiech
Maison Dieu Chapel (ruin)
Newmill of Inshewan
Fern
Careston
Noran Water
Dykehead
Cortachy
Burnside
Balintore
Memus
Tannadice
R South Esk
Brechin Castle & Pictavia
Inverquharity
Murthill
B957
Braes of Coul
Shielhill
Doocot
Finavon
Netherton
Camera Obscura
Crosston
Sculptured Stones
Kingoldrum
Oathlaw
Aberlemno
B951
Northmuir
Battledykes
Kinnordy
RSPB
A90
Bridgend of Lintrathen
Mains of Melgunds
B9134
Kirriemuir
Kemp's Castle
Westmuir
Southmuir
Ballinshoe
Lunanhead
Restenneth Priory
B9113
Kirkton of Airlie
A926
Padanaram
Reswallie
Littleton
Forfar Loch
Airlie
Craigton of Airlie
Roundyhill
Drumgley
A932
Burnside
Guthrie
Forfar
B954
St Orland's Stone
A928
Leys of Cossans
A94
Kingsmuir
Dunnichen
Pitmuies
Frockheim
River Isla
Letham
Ruthven
Dean Water
Eassie Sculptured Stone
Angus Folk Museum
Douglastown
Bowriefauld
Glamis
Craichie
B9127
Thornton
Charleston
B9128
Colliston
Balkeerie
Kirkinch
Eassie and Nevay
Inverarity
Whigstreet
Redford
Gateside
B961
Meigle
Sculptured Stone Museum
Kirkbuddo
B978
Greystone
Carmyllie
Newbigging
Hatton
Hayhillock
345 KINPURNEY HILL
Nether Handwick
379 GALLOW HILL
Gallowfauld
Elliot Water
Ardler
Newtyle
455 CRAIGOWL HILL
Petterden
259 CARROT HILL
Crombie
Bonnington
Tealing
Todhills
Monikie
Tealing Earth-House
Kirkton of Monikie
Bonnyton
Kirkton of Auchterhouse
Kirkton of Tealing
Tealing Dovecot
Newbigging
Craigton
Auchterhouse
Wellbank
Muirdrum
A92
Lundie
Kirkton of Strathmartine
Burnside of Duntrune
Carlungie Earth-House
Upper Victoria
East Haven
Mains of Fintry
Murroes
Ardestie Earth-House
Barry
Barry Mill
Panbride
West Haven
Carnoustie
Fowlis
Camperdown
Whitfield
B961
Baldovie
Douglas and Angus
B962
A930
0 1 2 3 4 miles
0 1 2 3 4 5 kilometres

Goosecruives
206
Drumlithie
Glenbervie
Bervie Water
Temple of Fiddes
Crawton
Fowlsheugh
Trelong Bay
Catterline
Todhead Point
Kinneff
465 GOYLE HILL
454 Cairn O'Mount
414 FINELLA HILL
Auchenblae
Mondynes
Fordoun
Pittarrow
Redmyre
Arbuthnott
B967
B966
A92
Inverbervie
Bervie Bay
Gourdon
Mains of Haulkerton
Laurencekirk
B9120
Bogmuir
B974
Sauchieburn
Redford
Benholm
Edzell Woods
Luthermuir
Dykelands
A90
A937
B974
River North Esk
Johnshaven
Marykirk
Logie Pert
Craigo
Lochside
Bush
Milton Ness
St Cyrus
Logie
Morphie
Hillside
A92
House of Dun
Dun
Montrose Air Station
A935
Montrose
Caledonian Railway
Haughs of Kinnaird
Montrose Basin
Barnhead
Scurdie Ness
Maryton
Ferryden
A934
Craig
Usan
Westerton of Rossie
Boddin Point
Braehead
132 WUDDY LAW
Lunan
Lunan Bay
Boysack
Inverkeilor
Red Head
Chapelton
Cauldcots
A92
Marywell
Auchmithie
St Vigeans
Carlingheugh Bay
The Deil's Head
Arbroath

208
447
BEINN BHREAC
Loch Eynort
434
AN CRUACHIN
Glenbritte House
Bualintur
Loch Brittle
Rudh' an Dùnain
CANNA
210
CÀRN A' GHAILL
Garrisdale Point
A'Chill
Canna Harbour
Sanday
Kilmory Bay
Rudha Shamhnan Insir
Sound of Canna
302
MULLACH MÒR
A Bhrideanach
570
ORVAL
Kinloch
Oigh-sgeir
RÙM
Harris Bay
810
ASKIVAL
763
SGÙRR NAN GILLEAN
The Small Isles
Rudha nam Meirleach
Eilean nan Each
MUCK
189
0 1 2 3 4 miles
0 1 2 3 4 5 kilometres
A B C D E F
1 2 3 4 5 6 7 8

ISLE OF SKYE
The Cuillin Hills
Cuillin Hills
Sligachan
Broadford
Corry
Broadford Bay
Waterloo
Lower Breakish
Upper Breakish
Harrapool
Skulamus
Kyleakin
Skye Bridge
Pabay
Dunan
Loch Ainort
Torrin
Loch Slapin
Kirkibost
Elgol
Glasnakille
Loch Scavaig
SOAY
Mol-chlach
Loch Coruisk
Loch na Crèitheach
Suisnish
Rudha Suisnish
Loch Eishort
Heast
Drumfearn
Duisdalemore
Isleornsay
Ornsay
Loch na Dal
Tokavaig
Ord River
Tarskavaig
Tarskavaig Bay
Achnacloich
Loch nam Uamph
Teangue
Knock
Knock Bay
Ferrindonald
Kilmore
Kilbeg
Clan Donald
Ardvasar
Armadale
Calligarry
Aird of Sleat
Ard Thurinish
Point of Sleat
SOUND OF SLEAT
Sandaig Island
Rudha Buidhe
Rudh' Ard Slisneach
Inverguseran
Glen Guseran
Airor
Sandaig
Sandaig Bay
Rudha Raonuill
Inverie Bay
Courteachan
Mallaigvaig
Mallaig (Malaig)
Glasnacardoch Bay
Loch an Nostaire
Beoraidbeg
Morar
Bracora
Bracorina
Tarbet
Swordland
Glenancross
Lettermorar
Bunacaimb
Eilean Ighe
Back of Keppoch
Arisaig
Loch nan Ceall
Luinga Mhòr
Rudh' Arisaig
Druimindarroch
Arisaig House
Prince Charlie's Cairn
Kinlochnanuagh
Loch nan Uamh
Polnish
Ardnish
Rudha Choalais
Loch Ailort
Inverailort
Lochailort
EIGG
Bay of Laig
Cleadale
Laig
Kildonnan
Sandavore
Eilean Chathastail
Rùm
A87
A851
A830
A861
B8083
B8008
209
200
190

200
Kyle of Lochalsh
(Caol Loch Aillse)
Skye Bridge
Kyleakin
Badicaul
Balmacara
Auchtertyre
Kirkton
Lochalsh Woodland Garden
Nostie
Conchra
Ardelve
Eilean Donan
Dornie
Carndu
Loch Long
Camas Luinie
Glen Elchaig
SGUMAN COINNTICH
Loch na Leitreach
River Elchaig
210
Loch Alsh
Keppoch
Letterfearn
Loch Duich
Inverinate
SGÙRR AN AIRGID
Morvich
Carn-gorm
Ault a' chruinn
Invershiel
Shiel Bridge
Ratagan
Mam Ratagan
Kintail
FIVE SISTERS
Glen Shiel
SGÙRR FHUARAN
A'GHLAS-BHEINN
BEN ATTOW
Pabay
Lower Breakish
Upper Breakish
SGURR NA COINNICH
Kyle Rhea
Otter Haven
Kylerhea
(Apr-Oct)
Bernera
Galltair
Glenelg
Glenelg Bay
Eilanreach
BEINN A'CHUIRN
BEINN A' CHAOINICH
Moyle
Balvraid
Glenelg Brochs
Glean Beag
BEN ASLAK
BEINN NA SEAMRAIG
Loch na Dal
Ornsay
Sandaig Island
SOUND OF SLEAT
Rudha Buidhe
BEINN SGRITHEAL
BEINN NAN CAORACH
THE SADDLE
SGURR NA-SGINE
Loch Hourn
Arnisdale
Corran
Glen Arnisdale
DRUM FADA
Rudh' Ard Slisneach
Inverguseran
BEINN NA CAILLICH
Barrisdale Bay
Kinloch Hourn
SGURR A MHAORAICH
199
Glen Guseran
LADHAR BHEINN
DRUIM NA CLUAIN-AIRIDHE
Sandaig
Sandaig Bay
Knoydart
KNOYDART
LUINNE BHEINN
Loch an Dubh-Lochain
Inverie
Inverie Bay
Rudha Raonuill
Loch Quoich
GAIRICH
SGURR MOR
Mallaigvaig
CÀRN A'GHOBHAIR
Loch an Nostaire
SGÙRR BHUIDHE
Loch Nevis
BEINN BHUIDHE
SGURR NA CICHE
SGURR MHURLAGAIN
Morar
Bracora
Bracorina
Kylesmorar
Tarbet
Swordland
SGURR BREAC
SGURR NAH-AIDE
Glen Dessarry
Murlaggan
Loch Morar
Glen Pean
Lettermorar
CÀRN A' DAIDH-RUAIDH
AN STAC
Meoble
MEITH BHEINN
SGURR NAN COIREACHAN
SGÙRR THUILM
GULVAIN
SIDHEAN MOR
River Meoble
Prince Charlie's Cairn
Arisaig House
Kinlochnanuagh
Loch Beoriad
SGÙRR AN UTHA
Glen Finnan
Gleann Dubhlighe
Gleann Fionnlighe
MEALL PHUBU
Polnish
Lochailort
Loch Eilt
A830
Glenfinnan Viaduct
Glenfinnan Visitor Centre
Glenfinnan Monument
190
191
Kinlocheil
Locheilside Station
Drimsallie
Fass
A87
A87
A861
0 1 2 3 4 miles
0 1 2 3 4 5 kilometres
1
2
3
4
5
6
7
8
A
B
C
D
E
F

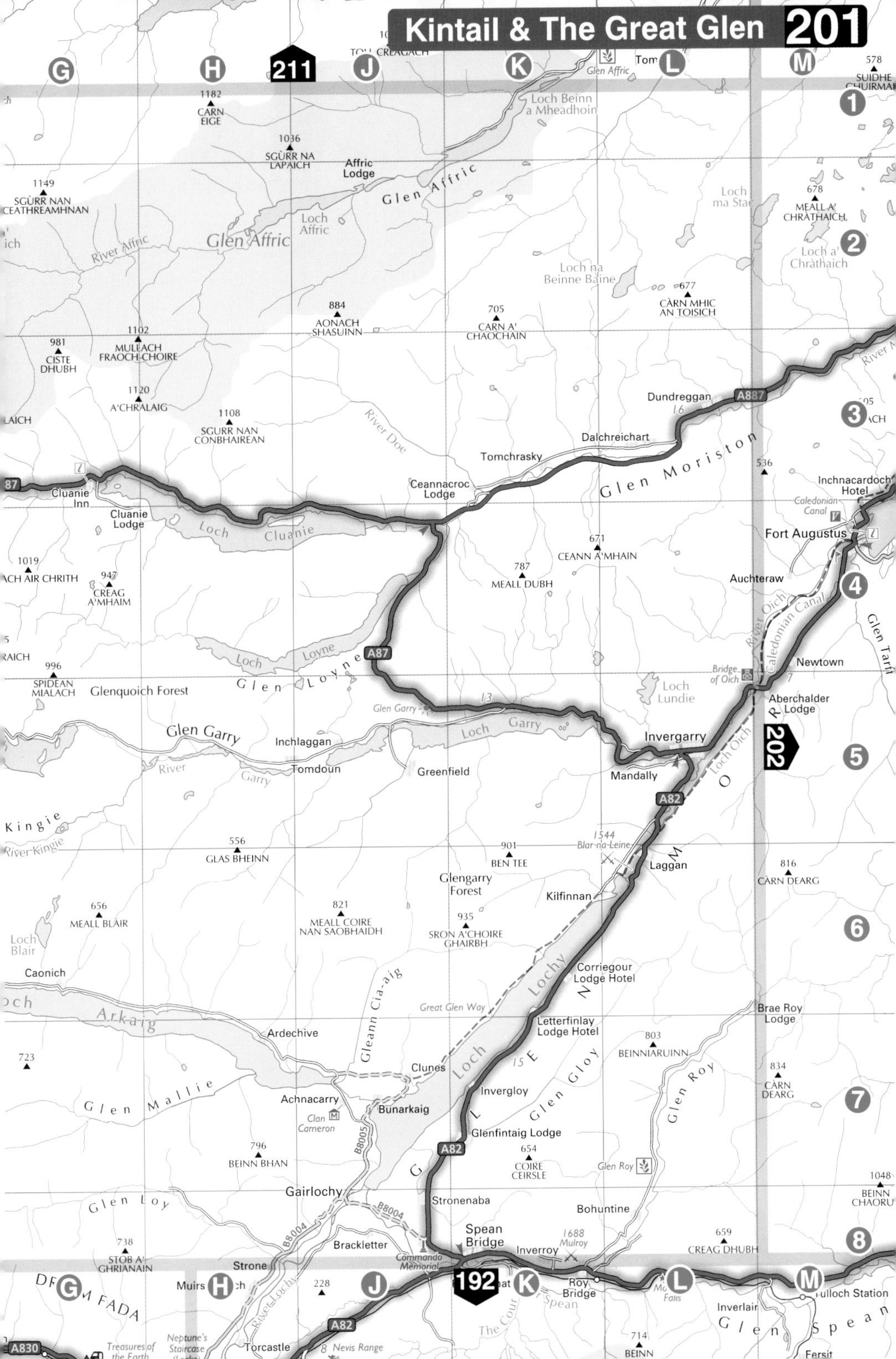

211
202
192
Carn Eige 1182
Sgùrr na Lapaich 1036
Affric Lodge
Glen Affric
Loch Affric
River Affric
Loch Beinn a Mheadhoin
Sgùrr nan Ceathreamhnan 1149
Loch ma Stac
Meall a' Chràthaich 678
Loch a' Chràthaich
Loch na Beinne Baine
Càrn Mhic an Toisich 677
Aonach Shasuinn 884
Carn a' Chaochain 705
Ciste Dhubh 981
Mullach Fraoch-choire 1102
A'Chralaig 1120
Sgurr nan Conbhairean 1108
River Doe
Dundreggan
Dalchreichart
Tomchrasky
Glen Moriston
Ceannacroc Lodge
Cluanie Inn
Cluanie Lodge
Loch Cluanie
Inchnacardoch Hotel
Caledonian Canal
Fort Augustus
Ceann a'Mhain 671
Meall Dubh 787
Creag a'Mhaim 947
Auchteraw
River Oich
Glen Tarff
Loch Loyne
Glen Loyne
Spidean Mialach 996
Glenquoich Forest
Bridge of Oich
Newtown
Loch Lundie
Aberchalder Lodge
Glen Garry
Inchlaggan
Loch Garry
Tomdoun
Greenfield
Invergarry
Mandally
Loch Oich
River Garry
Kingie
River Kingie
Glas Bheinn 556
Ben Tee 901
Blar-na-Leine 1544
Laggan
Càrn Dearg 816
Glengarry Forest
Kilfinnan
Meall Blàir 656
Meall Coire nan Saobhaidh 821
Sron a'Choire Ghairbh 935
Loch Blair
Caonich
Loch Arkaig
Gleann Cia-aig
Great Glen Way
Corriegour Lodge Hotel
Loch Lochy
Brae Roy Lodge
Ardechive
Letterfinlay Lodge Hotel
Beinniaruinn 803
Clunes
Glen Gloy
Glen Roy
Càrn Dearg 834
Glen Mallie
Achnacarry
Bunarkaig
Clan Cameron
Invergloy
Glenfintaig Lodge
Beinn Bhan 796
Coire Ceirsle 654
Glen Roy
Gairlochy
Glen Loy
Stronenaba
Bohuntine
Beinn Chaorunn 1048
Stob a' Ghrianain 738
Brackletter
Spean Bridge
Commando Memorial
Inverroy
Mulroy 1688
Creag Dhubh 659
Strone
Muirshearlich
Roy Bridge
Monessie Falls
Tulloch Station
Inverlair
Glen Spean
River Lochy
River Spean
The Cour
Treasures of the Earth
Neptune's Staircase (Locks)
Torcastle
Nevis Range
Fersit
A87
A887
A82
A830
B8005
B8004

Tomich
Loch Meiklie
Lewiston
Urquhart Castle
Falls of Divach
Strone
Lenie
212
SUIDHE GHUIRMAIN
578
Torness
Tullich
Loch Ruthven
Aberarder
LOCH NESS
Inverfarigaig
Aultnagoire
Farigaig
Loch ma Stac
678
MEALL A' CHRÀTHAICH
Loch a' Chràthaich
Loch nan Breac Deorga
696
A82
Errogie
Dunmaglass Lodge
Farraline
Foyers
Falls of Foyers
Gorthleck
Wester Aberchalder
686
BEINN DUBHCHARAIOH
677
CÀRN MHIC AN TOISICH
Achnaconeran
Invermoriston
Glebe
Loch Mhor
B862
B852
CÀRN
River Moriston
Great Glen Way
Loch Knockie
Whitebridge
810
CÀRN NA SAOBHAIDHE
Dundreggan
A887
605
BURACH
Glen Moriston
536
Inchnacardoch Hotel
Loch Killin
810
CÀRN NA LARAICHE MAOILE
Caledonian Canal
Glendoe Lodge
Fort Augustus
Monadhlia
Auchteraw
Glen Doe
Glen Tarff
River Oich
Caledonian Canal
778
CÀRN EASGANN BÀNA
855
SGARAMAN NAM FIADH
201
Newtown
Loch Lundie
Aberchalder Lodge
816
CÀRN A' CHUILINN
941
CÀRN BÀN
Invergarry
Loch Oich
891
CORRIEYAIRACK HILL
861
MEALL NA-H-AISRE
842
CÀRN AN LETH-CHOIN
925
GEAL CHÀRN
881
CÀRN LEAC
Laggan
816
CÀRN DEARG
Glen Markie
River Spey
Blargie
Laggan
Crathie
Loch Spey
Loch Crunachdan
Glenshero Lodge
563
BLACK CRAIG
A86
Catlodge
Strathmashie House
Brae Roy Lodge
803
1005
CÀRN LIATH
Kinlochlaggan
834
CÀRN DEARG
Gallovie
Loch Coaldair
Glen Roy
Creag Meagaidh
1128
CREAG MEAGAIDH
Loch Laggan
River Maghie
Distillery
1048
BEINN A' CHAORUNN
Dalwhinnie
River Pattack
Lochan na h-Earba
659
CREAG DHUBH
A86
Moy
747
BINNEIN SHUAS
1049
GEAL CHÀRN
Monessie Falls
192
193
CREAGAN MÒR
Inverlair
0 1 2 3 4 miles
0 1 2 3 4 5 kilometres
Loch Pattack
714
1088
Fersit

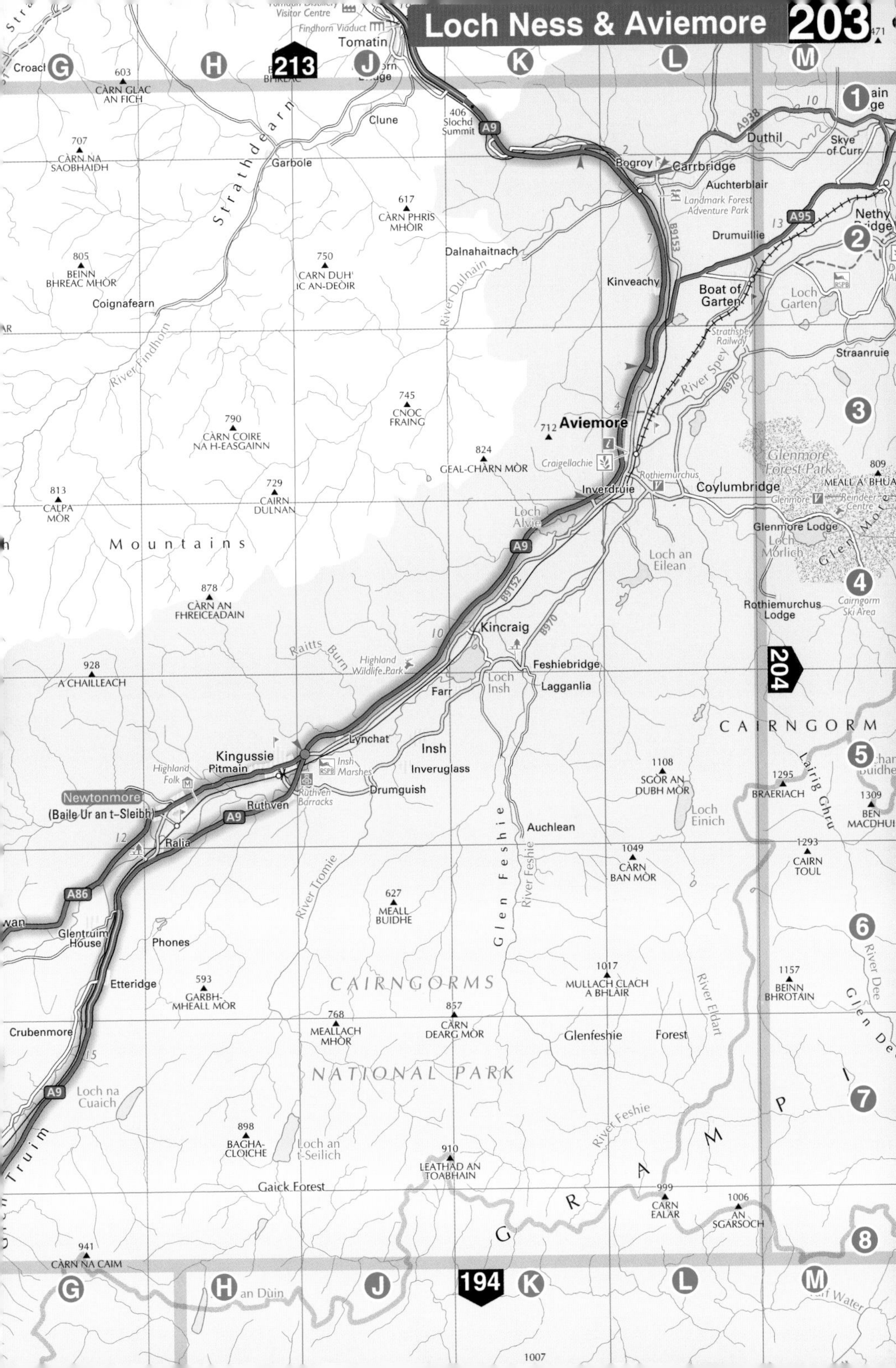

Tomatin
Findhorn Viaduct
213
Croach
603
CÀRN GLAC AN FICH
406 Slochd Summit
A9
Clune
707
CÀRN NA SAOBHAIDH
Garbole
Strathdearn
A938
Duthil
Skye of Curr
Bogroy
Carrbridge
Auchterblair
Landmark Forest Adventure Park
617
CÀRN PHRIS MHÒIR
A95
Nethy Bridge
B9153
Drumuillie
805
BEINN BHREAC MHÒR
750
CARN DUH' IC AN-DEÒIR
Dalnahaitnach
River Dulnain
Kinveachy
Boat of Garten
Loch Garten
RSPB
Coignafearn
River Findhorn
Strathspey Railway
River Spey
B970
Straanruie
745
CNOC FRAING
790
CÀRN COIRE NA H-EASGAINN
712
Aviemore
Craigellachie
824
GEAL-CHÀRN MÒR
Glenmore Forest Park
809
MEALL A' BHUA
729
CAIRN DULNAN
813
CALPA MÒR
Rothiemurchus
Inverdruie
Coylumbridge
Glenmore
Reindeer Centre
Loch Alvie
Glenmore Lodge
Loch Morlich
Glen More
Mountains
Loch an Eilean
B9152
878
CÀRN AN FHREICEADAIN
Rothiemurchus Lodge
Cairngorm Ski Area
Kincraig
Raitts Burn
Highland Wildlife Park
Feshiebridge
204
928
A CHAILLEACH
Farr
Loch Insh
Lagganlia
CAIRNGORM
Lynchat
Kingussie
Pitmain
Insh
Insh Marshes
Inveruglass
Highland Folk
1108
SGÒR AN DUBH MÒR
1295
BRAERIACH
Lairig Ghru
Newtonmore
(Baile Ur an t-Sleibh)
Ruthven
Ruthven Barracks
Drumguish
Loch Einich
1309
BEN MACDHUI
Ralia
Auchlean
1293
CAIRN TOUL
1049
CÀRN BAN MÒR
River Tromie
Glen Feshie
River Feshie
A86
627
MEALL BUIDHE
Glentruim House
Phones
River Dee
1017
MULLACH CLACH A BHLÀIR
1157
BEINN BHROTAIN
River Eidart
Etteridge
593
GARBH-MHEALL MÒR
CAIRNGORMS
Glen Dee
Crubenmore
768
MEALLACH MHÒR
857
CÀRN DEARG MÒR
Glenfeshie
Forest
NATIONAL PARK
Loch na Cuaich
898
BAGHA-CLOICHE
Loch an t-Seilich
910
LEATHAD AN TOABHAIN
GRAMPI
Truim
Gaick Forest
999
CARN EALAR
1006
AN SGARSOCH
941
CÀRN NA CAIM
194
an Dùin
1007

Grantown-on-Spey
Cromdale
214
Hills of Cromdale
Glenlivet
Shenval
Auchbreck
Glenlivet Distillery
Dulnain Bridge
Craggan
Speybridge
Tomnavoulin
Glen Livet
Strath Avon
Speyside Way
A938
Duthil
Skye of Curr
Bogroy
Carrbridge
Auchterblair
Landmark Forest Adventure Park
Auchnarrow
Clashn
B9008
B9136
Glen Lochy
459
CÀRN NA LOINNE
A939
B970
A95
B9153
Drumuillie
Nethy Bridge
Bridge of Brown
Tomintoul
Dell Wood (Abernethy)
Lettoch
Bridge of Avon
Milton
Glen Brown
Boat of Garten
Loch Garten
RSPB
Strathspey Railway
Dorback Lodge
Delnabo
River Nethy
River Spey
Straanruie
606
CÀRN TUADHAM
Glenmore Forest Park
821
GEAL CHÀRN
809
MEALL A' BHUACHAILLE
803
CARN BHEADHAIR
Lecht Ski Area
792
CARN EALASAID
710
CRAIG VEANN
Rothiemurchus
Coylumbridge
Glenmore
Reindeer Centre
Glenmore Lodge
Loch Morlich
Glen More
730
MAIM SUIM
Loch an Filean
741
BIG GARVOUN
River Avon
Cock Br
CAIRNGORMS
Glen Avon
Rothiemurchus Lodge
Cairngorm Ski Area
713
THE BRUACH
203
1245
CAIRN GORM
829
BROWN COW HILL
Loch Builg
NATIONAL
CAIRNGORM
1083
BEINN A CHAORRUINN
1171
BEN AVON
Lochan Buidhe
1196
NORTH TOP
River Gairn
SGÒR AN DUBH MÒR
1295
BRAERIACH
Lairig Ghru
1309
BEN MACDHUI
MOUNTAINS
1084
CÀRN EÀS
900
CULARDOCH
Loch Einich
PARK
1177
SOUTH TOP
1049
1293
CAIRN TOUL
930
BEINN BHREAC
Glen Derry
618
MEALL GORM
MOUNT
Quoich Water
Glen Lui
Linn of Dee
1157
BEINN BHROTAIN
River Dee
Glen Dee
813
SGOR MOR
Mar Lodge Estate
Allanaquoich
Braemar
Keiloch
A93
Inver
River Eldart
Forest
Inverey
859
MORRONE HILL
816
CARN LIATH
Clunie Water
GRAMPIAN
Loch Callater
1045
CARN TAGGART
999
CARN EALAR
1006
AN SGARSOCH
919
CARN BHAC
Glen Ey
886
SGOR MOR
Glen Clunie Lodge
195
1018
CÀRN AN TUIRC
Glenshee Ski Area
Baddoch Burn
957
TOM BUIDHE
0 1 2 3 4 miles
0 1 2 3 4 5 kilometres

Rhynie
Clatt
Duncanstone
Leslie
Aldivalloch
Aldunie
THE BUCK
HILL OF THREE STONES
MIRE OF MIDGATES
CORREEN HILLS
BRUX HILL
Lumsden
Ladder Hills
Badenyon
CREAG AN EUNAN
Mossat
Tullynessle
Scotsmill
Bridge of Alford
Montgarrie
Alford
CÀRN MÒR
MOSS HILL
Belnacraig
Kildrummy Castle
Kildrummy
Milltown
Glenbuchat Castle
Kirkton of Glenbuchat
THE SOCACH
Bellabeg
Glenkindie
Sinnarhard
Strathdon
Forbestown
Towie
Muir of Fowlis
Roughpark
Heughhead
Cushnie
Boltenstone
Garchory
Leochel-Cushnie
Craigievar Castle
Milltown
Colnabaichin
BROOM HILL
PRESSENDY
Corgarff
Crossroads
Migvie
MONA GOWAN
Tarland
CRAIGUCH
Corrachree
Culsh Earth-House
Logie Coldstone
CARN A' BHACAIN
MORVEN
Milton of Auchinhove
Tomnaverie Stone Circle
Coull
Auchlossan
Ordie
Loch Davan
Muir of Dinnet
Candacraig
Loch Kinord
Kincardine O'Neil
Cambus o' May
Dinnet
Aboyne
River Dee
GEALLAIG HILL
Bridge of Gairn
Milton of Tullich
Birsemore
Coilacriech
Pannanich Wells Hotel
Glen Tanar
Birse
Potarch
Marywell
Crathie
Littlemill
Ballater
BLACK CRAIG
Balnacroft
Birkhall
Glen Tanar
CARNFERG
Finzean
Water of Tanar
CREAG NAN GALL
THE COYLES OF MUICK
CAIRN LEUCHAN
CLACHAN YELL
HILL OF DUCHERY
Water of Feugh
Glen Muick
River Muick
COCK CAIRN
PETER HILL
MOUNT KEEN
HILL OF CAT
FASHEILACH
Spittal of Glenmuick
MOUNT BATTOCK
Water of Tarf
Loch Muick
Glen Mark
Glen Tennet
EASTERBALLOCH
Tarfside
Glen Lee
Loch Lee
Glenesk Folk

215 206 196

206
Kennethmont
Cottown
Clatt
Duncanstone
Insch
Dunnideer
Pitmachie
Old Rayne
216
Daviot
Oldmeldrum
Carnbrogie
Loanhead Stone Circle
A920
B992
B9002
A96
Whiteford
Kirkton
Archaeolink
Oyne
Pitcaple
Maiden Stone
Pittodrie House Hotel
Leslie
Auchleven
Chapel of Garioch
B9001
B9170
Kirktown of Bourtie
Whiterashes
484
MIRE OF MIDGATES
475
CORREEN HILLS
493
BENNACHIE
Mither Tap
518
The Bennachie Centre
Brandsbutt Symbol Stone
Inverurie
Nether Crimond
B993
Lethenty
Easter Aquhorthies Stone Circle
Port Elphinstone
Tullynessle
Kinmuck
Scotsmill
Keig
River Don
Burnhervie
Kinkell Church
Thainstone
Bridge of Alford
Montgarrie
Haughton House
Alford Valley Railway
Hatton of Fintray
B977
Pitfichie
B994
Kintore
Alford
Monymusk
Kemnay
Whitehouse
Pitmunie
Cottown
A980
Craigearn
Leylodge
B979
Muir of Fowlis
Kirkton of Tough
A944
Blackburn
Castle Fraser
Cushnie
Tillyfourie
Ordhead
Sauchen
Lyne of Skene
A96
Clinterty
Leochel-Cushnie
Craigievar Castle
Elrick
Corsindae
Skene House
Millbuie
494
BENAQUHALLIE
Dunecht
B9126
Brimmond Hill
Loch of Skene
Barmekin
Comers
Westhill
Crossroads
Tillybirloch
Marionburgh
Kirkton of Skene
Tornaveen
Carnie
Elrick
476
205
B9119
Garlogie
Culsh Earth-House
Lumphanan
Findrack House
Drumlasie
Echt
Redhill
B9119
Peel Ring of Lumphanan
Landerberry
Cullerlie Stone Circle
Easter Ord
Milltown of Learney
Cullerlie
Benthoul
Milton of Auchinhove
471
HILL OF FARE
B9125
Coull
Auchlossan
Craigton
Torphins
Milltown of Campfield
Hardgate
B977
Drum Castle
Peterculter
Mid Beltie
Hirn
West Park
Kincardine O'Neil
B993
A980
Brathens
Drumfrennie
Myrebird
River Dee
Aboyne
River Dee
Upper Lochton
The Neuk
Crathes Castle
Kirkton of Maryculter
B976
Birsemore
A93
A93
B993
Potarch
Bridge of Canny
Crathes
B9077
Birse
Marywell
Banchory
Durris
Denside
Woodlands
Bridge of Feugh
Royal Deeside Railway
310
TOM'S CAIRN
336
299
SCOLTY HILL
B974
Crossroads
525
CARNFERG
Baulds
Finzean
Waulkmill
B976
Strachan
556
Water of Feugh
Water of Aven
A957
376
MONGOUR
FETTERESSO FOREST
617
PETER HILL
Glen Dye
532
KERLOCH
507
MOUNT SHADE
579
CLACHNABEN
320
HILL OF TRUSTA
Bridge of Dye
390
LEACHIE HILL
Kirktown of Fetteresso
Elfhill
779
MOUNT BATTOCK
Water of Dye
Tannachie
Goosecruives
New Mill
B974
465
GOYLE HILL
475
HILL OF FINGRAY
Bervie Water
197
Drumlithie
Glenbervie
Temple of Fiddes
Mondynes
Glenesk Folk
0 1 2 3 4 miles
0 1 2 3 4 5 kilometres
414
FINELLA HILL
Auchenblae
544

Esslemont
Kirkton of Logie Buchan
Collieston
Pitmedden
Logierieve
217
Forvie
Housieside
Udny Green
Udny Station
Newburgh
Pettymuk
Culterculien
Foveran
Tillygreig
Delfrigs
Reisque
Causeyend
Whitecairns
Belhelvie
Balmedie
Kinmundy
Cothal
Potterton
Blackdog
Dyce
Middleton Park
Denmore
Kirkwall
Lerwick
Bankhead
Bucksburn
Bridge of Don
Northfield
Old Aberdeen
Kingswells
Kittybrewster
ABERDEEN
Ruthrieston
Torry
Nigg Bay
Mannofield
Cults
Bieldside
Kincorth
Nigg
Milton of Murtle
Banchory-Devenick
Altens Haven
Cove Bay
Kingcausie
Charlestown
Marywell
Hillside
Auchlee
Findon
Portlethen
Cammachmore Bay
Downies
Cammachmore
Newtonhill
Skateraw
Muchalls
Bridge of Muchalls
Doonie Point
Garron Point
Stonehaven Bay
Stonehaven
Dunnottar
Crawton
Fowlsheugh
Trelong Bay
A90
A920
A975
A956
A93
B999
B9000
B9005
B977
B979
B997
B9077
B9119
G
H
J
K
L
M
1
2
3
4
5
6
7
8

Duntulm
A855
Tairbeart (Tarbert)
Lùb Score
Skye Museum of Island
Borneskitaig
Heribusta
Kilmuir
Kilvaxter
Balgown
Loch nam Madadh (Lochmaddy)
218
Waternish Point
Linicro
Totscore
River Rha
Ascrib Islands
Idrigill
Uig (Uige)
Uig Bay
283 BEN GEARY
Geary
Trumpan
Loch Snizort
Earlish
Ardmore Point
Gillen
Hallin
A87
River Hinn
DUNVEGAN HEAD
Isay
Mingay
Stein
Lusta
Loch Bay
Kingsburgh
214 BEN DIUBAIG
Greshornish House Hotel
Loch Greshornish
Loch Snizort Beag
Loch Dunvegan
Claigan
Bay
Boreraig
327 BEINN BHREAC
B886
Uig
Treaslane
Flashader
A850
Loch Pooltiel
Upperglen
Feriniquarrie
Totaig
Edinbane
Bernisdale
Oisgill Bay
Milovaig
Glendale
Dunvegan
Tote
Waterstein
Lephin
B884
Colbost
Colbost Croft
Toy
Dunvegan
A850
Giant Angus MacAskill
Skeabost
Skinidin
Kilmuir
A864
Caroy River
Neist Point
Lonmore
265 BEN AKETIL
271 CRUACHAN BEINN A' CHEARCAILL
Uigshader
Moonen Bay
Roskhill
469 HEALAVAL MORE
Roag
Ramasaig
Orbost
Vatten
B885
Hoe Rape
ISLE OF
488 HEALAVAL BHEAG
Harlosh
Glen Ose
A863
Ose
Hoe Point
Loch Caroy
Colbost Point
368 BEINN NA BOINEID
Harlosh Island
Dun Beag
Bracadale
Loch Duagrich
Tarner Island
Coillore
Struan
Loch Bracadale
Ullinish Lodge Hotel
Wiay
Idrigill Point
Oronsay
439 ROINEV
Portnalong
Loch Harport
Fiskavaig
B8009
Rudha nan Clach
Fernilea
Drynoch
369 ARNAVAL
Carbost
Talisker Bay
Merkadale
Talisker
Glen Eynort
447 BEINN BHREAC
Grula
198
0 1 2 3 4 miles
0 1 2 3 4 5 kilometres
Loch Eynort

Kilmaluag
Flodigarry
Eilean Flodigarry
Poldorais
Staffin Bay
Staffin Island
542 MEAL NA SUIREAMACH
Digg
Brogaig
Stenscholl
Staffin
218
Kilt Rock Waterfall
Ellishader
Trotternish
Maligar
Marishader
Valtos
Rudha nam Brathairean
611 BEINN EDRA
Garros
Culnaknock
Lealt
Tote
A855
608 CREAG A' LAIN
Old Man of Storr
719 THE STORR
River Romesdal
River Haulton
Loch Leathan
Loch Fada
Borve
Drumuie
Glengrasco
312
Torvaig
Portree
Seafield
417 BEINN NA GREINE
Penifiler
412 BEN TIANAVAIG
Glenmore
Glenvarragill
A87
Mugeary
Camastianavaig
Tianavaig Bay
Ollach
B883
Glen Varragill
The Braes
444 BEN LEE
Peinchorran
Sconser
A863
SKYE
Sligachan
773 GLAMAIG
A87
Loch Ainort
Luib
Dunan
Caolas Scalpay
564 GLAS BHEIN MHÒRN
199
965 SGURR NAN GILLEAN
The Cuillin Hills
SOUND OF RAASAY
Loch a' Bhràige
RONA
Eilean Tigh
Eilean Fladday
Manish Point
Loch Arnish
Torran
Arnish
Brochel
RAASAY
444 DÙN CAAN
Rudha na' Leac
Oskaig
Clachan
310 BEINN NA LEAC
Inverarish
Eyre Point
Suisnish Point
INNER SOUND
SCALPAY
396 MULLACH NA CARN
67 Longay
27 Pabay
Corry
Broadford Bay
Broadford
Waterloo
Lower Breakish
Upper Breakish
732
708 BEINN NA
South Erradale
Redpoint
Red Point
Loch Torridon
Rudha na Fearn
Fearnmore
Òb Chuaig
Fearnbeg
Arrina
Kenmore
Cuaig
Callakille
Lonbain
492 AN GARBH-MHEALL
493 CROIC-BHEINN
River Applecross
210
Applecross Bay
Applecross
Milton
626 Pass of the Cattle
774 SGÙRR A' CHA
Camusteel
Camusterrach
Bealach-Na-Ba
Aird Dhubh
Culduie
Toscaig
River Toscaig
Caolas Mòr
Eilean Meadhonach
Eilean Mòr
CROWLIN ISLANDS
Loch Carron
Port-an-Eorna
Drumbuie
Badicaul
Kyle of Lochalsh (Caol Loch Aillse)
Skye Bridge
A87
Kyleakin
G H J K L M
1 2 3 4 5 6 7 8

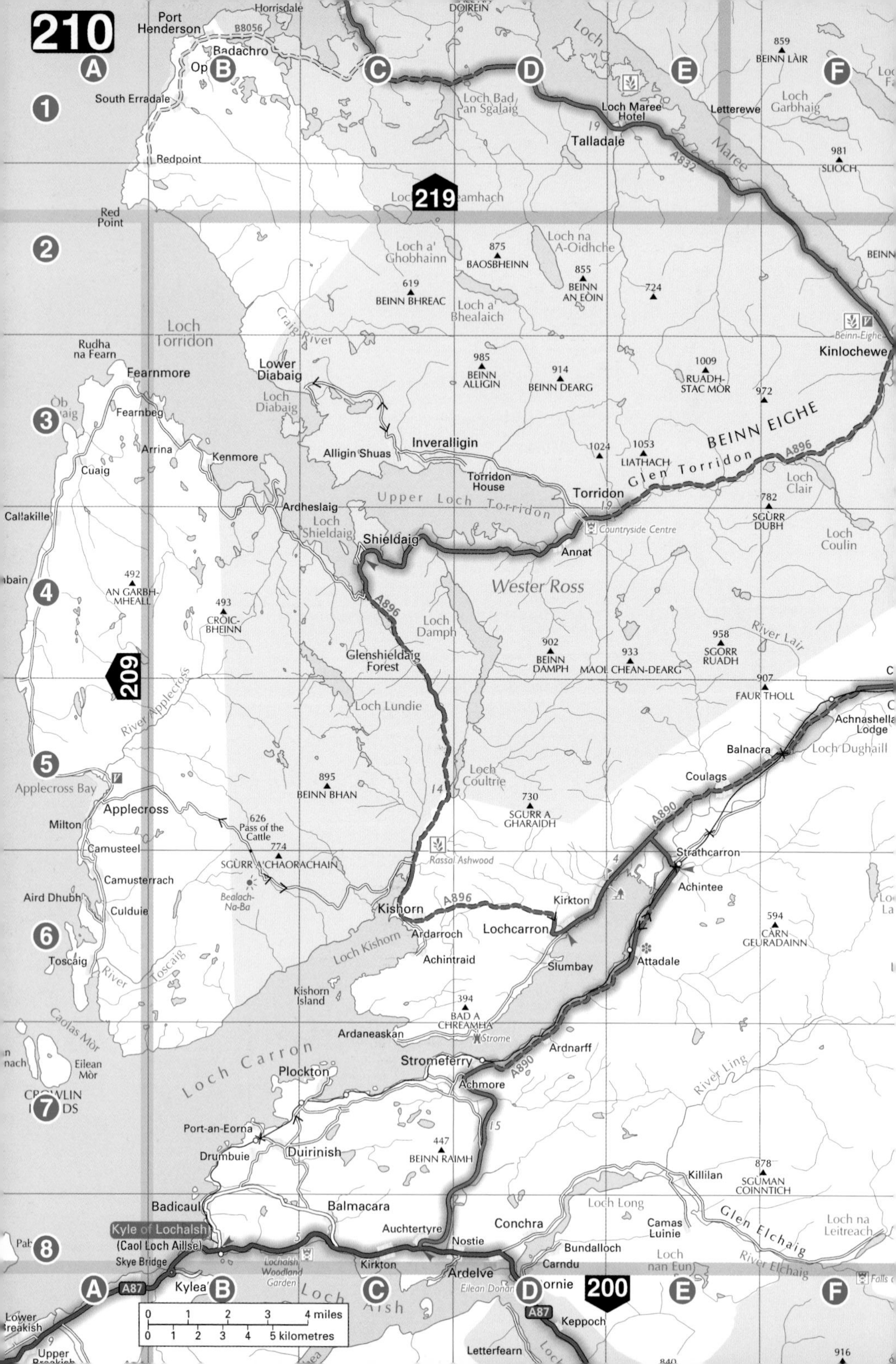

210
Port Henderson
Horrisdale
B8056
Badachro
Opinan
South Erradale
Redpoint
Red Point
DOIREIN
Loch Bad an Sgalaig
Loch Maree Hotel
Talladale
Loch Maree
A832
Letterewe
859
BEINN LÀIR
Loch Garbhaig
981
SLIOCH
219
Loch a' Ghobhainn
875
BAOSBHEINN
Loch na A-Oidhche
855
BEINN AN EÒIN
619
BEINN BHREAC
Loch a' Bhealaich
724
Craig River
Loch Torridon
Rudha na Fearn
Fearnmore
Lower Diabaig
Loch Diabaig
985
BEINN ALLIGIN
914
BEINN DEARG
1009
RUADH-STAC MÒR
Beinn-Eighe
Kinlochewe
972
BEINN EIGHE
Fearnbeg
Arrina
Kenmore
Cuaig
Alligin Shuas
Inveralligin
1024
1053
LIATHACH
Glen Torridon
A896
Loch Clair
Torridon House
Upper Loch Torridon
Torridon
Callakille
Ardheslaig
Loch Shieldaig
Shieldaig
Countryside Centre
782
SGÙRR DUBH
Loch Coulin
Annat
492
AN GARBH-MHEALL
493
CROIC-BHEINN
Wester Ross
Loch Damph
902
BEINN DAMPH
933
MAOL CHEAN-DEARG
958
SGORR RUADH
River Lair
Glenshieldaig Forest
209
907
FAUR THOLL
River Applecross
Loch Lundie
Achnashellach Lodge
Balnacra
Loch Dughaill
Coulags
Applecross Bay
895
BEINN BHAN
Loch Coultrie
Applecross
Milton
626
Pass of the Cattle
730
SGURR A GHARAIDH
A890
Camusteel
774
SGÙRR A' CHAORACHAIN
Rassal Ashwood
Strathcarron
Camusterrach
Bealach-Na-Ba
Aird Dhubh
Culduie
Kishorn
Kirkton
Achintee
594
CÀRN GEURADAINN
Ardarroch
Lochcarron
Toscaig
River Toscaig
Loch Kishorn
Achintraid
Slumbay
Attadale
Kishorn Island
394
BAD A CHREAMHA
Caolas Mòr
Ardaneaskan
Strome
Ardnarff
Eilean Mòr
Loch Carron
Plockton
Stromeferry
River Ling
CROWLIN
Achmore
Port-an-Eorna
Duirinish
Drumbuie
447
BEINN RAIMH
878
SGÙMAN COINNTICH
Killilan
Badicaul
Balmacara
Loch Long
Conchra
Camas Luinie
Glen Elchaig
Loch na Leitreach
Kyle of Lochalsh
(Caol Loch Aillse)
Auchtertyre
Nostie
Bundalloch
Loch nan Eun
River Elchaig
Skye Bridge
Lochalsh Woodland Garden
Kirkton
Ardelve
Carndu
Falls
A87
Loch Alsh
Eilean Donan
Dornie
200
Lower Breakish
Keppoch
Upper Breakish
Letterfearn
916
840
0 1 2 3 4 miles
0 1 2 3 4 5 kilometres

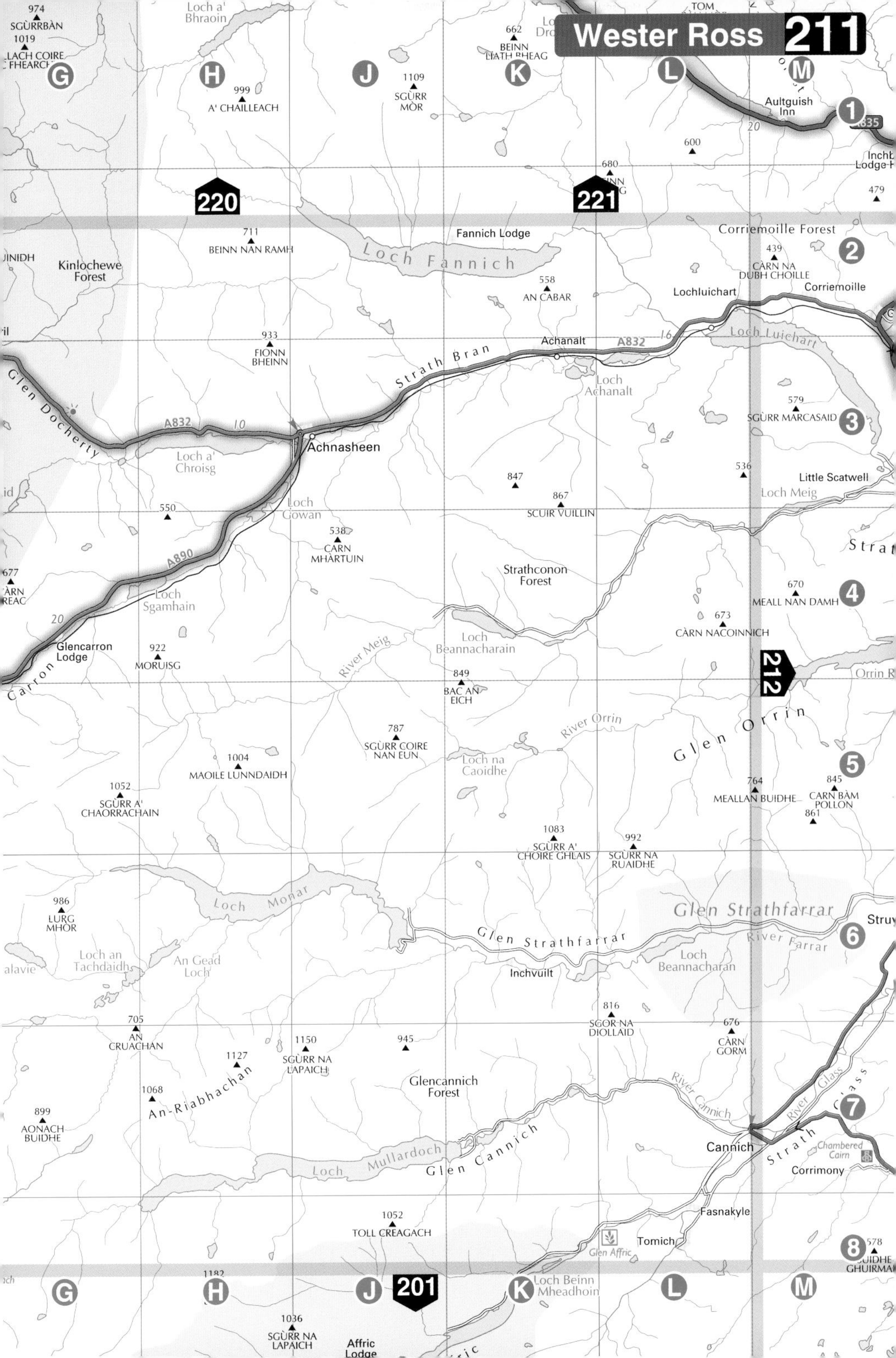

Loch a' Bhraoin
974 SGÙRRBÀN
1019
662 BEINN LIATH BHEAG
1109 SGÙRR MÒR
999 A' CHAILLEACH
Aultguish Inn
600
680
Inchbae Lodge
479
220
221
711 BEINN NAN RAMH
Fannich Lodge
Loch Fannich
Corriemoille Forest
439 CÀRN NA DUBH CHOILLE
Corriemoille
Lochluichart
Loch Luichart
Kinlochewe Forest
558 AN CABAR
933 FIONN BHEINN
Achanalt
A832
Strath Bran
Loch Achanalt
Glen Docherty
A832
Achnasheen
Loch a' Chroisg
579 SGÙRR MARCASAID
536
Little Scatwell
Loch Meig
847
867 SCUIR VUILLIN
550
Loch Gowan
538 CÀRN MHÀRTUIN
A890
Strathconon Forest
677
Loch Sgamhain
670 MEALL NAN DAMH
673 CÀRN NACOINNICH
Glencarron Lodge
922 MORUISG
River Meig
Loch Beannacharain
212
Orrin R
849 BAC AN EICH
Carron
River Orrin
Glen Orrin
787 SGÙRR COIRE NAN EUN
1004 MAOILE LUNNDAIDH
Loch na Caoidhe
764 MEALLAN BUIDHE
845 CÀRN BÀN POLLON
861
1052 SGÙRR A' CHAORRACHAIN
1083 SGÙRR A' CHOIRE GHLAIS
992 SGÙRR NA RUAIDHE
986 LURG MHOR
Loch Monar
Glen Strathfarrar
Struy
River Farrar
Loch an Tachdaidh
An Gead Loch
Inchvuilt
Loch Beannacharan
816 SGOR NA DIOLLAID
705 AN CRUACHAN
676 CÀRN GORM
1150 SGÙRR NA LAPAICH
945
1127
An-Riabhachan
1068
Glencannich Forest
River Cannich
River Glass
899 AONACH BUIDHE
Cannich
Strath Glass
Chambered Cairn
Corrimony
Loch Mullardoch
Glen Cannich
Fasnakyle
1052 TOLL CREAGACH
Tomich
Glen Affric
578
1182
201
Loch Beinn a' Mheadhoin
1036 SGÙRR NA LAPAICH
Affric Lodge
G H J K L M
1 2 3 4 5 6 7 8

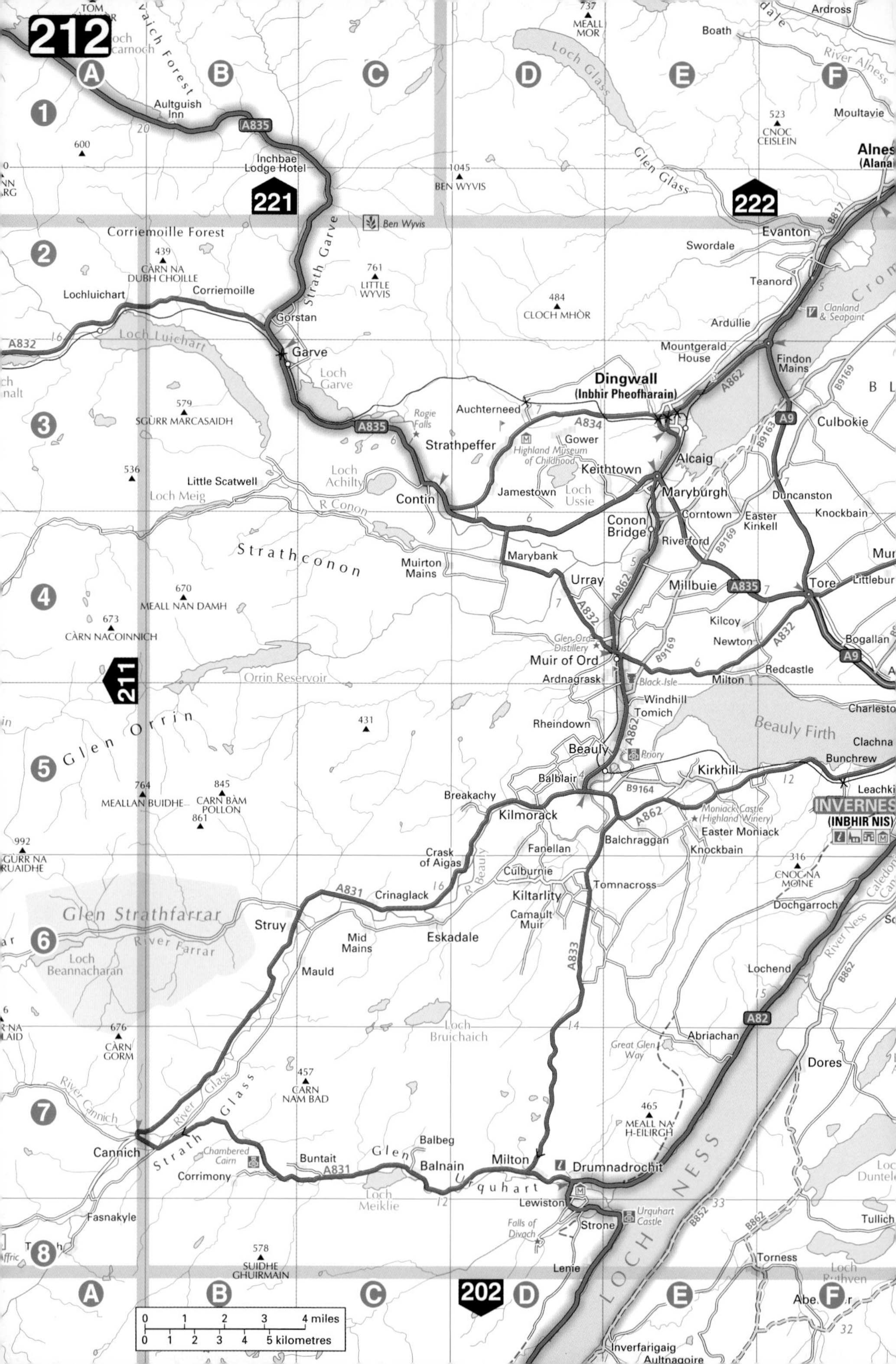

A
B
C
D
E
F
1
2
3
4
5
6
7
8
737
MEALL MOR
Loch Glass
Ardross
Boath
River Alness
Moultavie
523
CNOC CEISLEIN
Alness
(Alanais)
Aultguish Inn
A835
600
Inchbae Lodge Hotel
221
1045
BEN WYVIS
Glen Glass
222
Ben Wyvis
Evanton
B817
Swordale
Corriemoille Forest
439
CÀRN NA DUBH CHOILLE
Corriemoille
Lochluichart
Strath Garve
761
LITTLE WYVIS
Teanord
484
CLOCH MHÒR
Clanland & Seapoint
Cromarty
Ardullie
Gorstan
A832
Loch Luichart
Garve
Loch Garve
Mountgerald House
Findon Mains
Dingwall
(Inbhir Pheofharain)
A862
B9169
579
SGÙRR MARCASAIDH
Rogie Falls
Auchterneed
A834
A9
Culbokie
Strathpeffer
Highland Museum of Childhood
Gower
Alcaig
B9163
536
Little Scatwell
Loch Meig
Loch Achilty
Keithtown
Contin
Jamestown
Loch Ussie
Maryburgh
Duncanston
R Conon
Corntown
Easter Kinkell
Knockbain
Conon Bridge
Riverford
Strathconon
Marybank
Muirton Mains
Urray
Millbuie
Tore
Littlebur
670
MEALL NAN DAMH
673
CÀRN NACOINNICH
Kilcoy
Newton
Bogallan
211
Glen Ord Distillery
Muir of Ord
Redcastle
Ardnagrask
Black Isle
Milton
Orrin Reservoir
Windhill
Tomich
Charlesto
431
Rheindown
Beauly Firth
Glen Orrin
Beauly
Priory
Clachna
Bunchrew
Kirkhill
Balblair
B9164
Leachki
764
MEALLAN BUIDHE
845
CARN BÀM POLLON
861
Breakachy
Kilmorack
Moniack Castle (Highland Winery)
INVERNESS
(INBHIR NIS)
992
SGÙRR NA RUAIDHE
Crask of Aigas
R Beauly
Fanellan
Balchraggan
Easter Moniack
Knockbain
316
CNOC NA MOINE
Culburnie
Tomnacross
A831
Crinaglack
Kiltarlity
Dochgarroch
Caledonian Canal
Glen Strathfarrar
Camault Muir
Struy
River Farrar
Loch Beannacharan
Mid Mains
Eskadale
River Ness
A833
Mauld
Lochend
B862
676
CÀRN GORM
Loch Bruichaich
A82
Abriachan
Great Glen Way
Dores
River Cannich
River Glass
457
CARN NAM BAD
465
MEALL NA H-EILIRGH
Cannich
Strath Glass
Chambered Cairn
Balbeg
Glen Urquhart
Buntait
Balnain
Milton
Drumnadrochit
Corrimony
Loch Meiklie
Lewiston
Urquhart Castle
Loch Ness
Fasnakyle
Falls of Divach
Strone
B852
Tullich
578
SUIDHE GHUIRMAIN
Torness
Lenie
Loch Ruthven
202
Abe...r
0 1 2 3 4 miles
0 1 2 3 4 5 kilometres
Inverfarigaig
Aultnagoire

Shandwick Bay
Kildary
Milton
Kilmuir
Barbaraville
Pitcalnie
Nigg
Nigg Bay
Nigg Ferry
Rhicullen
Millcraig
Tomich
A9
Achnagarron
Balintraid
Saltburn
B817
Dalmore
Invergordon
223
Cromarty
Hugh Miller's Cottage
Balblair
Resolis
Udale Bay
Cromarty Bay
RSPB
Newton
B9163
Allerton
Navity
Jemimaville
Brae
Upper Eathie
MORAY FIRTH
A832
B9160
Raddery
Killen
RSPB
Rosemarkie
Cathedral
Groam House
Fort George
Whiteness Head
Nairn
(Inbhir Nàrann)
RSPB
Culbin Forest
Kintessack
Brodie Castle
Dyke
Brodie
A96
Fortrose
Chanonry Point
Avoch
A832
Munlochy Bay
Ardersier
B9092
B9006
Tradespark
Moss-side
Househill
Boath Doocot
Auldearn
1645
Foynesfield
Whitemire
Conicavel
Gollanfield
Lochside
B9039
Inverness
B9091
B9090
B9101
Righoul
Fornighty
Logie Steading
MORAY FIRTH
Fisherton
Kilmuir
Castle Stuart
Easter Dalziel
Clephanton
Cawdor
Piperhill
Culcharry
Littlemill
A939
214
Relugas
Alturlie Point
Tornagrain
Croy
River Nairn
North Kessock
Newton
Cantraywood
Balloch
Kirkton of Barevan
Clunas
Redburn
South Kessock
Culloden
Smithton
Resaurie
Culcabock
Culloden Viaduct
Culloden Battlefield & Visitor Centre
Clava Cairns
323 CÀRN MAOL
Ardclach Bell Tower
Ferness
B9177
B8082
401 CÀRN A' CHRASGIE
Knocknagael Boar Stone
Milton of Leys
A9
B851
Daviot House
Torbreck
Drummossie Muir
548 BEINN BHUIDHE MHOR
Bridge of Dulsie
Essich
Daviot
609 CÀRN NAN TRI-TIGHEARNAN
B861
B9154
464
Lochindorb
Lochindorb Lodge
Balnafoich
Loch Moy
Moy
483
B851
Farr
River Findhorn
633 CÀRN AN T-SEAN-LIATHANAICH
B9007
615 CÀRN NA H-EASGAINN
Strath Nairn
Balvraid
485 CÀRN SGRIOB
Tomatin Distillery Visitor Centre
659 CÀRN GLAS-CHOIRE
Findhorn Viaduct
Raigbeg
617
Tomatin
600 BEINN BHREAC
471
Croachy
603 CÀRN GLAC AN FICH
Findhorn Bridge
203
406 Slochd Summit
Clune
A938
Dulnain Bridge
Duthil
707 CÀRN NA SAOBHAIDH
Garbole
A9
Bogroy
Carrbridge
Skye of Curr

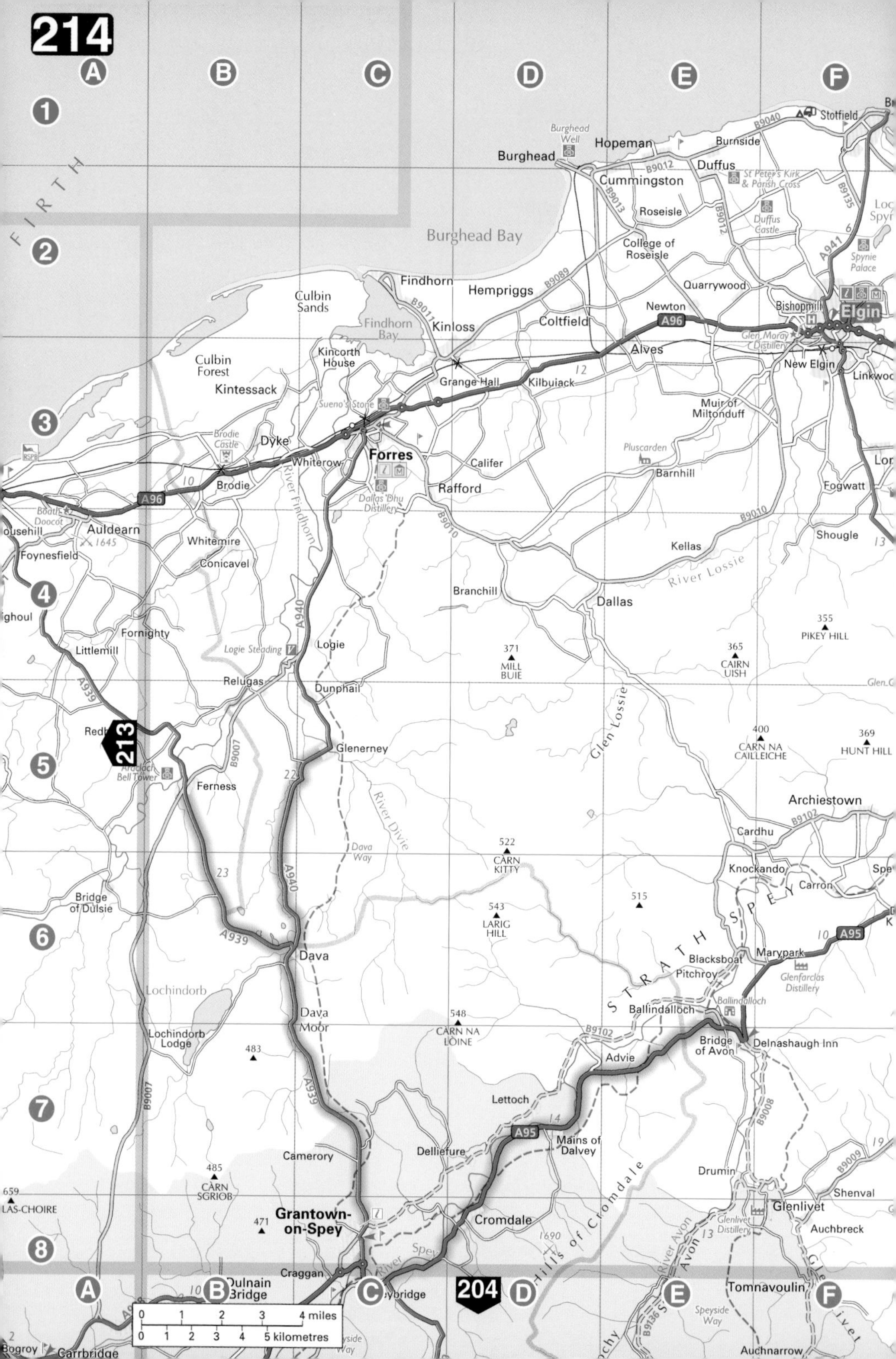
A
B
C
D
E
F
1
2
3
4
5
6
7
8
FIRTH
Burghead Bay
Burghead
Burghead Well
Hopeman
Stotfield
Burnside
Duffus
Cummingston
St Peter's Kirk & Parish Cross
Roseisle
Duffus Castle
College of Roseisle
Spynie Palace
Quarrywood
Findhorn
Hempriggs
Culbin Sands
Findhorn Bay
Kinloss
Coltfield
Newton
Bishopmill
Elgin
Glen Moray Distillery
Alves
New Elgin
Linkwood
Culbin Forest
Kincorth House
Grange Hall
Kilbuiack
Kintessack
Sueno's Stone
Muir of Miltonduff
Brodie Castle
Dyke
Whiterow
Forres
Pluscarden
Califer
Barnhill
Brodie
Rafford
Fogwatt
Dallas Dhu Distillery
Boath Doocot
Auldearn
1645
Shougle
Whitemire
Kellas
Foynesfield
Conicavel
River Lossie
River Findhorn
Branchill
Dallas
Fornighty
Littlemill
Logie Steading
Logie
371 MILL BUIE
365 CAIRN UISH
355 PIKEY HILL
Relugas
Dunphail
Glen Lossie
400 CARN NA CAILLEICHE
369 HUNT HILL
Glenerney
Ardclach Bell Tower
Ferness
River Divie
Archiestown
Cardhu
Dava Way
522 CARN KITTY
Knockando
Carron
515
Bridge of Dulsie
543 LARIG HILL
STRATH SPEY
Dava
Blacksboat
Marypark
Pitchroy
Glenfarclas Distillery
Lochindorb
Ballindalloch
Dava Moor
548 CARN NA LOINE
Lochindorb Lodge
483
Bridge of Avon
Delnashaugh Inn
Advie
Lettoch
Mains of Dalvey
Dellifure
Camerory
485 CARN SGRIOB
Drumin
Shenval
Glenlivet
Grantown-on-Spey
471
Cromdale
Hills of Cromdale
Glenlivet Distillery
Auchbreck
River Avon
River Spey
Craggan
Dulnain Bridge
Tomnavoulin
Speyside Way
Auchnarrow
Carrbridge
Bogroy
RSPB
A96
A940
A939
A941
A95
B9040
B9012
B9013
B9135
B9089
B9011
B9010
B9007
B9102
B9008
B9009
B9136
213
204
0 1 2 3 4 miles
0 1 2 3 4 5 kilometres

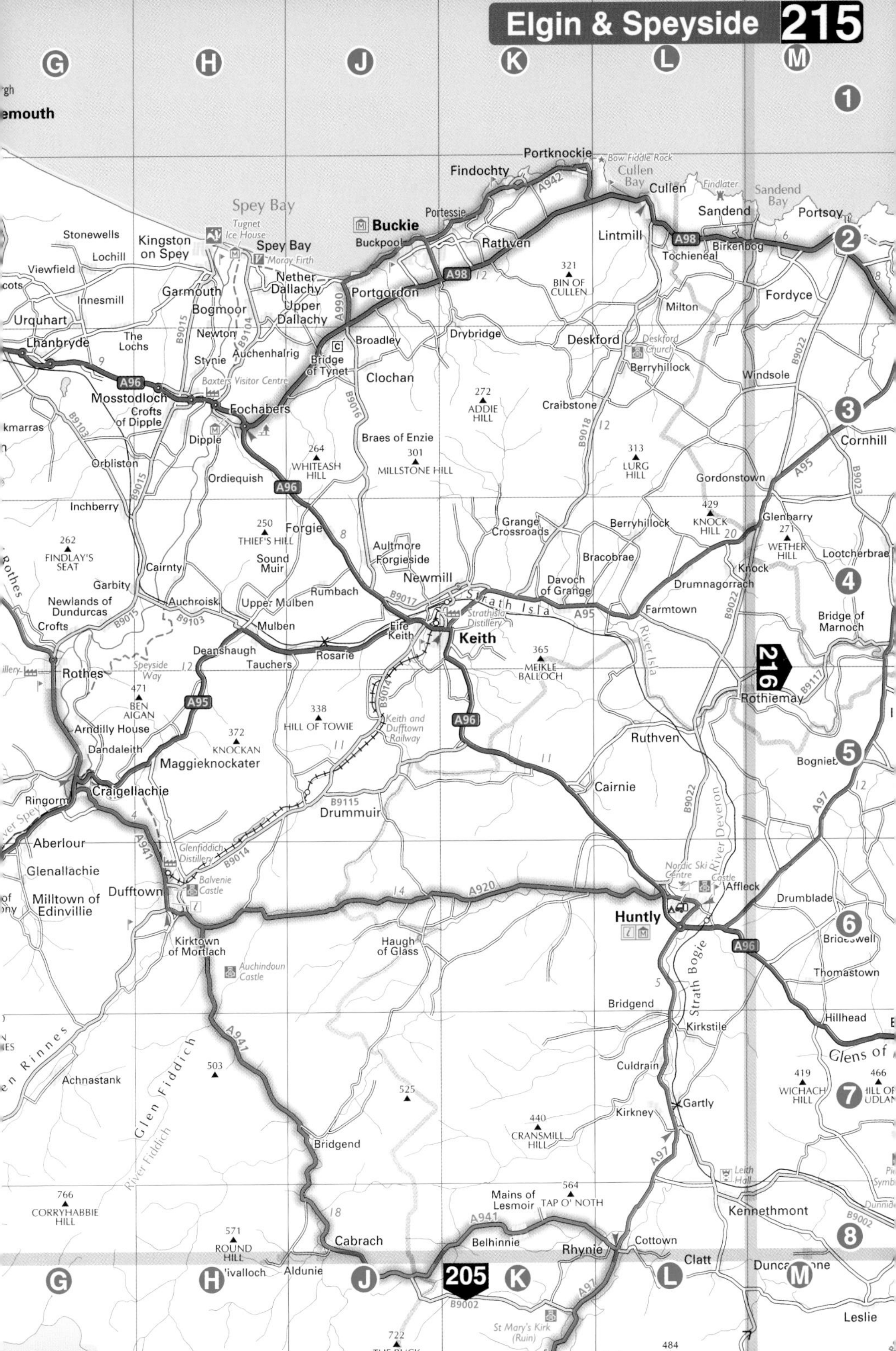

Portknockie
Findochty
Cullen
Cullen Bay
Sandend
Portsoy
Spey Bay
Buckie
Portessie
Buckpool
Rathven
Lintmill
Tochieneal
Birkenbog
Kingston on Spey
Garmouth
Portgordon
Fordyce
Deskford
Keith
Huntly
Rothes
Craigellachie
Aberlour
Dufftown
Fochabers
Mosstodloch
Lhanbryde
Urquhart
Newmill
Cornhill
Rothiemay
Drummuir
Cairnie
Kennethmont
Rhynie
Cabrach
Clatt
Gartly
A96
A98
A95
A941
A920
A97
A990
A942
216
205

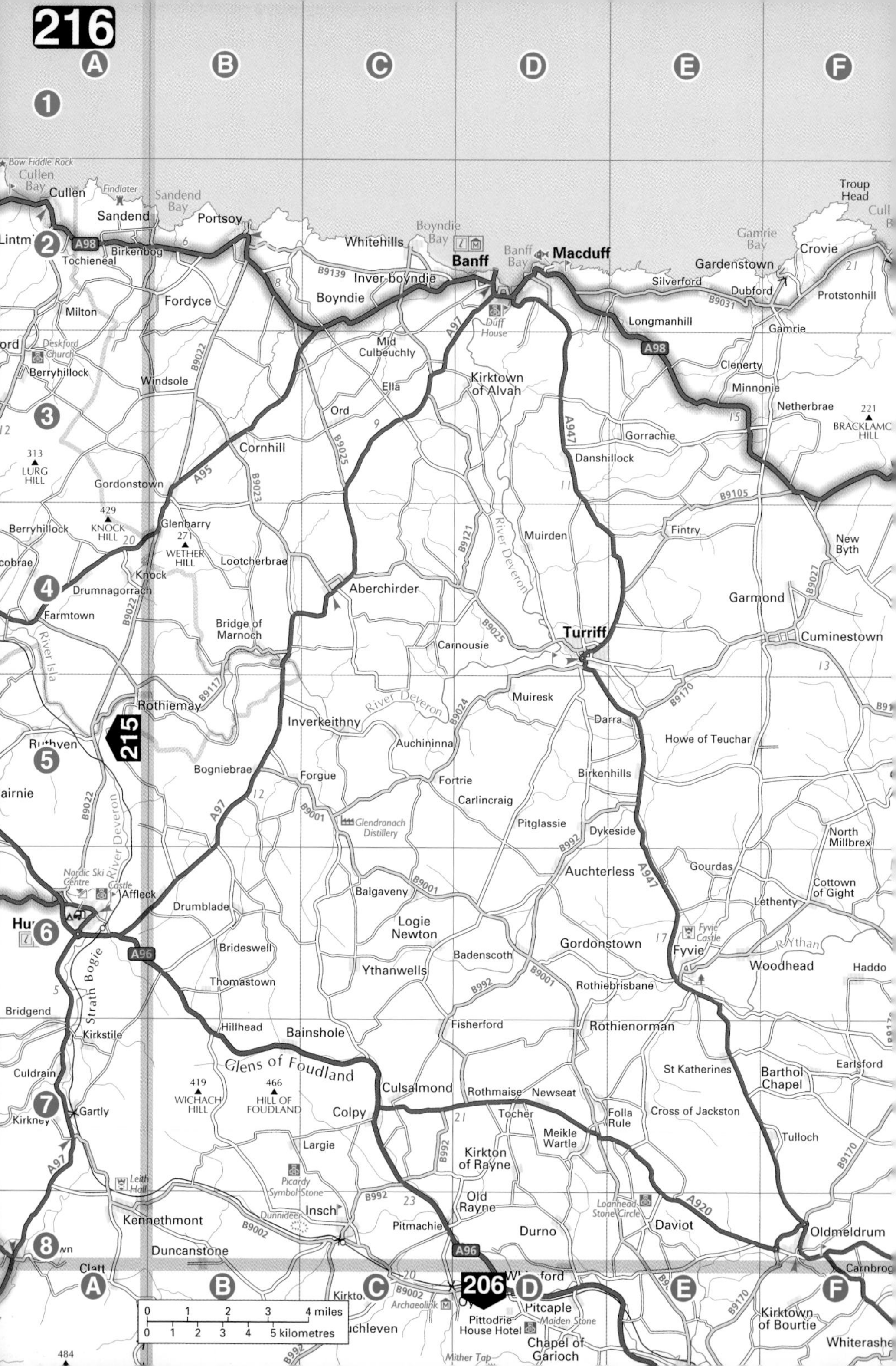
Bow Fiddle Rock
Cullen Bay
Cullen
Findlater
Sandend Bay
Sandend
Portsoy
A98
Tochieneal
Birkenbog
Boyndie Bay
Whitehills
Banff
Banff Bay
Macduff
Gamrie Bay
Troup Head
Crovie
Gardenstown
Silverford
Dubford
Protstonhill
B9139
Inver-boyndie
Boyndie
Fordyce
Milton
Deskford Church
Berryhillock
Duff House
Mid Culbeuchly
Longmanhill
B9031
Gamrie
Windsole
B9022
Ella
Kirktown of Alvah
Clenerty
Minnonie
Netherbrae
221 BRACKLAMORE HILL
Ord
A97
A947
Gorrachie
Danshillock
Cornhill
B9025
B9023
313 LURG HILL
A95
Gordonstown
B9105
429 KNOCK HILL
Berryhillock
Glenbarry
271 WETHER HILL
B9121
River Deveron
Muirden
Fintry
New Byth
Lootcherbrae
Knock
Drumnagorrach
Aberchirder
B9027
Garmond
Farmtown
Bridge of Marnoch
Carnousie
Turriff
Cuminestown
River Isla
B9117
Rothiemay
River Deveron
B9024
Muiresk
Darra
B9170
Inverkeithny
Howe of Teuchar
215
Ruthven
Auchininna
Birkenhills
Bogniebrae
Forgue
Fortrie
Carlincraig
B9022
B9001
Glendronach Distillery
Pitglassie
Dykeside
North Millbrex
River Deveron
B992
Auchterless
Gourdas
A947
Nordic Ski Centre
Castle
Affleck
Balgaveny
Cottown of Gight
Lethenty
Drumblade
Logie Newton
Fyvie Castle
R. Ythan
Gordonstown
Fyvie
Woodhead
Haddo
Brideswell
A96
Badenscoth
Ythanwells
Thomastown
B9001
Rothiebrisbane
Strath Bogie
Bridgend
B992
Fisherford
Rothienorman
Hillhead
Kirkstile
Bainshole
Earlsford
Glens of Foudland
St Katherines
Barthol Chapel
Culdrain
Culsalmond
419 WICHACH HILL
466 HILL OF FOUDLAND
Rothmaise
Newseat
Colpy
Tocher
Folla Rule
Cross of Jackson
Gartly
Kirkney
Meikle Wartle
Tulloch
Largie
B992
A97
Kirkton of Rayne
B9170
Leith Hall
Picardy Symbol Stone
Old Rayne
Loanhead Stone Circle
A920
Dunnideer
Insch
B992
Pitmachie
Kennethmont
Durno
Daviot
Oldmeldrum
B9002
Duncanstone
A96
Clatt
Carnbrogie
206
Whiteford
Kirkton
B9002
Archaeolink
Oyne
Pitcaple
Pittodrie House Hotel
Maiden Stone
B9170
Kirktown of Bourtie
Auchleven
B992
Chapel of Garioch
Mither Tap
Whiterashes
484
0 1 2 3 4 miles
0 1 2 3 4 5 kilometres

G
H
J
K
L
M
1
2
3
4
5
6
7
8
Castle Lighthouse & Museum
Kinnaird Head
Rosehearty
Sandhaven
Pittulie
Fraserburgh
Peathill
Fraserburgh Bay
Craigiefold
Kirktown
Cairnbulg
Aberdour Bay
Percyhorner
Inverallochy
Maggie's Hoosie
Whitelinks Bay
B9031
Coburby
Pitblae
Mid Ardlaw
A90
B9033
New Aberdour
Boyndlie
B9032
St Combs
Memsie
A98
Memsie Cairn
Rathen
Crofts of Savoch
A981
Newburgh
Lonmay
Rattray Head
234
WAUGHTON HILL
Loch of Strathbeg
RSPB
Crimond
Blackhill
A952
New Pitsligo
B9093
Strichen
New Leeds
Bonnykelly
B9093
Leys
Denhead
Backfolds
Kirktown
St Fergus
Fetterangus
Rora
A950
A981
A90
Deer Abbey
Dunshillock
River Ugie
Maud
B9106
Aden
Mintlaw
Longside
Inverugie
New Deer
B9029
B9029
Old Deer
Buchanhaven
Peterhead
Blackhill of Clackriach
A950
Peterhead
B9028
Inverquhomery
A948
Stuartfield
Drymuir
Bulwark
A982
Peterhead Bay
Millbreck
Nether Kinmundy
Hillhead of Cocklaw
Burnhaven
Nethermuir
B9170
Knaven
Clola
Buchan Ness
B9030
Kinnadie
Blackhill
Stirling
Boddam
Auchnagatt
Lendrum Terrace
Kinknockie
Cairnorrie
Brownhill
Longhaven
Inkhorn
A90
Ardallie
Coldwells
Bullers of Buchan
A952
Auchiries
Methlick
Hatton
North Haven
Slains
A948
Arthrath
Muirtack
R Ythan
Cruden Bay
Bogbrae
Chapel Hill
Bay of Cruden
B9005
A975
Ythanbank
Birness
Whinnyfold
The Skares
Auchedly
Altar Tomb of William Forbes
Artrochie
Kinharrachie
Ythsie
Ellon
P+R
Esslemont
B9005
Kirkton of Logie Buchan
Kirktown of Slains
B999
Tolquhon Castle
A920
Collieston
Pitmedden Garden
Pitmedden
32
Logierieve
Forvie
Housieside
207
B9000
Udny Station
B999
A90
Newburgh
Woodland
Pettymuk
Cultercullen
Foveran

Loch Shell
SOUND OF SHIANT
Loch Erisort
SHIANT ISLANDS
Fladda-chùain
Eilean Trodday
Rudha Hunish
North Duntulm
Duntulm
Kilmaluag
A855
Lùb Score
Skye Museum of Island Life
Flodigarry
Eilean Flodigarry
Poldorais
Tairbeart (Tarbert)
Borneskitaig
Heribusta
Kilmuir
Kilvaxter
542
MEAL NA SUIREAMACH
Digg
Staffin Bay
Staffin Island
Balgown
Brogaig
Stenscholl
Staffin
Linicro
Totscore
464
BIODA BUIDHE
River Rha
Trotternish
Kilt Rock Waterfall
Ellishader
Loch nam Madadh (Lochmaddy)
208
209
Maligar
Idrigill
Marishader
Valtos
Uig (Uige)
Uig Bay
River Conon
611
BEINN EDRA
Garros
Rudha nam Brathairean
Culnaknock
Loch Sport
Tote
0 1 2 3 4 miles
0 1 2 3 4 5 kilometres
608
CREAG A' LAIN
Peinlich

G
H
J
K
L
M
1
2
3
4
5
6
7
8
Tanera Beg
Tanera Mòr
Badentarbat Bay
Steornabhagh (Stornoway)
Glas-leac Beag
Eilean Dubh
Priest Island
Greenstone Point
Rudha Beag
Cailleach Head
Scoraig
Static Point
Mellon Udrigle
GRUINARD ISLAND
Badluarach
A832
Gruinard Bay
Laide
Foura
Rudha Reidh
Cove
Mellon Charles
Ormiscaig
Aultbea
Gruinard
296 AN CUAIDH
B8057
ISLE OF EWE
Little Gruinard River
Gruinard River
347 CREAG-MHEAL BEAG
Melvaig
Aultgrishin
Loch Ewe
Loch Fada
220
Inverasdale
293 CNOC BREAC
Naast
Inverewe Garden
13
250 MEALL NA MEINE
681 BEINN A' CHAISGEIN BEAG
B8021
North Erradale
Londubh
Poolewe
Fionn
Wester Ross
Big Sand
Strath
A832
Smithstown
Longa Island
Lonemore
Auchtercairn
Heritage
Dubh Loch
Loch Gairloch
Gairloch
791 BEINN AIRIDH CHARR
Loch
421 MEALL AN DOIREIN
Charlestown
Eilean Horrisdale
Port Henderson
B8056
Loch
859 BEINN LÀIR
Badachro
Opinan
South Erradale
Loch Bad an Sgalaig
Loch Maree Hotel
Letterewe
Loch Garbhaig
19
Talladale
Maree
981 SLIOCH
A832
Redpoint
Loch Ghaineamhach
Red Point
210
Loch na A-Oidhche
875 BAOSBHEINN
855 BEINN AN EÒIN
619 BEINN BHREAC
724
Loch a' Bhealaich
Loch Torridon
Craig River
Rudha na Fearn
Lower Diabaig
Loch Diabaig
ALLIGIN
914 BEINN DEARG
1009 RUADH-STAC MÒR
972
Kinloch
Òb Chuaig
Fearnbeg
BEINN EIGHE

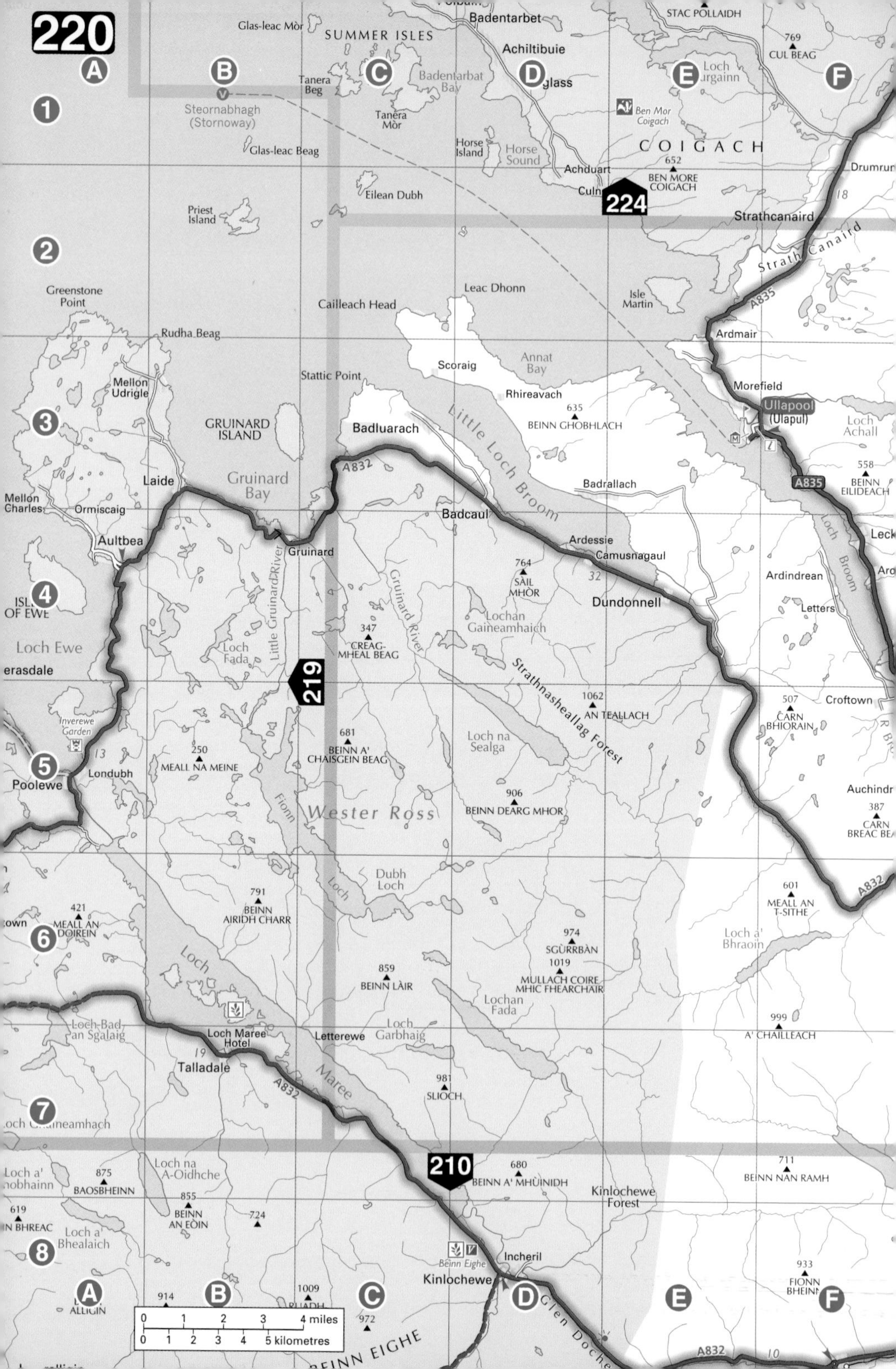

SUMMER ISLES
Glas-leac Mòr
Badentarbet
Achiltibuie
STAC POLLAIDH
769
CUL BEAG
Tanera Beg
Badentarbat Bay
Loch Lurgainn
Ben Mor Coigach
Steornabhagh (Stornoway)
Tanera Mòr
Horse Island
Horse Sound
COIGACH
Glas-leac Beag
Achduart
652
BEN MORE COIGACH
Drumrunie
Culn
224
Eilean Dubh
Priest Island
Strathcanaird
Strath Canaird
Greenstone Point
Cailleach Head
Leac Dhonn
Isle Martin
A835
Rudha Beag
Ardmair
Scoraig
Annat Bay
Mellon Udrigle
Stattic Point
Morefield
Rhireavach
Ullapool (Ulapul)
Loch Achall
635
BEINN GHOBHLACH
GRUINARD ISLAND
Badluarach
Little Loch Broom
A832
558
BEINN EILIDEACH
Laide
Gruinard Bay
Badrallach
A835
Mellon Charles
Ormiscaig
Badcaul
Aultbea
Gruinard
Ardessie
Camusnagaul
Loch Broom
Little Gruinard River
Gruinard River
764
SÀIL MHÒR
Ardindrean
ISLE OF EWE
Dundonnell
Letters
347
CREAG-MHEAL BEAG
Lochan Gaineamhaich
Loch Ewe
Loch Fada
Poolewe
Strathnasheallag Forest
219
1062
AN TEALLACH
507
CÀRN BHIORAIN
Croftown
Inverewe Garden
681
BEINN A' CHAISGEIN BEAG
Loch na Sealga
250
MEALL NA MEINE
Londubh
Poolewe
906
BEINN DEARG MHOR
Wester Ross
387
CARN BREAC
Fionn Loch
Dubh Loch
601
MEALL AN T-SITHE
A832
421
MEALL AN DOIREIN
791
BEINN AIRIDH CHARR
974
SGÙRR BÀN
Loch a' Bhraoin
1019
MULLACH COIRE MHIC FHEARCHAIR
859
BEINN LÀIR
Loch Maree
Lochan Fada
Loch Bad an Sgalaig
Loch Maree Hotel
Letterewe
Loch Garbhaig
999
A' CHAILLEACH
Talladale
A832
981
SLIOCH
Loch Gaineamhach
210
680
BEINN A' MHÙINIDH
711
BEINN NAN RAMH
Loch a' Ghobhainn
875
BAOSBHEINN
Loch na A-Oidhche
Kinlochewe Forest
619
BEINN BHREAC
855
BEINN AN EÒIN
724
Loch a' Bhealaich
Beinn Eighe
Incheril
933
FIONN BHEINN
Kinlochewe
914
1009
RUADH
972
Glen Docherty
BEINN EIGHE
A832
0 1 2 3 4 miles
0 1 2 3 4 5 kilometres

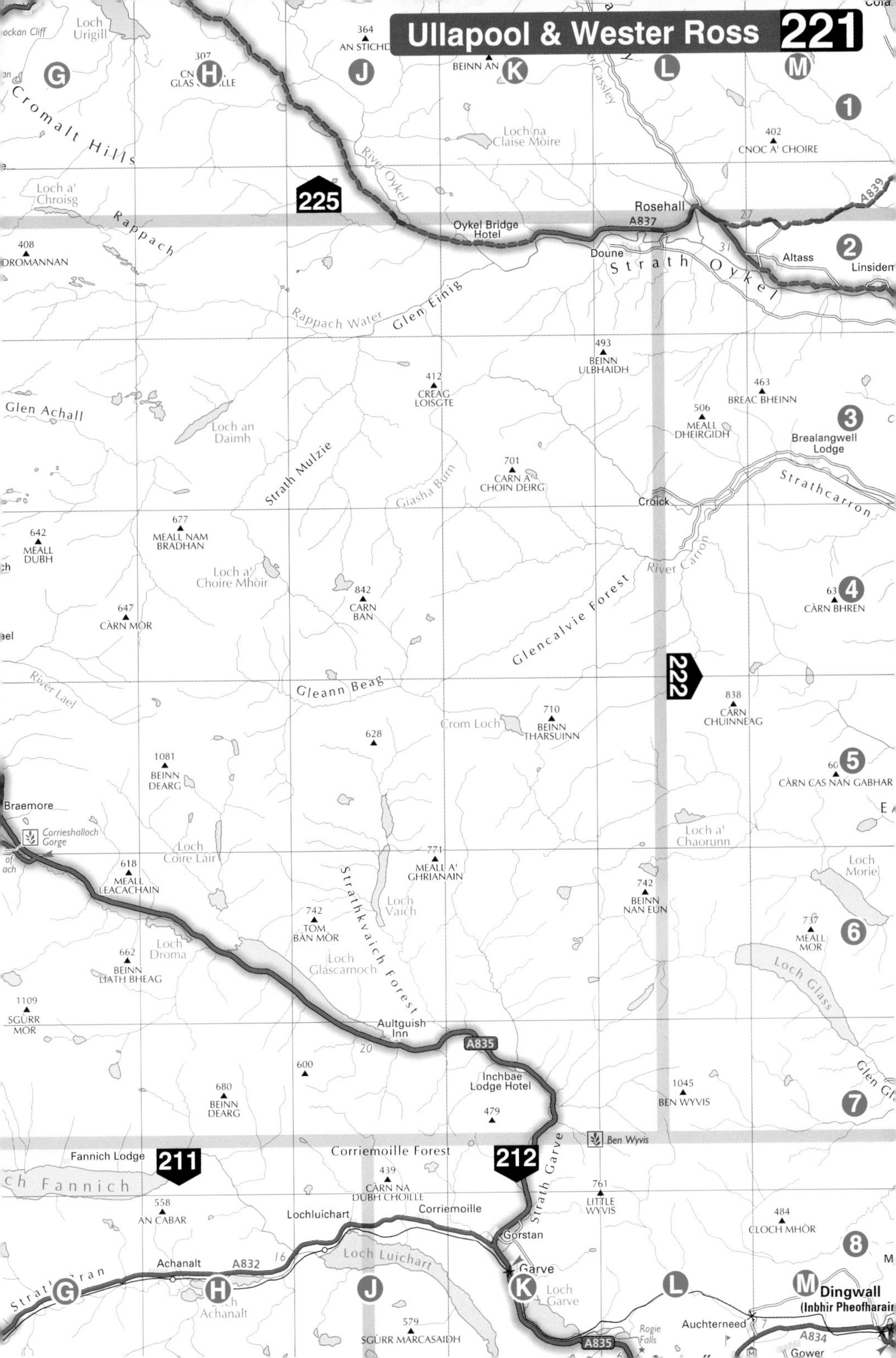
Loch Urigill
Cromalt Hills
Loch a' Chroisg
Rappach
225
River Oykel
Oykel Bridge Hotel
Rosehall
A837
Doune
Strath Oykel
Altass
A839
Rappach Water
Glen Einig
Loch na Claise Mòire
CNOC A' CHOIRE
BEINN ULBHAIDH
CREAG LOISGTE
BREAC BHEINN
MEALL DHEIRGIDH
Brealangwell Lodge
Strathcarron
Croick
River Carron
Glen Achall
Loch an Daimh
Strath Mulzie
Giasha Burn
CARN A' CHOIN DEIRG
MEALL NAM BRADHAN
MEALL DUBH
Loch a' Choire Mhòir
CARN BAN
CÀRN MOR
Glencalvie Forest
CÀRN BHREN
222
River Lael
Gleann Beag
Crom Loch
BEINN THARSUINN
CARN CHUINNEAG
CÀRN CAS NAN GABHAR
BEINN DEARG
Braemore
Corrieshalloch Gorge
Loch Coire Lair
Loch a' Chaorunn
MEALL LEACACHAIN
MEALL A' GHRIANAIN
Strathkvaich Forest
Loch Vaich
BEINN NAN EUN
Loch Morie
TOM BÀN MÒR
Loch Droma
Loch Glascarnoch
MEALL MOR
BEINN LIATH BHEAG
Loch Glass
SGÙRR MÒR
Aultguish Inn
A835
Inchbae Lodge Hotel
BEN WYVIS
Glen Glass
Ben Wyvis
Fannich Lodge
211
Loch Fannich
Corriemoille Forest
212
CÀRN NA DUBH CHOILLE
Strath Garve
LITTLE WYVIS
AN CABAR
Lochluichart
Corriemoille
Gorstan
CLOCH MHÒR
Achanalt
A832
Loch Luichart
Garve
Loch Garve
Strath Bran
Loch Achanalt
Dingwall
(Inbhir Pheofharain)
Auchterneed
Rogie Falls
SGÙRR MARCASAIDH
A834
Gower

222
Rosehall
Oykel Bridge Hotel
A837
Doune
Strath Oykel
Altass
Achany
Linsidemore
225
A839
Ferrycroft Countryside Centre
Lairg
Tomich
Torrobull
A836
B864
Falls of Shin
Inveran
Invershin
Culrain
1650 Carbisdale
Kyle of Sutherland
226
323 BEN DOULA
313 CREAGAN GLAS
333 MEALL EACHAINN
Loch Buidhe
Sleasdairidh
349 BEINN DONUILL
River Evelix
Loch na Claise Moire
402 CNOC A' CHOIRE
493 BEINN ULBHAIDH
412 CREAG
463 BREAC BHEINN
506 MEALL DHEIRGIDH
701 CARN A' CHOIN DEIRG
Brealangwell Lodge
Strathcarron
Croick
River Carron
Glencalvie Forest
Lower Gledfield
Dounie
Ardgay
Kincardine
Upper Ardchronie
Bonar Bridge
Loch Migdale
A949
Spinningdale
Dornoch
Ardmore
Struie Hill
Edderton
634 CÀRN BHREN
221
710 BEINN THARSUINN
Crom Loch
838 CÀRN CHUINNEAG
477 BEINN CLACH AN FHEADAIN
Aultnamain Inn
602 CÀRN CAS NAN GABHAR
EASTER ROSS
692 BEINN THARSUINN
Loch a' Chaorunn
379 CNOC AN T-SABHAIL
Loch Morie
742 BEINN NAN EUN
737 MEALL MOR
Strath Rusdale
B9176
Ardross
Boath
Loch Glass
River Alness
Achandunie
Rhicullen
Millcraig
Tomich
Moultavie
523 CNOC CEISLEIN
Achnagarron
Alness
(Alanais)
Dalmore
A835
Inchbae Lodge Hotel
479
1045 BEN WYVIS
Glen Glass
Ben Wyvis
Strath Garve
B817
Cromarty Firth
Evanton
212
Balblair
Resolis
B9163
761 LITTLE WYVIS
Teanord
Gorstan
484 CLOCH MHÒR
Clanland & Seapoint
Cullicudden
Brae
Ardullie
Garve
Mountgerald House
Findon Mains
Dingwall
(Inbhir Pheofharain)
B9169
BLACK ISLE
B9160
A834
A9
Culbokie
255 MOUNT
Raddery
Gower
0 1 2 3 4 miles
0 1 2 3 4 5 kilometres

River Brora
Dalreavoch Lodge
Loch Horn
520 BEN HORN
Golspie Burn
378 CAGAR FEOSAIG
Dalchalm
Brora
Doll
Backies
Carn Liath
A9
227
446 BEN LUNDIE
383 BEN BHRAGGIE
Rhives
Dunrobin Castle
Golspie
Torboll
Cambusavie Platform
Loch Fleet
Badninish
Skelbo
Skelbo Street
Fourpenny
Embo
Birichin
B9168
Embo Street
Pitgrudy
Evelix
A949
Royal Dornoch
Clashmore
Camore
Dornoch
Historylinks
Tarbat Ness
Cuthill
Wilkhaven
Dornoch Firth
Innis Mhor
Brucefield
Portmahomack
Glenmorangie Distillery
Morangie
Inver
Rockfield
Arboll
B9165
284
Tain (Baile Dhubhthaich)
Toulvaddie
Lochslin
Loch Eye
Rhynie
Hill of Fearn
Balmuchy
B9165
Newfield
Hilton of Cadboll Chapel (ruin)
Fearn
Tullich
B9166
Hilton
Arabella
Balintore
Ballchraggan
Shandwick
Shandwick Bay
Kildary
Ankerville
Milton
B9175
Kilmuir
Pitcalnie
Barbaraville
Nigg
Nigg Bay
Balintraid
Saltburn
Nigg Ferry
rgordon
Cromarty
Cromarty Bay
Hugh Miller's Cottage
213
214
Burghea
Newton
B9163
Allerton
Navity
Moray Firth
Findhorn
Culbin Sands
B9011
Findhorn Bay
Upper Eathie
Kincorth House
Culbin Forest
A832
Kintessack
Grange
Sueno's Stone
Whiteness Head
Brodie
Dyke

224
A
B
C
D
E
F
1
2
3
4
5
6
7
8
Scourie
A894
Scourie More
Badcall
Badcall Bay
Loch a' Mhuilinn
386
BEN AUSKAIRD
Rudh' a' Mhucard
228
17
Point of Stoer
Old Man of Stoer
OLDANY ISLAND
Eddrachillis Bay
Loch a' Chàirn Bhàin
419
BEN STROME
Kylestrome
Kylesku
Unapool
Culkein Drumbeg
Culkein
Clashnessie Bay
Oldany
Drumbeg
B869
Achnacarnin
Clashmore
Nedd
Clashnessie
Loch Poll
Glen Leirg
Loch an Leothaid
776
SAIL GHORM
809
QUINAG
Stoer
A894
Clachtoll
Bay of Clachtoll
B869
Loch Beannach
774
Achmelvich Bay
Rhicarn
A837
Achmelvich
Loch Assynt
Ardvreck
Baddidarrach
Soyea Island
Loch Inver
Lochinver
539
BEINN GHARBH
Strathan
Assynt - Coigach
Inverkirkaig
Loanan
River Kirkaig
Loch na Gainimh
847
CANISP
Stronchrubie
Rhu Coigach
Fionn Loch
732
SUILVEN
Eilean Mòr
Enard Bay
River
Loch Awe
Rubha Mòr
Reiff
Achnahaird
Càm Loch
Altandhu
Loch Sionascaig
Loch Veyatie
Eilean Mullagrach
849
CUL MÒR
Ledmore Junction
Loch Osgaig
Isle Ristol
Polbain
612
STAC POLLAIDH
Knockan
Elphin
Badentarbet
Knockan Cliff
Loch Urigill
SUMMER ISLES
Glas-leac Mòr
769
CUL BEAG
Achiltibuie
Knockan Crag
Badentarbat Bay
Loch Lurgainn
Tanera Beg
Polglass
Cromalt Hills
Steornabhagh (Stornoway)
Tanera Mòr
Ben Mor Coigach
Glas-leac Beag
Horse Island
Horse Sound
COIGACH
652
BEN MORE COIGACH
Achduart
Drumrunie Lodge
Culnacraig
Eilean Dubh
18
Loch a' Chroisg
Strathcanaird
220
Strath Canaird
408
NA DROMANNAN
Leac Dhonn
Cailleach Head
Isle Martin
A835
Ardmair
Annat Bay
Stattic Point
Scoraig
Morefield
0
1
2
3
4 miles
0
1
2
3
4
5 kilometres
635
Ullapool (Ulapul)
Loch Achall
Glen Achall
GRUINARD ISLAND
Badluarach

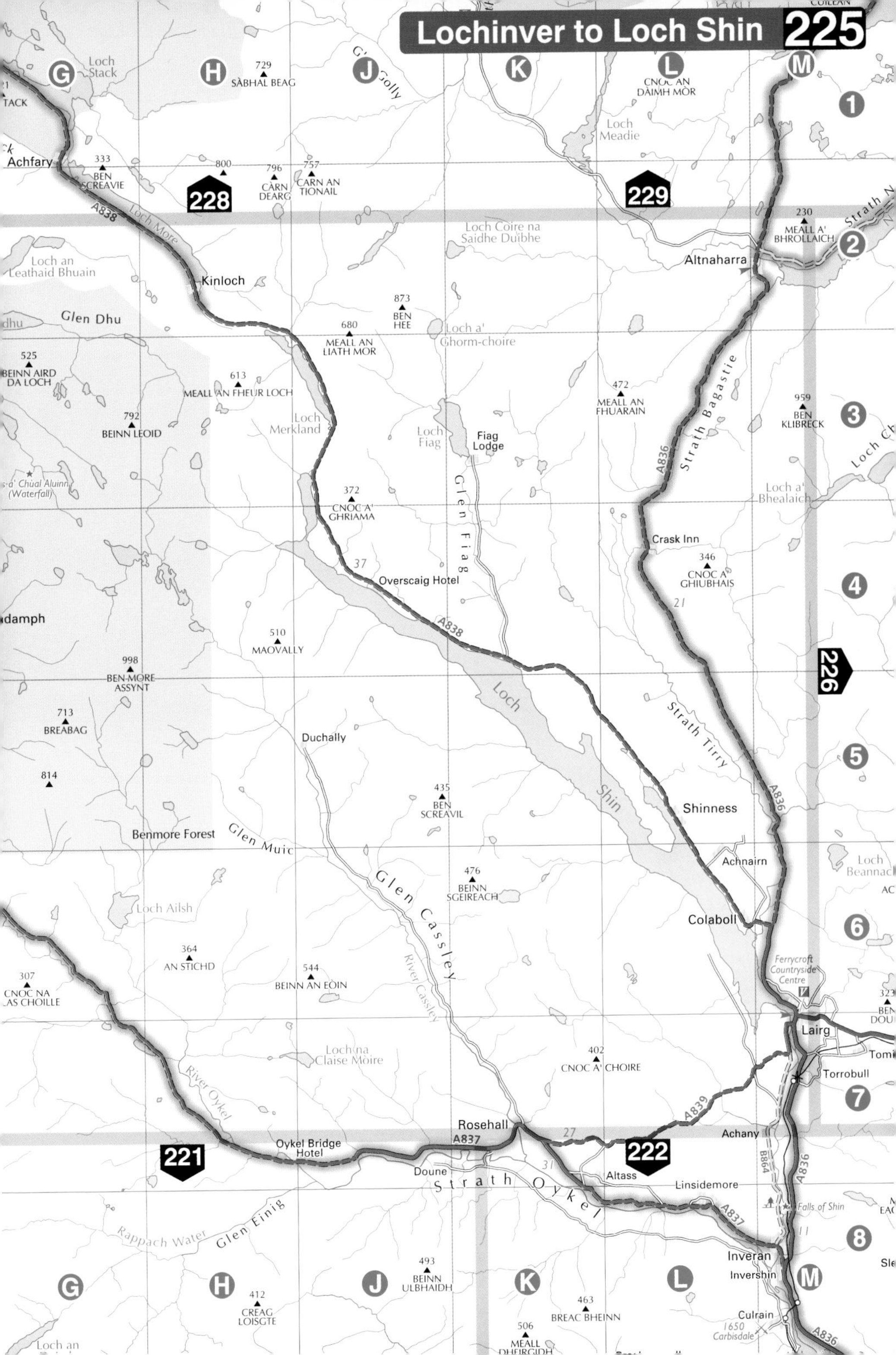
Loch Stack
729 SÀBHAL BEAG
Achfary
333 BEN SCREAVIE
800
796 CÀRN DEARG
757 CARN AN TIONAIL
228
229
CNOC AN DÀIMH MÒR
Loch Meadie
A838
Loch More
Loch an Leathaid Bhuain
Kinloch
Loch Coire na Saidhe Duibhe
230 MEALL A' BHROLLAICH
Altnaharra
Strath N
Glen Dhu
873 BEN HEE
680 MEALL AN LIATH MOR
Loch a' Ghorm-choire
525 BEINN AIRD DA LOCH
613 MEALL AN FHEUR LOCH
472 MEALL AN FHUARAIN
959 BEN KLIBRECK
Strath Bagastie
792 BEINN LEOID
Loch Merkland
Loch Fiag
Fiag Lodge
A836
Loch a' Bhealaich
(Waterfall)
Glen Fiag
372 CNOC A' GHRIAMA
Crask Inn
346 CNOC A' GHIUBHAIS
37
Overscaig Hotel
21
A838
510 MAOVALLY
998 BEN MORE ASSYNT
226
Loch
Strath Tirry
713 BREABAG
Duchally
814
435 BEN SCREAVIL
Shin
Shinness
A836
Benmore Forest
Glen Muic
Achnairn
476 BEINN SGEIREACH
Glen Cassley
Loch Ailsh
Colaboll
Ferrycroft Countryside Centre
364 AN STICHD
307 CNOC NA LAS CHOILLE
544 BEINN AN EOIN
River Cassley
Lairg
Loch na Claise Moire
402 CNOC A' CHOIRE
Torrobull
River Oykel
A839
Rosehall
27
Achany
221
Oykel Bridge Hotel
A837
222
Doune
31
Altass
B864
Strath Oykel
Linsidemore
A836
Falls of Shin
A837
Rappach Water
Glen Einig
11
Inveran
Invershin
493 BEINN ULBHAIDH
412 CREAG LOISGTE
463 BREAC BHEINN
Culrain
1650 Carbisdale
506 MEALL DHEIRGIDH
A836
Loch an

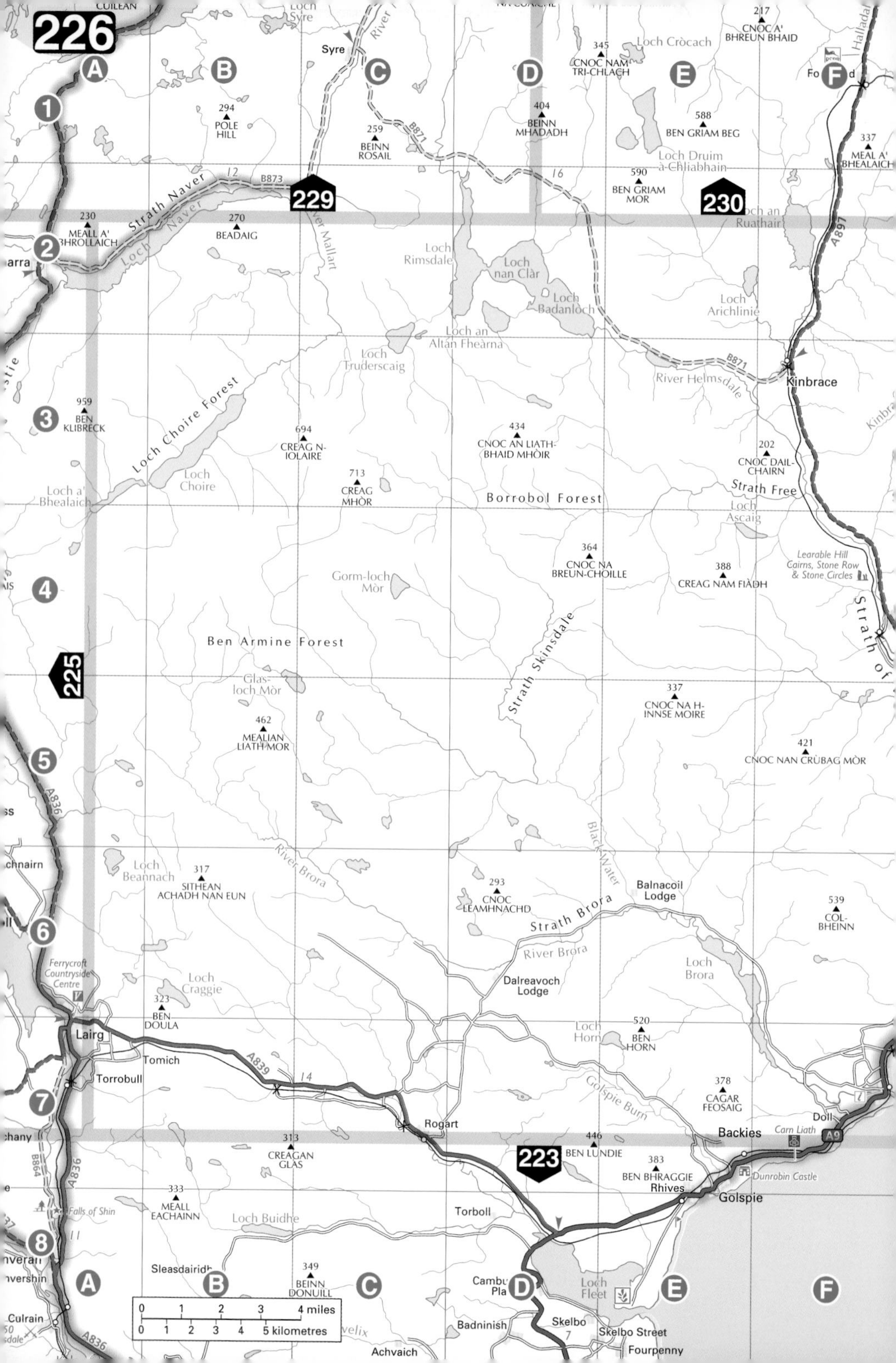
226
229
230
225
223
Syre
Strath Naver
Loch Naver
B873
B871
Loch Cròcach
Loch Druim a-Chliabhain
Loch Rimsdale
Loch nan Clàr
Loch Badanloch
Loch an Altan Fhearna
Loch Truderscaig
Loch Arichlinie
River Helmsdale
Kinbrace
A897
Loch Choire Forest
Loch Choire
Loch a' Bhealaich
Borrobol Forest
Strath Free
Loch Ascaig
Learable Hill Cairns, Stone Row & Stone Circles
Gorm-loch Mòr
Ben Armine Forest
Glas-loch Mòr
Strath Skinsdale
Black Water
River Brora
Strath Brora
Balnacoil Lodge
Loch Beannach
Loch Brora
Dalreavoch Lodge
Loch Craggie
Ferrycroft Countryside Centre
Lairg
Tomich
Torrobull
A839
Rogart
A836
B864
Falls of Shin
Loch Horn
Golspie Burn
Backies
Carn Liath
Doll
A9
Dunrobin Castle
Rhives
Golspie
Torboll
Loch Buidhe
Sleasdairidh
Loch Fleet
Skelbo
Skelbo Street
Fourpenny
Badninish
Achvaich
Culrain
Invershin
Loch Syre
294 POLE HILL
259 BEINN ROSAIL
404 BEINN MHADADH
345 CNOC NAM TRI-CHLACH
217 CNOC A' BHREUN BHAID
588 BEN GRIAM BEG
590 BEN GRIAM MOR
337 MEAL A' BHEALAICH
230 MEALL A' BHROLLAICH
270 BEADAIG
959 BEN KLIBRECK
694 CREAG N-IOLAIRE
713 CREAG MHÒR
434 CNOC AN LIATH-BHAID MHÒIR
202 CNOC DAIL-CHAIRN
364 CNOC NA BREUN-CHOILLE
388 CREAG NAM FIÀDH
462 MEALLAN LIATH MOR
337 CNOC NA H-INNSE MOIRE
421 CNOC NAN CRÙBAG MÒR
317 SITHEAN ACHADH NAN EUN
293 CNOC LEAMHNACHD
539 COL-BHEINN
323 BEN DOULA
520 BEN HORN
378 CAGAR FEOSAIG
313 CREAGAN GLAS
446 BEN LUNDIE
383 BEN BHRAGGIE
333 MEALL EACHAINN
349 BEINN DONUILL
0 1 2 3 4 miles
0 1 2 3 4 5 kilometres

Helmsdale
East Helmsdale
West Helmsdale
Navidale House Hotel
Timespan
Gartymore
Portgower
Lothmore
Lothbeg
Glen Loth
Torrish
River Helmsdale
A897
A9
Ord of Caithness
Badbea Historic Village
Berriedale
Langwell House
Newport
Borgue
Ramscraigs
Knockally
Dunbeath
Laidhay Croft
Janetstown
Latheron
Latheronwheel
Smerral
Landhallow
Houstry
Forse
Invershore
Lybster
Lybster Bay
Swiney
Upper Lybster
Achavanich
Loch Stemster
Stemster Hill
Loch Rangag
Coire na Beinn
Ben-a-Chielt
Loch Sand
Loch an Thulachan
Dalnawillan Lodge
Strathmore
Rumsdale Water
Glutt Water
Glutt Lodge
Ben Alisky
Cnocan Conachreag
Dunbeath Water
Berriedale Water
Braemore
Maiden Pap
Morven
Scaraben
Langwell Forest
Knockfin Heights
Cnoc nan Gall
Cnoc Loch Mhadadh
Cnoc Coire na Feàrna
Cnoc an Eireannaich
Creag Scalabsdale
Cnoc na Maoile
Beinn Dubhain
Creag Thoraraidh
Beinn na Mèilich
Dalchalm
230
231

CAPE WRATH
Kearvaig Bay
Cléit Dhubh
371 SGRIBHIS-BHEINN
297 CNOC A GHIUBHAIS
300 MAOVALLY
THE PARPH
Faraid Head
Balnakeil Bay
Balnakeil
Sango Bay
Durness
Smoo Cave
Sangomore
Smoo
Keoldale
Sangobeg
457 FASHVEN
Loch Airigh na Beinne
Sandwood Bay
Sandwood Loch
Kyle of Durness
Loch Meadaidh
485 CREAG RIABACH
468 BEINN DEARG MHÒR
464 MEALL NA MÒINE
Rudh' an Fhir Leithe
Strath Shinary
331 GHLAS-BHEINN
423 MEALL MEADHONACH
A838
Sheigra
Balchreick
Blairmore
Oldshoremore
521 FARVEALL
489 MEALL NA CRÀ
Laid
355 AN SOCACH
Kinlochbervie
Badcall
Loch Clash
773 BEINN SPIONNAIDH
801 CRANSTACKIE
Loch Inchard
B801
Achriesgill
Strath Dionard
River Dionard
Strath Beag
A838
520 AN LEAN-CHÀR
Rhiconich
Loch na Claise Càrnaich
Rudha Ruadh
908 FOINAVEN
Fanagmore
Skerricha
Loch Laxford
Tarbet
A838
Foindle
HANDA ISLAND
North-west Sutherland
Loch na Tuadh
Laxford Bridge
786 ARKLE
Scourie Bay
River Laxford
FEINNE-BH
A894
Scourie
Scourie More
Loch Stack
Glen Golly
729 SÀBHAL BEAG
Badcall
721 BEN STACK
Strath Stack
Badcall Bay
Loch a' Mhuilinn
386 BEN AUSKAIRD
Achfary
333 BEN SCREAVIE
800
796 CARN DEARG
757 CARN AN TIONAIL
Rudh' a' Mhucard
A838
Loch More
224
225
OLDANY ISLAND
Eddrachillis Bay
419 BEN STROME
Loch an Leathaid-Bhuain
Kinloch
Culkein Drumbeg
Loch a' Chàirn Bhàin
Kylestrome
Kylesku
Loch Glendhu
Glen Dhu
873 BEN HEE
Drumbeg
Unapool
680 MEALL AN LIATH...
B869
Nedd
Loch Glencoul
525 BEINN A' DA LOCH
613 MEALL AN FHEUR LOCH
Loch Poll
792 BEINN LEOID
QUINAG
Loch Merkland
0 1 2 3 4 miles
0 1 2 3 4 5 kilometres

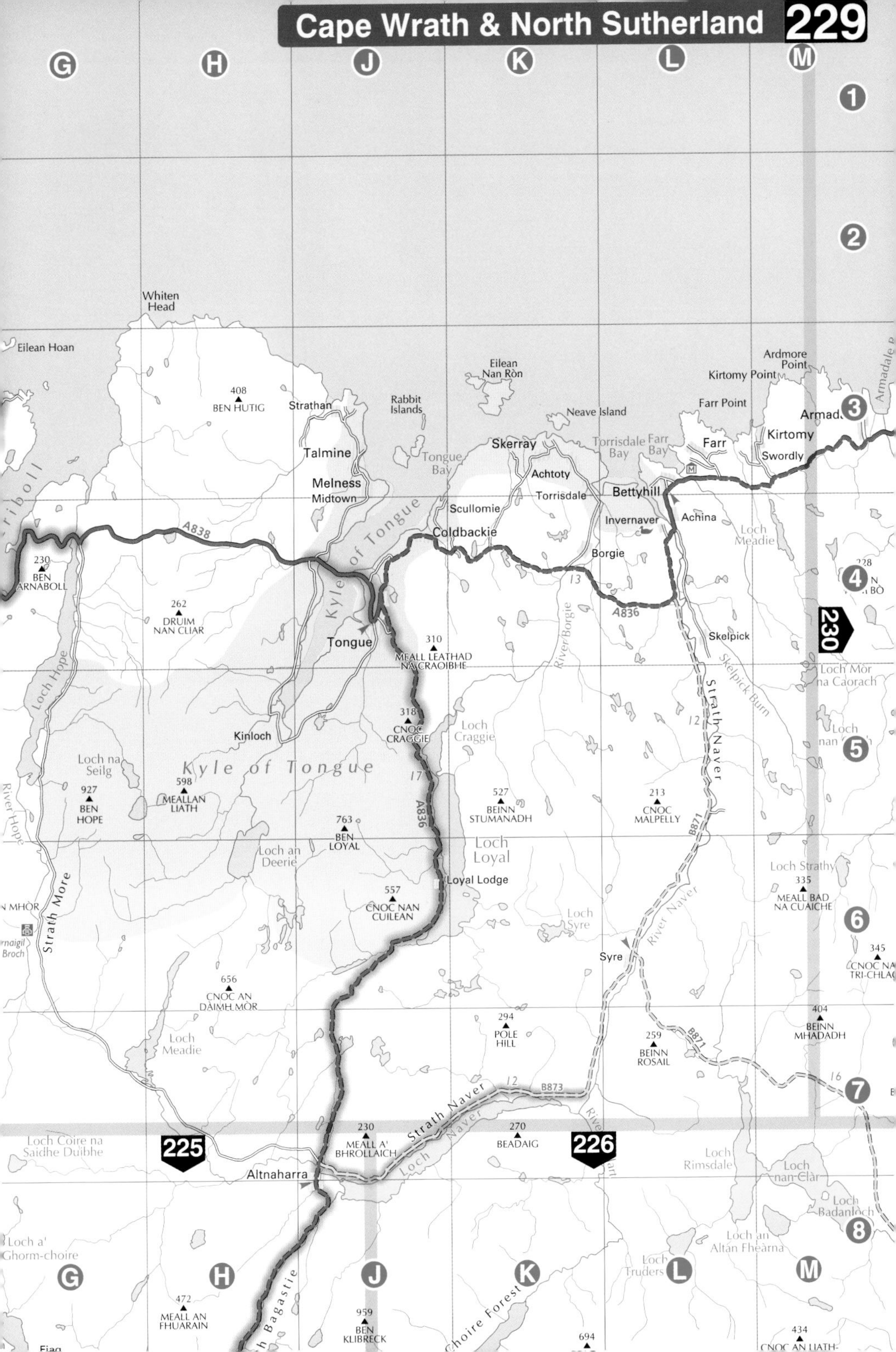
G
H
J
K
L
M
1
2
3
4
5
6
7
8
Whiten Head
Eilean Hoan
408 BEN HUTIG
Strathan
Talmine
Melness
Midtown
Rabbit Islands
Eilean Nan Ròn
Neave Island
Tongue Bay
Skerray
Achtoty
Torrisdale Bay
Farr Bay
Torrisdale
Bettyhill
Invernaver
Achina
Farr
Farr Point
Kirtomy Point
Ardmore Point
Kirtomy
Swordly
Armadale
Scullomie
Coldbackie
Borgie
Loch Meadie
Kyle of Tongue
A838
230 BEN ARNABOLL
262 DRUIM NAN CLIAR
Tongue
310 MEALL LEATHAD NA CRAOIBHE
A836
River Borgie
Skelpick
Skelpick Burn
230
Loch Mòr na Caorach
Loch Hope
318 CNOC CRAGGIE
Loch Craggie
Strath Naver
Kinloch
Loch na Seilg
927 BEN HOPE
598 MEALLAN LIATH
763 BEN LOYAL
River Hope
527 BEINN STUMANADH
213 CNOC MALPELLY
B871
Loch an Deerie
Loch Loyal
Loyal Lodge
557 CNOC NAN CUILEAN
Strath More
Loch Strathy
335 MEALL BAD NA CUAICHE
Loch Syre
River Naver
Syre
345 CNOC NA TRI-CHLAC
656 CNOC AN DÀIMH MÒR
Loch Meadie
294 POLE HILL
259 BEINN ROSAIL
404 BEINN MHADADH
B873
Loch Coire na Saidhe Duibhe
225
230 MEALL A' BHROLLAICH
270 BEADAIG
226
Altnaharra
Loch Naver
Loch Rimsdale
Loch nan Clàr
Loch Badanloch
Loch a' Ghorm-choire
Loch an Altan Fhèarna
Loch Truders
472 MEALL AN FHUARAIN
959 BEN KLIBRECK
434 CNOC AN LIATH-
694
Choire Forest

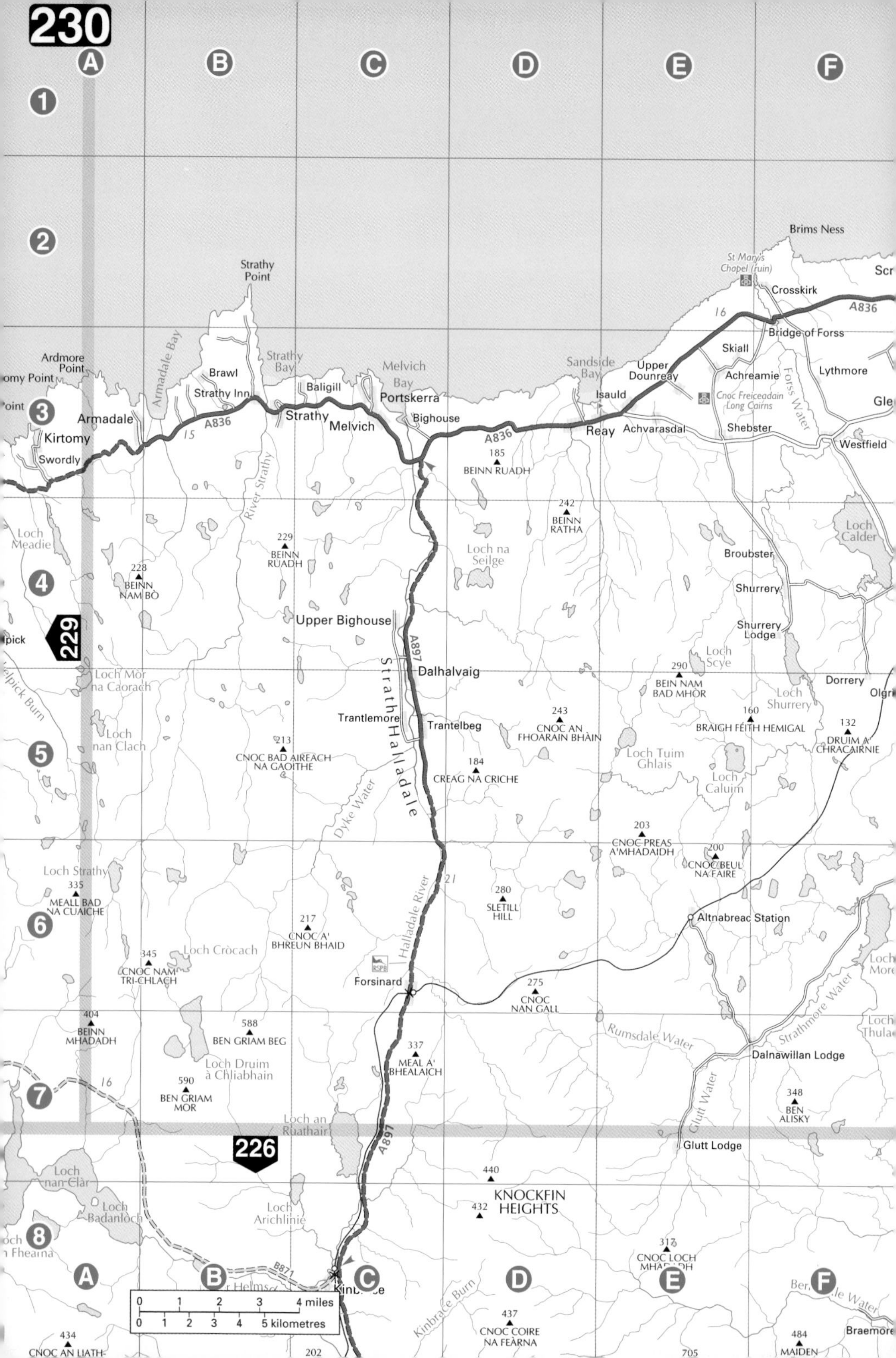
A
B
C
D
E
F
1
2
3
4
5
6
7
8
Brims Ness
St Mary's Chapel (ruin)
Crosskirk
Scr
A836
16
Bridge of Forss
Strathy Point
Ardmore Point
Armadale Bay
Strathy Bay
Melvich Bay
Sandside Bay
Upper Dounreay
Skiall
Achreamie
Lythmore
Brawl
Strathy Inn
Baligill
Portskerra
Isauld
Cnoc Freiceadain Long Cairns
Forss Water
Gle
Armadale
Strathy
Melvich
Bighouse
Reay
Achvarasdal
Shebster
Westfield
Kirtomy
Swordly
A836
15
A836
185
BEINN RUADH
242
BEINN RATHA
River Strathy
Loch Meadie
229
BEINN RUADH
Loch na Seilge
Loch Calder
Broubster
228
BEINN NAM BÒ
Shurrery
Upper Bighouse
Shurrery Lodge
229
A897
Loch Scye
Strath Halladale
Dalhalvaig
290
BEIN NAM BAD MHÒR
Dorrery
Loch Mòr na Caorach
Loch Shurrery
243
CNOC AN FHOARAIN BHÀIN
160
BRAIGH FÉITH HEMIGAL
132
DRUIM A' CHRACAIRNIE
Trantlemore
Trantelbeg
Loch nan Clach
213
CNOC BAD AIREACH NA GAOITHE
Loch Tuim Ghlais
184
CREAG NA CRICHE
Loch Caluim
Dyke Water
203
CNOC PREAS A'MHADAIDH
200
CNOC BEUL NA FAIRE
Loch Strathy
335
MEALL BAD NA CUAICHE
Halladale River
21
280
SLETILL HILL
217
CNOC A' BHREUN BHAID
Altnabreac Station
345
CNOC NAM TRI-CHLACH
Loch Cròcach
RSPB
Forsinard
275
CNOC NAN GALL
404
BEINN MHADADH
588
BEN GRIAM BEG
Rumsdale Water
Strathmore Water
337
MEAL A' BHEALAICH
Dalnawillan Lodge
Loch Druim à Chliabhain
590
BEN GRIAM MOR
16
348
BEN ALISKY
Glutt Water
Loch an Ruathair
226
A897
Glutt Lodge
Loch nan Clàr
440
KNOCKFIN HEIGHTS
432
Loch Badanloch
Loch Arichlinie
317
CNOC LOCH MHADADH
B871
Kinbrace
Kinbrace Burn
0 1 2 3 4 miles
0 1 2 3 4 5 kilometres
437
CNOC COIRE NA FEÀRNA
Braemore
434
CNOC AN LIATH-
202
705
484
MAIDEN

234
227
G
H
J
K
L
M
1
2
3
4
5
6
7
8
PENTLAND FIRTH
DUNNET HEAD
127
Briga Head
Stromness
Holborn Head
121
DUNNET HILL
Brough
B855
St John's Loch
West Dunnet
Dunnet Bay
Dunnet
Thurso Bay
Thurso
A9
A836
Murkle
Castlehill
Castletown
Scarfskerry
Castle of Mey
Loch Mey
Rattar
Mey
Barrock
Gills
Gills Bay
Nethertown
Mell Head
ISLAND OF STROMA
Uppertown
St John's Point
Inner Sound
St Margaret's Hope
DUNCANSBY HEAD
Huna
Kirkstyle
Muckle Stack
John o' Groats
Canisbay
Stacks of Duncansby
A99
Inkstack
Brabstermire
Loch Heilen
Greenland
Skirza
Gill Burn
Freswick
Freswick Bay
Ness Head
Slickly
Auckengill
Broch
Nybster
Kirk Burn
Olrig House
Tain
B876
Weydale
Hilliclay
Bowermadden
Sortat
Bower
Lyth
Howe
Brough Head
Sordale
Burn of Lyth
Knockdee
Roadside
B874
Loch Scarmclate
Halcro
Mireland
Keiss
Clayock
Gillock
Kirk
Halkirk
B870
Georgemas Junction Station
A882
Loch of Wester
Sinclair Bay
Scotscalder Station
Harpsdale
Loch Watten
Killimster
176
SPITTAL HILL
Reiss
Castle Girnigoe & Sinclair
Noss Head
Spittal
Watten
Winless
River Thurso
Wick River
Sibster
Ackergill
Wick John o' Groats
Staxigoe
Mybster
Bilbster
Loch of Toftingall
Janetstown
Papigoe
Westerdale
Haster
Milton
Wick
Wick Bay
Old Wick
South Head
Castle of Old Wick
Newton
Strath Beg
Achairn Burn
Badlipster
Whiterow
Loch Hempriggs
136
BEINN CHÀITEAG
Tannach
Thrumster
145
BALLHARN HILL
Grey Cairns of Camster
Loch Ruard
Sarclet
Loch Stemster
Achavanich
212
HILL OF YARROWS
Loch of Yarrows
248
STEMSTER HILL
Loch Sand
Loch Rangag
Cairn o'Get
Ulbster
Whaligoe
Whaligoe Steps
226
COIRE NA BEINN
Roster
Bruan
Hill o'Many Stanes
287
BEN-A-CHIELT
Upper Lybster
Mid Clyth
Halberry Head
264
CNOCAN CONACHREAG
Swiney
Clyth Ness
Occumster
Houstry
Invershore
Lybster
Land-hallow
Lybster Bay
Forse
Smerral
Latheron
Dunbeath Water
Latheronwheel
Janetstown
Laidhay Croft
Dunbeath
Knockally

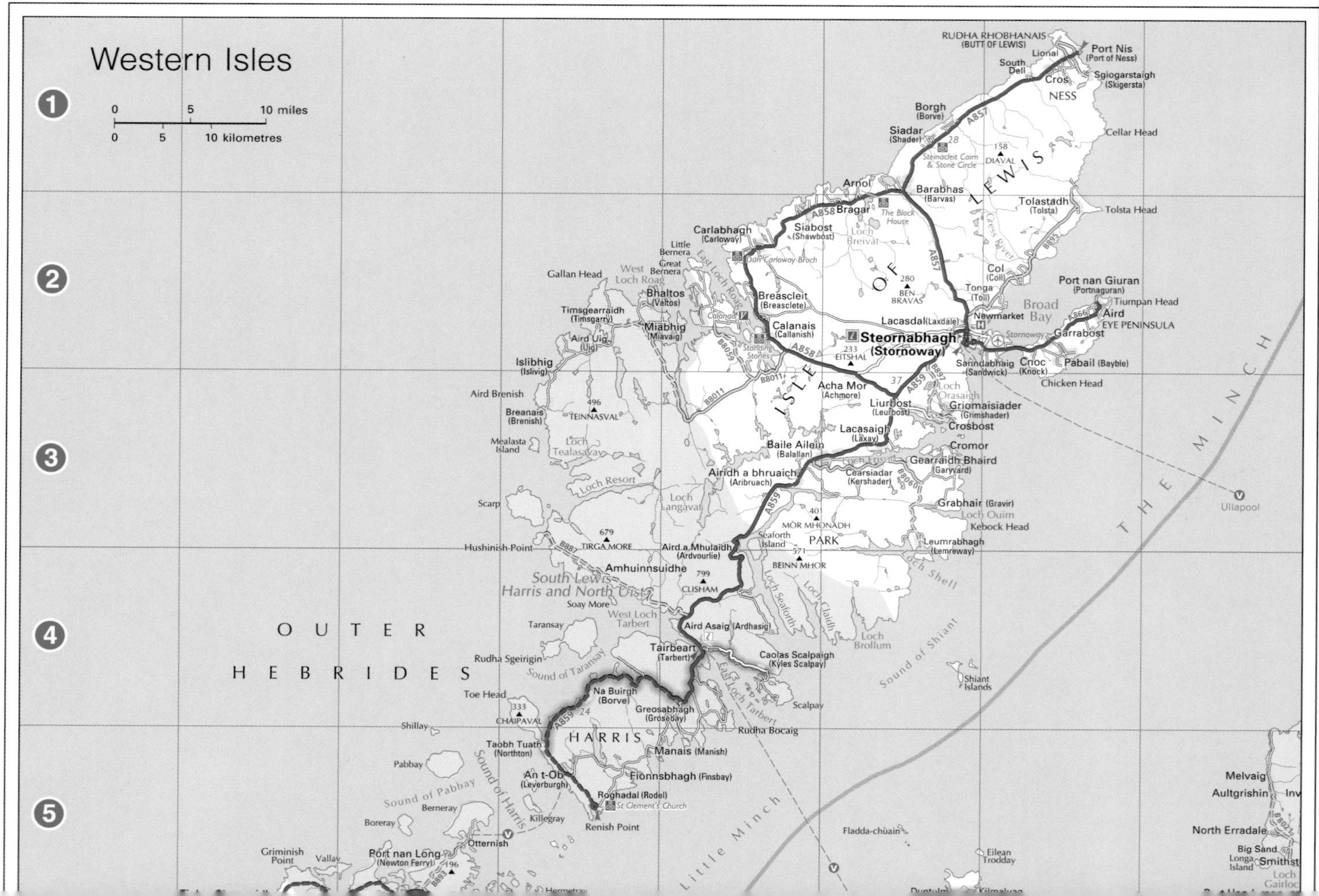

Western Isles

0 5 10 miles
0 5 10 kilometres

1
2
3
4
5

RUDHA RHOBHANAIS (BUTT OF LEWIS)
Port Nis (Port of Ness)
Lional
South Dell
Cros
Sgiogarstaigh (Skigersta)
NESS
Borgh (Borve)
Siadar (Shader)
Cellar Head
Steinacleit Cairn & Stone Circle
DIAVAL 158
ISLE OF LEWIS
Arnol
Barabhas (Barvas)
Tolastadh (Tolsta)
Tolsta Head
Bragar
The Black House
Carlabhagh (Carloway)
Siabost (Shawbost)
Loch Breivat
Gress River
Little Bernera
Great Bernera
Dun Carloway Broch
Gallan Head
West Loch Roag
East Loch Roag
Col (Coll)
Port nan Giuran (Portnaguran)
BEN BRAVAS 280
Tonga (Toll)
Broad Bay
Tiumpan Head
Bhaltos (Valtos)
Breascleit (Breasclete)
Timsgearraidh (Timsgarry)
Aird
EYE PENINSULA
Miabhig (Miavaig)
Calanais
Lacasdal (Laxdale)
Newmarket
Aird Uig (Uig)
Calanais (Callanish)
Steornabhagh (Stornoway)
Stornoway
Garrabost
Standing Stones
EITSHAL 233
Islibhig (Islivig)
Sanndabhaig (Sandwick)
Cnoc (Knock)
Pabail (Bayble)
Chicken Head
Acha Mor (Achmore)
Aird Brenish
Loch Orasaigh
Liurbost (Leurbost)
Griomaisiader (Grimshader)
TEINNASVAL 496
Breanais (Brenish)
Crosbost
Lacasaigh (Laxay)
Mealasta Island
Loch Tealasvay
Baile Ailein (Balallan)
Cromor
Loch Erisort
Gearraidh Bhaird (Garyvard)
Airidh a bhruaich (Aribruach)
Cearsiadar (Kershader)
Loch Resort
Scarp
Loch Langavat
Grabhair (Gravir)
Loch Ouirn
MOR MHONADH 401
Kebock Head
Ullapool
TIRGA MORE 679
Seaforth Island
PARK
Leumrabhagh (Lemreway)
Hushinish Point
Aird a Mhulaidh (Ardvourlie)
BEINN MHOR 571
Loch Shell
Amhuinnsuidhe
CLISHAM 799
South Lewis, Harris and North Uist
Soay More
Loch Seaforth
Loch Claidh
Taransay
West Loch Tarbert
Aird Asaig (Ardhasaig)
Loch Brollum
OUTER HEBRIDES
Tairbeart (Tarbert)
Caolas Scalpaigh (Kyles Scalpay)
Sound of Shiant
Rudha Sgeirigin
Sound of Taransay
Shiant Islands
Na Buirgh (Borve)
East Loch Tarbert
Toe Head
Greosabhagh (Grosebay)
Scalpay
CHAIPAVAL 333
Shillay
HARRIS
Rudha Bocaig
Taobh Tuath (Northton)
Manais (Manish)
Pabbay
Sound of Harris
An t-Ob (Leverburgh)
Fionnsbhagh (Finsbay)
Melvaig
Sound of Pabbay
Roghadal (Rodel)
St Clement's Church
Aultgrishin
Berneray
Boreray
Killegray
Renish Point
North Erradale
Fladda-chùain
Otternish
Griminish Point
Vallay
Port nan Long (Newton Ferry)
Eilean Trodday
Big Sand
Longa Island
Loch Gairloch
Little Minch
THE MINCH
A857
A858
A859
A866
B895
B897
B8011
B8059
B8060
B887
B893
B8021

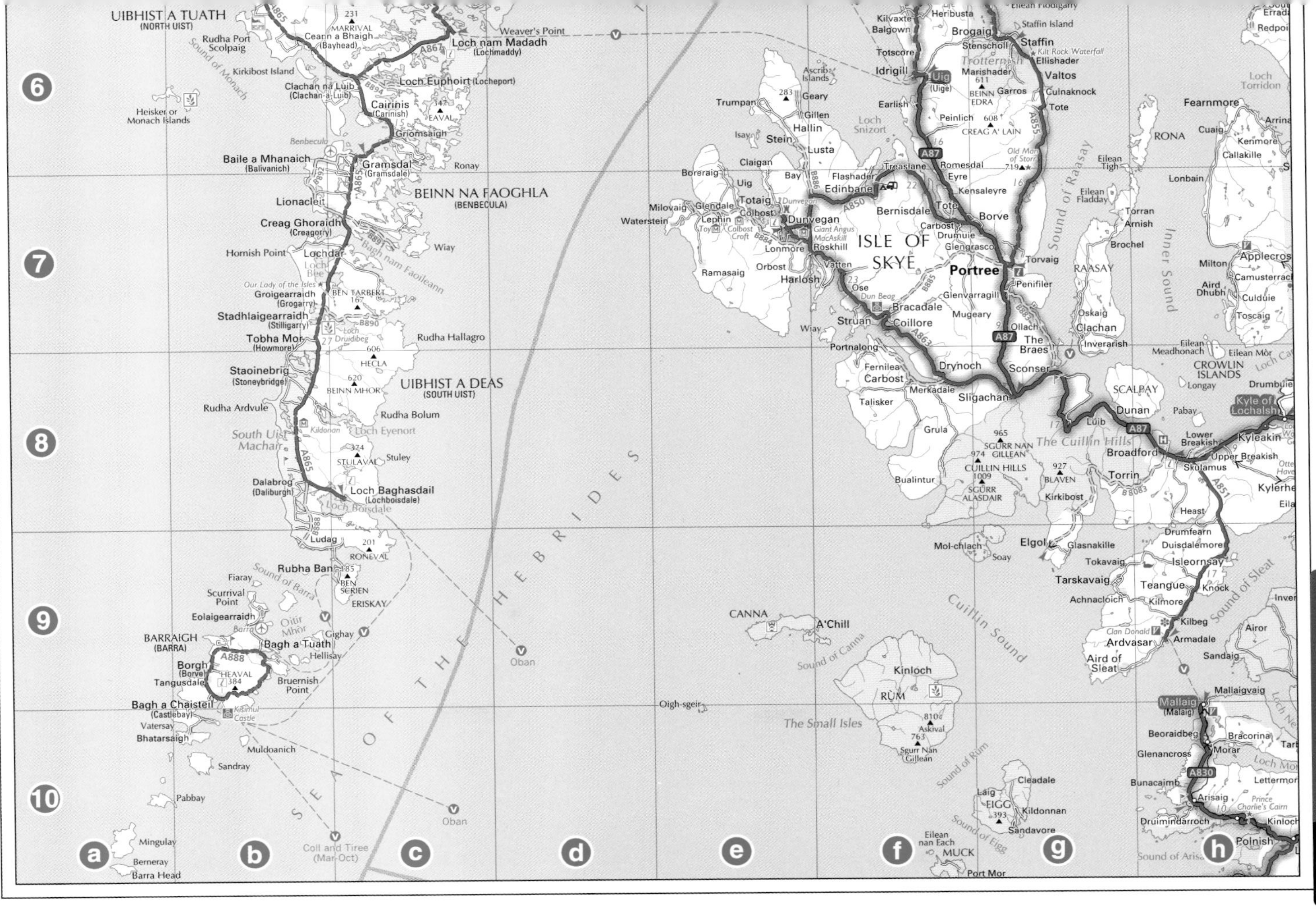
UIBHIST A TUATH (NORTH UIST)
Loch nam Madadh (Lochmaddy)
Weaver's Point
Loch Euphoirt (Locheport)
Cairinis (Carinish)
Griomsaigh
Heisker or Monach Islands
Sound of Monach
Baile a Mhanaich (Balivanich)
Gramsdal (Gramsdale)
BEINN NA FAOGHLA (BENBECULA)
Lionacleit
Creag Ghoraidh (Creagorry)
Lochdar
Stadhlaigearraidh (Stilligarry)
Tobha Mor (Howmore)
Staoinebrig (Stoneybridge)
UIBHIST A DEAS (SOUTH UIST)
Rudha Hallagro
Rudha Bolum
Loch Baghasdail (Lochboisdale)
Dalabrog (Daliburgh)
Ludag
ERISKAY
Rubha Ban
Sound of Barra
BARRAIGH (BARRA)
Bagh a Tuath
Borgh (Borve)
Bagh a Chaisteil (Castlebay)
Vatersay
Bhatarsaigh
Sandray
Pabbay
Mingulay
Berneray
Barra Head
Oban
Coll and Tiree (Mar-Oct)
SEA OF THE HEBRIDES
ISLE OF SKYE
Portree
Dunvegan
Uig
Staffin
Edinbane
Bracadale
Sligachan
Broadford
Kyleakin
Kyle of Lochalsh
The Cuillin Hills
Sound of Raasay
RAASAY
Inner Sound
RONA
SCALPAY
CROWLIN ISLANDS
Applecross
Elgol
Armadale
Sound of Sleat
Mallaig
CANNA
A'Chill
RÙM
Kinloch
The Small Isles
Cuillin Sound
EIGG
MUCK
6
7
8
9
10
a
b
c
d
e
f
g
h

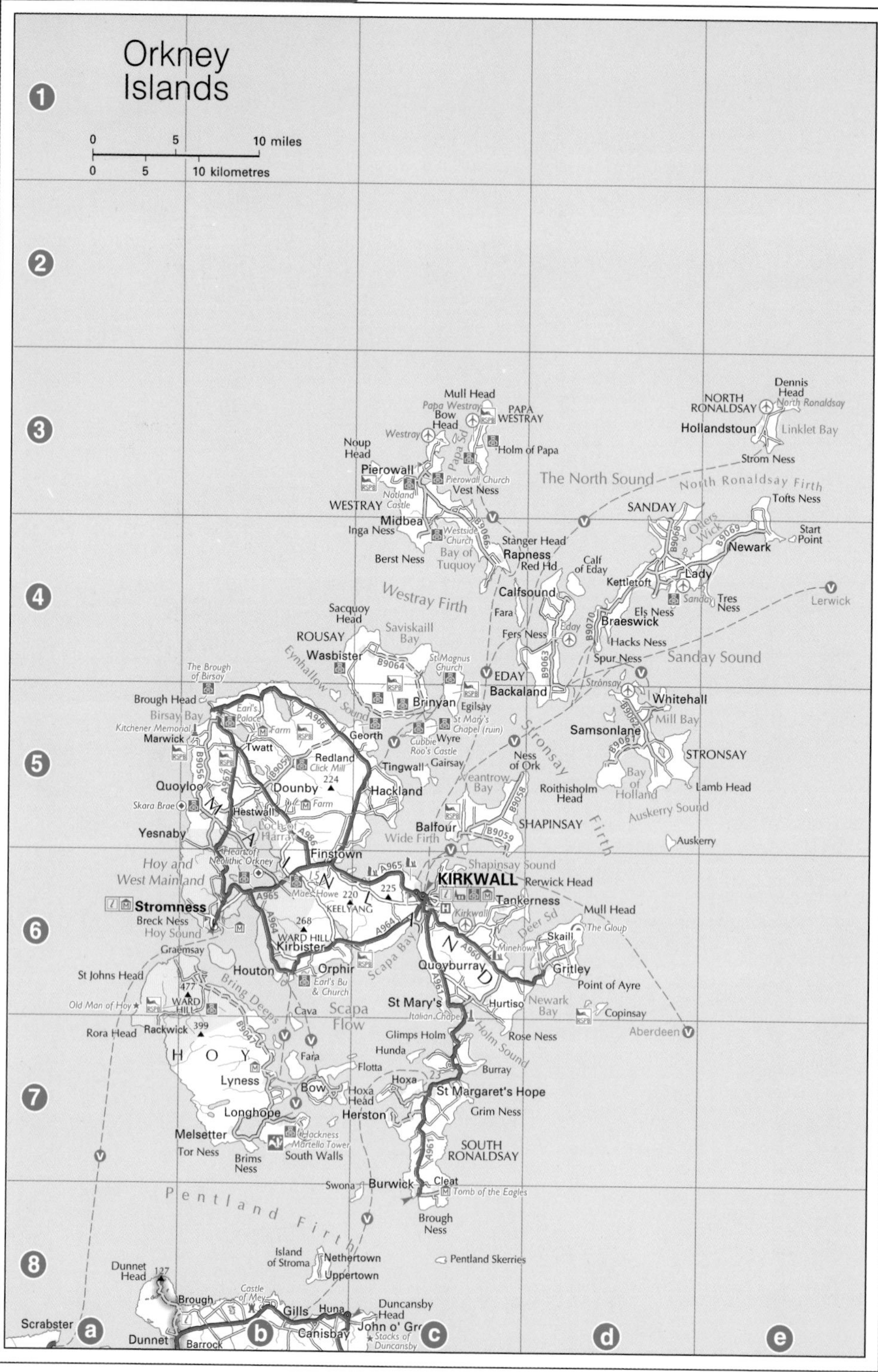
Orkney Islands
0 5 10 miles
0 5 10 kilometres
1
2
3
4
5
6
7
8
a
b
c
d
e
Mull Head
Papa Westray
PAPA WESTRAY
Bow Head
Westray
Holm of Papa
Noup Head
Pierowall
Pierowall Church
Vest Ness
Notland Castle
WESTRAY
Midbea
Inga Ness
Westside Church
Bay of Tuquoy
Berst Ness
Stanger Head
Rapness
Red Hd
Calf of Eday
Calfsound
Fara
Westray Firth
Fers Ness
Eday
EDAY
Backaland
NORTH RONALDSAY
Dennis Head
North Ronaldsay
Hollandstoun
Linklet Bay
Strom Ness
The North Sound
North Ronaldsay Firth
SANDAY
Tofts Ness
Otters Wick
Start Point
Newark
Lady
Kettletoft
Sanday
Tres Ness
Els Ness
Braeswick
Hacks Ness
Spur Ness
Sanday Sound
Lerwick
Stronsay
Whitehall
Mill Bay
Samsonlane
STRONSAY
Bay of Holland
Lamb Head
Auskerry Sound
Auskerry
Sacquoy Head
ROUSAY
Saviskaill Bay
Wasbister
Eynhallow Sound
St Magnus Church
Brinyan
Egilsay
St Mary's Chapel (ruin)
Wyre
Cubbie Roo's Castle
Gairsay
Georth
Tingwall
Hackland
The Brough of Birsay
Brough Head
Birsay Bay
Earl's Palace
Kitchener Memorial
Marwick
Farm
Twatt
Redland
Click Mill
224
Dounby
Quoyloo
Skara Brae
Hestwall
Loch of Harray
Yesnaby
MAINLAND
Heart of Neolithic Orkney
Finstown
Hoy and West Mainland
Stromness
Breck Ness
Hoy Sound
Maes Howe
220
225
KEELYANG
268
WARD HILL
Kirbister
Ness of Ork
Stronsay Firth
Veantrow Bay
Roithisholm Head
SHAPINSAY
Balfour
Wide Firth
Shapinsay Sound
KIRKWALL
Rerwick Head
Tankerness
Mull Head
The Gloup
Deer Sd
Skaill
Minehowe
Gritley
Point of Ayre
Newark Bay
Copinsay
Aberdeen
Graemsay
St Johns Head
Houton
Orphir
Earl's Bu & Church
Scapa Bay
Quoyburray
Bring Deeps
477
WARD HILL
Old Man of Hoy
Rora Head
Rackwick
399
Cava
Scapa Flow
St Mary's
Italian Chapel
Hurtiso
Holm Sound
Rose Ness
Glimps Holm
Hunda
HOY
Fara
Flotta
Burray
Lyness
Bow
Hoxa
Hoxa Head
St Margaret's Hope
Longhope
Herston
Grim Ness
Melsetter
Hackness Martello Tower
Tor Ness
Brims Ness
South Walls
SOUTH RONALDSAY
Swona
Burwick
Cleat
Tomb of the Eagles
Pentland Firth
Brough Ness
Island of Stroma
Nethertown
Uppertown
Pentland Skerries
Dunnet Head
127
Brough
Castle of Mey
Gills
Huna
Duncansby Head
Scrabster
Dunnet
Barrock
Canisbay
Stacks of Duncansby
A965
A966
A967
A986
A964
A960
A961
B9056
B9055
B9064
B9066
B9068
B9069
B9070
B9063
B9067
B9058
B9059
B9047
RSPB

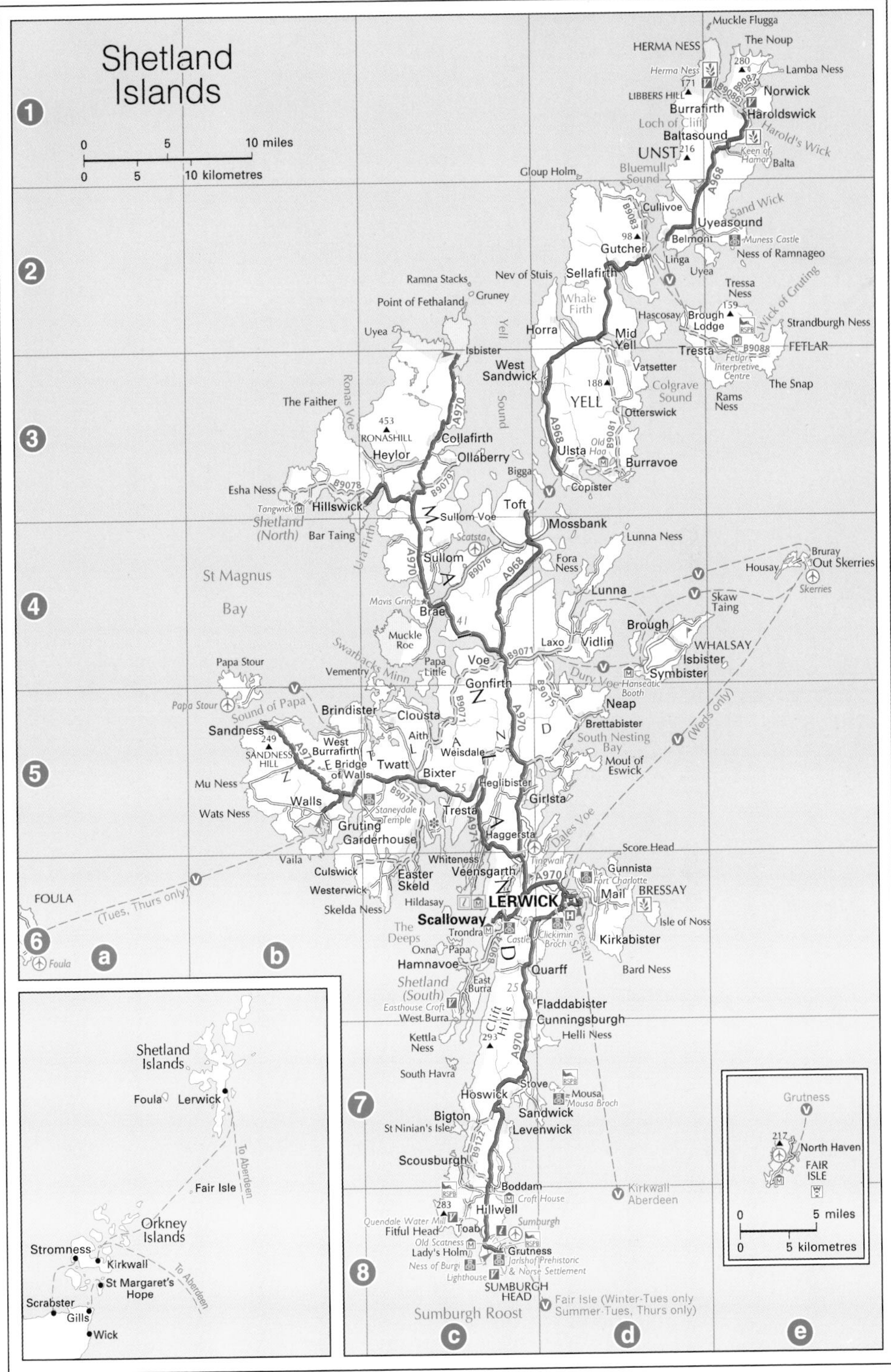
Shetland Islands
0 5 10 miles
0 5 10 kilometres
Muckle Flugga
HERMA NESS
The Noup
Lamba Ness
Norwick
Haroldswick
Burrafirth
Baltasound
UNST
Uyeasound
Belmont
Gutcher
Cullivoe
Sellafirth
Mid Yell
YELL
Ulsta
Burravoe
FETLAR
Tresta
Hillswick
Sullom Voe
Toft
Mossbank
Brae
Voe
Lunna
Vidlin
WHALSAY
Symbister
Out Skerries
St Magnus Bay
Papa Stour
Sandness
Walls
Aith
Bixter
Tresta
LERWICK
Scalloway
BRESSAY
FOULA
Sandwick
Sumburgh Head
Sumburgh Roost
Fair Isle (Winter-Tues only Summer-Tues, Thurs only)
FAIR ISLE
North Haven
Orkney Islands
Stromness
Kirkwall
St Margaret's Hope
Scrabster
Gills
Wick
To Aberdeen

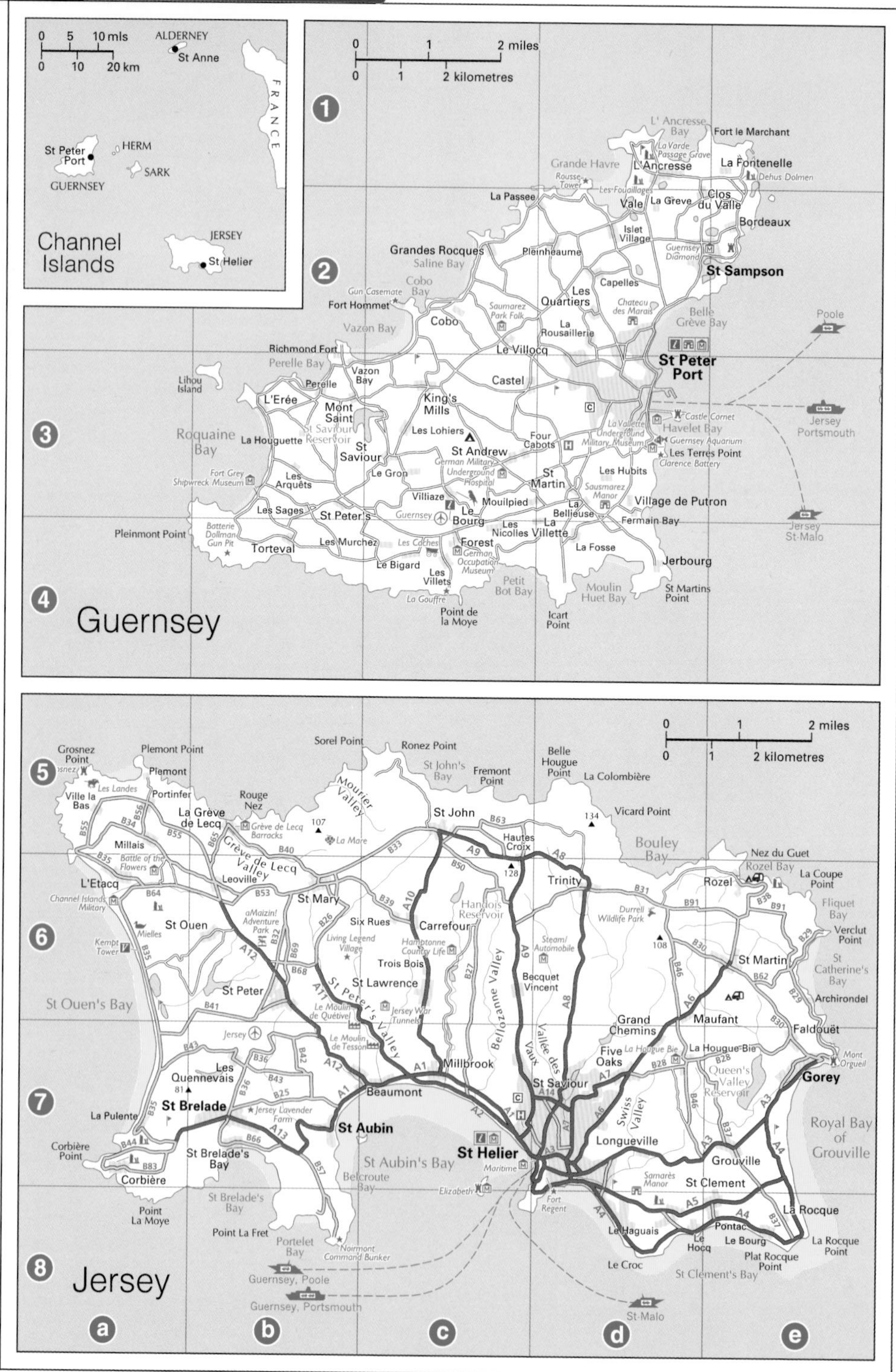
Channel Islands
ALDERNEY
St Anne
HERM
St Peter Port
SARK
GUERNSEY
JERSEY
St Helier
FRANCE
Guernsey
St Peter Port
St Sampson
L'Ancresse
La Fontenelle
Vale
Bordeaux
Grandes Rocques
Cobo
Castel
King's Mills
St Saviour
St Andrew
St Martin
St Peter's
Torteval
Forest
Le Bourg
Jerbourg
Pleinmont Point
Lihou Island
Roquaine Bay
Vazon Bay
Perelle Bay
Moulin Huet Bay
Petit Bot Bay
Icart Point
Fermain Bay
Havelet Bay
Belle Grève Bay
Jersey
St Helier
St Aubin
Gorey
St Brelade
St Ouen
St Peter
St Lawrence
St Mary
St John
Trinity
St Martin
St Saviour
St Clement
Grouville
Rozel
Beaumont
Millbrook
Carrefour
La Rocque
St Ouen's Bay
St Aubin's Bay
St Brelade's Bay
Bouley Bay
Royal Bay of Grouville
St Clement's Bay
Corbière
Grosnez Point
Sorel Point
Ronez Point
La Colombière
Guernsey, Poole
Guernsey, Portsmouth
St-Malo
0 1 2 miles
0 1 2 kilometres

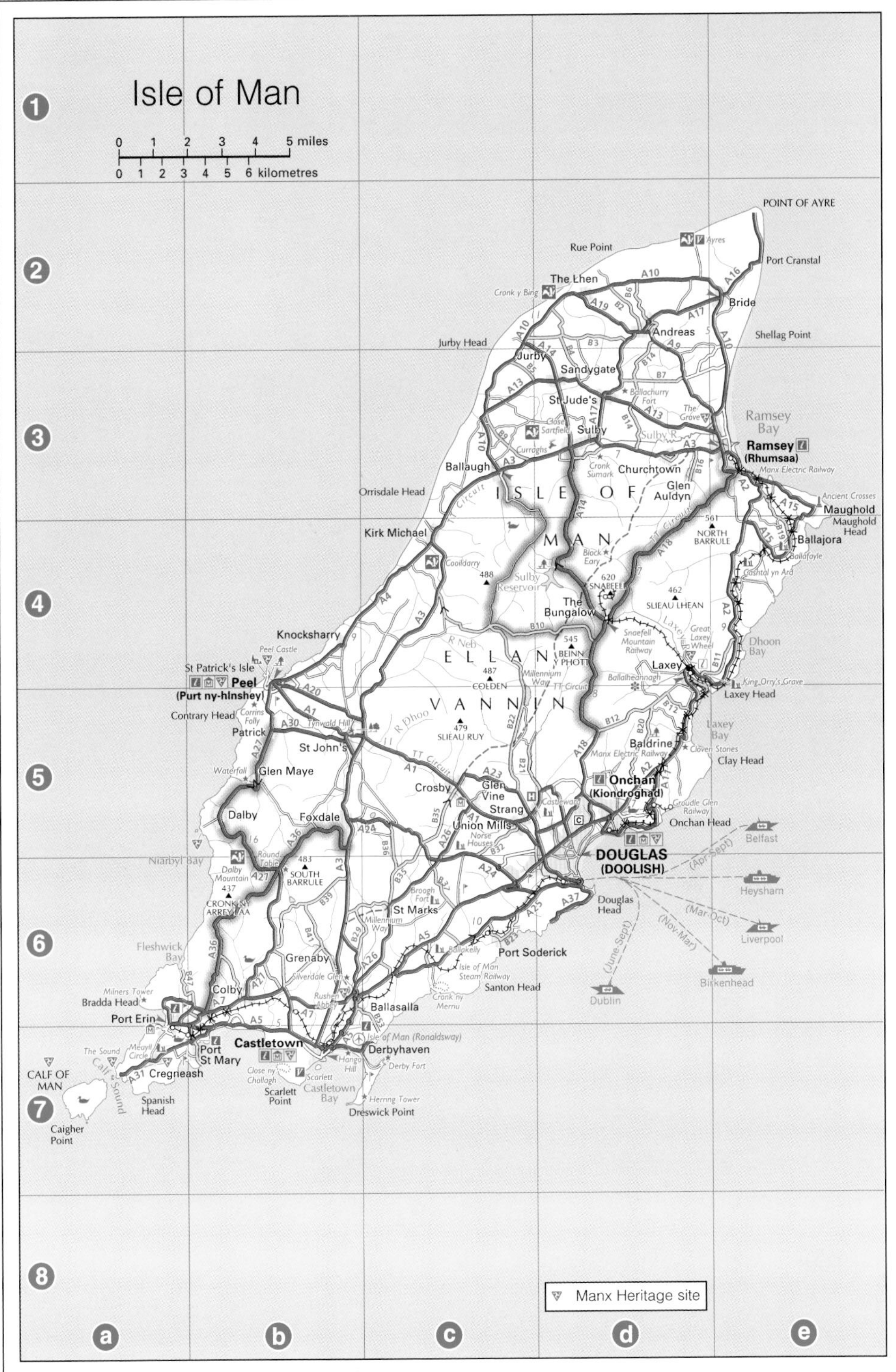
Isle of Man
0 1 2 3 4 5 miles
0 1 2 3 4 5 6 kilometres
POINT OF AYRE
Rue Point
Ayres
Port Cranstal
The Lhen
Cronk y Bing
Bride
Andreas
Shellag Point
Jurby Head
Jurby
Sandygate
St Jude's
Ballachurry Fort
The Grove
Ramsey Bay
Sulby
Curraghs
Ballaugh
Ramsey
(Rhumsaa)
Manx Electric Railway
Churchtown
Glen Auldyn
Orrisdale Head
ISLE OF MAN
Ancient Crosses
Maughold
Maughold Head
Ballajora
Kirk Michael
NORTH BARRULE
Cooildarry
Sulby Reservoir
Block Eary
SNAEFELL
SLIEAU LHEAN
The Bungalow
Knocksharry
Snaefell Mountain Railway
Great Laxey Wheel
Dhoon Bay
Peel Castle
St Patrick's Isle
Peel
(Purt ny-hInshey)
ELLAN VANNIN
BEINN Y PHOTT
COLDEN
Millennium Way
Laxey
Ballalheannagh
King Orry's Grave
Laxey Head
Contrary Head
Corrins Folly
Patrick
Tynwald Hill
SLIEAU RUY
St John's
Laxey Bay
Baldrine
Cloven Stones
Clay Head
Waterfall
Glen Maye
Crosby
Glen Vine
Onchan
(Kiondroghad)
Dalby
Foxdale
Strang
Union Mills
Groudle Glen Railway
Onchan Head
Norse Houses
Belfast
Niarbyl Bay
Round Table
SOUTH BARRULE
DOUGLAS
(DOOLISH)
Dalby Mountain
CRONK NY ARREY LAA
Brough Fort
St Marks
Heysham
Douglas Head
Millennium Way
Port Soderick
Liverpool
Fleshwick Bay
Grenaby
Ballakelly
Isle of Man Steam Railway
Santon Head
Silverdale Glen
Birkenhead
Milners Tower
Bradda Head
Colby
Rushen Abbey
Ballasalla
Cronk ny Merriu
Dublin
Port Erin
Castletown
Isle of Man (Ronaldsway)
Derbyhaven
The Sound
Meayll Circle
Port St Mary
Hango Hill
Derby Fort
CALF OF MAN
Calf Sound
Cregneash
Close ny Chollagh
Scarlett
Scarlett Point
Castletown Bay
Herring Tower
Spanish Head
Dreswick Point
Caigher Point
Manx Heritage site
(Apr-Sept)
(Mar-Oct)
(Nov-Mar)
(June-Sept)

Restricted junctions

Motorway and Primary Route junctions which have access or exit restrictions are shown on the map pages thus: 

M1 London - Leeds

Junction	Northbound	Southbound
2	Access only from A1 *(northbound)*	Exit only to A1 *(southbound)*
4	Access only from A41 *(northbound)*	Exit only to A41 *(southbound)*
6A	Access only from M25 (no link from A405)	Exit only to M25 (no link from A405)
7	Access only from A414	Exit only to A414
17	Exit only to M45	Access only from M45
19	Exit only to M6 *(northbound)*	Exit only to A14 *(sountbound)*
21A	Exit only, no access	Access only, no exit
23A	Access only from A42	No restriction
24A	Access only, no exit	Exit only, no access
35A	Exit only, no access	Access only, no exit
43	Exit only to M621	Access only from M621
48	Exit only to A1(M) *(northbound)*	Access only from A1(M) *(southbound)*

M2 Rochester - Faversham

Junction	Westbound	Eastbound
1	No exit to A2 *(eastbound)*	No access from A2 *(westbound)*

M3 Sunbury - Southampton

Junction	Northeastbound	Southwestbound
8	Access only from A303, no exit	Exit only to A303, no access
10	Exit only, no access	Access only, no exit
14	Access from M27 only, no exit	No access to M27 *(westbound)*

M4 London - South Wales

Junction	Westbound	Eastbound
1	Access only from A4 *(westbound)*	Exit only to A4 *(eastbound)*
21	Exit only to M48	Access only from M48
23	Access only from M48	Exit only to M48
25	Exit only, no access	Access only, no exit
25A	Exit only, no access	Access only, no exit
29	Exit only to A48(M)	Access only from A48(M)
38	Exit only, no access	No restriction
39	Access only, no exit	No access or exit

M5 Birmingham - Exeter

Junction	Northeastbound	Southwestbound
10	Access only, no exit	Exit only, no access
11A	Access only from A417 *(westbound)*	Exit only to A417 *(eastbound)*
18A	Exit only to M49	Access only from M49
18	Exit only, no access	Access only, no exit

M6 Toll Motorway

Junction	Northwestbound	Southeastbound
T1	Access only, no exit	No access or exit
T2	No access or exit	Exit only, no access
T3	Staggered junction, follow signs - access only from A38 *(northbound)*	Staggered junction, follow signs - access only from A38 *(southbound)*
T5	Access only, no exit	Exit only to A5148 *(northbound)*, no access
T7	Exit only, no access	Access only, no exit
T8	Exit only, no access	Access only, no exit

M6 Rugby - Carlisle

Junction	Northbound	Southbound
3A	Exit only to M6 Toll	Access only from M6 Toll
4A	Access only from M42 *(southbound)*	Exit only to M42
5	Exit only, no access	Access only, no exit
10A	Exit only to M54	Access only from M54
11A	Access only from M6 Toll	Exit only to M6 Toll
with M56 (jct 20A)	No restriction	Access only from M56 *(eastbound)*
20	Exit only to M56 (westbound)	Access only from M56 (eastbound)
24	Access only, no exit	Exit only, no access
25	Exit only, no access	Access only, no exit
30	Access only from M61	Exit only to M61
31A	Exit only, no access	Access only, no exit
45	Exit only, no access	Access only, no exit

M8 Edinburgh - Bishopton

Junction	Westbound	Eastbound
8	No access from M73 *(southbound)* or from A8 *(eastbound)* & A89	No exit to M73 *(northbound)* or to A8 *(westbound)* & A89
9	Access only, no exit	Exit only, no access
13	Access only from M80 *(southbound)*	Exit only to M80 *(northbound)*
14	Access only, no exit	Exit only, no access
16	Exit only to A804	Access only from A879
17	Exit only to A82	No restriction
18	Access only from A82 *(eastbound)*	Exit only to A814
19	No access from A814 *(westbound)*	Exit only to A814 *(westbound)*
20	Exit only, no access	Access only, no exit
21	Access only, no exit	Exit only to A8
22	Exit only to M77 *(southbound)*	Access only from M77 *(northbound)*
23	Exit only to B768	Access only from B768
25	No access or exit from or to A8	No access or exit from or to A8
25A	Exit only, no access	Access only, no exit
28	Exit only, no access	Access only, no exit
28A	Exit only to A737	Access only from A737

M9 Edinburgh - Dunblane

Junction	Northwestbound	Southeastbound
2	Access only, no exit	Exit only, no access
3	Exit only, no access	Access only, no exit
6	Access only, no exit	Exit only to A905
8	Exit only to M876 *(southwestbound)*	Access only from M876 *(northeastbound)*

M11 London - Cambridge

Junction	Northbound	Southbound
4	Access only from A406 *(eastbound)*	Exit only to A406
5	Exit only, no access	Access only, no exit
8A	Exit only, no access	No direct access, use jct 8
9	Exit only to A11	Access only from A11
13	Exit only, no access	Access only, no exit
14	Exit only, no access	Access only, no exit

M20 Swanley - Folkestone

Junction	Northwestbound	Southeastbound
2	Staggered junction; follow signs - access only	Staggered junction; follow signs - exit only
3	Exit only to M26 *(westbound)*	Access only from M26 *(eastbound)*
5	Access only from A20	For access follow signs - exit only to A20
6	No restriction	For exit follow signs
11A	Access only, no exit	Exit only, no access

M23 Hooley - Crawley

Junction	Northbound	Southbound
7	Exit only to A23 *(northbound)*	Access only from A23 *(southbound)*
10A	Access only, no exit	Exit only, no access

M25 London Orbital Motorway

Junction	Clockwise	Anticlockwise
1B	No direct access, use slip road to Jct 2. Exit only	Access only, no exit
5	No exit to M26 *(eastbound)*	No access from M26
19	Exit only, no access	Access only, no exit
21	Access only from M1 *(southbound)*. Exit only to M1 *(northbound)*	Access only from M1 *(southbound)*. Exit only to M1 *(northbound)*
31	No exit (use slip road via jct 30), access only	No access (use slip road via jct 30), exit only

M26 Sevenoaks - Wrotham

Junction	Westbound	Eastbound
with M25 (jct 5)	Exit only to clockwise M25 *(westbound)*	Access only from anticlockwise M25 *(eastbound)*
with M20 (jct 3)	Access only from M20 *(northwestbound)*	Exit only to M20 *(southeastbound)*

M27 Cadnam - Portsmouth

Junction	Westbound	Eastbound
4	Staggered junction; follow signs - access only from M3 *(southbound)*. Exit only to M3 *(northbound)*	Staggered junction; follow signs - access only from M3 *(southbound)*. Exit only to M3 *(northbound)*
10	Exit only, no access	Access only, no exit
12	Staggered junction; follow signs - exit only to M275 *(southbound)*	Staggered junction; follow signs - access only from M275 *(northbound)*

M40 London - Birmingham

Junction	Northwestbound	Southeastbound
3	Exit only, no access	Access only, no exit
7	Exit only, no access	Access only, no exit
8	Exit only to M40/A40	Access only from M40/A40
13	Exit only, no access	Access only, no exit
14	Access only, no exit	Exit only, no access
16	Access only, no exit	Exit only, no access

M42 Bromsgrove - Measham

Junction	Northeastbound	Southwestbound
1	Access only, no exit	Exit only, no access
7	Exit only to M6 *(northwestbound)*	Access only from M6 *(northwestbound)*
7A	Exit only to M6 *(southeastbound)*	No access or exit
8	Access only from M6 *(southeastbound)*	Exit only to M6 *(northwestbound)*

M45 Coventry - M1

Junction	Westbound	Eastbound
Dunchurch (unnumbered)	Access only from A45	Exit only, no access
with M1 (jct 17)	Access only from M1 *(northbound)*	Exit only to M1 *(southbound)*

M53 Mersey Tunnel - Chester

Junction	Northbound	Southbound
11	Access only from M56 *(westbound)*. Exit only to M56 *(eastbound)*	Access only from M56 *(westbound)*. Exit only to M56 *(eastbound)*

M54 Telford - Birmingham

Junction	Westbound	Eastbound
with M6 (jct 10A)	Access only from M6 *(northbound)*	Exit only to M6 *(southbound)*

M56 Chester - Manchester

Junction	Westbound	Eastbound
1	Access only from M60 *(westbound)*	Exit only to M60 *(eastbound)* & A34 *(northbound)*
2	Exit only, no access	Access only, no exit
3	Access only, no exit	Exit only, no access
4	Exit only, no access	Access only, no exit
7	Exit only, no access	No restriction
8	Access only, no exit	No access or exit
9	No exit to M6 *(southbound)*	No access from M6 *(northbound)*
15	Exit only to M53	Access only from M53
16	No access or exit	No restrictions

M57 Liverpool Outer Ring Road

Junction	Northwestbound	Southeastbound
3	Access only, no exit	Exit only, no access
5	Access only from A580 *(westbound)*	Exit only, no access

M58 Liverpool - Wigan

Junction	Westbound	Eastbound
1	Exit only, no access	Access only, no exit

M60 Manchester Orbital

Junction	Clockwise	Anticlockwise
2	Access only, no exit	Exit only, no access
3	No access from M56	Access only from A34 *(northbound)*
4	Access only from A34 *(northbound)*. Exit only to M56	Access only from M56 *(eastbound)*. Exit only to A34 *(southbound)*
5	Access and exit only from and to A5103 *(northbound)*	Access and exit only from and to A5103 *(southbound)*
7	No direct access, use slip road to jct 8. Exit only to A56	Access only from A56. No exit - use jct 8
14	Access from A580 *(eastbound)*	Exit only to A580 *(westbound)*
16	Access only, no exit	Exit only, no access
20	Exit only, no access	Access only, no exit
22	No restriction	Exit only, no access
25	Exit only, no access	No restriction
26	No restriction	Exit only, no access
27	Access only, no exit	Exit only, no access

M61 Manchester - Preston

Junction	Northwestbound	Southeastbound
3	No access or exit	Exit only, no access
with M6 (jct 30)	Exit only to M6 *(northbound)*	Access only from M6 *(southbound)*

M62 Liverpool - Kingston upon Hull

Junction	Westbound	Eastbound
23	Access only, no exit	Exit only, no access
32A	No access to A1(M) *(southbound)*	No restriction

M65 Preston - Colne

Junction	Northeastbound	Southwestbound
9	Exit only, no access	Access only, no exit
11	Access only, no exit	Exit only, no access

M66 Bury

Junction	Northbound	Southbound
with A56	Exit only to A56 *(northbound)*	Access only from A56 *(southbound)*
1	Exit only, no access	Access only, no exit

M67 Hyde Bypass

Junction	Westbound	Eastbound
1	Access only, no exit	Exit only, no access
2	Exit only, no access	Access only, no exit
3	Exit only, no access	No restriction

M69 Coventry - Leicester

Junction	Northbound	Southbound
2	Access only, no exit	Exit only, no access

M73 East of Glasgow

Junction	Northbound	Southbound
2	No access from or exit to A89. No access from M8 *(eastbound)*.	No access from or exit to A89. No exit to M8 *(westbound)*

M74 and A74(M) Glasgow - Gretna

Junction	Northbound	Southbound
3	Exit only, no access	Access only, no exit
3A	Access only, no exit	Exit only, no access
7	Access only, no exit	Exit only, no access
9	No access or exit	Exit only, no access
10	No restrictions	Access only, no exit
11	Access only, no exit	Exit only, no access
12	Exit only, no access	Access only, no exit
18	Exit only, no access	Access only, no exit

M77 Glasgow - Kilmarnock

Junction	Northbound	Southbound
with M8 (jct 22)	No exit to M8 *(westbound)*	No access from M8 *(eastbound)*
4	Access only, no exit	Exit only, no access
6	Access only, no exit	Exit only, no access
7	Access only, no exit	No restriction

M80 Glasgow - Stirling

Junction	Northbound	Southbound
4A	Exit only, no access	Access only, no exit
6A	Access only, no exit	Exit only, no access
8	Exit only to M876 *(northeastbound)*	Access only from M876 *(southwestbound)*

M90 Edinburgh - Perth

Junction	Northbound	Southbound
1	No exit, access only	Exit only to A90 *(eastbound)*
2A	Exit only to A92 *(eastbound)*	Access only from A92 *(westbound)*
7	Access only, no exit	Exit only, no access
8	Exit only, no access	Access only, no exit
10	No access from A912. No exit to A912 *(southbound)*	No access from A912 *(northbound)*. No exit to A912

M180 Doncaster - Grimsby

Junction	Westbound	Eastbound
1	Access only, no exit	Exit only, no access

M606 Bradford Spur

Junction	Northbound	Southbound
2	Exit only, no access	No restriction

M621 Leeds - M1

Junction	Clockwise	Anticlockwise
2A	Access only, no exit	Exit only, no access
4	No exit or access	No restriction
5	Access only, no exit	Exit only, no access
6	Exit only, no access	Access only, no exit
with M1 (jct 43)	Exit only to M1 *(southbound)*	Access only from M1 *(northbound)*

M876 Bonnybridge - Kincardine Bridge

Junction	Northeastbound	Southwestbound
with M80 (jct 5)	Access only from M80 *(northbound)*	Exit only to M80 *(southbound)*
with M9 (jct 8)	Exit only to M9 *(eastbound)*	Access only from M9 *(westbound)*

A1(M) South Mimms - Baldock

Junction	Northbound	Southbound
2	Exit only, no access	Access only, no exit
3	No restriction	Exit only, no access
5	Access only, no exit	No access or exit

A1(M) Pontefract - Bedale

Junction	Northbound	Southbound
41	No access to M62 *(eastbound)*	No restriction
43	Access only from M1 *(northbound)*	Exit only to M1 *(southbound)*

A1(M) Scotch Corner - Newcastle upon Tyne

Junction	Northbound	Southbound
57	Exit only to A66(M) *(eastbound)*	Access only from A66(M) *(westbound)*
65	No access. Exit only to A194(M) & A1 *(northbound)*	No exit. Access only from A194(M) & A1 *(southbound)*

A3(M) Horndean - Havant

Junction	Northbound	Southbound
1	Access only from A3	Exit only to A3
4	Exit only, no access	Access only, no exit

A48(M) Cardiff Spur

Junction	Westbound	Eastbound
29	Access only from M4 *(westbound)*	Exit only to M4 *(eastbound)*
29A	Exit only to A48 *(westbound)*	Access only from A48 *(eastbound)*

A66(M) Darlington Spur

Junction	Westbound	Eastbound
with A1(M) (jct 57)	Exit only to A1(M) *(southbound)*	Access only from A1(M) *(northbound)*

A194(M) Newcastle upon Tyne

Junction	Northbound	Southbound
with A1(M) (jct 65)	Access only from A1(M) *(northbound)*	Exit only to A1(M) *(southbound)*

A12 M25 - Ipswich

Junction	Northeastbound	Southwestbound
13	Access only, no exit	No restriction
14	Exit only, no access	Access only, no exit
20A	Exit only, no access	Access only, no exit
20B	Access only, no exit	Exit only, no access
21	No restriction	Access only, no exit
23	Exit only, no access	Access only, no exit
24	Access only, no exit	Exit only, no access
27	Exit only, no access	Access only, no exit
Dedham & Stratford St Mary (unnumbered)	Exit only	Access only

A14 M1 - Felixstowe

Junction	Westbound	Eastbound
with M1/M6 (jct19)	Exit only to M6 and M1 *(northbound)*	Access only from M6 and M1 *(southbound)*
4	Exit only, no access	Access only, no exit
31	Exit only to M11 *(for London)*	Access only, no exit
31A	Exit only to A14 (northbound)	Access only, no exit
34	Access only, no exit	Exit only, no access
36	Exit only to A11, access only from A1303	Access only from A11
38	Access only from A11	Exit only to A11
39	Exit only, no access	Access only, no exit
61	Access only, no exit	Exit only, no access

A55 Holyhead - Chester

Junction	Westbound	Eastbound
8A	Exit only, no access	Access only, no exit
23A	Access only, no exit	Exit only, no access
24A	Exit only, no access	No access or exit
33A	Exit only, no access	No access or exit
33B	Exit only, no access	Access only, no exit
36A	Exit only to A5104	Access only from A5104

Index to place names

This index lists places appearing in the main-map section of the atlas in alphabetical order. The reference following each name gives the atlas page number and grid reference of the square in which the place appears. The map shows counties and administrative areas, together with a list of the abbreviated name forms used in the index. The top 100 places of tourist interest are indexed in **red,** World Heritage sites in **green**, motorway service areas in **blue**, airports in blue *italic* and National Parks in green *italic*.

Scotland

Abers **Aberdeenshire**
Ag & B **Argyll and Bute**
Angus **Angus**
Border **Scottish Borders**
C Aber **City of Aberdeen**
C Dund **City of Dundee**
C Edin **City of Edinburgh**
C Glas **City of Glasgow**
Clacks **Clackmannanshire (1)**
D & G **Dumfries & Galloway**
E Ayrs **East Ayrshire**
E Duns **East Dunbartonshire (2)**
E Loth **East Lothian**
E Rens **East Renfrewshire (3)**
Falk **Falkirk**
Fife **Fife**
Highld **Highland**
Inver **Inverclyde (4)**
Mdloth **Midlothian (5)**
Moray **Moray**
N Ayrs **North Ayrshire**
N Lans **North Lanarkshire (6)**
Ork **Orkney Islands**
P & K **Perth & Kinross**
Rens **Renfrewshire (7)**
S Ayrs **South Ayrshire**
Shet **Shetland Islands**
S Lans **South Lanarkshire**
Stirlg **Stirling**
W Duns **West Dunbartonshire (8)**
W Isls **Western Isles (Na h-Eileanan an Iar)**
W Loth **West Lothian**

Wales

Blae G **Blaenau Gwent (9)**
Brdgnd **Bridgend (10)**
Caerph **Caerphilly (11)**
Cardif **Cardiff**
Carmth **Carmarthenshire**
Cerdgn **Ceredigion**
Conwy **Conwy**
Denbgs **Denbighshire**
Flints **Flintshire**
Gwynd **Gwynedd**
IoA **Isle of Anglesey**
Mons **Monmouthshire**
Myr Td **Merthyr Tydfil (12)**
Neath **Neath Port Talbot (13)**
Newpt **Newport (14)**
Pembks **Pembrokeshire**
Powys **Powys**
Rhondd **Rhondda Cynon Taff (15)**
Swans **Swansea**
Torfn **Torfaen (16)**
V Glam **Vale of Glamorgan (17)**
Wrexhm **Wrexham**

Channel Islands & Isle of Man

Guern **Guernsey**
Jersey **Jersey**
IoM **Isle of Man**

England

BaNES **Bath & N E Somerset (18)**
Barns **Barnsley (19)**
Bed **Bedford**
Birm **Birmingham**
Bl w D **Blackburn with Darwen (20)**
Bmouth **Bournemouth**
Bolton **Bolton (21)**
Bpool **Blackpool**
Br & H **Brighton & Hove (22)**
Br For **Bracknell Forest (23)**
Bristl **City of Bristol**
Bucks **Buckinghamshire**
Bury **Bury (24)**
C Beds **Central Bedfordshire**
C Brad **City of Bradford**
C Derb **City of Derby**
C KuH **City of Kingston upon Hull**
C Leic **City of Leicester**
C Nott **City of Nottingham**
C Pete **City of Peterborough**
C Plym **City of Plymouth**
C Port **City of Portsmouth**
C Sotn **City of Southampton**
C Stke **City of Stoke-on-Trent**
C York **City of York**
Calder **Calderdale (25)**
Cambs **Cambridgeshire**
Ches E **Cheshire East**
Ches W **Cheshire West and Chester**
Cnwll **Cornwall**
Covtry **Coventry**
Cumb **Cumbria**
Darltn **Darlington (26)**
Derbys **Derbyshire**
Devon **Devon**
Donc **Doncaster (27)**
Dorset **Dorset**
Dudley **Dudley (28)**
Dur **Durham**
E R Yk **East Riding of Yorkshire**
E Susx **East Sussex**
Essex **Essex**
Gatesd **Gateshead (29)**
Gloucs **Gloucestershire**
Gt Lon **Greater London**
Halton **Halton (30)**
Hants **Hampshire**
Hartpl **Hartlepool (31)**
Herefs **Herefordshire**
Herts **Hertfordshire**
IoS **Isles of Scilly**
IoW **Isle of Wight**
Kent **Kent**
Kirk **Kirklees (32)**
Knows **Knowsley (33)**
Lancs **Lancashire**
Leeds **Leeds**
Leics **Leicestershire**
Lincs **Lincolnshire**
Lpool **Liverpool**
Luton **Luton**
M Keyn **Milton Keynes**
Manch **Manchester**
Medway **Medway**
Middsb **Middlesbrough**
NE Lin **North East Lincolnshire**
N Linc **North Lincolnshire**
N Som **North Somerset (34)**
N Tyne **North Tyneside (35)**
N u Ty **Newcastle upon Tyne**
N York **North Yorkshire**
Nhants **Northamptonshire**
Norfk **Norfolk**
Notts **Nottinghamshire**
Nthumb **Northumberland**
Oldham **Oldham (36)**
Oxon **Oxfordshire**
Poole **Poole**
R & Cl **Redcar & Cleveland**
Readg **Reading**
Rochdl **Rochdale (37)**
Rothm **Rotherham (38)**
Rutlnd **Rutland**
S Glos **South Gloucestershire (39)**
S on T **Stockton-on-Tees (40)**
S Tyne **South Tyneside (41)**
Salfd **Salford (42)**
Sandw **Sandwell (43)**
Sefton **Sefton (44)**
Sheff **Sheffield**
Shrops **Shropshire**
Slough **Slough (45)**
Solhll **Solihull (46)**
Somset **Somerset**
St Hel **St Helens (47)**
Staffs **Staffordshire**
Sthend **Southend-on-Sea**
Stockp **Stockport (48)**
Suffk **Suffolk**
Sundld **Sunderland**
Surrey **Surrey**
Swindn **Swindon**
Tamesd **Tameside (49)**
Thurr **Thurrock (50)**
Torbay **Torbay**
Traffd **Trafford (51)**
W & M **Windsor and Maidenhead (52)**
W Berk **West Berkshire**
W Susx **West Sussex**
Wakefd **Wakefield (53)**
Warrtn **Warrington (54)**
Warwks **Warwickshire**
Wigan **Wigan (55)**
Wilts **Wiltshire**
Wirral **Wirral (56)**
Wokham **Wokingham (57)**
Wolves **Wolverhampton (58)**
Worcs **Worcestershire**
Wrekin **Telford & Wrekin (59)**
Wsall **Walsall (60)**

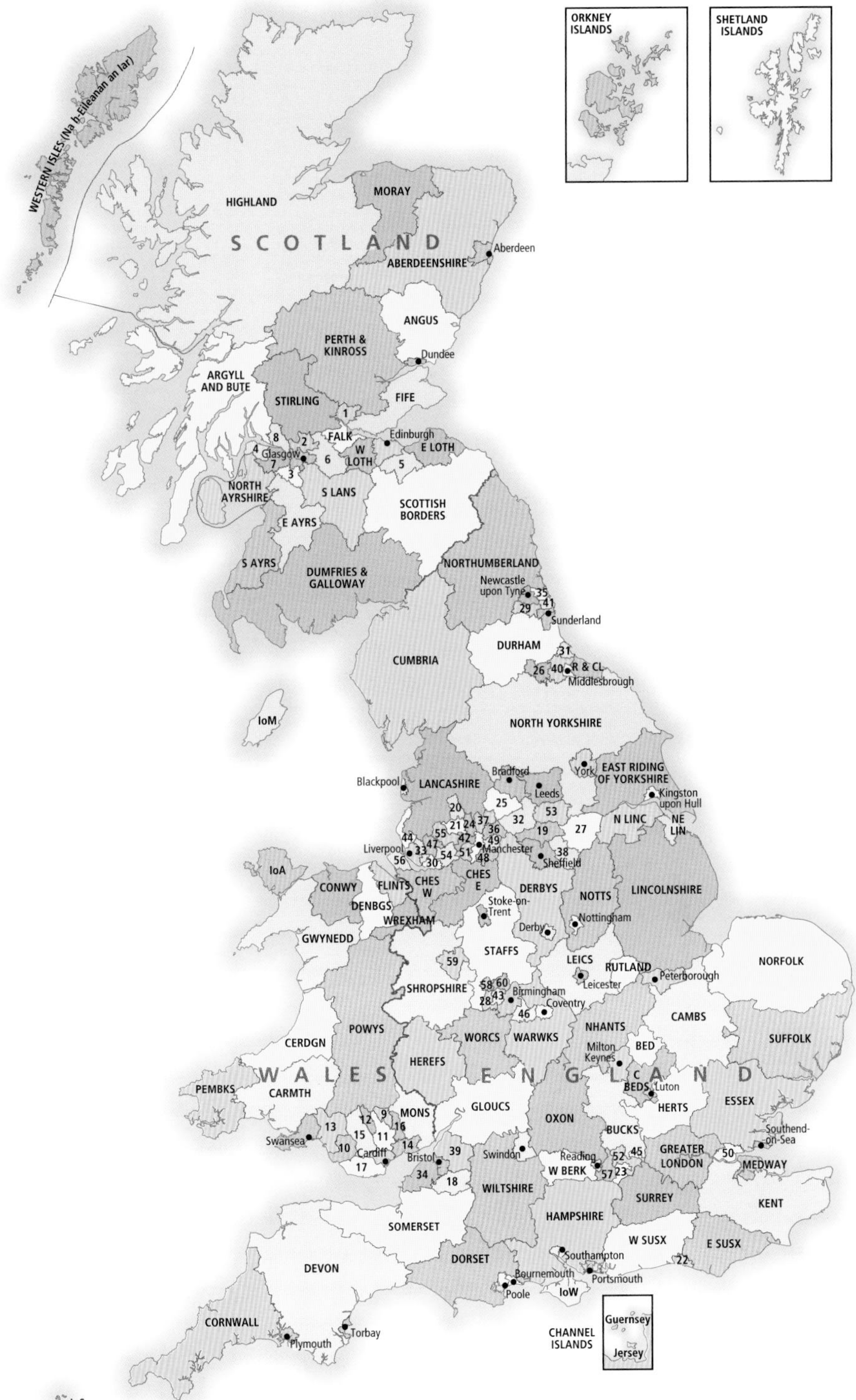
ORKNEY ISLANDS
SHETLAND ISLANDS
WESTERN ISLES (Na h-Eileanan an Iar)
HIGHLAND
MORAY
SCOTLAND
Aberdeen
ABERDEENSHIRE
ANGUS
PERTH & KINROSS
Dundee
ARGYLL AND BUTE
STIRLING
FIFE
FALK
Edinburgh
E LOTH
W LOTH
Glasgow
NORTH AYRSHIRE
S LANS
SCOTTISH BORDERS
E AYRS
S AYRS
DUMFRIES & GALLOWAY
NORTHUMBERLAND
Newcastle upon Tyne
Sunderland
DURHAM
CUMBRIA
R & CL
Middlesbrough
IoM
NORTH YORKSHIRE
Bradford
York
EAST RIDING OF YORKSHIRE
Blackpool
LANCASHIRE
Leeds
Kingston upon Hull
N LINC
NE LIN
Liverpool
Manchester
Sheffield
IoA
CONWY
FLINTS
CHES W
CHES E
DERBYS
NOTTS
LINCOLNSHIRE
DENBGS
WREXHAM
Stoke-on-Trent
Nottingham
Derby
GWYNEDD
STAFFS
LEICS
RUTLAND
Leicester
Peterborough
NORFOLK
SHROPSHIRE
Birmingham
Coventry
CAMBS
POWYS
NHANTS
CERDGN
WORCS
WARWKS
Milton Keynes
BED
SUFFOLK
HEREFS
WALES
ENGLAND
PEMBKS
CARMTH
C BEDS
Luton
HERTS
ESSEX
MONS
GLOUCS
OXON
Swansea
Cardiff
Bristol
Swindon
BUCKS
Reading
GREATER LONDON
Southend-on-Sea
MEDWAY
W BERK
WILTSHIRE
SURREY
KENT
SOMERSET
HAMPSHIRE
W SUSX
E SUSX
DORSET
Southampton
DEVON
Bournemouth
Portsmouth
Poole
IoW
CHANNEL ISLANDS
Guernsey
Jersey
CORNWALL
Plymouth
Torbay
IoS
1
2
3
4
5
6
7
8
9
10
11
12
13
14
15
16
17
18
19
20
21
22
23
24
25
26
27
28
29
30
31
32
33
34
35
36
37
38
39
40
41
42
43
44
45
46
47
48
49
50
51
52
53
54
55
56
57
58
59
60

A

Abbas Combe Somset 27 G6
Abberley Worcs 70 D2
Abberley Common Worcs 70 D2
Abberton Essex 62 B4
Abberton Worcs 71 H4
Abbess Roding Essex 60 F5
Abbeydale Sheff 114 F5
Abbey Dore Herefs 54 B3
Abbey Green Staffs 99 L2
Abbey St Bathans Border 178 F6
Abbeystead Lancs 130 B8
Abbey Town Cumb 147 L5
Abbey Valley Crematorium Derbys 101 H2
Abbey Village Lancs 121 J6
Abbey Wood Gt Lon 45 J4
Abbotrule Border 167 J6
Abbots Bickington Devon 9 K3
Abbots Bromley Staffs 100 B7
Abbotsbury Dorset 14 B5
Abbots Deuglie P & K 186 B5
Abbotsham Devon 22 F6
Abbotskerswell Devon 7 K3
Abbots Langley Herts 59 H7
Abbots Leigh N Som 38 D5
Abbotsley Cambs 75 J3
Abbots Morton Worcs 71 H4
Abbots Ripton Cambs 89 J7
Abbot's Salford Warwks 71 J4
Abbots Worthy Hants 29 J5
Abbotts Ann Hants 29 G3
Abbott Street Dorset 15 J3
Abdon Shrops 83 L6
Aberaeron Cerdgn 66 B3
Aberaman Rhondd 52 F7
Aberangell Gwynd 81 J2
Aberarder Highld 202 F1
Aberargie P & K 186 B4
Aberarth Cerdgn 66 B2
Aberavon Neath 51 L7
Abercanaid Myr Td 53 G7
Abercarn Caerph 37 K2
Abercastle Pembks 64 B7
Abercegir Powys 81 H3
Aberchalder Lodge Highld 202 B5
Aberchirder Abers 216 C4
Abercraf Powys 52 C5
Abercregan Neath 36 D2
Abercwmboi Rhondd 52 F7
Abercych Pembks 65 H6
Abercynon Rhondd 37 G2
Aberdalgie P & K 185 M4
Aberdare Rhondd 52 F7
Aberdaron Gwynd 94 C7
Aberdeen C Aber 207 H4
Aberdeen Airport C Aber 207 G3
Aberdeen Crematorium C Aber 207 G4
Aberdour Fife 177 G2
Aberdulais Neath 52 B7
Aberdyfi Gwynd 80 E4
Aberedw Powys 68 C5
Abereiddy Pembks 48 D2
Abererch Gwynd 95 G5
Aberfan Myr Td 53 G7
Aberfeldy P & K 194 D6
Aberffraw IoA 108 D7
Aberford Leeds 124 C3
Aberfoyle Stirlg 184 C7
Abergavenny Mons 53 L5
Abergele Conwy 110 C6
Abergorlech Carmth 66 D7
Abergwesyn Powys 67 J4
Abergwili Carmth 50 F2
Abergwynfi Neath 36 D2
Abergwyngregyn Gwynd 109 J6
Abergynolwyn Gwynd 80 F3
Aberkenfig Brdgnd 36 D4
Aberlady E Loth 178 B3
Aberlemno Angus 196 E5
Aberllefenni Gwynd 81 G2
Aberllynfi Powys 68 D6
Aberlour Moray 215 G5
Abermule Powys 82 D5
Abernant Carmth 50 D2
Aber-nant Rhondd 52 F7
Abernethy P & K 186 C4
Abernyte P & K 186 D2
Aberporth Cerdgn 65 J4
Abersoch Gwynd 94 E6
Abersychan Torfn 53 K7
Aberthin V Glam 36 F5
Abertillery Blae G 53 K7
Abertridwr Caerph 37 H3
Abertridwr Powys 97 G8
Aberuthven P & K 185 K4
Aberystwyth Cerdgn 80 D6
Aberystwyth Crematorium Cerdgn 80 E6
Abingdon-on-Thames Oxon 41 J2
Abinger Common Surrey 31 J3
Abinger Hammer Surrey 31 H2
Abington Nhants 73 L3
Abington S Lans 165 H5
Abington Pigotts Cambs 75 K5
Abington Services S Lans 165 H4
Abingworth W Susx 18 F3
Ab Kettleby Leics 102 B7
Ablington Gloucs 56 C6
Abney Derbys 114 D5
Aboyne Abers 205 L5
Abram Wigan 112 E2
Abriachan Highld 212 E7
Abridge Essex 45 J2
Abronhill N Lans 175 K3
Abson S Glos 39 G5
Abthorpe Nhants 73 J5
Aby Lincs 118 F5
Acaster Malbis C York 124 E2
Acaster Selby N York 124 E3
Accrington Lancs 121 L5
Accrington Crematorium Lancs 121 L5
Acha Ag & B 188 F5
Achahoish Ag & B 172 D3
Achalader P & K 195 H7
Achaleven Ag & B 182 D1
Acha Mor W Isls 232 f3
Achanalt Highld 211 K3
Achandunie Highld 222 E6
Achany Highld 222 D2
Acharacle Highld 190 D3
Acharn Highld 190 E6
Acharn P & K 194 B7
Achavanich Highld 231 H6
Achduart Highld 224 C7
Achfary Highld 228 D7
A'Chill Highld 198 D4
Achiltibuie Highld 224 C6
Achina Highld 229 L4
Achinhoan Ag & B 161 J6
Achintee Highld 210 E6
Achintraid Highld 210 C6
Achmelvich Highld 224 C4
Achmore Highld 210 D7
Achmore W Isls 232 f3
Achnacarnin Highld 224 C3
Achnacarry Highld 201 J7
Achnacloich Highld 199 J4
Achnaconeran Highld 202 C2
Achnacroish Ag & B 191 G7
Achnadrish House Ag & B 189 L6
Achnafauld P & K 185 J1
Achnagarron Highld 222 F7
Achnaha Highld 189 L3
Achnahaird Highld 224 B5
Achnairn Highld 225 L6
Achnalea Highld 191 G4
Achnamara Ag & B 172 D2
Achnasheen Highld 211 J3
Achnashellach Lodge Highld 210 F5
Achnastank Moray 215 G7
Achosnich Highld 189 K3
Achranich Highld 190 E6
Achreamie Highld 230 E3
Achriabhach Highld 192 B3
Achriesgill Highld 228 C5
Achtoty Highld 229 K3
Achurch Nhants 88 E6
Achvaich Highld 222 F3
Achvarasdal Highld 230 E3
Ackergill Highld 231 L5
Acklam Middsb 141 L4
Acklam N York 134 B7
Ackleton Shrops 84 D4
Acklington Nthumb 159 G2
Ackton Wakefd 124 C6
Ackworth Moor Top Wakefd 124 C7
Acle Norfk 93 J2
Acock's Green Birm 85 K6
Acol Kent 35 J2
Acomb C York 124 E1
Acomb Nthumb 150 B2
Aconbury Herefs 54 D2
Acton Ches E 98 F2
Acton Gt Lon 44 D4
Acton Staffs 99 J4
Acton Suffk 77 K5
Acton Beauchamp Herefs 70 C4
Acton Bridge Ches W 112 E6
Acton Burnell Shrops 83 K3
Acton Green Herefs 70 C4
Acton Park Wrexhm 97 M3
Acton Round Shrops 84 B4
Acton Scott Shrops 83 J5
Acton Trussell Staffs 99 L8
Acton Turville S Glos 39 J4
Adbaston Staffs 99 H6
Adber Dorset 26 E7
Adbolton Notts 101 L5
Adderbury Oxon 72 F7
Adderley Shrops 98 F4
Addiewell W Loth 176 D5
Addingham C Brad 123 G1
Addington Bucks 58 C3
Addington Gt Lon 45 G7
Addington Kent 33 H2
Addiscombe Gt Lon 45 G6
Addlestone Surrey 43 H7
Addlethorpe Lincs 119 H7
Adeyfield Herts 59 H6
Adfa Powys 82 B4
Adforton Herefs 69 H1
Adisham Kent 35 G4
Adlestrop Gloucs 56 E3
Adlingfleet E R Yk 125 K6
Adlington Lancs 121 J7
Admaston Staffs 100 B7
Admaston Wrekin 84 B2
Adpar Cerdgn 65 J6
Adsborough Somset 25 L5
Adscombe Somset 25 J4
Adstock Bucks 58 C3
Adstone Nhants 73 H4
Adversane W Susx 31 H6
Advie Highld 214 D7
Adwick le Street Donc 124 E8
Adwick upon Dearne Donc 115 J2
Ae D & G 155 H4
Ae Bridgend D & G 155 H5
Afan Forest Park Neath 36 D2
Affleck Abers 216 B6
Affpuddle Dorset 14 F4
Affric Lodge Highld 201 J2
Afon-wen Flints 110 F6
Afton IoW 16 D5
Agecroft Crematorium Salfd 113 J2
Agglethorpe N York 131 K3
Aigburth Lpool 111 L4
Aike E R Yk 126 C2
Aiketgate Cumb 148 E5
Aikton Cumb 148 B4
Ailsworth C Pete 89 G4
Ainderby Quernhow N York 132 E4
Ainderby Steeple N York 132 E2
Aingers Green Essex 62 D4
Ainsdale Sefton 120 D7
Ainstable Cumb 148 F5
Ainsworth Bury 121 L8
Ainthorpe N York 142 E5
Aintree Sefton 111 L2
Ainville W Loth 176 F5
Aird Ag & B 181 M7
Aird D & G 144 D3
Aird W Isls 232 g2
Aird a Mhulaidh W Isls 232 e3
Aird Asaig W Isls 232 e4
Aird Dhubh Highld 209 L6
Airdeny Ag & B 182 E2
Aird of Kinloch Ag & B 181 H2
Aird of Sleat Highld 199 J5
Airdrie N Lans 175 K5
Airdriehill N Lans 175 K5
Airds of Kells D & G 154 B7
Aird Uig W Isls 232 d2
Airidh a bhruaich W Isls 232 e3
Airieland D & G 146 D4
Airlie Angus 195 L6
Airmyn E R Yk 125 H5
Airntully P & K 186 A1
Airor Highld 199 L4
Airth Falk 176 B2
Airton N York 131 G7
Aisby Lincs 103 G5
Aisby Lincs 116 E3
Aish Devon 7 G4
Aish Devon 7 J4
Aisholt Somset 25 J4
Aiskew N York 132 D2
Aislaby N York 134 B3
Aislaby N York 143 H5
Aislaby S on T 141 J5
Aisthorpe Lincs 116 F5
Aith Shet 235 c5
Akeld Nthumb 168 E4
Akeley Bucks 73 K6
Albaston Cnwll 6 B2
Alberbury Shrops 83 G1
Albourne W Susx 19 H3
Albrighton Shrops 84 E3
Albrighton Shrops 98 C8
Alburgh Norfk 92 F6
Albury Herts 60 C3
Albury Surrey 31 H2
Albury Heath Surrey 31 H3
Alcaig Highld 212 E3
Alcaston Shrops 83 J6
Alcester Warwks 71 K3
Alcester Lane End Birm 85 J7
Alciston E Susx 20 B5
Alcombe Somset 24 F3
Alconbury Cambs 89 H7
Alconbury Weston Cambs 89 H7
Aldborough N York 132 F6
Aldborough Norfk 106 E5
Aldbourne Wilts 40 E5
Aldbrough E R Yk 127 G3
Aldbrough St John N York 140 F5
Aldbury Herts 58 F5

Aldcliffe Lancs 129 K7
Aldclune P & K 194 E4
Aldeburgh Suffk 79 K3
Aldeby Norfk 93 J5
Aldenham Herts 43 J2
Alderbury Wilts 28 D6
Alderford Norfk 106 D8
Alderholt Dorset 28 C8
Alderley Gloucs 39 H3
Alderley Edge Ches E 113 J5
Aldermans Green Covtry 86 D6
Aldermaston W Berk 41 L7
Alderminster Warwks 72 B5
Aldershot Hants 30 E2
Alderton Gloucs 55 M2
Alderton Nhants 73 K5
Alderton Suffk 79 H6
Alderton Wilts 39 J4
Aldfield N York 132 D5
Aldford Ches W 98 B2
Aldgate Rutlnd 88 E3
Aldham Essex 61 L3
Aldham Suffk 78 C5
Aldingbourne W Susx 18 C5
Aldingham Cumb 129 G5
Aldington Kent 34 E7
Aldington Worcs 71 J5
Aldington Corner Kent 34 E7
Aldivalloch Moray 205 H1
Aldochlay Ag & B 174 C1
Aldreth Cambs 90 C8
Aldridge Wsall 85 J4
Aldringham Suffk 79 J3
Aldsworth Gloucs 56 D6
Aldunie Moray 215 H8
Aldwark Derbys 100 E2
Aldwark N York 133 G6
Aldwick W Susx 18 C6
Aldwincle Nhants 88 E6
Aldworth W Berk 41 K4
Alexandria W Duns 174 D3
Aley Somset 25 J4
Alfington Devon 12 E3
Alfold Surrey 31 H5
Alfold Crossways Surrey 31 H4
Alford Abers 206 B3
Alford Lincs 118 F6
Alford Somset 26 E5
Alford Crematorium Lincs 118 F6
Alfreton Derbys 101 H2
Alfrick Worcs 70 D4
Alfrick Pound Worcs 70 D4
Alfriston E Susx 20 B5
Algarkirk Lincs 103 M5
Alhampton Somset 26 F4
Alkborough N Linc 125 K6
Alkham Kent 35 H6
Alkmonton Derbys 100 D5
Allaleigh Devon 7 J5
Allanaquoich Abers 204 D6
Allanbank N Lans 175 L6
Allanton Border 179 H7
Allanton N Lans 175 L6
Allanton S Lans 175 K7
Allaston Gloucs 54 F6
Allbrook Hants 29 J7
All Cannings Wilts 40 B7
Allendale Nthumb 149 L4
Allen End Warwks 85 L4
Allenheads Nthumb 149 L6
Allen's Green Herts 60 D5
Allensmore Herefs 69 J7
Allenton C Derb 101 G6
Aller Devon 24 B6
Aller Somset 26 B5
Allerby Cumb 147 J6
Allercombe Devon 12 D4
Allerford Somset 24 D3
Allerston N York 134 D3
Allerthorpe E R Yk 125 J2
Allerton C Brad 123 G4
Allerton Highld 213 H2
Allerton Lpool 111 L4
Allerton Bywater Leeds 124 C5
Allerton Mauleverer N York 132 F7
Allesley Covtry 86 C7
Allestree C Derb 101 G5
Allexton Leics 88 B4
Allgreave Ches E 113 L7
Allhallows Medway 46 D4
Alligin Shuas Highld 210 C3
Allington Dorset 13 L4
Allington Lincs 102 E4
Allington Wilts 28 D4
Allington Wilts 39 K5
Allington Wilts 40 B7
Allithwaite Cumb 129 J4
Alloa Clacks 185 J8
Allonby Cumb 147 J6
Alloway S Ayrs 163 J5
Allowenshay Somset 26 B8
All Stretton Shrops 83 J4
Alltchaorunn Highld 192 C6
Alltwalis Carmth 66 B7
Alltwen Neath 51 K5
Alltyblaca Cerdgn 66 C5
Allweston Dorset 26 F8
Almeley Herefs 69 G4
Almington Staffs 99 G5
Almondbank P & K 185 M3
Almondbury Kirk 123 H7
Almondsbury S Glos 38 E4
Alne N York 133 G6
Alness Highld 222 E7
Alnham Nthumb 168 E7
Alnmouth Nthumb 169 J7
Alnwick Nthumb 169 J6
Alperton Gt Lon 44 D4
Alphamstone Essex 77 K7
Alpheton Suffk 77 K4
Alphington Devon 11 L6
Alport Derbys 114 E8
Alpraham Ches E 98 E1
Alresford Essex 62 C4
Alrewas Staffs 85 L1
Alsager Ches E 99 H2
Alsop en le Dale Derbys 100 D2
Alston Cumb 149 J5
Alston Devon 13 H2
Alstone Gloucs 55 M2
Alstonefield Staffs 100 C2
Alston Sutton Somset 26 B2
Alswear Devon 23 L6
Altandhu Highld 224 B6
Altarnun Cnwll 9 G8
Altass Highld 222 C2
Altcreich Ag & B 190 D8
Altgaltraig Ag & B 173 H4
Althorne Essex 61 L7
Althorpe N Linc 125 K8
Altnabreac Station Highld 230 E6
Altnaharra Highld 225 M2
Alton Derbys 115 G8
Alton Hants 30 B4
Alton Staffs 100 B4
Alton Barnes Wilts 40 C7
Alton Pancras Dorset 14 D3
Alton Priors Wilts 40 C7
Alton Towers Staffs 100 B4
Altrincham Traffd 113 H4
Altrincham Crematorium Traffd 113 G4
Altskeith Hotel Stirlg 184 B6
Alva Clacks 185 J7
Alvanley Ches W 112 D6
Alvaston C Derb 101 H5
Alvechurch Worcs 85 J8
Alvecote Warwks 86 B3
Alvediston Wilts 27 L6
Alveley Shrops 84 D6
Alverdiscott Devon 23 H6
Alverstoke Hants 17 H3
Alverstone IoW 17 H5
Alverthorpe Wakefd 123 L6
Alverton Notts 102 C4
Alves Moray 214 E3
Alvescot Oxon 56 F6
Alveston S Glos 38 F3
Alveston Warwks 72 B3
Alvingham Lincs 118 E4
Alvington Gloucs 54 E7
Alwalton C Pete 89 G4
Alwinton Nthumb 168 D7
Alwoodley Leeds 123 K3
Alyth P & K 195 K6
Ambergate Derbys 101 G3
Amberley Gloucs 55 J7
Amberley W Susx 18 D3
Amble Nthumb 159 G2
Amblecote Dudley 84 F6
Ambler Thorn C Brad 123 G5
Ambleside Cumb 137 K6
Ambleston Pembks 49 G3
Ambrosden Oxon 57 L4
Amcotts N Linc 125 K7
Amersham Bucks 42 F2
Amersham Common Bucks 42 F2
Amersham Old Town Bucks 42 F2
Amersham on the Hill Bucks 58 F7
Amerton Railway & Farm Staffs 99 M6
Amesbury Wilts 28 D3
Amhuinnsuidhe W Isls 232 d4
Amington Staffs 86 B3
Amisfield D & G 155 H5
Amlwch IoA 108 F3
Ammanford Carmth 51 J3
Amotherby N York 134 B5
Ampfield Hants 29 H6
Ampleforth N York 133 J4
Ampney Crucis Gloucs 56 B7
Ampney St Mary Gloucs 56 C7
Ampney St Peter Gloucs 56 B7
Amport Hants 28 F3
Ampthill C Beds 74 F6
Ampton Suffk 77 J1
Amroth Pembks 49 K6
Amulree P & K 185 J1
Amwell Herts 59 K5
Anaheilt Highld 191 G4
Ancaster Lincs 103 G4
Ancroft Nthumb 168 E1
Ancrum Border 167 K4
Anderby Lincs 119 G6
Andover Hants 29 G3
Andoversford Gloucs 56 A4
Andreas IoM 237 d2
Anerley Gt Lon 45 G6
Anfield Lpool 111 K3
Anfield Crematorium Lpool 111 K3
Angarrack Cnwll 3 G4
Angelbank Shrops 83 L7
Angle Pembks 48 E6
Anglesey IoA 108 E5
Anglesey Abbey Cambs 76 D3
Angmering W Susx 18 E5
Angram N York 124 D2
Ankerville Highld 223 H6
Anlaby E R Yk 126 C5
Anmer Norfk 105 H6
Anmore Hants 17 J1
Annan D & G 147 L2
Annandale Water Services D & G 155 J4
Annat Highld 210 D4
Annathill N Lans 175 J4
Anna Valley Hants 29 G3
Annbank S Ayrs 163 K5
Anne Hathaway's Cottage Warwks 71 L4
Annfield Plain Dur 150 F5
Anniesland C Glas 174 F5
Ansdell Lancs 120 D5
Ansford Somset 26 F5
Ansley Warwks 86 C5
Anslow Staffs 100 E7
Anslow Gate Staffs 100 D7
Anstey Herts 60 C2
Anstey Leics 87 G2
Anstruther Fife 187 J6
Ansty W Susx 19 J2
Ansty Warwks 86 E6
Ansty Wilts 27 L6
Anthorn Cumb 147 L4
Antingham Norfk 106 F5
An t-Ob W Isls 232 d5
Antonine Wall Falk 175 L3
Anton's Gowt Lincs 103 M3
Antony Cnwll 6 B5
Antrobus Ches W 112 F5
Anwick Lincs 103 J3
Anwoth D & G 145 M4
Aperfield Gt Lon 32 D2
Apethorpe Nhants 88 E4
Apley Lincs 117 J6
Apperknowle Derbys 115 G5
Apperley Gloucs 55 K3
Appin Ag & B 191 J6
Appleby N Linc 126 B7
Appleby-in-Westmorland Cumb 139 G3
Appleby Magna Leics 86 C2
Appleby Parva Leics 86 C2
Applecross Highld 209 L5
Appledore Devon 23 G5
Appledore Devon 25 G8
Appledore Kent 34 C8
Appleford Oxon 41 K2
Applegarth Town D & G 155 J5
Appleshaw Hants 28 F2
Appleton Halton 112 D4
Appleton Oxon 57 H7
Appleton Warrtn 112 F5
Appleton-le-Moors N York 133 L3
Appleton-le-Street N York 134 B5
Appleton Roebuck N York 124 E3
Appleton Thorn Warrtn 112 F5
Appleton Wiske N York 141 J6
Appletreehall Border 167 H6
Appletreewick N York 131 K7
Appley Somset 25 G6
Appley Bridge Lancs 121 G8
Apse Heath IoW 17 G5
Apsley End C Beds 59 J2
Apuldram W Susx 18 A5
Arabella Highld 223 H6
Arbirlot Angus 196 F7
Arboll Highld 223 J5
Arborfield Wokham 42 C6
Arborfield Cross Wokham 42 C6
Arbourthorne Sheff 115 G4
Arbroath Angus 197 G7
Arbuthnott Abers 197 K2
Archddu Carmth 50 F5
Archdeacon Newton Darltn 141 G4
Archencarroch W Duns 174 D3
Archiestown Moray 214 F5
Archirondel Jersey 236 e6
Arclid Green Ches E 99 H1
Ardallie Abers 217 J6
Ardanaiseig Hotel Ag & B 182 F3
Ardaneaskan Highld 210 C7
Ardarroch Highld 210 C6
Ardbeg Ag & B 160 D1
Ardbeg Ag & B 173 J5
Ardbeg Ag & B 173 K2
Ardcharnich Highld 220 F4
Ardchiavaig Ag & B 180 E4
Ardchonnel Ag & B 182 D5

Ardchullarie More Stirlg 184 D5
Arddarroch Ag & B 183 J7
Arddleen Powys 82 F1
Ardechive Highld 201 H7
Ardeer N Ayrs 163 H2
Ardeley Herts 60 A3
Ardelve Highld 210 D8
Arden Ag & B 174 C2
Ardens Grafton Warwks 71 K4
Ardentallen Ag & B 182 B3
Ardentinny Ag & B 173 L2
Ardentraive Ag & B 173 H4
Ardeonaig Stirlg 184 E1
Ardersier Highld 213 J4
Ardessie Highld 220 D4
Ardfern Ag & B 182 A6
Ardfernal Ag & B 171 K4
Ardgartan Ag & B 183 J6
Ardgay Highld 222 D4
Ardgour Highld 191 K4
Ardgowan Inver 173 L4
Ardhallow Ag & B 173 K4
Ardhasig W Isls 232 e4
Ardheslaig Highld 210 B3
Ardindrean Highld 220 F4
Ardingly W Susx 32 C7
Ardington Oxon 41 H3
Ardlamont Ag & B 173 G5
Ardleigh Essex 62 C3
Ardleigh Heath Essex 62 C2
Ardler P & K 195 L7
Ardley Oxon 57 K3
Ardlui Ag & B 183 K4
Ardlussa Ag & B 172 B2
Ardmair Highld 220 E2
Ardmaleish Ag & B 173 J5
Ardminish Ag & B 172 B8
Ardmolich Highld 190 E3
Ardmore Ag & B 174 C3
Ardmore Highld 222 F4
Ardnadam Ag & B 173 K3
Ardnagrask Highld 212 E4
Ardnamurchan Highld 190 B3
Ardnarff Highld 210 D7
Ardnastang Highld 190 F4
Ardpatrick Ag & B 172 C6
Ardrishaig Ag & B 172 E2
Ardross Highld 222 E6
Ardrossan N Ayrs 163 G2
Ardsley East Leeds 123 K5
Ardslignish Highld 190 B4
Ardtalla Ag & B 171 J7
Ardtoe Highld 190 C3
Arduaine Ag & B 182 A5
Ardullie Highld 212 E2
Ardvasar Highld 199 K5
Ardvorlich P & K 184 D3
Ardvourlie W Isls 232 e3
Ardwell D & G 144 D5
Ardwick Manch 113 J3
Areley Kings Worcs 70 E1
Arevegaig Highld 190 D3
Arford Hants 30 D4
Argoed Caerph 53 J7
Argyll Forest Park Ag & B 183 J6
Aribruach W Isls 232 e3
Aridhglas Ag & B 180 D3
Arileod Ag & B 188 F5
Arinagour Ag & B 189 G5
Ariogan Ag & B 182 C3
Arisaig Highld 199 K7
Arisaig House Highld 199 L7
Arkendale N York 132 F7
Arkesden Essex 76 C7
Arkholme Lancs 130 B5
Arkleton D & G 156 C4
Arkley Gt Lon 44 E2
Arksey Donc 115 L1
Arkwright Town Derbys 115 H7
Arle Gloucs 55 L4
Arlecdon Cumb 136 E4
Arlesey C Beds 75 H7
Arleston Wrekin 84 B2
Arley Ches E 112 F5
Arley Warwks 86 C5
Arlingham Gloucs 55 G6
Arlington Devon 23 K4
Arlington E Susx 20 B4
Armadale Highld 199 K5
Armadale Highld 230 A3
Armadale W Loth 176 C5
Armathwaite Cumb 148 E5
Arminghall Norfk 92 F3
Armitage Staffs 85 J1
Armley Leeds 123 K4
Armscote Warwks 72 B5
Armthorpe Donc 115 L1
Arnabost Ag & B 188 F4
Arncliffe N York 131 H5
Arncroach Fife 187 H6
Arndilly House Moray 215 G5
Arne Dorset 15 H5
Arnesby Leics 87 H5
Arngask P & K 186 B5
Arnisdale Highld 200 C3
Arnish Highld 209 J5
Arniston Mdloth 177 K6
Arnol W Isls 232 f1
Arnold E R Yk 126 E3
Arnold Notts 101 L4
Arnprior Stirlg 184 D7
Arnside Cumb 129 K4
Aros Ag & B 190 B7
Arrad Foot Cumb 129 G4
Arram E R Yk 126 C2
Arran N Ayrs 162 B3
Arrathorne N York 132 C2
Arreton IoW 17 G5
Arrina Highld 210 B3
Arrington Cambs 75 K4
Arrochar Ag & B 183 K6
Arrow Warwks 71 J3
Arscott Shrops 83 J2
Artafallie Highld 212 F4
Arthington Leeds 123 K2
Arthingworth Nhants 87 L7
Arthrath Abers 217 H6
Artrochie Abers 217 J7
Arundel W Susx 18 D4
Asby Cumb 136 E3
Ascog Ag & B 173 J5
Ascot W & M 42 F6
Ascott-under-Wychwood Oxon 56 F4
Asenby N York 132 F4
Asfordby Leics 102 B8
Asfordby Hill Leics 102 B8
Asgarby Lincs 103 J4
Ash Kent 35 H3
Ash Kent 45 L6
Ash Somset 26 C7
Ash Surrey 30 E2
Ashampstead W Berk 41 K5
Ashbocking Suffk 78 E4
Ashbourne Derbys 100 D3
Ashbrittle Somset 25 G6
Ashburton Devon 7 H2
Ashbury Devon 10 D5
Ashbury Oxon 40 E4
Ashby N Linc 125 L8
Ashby by Partney Lincs 118 F7
Ashby cum Fenby NE Lin 118 C2
Ashby de la Launde Lincs 103 H2
Ashby-de-la-Zouch Leics 86 D1
Ashby Folville Leics 87 K2
Ashby Magna Leics 87 H5
Ashby Parva Leics 87 G5
Ashby Puerorum Lincs 118 D7
Ashby St Ledgers Nhants 73 H2
Ashby St Mary Norfk 93 G3
Ashchurch Gloucs 55 L2
Ashcombe Devon 11 L8
Ashcombe N Som 37 M7
Ashcott Somset 26 C4
Ashdon Essex 76 E6
Ashdown Forest E Susx 32 E6
Ashe Hants 29 K2
Asheldham Essex 62 A7
Ashen Essex 77 H6
Ashendon Bucks 58 B5
Asheridge Bucks 58 F6
Ashfield Stirlg 185 G6
Ashfield cum Thorpe Suffk 78 E3
Ashfield Green Suffk 92 F8
Ashford Devon 7 G6
Ashford Devon 23 H4
Ashford Kent 34 D6
Ashford Surrey 43 H6
Ashford Bowdler Shrops 69 K1
Ashford Carbonell Shrops 69 K1
Ashford Hill Hants 41 K7
Ashford in the Water Derbys 114 D7
Ashgill S Lans 175 K7
Ash Green Surrey 30 E2
Ash Green Warwks 86 D6
Ashill Devon 12 E1
Ashill Norfk 91 K3
Ashill Somset 25 L7
Ashingdon Essex 46 E2
Ashington Nthumb 159 G5
Ashington Somset 26 E6
Ashington W Susx 18 F3
Ashkirk Border 167 G5
Ashleworth Gloucs 55 J3
Ashleworth Quay Gloucs 55 J3
Ashley Cambs 77 G3
Ashley Ches E 113 H5
Ashley Devon 10 F3
Ashley Gloucs 39 L2
Ashley Hants 16 B4
Ashley Hants 29 G5
Ashley Kent 35 J5
Ashley Nhants 87 L5
Ashley Staffs 99 H5
Ashley Wilts 39 J6
Ashley Green Bucks 58 F6
Ash Magna Shrops 98 E4
Ashmansworth Hants 41 H8
Ashmansworthy Devon 22 E7
Ash Mill Devon 24 C6
Ashmore Dorset 27 K7
Ashmore Green W Berk 41 J6
Ashorne Warwks 72 C3
Ashover Derbys 115 G8
Ashow Warwks 72 C1
Ashperton Herefs 70 B6
Ashprington Devon 7 J4
Ash Priors Somset 25 J5
Ashreigney Devon 10 F3
Ash Street Suffk 78 B5
Ashtead Surrey 44 D8
Ash Thomas Devon 12 C1
Ashton Ches W 112 D7
Ashton Cnwll 3 G5
Ashton Devon 11 K7
Ashton Herefs 69 K2
Ashton Inver 173 L3
Ashton Nhants 73 L5
Ashton Nhants 88 F5
Ashton Common Wilts 39 K8
Ashton-in-Makerfield Wigan 112 E2
Ashton Keynes Wilts 40 B2
Ashton under Hill Worcs 71 H6
Ashton-under-Lyne Tamesd 113 L2
Ashurst Hants 16 D1
Ashurst Kent 32 F5
Ashurst Lancs 121 G8
Ashurst W Susx 19 G3
Ashurstwood W Susx 32 D5
Ash Vale Surrey 30 E2
Ashwater Devon 9 K5
Ashwell Herts 75 J6
Ashwell Rutlnd 88 C2
Ashwell End Herts 75 J6
Ashwellthorpe Norfk 92 D4
Ashwick Somset 26 F2
Ashwicken Norfk 105 H8
Askam in Furness Cumb 128 F4
Askern Donc 124 E7
Askerswell Dorset 14 A4
Askett Bucks 58 D6
Askham Cumb 138 D3
Askham Notts 116 C6
Askham Bryan C York 124 E2
Askham Richard C York 124 E2
Asknish Ag & B 172 F1
Askrigg N York 131 H2
Askwith N York 123 H2
Aslackby Lincs 103 H6
Aslacton Norfk 92 D5
Aslockton Notts 102 C4
Aspatria Cumb 147 K6
Aspenden Herts 60 B3
Aspley Guise C Beds 74 D7
Aspley Heath C Beds 74 D7
Aspull Wigan 121 J8
Asselby E R Yk 125 H5
Assington Suffk 77 L6
Assington Green Suffk 77 H4
Astbury Ches E 99 J1
Astcote Nhants 73 J4
Asterby Lincs 118 C5
Asterley Shrops 83 H3
Asterton Shrops 83 H5
Asthall Oxon 56 F5
Asthall Leigh Oxon 56 F5
Astle Highld 223 G3
Astley Shrops 98 D8
Astley Warwks 86 C5
Astley Wigan 113 G2
Astley Worcs 70 D2
Astley Abbots Shrops 84 C4
Astley Bridge Bolton 121 K7
Astley Cross Worcs 70 E1
Aston Birm 85 J5
Aston Ches E 98 E3
Aston Ches W 112 E5
Aston Derbys 114 D5
Aston Flints 111 J7
Aston Herts 59 L4
Aston Oxon 57 G7
Aston Rothm 115 J4
Aston Shrops 84 E5
Aston Shrops 98 D6
Aston Staffs 99 H4
Aston Staffs 99 K7
Aston Wokham 42 C4
Aston Wrekin 84 B2
Aston Abbotts Bucks 58 D4
Aston Botterell Shrops 84 B6
Aston-by-Stone Staffs 99 K6
Aston Cantlow Warwks 71 K3
Aston Clinton Bucks 58 E5
Aston Crews Herefs 54 F4
Aston End Herts 59 L3
Aston Fields Worcs 71 G1
Aston Flamville Leics 86 F5
Aston Ingham Herefs 55 G4
Aston le Walls Nhants 72 F4
Aston Magna Gloucs 71 L7
Aston Munslow Shrops 83 K6
Aston on Clun Shrops 83 H6
Aston Pigott Shrops 83 G3
Aston Rogers Shrops 83 G3
Aston Rowant Oxon 58 B7
Aston Somerville Worcs 71 J6
Aston-sub-Edge Gloucs 71 K6

Aston Tirrold Oxon 41 K3
Aston-upon-Trent Derbys 101 H6
Aston Upthorpe Oxon 41 K3
Astwick C Beds 75 J6
Astwood M Keyn 74 D5
Astwood Worcs 71 G2
Astwood Bank Worcs 71 J3
Aswarby Lincs 103 H4
Aswardby Lincs 118 E7
Atcham Shrops 83 K2
Athelhampton Dorset 14 E4
Athelington Suffk 78 E1
Athelney Somset 25 M5
Athelstaneford E Loth 178 C3
Atherington Devon 23 J6
Atherstone Warwks 86 C4
Atherstone on Stour Warwks 72 B4
Atherton Wigan 113 G2
Atlow Derbys 100 E3
Attadale Highld 210 E6
Atterby Lincs 117 G3
Attercliffe Sheff 115 G4
Atterton Leics 86 D4
Attingham Park Shrops 83 K2
Attleborough Norfk 92 C4
Attleborough Warwks 86 D5
Attlebridge Norfk 92 D1
Attleton Green Suffk 77 G4
Atwick E R Yk 126 F1
Atworth Wilts 39 J7
Aubourn Lincs 116 F8
Auchbreck Moray 214 F8
Auchedly Abers 217 G7
Auchenblae Abers 197 H1
Auchenbowie Stirlg 175 L2
Auchencairn D & G 146 D5
Auchencairn D & G 155 G5
Auchencairn N Ayrs 162 D4
Auchencrow Border 179 H6
Auchendinny Mdloth 177 H6
Auchengray S Lans 176 D7
Auchenhalrig Moray 215 J3
Auchenheath S Lans 164 F2
Auchenhessnane D & G 154 E3
Auchenlochan Ag & B 173 G4
Auchenmade N Ayrs 174 C8
Auchenmalg D & G 144 F4
Auchentiber N Ayrs 174 C8
Auchindrain Ag & B 182 E6
Auchindrean Highld 221 G5
Auchininna Abers 216 C5
Auchinleck E Ayrs 164 B5
Auchinloch N Lans 175 H4
Auchinstarry N Lans 175 J3
Auchintore Highld 191 L2
Auchiries Abers 217 K6
Auchlean Highld 203 K5
Auchlee Abers 207 G6
Auchleven Abers 206 C1
Auchlochan S Lans 164 F3
Auchlossan Abers 206 B5
Auchlyne Stirlg 184 B2
Auchmillan E Ayrs 164 A4
Auchmithie Angus 197 G7
Auchmuirbridge Fife 186 C6
Auchnacree Angus 196 D4
Auchnagatt Abers 217 H6
Auchnarrow Moray 204 F2
Auchnotteroch D & G 144 B3
Auchroisk Moray 215 H4
Auchterarder P & K 185 K5
Auchteraw Highld 202 B4
Auchterblair Highld 203 L2
Auchtercairn Highld 219 J6
Auchterderran Fife 186 C7
Auchterhouse Angus 196 B8
Auchterless Abers 216 D6
Auchtermuchty Fife 186 D5
Auchterneed Highld 212 D3
Auchtertool Fife 177 H1
Auchtertyre Highld 210 C8
Auchtubh Stirlg 184 C4
Auckengill Highld 231 L3
Auckley Donc 115 M2
Audenshaw Tamesd 113 K3
Audlem Ches E 98 F4
Audley Staffs 99 J3
Audley End Essex 76 D6
Audley End House & Gardens Essex 76 D6
Audnam Dudley 84 F6
Aughton E R Yk 125 G3
Aughton Lancs 111 L1
Aughton Lancs 129 L6
Aughton Rothm 115 J4
Aughton Wilts 28 E1
Aughton Park Lancs 112 B1
Auldearn Highld 213 L4
Aulden Herefs 69 J4
Auldgirth D & G 154 F5
Auldhouse S Lans 175 H7
Ault a' chruinn Highld 200 E2
Aultbea Highld 219 K4
Aultgrishin Highld 219 H4
Aultguish Inn Highld 221 J7
Ault Hucknall Derbys 115 J7
Aultmore Moray 215 J4
Aultnagoire Highld 202 E2
Aultnamain Inn Highld 222 F5
Aunsby Lincs 103 H5
Aust S Glos 38 E3
Austerfield Donc 116 A3
Austrey Warwks 86 C3
Austwick N York 130 E5
Authorpe Lincs 118 E5
Avebury Wilts 40 C6
Avebury Wilts 40 C6
Aveley Thurr 45 L4
Avening Gloucs 39 K2
Averham Notts 102 C2
Aveton Gifford Devon 7 G6
Aviemore Highld 203 L3
Avington W Berk 41 G6
Avoch Highld 213 G4
Avon Hants 15 L3
Avonbridge Falk 176 B4
Avon Dassett Warwks 72 E4
Avonmouth Bristl 38 D5
Avonwick Devon 7 G4
Awbridge Hants 28 F6
Awliscombe Devon 12 E3
Awre Gloucs 55 G6
Awsworth Notts 101 J4
Axbridge Somset 26 B1
Axford Hants 29 L3
Axford Wilts 40 E6
Axminster Devon 13 H3
Axmouth Devon 13 G4
Aycliffe Dur 141 G3
Aydon Nthumb 150 C2
Aylburton Gloucs 54 E7
Aylesbeare Devon 12 D4
Aylesbury Bucks 58 D5
Aylesbury Crematorium Bucks 58 D5
Aylesby NE Lin 126 F8
Aylesford Kent 33 J2
Aylesham Kent 35 H4
Aylestone C Leic 87 H4
Aylestone Park C Leic 87 H4
Aylmerton Norfk 106 E5
Aylsham Norfk 106 E6
Aylton Herefs 70 B6
Aylworth Gloucs 56 C4
Aymestrey Herefs 69 H2
Aynho Nhants 57 K2
Ayot St Lawrence Herts 59 K5
Ayr S Ayrs 163 J5
Aysgarth N York 131 J2
Ayshford Devon 25 G7
Ayside Cumb 129 J3
Ayston Rutlnd 88 C4
Ayton Border 179 J6
Azerley N York 132 C5

B

Babbacombe Torbay 7 L3
Babbs Green Herts 60 C5
Babcary Somset 26 E5
Babraham Cambs 76 D4
Babworth Notts 116 B5
Backaland Ork 234 d4
Backfolds Abers 217 J4
Backford Ches W 111 L6
Backies Highld 223 H2
Back of Keppoch Highld 199 K7
Backwell N Som 38 C6
Baconsthorpe Norfk 106 D5
Bacton Herefs 54 A2
Bacton Norfk 107 H5
Bacton Suffk 78 C2
Bacup Lancs 122 C6
Badachro Highld 219 J6
Badbury Swindn 40 D4
Badby Nhants 73 H3
Badcall Highld 228 B7
Badcall Highld 228 C4
Badcaul Highld 220 D3
Baddeley Edge C Stke 99 K3
Baddeley Green C Stke 99 K3
Baddesley Clinton Warwks 86 B8
Baddesley Ensor Warwks 86 C4
Baddidarrach Highld 224 D4
Baddinsgill Border 176 F7
Badenscoth Abers 216 D6
Badentarbet Highld 224 B6
Badenyon Abers 205 H2
Badger Shrops 84 D4
Badgeworth Gloucs 55 K4
Badgworth Somset 26 B2
Badicaul Highld 210 B8
Badingham Suffk 79 G2
Badlesmere Kent 34 D4
Badlieu Border 165 K5
Badlipster Highld 231 J5
Badluarach Highld 220 C3
Badninish Highld 223 G3
Badrallach Highld 220 D3
Badsey Worcs 71 J5
Badshot Lea Surrey 30 E2
Badsworth Wakefd 124 C7
Badwell Ash Suffk 78 B2
Bagber Dorset 27 H8
Bagby N York 133 G4
Bag Enderby Lincs 118 E6
Bagendon Gloucs 56 A6
Bagh a Chaisteil W Isls 233 b9
Bagh a Tuath W Isls 233 b9
Bagillt Flints 111 H6
Baginton Warwks 86 D8
Baglan Neath 51 L6
Bagley Shrops 98 B6
Bagley Somset 26 C3
Bagnall Staffs 99 L3
Bagshot Surrey 42 E7
Bagstone S Glos 39 G3
Bagworth Leics 86 F2
Bagwy Llydiart Herefs 54 C3
Baildon C Brad 123 H3
Baildon Green C Brad 123 H3
Baile Ailein W Isls 232 f3
Baile a Mhanaich W Isls 233 b6
Baile Mòr Ag & B 180 D3
Baillieston C Glas 175 J5
Bainbridge N York 131 H2
Bainshole Abers 216 B7
Bainton C Pete 89 G3
Bainton E R Yk 126 B1
Baintown Fife 186 F6
Bairnkine Border 167 K6
Bakewell Derbys 114 E7
Bala Gwynd 96 E5
Balallan W Isls 232 f3
Balbeg Highld 212 C7
Balbeggie P & K 186 C2
Balblair Highld 212 D5
Balblair Highld 213 G2
Balby Donc 115 K2
Balcary D & G 146 E5
Balchraggan Highld 212 E5
Balchreick Highld 228 B4
Balcombe W Susx 32 B6
Balcomie Links Fife 187 K5
Baldersby N York 132 E4
Baldersby St James N York 132 E4
Balderstone Lancs 121 J4
Balderton Notts 102 D3
Baldinnie Fife 187 G5
Baldinnies P & K 185 L4
Baldock Herts 75 J7
Baldock Services Herts 75 J6
Baldovie C Dund 187 G2
Baldrine IoM 237 d5
Baldslow E Susx 20 F3
Bale Norfk 106 B5
Baledgarno P & K 186 D2
Balemartine Ag & B 188 C7
Balerno C Edin 177 G5
Balfarg Fife 186 D6
Balfield Angus 196 E3
Balfour Ork 234 c5
Balfron Stirlg 174 F1
Balgaveny Abers 216 C6
Balgonar Fife 185 L8
Balgowan D & G 144 D6
Balgowan Highld 202 F6
Balgown Highld 218 B7
Balgracie D & G 144 B3
Balgray S Lans 165 H5
Balham Gt Lon 44 F5
Balhary P & K 195 L6
Balholmie P & K 186 B1
Baligill Highld 230 C3
Balintore Angus 195 L5
Balintore Highld 223 J6
Balintraid Highld 223 G7
Balivanich W Isls 233 b6
Balkeerie Angus 196 B7
Balkholme E R Yk 125 J5
Ballachulish Highld 191 L5
Ballajora IoM 237 e4
Ballanlay Ag & B 173 H6
Ballantrae S Ayrs 152 C5
Ballasalla IoM 237 b6
Ballater Abers 205 J6
Ballaugh IoM 237 c3
Ballchraggan Highld 223 G6
Ballencrieff E Loth 178 B3
Ballevullin Ag & B 188 B6
Ball Green C Stke 99 K3
Ballidon Derbys 100 D2
Balliekine N Ayrs 161 L2
Balliemore Ag & B 182 F7
Balligmorrie S Ayrs 152 F4
Ballimore Stirlg 184 C4
Ballindalloch Moray 214 E6
Ballindean P & K 186 D2
Ballinger Common Bucks 58 E7
Ballingham Herefs 54 E2
Ballingry Fife 186 C7
Ballinluig P & K 194 F6
Ballinshoe Angus 196 C5
Ballintuim P & K 195 H5
Balloch Highld 213 H5
Balloch N Lans 175 K4
Balloch P & K 185 H4
Balloch S Ayrs 153 G3
Balloch W Duns 174 D3
Balls Cross W Susx 31 G6
Balls Green E Susx 32 E6
Ballygown Ag & B 189 K7
Ballygrant Ag & B 171 G5
Ballyhaugh Ag & B 188 F5
Balmaclellan D & G 154 B6
Balmae D & G 146 C6
Balmaha Stirlg 174 D1
Balmalcolm Fife 186 E5

Balmangan D & G 146 B5
Balmedie Abers 207 H2
Balmerino Fife 186 F3
Balmichael N Ayrs 162 B3
Balmore E Duns 175 G4
Balmuchy Highld 223 J5
Balmule Fife 177 G2
Balmullo Fife 187 G4
Balnacoil Lodge Highld 226 E6
Balnacra Highld 210 F5
Balnacroft Abers 205 G6
Balnafoich Highld 213 G7
Balnaguard P & K 194 E6
Balnahard Ag & B 180 F1
Balnahard Ag & B 180 F7
Balnain Highld 212 C7
Balnakeil Highld 228 F2
Balne N York 124 F6
Balquharn P & K 185 L1
Balquhidder Stirlg 184 C3
Balsall Common Solhll 86 B7
Balsall Heath Birm 85 J6
Balscote Oxon 72 E6
Balsham Cambs 76 E4
Baltasound Shet 235 e1
Baltersan D & G 145 J3
Baltonsborough Somset 26 D4
Balvicar Ag & B 181 M4
Balvraid Highld 200 C3
Balvraid Highld 213 K7
Bamber Bridge Lancs 121 H5
Bamber's Green Essex 60 F4
Bamburgh Nthumb 169 H3
Bamburgh Castle Nthumb 169 H3
Bamford Derbys 114 E5
Bampton Cumb 138 D4
Bampton Devon 24 E6
Bampton Oxon 56 F7
Bampton Grange Cumb 138 D4
Banavie Highld 191 L2
Banbury Oxon 72 F6
Banbury Crematorium Oxon 72 F6
Bancffosfelen Carmth 50 F3
Banchory Abers 206 D6
Banchory-Devenick Abers 207 G5
Bancycapel Carmth 50 E3
Bancyfelin Carmth 50 D2
Bandirran P & K 186 C2
Banff Abers 216 D2
Bangor Gwynd 109 H6
Bangor Crematorium Gwynd 109 H6
Bangor-on-Dee Wrexhm 98 B4
Bangors Cnwll 9 G5
Banham Norfk 92 C6
Bank Hants 16 C2
Bankend D & G 147 H2
Bankfoot P & K 185 M1
Bankglen E Ayrs 164 C6
Bankhead C Aber 207 G4
Bankhead S Lans 165 J1
Banknock Falk 175 K3
Banks Lancs 120 E6
Bankshill D & G 155 L5
Banningham Norfk 106 F6
Bannister Green Essex 61 H4
Bannockburn Stirlg 175 L1
Banstead Surrey 44 E7
Bantham Devon 6 F6
Banton N Lans 175 K3
Banwell N Som 38 B8
Bapchild Kent 34 C3
Bapton Wilts 27 M4
Barabhas W Isls 232 f1
Barassie S Ayrs 163 J3
Barbaraville Highld 223 G6
Barbieston S Ayrs 163 K5
Barbon Cumb 130 C3
Barbrook Devon 23 L2
Barby Nhants 73 G1
Barcaldine Ag & B 191 J7
Barcombe E Susx 19 L3
Barcombe Cross E Susx 19 L3
Barden Park Kent 33 G4
Bardfield End Green Essex 61 G2
Bardfield Saling Essex 61 G3
Bardney Lincs 117 J7
Bardon Leics 86 F2
Bardon Mill Nthumb 149 K3
Bardowie E Duns 175 G4
Bardrainney Inver 174 C4
Bardsea Cumb 129 G5
Bardsey Leeds 124 B2
Bardsey Island Gwynd 94 B7
Bardwell Suffk 91 L8
Bare Lancs 129 K6
Barfad D & G 145 G2
Barford Norfk 92 D3
Barford Warwks 72 C3
Barford St John Oxon 57 H2
Barford St Martin Wilts 28 B5
Barford St Michael Oxon 57 H2
Barfrestone Kent 35 H5
Bargeddie N Lans 175 J5
Bargoed Caerph 53 J7
Bargrennan D & G 153 H6
Barham Cambs 89 G7
Barham Kent 35 G5
Barham Suffk 78 D4
Barham Crematorium Kent 35 G5
Bar Hill Cambs 75 L2
Barholm Lincs 88 F2
Barkby Leics 87 J2
Barkby Thorpe Leics 87 J2
Barkestone-le-Vale Leics 102 C5
Barkham Wokham 42 C6
Barking Gt Lon 45 H3
Barking Suffk 78 C4
Barkingside Gt Lon 45 H3
Barking Tye Suffk 78 C4
Barkisland Calder 122 F6
Barkla Shop Cnwll 3 J2
Barkston Lincs 102 F4
Barkston Ash N York 124 D4
Barkway Herts 75 L7
Barlanark C Glas 175 H5
Barlaston Staffs 99 K5
Barlavington W Susx 18 C3
Barlborough Derbys 115 J6
Barlby N York 124 F4
Barlestone Leics 86 E3
Barley Herts 76 B6
Barley Lancs 122 B3
Barleythorpe Rutlnd 88 B2
Barling Essex 46 F3
Barlings Lincs 117 H6
Barlochan D & G 146 E4
Barlow Derbys 115 G6
Barlow Gatesd 150 E3
Barlow N York 124 F5
Barmby Moor E R Yk 125 J2
Barmby on the Marsh E R Yk 125 G5
Barmollack Ag & B 161 K1
Barmouth Gwynd 80 E1
Barmpton Darltn 141 H4
Barmston E R Yk 135 J7
Barnacarry Ag & B 182 E8
Barnack C Pete 88 F3
Barnard Castle Dur 140 D4
Barnard Gate Oxon 57 H6
Barnardiston Suffk 77 G5
Barnbarroch D & G 146 E4
Barnburgh Donc 115 J2
Barnby Suffk 93 K5
Barnby Dun Donc 124 F8
Barnby in the Willows Notts 102 E3
Barnby Moor Notts 116 A5
Barncorkrie D & G 144 D7
Barnes Gt Lon 44 E5
Barnes Street Kent 33 H4
Barnet Gt Lon 44 E2
Barnetby le Wold N Linc 126 C8
Barney Norfk 106 B6
Barnham Suffk 91 K7
Barnham W Susx 18 C5
Barnham Broom Norfk 92 C3
Barnhead Angus 197 G5
Barnhill C Dund 187 H2
Barnhill Moray 214 E3
Barnhills D & G 152 B7
Barningham Dur 140 D5
Barningham Suffk 91 L7
Barnoldby le Beck NE Lin 118 C2
Barnoldswick Lancs 122 C2
Barns Green W Susx 31 J6
Barnsley Barns 115 G1
Barnsley Gloucs 56 B6
Barnsley Crematorium Barns 115 G1
Barnstaple Devon 23 J5
Barnston Essex 61 G4
Barnston Wirral 111 J5
Barnstone Notts 102 B5
Barnt Green Worcs 85 H8
Barnton C Edin 177 G4
Barnton Ches W 112 F6
Barnwell All Saints Nhants 88 F6
Barnwell St Andrew Nhants 88 F6
Barnwood Gloucs 55 K4
Barr S Ayrs 153 G4
Barra W Isls 233 b9
Barra Airport W Isls 233 b9
Barrachan D & G 145 H5
Barraigh W Isls 233 b9
Barrapoll Ag & B 188 B7
Barrasford Nthumb 158 A7
Barrhead E Rens 174 F6
Barrhill S Ayrs 152 F5
Barrington Cambs 76 B5
Barrington Somset 26 B7
Barripper Cnwll 3 H4
Barrmill N Ayrs 174 C7
Barrock Highld 231 J2
Barrow Gloucs 55 K3
Barrow Lancs 121 L3
Barrow Rutlnd 88 C1
Barrow Somset 27 G5
Barrow Suffk 77 H2
Barrowby Lincs 102 E5
Barrowden Rutlnd 88 D4
Barrowford Lancs 122 C3
Barrow Gurney N Som 38 D6
Barrow Haven N Linc 126 D6
Barrow-in-Furness Cumb 128 E5
Barrow Island Cumb 128 E5
Barrow-upon-Humber N Linc 126 D6
Barrow upon Soar Leics 101 L8
Barrow upon Trent Derbys 101 G6
Barry Angus 187 J1
Barry V Glam 37 H6
Barry Island V Glam 37 H6
Barsby Leics 87 K2
Barsham Suffk 93 H5
Barston Solhll 86 B7
Bartestree Herefs 69 L6
Barthol Chapel Abers 216 F7
Bartholomew Green Essex 61 H4
Barthomley Ches E 99 H3
Bartley Hants 28 F8
Bartley Green Birm 85 H6
Bartlow Cambs 76 E5
Barton Cambs 76 B4
Barton Ches W 98 C2
Barton Gloucs 56 C3
Barton Lancs 120 E8
Barton Lancs 121 G3
Barton N York 141 G5
Barton Oxon 57 K6
Barton Torbay 7 K3
Barton Bendish Norfk 91 G3
Barton End Gloucs 39 J2
Barton Hartshorn Bucks 57 M2
Barton in Fabis Notts 101 K6
Barton in the Beans Leics 86 E3
Barton-le-Clay C Beds 59 H2
Barton-le-Street N York 133 L5
Barton-le-Willows N York 133 L6
Barton Mills Suffk 91 G8
Barton-on-Sea Hants 16 B4
Barton-on-the-Heath Warwks 56 E2
Barton St David Somset 26 D5
Barton Seagrave Nhants 88 C7
Barton Stacey Hants 29 H3
Barton Town Devon 23 L4
Barton Turf Norfk 107 H7
Barton-under-Needwood Staffs 100 D8
Barton-upon-Humber N Linc 126 C6
Barton Waterside N Linc 126 C6
Barvas W Isls 232 f1
Barway Cambs 90 D7
Barwell Leics 86 F4
Barwick Devon 10 E4
Barwick Somset 26 E8
Barwick in Elmet Leeds 124 B3
Baschurch Shrops 98 B7
Bascote Warwks 72 E2
Bashall Eaves Lancs 121 K2
Basildon Essex 46 B3
Basildon & District Crematorium Essex 46 C3
Basingstoke Hants 29 M2
Basingstoke Crematorium Hants 29 K3
Baslow Derbys 114 E6
Bason Bridge Somset 25 M3
Bassaleg Newpt 37 L3
Bassendean Border 167 K1
Bassenthwaite Cumb 137 H2
Bassett C Sotn 29 H7
Bassingbourn-cum-Kneesworth Cambs 75 L5
Bassingham Lincs 102 E1
Bassingthorpe Lincs 102 F6
Bassus Green Herts 60 A3
Baston Lincs 89 G2
Bastwick Norfk 107 J8
Batchworth Herts 43 H2
Batcombe Dorset 14 C2
Batcombe Somset 27 G4
Batford Herts 59 J5
Bath BaNES 39 H7
Bathampton BaNES 39 H7
Bath, City of BaNES 39 H7
Bathealton Somset 25 G6
Batheaston BaNES 39 H6
Bathford BaNES 39 H6
Bathgate W Loth 176 D5
Bathley Notts 102 C2
Bathpool Cnwll 5 L2
Bathpool Somset 25 K6
Bath Side Essex 62 F2
Bathville W Loth 176 C5

Bathway Somset 26 E2
Batley Kirk 123 J5
Batsford Gloucs 71 L7
Battersby N York 142 D5
Battersea Gt Lon 44 F5
Battisford Tye Suffk 78 B4
Battle E Susx 20 F3
Battle Powys 52 F2
Battledykes Angus 196 D5
Battlesbridge Essex 46 C2
Battleton Somset 24 E6
Baughton Worcs 70 F6
Baughurst Hants 41 L7
Baulds Abers 206 B6
Baulking Oxon 40 F3
Baumber Lincs 117 L6
Baunton Gloucs 56 A6
Baverstock Wilts 28 B5
Bawburgh Norfk 92 D2
Bawdeswell Norfk 106 C7
Bawdrip Somset 25 M4
Bawdsey Suffk 79 H6
Bawtry Donc 115 M3
Baxenden Lancs 122 B5
Baxterley Warwks 86 C4
Bay Highld 208 D4
Bayble W Isls 232 g2
Baybridge Hants 29 K6
Baycliff Cumb 129 G5
Baydon Wilts 40 F5
Bayford Herts 60 A6
Bayford Somset 27 G5
Bayhead W Isls 233 b6
Baylham Suffk 78 D4
Baysham Herefs 54 E3
Bayston Hill Shrops 83 J2
Baythorne End Essex 77 G6
Bayton Worcs 84 C8
Bayworth Oxon 57 J7
Beachampton Bucks 73 L6
Beachamwell Norfk 91 H3
Beachy Head E Susx 20 C6
Beacon Devon 12 F2
Beacon End Essex 62 A3
Beacon Hill Notts 102 D2
Beacon Hill Surrey 30 E4
Beacon's Bottom Bucks 42 C2
Beaconsfield Bucks 42 F3
Beaconsfield Services Bucks 42 F3
Beadlam N York 133 K3
Beadlow C Beds 75 G6
Beadnell Nthumb 169 J4
Beaford Devon 10 E2
Beal N York 124 E5
Beal Nthumb 169 G2
Bealsmill Cnwll 6 A1
Beaminster Dorset 13 L3
Beamish Dur 150 F4
Beamish Museum Dur 150 F4
Beamsley N York 131 K8
Beanacre Wilts 39 K7
Beanley Nthumb 169 G5
Beardon Devon 10 D7
Beare Green Surrey 31 K3
Bearley Warwks 71 L3
Bearpark Dur 151 G6
Bearsden E Duns 174 F4
Bearsted Kent 33 K3
Bearstone Shrops 99 G5
Bearwood Birm 85 H6
Bearwood Herefs 69 H4
Bearwood Poole 15 K3
Beattock D & G 155 J2
Beauchamp Roding Essex 60 F6
Beaufort Blae G 53 J5
Beaulieu Hants 16 E3
Beauly Highld 212 E5
Beaumaris IoA 109 H6
Beaumaris Castle IoA 109 J6
Beaumont Cumb 148 C3
Beaumont Essex 62 E3
Beaumont Jersey 236 c7
Beausale Warwks 72 B1
Beauworth Hants 29 L6
Beaworthy Devon 10 C5
Beazley End Essex 61 H3
Bebington Wirral 111 K5
Beccles Suffk 93 J5
Becconsall Lancs 120 F6
Beckbury Shrops 84 D3
Beckenham Gt Lon 45 G6
Beckenham Crematorium Gt Lon 45 G6
Beckermet Cumb 136 E6
Beckfoot Cumb 147 J5
Beckford Worcs 71 H7
Beckhampton Wilts 40 C6
Beckingham Lincs 102 E2
Beckingham Notts 116 C4
Beckington Somset 27 J2
Beckjay Shrops 83 H7
Beckley E Susx 21 G2
Beckley Oxon 57 K5
Beck Row Suffk 91 G7
Beck Side Cumb 128 F3
Beckton Gt Lon 45 H4
Beckwithshaw N York 132 D8
Becontree Gt Lon 45 J3
Becquet Vincent Jersey 236 c6
Bedale N York 132 D2
Bedchester Dorset 27 J7
Beddau Rhondd 37 G4
Beddgelert Gwynd 95 K3
Beddingham E Susx 19 L4
Beddington Gt Lon 44 F6
Beddington Corner Gt Lon 44 F6
Bedfield Suffk 78 F2
Bedford Bed 74 F5
Bedford Crematorium Bed 75 G4
Bedhampton Hants 17 K2
Bedingfield Suffk 78 E2
Bedlam N York 132 D7
Bedlington Nthumb 159 G5
Bedlinog Myr Td 53 H7
Bedminster Bristl 38 E6
Bedminster Down Bristl 38 E6
Bedmond Herts 59 J7
Bednall Staffs 99 L8
Bedrule Border 167 J5
Bedstone Shrops 83 G7
Bedwas Caerph 37 J3
Bedwellty Caerph 53 J7
Bedworth Warwks 86 D6
Beeby Leics 87 J2
Beech Hants 30 B4
Beech Staffs 99 J5
Beech Hill W Berk 42 B7
Beechingstoke Wilts 40 C8
Beedon W Berk 41 J5
Beeford E R Yk 135 H8
Beeley Derbys 114 E7
Beelsby NE Lin 117 K2
Beenham W Berk 41 L6
Beer Devon 13 G5
Beer Somset 26 B5
Beercrocombe Somset 25 L7
Beer Hackett Dorset 14 B1
Beesands Devon 7 J7
Beesby Lincs 118 F5
Beeson Devon 7 J7
Beeston C Beds 75 H5
Beeston Ches W 98 D2
Beeston Leeds 123 K4
Beeston Norfk 91 K1
Beeston Notts 101 K5
Beeston Regis Norfk 106 E4
Beeswing D & G 146 F2
Beetham Cumb 129 K4
Beetham Somset 25 L8
Beetley Norfk 106 A8
Begbroke Oxon 57 J5
Begelly Pembks 49 J6
Beguildy Powys 82 D7
Beighton Norfk 93 H2
Beighton Sheff 115 H5
Beinn Na Faoghla W Isls 233 c7
Beith N Ayrs 174 C7
Bekesbourne Kent 35 G4
Belaugh Norfk 107 G8
Belbroughton Worcs 85 G7
Belchalwell Dorset 14 E1
Belchamp Otten Essex 77 J6
Belchamp St Paul Essex 77 H6
Belchamp Walter Essex 77 J6
Belchford Lincs 118 D6
Belford Nthumb 169 G3
Belgrave C Leic 87 H3
Belhaven E Loth 178 E3
Belhelvie Abers 207 H2
Belhinnie Abers 215 K8
Bellabeg Abers 205 H3
Bellanoch Ag & B 182 A8
Bellaty Angus 195 K4
Bell Busk N York 131 G7
Belleau Lincs 118 E5
Bell End Worcs 85 G7
Bellerby N York 131 L2
Belle Vue Cumb 148 C4
Belle Vue Wakefd 123 L6
Bellfield S Lans 164 F3
Bellfield S Lans 165 J5
Bellingdon Bucks 58 F6
Bellingham Nthumb 157 L5
Belloch Ag & B 161 H2
Bellochantuy Ag & B 161 H3
Bell o' th' Hill Ches W 98 D4
Bellshill N Lans 175 J6
Bellside N Lans 175 L6
Bellsquarry W Loth 176 E5
Bells Yew Green E Susx 33 G6
Belluton BaNES 38 E7
Belmaduthy Highld 213 G3
Belmont Bl w D 121 K7
Belmont Gt Lon 44 E7
Belmont S Ayrs 163 J5
Belmont Shet 235 d2
Belnacraig Abers 205 J3
Belper Derbys 101 G3
Belsay Nthumb 158 D6
Belses Border 167 J4
Belsford Devon 7 H4
Belsize Herts 59 G7
Belstead Suffk 78 D6
Belstone Devon 10 F6
Belthorn Lancs 121 L5
Beltinge Kent 47 K6
Beltingham Nthumb 149 K3
Beltoft N Linc 116 D1
Belton Leics 101 H7
Belton Lincs 102 F4
Belton N Linc 116 C1
Belton Norfk 93 K3
Belton Rutlnd 88 B3
Belton House Lincs 102 F5
Belvedere Gt Lon 45 J4
Belvoir Leics 102 D5
Bembridge IoW 17 J5
Bemerton Wilts 28 C5
Bempton E R Yk 135 J5
Benacre Suffk 93 K6
Benbecula W Isls 233 c7
Benbecula Airport W Isls 233 c6
Benbuie D & G 154 C3
Benderloch Ag & B 191 H8
Benenden Kent 33 K6
Benfieldside Dur 150 D4
Bengeo Herts 60 A5
Bengeworth Worcs 71 J5
Benhall Green Suffk 79 H3
Benhall Street Suffk 79 H3
Benholm Abers 197 K3
Beningbrough N York 133 H7
Benington Herts 59 M4
Benington Lincs 104 C3
Benllech IoA 109 G5
Benmore Ag & B 173 K2
Bennan N Ayrs 162 C5
Ben Nevis Highld 192 B3
Benniworth Lincs 117 K5
Benover Kent 33 J4
Ben Rhydding C Brad 123 H2
Benslie N Ayrs 163 J2
Benson Oxon 41 L3
Benthoul C Aber 206 F5
Bentley Donc 115 K1
Bentley E R Yk 126 C4
Bentley Hants 30 C3
Bentley Suffk 78 D6
Bentley Warwks 86 C4
Bentley Crematorium Essex 45 L2
Bentpath D & G 156 B4
Bentwichen Devon 24 B5
Bentworth Hants 30 A4
Benvie Angus 186 E2
Benville Dorset 14 A2
Benwick Cambs 89 L5
Beoley Worcs 71 J1
Beoraidbeg Highld 199 L6
Bepton W Susx 18 B3
Berden Essex 60 D3
Berea Pembks 48 D2
Bere Alston Devon 6 C3
Bere Ferrers Devon 6 C3
Bere Regis Dorset 14 F4
Bergh Apton Norfk 93 G4
Berinsfield Oxon 41 L2
Berkeley Gloucs 55 G7
Berkhamsted Herts 59 G6
Berkley Somset 27 J2
Berkswell Solhll 86 B7
Bermondsey Gt Lon 45 G4
Bernera Highld 200 C2
Bernisdale Highld 208 F4
Berrick Prior Oxon 41 L2
Berrick Salome Oxon 41 L2
Berriedale Highld 227 K4
Berrier Cumb 137 L2
Berriew Powys 82 D4
Berrington Shrops 83 K3
Berrington Worcs 69 L2
Berrington Green Worcs 69 L2
Berrow Somset 25 L2
Berrow Green Worcs 70 D3
Berryhillock Moray 215 L3
Berryhillock Moray 215 L4
Berrynarbor Devon 23 J3
Berry Pomeroy Devon 7 J4
Bersham Wrexhm 97 L3
Berwick E Susx 20 B5
Berwick Bassett Wilts 40 C5
Berwick Hill Nthumb 158 F6
Berwick St James Wilts 28 B4
Berwick St John Wilts 27 L6
Berwick St Leonard Wilts 27 L5
Berwick-upon-Tweed Nthumb 179 K7
Bescar Lancs 120 E7
Besford Worcs 71 G5
Bessacarr Donc 115 L2
Bessingby E R Yk 135 J6
Bessingham Norfk 106 E5
Besthorpe Norfk 92 C4
Besthorpe Notts 116 D8
Bestwood Village Notts 101 K3
Beswick E R Yk 126 C2
Betchworth Surrey 31 K2
Bethel Gwynd 109 G7
Bethel IoA 108 E7
Bethersden Kent 34 C6
Bethesda Gwynd 109 J7
Bethesda Pembks 49 J4
Bethlehem Carmth 51 K1
Bethnal Green Gt Lon 45 G4
Betley Staffs 99 H3
Betsham Kent 45 L5

Betteshanger Kent 35 J4
Bettiscombe Dorset 13 K3
Bettisfield Wrexhm 98 C5
Bettws Newpt 37 L3
Bettws Cedewain Powys 82 C4
Bettws Evan Cerdgn 65 J5
Bettws-Newydd Mons 54 A6
Bettyhill Highld 229 L3
Betws Brdgnd 36 D3
Betws Bledrws Cerdgn 66 D4
Betws Gwerfil Goch Denbgs 97 G3
Betws-y-Coed Conwy 96 C2
Betws-yn-Rhos Conwy 110 C6
Beulah Cerdgn 65 J5
Beulah Powys 67 K4
Bevercotes Notts 116 B6
Beverley E R Yk 126 C3
Beverston Gloucs 39 K2
Bewcastle Cumb 156 F7
Bewdley Worcs 84 D7
Bewerley N York 132 B6
Bewholme E R Yk 126 E1
Bexhill E Susx 20 E4
Bexley Gt Lon 45 J5
Bexleyheath Gt Lon 45 J5
Bexwell Norfk 90 F3
Beyton Suffk 77 L2
Beyton Green Suffk 77 L2
Bhaltos W Isls 232 d2
Bhatarsaigh W Isls 233 b10
Bibury Gloucs 56 C6
Bicester Oxon 57 L4
Bickenhill Solhll 85 L6
Bicker Lincs 103 L5
Bickerstaffe Lancs 112 C2
Bickerton N York 124 C1
Bickford Staffs 84 F2
Bickington Devon 7 J2
Bickington Devon 23 H5
Bickleigh Devon 6 D4
Bickleigh Devon 12 B2
Bickley Ches W 98 D3
Bickley Gt Lon 45 H6
Bickley N York 134 E2
Bicknacre Essex 61 J7
Bicknoller Somset 25 H4
Bicknor Kent 33 L2
Bicton Shrops 82 F6
Bicton Shrops 83 J1
Bidborough Kent 32 F5
Biddenden Kent 33 L5
Biddenham Bed 74 E4
Biddestone Wilts 39 K5
Biddisham Somset 26 B2
Biddlesden Bucks 73 J6
Biddulph Staffs 99 K2
Biddulph Moor Staffs 99 K2
Bideford Devon 23 G6
Bidford-on-Avon Warwks 71 K4
Bielby E R Yk 125 J2
Bieldside C Aber 207 G5
Bierley IoW 17 G6
Bierton Bucks 58 D5
Big Balcraig D & G 145 H6
Bigbury Devon 6 F6
Bigbury-on-Sea Devon 6 F6
Bigby Lincs 117 H1
Big Carlae D & G 154 B3
Biggar S Lans 165 K2
Biggin Derbys 100 D2
Biggin Hill Gt Lon 32 D2
Biggin Hill Airport Gt Lon 45 H7
Biggleswade C Beds 75 H5
Bigholms D & G 156 B6
Bighouse Highld 230 C3
Bighton Hants 29 L4
Biglands Cumb 148 A4
Bignor W Susx 18 D3
Bigrigg Cumb 136 D5
Big Sand Highld 219 H5
Bigton Shet 235 c7
Bilborough C Nott 101 K4
Bilbrook Somset 25 G3
Bilbrough N York 124 E2
Bilbster Highld 231 K5
Bildershaw Dur 140 F3
Bildeston Suffk 78 B5
Billericay Essex 46 B2
Billesdon Leics 87 K3
Billesley Warwks 71 K3
Billingborough Lincs 103 J5
Billinge St Hel 112 D2
Billingford Norfk 92 E7
Billingford Norfk 106 B7
Billingham S on T 141 K3
Billinghay Lincs 103 J2
Billingley Barns 115 H1
Billingshurst W Susx 31 H6
Billingsley Shrops 84 C6
Billington C Beds 58 F4
Billington Lancs 121 L4
Billockby Norfk 93 J2
Billy Row Dur 150 E7
Bilsborrow Lancs 121 G3
Bilsby Lincs 119 G6
Bilsham W Susx 18 D5
Bilsington Kent 34 D7
Bilsthorpe Notts 101 M1
Bilston Mdloth 177 H5
Bilston Wolves 85 G4
Bilstone Leics 86 D3
Bilton E R Yk 126 E4
Bilton N York 124 D1
Bilton N York 132 D7
Bilton Warwks 86 F8
Binbrook Lincs 117 K3
Bincombe Dorset 14 D5
Binegar Somset 26 E2
Binfield Br For 42 D6
Binfield Heath Oxon 42 C5
Bingfield Nthumb 158 B7
Bingham Notts 102 B4
Bingley C Brad 123 G3
Binham Norfk 106 B5
Binley Covtry 86 E7
Binley Hants 29 H2
Binley Woods Warwks 86 E7
Binnegar Dorset 15 G5
Binniehill Falk 176 B4
Binscombe Surrey 30 F3
Binstead IoW 17 H4
Binsted Hants 30 C3
Binsted W Susx 18 D4
Binton Warwks 71 K4
Bintree Norfk 106 B7
Birch Essex 61 M4
Bircham Newton Norfk 105 J5
Bircham Tofts Norfk 105 J6
Birchanger Essex 60 E4
Birchanger Green Services Essex 60 E4
Birch Cross Staffs 100 C6
Bircher Herefs 69 J2
Birchfield Birm 85 J5
Birch Green Essex 61 M4
Birchgrove Cardif 37 J4
Birchgrove Swans 51 K5
Birchgrove W Susx 32 D7
Birchington Kent 35 J2
Birchley Heath Warwks 86 C5
Birchover Derbys 100 E1
Birch Services Rochdl 122 C8
Birch Vale Derbys 114 A4
Birchwood Lincs 116 F7
Birch Wood Somset 25 K8
Birchwood Warrtn 112 F4
Bircotes Notts 115 M3
Birdbrook Essex 77 G6
Birdforth N York 133 G4
Birdham W Susx 17 M3
Birdingbury Warwks 72 E2
Birdlip Gloucs 55 L5
Birdsall N York 134 C6
Birds Edge Kirk 123 J8
Birds Green Essex 60 F6
Birdsgreen Shrops 84 D6
Birdsmoorgate Dorset 13 K3
Birdwell Barns 115 G2
Birgham Border 168 B2
Birichin Highld 223 G3
Birkby N York 141 H6
Birkdale Sefton 120 D7
Birkenbog Abers 215 L2
Birkenhead Wirral 111 K4
Birkenhills Abers 216 E5
Birkenshaw Kirk 123 J5
Birkhall Abers 205 H6
Birkhill Angus 186 F1
Birkhill D & G 166 B6
Birkin N York 124 E5
Birley Herefs 69 J4
Birley Carr Sheff 115 G3
Birling Kent 46 B7
Birlingham Worcs 71 G5
Birmingham Birm 85 J6
Birmingham Airport Solhll 85 L6
Birnam P & K 195 G7
Birness Abers 217 J7
Birse Abers 206 B6
Birsemore Abers 205 L5
Birstall Kirk 123 J5
Birstall Leics 87 H2
Birstwith N York 132 C7
Birtley Gatesd 151 G4
Birtley Herefs 69 G2
Birtley Nthumb 157 L6
Birtley Crematorium Gatesd 151 G4
Birts Street Worcs 70 D7
Bisbrooke Rutlnd 88 C4
Biscathorpe Lincs 118 C5
Bisham W & M 42 D4
Bishampton Worcs 71 H4
Bish Mill Devon 24 B6
Bishop Auckland Dur 140 F2
Bishopbridge Lincs 117 G4
Bishopbriggs E Duns 175 G4
Bishop Burton E R Yk 126 B3
Bishop Middleham Dur 141 H2
Bishopmill Moray 214 F2
Bishop Monkton N York 132 E6
Bishop Norton Lincs 117 G3
Bishopsbourne Kent 35 G4
Bishops Cannings Wilts 40 B7
Bishop's Castle Shrops 83 G5
Bishop's Caundle Dorset 27 G8
Bishop's Cleeve Gloucs 55 L3
Bishop's Frome Herefs 70 B5
Bishop's Green Essex 61 G4
Bishop's Hull Somset 25 J6
Bishop's Itchington Warwks 72 E3
Bishops Lydeard Somset 25 J5
Bishop's Norton Gloucs 55 J3
Bishop's Nympton Devon 24 B6
Bishop's Offley Staffs 99 H6
Bishop's Stortford Herts 60 D4
Bishop's Sutton Hants 29 L5
Bishop's Tachbrook Warwks 72 C3
Bishop's Tawton Devon 23 J5
Bishopsteignton Devon 7 K2
Bishopstoke Hants 29 J7
Bishopston Swans 51 H7
Bishopstone Bucks 58 D6
Bishopstone E Susx 19 M5
Bishopstone Herefs 69 H5
Bishopstone Kent 47 K6
Bishopstone Swindn 40 E4
Bishopstone Wilts 28 B6
Bishopstrow Wilts 27 K3
Bishop Sutton BaNES 38 E7
Bishop's Waltham Hants 29 K7
Bishopswood Somset 25 K8
Bishop's Wood Staffs 84 E2
Bishopsworth Bristl 38 E6
Bishop Thornton N York 132 D6
Bishopthorpe C York 124 F2
Bishopton Darltn 141 J3
Bishopton Rens 174 E4
Bishop Wilton E R Yk 134 C7
Bishton Newpt 38 B3
Bishton Staffs 100 A7
Bisley Gloucs 55 K6
Bisley Surrey 42 F8
Bissoe Cnwll 3 K3
Bisterne Hants 15 L3
Bitchfield Lincs 103 G6
Bittadon Devon 23 J3
Bittaford Devon 6 F4
Bitterley Shrops 83 L7
Bitterne C Sotn 29 J8
Bitteswell Leics 87 G6
Bitton S Glos 39 G6
Bix Oxon 42 B4
Bixter Shet 235 c5
Blaby Leics 87 H4
Blackadder Border 179 H7
Blackawton Devon 7 J5
Blackborough Devon 12 E1
Blackborough End Norfk 90 F1
Black Bourton Oxon 56 F6
Blackboys E Susx 20 B2
Blackbrook Derbys 101 G3
Blackbrook St Hel 112 D3
Blackbrook Staffs 99 H5
Blackburn Abers 206 F3
Blackburn Bl w D 121 K5
Blackburn W Loth 176 D5
Blackburn with Darwen Services Bl w D 121 K5
Black Callerton N u Ty 150 F2
Blackcraig E Ayrs 164 C7
Black Crofts Ag & B 182 D1
Blackdog Abers 207 H3
Black Dog Devon 11 J3
Blackdown Dorset 13 K2
Blacker Hill Barns 115 G2
Blackfen Gt Lon 45 J5
Blackfield Hants 16 E3
Blackford P & K 185 J5
Blackford Somset 26 B2
Blackford Somset 26 F6
Blackfordby Leics 101 G8
Blackhall C Edin 177 G4
Blackhall Colliery Dur 151 K6
Blackhall Mill Gatesd 150 E4
Blackhaugh Border 166 F2
Blackheath Gt Lon 45 G5
Blackheath Sandw 85 H6
Blackheath Suffk 93 J8
Blackheath Surrey 31 G3
Blackhill Abers 217 K3
Blackhill Abers 217 K5
Blackhill Dur 150 D5
Blackhill of Clackriach Abers 217 H5
Blackhorse Devon 12 C4
Blacklaw D & G 165 K7
Blackley Manch 113 J2
Blackley Crematorium Manch 113 J2
Blacklunans P & K 195 J4
Blackmarstone Herefs 69 K6
Blackmill Brdgnd 36 E3
Blackmoor Hants 30 C5

Blackmoor N Som 38 C7
Blackmoorfoot Kirk 123 G7
Blackmore Essex 60 F7
Blackmore End Essex 61 H2
Black Mountains 53 K3
Blackness Falk 176 E3
Blacknest Hants 30 D3
Black Notley Essex 61 J4
Blacko Lancs 122 C3
Black Pill Swans 51 J7
Blackpool Bpool 120 D4
Blackpool Devon 7 K6
Blackpool Airport Lancs 120 D4
Blackridge W Loth 176 B5
Blackrod Bolton 121 J7
Blacksboat Moray 214 E6
Blackshaw D & G 147 J2
Blackshaw Head Calder 122 E5
Blackstone W Susx 19 H3
Black Street Suffk 93 K6
Blackthorn Oxon 57 L4
Blackthorpe Suffk 77 K2
Blacktoft E R Yk 125 J5
Blacktop C Aber 207 G4
Black Torrington Devon 10 C4
Blackwall Derbys 100 E3
Blackwater Cnwll 3 J3
Blackwater Hants 42 D7
Blackwater IoW 17 G5
Blackwater Somset 25 K7
Blackwaterfoot N Ayrs 162 A4
Blackwell Cumb 148 D4
Blackwell Derbys 101 H2
Blackwell Derbys 114 C6
Blackwell Warwks 72 B5
Blackwell Worcs 71 H1
Blackwood Caerph 37 J2
Blackwood D & G 154 F5
Blackwood S Lans 164 F1
Blacon Ches W 111 L7
Bladnoch D & G 145 J4
Bladon Oxon 57 J5
Blaenannerch Cerdgn 65 H5
Blaenau Ffestiniog Gwynd 96 A4
Blaenavon Torfn 53 K6
Blaenavon Industrial Landscape Torfn 53 K6
Blaenffos Pembks 65 H6
Blaengarw Brdgnd 36 D2
Blaengwrach Neath 52 D6
Blaengwynfi Neath 36 D2
Blaenpennal Cerdgn 66 E2
Blaenplwyf Cerdgn 80 D7
Blaenporth Cerdgn 65 J5
Blaenrhondda Rhondd 52 E7
Blaenwaun Carmth 50 B1
Blaen-y-Coed Carmth 50 D1
Blaen-y-cwm Rhondd 52 E7
Blagdon N Som 38 D8
Blagdon Somset 25 K7
Blagdon Torbay 7 K4
Blagdon Hill Somset 25 K7
Blaich Highld 191 K2
Blain Highld 190 D3
Blaina Blae G 53 J6
Blair Atholl P & K 194 D4
Blair Drummond Stirlg 184 F7
Blairgowrie P & K 195 J7
Blairhall Fife 176 D2
Blairingone P & K 185 K7
Blairlogie Stirlg 185 H7
Blairmore Ag & B 173 L2
Blairmore Highld 228 C4
Blair's Ferry Ag & B 173 G4
Blaisdon Gloucs 55 G5
Blakebrook Worcs 84 E7
Blakedown Worcs 84 F7
Blake End Essex 61 H4
Blakemere Ches W 112 D7
Blakemere Herefs 69 G6
Blakenall Heath Wsall 85 H3
Blakeney Gloucs 54 F6
Blakeney Norfk 106 B4
Blakenhall Ches E 99 G3
Blakenhall Wolves 85 G4
Blakesley Nhants 73 J4
Blanchland Nthumb 150 B5
Blandford Forum Dorset 15 G2
Blandford St Mary Dorset 15 G2
Blanefield Stirlg 174 F3
Blankney Lincs 103 H1
Blantyre S Lans 175 J6
Blar a' Chaorainn Highld 191 L3
Blargie Highld 202 F6
Blarmachfoldach Highld 191 L3
Blaston Leics 88 B4
Blatherwycke Nhants 88 D4
Blawith Cumb 129 G2
Blawquhairn D & G 154 B5
Blaxhall Suffk 79 H3
Blaxton Donc 116 A2
Blaydon Gatesd 150 F3
Bleadney Somset 26 C3
Bleadon N Som 25 M1
Blean Kent 34 F3
Bleasby Notts 102 B3
Blebocraigs Fife 187 G4
Bleddfa Powys 68 E2
Bledington Gloucs 56 E4
Bledlow Bucks 58 C7
Bledlow Ridge Bucks 42 D2
Blegbie E Loth 178 B6
Blencarn Cumb 138 F2
Blencogo Cumb 147 L5
Blendworth Hants 30 B8
Blenheim Palace Oxon 57 H5
Blennerhasset Cumb 147 L6
Bletchingdon Oxon 57 J4
Bletchingley Surrey 32 B3
Bletchley M Keyn 58 E2
Bletchley Shrops 98 F5
Bletherston Pembks 49 H4
Bletsoe Bed 74 E3
Blewbury Oxon 41 K4
Blickling Norfk 106 E6
Blidworth Notts 101 L2
Blidworth Bottoms Notts 101 L2
Blindcrake Cumb 147 K7
Blindley Heath Surrey 32 C4
Blisland Cnwll 5 H2
Blissford Hants 28 D8
Bliss Gate Worcs 84 D8
Blisworth Nhants 73 K4
Blithbury Staffs 100 B8
Blockley Gloucs 71 L7
Blofield Norfk 93 G2
Blofield Heath Norfk 93 G2
Blo Norton Norfk 92 B7
Bloomfield Border 167 J4
Blore Staffs 100 C3
Bloxham Oxon 72 E7
Bloxholm Lincs 103 H2
Bloxwich Wsall 85 H3
Bloxworth Dorset 15 G4
Blubberhouses N York 132 B7
Blue Anchor Somset 24 F3
Blue Bell Hill Kent 46 C7
Blue John Cavern Derbys 114 C5
Blundellsands Sefton 111 J2
Blundeston Suffk 93 L4
Blunham C Beds 75 H4
Blunsdon St Andrew Swindn 40 C3
Bluntington Worcs 84 F8
Bluntisham Cambs 89 L8
Blurton C Stke 99 K4
Blyborough Lincs 116 F3
Blyford Suffk 93 J7
Blymhill Staffs 84 E2
Blyth Notts 115 L4
Blyth Nthumb 159 H5
Blyth Bridge Border 165 M1
Blythburgh Suffk 93 J7
Blyth Crematorium Nthumb 159 H5
Blythe Border 178 D7
Blyton Lincs 116 D3
Boarhills Fife 187 J5
Boarhunt Hants 17 H2
Boarstall Bucks 57 L5
Boath Highld 222 D6
Boat of Garten Highld 203 L2
Bobbing Kent 46 E6
Bobbington Staffs 84 E5
Bocking Essex 61 J4
Bocking Churchstreet Essex 61 J3
Boddam Abers 217 L6
Boddam Shet 235 c7
Boddington Gloucs 55 K3
Bodedern IoA 108 D5
Bodelwyddan Denbgs 110 D6
Bodenham Herefs 69 K4
Bodenham Wilts 28 D6
Bodenham Moor Herefs 69 K4
Bodewryd IoA 108 E4
Bodfari Denbgs 110 F7
Bodffordd IoA 108 F6
Bodfuan Gwynd 94 F5
Bodham Norfk 106 D4
Bodiam E Susx 33 K7
Bodicote Oxon 72 F6
Bodinnick Cnwll 5 H5
Bodle Street Green E Susx 20 D3
Bodmin Cnwll 5 G3
Bodmin Moor Cnwll 5 J1
Bodsham Kent 34 E5
Bodwen Cnwll 5 G4
Bogallan Highld 212 F4
Bogbrae Abers 217 J7
Bogend S Ayrs 163 K3
Boggs Holdings E Loth 177 L4
Boghall Mdloth 177 H5
Boghall W Loth 176 D5
Boghead S Lans 164 F2
Bogmoor Moray 215 H2
Bogmuir Abers 197 G3
Bogniebrae Abers 216 B5
Bognor Regis W Susx 18 C6
Bogroy Highld 203 L2
Bogue D & G 154 B6
Bohortha Cnwll 3 L5
Bohuntine Highld 201 L8
Bolam Dur 140 F3
Bolberry Devon 7 G7
Boldmere Birm 85 K5
Boldre Hants 16 C3
Boldron Dur 140 C4
Bole Notts 116 C4
Bolehill Derbys 100 F2
Bolham Devon 24 E7
Bolham Water Devon 25 J8
Bolingey Cnwll 3 K1
Bollington Ches E 113 L6
Bolney W Susx 31 L6
Bolnhurst Bed 74 F3
Bolnore W Susx 19 J2
Bolshan Angus 197 G6
Bolsover Derbys 115 J7
Bolsterstone Sheff 114 F3
Boltby N York 133 G3
Boltenstone Abers 205 J3
Bolton Bolton 121 L8
Bolton Cumb 138 F3
Bolton E Loth 178 B4
Bolton E R Yk 125 J1
Bolton Nthumb 169 G6
Bolton Abbey N York 131 K8
Bolton-by-Bowland Lancs 122 B1
Boltonfellend Cumb 148 E2
Boltongate Cumb 147 M6
Bolton-le-Sands Lancs 129 K6
Bolton Low Houses Cumb 147 M6
Bolton-on-Swale N York 141 G7
Bolton Percy N York 124 E3
Bolton upon Dearne Barns 115 J2
Bolventor Cnwll 5 J1
Bomere Heath Shrops 98 C8
Bonar Bridge Highld 222 E3
Bonawe Ag & B 182 E2
Bonby N Linc 126 C7
Boncath Pembks 65 H6
Bonchester Bridge Border 167 J6
Bondleigh Devon 10 F4
Bonds Lancs 121 G2
Bo'ness Falk 176 D3
Boney Hay Staffs 85 J2
Bonhill W Duns 174 D3
Boningale Shrops 84 E3
Bonjedward Border 167 K5
Bonkle N Lans 175 L6
Bonnington Angus 196 F7
Bonnington Kent 34 E7
Bonnybank Fife 186 F6
Bonnybridge Falk 175 L3
Bonnykelly Abers 217 G4
Bonnyrigg Mdloth 177 J5
Bonnyton Angus 196 B8
Bonsall Derbys 100 F2
Bonshaw Tower D & G 155 M7
Bont-Dolgadfan Powys 81 J4
Bont-goch Cerdgn 80 F6
Bontnewydd Cerdgn 66 E2
Bontnewydd Gwynd 95 H1
Bontuchel Denbgs 97 G2
Bonvilston V Glam 37 G5
Boode Devon 23 H4
Booker Bucks 42 D3
Boon Border 167 J1
Boosbeck R & Cl 142 E4
Boose's Green Essex 61 K2
Boot Cumb 137 G6
Booth Calder 122 F5
Boothby Graffoe Lincs 103 G2
Boothby Pagnell Lincs 102 F6
Boothferry E R Yk 125 H5
Boothstown Salfd 113 G2
Bootle Cumb 128 D2
Bootle Sefton 111 K3
Boraston Shrops 70 B1
Bordeaux Guern 236 e2
Borden Kent 34 B3
Borders Crematorium Border 167 H3
Boreham Essex 61 J6
Boreham Wilts 27 K3
Boreham Street E Susx 20 D4
Borehamwood Herts 44 D2
Boreland D & G 155 L4
Boreraig Highld 208 C4
Borgh W Isls 232 f1
Borgh W Isls 233 b9
Borgie Highld 229 K4
Borgue D & G 146 B5
Borgue Highld 227 K4
Borley Essex 77 J6
Borneskitaig Highld 218 B7
Borness D & G 146 A5
Boroughbridge N York 132 F6
Borough Green Kent 33 G2
Borrowash Derbys 101 H5
Borrowby N York 132 F2
Borrowstoun Falk 176 D3
Borstal Medway 46 B6
Borth Cerdgn 80 E5

Borthwickbrae Border 166 F6
Borthwickshiels Border 166 F6
Borth-y-Gest Gwynd 95 K5
Borve Highld 209 G5
Borve W Isls 232 d4
Borve W Isls 232 f1
Borve W Isls 233 b9
Borwick Lancs 129 L5
Bosbury Herefs 70 C5
Boscastle Cnwll 8 E6
Boscombe Bmouth 15 L4
Boscombe Wilts 28 D4
Bosham W Susx 17 L2
Bosherston Pembks 49 G8
Bosley Ches E 113 K7
Bossall N York 133 L7
Bossiney Cnwll 8 E6
Bossingham Kent 34 F5
Bossington Somset 24 D2
Bostock Green Ches W 112 F7
Boston Lincs 104 B4
Boston Crematorium Lincs 104 A4
Boston Spa Leeds 124 C2
Boswinger Cnwll 4 F7
Botallack Cnwll 2 C5
Botany Bay Gt Lon 59 M7
Botesdale Suffk 92 C7
Bothal Nthumb 159 G5
Bothamsall Notts 116 A6
Bothel Cumb 147 L6
Bothenhampton Dorset 13 L4
Bothwell S Lans 175 J6
Bothwell Services S Lans 175 J6
Botley Bucks 59 G7
Botley Hants 29 K8
Botley Oxon 57 J6
Botolph Claydon Bucks 58 B3
Botolphs W Susx 19 G4
Bottesford Leics 102 D5
Bottesford N Linc 125 K8
Bottisham Cambs 76 D3
Bottomcraig Fife 186 F3
Bottoms Calder 122 D6
Botusfleming Cnwll 6 B4
Botwnnog Gwynd 94 E6
Bough Beech Kent 32 E4
Boughrood Powys 68 C6
Boughton Nhants 73 L2
Boughton Norfk 91 G3
Boughton Notts 116 B7
Boughton Aluph Kent 34 D5
Boughton Green Kent 33 K3
Boughton Monchelsea Kent 33 K3
Boughton Street Kent 34 E3
Bouldon Shrops 83 K6
Boulmer Nthumb 169 K6
Boultham Lincs 116 F7
Bourn Cambs 75 K3
Bourne Lincs 103 H7
Bournebridge Essex 45 J2
Bournebrook Birm 85 J6
Bourne End Bucks 42 E3
Bourne End C Beds 74 D5
Bourne End Herts 59 G6
Bournemouth Bmouth 15 K4
Bournemouth Airport Dorset 15 L3
Bournemouth Crematorium Bmouth 15 L4
Bournes Green Sthend 46 E3
Bournheath Worcs 85 G8
Bournmoor Dur 151 H5
Bournville Birm 85 J7
Bourton Dorset 27 H5
Bourton Oxon 40 E3
Bourton Shrops 83 L4
Bourton Wilts 40 B7
Bourton on Dunsmore Warwks 72 E1
Bourton-on-the-Hill Gloucs 56 D2
Bourton-on-the-Water Gloucs 56 D4
Bousd Ag & B 189 G4
Bouth Cumb 129 H3
Bouthwaite N York 131 L5
Boveridge Dorset 28 B7
Bovey Tracey Devon 7 J1
Bovingdon Herts 59 G7
Bow Devon 11 G4
Bow Gt Lon 45 G4
Bow Ork 234 b7
Bow Brickhill M Keyn 74 C7
Bowbridge Gloucs 55 J6
Bowburn Dur 151 H7
Bowcombe IoW 16 F5
Bowd Devon 12 E4
Bowden Border 167 H4
Bowden Hill Wilts 39 L6
Bowdon Traffd 113 H4
Bower Highld 231 J3
Bowerchalke Wilts 28 A6
Bowermadden Highld 231 J3
Bowers Staffs 99 J5
Bowers Gifford Essex 46 C3
Bowershall Fife 176 F1
Bower's Row Leeds 124 B5
Bowes Dur 140 C4
Bowgreave Lancs 121 G2
Bowhouse D & G 147 H2
Bowland Border 167 G2
Bowley Herefs 69 K4
Bowlhead Green Surrey 30 E4
Bowling C Brad 123 H4
Bowling W Duns 174 E4
Bowmanstead Cumb 137 J7
Bowmore Ag & B 170 F6
Bowness-on-Solway Cumb 147 L3
Bowness-on-Windermere Cumb 137 L7
Bow of Fife Fife 186 E5
Bowriefauld Angus 196 E6
Bowsden Nthumb 168 E2
Bow Street Cerdgn 80 E6
Box Gloucs 55 K7
Box Wilts 39 J6
Boxford Suffk 77 L6
Boxford W Berk 41 H6
Boxgrove W Susx 18 B4
Boxley Kent 33 K2
Boxmoor Herts 59 H6
Boxted Essex 62 B2
Boxted Essex 62 B2
Boxted Suffk 77 J4
Boxted Cross Essex 62 B2
Boxworth Cambs 75 L2
Boyden Gate Kent 47 L6
Boylestone Derbys 100 D5
Boyndie Abers 216 C2
Boyndlie Abers 217 G2
Boynton E R Yk 135 H6
Boysack Angus 197 G6
Boyton Cnwll 9 J6
Boyton Suffk 79 H5
Boyton Wilts 27 L4
Boyton Cross Essex 61 G6
Boyton End Suffk 77 G5
Bozeat Nhants 74 C3
Brabourne Kent 34 E6
Brabourne Lees Kent 34 E6
Brabstermire Highld 231 K2
Bracadale Highld 208 E6
Braceborough Lincs 88 F2
Bracebridge Heath Lincs 117 G7
Bracebridge Low Fields Lincs 116 F7
Braceby Lincs 103 G5
Bracewell Lancs 122 C2
Brackenfield Derbys 101 G2
Brackenhirst N Lans 175 K5
Bracklesham W Susx 17 L3
Brackletter Highld 201 J8
Brackley Nhants 73 H6
Bracknell Br For 42 E6
Braco P & K 185 H5
Bracobrae Moray 215 L4
Bracon Ash Norfk 92 E4
Bracora Highld 199 L6
Bracorina Highld 199 L6
Bradbourne Derbys 100 D3
Bradbury Dur 141 H2
Bradden Nhants 73 J5
Bradeley C Stke 99 K3
Bradenham Bucks 42 D2
Bradenstoke Wilts 39 M4
Bradfield Devon 12 D1
Bradfield Essex 62 D2
Bradfield Norfk 106 F5
Bradfield Sheff 114 F3
Bradfield W Berk 41 L6
Bradfield Combust Suffk 77 K3
Bradfield Green Ches E 99 G2
Bradfield Heath Essex 62 D3
Bradfield St Clare Suffk 77 K3
Bradfield St George Suffk 77 K3
Bradford C Brad 123 H4
Bradford Devon 9 L4
Bradford Abbas Dorset 26 E8
Bradford Leigh Wilts 39 J7
Bradford-on-Avon Wilts 39 J7
Bradford-on-Tone Somset 25 J6
Bradford Peverell Dorset 14 C4
Bradiford Devon 23 J5
Brading IoW 17 H5
Bradley Derbys 100 E4
Bradley Hants 29 M3
Bradley NE Lin 118 C1
Bradley Staffs 99 K8
Bradley Wolves 85 G4
Bradley Worcs 71 H3
Bradley Green Worcs 71 H3
Bradley in the Moors Staffs 100 B4
Bradley Stoke S Glos 38 E4
Bradmore Notts 101 L6
Bradninch Devon 12 C2
Bradnop Staffs 100 A2
Bradpole Dorset 13 L4
Bradshaw Calder 123 G4
Bradstone Devon 9 K8
Bradwall Green Ches E 113 H8
Bradwell Derbys 114 D5
Bradwell Essex 61 J4
Bradwell M Keyn 74 B6
Bradwell Norfk 93 K3
Bradwell Crematorium Staffs 99 J3
Bradwell-on-Sea Essex 62 B6
Bradwell Waterside Essex 62 B6
Bradworthy Devon 9 J3
Brae Highld 213 G2
Brae Shet 235 c4
Braeface Falk 175 K3
Braehead Angus 197 H5
Braehead D & G 145 J4
Braehead S Lans 176 C7
Braemar Abers 204 E6
Braemore Highld 221 G5
Braemore Highld 227 J3
Brae Roy Lodge Highld 201 L6
Braeside Inver 173 L4
Braes of Coul Angus 195 L5
Braes of Enzie Moray 215 J3
Braeswick Ork 234 d4
Braevallich Ag & B 182 D6
Brafferton Darltn 141 H3
Brafferton N York 132 F5
Brafield-on-the-Green Nhants 74 B3
Bragar W Isls 232 f2
Bragbury End Herts 59 L4
Braidwood S Lans 175 L8
Brailsford Derbys 100 E4
Braintree Essex 61 J4
Braiseworth Suffk 78 D1
Braishfield Hants 29 G6
Braithwaite Cumb 137 H3
Braithwell Donc 115 K3
Bramber W Susx 19 G4
Bramcote Warwks 86 E5
Bramcote Crematorium Notts 101 J5
Bramdean Hants 29 L5
Bramerton Norfk 93 G3
Bramfield Herts 59 M5
Bramfield Suffk 93 H8
Bramford Suffk 78 D5
Bramhall Stockp 113 K5
Bramham Leeds 124 C2
Bramhope Leeds 123 K2
Bramley Hants 41 M8
Bramley Leeds 123 K4
Bramley Rothm 115 J3
Bramley Surrey 31 G3
Bramley Corner Hants 41 M8
Bramling Kent 35 G4
Brampford Speke Devon 11 L5
Brampton Cambs 75 J1
Brampton Cumb 138 F3
Brampton Cumb 148 F3
Brampton Lincs 116 D5
Brampton Norfk 106 F7
Brampton Rothm 115 H2
Brampton Suffk 93 J6
Brampton Abbotts Herefs 54 E3
Brampton Ash Nhants 87 L6
Brampton Bryan Herefs 83 G8
Brampton-en-le-Morthen Rothm 115 J4
Bramshall Staffs 100 B6
Bramshaw Hants 28 F7
Bramshott Hants 30 D5
Bramwell Somset 26 B5
Branault Highld 190 B3
Brancaster Norfk 105 J4
Brancaster Staithe Norfk 105 J4
Brancepeth Dur 150 F7
Branchill Moray 214 D4
Branderburgh Moray 214 F1
Brandesburton E R Yk 126 E2
Brandeston Suffk 78 F3
Brandiston Norfk 106 D7
Brandon Dur 151 G6
Brandon Lincs 102 E3
Brandon Suffk 91 H6
Brandon Warwks 86 E7
Brandon Parva Norfk 92 C2
Brandsby N York 133 J5
Brandy Wharf Lincs 117 G3
Bran End Essex 61 G3
Branksome Poole 15 K4
Branksome Park Poole 15 K4
Bransbury Hants 29 H3
Bransby Lincs 116 E5
Branscombe Devon 12 F5
Bransford Worcs 70 E4
Bransgore Hants 16 A3
Bransholme C KuH 126 D4
Bransley Shrops 84 B7
Branston Leics 102 D6

Branston Lincs 117 G7
Branston Staffs 100 E7
Branston Booths Lincs 117 H7
Branstone IoW 17 G5
Brant Broughton Lincs 102 E2
Brantham Suffk 78 D7
Branthwaite Cumb 136 E3
Branthwaite Cumb 148 B7
Brantingham E R Yk 125 L5
Branton Donc 115 M2
Branton Nthumb 168 F6
Branton Green N York 132 F6
Branxton Nthumb 168 D2
Brassington Derbys 100 E2
Brasted Kent 32 E3
Brasted Chart Kent 32 E3
Brathens Abers 206 D5
Bratoft Lincs 119 G8
Brattleby Lincs 116 F5
Bratton Wilts 27 K2
Bratton Wrekin 84 B2
Bratton Clovelly Devon 10 C6
Bratton Fleming Devon 23 K4
Bratton Seymour Somset 26 F5
Braughing Herts 60 C3
Braunston Nhants 73 G2
Braunston Rutlnd 88 B3
Braunton Devon 23 H4
Brawby N York 134 B4
Brawl Highld 230 B3
Bray W & M 42 E4
Braybrooke Nhants 87 L6
Brayford Devon 23 L4
Bray Shop Cnwll 5 M2
Brayton N York 124 F4
Braywick W & M 42 E4
Breachwood Green Herts 59 J4
Breadsall Derbys 101 G5
Breadstone Gloucs 55 G7
Breage Cnwll 3 G5
Breakachy Highld 212 D5
Breakspear Crematorium Gt Lon 43 H3
Brealangwell Lodge Highld 222 C3
Bream Gloucs 54 E6
Breamore Hants 28 D7
Brean Somset 25 L1
Breanais W Isls 232 d3
Brearton N York 132 E7
Breascleit W Isls 232 e2
Breasclete W Isls 232 e2
Breaston Derbys 101 J5
Brechfa Carmth 66 C7
Brechin Angus 196 F4
Breckles Norfk 91 L5
Brecon Powys 53 G3
Brecon Beacons National Park 52 F3
Bredbury Stockp 113 L3
Brede E Susx 21 G3
Bredenbury Herefs 69 L3
Bredfield Suffk 78 F4
Bredgar Kent 34 B3
Bredhurst Kent 46 D7
Bredon Worcs 71 G6
Bredon's Hardwick Worcs 71 G7
Bredon's Norton Worcs 71 G6
Bredwardine Herefs 69 G5
Breedon on the Hill Leics 101 H7
Breich W Loth 176 C6
Breightmet Bolton 121 L8
Breighton E R Yk 125 G4
Breinton Herefs 69 J6
Bremhill Wilts 39 L5
Brenchley Kent 33 H5
Brendon Devon 24 B2
Brenfield Ag & B 172 E2
Brenish W Isls 232 d3
Brent Cross Gt Lon 44 E3
Brent Eleigh Suffk 77 L5
Brentford Gt Lon 44 D5
Brentingby Leics 102 C8
Brent Knoll Somset 25 M2
Brent Mill Devon 7 G4
Brent Pelham Herts 60 C2
Brentwood Essex 45 L2
Brenzett Kent 21 K1
Brenzett Green Kent 34 D8
Brereton Staffs 85 J1
Brereton Green Ches E 113 H8
Bressay Shet 235 d6
Bressingham Norfk 92 C7
Bretby Derbys 100 F7
Bretby Crematorium Derbys 100 F7
Bretford Warwks 86 E7
Bretforton Worcs 71 K5
Bretherton Lancs 121 G6
Brettabister Shet 235 d5
Brettenham Norfk 91 L6
Brettenham Suffk 77 L4
Bretton Flints 111 K8
Brewood Staffs 84 F2
Briantspuddle Dorset 14 F4
Brickendon Herts 60 A6
Bricket Wood Herts 59 J7
Brick Houses Sheff 114 F5
Bricklehampton Worcs 71 H6
Bride IoM 237 e2
Bridekirk Cumb 147 K7
Bridestowe Devon 10 D6
Brideswell Abers 216 B6
Bridford Devon 11 J7
Bridge Kent 35 G4
Bridgehampton Somset 26 E6
Bridge Hewick N York 132 E5
Bridgehill Dur 150 D5
Bridgemary Hants 17 H2
Bridgend Abers 215 L7
Bridgend Ag & B 161 K2
Bridgend Ag & B 171 G6
Bridgend Angus 196 E3
Bridgend Brdgnd 36 E4
Bridgend D & G 165 L7
Bridgend Devon 6 E6
Bridgend Fife 186 F5
Bridgend Moray 215 J7
Bridgend P & K 186 B3
Bridgend W Loth 176 E3
Bridgend of Lintrathen Angus 195 L5
Bridge of Alford Abers 206 B2
Bridge of Allan Stirlg 185 G7
Bridge of Avon Moray 204 E2
Bridge of Avon Moray 214 E7
Bridge of Balgie P & K 193 J6
Bridge of Brewlands Angus 195 J4
Bridge of Brown Highld 204 D2
Bridge of Cally P & K 195 J6
Bridge of Canny Abers 206 C6
Bridge of Craigisla Angus 195 K5
Bridge of Dee D & G 146 C3
Bridge of Don C Aber 207 H4
Bridge of Dulsie Highld 213 L6
Bridge of Dye Abers 206 C7
Bridge of Earn P & K 186 B4
Bridge of Ericht P & K 193 H5
Bridge of Feugh Abers 206 D6
Bridge of Forss Highld 230 F2
Bridge of Gairn Abers 205 H6
Bridge of Gaur P & K 193 H5
Bridge of Marnoch Abers 216 B4
Bridge of Muchalls Abers 207 G6
Bridge of Orchy Ag & B 192 E7
Bridge of Tilt P & K 194 D4
Bridge of Tynet Moray 215 J3
Bridge of Walls Shet 235 b5
Bridge of Weir Rens 174 D5
Bridgerule Devon 9 H4
Bridge Sollers Herefs 69 H6
Bridge Street Suffk 77 K5
Bridgetown Somset 24 E5
Bridge Trafford Ches W 112 C7
Bridgham Norfk 91 L6
Bridgnorth Shrops 84 C5
Bridgwater Somset 25 L4
Bridgwater Services Somset 25 L4
Bridlington E R Yk 135 J6
Bridport Dorset 13 L4
Bridstow Herefs 54 E3
Brierfield Lancs 122 C3
Brierley Barns 124 C7
Brierley Gloucs 54 F5
Brierley Hill Dudley 85 G6
Brigg N Linc 117 G1
Briggate Norfk 107 G6
Briggswath N York 143 H5
Brigham Cumb 136 F2
Brigham E R Yk 135 G8
Brighouse Calder 123 H6
Brighstone IoW 16 E5
Brighthampton Oxon 57 G7
Brightley Devon 10 E5
Brightling E Susx 20 D2
Brightlingsea Essex 62 C5
Brighton Br & H 19 J5
Brighton le Sands Sefton 111 J2
Brightons Falk 176 C3
Brightwalton W Berk 41 H5
Brightwell Suffk 78 F5
Brightwell Baldwin Oxon 41 M2
Brightwell-cum-Sotwell Oxon 41 L3
Brightwell Upperton Oxon 42 A2
Brignall Dur 140 D5
Brig o'Turk Stirlg 184 C6
Brigsley NE Lin 118 C2
Brigsteer Cumb 129 K2
Brigstock Nhants 88 D6
Brill Bucks 58 A5
Brill Cnwll 3 J5
Brilley Herefs 68 F5
Brimfield Herefs 69 K2
Brimfield Cross Herefs 69 K2
Brimington Derbys 115 H6
Brimley Devon 7 J1
Brimpsfield Gloucs 55 L5
Brimpton W Berk 41 K7
Brimscombe Gloucs 55 K7
Brimstage Wirral 111 J5
Brincliffe Sheff 115 F4
Brind E R Yk 125 H4
Brindister Shet 235 c5
Brindle Lancs 121 J5
Brineton Staffs 84 E2
Bringhurst Leics 88 B5
Bringsty Common Herefs 70 C4
Brington Cambs 88 F7
Briningham Norfk 106 C5
Brinkhill Lincs 118 E6
Brinkley Cambs 76 F4
Brinklow Warwks 86 E7
Brinkworth Wilts 40 A4
Brinscall Lancs 121 J6
Brinsley Notts 101 J3
Brinsworth Rothm 115 H4
Brinton Norfk 106 C5
Brinyan Ork 234 c5
Brisley Norfk 105 M7
Brislington Bristl 38 F6
Brissenden Green Kent 34 C6
Bristol Bristl 38 E5
Bristol Airport N Som 38 D7
Bristol Zoo Gardens Bristl 38 E5
Briston Norfk 106 C6
Britford Wilts 28 D5
Brithdir Caerph 53 J7
Brithdir Gwynd 96 B8
British Legion Village Kent 33 J2
Briton Ferry Neath 51 L6
Britwell Salome Oxon 42 A2
Brixham Torbay 7 L5
Brixton Devon 6 E5
Brixton Gt Lon 44 F5
Brixton Deverill Wilts 27 K4
Brixworth Nhants 73 L1
Brize Norton Oxon 56 F6
Brize Norton Airport Oxon 56 F6
Broad Alley Worcs 70 F2
Broad Blunsdon Swindn 40 D3
Broadbottom Tamesd 113 M3
Broadbridge W Susx 17 M2
Broadbridge Heath W Susx 31 J5
Broad Campden Gloucs 71 L6
Broad Carr Calder 123 G6
Broad Chalke Wilts 28 B6
Broadclyst Devon 12 C3
Broadfield Inver 174 C4
Broadford Highld 199 K2
Broadford Bridge W Susx 31 H6
Broadgairhill Border 166 C7
Broad Green Worcs 70 D4
Broadhaugh Border 179 H7
Broad Haven Pembks 48 E5
Broadheath Traffd 113 H4
Broadhembury Devon 12 E2
Broadhempston Devon 7 J3
Broad Hinton Wilts 40 C5
Broadland Row E Susx 21 G2
Broad Layings Hants 41 H7
Broadley Moray 215 J3
Broad Marston Worcs 71 K5
Broadmayne Dorset 14 D5
Broad Meadow Staffs 99 J3
Broadmoor Pembks 49 J6
Broadoak Dorset 13 K3
Broad Oak E Susx 20 C2
Broad Oak E Susx 21 G2
Broad Oak Herefs 54 C4
Broad Oak Kent 35 G3
Broad Oak St Hel 112 D3
Broad's Green Essex 61 H5
Broadstairs Kent 35 K2
Broadstone Poole 15 J4
Broadstone Shrops 83 K5
Broad Street E Susx 21 H3
Broad Street Kent 33 L2
Broad Town Wilts 40 C5
Broadwas Worcs 70 D4
Broadwater Herts 59 L4
Broadwater W Susx 18 F5
Broadwaters Worcs 84 E7
Broadway Pembks 48 E5
Broadway Somset 25 L7
Broadway Worcs 71 K6
Broadwell Gloucs 54 E5
Broadwell Gloucs 56 D3
Broadwell Oxon 56 E6
Broadwell Warwks 72 F2
Broadwindsor Dorset 13 K2
Broadwood Kelly Devon 10 F4

Broadwoodwidger Devon 9 K6
Brochel Highld 209 J5
Brochroy Ag & B 182 E2
Brockamin Worcs 70 D4
Brockbridge Hants 29 L7
Brockdish Norfk 92 E7
Brockenhurst Hants 16 C3
Brocketsbrae S Lans 164 F2
Brockford Street Suffk 78 D2
Brockhall Nhants 73 J2
Brockham Surrey 31 K2
Brockhampton Gloucs 56 B4
Brockhampton Hants 17 K2
Brockhampton Herefs 54 E2
Brockholes Kirk 123 H7
Brocklesby Lincs 126 E7
Brockley N Som 38 C6
Brockley Suffk 77 J1
Brockley Green Suffk 77 G5
Brockley Green Suffk 77 J4
Brockmoor Dudley 84 F5
Brockton Shrops 83 G3
Brockton Shrops 83 G6
Brockton Shrops 83 L5
Brockweir Gloucs 54 D7
Brockworth Gloucs 55 K5
Brocton Staffs 99 L8
Brodick N Ayrs 162 C3
Brodie Moray 214 B3
Brodsworth Donc 115 J1
Brogaig Highld 218 C7
Brokenborough Wilts 39 K3
Broken Cross Ches E 113 K6
Brokerswood Wilts 27 J2
Bromborough Wirral 111 K5
Brome Suffk 92 D7
Brome Street Suffk 92 D7
Bromeswell Suffk 79 G4
Bromfield Cumb 147 L5
Bromfield Shrops 83 J7
Bromham Bed 74 E4
Bromham Wilts 39 L7
Bromley Dudley 85 G6
Bromley Gt Lon 45 H6
Bromley Shrops 84 D4
Bromley Cross Bolton 121 L7
Brompton Medway 46 C6
Brompton N York 141 J7
Brompton-by-Sawdon N York 134 E3
Brompton-on-Swale N York 140 F7
Brompton Ralph Somset 25 G5
Brompton Regis Somset 24 E5
Bromsberrow Gloucs 70 D7
Bromsberrow Heath Gloucs 55 G2
Bromsgrove Worcs 71 G1
Bromyard Herefs 70 B4
Bronant Cerdgn 66 E2
Brongest Cerdgn 65 K5
Bronington Wrexhm 98 C4
Bronllys Powys 68 D7
Bronwydd Carmth 50 E2
Bronygarth Shrops 97 K5
Brook Hants 28 F8
Brook IoW 16 E5
Brook Kent 34 E6
Brook Surrey 30 F4
Brooke Norfk 93 G4
Brooke Rutlnd 88 B3
Brookenby Lincs 117 K3
Brookfield Rens 174 D5
Brookhampton Somset 26 F5
Brook Hill Hants 28 F8
Brookhouse Lancs 129 L6
Brookhouse Rothm 115 K4
Brookhouse Green Ches E 99 J1
Brookhouses Derbys 114 B4
Brookland Kent 21 K1
Brooklands Traffd 113 H4
Brookmans Park Herts 59 L7
Brook Street Essex 45 L2
Brook Street Kent 34 C7
Brookthorpe Gloucs 55 J5
Brookwood Surrey 42 F8
Broom C Beds 75 H6
Broom Rothm 115 H3
Broom Warwks 71 K4
Broome Norfk 93 H5
Broome Shrops 83 H7
Broome Worcs 84 F7
Broomedge Warrtn 113 G4
Broomfield Essex 61 H5
Broomfield Kent 33 L3
Broomfield Kent 47 K6
Broomfield Somset 25 K5
Broomfleet E R Yk 125 K5
Broomhaugh Nthumb 150 C3
Broom Hill Barns 115 H2
Broom Hill Notts 101 K3
Broomhill Nthumb 159 G3
Broompark Dur 151 G6
Brora Highld 226 F7
Broseley Shrops 84 C3
Brotherlee Dur 150 A7
Brotherton N York 124 D5
Brotton R & Cl 142 E4
Broubster Highld 230 F4
Brough Cumb 139 H4
Brough E R Yk 125 L5
Brough Highld 231 J2
Brough Notts 102 D2
Brough Shet 235 d4
Broughall Shrops 98 E4
Brough Lodge Shet 235 d2
Brough Sowerby Cumb 139 H5
Broughton Border 165 L3
Broughton Cambs 89 K7
Broughton Flints 111 K8
Broughton Hants 28 F5
Broughton Lancs 121 G4
Broughton M Keyn 74 C6
Broughton N Linc 126 B8
Broughton N York 122 D1
Broughton N York 134 B5
Broughton Nhants 88 B7
Broughton Oxon 72 E6
Broughton Salfd 113 J2
Broughton V Glam 36 E6
Broughton Astley Leics 87 G5
Broughton Gifford Wilts 39 K7
Broughton Green Worcs 71 G3
Broughton Hackett Worcs 71 G4
Broughton-in-Furness Cumb 128 F3
Broughton Mains D & G 145 J6
Broughton Mills Cumb 128 F2
Broughton Moor Cumb 147 J7
Broughton Poggs Oxon 56 E7
Broughty Ferry C Dund 187 H2
Brown Candover Hants 29 L4
Brown Edge Staffs 99 K2
Brownhill Abers 217 G6
Brownhills Fife 187 H4
Brownhills Wsall 85 J3
Browninghill Green Hants 41 L7
Brown Lees Staffs 99 K2
Brownsea Island Dorset 15 J5
Brown's Green Birm 85 J5
Browns Hill Gloucs 55 K7
Brownston Devon 7 G5
Broxa N York 134 E2
Broxbourne Herts 60 B6
Broxburn E Loth 178 E3
Broxburn W Loth 176 E4
Broxted Essex 60 F3
Bruan Highld 231 K7
Bruar P & K 194 C3
Brucefield Highld 223 K4
Bruchag Ag & B 173 J6
Bruichladdich Ag & B 170 E6
Bruisyard Suffk 79 G2
Bruisyard Street Suffk 79 G2
Brumby N Linc 125 K8
Brund Staffs 100 C1
Brundall Norfk 93 G2
Brundish Suffk 78 F1
Brundish Street Suffk 78 F1
Brunery Highld 190 E3
Brunswick Village N u Ty 159 G7
Brunthwaite C Brad 122 F2
Bruntingthorpe Leics 87 H5
Brunton Fife 186 E3
Brunton Wilts 28 E1
Brushford Devon 11 G4
Brushford Somset 24 E6
Bruton Somset 27 G4
Bryan's Green Worcs 70 F2
Bryanston Dorset 15 G2
Brydekirk D & G 155 L7
Bryher IoS 2 a1
Brympton Somset 26 D7
Bryn Carmth 51 G5
Bryn Neath 36 C3
Brynamman Carmth 51 K3
Brynberian Pembks 64 F7
Bryncir Gwynd 95 H4
Bryn-côch Neath 51 L5
Bryncroes Gwynd 94 D6
Bryncrug Gwynd 80 E3
Bryneglwys Denbgs 97 H3
Brynford Flints 111 G6
Bryn Gates Wigan 112 E2
Bryngwran IoA 108 D6
Bryngwyn Mons 54 B6
Bryngwyn Powys 68 D5
Bryn-Henllan Pembks 64 E6
Brynhoffnant Cerdgn 65 K4
Brynmawr Blae G 53 J5
Bryn-mawr Gwynd 94 D5
Brynmenyn Brdgnd 36 D4
Brynmill Swans 51 J6
Brynna Rhondd 36 F4
Brynrefail Gwynd 109 H8
Brynsadler Rhondd 37 G4
Bryn Saith Marchog Denbgs 97 G3
Brynsiencyn IoA 108 F7
Brynteg IoA 109 G5
Bryn-y-Maen Conwy 110 B6
Bualintur Highld 198 F2
Bubbenhall Warwks 86 D8
Bubwith E R Yk 125 H4
Buccleuch Border 166 E6
Buchanan Smithy Stirlg 174 E1
Buchanhaven Abers 217 L5
Buchanty P & K 185 J2
Buchany Stirlg 184 F6
Buchlyvie Stirlg 184 C8
Buckabank Cumb 148 C5
Buckden Cambs 75 H2
Buckden N York 131 H4
Buckenham Norfk 93 H3
Buckerell Devon 12 E3
Buckfast Devon 7 H3
Buckfastleigh Devon 7 H3
Buckhaven Fife 186 F7
Buckholt Mons 54 D5
Buckhorn Weston Dorset 27 H6
Buckhurst Hill Essex 45 H2
Buckie Moray 215 J2
Buckingham Bucks 73 K7
Buckland Bucks 58 E5
Buckland Devon 7 G6
Buckland Gloucs 71 J7
Buckland Herts 75 L7
Buckland Kent 35 J6
Buckland Oxon 41 G2
Buckland Surrey 31 K2
Buckland Brewer Devon 22 F7
Buckland Common Bucks 58 F6
Buckland Dinham Somset 27 H2
Buckland Filleigh Devon 10 C3
Buckland in the Moor Devon 7 G2
Buckland Monachorum Devon 6 D3
Buckland Newton Dorset 14 D2
Buckland Ripers Dorset 14 C6
Buckland St Mary Somset 25 L8
Buckland-Tout-Saints Devon 7 H6
Bucklebury W Berk 41 K6
Bucklers Hard Hants 16 E3
Bucklesham Suffk 78 F6
Buckley Flints 111 J8
Bucklow Hill Ches E 113 G5
Buckminster Leics 102 E7
Bucknall C Stke 99 K3
Bucknall Lincs 117 K7
Bucknell Oxon 57 K3
Bucknell Shrops 83 G8
Buckpool Moray 215 J2
Bucksburn C Aber 207 G4
Buck's Cross Devon 22 E6
Bucks Green W Susx 31 H5
Buckshaw Village Lancs 121 H6
Bucks Horn Oak Hants 30 D3
Buck's Mills Devon 22 E6
Buckton E R Yk 135 J5
Buckton Nthumb 169 G2
Buckworth Cambs 89 G7
Budby Notts 115 L7
Bude Cnwll 9 G4
Budge's Shop Cnwll 5 M4
Budleigh Salterton Devon 12 D6
Budock Water Cnwll 3 K5
Buerton Ches E 99 G4
Bugbrooke Nhants 73 J3
Bugle Cnwll 4 F4
Bugley Dorset 27 H6
Bugthorpe E R Yk 134 B7
Buildwas Shrops 84 B3
Builth Wells Powys 68 B4
Bulbridge Wilts 28 C5
Bulford Wilts 28 D3
Bulkeley Ches E 98 D2
Bulkington Warwks 86 E6
Bulkington Wilts 39 L8
Bulkworthy Devon 9 K3
Bullbrook Br For 42 E6
Bullington Hants 29 J3
Bullington Lincs 117 H6
Bulmer Essex 77 J6
Bulmer N York 133 L6
Bulmer Tye Essex 77 J6
Bulphan Thurr 45 M3
Bulwark Abers 217 H5
Bulwell C Nott 101 K4
Bulwick Nhants 88 D5
Bumble's Green Essex 60 C6
Bunacaimb Highld 199 K7
Bunarkaig Highld 201 J7
Bunbury Ches E 98 E2
Bunchrew Highld 212 F5
Bundalloch Highld 210 D8
Bunessan Ag & B 180 E3
Bungay Suffk 93 G5

Bunnahabhain Ag & B....171 H4
Bunny Notts....101 L6
Buntait Highld....212 C7
Buntingford Herts....60 B3
Bunwell Norfk....92 D5
Burbage Leics....86 F5
Burbage Wilts....40 E7
Burchett's Green W & M....42 D4
Burcombe Wilts....28 B5
Burcott Bucks....58 E4
Bures Essex....77 K7
Burford Oxon....56 E5
Burford Shrops....69 L2
Burg Ag & B....189 J7
Burgates Hants....30 C5
Burgess Hill W Susx....19 J2
Burgh Suffk....78 F4
Burgh by Sands Cumb....148 B3
Burgh Castle Norfk....93 K3
Burghclere Hants....41 J7
Burghead Moray....214 D1
Burghfield W Berk....42 A6
Burghfield Common W Berk....42 A6
Burgh Heath Surrey....44 E7
Burghill Herefs....69 J5
Burgh Island Devon....6 F6
Burgh le Marsh Lincs....119 G7
Burgh next Aylsham Norfk....106 F7
Burgh on Bain Lincs....117 L4
Burgh St Margaret Norfk....93 J2
Burgh St Peter Norfk....93 K5
Burghwallis Donc....124 E7
Burham Kent....46 B7
Buriton Hants....30 C7
Burland Ches E....98 E2
Burlawn Cnwll....4 F2
Burleigh Gloucs....55 K7
Burlescombe Devon....25 G7
Burleston Dorset....14 E4
Burley Hants....16 B2
Burley Rutlnd....88 C2
Burleydam Ches E....98 E4
Burley Gate Herefs....69 L5
Burley in Wharfedale C Brad....123 H2
Burley Street Hants....16 B2
Burley Wood Head C Brad....123 H2
Burlton Shrops....98 C7
Burmarsh Kent....34 E7
Burmington Warwks....72 C6
Burn N York....124 F5
Burnage Manch....113 K3
Burnaston Derbys....100 F6
Burnbrae N Lans....176 B6
Burnby E R Yk....125 K2
Burneside Cumb....138 D7
Burneston N York....132 D3
Burnett BaNES....38 F7
Burnfoot Border....166 F6
Burnfoot Border....167 H6
Burnfoot D & G....155 G4
Burnfoot D & G....156 C3
Burnfoot D & G....156 C4
Burnfoot P & K....185 K6
Burnham Bucks....42 F4
Burnham Deepdale Norfk....105 J4
Burnham Market Norfk....105 K4
Burnham Norton Norfk....105 K4
Burnham-on-Crouch Essex....46 F2
Burnham-on-Sea Somset....25 L2
Burnham Overy Norfk....105 K4
Burnham Overy Staithe Norfk....105 K4
Burnham Thorpe Norfk....105 K4
Burnhaven Abers....217 L5
Burnhead D & G....154 E3
Burnhervie Abers....206 D2
Burnhill Green Staffs....84 E4
Burnhope Dur....150 F5
Burnhouse N Ayrs....174 D7
Burniston N York....134 F2
Burnley Lancs....122 C4
Burnley Crematorium Lancs....122 B4
Burnmouth Border....179 K6
Burn of Cambus Stirlg....184 F6
Burnopfield Dur....150 F4
Burnsall N York....131 J7
Burnside Angus....196 C4
Burnside Angus....196 E6
Burnside Fife....186 B5
Burnside Moray....214 E1
Burnside W Loth....176 E3
Burnside of Duntrune Angus....187 G1
Burntisland Fife....177 H2
Burntwood Staffs....85 J2
Burntwood Green Staffs....85 J2
Burnt Yates N York....132 C7
Burnworthy Somset....25 J7
Burpham Surrey....31 G2
Burpham W Susx....18 E4
Burradon Nthumb....168 E7
Burrafirth Shet....235 e1
Burravoe Shet....235 d3
Burrells Cumb....138 F4
Burrelton P & K....195 K8
Burridge Devon....13 H2
Burridge Hants....17 G1
Burrill N York....132 C3
Burringham N Linc....125 K8
Burrington Devon....10 F2
Burrington Herefs....69 J1
Burrington N Som....38 C8
Burrough Green Cambs....76 F4
Burrough on the Hill Leics....87 L2
Burrow Lancs....130 C4
Burrow Somset....24 E3
Burrow Bridge Somset....26 A5
Burrowhill Surrey....42 F7
Burry Green Swans....50 F7
Burry Port Carmth....50 F5
Burscough Lancs....120 F7
Burscough Bridge Lancs....120 F7
Bursea E R Yk....125 J4
Bursledon Hants....16 F1
Burstall Suffk....78 D5
Burstock Dorset....13 K2
Burston Norfk....92 D6
Burstow Surrey....32 B5
Burstwick E R Yk....126 F5
Burtersett N York....131 G2
Burtholme Cumb....148 F3
Burthorpe Green Suffk....77 H2
Burtoft Lincs....103 L5
Burton Ches W....111 K6
Burton Ches W....112 D8
Burton Dorset....15 M4
Burton Lincs....116 F6
Burton Pembks....49 G6
Burton Somset....25 J3
Burton Wilts....39 J4
Burton Agnes E R Yk....135 H6
Burton Bradstock Dorset....13 L4
Burton Coggles Lincs....103 G7
Burton End Essex....60 E4
Burton Fleming E R Yk....135 G5
Burton Hastings Warwks....86 E5
Burton-in-Kendal Cumb....129 L4
Burton-in-Kendal Services Cumb....129 L4
Burton in Lonsdale N York....130 C5
Burton Joyce Notts....101 M4
Burton Latimer Nhants....88 C8
Burton Lazars Leics....87 L1
Burton Leonard N York....132 E6
Burton on the Wolds Leics....101 L7
Burton Overy Leics....87 J4
Burton Pedwardine Lincs....103 J4
Burton Pidsea E R Yk....127 G4
Burton Salmon N York....124 D5
Burton's Green Essex....61 K3
Burton upon Stather N Linc....125 K6
Burton upon Trent Staffs....100 E7
Burton Waters Lincs....116 F6
Burtonwood Warrtn....112 E3
Burtonwood Services Warrtn....112 E4
Burwardsley Ches W....98 D2
Burwarton Shrops....84 B6
Burwash E Susx....33 H7
Burwash Common E Susx....20 D2
Burwash Weald E Susx....20 D2
Burwell Cambs....76 E2
Burwell Lincs....118 E5
Burwen IoA....108 E3
Burwick Ork....234 c8
Bury Bury....122 B7
Bury Cambs....89 K6
Bury Somset....24 E6
Bury W Susx....18 D3
Bury Green Herts....60 D4
Bury St Edmunds Suffk....77 J2
Burythorpe N York....134 C6
Busby E Rens....175 G6
Buscot Oxon....40 E2
Bush Abers....197 J4
Bush Bank Herefs....69 J4
Bushbury Wolves....85 G3
Bushbury Crematorium Wolves....85 G3
Bushey Herts....43 J2
Bushey Heath Herts....43 J2
Bush Hill Park Gt Lon....45 G2
Bushley Worcs....70 F7
Bushmoor Shrops....83 J6
Bushton Wilts....40 B5
Bussage Gloucs....55 K7
Bussex Somset....26 A4
Butcombe N Som....38 D7
Bute Ag & B....173 H4
Butleigh Somset....26 D5
Butleigh Wootton Somset....26 D4
Butlers Marston Warwks....72 D4
Butley Suffk....79 H4
Buttercrambe N York....133 L7
Butterdean Border....179 G5
Butterknowle Dur....140 E3
Butterleigh Devon....12 C2
Buttermere Cumb....137 G4
Buttershaw C Brad....123 H5
Butterstone P & K....195 G7
Butterton Staffs....99 J4
Butterton Staffs....100 B2
Butterwick Lincs....104 C4
Butterwick N York....133 L4
Butterwick N York....134 F5
Buttington Powys....82 E2
Buttonoak Shrops....84 D7
Buxhall Suffk....78 B3
Buxted E Susx....20 A2
Buxton Derbys....114 B6
Buxton Norfk....106 F7
Buxton Heath Norfk....106 E7
Bwlch Powys....53 J4
Bwlchgwyn Wrexhm....97 K2
Bwlchllan Cerdgn....66 D3
Bwlchtocyn Gwynd....94 E7
Bwlch-y-cibau Powys....97 J8
Bwlch-y-ffridd Powys....82 B4
Bwlch-y-groes Pembks....65 H7
Bwlch-y-sarnau Powys....82 B8
Byers Green Dur....150 F7
Byfield Nhants....73 G4
Byfleet Surrey....43 H7
Byford Herefs....69 H6
Byker N u Ty....151 G3
Bylchau Conwy....110 D8
Byley Ches W....113 G7
Byrness Nthumb....157 K2
Bystock Devon....12 D5
Bythorn Cambs....88 F7
Byton Herefs....69 G2
Bywell Nthumb....150 D3
Byworth W Susx....31 G7

C

Cabourne Lincs....117 J2
Cabrach Ag & B....171 J5
Cabrach Moray....215 J8
Cabus Lancs....121 G2
Cadbury Devon....11 L4
Cadbury World Birm....85 J7
Cadder E Duns....175 G4
Caddington C Beds....59 H4
Caddonfoot Border....167 G3
Cadeby Donc....115 K2
Cadeby Leics....86 E3
Cadeleigh Devon....11 L4
Cade Street E Susx....20 C2
Cadgwith Cnwll....3 J7
Cadham Fife....186 D6
Cadishead Salfd....113 G3
Cadle Swans....51 J6
Cadley Lancs....121 G4
Cadley Wilts....28 E2
Cadley Wilts....40 E6
Cadmore End Bucks....42 C3
Cadnam Hants....28 F8
Cadney N Linc....117 G2
Cadoxton V Glam....37 H6
Cadoxton Juxta-Neath Neath....51 L5
Caeathro Gwynd....95 J1
Caenby Lincs....117 G4
Caeo Carmth....66 F6
Caerau Brdgnd....36 D2
Caerau Cardif....37 H5
Caer Farchell Pembks....48 D3
Caergeiliog IoA....108 D5
Caergwrle Flints....97 L2
Caerlanrig Border....156 D2
Caerleon Newpt....37 M3
Caernarfon Gwynd....108 F8
Caernarfon Castle Gwynd....108 F8
Caerphilly Caerph....37 J3
Caersws Powys....82 B5
Caerwedros Cerdgn....65 L4
Caerwent Mons....38 C3
Caerwys Flints....110 F6
Cairinis W Isls....233 c6
Cairnbaan Ag & B....172 E1
Cairnbulg Abers....217 J2
Cairncross Border....179 J5
Cairncurran Inver....174 C4
Cairndow Ag & B....183 H5
Cairneyhill Fife....176 E2
Cairngarroch D & G....144 C5
Cairngorms National Park....204 C5
Cairnie Abers....215 K5

Cairnorrie Abers 217 G6
Cairnryan D & G 144 C2
Cairnty Moray 215 H4
Caister-on-Sea Norfk 93 L2
Caistor Lincs 117 J2
Caistor St Edmund Norfk 92 F3
Calanais W Isls 232 e2
Calbourne IoW 16 E5
Calcot Flints 111 G6
Calcot Gloucs 56 C6
Calcot Row W Berk 42 A6
Calcots Moray 215 G2
Caldbeck Cumb 148 B6
Caldecote Cambs 75 L3
Caldecote Cambs 89 G5
Caldecote Highfields Cambs 75 L3
Caldecott Nhants 74 E2
Caldecott Oxon 41 J2
Caldecott Rutlnd 88 C5
Calderbank N Lans 175 K5
Calder Bridge Cumb 136 E6
Caldercruix N Lans 175 L5
Calder Grove Wakefd 123 L6
Caldermill S Lans 164 D2
Calder Vale Lancs 121 G2
Calderwood S Lans 175 H7
Caldey Island Pembks 49 K7
Caldicot Mons 38 C3
Caldmore Wsall 85 H4
Caldwell N York 140 E5
Calf of Man IoM 237 a7
Calfsound Ork 234 d4
Calgary Ag & B 189 J6
Califer Moray 214 D3
California Falk 176 B3
California Norfk 93 K1
Calke Derbys 101 G7
Calke Abbey Derbys 101 G7
Callakille Highld 209 L4
Callander Stirlg 184 D5
Callanish W Isls 232 e2
Callestick Cnwll 3 K2
Calligarry Highld 199 K5
Callington Cnwll 6 A3
Callow Herefs 69 J7
Callow End Worcs 70 E4
Callow Hill Wilts 40 B4
Calmore Hants 29 G7
Calmsden Gloucs 56 B6
Calne Wilts 39 M6
Calshot Hants 16 F3
Calstock Cnwll 6 C3
Calstone Wellington Wilts 40 B6
Calthorpe Norfk 106 E6
Calthorpe Street Norfk 107 J7
Calthwaite Cumb 148 E6
Calton Staffs 100 C3
Calveley Ches E 98 E2
Calver Derbys 114 E6
Calverhall Shrops 98 E5
Calverleigh Devon 11 L3
Calverton M Keyn 73 L6
Calverton Notts 101 L3
Calvine P & K 194 C3
Calzeat Border 165 L3
Cam Gloucs 55 H7
Camasachoirce Highld 190 F4
Camasine Highld 190 F4
Camas Luinie Highld 210 E8
Camastianavaig Highld 209 H6
Camault Muir Highld 212 D6
Camber E Susx 21 J2
Camberley Surrey 42 E7
Camberwell Gt Lon 44 F5
Camblesforth N York 124 F5
Cambo Nthumb 158 C5
Camborne Cnwll 3 H4
Camborne and Redruth Mining District Cnwll 3 H4
Cambourne Cambs 75 K3
Cambridge Cambs 76 C3
Cambridge Gloucs 55 H7
Cambridge Airport Cambs 76 C3
Cambridge City Crematorium Cambs 76 B3
Cambrose Cnwll 3 H3
Cambus Clacks 185 H8
Cambusavie Platform Highld 223 G3
Cambusbarron Stirlg 185 G8
Cambuskenneth Stirlg 185 G8
Cambuslang S Lans 175 H6
Cambus o' May Abers 205 J5
Cambuswallace S Lans 165 K2
Camden Town Gt Lon 44 F4
Cameley BaNES 38 E8
Camelford Cnwll 8 E7
Camelon Falk 176 B3
Camerory Highld 214 C7
Camerton BaNES 39 G8
Camerton Cumb 136 E2
Camghouran P & K 193 J5
Camieston Border 167 J4
Cammachmore Abers 207 G6
Cammeringham Lincs 116 F5
Camore Highld 223 G4
Campbeltown Ag & B 161 J5
Campbeltown Airport Ag & B 161 H5
Cample D & G 154 F4
Campmuir P & K 195 K8
Camps W Loth 176 E5
Campsall Donc 124 E7
Campsea Ash Suffk 79 G4
Campton C Beds 75 G6
Camptown Border 167 K6
Camrose Pembks 48 F4
Camserney P & K 194 C6
Camusnagaul Highld 191 L2
Camusnagaul Highld 220 D4
Camusteel Highld 209 L6
Camusterrach Highld 209 L6
Canada Hants 28 F7
Candacraig Abers 205 H5
Candlesby Lincs 118 F7
Candy Mill Border 165 L2
Cane End Oxon 42 B4
Canewdon Essex 46 E2
Canford Cliffs Poole 15 K5
Canford Crematorium Bristl 38 E5
Canford Heath Poole 15 J4
Canisbay Highld 231 L2
Canley Covtry 86 C7
Canley Crematorium Covtry 86 C7
Cann Dorset 27 K7
Canna Highld 198 C4
Cann Common Dorset 27 K7
Cannich Highld 211 L7
Cannington Somset 25 K4
Canning Town Gt Lon 45 H4
Cannock Staffs 85 H2
Cannock Chase Staffs 99 M8
Cannon Bridge Herefs 69 H6
Canonbie D & G 156 C6
Canon Frome Herefs 70 B5
Canon Pyon Herefs 69 J5
Canons Ashby Nhants 73 H4
Canonstown Cnwll 2 F4
Canterbury Kent 34 F3
Canterbury Cathedral Kent 34 F3
Cantley Norfk 93 H3
Canton Cardif 37 J5
Cantraywood Highld 213 J5
Cantsfield Lancs 130 C5
Canvey Island Essex 46 D4
Canwick Lincs 117 G7
Canworthy Water Cnwll 9 G6
Caol Highld 191 L2
Caolas Scalpaigh W Isls 232 e4
Caoles Ag & B 188 D6
Caonich Highld 201 G6
Capel Kent 33 H4
Capel Surrey 31 K4
Capel Bangor Cerdgn 80 E7
Capel Coch IoA 108 F5
Capel Curig Conwy 96 A2
Capel Dewi Carmth 50 F2
Capel Dewi Cerdgn 66 B6
Capel-Dewi Cerdgn 80 E6
Capel Garmon Conwy 96 C2
Capel Hendre Carmth 51 H4
Capel Iwan Carmth 65 J7
Capel le Ferne Kent 35 H6
Capelles Guern 236 d2
Capel Parc IoA 108 F4
Capel St Andrew Suffk 79 H5
Capel St Mary Suffk 78 C6
Capel Seion Cerdgn 80 E7
Capelulo Conwy 109 L6
Capenhurst Ches W 111 K6
Cape Wrath Highld 228 D1
Capheaton Nthumb 158 C6
Caplaw E Rens 174 E6
Cappercleuch Border 166 C5
Capton Devon 7 J5
Caputh P & K 195 H7
Caradon Mining District Cnwll 5 L2
Carbeth Inn Stirlg 174 F3
Carbis Bay Cnwll 2 F4
Carbost Highld 208 F5
Carbost Highld 208 F7
Carbrook Sheff 115 G4
Carbrooke Norfk 91 L3
Car Colston Notts 102 B4
Carcroft Donc 124 E8
Cardenden Fife 186 C7
Cardhu Moray 214 F5
Cardiff Cardif 37 J5
Cardiff Airport V Glam 37 G6
Cardiff & Glamorgan Crematorium Cardif 37 J4
Cardiff Gate Services Cardif 37 K4
Cardiff West Services Cardif 37 H4
Cardigan Cerdgn 65 G5
Cardington Bed 74 F5
Cardington Shrops 83 K4
Cardinham Cnwll 5 H3
Cardrain D & G 144 D8
Cardrona Border 166 D2
Cardross Ag & B 174 C3
Cardross Crematorium Ag & B 174 C3
Cardryne D & G 144 D7
Cardurnock Cumb 147 L3
Careby Lincs 88 E1
Careston Angus 196 E4
Carew Pembks 49 H6
Carew Cheriton Pembks 49 H6
Carew Newton Pembks 49 H6
Carey Herefs 54 E2
Carfin N Lans 175 K6
Carfraemill Border 178 B7
Cargate Green Norfk 93 H2
Cargenbridge D & G 155 G7
Cargill P & K 195 J8
Cargo Cumb 148 C3
Cargreen Cnwll 6 C4
Carham Nthumb 168 B2
Carhampton Somset 24 F3
Carharrack Cnwll 3 J3
Carie P & K 193 K5
Carinish W Isls 233 c6
Carisbrooke IoW 16 F5
Cark Cumb 129 H4
Carkeel Cnwll 6 B4
Carlabhagh W Isls 232 e2
Carlbury Darltn 140 F4
Carlby Lincs 88 F2
Carleen Cnwll 3 G5
Carleton N York 122 E1
Carleton Crematorium Bpool 120 D3
Carleton Forehoe Norfk 92 C3
Carleton Rode Norfk 92 D5
Carleton St Peter Norfk 93 H3
Carlincraig Abers 216 D5
Carlingcott BaNES 39 G8
Carlisle Cumb 148 D4
Carlisle Airport Cumb 148 E3
Carlisle Crematorium Cumb 148 C4
Carlops Border 177 G6
Carloway W Isls 232 e2
Carlton Barns 124 B7
Carlton Bed 74 D4
Carlton Cambs 76 F4
Carlton Leeds 123 L5
Carlton Leics 86 E3
Carlton N York 124 F5
Carlton N York 131 K3
Carlton N York 133 J3
Carlton Notts 101 L4
Carlton S on T 141 J3
Carlton Suffk 79 H2
Carlton Colville Suffk 93 K5
Carlton Curlieu Leics 87 K4
Carlton Green Cambs 76 F4
Carlton Husthwaite N York 133 G4
Carlton-in-Cleveland N York 142 B6
Carlton in Lindrick Notts 115 L5
Carlton-le-Moorland Lincs 102 E2
Carlton Miniott N York 132 F4
Carlton-on-Trent Notts 116 D8
Carlton Scroop Lincs 102 F4
Carluke S Lans 175 L7
Carmacoup S Lans 164 F4
Carmarthen Carmth 50 E2
Carmel Carmth 51 H3
Carmel Flints 111 G6
Carmel Gwynd 95 H2
Carmichael S Lans 165 H2
Carmountside Crematorium C Stke 99 K3
Carmunnock C Glas 175 G6
Carmyle C Glas 175 H6
Carmyllie Angus 196 E7
Carnaby E R Yk 135 H6
Carnbee Fife 187 J6
Carnbo P & K 185 L6
Carn Brea Cnwll 3 H3
Carnbrogie Abers 216 F8
Carndu Highld 210 D8
Carnduff S Lans 164 D1
Carnell E Ayrs 163 L3
Carnforth Lancs 129 K5
Carn-gorm Highld 200 E2
Carnhell Green Cnwll 3 G4
Carnie Abers 206 F4
Carnkie Cnwll 3 H4
Carnkie Cnwll 3 J4
Carno Powys 81 K4
Carnock Fife 176 E1
Carnon Downs Cnwll 4 C7
Carnousie Abers 216 C4
Carnoustie Angus 187 J1
Carnwath S Lans 165 J1
Carol Green Solhll 86 C7
Carperby N York 131 J2
Carradale Ag & B 161 K2
Carrbridge Highld 203 L2
Carrefour Jersey 236 c6
Carreglefn IoA 108 E4
Carr Gate Wakefd 123 L5

Carrhouse N Linc 116 C1
Carrick Ag & B 172 F2
Carrick Castle Ag & B 183 H8
Carriden Falk 176 D3
Carrington Mdloth 177 J6
Carrington Traffd 113 H3
Carrog Denbgs 97 H4
Carron Falk 176 B2
Carron Moray 214 F6
Carronbridge D & G 154 F3
Carron Bridge Stirlg 175 K2
Carronshore Falk 176 B2
Carr Shield Nthumb 149 K5
Carrutherstown D & G 155 J7
Carruth House Inver 174 C5
Carrville Dur 151 H6
Carsaig Ag & B 181 H3
Carseriggan D & G 145 G2
Carsethorn D & G 147 H3
Carshalton Gt Lon 44 F6
Carsington Derbys 100 E2
Carskey Ag & B 161 H7
Carsluith D & G 145 K4
Carsphairn D & G 153 L4
Carstairs S Lans 165 H1
Carstairs Junction S Lans 165 J1
Carterton Oxon 56 F6
Carthew Cnwll 4 F5
Carthorpe N York 132 D3
Cartland S Lans 165 G1
Cartmel Cumb 129 H4
Carway Carmth 50 F4
Cashe's Green Gloucs 55 J6
Cassington Oxon 57 J5
Cassop Colliery Dur 151 J7
Castel Guern 236 c3
Casterton Cumb 130 C4
Castle Acre Norfk 91 J1
Castle Ashby Nhants 74 C3
Castlebay W Isls 233 b9
Castle Bolton N York 131 J2
Castle Bromwich Solhll 85 K5
Castle Bytham Lincs 103 G8
Castlebythe Pembks 49 H2
Castle Caereinion Powys 82 D3
Castle Camps Cambs 76 F6
Castle Carrock Cumb 148 F4
Castlecary Falk 175 K3
Castle Cary Somset 26 F5
Castle Combe Wilts 39 J5
Castle Donington Leics 101 H6
Castle Douglas D & G 146 D3
Castle Eaton Swindn 40 C2
Castle Eden Dur 151 K7
Castleford Wakefd 124 C5
Castle Frome Herefs 70 C5
Castle Gresley Derbys 100 F8
Castle Hedingham Essex 77 H7
Castlehill Border 166 C3
Castlehill Highld 231 H2
Castle Hill Suffk 78 D5
Castlehill W Duns 174 D3
Castle Howard N York 133 L5
Castle Kennedy D & G 144 D3
Castle Lachlan Ag & B 182 E7
Castlemartin Pembks 48 F7
Castlemilk C Glas 175 G6
Castlemorton Worcs 70 E6
Castlemorton Common Worcs 70 E6
Castle O'er D & G 156 A4
Castle Pulverbatch Shrops 83 H3
Castle Rising Norfk 105 G7
Castleside Dur 150 D5
Castle Stuart Highld 213 H4
Castlethorpe M Keyn 74 B5
Castleton Border 156 E4
Castleton Derbys 114 D5
Castleton N York 142 E5
Castleton Newpt 37 K4
Castleton Rochdl 122 D7
Castletown Highld 231 H3
Castletown IoM 237 b7
Castletown Sundld 151 J4
Castley N York 123 K2
Caston Norfk 91 L4
Castor C Pete 89 G4
Catacol N Ayrs 172 F7
Catcliffe Rothm 115 H4
Catcomb Wilts 40 A5
Catcott Somset 26 B4
Catcott Burtle Somset 26 B3
Caterham Surrey 32 C3
Catfield Norfk 107 H7
Catford Gt Lon 45 G5
Catforth Lancs 121 G4
Cathcart C Glas 175 G6
Cathedine Powys 53 H3
Catherington Hants 30 B8
Catherston Leweston Dorset 13 J4
Catisfield Hants 17 G2
Catlodge Highld 202 F6
Catmere End Essex 76 C6
Catmore W Berk 41 J4
Caton Lancs 129 L6
Caton Green Lancs 129 L6
Catrine E Ayrs 164 B4
Catsfield E Susx 20 E3
Catsgore Somset 26 D6
Catshill Worcs 85 G8
Cattadale Ag & B 161 H7
Cattal N York 133 G8
Cattawade Suffk 62 D2
Catterall Lancs 121 G3
Catterick N York 141 G7
Catterick Bridge N York 141 G7
Catterlen Cumb 148 E7
Catterline Abers 197 L2
Catterton N York 124 D2
Catteshall Surrey 31 G3
Catthorpe Leics 87 G7
Cattistock Dorset 14 B3
Catton N York 132 E4
Catton Nthumb 149 L4
Catwick E R Yk 126 E2
Catworth Cambs 88 F8
Caudle Green Gloucs 55 L6
Caulcott Oxon 57 K3
Cauldcots Angus 197 G6
Cauldhame Stirlg 184 E8
Cauldmill Border 167 H6
Cauldon Staffs 100 B3
Cauldwell Derbys 86 B1
Caulkerbush D & G 147 G4
Caulside D & G 156 D6
Caundle Marsh Dorset 27 G8
Caunton Notts 102 C1
Causeway End D & G 145 J3
Causeway End Essex 61 G4
Causewayend S Lans 165 K3
Causewayhead Stirlg 185 G7
Causeyend Abers 207 H2
Causey Park Bridge Nthumb 158 F3
Cavendish Suffk 77 J5
Cavenham Suffk 77 H1
Caversfield Oxon 57 L3
Caversham Readg 42 B5
Caverswall Staffs 99 L4
Caverton Mill Border 167 M4
Cawdor Highld 213 K4
Cawood N York 124 E3
Cawsand Cnwll 6 C5
Cawston Norfk 106 D7
Cawthorne Barns 123 K8
Caxton Cambs 75 K3
Caynham Shrops 83 K8
Caythorpe Lincs 102 F3
Caythorpe Notts 102 B4
Cayton N York 135 G3
Ceann a Bhaigh W Isls 233 b6
Ceannacroc Lodge Highld 201 K3
Cearsiadar W Isls 232 f3
Cefn Newpt 37 L3
Cefn-brith Conwy 96 E3
Cefn-bryn-brain Carmth 51 L3
Cefn Cribwr Brdgnd 36 D4
Cefneithin Carmth 51 G3
Cefngorwydd Powys 67 J5
Cefn-mawr Wrexhm 97 L4
Cefn-y-pant Carmth 49 K3
Cellardyke Fife 187 J6
Cellarhead Staffs 99 L3
Cemaes IoA 108 E3
Cemmaes Powys 81 H3
Cemmaes Road Powys 81 H3
Cenarth Cerdgn 65 J6
Ceres Fife 186 F5
Cerne Abbas Dorset 14 C3
Cerney Wick Gloucs 40 B2
Cerrigydrudion Conwy 96 E3
Ceunant Gwynd 95 J1
Chaceley Gloucs 55 J2
Chacewater Cnwll 3 K3
Chackmore Bucks 73 K7
Chacombe Nhants 72 F5
Chadbury Worcs 71 H5
Chadderton Oldham 113 K1
Chaddesden C Derb 101 G5
Chaddesley Corbett Worcs 84 F8
Chaddlehanger Devon 6 C1
Chaddleworth W Berk 41 H5
Chadlington Oxon 57 G4
Chadshunt Warwks 72 D4
Chadwell Leics 102 C7
Chadwell Heath Gt Lon 45 J3
Chadwell St Mary Thurr 45 M4
Chadwick Worcs 70 E2
Chadwick End Solhll 86 B8
Chaffcombe Somset 13 J1
Chagford Devon 11 G7
Chailey E Susx 19 K2
Chainhurst Kent 33 J4
Chaldon Surrey 32 B3
Chale IoW 16 F6
Chale Green IoW 16 F6
Chalfont Common Bucks 43 G3
Chalfont St Giles Bucks 43 G2
Chalfont St Peter Bucks 43 G3
Chalford Gloucs 55 K7
Chalford Wilts 27 K2
Chalgrove Oxon 41 M2
Chalk Kent 46 A5
Chalkwell Kent 34 B2
Challacombe Devon 23 L3
Challoch D & G 145 H2
Challock Kent 34 D5
Chalton C Beds 59 G3
Chalton Hants 30 B7
Chalvey Slough 42 F4
Chalvington E Susx 20 B4
Chandler's Cross Herts 43 H2
Chandler's Ford Hants 29 H7
Channel Tunnel Terminal Kent 35 G6
Chanterlands Crematorium C KuH 126 D4
Chantry Somset 27 G3
Chantry Suffk 78 D5
Chapel Fife 186 D8
Chapel Allerton Leeds 123 L3
Chapel Allerton Somset 26 B2
Chapel Amble Cnwll 4 F2
Chapel Brampton Nhants 73 K2
Chapel Chorlton Staffs 99 J5
Chapelend Way Essex 77 G6
Chapel-en-le-Frith Derbys 114 B5
Chapel Green Warwks 72 F3
Chapel Haddlesey N York 124 E5
Chapelhall N Lans 175 K5
Chapel Hill Abers 217 K7
Chapel Hill Lincs 103 K2
Chapel Hill Mons 54 D7
Chapel Hill N York 123 L2
Chapelhope Border 166 C5
Chapelknowe D & G 156 B7
Chapel Lawn Shrops 82 F7
Chapel-le-Dale N York 130 E4
Chapel Leigh Somset 25 H5
Chapel of Garioch Abers 206 D1
Chapel Rossan D & G 144 D6
Chapel Row W Berk 41 L6
Chapel St Leonards Lincs 119 H6
Chapel Stile Cumb 137 K6
Chapelton Angus 197 G6
Chapelton Devon 23 J6
Chapelton S Lans 175 J8
Chapeltown Bl w D 121 L7
Chapeltown Moray 204 F2
Chapeltown Sheff 115 G3
Chapmanslade Wilts 27 J2
Chapmans Well Devon 9 J6
Chapmore End Herts 60 B5
Chappel Essex 61 L3
Chard Somset 13 H2
Chard Junction Somset 13 J2
Chardleigh Green Somset 13 H1
Chardstock Devon 13 H2
Charfield S Glos 39 G3
Charing Kent 34 C5
Charing Crematorium Kent 34 C5
Charingworth Gloucs 71 L6
Charlbury Oxon 57 G4
Charlcombe BaNES 39 H6
Charlcutt Wilts 39 M5
Charlecote Warwks 72 C3
Charlemont Sandw 85 H5
Charles Devon 23 L5
Charleston Angus 196 C7
Charlestown C Aber 207 H5
Charlestown C Brad 123 H3
Charlestown Calder 122 E5
Charlestown Cnwll 5 G5
Charlestown Fife 176 E2
Charlestown Highld 213 G5
Charlestown Highld 219 J6
Charlestown Salfd 113 J2
Charles Tye Suffk 78 B4
Charlesworth Derbys 114 A3
Charlinch Somset 25 K4
Charlottetown Fife 186 E5
Charlton Gt Lon 45 H4
Charlton Nhants 73 G7
Charlton Nthumb 157 K5
Charlton Oxon 41 H3
Charlton Somset 25 L6
Charlton Somset 27 G2
Charlton W Susx 18 B3
Charlton Wilts 27 K6
Charlton Wilts 39 L3
Charlton Worcs 71 H5
Charlton Wrekin 83 L2
Charlton Abbots Gloucs 56 B3
Charlton Adam Somset 26 D5
Charlton All Saints Wilts 28 D6
Charlton Down Dorset 14 D4

Charlton Horethorne Somset 26 F6
Charlton Kings Gloucs 55 L4
Charlton Mackrell Somset 26 D5
Charlton Marshall Dorset 15 G2
Charlton Musgrove Somset 27 G5
Charlton-on-Otmoor Oxon 57 K5
Charlton on the Hill Dorset 15 G2
Charlton St Peter Wilts 28 C1
Charlwood Hants 30 A5
Charlwood Surrey 31 L3
Charminster Dorset 14 D4
Charmouth Dorset 13 J4
Charndon Bucks 58 A3
Charney Bassett Oxon 41 G2
Charnock Richard Lancs 121 H7
Charnock Richard Crematorium Lancs 121 H6
Charnock Richard Services Lancs 121 H7
Charsfield Suffk 78 F3
Charter Alley Hants 41 L8
Charterhall Border 179 G8
Charterhouse Somset 26 D1
Chartershall Stirlg 175 K1
Chartham Kent 34 E4
Chartham Hatch Kent 34 E4
Chartridge Bucks 58 F7
Chart Sutton Kent 33 K4
Charvil Wokham 42 C5
Charwelton Nhants 73 G4
Chase Terrace Staffs 85 J2
Chasetown Staffs 85 J2
Chastleton Oxon 56 E3
Chasty Devon 9 J4
Chatburn Lancs 121 L2
Chatcull Staffs 99 H5
Chatham Medway 46 C6
Chatham Green Essex 61 H5
Chathill Nthumb 169 J4
Chatsworth House Derbys 114 E7
Chattenden Medway 46 C5
Chatteris Cambs 90 B6
Chatterton Lancs 122 B6
Chattisham Suffk 78 C6
Chatto Border 168 B5
Chatton Nthumb 168 F4
Chawleigh Devon 11 G3
Chawton Hants 30 B4
Cheadle Staffs 100 A4
Cheadle Stockp 113 K4
Cheadle Hulme Stockp 113 K4
Cheam Gt Lon 44 E7
Chearsley Bucks 58 B6
Chebsey Staffs 99 J6
Checkendon Oxon 42 A4
Checkley Ches E 99 G4
Checkley Staffs 100 B5
Chedburgh Suffk 77 H3
Cheddar Somset 26 C2
Cheddington Bucks 58 F4
Cheddleton Staffs 99 L3
Cheddon Fitzpaine Somset 25 K6
Chedgrave Norfk 93 H4
Chedington Dorset 13 L2
Chediston Suffk 93 H7
Chedworth Gloucs 56 B5
Chedzoy Somset 25 M4
Cheetham Hill Manch 113 J2
Cheldon Devon 11 H3
Chelford Ches E 113 J6
Chellaston C Derb 101 G6
Chellington Bed 74 D4
Chelmarsh Shrops 84 C5
Chelmondiston Suffk 78 E6
Chelmorton Derbys 114 C7
Chelmsford Essex 61 H6
Chelmsford Crematorium Essex 61 H6
Chelmsley Wood Solhll 85 L6
Chelsea Gt Lon 44 F4
Chelsfield Gt Lon 45 J7
Chelsworth Suffk 77 L5
Cheltenham Gloucs 55 L4
Cheltenham Crematorium Gloucs 55 L4
Chelveston Nhants 74 E1
Chelvey N Som 38 C6
Chelwood BaNES 38 F7
Chelwood Gate E Susx 32 D6
Cheney Longville Shrops 83 H6
Chenies Bucks 43 G2
Chepstow Mons 38 D2
Cherhill Wilts 40 B6
Cherington Gloucs 55 K7
Cherington Warwks 72 C6
Cheriton Hants 29 L5
Cheriton Kent 35 G7
Cheriton Swans 50 F6
Cheriton Bishop Devon 11 H6
Cheriton Fitzpaine Devon 11 K4
Cheriton or Stackpole Elidor Pembks 49 G7
Cherrington Wrekin 98 F8
Cherry Burton E R Yk 126 B3
Cherry Hinton Cambs 76 C3
Cherry Orchard Worcs 70 F4
Cherry Willingham Lincs 117 G6
Chertsey Surrey 43 H6
Cherwell Valley Services Oxon 57 K3
Cheselbourne Dorset 14 E3
Chesham Bucks 58 F7
Chesham Bury 122 B7
Chesham Bois Bucks 58 F7
Cheshire Farm Ice Cream Ches W 98 D2
Cheshunt Herts 60 B7
Chesil Beach Dorset 14 B6
Cheslyn Hay Staffs 85 H3
Chessetts Wood Warwks 85 L8
Chessington Gt Lon 44 D7
Chessington World of Adventures Gt Lon 44 D7
Chester Ches W 112 B7
Chesterblade Somset 26 F3
Chester Crematorium Ches W 111 L7
Chesterfield Derbys 115 G7
Chesterfield Crematorium Derbys 115 H6
Chesterhill Mdloth 177 K5
Chester-le-Street Dur 151 G5
Chester Moor Dur 151 G5
Chesters Border 167 J5
Chesters Border 167 K7
Chester Services Ches W 112 C6
Chesterton Cambs 76 C3
Chesterton Cambs 89 G4
Chesterton Gloucs 56 A7
Chesterton Oxon 57 K4
Chesterton Shrops 84 D4
Chesterton Staffs 99 J3
Chesterton Green Warwks 72 D3
Chesterwood Nthumb 149 L2
Chester Zoo Ches W 112 B7
Chestfield Kent 47 J6
Cheston Devon 7 G4
Cheswardine Shrops 99 G6
Cheswick Nthumb 168 F1
Chetnole Dorset 14 B2
Chettisham Cambs 90 D6
Chettle Dorset 27 L8
Chetton Shrops 84 B5
Chetwynd Wrekin 99 G7
Chetwynd Aston Wrekin 99 H8
Cheveley Cambs 76 F3
Chevening Kent 32 E2
Chevington Suffk 77 H3
Cheviot Hills 168 A7
Chevithorne Devon 24 F7
Chew Magna BaNES 38 E7
Chew Stoke BaNES 38 E7
Chewton Keynsham BaNES 38 F6
Chewton Mendip Somset 26 E2
Chicheley M Keyn 74 C5
Chichester W Susx 18 B5
Chichester Crematorium W Susx 18 B4
Chickerell Dorset 14 C6
Chicklade Wilts 27 K4
Chidden Hants 30 A7
Chiddingfold Surrey 30 F4
Chiddingly E Susx 20 B3
Chiddingstone Kent 32 E4
Chiddingstone Causeway Kent 32 F4
Chideock Dorset 13 K4
Chidham W Susx 17 L2
Chidswell Kirk 123 K6
Chieveley W Berk 41 J5
Chieveley Services W Berk 41 J6
Chignall St James Essex 61 G6
Chignall Smealy Essex 61 G5
Chigwell Essex 45 H2
Chigwell Row Essex 45 J2
Chilbolton Hants 29 H4
Chilcomb Hants 29 J5
Chilcombe Dorset 13 M4
Chilcompton Somset 26 F2
Chilcote Leics 86 C2
Childer Thornton Ches W 111 K6
Child Okeford Dorset 27 J8
Childrey Oxon 41 G3
Child's Ercall Shrops 98 F7
Childswickham Worcs 71 J6
Childwall Lpool 112 B4
Chilfrome Dorset 14 B3
Chilgrove W Susx 18 A3
Chilham Kent 34 E4
Chillaton Devon 10 C8
Chillenden Kent 35 H4
Chillerton IoW 16 F5
Chillesford Suffk 79 H4
Chillington Devon 7 J7
Chillington Somset 13 K1
Chilmark Wilts 27 L5
Chilmington Green Kent 34 C6
Chilson Oxon 56 F4
Chilsworthy Cnwll 6 B2
Chilsworthy Devon 9 J4
Chiltern Hills 42 C2
Chilterns Crematorium Bucks 42 F2
Chilthorne Domer Somset 26 D7
Chilton Bucks 58 B5
Chilton Dur 141 H2
Chilton Oxon 41 J4
Chilton Candover Hants 29 L4
Chilton Cantelo Somset 26 E6
Chilton Foliat Wilts 40 F6
Chilton Polden Somset 26 B4
Chilton Street Suffk 77 H5
Chilton Trinity Somset 25 L4
Chilwell Notts 101 K5
Chilworth Hants 29 H7
Chilworth Surrey 31 G3
Chimney Oxon 57 G7
Chineham Hants 30 A1
Chingford Gt Lon 45 G2
Chinley Derbys 114 B5
Chinnor Oxon 58 C7
Chipnall Shrops 99 G6
Chippenham Cambs 76 F1
Chippenham Wilts 39 L5
Chipperfield Herts 59 H7
Chipping Herts 60 B2
Chipping Lancs 121 J2
Chipping Campden Gloucs 71 L6
Chipping Norton Oxon 56 F3
Chipping Ongar Essex 60 E7
Chipping Sodbury S Glos 39 G4
Chipping Warden Nhants 72 F5
Chipstable Somset 25 G6
Chipstead Kent 32 E3
Chipstead Surrey 32 B2
Chirbury Shrops 82 F4
Chirk Wrexhm 97 L5
Chirnside Border 179 H6
Chirnsidebridge Border 179 H7
Chirton Wilts 40 B8
Chisbury Wilts 40 F6
Chiselborough Somset 26 C8
Chiseldon Swindn 40 D4
Chiselhampton Oxon 57 L7
Chisholme Border 166 F6
Chislehurst Gt Lon 45 H6
Chislet Kent 47 L6
Chisley Calder 122 F5
Chiswell Green Herts 59 J6
Chiswick Gt Lon 44 E4
Chisworth Derbys 113 M3
Chithurst W Susx 30 D6
Chittering Cambs 76 C1
Chitterne Wilts 27 M3
Chittlehamholt Devon 23 K7
Chittlehampton Devon 23 K6
Chittoe Wilts 39 L6
Chivelstone Devon 7 H7
Chivenor Devon 23 H4
Chlenry D & G 144 D3
Chobham Surrey 42 F7
Cholderton Wilts 28 E3
Cholesbury Bucks 58 F6
Chollerton Nthumb 158 B7
Cholsey Oxon 41 L3
Cholstrey Herefs 69 J3
Chop Gate N York 142 C7
Choppington Nthumb 159 G5
Chopwell Gatesd 150 E4
Chorley Ches E 98 E3
Chorley Lancs 121 H6
Chorley Shrops 84 C6
Chorleywood Herts 43 H2
Chorleywood West Herts 43 G2
Chorlton Ches E 99 G3
Chorlton-cum-Hardy Manch 113 J3
Chorlton Lane Ches W 98 C3
Choulton Shrops 83 H5
Chrishall Essex 76 C6
Chrisswell Inver 173 L4
Christchurch Cambs 90 C4
Christchurch Dorset 15 M4
Christchurch Newpt 37 M3

Christian Malford Wilts 39 L5
Christon N Som 38 B8
Christon Bank Nthumb 169 J5
Christow Devon 11 J7
Chudleigh Devon 11 K8
Chudleigh Knighton Devon 7 J1
Chulmleigh Devon 11 G3
Church Lancs 121 L5
Churcham Gloucs 55 H4
Church Aston Wrekin 99 H8
Church Brampton Nhants 73 K2
Church Broughton Derbys 100 D5
Church Cove Cnwll 3 J8
Church Crookham Hants 30 D2
Churchdown Gloucs 55 K4
Church Eaton Staffs 99 J8
Church End C Beds 75 H6
Churchend Essex 47 G2
Church End Essex 61 H3
Church End Gt Lon 44 E3
Church Enstone Oxon 57 G3
Church Fenton N York 124 D3
Churchfield Sandw 85 H5
Church Green Devon 12 F3
Church Hanborough Oxon 57 H5
Church Houses N York 142 E7
Churchill Devon 13 H3
Churchill N Som 38 C7
Churchill Oxon 56 F3
Churchill Worcs 71 G4
Churchill Worcs 84 F7
Churchinford Somset 25 K8
Church Knowle Dorset 15 H6
Church Langton Leics 87 K5
Church Lawford Warwks 86 F7
Church Leigh Staffs 100 A5
Church Lench Worcs 71 H4
Church Mayfield Staffs 100 D4
Church Minshull Ches E 98 F1
Church Norton W Susx 18 B6
Churchover Warwks 87 G7
Church Preen Shrops 83 K4
Church Pulverbatch Shrops 83 H3
Churchstanton Somset 25 J8
Churchstoke Powys 82 F5
Churchstow Devon 7 G6
Church Stowe Nhants 73 J3
Church Street Kent 46 B5
Church Stretton Shrops 83 J5
Churchtown Cnwll 5 H1
Churchtown Derbys 114 E8
Churchtown IoM 237 d3
Churchtown Lancs 121 G2
Church Village Rhondd 37 G3
Church Warsop Notts 115 K7
Churston Ferrers Torbay 7 K5
Churt Surrey 30 D4
Churton Ches W 98 B2
Churwell Leeds 123 K5
Chwilog Gwynd 95 G5
Chyandour Cnwll 2 E5
Cilcain Flints 111 G7
Cilcennin Cerdgn 66 C3
Cilfrew Neath 52 B7
Cilfynydd Rhondd 37 G3
Cilgerran Pembks 65 H6
Cilmaengwyn Neath 51 L4
Cilmery Powys 67 L4
Cilsan Carmth 51 H2
Ciltalgarth Gwynd 96 D4
Cilycwm Carmth 67 G6
Cimla Neath 36 B2
Cinderford Gloucs 54 F5
Cinder Hill Wolves 85 G5
Cippenham Slough 42 F4
Cirencester Gloucs 56 A7
City Gt Lon 45 G4
City Airport Gt Lon 45 H4
City of London Crematorium Gt Lon 45 H3
Clabhach Ag & B 188 F5
Clachaig Ag & B 173 J3
Clachan Ag & B 172 C6
Clachan Ag & B 182 A4
Clachan Ag & B 191 G7
Clachan Highld 209 H6
Clachan-a-Luib W Isls 233 c6
Clachan Mor Ag & B 188 C6
Clachan na Luib W Isls 233 c6
Clachan of Campsie E Duns 175 G3
Clachan-Seil Ag & B 181 M4
Clachnaharry Highld 213 G5
Clachtoll Highld 224 C3
Clackavoid P & K 195 J4
Clacket Lane Services Surrey 32 D3
Clackmannan Clacks 185 J8
Clackmannanshire Bridge Fife 176 C2
Clackmarras Moray 214 F3
Clacton-on-Sea Essex 62 E5
Cladich Ag & B 182 F3
Cladswell Worcs 71 J3
Claggan Highld 190 E6
Claigan Highld 208 C4
Clanfield Hants 30 B7
Clanfield Oxon 56 F7
Clanville Hants 28 F2
Clanville Somset 26 F5
Claonaig Ag & B 172 E6
Clapgate Herts 60 C3
Clapham Bed 74 F4
Clapham Gt Lon 44 F5
Clapham N York 130 E5
Clapham W Susx 18 F4
Clapton Somset 13 K2
Clapton Somset 26 F2
Clapton-in-Gordano N Som 38 C5
Clapton-on-the-Hill Gloucs 56 D4
Claravale Gatesd 150 E3
Clarbeston Pembks 49 H3
Clarbeston Road Pembks 49 H4
Clarborough Notts 116 B5
Clare Suffk 77 H5
Clarebrand D & G 146 D2
Clarencefield D & G 147 J2
Clarilaw Border 167 H5
Clarkston E Rens 175 G6
Clashmore Highld 223 G4
Clashmore Highld 224 C3
Clashnessie Highld 224 C3
Clashnoir Moray 204 F2
Clathy P & K 185 K4
Clathymore P & K 185 L3
Clatt Abers 205 L1
Clatter Powys 81 L5
Clatworthy Somset 25 G5
Claughton Lancs 121 G3
Claughton Lancs 130 B6
Claughton Wirral 111 J4
Claverdon Warwks 71 L2
Claverham N Som 38 C6
Clavering Essex 60 D2
Claverley Shrops 84 E5
Claverton BaNES 39 H7
Clawdd-coch V Glam 37 G5
Clawdd-newydd Denbgs 97 G3
Clawton Devon 9 J5
Claxby Lincs 117 J3
Claxton N York 133 L7
Claxton Norfk 93 H3
Claybrooke Magna Leics 86 F5
Clay Coton Nhants 87 H7
Clay Cross Derbys 115 H8
Claydon Oxon 72 F4
Claydon Suffk 78 D5
Claygate D & G 156 D6
Claygate Kent 33 J4
Claygate Surrey 44 D7
Clayhall Gt Lon 45 H3
Clayhanger Devon 24 F6
Clayhidon Devon 25 J7
Clayhill E Susx 21 G2
Clayock Highld 231 H4
Claypits Gloucs 55 H6
Claypole Lincs 102 D3
Clayton C Brad 123 G4
Clayton Donc 124 C8
Clayton W Susx 19 J3
Clayton-le-Moors Lancs 121 L4
Clayton-le-Woods Lancs 121 H6
Clayton West Kirk 123 K7
Clayworth Notts 116 B4
Cleadale Highld 199 G7
Cleadon S Tyne 151 J3
Clearbrook Devon 6 D3
Clearwell Gloucs 54 E6
Cleasby N York 141 G5
Cleat Ork 234 c8
Cleatlam Dur 140 E4
Cleator Cumb 136 D4
Cleator Moor Cumb 136 E4
Cleckheaton Kirk 123 J5
Cleehill Shrops 83 L7
Cleekhimin N Lans 175 K6
Clee St Margaret Shrops 83 L6
Cleethorpes NE Lin 127 H8
Cleeton St Mary Shrops 84 B7
Cleeve N Som 38 C7
Cleeve Oxon 41 L4
Cleeve Hill Gloucs 55 M3
Cleeve Prior Worcs 71 J5
Cleghornie E Loth 178 D2
Clehonger Herefs 69 J6
Cleish P & K 186 A7
Cleland N Lans 175 L6
Clenamacrie Ag & B 182 C2
Clenchwarton Norfk 104 F7
Clenerty Abers 216 E3
Clent Worcs 85 G7
Cleobury Mortimer Shrops 84 C7
Cleobury North Shrops 84 B6
Cleongart Ag & B 161 H3
Clephanton Highld 213 J4
Clerkhill D & G 156 A3
Cleuch-head D & G 154 E3
Clevancy Wilts 40 B5
Clevedon N Som 38 B6
Cleveleys Lancs 120 D2
Cleverton Wilts 39 L4
Clewer Somset 26 C2
Cley next the Sea Norfk 106 C4
Cliburn Cumb 138 E3
Cliddesden Hants 29 M2
Cliffe Medway 46 C5
Cliffe N York 125 G4
Cliff End E Susx 21 H3
Cliffe Woods Medway 46 C5
Clifford Herefs 68 E5
Clifford Leeds 124 C2
Clifford Chambers Warwks 71 L4
Clifford's Mesne Gloucs 55 G4
Clifton Bristl 38 E5
Clifton C Beds 75 H6
Clifton C Nott 101 K5
Clifton C York 133 J8
Clifton Calder 123 H6
Clifton Cumb 138 D2
Clifton Derbys 100 D4
Clifton Devon 23 J3
Clifton Donc 115 K3
Clifton Lancs 120 F4
Clifton N York 123 J2
Clifton Oxon 57 J2
Clifton Worcs 70 F5
Clifton Campville Staffs 86 B2
Clifton Hampden Oxon 41 K2
Clifton Reynes M Keyn 74 C4
Clifton upon Dunsmore Warwks 87 G7
Clifton upon Teme Worcs 70 C3
Cliftonville Kent 35 K1
Climping W Susx 18 D5
Clink Somset 27 H2
Clint N York 132 D7
Clinterty C Aber 206 F3
Clint Green Norfk 92 B2
Clintmains Border 167 J3
Clippesby Norfk 93 J2
Clipsham Rutlnd 88 D1
Clipston Nhants 87 K7
Clipston Notts 101 M5
Clipstone C Beds 58 F3
Clitheroe Lancs 121 L3
Clive Shrops 98 D7
Cliveden Bucks 42 E4
Clixby Lincs 117 J2
Cloatley Wilts 39 M3
Clocaenog Denbgs 97 G2
Clochan Moray 215 J3
Clodock Herefs 53 L3
Clola Abers 217 J5
Clophill C Beds 74 F6
Clopton Nhants 88 F7
Clopton Suffk 78 F4
Clopton Corner Suffk 78 F4
Clos du Valle Guern 236 d2
Closeburn D & G 154 F4
Closeburnmill D & G 154 F3
Closworth Somset 14 B1
Clothall Herts 59 L2
Clotton Ches W 112 D8
Clough Foot Calder 122 D5
Clough Head Calder 123 G6
Cloughton N York 143 K7
Clousta Shet 235 c5
Clova Angus 196 B2
Clovelly Devon 22 E6
Clovenfords Border 167 G3
Clovulin Highld 191 K4
Clowne Derbys 115 J6
Clows Top Worcs 70 C1
Cluanie Inn Highld 201 G3
Cluanie Lodge Highld 201 G3
Clugston D & G 145 H4
Clun Shrops 82 F7
Clunas Highld 213 K5
Clunbury Shrops 83 G7
Clunderwen Carmth 49 J4
Clune Highld 203 J1
Clunes Highld 201 J7
Clungunford Shrops 83 H7
Clunie P & K 195 H7
Clunton Shrops 83 G7
Cluny Fife 186 D7
Clutton BaNES 38 F8
Clutton Ches W 98 C2
Clutton Hill BaNES 38 F8
Clydach Mons 53 K5
Clydach Swans 51 K5
Clydach Vale Rhondd 36 F2
Clydebank W Duns 174 F4
Clydebank Crematorium W Duns 174 E4
Clyffe Pypard Wilts 40 B5
Clynder Ag & B 174 A2
Clyne Neath 52 C7
Clynnog-fawr Gwynd 95 G3

Clyro Powys 68 E5
Clyst Honiton Devon 12 C4
Clyst Hydon Devon 12 D3
Clyst St George Devon 12 C5
Clyst St Lawrence Devon 12 D3
Clyst St Mary Devon 12 C4
Cnoc W Isls 232 g2
Cnwch Coch Cerdgn 80 F8
Coad's Green Cnwll 5 L1
Coalburn S Lans 164 F3
Coalburns Gatesd 150 E3
Coaley Gloucs 55 H7
Coalhill Essex 61 J7
Coalpit Heath S Glos 38 F4
Coal Pool Wsall 85 H4
Coalport Wrekin 84 C3
Coalsnaughton Clacks 185 J7
Coaltown of Balgonie Fife 186 E7
Coaltown of Wemyss Fife 186 E7
Coalville Leics 86 E2
Coanwood Nthumb 149 H3
Coat Somset 26 C7
Coatbridge N Lans 175 J5
Coatdyke N Lans 175 K5
Coate Swindn 40 D4
Coate Wilts 40 B7
Coates Cambs 89 K4
Coates Gloucs 55 L7
Coates Lincs 116 E5
Coates W Susx 18 D3
Cobbaton Devon 23 K6
Coberley Gloucs 55 L5
Cobham Kent 46 A6
Cobham Surrey 43 J7
Cobham Services Surrey 43 J8
Cobnash Herefs 69 J3
Cobo Guern 236 c2
Cobridge C Stke 99 K3
Coburby Abers 217 H2
Cockayne Hatley C Beds 75 J5
Cock Bridge Abers 205 G4
Cockburnspath Border 179 G4
Cock Clarks Essex 61 K7
Cockenzie and Port Seton E Loth 177 L4
Cockerham Lancs 120 F1
Cockermouth Cumb 136 F2
Cockernhoe Herts 59 J4
Cockett Swans 51 J6
Cockfield Dur 140 E3
Cockfield Suffk 77 K4
Cockfosters Gt Lon 44 F2
Cock Green Essex 61 H4
Cocking W Susx 18 B3
Cocking Causeway W Susx 18 B2
Cockington Torbay 7 K3
Cocklake Somset 26 C2
Cockley Cley Norfk 91 H3
Cock Marling E Susx 21 H2
Cockpole Green Wokham 42 D4
Cockshutt Shrops 98 B6
Cockthorpe Norfk 106 B4
Cockwood Devon 12 C6
Cockyard Derbys 114 B5
Coddenham Suffk 78 D4
Coddington Herefs 70 C6
Coddington Notts 102 D2
Codford St Mary Wilts 27 L4
Codford St Peter Wilts 27 L4
Codicote Herts 59 K4
Codmore Hill W Susx 31 H7
Codnor Derbys 101 H3
Codrington S Glos 39 G5
Codsall Staffs 84 F3
Codsall Wood Staffs 84 F3
Coedpoeth Wrexhm 97 L3
Coed Talon Flints 97 L2
Coed-y-paen Mons 53 M7
Coffinswell Devon 7 K3
Cofton Devon 12 C6
Cofton Hackett Worcs 85 H7
Cogan V Glam 37 J6
Cogenhoe Nhants 74 B3
Coggeshall Essex 61 K4
Coignafearn Highld 203 H2
Coilacriech Abers 205 H6
Coilantogle Stirlg 184 D6
Coillore Highld 208 E6
Coity Brdgnd 36 E4
Col W Isls 232 g2
Colaboll Highld 225 L6
Colan Cnwll 4 D4
Colaton Raleigh Devon 12 D5
Colbost Highld 208 C5
Colburn N York 140 F7
Colby Cumb 138 F3
Colby IoM 237 b6
Colchester Essex 62 B3
Colchester Crematorium Essex 62 B4
Colchester Zoo Essex 62 A4
Cold Ash W Berk 41 K6
Cold Ashby Nhants 87 J7
Cold Ashton S Glos 39 H6
Cold Aston Gloucs 56 C4
Coldbackie Highld 229 J4
Cold Brayfield M Keyn 74 D4
Coldean Br & H 19 J4
Coldeast Devon 7 J2
Colden Calder 122 E5
Colden Common Hants 29 J6
Cold Hanworth Lincs 117 G5
Coldharbour Surrey 31 J3
Cold Higham Nhants 73 J4
Coldingham Border 179 J5
Cold Kirby N York 133 H3
Coldmeece Staffs 99 J6
Cold Norton Essex 61 K7
Cold Overton Leics 88 B2
Coldred Kent 35 H5
Coldridge Devon 11 G4
Coldstream Border 168 C2
Coldwaltham W Susx 18 D3
Coldwell Herefs 69 H7
Coldwells Abers 217 H6
Cole Somset 26 F5
Colebatch Shrops 83 G6
Colebrook Devon 12 C2
Colebrooke Devon 11 H5
Coleby Lincs 102 F1
Coleby N Linc 125 L6
Coleford Devon 11 H5
Coleford Gloucs 54 E6
Coleford Somset 27 G2
Colegate End Norfk 92 E6
Colehill Dorset 15 J3
Coleman's Hatch E Susx 32 D6
Colemere Shrops 98 B6
Colemore Hants 30 B5
Colenden P & K 186 B2
Colerne Wilts 39 J6
Colesbourne Gloucs 56 A5
Coleshill Bucks 42 F2
Coleshill Oxon 40 E2
Coleshill Warwks 85 L5
Coley BaNES 26 E1
Colgate W Susx 31 L5
Colinsburgh Fife 187 H6
Colinton C Edin 177 H5
Colintraive Ag & B 173 H4
Colkirk Norfk 105 L7
Coll Ag & B 189 G5
Coll W Isls 232 g2
Collace P & K 186 C2
Collafirth Shet 235 c3
Coll Airport Ag & B 188 F5
Collaton Devon 7 G7
Collaton St Mary Torbay 7 K4
College of Roseisle Moray 214 E2
College Town Br For 42 D7
Collessie Fife 186 E5
Collier Row Gt Lon 45 J2
Collier's End Herts 60 B4
Collier Street Kent 33 J4
Collieston Abers 217 K8
Collin D & G 155 H6
Collingbourne Ducis Wilts 28 E2
Collingbourne Kingston Wilts 28 E1
Collingham Leeds 124 B2
Collingham Notts 102 D1
Collington Herefs 70 B3
Collingtree Nhants 73 L4
Collins Green Warrtn 112 E3
Colliston Angus 196 F7
Colliton Devon 12 E2
Collyweston Nhants 88 E3
Colmonell S Ayrs 152 D5
Colmworth Bed 75 G3
Colnabaichin Abers 205 G4
Colnbrook Slough 43 G5
Colne Cambs 89 L7
Colne Lancs 122 D3
Colne Engaine Essex 61 K3
Colney Norfk 92 E3
Colney Heath Herts 59 K6
Coln Rogers Gloucs 56 B6
Coln St Aldwyns Gloucs 56 C6
Coln St Dennis Gloucs 56 B5
Colonsay Ag & B 180 E7
Colonsay Airport Ag & B 180 E8
Colpy Abers 216 C7
Colquhar Border 166 E2
Colsterworth Lincs 102 F7
Colston Bassett Notts 102 B5
Coltfield Moray 214 D2
Coltishall Norfk 106 F8
Colton Cumb 129 G3
Colton Leeds 124 B4
Colton N York 124 E2
Colton Norfk 92 D2
Colton Staffs 100 B7
Colt's Hill Kent 33 H4
Colvend D & G 146 F4
Colwall Herefs 70 D6
Colwell Nthumb 158 B6
Colwich Staffs 100 A7
Colwinston V Glam 36 E5
Colworth W Susx 18 C5
Colwyn Bay Conwy 110 B5
Colwyn Bay Crematorium Conwy 110 A5
Colyford Devon 13 G4
Colyton Devon 13 G4
Combe Oxon 57 H5
Combe W Berk 41 G7
Combe Down BaNES 39 H7
Combe Fishacre Devon 7 J3
Combe Florey Somset 25 J5
Combe Hay BaNES 39 G7
Combeinteignhead Devon 7 K2
Combe Martin Devon 23 J3
Combe Raleigh Devon 12 F3
Comberbach Ches W 112 F6
Comberford Staffs 85 L3
Comberton Cambs 75 L4
Comberton Herefs 69 K2
Combe St Nicholas Somset 13 H1
Combrook Warwks 72 C4
Combs Derbys 114 B6
Combs Suffk 78 C3
Combs Ford Suffk 78 C3
Combwich Somset 25 K3
Comers Abers 206 D4
Comhampton Worcs 70 E2
Commins Coch Powys 81 J3
Commondale N York 142 E5
Common End Cumb 136 D3
Common Moor Cnwll 5 K2
Compstall Stockp 113 L4
Compstonend D & G 146 B4
Compton Devon 7 K3
Compton Hants 29 J6
Compton Staffs 84 E6
Compton Surrey 30 F3
Compton W Berk 41 K4
Compton W Susx 30 C7
Compton Wilts 28 C2
Compton Abbas Dorset 27 K7
Compton Abdale Gloucs 56 B5
Compton Bassett Wilts 40 B6
Compton Beauchamp Oxon 40 F3
Compton Bishop Somset 26 B1
Compton Chamberlayne Wilts 28 B5
Compton Dando BaNES 38 F7
Compton Dundon Somset 26 C5
Compton Durville Somset 26 B7
Compton Greenfield S Glos 38 E4
Compton Martin BaNES 38 D8
Compton Pauncefoot Somset 26 F6
Compton Valence Dorset 14 B4
Comrie Fife 176 D1
Comrie P & K 185 G3
Conaglen House Highld 191 K3
Conchra Highld 210 D8
Concraigie P & K 195 H7
Conderton Worcs 71 G6
Condicote Gloucs 56 D3
Condorrat N Lans 175 K4
Condover Shrops 83 J3
Coney Hill Gloucs 55 J4
Coneyhurst Common W Susx 31 J6
Coneysthorpe N York 133 L5
Coney Weston Suffk 91 L7
Congerstone Leics 86 D3
Congham Norfk 105 H7
Congleton Ches E 113 J8
Congresbury N Som 38 C7
Conheath D & G 147 H2
Conicavel Moray 214 B4
Coningsby Lincs 103 L2
Conington Cambs 75 K2
Conington Cambs 89 H6
Conisbrough Donc 115 K2
Conisholme Lincs 118 E3
Coniston Cumb 137 J7
Coniston E R Yk 126 E4
Coniston Cold N York 131 G8
Conistone N York 131 J6
Connah's Quay Flints 111 J7
Connel Ag & B 182 C1
Connel Park E Ayrs 164 C6
Connor Downs Cnwll 3 G4
Conon Bridge Highld 212 E4
Cononley N York 122 E2
Consall Staffs 99 M3
Consett Dur 150 E5
Constable Burton N York 132 B2
Constable Lee Lancs 122 B5
Constantine Cnwll 3 J5
Constantine Bay Cnwll 4 D2
Contin Highld 212 C3
Conwy Conwy 109 L6
Conwy Castle Conwy 109 L6

Conyer's Green Suffk......77 K2
Cooden E Susx......20 E4
Cookbury Devon......9 K4
Cookham W & M......42 E4
Cookham Dean W & M......42 E4
Cookham Rise W & M......42 E4
Cookhill Worcs......71 J3
Cookley Suffk......93 H7
Cookley Worcs......84 E7
Cookley Green Oxon......42 B3
Cookney Abers......207 G6
Cook's Green Essex......62 E4
Cooks Green Suffk......77 L4
Cooksmill Green Essex......61 G6
Coolham W Susx......31 J6
Cooling Medway......46 C5
Coombe Cnwll......4 E5
Coombe Devon......7 L2
Coombe Devon......12 E4
Coombe Gloucs......39 H2
Coombe Hants......30 A7
Coombe Abbey Warwks......86 E7
Coombe Bissett Wilts......28 C6
Coombe Cellars Devon......7 K2
Coombe Hill Gloucs......55 K3
Coombe Keynes Dorset......14 F5
Coombe Pafford Torbay......7 L3
Coombes W Susx......19 G4
Coombes-Moor Herefs......69 G2
Coombeswood Dudley......85 H6
Coopersale Common Essex......60 D7
Copdock Suffk......78 D6
Copford Green Essex......61 L4
Copgrove N York......132 E6
Copister Shet......235 d3
Cople Bed......75 G5
Copley Dur......140 D3
Copmanthorpe C York......124 E2
Copmere End Staffs......99 J6
Copp Lancs......120 F3
Coppenhall Staffs......99 K8
Copperhouse Cnwll......2 F4
Coppingford Cambs......89 H7
Copplestone Devon......11 H4
Coppull Lancs......121 H7
Copsale W Susx......31 K6
Copster Green Lancs......121 K4
Copston Magna Warwks......86 F5
Cop Street Kent......35 J3
Copt Hewick N York......132 E5
Copthorne W Susx......32 B5
Copt Oak Leics......86 F2
Copythorne Hants......28 F8
Corbets Tey Gt Lon......45 K3
Corbière Jersey......236 a7
Corbridge Nthumb......150 C3
Corby Nhants......88 C5
Corby Glen Lincs......103 G7
Cordon N Ayrs......162 D4
Coreley Shrops......84 B8
Corfe Somset......25 K7
Corfe Castle Dorset......15 H6
Corfe Mullen Dorset......15 J3
Corfton Shrops......83 J6
Corgarff Abers......205 G4
Corhampton Hants......29 L7
Corley Warwks......86 C6
Corley Services Warwks......86 C6
Cormuir Angus......195 L3
Cornard Tye Suffk......77 K6
Cornforth Dur......151 H7
Cornhill Abers......216 B3
Cornhill-on-Tweed Nthumb......168 C2
Cornholme Calder......122 D5
Cornoigmore Ag & B......188 C6
Cornsay Dur......150 E6
Cornsay Colliery Dur......150 F6
Corntown Highld......212 E3
Corntown V Glam......36 E5
Cornwell Oxon......56 F3
Cornwood Devon......6 E4
Cornworthy Devon......7 J5
Corpach Highld......191 L2
Corpusty Norfk......106 D6
Corrachree Abers......205 K4
Corran Highld......191 K4
Corran Highld......200 C4
Corrie D & G......155 L5
Corrie N Ayrs......162 C2
Corriecravie N Ayrs......162 B5
Corriegills N Ayrs......162 D3
Corriegour Lodge Hotel Highld......201 K6
Corriemoille Highld......212 B2
Corrimony Highld......212 B7
Corringham Lincs......116 E4
Corringham Thurr......46 B4
Corris Gwynd......81 G2
Corris Uchaf Gwynd......81 G2
Corrow Ag & B......183 H7
Corry Highld......199 K1
Corscombe Devon......10 F5
Corscombe Dorset......13 M2
Corse Gloucs......55 H3
Corse Lawn Gloucs......55 J2
Corsham Wilts......39 K6
Corsindae Abers......206 D4
Corsley Wilts......27 J3
Corsley Heath Wilts......27 J3
Corsock D & G......154 D6
Corston BaNES......39 G7
Corston Wilts......39 L4
Corstorphine C Edin......177 G4
Cortachy Angus......196 C4
Corton Suffk......93 L4
Corton Wilts......27 L4
Corton Denham Somset......26 F6
Coruanan Highld......191 L3
Corwen Denbgs......97 G4
Coryton Devon......10 C7
Coryton Thurr......46 C4
Cosby Leics......87 G4
Coseley Dudley......85 G5
Cosgrove Nhants......73 L6
Cosham C Port......17 J2
Cosheston Pembks......49 G6
Coshieville P & K......194 C6
Cossall Notts......101 J4
Cossington Leics......87 H2
Cossington Somset......26 A4
Costessey Norfk......92 E2
Costock Notts......101 L7
Coston Leics......102 D7
Coston Norfk......92 C3
Cote Oxon......57 G7
Cotebrook Ches W......112 E7
Cotehill Cumb......148 E5
Cotes Leics......101 K7
Cotesbach Leics......87 G6
Cotford St Luke Somset......25 J6
Cotgrave Notts......101 M5
Cothal Abers......207 G3
Cotham Notts......102 C3
Cotherstone Dur......140 C4
Cothill Oxon......57 J7
Cotleigh Devon......13 G3
Cotmanhay Derbys......101 J4
Coton Cambs......76 B3
Coton Nhants......73 J1
Coton Staffs......99 J7
Coton Clanford Staffs......99 K7
Coton Hill Shrops......83 J2
Coton in the Elms Derbys......86 B1
Cotswolds......55 M6
Cotswold Wildlife Park & Gardens Oxon......56 E6
Cott Devon......7 H4
Cottam Lancs......121 G4
Cottam Notts......116 D5
Cottenham Cambs......76 C2
Cottered Herts......60 A3
Cotteridge Birm......85 J7
Cotterstock Nhants......88 F5
Cottesbrooke Nhants......87 K8
Cottesmore Rutlnd......88 C2
Cottingham E R Yk......126 C4
Cottingham Nhants......88 B5
Cottingley C Brad......123 G3
Cottingley Hall Crematorium Leeds......123 K4
Cottisford Oxon......57 L2
Cotton Suffk......78 C2
Cottown Abers......206 E3
Cottown Abers......215 L8
Cottown of Gight Abers......216 F6
Cotts Devon......6 C3
Coughton Warwks......71 J3
Coulaghailtro Ag & B......172 C5
Coulags Highld......210 E5
Coull Abers......205 L5
Coulport Ag & B......173 L2
Coulsdon Gt Lon......32 B2
Coulston Wilts......27 L2
Coulter S Lans......165 K3
Coulton N York......133 K5
Coultra Fife......186 F3
Cound Shrops......83 L3
Coundon Dur......141 G2
Countersett N York......131 H2
Countess Wear Devon......12 B4
Countesthorpe Leics......87 H4
Countisbury Devon......24 B2
Coupar Angus P & K......195 K7
Coupland Nthumb......168 D3
Cour Ag & B......172 D8
Courteachan Highld......199 L6
Courteenhall Nhants......73 L4
Court Henry Carmth......51 H2
Courtsend Essex......47 G2
Courtway Somset......25 J5
Cousland Mdloth......177 K5
Cousley Wood E Susx......33 H6
Cove Ag & B......173 L2
Cove Border......179 G4
Cove Devon......24 E7
Cove Hants......30 E1
Cove Highld......219 J3
Cove Bay C Aber......207 H5
Covehithe Suffk......93 L6
Coven Staffs......85 G3
Coveney Cambs......90 C6
Covenham St Bartholomew Lincs......118 D3
Covenham St Mary Lincs......118 D3
Coventry Covtry......86 D7
Coventry Airport Warwks......86 D8
Coverack Cnwll......3 K7
Coverack Bridges Cnwll......3 H5
Coverham N York......131 L3
Covington Cambs......74 F1
Covington S Lans......165 J2
Cowan Bridge Lancs......130 C4
Cowbeech E Susx......20 C3
Cowbit Lincs......103 L8
Cowbridge V Glam......36 F5
Cowden Kent......32 E5
Cowdenbeath Fife......177 G1
Cowers Lane Derbys......100 F3
Cowes IoW......16 F3
Cowesby N York......133 G2
Cowfold W Susx......31 K6
Cowhill S Glos......38 E3
Cowie Stirlg......175 L1
Cowley Devon......11 K5
Cowley Gloucs......55 L5
Cowley Gt Lon......43 H4
Cowley Oxon......57 K7
Cowling Lancs......121 H6
Cowling N York......122 E2
Cowling N York......132 C3
Cowlinge Suffk......77 G4
Cowpen Nthumb......159 H5
Cowplain Hants......17 K1
Cowshill Dur......149 L6
Cowslip Green N Som......38 C7
Cowthorpe N York......132 F8
Coxbank Ches E......98 F4
Coxbench Derbys......101 G4
Coxford Cnwll......8 F5
Coxford Norfk......105 K6
Coxheath Kent......33 J3
Coxhoe Dur......151 H7
Coxley Somset......26 D3
Coxley Wick Somset......26 D3
Coxtie Green Essex......45 K2
Coxwold N York......133 H4
Coychurch Brdgnd......36 E4
Coychurch Crematorium Brdgnd......36 E4
Coylton S Ayrs......163 K5
Coylumbridge Highld......203 L3
Coytrahen Brdgnd......36 D4
Crabbs Cross Worcs......71 J2
Crabtree W Susx......31 K6
Crackenthorpe Cumb......138 F3
Crackington Haven Cnwll......8 F5
Crackley Staffs......99 J3
Crackleybank Shrops......84 D2
Cracoe N York......131 J7
Craddock Devon......25 G8
Cradley Dudley......85 G6
Cradley Herefs......70 D5
Cradley Heath Sandw......85 G6
Cradoc Powys......52 F2
Crafthole Cnwll......6 B5
Craggan Highld......204 C1
Craghead Dur......150 F5
Cragside House & Garden Nthumb......158 D2
Crai Powys......52 D3
Craibstone Moray......215 L3
Craichie Angus......196 E6
Craig Angus......197 H5
Craig Highld......211 G4
Craigbank E Ayrs......164 C6
Craigburn Border......177 H7
Craigcleuch D & G......156 C5
Craigdam Abers......216 F7
Craigdhu Ag & B......182 B6
Craigearn Abers......206 D3
Craigellachie Moray......215 G5
Craigend P & K......186 B4
Craigend Rens......174 E4
Craigendoran Ag & B......174 C3
Craigends Rens......174 D5
Craighlaw D & G......145 G3
Craighouse Ag & B......171 K5
Craigie P & K......195 H7
Craigie S Ayrs......163 K3
Craigiefold Abers......217 H2
Craigley D & G......146 D4
Craig Llangiwg Neath......51 K4
Craiglockhart C Edin......177 H4
Craigmillar C Edin......177 J4
Craigneston D & G......154 D5
Craigneuk N Lans......175 K5
Craigneuk N Lans......175 K6
Craignure Ag & B......190 E8
Craigo Angus......197 H4
Craigrothie Fife......186 F5
Craigruie Stirlg......184 B4
Craigton Angus......196 E8
Craigton C Aber......206 F5
Craigton E Rens......174 F7
Craigton Crematorium C Glas......174 F5
Craigton of Airlie Angus......196 B6
Crail Fife......187 K5
Crailing Border......167 L4
Craiselound N Linc......116 C2

Crakehall N York 132 C2
Crambe N York 133 L6
Cramlington Nthumb 159 G6
Cramond C Edin 177 G3
Cramond Bridge C Edin 177 G4
Cranage Ches E 113 H7
Cranberry Staffs 99 J5
Cranborne Dorset 28 B8
Cranbourne Br For 42 F5
Cranbrook Devon 12 C4
Cranbrook Kent 33 K6
Cranfield C Beds 74 D6
Cranford Gt Lon 43 J5
Cranford St Andrew Nhants 88 D7
Cranford St John Nhants 88 D7
Cranham Gloucs 55 K5
Crank St Hel 112 D2
Cranleigh Surrey 31 H4
Cranmore Somset 26 F3
Cranoe Leics 87 L4
Cransford Suffk 79 G2
Cranshaws Border 178 E6
Crantock Cnwll 4 C4
Cranwell Lincs 103 G3
Cranwich Norfk 91 H4
Cranworth Norfk 92 B3
Craobh Haven Ag & B 182 A6
Crarae Ag & B 182 E7
Crask Inn Highld 225 L4
Crask of Aigas Highld 212 D6
Craster Nthumb 169 K5
Cratfield Suffk 93 G7
Crathes Abers 206 E6
Crathes Crematorium Abers 206 E6
Crathie Abers 205 G6
Crathie Highld 202 E6
Crathorne N York 141 K5
Craven Arms Shrops 83 H6
Crawcrook Gatesd 150 E3
Crawford S Lans 165 J5
Crawfordjohn S Lans 165 G5
Crawley Hants 29 H4
Crawley Oxon 57 G5
Crawley W Susx 31 L4
Crawley Down W Susx 32 C5
Crawton Abers 197 L1
Cray N York 131 H4
Crayford Gt Lon 45 K5
Crayke N York 133 H5
Crays Hill Essex 46 B2
Creacombe Devon 24 C7
Creagan Inn Ag & B 191 J7
Creag Ghoraidh W Isls 233 c7
Creagorry W Isls 233 c7
Creaguaineach Lodge Highld 192 E3
Creaton Nhants 73 K1
Creca D & G 155 M7
Credenhill Herefs 69 J5
Crediton Devon 11 J5
Creebank D & G 153 H6
Creebridge D & G 145 J2
Creech Heathfield Somset 25 L6
Creech St Michael Somset 25 L6
Creed Cnwll 4 E6
Creekmouth Gt Lon 45 J4
Creeting St Mary Suffk 78 D3
Creeton Lincs 103 G8
Creetown D & G 145 K3
Cregneash IoM 237 a7
Creich Fife 186 E3
Creigiau Cardif 37 G4
Cremyll Cnwll 6 C5
Cressage Shrops 83 L3
Cressbrook Derbys 114 D6
Cresselly Pembks 49 H6
Cressex Bucks 42 D3
Cressing Essex 61 J4
Cresswell Nthumb 159 H4
Cresswell Pembks 49 H6
Cresswell Staffs 99 L5
Creswell Derbys 115 K6
Cretingham Suffk 78 F3
Cretshengan Ag & B 172 C5
Crewe Ches E 99 G2
Crewe-by-Farndon Ches W 98 B2
Crewe Crematorium Ches E 99 G2
Crewe Green Ches E 99 G2
Crew Green Powys 83 G1
Crewkerne Somset 13 K1
Crewton C Derb 101 G5
Crianlarich Stirlg 183 L3
Cribyn Cerdgn 66 C4
Criccieth Gwynd 95 J5
Crich Derbys 101 G2
Crichton Mdloth 177 K6
Crick Nhants 87 H8
Crickadarn Powys 68 C6
Cricket St Thomas Somset 13 J2
Crickhowell Powys 53 K4
Cricklade Wilts 40 C2
Cricklewood Gt Lon 44 E3
Crieff P & K 185 H3
Criggion Powys 82 F1
Crigglestone Wakefd 123 L7
Crimond Abers 217 K3
Crimplesham Norfk 90 F3
Crimscote Warwks 72 B5
Crinaglack Highld 212 C6
Crinan Ag & B 182 A8
Crindledyke N Lans 175 L6
Cringleford Norfk 92 E3
Crinow Pembks 49 J5
Croachy Highld 213 G8
Crockenhill Kent 45 J6
Crocker End Oxon 42 B3
Crockernwell Devon 11 H6
Crockerton Wilts 27 K3
Crocketford D & G 154 E7
Crockham Hill Kent 32 D3
Croeserw Neath 36 D2
Croes-goch Pembks 48 D2
Croes-lan Cerdgn 65 L5
Croesor Gwynd 95 L4
Croesyceiliog Carmth 50 E3
Croesyceiliog Torfn 37 L2
Croft Leics 87 G4
Croft Lincs 104 E1
Croft Warrtn 112 F3
Croftamie Stirlg 174 E2
Crofton Wakefd 124 B6
Croft-on-Tees N York 141 H5
Croftown Highld 220 F5
Crofts Moray 215 G4
Crofts of Dipple Moray 215 H3
Crofts of Savoch Abers 217 K3
Crofty Swans 51 G6
Croggan Ag & B 181 L3
Croglin Cumb 148 F5
Croick Highld 222 B3
Cromarty Highld 223 H7
Crombie Fife 176 E2
Cromdale Highld 214 D8
Cromer Herts 59 M3
Cromer Norfk 106 F4
Cromford Derbys 100 F2
Cromhall S Glos 39 G3
Cromor W Isls 232 f3
Cromwell Notts 102 D1
Cronberry E Ayrs 164 C5
Crondall Hants 30 C2
Cronton Knows 112 C4
Crook Cumb 138 C7
Crook Dur 150 E7
Crookedholm E Ayrs 163 L3
Crookham Nthumb 168 D2
Crookham W Berk 41 K7
Crookham Village Hants 30 C2
Crook Inn Border 165 L4
Crooklands Cumb 129 L3
Crook of Devon P & K 185 L7
Cropredy Oxon 72 F5
Cropston Leics 87 G2
Cropthorne Worcs 71 H5
Cropton N York 134 B2
Cropwell Bishop Notts 102 B5
Cropwell Butler Notts 102 B5
Cros W Isls 232 g1
Crosbost W Isls 232 f3
Crosby Cumb 147 J7
Crosby IoM 237 c5
Crosby N Linc 125 K7
Crosby Sefton 111 J2
Crosby Garret Cumb 139 G5
Crosby Ravensworth Cumb 138 F4
Croscombe Somset 26 E3
Cross Somset 26 B1
Crossaig Ag & B 172 E7
Crossapoll Ag & B 188 C7
Cross Ash Mons 54 B4
Cross-at-Hand Kent 33 K4
Crosscanonby Cumb 147 J6
Crossdale Street Norfk 106 F5
Cross Flatts C Brad 123 G3
Crossford Fife 176 E2
Crossford S Lans 175 L8
Crossgatehall E Loth 177 K5
Crossgates E Ayrs 163 J1
Crossgates Fife 176 F1
Cross Gates Leeds 124 B4
Crossgates N York 134 F3
Crossgill Lancs 129 L6
Cross Green Leeds 123 L4
Cross Green Suffk 77 K4
Cross Green Suffk 78 B4
Cross Hands Carmth 51 H3
Crosshands E Ayrs 163 L4
Crosshill Fife 186 C7
Crosshill S Ayrs 163 J7
Crosshouse E Ayrs 163 K2
Cross Houses Shrops 83 K3
Cross in Hand E Susx 20 B2
Cross Inn Cerdgn 65 L3
Cross Keys Ag & B 174 C2
Crosskeys Caerph 37 K3
Crosskirk Highld 230 F2
Cross Lane IoW 17 G4
Cross Lane Head Shrops 84 C4
Crosslee Rens 174 D5
Crossmichael D & G 146 C2
Cross of Jackston Abers 216 E7
Cross o' th' hands Derbys 100 F4
Crossroads Abers 206 B4
Crossroads Abers 206 E6
Cross Street Suffk 92 E7
Crosston Angus 196 E5
Cross Town Ches E 113 H5
Crossway Green Worcs 70 E2
Crossways Dorset 14 E5
Crosswell Pembks 64 F6
Crosthwaite Cumb 129 J2
Croston Lancs 121 G6
Crostwick Norfk 92 F1
Crouch End Gt Lon 44 F3
Croucheston Wilts 28 B6
Crouch Hill Dorset 14 D1
Croughton Nhants 73 G7
Crovie Abers 216 F2
Crowan Cnwll 3 H4
Crowborough E Susx 32 F6
Crowcombe Somset 25 H4
Crowdecote Derbys 114 C7
Crowden Derbys 114 B2
Crow Edge Barns 114 D2
Crowell Oxon 58 C7
Crowfield Suffk 78 D3
Crowhill E Loth 178 F4
Crow Hill Herefs 54 F3
Crowhurst E Susx 20 F3
Crowhurst Surrey 32 D4
Crowland Lincs 89 J2
Crowland Suffk 78 B1
Crowlas Cnwll 2 F5
Crowle N Linc 125 J7
Crowle Worcs 71 G4
Crowle Green Worcs 71 G3
Crowmarsh Gifford Oxon 41 L3
Crown Corner Suffk 78 F1
Crownhill C Plym 6 C4
Crownhill Crematorium M Keyn 74 B6
Crownthorpe Norfk 92 C3
Crowntown Cnwll 3 H5
Crows-an-Wra Cnwll 2 D5
Crowthorne Wokham 42 D7
Crowton Ches W 112 E6
Croxdale Dur 151 G7
Croxden Staffs 100 B5
Croxley Green Herts 43 H2
Croxteth Lpool 111 L3
Croxton Cambs 75 J3
Croxton N Linc 126 D7
Croxton Norfk 91 K6
Croxton Norfk 106 B6
Croxton Staffs 99 H6
Croxton Kerrial Leics 102 D6
Croy Highld 213 J4
Croy N Lans 175 J3
Croyde Devon 23 G4
Croydon Cambs 75 K5
Croydon Gt Lon 44 F6
Croydon Crematorium Gt Lon 44 F6
Crubenmore Highld 203 G7
Cruckmeole Shrops 83 H2
Cruckton Shrops 83 H2
Cruden Bay Abers 217 K6
Crudgington Wrekin 98 F8
Crudwell Wilts 39 L2
Crumlin Caerph 37 K2
Crumplehorn Cnwll 5 K5
Crumpsall Manch 113 J2
Crundale Kent 34 E5
Crunwear Pembks 49 K5
Crux Easton Hants 29 H1
Crwbin Carmth 50 F3
Cryers Hill Bucks 42 E2
Crymych Pembks 65 G7
Crynant Neath 52 C6
Crystal Palace Gt Lon 45 G5
Cuaig Highld 209 L3
Cuan Ag & B 181 L4
Cubert Cnwll 4 C4
Cublington Bucks 58 D4
Cublington Herefs 69 H6
Cuckfield W Susx 32 B7
Cucklington Somset 27 H6
Cuckney Notts 115 K7
Cuddesdon Oxon 57 L7
Cuddington Bucks 58 C5
Cuddington Ches W 112 E7
Cuddington Heath Ches W 98 C3
Cudham Gt Lon 32 D2
Cudliptown Devon 10 D8
Cudnell Bmouth 15 K3
Cudworth Barns 124 B8
Cudworth Somset 13 J1
Cuffley Herts 59 M7
Cuil Highld 191 J5
Culbokie Highld 212 F3
Culburnie Highld 212 D6
Culcabock Highld 213 G5
Culcharry Highld 213 K4
Culcheth Warrtn 112 F3
Culdrain Abers 215 L7
Culduie Highld 209 L6
Culford Suffk 77 J1
Culgaith Cumb 138 E2
Culham Oxon 41 J2
Culkein Highld 224 C2
Culkein Drumbeg Highld 224 D2

Culkerton Gloucs 39 L2
Cullen Moray 215 L2
Cullercoats N Tyne 159 J7
Cullerlie Abers 206 E5
Cullicudden Highld 213 G2
Cullingworth C Brad 123 G3
Cuillin Hills Highld 199 G2
Cullipool Ag & B 181 L5
Cullivoe Shet 235 d2
Culloden Highld 213 H5
Cullompton Devon 12 C2
Cullompton Services Devon 12 D2
Culm Davy Devon 25 H7
Culmington Shrops 83 J6
Culmstock Devon 25 H8
Culnacraig Highld 224 C7
Culnaightrie D & G 146 D5
Culnaknock Highld 209 H2
Culrain Highld 222 D3
Culross Fife 176 D2
Culroy S Ayrs 163 H6
Culsalmond Abers 216 C7
Culscadden D & G 145 K5
Culshabbin D & G 145 G5
Culswick Shet 235 b6
Cultercullen Abers 207 H1
Cults C Aber 207 G5
Culverstone Green Kent 45 M7
Culverthorpe Lincs 103 G4
Culworth Nhants 73 G5
Culzean Castle & Country Park S Ayrs 163 G7
Cumbernauld N Lans 175 K4
Cumbernauld Village N Lans 175 K3
Cumberworth Lincs 119 G6
Cuminestown Abers 216 F4
Cumledge Border 179 G6
Cummersdale Cumb 148 D4
Cummertrees D & G 147 K2
Cummingston Moray 214 E1
Cumnock E Ayrs 164 B5
Cumnor Oxon 57 J7
Cumrew Cumb 148 F5
Cumrue D & G 155 J5
Cumwhinton Cumb 148 D4
Cumwhitton Cumb 148 E4
Cundall N York 132 F5
Cunninghamhead N Ayrs 163 J2
Cunningsburgh Shet 235 c7
Cupar Fife 186 F4
Cupar Muir Fife 186 F5
Curbar Derbys 114 E6
Curbridge Hants 17 G1
Curbridge Oxon 57 G6
Curdridge Hants 29 K8
Curdworth Warwks 85 L5
Curland Somset 25 L7
Curridge W Berk 41 J6
Currie C Edin 177 G5
Curry Mallet Somset 25 L6
Curry Rivel Somset 26 B6
Curtisden Green Kent 33 J5
Curtisknowle Devon 7 H5
Cury Cnwll 3 H6
Cushnie Abers 205 L3
Cusworth Donc 115 K2
Cutcloy D & G 145 J7
Cutcombe Somset 24 E4
Cuthill Highld 223 G4
Cutnall Green Worcs 70 F2
Cutsdean Gloucs 56 C3
Cutthorpe Derbys 115 G6
Cuxham Oxon 42 A2
Cuxton Medway 46 B6
Cuxwold Lincs 117 K2
Cwm Denbgs 110 E6
Cwmafan Neath 36 B3
Cwmaman Rhondd 52 F7
Cwmbach Carmth 50 B1
Cwmbach Powys 68 D6
Cwmbach Rhondd 52 F7
Cwmbach Llechrhyd Powys 68 B4
Cwmbran Torfn 37 L2
Cwmcarn Caerph 37 K2
Cwmcarvan Mons 54 C6
Cwm-cou Cerdgn 65 J6
Cwm Crawnon Powys 53 H4
Cwmdare Rhondd 52 F7
Cwmdu Powys 53 J4
Cwmdu Swans 51 J6
Cwmduad Carmth 65 L7
Cwmfelin Brdgnd 36 D3
Cwmfelin Myr Td 53 H7
Cwmfelin Boeth Carmth 49 K4
Cwmfelinfach Caerph 37 J3
Cwmffrwd Carmth 50 E3
Cwmgiedd Powys 52 C5
Cwmgorse Carmth 51 K4
Cwmgwili Carmth 51 H4
Cwmhiraeth Carmth 65 K6
Cwm Llinau Powys 81 J2
Cwmllynfell Neath 51 L3
Cwmmawr Carmth 51 G3
Cwmparc Rhondd 36 E2
Cwmpengraig Carmth 65 K6
Cwmtillery Blae G 53 K6
Cwm-twrch Isaf Powys 52 B6
Cwm-twrch Uchaf Powys 51 L4
Cwm-y-glo Gwynd 109 H8
Cwmystwyth Cerdgn 81 H8
Cwrt-newydd Cerdgn 66 C5
Cyfarthfa Castle Museum Myr Td 53 G6
Cylibebyll Neath 51 L5
Cymer Neath 36 D2
Cymmer Rhondd 36 F3
Cynghordy Carmth 67 H6
Cynonville Neath 36 C2
Cynwyd Denbgs 97 G4
Cynwyl Elfed Carmth 65 L8

D

Daccombe Devon 7 K3
Dacre Cumb 138 C2
Dacre N York 132 B7
Dacre Banks N York 132 B6
Daddry Shield Dur 149 M7
Dadford Bucks 73 J6
Dadlington Leics 86 E4
Dagenham Gt Lon 45 J3
Daglingworth Gloucs 55 M6
Dagnall Bucks 59 G5
Dailly S Ayrs 152 F2
Dairsie Fife 187 G4
Dalabrog W Isls 233 b8
Dalavich Ag & B 182 D5
Dalbeattie D & G 146 E3
Dalby IoM 237 b5
Dalby N York 133 K5
Dalcapon P & K 194 F5
Dalchalm Highld 226 F7
Dalchreichart Highld 201 L3
Dalchruin P & K 184 F4
Dalcrue P & K 185 L2
Dalditch Devon 12 D5
Daldowie Crematorium C Glas 175 J6
Dale Derbys 101 H5
Dale Pembks 48 D6
Dalelia Highld 190 E3
Dalgarven N Ayrs 163 H1
Dalgety Bay Fife 177 G2
Dalgig E Ayrs 164 B6
Dalginross P & K 185 G3
Dalguise P & K 194 F6
Dalhalvaig Highld 230 C5
Dalham Suffk 77 G3
Daliburgh W Isls 233 b8
Dalkeith Mdloth 177 K5
Dallas Moray 214 D4
Dallinghoo Suffk 78 F4
Dallington E Susx 20 D2
Dallington Nhants 73 K3
Dalmally Ag & B 183 H3
Dalmary Stirlg 184 C7
Dalmellington E Ayrs 153 K2
Dalmeny C Edin 176 F3
Dalmore Highld 222 F7
Dalmuir W Duns 174 E4
Dalnabreck Highld 190 E3
Dalnacardoch P & K 194 B3
Dalnahaitnach Highld 203 K2
Dalnaspidal P & K 193 K2
Dalnawillan Lodge Highld 230 F7
Daloist P & K 194 C5
Dalqueich P & K 186 A6
Dalquhairn S Ayrs 153 G3
Dalreavoch Lodge Highld 226 D6
Dalry N Ayrs 174 B7
Dalrymple E Ayrs 163 J6
Dalserf S Lans 175 L7
Dalsmeran Ag & B 161 G6
Dalston Cumb 148 C5
Dalston Gt Lon 45 G3
Dalswinton D & G 155 G5
Dalton D & G 155 K7
Dalton N York 132 F4
Dalton N York 140 E5
Dalton Nthumb 158 E7
Dalton-in-Furness Cumb 128 F5
Dalton-le-Dale Dur 151 K5
Dalton-on-Tees N York 141 H5
Dalton Piercy Hartpl 141 L2
Dalveich Stirlg 184 D3
Dalwhinnie Highld 202 F7
Dalwood Devon 13 G3
Damerham Hants 28 C7
Damgate Norfk 93 J2
Damnaglaur D & G 144 D7
Danbury Essex 61 J6
Danby N York 142 F5
Danby Wiske N York 141 H7
Dandaleith Moray 215 G5
Danderhall Mdloth 177 J4
Danebridge Ches E 113 L7
Dane End Herts 60 B4
Danehill E Susx 32 D7
Dane Hills C Leic 87 H3
Dane Street Kent 34 E4
Danshillock Abers 216 D3
Danskine E Loth 178 C5
Darenth Kent 45 K5
Daresbury Halton 112 E5
Darfield Barns 115 H1
Dargate Kent 34 E3
Darite Cnwll 5 K3
Darlaston Wsall 85 H4
Darlaston Green Wsall 85 H4
Darley N York 132 C7
Darley Abbey C Derb 101 G5
Darley Bridge Derbys 100 E1
Darley Dale Derbys 114 F8
Darley Green Solhll 85 L8
Darleyhall Herts 59 J4
Darley Head N York 132 B7
Darlingscott Warwks 72 B6
Darlington Darltn 141 H4
Darlington Crematorium Darltn 141 G4
Darlton Notts 116 C6
Darnick Border 167 H3
Darowen Powys 81 H3
Darra Abers 216 E5
Darracott Devon 9 G2
Darracott Devon 23 G4
Darras Hall Nthumb 158 E7
Darrington Wakefd 124 D6
Darsham Suffk 79 J1
Darshill Somset 26 E3
Dartford Kent 45 K5
Dartford Crossing Kent 45 K5
Dartington Devon 7 H4
Dartmoor National Park Devon 11 G8
Dartmouth Devon 7 K5
Darton Barns 123 L7
Darvel E Ayrs 164 B2
Darwen Bl w D 121 K6
Datchet W & M 43 G5
Datchworth Herts 59 L4
Daubhill Bolton 121 K8
Daugh of Kinermony Moray 214 F6
Dauntsey Wilts 39 M4
Dava Highld 214 C6
Davenham Ches W 112 F7
Daventry Nhants 73 H3
Davidson's Mains C Edin 177 G4
Davidstow Cnwll 8 F7
Davington D & G 155 M2
Davington Hill Kent 34 D3
Daviot Abers 216 E8
Daviot Highld 213 H6
Daviot House Highld 213 H6
Davoch of Grange Moray 215 K4
Daw End Wsall 85 J4
Dawesgreen Surrey 31 K3
Dawley Wrekin 84 C2
Dawlish Devon 12 B6
Dawlish Warren Devon 12 C6
Daybrook Notts 101 L4
Daylesford Gloucs 56 E3
Deal Kent 35 K4
Dean Cumb 136 E3
Dean Devon 7 H3
Dean Devon 23 L2
Dean Hants 29 K7
Dean Oxon 57 G4
Dean Somset 26 F3
Dean Bottom Kent 45 L6
Deanburnhaugh Border 166 F6
Deancombe Devon 7 G3
Dean Court Oxon 57 J6
Deane Bolton 121 K8
Deane Hants 29 K2
Deanhead Kirk 122 F7
Deanland Dorset 27 M7
Dean Prior Devon 7 H3
Deanraw Nthumb 149 L3
Deans W Loth 176 D5
Deanscales Cumb 136 F2
Deanshanger Nhants 73 L6
Deanshaugh Moray 215 H4
Deanston Stirlg 184 F6
Dearham Cumb 147 J7
Debach Suffk 78 F4
Debden Essex 45 H2
Debden Essex 60 E2
Debenham Suffk 78 E2
Deblin's Green Worcs 70 E5
Dechmont W Loth 176 E4
Dechmont Road W Loth 176 D4
Deddington Oxon 57 J2
Dedham Essex 62 C2
Dedworth W & M 42 F5
Deene Nhants 88 D5
Deenethorpe Nhants 88 D5
Deepcar Sheff 114 F3
Deeping Gate C Pete 89 G2
Deeping St James Lincs 89 H2
Deeping St Nicholas Lincs 89 J1
Deerhurst Gloucs 55 K3
Defford Worcs 71 G5
Defynnog Powys 52 E3
Deganwy Conwy 109 L5
Degnish Ag & B 182 A5
Deighton C York 124 F2
Deighton N York 141 J6
Deiniolen Gwynd 109 H8

Delabole Cnwll 8 E7
Delamere Ches W 112 E7
Delfrigs Abers 207 H2
Delliefure Highld 214 D7
Dell Quay W Susx 18 A5
Delnabo Moray 204 E3
Delnashaugh Inn Moray 214 E7
Delny Highld 223 G6
Delph Oldham 122 E8
Delves Dur 150 E5
Dembleby Lincs 103 H5
Denaby Donc 115 J2
Denbigh Denbgs 110 E7
Denbighshire Crematorium Denbgs 110 E6
Denbrae Fife 186 F4
Denbury Devon 7 J3
Denby Derbys 101 H4
Denby Dale Kirk 123 J8
Denchworth Oxon 41 G3
Dendron Cumb 128 F5
Denfield P & K 185 K4
Denford Nhants 88 E7
Dengie Essex 62 B7
Denham Bucks 43 H3
Denham Suffk 77 H3
Denham Suffk 92 E8
Denham Green Bucks 43 H3
Denhead Abers 217 J4
Denhead Fife 187 G5
Denhead of Gray C Dund 186 F2
Denholm Border 167 J5
Denholme C Brad 123 G4
Denmead Hants 30 A8
Denmore C Aber 207 H3
Dennington Suffk 79 G2
Denny Falk 175 L2
Dennyloanhead Falk 175 L3
Den of Lindores Fife 186 D4
Denshaw Oldham 122 E7
Denside Abers 206 F6
Densole Kent 35 G6
Denston Suffk 77 H4
Denstone Staffs 100 C4
Denstroude Kent 34 E3
Dent Cumb 130 D3
Denton Cambs 89 G6
Denton Darltn 140 F4
Denton E Susx 19 L5
Denton Kent 35 G5
Denton Lincs 102 E6
Denton N York 123 H2
Denton Nhants 74 B3
Denton Norfk 93 G5
Denton Tamesd 113 L3
Denver Norfk 90 E3
Denwick Nthumb 169 J6
Deopham Norfk 92 C4
Deopham Green Norfk 92 C4
Depden Suffk 77 H3
Deptford Gt Lon 45 G4
Deptford Wilts 28 A4
Derby C Derb 101 G5
Derby Devon 23 J5
Derbyhaven IoM 237 b7
Derculich P & K 194 D5
Dereham Norfk 92 B2
Deri Caerph 53 H7
Derringstone Kent 35 G5
Derrington Staffs 99 K7
Derry Hill Wilts 39 L6
Derrythorpe N Linc 125 J8
Dersingham Norfk 105 H6
Dervaig Ag & B 189 K6
Derwen Denbgs 97 G3
Derwenlas Powys 80 F4
Derwent Valley Mills Derbys 100 F2
Derwentwater Cumb 137 J3
Desborough Nhants 88 B6
Desford Leics 86 F3
Deskford Moray 215 L3
Detling Kent 33 K2
Devauden Mons 54 C7
Devil's Bridge Cerdgn 81 G7
Devizes Wilts 40 A7
Devonport C Plym 6 C5
Devonside Clacks 185 J7
Devoran Cnwll 4 C7
Devoran & Perran Cnwll 3 K4
Dewarton Mdloth 177 K5
Dewlish Dorset 14 E3
Dewsbury Kirk 123 K6
Dewsbury Moor Crematorium Kirk 123 J6
Deytheur Powys 97 K8
Dibden Hants 16 E2
Dibden Purlieu Hants 16 E2
Dickleburgh Norfk 92 E6
Didbrook Gloucs 56 B2
Didcot Oxon 41 K3
Diddington Cambs 75 H2
Diddlebury Shrops 83 K6
Didling W Susx 18 A3
Didmarton Gloucs 39 J3
Didsbury Manch 113 J3
Digby Lincs 103 H2
Digg Highld 218 C7
Diggle Oldham 122 F8
Digmoor Lancs 112 C1
Dihewyd Cerdgn 66 C4
Dilham Norfk 107 G7
Dilhorne Staffs 99 L4
Dill Hall Lancs 121 L4
Dillington Cambs 75 G2
Dilston Nthumb 150 B3
Dilton Wilts 27 K2
Dilton Marsh Wilts 27 J2
Dilwyn Herefs 69 H4
Dinas Gwynd 94 E5
Dinas Pembks 64 E6
Dinas-Mawddwy Gwynd 81 J1
Dinas Powys V Glam 37 J6
Dinder Somset 26 E3
Dinedor Herefs 69 K6
Dingestow Mons 54 C6
Dingle Lpool 111 K4
Dingley Nhants 87 L6
Dingwall Highld 212 E3
Dinnet Abers 205 K5
Dinnington N u Ty 158 F7
Dinnington Rothm 115 K4
Dinnington Somset 26 B8
Dinorwic Gwynd 95 K1
Dinton Bucks 58 C5
Dinton Wilts 28 A5
Dinwoodie D & G 155 K4
Dinworthy Devon 9 J2
Dipford Somset 25 J6
Dippen Ag & B 161 K2
Dippen N Ayrs 162 D5
Dippertown Devon 10 C7
Dipple Moray 215 H3
Dipple S Ayrs 152 E2
Diptford Devon 7 G4
Dipton Dur 150 E4
Dirleton E Loth 178 B2
Dirt Pot Nthumb 149 L5
Diseworth Leics 101 J7
Dishforth N York 132 F5
Disley Ches E 113 L5
Diss Norfk 92 D7
Distington Cumb 136 D3
Distington Hall Crematorium Cumb 136 E3
Ditchampton Wilts 28 C5
Ditcheat Somset 26 F4
Ditchingham Norfk 93 G5
Ditchling E Susx 19 J3
Ditherington Shrops 83 K2
Ditteridge Wilts 39 J6
Dittisham Devon 7 K5
Ditton Kent 33 J2
Ditton Green Cambs 76 F3
Ditton Priors Shrops 83 L5
Dixton Mons 54 D5
Dobcross Oldham 113 M1
Dobwalls Cnwll 5 K3
Doccombe Devon 11 H7
Dochgarroch Highld 212 F6
Docking Norfk 105 J5
Docklow Herefs 69 L3
Dockray Cumb 137 L3
Doddinghurst Essex 60 F7
Doddington Cambs 90 B5
Doddington Kent 34 C4
Doddington Lincs 116 E7
Doddington Nthumb 168 E3
Doddington Shrops 84 B7
Doddiscombsleigh Devon 11 K7
Dodd's Green Ches E 98 E4
Dodford Nhants 73 H3
Dodford Worcs 85 G8
Dodington S Glos 39 H4
Dodington Somset 25 J4
Dodleston Ches W 98 A1
Dodside E Rens 174 F7
Dod's Leigh Staffs 100 A5
Dodworth Barns 114 F1
Doe Bank Birm 85 K4
Dogdyke Lincs 103 K2
Dogmersfield Hants 30 C2
Dolanog Powys 82 B2
Dolbenmaen Gwynd 95 J4
Dolfach Powys 81 K3
Dolfor Powys 82 C6
Dolgarrog Conwy 109 L7
Dolgellau Gwynd 96 B8
Doll Highld 226 F7
Dollar Clacks 185 K7
Dollarfield Clacks 185 K7
Dolphin Flints 111 H6
Dolphinholme Lancs 129 L8
Dolphinton S Lans 176 F8
Dolton Devon 10 E3
Dolwen Conwy 110 B6
Dolwyddelan Conwy 96 B3
Domgay Powys 97 L8
Doncaster Donc 115 L2
Doncaster North Services Donc 125 G7
Donhead St Andrew Wilts 27 K6
Donhead St Mary Wilts 27 K6
Donibristle Fife 177 G2
Doniford Somset 25 G3
Donington Lincs 103 K5
Donington on Bain Lincs 118 C5
Donington Park Services Leics 101 J7
Donisthorpe Leics 86 C2
Donnington Gloucs 56 D3
Donnington Shrops 83 L2
Donnington W Berk 41 J6
Donnington W Susx 18 B5
Donnington Wrekin 84 C2
Donnington Wood Wrekin 84 C2
Donyatt Somset 25 M8
Doonfoot S Ayrs 163 H5
Dorback Lodge Highld 204 D3
Dorchester Dorset 14 D4
Dorchester Oxon 41 L2
Dordon Warwks 86 C4
Dore Sheff 114 F5
Dores Highld 212 F7
Dorking Surrey 31 K2
Dormansland Surrey 32 D5
Dormington Herefs 69 L6
Dormston Worcs 71 H3
Dorney Bucks 42 F5
Dornie Highld 200 D1
Dornoch Highld 223 H4
Dornock D & G 147 M2
Dorrery Highld 230 F5
Dorridge Solhll 85 L8
Dorrington Lincs 103 H2
Dorrington Shrops 83 J3
Dorrington Shrops 99 G4
Dorsington Warwks 71 K4
Dorstone Herefs 69 G6
Dorton Bucks 58 B5
Douglas IoM 237 d6
Douglas S Lans 165 G4
Douglas and Angus C Dund 187 G2
Douglas Crematorium IoM 237 d5
Douglas Pier Ag & B 183 H7
Douglastown Angus 196 C6
Douglas Water S Lans 165 G3
Douglas West S Lans 164 F3
Doulting Somset 26 F3
Dounby Ork 234 b5
Doune Highld 221 L2
Doune Stirlg 184 F6
Dounepark S Ayrs 152 E3
Dounie Highld 222 D4
Dousland Devon 6 D3
Dove Dale Derbys 100 D3
Dove Holes Derbys 114 B6
Dovenby Cumb 147 J7
Dover Kent 35 J6
Dover Castle Kent 35 J6
Dovercourt Essex 62 F2
Doverdale Worcs 70 F2
Doveridge Derbys 100 C5
Doversgreen Surrey 31 L2
Dowally P & K 194 F6
Dowdeswell Gloucs 55 M4
Dowlais Myr Td 53 G6
Dowland Devon 10 E3
Dowlish Wake Somset 26 A8
Down Ampney Gloucs 40 C2
Downderry Cnwll 5 L5
Downe Gt Lon 45 H7
Downend Gloucs 39 J2
Downend S Glos 38 F5
Downfield C Dund 186 F2
Downgate Cnwll 6 A2
Downham Essex 46 B2
Downham Gt Lon 45 H5
Downham Lancs 122 B2
Downham Market Norfk 90 E3
Down Hatherley Gloucs 55 K4
Downhead Somset 26 E6
Downhead Somset 27 G3
Downhill P & K 186 A2
Downholme N York 140 E7
Downies Abers 207 H6
Downley Bucks 42 D2
Down St Mary Devon 11 H4
Downs Crematorium Br & H 19 J4
Downside Surrey 43 J8
Down Thomas Devon 6 D6
Downton Wilts 28 D6
Dowsby Lincs 103 J6
Doynton S Glos 39 G5
Draethen Caerph 37 K3
Draffan S Lans 164 F1
Drakeholes Notts 116 B4
Drakemyre N Ayrs 174 B7
Drakes Broughton Worcs 71 G5
Draughton N York 131 K8
Draughton Nhants 87 L7
Drax N York 125 G5
Draycote Warwks 72 F1
Draycott Gloucs 71 L7
Draycott Somset 26 C2
Draycott in the Clay Staffs 100 D6
Draycott in the Moors Staffs 99 M4
Drayton C Port 17 J2
Drayton Leics 88 B5
Drayton Norfk 92 E2
Drayton Oxon 41 J2
Drayton Oxon 72 E6
Drayton Somset 26 B6
Drayton Worcs 85 G7
Drayton Bassett Staffs 85 L4

Drayton Beauchamp Bucks 58 E5
Drayton Manor Park Staffs 85 L4
Drayton Parslow Bucks 58 D3
Drayton St Leonard Oxon 41 L2
Dreen Hill Pembks 48 F5
Drefach Carmth 51 G3
Drefach Carmth 65 K6
Drefach Cerdgn 66 C5
Dreghorn N Ayrs 163 J2
Drellingore Kent 35 H6
Drem E Loth 178 B3
Dresden C Stke 99 K4
Drewsteignton Devon 11 H6
Driffield E R Yk 134 F7
Driffield Gloucs 56 B7
Drift Cnwll 2 D5
Drigg Cumb 136 E7
Drighlington Leeds 123 J5
Drimnin Highld 190 B5
Drimpton Dorset 13 K2
Drimsallie Highld 191 J1
Dringhouses C York 124 E2
Drinkstone Suffk 77 L3
Drinkstone Green Suffk 77 L3
Drointon Staffs 100 A6
Droitwich Spa Worcs 70 F2
Dron P & K 186 B4
Dronfield Derbys 115 G5
Drongan E Ayrs 163 K5
Dronley Angus 186 E1
Droop Dorset 14 E2
Droxford Hants 29 L7
Droylsden Tamesd 113 K2
Druid Denbgs 97 G4
Druidston Pembks 48 E4
Druimarbin Highld 191 L3
Druimavuic Ag & B 191 K7
Druimdrishaig Ag & B 172 C4
Druimindarroch Highld 199 L7
Drum Ag & B 172 F3
Drum P & K 185 L7
Drumalbin S Lans 165 H2
Drumbeg Highld 224 D3
Drumblade Abers 216 B6
Drumbreddon D & G 144 C6
Drumbuie Highld 210 B7
Drumburgh Cumb 148 A3
Drumburn D & G 146 F4
Drumchapel C Glas 174 F4
Drumchastle P & K 193 L5
Drumclog S Lans 164 C2
Drumeldrie Fife 187 G6
Drumelzier Border 165 M3
Drumfearn Highld 199 L3
Drumfrennie Abers 206 D5
Drumgley Angus 196 C6
Drumguish Highld 203 J5
Drumin Moray 214 E7
Drumjohn D & G 153 L3
Drumlamford S Ayrs 153 G6
Drumlasie Abers 206 C4
Drumleaning Cumb 148 A5
Drumlemble Ag & B 161 H5
Drumlithie Abers 197 J1
Drummoddie D & G 145 H6
Drummore D & G 144 D7
Drummuir Moray 215 J5
Drumnadrochit Highld 212 D7
Drumnagorrach Moray 215 L4
Drumpark D & G 154 F6
Drumrunie Lodge Highld 224 E7
Drumshang S Ayrs 163 G6
Drumuie Highld 209 G5
Drumuillie Highld 204 B2
Drumvaich Stirlg 184 E6
Drunzie P & K 186 B5
Drybeck Cumb 138 F4
Drybridge Moray 215 K2
Drybridge N Ayrs 163 J3
Drybrook Gloucs 54 F4
Dryburgh Border 167 J3
Dry Doddington Lincs 102 D3
Dry Drayton Cambs 75 L3
Drymen Stirlg 174 E2
Drymuir Abers 217 G5
Drynoch Highld 208 F7
Dubford Abers 216 F2
Duchally Highld 225 J5
Ducklington Oxon 57 G6
Duddenhoe End Essex 76 C7
Duddingston C Edin 177 J4
Duddington Nhants 88 E4
Duddlestone Somset 25 K7
Duddo Nthumb 168 D2
Duddon Ches W 112 D8
Dudleston Shrops 97 M5
Dudleston Heath Shrops 98 A5
Dudley Dudley 85 G5
Dudley N Tyne 159 G7
Dudley Port Sandw 85 G5
Dudsbury Dorset 15 K3
Duffield Derbys 101 G4
Duffryn Neath 36 C2
Dufftown Moray 215 H6
Duffus Moray 214 E2
Dufton Cumb 139 G3
Duggleby N York 134 D6
Duirinish Highld 210 B7
Duisdalemore Highld 199 L3
Duisky Highld 191 K2
Duke Street Suffk 78 C6
Dukinfield Tamesd 113 L2
Dukinfield Crematorium Tamesd 113 L2
Dulcote Somset 26 E3
Dulford Devon 12 D2
Dull P & K 194 C6
Dullatur N Lans 175 K3
Dullingham Cambs 76 F3
Dulnain Bridge Highld 204 B1
Duloe Bed 75 H3
Duloe Cnwll 5 K4
Dulverton Somset 24 E5
Dulwich Gt Lon 45 G5
Dumbarton W Duns 174 D4
Dumbleton Gloucs 71 H7
Dumfries D & G 155 G6
Dumgoyne Stirlg 174 F2
Dummer Hants 29 L3
Dumpton Kent 35 K2
Dun Angus 197 G4
Dunalastair P & K 193 L5
Dunan Ag & B 173 K4
Dunan Highld 209 J8
Dunan P & K 193 G5
Dunaverty Ag & B 161 H7
Dunball Somset 25 L3
Dunbar E Loth 178 E3
Dunbeath Highld 227 L3
Dunbeg Ag & B 182 C2
Dunblane Stirlg 185 G6
Dunbog Fife 186 E4
Duncanston Highld 212 F3
Duncanstone Abers 216 B8
Dunchideock Devon 11 K7
Dunchurch Warwks 72 F1
Duncow D & G 155 G5
Duncrievie P & K 186 B5
Duncton W Susx 18 C3
Dundee C Dund 186 F2
Dundee Airport C Dund 186 F2
Dundee Crematorium C Dund 186 F2
Dundon Somset 26 C5
Dundonald S Ayrs 163 J3
Dundonnell Highld 220 E4
Dundraw Cumb 147 L5
Dundreggan Highld 201 L3
Dundrennan D & G 146 D5
Dundry N Som 38 E6
Dunecht Abers 206 E4
Dunfermline Fife 176 F2
Dunfermline Crematorium Fife 176 F2
Dunfield Gloucs 40 C2
Dungavel S Lans 164 D3
Dungeness Kent 21 L3
Dunham-on-the-Hill Ches W 112 C6
Dunham-on-Trent Notts 116 D6
Dunhampton Worcs 70 F2
Dunham Town Traffd 113 H4
Dunham Woodhouses Traffd 113 G4
Dunholme Lincs 117 G5
Dunino Fife 187 J5
Dunipace Falk 175 L2
Dunkeld P & K 195 G7
Dunkerton BaNES 39 G8
Dunkeswell Devon 12 E2
Dunkeswick N York 123 L2
Dunkirk Kent 34 E3
Dunkirk S Glos 39 H4
Dunk's Green Kent 33 G3
Dunlappie Angus 196 F3
Dunley Worcs 70 E2
Dunlop E Ayrs 174 D8
Dunmaglass Highld 202 F2
Dunmore Falk 176 B1
Dunnet Highld 231 J2
Dunnichen Angus 196 E6
Dunning P & K 185 L4
Dunnington C York 133 K8
Dunnington E R Yk 126 E1
Dunnington Warwks 71 J4
Dunoon Ag & B 173 K3
Dunphail Moray 214 C5
Dunragit D & G 144 E4
Duns Border 179 G7
Dunsby Lincs 103 J6
Dunscore D & G 154 F5
Dunscroft Donc 124 F8
Dunsdale R & Cl 142 D4
Dunsden Green Oxon 42 C5
Dunsdon Devon 9 J3
Dunsfold Surrey 31 G4
Dunsford Devon 11 J6
Dunshalt Fife 186 D5
Dunshillock Abers 217 J5
Dunsill Notts 101 J1
Dunsley N York 143 H5
Dunsley Staffs 84 F6
Dunsmore Bucks 58 E6
Dunsop Bridge Lancs 121 K1
Dunstable C Beds 59 G4
Dunstall Staffs 100 D7
Dunstan Nthumb 169 K5
Dunster Somset 24 F3
Duns Tew Oxon 57 J3
Dunston Gatesd 151 G3
Dunston Lincs 117 H8
Dunston Norfk 92 F3
Dunston Staffs 99 L8
Dunstone Devon 6 E5
Dunstone Devon 7 G2
Dunsville Donc 124 F8
Dunswell E R Yk 126 D4
Dunsyre S Lans 176 E8
Dunterton Devon 6 B1
Duntisbourne Abbots Gloucs 55 L6
Duntisbourne Rouse Gloucs 55 M6
Duntish Dorset 14 D2
Duntocher W Duns 174 E4
Dunton Bucks 58 D3
Dunton C Beds 75 J5
Dunton Norfk 105 L6
Dunton Bassett Leics 87 G5
Dunton Green Kent 32 F2
Duntulm Highld 218 C6
Dunure S Ayrs 163 G6
Dunvant Swans 51 H6
Dunvegan Highld 208 D5
Dunwich Suffk 79 K1
Durgan Cnwll 3 K5
Durham Dur 151 G6
Durham Cathedral Dur 151 G6
Durham Crematorium Dur 151 G6
Durham Services Dur 151 H7
Durham Tees Valley Airport S on T 141 J5
Durisdeer D & G 154 F2
Durisdeermill D & G 154 F2
Durleigh Somset 25 L4
Durley Hants 29 K7
Durley Wilts 40 E7
Durley Street Hants 29 K7
Durlock Kent 35 H3
Durlock Kent 35 J2
Durness Highld 228 F3
Durno Abers 216 D8
Duror Highld 191 K5
Durran Ag & B 182 D5
Durrington W Susx 18 F5
Durrington Wilts 28 D3
Durris Abers 206 E6
Dursley Gloucs 39 H2
Dursley Cross Gloucs 55 G4
Durston Somset 25 L5
Durweston Dorset 15 G2
Duston Nhants 73 K3
Duthil Highld 203 L1
Dutton Ches W 112 E5
Duxford Cambs 76 C5
Duxford Oxon 57 G7
Duxford IWM Cambs 76 C5
Dwygyfylchi Conwy 109 L6
Dwyran IoA 108 F7
Dyce C Aber 207 G3
Dyffryn Ardudwy Gwynd 95 K7
Dyffryn Cellwen Neath 52 D6
Dyke Lincs 103 J7
Dyke Moray 214 B3
Dykehead Angus 195 K5
Dykehead Angus 196 C4
Dykehead N Lans 176 B6
Dykehead Stirlg 184 D7
Dykelands Abers 197 H3
Dykends Angus 195 K5
Dykeside Abers 216 D5
Dymchurch Kent 34 E8
Dymock Gloucs 55 G2
Dyrham S Glos 39 H5
Dysart Fife 186 E8
Dyserth Denbgs 110 E5

E

Eagland Hill Lancs 120 F2
Eagle Lincs 116 E7
Eaglesfield Cumb 136 F2
Eaglesfield D & G 155 M7
Eaglesham E Rens 175 G7
Eagley Bolton 121 L7
Eakring Notts 102 A1
Ealand N Linc 125 J7
Ealing Gt Lon 44 D4
Eals Nthumb 149 H4
Eamont Bridge Cumb 138 D2
Earby Lancs 122 D2
Eardington Shrops 84 C5
Eardisland Herefs 69 H3
Eardisley Herefs 68 F5
Eardiston Shrops 98 A7
Eardiston Worcs 70 C2
Earith Cambs 89 L8
Earlestown St Hel 112 E3
Earley Wokham 42 C6
Earlham Norfk 92 E2
Earlham Crematorium Norfk 92 E2
Earlish Highld 208 F3
Earls Barton Nhants 74 C2

Earls Colne Essex 61 K3
Earls Common Worcs 71 G3
Earl's Croome Worcs 70 F6
Earlsdon Covtry 86 D7
Earlsferry Fife 187 H7
Earlsfield Gt Lon 44 E5
Earlsford Abers 216 F7
Earlsheaton Kirk 123 K6
Earl Shilton Leics 86 F4
Earl Soham Suffk 78 F2
Earl Sterndale Derbys 114 C7
Earlston Border 167 J2
Earlston E Ayrs 163 K3
Earlswood Surrey 32 B4
Earlswood Warwks 85 K8
Earnley W Susx 17 M3
Earsdon N Tyne 159 H7
Earsham Norfk 93 G5
Eartham W Susx 18 C4
Easby N York 142 C5
Easdale Ag & B 181 L4
Easebourne W Susx 30 E6
Easenhall Warwks 86 F7
Eashing Surrey 30 F3
Easington Bucks 58 B6
Easington Dur 151 K6
Easington E R Yk 127 J6
Easington R & Cl 142 F4
Easington Colliery Dur 151 K6
Easington Lane Sundld 151 J5
Easingwold N York 133 H5
Eassie and Nevay Angus 196 B7
East Aberthaw V Glam 37 G6
East Allington Devon 7 H6
East Anstey Devon 24 D6
East Ashey IoW 17 H5
East Ashling W Susx 17 M2
East Ayton N York 134 F3
East Barkwith Lincs 117 K5
East Barming Kent 33 J3
East Barnby N York 143 G5
East Barnet Gt Lon 44 F2
East Barns E Loth 178 F3
East Barsham Norfk 105 L5
East Beckham Norfk 106 E4
East Bedfont Gt Lon 43 H5
East Bergholt Suffk 78 C7
East Bilney Norfk 106 A8
East Blatchington E Susx 20 A5
East Boldon S Tyne 151 J3
East Boldre Hants 16 D3
Eastbourne Darltn 141 H4
Eastbourne E Susx 20 C5
Eastbourne Crematorium E Susx 20 D5
East Bradenham Norfk 91 L2
East Brent Somset 25 M2
Eastbridge Suffk 79 J2
East Bridgford Notts 102 B4
East Buckland Devon 23 L5
East Budleigh Devon 12 D5
Eastburn C Brad 122 F2
Eastbury Herts 43 J2
Eastbury W Berk 41 G5
East Butterwick N Linc 116 D1
Eastby N York 131 J8
East Calder W Loth 176 E5
East Carleton Norfk 92 E3
East Carlton Leeds 123 J2
East Carlton Nhants 88 B5
East Chaldon (Chaldon Herring) Dorset 14 E5
East Challow Oxon 41 G3
East Charleton Devon 7 H7
East Chelborough Dorset 14 A2
East Chiltington E Susx 19 K3
East Chinnock Somset 26 C8
East Chisenbury Wilts 28 C2
Eastchurch Kent 47 G5
East Clandon Surrey 31 H2
East Claydon Bucks 58 C3
East Coker Somset 26 D8
Eastcombe Gloucs 55 K6
East Compton Somset 26 E3
East Cornworthy Devon 7 J5
Eastcote Gt Lon 43 J3
Eastcote Nhants 73 K4
Eastcote Solhll 85 L7
Eastcott Wilts 28 A1
East Cottingwith E R Yk 125 G3
Eastcourt Wilts 40 E7
East Cowes IoW 16 F4
East Cowick E R Yk 125 G6
East Cowton N York 141 H6
East Cranmore Somset 27 G3
East Dean E Susx 20 B6
East Dean Gloucs 54 F4
East Dean Hants 28 F6
East Dean W Susx 18 B3
East Devon Crematorium Devon 12 D4
East Drayton Notts 116 C6
East Dulwich Gt Lon 45 G5
East Dundry N Som 38 E7
East Ella C KuH 126 C5
Eastend Essex 46 F2
East End Hants 16 D3
East End Hants 41 H7
East End Kent 33 L6
East End Oxon 57 H5
East End Somset 26 F3
Easter Balmoral Abers 205 G6
Easter Compton S Glos 38 E4
Easter Dalziel Highld 213 H4
Eastergate W Susx 18 C5
Easterhouse C Glas 175 J5
Easter Howgate Mdloth 177 H5
Easter Kinkell Highld 212 E4
Easter Moniack Highld 212 E5
Eastern Green Covtry 86 C7
Easter Ord Abers 206 F4
Easter Pitkierie Fife 187 J6
Easter Skeld Shet 235 c6
Easter Softlaw Border 168 A3
Easterton Wilts 28 A1
East Everleigh Wilts 28 D2
East Farleigh Kent 33 J3
East Farndon Nhants 87 K6
East Ferry Lincs 116 D2
Eastfield N Lans 176 B5
Eastfield N York 135 G3
East Fortune E Loth 178 C3
East Garston W Berk 41 G5
Eastgate Dur 150 B7
Eastgate Norfk 106 D7
East Goscote Leics 87 J2
East Grafton Wilts 40 E7
East Grimstead Wilts 28 E5
East Grinstead W Susx 32 D5
East Guldeford E Susx 21 J2
East Haddon Nhants 73 J2
East Hagbourne Oxon 41 K3
East Halton N Linc 126 E6
East Ham Gt Lon 45 H4
Easthampstead Park Crematorium Br For 42 D6
Easthampton Herefs 69 H2
East Hanney Oxon 41 H2
East Hanningfield Essex 61 J7
East Hardwick Wakefd 124 C6
East Harling Norfk 92 B6
East Harlsey N York 141 K7
East Harnham Wilts 28 C5
East Harptree BaNES 26 E1
East Harting W Susx 30 D7
East Hatch Wilts 27 L5
East Hatley Cambs 75 K4
East Hauxwell N York 132 B2
East Haven Angus 187 J1
East Heckington Lincs 103 K4
East Hedleyhope Dur 150 E6
East Helmsdale Highld 227 H5
East Hendred Oxon 41 J3
East Heslerton N York 134 E4
East Hoathly E Susx 20 B3
East Holme Dorset 15 G5
Easthope Shrops 83 L4
Easthorpe Essex 61 L4
East Horrington Somset 26 E3
East Horsley Surrey 31 H2
East Howe Bmouth 15 K4
East Huntington C York 133 J7
East Huntspill Somset 25 M3
East Ilsley W Berk 41 J4
Eastington Devon 11 H3
Eastington Gloucs 55 H6
Eastington Gloucs 56 C5
East Keal Lincs 118 E8
East Kennett Wilts 40 C6
East Keswick Leeds 124 B2
East Kilbride S Lans 175 H7
East Kirkby Lincs 118 D8
East Knighton Dorset 14 F5
East Knoyle Wilts 27 K5
East Lambrook Somset 26 B7
East Lancashire Crematorium Bury 122 B8
Eastlands D & G 154 E7
East Langdon Kent 35 J5
East Langton Leics 87 K5
East Lavant W Susx 18 B4
East Lavington W Susx 18 C3
East Layton N York 140 E5
Eastleach Martin Gloucs 56 D6
Eastleach Turville Gloucs 56 D6
East Leake Notts 101 K7
Eastleigh Devon 23 H5
Eastleigh Hants 29 J7
East Lexham Norfk 105 K8
Eastling Kent 34 C4
East Linton E Loth 178 D3
East Lockinge Oxon 41 H3
East London Crematorium Gt Lon 45 H4
East Lound N Linc 116 C2
East Lulworth Dorset 15 G6
East Lutton N York 134 E5
East Lydford Somset 26 E5
East Malling Kent 33 J2
East Marden W Susx 30 D8
East Markham Notts 116 C6
East Martin Hants 28 B7
East Marton N York 122 D1
East Meon Hants 30 B6
East Mersea Essex 62 C5
East Midlands Airport Leics 101 J7
East Molesey Surrey 43 J6
East Morden Dorset 15 G4
East Morton C Brad 123 G3
East Morton D & G 154 F3
East Ness N York 133 L4
Eastney C Port 17 J3
Eastnor Herefs 70 D6
East Norton Leics 87 L4
Eastoft N Linc 125 J7
East Ogwell Devon 7 J2
Easton Cambs 75 G1
Easton Devon 11 G6
Easton Dorset 14 D7
Easton Hants 29 K5
Easton Lincs 102 F6
Easton Norfk 92 D2
Easton Somset 26 D3
Easton Suffk 79 G3
Easton Wilts 39 K6
Easton Grey Wilts 39 K3
Easton-in-Gordano N Som 38 D5
Easton Maudit Nhants 74 C3
Easton-on-the-Hill Nhants 88 E3
Easton Royal Wilts 40 D7
East Orchard Dorset 27 J7
East Peckham Kent 33 H4
East Pennar Pembks 49 G6
East Pennard Somset 26 E4
East Perry Cambs 75 G2
East Portlemouth Devon 7 H7
East Prawle Devon 7 H8
East Preston W Susx 18 E5
East Putford Devon 9 K2
East Quantoxhead Somset 25 H3
East Rainton Sundld 151 H5
East Ravendale NE Lin 118 C2
East Raynham Norfk 105 L7
Eastrea Cambs 89 K4
East Riding Crematorium E R Yk 134 F5
Eastriggs D & G 147 M2
East Rigton Leeds 124 B2
Eastrington E R Yk 125 J4
Eastrop Swindn 40 D2
East Rounton N York 141 K6
East Rudham Norfk 105 K6
East Runton Norfk 106 E4
East Ruston Norfk 107 H6
Eastry Kent 35 J4
East Saltoun E Loth 178 B5
East Sheen Gt Lon 44 D5
East Shefford W Berk 41 H5
East Stockwith Lincs 116 C3
East Stoke Dorset 15 G5
East Stoke Notts 102 C3
East Stour Dorset 27 J6
East Stourmouth Kent 35 H3
East Stowford Devon 23 K6
East Stratton Hants 29 K4
East Studdal Kent 35 J5
East Taphouse Cnwll 5 J3
East-the-Water Devon 23 G6
East Thirston Nthumb 158 F3
East Tilbury Thurr 46 B5
East Tisted Hants 30 B5
East Torrington Lincs 117 J5
East Tuddenham Norfk 92 C2
East Tytherley Hants 28 F5
East Tytherton Wilts 39 L5
East Village Devon 11 J4
Eastville Bristl 38 E5
Eastville Lincs 104 C2
East Walton Norfk 91 G1
East Week Devon 10 F6
Eastwell Leics 102 C6
East Wellow Hants 28 F7
East Wemyss Fife 186 E7
East Whitburn W Loth 176 C5
Eastwick Herts 60 C5
East Wickham Gt Lon 45 J5
East Williamston Pembks 49 J6

East Winch Norfk 91 G1
East Winterslow Wilts 28 E5
East Wittering W Susx 17 L3
East Witton N York 131 L3
Eastwood Notts 101 J3
Eastwood Sthend 46 D3
East Woodburn Nthumb 158 A5
East Woodhay Hants 41 H7
East Worldham Hants 30 C4
East Wretham Norfk 91 K5
East Youlstone Devon 9 H2
Eathorpe Warwks 72 E2
Eaton Ches E 113 K7
Eaton Ches W 112 E8
Eaton Leics 102 D6
Eaton Norfk 92 E3
Eaton Notts 116 B6
Eaton Oxon 57 H7
Eaton Shrops 83 K5
Eaton Bray C Beds 58 F4
Eaton Constantine Shrops 83 L3
Eaton Green C Beds 58 F4
Eaton Hastings Oxon 56 E7
Eaton Mascott Shrops 83 K3
Eaton Socon Cambs 75 H3
Eaton upon Tern Shrops 98 F7
Ebberston N York 134 D3
Ebbesborne Wake Wilts 27 M6
Ebbw Vale Blae G 53 J6
Ebchester Dur 150 D4
Ebford Devon 12 C5
Ebley Gloucs 55 J6
Ebnal Ches W 98 C3
Ebrington Gloucs 71 L6
Ecchinswell Hants 41 J8
Ecclaw Border 178 F5
Ecclefechan D & G 155 L7
Eccles Border 168 A2
Eccles Kent 46 B7
Eccles Salfd 113 H2
Ecclesall Sheff 114 F5
Ecclesfield Sheff 115 G3
Eccleshall Staffs 99 J6
Eccleshill C Brad 123 H4
Ecclesmachan W Loth 176 E4
Eccles Road Norfk 92 B5
Eccleston Ches W 112 B8
Eccleston Lancs 121 G6
Eccleston St Hel 112 C3
Echt Abers 206 E4
Eckford Border 167 L4
Eckington Derbys 115 H5
Eckington Worcs 71 G6
Ecton Nhants 74 B2
Edale Derbys 114 C4
Eday Ork 234 d4
Eday Airport Ork 234 d4
Edburton W Susx 19 H4
Edderton Highld 222 F4
Eddleston Border 177 H8
Eddlewood S Lans 175 J7
Edenbridge Kent 32 D4
Edenfield Lancs 122 B6
Edenhall Cumb 138 E2
Edenham Lincs 103 H7
Eden Park Gt Lon 45 G6
Eden Project Cnwll 5 G5
Edensor Derbys 114 E7
Edentaggart Ag & B 183 K8
Edenthorpe Donc 115 L1
Edern Gwynd 94 E5
Edgbaston Birm 85 J6
Edgcott Bucks 58 B4
Edgcott Somset 24 D4
Edge Gloucs 55 J6
Edgefield Norfk 106 C5
Edgefield Green Norfk 106 D5
Edgerton Kirk 123 H6
Edgeworth Gloucs 55 L6
Edgmond Wrekin 99 G8
Edgton Shrops 83 H6
Edgware Gt Lon 44 D2
Edgworth Bl w D 121 L6
Edinbane Highld 208 E4
Edinburgh C Edin 177 H4
Edinburgh Airport C Edin 176 F4
Edinburgh Castle C Edin 177 H4
Edinburgh Old & New Town C Edin 177 H4
Edinburgh Royal Botanic Gardens C Edin 177 H4
Edinburgh Zoo C Edin 177 G4
Edingale Staffs 86 B2
Edingham D & G 146 E3
Edingley Notts 102 A2
Edingthorpe Norfk 107 G6
Edingthorpe Green Norfk 107 G6
Edington Border 179 J7
Edington Nthumb 158 E5
Edington Somset 26 B4
Edington Wilts 27 L2
Edington Burtle Somset 26 B3
Edingworth Somset 26 A2
Edithmead Somset 25 L2
Edith Weston Rutlnd 88 D3
Edlesborough Bucks 58 F4
Edlingham Nthumb 169 G7
Edlington Lincs 118 C7
Edmondsham Dorset 15 K1
Edmondsley Dur 151 G5
Edmondthorpe Leics 102 E8
Edmonton Gt Lon 45 G2
Edmundbyers Dur 150 C5
Ednam Border 167 L2
Edradynate P & K 194 D6
Edrom Border 179 H7
Edstaston Shrops 98 D6
Edstone Warwks 71 L3
Edwalton Notts 101 L5
Edwinstowe Notts 115 L7
Edworth C Beds 75 J6
Edwyn Ralph Herefs 70 B3
Edzell Angus 196 F3
Edzell Woods Abers 197 G3
Efail-fach Neath 36 B2
Efail Isaf Rhondd 37 G4
Efailnewydd Gwynd 94 F5
Efailwen Carmth 49 K3
Efenechtyd Denbgs 97 H2
Effgill D & G 156 B4
Effingham Surrey 31 J2
Efford Crematorium C Plym 6 D4
Egerton Bolton 121 K7
Egerton Kent 34 B5
Eggborough N York 124 E5
Eggbuckland C Plym 6 D4
Eggesford Devon 11 G3
Eggington C Beds 58 F3
Egginton Derbys 100 E6
Eggleston Dur 140 C3
Egham Surrey 43 G6
Egleton Rutlnd 88 C3
Eglingham Nthumb 169 G5
Egloshayle Cnwll 4 F2
Egloskerry Cnwll 9 H7
Eglwysbach Conwy 109 M7
Eglwys Cross Wrexhm 98 C4
Eglwyswrw Pembks 65 G6
Egmanton Notts 116 B7
Egremont Cumb 136 D5
Egremont Wirral 111 K3
Egton N York 143 G6
Egton Bridge N York 143 G6
Egypt Bucks 42 F3
Eigg Highld 199 G7
Eight Ash Green Essex 61 M3
Eilanreach Highld 200 C2
Eilean Donan Castle Highld 200 D1
Elan Valley Powys 67 J2
Elan Village Powys 67 K2
Elberton S Glos 38 E3
Elburton C Plym 6 D5
Elcombe Swindn 40 C4
Eldersfield Worcs 55 H2
Elderslie Rens 174 E5
Eldon Dur 141 G2
Elerch Cerdgn 80 F6
Elfhill Abers 206 F7
Elford Staffs 85 L2
Elgin Moray 214 F2
Elgol Highld 199 H3
Elham Kent 35 G6
Elie Fife 187 H7
Elim IoA 108 D4
Eling Hants 29 G8
Elkesley Notts 116 B6
Elkstone Gloucs 55 L5
Ella Abers 216 C3
Ellacombe Torbay 7 L3
Elland Calder 123 G6
Ellary Ag & B 172 C3
Ellastone Staffs 100 C4
Ellel Lancs 129 K7
Ellemford Border 178 F6
Ellenabeich Ag & B 181 L4
Ellenhall Staffs 99 J7
Ellen's Green Surrey 31 H4
Ellerbeck N York 141 K7
Ellerby N York 143 G4
Ellerdine Heath Wrekin 98 F7
Elleric Ag & B 191 K6
Ellerker E R Yk 125 L5
Ellerton E R Yk 125 G3
Ellerton N York 141 G7
Ellesborough Bucks 58 D6
Ellesmere Shrops 98 B5
Ellesmere Port Ches W 111 L6
Ellingham Norfk 93 H5
Ellingham Nthumb 169 H4
Ellingstring N York 132 B3
Ellington Cambs 75 H1
Ellington Nthumb 159 G4
Elliots Green Somset 27 J3
Ellisfield Hants 29 M3
Ellishader Highld 209 H2
Ellistown Leics 86 E2
Ellon Abers 217 H7
Ellonby Cumb 148 D7
Elloughton E R Yk 126 B5
Ellwood Gloucs 54 E6
Elm Cambs 90 C3
Elmbridge Worcs 70 F2
Elmdon Essex 76 C6
Elmdon Solhll 85 L6
Elmers End Gt Lon 45 G6
Elmer's Green Lancs 112 D1
Elmesthorpe Leics 86 F4
Elmhurst Staffs 85 K2
Elmley Castle Worcs 71 H6
Elmley Lovett Worcs 70 F1
Elmore Gloucs 55 H5
Elmore Back Gloucs 55 H5
Elm Park Gt Lon 45 K3
Elmsett Suffk 78 C5
Elmstead Market Essex 62 C3
Elmsted Kent 34 F5
Elmstone Kent 35 H3
Elmstone Hardwicke Gloucs 55 K3
Elmswell E R Yk 134 F7
Elmswell Suffk 78 B2
Elmton Derbys 115 J6
Elphin Highld 224 F6
Elphinstone E Loth 177 K4
Elrick Abers 206 F4
Elrig D & G 145 G5
Elrington Nthumb 149 L3
Elsdon Nthumb 158 B4
Elsenham Essex 60 E3
Elsfield Oxon 57 K6
Elsham N Linc 126 C7
Elsing Norfk 92 C1
Elslack N York 122 D2
Elson Hants 17 H3
Elsrickle S Lans 165 K2
Elstead Surrey 30 E3
Elsted W Susx 30 D7
Elsthorpe Lincs 103 H7
Elston Notts 102 C3
Elstow Bed 74 F5
Elstree Herts 44 D2
Elstronwick E R Yk 126 F4
Elswick Lancs 120 F3
Elswick N u Ty 151 G3
Elsworth Cambs 75 K2
Elterwater Cumb 137 K6
Eltham Gt Lon 45 H5
Eltham Crematorium Gt Lon 45 J5
Eltisley Cambs 75 J3
Elton Cambs 88 F5
Elton Ches W 112 C6
Elton Derbys 100 E1
Elton Herefs 69 J1
Elton Notts 102 C5
Elton S on T 141 J4
Eltringham Nthumb 150 D3
Elvanfoot S Lans 165 J6
Elvaston Derbys 101 H6
Elveden Suffk 91 J7
Elvetham Heath Hants 30 D1
Elvingston E Loth 178 A4
Elvington C York 125 G2
Elvington Kent 35 H5
Elwick Hartpl 141 K2
Elworth Ches E 99 H1
Elworthy Somset 25 G4
Ely Cambs 90 D7
Ely Cardif 37 H5
Emberton M Keyn 74 C5
Embleton Cumb 137 G2
Embleton Nthumb 169 J5
Embo Highld 223 H3
Emborough Somset 26 E2
Embo Street Highld 223 H3
Embsay N York 131 J8
Emery Down Hants 16 C2
Emley Kirk 123 K7
Emmington Oxon 58 C7
Emneth Norfk 90 C3
Emneth Hungate Norfk 90 D3
Empingham Rutlnd 88 D2
Empshott Hants 30 C5
Emstrey Crematorium Shrops 83 K2
Emsworth Hants 17 K2
Enborne W Berk 41 H7
Enborne Row W Berk 41 H7
Enderby Leics 87 G4
Endmoor Cumb 129 L3
Endon Staffs 99 L2
Endon Bank Staffs 99 L2
Enfield Gt Lon 60 B7
Enfield Crematorium Gt Lon 60 B7
Enfield Lock Gt Lon 60 B7
Enfield Wash Gt Lon 60 B7
Enford Wilts 28 C2
Engine Common S Glos 39 G4
Englefield W Berk 41 L6
Englefield Green Surrey 43 G6
English Bicknor Gloucs 54 E5
Englishcombe BaNES 39 G7
English Frankton Shrops 98 C6
Enham-Alamein Hants 29 G2
Enmore Somset 25 K4
Enmore Green Dorset 27 J6
Ennerdale Bridge Cumb 136 E4
Enochdhu P & K 195 G4
Ensay Ag & B 189 J6
Ensbury Bmouth 15 K3
Ensdon Shrops 83 H1

Enstone Oxon 57 G3
Enterkinfoot D & G 154 E2
Enville Staffs 84 E6
Eolaigearraidh W Isls 233 b9
Epney Gloucs 55 H5
Epperstone Notts 101 M3
Epping Essex 60 D7
Epping Green Essex 60 C6
Epping Upland Essex 60 C6
Eppleby N York 140 F5
Epsom Surrey 44 E7
Epwell Oxon 72 D6
Epworth N Linc 116 C2
Erbistock Wrexhm 97 M4
Erdington Birm 85 K5
Eridge Green E Susx 32 F6
Erines Ag & B 172 E4
Eriska Ag & B 191 H7
Eriskay W Isls 233 c9
Eriswell Suffk 91 G7
Erith Gt Lon 45 K4
Erlestoke Wilts 27 L2
Ermington Devon 6 F5
Erpingham Norfk 106 E6
Errogie Highld 202 E2
Errol P & K 186 D3
Erskine Rens 174 E4
Erskine Bridge Rens 174 E4
Ervie D & G 144 B2
Erwarton Suffk 78 F7
Erwood Powys 68 C6
Eryholme N York 141 H5
Eryrys Denbgs 97 J2
Escomb Dur 140 F2
Escrick N York 124 F2
Esgairgeiliog Powys 81 G3
Esh Dur 150 F6
Esher Surrey 43 J7
Eshott Nthumb 158 F3
Esh Winning Dur 150 F6
Eskadale Highld 212 C6
Eskbank Mdloth 177 J5
Eskdale Green Cumb 137 G6
Eskdalemuir D & G 156 A3
Esprick Lancs 120 E3
Essendine Rutlnd 88 F2
Essendon Herts 59 L6
Essich Highld 213 G6
Essington Staffs 85 G3
Esslemont Abers 217 H7
Eston R & Cl 142 C4
Etal Nthumb 168 D2
Etchilhampton Wilts 40 B7
Etchingham E Susx 33 J7
Etchinghill Kent 34 F6
Etchinghill Staffs 100 B8
Eton W & M 42 F5
Eton Wick W & M 42 F5
Etruria C Stke 99 K3
Etteridge Highld 203 G6
Ettersgill Dur 139 K2
Ettiley Heath Ches E 99 G1
Ettingshall Wolves 85 G4
Ettington Warwks 72 C5
Etton C Pete 89 G3
Etton E R Yk 126 B2
Ettrick Border 166 D6
Ettrickbridge Border 166 F4
Ettrickhill Border 166 C6
Etwall Derbys 100 F6
Euston Suffk 91 K7
Euxton Lancs 121 H6
Evanton Highld 212 F2
Evedon Lincs 103 H3
Evelix Highld 223 G4
Evenjobb Powys 68 F3
Evenley Nhants 73 H7
Evenlode Gloucs 56 E3
Evenwood Dur 140 E3
Evercreech Somset 26 F4
Everingham E R Yk 125 J3
Everleigh Wilts 28 D2
Eversholt C Beds 59 G2
Evershot Dorset 14 B2
Eversley Hants 42 C7
Eversley Cross Hants 42 C7
Everthorpe E R Yk 125 L4
Everton C Beds 75 H4
Everton Hants 16 C4
Everton Lpool 111 K3
Everton Notts 116 B4
Evertown D & G 156 C6
Evesbatch Herefs 70 C5
Evesham Worcs 71 J5
Evington C Leic 87 J3
Ewden Village Sheff 114 F3
Ewell Surrey 44 E7
Ewell Minnis Kent 35 H6
Ewelme Oxon 41 M3
Ewen Gloucs 40 A2
Ewenny V Glam 36 D5
Ewerby Lincs 103 J3
Ewhurst Surrey 31 H4
Ewhurst Green E Susx 20 F2
Ewhurst Green Surrey 31 H4
Ewloe Flints 111 J7
Eworthy Devon 10 C6
Ewshot Hants 30 D2
Ewyas Harold Herefs 54 B3
Exbourne Devon 10 E4
Exbury Hants 16 E3
Exebridge Somset 24 E6
Exelby N York 132 D3
Exeter Devon 11 L6
Exeter Airport Devon 12 C4
Exeter & Devon Crematorium Devon 12 B4
Exeter Services Devon 12 C4
Exford Somset 24 D4
Exfordsgreen Shrops 83 J3
Exhall Warwks 71 K4
Exhall Warwks 86 D6
Exlade Street Oxon 42 A4
Exminster Devon 12 B5
Exmoor National Park 24 D4
Exmouth Devon 12 C6
Exning Suffk 76 E2
Exton Devon 12 C5
Exton Hants 29 L7
Exton Rutlnd 88 D2
Exton Somset 24 E5
Exwick Devon 11 K6
Eyam Derbys 114 E6
Eydon Nhants 73 G4
Eye C Pete 89 J3
Eye Herefs 69 J2
Eye Suffk 92 D8
Eyemouth Border 179 K5
Eyeworth C Beds 75 J5
Eyhorne Street Kent 33 L3
Eyke Suffk 79 G4
Eynesbury Cambs 75 H3
Eynsford Kent 45 K6
Eynsham Oxon 57 H6
Eype Dorset 13 L4
Eyre Highld 208 F4
Eythorne Kent 35 H5
Eyton Herefs 69 J3
Eyton Shrops 98 C7
Eyton on Severn Shrops 83 L3
Eyton upon the Weald Moors Wrekin 84 B1

F

Faccombe Hants 41 H8
Faceby N York 141 L6
Fachwen Powys 82 B1
Faddiley Ches E 98 E3
Fadmoor N York 133 K2
Faerdre Swans 51 K5
Faifley W Duns 174 F4
Failand N Som 38 D6
Failford S Ayrs 163 L4
Failsworth Oldham 113 K2
Fairbourne Gwynd 80 E2
Fairburn N York 124 D5
Fairfield Derbys 114 B6
Fairfield Worcs 85 G7
Fairford Gloucs 56 D7
Fairgirth D & G 146 F4
Fair Green Norfk 90 F1
Fairhaven Lancs 120 D5
Fair Isle Shet 235 e7
Fair Isle Airport Shet 235 e7
Fairlands Surrey 30 F2
Fairlie N Ayrs 173 L7
Fairlight E Susx 21 G4
Fairmile Devon 12 E3
Fairmile Surrey 43 J7
Fairnilee Border 167 G3
Fair Oak Hants 29 J7
Fairoak Staffs 99 H6
Fair Oak Green Hants 42 A7
Fairseat Kent 45 L7
Fairstead Essex 61 J5
Fairstead Norfk 105 G8
Fairwarp E Susx 32 E7
Fairwater Cardif 37 H5
Fairy Cross Devon 22 F6
Fakenham Norfk 105 L6
Fakenham Magna Suffk 91 K7
Fala Mdloth 177 L6
Fala Dam Mdloth 177 L6
Faldingworth Lincs 117 H5
Faldouët Jersey 236 e7
Falfield S Glos 39 G2
Falkenham Suffk 79 G6
Falkirk Falk 176 B3
Falkirk Crematorium Falk 176 B3
Falkirk Wheel Falk 176 A3
Falkland Fife 186 D6
Fallburn S Lans 165 J2
Fallin Stirlg 185 H8
Fallodon Nthumb 169 J5
Fallowfield Manch 113 J3
Fallowfield Nthumb 150 B2
Falls of Blarghour Ag & B 182 E5
Falmer E Susx 19 K4
Falmouth Cnwll 3 K5
Falnash Border 156 D2
Falsgrave N York 134 F2
Falstone Nthumb 157 J5
Fanagmore Highld 228 B5
Fancott C Beds 59 G3
Fanellan Highld 212 D5
Fangdale Beck N York 142 C7
Fangfoss E R Yk 134 B8
Fanmore Ag & B 189 K7
Fannich Lodge Highld 211 K2
Fans Border 167 J2
Far Bletchley M Keyn 74 C7
Farcet Cambs 89 H5
Far Cotton Nhants 73 L3
Fareham Hants 17 H2
Far End Cumb 137 J7
Farewell Staffs 85 J2
Faringdon Oxon 40 F2
Farington Lancs 121 H5
Farlam Cumb 148 F3
Farleigh N Som 38 D6
Farleigh Surrey 32 C2
Farleigh Hungerford Somset 39 J8
Farleigh Wallop Hants 29 L3
Farlesthorpe Lincs 119 G6
Farleton Cumb 129 L4
Farleton Lancs 130 B6
Farley Staffs 100 B4
Farley Wilts 28 E5
Farley Green Surrey 31 H3
Farley Hill Wokham 42 C7
Farleys End Gloucs 55 H5
Farlington C Port 17 J2
Farlington N York 133 J6
Farlow Shrops 84 B7
Farmborough BaNES 38 F7
Farmcote Gloucs 56 B3
Farmers Carmth 66 E5
Farmington Gloucs 56 C5
Farmoor Oxon 57 J6
Far Moor Wigan 112 D2
Farmtown Moray 215 L4
Farnborough Gt Lon 45 H7
Farnborough Hants 30 E2
Farnborough W Berk 41 H4
Farnborough Warwks 72 E5
Farnborough Park Hants 30 E1
Farnborough Street Hants 30 E1
Farncombe Surrey 31 G3
Farndish Bed 74 D2
Farndon Ches W 98 B2
Farndon Notts 102 C3
Farne Islands Nthumb 169 J2
Farnell Angus 197 G5
Farnham Dorset 27 L7
Farnham Essex 60 D3
Farnham N York 132 E7
Farnham Suffk 79 H3
Farnham Surrey 30 D3
Farnham Common Bucks 42 F4
Farnham Royal Bucks 42 F4
Farningham Kent 45 K6
Farnley Leeds 123 K4
Farnley N York 123 J2
Farnley Tyas Kirk 123 H7
Farnsfield Notts 101 M2
Farnworth Bolton 113 G1
Farnworth Halton 112 D4
Far Oakridge Gloucs 55 L7
Farr Highld 203 K5
Farr Highld 213 G7
Farr Highld 229 L3
Farraline Highld 202 E2
Farringdon Devon 12 C4
Farrington Gurney BaNES 26 F1
Far Sawrey Cumb 137 K7
Farthinghoe Nhants 73 G6
Farthingstone Nhants 73 H4
Fartown Kirk 123 H6
Fartown Leeds 123 J4
Fasnacloich Ag & B 191 K6
Fasnakyle Highld 211 L8
Fassfern Highld 191 K2
Fatfield Sundld 151 H4
Fauldhouse W Loth 176 C6
Faulkbourne Essex 61 J5
Faulkland Somset 27 H1
Fauls Shrops 98 E6
Faversham Kent 34 D3
Fawdington N York 132 F5
Fawdon N u Ty 151 G2
Fawkham Green Kent 45 L6
Fawler Oxon 57 G4
Fawley Bucks 42 C3
Fawley Hants 16 F2
Fawley W Berk 41 H4
Faxfleet E R Yk 125 K5
Faygate W Susx 31 K5
Fazakerley Lpool 111 K3
Fazeley Staffs 85 L3
Fearby N York 132 B4
Fearn Highld 223 H6
Fearnan P & K 194 B7
Fearnbeg Highld 210 B3
Fearnmore Highld 209 L3
Fearnoch Ag & B 172 F3
Featherstone Staffs 85 G3
Featherstone Wakefd 124 C6
Feckenham Worcs 71 H3
Feering Essex 61 L4
Feetham N York 140 C7
Felbridge Surrey 32 C5
Felbrigg Norfk 106 E5
Felcourt Surrey 32 C5
Felindre Carmth 51 G2
Felindre Carmth 65 K6
Felindre Powys 82 D7
Felindre Swans 51 J5
Felindre Farchog Pembks 64 F6

Felingwm Isaf Carmth 51 G2
Felingwm Uchaf Carmth 51 G1
Felixkirk N York 133 G3
Felixstowe Suffk 79 G7
Felling Gatesd 151 G3
Felmersham Bed 74 E3
Felmingham Norfk 106 F6
Felpham W Susx 18 C5
Felsham Suffk 77 L3
Felsted Essex 61 G4
Feltham Gt Lon 43 J5
Felthamhill Surrey 43 H6
Felthorpe Norfk 106 E8
Felton Herefs 69 L5
Felton N Som 38 D7
Felton Nthumb 158 F3
Felton Butler Shrops 98 B8
Feltwell Norfk 91 G5
Fence Lancs 122 C3
Fence Rothm 115 H4
Fencott Oxon 57 L5
Fendike Corner Lincs 104 D1
Fen Ditton Cambs 76 C3
Fen Drayton Cambs 75 L2
Feniscowles Bl w D 121 J5
Feniton Devon 12 E3
Fenland Crematorium Cambs 90 B5
Fenn Green Shrops 84 D6
Fenn Street Medway 46 D5
Fenny Bentley Derbys 100 D3
Fenny Bridges Devon 12 E3
Fenny Compton Warwks 72 E4
Fenny Drayton Leics 86 D4
Fenstanton Cambs 75 K2
Fen Street Norfk 92 B4
Fenton Cambs 89 K7
Fenton Cumb 148 E4
Fenton Lincs 102 E3
Fenton Lincs 116 D6
Fenton Notts 116 C5
Fenton Nthumb 168 E3
Fenton Barns E Loth 178 B3
Fenwick Donc 124 F7
Fenwick E Ayrs 163 L2
Fenwick Nthumb 158 D7
Fenwick Nthumb 169 G2
Feock Cnwll 4 C7
Feolin Ferry Ag & B 171 H4
Fergushill N Ayrs 163 J2
Feriniquarrie Highld 208 B4
Fermain Bay Guern 236 d3
Fern Angus 196 D4
Ferndale Rhondd 36 F2
Ferndown Dorset 15 K3
Ferness Highld 214 B5
Fernham Oxon 40 F3
Fernhill Heath Worcs 70 F3
Fernhurst W Susx 30 E5
Fernie Fife 186 E4
Ferniegair S Lans 175 K7
Fernilea Highld 208 F7
Fernilee Derbys 114 A5
Fernwood Notts 102 D3
Ferrensby N York 132 E7
Ferrindonald Highld 199 K4
Ferring W Susx 18 F5
Ferrybridge Services Wakefd 124 D6
Ferryden Angus 197 H5
Ferryhill Dur 141 H2
Ferryhill Station Dur 141 H2
Ferry Point Highld 223 G4
Ferryside Carmth 50 D4
Ferrytown Highld 223 G4
Fersfield Norfk 92 C6
Fersit Highld 192 F2
Feshiebridge Highld 203 K4
Fetcham Surrey 31 J1
Fetlar Shet 235 e2
Fetterangus Abers 217 J4
Fettercairn Abers 197 G2
Fewston N York 132 B8
Ffairfach Carmth 51 J2
Ffair Rhos Cerdgn 67 G2
Ffestiniog Gwynd 96 A4
Ffestiniog Railway Gwynd 95 L4
Fforest Carmth 51 H5
Fforest Fach Swans 51 J6
Ffostrasol Cerdgn 65 L5
Ffrith Flints 97 L2
Ffynnongroyw Flints 111 G5
Fiag Lodge Highld 225 K3
Fickleshole Surrey 32 C2
Fiddington Somset 25 K4
Fiddleford Dorset 27 J8
Fiddlers Green Cnwll 4 C5
Field Staffs 100 A5
Field Dalling Norfk 106 B5
Field Head Leics 86 F2
Fifehead Magdalen Dorset 27 H6
Fifehead Neville Dorset 14 E1
Fifehead St Quintin Dorset 14 E1
Fife Keith Moray 215 J4
Fifield Oxon 56 E4
Fifield W & M 42 E5
Figheldean Wilts 28 D3
Filby Norfk 93 K2
Filey N York 135 H4
Filgrave M Keyn 74 C5
Filkins Oxon 56 E6
Filleigh Devon 23 K5
Fillingham Lincs 116 F4
Fillongley Warwks 86 C6
Filton S Glos 38 E5
Fimber E R Yk 134 D7
Finavon Angus 196 D5
Fincham Norfk 91 G3
Finchampstead Wokham 42 D7
Fincharn Ag & B 182 C6
Finchdean Hants 30 C8
Finchingfield Essex 61 G2
Finchley Gt Lon 44 F2
Findern Derbys 100 F6
Findhorn Moray 214 C2
Findhorn Bridge Highld 213 J8
Findochty Moray 215 K2
Findo Gask P & K 185 L4
Findon Abers 207 H6
Findon W Susx 18 F4
Findon Mains Highld 212 F3
Findrack House Abers 206 B4
Finedon Nhants 74 D1
Fingask P & K 186 C4
Fingest Bucks 42 C3
Finghall N York 132 B2
Fingland D & G 164 E6
Finglesham Kent 35 J4
Fingringhoe Essex 62 B4
Finlarig Stirlg 184 C1
Finmere Oxon 57 M2
Finnart P & K 193 H5
Finningham Suffk 78 C1
Finningley Donc 116 A2
Finsbay W Isls 232 d5
Finstall Worcs 71 H1
Finsthwaite Cumb 129 H2
Finstock Oxon 57 G5
Finstown Ork 234 b6
Fintry Abers 216 E4
Fintry Stirlg 175 H2
Finzean Abers 206 B6
Fionnphort Ag & B 180 D3
Fionnsbhagh W Isls 232 d5
Firbank Cumb 130 C2
Firbeck Rothm 115 K4
Firby N York 132 D3
Firby N York 134 B6
Firle E Susx 19 M4
Firsby Lincs 118 F8
Fir Tree Dur 150 E7
Fishbourne IoW 17 G4
Fishbourne W Susx 18 A5
Fishburn Dur 141 J2
Fishcross Clacks 185 J7
Fisherford Abers 216 C7
Fisherrow E Loth 177 K4
Fisher's Pond Hants 29 J7
Fisherton Highld 213 H4
Fisherton S Ayrs 163 H6
Fisherton de la Mere Wilts 27 M4
Fishguard Pembks 64 D6
Fishlake Donc 125 G7
Fishnish Pier Ag & B 190 D7
Fishponds Bristl 38 F5
Fishtoft Lincs 104 B4
Fishtoft Drove Lincs 104 A3
Fiskavaig Highld 208 E7
Fiskerton Lincs 117 H6
Fiskerton Notts 102 C3
Fittleton Wilts 28 D2
Fittleworth W Susx 18 D2
Fitz Shrops 98 C8
Fitzhead Somset 25 H5
Fitzwilliam Wakefd 124 C7
Five Ash Down E Susx 19 M2
Five Ashes E Susx 32 F7
Fivehead Somset 26 A6
Fivelanes Cnwll 9 G8
Five Oak Green Kent 33 H4
Five Oaks Jersey 236 d7
Five Oaks W Susx 31 H5
Five Roads Carmth 50 F4
Flackwell Heath Bucks 42 E3
Fladbury Worcs 71 H5
Fladdabister Shet 235 c6
Flagg Derbys 114 C7
Flamborough E R Yk 135 K5
Flamborough Head E R Yk 135 K5
Flamingo Land Theme Park N York 134 B4
Flamstead Herts 59 H5
Flansham W Susx 18 C5
Flanshaw Wakefd 123 L6
Flasby N York 131 H7
Flash Staffs 114 A7
Flashader Highld 208 E4
Flaunden Herts 59 G7
Flawborough Notts 102 C4
Flawith N York 133 G6
Flax Bourton N Som 38 D6
Flaxby N York 132 F7
Flaxley Gloucs 55 G5
Flaxpool Somset 25 H4
Flaxton N York 133 K6
Fleckney Leics 87 J5
Flecknoe Warwks 73 G2
Fledborough Notts 116 D6
Fleet Dorset 14 C6
Fleet Hants 30 D2
Fleet Lincs 104 C7
Fleet Hargate Lincs 104 C7
Fleet Services Hants 30 D1
Fleetwood Lancs 120 D2
Flemingston V Glam 36 F6
Flemington S Lans 175 H6
Flempton Suffk 77 J1
Fletchertown Cumb 147 L6
Fletching E Susx 19 L2
Flexbury Cnwll 9 G4
Flexford Surrey 30 F2
Flimby Cumb 147 H7
Flimwell E Susx 33 J6
Flint Flints 111 H6
Flintham Notts 102 C4
Flinton E R Yk 126 F4
Flitcham Norfk 105 H6
Flitton C Beds 74 F7
Flitwick C Beds 74 F7
Flixborough N Linc 125 K7
Flixborough Stather N Linc 125 K7
Flixton N York 135 G4
Flixton Suffk 93 G6
Flixton Traffd 113 H3
Flockton Kirk 123 J7
Flockton Green Kirk 123 K7
Flodigarry Highld 218 C6
Flookburgh Cumb 129 H4
Flordon Norfk 92 E4
Flore Nhants 73 J3
Flowton Suffk 78 C5
Flushing Cnwll 3 L4
Fluxton Devon 12 E4
Flyford Flavell Worcs 71 H4
Fobbing Thurr 46 B4
Fochabers Moray 215 H3
Fochriw Caerph 53 H6
Fockerby N Linc 125 K6
Foddington Somset 26 E5
Foel Powys 81 L2
Foggathorpe E R Yk 125 H3
Fogo Border 179 G8
Fogwatt Moray 214 F3
Foindle Highld 228 B5
Folda Angus 195 J4
Fole Staffs 100 B5
Foleshill Covtry 86 D6
Folke Dorset 26 F8
Folkestone Kent 35 H7
Folkingham Lincs 103 H5
Folkington E Susx 20 B5
Folksworth Cambs 89 G5
Folkton N York 135 G4
Folla Rule Abers 216 D7
Follifoot N York 132 E8
Folly Gate Devon 10 E5
Fonthill Bishop Wilts 27 L5
Fonthill Gifford Wilts 27 L5
Fontmell Magna Dorset 27 K7
Fontmell Parva Dorset 27 J8
Fontwell W Susx 18 C4
Foolow Derbys 114 D6
Forbestown Abers 205 H3
Forcett N York 140 F5
Ford Ag & B 182 C6
Ford Bucks 58 C6
Ford Derbys 115 H5
Ford Devon 22 F6
Ford Gloucs 56 C3
Ford Nthumb 168 E2
Ford Somset 25 H5
Ford Staffs 100 B2
Ford W Susx 18 D5
Ford Wilts 39 J5
Fordcombe Kent 32 F5
Fordell Fife 177 G2
Forden Powys 82 E4
Ford End Essex 61 G5
Forder Green Devon 7 H3
Fordham Cambs 76 F1
Fordham Essex 61 L3
Fordham Norfk 90 E4
Fordingbridge Hants 28 D8
Fordon E R Yk 135 G4
Fordoun Abers 197 J2
Fordstreet Essex 61 L3
Ford Street Somset 25 J7
Fordwich Kent 35 G3
Fordyce Abers 216 B2
Forebridge Staffs 99 L7
Forest Guern 236 c4
Forest Chapel Ches E 113 L6
Forest Gate Gt Lon 45 H3
Forest Green Surrey 31 J3
Forest Hall N Tyne 151 G2
Forest Hill Gt Lon 45 G5
Forest Hill Oxon 57 L6
Forest Lane Head N York 132 E7
Forest Mill Clacks 185 K8
Forest of Bowland Lancs 130 C8
Forest of Dean Gloucs 54 F5
Forest of Dean Crematorium Gloucs 54 F5
Forest Park Crematorium Gt Lon 45 J2
Forest Row E Susx 32 D6

Forestside W Susx 30 C8
Forfar Angus 196 D6
Forgandenny P & K 186 A4
Forge Hammer Torfn 37 L2
Forgie Moray 215 J4
Forgieside Moray 215 J4
Forgue Abers 216 B5
Formby Sefton 111 J1
Forncett End Norfk 92 D5
Forncett St Mary Norfk 92 E5
Forncett St Peter Norfk 92 E5
Fornham All Saints Suffk 77 J2
Fornham St Martin Suffk 77 J2
Fornighty Highld 213 L4
Forres Moray 214 C3
Forsbrook Staffs 99 L4
Forse Highld 227 M2
Forsinard Highld 230 C6
Fort Augustus Highld 202 B4
Forteviot P & K 185 L4
Forth S Lans 176 C7
Forthampton Gloucs 55 K2
Fort Hommet Guern 236 c2
Forth Rail Bridge C Edin 176 F3
Forth Road Bridge Fife 176 F3
Fortingall P & K 194 B6
Fort le Marchant Guern 236 d1
Forton Hants 29 H3
Forton Lancs 121 G1
Forton Shrops 83 H1
Forton Somset 13 J2
Forton Staffs 99 H7
Fortrie Abers 216 C5
Fortrose Highld 213 H3
Fortuneswell Dorset 14 D7
Fort William Highld 191 L2
Forty Hill Gt Lon 60 B7
Fosbury Wilts 40 F8
Foscot Oxon 56 E4
Fosdyke Lincs 104 A5
Foss P & K 194 C5
Fossebridge Gloucs 56 B5
Foster Street Essex 60 D6
Foston Derbys 100 D6
Foston Leics 87 H4
Foston Lincs 102 E4
Foston N York 133 L6
Foston on the Wolds E R Yk 135 H7
Fotherby Lincs 118 D3
Fotheringhay Nhants 88 F5
Foula Shet 235 a6
Foula Airport Shet 235 a6
Foulden Border 179 J7
Foulden Norfk 91 H4
Foul End Warwks 86 B4
Foulness Island Essex 47 G2
Foulon Vale Crematorium Guern 236 d3
Foulridge Lancs 122 D3
Foulsham Norfk 106 B7
Fountainhall Border 177 L8
Four Ashes Suffk 78 B1
Four Cabots Guern 236 c3
Four Crosses Powys 97 K8
Four Elms Kent 32 E4
Four Forks Somset 25 K4
Four Gotes Cambs 90 C1
Four Lanes Cnwll 3 J4
Four Marks Hants 30 A4
Four Mile Bridge IoA 108 C5
Four Oaks Birm 85 K4
Four Oaks Solhll 86 B7
Fourpenny Highld 223 H3
Four Roads Carmth 50 F4
Fourstones Nthumb 149 M2
Four Throws Kent 33 K7
Fovant Wilts 28 A5
Foveran Abers 207 H2
Fowey Cnwll 5 H5
Fowlhall Kent 33 J4
Fowlis Angus 186 E2
Fowlis Wester P & K 185 J3
Fowlmere Cambs 76 B5
Fownhope Herefs 69 L7
Foxbar Rens 174 E6
Foxcote Somset 27 G1
Foxdale IoM 237 b5
Foxearth Essex 77 J5
Foxfield Cumb 128 F3
Foxhole Cnwll 4 F5
Foxholes N York 134 F5
Foxley Norfk 106 C7
Foxt Staffs 100 B3
Foxton Cambs 76 B5
Foxton Leics 87 K5
Foxton N York 141 K7
Foxwood Shrops 84 B7
Foy Herefs 54 E3
Foyers Highld 202 D2
Foynesfield Highld 213 L4
Fraddon Cnwll 4 E4
Fradley Staffs 85 L2
Fradswell Staffs 99 M6
Fraisthorpe E R Yk 135 J7
Framfield E Susx 20 A2
Framingham Earl Norfk 92 F3
Framingham Pigot Norfk 92 F3
Framlingham Suffk 79 G2
Frampton Dorset 14 C4
Frampton Lincs 104 B5
Frampton Cotterell S Glos 38 F4
Frampton Mansell Gloucs 55 L7
Frampton-on-Severn Gloucs 55 H6
Framsden Suffk 78 E3
Framwellgate Moor Dur 151 G6
Franche Worcs 84 E7
Frankby Wirral 111 H4
Frankley Worcs 85 H7
Frankley Services Worcs 85 H7
Frankton Warwks 72 E1
Frant E Susx 33 G6
Fraserburgh Abers 217 J2
Frating Essex 62 C4
Frating Green Essex 62 C4
Fratton C Port 17 J3
Freathy Cnwll 6 B5
Freckenham Suffk 76 F1
Freckleton Lancs 120 F5
Freeby Leics 102 D7
Freefolk Hants 29 J2
Freeland Oxon 57 H5
Freethorpe Norfk 93 J3
Freethorpe Common Norfk 93 J3
Freiston Lincs 104 B4
Fremington Devon 23 H5
Fremington N York 140 D7
Frenchay S Glos 38 F5
Frenich P & K 194 C5
Frensham Surrey 30 D3
Freshfield Sefton 120 C8
Freshford Wilts 39 H7
Freshwater IoW 16 D5
Fressingfield Suffk 92 F7
Freston Suffk 78 E6
Freswick Highld 231 L3
Fretherne Gloucs 55 G6
Frettenham Norfk 106 F8
Freuchie Fife 186 E6
Freystrop Pembks 49 G5
Friar Park Sandw 85 H4
Friday Bridge Cambs 90 C3
Friday Street Suffk 79 H3
Fridaythorpe E R Yk 134 D7
Friern Barnet Gt Lon 44 F2
Friesthorpe Lincs 117 H5
Frieston Lincs 102 F3
Frieth Bucks 42 D3
Frilford Oxon 41 H2
Frilsham W Berk 41 K5
Frimley Surrey 42 E8
Frindsbury Medway 46 C6
Fring Norfk 105 H5
Fringford Oxon 57 L3
Frinsted Kent 34 B4
Frinton-on-Sea Essex 62 F4
Friockheim Angus 196 F6
Frisby on the Wreake Leics 102 B8
Friskney Lincs 104 D2
Friston E Susx 20 B6
Friston Suffk 79 J3
Fritchley Derbys 101 G3
Fritham Hants 28 E8
Frithelstock Devon 23 G7
Frithelstock Stone Devon 23 G7
Frithville Lincs 104 A3
Frittenden Kent 33 K5
Frittiscombe Devon 7 J6
Fritton Norfk 92 F5
Fritton Norfk 93 K4
Fritwell Oxon 57 K3
Frizinghall C Brad 123 H4
Frizington Cumb 136 E4
Frocester Gloucs 55 H7
Frodesley Shrops 83 K3
Frodsham Ches W 112 D6
Frogden Border 168 B4
Frog End Cambs 76 B5
Froggatt Derbys 114 E6
Froghall Staffs 100 A3
Frogmore Devon 7 H7
Frognall Lincs 89 H2
Frog Pool Worcs 70 E2
Frogwell Cnwll 6 A3
Frolesworth Leics 87 G5
Frome Somset 27 H2
Frome St Quintin Dorset 14 B2
Fromes Hill Herefs 70 C5
Froncysyllte Denbgs 97 K4
Fron-goch Gwynd 96 D5
Fron Isaf Wrexhm 97 L4
Frosterley Dur 150 C7
Froxfield Wilts 40 F6
Froxfield Green Hants 30 B6
Fryern Hill Hants 29 H7
Fryerning Essex 61 G7
Fuinary Highld 190 C6
Fulbeck Lincs 102 F3
Fulbourn Cambs 76 D4
Fulbrook Oxon 56 E5
Fulflood Hants 29 J5
Fulford C York 124 F2
Fulford Somset 25 K5
Fulford Staffs 99 L5
Fulham Gt Lon 44 E5
Fulking W Susx 19 H4
Fullarton N Ayrs 163 H2
Fuller Street Essex 61 H5
Fullerton Hants 29 G4
Fulletby Lincs 118 D6
Fullready Warwks 72 C5
Full Sutton E R Yk 134 B7
Fullwood E Ayrs 174 E7
Fulmer Bucks 43 G4
Fulmodeston Norfk 106 B6
Fulnetby Lincs 117 H5
Fulney Lincs 103 L7
Fulstow Lincs 118 D3
Fulwell Sundld 151 J3
Fulwood Lancs 121 H4
Fulwood Sheff 114 F4
Fundenhall Norfk 92 D4
Funtington W Susx 17 L2
Funtullich P & K 184 F3
Furley Devon 13 H2
Furnace Ag & B 182 E7
Furnace Carmth 51 G5
Furness Vale Derbys 114 A5
Furneux Pelham Herts 60 C3
Furzley Hants 28 F7
Fyfield Essex 60 F6
Fyfield Hants 28 F3
Fyfield Oxon 57 H7
Fyfield Wilts 40 C6
Fyfield Wilts 40 D7
Fylingthorpe N York 143 J6
Fyning W Susx 30 D6
Fyvie Abers 216 E6

G

Gabroc Hill E Ayrs 174 E7
Gaddesby Leics 87 K2
Gaddesden Row Herts 59 H5
Gadgirth S Ayrs 163 K5
Gaerllwyd Mons 38 C2
Gaerwen IoA 108 F7
Gailes N Ayrs 163 H3
Gailey Staffs 85 G2
Gainford Dur 140 F4
Gainsborough Lincs 116 D4
Gainsford End Essex 77 G7
Gairloch Highld 219 J6
Gairlochy Highld 201 J8
Gairneybridge P & K 186 B7
Gaitsgill Cumb 148 C5
Galashiels Border 167 G3
Galgate Lancs 129 K7
Galhampton Somset 26 F5
Gallanachbeg Ag & B 182 B2
Gallanachmore Ag & B 182 B3
Gallatown Fife 186 E8
Galleywood Essex 61 H7
Gallovie Highld 202 E7
Galloway Forest Park 153 J5
Gallowfauld Angus 196 D7
Gallowhill P & K 186 B1
Galltair Highld 200 C2
Galmpton Devon 7 G7
Galmpton Torbay 7 K5
Galphay N York 132 C5
Galston E Ayrs 163 L3
Gamblesby Cumb 149 G6
Gamlingay Cambs 75 J4
Gamlingay Great Heath Cambs 75 J4
Gamrie Abers 216 F2
Gamston Notts 101 L5
Gamston Notts 116 B6
Ganavan Bay Ag & B 182 B2
Ganllwyd Gwynd 96 B7
Gannachy Angus 196 F3
Ganstead E R Yk 126 E4
Ganthorpe N York 133 L5
Ganton N York 134 F4
Garbity Moray 215 H4
Garboldisham Norfk 92 B7
Garbole Highld 203 H1
Garchory Abers 205 G4
Gardeners Green Wokham 42 D6
Gardenstown Abers 216 F2
Garden Village Sheff 114 E2
Garderhouse Shet 235 c5
Gare Hill Somset 27 H4
Garelochhead Ag & B 173 L1
Garford Oxon 41 H2
Garforth Leeds 124 B4
Gargrave N York 131 H8
Gargunnock Stirlg 184 F8
Garlic Street Norfk 92 E6
Garlieston D & G 145 K5
Garlinge Kent 35 J2
Garlinge Green Kent 34 F4
Garlogie Abers 206 E4
Garmond Abers 216 F4
Garmouth Moray 215 H2
Garmston Shrops 83 L3
Garn-Dolbenmaen Gwynd 95 J4
Garnkirk N Lans 175 J5
Garrabost W Isls 232 g2
Garrallan E Ayrs 164 B5

Garras Cnwll 3 J6
Garreg Gwynd 95 K4
Garrigill Cumb 149 J6
Garroch D & G 153 M6
Garrochtrie D & G 144 D7
Garrochty Ag & B 173 J7
Garros Highld 209 H2
Garsdale Head Cumb 130 E2
Garsdon Wilts 39 L3
Garshall Green Staffs 99 L5
Garsington Oxon 57 L7
Garstang Lancs 121 G2
Garston Herts 59 J7
Garston Lpool 112 B5
Gartachossan Ag & B 171 G6
Gartcosh N Lans 175 J5
Garth Powys 67 K5
Garth Wrexhm 97 K4
Garthamlock C Glas 175 H5
Garthmyl Powys 82 E4
Garthorpe Leics 102 D7
Garthorpe N Linc 125 K6
Garth Row Cumb 138 D7
Gartly Abers 215 L7
Gartmore Stirlg 184 C7
Gartness N Lans 175 K5
Gartness Stirlg 174 F2
Gartocharn W Duns 174 D2
Garton-on-the-Wolds E R Yk 134 F7
Gartymore Highld 227 H5
Garvald E Loth 178 D4
Garvan Highld 191 J2
Garvard Ag & B 171 G1
Garve Highld 212 B3
Garvellachs Ag & B 181 K5
Garvestone Norfk 92 B3
Garvock Inver 174 B4
Garway Herefs 54 C4
Garyvard W Isls 232 f3
Gasper Wilts 27 H5
Gastard Wilts 39 K6
Gasthorpe Norfk 91 L7
Gaston Green Essex 60 D5
Gatcombe IoW 16 F5
Gate Burton Lincs 116 D5
Gateforth N York 124 E5
Gatehead E Ayrs 163 K3
Gate Helmsley N York 133 L7
Gatehouse Nthumb 157 K4
Gatehouse of Fleet D & G 145 M4
Gateley Norfk 106 A7
Gatenby N York 132 E3
Gateshaw Border 168 B5
Gateshead Gatesd 151 G3
Gateside Angus 196 D7
Gateside E Rens 174 E6
Gateside Fife 186 C5
Gateside N Ayrs 174 C7
Gateslack D & G 154 F2
Gatley Stockp 113 J4
Gattonside Border 167 H3
Gatwick Airport W Susx 32 B5
Gaulby Leics 87 K4
Gauldry Fife 186 F3
Gauldswell P & K 195 K6
Gautby Lincs 117 K6
Gavinton Border 179 G7
Gawcott Bucks 58 B2
Gawsworth Ches E 113 K7
Gawthrop Cumb 130 D3
Gawthwaite Cumb 129 G3
Gaydon Warwks 72 D4
Gayhurst M Keyn 74 B5
Gayle N York 131 G2
Gayles N York 140 E5
Gayton Nhants 73 K4
Gayton Norfk 105 H8
Gayton Staffs 99 M6
Gayton le Marsh Lincs 118 F5
Gayton Thorpe Norfk 105 H8
Gaywood Norfk 105 G7
Gazeley Suffk 77 G2
Gearraidh Bhaird W Isls 232 f3
Geary Highld 208 D3
Gedding Suffk 77 L3
Geddington Nhants 88 C6
Gedling Notts 101 L4
Gedney Lincs 104 C7
Gedney Broadgate Lincs 104 C7
Gedney Drove End Lincs 104 D6
Gedney Dyke Lincs 104 C7
Gedney Hill Lincs 89 L2
Geeston Rutlnd 88 E3
Geldeston Norfk 93 H5
Gellifor Denbgs 110 F8
Gelligaer Caerph 37 H2
Gellilydan Gwynd 95 M4
Gellinudd Neath 51 K5
Gellyburn P & K 195 H8
Gellywen Carmth 50 C2
Gelston D & G 146 D3
Gelston Lincs 102 E4
Gembling E R Yk 135 H7
Gentleshaw Staffs 85 J2
Georgefield D & G 156 B4
George Green Bucks 43 G4
Georgeham Devon 23 G4
Georgemas Junction Station Highld 231 H4
George Nympton Devon 23 L6
Georth Ork 234 b5
Germansweek Devon 10 C6
Gerrans Cnwll 4 D8
Gerrards Cross Bucks 43 G3
Gerrick R & Cl 142 E5
Gestingthorpe Essex 77 J6
Geuffordd Powys 82 E2
Gidea Park Gt Lon 45 K3
Giffnock E Rens 175 G6
Gifford E Loth 178 C5
Giffordtown Fife 186 E5
Giggleswick N York 130 F6
Gigha Ag & B 171 L7
Gilberdyke E R Yk 125 K5
Gilchriston E Loth 178 B5
Gilcrux Cumb 147 K7
Gildersome Leeds 123 K5
Gildingwells Rothm 115 K4
Gilesgate Moor Dur 151 H6
Gileston V Glam 36 F6
Gilfach Caerph 53 J7
Gilfach Goch Brdgnd 36 F3
Gilfachrheda Cerdgn 65 L3
Gilgarran Cumb 136 E3
Gillamoor N York 133 K2
Gillen Highld 208 D3
Gillesbie D & G 155 K4
Gilling East N York 133 J4
Gillingham Dorset 27 J6
Gillingham Medway 46 C6
Gillingham Norfk 93 J5
Gilling West N York 140 F6
Gillock Highld 231 J4
Gills Highld 231 K2
Gilmanscleuch Border 166 E5
Gilmerton C Edin 177 J5
Gilmerton P & K 185 J3
Gilmonby Dur 140 C5
Gilmorton Leics 87 H6
Gilroes Crematorium C Leic 87 H3
Gilsland Nthumb 149 G2
Gilston Border 177 L6
Gilston Herts 60 D5
Gilwern Mons 53 K5
Gimingham Norfk 107 G5
Gipping Suffk 78 C2
Gipsey Bridge Lincs 103 M3
Girdle Toll N Ayrs 163 J2
Girlsta Shet 235 c5
Girsby N York 141 J5
Girthon D & G 146 A4
Girton Cambs 76 B3
Girton Notts 116 D7
Girvan S Ayrs 152 E3
Gisburn Lancs 122 C2
Gisleham Suffk 93 K5
Gislingham Suffk 78 C1
Gissing Norfk 92 D6
Gittisham Devon 12 E3
Gladestry Powys 68 E4
Gladsmuir E Loth 177 M4
Glais Swans 51 K5
Glaisdale N York 143 G6
Glamis Angus 196 C6
Glanaman Carmth 51 J3
Glandford Norfk 106 C4
Glandwr Pembks 49 K2
Glandyfi Cerdgn 80 F4
Glanllynfi Brdgnd 36 D3
Glan-rhyd Powys 52 B6
Glanton Nthumb 169 G6
Glanvilles Wootton Dorset 14 D2
Glan-y-don Flints 111 G5
Glapthorn Nhants 88 E5
Glapwell Derbys 115 J7
Glasbury Powys 68 D6
Glascwm Powys 68 D4
Glasfryn Conwy 96 E3
Glasgow C Glas 175 G5
Glasgow Airport Rens 174 E5
Glasgow Science Centre C Glas 175 G5
Glasinfryn Gwynd 109 H7
Glasnacardoch Bay Highld 199 L6
Glasnakille Highld 199 H3
Glassford S Lans 175 J8
Glasshouse Gloucs 55 G4
Glasshouses N York 132 B6
Glasson Cumb 148 A3
Glasson Lancs 129 K7
Glassonby Cumb 149 G7
Glasterlaw Angus 196 F6
Glaston Rutlnd 88 C4
Glastonbury Somset 26 D4
Glatton Cambs 89 H6
Glazebrook Warrtn 113 G3
Glazebury Warrtn 112 F3
Glazeley Shrops 84 C5
Gleaston Cumb 128 F5
Glebe Highld 202 D2
Gledhow Leeds 123 L3
Gledpark D & G 146 B5
Gledrid Shrops 97 L5
Glemsford Suffk 77 J5
Glenallachie Moray 215 G6
Glenancross Highld 199 K6
Glenaros House Ag & B 190 B7
Glen Auldyn IoM 237 d3
Glenbarr Ag & B 161 H3
Glenbarry Abers 216 B4
Glenbeg Highld 190 C4
Glenbervie Abers 197 J1
Glenboig N Lans 175 J5
Glenborrodale Highld 190 C4
Glenbranter Ag & B 183 G7
Glenbreck Border 165 K5
Glenbrittle House Highld 198 F2
Glenbuck E Ayrs 164 E4
Glencally Angus 196 B4
Glencaple D & G 147 H2
Glencarron Lodge Highld 211 G4
Glencarse P & K 186 C3
Glen Clunie Lodge Abers 204 E8
Glencoe Highld 191 L5
Glencothe Border 165 L4
Glencraig Fife 186 C7
Glencrosh D & G 154 D4
Glendale Highld 208 B4
Glendaruel Ag & B 173 G2
Glendevon P & K 185 K6
Glendoe Lodge Highld 202 C4
Glendoick P & K 186 C3
Glenduckie Fife 186 D4
Glenegedale Ag & B 170 F7
Glenelg Highld 200 C2
Glenerney Moray 214 C5
Glenfarg P & K 186 B5
Glenfield Leics 87 G3
Glenfinnan Highld 191 H1
Glenfintaig Lodge Highld 201 K7
Glenfoot P & K 186 C4
Glenfyne Lodge Ag & B 183 H4
Glengarnock N Ayrs 174 C7
Glengolly Highld 231 G3
Glengorm Castle Ag & B 189 K5
Glengrasco Highld 209 G5
Glenholm Border 165 L3
Glenhoul D & G 154 A5
Glenisla Angus 195 K4
Glenkin Ag & B 173 K3
Glenkindie Abers 205 K3
Glenlivet Moray 214 F8
Glenlochar D & G 146 C3
Glenlomond P & K 186 C6
Glenluce D & G 144 E4
Glenmassen Ag & B 173 J2
Glenmavis N Lans 175 K5
Glen Maye IoM 237 b5
Glenmore Highld 209 G6
Glenmore Lodge Highld 204 B4
Glen Nevis House Highld 192 B3
Glenochil Clacks 185 H7
Glen Parva Leics 87 H4
Glenquiech Angus 196 C4
Glenralloch Ag & B 172 E5
Glenridding Cumb 137 L4
Glenrothes Fife 186 D7
Glenshero Lodge Highld 202 E6
Glenstriven Ag & B 173 J3
Glentham Lincs 117 G4
Glentrool D & G 153 H6
Glen Trool Lodge D & G 153 J6
Glentruim House Highld 203 G6
Glentworth Lincs 116 F4
Glenuig Highld 190 D2
Glenvarragill Highld 209 G6
Glen Vine IoM 237 c5
Glenwhilly D & G 152 E7
Glespin S Lans 164 F4
Glewstone Herefs 54 E4
Glinton C Pete 89 H3
Glooston Leics 87 L4
Glossop Derbys 114 B3
Gloster Hill Nthumb 159 G2
Gloucester Gloucs 55 J4
Gloucester Crematorium Gloucs 55 J5
Gloucester Services Gloucs 55 J5
Gloucestershire Airport Gloucs 55 K4
Glusburn N York 122 F2
Glutt Lodge Highld 227 H2
Glympton Oxon 57 H4
Glynarthen Cerdgn 65 K5
Glyn Ceiriog Wrexhm 97 J5
Glyncorrwg Neath 52 D7
Glynde E Susx 19 L4
Glyndyfrdwy Denbgs 97 J4
Glynneath Neath 52 D6
Glynn Valley Crematorium Cnwll 5 H3
Glyntaff Crematorium Rhondd 37 H3
Glyntawe Powys 52 D5
Glynteg Carmth 65 K6
Gnosall Staffs 99 J7
Gnosall Heath Staffs 99 J7
Goadby Leics 87 L4
Goadby Marwood Leics 102 C7
Goatacre Wilts 40 A5
Goathill Dorset 26 F7

Goathland N York 143 H6
Goathurst Somset 25 K5
Gobowen Shrops 97 L5
Godalming Surrey 30 F3
Goddard's Green Kent 33 L6
Godmanchester Cambs 75 J1
Godmanstone Dorset 14 C3
Godmersham Kent 34 E5
Godney Somset 26 C3
Godolphin Cross Cnwll 3 G5
Godre'r-graig Neath 51 L4
Godshill IoW 17 G6
Godstone Surrey 32 C3
Goetre Mons 53 L6
Goff's Oak Herts 60 B7
Gogar C Edin 177 G4
Goginan Cerdgn 80 F7
Golan Gwynd 95 J4
Golant Cnwll 5 H5
Golberdon Cnwll 5 M2
Golborne Wigan 112 E3
Golcar Kirk 123 G7
Goldcliff Newpt 38 A4
Golden Green Kent 33 H4
Goldenhill C Stke 99 J2
Golden Pot Hants 30 B3
Golders Green Gt Lon 44 E3
Golders Green Crematorium Gt Lon 44 E3
Goldhanger Essex 61 L6
Goldington Bed 74 F4
Goldsborough N York 132 F7
Goldsborough N York 143 H4
Golds Green Sandw 85 H5
Goldsithney Cnwll 2 F5
Goldsworth Park Surrey 43 G8
Goldthorpe Barns 115 J2
Goldworthy Devon 22 F6
Gollanfield Highld 213 J4
Golspie Highld 223 H2
Gomeldon Wilts 28 D4
Gomshall Surrey 31 H2
Gonalston Notts 102 B3
Gonerby Hill Foot Lincs 102 E5
Gonfirth Shet 235 c4
Good Easter Essex 60 F5
Gooderstone Norfk 91 H3
Goodleigh Devon 23 J5
Goodmanham E R Yk 125 K2
Goodmayes Gt Lon 45 J3
Goodnestone Kent 34 D3
Goodnestone Kent 35 H4
Goodrich Herefs 54 E4
Goodrington Torbay 7 K4
Goodshaw Lancs 122 B5
Goodwick Pembks 64 C6
Goodworth Clatford Hants 29 G3
Goole E R Yk 125 H5
Goom's Hill Worcs 71 H4
Goonbell Cnwll 3 J2
Goonhavern Cnwll 3 K1
Goonvrea Cnwll 3 J2
Goosecruives Abers 206 E8
Gooseford Devon 11 G6
Goose Green Essex 62 D3
Goose Green S Glos 38 F5
Gooseham Cnwll 9 G2
Goosey Oxon 41 G3
Goosnargh Lancs 121 H3
Goostrey Ches E 113 H7
Gordano Services N Som 38 D5
Gordon Border 167 K2
Gordon Arms Hotel Border 166 D4
Gordonstown Abers 216 B3
Gordonstown Abers 216 D6
Gorebridge Mdloth 177 K6
Gorefield Cambs 90 B2
Gores Wilts 40 C8
Gorey Jersey 236 e7
Goring Oxon 41 L4
Goring-by-Sea W Susx 18 F5
Gorleston on Sea Norfk 93 L3
Gornal Wood Crematorium Dudley 85 G5
Gorrachie Abers 216 E3
Gorran Churchtown Cnwll 4 F7
Gorran Haven Cnwll 4 F7
Gorsedd Flints 111 G6
Gorse Hill Swindn 40 D3
Gorseinon Swans 51 H5
Gorsgoch Cerdgn 66 C4
Gorslas Carmth 51 H3
Gorsley Gloucs 55 G3
Gorsley Common Herefs 54 F3
Gorstan Highld 212 B2
Gorsty Hill Staffs 100 C6
Gorten Ag & B 181 L2
Gorthleck Highld 202 E2
Gorton Manch 113 K3
Gosbeck Suffk 78 D4
Gosberton Lincs 103 L6
Gosfield Essex 61 J3
Gosforth Cumb 136 E6
Gosforth N u Ty 151 G2
Gospel End Staffs 84 F5
Gosport Hants 17 H3
Gossington Gloucs 55 H7
Gotham Notts 101 K6
Gotherington Gloucs 55 L3
Gotton Somset 25 K5
Goudhurst Kent 33 J5
Goulceby Lincs 118 C5
Gourdas Abers 216 E6
Gourdie C Dund 186 F2
Gourdon Abers 197 K3
Gourock Inver 173 L3
Govan C Glas 174 F5
Goveton Devon 7 H6
Govilon Mons 53 K5
Gowdall E R Yk 124 F6
Gower Highld 212 D3
Gower Swans 51 G7
Gowerton Swans 51 H6
Gowkhall Fife 176 E1
Goxhill E R Yk 126 F2
Goxhill N Linc 126 D6
Grabhair W Isls 232 f3
Graffham W Susx 18 C3
Grafham Cambs 75 H2
Grafham Surrey 31 G3
Grafton N York 132 F6
Grafton Oxon 56 F7
Grafton Shrops 98 B8
Grafton Worcs 71 H6
Grafton Flyford Worcs 71 G4
Grafton Regis Nhants 73 L5
Grafton Underwood Nhants 88 D7
Grafty Green Kent 34 B5
Graig Conwy 109 M6
Graig-fechan Denbgs 97 J2
Grain Medway 46 E5
Grainsby Lincs 118 C2
Grainthorpe Lincs 118 E3
Grampound Cnwll 4 E6
Grampound Road Cnwll 4 E5
Gramsdal W Isls 233 c6
Gramsdale W Isls 233 c6
Granborough Bucks 58 C3
Granby Notts 102 C5
Grandborough Warwks 72 F2
Grand Chemins Jersey 236 d7
Grandes Rocques Guern 236 c2
Grandtully P & K 194 E5
Grange Cumb 137 H4
Grange Medway 46 D6
Grange P & K 186 D3
Grange Crossroads Moray 215 K4
Grange Hall Moray 214 C3
Grangehall S Lans 165 J2
Grange Hill Essex 45 H2
Grangemill Derbys 100 E2
Grange Moor Kirk 123 J7
Grangemouth Falk 176 C3
Grange of Lindores Fife 186 D4
Grange-over-Sands Cumb 129 J4
Grangepans Falk 176 D3
Grangetown R & Cl 142 C3
Grangetown Sundld 151 K4
Grange Villa Dur 151 G4
Gransmoor E R Yk 135 H7
Granston Pembks 64 C7
Grantchester Cambs 76 B4
Grantham Lincs 102 E5
Grantham Crematorium Lincs 102 F5
Granton C Edin 177 H3
Grantown-on-Spey Highld 214 C8
Grantshouse Border 179 G5
Grasby Lincs 117 H1
Grasmere Cumb 137 K5
Grasscroft Oldham 113 L1
Grassendale Lpool 111 L4
Grassington N York 131 J6
Grassmoor Derbys 115 H7
Grassthorpe Notts 116 C7
Grateley Hants 28 F3
Graveley Cambs 75 J2
Graveley Herts 59 L3
Gravelly Hill Birm 85 K5
Graveney Kent 34 E3
Gravesend Kent 46 A5
Gravir W Isls 232 f3
Grayingham Lincs 116 F3
Grayrigg Cumb 138 E7
Grays Thurr 45 L4
Grayshott Hants 30 E4
Grayswood Surrey 30 E4
Greasbrough Rothm 115 H3
Greasby Wirral 111 H4
Great Abington Cambs 76 D5
Great Addington Nhants 88 D7
Great Alne Warwks 71 K3
Great Altcar Lancs 111 K1
Great Amwell Herts 60 B5
Great Asby Cumb 138 F5
Great Ashfield Suffk 78 B2
Great Ayton N York 142 C5
Great Baddow Essex 61 H6
Great Badminton S Glos 39 J4
Great Bardfield Essex 61 G2
Great Barford Bed 75 G4
Great Barr Sandw 85 J4
Great Barrington Gloucs 56 E5
Great Barrow Ches W 112 C7
Great Barton Suffk 77 K2
Great Barugh N York 134 B4
Great Bavington Nthumb 158 C6
Great Bealings Suffk 78 F5
Great Bedwyn Wilts 40 F7
Great Bentley Essex 62 D4
Great Billing Nhants 74 B3
Great Bircham Norfk 105 J6
Great Blakenham Suffk 78 D4
Great Blencow Cumb 138 C2
Great Bolas Wrekin 98 F7
Great Bookham Surrey 31 J1
Great Bourton Oxon 72 F5
Great Bowden Leics 87 L5
Great Bradley Suffk 76 F4
Great Braxted Essex 61 K5
Great Bricett Suffk 78 C4
Great Brickhill Bucks 58 E3
Great Bridgeford Staffs 99 K6
Great Brington Nhants 73 J2
Great Bromley Essex 62 C3
Great Broughton Cumb 136 E2
Great Broughton N York 142 C6
Great Budworth Ches W 112 F6
Great Burdon Darltn 141 H4
Great Burstead Essex 46 B2
Great Busby N York 142 B6
Great Carlton Lincs 118 E4
Great Casterton Rutlnd 88 E2
Great Chalfield Wilts 39 K7
Great Chart Kent 34 C6
Great Chatwell Staffs 84 E1
Great Chell C Stke 99 K3
Great Chesterford Essex 76 D6
Great Cheverell Wilts 27 M1
Great Chishill Cambs 76 B6
Great Clacton Essex 62 E5
Great Clifton Cumb 136 E2
Great Coates NE Lin 126 F8
Great Comberton Worcs 71 G6
Great Corby Cumb 148 E4
Great Cornard Suffk 77 K6
Great Cowden E R Yk 126 F3
Great Coxwell Oxon 40 F2
Great Cransley Nhants 88 B7
Great Cressingham Norfk 91 J3
Great Crosthwaite Cumb 137 J3
Great Cubley Derbys 100 D5
Great Cumbrae Island N Ayrs 173 K6
Great Dalby Leics 87 L2
Great Doddington Nhants 74 C2
Great Dunham Norfk 91 K1
Great Dunmow Essex 61 G4
Great Durnford Wilts 28 C4
Great Easton Essex 60 F3
Great Easton Leics 88 B5
Great Eccleston Lancs 120 F3
Great Ellingham Norfk 92 B4
Great Elm Somset 27 H2
Great Everdon Nhants 73 H3
Great Eversden Cambs 75 L4
Great Fencote N York 132 D2
Great Finborough Suffk 78 B3
Greatford Lincs 88 F2
Great Fransham Norfk 91 K2
Great Gaddesden Herts 59 G5
Greatgate Staffs 100 B4
Great Gidding Cambs 89 G6
Great Givendale E R Yk 134 C8
Great Glemham Suffk 79 H3
Great Glen Leics 87 J4
Great Gonerby Lincs 102 E5
Great Gransden Cambs 75 J4
Great Green Cambs 75 K5
Great Green Suffk 77 K4
Great Habton N York 134 B4
Great Hale Lincs 103 J4
Great Hallingbury Essex 60 E4
Greatham Hants 30 C5
Greatham Hartpl 141 L2
Greatham W Susx 18 E3

Great Hampden Bucks 58 D7
Great Harrowden Nhants 74 C1
Great Harwood Lancs 121 L4
Great Haseley Oxon 57 M7
Great Hatfield E R Yk 126 F3
Great Haywood Staffs 99 M7
Great Heck N York 124 E6
Great Henny Essex 77 K6
Great Hinton Wilts 39 K8
Great Hockham Norfk 91 L5
Great Holland Essex 62 E4
Great Hollands Br For 42 E6
Great Horkesley Essex 62 B2
Great Hormead Herts 60 C3
Great Horton C Brad 123 H4
Great Horwood Bucks 58 C2
Great Houghton Barns 115 H1
Great Houghton Nhants 73 L3
Great Hucklow Derbys 114 D6
Great Kelk E R Yk 135 H7
Great Kimble Bucks 58 D6
Great Kingshill Bucks 42 E2
Great Langdale Cumb 137 J6
Great Langton N York 141 H7
Great Leighs Essex 61 H4
Great Limber Lincs 126 E8
Great Linford M Keyn 74 C6
Great Livermere Suffk 77 K1
Great Longstone Derbys 114 D6
Great Lumley Dur 151 H5
Great Malvern Worcs 70 D5
Great Maplestead Essex 77 J7
Great Marton Bpool 120 D4
Great Massingham Norfk 105 J7
Great Milton Oxon 57 L7
Great Missenden Bucks 58 E7
Great Mitton Lancs 121 K3
Great Mongeham Kent 35 K4
Great Moulton Norfk 92 E5
Great Musgrave Cumb 139 H4
Great Ness Shrops 98 B8
Great Notley Essex 61 H4
Great Oak Mons 54 B6
Great Oakley Essex 62 E3
Great Oakley Nhants 88 C6
Great Offley Herts 59 J3
Great Ormside Cumb 139 G4
Great Orton Cumb 148 B4
Great Ouseburn N York 133 G6
Great Oxendon Nhants 87 K6
Great Paxton Cambs 75 H2
Great Plumpton Lancs 120 E4
Great Plumstead Norfk 93 G2
Great Ponton Lincs 102 F6
Great Preston Leeds 124 B5
Great Raveley Cambs 89 J7
Great Rissington Gloucs 56 D5
Great Rollright Oxon 56 F2
Great Ryburgh Norfk 106 A6
Great Ryton Shrops 83 J3
Great Saling Essex 61 H3
Great Salkeld Cumb 148 F7
Great Sampford Essex 76 F7
Great Saughall Ches W 111 K7
Great Shefford W Berk 41 G5
Great Shelford Cambs 76 C4
Great Smeaton N York 141 H6
Great Snoring Norfk 105 M5
Great Somerford Wilts 39 L4
Great Soudley Shrops 99 G6
Great Stainton Darltn 141 H3
Great Stambridge Essex 46 E2
Great Staughton Cambs 75 G2
Great Steeping Lincs 118 F8
Great Stoke S Glos 38 F4
Greatstone-on-Sea Kent 21 L2
Great Strickland Cumb 138 D3
Great Stukeley Cambs 89 J8
Great Sturton Lincs 117 K6
Great Swinburne Nthumb 158 B6
Great Tew Oxon 57 H3
Great Tey Essex 61 L3
Great Thurlow Suffk 76 F4
Great Torrington Devon 23 H7
Great Tosson Nthumb 158 C3
Great Totham Essex 61 K5
Great Totham Essex 61 L5
Great Urswick Cumb 129 G5
Great Wakering Essex 46 F3
Great Waldingfield Suffk 77 K5
Great Walsingham Norfk 105 M5
Great Waltham Essex 61 H5
Great Warley Essex 45 L2
Great Washbourne Gloucs 71 H7
Great Weeke Devon 11 G7
Great Wenham Suffk 78 C6
Great Whittington Nthumb 158 C7
Great Wigborough Essex 62 A5
Great Wilbraham Cambs 76 D3
Great Wishford Wilts 28 B4
Great Witcombe Gloucs 55 K5
Great Witley Worcs 70 D2
Great Wolford Warwks 72 B7
Greatworth Nhants 73 G6
Great Wratting Suffk 77 G5
Great Wymondley Herts 59 K3
Great Wyrley Staffs 85 H3
Great Yarmouth Norfk 93 L3
Great Yarmouth Crematorium Norfk 93 K3
Great Yeldham Essex 77 H6
Greenburn W Loth 176 C6
Green End Herts 60 B2
Green End Herts 60 B4
Greenfield Ag & B 173 M1
Greenfield C Beds 74 F7
Greenfield Flints 111 H6
Greenfield Highld 201 J5
Greenfield Oldham 113 M2
Greenford Gt Lon 43 J4
Greengairs N Lans 175 K4
Greengates C Brad 123 J3
Greenham Somset 25 G7
Green Hammerton N York 133 G7
Greenhaugh Nthumb 157 K5
Greenhead Nthumb 149 H3
Green Heath Staffs 85 H2
Greenhill D & G 155 J6
Greenhill Falk 175 L3
Greenhill Kent 47 K6
Greenhill S Lans 165 H3
Greenhithe Kent 45 L5
Greenholm E Ayrs 164 B3
Greenhouse Border 167 H5
Greenhow Hill N York 131 L6
Greenland Highld 231 J3
Greenland Sheff 115 H4
Greenlaw Border 167 L1
Greenlea D & G 155 H6
Greenloaning P & K 185 H6
Greenmount Bury 122 B7
Greenock Inver 174 B3
Greenodd Cumb 129 G3
Green Ore Somset 26 E2
Green Quarter Cumb 138 C6
Greenshields S Lans 165 K2
Greenside Gatesd 150 E3
Greenside Kirk 123 H7
Greens Norton Nhants 73 J4
Greenstead Green Essex 61 K3
Green Street Herts 59 K7
Green Street Herts 60 D4
Green Street Green Kent 45 L6
Green Tye Herts 60 C4
Greenway Somset 25 L6
Greenwich Gt Lon 45 G4
Greenwich Maritime Gt Lon 45 H4
Greet Gloucs 56 B3
Greete Shrops 69 L1
Greetham Lincs 118 D7
Greetham Rutlnd 88 D2
Greetland Calder 123 G6
Greinton Somset 26 B4
Grenaby IoM 237 b6
Grendon Nhants 74 C3
Grendon Warwks 86 C4
Grendon Underwood Bucks 58 B4
Grenoside Sheff 115 G3
Grenoside Crematorium Sheff 114 F3
Greosabhagh W Isls 232 e4
Gresford Wrexhm 97 M2
Gresham Norfk 106 E5
Greshornish House Hotel Highld 208 E4
Gressenhall Norfk 91 L1
Gressenhall Green Norfk 91 L1
Gressingham Lancs 130 B5
Greta Bridge Dur 140 D5
Gretna D & G 148 B2
Gretna Green D & G 148 B2
Gretna Services D & G 148 B2
Gretton Gloucs 56 A2
Gretton Nhants 88 C5
Gretton Shrops 83 K4
Grewelthorpe N York 132 C4
Greyrigg D & G 155 J4
Greys Green Oxon 42 B4
Greysouthen Cumb 136 E2
Greystoke Cumb 138 B2
Greystone Angus 196 E7
Greywell Hants 30 B2
Griff Warwks 86 D5
Griffithstown Torfn 53 L7
Grimeford Village Lancs 121 J7
Grimesthorpe Sheff 115 G4
Grimethorpe Barns 124 C8
Grimley Worcs 70 E3
Grimmet S Ayrs 163 H7
Grimoldby Lincs 118 E4
Grimpo Shrops 98 A7
Grimsargh Lancs 121 H4
Grimsby NE Lin 127 G7
Grimsby Crematorium NE Lin 118 C1
Grimscote Nhants 73 J4
Grimscott Cnwll 9 H4
Grimshader W Isls 232 f3
Grimsthorpe Lincs 103 H7
Grimston Leics 102 B7
Grimston Norfk 105 H7
Grimstone Dorset 14 C4
Grimstone End Suffk 77 L2
Grindale E R Yk 135 H5
Grindleford Derbys 114 E6
Grindleton Lancs 121 L2
Grindley Brook Shrops 98 D4
Grindlow Derbys 114 D6
Grindon Staffs 100 B2
Gringley on the Hill Notts 116 C4
Grinsdale Cumb 148 C4
Grinshill Shrops 98 D7
Grinton N York 140 D7
Griomaisiader W Isls 232 f3
Griomsaigh W Isls 233 c6
Grishipoll Ag & B 188 F4
Gristhorpe N York 135 H3
Griston Norfk 91 L4
Gritley Ork 234 d6
Grittenham Wilts 40 B4
Grittleton Wilts 39 K4
Grizebeck Cumb 128 F3
Grizedale Cumb 137 K7
Groby Leics 87 G3
Groes Conwy 110 D8
Groes-faen Rhondd 37 G4
Groeslon Gwynd 95 H2
Groes-Wen Caerph 37 H3
Grogarry W Isls 233 b7
Grogport Ag & B 161 K1
Groigearraidh W Isls 233 b7
Gronant Flints 110 F5
Groombridge E Susx 32 F5
Grosebay W Isls 232 e4
Grosmont Mons 54 B3
Grosmont N York 143 H6
Groton Suffk 77 L6
Grouville Jersey 236 e7
Grove Notts 116 C5
Grove Oxon 41 H3
Grove Green Kent 33 K3
Grove Park Gt Lon 45 H5
Grovesend Swans 51 H5
Gruinard Highld 219 L4
Gruinart Ag & B 170 F5
Grula Highld 208 F8
Gruline Ag & B 190 B7
Grundisburgh Suffk 78 F4
Gruting Shet 235 c5
Grutness Shet 235 c8
Gualachulain Highld 192 B7
Guardbridge Fife 187 G4
Guarlford Worcs 70 E5
Guay P & K 194 F6
Guernsey Guern 236 c3
Guernsey Airport Guern 236 c3
Guestling Green E Susx 21 G3
Guestling Thorn E Susx 21 G3
Guestwick Norfk 106 C6
Guide Bridge Tamesd 113 L3
Guilden Morden Cambs 75 K5
Guilden Sutton Ches W 112 C7
Guildford Surrey 31 G2
Guildford Crematorium Surrey 31 G3
Guildtown P & K 186 B2
Guilsborough Nhants 87 J8
Guilsfield Powys 82 E2
Guiltreehill S Ayrs 163 J7
Guineaford Devon 23 J4
Guisborough R & Cl 142 D4
Guiseley Leeds 123 J3
Guist Norfk 106 B7
Guiting Power Gloucs 56 C3
Gullane E Loth 178 B2
Gulval Cnwll 2 E5
Gulworthy Devon 6 C2
Gumfreston Pembks 49 J7
Gumley Leics 87 K5

Gunby Lincs....102 E7
Gunby Lincs....118 F7
Gundleton Hants....29 L5
Gun Hill E Susx....20 C3
Gunn Devon....23 K5
Gunnerside N York....139 L7
Gunnerton Nthumb....158 A7
Gunness N Linc....125 K7
Gunnislake Cnwll....6 C2
Gunnista Shet....235 d6
Gunthorpe N Linc....116 D3
Gunthorpe Norfk....106 B5
Gunthorpe Notts....102 B4
Gunwalloe Cnwll....3 H6
Gurnard IoW....16 F4
Gurney Slade Somset....26 F2
Gurnos Powys....52 B6
Gussage All Saints Dorset....15 J1
Gussage St Andrew Dorset....27 L8
Gussage St Michael Dorset....15 J1
Guston Kent....35 J5
Gutcher Shet....235 d2
Guthrie Angus....196 F6
Guyhirn Cambs....90 B3
Guyzance Nthumb....158 F2
Gwaenysgor Flints....110 F5
Gwalchmai IoA....108 E6
Gwaun-Cae-Gurwen Carmth....51 K3
Gweek Cnwll....3 J6
Gwenddwr Powys....68 B6
Gwennap Cnwll....3 J4
Gwennap Mining District Cnwll....3 K3
Gwent Crematorium Mons....37 L2
Gwernaffield Flints....111 H7
Gwernesney Mons....54 B7
Gwernogle Carmth....66 C7
Gwernymynydd Flints....111 H8
Gwespyr Flints....110 F5
Gwinear Cnwll....3 G4
Gwithian Cnwll....3 G3
Gwyddelwern Denbgs....97 G3
Gwyddgrug Carmth....66 B7
Gwytherin Conwy....96 D1

H

Habberley Shrops....83 H3
Habberley Worcs....84 E7
Habergham Lancs....122 B4
Habertoft Lincs....119 G7
Habrough NE Lin....126 E7
Hacconby Lincs....103 J7
Haceby Lincs....103 G5
Hacheston Suffk....79 G3
Hackbridge Gt Lon....44 F6
Hackenthorpe Sheff....115 H5
Hackford Norfk....92 C3
Hackforth N York....132 C2
Hackland Ork....234 c5
Hackleton Nhants....74 B4
Hacklinge Kent....35 J4
Hackness N York....134 F2
Hackney Gt Lon....45 G3
Hackthorn Lincs....117 G5
Hackthorpe Cumb....138 D3
Hadden Border....168 B3
Haddenham Bucks....58 C6
Haddenham Cambs....90 C7
Haddington E Loth....178 B4
Haddington Lincs....116 E8
Haddiscoe Norfk....93 J4
Haddo Abers....216 F6
Haddon Cambs....89 G5
Hadfield Derbys....114 A3
Hadham Ford Herts....60 C4
Hadleigh Essex....46 D3
Hadleigh Suffk....78 B6
Hadley Worcs....70 F2
Hadley Wrekin....84 C2
Hadley End Staffs....100 C7
Hadley Wood Gt Lon....44 E1
Hadlow Kent....33 H3
Hadlow Down E Susx....20 B2
Hadnall Shrops....98 D7
Hadrian's Wall Nthumb....150 B2
Hadstock Essex....76 D5
Hadzor Worcs....71 G3
Haggersta Shet....235 c5
Haggerston Nthumb....168 F2
Haggs Falk....175 L3
Hagley Herefs....69 L6
Hagley Worcs....85 G7
Hagworthingham Lincs....118 D7
Haile Cumb....136 E5
Hailey Oxon....57 G5
Hailsham E Susx....20 C4
Hail Weston Cambs....75 H3
Hainault Gt Lon....45 J2
Hainford Norfk....106 F8
Hainton Lincs....117 K5
Haisthorpe E R Yk....135 H6
Hakin Pembks....48 F6
Halam Notts....102 B2
Halbeath Fife....176 F1
Halberton Devon....24 F8
Halcro Highld....231 J4
Hale Cumb....129 K4
Hale Halton....112 C5
Hale Hants....28 D7
Hale Surrey....30 D2
Hale Traffd....113 H4
Halebarns Traffd....113 H4
Hales Norfk....93 H4
Hales Staffs....99 G5
Halesowen Dudley....85 G6
Hales Place Kent....34 F3
Hale Street Kent....33 H4
Halesworth Suffk....93 H7
Halewood Knows....112 C4
Halford Devon....7 J2
Halford Warwks....72 C5
Halfpenny Green Staffs....84 E5
Halfway House Shrops....83 G2
Halfway Houses Kent....46 F5
Halifax Calder....123 G5
Halket E Ayrs....174 D7
Halkirk Highld....231 G4
Halkyn Flints....111 H7
Hall E Rens....174 D7
Halland E Susx....20 A3
Hallaton Leics....87 L4
Hallatrow BaNES....38 F8
Hallbankgate Cumb....149 G3
Hall Dunnerdale Cumb....137 H7
Hallen S Glos....38 D4
Hallgarth Dur....151 H6
Hall Glen Falk....176 B3
Hall Green Birm....85 K7
Hallin Highld....208 D3
Halling Medway....46 B7
Hallington Lincs....118 D4
Hallington Nthumb....158 C6
Halliwell Bolton....121 K7
Halloughton Notts....102 B3
Hallow Worcs....70 E3
Hall's Green Herts....59 L3
Hallyne Border....166 B2
Halmore Gloucs....55 G7
Halnaker W Susx....18 B4
Halsall Lancs....120 E7
Halse Nhants....73 H6
Halse Somset....25 H5
Halsetown Cnwll....2 E4
Halsham E R Yk....127 G5
Halstead Essex....61 K2
Halstead Kent....45 J7
Halstead Leics....87 L3
Halstock Dorset....14 A2
Haltemprice Crematorium E R Yk....126 C4
Haltham Lincs....118 C8
Halton Bucks....58 E6
Halton Halton....112 D5
Halton Lancs....129 K6
Halton Leeds....123 L4
Halton Nthumb....150 C2
Halton Wrexhm....97 L4
Halton East N York....131 K8
Halton Gill N York....131 G4
Halton Holegate Lincs....118 F7
Halton Lea Gate Nthumb....149 H4
Halton Shields Nthumb....150 C2
Halton West N York....130 F8
Haltwhistle Nthumb....149 J3
Halvergate Norfk....93 J3
Halwell Devon....7 H5
Halwill Devon....10 C5
Halwill Junction Devon....10 C5
Ham Devon....13 G3
Ham Gloucs....55 G7
Ham Gt Lon....44 D5
Ham Kent....35 J4
Ham Somset....25 L6
Ham Wilts....41 G7
Hambleden Bucks....42 C3
Hambledon Hants....29 M7
Hambledon Surrey....30 F4
Hamble-le-Rice Hants....16 F2
Hambleton Lancs....120 E3
Hambleton N York....124 E4
Hambridge Somset....26 B6
Hambrook W Susx....17 L2
Hameringham Lincs....118 D7
Hamerton Cambs....89 G7
Ham Green Worcs....71 H2
Hamilton S Lans....175 J7
Hamilton Services S Lans....175 J6
Hamlet Dorset....14 B2
Hammersmith Gt Lon....44 E4
Hammerwich Staffs....85 J3
Hammoon Dorset....27 J8
Hamnavoe Shet....235 c6
Hampden Park E Susx....20 C5
Hampnett Gloucs....56 C5
Hampole Donc....124 D7
Hampreston Dorset....15 K3
Hampstead Gt Lon....44 E3
Hampstead Norreys W Berk....41 K5
Hampsthwaite N York....132 C7
Hampton C Pete....89 H5
Hampton Gt Lon....43 J6
Hampton Kent....47 K6
Hampton Shrops....84 D6
Hampton Swindn....40 D3
Hampton Worcs....71 H5
Hampton Bishop Herefs....69 L6
Hampton Court Palace Gt Lon....44 D6
Hampton Heath Ches W....98 D3
Hampton-in-Arden Solhll....86 B7
Hampton Lovett Worcs....70 F2
Hampton Lucy Warwks....72 B3
Hampton Magna Warwks....72 C2
Hampton Poyle Oxon....57 J5
Hampton Wick Gt Lon....44 D6
Hamptworth Wilts....28 E7
Hamsey E Susx....19 L3
Hamstall Ridware Staffs....100 C8
Hamstead Birm....85 J5
Hamstead Marshall W Berk....41 H7
Hamsterley Dur....140 E2
Hamsterley Dur....150 E4
Hamstreet Kent....34 D7
Ham Street Somset....26 D4
Hamworthy Poole....15 J4
Hanbury Staffs....100 D6
Hanbury Worcs....71 G2
Hanchurch Staffs....99 J4
Handa Island Highld....228 A6
Hand and Pen Devon....12 D4
Handbridge Ches W....112 B7
Handcross W Susx....31 L5
Handforth Ches E....113 J5
Handley Ches W....98 C2
Handley Derbys....101 G1
Handsworth Birm....85 J5
Handsworth Sheff....115 H4
Hanford C Stke....99 K4
Hanging Heaton Kirk....123 K6
Hanging Houghton Nhants....87 L8
Hanging Langford Wilts....28 B4
Hangleton Br & H....19 H4
Hanham S Glos....38 F6
Hankelow Ches E....98 F4
Hankerton Wilts....39 L3
Hanley C Stke....99 K3
Hanley Castle Worcs....70 E6
Hanley Child Worcs....70 B2
Hanley Swan Worcs....70 E6
Hanley William Worcs....70 C2
Hanlith N York....131 G7
Hanmer Wrexhm....98 C4
Hannaford Devon....23 J5
Hannington Hants....29 K1
Hannington Nhants....74 B1
Hannington Swindn....40 D2
Hannington Wick Swindn....40 D2
Hanslope M Keyn....74 B5
Hanthorpe Lincs....103 H7
Hanwell Gt Lon....44 D4
Hanwell Oxon....72 E5
Hanwood Shrops....83 J2
Hanworth Gt Lon....43 J6
Hanworth Norfk....106 E5
Happendon S Lans....165 G3
Happendon Services S Lans....165 G3
Happisburgh Norfk....107 H6
Happisburgh Common Norfk....107 H6
Hapsford Ches W....112 C6
Hapton Lancs....122 B4
Hapton Norfk....92 E4
Harberton Devon....7 H4
Harbertonford Devon....7 H5
Harbledown Kent....34 F3
Harborne Birm....85 H6
Harborough Magna Warwks....86 F7
Harbottle Nthumb....158 B2
Harbourneford Devon....7 G4
Harbury Warwks....72 D3
Harby Leics....102 C6
Harby Notts....116 E7
Harcombe Devon....11 K8
Harcombe Devon....12 F4
Harcombe Bottom Devon....13 J4
Harden C Brad....123 G3
Harden Wsall....85 H4
Hardenhuish Wilts....39 K5
Hardgate Abers....206 E5
Hardgate D & G....146 E2
Hardgate W Duns....174 F4
Hardham W Susx....18 E3
Hardingham Norfk....92 C3
Hardingstone Nhants....73 L3
Hardington Somset....27 H2
Hardington Mandeville Somset....13 M1
Hardington Marsh Somset....13 M1

Hardington Moor Somset 26 D8
Hardisworthy Devon 22 C7
Hardley Hants 16 E2
Hardley Street Norfk 93 H4
Hardraw N York 131 G2
Hardstoft Derbys 115 H8
Hardway Hants 17 H3
Hardway Somset 27 G5
Hardwick Bucks 58 D4
Hardwick Cambs 75 L3
Hardwick Nhants 74 B1
Hardwick Norfk 92 F5
Hardwick Oxon 57 G6
Hardwick Oxon 57 L3
Hardwick Wsall 85 J4
Hardwicke Gloucs 55 H5
Hardwicke Gloucs 55 K3
Hardwick Hall Dur 141 H2
Hardy's Green Essex 61 M4
Hare Croft C Brad 123 G4
Harefield Gt Lon 43 H3
Hare Green Essex 62 D3
Hare Hatch Wokham 42 D5
Harehill Derbys 100 D5
Harehills Leeds 123 L4
Harelaw Border 167 H5
Harelaw D & G 156 D6
Harescombe Gloucs 55 J6
Haresfield Gloucs 55 J6
Harestock Hants 29 J5
Hare Street Essex 60 C6
Hare Street Herts 60 C3
Harewood Leeds 123 L2
Harewood End Herefs 54 D3
Harford Devon 6 F4
Hargrave Ches W 98 C1
Hargrave Nhants 74 F1
Hargrave Suffk 77 H3
Harkstead Suffk 78 E7
Harlaston Staffs 86 B2
Harlaxton Lincs 102 E6
Harlech Gwynd 95 K6
Harlech Castle Gwynd 95 K6
Harlescott Shrops 83 K1
Harlesden Gt Lon 44 E4
Harlesthorpe Derbys 115 J6
Harleston Devon 7 J6
Harleston Norfk 92 F6
Harleston Suffk 78 B3
Harlestone Nhants 73 K2
Harle Syke Lancs 122 C4
Harley Rothm 115 G2
Harley Shrops 83 L3
Harlington C Beds 59 G2
Harlington Donc 115 J2
Harlington Gt Lon 43 H5
Harlosh Highld 208 D6
Harlow Essex 60 D6
Harlow Carr RHS N York 132 D8
Harlow Hill Nthumb 150 D2
Harlthorpe E R Yk 125 H3
Harlton Cambs 75 L4
Harlyn Cnwll 4 D2
Harman's Cross Dorset 15 J6
Harmby N York 131 L2
Harmer Green Herts 59 L5
Harmer Hill Shrops 98 C7
Harmston Lincs 116 F8
Harnage Shrops 83 L3
Harnhill Gloucs 56 B7
Harold Hill Gt Lon 45 K2
Haroldston West Pembks 48 E4
Haroldswick Shet 235 e1
Harold Wood Gt Lon 45 K3
Harome N York 133 K3
Harpenden Herts 59 J5
Harpford Devon 12 E4
Harpham E R Yk 135 H7
Harpley Norfk 105 J7
Harpley Worcs 70 C3
Harpole Nhants 73 K3
Harpsdale Highld 231 G4
Harpswell Lincs 116 F4
Harpurhey Manch 113 K2
Harraby Cumb 148 D4
Harracott Devon 23 J6
Harrapool Highld 199 K2
Harrietfield P & K 185 K2
Harrietsham Kent 33 L3
Harringay Gt Lon 44 F3
Harrington Cumb 136 D3
Harrington Lincs 118 E6
Harrington Nhants 87 L7
Harringworth Nhants 88 D4
Harris W Isls 232 d4
Harrogate N York 132 D7
Harrogate Crematorium N York 132 E8
Harrold Bed 74 D3
Harrow Gt Lon 44 D3
Harrowbarrow Cnwll 6 B2
Harrowgate Village Darltn 141 H4
Harrow Green Suffk 77 J4
Harrow on the Hill Gt Lon 44 D3
Harrow Weald Gt Lon 44 D2
Harston Cambs 76 B4
Harston Leics 102 D6
Harswell E R Yk 125 J3
Hart Hartpl 151 L7
Hartburn Nthumb 158 D5
Hartburn S on T 141 K4
Hartest Suffk 77 J4
Hartfield E Susx 32 E6
Hartford Cambs 89 J8
Hartford Ches W 112 F6
Hartfordbridge Hants 42 C8
Hartford End Essex 61 G4
Hartforth N York 140 F6
Hartgrove Dorset 27 J7
Harthill Ches W 98 D2
Harthill N Lans 176 B5
Harthill Rothm 115 J5
Hartington Derbys 100 C1
Hartland Devon 22 D6
Hartland Quay Devon 22 C6
Hartlebury Worcs 70 E1
Hartlepool Hartpl 151 L7
Hartlepool Crematorium Hartpl 142 B2
Hartley Cumb 139 H5
Hartley Kent 33 K6
Hartley Kent 45 L6
Hartley Wespall Hants 42 B8
Hartley Wintney Hants 30 C1
Hartlip Kent 46 D7
Harton N York 133 L6
Harton S Tyne 151 J2
Hartpury Gloucs 55 J3
Hartshead Kirk 123 J6
Hartshead Moor Services Calder 123 H5
Hartshill C Stke 99 K4
Hartshill Warwks 86 D5
Hartshorne Derbys 100 F7
Hartwell Nhants 73 L4
Hartwith N York 132 C6
Hartwood N Lans 175 L6
Hartwoodmyres Border 166 F4
Harvel Kent 46 A7
Harvington Worcs 71 J5
Harvington Worcs 84 F8
Harwell Notts 116 B3
Harwell Oxon 41 J3
Harwich Essex 62 F2
Harwood Dale N York 143 K7
Harwood Park Crematorium Herts 59 L4
Harworth Notts 115 L3
Hasbury Dudley 85 G6
Hascombe Surrey 31 G4
Haselbech Nhants 87 K7
Haselbury Plucknett Somset 13 L1
Haseley Warwks 72 B2
Haselor Warwks 71 K3
Hasfield Gloucs 55 J3
Haskayne Lancs 120 E8
Hasketon Suffk 78 F4
Haslemere Surrey 30 E5
Haslingden Lancs 122 B6
Haslingfield Cambs 76 B4
Haslington Ches E 99 G2
Hassingham Norfk 93 H3
Hassocks W Susx 19 J3
Hassop Derbys 114 E6
Haster Highld 231 K5
Hastingleigh Kent 34 E5
Hastings E Susx 21 G4
Hastings Crematorium E Susx 21 G3
Hastingwood Essex 60 D6
Hastoe Herts 58 F6
Haswell Dur 151 J6
Haswell Plough Dur 151 J6
Hatch Beauchamp Somset 25 L7
Hatch End Gt Lon 43 J3
Hatchmere Ches W 112 D6
Hatcliffe NE Lin 117 K2
Hatfield Donc 125 G8
Hatfield Herefs 69 L3
Hatfield Herts 59 L6
Hatfield Broad Oak Essex 60 E5
Hatfield Heath Essex 60 E5
Hatfield Peverel Essex 61 J5
Hatfield Woodhouse Donc 125 G8
Hatford Oxon 41 G2
Hatherden Hants 29 G2
Hatherleigh Devon 10 D4
Hathern Leics 101 J7
Hatherop Gloucs 56 D6
Hathersage Derbys 114 E5
Hathersage Booths Derbys 114 E5
Hatherton Ches E 99 G3
Hatherton Staffs 85 G2
Hatley St George Cambs 75 K4
Hatt Cnwll 6 B4
Hattersley Tamesd 113 M3
Hatton Abers 217 K6
Hatton Angus 196 D7
Hatton Derbys 100 E6
Hatton Gt Lon 43 J5
Hatton Lincs 117 K6
Hatton Shrops 83 J5
Hatton Warrtn 112 E5
Hatton Warwks 72 B2
Hatton of Fintray Abers 206 F3
Haugh E Ayrs 163 L4
Haugham Lincs 118 D5
Haughhead E Duns 175 G3
Haughley Suffk 78 B3
Haughley Green Suffk 78 B2
Haugh of Glass Moray 215 J6
Haugh of Urr D & G 146 E2
Haughs of Kinnaird Angus 197 G5
Haughton Ches E 98 E2
Haughton Shrops 98 B6
Haughton Staffs 99 K7
Haughton le Skerne Darltn 141 H4
Haultwick Herts 60 B4
Haunton Staffs 86 B2
Hautes Croix Jersey 236 c6
Hauxton Cambs 76 B4
Havant Hants 17 K2
Havant Crematorium Hants 17 K2
Havenstreet IoW 17 G4
Havercroft Wakefd 124 B7
Haverfordwest Pembks 48 F4
Haverhill Suffk 76 F5
Haverigg Cumb 128 E4
Havering-atte-Bower Gt Lon 45 K2
Haversham M Keyn 74 B6
Haverthwaite Cumb 129 H3
Havyat N Som 38 C7
Hawarden Flints 111 J7
Hawbush Green Essex 61 J4
Hawen Cerdgn 65 K5
Hawes N York 131 G2
Hawe's Green Norfk 92 F4
Hawford Worcs 70 E3
Hawick Border 167 G6
Hawkchurch Devon 13 J3
Hawkedon Suffk 77 H4
Hawkeridge Wilts 27 K2
Hawkesbury S Glos 39 H3
Hawkesbury Upton S Glos 39 H3
Hawkhurst Kent 33 K6
Hawkinge Kent 35 G6
Hawkinge Crematorium Kent 35 G6
Hawkley Hants 30 C5
Hawkridge Somset 24 D5
Hawkshead Cumb 137 K7
Hawkshead Hill Cumb 137 K7
Hawksland S Lans 165 G2
Hawkstone Shrops 98 E6
Hawkswick N York 131 H5
Hawksworth Leeds 123 H3
Hawksworth Notts 102 C4
Hawkwell Essex 46 E2
Hawley Hants 42 E8
Hawling Gloucs 56 B4
Hawnby N York 133 H2
Haworth C Brad 122 F3
Hawstead Suffk 77 J3
Hawthorn Dur 151 K5
Hawthorn Hill Lincs 103 K2
Hawton Notts 102 C3
Haxby C York 133 J7
Haxey N Linc 116 C2
Haycombe Crematorium BaNES 39 G7
Haydock St Hel 112 E3
Haydon Bridge Nthumb 149 L3
Haydon Wick Swindn 40 C3
Hayes Gt Lon 43 J4
Hayes Gt Lon 45 H6
Hayes End Gt Lon 43 H4
Hayfield Ag & B 182 F3
Hayfield Derbys 114 B4
Hayhillock Angus 196 E7
Hayle Cnwll 2 F4
Hayle Port Cnwll 2 F4
Hayley Green Dudley 85 G6
Hayling Island Hants 17 K3
Hayne Devon 11 H7
Haynes (Church End) C Beds 74 F6
Haynes (Northwood End) C Beds 75 G6
Haynes (Silver End) C Beds 75 G6
Haynes (West End) C Beds 74 F6
Hay-on-Wye Powys 68 E6
Hayscastle Pembks 48 F3
Hayscastle Cross Pembks 48 F3
Hay Street Herts 60 C3
Hayton Cumb 147 K6
Hayton Cumb 148 E4
Hayton E R Yk 125 J2
Hayton Notts 116 B5
Haytor Vale Devon 7 H1
Haytown Devon 9 K3

Haywards Heath W Susx 19 J2
Haywood Donc 124 E7
Hazelbank S Lans 165 G1
Hazelbury Bryan Dorset 14 E2
Hazeleigh Essex 61 K7
Hazel Grove Stockp 113 L4
Hazelton Walls Fife 186 E3
Hazelwood Derbys 101 G4
Hazlemere Bucks 42 E2
Hazlerigg N u Ty 159 G7
Hazleton Gloucs 56 B4
Heacham Norfk 105 G5
Headbourne Worthy Hants 29 J5
Headcorn Kent 33 L4
Headingley Leeds 123 K4
Headington Oxon 57 K6
Headlam Dur 140 F4
Headlesscross N Lans 176 B6
Headless Cross Worcs 71 J2
Headley Hants 30 D4
Headley Hants 41 K7
Headley Surrey 31 K1
Headley Down Hants 30 D4
Headon Notts 116 C6
Heads Nook Cumb 148 E4
Heage Derbys 101 G3
Healaugh N York 124 D2
Healaugh N York 140 C7
Heald Green Stockp 113 J4
Heale Somset 25 K7
Heale Somset 26 B6
Healey N York 132 B4
Healeyfield Dur 150 D5
Healing NE Lin 126 F7
Heamoor Cnwll 2 E5
Heanor Derbys 101 H3
Heanton Punchardon Devon 23 H4
Heapham Lincs 116 E4
Heart of England Crematorium Warwks 86 E5
Heart of Scotland Services N Lans 176 B5
Heasley Mill Devon 24 B5
Heast Highld 199 K2
Heath Derbys 115 J7
Heath Wakefd 123 L6
Heath and Reach C Beds 58 F3
Heathcote Derbys 100 D1
Heather Leics 86 E2
Heathfield E Susx 20 C2
Heathfield Somset 25 J6
Heath Green Worcs 71 J1
Heath Hall D & G 155 H6
Heath Hayes & Wimblebury Staffs 85 H2
Heath Hill Shrops 84 D2
Heathrow Airport Gt Lon 43 H5
Heathton Shrops 84 E5
Heath Town Wolves 85 G4
Heatley Warrtn 113 G4
Heaton C Brad 123 H4
Heaton N u Ty 151 G2
Heaton Staffs 113 L8
Heaton Chapel Stockp 113 K3
Heaton Mersey Stockp 113 K4
Heaton Norris Stockp 113 K4
Heaton's Bridge Lancs 120 E7
Heaverham Kent 33 G2
Heavitree Devon 12 B4
Hebburn S Tyne 151 H3
Hebden N York 131 J6
Hebden Bridge Calder 122 E5
Hebing End Herts 60 A4
Hebron Carmth 49 K3
Hebron Nthumb 158 F4
Heckfield Hants 42 B7
Heckfield Green Suffk 92 E7
Heckfordbridge Essex 61 M4
Heckington Lincs 103 J4
Heckmondwike Kirk 123 J5
Heddington Wilts 39 M6
Heddon-on-the-Wall Nthumb 150 E2
Hedenham Norfk 93 G5
Hedge End Hants 29 J8
Hedgerley Bucks 42 F3
Hedging Somset 25 L5
Hedley on the Hill Nthumb 150 D3
Hednesford Staffs 85 H2
Hedon E R Yk 126 F5
Hedsor Bucks 42 E3
Heglibister Shet 235 c5
Heighington Darltn 141 G3
Heighington Lincs 117 G7
Heightington Worcs 70 D1
Heiton Border 167 L4
Hele Devon 12 C2
Hele Devon 23 H3
Helensburgh Ag & B 174 B2
Helenton S Ayrs 163 K3
Helford Cnwll 3 K6
Helford Passage Cnwll 3 K6
Helhoughton Norfk 105 K7
Helions Bumpstead Essex 76 F6
Helland Cnwll 5 G2
Hellescott Cnwll 9 H6
Hellesdon Norfk 92 E2
Hellidon Nhants 73 G3
Hellifield N York 131 G7
Hellingly E Susx 20 C4
Helmdon Nhants 73 H5
Helme Kirk 123 G7
Helmingham Suffk 78 E3
Helmsdale Highld 227 H5
Helmshore Lancs 122 B6
Helmsley N York 133 J3
Helperby N York 133 G5
Helperthorpe N York 134 E5
Helpringham Lincs 103 J4
Helpston C Pete 89 G3
Helsby Ches W 112 C6
Helston Cnwll 3 H5
Helstone Cnwll 8 E8
Helton Cumb 138 D3
Hemel Hempstead Herts 59 H6
Hemerdon Devon 6 E4
Hemingbrough N York 125 G4
Hemingby Lincs 118 C6
Hemingford Abbots Cambs 75 K1
Hemingford Grey Cambs 75 K1
Hemingstone Suffk 78 D4
Hemington Leics 101 J6
Hemington Nhants 88 F6
Hemington Somset 27 G2
Hemley Suffk 79 G6
Hemlington Middsb 142 B4
Hempnall Norfk 92 F5
Hempnall Green Norfk 92 F5
Hempriggs Moray 214 D2
Hempstead Essex 76 F6
Hempstead Norfk 106 D5
Hempstead Norfk 107 J6
Hempton Norfk 105 L6
Hempton Oxon 57 H2
Hemsby Norfk 107 K8
Hemswell Lincs 116 F4
Hemswell Cliff Lincs 116 F4
Hemsworth Wakefd 124 C7
Hemyock Devon 25 H8
Hendon Gt Lon 44 E3
Hendon Sundld 151 K4
Hendon Crematorium Gt Lon 44 E2
Hendy Carmth 51 H5
Henfield W Susx 19 G3
Hengoed Caerph 37 J2
Hengoed Powys 68 E4
Hengrave Suffk 77 J2
Henham Essex 60 E3
Heniarth Powys 82 C2
Henlade Somset 25 L6
Henley Dorset 14 D2
Henley Somset 26 B5
Henley Suffk 78 E4
Henley W Susx 30 E6
Henley-in-Arden Warwks 71 L2
Henley-on-Thames Oxon 42 C4
Henley's Down E Susx 20 E3
Henllan Cerdgn 65 K6
Henllan Denbgs 110 E7
Henllys Torfn 37 K3
Henlow C Beds 75 H6
Hennock Devon 11 J8
Henny Street Essex 77 K6
Henryd Conwy 109 L6
Henry's Moat (Castell Hendre) Pembks 49 H3
Hensall N York 124 F5
Henshaw Nthumb 149 J3
Hensingham Cumb 136 D4
Henstead Suffk 93 K6
Hensting Hants 29 J6
Henstridge Somset 27 G7
Henstridge Ash Somset 27 G7
Henton Oxon 58 C7
Henton Somset 26 C3
Henwick Worcs 70 E4
Henwood Cnwll 5 L2
Heol-y-Cyw Brdgnd 36 E4
Hepple Nthumb 158 C2
Hepscott Nthumb 158 F5
Heptonstall Calder 122 E5
Hepworth Kirk 114 D1
Hepworth Suffk 92 B8
Herbrandston Pembks 48 E6
Hereford Herefs 69 K6
Hereford Crematorium Herefs 69 J6
Hereson Kent 35 K2
Heribusta Highld 218 B7
Heriot Border 177 L7
Hermiston C Edin 177 G4
Hermitage Border 156 E3
Hermitage Dorset 14 C2
Hermitage W Berk 41 J5
Hermon Carmth 65 K7
Hermon Pembks 49 L2
Herne Kent 47 K6
Herne Bay Kent 47 K6
Herne Hill Gt Lon 44 F5
Herne Pound Kent 33 H3
Hernhill Kent 34 E3
Herodsfoot Cnwll 5 K4
Heronsford S Ayrs 152 D5
Herriard Hants 30 A3
Herringfleet Suffk 93 K4
Herringswell Suffk 77 G1
Herringthorpe Rothm 115 J3
Herrington Sundld 151 J4
Hersden Kent 35 G3
Hersham Surrey 43 J7
Herstmonceux E Susx 20 D3
Herston Ork 234 c7
Hertford Herts 60 B5
Hertford Heath Herts 60 B5
Hertingfordbury Herts 60 A5
Hesketh Bank Lancs 120 F5
Hesketh Lane Lancs 121 J3
Hesket Newmarket Cumb 148 C7
Hesleden Dur 151 K7
Heslington C York 124 F1
Hessay C York 133 H8
Hessenford Cnwll 5 L4
Hessett Suffk 77 L3
Hessle E R Yk 126 C5
Hessle Wakefd 124 C6
Hest Bank Lancs 129 K6
Heston Gt Lon 43 J5
Heston Services Gt Lon 43 J5
Hestwall Ork 234 b5
Heswall Wirral 111 J5
Hethe Oxon 57 L3
Hethersett Norfk 92 D3
Hethersgill Cumb 148 E2
Hett Dur 151 G7
Hetton N York 131 H7
Hetton-le-Hole Sundld 151 J5
Heugh Nthumb 158 D7
Heughhead Abers 205 J3
Heugh Head Border 179 H6
Heveningham Suffk 93 G8
Hever Kent 32 E4
Heversham Cumb 129 K3
Hevingham Norfk 106 E7
Hewas Water Cnwll 4 F6
Hewelsfield Gloucs 54 E7
Hewish Somset 13 K2
Hewood Dorset 13 J2
Hexham Nthumb 150 B3
Hextable Kent 45 K6
Hexthorpe Donc 115 K2
Hexton Herts 59 J2
Hexworthy Cnwll 9 K8
Hexworthy Devon 6 F2
Heybridge Essex 61 G7
Heybridge Essex 61 K6
Heybrook Bay Devon 6 D6
Heydon Cambs 76 B6
Heydon Norfk 106 D6
Heydour Lincs 103 G5
Heylipoll Ag & B 188 C7
Heylor Shet 235 c3
Heysham Lancs 129 J7
Heyshott W Susx 18 B3
Heytesbury Wilts 27 L3
Heythrop Oxon 57 G3
Heywood Rochdl 122 C7
Heywood Wilts 27 K2
Hibaldstow N Linc 116 F2
Hickleton Donc 115 J1
Hickling Norfk 107 J7
Hickling Notts 102 B6
Hickling Green Norfk 107 J7
Hickstead W Susx 31 L7
Hidcote Bartrim Gloucs 71 L6
Hidcote Boyce Gloucs 71 L6
High Ackworth Wakefd 124 C6
Higham Barns 114 F1
Higham Derbys 101 H2
Higham Kent 33 G4
Higham Kent 46 B5
Higham Lancs 122 B3
Higham Suffk 77 H2
Higham Suffk 78 B7
Higham Ferrers Nhants 74 D2
Higham Gobion C Beds 59 J2
Higham Hill Gt Lon 45 G3
Higham on the Hill Leics 86 E4
Highampton Devon 10 C4
Highams Park Gt Lon 45 H2
High Ardwell D & G 144 C6
High Auldgirth D & G 154 F5
High Bankhill Cumb 148 F6
High Beach Essex 60 C7
High Bentham N York 130 C5
High Bickington Devon 23 J7
High Biggins Cumb 130 B4
High Blantyre S Lans 175 J6
High Bonnybridge Falk 175 L3
High Bray Devon 23 L5
Highbridge Somset 25 L3

Highbrook W Susx 32 C7
High Brooms Kent 33 G5
Highburton Kirk 123 J7
Highbury Gt Lon 44 F3
Highbury Somset 27 G2
High Casterton Cumb 130 C4
High Catton E R Yk 133 L8
Highclere Hants 41 H8
Highcliffe Dorset 16 B4
High Coniscliffe Darltn 141 G4
High Crosby Cumb 148 E3
High Cross E Ayrs 163 K1
High Cross Hants 30 B6
High Cross Herts 60 B4
High Cross Warwks 71 L2
High Drummore D & G 144 D7
High Easter Essex 60 F5
High Ellington N York 132 B3
Higher Ansty Dorset 14 E2
Higher Bartle Lancs 121 G4
Higher Bockhampton Dorset 14 D4
Higher Brixham Torbay 7 L5
High Ercall Wrekin 98 E8
Higher Chillington Somset 13 K1
Higher Folds Wigan 113 G2
Higher Gabwell Devon 7 L3
Higher Heysham Lancs 129 J7
Higher Irlam Salfd 113 G3
Higher Kinnerton Flints 97 L1
Higher Muddiford Devon 23 J4
Higher Penwortham Lancs 121 G5
Higher Prestacott Devon 9 K5
Higher Town Cnwll 4 C6
Higher Town Cnwll 4 F4
Higher Town IoS 2 b1
Higher Walton Lancs 121 H5
Higher Walton Warrtn 112 E4
Higher Wambrook Somset 13 H2
Higher Waterston Dorset 14 D4
Higher Wheelton Lancs 121 J6
Higher Whitley Ches W 112 F5
Higher Wincham Ches W 113 G6
Higher Wraxhall Dorset 14 B3
Higher Wych Ches W 98 C4
High Etherley Dur 140 F2
Highfield Gatesd 150 E3
Highfield N Ayrs 174 C7
High Garrett Essex 61 J3
Highgate Gt Lon 44 F3
High Grantley N York 132 C5
High Green Norfk 92 D3
High Green Norfk 92 E5
High Green Sheff 115 G3
High Halden Kent 34 B7
High Halstow Medway 46 C5
High Ham Somset 26 B5
High Harrogate N York 132 D7
High Hatton Shrops 98 E7
High Hauxley Nthumb 159 G2
High Hawsker N York 143 J5
High Hesket Cumb 148 E6
High Hoyland Barns 123 K8
High Hurstwood E Susx 32 E7
High Hutton N York 134 B5
High Ireby Cumb 147 M7
High Kilburn N York 133 H4
High Lands Dur 140 E3
Highlane Derbys 115 H5
High Lane Stockp 113 L4
High Lanes Cnwll 3 G4
Highleadon Gloucs 55 H4
High Legh Ches E 113 G5
Highleigh W Susx 18 A6
High Leven S on T 141 K5
Highley Shrops 84 D6
High Littleton BaNES 38 F8
High Lorton Cumb 137 G3
High Marnham Notts 116 D7
High Melton Donc 115 K2
High Mickley Nthumb 150 D3
Highmoor Oxon 42 B4
Highmoor Cross Oxon 42 B4
Highnam Gloucs 55 H4
High Newport Sundld 151 J4
High Newton Cumb 129 J3
High Nibthwaite Cumb 129 G2
High Offley Staffs 99 H7
High Ongar Essex 60 E7
High Onn Staffs 84 E1
High Park Corner Essex 62 C4
High Pennyvenie E Ayrs 163 L7
High Roding Essex 60 F4
High Salvington W Susx 18 F4
High Spen Gatesd 150 E3
Highsted Kent 34 B3
High Street Cnwll 4 F5
Highstreet Kent 34 E3
Highstreet Green Surrey 31 G4
Hightae D & G 155 J6
Highter's Heath Birm 85 J7
Hightown Sefton 111 J2
Hightown Green Suffk 77 L4
High Toynton Lincs 118 C7
High Valleyfield Fife 176 D2
Highweek Devon 7 J2
Highwood Hill Gt Lon 44 E2
Highworth Swindn 40 D2
High Wray Cumb 137 K7
High Wych Herts 60 D5
High Wycombe Bucks 42 E2
Hilborough Norfk 91 J4
Hilcott Wilts 40 C8
Hildenborough Kent 32 F4
Hilden Park Kent 33 G4
Hildersham Cambs 76 D5
Hilderstone Staffs 99 L5
Hilderthorpe E R Yk 135 J6
Hilgay Norfk 90 E4
Hill S Glos 38 F2
Hill Warwks 72 F2
Hillam N York 124 D5
Hill Brow Hants 30 C6
Hillbutts Dorset 15 J3
Hill Chorlton Staffs 99 H5
Hillcliffiane Derbys 100 F3
Hill Common Somset 25 H6
Hilldyke Lincs 104 B3
Hillend Fife 176 F2
Hill End Fife 185 L7
Hill End Gloucs 70 F6
Hillend Mdloth 177 H5
Hillend N Lans 175 L5
Hillesden Bucks 58 B3
Hillesley Gloucs 39 H3
Hillfarrance Somset 25 J6
Hill Green Kent 46 D7
Hillhead Abers 216 B7
Hill Head Hants 17 G2
Hillhead S Lans 165 J2
Hillhead of Cocklaw Abers 217 K5
Hilliclay Highld 231 H3
Hillingdon Gt Lon 43 H4
Hillington C Glas 174 F5
Hillington Norfk 105 H7
Hillmorton Warwks 87 G8
Hill of Beath Fife 176 F1
Hill of Fearn Highld 223 H5
Hillowton D & G 146 D3
Hill Ridware Staffs 100 B8
Hillside Abers 207 H5
Hillside Angus 197 H4
Hill Side Kirk 123 H6
Hills Town Derbys 115 J7
Hillstreet Hants 29 G7
Hillswick Shet 235 c3
Hill Top Sandw 85 H5
Hill Top Wakefd 123 L7
Hillwell Shet 235 c8
Hilmarton Wilts 40 A5
Hilperton Wilts 39 K8
Hilsea C Port 17 J2
Hilston E R Yk 127 G4
Hilton Border 179 H7
Hilton Cambs 75 K2
Hilton Cumb 139 G3
Hilton Derbys 100 E6
Hilton Dorset 14 E2
Hilton Dur 140 F3
Hilton Highld 223 J6
Hilton S on T 141 K5
Hilton Shrops 84 D4
Hilton Park Services Staffs 85 G3
Himbleton Worcs 71 G3
Himley Staffs 84 F5
Hincaster Cumb 129 L3
Hinchley Wood Surrey 44 D6
Hinckley Leics 86 E5
Hinderclay Suffk 92 B7
Hinderwell N York 143 G4
Hindhead Surrey 30 E4
Hindley Wigan 112 F1
Hindlip Worcs 70 F3
Hindolveston Norfk 106 C6
Hindon Wilts 27 K5
Hindringham Norfk 106 B5
Hingham Norfk 92 B3
Hinstock Shrops 99 G7
Hintlesham Suffk 78 C5
Hinton Herefs 69 G6
Hinton S Glos 39 G5
Hinton Shrops 83 H2
Hinton Ampner Hants 29 L6
Hinton Blewett BaNES 26 E1
Hinton Charterhouse BaNES 39 H8
Hinton-in-the-Hedges Nhants 73 H6
Hinton Martell Dorset 15 J2
Hinton on the Green Worcs 71 H6
Hinton Parva Swindn 40 E4
Hinton St George Somset 26 B8
Hinton St Mary Dorset 27 H7
Hinton Waldrist Oxon 57 G7
Hints Staffs 85 L3
Hinwick Bed 74 D3
Hinxhill Kent 34 D6
Hinxton Cambs 76 C5
Hinxworth Herts 75 J6
Hipperholme Calder 123 H5
Hipswell N York 140 F7
Hirn Abers 206 D5
Hirnant Powys 97 G7
Hirst Nthumb 159 G5
Hirst Courtney N York 124 F5
Hirwaun Rhondd 52 E6
Hiscott Devon 23 J6
Histon Cambs 76 B2
Hitcham Suffk 78 B4
Hitcham Causeway Suffk 78 B4
Hitcham Street Suffk 78 B4
Hitchin Herts 59 K3
Hither Green Gt Lon 45 H5
Hittisleigh Devon 11 H5
Hive E R Yk 125 J4
Hixon Staffs 100 A7
Hoaden Kent 35 H3
Hoar Cross Staffs 100 C7
Hoarwithy Herefs 54 D3
Hoath Kent 47 K7
Hobarris Shrops 82 F7
Hobkirk Border 167 J7
Hobson Dur 150 F4
Hoby Leics 102 A8
Hockering Norfk 92 C2
Hockerton Notts 102 B2
Hockley Essex 46 D2
Hockley Heath Solhll 85 L8
Hockliffe C Beds 58 F3
Hockwold cum Wilton Norfk 91 G6
Hockworthy Devon 25 G7
Hoddesdon Herts 60 B6
Hoddlesden Bl w D 121 L6
Hoddom Cross D & G 155 L7
Hoddom Mains D & G 155 K7
Hodgeston Pembks 49 H7
Hodnet Shrops 98 E6
Hodsock Notts 115 L4
Hodsoll Street Kent 45 M7
Hodson Swindn 40 D4
Hodthorpe Derbys 115 K6
Hoe Norfk 92 B1
Hogben's Hill Kent 34 D4
Hoggeston Bucks 58 D3
Hoggrill's End Warwks 86 B5
Hoghton Lancs 121 J5
Hognaston Derbys 100 E3
Hogsthorpe Lincs 119 H6
Holbeach Lincs 104 B7
Holbeach Bank Lincs 104 B6
Holbeach Clough Lincs 104 B6
Holbeach Drove Lincs 89 K2
Holbeach Hurn Lincs 104 C6
Holbeach St Johns Lincs 104 B8
Holbeach St Mark's Lincs 104 B6
Holbeach St Matthew Lincs 104 C6
Holbeck Notts 115 K6
Holberrow Green Worcs 71 H3
Holbeton Devon 6 F5
Holborn Gt Lon 44 F4
Holbrook Derbys 101 G4
Holbrook Suffk 78 E6
Holbrooks Covtry 86 D6
Holbury Hants 16 E2
Holcombe Devon 12 B7
Holcombe Somset 26 F2
Holcombe Rogus Devon 25 G7
Holcot Nhants 73 L1
Holden Lancs 122 B1
Holdenby Nhants 73 K2
Holder's Green Essex 61 G3
Holdgate Shrops 83 L5
Holdingham Lincs 103 H3
Holditch Dorset 13 J2
Holemoor Devon 10 B4
Holford Somset 25 J3
Holgate C York 124 E1
Holker Cumb 129 H4
Holkham Norfk 105 L4
Hollacombe Devon 9 K4
Holland Fen Lincs 103 L3
Holland-on-Sea Essex 62 E5
Hollandstoun Ork 234 e3
Hollee D & G 148 A2
Hollesley Suffk 79 H5
Hollicombe Torbay 7 K4
Hollingbourne Kent 33 L3
Hollingbury Br & H 19 J4
Hollingdon Bucks 58 E3
Hollington Derbys 100 E5
Hollington Staffs 100 B5
Hollingworth Tamesd 114 A3
Hollinsclough Staffs 114 B7
Hollins End Sheff 115 G5
Hollins Green Warrtn 113 G4
Hollinswood Wrekin 84 C2

Hollocombe Devon 10 F3
Holloway Derbys 100 F2
Holloway Gt Lon 44 F3
Hollowell Nhants 73 K1
Hollowmoor Heath Ches W 112 C7
Hollows D & G 156 C6
Hollybush Caerph 53 J7
Hollybush E Ayrs 163 K6
Hollybush Herefs 70 D6
Hollym E R Yk 127 H5
Holmbridge Kirk 114 C1
Holmbury St Mary Surrey 31 J3
Holmbush Cnwll 5 G5
Holmcroft Staffs 99 K7
Holme Cambs 89 H6
Holme Cumb 129 L4
Holme Kirk 114 C1
Holme N York 132 E3
Holme Notts 102 D2
Holme Chapel Lancs 122 C5
Holme Hale Norfk 91 K3
Holme Lacy Herefs 69 L7
Holme Marsh Herefs 69 G4
Holme next the Sea Norfk 105 H4
Holme on the Wolds E R Yk 126 B2
Holme Pierrepont Notts 101 L5
Holmer Herefs 69 K6
Holmer Green Bucks 42 E2
Holme St Cuthbert Cumb 147 J5
Holmes Chapel Ches E 113 H7
Holmesfield Derbys 114 F6
Holmeswood Lancs 120 F6
Holmethorpe Surrey 32 B3
Holme upon Spalding Moor E R Yk 125 J3
Holmewood Derbys 115 H7
Holmfirth Kirk 123 H8
Holmhead E Ayrs 164 B5
Holmpton E R Yk 127 J5
Holmrook Cumb 136 E7
Holmsford Bridge Crematorium N Ayrs 163 J2
Holmside Dur 150 F5
Holne Devon 7 G3
Holnicote Somset 24 E3
Holsworthy Devon 9 J4
Holsworthy Beacon Devon 9 K3
Holt Dorset 15 J2
Holt Norfk 106 C5
Holt Wilts 39 K7
Holt Worcs 70 E3
Holt Wrexhm 98 B2
Holtby C York 133 K8
Holt End Worcs 71 J1
Holt Heath Worcs 70 E2
Holton Oxon 57 L6
Holton Somset 27 G6
Holton Suffk 93 J7
Holton cum Beckering Lincs 117 J5
Holton le Clay Lincs 118 C2
Holton le Moor Lincs 117 H3
Holton St Mary Suffk 78 C6
Holwell Dorset 14 D1
Holwell Herts 59 K2
Holwell Leics 102 B7
Holwell Oxon 56 E6
Holwick Dur 139 K2
Holybourne Hants 30 B4
Holyhead IoA 108 C5
Holy Island IoA 108 C5
Holy Island Nthumb 169 H2
Holy Island Nthumb 169 H2
Holymoorside Derbys 115 G7
Holyport W & M 42 E5
Holystone Nthumb 158 B2
Holytown N Lans 175 K6
Holytown Crematorium N Lans 175 K6
Holywell C Beds 59 G5
Holywell Cambs 75 L1
Holywell Cnwll 4 B4
Holywell Dorset 14 B2
Holywell Flints 111 G6
Holywell Green Calder 123 G6
Holywell Lake Somset 25 H7
Holywell Row Suffk 91 G7
Holywood D & G 155 G6
Holywood Village D & G 155 G6
Homer Shrops 84 B3
Homer Green Sefton 111 K2
Homersfield Suffk 93 G6
Homington Wilts 28 C6
Honeybourne Worcs 71 K5
Honeychurch Devon 10 F4
Honeystreet Wilts 40 C7
Honey Tye Suffk 77 L7
Honiley Warwks 86 B8
Honing Norfk 107 G6
Honingham Norfk 92 D2
Honington Lincs 102 F4
Honington Suffk 91 K8
Honington Warwks 72 C6
Honiton Devon 12 F3
Honley Kirk 123 H7
Honor Oak Crematorium Gt Lon 45 G5
Hooe C Plym 6 D5
Hooe E Susx 20 E4
Hoo Green Ches E 113 G5
Hoohill Bpool 120 D3
Hook E R Yk 125 H5
Hook Gt Lon 44 D7
Hook Hants 30 B1
Hook Pembks 49 G5
Hook Wilts 40 B4
Hooke Dorset 14 A3
Hook Green Kent 33 H6
Hook Green Kent 45 L6
Hook Norton Oxon 57 G2
Hookway Devon 11 K5
Hooley Surrey 32 B3
Hoo St Werburgh Medway 46 C5
Hooton Levitt Rothm 115 K3
Hooton Pagnell Donc 124 D8
Hooton Roberts Rothm 115 J3
Hope Derbys 114 D5
Hope Devon 7 G7
Hope Flints 97 L2
Hope Staffs 100 C2
Hope Bagot Shrops 83 L8
Hope Bowdler Shrops 83 J5
Hopehouse Border 166 D6
Hopeman Moray 214 E1
Hope Mansell Herefs 54 F4
Hopesay Shrops 83 H6
Hope under Dinmore Herefs 69 K4
Hopgrove C York 133 K8
Hopperton N York 132 F7
Hopstone Shrops 84 D5
Hopton Derbys 100 E2
Hopton Staffs 99 L7
Hopton Suffk 92 B7
Hopton Cangeford Shrops 83 K7
Hopton Castle Shrops 83 G7
Hoptonheath Shrops 83 H7
Hopton on Sea Norfk 93 L4
Hopton Wafers Shrops 84 B7
Hopwas Staffs 85 L3
Hopwood Worcs 85 J7
Hopwood Park Services Worcs 85 J8
Horam E Susx 20 C3
Horbling Lincs 103 J5
Horbury Wakefd 123 K6
Horden Dur 151 K6
Hordle Hants 16 C4
Hordley Shrops 98 B6
Horfield Bristl 38 E5
Horham Suffk 92 E8
Horkesley Heath Essex 62 B3
Horkstow N Linc 126 B6
Horley Oxon 72 E5
Horley Surrey 32 B5
Hornblotton Green Somset 26 E5
Hornby Lancs 130 B5
Hornby N York 132 C2
Hornby N York 141 J6
Horncastle Lincs 118 C7
Hornchurch Gt Lon 45 K3
Horncliffe Nthumb 179 J7
Horndean Border 179 J8
Horndean Hants 30 B8
Horndon Devon 10 D8
Horndon on the Hill Thurr 46 A4
Horne Surrey 32 C4
Horner Somset 24 D3
Horning Norfk 107 H8
Horninghold Leics 88 B4
Horninglow Staffs 100 E7
Horningsea Cambs 76 C3
Horningsham Wilts 27 J3
Horningtoft Norfk 105 M7
Horns Cross Devon 22 F6
Hornsea E R Yk 126 F2
Hornsey Gt Lon 44 F3
Hornton Oxon 72 E5
Horra Shet 235 d2
Horrabridge Devon 6 D2
Horringer Suffk 77 J3
Horrocksford Lancs 121 L2
Horsebridge Devon 6 B2
Horsebridge E Susx 20 C4
Horsebridge Hants 29 G5
Horsehay Wrekin 84 C3
Horseheath Cambs 76 E5
Horsehouse N York 131 K4
Horsell Surrey 43 G8
Horseman's Green Wrexhm 98 C4
Horsey Norfk 107 K7
Horsey Somset 25 L4
Horsford Norfk 92 E1
Horsforth Leeds 123 J3
Horsham W Susx 31 K5
Horsham Worcs 70 D3
Horsham St Faith Norfk 92 E1
Horsington Lincs 117 K7
Horsington Somset 27 G6
Horsley Derbys 101 G4
Horsley Gloucs 39 J2
Horsley Nthumb 150 D2
Horsley Nthumb 157 L3
Horsleycross Street Essex 62 D3
Horsleyhill Border 167 H5
Horsley Woodhouse Derbys 101 H4
Horsmonden Kent 33 J5
Horspath Oxon 57 L6
Horstead Norfk 106 F8
Horsted Keynes W Susx 32 C7
Horton Bucks 58 F4
Horton Dorset 15 J2
Horton Lancs 122 C1
Horton Nhants 74 B4
Horton S Glos 39 H4
Horton Somset 25 L7
Horton Staffs 99 L2
Horton Swans 50 F7
Horton W & M 43 G5
Horton Wilts 40 B7
Horton Wrekin 84 C1
Horton-cum-Studley Oxon 57 L5
Horton Green Ches W 98 C3
Horton-in-Ribblesdale N York 130 F5
Horton Kirby Kent 45 K6
Horwich Bolton 121 J7
Horwood Devon 23 H6
Hoscote Border 166 F6
Hose Leics 102 B6
Hosh P & K 185 H3
Hoswick Shet 235 c7
Hotham E R Yk 125 L4
Hothfield Kent 34 C5
Hoton Leics 101 L7
Hough Ches E 99 G3
Hougham Lincs 102 E4
Hough Green Halton 112 C4
Hough-on-the-Hill Lincs 102 F3
Houghton Cambs 75 K1
Houghton Hants 29 G5
Houghton Pembks 49 G6
Houghton W Susx 18 D4
Houghton Conquest C Beds 74 F6
Houghton Green E Susx 21 H2
Houghton-le-Spring Sundld 151 H5
Houghton on the Hill Leics 87 J3
Houghton Regis C Beds 59 G4
Houghton St Giles Norfk 105 L5
Hound Green Hants 42 B8
Houndslow Border 178 D8
Houndwood Border 179 H5
Hounslow Gt Lon 43 J5
Househill Highld 213 L4
Houses Hill Kirk 123 J6
Housieside Abers 207 G1
Houston Rens 174 D5
Houstry Highld 227 K2
Houton Ork 234 b6
Hove Br & H 19 J5
Hoveringham Notts 102 B3
Hoveton Norfk 107 G8
Hovingham N York 133 K4
How Caple Herefs 54 E3
Howden E R Yk 125 H5
Howden-le-Wear Dur 150 E7
Howe Highld 231 K3
Howe N York 132 E4
Howe Norfk 92 F4
Howe Bridge Crematorium Wigan 112 F2
Howe Green Essex 61 J7
Howegreen Essex 61 K7
Howell Lincs 103 J4
Howe of Teuchar Abers 216 E5
Howes D & G 147 L2
Howe Street Essex 61 H5
Howe Street Essex 77 G7
Howey Powys 68 B3
Howgate Cumb 136 D3
Howgate Mdloth 177 H6
Howick Nthumb 169 K5
Howlett End Essex 76 E7
Howley Somset 13 H1
How Mill Cumb 148 E4
Howmore W Isls 233 b7
Hownam Border 168 B5
Howsham N Linc 117 H2
Howsham N York 133 L6
Howtel Nthumb 168 D3
How Wood Herts 59 J7
Howwood Rens 174 D6
Hoxa Ork 234 c7
Hoxne Suffk 92 E7
Hoy Ork 234 b7
Hoylake Wirral 111 H4
Hoyland Nether Barns 115 G2
Hoyland Swaine Barns 114 E1

Hubberston Pembks....48 E6
Huby N York....123 K2
Huby N York....133 J6
Hucclecote Gloucs....55 K4
Hucking Kent....33 L2
Hucknall Notts....101 K3
Huddersfield Kirk....123 H7
Huddersfield Crematorium Kirk....123 H6
Huddington Worcs....71 G3
Hudswell N York....140 E7
Huggate E R Yk....134 D7
Hughenden Valley Bucks....42 E2
Hughley Shrops....83 L4
Hugh Town IoS....2 b2
Huish Devon....10 D3
Huish Wilts....40 C7
Huish Champflower Somset....25 G5
Huish Episcopi Somset....26 B6
Hulcott Bucks....58 D5
Hulham Devon....12 C5
Hulland Derbys....100 E3
Hulland Ward Derbys....100 E3
Hullavington Wilts....39 K4
Hullbridge Essex....46 D2
Hull, Kingston upon C KuH....126 D5
Hulme Manch....113 J3
Hulme Staffs....99 L4
Hulme Warrtn....112 E4
Hulme End Staffs....100 C2
Hulme Walfield Ches E....113 J7
Hulverstone IoW....16 E5
Hulver Street Suffk....93 K6
Humber Bridge N Linc....126 C5
Humberside Airport N Linc....126 D7
Humberston NE Lin....118 D1
Humberstone C Leic....87 J3
Humbie E Loth....178 B5
Humbleton E R Yk....126 F4
Humby Lincs....103 G6
Hume Border....167 L2
Humshaugh Nthumb....158 A7
Huna Highld....231 L2
Huncote Leics....87 G4
Hundalee Border....167 K5
Hunderthwaite Dur....140 C3
Hundleby Lincs....118 E7
Hundleton Pembks....49 G7
Hundon Suffk....77 G5
Hundred House Powys....68 C4
Hungarton Leics....87 K3
Hungerford Somset....25 G4
Hungerford W Berk....41 G6
Hungerford Newtown W Berk....41 G6
Hungerstone Herefs....69 J7
Hunmanby N York....135 H4
Hunningham Warwks....72 D2
Hunsbury Hill Nhants....73 K3
Hunsdon Herts....60 C5
Hunsingore N York....132 F8
Hunslet Leeds....123 L4
Hunsonby Cumb....149 G7
Hunstanton Norfk....105 G4
Hunstanworth Dur....150 B5
Hunsterson Ches E....99 G4
Hunston Suffk....77 L2
Hunston W Susx....18 B5
Hunstrete BaNES....38 F7
Hunsworth Kirk....123 J5
Hunter's Quay Ag & B....173 K3
Huntham Somset....25 M6
Hunthill Lodge Angus....196 D3
Huntingdon Cambs....89 J8
Huntingfield Suffk....93 G8
Huntington C York....133 J7
Huntington Ches W....112 B8
Huntington E Loth....178 B4
Huntington Herefs....68 E4
Huntington Staffs....85 H2
Huntley Gloucs....55 G4
Huntly Abers....215 L6
Hunton Kent....33 J4
Hunton N York....132 B2
Huntscott Somset....24 E3
Huntsham Devon....24 F7
Huntshaw Devon....23 H6
Huntspill Somset....25 L3
Huntstile Somset....25 K5
Huntworth Somset....25 L4
Hunwick Dur....140 F2
Hunworth Norfk....106 C5
Hurdcott Wilts....28 D5
Hurdsfield Ches E....113 L6
Hurley W & M....42 D4
Hurley Warwks....86 B4
Hurley Common Warwks....86 B4
Hurlford E Ayrs....163 L3
Hurn Dorset....15 L3
Hursley Hants....29 H6
Hurst Wokham....42 C5
Hurstbourne Priors Hants....29 H3
Hurstbourne Tarrant Hants....29 G2
Hurst Green E Susx....33 J7
Hurst Green Essex....62 C5
Hurst Green Lancs....121 K3
Hurst Green Surrey....32 D3
Hurst Hill Dudley....85 G5
Hurstpierpoint W Susx....19 J3
Hurstwood Lancs....122 C4
Hurtiso Ork....234 c6
Hurworth-on-Tees Darltn....141 H5
Hurworth Place Darltn....141 H5
Husbands Bosworth Leics....87 J6
Husborne Crawley C Beds....74 D7
Husthwaite N York....133 H4
Hutcliffe Wood Crematorium Sheff....115 G5
Huthwaite Notts....101 J2
Huttoft Lincs....119 G6
Hutton Border....179 J7
Hutton E R Yk....134 F8
Hutton Essex....45 M2
Hutton Lancs....121 G5
Hutton N Som....37 M8
Hutton Buscel N York....134 F3
Hutton Conyers N York....132 E5
Hutton Cranswick E R Yk....126 C1
Hutton End Cumb....148 D7
Hutton Henry Dur....151 K7
Hutton-le-Hole N York....133 L2
Hutton Lowcross R & Cl....142 D4
Hutton Magna Dur....140 E5
Hutton Roof Cumb....130 B4
Hutton Roof Cumb....148 C7
Hutton Rudby N York....141 K6
Hutton Sessay N York....133 G4
Hutton Wandesley N York....124 D1
Huxham Devon....12 B3
Huxley Ches W....98 D1
Huyton Knows....112 C4
Hycemoor Cumb....128 D2
Hyde Tamesd....113 L3
Hyde Heath Bucks....58 F7
Hyde Lea Staffs....99 K8
Hylands House & Park Essex....61 G7
Hyndford Bridge S Lans....165 H2
Hynish Ag & B....188 C8
Hyssington Powys....82 F5
Hythe Essex....62 B3
Hythe Hants....16 E2
Hythe Kent....34 F7
Hythe End W & M....43 G6

I

Ibberton Dorset....14 E2
Ible Derbys....100 E2
Ibsley Hants....15 L1
Ibstock Leics....86 E2
Ibstone Bucks....42 C2
Ibthorpe Hants....29 G2
Iburndale N York....143 H5
Ibworth Hants....29 K1
Ichrachan Ag & B....182 E2
Ickburgh Norfk....91 J4
Ickenham Gt Lon....43 H3
Ickford Bucks....57 M6
Ickham Kent....35 G3
Ickleford Herts....59 K2
Icklesham E Susx....21 H3
Ickleton Cambs....76 C5
Icklingham Suffk....91 H8
Ickornshaw N York....122 E2
Ickwell Green C Beds....75 G5
Icomb Gloucs....56 E4
Idbury Oxon....56 E4
Iddesleigh Devon....10 E3
Ide Devon....11 K6
Ideford Devon....7 K1
Ide Hill Kent....32 E3
Iden E Susx....21 H2
Iden Green Kent....33 J5
Iden Green Kent....33 K6
Idle C Brad....123 H3
Idless Cnwll....4 C6
Idlicote Warwks....72 C5
Idmiston Wilts....28 D4
Idole Carmth....50 E3
Idridgehay Derbys....100 F3
Idrigill Highld....208 F2
Idstone Oxon....40 E4
Iffley Oxon....57 K7
Ifield W Susx....31 L4
Ifold W Susx....31 G5
Iford Bmouth....15 L4
Iford E Susx....19 L4
Ifton Mons....38 C3
Ightfield Shrops....98 E5
Ightham Kent....33 G2
Ilam Staffs....100 C3
Ilchester Somset....26 D6
Ilderton Nthumb....168 F5
Ilford Gt Lon....45 H3
Ilford Somset....26 A7
Ilfracombe Devon....23 H2
Ilkeston Derbys....101 J4
Ilketshall St Andrew Suffk....93 H6
Ilketshall St Margaret Suffk....93 H6
Ilkley C Brad....123 G2
Illand Cnwll....5 L1
Illey Dudley....85 H7
Illogan Cnwll....3 H3
Illston on the Hill Leics....87 K4
Ilmer Bucks....58 C6
Ilmington Warwks....72 B5
Ilminster Somset....26 A8
Ilsington Devon....7 H2
Ilston Swans....51 H7
Ilton N York....132 B4
Ilton Somset....25 M7
Imachar N Ayrs....161 L2
Immingham NE Lin....126 F7
Immingham Dock NE Lin....126 F7
Impington Cambs....76 C2
Ince Ches W....112 C6
Ince Blundell Sefton....111 K2
Ince-in-Makerfield Wigan....112 E1
Inchbae Lodge Hotel Highld....221 K7
Inchbare Angus....196 F4
Inchberry Moray....215 G4
Incheril Highld....211 G3
Inchinnan Rens....174 E5
Inchlaggan Highld....201 J5
Inchmichael P & K....186 D3
Inchnacardoch Hotel Highld....202 B3
Inchnadamph Highld....224 F4
Inchture P & K....186 D2
Inchvuilt Highld....211 K6
Inchyra P & K....186 C4
Indian Queens Cnwll....4 E4
Ingatestone Essex....61 G7
Ingbirchworth Barns....114 E1
Ingestre Staffs....99 L7
Ingham Lincs....116 F5
Ingham Norfk....107 H7
Ingham Suffk....77 J1
Ingham Corner Norfk....107 H6
Ingleby Derbys....101 G6
Ingleby Arncliffe N York....141 K6
Ingleby Barwick S on T....141 K4
Ingleby Greenhow N York....142 C6
Ingleigh Green Devon....10 E4
Inglesbatch BaNES....39 G7
Inglesham Swindn....56 D7
Ingleston D & G....147 G2
Ingleton Dur....140 F3
Ingleton N York....130 D5
Inglewhite Lancs....121 H3
Ingoe Nthumb....158 C7
Ingol Lancs....121 G4
Ingoldisthorpe Norfk....105 G6
Ingoldmells Lincs....119 H7
Ingoldsby Lincs....103 G6
Ingram Nthumb....168 F6
Ingrave Essex....45 M2
Ingrow C Brad....122 F3
Ings Cumb....138 C7
Ingst S Glos....38 E3
Ingthorpe Rutlnd....88 E2
Ingworth Norfk....106 E6
Inkberrow Worcs....71 H3
Inkhorn Abers....217 H6
Inkpen W Berk....41 G7
Inkstack Highld....231 J2
Innellan Ag & B....173 K4
Innerleithen Border....166 E3
Innerleven Fife....186 F7
Innermessan D & G....144 C3
Innerwick E Loth....178 F4
Innesmill Moray....215 G2
Insch Abers....216 C8
Insh Highld....203 J5
Inskip Lancs....120 F3
Instow Devon....23 G5
Intake Sheff....115 H5
Inver Abers....204 F6
Inver Highld....223 J5
Inver P & K....194 F7
Inverailort Highld....190 F1
Inveralligin Highld....210 C3
Inverallochy Abers....217 K2
Inveran Highld....222 D2
Inveraray Ag & B....182 F5
Inverarish Highld....209 J7
Inverarity Angus....196 D7
Inverarnan Stirlg....183 K4
Inverasdale Highld....219 J4
Inverbeg Ag & B....183 K7
Inverbervie Abers....197 K2
Inver-boyndie Abers....216 C2
Invercreran House Hotel Ag & B....191 K6
Inverdruie Highld....203 L3
Inveresk E Loth....177 K4
Inveresragan Ag & B....182 E1
Inverey Abers....204 D7
Inverfarigaig Highld....202 D2
Inverfolla Ag & B....191 J7
Invergarry Highld....201 L5

Invergeldie P & K 184 F2
Invergloy Highld 201 K7
Invergordon Highld 222 F7
Invergowrie P & K 186 F2
Inverguseran Highld 200 B4
Inverhadden P & K 193 L5
Inverherive Hotel Stirlg 183 L3
Inverie Highld 200 B5
Inverinan Ag & B 182 E4
Inverinate Highld 200 E2
Inverkeilor Angus 197 G6
Inverkeithing Fife 176 F2
Inverkeithny Abers 216 C5
Inverkip Inver 173 L4
Inverkirkaig Highld 224 C4
Inverlael Highld 220 F4
Inverlair Highld 192 E1
Inverliever Lodge Ag & B 182 C6
Inverlochy Ag & B 183 H2
Invermark Angus 196 D1
Invermoriston Highld 202 C3
Invernaver Highld 229 L4
Inverness Highld 213 G5
Inverness Airport Highld 213 J4
Inverness Crematorium Highld 212 F5
Invernoaden Ag & B 183 G7
Inveroran Hotel Ag & B 192 D7
Inverquharity Angus 196 C5
Inverquhomery Abers 217 J5
Inverroy Highld 201 K8
Inversanda Highld 191 J4
Invershiel Highld 200 E2
Invershin Highld 222 D3
Invershore Highld 231 J8
Inversnaid Hotel Stirlg 183 K5
Inverugie Abers 217 L5
Inveruglas Ag & B 183 K5
Inveruglass Highld 203 J5
Inverurie Abers 206 E2
Inwardleigh Devon 10 E5
Inworth Essex 61 L4
Iona Ag & B 180 D3
Iping W Susx 30 D6
Ipplepen Devon 7 J3
Ipsden Oxon 41 M4
Ipstones Staffs 100 A3
Ipswich Suffk 78 E5
Ipswich Crematorium Suffk 78 E5
Irby Wirral 111 J5
Irby in the Marsh Lincs 118 F8
Irby upon Humber NE Lin 117 K1
Irchester Nhants 74 D2
Ireby Cumb 147 M7
Ireby Lancs 130 C4
Ireleth Cumb 128 F4
Ireshopeburn Dur 149 L7
Irlam Salfd 113 G3
Irnham Lincs 103 G7
Iron Acton S Glos 39 G4
Ironbridge Wrekin 84 C3
Ironbridge Gorge Wrekin 84 C3
Ironmacannie D & G 154 B6
Ironville Derbys 101 H3
Irstead Norfk 107 H7
Irthington Cumb 148 E3
Irthlingborough Nhants 74 D1
Irton N York 134 F3
Irvine N Ayrs 163 H2
Isauld Highld 230 E3
Isbister Shet 235 c2
Isbister Shet 235 d4
Isfield E Susx 19 L3
Isham Nhants 88 C8
Isington Hants 30 C3
Islay Ag & B 171 G4
Islay Airport Ag & B 170 F7
Isle Abbotts Somset 26 A7
Isle Brewers Somset 26 A7
Isleham Cambs 90 F8
Isle of Dogs Gt Lon 45 G4
Isle of Grain Medway 46 E5
Isle of Lewis W Isls 232 f2
Isle of Man IoM 237 c4
Isle of Man Ronaldsway Airport IoM 237 b7
Isle of Mull Ag & B 181 J1
Isle of Purbeck Dorset 15 J5
Isle of Sheppey Kent 46 F6
Isle of Skye Highld 208 F6
Isle of Thanet Kent 35 J2
Isle of Walney Cumb 128 E6
Isle of Whithorn D & G 145 K7
Isle of Wight IoW 17 G5
Isle of Wight Crematorium IoW 17 G4
Isleornsay Highld 199 L3
Isles of Scilly IoS 2 b1
Isles of Scilly St Mary's Airport IoS 2 b2
Islesteps D & G 155 G7
Islet Village Guern 236 d2
Isleworth Gt Lon 44 D5
Isley Walton Leics 101 H7
Islibhig W Isls 232 d3
Islington Gt Lon 44 F3
Islington Crematorium Gt Lon 44 F3
Islip Nhants 88 E7
Islip Oxon 57 K5
Islivig W Isls 232 d3
Isombridge Wrekin 83 L2
Itchen Abbas Hants 29 K5
Itchen Stoke Hants 29 K5
Itchingfield W Susx 31 J5
Itteringham Norfk 106 D6
Itton Mons 38 C2
Itton Common Mons 38 C2
Ivegill Cumb 148 D6
Iver Bucks 43 G4
Iver Heath Bucks 43 G4
Iveston Dur 150 E5
Ivinghoe Bucks 58 F5
Ivinghoe Aston Bucks 58 F4
Ivington Herefs 69 J3
Ivybridge Devon 6 F5
Ivychurch Kent 21 K1
Ivy Hatch Kent 33 G3
Iwade Kent 46 E6
Iwerne Courtney or Shroton Dorset 27 K8
Iwerne Minster Dorset 27 K8
Ixworth Suffk 77 L1
Ixworth Thorpe Suffk 91 K8

J

Jack-in-the-Green Devon 12 C4
Jackton S Lans 175 G7
Jacobstow Cnwll 9 G5
Jacobstowe Devon 10 E4
Jameston Pembks 49 H7
Jamestown Highld 212 D3
Jamestown W Duns 174 D3
Janetstown Highld 227 L3
Janetstown Highld 231 L5
Jardine Hall D & G 155 J5
Jarrow S Tyne 151 H3
Jasper's Green Essex 61 H3
Jawcraig Falk 175 L4
Jaywick Essex 62 D5
Jedburgh Border 167 K5
Jeffreyston Pembks 49 J6
Jemimaville Highld 213 H2
Jerbourg Guern 236 d4
Jersey Jersey 236 c6
Jersey Airport Jersey 236 b7
Jersey Crematorium Jersey 236 c7
Jesmond N u Ty 151 G2
Jevington E Susx 20 B5
Jockey End Herts 59 H5
Johnby Cumb 148 D7
John Lennon Airport Lpool 112 B5
John o' Groats Highld 231 L2
Johnshaven Abers 197 J3
Johnston Pembks 48 F5
Johnstone D & G 155 M3
Johnstone Rens 174 D5
Johnstonebridge D & G 155 J4
Johnstown Carmth 50 E2
Johnstown Wrexhm 97 L4
Joppa C Edin 177 J4
Joppa Cerdgn 66 D2
Joppa S Ayrs 163 K5
Jordanston Pembks 64 C7
Joyden's Wood Kent 45 K5
Juniper Nthumb 150 B3
Juniper Green C Edin 177 G5
Jura Ag & B 171 J2
Jurassic Coast Devon 13 H4
Jurby IoM 237 c2

K

Kaber Cumb 139 H5
Kaimend S Lans 165 J1
Kames Ag & B 173 G4
Kames E Ayrs 164 D4
Kea Cnwll 4 C7
Keadby N Linc 125 K7
Keal Cotes Lincs 104 B1
Kearsley Bolton 113 H1
Kearsney Kent 35 H6
Kearstwick Cumb 130 B4
Kedington Suffk 77 G5
Kedleston Derbys 100 F4
Keelby Lincs 126 E8
Keele Staffs 99 J4
Keele Services Staffs 99 J4
Keelham C Brad 123 G4
Keeston Pembks 48 F4
Keevil Wilts 39 L8
Kegworth Leics 101 J7
Kehelland Cnwll 3 G3
Keig Abers 206 B2
Keighley C Brad 122 F3
Keighley Crematorium C Brad 122 F3
Keilarsbrae Clacks 185 J8
Keillour P & K 185 K3
Keiloch Abers 204 E6
Keils Ag & B 171 K5
Keinton Mandeville Somset 26 D5
Keir Mill D & G 154 E4
Keisley Cumb 139 G3
Keiss Highld 231 L4
Keith Moray 215 J4
Keithick P & K 195 K8
Keithock Angus 196 F4
Keithtown Highld 212 E3
Kelbrook Lancs 122 D2
Kelby Lincs 103 G4
Keld N York 139 K6
Kelfield N York 124 F3
Kelham Notts 102 C2
Kelhead D & G 147 K2
Kellamergh Lancs 120 E5
Kellas Angus 187 G1
Kellas Moray 214 E4
Kellaton Devon 7 J7
Kelling Norfk 106 C4
Kellington N York 124 E5
Kelloe Dur 151 J7
Kelloholm D & G 164 E6
Kelly Devon 9 K8
Kelmarsh Nhants 87 K7
Kelmscott Oxon 56 E7
Kelsale Suffk 79 H2
Kelsall Ches W 112 D7
Kelshall Herts 75 K7
Kelsick Cumb 147 L5
Kelso Border 167 L3
Kelstedge Derbys 115 G8
Kelstern Lincs 118 C4
Kelston BaNES 39 G6
Keltneyburn P & K 194 B6
Kelton D & G 155 H7
Kelty Fife 186 B8
Kelvedon Essex 61 K4
Kelvedon Hatch Essex 60 F7
Kelynack Cnwll 2 C5
Kemback Fife 187 G4
Kemberton Shrops 84 D3
Kemble Gloucs 39 M2
Kemerton Worcs 71 G6
Kemeys Commander Mons 53 M6
Kemnay Abers 206 E3
Kempley Gloucs 54 F3
Kempley Green Gloucs 55 G3
Kempsey Worcs 70 F5
Kempsford Gloucs 40 D2
Kempshott Hants 29 L2
Kempston Bed 74 F5
Kempton Shrops 83 G6
Kemp Town Br & H 19 J5
Kemsing Kent 32 F2
Kenardington Kent 34 C7
Kenchester Herefs 69 J6
Kencot Oxon 56 E6
Kendal Cumb 129 L2
Kenfig Brdgnd 36 C4
Kenilworth Warwks 72 C1
Kenley Gt Lon 32 B2
Kenley Shrops 83 L4
Kenmore Highld 210 B3
Kenmore P & K 194 B7
Kenn Devon 11 L7
Kenn N Som 38 B6
Kennacraig Ag & B 172 D5
Kennall Vale Cnwll 3 J4
Kennerleigh Devon 11 J4
Kennessee Green Sefton 111 L2
Kennet Clacks 176 C1
Kennethmont Abers 215 L8
Kennett Cambs 77 G2
Kennford Devon 11 L7
Kenninghall Norfk 92 C6
Kennington Kent 34 D5
Kennington Oxon 57 K7
Kennoway Fife 186 F6
Kenny Somset 25 L7
Kennyhill Suffk 90 F7
Kennythorpe N York 134 C6
Kenovay Ag & B 188 C6
Kensaleyre Highld 208 F4
Kensington Gt Lon 44 E4
Kensington Palace Gt Lon 44 E4
Kensworth Common C Beds 59 G4
Kentallen Highld 191 K5
Kent and Sussex Crematorium Kent 33 G5
Kentchurch Herefs 54 B3
Kentford Suffk 77 G2
Kentisbeare Devon 12 D2
Kentisbury Devon 23 K3
Kentish Town Gt Lon 44 F3
Kentmere Cumb 138 C6
Kenton Devon 12 B5
Kenton Gt Lon 44 D3
Kenton N u Ty 150 F2
Kenton Suffk 78 E2
Kenton Bankfoot N u Ty 150 F2

Kentra Highld 190 D3
Kent's Green Gloucs 55 H4
Kent's Oak Hants 28 F6
Kenwyn Cnwll 4 C6
Keoldale Highld 228 F3
Keppoch Highld 200 D1
Kepwick N York 133 G2
Keresley Covtry 86 D6
Kerrera Ag & B 182 B2
Kerris Cnwll 2 D5
Kerry Powys 82 D5
Kerrycroy Ag & B 173 J6
Kersall Notts 116 B8
Kersbrook Devon 12 D5
Kersey Suffk 78 B5
Kershader W Isls 232 f3
Kerswell Devon 12 D2
Kerswell Green Worcs 70 F5
Kesgrave Suffk 78 F5
Kessingland Suffk 93 L6
Kestle Cnwll 4 F6
Kestle Mill Cnwll 4 D4
Keston Gt Lon 45 H7
Keswick Cumb 137 J3
Keswick Norfk 92 E3
Kettering Nhants 88 C7
Kettering Crematorium Nhants 88 C7
Ketteringham Norfk 92 E3
Kettins P & K 195 K8
Kettlebaston Suffk 77 L4
Kettlebridge Fife 186 E6
Kettlebrook Staffs 86 B3
Kettleburgh Suffk 78 F3
Kettleholm D & G 155 K6
Kettleshulme Ches E 113 M5
Kettlesing N York 132 C7
Kettlesing Bottom N York 132 C7
Kettlestone Norfk 106 A6
Kettlethorpe Lincs 116 D6
Kettletoft Ork 234 d4
Kettlewell N York 131 H5
Ketton Rutlnd 88 E3
Kew Gt Lon 44 D5
Kew Royal Botanic Gardens Gt Lon 44 D5
Kewstoke N Som 37 M7
Kexby C York 125 G1
Kexby Lincs 116 E4
Key Green Ches E 113 K8
Keyham Leics 87 J3
Keyhaven Hants 16 C4
Keyingham E R Yk 127 G5
Keymer W Susx 19 J3
Keynsham BaNES 38 F6
Keysoe Bed 74 F3
Keysoe Row Bed 74 F3
Keyston Cambs 88 F7
Keyworth Notts 101 L6
Kibblesworth Gatesd 151 G4
Kibworth Beauchamp Leics 87 K5
Kibworth Harcourt Leics 87 K5
Kidbrooke Gt Lon 45 H5
Kidderminster Worcs 84 E7
Kidlington Oxon 57 J5
Kidmore End Oxon 42 B5
Kidsdale D & G 145 J7
Kidsgrove Staffs 99 J2
Kidwelly Carmth 50 E4
Kiel Crofts Ag & B 191 H8
Kielder Nthumb 157 G4
Kielder Forest 157 G5
Kiells Ag & B 171 H5
Kilbarchan Rens 174 D5
Kilbeg Highld 199 K4
Kilberry Ag & B 172 C5
Kilbirnie N Ayrs 174 C7
Kilbride Ag & B 172 C3
Kilbride Ag & B 173 H5
Kilbuiack Moray 214 D3
Kilburn Derbys 101 G4
Kilburn Gt Lon 44 E4
Kilburn N York 133 H4
Kilby Leics 87 J4
Kilchamaig Ag & B 172 D6
Kilchattan Ag & B 173 J7
Kilchattan Ag & B 180 E7
Kilcheran Ag & B 191 G8
Kilchoan Highld 189 L4
Kilchoman Ag & B 170 D5
Kilchrenan Ag & B 182 E3
Kilconquhar Fife 187 H6
Kilcot Gloucs 55 G3
Kilcoy Highld 212 E4
Kilcreggan Ag & B 173 L3
Kildale N York 142 D5
Kildalloig Ag & B 161 J5
Kildary Highld 223 G6
Kildavaig Ag & B 173 G5
Kildavanan Ag & B 173 H5
Kildonan Highld 227 G4
Kildonan N Ayrs 162 D5
Kildonan Lodge Highld 226 F4
Kildonnan Highld 199 G7
Kildrochet House D & G 144 C4
Kildrummy Abers 205 K2
Kildwick N York 122 F2
Kilfinan Ag & B 172 F3
Kilfinnan Highld 201 K6
Kilgetty Pembks 49 J6
Kilgrammie S Ayrs 152 F2
Kilgwrrwg Common Mons 38 C2
Kilham E R Yk 135 G6
Kilkenneth Ag & B 188 B7
Kilkenzie Ag & B 161 H4
Kilkerran Ag & B 161 J5
Kilkhampton Cnwll 9 H3
Killamarsh Derbys 115 J5
Killay Swans 51 H6
Killearn Stirlg 174 F2
Killen Highld 213 G3
Killerby Darltn 140 F3
Killerton Devon 12 C3
Killichonan P & K 193 J5
Killiechonate Highld 192 D1
Killiechronan Ag & B 190 B7
Killiecrankie P & K 194 E4
Killilan Highld 210 E7
Killimster Highld 231 K4
Killin Stirlg 184 C2
Killinghall N York 132 D7
Killington Cumb 130 C2
Killington Lake Services Cumb 130 B2
Killingworth N Tyne 159 G7
Killochyett Border 167 G1
Kilmacolm Inver 174 C4
Kilmahog Stirlg 184 D5
Kilmahumaig Ag & B 182 A8
Kilmaluag Highld 218 C6
Kilmany Fife 186 F3
Kilmarnock E Ayrs 163 K2
Kilmartin Ag & B 182 B7
Kilmaurs E Ayrs 163 K2
Kilmelford Ag & B 182 B5
Kilmersdon Somset 27 G2
Kilmeston Hants 29 L6
Kilmichael Ag & B 161 H5
Kilmichael Glassary Ag & B 182 B8
Kilmichael of Inverlussa Ag & B 172 D2
Kilmington Devon 13 H3
Kilmington Wilts 27 H4
Kilmington Common Wilts 27 H4
Kilmington Street Wilts 27 H4
Kilmorack Highld 212 D5
Kilmore Ag & B 182 C3
Kilmore Highld 199 K4
Kilmory Ag & B 172 C4
Kilmory Highld 190 B3
Kilmory N Ayrs 162 B5
Kilmuir Highld 208 D5
Kilmuir Highld 213 G4
Kilmuir Highld 218 B7
Kilmuir Highld 223 G6
Kilmun Ag & B 173 K3
Kilnave Ag & B 170 F4
Kilncadzow S Lans 176 B8
Kilndown Kent 33 J6
Kilninver Ag & B 182 B3
Kilnsea E R Yk 127 J7
Kilnsey N York 131 H6
Kilnwick E R Yk 126 C1
Kiloran Ag & B 180 E7
Kilpatrick N Ayrs 162 A4
Kilpeck Herefs 54 C3
Kilpin E R Yk 125 J5
Kilrenny Fife 187 J6
Kilsby Nhants 73 H1
Kilspindie P & K 186 C3
Kilstay D & G 144 D7
Kilsyth N Lans 175 J3
Kiltarlity Highld 212 D6
Kilton R & Cl 142 E4
Kilton Thorpe R & Cl 142 E4
Kilvaxter Highld 218 B7
Kilve Somset 25 H3
Kilvington Notts 102 D4
Kilwinning N Ayrs 163 H2
Kimberley Norfk 92 C3
Kimberley Notts 101 J4
Kimberworth Rothm 115 H3
Kimblesworth Dur 151 G5
Kimbolton Cambs 75 G2
Kimbolton Herefs 69 K3
Kimcote Leics 87 H6
Kimmeridge Dorset 15 H6
Kimpton Hants 28 F3
Kimpton Herts 59 K4
Kinbrace Highld 226 F3
Kinbuck Stirlg 185 G6
Kincaple Fife 187 G4
Kincardine Fife 176 C2
Kincardine Highld 222 E4
Kincardine Bridge Fife 176 C2
Kincardine O'Neil Abers 206 B5
Kinclaven P & K 195 J8
Kincorth C Aber 207 H5
Kincorth House Moray 214 C3
Kincraig Highld 203 K4
Kincraigie P & K 194 F6
Kindallachan P & K 194 F6
Kinerarach Ag & B 172 B7
Kineton Gloucs 56 C3
Kineton Warwks 72 D4
Kinfauns P & K 186 C3
Kingarth Ag & B 173 J6
Kingcausie Abers 207 G5
Kingcoed Mons 54 B6
Kingerby Lincs 117 H3
Kingham Oxon 56 E3
Kingholm Quay D & G 155 G7
Kinghorn Fife 177 H2
Kinglassie Fife 186 D7
Kingoldrum Angus 196 B5
Kingoodie P & K 186 E2
Kingsand Cnwll 6 C5
Kingsbarns Fife 187 K5
Kingsbridge Devon 7 H6
Kingsbridge Somset 24 F4
King's Bromley Staffs 85 K1
Kingsburgh Highld 208 F4
Kingsbury Gt Lon 44 D3
Kingsbury Warwks 86 B4
Kingsbury Episcopi Somset 26 B7
King's Caple Herefs 54 E3
Kingsclere Hants 41 K8
King's Cliffe Nhants 88 E4
Kings Clipstone Notts 115 L8
Kingscote Gloucs 39 J2
Kingscott Devon 23 H7
King's Coughton Warwks 71 J3
Kingscross N Ayrs 162 D4
Kingsdon Somset 26 D6
Kingsdown Kent 35 K5
Kingsdown Swindn 40 D3
Kingsdown Wilts 39 J6
Kingsdown Crematorium Swindn 40 D3
Kingseat Fife 176 F1
Kingsey Bucks 58 C6
Kingsfold W Susx 31 K4
Kingsford C Aber 206 F4
Kingsford E Ayrs 174 E8
Kingsgate Kent 35 K1
Kingshall Street Suffk 77 K3
King's Heath Birm 85 J7
Kings Hill Kent 33 H3
King's Hill Wsall 85 H4
Kings House Hotel Highld 192 D5
Kingshouse Hotel Stirlg 184 C4
Kingshurst Solhll 85 L6
Kingskerswell Devon 7 K3
Kingskettle Fife 186 E5
Kingsland Herefs 69 J3
Kingsland IoA 108 C5
Kings Langley Herts 59 H7
Kingsley Ches W 112 D6
Kingsley Hants 30 C4
Kingsley Staffs 100 A3
Kingsley Green W Susx 30 E5
Kingsley Park Nhants 73 L3
King's Lynn Norfk 104 F8
Kings Meaburn Cumb 138 E3
King's Mills Guern 236 c3
Kingsmuir Angus 196 D6
Kings Muir Border 166 C2
Kingsmuir Fife 187 J5
Kingsnorth Kent 34 D6
King's Norton Birm 85 J7
King's Norton Leics 87 K4
Kings Nympton Devon 23 L7
King's Pyon Herefs 69 J4
Kings Ripton Cambs 89 J7
King's Somborne Hants 29 G5
King's Stag Dorset 14 D1
King's Stanley Gloucs 55 J7
King's Sutton Nhants 72 F7
Kingstanding Birm 85 J4
Kingsteignton Devon 7 K2
Kingsthorne Herefs 54 D2
Kingsthorpe Nhants 73 L2
Kingston Cambs 75 L4
Kingston Cnwll 6 A2
Kingston Devon 6 F6
Kingston Dorset 14 E1
Kingston Dorset 15 H6
Kingston E Loth 178 C3
Kingston IoW 16 F6
Kingston Kent 35 G4
Kingston Bagpuize Oxon 57 H7
Kingston Blount Oxon 58 C7
Kingston Deverill Wilts 27 J4
Kingstone Herefs 69 H7
Kingstone Somset 26 B8
Kingstone Staffs 100 B6
Kingston Lacy House & Gardens Dorset 15 J3
Kingston Lisle Oxon 40 F3
Kingston near Lewes E Susx 19 K4
Kingston on Soar Notts 101 J6
Kingston on Spey Moray 215 H2
Kingston Russell Dorset 14 B4
Kingston St Mary Somset 25 K5
Kingston Seymour N Som 38 B6
Kingston upon Hull C KuH 126 D5

Kingston upon Thames Gt Lon 44 D6
Kingston upon Thames Crematorium Gt Lon 44 D6
King's Walden Herts 59 K4
Kingswear Devon 7 K5
Kingswells C Aber 207 G4
Kings Weston Bristl 38 D5
Kingswinford Dudley 84 F5
Kingswood Bucks 58 B4
Kingswood Gloucs 39 H3
Kingswood S Glos 38 F5
Kingswood Somset 25 H4
Kingswood Surrey 31 L1
Kingswood Warwks 71 L1
Kingswood Common Staffs 84 E3
Kings Worthy Hants 29 J5
Kingthorpe Lincs 117 J6
Kington Herefs 68 F3
Kington S Glos 38 F3
Kington Worcs 71 H4
Kington Langley Wilts 39 L5
Kington Magna Dorset 27 H6
Kington St Michael Wilts 39 K5
Kingussie Highld 203 H5
Kingweston Somset 26 D5
Kinharrachie Abers 217 H7
Kinharvie D & G 147 G2
Kinkell Bridge P & K 185 J4
Kinknockie Abers 217 J6
Kinleith C Edin 177 G5
Kinlet Shrops 84 C7
Kinloch Highld 198 F5
Kinloch Highld 225 H2
Kinloch Highld 229 H5
Kinloch P & K 195 J7
Kinlochard Stirlg 184 B6
Kinlochbervie Highld 228 C4
Kinlocheil Highld 191 J1
Kinlochewe Highld 210 F3
Kinloch Hourn Highld 200 E4
Kinlochlaggan Highld 202 E7
Kinlochleven Highld 192 C4
Kinlochmoidart Highld 190 E2
Kinlochnanuagh Highld 200 B8
Kinloch Rannoch P & K 193 L5
Kinloss Moray 214 C3
Kinmel Bay Conwy 110 D5
Kinmuck Abers 206 F2
Kinmundy Abers 207 G2
Kinnabus Ag & B 160 B2
Kinnadie Abers 217 H5
Kinnaird P & K 194 F5
Kinneff Abers 197 K2
Kinnelhead D & G 155 H2
Kinnell Angus 196 F6
Kinnerley Shrops 97 M7
Kinnersley Herefs 69 G5
Kinnersley Worcs 70 F5
Kinnerton Powys 68 E2
Kinnesswood P & K 186 C6
Kinnordy Angus 196 B5
Kinoulton Notts 102 B6
Kinross P & K 186 B6
Kinrossie P & K 186 C2
Kinross Services P & K 186 B6
Kinsham Herefs 69 G2
Kinsham Worcs 71 G7
Kinsley Wakefd 124 C7
Kinson Bmouth 15 K3
Kintail Highld 200 F2
Kintbury W Berk 41 G6
Kintessack Moray 214 B3
Kintillo P & K 186 B4
Kinton Herefs 83 H8
Kinton Shrops 98 A8
Kintore Abers 206 E3
Kintour Ag & B 171 H7
Kintra Ag & B 170 F8
Kintra Ag & B 180 D3
Kintraw Ag & B 182 B6
Kintyre Ag & B 161 J2
Kinveachy Highld 203 L2
Kinver Staffs 84 E6
Kippax Leeds 124 C4
Kippen Stirlg 184 E7
Kippford or Scaur D & G 146 E4
Kipping's Cross Kent 33 H5
Kirbister Ork 234 b6
Kirby Bedon Norfk 93 G3
Kirby Bellars Leics 102 B8
Kirby Cane Norfk 93 H5
Kirby Cross Essex 62 E4
Kirby Grindalythe N York 134 D6
Kirby Hill N York 132 F5
Kirby Hill N York 140 E6
Kirby Knowle N York 133 G3
Kirby-le-Soken Essex 62 F4
Kirby Misperton N York 134 B4
Kirby Muxloe Leics 87 G3
Kirby Underdale E R Yk 134 C7
Kirby Wiske N York 132 E3
Kirdford W Susx 31 G6
Kirk Highld 231 K4
Kirkabister Shet 235 d6
Kirkandrews D & G 146 A5
Kirkandrews upon Eden Cumb 148 C4
Kirkbampton Cumb 148 B4
Kirkbean D & G 147 G3
Kirk Bramwith Donc 124 F7
Kirkbride Cumb 147 M4
Kirkbuddo Angus 196 E7
Kirkburn Border 166 D2
Kirkburn E R Yk 134 F7
Kirkburton Kirk 123 J7
Kirkby Knows 111 L2
Kirkby Lincs 117 H3
Kirkby N York 142 C6
Kirkby Fleetham N York 141 G7
Kirkby Green Lincs 103 H2
Kirkby-in-Ashfield Notts 101 J2
Kirkby-in-Furness Cumb 128 F3
Kirkby la Thorpe Lincs 103 J4
Kirkby Lonsdale Cumb 130 B4
Kirkby Malham N York 131 G7
Kirkby Mallory Leics 86 F4
Kirkby Malzeard N York 132 C5
Kirkbymoorside N York 133 L3
Kirkby on Bain Lincs 118 C8
Kirkby Overblow N York 123 L2
Kirkby Stephen Cumb 139 H5
Kirkby Thore Cumb 138 F3
Kirkby Underwood Lincs 103 H6
Kirkby Wharf N York 124 D3
Kirkcaldy Fife 186 D8
Kirkcaldy Crematorium Fife 186 D8
Kirkcambeck Cumb 148 F2
Kirkchrist D & G 146 B5
Kirkcolm D & G 144 B2
Kirkconnel D & G 164 E6
Kirkconnell D & G 147 G2
Kirkcowan D & G 145 G3
Kirkcudbright D & G 146 B5
Kirkdale Lpool 111 K3
Kirk Deighton N York 124 B1
Kirk Ella E R Yk 126 C5
Kirkfieldbank S Lans 165 G2
Kirkgunzeon D & G 146 F2
Kirk Hallam Derbys 101 J4
Kirkham Lancs 120 F4
Kirkham N York 134 B6
Kirkhamgate Wakefd 123 K6
Kirk Hammerton N York 133 G7
Kirkhaugh Nthumb 149 H5
Kirkheaton Kirk 123 H6
Kirkheaton Nthumb 158 C6
Kirkhill Highld 212 E5
Kirkhope S Lans 165 J7
Kirkibost Highld 199 H2
Kirkinch P & K 195 L7
Kirkinner D & G 145 J5
Kirkintilloch E Duns 175 H4
Kirk Ireton Derbys 100 E3
Kirkland Cumb 136 E4
Kirkland D & G 154 E4
Kirkland D & G 155 H4
Kirkland D & G 164 E6
Kirk Langley Derbys 100 F5
Kirkleatham R & Cl 142 D3
Kirkleatham Crematorium R & Cl 142 D3
Kirklevington S on T 141 K5
Kirkley Suffk 93 L5
Kirklington N York 132 D4
Kirklington Notts 102 B2
Kirklinton Cumb 148 D2
Kirkliston C Edin 176 F4
Kirkmabreck D & G 145 K4
Kirkmaiden D & G 144 D7
Kirk Merrington Dur 141 G2
Kirk Michael IoM 237 c4
Kirkmichael P & K 195 H4
Kirkmichael S Ayrs 163 J7
Kirkmuirhill S Lans 164 F2
Kirknewton Nthumb 168 D4
Kirknewton W Loth 176 F5
Kirkney Abers 215 L7
Kirk of Shotts N Lans 175 L5
Kirkoswald Cumb 148 F6
Kirkoswald S Ayrs 163 G7
Kirkpatrick D & G 154 F4
Kirkpatrick Durham D & G 154 D7
Kirkpatrick-Fleming D & G 156 B7
Kirk Sandall Donc 124 F8
Kirksanton Cumb 128 D4
Kirk Smeaton N York 124 D7
Kirkstall Leeds 123 K4
Kirkstead Lincs 103 K1
Kirkstile Abers 215 L7
Kirkstile D & G 156 C4
Kirkstyle Highld 231 L2
Kirkthorpe Wakefd 124 B6
Kirkton Abers 206 C1
Kirkton D & G 155 G6
Kirkton Fife 186 F3
Kirkton Highld 210 C8
Kirkton Highld 210 D6
Kirkton P & K 185 K4
Kirkton Manor Border 166 C2
Kirkton of Airlie Angus 195 L6
Kirkton of Auchterhouse Angus 196 B8
Kirkton of Barevan Highld 213 K5
Kirkton of Collace P & K 186 C2
Kirkton of Glenbuchat Abers 205 J3
Kirkton of Logie Buchan Abers 217 J7
Kirkton of Maryculter Abers 207 G5
Kirkton of Menmuir Angus 196 E4
Kirkton of Monikie Angus 196 E8
Kirkton of Rayne Abers 216 D7
Kirkton of Skene Abers 206 F4
Kirkton of Strathmartine Angus 186 F1
Kirkton of Tealing Angus 196 C8
Kirkton of Tough Abers 206 C3
Kirktown Abers 217 J2
Kirktown Abers 217 K4
Kirktown of Alvah Abers 216 D3
Kirktown of Bourtie Abers 206 F1
Kirktown of Fetteresso Abers 206 F7
Kirktown of Mortlach Moray 215 H6
Kirktown of Slains Abers 217 K8
Kirkurd Border 165 M1
Kirkwall Ork 234 c6
Kirkwall Airport Ork 234 c6
Kirkwhelpington Nthumb 158 C5
Kirk Yetholm Border 168 C4
Kirmington N Linc 126 D7
Kirmond le Mire Lincs 117 K3
Kirn Ag & B 173 K3
Kirriemuir Angus 196 C5
Kirstead Green Norfk 93 G4
Kirtlebridge D & G 155 M7
Kirtling Cambs 77 G3
Kirtling Green Cambs 76 F4
Kirtlington Oxon 57 J4
Kirtomy Highld 229 M3
Kirton Lincs 104 A5
Kirton Notts 116 B7
Kirton Suffk 78 F6
Kirtonhill W Duns 174 D4
Kirton in Lindsey N Linc 116 F2
Kirwaugh D & G 145 J4
Kishorn Highld 210 C6
Kislingbury Nhants 73 K3
Kittisford Somset 25 G6
Kitt's Green Birm 85 L6
Kittybrewster C Aber 207 H4
Kivernoll Herefs 54 C2
Kiveton Park Rothm 115 J5
Knaith Lincs 116 D5
Knap Corner Dorset 27 J6
Knaphill Surrey 42 F8
Knapp Somset 25 L6
Knapton C York 124 E1
Knapton N York 134 D4
Knapton Norfk 107 G5
Knapwell Cambs 75 K2
Knaresborough N York 132 E7
Knarsdale Nthumb 149 H4
Knaven Abers 217 G5
Knayton N York 132 F2
Knebworth Herts 59 L4
Knedlington E R Yk 125 H5
Kneesall Notts 116 B8
Kneeton Notts 102 B4
Knelston Swans 50 F7
Knenhall Staffs 99 L5
Knightcote Warwks 72 E4
Knightley Staffs 99 J7
Knighton C Leic 87 H4
Knighton Dorset 14 C1
Knighton Powys 82 F8
Knighton Somset 25 J3
Knighton Staffs 99 G4
Knighton Staffs 99 H6
Knighton on Teme Worcs 70 B1
Knightwick Worcs 70 D4
Knill Herefs 68 F3
Knipton Leics 102 D6
Kniveton Derbys 100 E3
Knock Cumb 138 F2
Knock Highld 199 K4
Knock Moray 215 L4

Knock W Isls 232 g2
Knockally Highld 227 K3
Knockan Highld 224 F6
Knockando Moray 214 F6
Knockbain Highld 212 E5
Knockbain Highld 212 F3
Knock Castle N Ayrs 173 L5
Knockdee Highld 231 H4
Knockdow Ag & B 173 J4
Knockdown Wilts 39 J3
Knockeen S Ayrs 153 G3
Knockenkelly N Ayrs 162 D4
Knockentiber E Ayrs 163 K2
Knockholt Kent 32 E2
Knockholt Pound Kent 32 E2
Knockin Shrops 97 M7
Knockinlaw E Ayrs 163 K2
Knocknain D & G 144 B3
Knockrome Ag & B 171 K4
Knocksharry IoM 237 b4
Knocksheen D & G 153 M5
Knockvennie Smithy D & G 154 D7
Knodishall Suffk 79 J3
Knodishall Common Suffk 79 J3
Knole Somset 26 C6
Knolls Green Ches E 113 J5
Knolton Wrexhm 98 B5
Knook Wilts 27 L3
Knossington Leics 88 B2
Knott End-on-Sea Lancs 120 E2
Knotting Bed 74 E2
Knotting Green Bed 74 E3
Knottingley Wakefd 124 D5
Knotty Ash Lpool 112 B3
Knowbury Shrops 83 L7
Knowe D & G 153 G7
Knowehead D & G 154 A4
Knoweside S Ayrs 163 G6
Knowle Bristl 38 E6
Knowle Devon 11 H5
Knowle Devon 12 C2
Knowle Devon 12 D6
Knowle Devon 23 H4
Knowle Shrops 83 L8
Knowle Solhll 85 L7
Knowle Somset 24 E3
Knowlefield Cumb 148 D4
Knowle Green Lancs 121 J3
Knowle St Giles Somset 13 J1
Knowl Hill W & M 42 D4
Knowsley Knows 112 C3
Knowsley Safari Park Knows 112 C3
Knowstone Devon 24 C6
Knox Bridge Kent 33 K5
Knoydart Highld 200 C5
Knucklas Powys 82 F8
Knuston Nhants 74 D2
Knutsford Ches E 113 H5
Knutsford Services Ches E 113 G6
Krumlin Calder 122 F6
Kuggar Cnwll 3 J7
Kyleakin Highld 200 B1
Kyle of Lochalsh Highld 210 B8
Kylerhea Highld 200 B2
Kylesku Highld 224 F2
Kylesmorar Highld 200 C6
Kyles Scalpay W Isls 232 e4
Kylestrome Highld 224 F2
Kynnersley Wrekin 84 C1
Kyrewood Worcs 69 L2

L

La Bellieuse Guern 236 d3
Lacasaigh W Isls 232 f3
Lacasdal W Isls 232 f2
Laceby NE Lin 117 K1
Lacey Green Bucks 58 D7
Lach Dennis Ches W 113 G6
Lackford Suffk 77 H1
Lackford Green Suffk 77 H1
Lacock Wilts 39 K6
Ladbroke Warwks 72 E3
Laddingford Kent 33 J4
Ladock Cnwll 4 D5
Lady Ork 234 d4
Ladybank Fife 186 E5
Ladygill S Lans 165 H4
Lady Hall Cumb 128 E3
Ladykirk Border 179 J8
Ladywood Birm 85 J6
Ladywood Worcs 70 F3
La Fontenelle Guern 236 e1
La Fosse Guern 236 d4
Lag D & G 154 F5
Laga Highld 190 D4
Lagavulin Ag & B 160 C1
Lagg N Ayrs 162 B5
Laggan Highld 201 L6
Laggan Highld 202 F6
Lagganlia Highld 203 K5
La Greve Guern 236 d2
La Grève de Lecq Jersey 236 b5
La Hougue Bie Jersey 236 d7
La Houguette Guern 236 b3
Laid Highld 228 F4
Laide Highld 219 L3
Laig Highld 199 G7
Laigh Clunch E Ayrs 174 E8
Laigh Fenwick E Ayrs 163 L2
Laigh Glenmuir E Ayrs 164 C5
Laighstonehall S Lans 175 J7
Laindon Essex 46 B3
Lairg Highld 225 M7
Laisterdyke C Brad 123 J4
Lake IoW 17 H5
Lake Wilts 28 C4
Lake District National Park Cumb 137 H5
Lakenheath Suffk 91 G6
Lakesend Norfk 90 D4
Laleston Brdgnd 36 D4
Lamarsh Essex 77 K7
Lamas Norfk 106 F7
Lambden Border 167 L2
Lamberhurst Kent 33 H6
Lamberhurst Down Kent 33 H6
Lamberton Border 179 K6
Lambeth Gt Lon 44 F4
Lambeth Crematorium Gt Lon 44 F5
Lambfair Green Suffk 77 G4
Lambley Notts 101 M4
Lambley Nthumb 149 H4
Lambourn W Berk 40 F5
Lambourne End Essex 45 J2
Lambs Green W Susx 31 L4
Lamerton Devon 6 C1
Lamesley Gatesd 151 G4
Lamington S Lans 165 J3
Lamlash N Ayrs 162 C3
Lamonby Cumb 148 D7
Lamorna Cnwll 2 E6
Lamorran Cnwll 4 D7
Lampeter Cerdgn 66 D5
Lampeter Velfrey Pembks 49 K5
Lamphey Pembks 49 H7
Lamplugh Cumb 136 F3
Lamport Nhants 87 L8
Lamyatt Somset 26 F4
Lanark S Lans 165 G2
Lancaster Lancs 129 K7
Lancaster & Morecambe Crematorium Lancs 129 K6
Lancaster Services Lancs 121 G1
Lanchester Dur 150 F5
Lancing W Susx 19 G5
L'Ancresse Guern 236 d1
Landbeach Cambs 76 C2
Landcross Devon 23 G6
Landerberry Abers 206 E4
Landford Wilts 28 E7
Land-hallow Highld 227 L2
Landican Crematorium Wirral 111 J4
Landimore Swans 50 F6
Landkey Devon 23 J5
Landore Swans 51 J6
Landrake Cnwll 6 B4
Land's End Airport Cnwll 2 C5
Landulph Cnwll 6 C4
Lane Cnwll 4 C4
Laneast Cnwll 9 G7
Lane End Bucks 42 D3
Lane End Wilts 27 J3
Lane Ends Derbys 100 E5
Laneham Notts 116 D6
Lane Head Dur 140 E5
Lanehead Dur 149 L6
Lane Head Wsall 85 H4
Langaller Somset 25 K6
Langar Notts 102 B5
Langbank Rens 174 D4
Langbar N York 123 G1
Langcliffe N York 130 F6
Langdale End N York 134 E2
Langdown Hants 16 E2
Langdyke Fife 186 E6
Langenhoe Essex 62 B4
Langford C Beds 75 H6
Langford Devon 12 D2
Langford Essex 61 K6
Langford Notts 102 D2
Langford Oxon 56 E7
Langford Budville Somset 25 H6
Langham Essex 62 B2
Langham Norfk 106 B4
Langham Rutlnd 88 B2
Langham Suffk 77 L1
Langho Lancs 121 K4
Langholm D & G 156 C5
Langlee Border 167 H3
Langley Hants 16 F3
Langley Herts 59 K4
Langley Kent 33 K3
Langley Nthumb 149 L3
Langley Slough 43 G5
Langley Somset 25 G5
Langley W Susx 30 D5
Langley Warwks 71 L3
Langley Burrell Wilts 39 L5
Langley Green Essex 61 L4
Langley Marsh Somset 25 G5
Langley Park Dur 150 F6
Langley Street Norfk 93 H3
Langley Upper Green Essex 76 C7
Langney E Susx 20 D5
Langold Notts 115 L4
Langore Cnwll 9 J7
Langport Somset 26 B6
Langrick Lincs 103 L3
Langridge BaNES 39 H6
Langrigg Cumb 147 K5
Langrish Hants 30 B6
Langsett Barns 114 E2
Langside P & K 185 G5
Langstone Hants 17 K2
Langthorne N York 132 C2
Langthorpe N York 132 F6
Langthwaite N York 140 C6
Langtoft E R Yk 134 F6
Langtoft Lincs 89 G2
Langton Dur 140 F4
Langton Lincs 118 C7
Langton Lincs 118 E7
Langton N York 134 C6
Langton by Wragby Lincs 117 J6
Langton Green Kent 32 F5
Langton Herring Dorset 14 C6
Langton Matravers Dorset 15 J6
Langtree Devon 10 C2
Langwathby Cumb 148 F7
Langwell House Highld 227 K4
Langwith Derbys 115 K7
Langwith Junction Derbys 115 K7
Langworth Lincs 117 H6
Lanhydrock House & Gardens Cnwll 5 H3
Lanivet Cnwll 5 G3
Lanlivery Cnwll 5 G4
Lanner Cnwll 3 J4
Lanreath Cnwll 5 J4
Lansallos Cnwll 5 J5
Lanteglos Cnwll 8 E7
Lanteglos Highway Cnwll 5 J5
Lanton Border 167 J5
Lanton Nthumb 168 D3
La Passee Guern 236 d2
Lapford Devon 11 H3
Laphroaig Ag & B 160 C1
Lapley Staffs 84 F2
La Pulente Jersey 236 a7
Lapworth Warwks 71 L1
Larachbeg Highld 190 E6
Larbert Falk 176 B3
Largie Abers 216 B7
Largiemore Ag & B 172 F2
Largoward Fife 187 H5
Largs N Ayrs 173 L6
Largybeg N Ayrs 162 D5
Largymore N Ayrs 162 D4
Larkfield Inver 173 L4
Larkfield Kent 33 J2
Larkhall S Lans 175 K7
Larkhill Wilts 28 C3
Larling Norfk 92 B5
La Rocque Jersey 236 e8
La Rousaillerie Guern 236 d2
Lartington Dur 140 C4
Lasham Hants 30 A3
Lasswade Mdloth 177 J5
Lastingham N York 133 L2
Latchingdon Essex 61 L7
Latchley Cnwll 6 B2
Lathbury M Keyn 74 C5
Latheron Highld 227 L2
Latheronwheel Highld 227 L3
Lathones Fife 187 H5
Latimer Bucks 59 G7
Latteridge S Glos 38 F4
Lattiford Somset 27 G6
Latton Wilts 40 C2
Lauder Border 178 C8
Laugharne Carmth 50 C4
Laughterton Lincs 116 D6
Laughton E Susx 20 A3
Laughton Leics 87 J5
Laughton Lincs 103 H6
Laughton Lincs 116 D3
Laughton-en-le-Morthen Rothm 115 K4
Launcells Cnwll 9 H4
Launceston Cnwll 9 J7
Launton Oxon 57 L4
Laurencekirk Abers 197 H3
Laurieston D & G 146 B3
Laurieston Falk 176 B3
Lavendon M Keyn 74 D4
Lavenham Suffk 77 K5
Lavernock V Glam 37 J6
Laversdale Cumb 148 E3
Laverstock Wilts 28 D5
Laverstoke Hants 29 J2
Laverton Gloucs 71 J7
Laverton N York 132 C5
Laverton Somset 27 H2
La Villette Guern 236 d4
Lavister Wrexhm 98 A2

Law S Lans 175 L7
Lawers P & K 193 L7
Lawford Essex 62 C2
Lawford Somset 25 H4
Law Hill S Lans 175 L7
Lawhitton Cnwll 9 J7
Lawkland N York 130 E6
Lawns Wood Crematorium Leeds 123 K3
Lawrenny Pembks 49 H6
Lawshall Suffk 77 K4
Laxay W Isls 232 f3
Laxdale W Isls 232 f2
Laxey IoM 237 d4
Laxfield Suffk 93 G8
Laxford Bridge Highld 228 C6
Laxo Shet 235 d4
Laxton E R Yk 125 J5
Laxton Nhants 88 D4
Laxton Notts 116 B7
Laycock C Brad 122 F3
Layer Breton Essex 61 M4
Layer-de-la-Haye Essex 62 A4
Layer Marney Essex 61 L4
Layham Suffk 78 B6
Laymore Dorset 13 K2
Laytham E R Yk 125 H3
Lazonby Cumb 148 F6
Lea Derbys 101 G2
Lea Herefs 54 F4
Lea Lincs 116 D4
Lea Shrops 83 G5
Lea Wilts 39 L3
Leachkin Highld 212 F5
Leadburn Border 177 H7
Leadenham Lincs 102 F3
Leaden Roding Essex 60 F5
Leadgate Dur 150 E5
Leadhills S Lans 165 G6
Leafield Oxon 56 F5
Leagrave Luton 59 H4
Leake Common Side Lincs 104 C3
Lealholm N York 142 F5
Lealt Highld 209 H3
Lea Marston Warwks 86 B5
Leamington Hastings Warwks 72 F2
Leamington Spa Warwks 72 D2
Leap Cross E Susx 20 C4
Leasgill Cumb 129 K3
Leasingham Lincs 103 H3
Leasingthorne Dur 141 G2
Leatherhead Surrey 31 K1
Leathley N York 123 J2
Leaton Shrops 98 C8
Leaveland Kent 34 D4
Leavenheath Suffk 77 L6
Leavening N York 134 C6
Leaves Green Gt Lon 45 H7
Lebberston N York 135 G3
Le Bigard Guern 236 c4
Le Bourg Guern 236 c4
Le Bourg Jersey 236 e8
Lechlade on Thames Gloucs 56 E7
Lecht Gruinart Ag & B 170 E5
Leck Lancs 130 C4
Leckbuie P & K 193 L7
Leckford Hants 29 G4
Leckhampstead Bucks 73 K6
Leckhampstead W Berk 41 H5
Leckhampstead Thicket W Berk 41 H5
Leckhampton Gloucs 55 L4
Leckmelm Highld 220 F4
Leconfield E R Yk 126 C2
Ledaig Ag & B 191 H8
Ledburn Bucks 58 E4
Ledbury Herefs 70 C6
Ledgemoor Herefs 69 H4
Ledmore Junction Highld 224 F6
Ledsham Leeds 124 C4
Ledston Leeds 124 C5
Ledwell Oxon 57 H3
Lee Devon 23 H3
Lee Gt Lon 45 H5
Leebotwood Shrops 83 J4
Lee Brockhurst Shrops 98 D6
Leece Cumb 128 F5
Lee Chapel Essex 46 B3
Lee Clump Bucks 58 E6
Leeds Kent 33 L3
Leeds Leeds 123 K4
Leeds Bradford Airport Leeds 123 J3
Leeds Castle Kent 33 L3
Leedstown Cnwll 3 G4
Leek Staffs 99 M2
Leek Wootton Warwks 72 C2
Lee Mill Devon 6 E5
Leeming N York 132 D2
Leeming Bar N York 132 D2
Lee-on-the-Solent Hants 17 G3
Lees Derbys 100 E5
Lees Oldham 113 L2
Lees Green Derbys 100 E5
Leesthorpe Leics 87 L2
Leeswood Flints 97 K1
Leetown P & K 186 C3
Leftwich Ches W 112 F6
Legbourne Lincs 118 E5
Legerwood Border 167 J2
Legoland W & M 42 F5
Le Gron Guern 236 c3
Legsby Lincs 117 J4
Le Haguais Jersey 236 d8
Le Hocq Jersey 236 d8
Leicester C Leic 87 H3
Leicester Forest East Services Leics 87 G3
Leigh Dorset 14 C2
Leigh Gloucs 55 K3
Leigh Kent 32 F4
Leigh Surrey 31 L3
Leigh Wigan 112 F2
Leigh Wilts 40 B3
Leigh Worcs 70 D4
Leigh Beck Essex 46 D4
Leigh Delamere Wilts 39 K5
Leigh Delamere Services Wilts 39 K5
Leigh Green Kent 34 B7
Leigh Knoweglass S Lans 175 H7
Leigh-on-Sea Sthend 46 D3
Leigh Park Dorset 15 J3
Leigh Sinton Worcs 70 D4
Leighswood Wsall 85 J3
Leighterton Gloucs 39 J3
Leighton Powys 82 E3
Leighton Shrops 84 B3
Leighton Bromswold Cambs 89 G7
Leighton Buzzard C Beds 58 F3
Leigh upon Mendip Somset 27 G3
Leigh Woods N Som 38 E6
Leinthall Earls Herefs 69 J2
Leinthall Starkes Herefs 69 J1
Leintwardine Herefs 83 H8
Leire Leics 87 G5
Leiston Suffk 79 J3
Leith C Edin 177 H3
Leitholm Border 168 B1
Lelant Cnwll 2 F4
Lelley E R Yk 126 F4
Lempitlaw Border 168 B3
Lemreway W Isls 232 f3
Lemsford Herts 59 L5
Lenchwick Worcs 71 J5
Lendalfoot S Ayrs 152 D4
Lendrick Stirlg 184 C6
Lendrum Terrace Abers 217 L6
Lenham Kent 34 B4
Lenham Heath Kent 34 B5
Lenie Highld 202 D1
Lennel Border 168 C2
Lennox Plunton D & G 146 A5
Lennoxtown E Duns 175 H3
Lenton C Nott 101 K5
Lenton Lincs 103 G6
Lenwade Norfk 106 D8
Lenzie E Duns 175 H4
Leochel-Cushnie Abers 205 L4
Leominster Herefs 69 K3
Leonard Stanley Gloucs 55 J7
Leoville Jersey 236 b6
Lephin Highld 208 B4
Leppington N York 134 B7
Lepton Kirk 123 J7
Lerags Ag & B 182 B3
L'Erée Guern 236 b3
Lerryn Cnwll 5 J4
Lerwick Shet 235 d6
Les Arquets Guern 236 b3
Lesbury Nthumb 169 J6
Les Hubits Guern 236 d3
Leslie Abers 206 B1
Leslie Fife 186 D6
Les Lohiers Guern 236 c3
Lesmahagow S Lans 164 F2
Les Murchez Guern 236 c4
Lesnewth Cnwll 8 F6
Les Nicolles Guern 236 c4
Les Quartiers Guern 236 d2
Les Quennevais Jersey 236 b7
Les Sages Guern 236 b3
Lessingham Norfk 107 H6
Lessonhall Cumb 147 L5
Les Villets Guern 236 c4
Leswalt D & G 144 B3
L'Etacq Jersey 236 a6
Letchmore Heath Herts 43 J2
Letchworth Garden City Herts 59 L2
Letcombe Bassett Oxon 41 G4
Letcombe Regis Oxon 41 G3
Letham Angus 196 E6
Letham Border 167 K7
Letham Falk 176 B2
Letham Fife 186 E4
Letham Grange Angus 197 G7
Lethendy P & K 195 H7
Lethenty Abers 206 B2
Lethenty Abers 216 F6
Letheringham Suffk 78 F3
Letheringsett Norfk 106 C5
Letterewe Highld 219 L7
Letterfearn Highld 200 D2
Letterfinlay Lodge Hotel Highld 201 K6
Lettermorar Highld 199 M7
Letters Highld 220 F4
Lettershaw S Lans 165 H5
Letterston Pembks 48 F2
Lettoch Highld 204 C2
Lettoch Highld 214 D7
Letton Herefs 69 G5
Letty Green Herts 59 M5
Letwell Rothm 115 K4
Leuchars Fife 187 G3
Leumrabhagh W Isls 232 f3
Leurbost W Isls 232 f3
Levedale Staffs 84 F1
Leven E R Yk 126 D2
Leven Fife 186 F7
Levens Cumb 129 K3
Levens Green Herts 60 B4
Levenshulme Manch 113 K3
Levenwick Shet 235 c7
Leverburgh W Isls 232 d5
Leverington Cambs 90 C2
Leverstock Green Herts 59 H6
Leverton Lincs 104 C3
Le Villocq Guern 236 c2
Levington Suffk 78 F6
Levisham N York 134 C2
Lew Oxon 56 F6
Lewannick Cnwll 9 H8
Lewdown Devon 10 C7
Lewes E Susx 19 L4
Leweston Pembks 48 F3
Lewisham Gt Lon 45 G5
Lewisham Crematorium Gt Lon 45 H5
Lewiston Highld 212 D8
Lewistown Brdgnd 36 E3
Lewknor Oxon 42 B2
Lewson Street Kent 34 C3
Lewtrenchard Devon 10 C7
Lexden Essex 62 A3
Lexworthy Somset 25 K4
Leybourne Kent 33 H2
Leyburn N York 131 L2
Leygreen Herts 59 K3
Ley Hill Bucks 59 G7
Leyland Lancs 121 H6
Leylodge Abers 206 E3
Leys Abers 217 J4
Leys P & K 195 K8
Leysdown-on-Sea Kent 47 G6
Leysmill Angus 196 F6
Leys of Cossans Angus 196 C6
Leysters Herefs 69 L2
Leyton Gt Lon 45 G3
Leytonstone Gt Lon 45 H3
Lezant Cnwll 5 M1
Lhanbryde Moray 215 G3
Libanus Powys 52 F3
Libberton S Lans 165 J2
Liberton C Edin 177 J4
Lichfield Staffs 85 K2
Lichfield & District Crematorium Staffs 85 L2
Lickey Worcs 85 H7
Lickey End Worcs 85 H8
Lickfold W Susx 30 F6
Liddesdale Highld 190 F4
Liddington Swindn 40 E4
Lidgate Suffk 77 G3
Lidlington C Beds 74 E6
Liff Angus 186 E2
Lifford Birm 85 J7
Lifton Devon 9 K7
Liftondown Devon 9 K7
Lighthorne Warwks 72 D4
Lighthorne Heath Warwks 72 D4
Lightwater Surrey 42 F7
Lightwater Valley Theme Park N York 132 D4
Lightwood C Stke 99 L4
Lilbourne Nhants 87 H7
Lilleshall Wrekin 84 D1
Lilley Herts 59 J3
Lilliesleaf Border 167 H4
Lillingstone Dayrell Bucks 73 K6
Lillingstone Lovell Bucks 73 K6
Lillington Dorset 26 F8
Lilliput Poole 15 K4
Lilstock Somset 25 J3
Limbury Luton 59 H3
Limekilnburn S Lans 175 J7
Limekilns Fife 176 E2
Limerigg Falk 176 B4
Limerstone IoW 16 E6
Lime Street Worcs 55 J2
Limington Somset 26 D6
Limmerhaugh E Ayrs 164 C4

Limpenhoe Norfk 93 H3
Limpley Stoke Wilts 39 H7
Limpsfield Surrey 32 D3
Limpsfield Chart Surrey 32 D3
Linby Notts 101 K3
Linchmere W Susx 30 E5
Lincluden D & G 155 G6
Lincoln Lincs 116 F7
Lincoln Crematorium Lincs 117 G7
Lincomb Worcs 70 E2
Lindale Cumb 129 J4
Lindal in Furness Cumb 128 F4
Lindfield W Susx 32 C7
Lindford Hants 30 D4
Lindley Kirk 123 G6
Lindores Fife 186 D4
Lindridge Worcs 70 C2
Lindsell Essex 61 G3
Lindsey Suffk 77 L5
Lindsey Tye Suffk 78 B5
Lingdale R & Cl 142 E4
Lingen Herefs 69 G2
Lingfield Surrey 32 C4
Lingwood Norfk 93 H2
Linicro Highld 218 B7
Linkend Worcs 55 J2
Linkenholt Hants 41 G8
Linkinhorne Cnwll 5 L2
Linktown Fife 177 J1
Linkwood Moray 214 F3
Linley Shrops 83 G5
Linley Green Herefs 70 C4
Linlithgow W Loth 176 D3
Linn Crematorium E Rens 175 G6
Linsidemore Highld 222 D2
Linslade C Beds 58 E3
Linstead Parva Suffk 93 G7
Linstock Cumb 148 D4
Linthurst Worcs 85 H8
Linthwaite Kirk 123 G7
Lintlaw Border 179 H6
Lintmill Moray 215 L2
Linton Border 168 B4
Linton Cambs 76 E5
Linton Derbys 86 C1
Linton Herefs 54 F3
Linton Kent 33 K3
Linton Leeds 124 B2
Linton N York 131 J6
Linton Hill Herefs 54 F3
Linton-on-Ouse N York 133 G7
Linwood Lincs 117 J4
Linwood Rens 174 E5
Lionacleit W Isls 233 b7
Lional W Isls 232 g1
Liphook Hants 30 D5
Liscard Wirral 111 J3
Liscombe Somset 24 D5
Liskeard Cnwll 5 K3
Lismore Ag & B 191 G7
Liss Hants 30 C5
Lissett E R Yk 135 H7
Lissington Lincs 117 J5
Lisvane Cardif 37 J4
Liswerry Newpt 37 M3
Litcham Norfk 105 L8
Litchborough Nhants 73 J4
Litchfield Hants 29 J2
Litherland Sefton 111 K2
Litlington Cambs 75 K6
Litlington E Susx 20 B5
Little Abington Cambs 76 D5
Little Addington Nhants 88 D8
Little Airies D & G 145 J5
Little Alne Warwks 71 K3
Little Altcar Sefton 111 J1
Little Amwell Herts 60 B5
Little Aston Staffs 85 K4
Little Ayton N York 142 C5
Little Baddow Essex 61 J6
Little Badminton S Glos 39 J4
Little Bampton Cumb 148 A4
Little Bardfield Essex 61 G2
Little Barford Bed 75 H3
Little Barningham Norfk 106 D5
Little Barrington Gloucs 56 D5
Little Barrow Ches W 112 C7
Little Bavington Nthumb 158 C6
Little Bedwyn Wilts 40 F7
Little Bentley Essex 62 D3
Little Berkhamsted Herts 59 M6
Little Billing Nhants 74 B3
Little Billington C Beds 58 F4
Little Birch Herefs 54 D2
Little Blakenham Suffk 78 D5
Little Blencow Cumb 148 E7
Little Bognor W Susx 31 G7
Little Bollington Ches E 113 G4
Little Bookham Surrey 31 J1
Littleborough Notts 116 D5
Littleborough Rochdl 122 D7
Littlebourne Kent 35 G3
Little Bourton Oxon 72 F5
Little Braxted Essex 61 K5
Little Brechin Angus 196 F4
Littlebredy Dorset 14 B5
Little Brickhill M Keyn 58 E2
Little Brington Nhants 73 J2
Little Bromley Essex 62 C3
Little Budworth Ches W 112 E7
Littleburn Highld 212 F4
Little Burstead Essex 46 A2
Littlebury Essex 76 D6
Littlebury Green Essex 76 C6
Little Bytham Lincs 103 G8
Little Carlton Lincs 118 E4
Little Casterton Rutlnd 88 E2
Little Cawthorpe Lincs 118 E5
Little Chalfont Bucks 43 G2
Little Chart Kent 34 C5
Little Chesterford Essex 76 D6
Little Cheverell Wilts 27 M2
Little Chishill Cambs 76 B6
Little Clacton Essex 62 E4
Little Clifton Cumb 136 E2
Little Coates NE Lin 127 G8
Little Comberton Worcs 71 G5
Little Common E Susx 20 E4
Little Compton Warwks 56 E3
Little Cornard Suffk 77 K6
Little Cowarne Herefs 69 L4
Little Coxwell Oxon 40 F2
Little Crakehall N York 132 C2
Little Cressingham Norfk 91 K4
Little Crosby Sefton 111 K2
Little Cubley Derbys 100 D5
Little Dalby Leics 87 L2
Littledean Gloucs 54 F5
Little Dewchurch Herefs 54 D2
Little Ditton Cambs 76 F3
Little Downham Cambs 90 D6
Little Driffield E R Yk 134 F7
Little Dunham Norfk 91 K2
Little Dunkeld P & K 195 G7
Little Dunmow Essex 61 G4
Little Durnford Wilts 28 C5
Little Easton Essex 60 F3
Little Eaton Derbys 101 G4
Little Ellingham Norfk 92 B4
Little Everdon Nhants 73 H3
Little Eversden Cambs 75 L4
Little Faringdon Oxon 56 E7
Little Fencote N York 132 D2
Little Fenton N York 124 D4
Little Fransham Norfk 91 K2
Little Gaddesden Herts 59 G5
Little Glemham Suffk 79 H3
Little Gorsley Herefs 55 G3
Little Gransden Cambs 75 J4
Little Green Somset 27 G2
Little Hadham Herts 60 C4
Little Hale Lincs 103 J4
Little Hallam Derbys 101 J4
Little Hallingbury Essex 60 D4
Littleham Devon 12 D6
Littleham Devon 23 G6
Littlehampton W Susx 18 D5
Little Harrowden Nhants 74 C1
Little Haseley Oxon 57 M7
Little Haven Pembks 48 E5
Littlehaven W Susx 31 K5
Little Hay Staffs 85 K3
Little Haywood Staffs 100 A7
Littlehempston Devon 7 J4
Little Hereford Herefs 69 K2
Little Horkesley Essex 62 A2
Little Hormead Herts 60 C3
Little Horsted E Susx 19 M3
Little Horton C Brad 123 H4
Little Horwood Bucks 58 C2
Little Houghton Barns 115 H1
Little Houghton Nhants 74 B3
Little Hucklow Derbys 114 D5
Little Hutton N York 133 G4
Little Irchester Nhants 74 C2
Little Keyford Somset 27 H3
Little Kimble Bucks 58 D6
Little Kineton Warwks 72 D4
Little Kingshill Bucks 58 E7
Little Knox D & G 146 E3
Little Langdale Cumb 137 J6
Little Langford Wilts 28 B4
Little Leigh Ches W 112 F6
Little Leighs Essex 61 H5
Little Lever Bolton 121 L8
Little Linford M Keyn 74 B5
Little Load Somset 26 C6
Little London E Susx 20 C2
Little London Hants 29 G2
Little London Hants 41 L8
Little Longstone Derbys 114 D6
Little Maplestead Essex 77 J7
Little Marcle Herefs 70 C7
Little Marlow Bucks 42 E3
Little Massingham Norfk 105 J7
Little Melton Norfk 92 E3
Littlemill Abers 205 H6
Littlemill Highld 213 L4
Little Mill Mons 53 L7
Little Milton Oxon 57 L7
Little Missenden Bucks 58 F7
Littlemore Oxon 57 K7
Little Musgrave Cumb 139 H5
Little Ness Shrops 98 B8
Little Newcastle Pembks 49 G2
Little Newsham Dur 140 E4
Little Norton Somset 26 C7
Little Oakley Essex 62 F3
Little Oakley Nhants 88 C6
Little Orton Cumb 148 C4
Littleover C Derb 101 G5
Little Packington Warwks 86 B6
Little Paxton Cambs 75 H3
Little Petherick Cnwll 4 E2
Little Plumstead Norfk 93 G2
Little Ponton Lincs 102 F6
Littleport Cambs 90 E6
Little Preston Nhants 73 H4
Little Raveley Cambs 89 J7
Little Reedness E R Yk 125 J6
Little Ribston N York 132 F8
Little Rissington Gloucs 56 D4
Little Rollright Oxon 56 F3
Little Ryburgh Norfk 106 A6
Little Salkeld Cumb 148 F7
Little Sampford Essex 76 F7
Little Saughall Ches W 111 K7
Little Saxham Suffk 77 H2
Little Scatwell Highld 212 B3
Little Shelford Cambs 76 C4
Little Singleton Lancs 120 E3
Little Skipwith N York 125 G3
Little Smeaton N York 124 D6
Little Snoring Norfk 106 A6
Little Sodbury S Glos 39 H4
Little Somborne Hants 29 G5
Little Somerford Wilts 39 L4
Little Soudley Shrops 99 G6
Little Stainton Darltn 141 J3
Little Stanney Ches W 112 B6
Little Staughton Bed 75 G3
Little Steeping Lincs 118 F8
Little Stoke Staffs 99 K6
Littlestone-on-Sea Kent 21 L2
Little Stonham Suffk 78 D3
Little Stretton Leics 87 J4
Little Stretton Shrops 83 J5
Little Strickland Cumb 138 E4
Little Stukeley Cambs 89 H7
Little Sugnall Staffs 99 J6
Little Swinburne Nthumb 158 B6
Little Sypland D & G 146 C4
Little Tew Oxon 57 G3
Little Tey Essex 61 L4
Little Thetford Cambs 90 D7
Little Thorpe Dur 151 K6
Littlethorpe Leics 87 G4
Littlethorpe N York 132 E5
Little Thurlow Suffk 76 F4
Little Thurrock Thurr 45 L4
Littleton Angus 196 B6
Littleton Ches W 112 C7
Littleton D & G 146 B4
Littleton Hants 29 J5
Littleton Somset 26 C5
Littleton Surrey 43 H6
Littleton Drew Wilts 39 J4
Littleton-on-Severn S Glos 38 E3
Littleton Pannell Wilts 27 M2
Little Torrington Devon 10 D2
Littletown Dur 151 H6
Little Town Lancs 121 K4
Little Urswick Cumb 128 F5
Little Wakering Essex 46 F3
Little Walden Essex 76 D6
Little Waldingfield Suffk 77 K5
Little Walsingham Norfk 105 M5
Little Waltham Essex 61 H5
Little Weighton E R Yk 126 B4
Little Wenlock Wrekin 84 B3

Little Weston Somset 26 F6
Little Whitefield IoW 17 H4
Littlewick Green W & M 42 D4
Little Wilbraham Cambs 76 D3
Little Witcombe Gloucs 55 K5
Little Witley Worcs 70 D2
Little Wittenham Oxon 41 K2
Little Wolford Warwks 72 C7
Little Woodcote Gt Lon 44 F7
Littleworth Oxon 40 F2
Littleworth Staffs 99 L7
Littleworth Worcs 70 F4
Little Wymington Bed 74 D2
Little Wymondley Herts 59 K3
Little Wyrley Staffs 85 H3
Little Yeldham Essex 77 H6
Littley Green Essex 61 H4
Litton Derbys 114 D6
Litton N York 131 G5
Litton Somset 26 E1
Litton Cheney Dorset 14 A4
Liurbost W Isls 232 f3
Liverpool Lpool 111 K4
Liverpool Maritime Mercantile City Lpool 111 K4
Liversedge Kirk 123 J5
Liverton Devon 7 J2
Liverton R & Cl 142 F4
Livingston W Loth 176 E5
Livingston Village W Loth 176 E5
Lixwm Flints 111 G7
Lizard Cnwll 3 J8
Llanaelhaearn Gwynd 95 G4
Llanafan Cerdgn 66 F1
Llanafan-Fawr Powys 67 L4
Llanallgo IoA 109 G4
Llanarmon Dyffryn Ceiriog Wrexhm 97 J6
Llanarmon-yn-Ial Denbgs 97 J2
Llanarth Cerdgn 65 L3
Llanarth Mons 54 B5
Llanarthne Carmth 51 G2
Llanasa Flints 110 F5
Llanbadarn Fawr Cerdgn 80 E7
Llanbadarn Fynydd Powys 82 C7
Llanbadoc Mons 54 B7
Llanbeder Newpt 38 B3
Llanbedr Gwynd 95 K7
Llanbedr Powys 53 K4
Llanbedr-Dyffryn-Clwyd Denbgs 97 H2
Llanbedrgoch IoA 109 G5
Llanbedrog Gwynd 94 F6
Llanbedr-y-Cennin Conwy 109 L7
Llanberis Gwynd 95 K1
Llanbethery V Glam 37 G6
Llanbister Powys 82 C8
Llanblethian V Glam 36 F5
Llanboidy Carmth 49 L3
Llanbradach Caerph 37 J3
Llanbrynmair Powys 81 J3
Llancadle V Glam 37 G6
Llancarfan V Glam 37 G6
Llancloudy Herefs 54 D4
Llandaff Cardif 37 J5
Llandanwg Gwynd 95 K6
Llanddaniel Fab IoA 109 G7
Llanddarog Carmth 51 G3
Llanddeiniol Cerdgn 66 D1
Llanddeiniolen Gwynd 109 H7
Llandderfel Gwynd 96 F5
Llanddeusant IoA 108 D4
Llanddew Powys 53 G2
Llanddewi Swans 50 F7
Llanddewi Brefi Cerdgn 66 F4
Llanddewi Rhydderch Mons 53 M5
Llanddewi Velfrey Pembks 49 K4
Llanddewi Ystradenni Powys 68 C2
Llanddoget Conwy 109 M8
Llanddona IoA 109 H5
Llanddowror Carmth 50 B3
Llanddulas Conwy 110 C6
Llanddwywe Gwynd 95 K7
Llanddyfnan IoA 109 G5
Llandefaelog-Tre'r-Graig Powys 53 H3
Llandefalle Powys 68 C7
Llandegfan IoA 109 H6
Llandegla Denbgs 97 J3
Llandegley Powys 68 D2
Llandegveth Mons 37 M2
Llandeilo Carmth 51 J2
Llandeilo Graban Powys 68 C5
Llandeloy Pembks 48 E3
Llandenny Mons 54 B7
Llandevaud Newpt 38 B3
Llandevenny Mons 38 B3
Llandinam Powys 82 B5
Llandissilio Pembks 49 J3
Llandogo Mons 54 D7
Llandough V Glam 36 F6
Llandough V Glam 37 J5
Llandovery Carmth 67 G7
Llandow V Glam 36 E5
Llandre Carmth 66 F6
Llandre Cerdgn 80 E6
Llandre Isaf Pembks 49 J2
Llandrillo Denbgs 97 G5
Llandrillo-yn-Rhos Conwy 110 B5
Llandrindod Wells Powys 68 B3
Llandrinio Powys 97 L8
Llandudno Conwy 109 L5
Llandudno Junction Conwy 109 M6
Llandulas Powys 67 J6
Llandwrog Gwynd 95 H2
Llandybie Carmth 51 J3
Llandyfaelog Carmth 50 E3
Llandyfriog Cerdgn 65 K6
Llandygai Gwynd 109 H7
Llandygwydd Cerdgn 65 H5
Llandyrnog Denbgs 110 F8
Llandyssil Powys 82 E4
Llandysul Cerdgn 65 L6
Llanedeyrn Cardif 37 K4
Llaneglwys Powys 68 B6
Llanegryn Gwynd 80 D3
Llanegwad Carmth 51 G2
Llaneilian IoA 108 F3
Llanelian-yn-Rhôs Conwy 110 B6
Llanelidan Denbgs 97 H3
Llanelieu Powys 68 D7
Llanellen Mons 53 L5
Llanelli Carmth 51 G5
Llanelli Crematorium Carmth 51 G5
Llanelltyd Gwynd 96 A8
Llanelwedd Powys 68 B4
Llanenddwyn Gwynd 95 K7
Llanengan Gwynd 94 E6
Llanerchymedd IoA 108 E5
Llanerfyl Powys 82 B2
Llanfachraeth IoA 108 D5
Llanfachreth Gwynd 96 B7
Llanfaelog IoA 108 D6
Llanfaelrhys Gwynd 94 D6
Llanfaethlu IoA 108 D4
Llanfair Gwynd 95 K6
Llanfair Caereinion Powys 82 C3
Llanfair Clydogau Cerdgn 66 E4
Llanfair Dyffryn Clwyd Denbgs 97 H2
Llanfairfechan Conwy 109 K6
Llanfairpwllgwyngyll IoA 109 G6
Llanfair Talhaiarn Conwy 110 C7
Llanfair Waterdine Shrops 82 E7
Llanfairynghornwy IoA 108 D4
Llanfair-yn-Neubwll IoA 108 C6
Llanfallteg Carmth 49 K4
Llanfallteg West Carmth 49 K4
Llanfarian Cerdgn 80 D7
Llanfechain Powys 97 J7
Llanfechell IoA 108 E3
Llanferres Denbgs 97 J1
Llanfihangel-ar-arth Carmth 66 B6
Llanfihangel Glyn Myfyr Conwy 96 F3
Llanfihangel Nant Bran Powys 67 K7
Llanfihangel Rhydithon Powys 68 D2
Llanfihangel Rogiet Mons 38 C3
Llanfihangel-y-Creuddyn Cerdgn 80 F7
Llanfihangel-yng-Ngwynfa Powys 82 C1
Llanfihangel yn Nhowyn IoA 108 D6
Llanfihangel-y-traethau Gwynd 95 K5
Llanfilo Powys 53 H2
Llanfoist Mons 53 L5
Llanfor Gwynd 96 E5
Llanfrechfa Torfn 37 L2
Llanfrynach Powys 53 G3
Llanfwrog Denbgs 97 H2
Llanfwrog IoA 108 C5
Llanfyllin Powys 97 H8
Llanfynydd Carmth 66 D8
Llanfynydd Flints 97 L2
Llanfyrnach Pembks 49 L2
Llangadfan Powys 81 L2
Llangadog Carmth 66 F8
Llangadwaladr IoA 108 E7
Llangaffo IoA 108 F7
Llangammarch Wells Powys 67 K5
Llangan V Glam 36 E5
Llangarron Herefs 54 D4
Llangathen Carmth 51 H2
Llangattock Powys 53 K4
Llangattock Lingoed Mons 54 A4
Llangedwyn Powys 97 J7
Llangefni IoA 108 F6
Llangeinor Brdgnd 36 E3
Llangeitho Cerdgn 66 E3
Llangeler Carmth 65 L6
Llangelynin Gwynd 80 D3
Llangendeirne Carmth 50 F3
Llangennech Carmth 51 H5
Llangennith Swans 50 E7
Llangernyw Conwy 110 B7
Llangian Gwynd 94 E6
Llangloffan Pembks 64 C7
Llanglydwen Carmth 49 K3
Llangoed IoA 109 J5
Llangollen Denbgs 97 K4
Llangolman Pembks 49 J3
Llangors Powys 53 H3
Llangower Gwynd 96 D6
Llangrannog Cerdgn 65 K4
Llangristiolus IoA 108 F6
Llangrove Herefs 54 D4
Llangunllo Powys 68 E1
Llangunnor Carmth 50 E2
Llangurig Powys 81 K7
Llangwm Conwy 96 F4
Llangwm Mons 54 B7
Llangwm Pembks 49 G5
Llangwnnadl Gwynd 94 D6
Llangwyryfon Cerdgn 66 D1
Llangybi Cerdgn 66 E4
Llangybi Gwynd 95 G4
Llangybi Mons 38 A2
Llangynhafal Denbgs 110 F8
Llangynidr Powys 53 J4
Llangynin Carmth 50 B2
Llangynog Carmth 50 D3
Llangynog Powys 97 G7
Llangynwyd Brdgnd 36 D3
Llanhamlach Powys 53 H3
Llanharan Rhondd 36 F4
Llanharry Rhondd 36 F4
Llanhennock Mons 38 A2
Llanhilleth Blae G 53 K7
Llanidloes Powys 81 K6
Llaniestyn Gwynd 94 E5
Llanigon Powys 68 E6
Llanilar Cerdgn 80 E8
Llanilid Rhondd 36 F4
Llanina Cerdgn 65 L3
Llanishen Cardif 37 J4
Llanishen Mons 54 C7
Llanllechid Gwynd 109 J7
Llanllowell Mons 54 B7
Llanllugan Powys 82 B3
Llanllwch Carmth 50 E2
Llanllwchaiarn Powys 82 C5
Llanllwni Carmth 66 C6
Llanllyfni Gwynd 95 H3
Llanmadoc Swans 50 F6
Llanmaes V Glam 36 F6
Llanmartin Newpt 38 B3
Llanmiloe Carmth 50 B4
Llannefydd Conwy 110 D7
Llannon Carmth 51 G4
Llannor Gwynd 94 F5
Llanon Cerdgn 66 C2
Llanover Mons 53 L6
Llanpumsaint Carmth 65 L8
Llanrhaeadr-ym-Mochnant Powys 97 H7
Llanrhian Pembks 48 D2
Llanrhidian Swans 50 F6
Llanrhychwyn Conwy 96 B1
Llanrhyddlad IoA 108 D4
Llanrhystud Cerdgn 66 C1
Llanrug Gwynd 109 G8
Llanrumney Cardif 37 K4
Llanrwst Conwy 96 C1
Llansadurnen Carmth 50 C4
Llansadwrn Carmth 66 F7
Llansadwrn IoA 109 H6
Llansaint Carmth 50 E4
Llansamlet Swans 51 K6
Llansanffraid Glan Conwy Conwy 109 M6
Llansannan Conwy 110 C7
Llansantffraed Powys 53 H4
Llansantffraed-Cwmdeuddwr Powys 67 L2
Llansantffraed-in-Elvel Powys 68 C4
Llansantffraid Cerdgn 66 C2
Llansantffraid-ym-Mechain Powys 97 K7
Llansawel Carmth 66 E7
Llansilin Powys 97 K6
Llansoy Mons 54 C7
Llanspyddid Powys 52 F3
Llanstadwell Pembks 48 F6
Llansteffan Carmth 50 D4
Llantarnam Torfn 37 L2
Llanteg Pembks 49 K5
Llanthewy Skirrid Mons 53 M5
Llanthony Mons 53 L3
Llantilio-Crossenny Mons 54 B5
Llantilio Pertholey Mons 53 L5
Llantrisant Mons 38 B2

Llantrisant Rhondd 37 G4
Llantrithyd V Glam 37 G6
Llantwit Fardre Rhondd 37 G3
Llantwit Major V Glam 36 F6
Llanuwchllyn Gwynd 96 D6
Llanvaches Newpt 38 B3
Llanvair Discoed Mons 38 C3
Llanvapley Mons 54 A5
Llanvetherine Mons 54 A5
Llanvihangel Crucorney Mons 53 L4
Llanwddyn Powys 96 F8
Llanwenog Cerdgn 66 C5
Llanwern Newpt 38 A3
Llanwinio Carmth 50 C1
Llanwnda Gwynd 95 H2
Llanwnda Pembks 64 C6
Llanwnnen Cerdgn 66 C5
Llanwnog Powys 82 B5
Llanwrda Carmth 66 F7
Llanwrin Powys 81 H3
Llanwrthwl Powys 67 L2
Llanwrtyd Wells Powys 67 J5
Llanwyddelan Powys 82 C4
Llanyblodwel Shrops 97 K7
Llanybri Carmth 50 D3
Llanybydder Carmth 66 C5
Llanycefn Pembks 49 J3
Llanychaer Pembks 64 D7
Llanymawddwy Gwynd 96 D8
Llanymynech Powys 97 K7
Llanynghenedl IoA 108 D5
Llanynys Denbgs 110 F8
Llanyre Powys 68 B3
Llanystumdwy Gwynd 95 H5
Llanywern Powys 53 H3
Llawhaden Pembks 49 H4
Llawryglyn Powys 81 K5
Llay Wrexhm 97 M2
Llechrhyd Caerph 53 H6
Llechryd Cerdgn 65 H5
Lledrod Cerdgn 66 E1
Lleyn Peninsula Gwynd 94 E5
Llithfaen Gwynd 94 F4
Lloc Flints 111 G6
Llowes Powys 68 D6
Llwydcoed Rhondd 52 F6
Llwydcoed Crematorium Rhondd 52 F6
Llwydiarth Powys 82 B1
Llwyncelyn Cerdgn 66 B3
Llwyndafydd Cerdgn 65 L4
Llwyngwril Gwynd 80 D2
Llwynmawr Wrexhm 97 K5
Llwynypia Rhondd 36 F2
Llynclys Shrops 97 L7
Llynfaes IoA 108 E5
Llysfaen Conwy 110 B6
Llyswen Powys 68 C6
Llysworney V Glam 36 E5
Llys-y-frân Pembks 49 H3
Llywel Powys 52 D3
Loan Falk 176 C3
Loanhead Mdloth 177 J5
Loaningfoot D & G 147 G4
Loans S Ayrs 163 J3
Lobhillcross Devon 10 C7
Lochailort Highld 200 B8
Lochaline Highld 190 D7
Lochans D & G 144 C4
Locharbriggs D & G 155 H6
Lochavich Ag & B 182 D4
Lochawe Ag & B 183 G2
Loch Baghasdail W Isls 233 c8
Lochboisdale W Isls 233 c8
Lochbuie Ag & B 181 J3
Lochcarron Highld 210 D6
Lochdar W Isls 233 b7
Lochdon Ag & B 181 L2
Lochdonhead Ag & B 181 L2
Lochead Ag & B 172 D3
Lochearnhead Stirlg 184 D3
Lochee C Dund 186 F2
Locheilside Station Highld 191 K2
Lochend Highld 212 F6
Locheport W Isls 233 c6
Loch Euphoirt W Isls 233 c6
Lochfoot D & G 154 F7
Lochgair Ag & B 172 F1
Lochgelly Fife 186 C8
Lochgilphead Ag & B 172 E2
Lochgoilhead Ag & B 183 H6
Lochieheads Fife 186 D5
Lochill Moray 215 G2
Lochindorb Lodge Highld 214 B7
Lochinver Highld 224 D4
Loch Lomond and The Trossachs National Park 184 A5
Lochluichart Highld 211 L2
Lochmaben D & G 155 J5
Lochmaddy W Isls 233 c6
Loch Maree Hotel Highld 219 L7
Loch nam Madadh W Isls 233 c6
Loch Ness Highld 202 E1
Lochore Fife 186 C7
Lochranza N Ayrs 172 F7
Lochside Abers 197 H4
Lochside D & G 155 G6
Lochside Highld 213 J4
Lochslin Highld 223 J5
Lochton S Ayrs 152 F6
Lochty Angus 196 E4
Lochty Fife 187 H5
Lochuisge Highld 190 F5
Lochwinnoch Rens 174 C6
Lochwood D & G 155 J3
Lockengate Cnwll 5 G4
Lockerbie D & G 155 K5
Lockeridge Wilts 40 C6
Lockerley Hants 28 F6
Locking N Som 38 A8
Locking Stumps Warrtn 112 F3
Lockington E R Yk 126 B2
Lockleywood Shrops 99 G6
Locksbottom Gt Lon 45 H6
Locks Heath Hants 17 G2
Lockton N York 134 C2
Loddington Leics 87 L3
Loddington Nhants 88 B7
Loddiswell Devon 7 G6
Loddon Norfk 93 H4
Lode Cambs 76 D3
Lode Heath Solhll 85 L7
Loders Dorset 13 L4
Lodge Hill Crematorium Birm 85 H6
Lodsworth W Susx 30 F6
Lofthouse Leeds 123 L5
Lofthouse N York 131 L5
Lofthouse Gate Wakefd 123 L5
Loftus R & Cl 142 F4
Logan E Ayrs 164 C5
Loganlea W Loth 176 C6
Loggerheads Staffs 99 G5
Logie Angus 197 H4
Logie Fife 186 F4
Logie Moray 214 C4
Logie Coldstone Abers 205 K4
Logie Newton Abers 216 C6
Logie Pert Angus 197 G4
Logierait P & K 194 F6
Logierieve Abers 217 H8
Login Carmth 49 K3
Lolworth Cambs 75 L2
Lonbain Highld 209 L4
Londesborough E R Yk 125 K2
London Gt Lon 44 F4
London Apprentice Cnwll 4 F6
London Colney Herts 59 K7
Londonderry N York 132 D3
London Gateway Services Gt Lon 44 D2
Londonthorpe Lincs 102 F5
London Zoo ZSL Gt Lon 44 F4
Londubh Highld 219 K5
Lonemore Highld 219 J6
Long Ashton N Som 38 D6
Long Bank Worcs 84 D8
Long Bennington Lincs 102 D4
Longbenton N Tyne 151 G2
Longborough Gloucs 56 D3
Long Bredy Dorset 14 B4
Longbridge Birm 85 H7
Longbridge Deverill Wilts 27 K4
Long Buckby Nhants 73 J2
Longburton Dorset 26 F8
Long Clawson Leics 102 B6
Longcliffe Derbys 100 E2
Longcombe Devon 7 J4
Long Compton Staffs 99 J7
Long Compton Warwks 56 F2
Longcot Oxon 40 F3
Long Crendon Bucks 58 B6
Long Crichel Dorset 15 J1
Longden Shrops 83 J3
Long Ditton Surrey 44 D6
Longdon Staffs 85 J2
Longdon Worcs 70 E7
Longdon Green Staffs 85 J2
Longdon upon Tern Wrekin 84 B1
Longdown Devon 11 K6
Longdowns Cnwll 3 J4
Long Duckmanton Derbys 115 H7
Long Eaton Derbys 101 J5
Longfield Kent 45 L6
Longford Covtry 86 D6
Longford Derbys 100 E5
Longford Gloucs 55 J4
Longford Shrops 98 F5
Longford Wrekin 99 G8
Longforgan P & K 186 E2
Longformacus Border 178 E6
Longframlington Nthumb 158 E3
Long Green Ches W 112 C7
Longham Dorset 15 K3
Longham Norfk 91 L1
Long Hanborough Oxon 57 H5
Longhaven Abers 217 L6
Longhirst Nthumb 158 F4
Longhope Gloucs 55 G4
Longhope Ork 234 b7
Longhorsley Nthumb 158 E4
Longhoughton Nthumb 169 J6
Long Itchington Warwks 72 E2
Longlane Derbys 100 E5
Long Lawford Warwks 86 F7
Longleat Safari & Adventure Park Wilts 27 J3
Longlevens Gloucs 55 J4
Longleys P & K 195 L7
Long Load Somset 26 C6
Longmanhill Abers 216 E2
Long Marston Herts 58 E5
Long Marston N York 124 D1
Long Marston Warwks 71 L5
Long Marton Cumb 138 F3
Long Melford Suffk 77 J5
Longmoor Camp Hants 30 C5
Longmorn Moray 214 F3
Longmoss Ches E 113 K6
Long Newnton Gloucs 39 K3
Longnewton Border 167 J4
Long Newton E Loth 178 B5
Longnewton S on T 141 J4
Longney Gloucs 55 H5
Longniddry E Loth 177 L3
Longnor Shrops 83 J4
Longnor Staffs 114 C8
Longparish Hants 29 H3
Long Preston N York 130 F7
Longridge Lancs 121 J3
Longridge W Loth 176 C5
Longriggend N Lans 175 L4
Long Riston E R Yk 126 E3
Longrock Cnwll 2 E5
Longsdon Staffs 99 L2
Longside Abers 217 K5
Longstanton Cambs 76 B2
Longstock Hants 29 G4
Longstowe Cambs 75 K4
Long Stratton Norfk 92 E5
Long Street M Keyn 74 B5
Longstreet Wilts 28 C2
Long Sutton Hants 30 C3
Long Sutton Lincs 104 C7
Long Sutton Somset 26 C6
Longthorpe C Pete 89 H4
Long Thurlow Suffk 78 B2
Longthwaite Cumb 138 B3
Longton Lancs 121 G5
Longtown Cumb 148 C2
Longtown Herefs 53 L3
Longueville Jersey 236 d7
Longville in the Dale Shrops 83 K5
Long Waste Wrekin 84 B1
Long Whatton Leics 101 J7
Longwick Bucks 58 C6
Long Wittenham Oxon 41 K2
Longwitton Nthumb 158 D4
Longwood D & G 146 C3
Longworth Oxon 57 G7
Longyester E Loth 178 C5
Lonmay Abers 217 J3
Lonmore Highld 208 D5
Looe Cnwll 5 K5
Loose Kent 33 K3
Loosley Row Bucks 58 D7
Lootcherbrae Abers 216 B4
Lopen Somset 26 B8
Loppington Shrops 98 C6
Lordshill C Sotn 29 H7
Lords Wood Medway 46 C7
Lornty P & K 195 J6
Loscoe Derbys 101 H3
Lossiemouth Moray 214 F1
Lostock Gralam Ches W 113 G6
Lostock Green Ches W 113 G6
Lostwithiel Cnwll 5 H4
Lothbeg Highld 227 G6
Lothersdale N York 122 E2
Lothmore Highld 227 G6
Loudwater Bucks 42 E3
Loughborough Leics 101 K8
Loughborough Crematorium Leics 101 K8
Loughor Swans 51 H6
Loughton Essex 45 H2
Loughton M Keyn 74 B6
Lound Lincs 103 H8
Lound Notts 116 B4
Lound Suffk 93 K4
Lount Leics 101 G8
Louth Lincs 118 D4
Lovedean Hants 30 B8
Lover Wilts 28 E7
Loversall Donc 115 L2
Loves Green Essex 61 G6
Loveston Pembks 49 J5
Lovington Somset 26 E5

Low Ackworth Wakefd 124 C6
Low Barbeth D & G 144 B2
Low Bentham N York 130 C5
Low Biggins Cumb 130 B4
Low Borrowbridge Cumb 138 E6
Low Bradfield Sheff 114 E3
Low Bradley N York 122 F2
Low Burnham N Linc 116 C2
Lowca Cumb 136 D3
Low Catton E R Yk 133 L8
Low Crosby Cumb 148 D3
Lowdham Notts 102 A3
Low Dinsdale Darltn 141 J5
Lower Aisholt Somset 25 J4
Lower Ansty Dorset 14 E2
Lower Apperley Gloucs 55 J3
Lower Ashton Devon 11 J7
Lower Assendon Oxon 42 C4
Lower Bartle Lancs 121 G4
Lower Basildon W Berk 41 L5
Lower Beeding W Susx 31 L6
Lower Benefield Nhants 88 E5
Lower Bentley Worcs 71 H2
Lower Boddington Nhants 72 F4
Lower Bourne Surrey 30 D3
Lower Brailes Warwks 72 C6
Lower Breakish Highld 199 L2
Lower Broadheath Worcs 70 E3
Lower Broxwood Herefs 69 G4
Lower Bullingham Herefs 69 K6
Lower Burgate Hants 28 D7
Lower Caldecote C Beds 75 H5
Lower Chapel Powys 68 B7
Lower Chicksgrove Wilts 27 L5
Lower Chute Wilts 28 F2
Lower Clapton Gt Lon 45 G3
Lower Clent Worcs 85 G7
Lower Cumberworth Kirk 123 J8
Lower Dean Bed 74 F2
Lower Diabaig Highld 210 C3
Lower Dicker E Susx 20 B4
Lower Down Shrops 83 G6
Lower Dunsforth N York 133 G6
Lower Egleton Herefs 70 B5
Lower End M Keyn 74 D6
Lower Eythorne Kent 35 H5
Lower Failand N Som 38 D5
Lower Farringdon Hants 30 B4
Lower Feltham Gt Lon 43 H6
Lower Froyle Hants 30 C3
Lower Gabwell Devon 7 L2
Lower Gledfield Highld 222 D4
Lower Godney Somset 26 C3
Lower Gornal Dudley 85 G5
Lower Gravenhurst C Beds 75 G7
Lower Green Kent 32 F5
Lower Green Kent 33 G5
Lower Halliford Surrey 43 H6
Lower Halstow Kent 46 E6
Lower Hamworthy Poole 15 J4
Lower Hardres Kent 34 F4
Lower Hartwell Bucks 58 C5
Lower Hergest Herefs 68 F4
Lower Heyford Oxon 57 J3
Lower Heysham Lancs 129 J7
Lower Houses Kirk 123 H7
Lower Irlam Salfd 113 G3
Lower Killeyan Ag & B 160 A2
Lower Langford N Som 38 C7
Lower Largo Fife 187 G6
Lower Leigh Staffs 100 A5
Lower Loxhore Devon 23 K4
Lower Lydbrook Gloucs 54 E5
Lower Lye Herefs 69 H2
Lower Machen Newpt 37 K3
Lower Merridge Somset 25 J4
Lower Middleton Cheney Nhants 73 G6
Lower Moor Worcs 71 H5
Lower Morton S Glos 38 F3
Lower Nazeing Essex 60 C6
Lower Penarth V Glam 37 J6
Lower Penn Staffs 84 F4
Lower Peover Ches E 113 H6
Lower Quinton Warwks 71 L5
Lower Raydon Suffk 78 C6
Lower Roadwater Somset 25 G4
Lower Seagry Wilts 39 L4
Lower Shelton C Beds 74 E6
Lower Shiplake Oxon 42 C4
Lower Shuckburgh Warwks 72 F3
Lower Slaughter Gloucs 56 D4
Lower Standen Kent 35 H6
Lower Stanton St Quintin Wilts 39 L4
Lower Stoke Medway 46 D5
Lower Stone Gloucs 38 F2
Lower Stow Bedon Norfk 91 L5
Lower Street Norfk 106 F5
Lower Street Suffk 78 D4
Lower Swanwick Hants 16 F1
Lower Swell Gloucs 56 D3
Lower Tean Staffs 100 A5
Lower Town Devon 7 G2
Lower Town Pembks 64 D6
Lower Upcott Devon 11 K8
Lower Upham Hants 29 K7
Lower Weare Somset 26 B2
Lower Welson Herefs 68 F4
Lower Westmancote Worcs 71 G6
Lower Whatley Somset 27 H3
Lower Whitley Ches W 112 E5
Lower Wield Hants 29 M4
Lower Willingdon E Susx 20 C5
Lower Withington Ches E 113 J7
Lower Woodford Wilts 28 C4
Lower Wraxhall Dorset 14 B3
Lowesby Leics 87 K3
Lowestoft Suffk 93 L5
Loweswater Cumb 137 G3
Low Fell Gatesd 151 G3
Lowfield Heath W Susx 31 L4
Low Gartachorrans Stirlg 174 E2
Low Grantley N York 132 C5
Low Ham Somset 26 B5
Low Harrogate N York 132 D7
Low Hesket Cumb 148 E5
Low Hutton N York 134 B6
Lowick Nhants 88 E7
Lowick Nthumb 168 F2
Lowick Green Cumb 129 G3
Low Lorton Cumb 137 G3
Low Marnham Notts 116 D7
Low Mill N York 142 E7
Low Moorsley Sundld 151 H5
Low Moresby Cumb 136 D3
Low Newton Cumb 129 J3
Low Row Cumb 149 G3
Low Row N York 140 B7
Low Salchrie D & G 144 B2
Low Santon N Linc 125 L7
Lowsonford Warwks 71 L2
Low Tharston Norfk 92 E4
Lowther Cumb 138 D3
Lowthorpe E R Yk 135 G7
Lowton Somset 25 J7
Low Torry Fife 176 D2
Low Worsall N York 141 J5
Low Wray Cumb 137 K6
Loxbeare Devon 11 L2
Loxhill Surrey 31 G4
Loxhore Devon 23 K4
Loxley Warwks 72 C4
Loxton N Som 26 A1
Loxwood W Susx 31 H5
Loyal Lodge Highld 229 J6
Lubenham Leics 87 K6
Luccombe Somset 24 E3
Luccombe Village IoW 17 H6
Lucker Nthumb 169 H4
Luckett Cnwll 6 B2
Lucking Street Essex 77 J7
Luckington Wilts 39 J4
Lucklawhill Fife 187 G3
Luckwell Bridge Somset 24 E4
Lucton Herefs 69 J2
Ludag W Isls 233 b9
Ludborough Lincs 118 D3
Ludbrook Devon 6 F5
Ludchurch Pembks 49 K5
Luddenden Calder 122 F5
Luddenden Foot Calder 122 F5
Luddesdown Kent 46 A6
Luddington N Linc 125 J7
Luddington Warwks 71 L4
Luddington in the Brook Nhants 89 G6
Ludford Lincs 117 K4
Ludford Shrops 83 K8
Ludgershall Bucks 58 A4
Ludgershall Wilts 28 E2
Ludgvan Cnwll 2 E5
Ludham Norfk 107 H8
Ludlow Shrops 83 K7
Ludney Somset 26 B8
Ludwell Wilts 27 K6
Ludworth Dur 151 J6
Luffness E Loth 178 B3
Lugar E Ayrs 164 C5
Luggate Burn E Loth 178 D4
Luggiebank N Lans 175 K4
Lugton E Ayrs 174 D7
Lugwardine Herefs 69 K6
Luib Highld 209 J8
Luing Ag & B 181 L5
Lulham Herefs 69 H6
Lullington Derbys 86 B2
Lullington Somset 27 H2
Lulsgate Bottom N Som 38 D7
Lulsley Worcs 70 D4
Lumb Calder 122 F6
Lumby N York 124 D4
Lumloch E Duns 175 H4
Lumphanan Abers 206 B4
Lumphinnans Fife 186 C8
Lumsden Abers 205 K2
Lunan Angus 197 H6
Lunanhead Angus 196 D6
Luncarty P & K 186 A2
Lund E R Yk 126 B2
Lund N York 125 G4
Lundie Angus 186 E1
Lundin Links Fife 187 G6
Lundin Mill Fife 187 G6
Lundy Devon 22 B3
Lunga Ag & B 181 L5
Lunna Shet 235 d4
Lunsford Kent 33 J2
Lunsford's Cross E Susx 20 E4
Lunt Sefton 111 K2
Luppitt Devon 12 F2
Lupset Wakefd 123 L6
Lupton Cumb 129 L4
Lurgashall W Susx 30 F6
Lurley Devon 11 L2
Luscombe Devon 7 J4
Luss Ag & B 183 L8
Lussagiven Ag & B 171 L2
Lusta Highld 208 D3
Lustleigh Devon 11 H8
Luston Herefs 69 J2
Luthermuir Abers 197 G3
Luthrie Fife 186 E4
Luton Devon 7 K1
Luton Devon 12 D2
Luton Luton 59 H4
Luton Medway 46 C6
Luton Airport Luton 59 J4
Lutterworth Leics 87 G6
Lutton Devon 6 E4
Lutton Devon 7 G4
Lutton Lincs 104 C7
Lutton Nhants 89 G6
Luxborough Somset 24 F4
Luxulyan Cnwll 5 G4
Luxulyan Valley Cnwll 5 G4
Lybster Highld 231 J7
Lydbury North Shrops 83 G6
Lydd Kent 21 K2
Lydd Airport Kent 21 L2
Lydden Kent 35 H5
Lydden Kent 35 K2
Lyddington Rutlnd 88 C4
Lydeard St Lawrence Somset 25 H5
Lydford Devon 10 D7
Lydford on Fosse Somset 26 E5
Lydgate Calder 122 D5
Lydham Shrops 83 G5
Lydiard Millicent Wilts 40 C3
Lydiard Tregoze Swindn 40 C4
Lydiate Sefton 111 K2
Lydiate Ash Worcs 85 H7
Lydlinch Dorset 27 H8
Lydney Gloucs 54 F7
Lydstep Pembks 49 J7
Lye Dudley 85 G6
Lye Green E Susx 32 F6
Lye Green Warwks 71 L2
Lye's Green Wilts 27 J3
Lyford Oxon 41 H2
Lymbridge Green Kent 34 F6
Lyme Regis Dorset 13 J4
Lyminge Kent 34 F6
Lymington Hants 16 C4
Lyminster W Susx 18 D5
Lymm Warrtn 113 G4
Lymm Services Warrtn 112 F4
Lympne Kent 34 F7
Lympsham Somset 25 M1
Lympstone Devon 12 C5
Lynchat Highld 203 J5
Lynch Green Norfk 92 D3
Lyndhurst Hants 16 C2
Lyndon Rutlnd 88 C3
Lyndon Green Birm 85 K6
Lyne Border 166 B2
Lyne Surrey 43 G7
Lyneal Shrops 98 C6
Lyneham Oxon 56 F4
Lyneham Wilts 40 A5
Lynemouth Nthumb 159 H4
Lyne of Skene Abers 206 E4
Lyness Ork 234 b7

Lyng Norfk 106 C8
Lyng Somset 25 M5
Lynmouth Devon 23 L2
Lynsted Kent 34 C3
Lynton Devon 23 L2
Lyon's Gate Dorset 14 C2
Lyonshall Herefs 69 G4
Lytchett Matravers Dorset 15 H4
Lytchett Minster Dorset 15 H4
Lyth Highld 231 K3
Lytham Lancs 120 E5
Lytham St Anne's Lancs 120 D5
Lythe N York 143 H5
Lythmore Highld 230 F3

M

Mabe Burnthouse Cnwll 3 K4
Mablethorpe Lincs 119 G4
Macclesfield Ches E 113 K6
Macclesfield Crematorium Ches E 113 K6
Macduff Abers 216 D2
Macharioch Ag & B 161 J7
Machen Caerph 37 K3
Machrie N Ayrs 162 A3
Machrihanish Ag & B 161 G5
Machrins Ag & B 180 E8
Machynlleth Powys 81 G4
Machynys Carmth 51 G5
Mackworth Derbys 100 F5
Macmerry E Loth 177 L4
Madderty P & K 185 K3
Maddiston Falk 176 C3
Madeley Staffs 99 H4
Madeley Wrekin 84 C3
Madingley Cambs 76 B3
Madley Herefs 69 H6
Madresfield Worcs 70 E5
Madron Cnwll 2 E5
Maenclochog Pembks 49 J3
Maendy V Glam 36 F5
Maentwrog Gwynd 95 L4
Maen-y-groes Cerdgn 65 L3
Maer Staffs 99 H5
Maerdy Rhondd 36 F2
Maesbrook Shrops 97 L7
Maesbury Shrops 97 L7
Maesbury Marsh Shrops 97 L7
Maesllyn Cerdgn 65 K5
Maesteg Brdgnd 36 D3
Maesybont Carmth 51 H3
Maesycwmmer Caerph 37 J2
Maggieknockater Moray 215 H5
Magham Down E Susx 20 C4
Maghull Sefton 111 K2
Magna Park Leics 87 G6
Magor Mons 38 B3
Magor Services Mons 38 B3
Maidenbower W Susx 32 B6
Maiden Bradley Wilts 27 J4
Maidencombe Torbay 7 L3
Maidenhayne Devon 13 H4
Maiden Head N Som 38 E6
Maidenhead W & M 42 E4
Maiden Newton Dorset 14 B3
Maidens S Ayrs 163 G7
Maiden's Green Br For 42 E5
Maiden Wells Pembks 49 G7
Maidford Nhants 73 H4
Maids Moreton Bucks 73 K7
Maidstone Kent 33 K3
Maidstone Services Kent 33 L3
Maidwell Nhants 87 L7
Mail Shet 235 d6
Maindee Newpt 37 L3
Mainland Ork 234 c6
Mainland Shet 235 c5
Mainsforth Dur 141 H2
Mains of Balhall Angus 196 E4
Mains of Balnakettle Abers 197 G2
Mains of Dalvey Highld 214 D7
Mains of Haulkerton Abers 197 H2
Mains of Lesmoir Abers 215 K8
Mains of Melgunds Angus 196 E5
Mainsriddle D & G 147 G4
Mainstone Shrops 82 F6
Maisemore Gloucs 55 J4
Major's Green Worcs 85 K7
Malborough Devon 7 G7
Maldon Essex 61 K6
Malham N York 131 G6
Maligar Highld 209 G2
Mallaig Highld 199 L6
Mallaigvaig Highld 199 L5
Malleny Mills C Edin 177 G5
Malltraeth IoA 108 E7
Mallwyd Gwynd 81 J2
Malmesbury Wilts 39 L3
Malmsmead Devon 24 C2
Malpas Ches W 98 C3
Malpas Cnwll 4 D7
Malpas Newpt 37 L3
Maltby Rothm 115 K3
Maltby S on T 141 L5
Maltby le Marsh Lincs 118 F5
Maltman's Hill Kent 34 B6
Malton N York 134 C5
Malvern Hills 70 D5
Malvern Link Worcs 70 E5
Malvern Wells Worcs 70 D6
Mamble Worcs 70 C1
Mamhilad Mons 53 L7
Manaccan Cnwll 3 K6
Manafon Powys 82 C3
Manais W Isls 232 d5
Manaton Devon 11 H8
Manby Lincs 118 E4
Mancetter Warwks 86 D4
Manchester Manch 113 J3
Manchester Airport Manch 113 J5
Manchester Cathedral Salfd 113 J2
Manchester Crematorium Manch 113 J3
Mancot Flints 111 K7
Mandally Highld 201 L5
Manea Cambs 90 C5
Maney Birm 85 K4
Manfield N York 140 F4
Mangotsfield S Glos 38 F5
Manish W Isls 232 d5
Manley Ches W 112 D7
Manmoel Caerph 53 J7
Mannel Ag & B 188 C7
Manningford Bohune Wilts 40 C8
Manningford Bruce Wilts 40 C8
Manningham C Brad 123 H4
Manning's Heath W Susx 31 K5
Mannington Dorset 15 K2
Manningtree Essex 62 D2
Mannofield C Aber 207 H4
Manorbier Pembks 49 H7
Manorbier Newton Pembks 49 H7
Manorhill Border 167 K3
Manorowen Pembks 64 C7
Manor Park Gt Lon 45 H3
Manor Park Crematorium Gt Lon 45 H3
Mansell Gamage Herefs 69 H5
Mansell Lacy Herefs 69 H5
Mansfield E Ayrs 164 C6
Mansfield Notts 101 K1
Mansfield & District Crematorium Notts 101 K2
Mansfield Woodhouse Notts 115 K8
Manston Dorset 27 J7
Manston Kent 35 J2
Manston Leeds 124 B4
Manswood Dorset 15 J2
Manthorpe Lincs 88 F1
Manton N Linc 116 F2
Manton Rutlnd 88 C3
Manton Wilts 40 D6
Manuden Essex 60 D3
Maperton Somset 26 F6
Maplebeck Notts 102 B1
Mapledurham Oxon 42 A5
Mapledurwell Hants 30 B2
Maplehurst W Susx 31 K6
Maplescombe Kent 45 K7
Mapleton Derbys 100 D3
Mapperley Derbys 101 H4
Mapperley Park C Nott 101 L4
Mapperton Dorset 13 L3
Mappleborough Green Warwks 71 J2
Mappleton E R Yk 126 F2
Mapplewell Barns 123 L7
Mappowder Dorset 14 E2
Marazanvose Cnwll 4 C5
Marazion Cnwll 2 F5
Marbury Ches E 98 E4
March Cambs 90 B4
March S Lans 165 J6
Marcham Oxon 41 J2
Marchamley Shrops 98 E6
Marchington Staffs 100 C6
Marchros Gwynd 94 F7
Marchwiel Wrexhm 98 A3
Marchwood Hants 16 D1
Marcross V Glam 36 E6
Marden Herefs 69 K5
Marden Kent 33 J4
Marden Wilts 40 C8
Marden Thorn Kent 33 K5
Mardy Mons 53 L5
Mareham le Fen Lincs 103 L1
Mareham on the Hill Lincs 118 C7
Marehill W Susx 18 E3
Maresfield E Susx 19 M2
Marfleet C KuH 126 E5
Marford Wrexhm 98 A2
Margam Neath 36 B3
Margam Crematorium Neath 36 C4
Margaret Marsh Dorset 27 J7
Margaretting Essex 61 G7
Margaretting Tye Essex 61 G7
Margate Kent 35 K1
Margnaheglish N Ayrs 162 D3
Margrie D & G 145 M5
Margrove Park R & Cl 142 E4
Marham Norfk 91 G2
Marhamchurch Cnwll 9 G4
Marholm C Pete 89 G3
Mariansleigh Devon 24 B6
Marine Town Kent 46 F5
Marionburgh Abers 206 D4
Marishader Highld 209 H2
Maristow Devon 6 C3
Marjoriebanks D & G 155 J5
Mark Somset 26 B2
Markbeech Kent 32 E5
Markby Lincs 119 G5
Mark Cross E Susx 33 G6
Markeaton Crematorium C Derb 100 F5
Market Bosworth Leics 86 E3
Market Deeping Lincs 89 G2
Market Drayton Shrops 98 F5
Market Harborough Leics 87 K6
Market Lavington Wilts 28 A1
Market Overton Rutlnd 88 C1
Market Rasen Lincs 117 J4
Market Stainton Lincs 118 C5
Market Warsop Notts 115 K7
Market Weighton E R Yk 125 K3
Market Weston Suffk 92 B7
Markfield Leics 86 F2
Markham Caerph 53 J7
Markham Moor Notts 116 B6
Markinch Fife 186 E6
Markington N York 132 D6
Markle E Loth 178 C3
Marksbury BaNES 38 F7
Marks Tey Essex 61 L4
Markyate Herts 59 H5
Marlborough Wilts 40 D6
Marlcliff Warwks 71 K4
Marldon Devon 7 K3
Marlesford Suffk 79 G3
Marlingford Norfk 92 D2
Marloes Pembks 48 D5
Marlow Bucks 42 D3
Marlow Bottom Bucks 42 D3
Marlpit Hill Kent 32 D4
Marnhull Dorset 27 H7
Marple Stockp 113 L4
Marr Donc 115 K1
Marrick N York 140 D7
Marsden Kirk 122 F7
Marsden S Tyne 151 J3
Marshalswick Herts 59 K6
Marsham Norfk 106 E7
Marsh Baldon Oxon 57 K7
Marshborough Kent 35 J3
Marshbrook Shrops 83 J5
Marshchapel Lincs 118 E2
Marsh Farm Luton 59 H3
Marshfield Newpt 37 K4
Marshfield S Glos 39 H5
Marshgate Cnwll 8 F6
Marsh Gibbon Bucks 57 M4
Marsh Green Devon 12 D4
Marsh Green Kent 32 D4
Marshland St James Norfk 90 D2
Marsh Lane Derbys 115 H5
Marsh Street Somset 24 F3
Marshwood Dorset 13 J3
Marske N York 140 D6
Marske-by-the-Sea R & Cl 142 D3
Marston Herefs 69 G3
Marston Lincs 102 E4
Marston Oxon 57 K6
Marston Staffs 99 L6
Marston Wilts 27 L1
Marston Green Solhll 85 L6
Marston Magna Somset 26 E6
Marston Meysey Wilts 40 C2
Marston Montgomery Derbys 100 C5
Marston Moretaine C Beds 74 E6
Marston on Dove Derbys 100 E6
Marston St Lawrence Nhants 73 G6
Marston Trussell Nhants 87 K6

Marstow Herefs 54 D4
Marsworth Bucks 58 F5
Marten Wilts 40 F7
Martham Norfk 107 J8
Martin Hants 28 B7
Martin Kent 35 J5
Martin Lincs 103 J1
Martinhoe Devon 23 L2
Martin Hussingtree Worcs 70 F3
Martinstown Dorset 14 C5
Martlesham Suffk 78 F5
Martlesham Heath Suffk 78 F5
Martletwy Pembks 49 H5
Martley Worcs 70 D3
Martock Somset 26 C7
Marton Ches E 113 J7
Marton E R Yk 126 F3
Marton Lincs 116 D5
Marton Middsb 142 B4
Marton N York 132 F6
Marton N York 134 B3
Marton Shrops 82 F3
Marton Warwks 72 E2
Marton-le-Moor N York 132 E5
Martyr Worthy Hants 29 K5
Marwell Wildlife Hants 29 J6
Marwick Ork 234 b5
Marwood Devon 23 H4
Marybank Highld 212 D4
Maryburgh Highld 212 E3
Marygold Border 179 G6
Maryhill C Glas 175 G4
Maryhill Crematorium C Glas 175 G4
Marykirk Abers 197 H3
Marylebone Gt Lon 44 F4
Marylebone Wigan 121 H8
Marypark Moray 214 F6
Maryport Cumb 147 H7
Maryport D & G 144 D7
Marystow Devon 10 C7
Mary Tavy Devon 6 D1
Maryton Angus 197 H5
Marywell Abers 206 B6
Marywell Abers 207 H5
Marywell Angus 197 G7
Masham N York 132 C4
Masongill N York 130 C4
Masonhill Crematorium S Ayrs 163 J5
Mastin Moor Derbys 115 J6
Matching Green Essex 60 E5
Matching Tye Essex 60 E5
Matfen Nthumb 158 C7
Matfield Kent 33 H5
Mathern Mons 38 D3
Mathon Herefs 70 D5
Mathry Pembks 48 E2
Matlask Norfk 106 D5
Matlock Derbys 100 F1
Matlock Bath Derbys 100 F2
Matson Gloucs 55 J5
Mattersey Notts 116 B4
Mattingley Hants 42 B8
Mattishall Norfk 92 C2
Mattishall Burgh Norfk 92 C2
Mauchline E Ayrs 163 L4
Maud Abers 217 H5
Maufant Jersey 236 d6
Maugersbury Gloucs 56 D3
Maughold IoM 237 e3
Mauld Highld 212 C6
Maulden C Beds 74 F6
Maulds Meaburn Cumb 138 F4
Maunby N York 132 E3
Maundown Somset 25 G5
Mautby Norfk 93 K2
Mavesyn Ridware Staffs 85 J1
Mavis Enderby Lincs 118 E7
Mawbray Cumb 147 J5
Mawdesley Lancs 121 G7
Mawdlam Brdgnd 36 C4
Mawgan Cnwll 3 J6
Mawgan Porth Cnwll 4 D3
Mawla Cnwll 3 J3
Mawnan Cnwll 3 K5
Mawnan Smith Cnwll 3 K5
Mawsley Nhants 88 B7
Maxey C Pete 89 G2
Maxstoke Warwks 86 B6
Maxton Border 167 J4
Maxton Kent 35 J6
Maxwell Town D & G 155 G6
Maxworthy Cnwll 9 H6
May Bank Staffs 99 J3
Maybole S Ayrs 163 H7
Maybury Surrey 43 G8
Mayfield E Susx 33 G7
Mayfield Mdloth 177 K5
Mayfield Staffs 100 D4
Mayford Surrey 31 G1
May Hill Gloucs 55 G4
Mayland Essex 61 L7
Maylandsea Essex 61 L7
Maynard's Green E Susx 20 C3
Maypole Birm 85 J7
Maypole Green Norfk 93 J4
Maypole Green Suffk 77 K3
Meadgate BaNES 39 G8
Meadle Bucks 58 D6
Meadowfield Dur 151 G6
Meadwell Devon 9 K8
Meanwood Leeds 123 K3
Meare Somset 26 C3
Meare Green Somset 25 L6
Meare Green Somset 25 M6
Mearns E Rens 174 F7
Mears Ashby Nhants 74 B2
Measham Leics 86 D2
Meathop Cumb 129 J4
Meavy Devon 6 D3
Medbourne Leics 88 B5
Meddon Devon 9 H2
Meden Vale Notts 115 L7
Medmenham Bucks 42 D4
Medomsley Dur 150 E4
Medstead Hants 30 A4
Medway Crematorium Kent 46 C7
Medway Services Medway 46 D7
Meerbrook Staffs 99 M1
Meesden Herts 60 C2
Meeth Devon 10 E3
Meeting House Hill Norfk 107 G6
Meidrim Carmth 50 C2
Meifod Powys 82 D2
Meigle P & K 195 L7
Meikle Carco D & G 164 F6
Meikle Earnock S Lans 175 J7
Meikle Kilmory Ag & B 173 H6
Meikle Obney P & K 195 G8
Meikleour P & K 195 J7
Meikle Wartle Abers 216 D7
Meinciau Carmth 50 F4
Meir C Stke 99 L4
Melbourn Cambs 75 L5
Melbourne Derbys 101 G7
Melbourne E R Yk 125 H2
Melbury Abbas Dorset 27 K7
Melbury Bubb Dorset 14 B2
Melbury Osmond Dorset 14 B2
Melchbourne Bed 74 E2
Melcombe Bingham Dorset 14 E2
Meldon Devon 10 E6
Meldon Nthumb 158 E5
Meldreth Cambs 75 L5
Meldrum Stirlg 184 F7
Melfort Ag & B 182 B5
Meliden Denbgs 110 E5
Melin-y-wig Denbgs 97 G3
Melkinthorpe Cumb 138 D3
Melkridge Nthumb 149 J3
Melksham Wilts 39 K7
Melling Lancs 130 B5
Melling Sefton 111 L2
Mellis Suffk 92 C8
Mellon Charles Highld 219 K3
Mellon Udrigle Highld 219 K3
Mellor Lancs 121 J4
Mellor Stockp 113 M4
Mellor Brook Lancs 121 J4
Mells Somset 27 G2
Melmerby Cumb 149 G7
Melmerby N York 131 K3
Melmerby N York 132 E4
Melness Highld 229 J3
Melplash Dorset 13 L3
Melrose Border 167 H3
Melsetter Ork 234 b7
Melsonby N York 140 F5
Meltham Kirk 123 G7
Melton E R Yk 126 B5
Melton Suffk 79 G4
Melton Constable Norfk 106 C6
Melton Mowbray Leics 102 C8
Melton Ross N Linc 126 D7
Melvaig Highld 219 H4
Melverley Shrops 83 G1
Melvich Highld 230 C3
Membury Devon 13 H2
Membury Services W Berk 40 F5
Memsie Abers 217 H2
Memus Angus 196 C5
Menai Bridge IoA 109 H6
Mendham Suffk 92 F6
Mendip Crematorium Somset 26 E3
Mendip Hills 26 D2
Mendlesham Suffk 78 D2
Mendlesham Green Suffk 78 D2
Menheniot Cnwll 5 L4
Mennock D & G 164 F7
Menston C Brad 123 H2
Menstrie Clacks 185 H7
Mentmore Bucks 58 E4
Meoble Highld 200 C7
Meole Brace Shrops 83 J2
Meonstoke Hants 29 L7
Meopham Kent 45 M6
Mepal Cambs 90 B7
Meppershall C Beds 75 G7
Mere Ches E 113 G5
Mere Wilts 27 J5
Mere Brow Lancs 120 F6
Mereclough Lancs 122 C4
Mere Green Birm 85 K4
Mereworth Kent 33 H3
Meriden Solhll 86 B6
Merkadale Highld 208 F7
Merley Poole 15 J3
Merrion Pembks 48 F7
Merriott Somset 26 C8
Merrow Surrey 31 G2
Merry Hill Herts 43 J2
Merryhill Wolves 84 F4
Merrymeet Cnwll 5 L3
Mersea Island Essex 62 B5
Mersham Kent 34 E6
Merstham Surrey 32 B3
Merston W Susx 18 B5
Merstone IoW 17 G5
Merthyr Cynog Powys 67 L6
Merthyr Mawr Brdgnd 36 D5
Merthyr Tydfil Myr Td 53 G6
Merthyr Vale Myr Td 53 G7
Merton Devon 10 D3
Merton Gt Lon 44 E6
Merton Norfk 91 K4
Merton Oxon 57 L4
Meshaw Devon 24 B7
Messing Essex 61 L4
Messingham N Linc 116 E2
Metfield Suffk 93 G7
Metherell Cnwll 6 B3
Metheringham Lincs 103 H1
Methil Fife 186 F7
Methilhill Fife 186 F7
Methlick Abers 217 G6
Methven P & K 185 L3
Methwold Norfk 91 G4
Methwold Hythe Norfk 91 G4
Mettingham Suffk 93 H5
Metton Norfk 106 E5
Mevagissey Cnwll 4 F6
Mexborough Donc 115 J2
Mey Highld 231 K2
Meylltyrn Gwynd 94 D6
Meysey Hampton Gloucs 56 C7
Miabhig W Isls 232 d2
Miavaig W Isls 232 d2
Michaelchurch Herefs 54 D3
Michaelchurch Escley Herefs 69 G7
Michaelstone-y-Fedw Newpt 37 K4
Michaelston-le-Pit V Glam 37 J5
Michaelstow Cnwll 5 G1
Michaelwood Services Gloucs 39 G2
Micheldever Hants 29 K4
Micheldever Station Hants 29 K3
Michelmersh Hants 29 G6
Mickfield Suffk 78 D3
Micklebring Donc 115 K3
Mickleby N York 143 G5
Micklefield Leeds 124 C4
Mickleham Surrey 31 K2
Mickleover C Derb 100 F5
Mickleton Dur 140 B3
Mickleton Gloucs 71 L5
Mickletown Leeds 124 B5
Mickle Trafford Ches W 112 C7
Mickley N York 132 C4
Mickley Square Nthumb 150 D3
Mid Ardlaw Abers 217 H2
Midbea Ork 234 c4
Mid Beltie Abers 206 C5
Mid Calder W Loth 176 E5
Mid Clyth Highld 231 K7
Mid Culbeuchly Abers 216 C3
Middle Aston Oxon 57 J3
Middle Barton Oxon 57 H3
Middlebie D & G 155 L6
Middlebridge P & K 194 D3
Middle Chinnock Somset 26 C8
Middle Claydon Bucks 58 B3
Middleham N York 131 L3
Middle Handley Derbys 115 H6
Middlehill Wilts 39 J6
Middlehope Shrops 83 K5
Middle Kames Ag & B 172 F1
Middle Littleton Worcs 71 J5
Middlemarsh Dorset 14 C2
Middle Mayfield Staffs 100 C4
Middle Rasen Lincs 117 H4
Middle Rocombe Devon 7 K2
Middlesbrough Middsb 141 L4
Middleshaw Cumb 129 L2
Middlesmoor N York 131 K5
Middle Stoke Medway 46 D5
Middlestone Dur 141 G2

Middlestown Wakefd 123 K6
Middlethird Border 167 K2
Middleton Ag & B 188 B7
Middleton Derbys 100 F2
Middleton Derbys 114 D8
Middleton Essex 77 K6
Middleton Hants 29 H3
Middleton Herefs 69 K1
Middleton Leeds 123 L5
Middleton N York 123 G2
Middleton N York 134 B3
Middleton Nhants 88 B5
Middleton Norfk 90 F1
Middleton Nthumb 158 D5
Middleton P & K 186 B6
Middleton Rochdl 113 K1
Middleton Shrops 83 K7
Middleton Suffk 79 J2
Middleton Swans 50 E7
Middleton Warwks 85 L4
Middleton Cheney Nhants 73 G6
Middleton Crematorium Rochdl 113 K1
Middleton-in-Teesdale Dur 139 L3
Middleton Moor Suffk 79 J2
Middleton One Row Darltn 141 J5
Middleton-on-Sea W Susx 18 C5
Middleton on the Hill Herefs 69 K2
Middleton on the Wolds E R Yk 125 L2
Middleton Park C Aber 207 H3
Middleton Quernhow N York 132 E4
Middleton St George Darltn 141 J5
Middleton Scriven Shrops 84 C6
Middleton Stoney Oxon 57 K4
Middleton Tyas N York 141 G6
Middle Town IoS 2 a2
Middletown Powys 82 F2
Middle Tysoe Warwks 72 D5
Middle Wallop Hants 28 F4
Middlewich Ches E 113 G7
Middle Winterslow Wilts 28 E5
Middlewood Cnwll 5 L2
Middle Woodford Wilts 28 C4
Middlewood Green Suffk 78 D3
Middleyard E Ayrs 163 M3
Middlezoy Somset 26 B5
Midford BaNES 39 H7
Midgham W Berk 41 K6
Midgley Calder 122 F5
Midgley Wakefd 123 K7
Midhopestones Sheff 114 E2
Midhurst W Susx 30 E6
Mid Lavant W Susx 18 B4
Midlem Border 167 H4
Mid Mains Highld 212 C6
Midpark Ag & B 173 H6
Midsomer Norton BaNES 26 F1
Midtown Highld 229 J4
Mid Warwickshire Crematorium Warwks 72 C3
Mid Yell Shet 235 d3
Migvie Abers 205 K4
Milborne Port Somset 26 F7
Milborne St Andrew Dorset 14 F3
Milborne Wick Somset 26 F7
Milbourne Nthumb 158 E6
Milbourne Wilts 39 L3
Milburn Cumb 138 F2
Milbury Heath S Glos 38 F3
Milby N York 132 F6
Milcombe Oxon 72 E7
Milden Suffk 77 L5
Mildenhall Suffk 91 G8
Mildenhall Wilts 40 E6
Mileham Norfk 105 L8
Mile Oak Br & H 19 H4
Milesmark Fife 176 E2
Miles Platting Manch 113 J2
Mile Town Kent 46 F5
Milfield Nthumb 168 D3
Milford Derbys 101 G4
Milford Devon 22 C6
Milford Staffs 99 L7
Milford Surrey 30 F3
Milford Haven Pembks 48 F6
Milford on Sea Hants 16 C4
Milkwall Gloucs 54 E6
Millais Jersey 236 a5
Milland W Susx 30 D5
Mill Bank Calder 122 F6
Millbreck Abers 217 J5
Millbridge Surrey 30 D3
Millbrook C Beds 74 E6
Millbrook C Sotn 29 G8
Millbrook Cnwll 6 B5
Millbrook Jersey 236 c7
Mill Brow Stockp 113 L4
Millbuie Abers 206 F4
Millbuie Highld 212 E4
Millcorner E Susx 21 G2
Millcraig Highld 222 E7
Milldale Staffs 100 C2
Mill End Bucks 42 C4
Mill End Herts 60 B2
Millerhill Mdloth 177 J4
Miller's Dale Derbys 114 C6
Millerston C Glas 175 H5
Mill Green Cambs 76 F5
Mill Green Essex 61 G7
Mill Green Lincs 103 L7
Mill Green Suffk 77 L6
Mill Green Suffk 78 B3
Mill Green Suffk 78 D3
Millhalf Herefs 68 F5
Millheugh S Lans 175 K7
Mill Hill Gt Lon 44 E2
Millhouse Ag & B 173 G4
Millhousebridge D & G 155 K5
Millhouse Green Barns 114 E2
Millhouses Sheff 115 G5
Milliken Park Rens 174 D6
Millington E R Yk 125 J1
Millmeece Staffs 99 J5
Mill of Drummond P & K 185 H4
Mill of Haldane W Duns 174 D2
Millom Cumb 128 E4
Millport N Ayrs 173 K7
Mill Street Suffk 78 C1
Millthrop Cumb 130 C2
Milltimber C Aber 207 G5
Milltown Abers 205 G4
Milltown Abers 205 K3
Milltown D & G 156 C6
Milltown Devon 23 J4
Milltown of Campfield Abers 206 C5
Milltown of Edinvillie Moray 215 G6
Milltown of Learney Abers 206 C5
Milnathort P & K 186 B6
Milngavie E Duns 175 G4
Milnrow Rochdl 122 D7
Milnthorpe Cumb 129 K3
Milovaig Highld 208 B4
Milson Shrops 84 B8
Milstead Kent 34 B3
Milston Wilts 28 D3
Milthorpe Nhants 73 H5
Milton C Stke 99 K3
Milton Cambs 76 C2
Milton Cumb 148 F3
Milton D & G 144 F4
Milton D & G 154 E7
Milton Derbys 100 F7
Milton Highld 209 L5
Milton Highld 212 D7
Milton Highld 212 E4
Milton Highld 223 G6
Milton Highld 231 L5
Milton Inver 174 C5
Milton Kent 46 A5
Milton Moray 204 E2
Milton Moray 215 L2
Milton N Som 37 M7
Milton Notts 116 B6
Milton Oxon 41 J3
Milton Oxon 72 F7
Milton P & K 195 G4
Milton Pembks 49 H6
Milton Somset 26 C6
Milton Stirlg 184 B6
Milton W Duns 174 D4
Milton Abbas Dorset 14 F3
Milton Abbot Devon 9 K8
Milton Bridge Mdloth 177 H5
Milton Bryan C Beds 58 F3
Milton Clevedon Somset 26 F4
Milton Combe Devon 6 D3
Milton Damerel Devon 9 K3
Milton Ernest Bed 74 E4
Milton Green Ches W 98 C2
Milton Hill Oxon 41 J3
Milton Keynes M Keyn 74 C6
Milton Lilbourne Wilts 40 D7
Milton Malsor Nhants 73 K4
Milton Morenish P & K 184 D1
Milton of Auchinhove Abers 206 B5
Milton of Balgonie Fife 186 E7
Milton of Buchanan Stirlg 174 E1
Milton of Campsie E Duns 175 H3
Milton of Leys Highld 213 G6
Milton of Murtle C Aber 207 G5
Milton of Tullich Abers 205 J6
Milton on Stour Dorset 27 J5
Milton Regis Kent 46 E6
Milton-under-Wychwood Oxon 56 E4
Milverton Somset 25 H6
Milverton Warwks 72 C2
Milwich Staffs 99 L6
Minard Ag & B 182 D7
Minchinhampton Gloucs 55 K7
Minehead Somset 24 F3
Minera Wrexhm 97 L3
Minety Wilts 40 A3
Minffordd Gwynd 95 K5
Mingarrypark Highld 190 D3
Miningsby Lincs 118 D8
Minions Cnwll 5 L2
Minishant S Ayrs 163 J6
Minllyn Gwynd 81 J2
Minnigaff D & G 145 J2
Minnonie Abers 216 E3
Minskip N York 132 F6
Minstead Hants 16 C1
Minsted W Susx 30 D7
Minster Kent 35 J2
Minster Kent 46 F5
Minsterley Shrops 83 G3
Minster Lovell Oxon 56 F5
Minsterworth Gloucs 55 H5
Minterne Magna Dorset 14 C2
Minting Lincs 117 K6
Mintlaw Abers 217 J5
Mintlyn Crematorium Norfk 105 G8
Minto Border 167 H5
Minton Shrops 83 H5
Mirehouse Cumb 136 D4
Mireland Highld 231 K4
Mirfield Kirk 123 J6
Miserden Gloucs 55 L6
Miskin Rhondd 37 G4
Misson Notts 116 B3
Misterton Leics 87 G6
Misterton Notts 116 C3
Misterton Somset 13 L2
Mistley Essex 62 D2
Mitcham Gt Lon 44 F6
Mitcheldean Gloucs 54 F4
Mitchell Cnwll 4 D5
Mitchellslacks D & G 155 G3
Mitchel Troy Mons 54 C6
Mitford Nthumb 158 F5
Mithian Cnwll 3 J2
Mixbury Oxon 73 H7
Mobberley Ches E 113 H5
Mobberley Staffs 100 A4
Mochdre Powys 82 B5
Mochrum D & G 145 H5
Mockbeggar Kent 33 J4
Mockerkin Cumb 136 F3
Modbury Devon 6 F5
Moddershall Staffs 99 L5
Moelfre IoA 109 G4
Moelfre Powys 97 J6
Moffat D & G 155 J2
Moggerhanger C Beds 75 G5
Moira Leics 86 C1
Molash Kent 34 D4
Mol-chlach Highld 199 G3
Mold Flints 111 H8
Moldgreen Kirk 123 H7
Molehill Green Essex 60 E3
Molescroft E R Yk 126 C3
Molesworth Cambs 88 F7
Molland Devon 24 C5
Mollington Ches W 111 L7
Mollington Oxon 72 F5
Mollinsburn N Lans 175 J4
Mondynes Abers 197 J1
Monewden Suffk 78 F3
Moneydie P & K 185 M2
Moniaive D & G 154 D4
Monifieth Angus 187 H2
Monikie Angus 196 E8
Monimail Fife 186 E5
Monken Hadley Gt Lon 44 E1
Monk Fryston N York 124 D5
Monkhide Herefs 70 B5
Monkhill Cumb 148 C3
Monkhopton Shrops 84 B5
Monkland Herefs 69 J3
Monkleigh Devon 23 G7
Monknash V Glam 36 E6
Monkokehampton Devon 10 E4
Monkseaton N Tyne 159 H7
Monks Eleigh Suffk 77 L5
Monk's Gate W Susx 31 K6
Monks Heath Ches E 113 J6
Monk Sherborne Hants 29 L1
Monksilver Somset 25 G4
Monks Kirby Warwks 86 F6
Monk Soham Suffk 78 E2
Monks Risborough Bucks 58 D6
Monksthorpe Lincs 118 F7
Monk Street Essex 60 F3
Monkswood Mons 53 M7
Monkton Devon 12 F2
Monkton Kent 47 M6
Monkton S Ayrs 163 J4
Monkton S Tyne 151 H3
Monkton Combe BaNES 39 H7

Monkton Deverill Wilts 27 J4
Monkton Farleigh Wilts 39 J7
Monkton Heathfield Somset 25 K6
Monkton Wyld Dorset 13 J3
Monkwearmouth Sundld 151 J4
Monkwood Hants 30 A5
Monmore Green Wolves 85 G4
Monmouth Mons 54 D5
Monnington on Wye Herefs 69 G5
Monreith D & G 145 H6
Montacute Somset 26 D7
Montford Shrops 83 H1
Montford Bridge Shrops 83 H1
Montgarrie Abers 206 B2
Montgomery Powys 82 E4
Montrose Angus 197 H5
Mont Saint Guern 236 b3
Monxton Hants 28 F3
Monyash Derbys 114 D7
Monymusk Abers 206 D3
Monzie P & K 185 H3
Moodiesburn N Lans 175 J4
Moonzie Fife 186 E4
Moor Allerton Leeds 123 L3
Moorby Lincs 118 D8
Moor Crichel Dorset 15 J2
Moordown Bmouth 15 K4
Moore Halton 112 E5
Moor End Calder 122 F5
Moorends Donc 125 G7
Moorhead C Brad 123 H3
Moorhouse Cumb 148 B4
Moorhouse Notts 116 C7
Moorhouse Bank Surrey 32 D3
Moorlinch Somset 26 B4
Moor Monkton N York 133 H7
Moorsholm R & Cl 142 E4
Moorside Dorset 27 H7
Moor Street Birm 85 H6
Moorswater Cnwll 5 K3
Moorthorpe Wakefd 124 C7
Moortown Leeds 123 K3
Moortown Lincs 117 H2
Morangie Highld 223 G5
Morar Highld 199 L6
Moray Crematorium Moray 215 J3
Morborne Cambs 89 G5
Morchard Bishop Devon 11 H4
Morcombelake Dorset 13 K4
Morcott Rutlnd 88 D4
Morda Shrops 97 L6
Morden Dorset 15 H4
Morden Gt Lon 44 E6
Mordiford Herefs 69 L6
Mordon Dur 141 H2
More Shrops 83 G5
Morebath Devon 24 E6
Morebattle Border 168 B4
Morecambe Lancs 129 J6
Moredon Swindn 40 C3
Morefield Highld 220 E3
Morehall Kent 35 G7
Moreleigh Devon 7 H5
Morenish P & K 184 D1
Morestead Hants 29 K6
Moreton Dorset 14 F4
Moreton Essex 60 E6
Moreton Herefs 69 K2
Moreton Oxon 58 B6
Moreton Wirral 111 J4
Moreton Corbet Shrops 98 E7
Moretonhampstead Devon 11 H7
Moreton-in-Marsh Gloucs 56 D2
Moreton Jeffries Herefs 69 L5
Moreton Morrell Warwks 72 C4
Moreton on Lugg Herefs 69 K5
Moreton Pinkney Nhants 73 H5
Moreton Say Shrops 98 F5
Moreton Valence Gloucs 55 H6
Morfa Nefyn Gwynd 94 E4
Morham E Loth 178 C4
Morland Cumb 138 E3
Morley Ches E 113 J5
Morley Derbys 101 H4
Morley Leeds 123 K5
Morley Green Ches E 113 J5
Morley St Botolph Norfk 92 C4
Morningside C Edin 177 H4
Morningside N Lans 175 L7
Morningthorpe Norfk 92 F5
Morpeth Nthumb 158 F5
Morphie Abers 197 H4
Morrey Staffs 100 C8
Morriston Swans 51 J6
Morston Norfk 106 B4
Mortehoe Devon 23 G3
Morthen Rothm 115 J4
Mortimer W Berk 41 M7
Mortimer West End Hants 41 M7
Mortlake Gt Lon 44 E5
Mortlake Crematorium Gt Lon 44 D5
Morton Cumb 148 C4
Morton Derbys 101 H1
Morton Lincs 103 H7
Morton Lincs 116 D3
Morton Notts 102 B3
Morton Shrops 97 L7
Mortonhall Crematorium C Edin 177 H5
Morton-on-Swale N York 132 E2
Morton on the Hill Norfk 92 D1
Morvah Cnwll 2 D4
Morvich Highld 200 E2
Morville Shrops 84 C5
Morwenstow Cnwll 9 G2
Mosborough Sheff 115 H5
Moscow E Ayrs 163 L2
Moseley Birm 85 J6
Moseley Wolves 85 G4
Moseley Worcs 70 E3
Moss Ag & B 188 B7
Moss Donc 124 F7
Mossat Abers 205 K2
Mossbank Shet 235 d4
Moss Bank St Hel 112 D3
Mossbay Cumb 136 D2
Mossblown S Ayrs 163 K4
Mossburnford Border 167 K6
Mossdale D & G 154 B7
Mossdale E Ayrs 153 K2
Moss Edge Lancs 120 F2
Mossend N Lans 175 K6
Mossley Tamesd 113 L2
Mosspaul Hotel Border 156 D3
Moss-side Highld 213 K4
Mosstodloch Moray 215 H3
Mossyard D & G 145 L5
Mossy Lea Lancs 121 H7
Mosterton Dorset 13 L2
Moston Manch 113 K2
Mostyn Flints 111 G5
Motcombe Dorset 27 J6
Mothecombe Devon 6 F6
Motherby Cumb 138 B2
Motherwell N Lans 175 K6
Motspur Park Gt Lon 44 E6
Mottingham Gt Lon 45 H5
Mottisfont Hants 28 F6
Mottistone IoW 16 E5
Mottram in Longdendale Tamesd 113 M3
Mottram St Andrew Ches E 113 K5
Mouilpied Guern 236 c3
Mouldsworth Ches W 112 D7
Moulin P & K 194 E4
Moulsecoomb Br & H 19 J4
Moulsford Oxon 41 L4
Moulsoe M Keyn 74 C6
Moultavie Highld 222 E7
Moulton Ches W 112 F7
Moulton Lincs 104 A7
Moulton N York 141 G6
Moulton Nhants 73 L2
Moulton Suffk 77 G2
Moulton V Glam 37 G6
Moulton Chapel Lincs 103 M8
Moulton St Mary Norfk 93 H3
Moulton Seas End Lincs 104 A6
Mount Cnwll 5 J3
Mountain C Brad 123 G4
Mountain Ash Rhondd 53 G7
Mountain Cross Border 176 F8
Mount Ambrose Cnwll 3 J3
Mount Bures Essex 61 L2
Mountfield E Susx 20 E2
Mountgerald House Highld 212 E3
Mount Hawke Cnwll 3 J2
Mountjoy Cnwll 4 D4
Mount Lothian Mdloth 177 H6
Mountnessing Essex 60 F8
Mounton Mons 38 D2
Mount Pleasant Derbys 101 G3
Mount Pleasant Suffk 77 G5
Mountsett Crematorium Dur 150 E4
Mountsorrel Leics 87 H2
Mount Tabor Calder 122 F5
Mousehole Cnwll 2 E6
Mouswald D & G 155 J7
Mow Cop Ches E 99 J2
Mowhaugh Border 168 B5
Mowmacre Hill C Leic 87 H3
Mowsley Leics 87 J5
Moy Highld 202 C8
Moy Highld 213 J7
Moyle Highld 200 D2
Moylegrove Pembks 64 F5
Muasdale Ag & B 161 H2
Muchalls Abers 207 G6
Much Birch Herefs 54 D3
Much Cowarne Herefs 70 B5
Much Dewchurch Herefs 54 C2
Muchelney Somset 26 B6
Muchelney Ham Somset 26 C6
Much Hadham Herts 60 C4
Much Hoole Lancs 120 F6
Muchlarnick Cnwll 5 K5
Much Marcle Herefs 54 F2
Much Wenlock Shrops 84 B4
Muck Highld 189 K1
Muckleburgh Collection Norfk 106 D4
Mucklestone Staffs 99 G5
Muckton Lincs 118 E5
Muddiford Devon 23 J4
Muddles Green E Susx 20 B3
Mudeford Dorset 16 A4
Mudford Somset 26 E7
Mudford Sock Somset 26 E7
Mugdock Stirlg 175 G3
Mugeary Highld 209 G6
Mugginton Derbys 100 F4
Muirden Abers 216 D4
Muirdrum Angus 196 F8
Muiresk Abers 216 D5
Muirhead Angus 186 E1
Muirhead Fife 186 E6
Muirhead N Lans 175 J4
Muirkirk E Ayrs 164 D4
Muirmill Stirlg 175 J2
Muir of Fowlis Abers 206 B3
Muir of Miltonduff Moray 214 E3
Muir of Ord Highld 212 E4
Muirshearlich Highld 192 B1
Muirtack Abers 217 J6
Muirton P & K 185 J5
Muirton Mains Highld 212 C4
Muirton of Ardblair P & K 195 J7
Muker N York 139 K7
Mulbarton Norfk 92 E4
Mulben Moray 215 H4
Mull Ag & B 181 J1
Mullion Cnwll 3 H7
Mullion Cove Cnwll 3 H7
Mumby Lincs 119 G6
Munderfield Row Herefs 70 B4
Munderfield Stocks Herefs 70 B4
Mundesley Norfk 107 G5
Mundford Norfk 91 H5
Mundham Norfk 93 G4
Mundon Hill Essex 61 K7
Mungrisdale Cumb 137 K2
Munlochy Highld 213 G4
Munnoch N Ayrs 174 B8
Munsley Herefs 70 B6
Munslow Shrops 83 K6
Murchington Devon 11 G7
Murcott Oxon 57 L5
Murkle Highld 231 H2
Murlaggan Highld 200 F6
Murroes Angus 187 G1
Murrow Cambs 89 L3
Mursley Bucks 58 D3
Murthill Angus 196 D5
Murthly P & K 195 H8
Murton C York 133 K8
Murton Cumb 139 G3
Murton Dur 151 J5
Murton Nthumb 179 K8
Musbury Devon 13 H4
Musselburgh E Loth 177 K4
Muston Leics 102 D5
Muston N York 135 H4
Muswell Hill Gt Lon 44 F3
Mutehill D & G 146 C5
Mutford Suffk 93 K6
Muthill P & K 185 H4
Mybster Highld 231 H5
Myddfai Carmth 52 B3
Myddle Shrops 98 C7
Mydroilyn Cerdgn 66 B4
Mylor Cnwll 4 C8
Mylor Bridge Cnwll 4 C8
Mynachlog ddu Pembks 49 K2
Mynydd-bach Mons 38 C2
Mynydd-Bach Swans 51 J6
Mynyddgarreg Carmth 50 E4
Mynydd Isa Flints 111 J8
Myrebird Abers 206 E5
Myredykes Border 157 G3
Mytchett Surrey 30 E1
Mytholm Calder 122 E5
Mytholmroyd Calder 122 F5
Myton-on-Swale N York 132 F6

N

Naast Highld 219 J5
Na Buirgh W Isls 232 d4
Naburn C York 124 F2
Nab Wood Crematorium C Brad 123 H3
Nackington Kent 34 F4
Nacton Suffk 78 F6
Nafferton E R Yk 135 G7
Nailsbourne Somset 25 K5
Nailsea N Som 38 C6
Nailstone Leics 86 E3
Nailsworth Gloucs 55 J7
Nairn Highld 213 K3
Nannerch Flints 111 G7
Nanpantan Leics 87 G1
Nanpean Cnwll 4 F5
Nanstallon Cnwll 5 G3
Nanternis Cerdgn 65 L3
Nantgaredig Carmth 50 F2
Nantglyn Denbgs 96 F1
Nantmel Powys 68 B2
Nantmor Gwynd 95 K4
Nant Peris Gwynd 95 K2
Nantwich Ches E 98 F3
Nantyglo Blae G 53 J6
Nant-y-moel Brdgnd 36 E2
Naphill Bucks 42 D2
Napton on the Hill Warwks 72 F3
Narberth Pembks 49 J4
Narborough Leics 87 G4
Narborough Norfk 91 H2
Nasareth Gwynd 95 H3
Naseby Nhants 87 K7
Nash Bucks 73 L7
Nash Newpt 37 M4
Nash Shrops 69 L1
Nassington Nhants 88 F4
Nateby Cumb 139 H6
Nateby Lancs 120 F2
National Memorial Arboretum Staffs 85 L1
National Motor Museum (Beaulieu) Hants 16 E2
National Space Science Centre C Leic 87 H3
Natland Cumb 129 L2
Naughton Suffk 78 B5
Naunton Gloucs 56 C4
Naunton Worcs 70 F6
Naunton Beauchamp Worcs 71 G4
Navenby Lincs 103 G2
Navestock Essex 45 K1
Navestock Side Essex 60 E8
Navidale House Hotel Highld 227 J5
Navity Highld 213 J2
Nawton N York 133 K3
Nayland Suffk 77 L7
Nazeing Essex 60 C6
Neap Shet 235 d5
Near Cotton Staffs 100 B4
Near Sawrey Cumb 137 K7
Neasden Gt Lon 44 E3
Neasham Darltn 141 H5
Neath Neath 51 L6
Neatham Hants 30 C4
Neatishead Norfk 107 H7
Nebo Cerdgn 66 D2
Nebo Conwy 96 C2
Nebo Gwynd 95 H3
Nebo IoA 108 F4
Necton Norfk 91 K2
Nedd Highld 224 D3
Nedging Suffk 78 B5
Nedging Tye Suffk 78 B4
Needham Norfk 92 F6
Needham Lake & Nature Reserve Suffk 78 C4
Needham Market Suffk 78 C4
Needingworth Cambs 75 L1
Neen Savage Shrops 84 C7
Neen Sollars Shrops 84 B8
Neenton Shrops 84 B6
Nefyn Gwynd 94 E4
Neilston E Rens 174 E6
Nelson Caerph 37 H2
Nelson Lancs 122 C3
Nemphlar S Lans 165 G1
Nempnett Thrubwell BaNES 38 D7
Nenthead Cumb 149 K6
Nenthorn Border 167 K2
Nercwys Flints 97 K1
Nereabolls Ag & B 170 E7
Nerston S Lans 175 H6
Nesbit Nthumb 168 E3
Nesfield N York 123 G1
Nesscliffe Shrops 98 B8
Neston Ches W 111 J6
Neston Wilts 39 K6
Netchwood Shrops 84 B5
Nether Alderley Ches E 113 J6
Netheravon Wilts 28 D2
Nether Blainslie Border 167 H2
Netherbrae Abers 216 F3
Nether Broughton Leics 102 B7
Netherburn S Lans 175 L8
Netherbury Dorset 13 L3
Netherby N York 123 L2
Nether Cerne Dorset 14 C3
Nethercleuch D & G 155 K5
Nether Compton Dorset 26 E7
Nether Crimond Abers 206 F2
Nether Dallachy Moray 215 H2
Netherend Gloucs 54 E7
Netherfield E Susx 20 E2
Netherfield Notts 101 L4
Nether Fingland S Lans 165 H7
Netherhampton Wilts 28 C5
Nether Handwick Angus 196 B7
Nether Haugh Rothm 115 H3
Netherhay Dorset 13 K2
Nether Headon Notts 116 C6
Nether Heage Derbys 101 G3
Nether Heyford Nhants 73 J3
Nether Howcleugh S Lans 165 K6
Nether Kellet Lancs 129 K6
Nether Kinmundy Abers 217 K5
Nether Langwith Notts 115 K7
Netherlaw D & G 146 C6
Netherley Abers 207 G6
Nethermill D & G 155 H5
Nethermuir Abers 217 G5
Netherne-on-the-Hill Surrey 32 B3
Netheroyd Hill Kirk 123 H6
Nether Padley Derbys 114 E6
Netherplace E Rens 174 F7
Nether Poppleton C York 133 J8
Netherseal Derbys 86 C2
Nether Silton N York 133 G2
Nether Stowey Somset 25 J4
Netherthong Kirk 123 H8
Netherton Angus 196 E5
Netherton Devon 7 K2
Netherton Dudley 85 G6
Netherton Kirk 123 H7
Netherton N Lans 175 K7
Netherton Nthumb 168 E7
Netherton P & K 195 J6
Netherton Sefton 111 K2
Netherton Stirlg 175 G3
Netherton Wakefd 123 K6
Nethertown Cumb 136 D5
Nethertown Highld 231 L1
Nethertown Staffs 100 C8
Netherurd Border 165 L1
Nether Wallop Hants 28 F4
Nether Wasdale Cumb 136 F6
Nether Westcote Gloucs 56 E4
Nether Whitacre Warwks 86 B5
Nether Whitecleuch S Lans 165 G5
Nether Winchendon Bucks 58 B5
Netherwitton Nthumb 158 D4
Nethy Bridge Highld 204 B2
Netley Hants 16 F2
Netley Marsh Hants 29 G8
Nettlebed Oxon 42 B3
Nettlebridge Somset 26 F2
Nettlecombe Dorset 13 M4
Nettleden Herts 59 G6
Nettleham Lincs 117 G6
Nettlestead Kent 33 H3
Nettlestead Green Kent 33 H3
Nettlestone IoW 17 H4
Nettlesworth Dur 151 G5
Nettleton Lincs 117 J2
Nettleton Wilts 39 J5
Netton Wilts 28 C4
Nevern Pembks 64 F6
Nevill Holt Leics 88 B5
New Abbey D & G 147 G2
New Aberdour Abers 217 G2
New Addington Gt Lon 45 G7
Newall Leeds 123 J2
New Alresford Hants 29 L5
New Alyth P & K 195 K6
Newark Ork 234 e4
Newark-on-Trent Notts 102 D2
Newarthill N Lans 175 K6
New Ash Green Kent 45 L6
New Balderton Notts 102 D3
New Barn Kent 45 L6
New Barnet Gt Lon 44 F2
Newbattle Mdloth 177 J5
New Bewick Nthumb 169 G5
Newbie D & G 147 L3
Newbiggin Cumb 138 C2
Newbiggin Cumb 138 F2
Newbiggin Cumb 148 F5
Newbiggin Dur 139 K2
Newbiggin N York 131 J3
Newbiggin-by-the-Sea Nthumb 159 H5
Newbigging Angus 187 H1
Newbigging Angus 195 L7
Newbigging Angus 196 C8
Newbigging S Lans 165 K1
Newbiggin-on-Lune Cumb 139 G6
New Bilton Warwks 86 F7
Newbold Derbys 115 G6
Newbold on Avon Warwks 86 F7
Newbold on Stour Warwks 72 B5
Newbold Pacey Warwks 72 C3
Newbold Verdon Leics 86 F3
New Bolingbroke Lincs 104 A2
Newborough C Pete 89 H3
Newborough IoA 108 E7
Newborough Staffs 100 C7
New Boultham Lincs 116 F7
Newbourne Suffk 78 F6
New Bradwell M Keyn 74 B6
New Brampton Derbys 115 G7
New Brancepeth Dur 151 G6
Newbridge C Edin 176 F4
Newbridge Caerph 37 K2
Newbridge Cnwll 2 D5
Newbridge D & G 155 G6
Newbridge Hants 28 F7
Newbridge IoW 16 E5
Newbridge Green Worcs 70 E6
Newbridge-on-Wye Powys 67 L3
New Brighton Wirral 111 J3
Newbrough Nthumb 149 L2
New Buckenham Norfk 92 C5
Newbuildings Devon 11 J4
Newburgh Abers 207 J1
Newburgh Abers 217 H3
Newburgh Fife 186 D4
Newburgh Lancs 121 G7
Newburgh Priory N York 133 H4
Newburn N u Ty 150 F2
Newbury Somset 27 G2
Newbury W Berk 41 J6
Newbury Park Gt Lon 45 J3
Newby Cumb 138 E3
Newby Lancs 122 B2
Newby N York 130 D5
Newby N York 142 B5
Newby Bridge Cumb 129 H3
Newby East Cumb 148 E4
New Byth Abers 216 F4
Newby West Cumb 148 C4
Newcastle Mons 54 C5
Newcastle Shrops 82 E6
Newcastle Airport Nthumb 158 F7
Newcastle Emlyn Carmth 65 J6
Newcastleton Border 156 E5
Newcastle-under-Lyme Staffs 99 J4
Newcastle upon Tyne N u Ty 151 G3
Newchapel Pembks 65 H6
Newchapel Surrey 32 C5
Newchurch IoW 17 G5
Newchurch Kent 34 E7
Newchurch Mons 38 C2
Newchurch Powys 68 E4
Newchurch Staffs 100 D7
New Costessey Norfk 92 E2
Newcraighall C Edin 177 J4
New Crofton Wakefd 124 B6
New Cross Gt Lon 45 G5
New Cross Somset 26 B7
New Cumnock E Ayrs 164 C6
New Deer Abers 217 G5
New Denham Bucks 43 H4
Newdigate Surrey 31 K3
New Duston Nhants 73 K3
New Earswick C York 133 J7
New Edlington Donc 115 K2
New Elgin Moray 214 F3
New Ellerby E R Yk 126 E3
Newell Green Br For 42 E6
New Eltham Gt Lon 45 H5
New End Worcs 71 J3
Newenden Kent 33 L7
New England C Pete 89 H4
Newent Gloucs 55 G3
Newfield Dur 150 F7
Newfield Highld 223 H6
New Fletton C Pete 89 H4
New Forest National Park 16 C2
Newgale Pembks 48 E3
New Galloway D & G 154 B6
Newgate Street Herts 59 M6
New Gilston Fife 187 G5
New Grimsby IoS 2 a1
Newhall Ches E 98 E4
New Hartley Nthumb 159 H6
Newhaven C Edin 177 H3

Newhaven E Susx 19 L5
New Haw Surrey 43 H7
New Hedges Pembks 49 J6
New Holland N Linc 126 D5
Newholm N York 143 H5
New Houghton Derbys 115 J7
New Houghton Norfk 105 J6
Newhouse N Lans 175 L6
New Hutton Cumb 130 B2
Newick E Susx 19 L2
Newington Kent 35 G6
Newington Kent 46 E6
Newington Oxon 41 L2
New Inn Carmth 66 B6
New Inn Torfn 53 L7
New Invention Shrops 82 F7
New Lakenham Norfk 92 F3
New Lanark S Lans 165 G2
New Lanark Village S Lans 165 G2
Newland C KuH 126 D4
Newland Gloucs 54 D6
Newland N York 125 G5
Newland Somset 24 C4
Newland Worcs 70 E5
Newlandrig Mdloth 177 K6
Newlands Border 156 E4
Newlands Nthumb 150 D4
Newlands of Dundurcas Moray 215 G4
New Langholm D & G 156 C5
New Leake Lincs 104 C2
New Leeds Abers 217 J4
New Lodge Barns 123 L8
New Longton Lancs 121 G5
New Luce D & G 144 E3
Newlyn Cnwll 2 E5
Newmachar Abers 207 G2
Newmains N Lans 175 L6
New Malden Gt Lon 44 E6
Newman's Green Suffk 77 K5
Newmarket Suffk 76 F2
Newmarket W Isls 232 f2
New Marske R & Cl 142 D3
New Marston Oxon 57 K6
New Mill Abers 206 E8
Newmill Border 167 G7
New Mill Cnwll 2 E4
New Mill Kirk 123 H8
Newmill Moray 215 K4
Newmillerdam Wakefd 123 L7
Newmill of Inshewan Angus 196 C4
Newmills C Edin 177 G5
New Mills Derbys 113 M4
Newmills Fife 176 D2
Newmills Mons 54 D6
New Mills Powys 82 C4
Newmiln P & K 186 B2
Newmilns E Ayrs 164 B2
New Milton Hants 16 B4
New Mistley Essex 62 D2
New Moat Pembks 49 H3
Newney Green Essex 61 G6
Newnham Gloucs 55 G5
Newnham Hants 30 B2
Newnham Herts 75 J6
Newnham Kent 34 C3
Newnham Nhants 73 H3
Newnham Worcs 70 B2
New Ollerton Notts 116 A7
New Oscott Birm 85 K5
New Pitsligo Abers 217 G3
Newport Cnwll 9 J7
Newport E R Yk 125 K4
Newport Essex 76 D7
Newport Gloucs 39 G2
Newport Highld 227 K4
Newport IoW 16 F5
Newport Newpt 37 L3
Newport Pembks 64 E6
Newport Wrekin 99 H8
Newport-on-Tay Fife 187 G2
Newport Pagnell M Keyn 74 C5
Newport Pagnell Services M Keyn 74 C5
New Prestwick S Ayrs 163 J4
New Quay Cerdgn 65 L3
Newquay Cnwll 4 C4
Newquay Airport Cnwll 4 D3
New Rackheath Norfk 93 G2
New Radnor Powys 68 E3
New Ridley Nthumb 150 D3
New Romney Kent 21 L2
New Rossington Donc 115 L2
New Sauchie Clacks 185 J7
Newseat Abers 216 D7
Newsham Lancs 121 G4
Newsham N York 132 E3
Newsham N York 140 E5
Newsham Nthumb 159 H6
New Sharlston Wakefd 124 B6
Newsholme E R Yk 125 H5
New Silksworth Sundld 151 J4
Newsome Kirk 123 H7
New Somerby Lincs 102 F5
New Southgate Crematorium Gt Lon 44 F2
Newstead Border 167 H3
Newstead Notts 101 K3
Newstead Nthumb 169 H4
New Stevenston N Lans 175 K6
Newthorpe Notts 101 J4
Newton Ag & B 182 F7
Newton Border 167 J5
Newton Brdgnd 36 C5
Newton C Beds 75 J5
Newton Cambs 76 B5
Newton Cambs 90 B1
Newton Ches W 98 D1
Newton Ches W 112 B7
Newton Cumb 128 F5
Newton Derbys 101 H2
Newton Herefs 53 M2
Newton Herefs 69 K4
Newton Highld 212 F4
Newton Highld 213 H5
Newton Highld 213 J2
Newton Highld 231 L5
Newton Lincs 103 H5
Newton Mdloth 177 J4
Newton Moray 214 E2
Newton Moray 215 H2
Newton Nhants 88 C6
Newton Norfk 91 J1
Newton Notts 102 B4
Newton Nthumb 150 C3
Newton S Lans 165 H3
Newton S Lans 175 H6
Newton Sandw 85 J5
Newton Staffs 100 B7
Newton Suffk 77 K6
Newton W Loth 176 E3
Newton Warwks 87 G7
Newton Abbot Devon 7 K2
Newton Arlosh Cumb 147 L4
Newton Aycliffe Dur 141 G3
Newton Bewley Hartpl 141 K2
Newton Blossomville M Keyn 74 D4
Newton Bromswold Nhants 74 E2
Newton Burgoland Leics 86 D2
Newton-by-the-Sea Nthumb 169 J4
Newton by Toft Lincs 117 H4
Newton Ferrers Devon 6 E6
Newton Ferry W Isls 232 c5
Newton Flotman Norfk 92 E4
Newtongrange Mdloth 177 J5
Newton Green Mons 38 D3
Newton Harcourt Leics 87 J4
Newton Heath Manch 113 K2
Newtonhill Abers 207 G6
Newton-in-Bowland Lancs 121 K1
Newton Kyme N York 124 C2
Newton-le-Willows N York 132 C2
Newton-le-Willows St Hel 112 E3
Newtonloan Mdloth 177 J5
Newton Longville Bucks 58 D2
Newton Mearns E Rens 174 F7
Newtonmill Angus 196 F4
Newtonmore Highld 203 H5
Newton Morrell N York 141 G5
Newton of Balcanquhal P & K 186 B5
Newton of Balcormo Fife 187 H6
Newton-on-Ouse N York 133 H7
Newton-on-Rawcliffe N York 134 C2
Newton-on-the-Moor Nthumb 158 F2
Newton on Trent Lincs 116 D6
Newton Poppleford Devon 12 E4
Newton Purcell Oxon 57 L3
Newton Regis Warwks 86 C3
Newton Reigny Cumb 138 C2
Newton St Cyres Devon 11 K5
Newton St Faith Norfk 92 F1
Newton St Loe BaNES 39 G7
Newton St Petrock Devon 9 K3
Newton Solney Derbys 100 F7
Newton Stacey Hants 29 H4
Newton Stewart D & G 145 J3
Newton Tony Wilts 28 E4
Newton Tracey Devon 23 H6
Newton under Roseberry R & Cl 142 C5
Newton upon Derwent E R Yk 125 H2
Newton Valence Hants 30 B5
Newton Wamphray D & G 155 K3
Newton with Scales Lancs 120 F4
Newtown Cumb 147 J5
Newtown Cumb 148 E3
Newtown D & G 164 F7
Newtown Devon 12 D3
Newtown Devon 24 B6
New Town Dorset 27 L7
New Town Dorset 27 M7
New Town E Susx 19 M2
Newtown Gloucs 54 F7
Newtown Hants 29 L8
Newtown Herefs 70 B5
Newtown Herefs 70 C6
Newtown Highld 202 B4
Newtown IoW 16 E4
Newtown Nthumb 168 F4
Newtown Poole 15 K4
Newtown Powys 82 C5
Newtown Shrops 98 B7
Newtown Shrops 98 C6
Newtown Somset 25 L8
Newtown Staffs 99 K1
Newtown Wigan 112 E1
Newtown Worcs 70 F4
Newtown Linford Leics 87 G2
Newtown of Beltrees Rens 174 D6
Newtown St Boswells Border 167 J3
New Tredegar Caerph 53 H7
New Trows S Lans 164 F2
Newtyle Angus 195 L7
New Walsoken Cambs 90 C2
New Waltham NE Lin 118 C1
New Winton E Loth 177 L4
Newyork Ag & B 182 D5
New York Lincs 103 L2
Neyland Pembks 49 G6
Nicholashayne Devon 25 H7
Nicholaston Swans 51 G7
Nidd N York 132 D7
Nigg C Aber 207 H5
Nigg Highld 223 H6
Nigg Ferry Highld 223 H7
Ninebanks Nthumb 149 K4
Nine Elms Swindn 40 C3
Ninfield E Susx 20 E3
Ningwood IoW 16 E5
Nisbet Border 167 K4
Nisbet Hill Border 179 G7
Niton IoW 17 F6
Nitshill C Glas 174 F6
Nocton Lincs 117 H8
Noke Oxon 57 K5
Nolton Pembks 48 E4
Nolton Haven Pembks 48 E4
No Man's Heath Ches W 98 D3
No Man's Heath Warwks 86 C2
Nomansland Devon 11 J3
Nomansland Wilts 28 E7
Noneley Shrops 98 C6
Nonington Kent 35 H4
Nook Cumb 129 L3
Norbiton Gt Lon 44 D6
Norbury Ches E 98 E3
Norbury Derbys 100 C4
Norbury Gt Lon 44 F6
Norbury Shrops 83 G5
Norbury Staffs 99 H7
Norchard Worcs 70 F2
Nordelph Norfk 90 D4
Nordley Shrops 84 C4
Norfolk Broads Norfk 93 K2
Norham Nthumb 179 J8
Norley Ches W 112 E6
Norleywood Hants 16 D3
Normanby Lincs 117 G4
Normanby N Linc 125 K7
Normanby N York 134 B3
Normanby R & Cl 142 C4
Normanby le Wold Lincs 117 J3
Normandy Surrey 30 F2
Norman's Green Devon 12 D2
Normanton C Derb 101 G5
Normanton Leics 102 D4
Normanton Notts 102 B2
Normanton Wakefd 124 B6
Normanton le Heath Leics 86 D2
Normanton on Cliffe Lincs 102 F4
Normanton on Soar Notts 101 K7
Normanton on the Wolds Notts 101 L6
Normanton on Trent Notts 116 C7
Norris Green Lpool 111 L3
Norris Hill Leics 86 D1

Norristhorpe Kirk 123 J6
Northall Bucks 58 F4
Northallerton N York 141 J7
Northam C Sotn 29 H8
Northam Devon 23 G5
Northampton Nhants 73 L3
Northampton Worcs 70 E2
Northampton Services Nhants 73 K3
North Anston Rothm 115 K5
North Ascot Br For 42 E6
North Aston Oxon 57 J3
Northaw Herts 59 L7
Northay Somset 13 H1
North Baddesley Hants 29 H7
North Ballachulish Highld 191 L4
North Barrow Somset 26 E5
North Barsham Norfk 105 L5
North Benfleet Essex 46 C3
North Bersted W Susx 18 C5
North Berwick E Loth 178 C2
North Boarhunt Hants 17 H1
Northborough C Pete 89 H3
Northbourne Kent 35 J4
North Bovey Devon 11 H7
North Bradley Wilts 27 J1
North Brentor Devon 10 C8
North Brewham Somset 27 G4
Northbrook Hants 29 K4
North Buckland Devon 23 G4
North Burlingham Norfk 93 H2
North Cadbury Somset 26 F6
North Carlton Lincs 116 F6
North Carlton Notts 115 L4
North Cave E R Yk 125 K4
North Cerney Gloucs 56 A6
North Chailey E Susx 19 K2
Northchapel W Susx 30 F5
North Charford Hants 28 D7
North Charlton Nthumb 169 H5
North Cheam Gt Lon 44 E6
North Cheriton Somset 27 G6
North Chideock Dorset 13 K4
Northchurch Herts 58 F6
North Cliffe E R Yk 125 K3
North Clifton Notts 116 D6
North Cockerington Lincs 118 E4
North Connel Ag & B 182 C1
North Cornelly Brdgnd 36 C4
North Cotes Lincs 118 E2
Northcott Devon 9 J6
Northcourt Oxon 57 J7
North Cove Suffk 93 K5
North Cowton N York 141 G6
North Crawley M Keyn 74 D5
North Creake Norfk 105 K5
North Curry Somset 25 L6
North Dalton E R Yk 125 L1
North Deighton N York 124 B1
North Devon Crematorium Devon 23 H5
Northdown Kent 35 K2
North Downs 34 B4
North Duffield N York 125 G3
North Duntulm Highld 218 C6
North East Surrey Crematorium Gt Lon 44 E6
North Elmham Norfk 106 B7
North Elmsall Wakefd 124 D7
North End C Port 17 J3
North End Essex 61 G4
North End Hants 28 C7
North End Nhants 74 D2
North End W Susx 18 D5
Northend Warwks 72 E4
Northenden Manch 113 J4
North Erradale Highld 219 H5
North Evington C Leic 87 J3
North Fambridge Essex 61 K7
North Ferriby E R Yk 126 B5
Northfield Birm 85 H7
Northfield C Aber 207 G4
Northfield E R Yk 126 C5
Northfields Lincs 88 E2
Northfleet Kent 45 M5
North Frodingham E R Yk 135 H8
North Gorley Hants 15 M1
North Green Suffk 79 G3
North Greetwell Lincs 117 G6
North Grimston N York 134 C6
North Haven Shet 235 e7
North Hayling Hants 17 K2
North Hill Cnwll 5 L1
North Hillingdon Gt Lon 43 H4
North Hinksey Village Oxon 57 J6
North Holmwood Surrey 31 K3
North Huish Devon 7 G5
North Hykeham Lincs 116 F7
Northiam E Susx 21 G2
Northill C Beds 75 G5
Northington Hants 29 K4
North Kelsey Lincs 117 H2
North Kessock Highld 213 G5
North Killingholme N Linc 126 E6
North Kilvington N York 132 F3
North Kilworth Leics 87 H6
North Kyme Lincs 103 J3
North Landing E R Yk 135 K5
Northlands Lincs 104 B2
Northleach Gloucs 56 C5
North Lee Bucks 58 D6
Northleigh Devon 12 F3
North Leigh Oxon 57 H5
North Leverton with Habblesthorpe Notts 116 C5
Northlew Devon 10 D5
North Littleton Worcs 71 J5
North Lopham Norfk 92 C6
North Luffenham Rutlnd 88 D3
North Marden W Susx 30 D7
North Marston Bucks 58 C4
North Middleton Mdloth 177 K6
North Millbrex Abers 216 F5
North Milmain D & G 144 C4
North Molton Devon 24 B5
Northmoor Oxon 57 H7
North Moreton Oxon 41 K3
Northmuir Angus 196 C5
North Mundham W Susx 18 B5
North Muskham Notts 102 D2
North Newbald E R Yk 125 L3
North Newington Oxon 72 E6
North Newnton Wilts 40 C8
North Newton Somset 25 L5
Northney Hants 17 K2
North Nibley Gloucs 39 H2
Northolt Gt Lon 43 J4
Northop Flints 111 H7
Northop Hall Flints 111 J7
North Ormesby Middsb 142 B4
North Ormsby Lincs 118 C3
Northorpe Kirk 123 J6
Northorpe Lincs 103 K5
Northorpe Lincs 116 E3
North Otterington N York 132 E2
North Owersby Lincs 117 H3
Northowram Calder 123 G5
North Perrott Somset 13 L1
North Petherton Somset 25 L5
North Petherwin Cnwll 9 H6
North Pickenham Norfk 91 J3
North Piddle Worcs 71 G4
North Poorton Dorset 13 M3
Northport Dorset 15 H5
North Queensferry Fife 176 F3
North Rauceby Lincs 103 G3
Northrepps Norfk 106 F5
North Reston Lincs 118 E5
North Rigton N York 123 K1
North Rode Ches E 113 K7
North Ronaldsay Ork 234 e3
North Ronaldsay Airport Ork 234 e3
North Runcton Norfk 90 F1
North Scarle Lincs 116 D7
North Shian Ag & B 191 H7
North Shields N Tyne 151 J2
North Shoebury Sthend 46 F3
North Shore Bpool 120 D3
North Side C Pete 89 K4
North Somercotes Lincs 118 F3
North Stainley N York 132 D4
North Stifford Thurr 45 L4
North Stoke BaNES 39 G6
North Stoke Oxon 41 L3
North Stoke W Susx 18 D4
North Street Kent 34 D3
North Street W Berk 41 M6
North Sunderland Nthumb 169 J3
North Tamerton Cnwll 9 J5
North Tawton Devon 10 F4
North Third Stirlg 175 K1
North Thoresby Lincs 118 D2
Northton W Isls 232 d5
North Town Devon 10 D3
North Town Somset 26 E3
North Town W & M 42 E4
North Tuddenham Norfk 92 C2
North Uist W Isls 233 b6
Northumberland National Park Nthumb 157 L3
North Walsham Norfk 107 G6
North Waltham Hants 29 K3
North Warnborough Hants 30 B2
North Weald Bassett Essex 60 D7
North Wheatley Notts 116 C4
Northwich Ches W 112 F6
Northwick Worcs 70 E3
North Widcombe BaNES 38 E8
North Willingham Lincs 117 K4
North Wingfield Derbys 115 H8
North Witham Lincs 102 F7
Northwold Norfk 91 H4
Northwood C Stke 99 K3
Northwood Gt Lon 43 H3
Northwood IoW 16 F4
Northwood Shrops 98 C6
Northwood Green Gloucs 55 G5
North Wootton Dorset 26 F8
North Wootton Norfk 105 G7
North Wootton Somset 26 E3
North Wraxall Wilts 39 J5
North York Moors National Park 142 F6
Norton Donc 124 E7
Norton E Susx 19 M5
Norton Gloucs 55 J3
Norton Halton 112 D5
Norton Nhants 73 H2
Norton Notts 115 L6
Norton Powys 68 F2
Norton S on T 141 K3
Norton Shrops 84 D4
Norton Suffk 77 L2
Norton W Susx 18 C4
Norton Wilts 39 K4
Norton Worcs 70 F4
Norton Worcs 71 J5
Norton Bavant Wilts 27 K3
Norton Bridge Staffs 99 K6
Norton Canes Staffs 85 H2
Norton Canes Services Staffs 85 H3
Norton Canon Herefs 69 H5
Norton Disney Lincs 102 E2
Norton Fitzwarren Somset 25 J6
Norton Green IoW 16 D5
Norton Hawkfield BaNES 38 E7
Norton Heath Essex 60 F6
Norton in Hales Shrops 99 G5
Norton in the Moors C Stke 99 K3
Norton-Juxta-Twycross Leics 86 D3
Norton-le-Clay N York 132 F5
Norton Lindsey Warwks 72 B2
Norton Little Green Suffk 77 L2
Norton Malreward BaNES 38 E7
Norton-on-Derwent N York 134 C5
Norton St Philip Somset 27 H1
Norton Subcourse Norfk 93 J4
Norton sub Hamdon Somset 26 C7
Norwell Notts 102 C1
Norwell Woodhouse Notts 116 B8
Norwich Norfk 92 F2
Norwich Airport Norfk 92 E2
Norwich (St Faith) Crematorium Norfk 92 F1
Norwick Shet 235 e1
Norwood Clacks 185 J8
Norwood Green Gt Lon 43 J5
Norwood Hill Surrey 31 L3
Noss Mayo Devon 6 E6
Nosterfield N York 132 D4
Nostie Highld 210 D8
Notgrove Gloucs 56 C4
Nottage Brdgnd 36 C5
Nottingham C Nott 101 L5
Notton Wakefd 123 L7
Notton Wilts 39 K6
Noutard's Green Worcs 70 E2
Nuffield Oxon 42 A3
Nunburnholme E R Yk 125 K2
Nuneaton Warwks 86 D5
Nunhead Gt Lon 45 G5
Nun Monkton N York 133 H7
Nunney Somset 27 G3
Nunnington N York 133 K4
Nunsthorpe NE Lin 127 G8
Nunthorpe C York 124 F1

Nunthorpe Middsb 142 C4
Nunthorpe Village Middsb 142 C5
Nunton Wilts 28 D6
Nunwick N York 132 E5
Nursling Hants 29 G7
Nutbourne W Susx 17 L2
Nutbourne W Susx 18 E3
Nutfield Surrey 32 B3
Nuthall Notts 101 K4
Nuthampstead Herts 76 B7
Nuthurst W Susx 31 K6
Nutley E Susx 32 D7
Nuttall Bury 122 B7
Nybster Highld 231 L3
Nyetimber W Susx 18 B6
Nyewood W Susx 30 D6
Nymans W Susx 31 L5
Nymet Rowland Devon 11 G4
Nymet Tracey Devon 11 G5
Nympsfield Gloucs 55 J7
Nynehead Somset 25 H6
Nyton W Susx 18 C5

O

Oadby Leics 87 J4
Oad Street Kent 34 B3
Oakamoor Staffs 100 B4
Oakbank W Loth 176 E5
Oak Cross Devon 10 D5
Oakdale Caerph 37 J2
Oake Somset 25 J6
Oaken Staffs 84 F3
Oakenclough Lancs 121 H2
Oakengates Wrekin 84 C2
Oakenshaw Dur 150 F7
Oakenshaw Kirk 123 H5
Oakford Cerdgn 66 B3
Oakford Devon 24 E6
Oakham Rutlnd 88 C2
Oakhanger Hants 30 C4
Oakhill Somset 26 F3
Oakington Cambs 76 B2
Oakle Street Gloucs 55 H4
Oakley Bed 74 E4
Oakley Bucks 57 M5
Oakley Fife 176 D1
Oakley Hants 29 K2
Oakley Suffk 92 E7
Oakridge Lynch Gloucs 55 K7
Oaksey Wilts 39 M2
Oakthorpe Leics 86 D2
Oakwood C Derb 101 G5
Oakworth C Brad 122 F3
Oare Kent 34 D3
Oare Somset 24 C3
Oare Wilts 40 D7
Oasby Lincs 103 G5
Oath Somset 26 B6
Oathlaw Angus 196 D5
Oatlands Park Surrey 43 H7
Oban Ag & B 182 B2
Oban Airport Ag & B 182 C1
Obley Shrops 83 G7
Obney P & K 195 G8
Oborne Dorset 26 F7
Occold Suffk 78 D1
Occumster Highld 231 J7
Ochiltree E Ayrs 163 L5
Ockbrook Derbys 101 H5
Ocker Hill Sandw 85 H5
Ockham Surrey 31 H1
Ockle Highld 190 B3
Ockley Surrey 31 J4
Ocle Pychard Herefs 69 L5
Odcombe Somset 26 D7
Odd Down BaNES 39 H7
Oddingley Worcs 71 G3
Oddington Gloucs 56 E3
Oddington Oxon 57 K5
Odell Bed 74 D3
Odiham Hants 30 C2
Odsal C Brad 123 H5
Odsey Cambs 75 K6
Odstock Wilts 28 D6
Odstone Leics 86 E3
Offchurch Warwks 72 D2
Offenham Worcs 71 J5
Offerton Stockp 113 K4
Offham E Susx 19 L3
Offham Kent 33 H2
Offham W Susx 18 D4
Offord Cluny Cambs 75 J2
Offord D'Arcy Cambs 75 J2
Offton Suffk 78 C5
Offwell Devon 12 F3
Ogbourne Maizey Wilts 40 D6
Ogbourne St Andrew Wilts 40 D6
Ogbourne St George Wilts 40 D5
Ogle Nthumb 158 E6
Oglet Lpool 112 C5
Ogmore V Glam 36 D5
Ogmore-by-Sea V Glam 36 D5
Ogmore Vale Brdgnd 36 E3
Okeford Fitzpaine Dorset 14 F1
Okehampton Devon 10 E5
Oker Side Derbys 100 F1
Okewood Hill Surrey 31 J4
Old Nhants 87 L8
Old Aberdeen C Aber 207 H4
Old Alresford Hants 29 L5
Oldany Highld 224 D2
Old Auchenbrack D & G 154 D3
Old Basford C Nott 101 K4
Old Basing Hants 30 A2
Old Beetley Norfk 106 A8
Oldberrow Warwks 71 K2
Old Bewick Nthumb 169 G5
Old Bolingbroke Lincs 118 E8
Old Bramhope Leeds 123 J2
Old Brampton Derbys 115 G6
Old Bridge of Urr D & G 146 D2
Old Buckenham Norfk 92 C5
Old Burghclere Hants 41 J8
Oldbury Sandw 85 H5
Oldbury Shrops 84 C5
Oldbury Warwks 86 C5
Oldbury-on-Severn S Glos 38 E2
Oldbury on the Hill Gloucs 39 J3
Old Byland N York 133 H3
Old Cantley Donc 115 L2
Oldcastle Mons 53 L3
Old Catton Norfk 92 F2
Old Clee NE Lin 127 G8
Old Cleeve Somset 25 G3
Old Colwyn Conwy 110 B6
Oldcotes Notts 115 L4
Old Dailly S Ayrs 152 F3
Old Dalby Leics 102 A7
Old Deer Abers 217 J5
Old Edlington Donc 115 K3
Old Ellerby E R Yk 126 E3
Old Felixstowe Suffk 79 G7
Oldfield Worcs 70 E2
Old Fletton C Pete 89 H4
Oldford Somset 27 H2
Old Forge Herefs 54 E4
Old Grimsby IoS 2 a1
Old Hall Green Herts 60 B4
Oldham Oldham 113 L1
Oldham Crematorium Oldham 113 K2
Oldhamstocks E Loth 178 F4
Old Harlow Essex 60 D5
Old Hunstanton Norfk 105 G4
Old Hurst Cambs 89 K7
Old Hutton Cumb 130 B2
Old Inns Services N Lans 175 K3
Old Kilpatrick W Duns 174 E4
Old Knebworth Herts 59 L4
Old Lakenham Norfk 92 F3
Oldland S Glos 38 F6
Old Langho Lancs 121 K4
Old Leake Lincs 104 C3
Old Malton N York 134 C5
Oldmeldrum Abers 216 F8
Oldmill Cnwll 6 B2
Old Milverton Warwks 72 C2
Oldmixon N Som 37 M8
Old Newton Suffk 78 C3
Old Radford C Nott 101 K4
Old Radnor Powys 68 E3
Old Rayne Abers 216 D8
Old Romney Kent 21 K2
Old Shoreham W Susx 19 G4
Oldshoremore Highld 228 C4
Old Sodbury S Glos 39 H4
Old Somerby Lincs 102 F5
Oldstead N York 133 H4
Old Stratford Nhants 73 L6
Old Struan P & K 194 C4
Old Swinford Dudley 84 F6
Old Thirsk N York 132 F3
Old Town Cumb 130 B3
Old Town E Susx 20 C5
Old Town IoS 2 b2
Old Trafford Traffd 113 J3
Oldwall Cumb 148 E3
Oldwalls Swans 50 F6
Old Warden C Beds 75 G5
Old Weston Cambs 89 G7
Old Wick Highld 231 L5
Old Windsor W & M 43 G5
Old Wives Lees Kent 34 E4
Old Woking Surrey 43 G8
Olgrinmore Highld 231 G5
Olive Green Staffs 100 C8
Oliver's Battery Hants 29 J6
Ollaberry Shet 235 c3
Ollach Highld 209 H6
Ollerton Ches E 113 H6
Ollerton Notts 116 A7
Ollerton Shrops 98 F7
Olney M Keyn 74 C4
Olrig House Highld 231 H3
Olton Solhll 85 K6
Olveston S Glos 38 E3
Ombersley Worcs 70 E2
Ompton Notts 116 B7
Onchan IoM 237 d5
Onecote Staffs 100 B2
Onibury Shrops 83 J7
Onich Highld 191 K4
Onllwyn Neath 52 C6
Onneley Staffs 99 H4
Onslow Green Essex 61 G4
Onslow Village Surrey 31 G2
Onston Ches W 112 E6
Opinan Highld 219 H6
Orbliston Moray 215 G3
Orbost Highld 208 D5
Orby Lincs 119 G7
Orchard Portman Somset 25 K6
Orcheston Wilts 28 B3
Orcop Herefs 54 C3
Orcop Hill Herefs 54 C3
Ord Abers 216 C3
Ordhead Abers 206 C3
Ordie Abers 205 K5
Ordiequish Moray 215 H3
Ordsall Notts 116 B5
Ore E Susx 21 G4
Orford Suffk 79 J4
Orford Warrtn 112 E4
Organford Dorset 15 H4
Orkney Islands Ork 234 c6
Orkney Neolithic Ork 234 b6
Orlestone Kent 34 D7
Orleton Herefs 69 J2
Orleton Worcs 70 C2
Orlingbury Nhants 74 C1
Ormesby R & Cl 142 C4
Ormesby St Margaret Norfk 93 K1
Ormesby St Michael Norfk 93 K1
Ormiscaig Highld 219 K4
Ormiston E Loth 177 L4
Ormsaigmore Highld 189 L4
Ormsary Ag & B 172 C4
Ormskirk Lancs 120 F8
Oronsay Ag & B 171 G2
Orphir Ork 234 b6
Orpington Gt Lon 45 J6
Orrell Sefton 111 K3
Orrell Wigan 112 D2
Orroland D & G 146 D5
Orsett Thurr 45 M4
Orslow Staffs 84 E1
Orston Notts 102 C4
Orton Cumb 138 F5
Orton Nhants 88 B7
Orton Staffs 84 F4
Orton Longueville C Pete 89 H4
Orton-on-the-Hill Leics 86 C3
Orton Waterville C Pete 89 H4
Orwell Cambs 75 L4
Osbaldeston Lancs 121 J4
Osbaldwick C York 124 F1
Osbaston Leics 86 E3
Osbaston Shrops 97 L7
Osborne House IoW 17 G4
Osbournby Lincs 103 H5
Oscroft Ches W 112 D7
Ose Highld 208 E6
Osgathorpe Leics 101 H8
Osgodby Lincs 117 H3
Osgodby N York 124 F4
Osgodby N York 135 G3
Oskaig Highld 209 H6
Oskamull Ag & B 189 L7
Osmaston Derbys 100 D4
Osmington Dorset 14 D5
Osmington Mills Dorset 14 E6
Osmondthorpe Leeds 123 L4
Osmotherley N York 141 K7
Osney Oxon 57 J6
Ospringe Kent 34 D3
Ossett Wakefd 123 K6
Ossington Notts 116 C8
Osterley Gt Lon 44 D5
Oswaldkirk N York 133 K4
Oswaldtwistle Lancs 121 L5
Oswestry Shrops 97 L6
Otford Kent 32 F2
Otham Kent 33 K3
Othery Somset 26 B5
Otley Leeds 123 J2
Otley Suffk 78 E4
Otterbourne Hants 29 J6
Otterburn N York 131 G7
Otterburn Nthumb 157 M4
Otter Ferry Ag & B 172 F2
Otterham Cnwll 8 F6
Otterhampton Somset 25 K3
Otternish W Isls 232 c5
Ottershaw Surrey 43 G7
Otterswick Shet 235 d3
Otterton Devon 12 E5
Ottery St Mary Devon 12 E4
Ottinge Kent 34 F6
Ottringham E R Yk 127 G5
Oughterside Cumb 147 K6
Oughtibridge Sheff 114 F3
Oughtrington Warrtn 113 G4
Oulston N York 133 H5
Oulton Cumb 147 M5
Oulton Norfk 106 D6
Oulton Staffs 99 K5
Oulton Suffk 93 L5
Oulton Broad Suffk 93 L5
Oulton Street Norfk 106 D6
Oundle Nhants 88 F6
Ounsdale Staffs 84 F5

Our Dynamic Earth C Edin 177 H4
Ousby Cumb 149 G7
Ousden Suffk 77 G3
Ousefleet E R Yk 125 K6
Ouston Dur 151 G4
Outgate Cumb 137 K7
Outhgill Cumb 139 H6
Outhill Warwks 71 K2
Outlane Kirk 123 G6
Out Rawcliffe Lancs 120 E3
Outwell Norfk 90 D3
Outwood Surrey 32 B4
Outwoods Staffs 99 H8
Ouzlewell Green Leeds 123 L5
Over Cambs 75 L1
Overbury Worcs 71 G6
Overcombe Dorset 14 D6
Over Compton Dorset 26 E7
Overdale Crematorium Bolton 121 K8
Over Haddon Derbys 114 D7
Over Kellet Lancs 129 L5
Over Kiddington Oxon 57 H4
Overleigh Somset 26 C4
Over Norton Oxon 56 F3
Over Peover Ches E 113 H6
Overpool Ches W 111 L6
Overscaig Hotel Highld 225 J4
Overseal Derbys 86 C1
Over Silton N York 133 G2
Oversland Kent 34 E3
Overstone Nhants 74 B2
Over Stowey Somset 25 J4
Overstrand Norfk 106 F4
Over Stratton Somset 26 B7
Overthorpe Nhants 72 F6
Overton C Aber 207 G3
Overton Hants 29 K2
Overton Lancs 129 J7
Overton N York 133 H7
Overton Shrops 69 K1
Overton Swans 50 F7
Overton Wakefd 123 K7
Overton Wrexhm 98 A4
Overtown N Lans 175 L7
Over Wallop Hants 28 F4
Over Whitacre Warwks 86 B5
Over Worton Oxon 57 H3
Oving Bucks 58 C4
Oving W Susx 18 B5
Ovingdean Br & H 19 K5
Ovingham Nthumb 150 D3
Ovington Dur 140 E4
Ovington Essex 77 H6
Ovington Hants 29 K5
Ovington Norfk 91 K3
Ovington Nthumb 150 D3
Ower Hants 28 F7
Owermoigne Dorset 14 E5
Owlerton Sheff 115 G4
Owlsmoor Br For 42 D7
Owlswick Bucks 58 C6
Owmby Lincs 117 G4
Owmby Lincs 117 H1
Owslebury Hants 29 K6
Owston Donc 124 E7
Owston Leics 87 L3
Owston Ferry N Linc 116 D2
Owstwick E R Yk 127 G4
Owthorne E R Yk 127 H5
Owthorpe Notts 102 A5
Owton Manor Hartpl 141 L2
Oxborough Norfk 91 G3
Oxcombe Lincs 118 D6
Oxenholme Cumb 129 L2
Oxenhope C Brad 122 F4
Oxen Park Cumb 129 G3
Oxenpill Somset 26 C3
Oxenton Gloucs 55 L2
Oxenwood Wilts 40 F8
Oxford Oxon 57 K6
Oxford Airport Oxon 57 J5
Oxford Crematorium Oxon 57 K6
Oxford Services Oxon 57 L6
Oxhey Herts 43 J2
Oxhill Warwks 72 C5
Oxley Wolves 84 F3
Oxley Green Essex 61 L5
Oxlode Cambs 90 C6
Oxnam Border 167 L5
Oxnead Norfk 106 F7
Oxshott Surrey 43 J7
Oxspring Barns 114 F2
Oxted Surrey 32 C3
Oxton Border 178 B7
Oxton N York 124 D2
Oxton Notts 101 M3
Oxwich Swans 51 G7
Oxwich Green Swans 50 F7
Oykel Bridge Hotel Highld 221 K2
Oyne Abers 206 D1
Oystermouth Swans 51 H7

P

Pabail W Isls 232 g2
Packington Leics 86 D1
Packmoor C Stke 99 K2
Padanaram Angus 196 C6
Padbury Bucks 58 B2
Paddington Gt Lon 44 F4
Paddlesworth Kent 35 G6
Paddlesworth Kent 46 B7
Paddock Wood Kent 33 H4
Padiham Lancs 122 B4
Padside N York 132 B7
Padstow Cnwll 4 E2
Padworth W Berk 41 L7
Pagham W Susx 18 B6
Paglesham Essex 46 F2
Paignton Torbay 7 K4
Pailton Warwks 86 F6
Painscastle Powys 68 D5
Painshawfield Nthumb 150 D3
Painsthorpe E R Yk 134 C7
Painswick Gloucs 55 K6
Painter's Forstal Kent 34 D3
Paisley Rens 174 E5
Paisley Woodside Crematorium Rens 174 E5
Pakefield Suffk 93 L5
Pakenham Suffk 77 L2
Paley Street W & M 42 E5
Palfrey Wsall 85 H4
Palgrave Suffk 92 D7
Pallington Dorset 14 E4
Palmerston E Ayrs 163 L5
Palnackie D & G 146 E4
Palnure D & G 145 J3
Palterton Derbys 115 J7
Pamber End Hants 41 L8
Pamber Green Hants 41 L8
Pamber Heath Hants 41 L7
Pamington Gloucs 55 L2
Pamphill Dorset 15 J3
Pampisford Cambs 76 C5
Panbride Angus 187 J1
Pancrasweek Devon 9 H4
Pandy Mons 53 M4
Pandy Tudur Conwy 110 B8
Panfield Essex 61 H3
Pangbourne W Berk 41 M5
Pangdean W Susx 19 J4
Pannal N York 123 L1
Pannal Ash N York 132 D8
Pannanich Wells Hotel Abers 205 J6
Pant Shrops 97 L7
Pantasaph Flints 111 G6
Pant-ffrwyth Brdgnd 36 E4
Pant Glas Gwynd 95 H3
Pantglas Powys 81 G4
Panton Lincs 117 K5
Pant-y-dwr Powys 81 L8
Pant-y-mwyn Flints 111 H8
Panxworth Norfk 93 H2
Papa Stour Airport Shet 235 b5
Papa Westray Airport Ork 234 c3
Papcastle Cumb 136 F2
Papigoe Highld 231 L5
Papple E Loth 178 D4
Papplewick Notts 101 K3
Papworth Everard Cambs 75 K3
Papworth St Agnes Cambs 75 J2
Par Cnwll 5 G5
Parbold Lancs 121 G7
Parbrook Somset 26 E4
Parc Gwynd 96 D5
Parc Gwyn Crematorium Pembks 49 K5
Parc Seymour Newpt 38 B3
Pardshaw Cumb 136 F3
Parham Suffk 79 G3
Park D & G 154 F4
Park Nthumb 149 H3
Park Corner Oxon 42 B3
Park Crematorium Lancs 120 E5
Parkend Gloucs 54 E6
Parkers Green Kent 33 G4
Park Farm Kent 34 D6
Parkgate Ches W 111 J6
Parkgate D & G 155 H4
Park Gate Hants 17 G2
Park Gate Leeds 123 J3
Parkgate Surrey 31 K3
Parkgrove Crematorium Angus 196 F6
Parkhall W Duns 174 E4
Parkham Devon 22 F6
Parkmill Swans 51 G7
Park Royal Gt Lon 44 D4
Parkside Dur 151 K5
Parkside N Lans 175 L6
Parkstone Poole 15 J4
Park Street Herts 59 J6
Park Wood Crematorium Calder 123 G6
Parndon Essex 60 C6
Parndon Wood Crematorium Essex 60 C6
Parracombe Devon 23 L3
Parson Drove Cambs 89 L2
Parson's Heath Essex 62 B3
Partick C Glas 174 F5
Partington Traffd 113 G3
Partney Lincs 118 F7
Parton Cumb 136 D3
Partridge Green W Susx 19 G2
Parwich Derbys 100 D2
Passenham Nhants 73 L6
Paston Norfk 107 G5
Patcham Br & H 19 J4
Patching W Susx 18 E4
Patchway S Glos 38 E4
Pateley Bridge N York 132 B6
Pathhead Fife 186 E8
Pathhead Mdloth 177 K5
Path of Condie P & K 185 M5
Patna E Ayrs 163 K7
Patney Wilts 40 B8
Patrick IoM 237 b5
Patrick Brompton N York 132 C2
Patricroft Salfd 113 H2
Patrington E R Yk 127 H6
Patrington Haven E R Yk 127 H6
Patrixbourne Kent 35 G4
Patterdale Cumb 137 L4
Pattingham Staffs 84 E4
Pattishall Nhants 73 J4
Pattiswick Green Essex 61 K3
Paul Cnwll 2 E5
Paulerspury Nhants 73 K5
Paull E R Yk 126 E5
Paul's Dene Wilts 28 C5
Paulton BaNES 26 F1
Pauperhaugh Nthumb 158 D3
Pavenham Bed 74 E4
Pawlett Somset 25 L3
Paxford Gloucs 71 L6
Paxton Border 179 J7
Payhembury Devon 12 E3
Paythorne Lancs 122 C1
Peacehaven E Susx 19 L5
Peak District National Park 114 D3
Peak Forest Derbys 114 C5
Peakirk C Pete 89 H3
Peasedown St John BaNES 39 G8
Peaseland Green Norfk 92 C1
Peasemore W Berk 41 J5
Peasenhall Suffk 79 H2
Pease Pottage W Susx 31 L5
Peaslake Surrey 31 H3
Peasley Cross St Hel 112 D3
Peasmarsh E Susx 21 H2
Peathill Abers 217 H2
Peat Inn Fife 187 G5
Peatling Magna Leics 87 H5
Peatling Parva Leics 87 H5
Pebmarsh Essex 77 J7
Pebworth Worcs 71 K5
Pecket Well Calder 122 E5
Peckforton Ches E 98 D2
Peckham Gt Lon 45 G5
Peckleton Leics 86 F4
Pedlinge Kent 34 F7
Pedmore Dudley 85 G6
Pedwell Somset 26 B4
Peebles Border 166 C2
Peel IoM 237 b4
Peel Green Crematorium Salfd 113 H3
Peene Kent 35 G6
Pegsdon C Beds 59 J2
Pegswood Nthumb 159 G5
Pegwell Kent 35 K2
Peinchorran Highld 209 H7
Peinlich Highld 208 F3
Peldon Essex 62 B5
Pelsall Wsall 85 H3
Pelton Dur 151 G4
Pelynt Cnwll 5 K5
Pemberton Carmth 51 G5
Pemberton Wigan 112 D2
Pembrey Carmth 50 E5
Pembridge Herefs 69 H3
Pembroke Pembks 49 G7
Pembroke Dock Pembks 49 G6
Pembrokeshire Coast National Park Pembks 48 E4
Pembury Kent 33 G5
Pen-allt Herefs 54 E3
Penallt Mons 54 D6
Penally Pembks 49 J7
Penarth V Glam 37 J6
Pen-bont Rhydybeddau Cerdgn 80 F6
Penbryn Cerdgn 65 J4
Pencader Carmth 66 B7
Pencaitland E Loth 177 L5
Pencarnisiog IoA 108 D6
Pencarreg Carmth 66 C5
Pencelli Powys 53 H3
Penclawdd Swans 51 G6
Pencoed Brdgnd 36 E4

Pencombe Herefs 69 L4
Pencraig Herefs 54 E4
Pencraig Powys 97 G6
Pendeen Cnwll 2 C4
Penderyn Rhondd 52 E6
Pendine Carmth 50 B4
Pendlebury Salfd 113 H2
Pendleton Lancs 121 L3
Pendock Worcs 55 H2
Pendoggett Cnwll 8 D8
Pendomer Somset 13 M1
Pendoylan V Glam 37 G5
Penegoes Powys 81 G4
Pen-ffordd Pembks 49 J3
Pengam Caerph 37 J2
Pengam Cardif 37 K5
Penge Gt Lon 45 G6
Pengelly Cnwll 8 E7
Penhallow Cnwll 3 K2
Penhalvean Cnwll 3 J4
Penhill Swindn 40 D3
Penhow Newpt 38 B3
Penicuik Mdloth 177 H6
Penifiler Highld 209 G6
Peninver Ag & B 161 J4
Penistone Barns 114 E2
Penkill S Ayrs 152 F3
Penkridge Staffs 85 G2
Penley Wrexhm 98 B4
Penllyn V Glam 36 F5
Penmachno Conwy 96 C3
Penmaen Caerph 37 J2
Penmaen Swans 51 G7
Penmaenmawr Conwy 109 K6
Penmaenpool Gwynd 95 M8
Penmark V Glam 37 G6
Penmount Crematorium Cnwll 4 C6
Penmynydd IoA 109 G6
Pennal Gwynd 80 F4
Pennan Abers 216 F2
Pennant Powys 81 J4
Pennerley Shrops 83 G4
Pennines 122 E4
Pennington Cumb 128 F4
Pennorth Powys 53 H3
Penn Street Bucks 42 F2
Penny Bridge Cumb 129 G3
Pennycross Ag & B 181 G3
Pennyghael Ag & B 181 H3
Pennyglen S Ayrs 163 H7
Pennymoor Devon 11 K3
Pennywell Sundld 151 J4
Penparc Cerdgn 65 H5
Penperlleni Mons 53 L6
Penpoll Cnwll 5 J5
Penponds Cnwll 3 H4
Penpont D & G 154 E4
Pen-rhiw Pembks 65 H6
Penrhiwceiber Rhondd 37 G2
Pen Rhiwfawr Neath 51 L4
Penrhiw-llan Cerdgn 65 K6
Penrhiw-pal Cerdgn 65 K5
Penrhos Gwynd 94 F5
Penrhos Mons 54 B5
Penrhyn Bay Conwy 110 A5
Penrhyn-coch Cerdgn 80 E6
Penrhyndeudraeth Gwynd 95 K5
Penrice Swans 50 F7
Penrioch N Ayrs 161 L1
Penrith Cumb 138 D2
Penrose Cnwll 4 D2
Penruddock Cumb 138 B2
Penryn Cnwll 3 K4
Pensarn Conwy 110 C5
Pensax Worcs 70 C2
Penselwood Somset 27 H5
Pensford BaNES 38 F7
Pensham Worcs 71 G5
Penshaw Sundld 151 H4
Penshurst Kent 32 F4
Pensilva Cnwll 5 L2
Pensnett Dudley 85 G5
Pentewan Cnwll 4 F6
Pentir Gwynd 109 H7
Pentire Cnwll 4 C4
Pentlow Essex 77 J5
Pentney Norfk 91 G2
Pentonbridge Cumb 156 D6
Penton Mewsey Hants 29 G3
Pentraeth IoA 109 G5
Pentre Mons 54 B7
Pentre Rhondd 36 F2
Pentre Shrops 98 A8
Pentrebach Myr Td 53 G7
Pentre-bach Powys 52 E2
Pentre Berw IoA 108 F6
Pentrebychan Crematorium Wrexhm 97 L3
Pentre-celyn Denbgs 97 J2
Pentre-celyn Powys 81 J3
Pentre-chwyth Swans 51 J6
Pentre-cwrt Carmth 65 L6
Pentredwr Denbgs 97 J3
Pentrefelin Gwynd 95 J5
Pentrefoelas Conwy 96 D3
Pentregat Cerdgn 65 K4
Pentre-Gwenlais Carmth 51 H3
Pentre Hodrey Shrops 83 G7
Pentre Llanrhaeadr Denbgs 110 F8
Pentre Meyrick V Glam 36 E5
Pentre-tafarn-y-fedw Conwy 96 C1
Pentrich Derbys 101 G3
Pentridge Dorset 28 B7
Pen-twyn Mons 54 D6
Pentwynmaur Caerph 37 J2
Pentyrch Cardif 37 H4
Penwithick Cnwll 5 G5
Penybanc Carmth 51 H2
Penybont Powys 68 C2
Pen-y-bont Powys 97 K7
Pen-y-bont-fawr Powys 97 G7
Pen-y-bryn Pembks 65 G6
Penycae Wrexhm 97 L4
Pen-y-clawdd Mons 54 C6
Pen-y-coedcae Rhondd 37 G3
Penycwn Pembks 48 E3
Pen-y-felin Flints 111 G7
Penyffordd Flints 97 L1
Pen-y-Garnedd Powys 97 H7
Pen-y-graig Gwynd 94 D5
Penygraig Rhondd 36 F3
Penygroes Carmth 51 H3
Penygroes Gwynd 95 H2
Pen-y-Mynydd Carmth 50 F5
Penymynydd Flints 97 L1
Penysarn IoA 108 F4
Pen-y-stryt Denbgs 97 J3
Penywaun Rhondd 52 F6
Penzance Cnwll 2 E5
Peopleton Worcs 71 G4
Peplow Shrops 98 F7
Perceton N Ayrs 163 J2
Percyhorner Abers 217 H2
Perelle Guern 236 b3
Perham Down Wilts 28 E2
Periton Somset 24 E3
Perivale Gt Lon 44 D4
Perkins Village Devon 12 D4
Perlethorpe Notts 115 M7
Perranarworthal Cnwll 3 K4
Perranporth Cnwll 3 K1
Perranuthnoe Cnwll 2 F5
Perranwell Cnwll 3 K4
Perranzabuloe Cnwll 3 K2
Perry Birm 85 J5
Perry Barr Birm 85 J5
Perry Barr Crematorium Birm 85 J5
Perry Green Wilts 39 L3
Pershall Staffs 99 J6
Pershore Worcs 71 G5
Pertenhall Bed 74 F2
Perth P & K 186 B3
Perth Crematorium P & K 186 A3
Perthy Shrops 98 A5
Perton Herefs 69 L6
Perton Staffs 84 F4
Peterborough C Pete 89 H4
Peterborough Crematorium C Pete 89 H3
Peterborough Services Cambs 89 G5
Peterchurch Herefs 69 G6
Peterculter C Aber 206 F5
Peterhead Abers 217 L5
Peterlee Dur 151 K6
Petersfield Hants 30 C6
Peter's Green Herts 59 J4
Petersham Gt Lon 44 D5
Peters Marland Devon 10 C3
Peterstone Wentlooge Newpt 37 K4
Peterston-super-Ely V Glam 37 G5
Peterstow Herefs 54 E3
Peter Tavy Devon 6 D1
Petham Kent 34 F4
Petherwin Gate Cnwll 9 H6
Petrockstow Devon 10 D3
Pett E Susx 21 H3
Pettaugh Suffk 78 E3
Petterden Angus 196 C7
Pettinain S Lans 165 J2
Pettistree Suffk 79 G4
Petton Devon 24 F6
Petts Wood Gt Lon 45 J6
Pettycur Fife 177 H2
Pettymuk Abers 207 G1
Petworth W Susx 31 G6
Pevensey E Susx 20 D5
Pevensey Bay E Susx 20 D5
Pewsey Wilts 40 D7
Phepson Worcs 71 G3
Philham Devon 22 D6
Philiphaugh Border 166 F4
Phillack Cnwll 2 F4
Philleigh Cnwll 4 D7
Philpstoun W Loth 176 E3
Phoenix Green Hants 30 C1
Phones Highld 203 G6
Pibsbury Somset 26 C6
Pickburn Donc 115 K1
Pickering N York 134 C3
Pickford Covtry 86 C6
Pickhill N York 132 E3
Picklescott Shrops 83 J4
Pickmere Ches E 113 G6
Pickney Somset 25 J5
Pickwell Leics 87 L2
Pickworth Lincs 103 H5
Pickworth Rutlnd 88 E2
Picton Ches W 112 B7
Picton N York 141 K5
Piddinghoe E Susx 19 L5
Piddington Nhants 74 B4
Piddington Oxon 57 M5
Piddlehinton Dorset 14 D3
Piddletrenthide Dorset 14 D3
Pidley Cambs 89 K7
Piercebridge Darltn 140 F4
Pierowall Ork 234 c3
Pilgrims Hatch Essex 45 L2
Pilham Lincs 116 E3
Pillaton Cnwll 6 A3
Pillerton Hersey Warwks 72 C5
Pillerton Priors Warwks 72 C5
Pilley Barns 115 G2
Pilley Hants 16 D3
Pilling Lancs 120 E2
Pilning S Glos 38 D4
Pilsbury Derbys 114 C8
Pilsdon Dorset 13 K3
Pilsley Derbys 101 H1
Pilsley Derbys 114 E7
Pilson Green Norfk 93 H2
Piltdown E Susx 19 L2
Pilton Devon 23 J5
Pilton Nhants 88 E6
Pilton Rutlnd 88 D3
Pilton Somset 26 E3
Pimperne Dorset 15 G1
Pinchbeck Lincs 103 L7
Pin Green Herts 59 L3
Pinhoe Devon 12 C4
Pinley Green Warwks 72 B2
Pinminnoch S Ayrs 152 E4
Pinmore S Ayrs 152 E4
Pinn Devon 12 E5
Pinner Gt Lon 43 J3
Pinner Green Gt Lon 43 J3
Pinvin Worcs 71 G5
Pinwherry S Ayrs 152 E5
Pinxton Derbys 101 J2
Pipe and Lyde Herefs 69 K5
Pipe Aston Herefs 69 J1
Pipe Gate Shrops 99 G4
Piperhill Highld 213 K4
Pipewell Nhants 88 B6
Pirbright Surrey 30 F1
Pirnie Border 167 K4
Pirnmill N Ayrs 161 L1
Pirton Herts 59 J2
Pishill Oxon 42 B3
Pistyll Gwynd 94 F4
Pitagowan P & K 194 C3
Pitblae Abers 217 J2
Pitcairngreen P & K 185 M3
Pitcalnie Highld 223 H6
Pitcaple Abers 206 D1
Pitcarity Angus 196 B4
Pitchcombe Gloucs 55 J6
Pitchcott Bucks 58 C4
Pitchford Shrops 83 K3
Pitch Green Bucks 58 C7
Pitchroy Moray 214 E6
Pitcombe Somset 26 F5
Pitcox E Loth 178 E4
Pitfichie Abers 206 D3
Pitglassie Abers 216 D5
Pitgrudy Highld 223 H3
Pitlessie Fife 186 E5
Pitlochry P & K 194 E5
Pitmachie Abers 216 C8
Pitmain Highld 203 H5
Pitmedden Abers 217 G8
Pitmedden Garden Abers 217 G8
Pitminster Somset 25 K7
Pitmuies Angus 196 F6
Pitmunie Abers 206 C3
Pitney Somset 26 C5
Pitroddie P & K 186 C3
Pitscottie Fife 187 G5
Pitsea Essex 46 C3
Pitsford Nhants 73 L2
Pitstone Bucks 58 F5
Pittarrow Abers 197 H2
Pittenweem Fife 187 J6
Pitteuchar Fife 186 D7
Pittington Dur 151 H6
Pittodrie House Hotel Abers 206 D1
Pitton Wilts 28 E5
Pittulie Abers 217 H2
Pity Me Dur 151 G5
Pixham Surrey 31 K2
Plains N Lans 175 L5
Plaish Shrops 83 K4
Plaistow Gt Lon 45 H4
Plaistow W Susx 31 G5
Plaitford Hants 28 F7

Platt Kent 33 G2
Plawsworth Dur 151 G5
Plaxtol Kent 33 G3
Playden E Susx 21 H2
Playford Suffk 78 F5
Play Hatch Oxon 42 C5
Playing Place Cnwll 4 C7
Playley Green Gloucs 55 H2
Plealey Shrops 83 H3
Plean Stirlg 175 L2
Pleasance Fife 186 D5
Pleasington Bl w D 121 J5
Pleasington Crematorium Bl w D 121 J5
Pleasley Derbys 115 J8
Pleinheaume Guern 236 d2
Plemont Jersey 236 a5
Plemstall Ches W 112 C7
Pleshey Essex 61 G5
Plockton Highld 210 C7
Plowden Shrops 83 H6
Pluckley Kent 34 B5
Pluckley Thorne Kent 34 B5
Plumbland Cumb 147 K6
Plumley Ches E 113 G6
Plumpton Cumb 148 E7
Plumpton E Susx 19 K3
Plumpton Nhants 73 H5
Plumpton Green E Susx 19 K3
Plumstead Gt Lon 45 J4
Plumstead Norfk 106 D5
Plumtree Notts 101 L6
Plungar Leics 102 C5
Plurenden Kent 34 C7
Plush Dorset 14 D3
Plwmp Cerdgn 65 K4
Plymouth C Plym 6 C5
Plymouth Airport C Plym 6 D4
Plympton C Plym 6 D5
Plymstock C Plym 6 D5
Plymtree Devon 12 D2
Pockley N York 133 K3
Pocklington E R Yk 125 J2
Podimore Somset 26 D6
Podington Bed 74 D3
Podmore Staffs 99 H5
Pointon Lincs 103 J6
Pokesdown Bmouth 15 L4
Polbain Highld 224 B6
Polbathic Cnwll 6 A4
Polbeth W Loth 176 D5
Poldark Mine Cnwll 3 H5
Polebrook Nhants 88 F6
Polegate E Susx 20 C5
Polesden Lacey Surrey 31 J2
Polesworth Warwks 86 C3
Polglass Highld 224 C6
Polgooth Cnwll 4 F5
Polgown D & G 154 C2
Poling W Susx 18 E5
Poling Corner W Susx 18 E5
Polkerris Cnwll 5 H5
Pollington E R Yk 124 F6
Polloch Highld 190 F3
Pollokshaws C Glas 175 G6
Pollokshields C Glas 175 G5
Polmassick Cnwll 4 F6
Polmont Falk 176 C3
Polnish Highld 200 B8
Polperro Cnwll 5 K5
Polruan Cnwll 5 H5
Polstead Suffk 78 B6
Poltalloch Ag & B 182 B7
Poltimore Devon 12 C3
Polton Mdloth 177 J5
Polwarth Border 178 F7
Polyphant Cnwll 9 H7
Polzeath Cnwll 4 E1
Pomathorn Mdloth 177 H6
Pondersbridge Cambs 89 J5
Ponders End Gt Lon 45 G2
Ponsanooth Cnwll 3 K4
Ponsworthy Devon 7 G2
Pont Abraham Services Carmth 51 H4
Pontac Jersey 236 e8
Pontantwn Carmth 50 F3
Pontardawe Neath 51 K5
Pontarddulais Swans 51 H5
Pont-ar-gothi Carmth 51 G2
Pontarsais Carmth 66 B8
Pontblyddyn Flints 97 L1
Pontcysyllte Aqueduct Wrexhm 97 L4
Pontefract Wakefd 124 C6
Pontefract Crematorium Wakefd 124 C6
Ponteland Nthumb 158 F7
Ponterwyd Cerdgn 81 G7
Pontesbury Shrops 83 H3
Pontesford Shrops 83 H3
Pontfadog Wrexhm 97 K5
Pontfaen Pembks 64 E7
Pont-faen Powys 67 L7
Pontgarreg Cerdgn 65 K4
Ponthenry Carmth 50 F4
Ponthir Torfn 37 M2
Ponthirwaun Cerdgn 65 J5
Pontllanfraith Caerph 37 J2
Pontlliw Swans 51 H5
Pontlottyn Caerph 53 H6
Pontlyfni Gwynd 95 G3
Pontneddfechan Neath 52 D6
Pontnewydd Torfn 37 L2
Pontrhydfendigaid Cerdgn 67 G2
Pont-rhyd-y-fen Neath 36 C2
Pontrhydygroes Cerdgn 81 G8
Pontrilas Herefs 54 B3
Pont Robert Powys 82 C2
Pontshaen Cerdgn 66 B5
Pontsticill Myr Td 53 G5
Pontwelly Carmth 65 L6
Pontyates Carmth 50 F4
Pontyberem Carmth 51 G4
Pontybodkin Flints 97 L2
Pontyclun Rhondd 37 G4
Pontycymer Brdgnd 36 D3
Pont-y-pant Conwy 96 B2
Pontypool Torfn 53 L7
Pontypridd Rhondd 37 G3
Pontywaun Caerph 37 K2
Pool Cnwll 3 H3
Pool Leeds 123 J2
Poole Poole 15 J4
Poole Crematorium Poole 15 J3
Poole Keynes Gloucs 39 M2
Poolewe Highld 219 K5
Pooley Bridge Cumb 138 C3
Poolfold Staffs 99 K1
Poolhill Gloucs 55 G3
Pool of Muckhart Clacks 185 L7
Pool Street Essex 77 H6
Poplar Gt Lon 45 G4
Porchfield IoW 16 F4
Poringland Norfk 92 F3
Porkellis Cnwll 3 J5
Porlock Somset 24 D3
Porlock Weir Somset 24 D2
Portachoillan Ag & B 172 C6
Port-an-Eorna Highld 210 B7
Port Appin Ag & B 191 H7
Port Askaig Ag & B 171 H5
Portavadie Ag & B 172 F4
Port Bannatyne Ag & B 173 J5
Portbury N Som 38 D5
Port Carlisle Cumb 147 M3
Port Charlotte Ag & B 170 E6
Portchester Hants 17 H2
Portchester Crematorium Hants 17 H2
Port Driseach Ag & B 173 G4
Port Ellen Ag & B 160 C1
Port Elphinstone Abers 206 E2
Portencalzie D & G 152 B7
Portencross N Ayrs 173 K8
Port Erin IoM 237 a6
Portesham Dorset 14 B5
Portessie Moray 215 K2
Port Eynon Swans 50 F7
Portfield Gate Pembks 48 F4
Portgate Devon 10 B7
Port Gaverne Cnwll 8 D8
Port Glasgow Inver 174 C4
Portgordon Moray 215 J2
Portgower Highld 227 H5
Porth Cnwll 4 C4
Porth Rhondd 36 F3
Porthallow Cnwll 3 K6
Porthallow Cnwll 5 K5
Porthcawl Brdgnd 36 C5
Porthcothan Cnwll 4 D2
Porthcurno Cnwll 2 C6
Port Henderson Highld 219 H6
Porthgain Pembks 64 A7
Porthgwarra Cnwll 2 C6
Porthill Staffs 99 J3
Porthkerry V Glam 37 G6
Porthleven Cnwll 3 H6
Porthmadog Gwynd 95 K5
Porth Navas Cnwll 3 K5
Porthoustock Cnwll 3 K6
Porthpean Cnwll 5 G5
Porthtowan Cnwll 3 J2
Porthyrhyd Carmth 51 G3
Portincaple Ag & B 183 J8
Portinfer Jersey 236 a5
Portington E R Yk 125 J4
Portinnisherrich Ag & B 182 D5
Portinscale Cumb 137 H3
Port Isaac Cnwll 8 D8
Portishead N Som 38 C5
Portknockie Moray 215 K2
Portland Dorset 14 D7
Portlethen Abers 207 H6
Portling D & G 146 F4
Portloe Cnwll 4 E7
Port Logan D & G 144 D6
Portmahomack Highld 223 K5
Portmeirion Gwynd 95 K5
Portmellon Cnwll 4 F6
Port Mor Highld 189 K1
Portnacroish Ag & B 191 H6
Portnaguran W Isls 232 g2
Portnahaven Ag & B 170 D7
Portnalong Highld 208 E7
Port nan Giuran W Isls 232 g2
Port nan Long W Isls 232 c5
Port Nis W Isls 232 g1
Portobello C Edin 177 J4
Portobello Wolves 85 G4
Port of Menteith Stirlg 184 D6
Port of Ness W Isls 232 g1
Porton Wilts 28 D4
Portpatrick D & G 144 B4
Port Quin Cnwll 8 C8
Port Ramsay Ag & B 191 H7
Portreath Cnwll 3 H3
Portreath Harbour Cnwll 3 H3
Portree Highld 209 G5
Port St Mary IoM 237 b7
Portscatho Cnwll 4 D8
Portsea C Port 17 J3
Portskerra Highld 230 C3
Portskewett Mons 38 D3
Portslade Br & H 19 H4
Portslade-by-Sea Br & H 19 H5
Portslogan D & G 144 B3
Portsmouth C Port 17 J3
Portsmouth Calder 122 D5
Portsmouth Dockyard C Port 17 J3
Port Soderick IoM 237 c6
Portsonachan Hotel Ag & B 182 F3
Portsoy Abers 216 B2
Port Sunlight Wirral 111 K5
Portswood C Sotn 29 H8
Port Talbot Neath 36 B3
Portuairk Highld 189 K3
Portway Sandw 85 H6
Portway Worcs 85 J8
Port Wemyss Ag & B 170 D7
Port William D & G 145 H6
Portwrinkle Cnwll 6 A5
Portyerrock D & G 145 K7
Poslingford Suffk 77 H5
Posso Border 166 B3
Postbridge Devon 10 F8
Postcombe Oxon 58 B7
Postling Kent 34 F6
Postwick Norfk 93 G2
Potarch Abers 206 B6
Potten End Herts 59 G6
Potter Brompton N York 134 F4
Potterhanworth Lincs 117 H7
Potterhanworth Booths Lincs 117 H7
Potter Heigham Norfk 107 J8
Potterne Wilts 39 M8
Potterne Wick Wilts 39 M8
Potters Bar Herts 59 L7
Potters Crouch Herts 59 J6
Potters Green Covtry 86 D6
Potters Marston Leics 87 G4
Potterspury Nhants 73 L6
Potterton Abers 207 H3
Potto N York 141 L6
Potton C Beds 75 J5
Pott Shrigley Ches E 113 L5
Poughill Cnwll 9 G4
Poughill Devon 11 K3
Poulner Hants 15 M2
Poulshot Wilts 39 L7
Poulton Gloucs 56 C7
Poulton Wirral 111 J4
Poulton-le-Fylde Lancs 120 D3
Poundbury Dorset 14 D4
Poundffald Swans 51 H6
Pound Green E Susx 20 B2
Pound Green Suffk 77 G4
Pound Hill W Susx 32 B5
Poundon Bucks 57 M3
Poundsgate Devon 7 G2
Poundstock Cnwll 9 G5
Pouton D & G 145 K5
Povey Cross Surrey 31 L3
Powburn Nthumb 168 F6
Powderham Devon 12 C5
Powerstock Dorset 13 M3
Powfoot D & G 147 K2
Powick Worcs 70 E4
Powmill P & K 185 L7
Poxwell Dorset 14 E5
Poyle Slough 43 G5
Poynings W Susx 19 H4
Poyntington Dorset 26 F7
Poynton Ches E 113 L5
Poynton Green Wrekin 98 E8
Praa Sands Cnwll 3 G5
Praze-an-Beeble Cnwll 3 H4
Prees Shrops 98 D5
Preesall Lancs 120 E2
Prees Green Shrops 98 E6
Prees Heath Shrops 98 E5

Prees Higher Heath Shrops 98 E5
Pren-gwyn Cerdgn 65 L5
Prenteg Gwynd 95 K4
Prescot Knows 112 C3
Prescott Devon 25 H8
Presnerb Angus 195 J3
Prestatyn Denbgs 110 E5
Prestbury Ches E 113 K6
Prestbury Gloucs 55 L4
Presteigne Powys 69 G2
Prestleigh Somset 26 F4
Preston Border 179 G6
Preston Br & H 19 J4
Preston Devon 7 K2
Preston Dorset 14 D5
Preston E R Yk 126 F4
Preston Gloucs 56 B7
Preston Herts 59 K3
Preston Kent 34 D3
Preston Kent 35 H3
Preston Lancs 121 H4
Preston Nthumb 169 H4
Preston Rutlnd 88 C3
Preston Somset 25 H4
Preston Suffk 77 L4
Preston Torbay 7 K4
Preston Wilts 40 B5
Preston Bagot Warwks 71 L2
Preston Bissett Bucks 58 A3
Preston Bowyer Somset 25 H6
Preston Brockhurst Shrops 98 D7
Preston Brook Halton 112 E5
Preston Candover Hants 29 L3
Preston Capes Nhants 73 H4
Preston Crematorium Lancs 121 H4
Preston Green Warwks 71 L2
Preston Gubbals Shrops 98 C8
Preston on Stour Warwks 72 B4
Preston on the Hill Halton 112 E5
Preston on Wye Herefs 69 H6
Prestonpans E Loth 177 K4
Preston Patrick Cumb 129 L3
Preston Plucknett Somset 26 D7
Preston-under-Scar N York 131 K2
Preston upon the Weald Moors Wrekin 84 C1
Preston Wynne Herefs 69 L5
Prestwich Bury 113 J1
Prestwick S Ayrs 163 J4
Prestwick Airport S Ayrs 163 J4
Prestwood Bucks 58 E7
Prickwillow Cambs 90 E6
Priddy Somset 26 D2
Priest Hutton Lancs 129 L5
Priestland E Ayrs 164 B2
Priest Weston Shrops 82 F4
Primrosehill Border 179 G6
Primrose Hill Dudley 85 G6
Primsidemill Border 168 B4
Princes Risborough Bucks 58 D7
Princethorpe Warwks 72 E1
Princetown Devon 6 E2
Priors Hardwick Warwks 72 F4
Priorslee Wrekin 84 C2
Priors Marston Warwks 72 F3
Priors Norton Gloucs 55 K3
Priory Vale Swindn 40 C3
Priston BaNES 39 G7
Prittlewell Sthend 46 E3
Privett Hants 30 B6
Prixford Devon 23 J4
Probus Cnwll 4 E6
Prora E Loth 178 C3
Prospect Cumb 147 K6
Prospidnick Cnwll 3 H5
Protstonhill Abers 216 F2
Prudhoe Nthumb 150 D3
Publow BaNES 38 F7
Puckeridge Herts 60 C4
Puckington Somset 26 B7
Pucklechurch S Glos 39 G5
Puddington Ches W 111 K6
Puddington Devon 11 J3
Puddletown Dorset 14 E4
Pudsey Leeds 123 J4
Pulborough W Susx 18 E3
Pulford Ches W 98 A2
Pulham Dorset 14 D2
Pulham Market Norfk 92 E6
Pulham St Mary Norfk 92 E6
Pulloxhill C Beds 74 F7
Pumpherston W Loth 176 E4
Pumsaint Carmth 66 E6
Puncheston Pembks 49 G2
Puncknowle Dorset 14 A5
Punnett's Town E Susx 20 C2
Purbrook Hants 17 J2
Purfleet Thurr 45 K4
Puriton Somset 25 L3
Purleigh Essex 61 K7
Purley Gt Lon 44 F7
Purley W Berk 42 A5
Purse Caundle Dorset 27 G7
Purtington Somset 13 K2
Purton Gloucs 54 F6
Purton Gloucs 55 G7
Purton Wilts 40 C3
Purton Stoke Wilts 40 C3
Pury End Nhants 73 K5
Pusey Oxon 41 G2
Putley Herefs 70 B6
Putley Green Herefs 70 B6
Putney Gt Lon 44 E5
Putney Vale Crematorium Gt Lon 44 E5
Puttenham Surrey 30 F2
Puxley Nhants 73 L6
Puxton N Som 38 B7
Pwll Carmth 50 F5
Pwll-glâs Denbgs 97 H2
Pwllgloyw Powys 68 B7
Pwllheli Gwynd 94 F5
Pwllmeyric Mons 38 D2
Pwll Trap Carmth 50 C3
Pwll-y-glaw Neath 36 C2
Pye Bridge Derbys 101 H3
Pyecombe W Susx 19 J3
Pyle Brdgnd 36 C4
Pyleigh Somset 25 H5
Pylle Somset 26 E4
Pymoor Cambs 90 C6
Pymore Dorset 13 L4
Pyrford Surrey 43 H8
Pyrton Oxon 42 B2
Pytchley Nhants 88 C8
Pyworthy Devon 9 J4

Q

Quadring Lincs 103 L6
Quadring Eaudike Lincs 103 L5
Quainton Bucks 58 C4
Quantock Hills Somset 25 J4
Quarff Shet 235 c6
Quarley Hants 28 F3
Quarndon Derbys 101 G4
Quarrier's Village Inver 174 C5
Quarrington Lincs 103 H4
Quarrington Hill Dur 151 H7
Quarry Bank Dudley 85 G6
Quarrywood Moray 214 E2
Quarter N Ayrs 173 L6
Quarter S Lans 175 J7
Quatford Shrops 84 D5
Quatt Shrops 84 D6
Quebec Dur 150 F6
Quedgeley Gloucs 55 J5
Queen Adelaide Cambs 90 E7
Queen Camel Somset 26 E6
Queen Charlton BaNES 38 F6
Queen Elizabeth Forest Park Stirlg 184 B6
Queenhill Worcs 70 F6
Queen Oak Dorset 27 H5
Queen's Bower IoW 17 H5
Queensbury C Brad 123 G4
Queensferry Flints 111 K7
Queensferry Crossing Fife 176 F3
Queenslie C Glas 175 H5
Queenzieburn N Lans 175 J3
Quendon Essex 60 E3
Queniborough Leics 87 J2
Quenington Gloucs 56 C7
Queslett Birm 85 J4
Quethiock Cnwll 5 L3
Quidenham Norfk 92 B6
Quidhampton Wilts 28 C5
Quinton Nhants 73 L4
Quintrell Downs Cnwll 4 D4
Quixwood Border 179 G5
Quoig P & K 185 H3
Quorn Leics 87 H1
Quothquan S Lans 165 J2
Quoyburray Ork 234 c6
Quoyloo Ork 234 b5

R

Raasay Highld 209 J5
Rachan Mill Border 165 L3
Rachub Gwynd 109 J7
Rackenford Devon 24 D7
Rackham W Susx 18 E3
Rackheath Norfk 93 G1
Racks D & G 155 H7
Rackwick Ork 234 a7
Radbourne Derbys 100 F5
Radcliffe Bury 113 H1
Radcliffe on Trent Notts 101 M5
Radclive Bucks 73 J7
Raddery Highld 213 H3
Radernie Fife 187 G5
Radford Covtry 86 D7
Radford Semele Warwks 72 D2
Radlett Herts 59 K7
Radley Oxon 57 K7
Radley Green Essex 60 F6
Radnage Bucks 42 C2
Radstock BaNES 27 G1
Radstone Nhants 73 H6
Radway Warwks 72 D5
Radwell Bed 74 E3
Radwell Herts 75 J7
Radwinter Essex 76 E6
Radyr Cardif 37 H4
Rafford Moray 214 C3
RAF Museum Cosford Shrops 84 E3
RAF Museum Hendon Gt Lon 44 E3
Ragdale Leics 102 A8
Raglan Mons 54 B6
Ragnall Notts 116 D6
Raigbeg Highld 213 J8
Rainbow Hill Worcs 70 F4
Rainford St Hel 112 C2
Rainham Gt Lon 45 K4
Rainham Medway 46 D6
Rainhill St Hel 112 C4
Rainhill Stoops St Hel 112 D4
Rainow Ches E 113 L6
Rainsbrook Crematorium Warwks 87 G8
Rainton N York 132 E4
Rainworth Notts 101 L2
Rait P & K 186 D3
Raithby Lincs 118 D5
Raithby Lincs 118 E7
Rake Hants 30 D5
Ralia Highld 203 H5
Ramasaig Highld 208 B5
Rame Cnwll 3 J4
Rame Cnwll 6 B6
Rampisham Dorset 14 B3
Rampside Cumb 128 F6
Rampton Cambs 76 B2
Rampton Notts 116 D5
Ramsbottom Bury 122 B6
Ramsbury Wilts 40 F6
Ramscraigs Highld 227 K3
Ramsdean Hants 30 B6
Ramsdell Hants 41 L8
Ramsden Oxon 57 G5
Ramsden Bellhouse Essex 46 B2
Ramsey Cambs 89 K6
Ramsey Essex 62 E2
Ramsey IoM 237 e3
Ramsey Forty Foot Cambs 89 K6
Ramsey Heights Cambs 89 J6
Ramsey Island Essex 61 M6
Ramsey Island Pembks 48 B3
Ramsey Mereside Cambs 89 K5
Ramsey St Mary's Cambs 89 J6
Ramsgate Kent 35 K2
Ramsgill N York 131 L5
Ramshope Nthumb 157 J2
Ramshorn Staffs 100 B4
Ramsnest Common Surrey 30 F5
Ranby Lincs 118 B5
Ranby Notts 116 A5
Rand Lincs 117 J5
Randalls Park Crematorium Surrey 44 D8
Randwick Gloucs 55 J6
Ranfurly Rens 174 D5
Rangemore Staffs 100 D7
Rangeworthy S Glos 39 G3
Rankinston E Ayrs 163 L6
Rannoch Station P & K 193 G5
Ranscombe Somset 24 E3
Ranskill Notts 116 A4
Ranton Staffs 99 J7
Ranton Green Staffs 99 J7
Ranworth Norfk 93 H1
Raploch Stirlg 185 G7
Rapness Ork 234 c4
Rascarrel D & G 146 D5
Rashfield Ag & B 173 K2
Rashwood Worcs 71 G2
Raskelf N York 133 G5
Rastrick Calder 123 H6
Ratagan Highld 200 E2
Ratby Leics 87 G3
Ratcliffe Culey Leics 86 D4
Ratcliffe on Soar Notts 101 J6
Ratcliffe on the Wreake Leics 87 J1
Rathen Abers 217 J3
Rathillet Fife 186 F3

Rathmell N York 130 F7
Ratho C Edin 176 F4
Ratho Station C Edin 176 F4
Rathven Moray 215 K2
Ratley Warwks 72 E5
Ratling Kent 35 H4
Ratlinghope Shrops 83 H4
Rattar Highld 231 J2
Rattery Devon 7 H4
Rattlesden Suffk 77 L3
Ratton Village E Susx 20 C5
Rattray P & K 195 J7
Raunds Nhants 88 E8
Ravenfield Rothm 115 J3
Ravenglass Cumb 136 F7
Raveningham Norfk 93 H4
Ravenscar N York 143 K6
Ravenscraig N Lans 175 K6
Ravensden Bed 74 F4
Ravenshead Notts 101 K2
Ravensthorpe Kirk 123 J6
Ravensthorpe Nhants 73 J1
Ravenstone Leics 86 E2
Ravenstone M Keyn 74 B4
Ravenstonedale Cumb 139 G6
Ravenstruther S Lans 165 H1
Ravensworth N York 140 E5
Rawcliffe C York 133 J8
Rawcliffe E R Yk 125 G6
Rawdon Leeds 123 J3
Rawdon Crematorium Leeds 123 J3
Rawling Street Kent 34 B3
Rawmarsh Rothm 115 H3
Rawreth Essex 46 C2
Rawridge Devon 12 F2
Rawtenstall Lancs 122 B6
Raydon Suffk 78 C6
Rayleigh Essex 46 D2
Rayne Essex 61 H4
Raynes Park Gt Lon 44 E6
Reach Cambs 76 E2
Read Lancs 122 B4
Reading Readg 42 B5
Reading Crematorium Readg 42 B5
Reading Services W Berk 42 A6
Reading Street Kent 34 B8
Reading Street Kent 35 K2
Reagill Cumb 138 E4
Realwa Cnwll 3 G4
Rearquhar Highld 223 G3
Rearsby Leics 87 J2
Reay Highld 230 D3
Reculver Kent 47 L6
Red Ball Devon 25 H7
Redberth Pembks 49 J6
Redbourn Herts 59 J5
Redbourne N Linc 116 F2
Redbrook Gloucs 54 D6
Redbrook Wrexhm 98 D4
Redbrook Street Kent 34 C7
Redburn Highld 213 L5
Redcar R & Cl 142 D3
Redcastle D & G 146 E2
Redcastle Highld 212 E4
Redding Falk 176 C3
Reddingmuirhead Falk 176 C3
Reddish Stockp 113 K3
Redditch Worcs 71 J2
Redditch Crematorium Worcs 71 J2
Rede Suffk 77 J4
Redenhall Norfk 92 F6
Redesmouth Nthumb 157 L5
Redford Abers 197 J3
Redford Angus 196 F7
Redford W Susx 30 E6
Redfordgreen Border 166 E6
Redgorton P & K 186 A2
Redgrave Suffk 92 C7
Redhill Abers 206 E4
Red Hill Bmouth 15 K4
Redhill Herts 59 M2
Redhill N Som 38 D7
Redhill Surrey 32 B3
Redisham Suffk 93 J6
Redland Bristl 38 E5
Redland Ork 234 b5
Redlingfield Suffk 78 E1
Redlingfield Green Suffk 78 E1
Red Lodge Suffk 77 G1
Redlynch Somset 27 G5
Redlynch Wilts 28 D7
Redmarley Worcs 70 D2
Redmarley D'Abitot Gloucs 55 H2
Redmarshall S on T 141 J3
Redmile Leics 102 D5
Redmire N York 131 K2
Redmyre Abers 197 J2
Rednal Shrops 98 A6
Redpath Border 167 J3
Redpoint Highld 219 H7
Red Roses Carmth 49 L5
Red Row Nthumb 159 G3
Redruth Cnwll 3 J3
Redstone P & K 186 C1
Red Street Staffs 99 J3
Red Wharf Bay IoA 109 G5
Redwick Newpt 38 B4
Redwick S Glos 38 D3
Redworth Darltn 141 G3
Reed Herts 75 L7
Reedham Norfk 93 J3
Reedness E R Yk 125 J6
Reeds Holme Lancs 122 B5
Reepham Lincs 117 H6
Reepham Norfk 106 D7
Reeth N York 140 C7
Reeves Green Solhll 86 C7
Regil N Som 38 D7
Reiff Highld 224 B5
Reigate Surrey 31 L2
Reighton N York 135 H4
Reisque Abers 207 G2
Reiss Highld 231 L5
Relubbus Cnwll 2 F5
Relugas Moray 214 B5
Remenham Wokham 42 C4
Remenham Hill Wokham 42 C4
Rempstone Notts 101 L7
Rendcomb Gloucs 56 A6
Rendham Suffk 79 H2
Rendlesham Suffk 79 H4
Renfrew Rens 174 F5
Renhold Bed 74 F4
Renishaw Derbys 115 J6
Rennington Nthumb 169 J5
Renton W Duns 174 D3
Renwick Cumb 149 G6
Repps Norfk 93 J1
Repton Derbys 100 F6
Resaurie Highld 213 H5
Resipole Highld 190 E4
Reskadinnick Cnwll 3 H3
Resolis Highld 213 G2
Resolven Neath 52 C7
Rest and be thankful Ag & B 183 J6
Reston Border 179 H6
Reswallie Angus 196 E6
Retford Notts 116 B5
Rettendon Essex 61 J7
Revesby Lincs 103 M1
Rewe Devon 12 B3
Rew Street IoW 16 F4
Reymerston Norfk 92 B3
Reynalton Pembks 49 J5
Reynoldston Swans 50 F7
Rezare Cnwll 6 A1
Rhandirmwyn Carmth 67 H5
Rhayader Powys 67 L2
Rheindown Highld 212 D5
Rhes-y-cae Flints 111 G7
Rhewl Denbgs 97 H1
Rhewl Denbgs 97 J4
Rhicarn Highld 224 D4
Rhiconich Highld 228 C5
Rhicullen Highld 222 F6
Rhigos Rhondd 52 E6
Rhireavach Highld 220 D3
Rhives Highld 223 H2
Rhiwbina Cardif 37 J4
Rhiwderyn Newpt 37 K3
Rhiwlas Gwynd 109 H7
Rhoden Green Kent 33 H4
Rhodes Minnis Kent 34 F6
Rhodiad-y-brenin Pembks 48 C3
Rhonehouse D & G 146 C3
Rhoose V Glam 37 G6
Rhos Carmth 65 L7
Rhos Neath 51 L5
Rhoscolyn IoA 108 C6
Rhoscrowther Pembks 48 F6
Rhosesmor Flints 111 H7
Rhosgoch Powys 68 D5
Rhoshill Pembks 65 H6
Rhoshirwaun Gwynd 94 D6
Rhoslefain Gwynd 80 D3
Rhosllanerchrugog Wrexhm 97 L3
Rhosmeirch IoA 108 F6
Rhosneigr IoA 108 D6
Rhosnesni Wrexhm 97 M3
Rhôs-on-Sea Conwy 110 B5
Rhossili Swans 50 E7
Rhostryfan Gwynd 95 H2
Rhostyllen Wrexhm 97 L3
Rhosybol IoA 108 F4
Rhos-y-gwaliau Gwynd 96 E5
Rhosymedre Wrexhm 97 L4
Rhu Ag & B 174 B2
Rhuallt Denbgs 110 F6
Rhubodach Ag & B 173 H4
Rhuddlan Denbgs 110 E6
Rhunahaorine Ag & B 172 C8
Rhyd Gwynd 95 L4
Rhydargaeau Carmth 50 F1
Rhydcymerau Carmth 66 D6
Rhyd-Ddu Gwynd 95 K3
Rhydlewis Cerdgn 65 K5
Rhydowen Cerdgn 66 B5
Rhyd-uchaf Gwynd 96 D5
Rhyd-y-clafdy Gwynd 94 F5
Rhyd-y-foel Conwy 110 C6
Rhydyfro Neath 51 K4
Rhyd-y-groes Gwynd 109 H7
Rhyd-y-pennau Cerdgn 80 E6
Rhyl Denbgs 110 D5
Rhymney Caerph 53 H6
Rhynd P & K 186 B4
Rhynie Abers 215 L8
Rhynie Highld 223 J5
Ribbesford Worcs 84 D8
Ribbleton Lancs 121 H4
Ribchester Lancs 121 J4
Riby Lincs 126 F8
Riccall N York 124 F3
Riccarton Border 156 F3
Riccarton E Ayrs 163 K3
Richards Castle Herefs 69 J1
Richmond Gt Lon 44 D5
Richmond N York 140 F6
Richmond Sheff 115 H4
Richmond Fort Guern 236 b3
Rickerscote Staffs 99 L7
Rickford N Som 38 C8
Rickham Devon 7 H7
Rickinghall Suffk 92 C7
Rickling Green Essex 60 E3
Rickmansworth Herts 43 H2
Riddell Border 167 H4
Riddlecombe Devon 10 F3
Riddlesden C Brad 123 G3
Ridge Dorset 15 H5
Ridge Herts 59 K7
Ridge Wilts 27 L5
Ridge Lane Warwks 86 C4
Ridgeway Derbys 115 H5
Ridgewell Essex 77 G6
Ridgewood E Susx 19 M2
Ridgmont C Beds 74 E7
Riding Mill Nthumb 150 C3
Ridlington Norfk 107 H6
Ridlington RutInd 88 B3
Ridsdale Nthumb 158 A5
Rievaulx N York 133 J3
Rigg D & G 148 B2
Riggend N Lans 175 K4
Righoul Highld 213 K4
Rigsby Lincs 118 F6
Rigside S Lans 165 G3
Riley Green Lancs 121 J5
Rilla Mill Cnwll 5 L2
Rillington N York 134 D5
Rimington Lancs 122 B2
Rimpton Somset 26 E6
Rimswell E R Yk 127 H5
Rinaston Pembks 49 G3
Rindleford Shrops 84 D4
Ringford D & G 146 C4
Ringland Norfk 92 D2
Ringmer E Susx 19 L3
Ringmore Devon 6 F6
Ringmore Devon 7 L2
Ringorm Moray 215 G5
Ringsfield Suffk 93 J5
Ringsfield Corner Suffk 93 J6
Ringshall Herts 59 G5
Ringshall Suffk 78 C4
Ringshall Stocks Suffk 78 C4
Ringstead Nhants 88 E7
Ringstead Norfk 105 H4
Ringwood Hants 15 L2
Ringwould Kent 35 K5
Ripe E Susx 20 B4
Ripley Derbys 101 H3
Ripley Hants 15 M3
Ripley N York 132 D7
Ripley Surrey 31 H1
Riplington Hants 30 A6
Ripon N York 132 D5
Rippingale Lincs 103 H6
Ripple Kent 35 J5
Ripple Worcs 70 F6
Ripponden Calder 122 F6
Risabus Ag & B 160 B2
Risbury Herefs 69 K4
Risby Suffk 77 H2
Risca Caerph 37 K3
Rise E R Yk 126 E3
Risegate Lincs 103 K6
Riseley Bed 74 F3
Riseley Wokham 42 B7
Rishangles Suffk 78 E2
Rishton Lancs 121 L4
Rishworth Calder 122 F6
Risley Derbys 101 J5
Risley Warrtn 112 F3
Risplith N York 132 C5
River Kent 35 J6
River W Susx 30 F6
Riverford Highld 212 E4
Riverhead Kent 32 F3
Rivington Lancs 121 J7
Rivington Services Lancs 121 J7
Roade Nhants 73 L4
Roadmeetings S Lans 176 B7
Roadside E Ayrs 164 B5
Roadside Highld 231 H4
Roadwater Somset 25 G4
Roag Highld 208 D5
Roan of Craigoch S Ayrs 153 G2
Roath Cardif 37 J5
Roberton Border 166 F6
Roberton S Lans 165 H4
Robertsbridge E Susx 20 E2
Roberttown Kirk 123 J6

Robeston Wathen Pembks 49 J4
Robgill Tower D & G 155 M7
Robin Hood Crematorium Solhll 85 K7
Robin Hood Doncaster Sheffield Airport Donc 115 M2
Robin Hood's Bay N York 143 K6
Roborough Devon 6 D4
Roborough Devon 10 E2
Roby Knows 112 B4
Rocester Staffs 100 C5
Roch Pembks 48 E3
Rochdale Rochdl 122 D7
Rochdale Crematorium Rochdl 122 C7
Roche Cnwll 4 F4
Rochester Medway 46 C6
Rochester Nthumb 157 L3
Rochford Essex 46 E3
Rochford Worcs 70 B2
Rock Cnwll 4 E2
Rock Nthumb 169 J5
Rock Worcs 70 D1
Rockbeare Devon 12 C4
Rockbourne Hants 28 C7
Rockcliffe Cumb 148 C3
Rockcliffe D & G 146 E4
Rockend Torbay 7 L4
Rock Ferry Wirral 111 K4
Rockfield Highld 223 K5
Rockfield Mons 54 C5
Rockford Devon 24 B2
Rockhampton S Glos 38 F2
Rockhill Shrops 82 F7
Rockingham Nhants 88 C5
Rockland All Saints Norfk 92 B4
Rockland St Mary Norfk 93 G3
Rockland St Peter Norfk 92 B4
Rockley Notts 116 B6
Rockville Ag & B 173 L1
Rockwell End Bucks 42 D3
Rodborough Gloucs 55 J6
Rodbourne Swindn 40 C4
Rodbourne Wilts 39 L4
Rodden Dorset 14 B5
Rode Somset 27 J2
Rode Heath Ches E 99 J2
Rodel W Isls 232 d5
Roden Wrekin 83 L1
Rodhuish Somset 24 F4
Rodington Wrekin 83 L1
Rodington Heath Wrekin 83 L1
Rodley Gloucs 55 H5
Rodmarton Gloucs 39 L2
Rodmell E Susx 19 L4
Rodmersham Kent 34 B3
Rodmersham Green Kent 34 B3
Rodney Stoke Somset 26 C2
Rodsley Derbys 100 D4
Roecliffe N York 132 E6
Roe Green Herts 59 K6
Roe Green Herts 75 K7
Roehampton Gt Lon 44 E5
Roffey W Susx 31 K5
Rogart Highld 226 C7
Rogate W Susx 30 D6
Rogerstone Newpt 37 L3
Roghadal W Isls 232 d5
Rogiet Mons 38 C3
Roke Oxon 41 L2
Roker Sundld 151 J3
Rollesby Norfk 93 J1
Rolleston Leics 87 K4
Rolleston Notts 102 C3
Rolleston on Dove Staffs 100 E6
Rolston E R Yk 126 F2
Rolvenden Kent 33 L6
Rolvenden Layne Kent 33 L7
Romaldkirk Dur 140 C3
Romanby N York 132 E2
Romanno Bridge Border 177 G8
Romansleigh Devon 24 B7
Romesdal Highld 208 F4
Romford Dorset 15 K1
Romford Gt Lon 45 K3
Romiley Stockp 113 L4
Romsey Cambs 76 C3
Romsey Hants 29 G6
Romsley Shrops 84 D6
Romsley Worcs 85 G7
Rona Highld 209 K3
Ronachan Ag & B 172 C7
Rookhope Dur 150 B6
Rookley IoW 17 G5
Rooks Bridge Somset 26 A2
Rooks Nest Somset 25 H5
Rookwith N York 132 C3
Roos E R Yk 127 G4
Roothams Green Bed 75 G3
Ropley Hants 29 M5
Ropley Dean Hants 29 L5
Ropsley Lincs 103 G5
Rora Abers 217 K4
Rorrington Shrops 82 F4
Rosarie Moray 215 J4
Rose Cnwll 3 K1
Rose Ash Devon 24 C6
Rosebank S Lans 175 L7
Rosebush Pembks 49 J2
Rosedale Abbey N York 142 F7
Rose Green Essex 61 L3
Rose Green Suffk 77 L5
Rose Green Suffk 77 L6
Rose Green W Susx 18 B5
Rosehall Highld 225 K7
Rosehearty Abers 217 H2
Rose Hill Lancs 122 C4
Rose Hill Crematorium Donc 115 L2
Roseisle Moray 214 E2
Roselands E Susx 20 C5
Rosemarket Pembks 49 G5
Rosemarkie Highld 213 H3
Rosemary Lane Devon 25 J7
Rosemount P & K 195 J7
Rosenannon Cnwll 4 E3
Rosewell Mdloth 177 J6
Roseworth S on T 141 K3
Rosgill Cumb 138 D4
Roskhill Highld 208 D5
Rosley Cumb 148 B6
Roslin Mdloth 177 H5
Rosliston Derbys 86 B1
Rosneath Ag & B 174 B2
Ross D & G 146 B6
Rossett Wrexhm 98 A2
Rossett Green N York 132 D8
Rossington Donc 115 L2
Rossland Rens 174 E4
Ross-on-Wye Herefs 54 E4
Roster Highld 231 J7
Rostherne Ches E 113 H5
Rosthwaite Cumb 137 H4
Roston Derbys 100 C4
Rosyth Fife 176 F2
Rothbury Nthumb 158 D2
Rotherby Leics 87 J1
Rotherfield E Susx 32 F7
Rotherfield Greys Oxon 42 B4
Rotherfield Peppard Oxon 42 B4
Rotherham Rothm 115 H3
Rotherham Crematorium Rothm 115 J3
Rothersthorpe Nhants 73 K3
Rotherwick Hants 30 B1
Rothes Moray 215 G4
Rothesay Ag & B 173 J5
Rothiebrisbane Abers 216 E6
Rothiemay Moray 215 M5
Rothiemurchus Lodge Highld 204 B4
Rothiemurchus Visitor Centre Highld 203 L3
Rothienorman Abers 216 D7
Rothley Leics 87 H2
Rothmaise Abers 216 D7
Rothwell Leeds 123 L5
Rothwell Lincs 117 J2
Rothwell Nhants 88 B7
Rottal Lodge Angus 196 B3
Rottingdean Br & H 19 K5
Rottington Cumb 136 D5
Roucan D & G 155 H6
Roucan Loch Crematorium D & G 155 H6
Rougham Norfk 105 K7
Rougham Suffk 77 K3
Rough Common Kent 34 F3
Roughpark Abers 205 H3
Roughton Lincs 118 C8
Roughton Norfk 106 F5
Roughton Shrops 84 D5
Roundbush Green Essex 60 F5
Round Green Luton 59 J4
Roundham Somset 13 K1
Roundhay Leeds 123 L3
Rounds Green Sandw 85 H5
Roundswell Devon 23 H5
Roundway Wilts 40 A7
Roundyhill Angus 196 C6
Rousay Ork 234 c4
Rousdon Devon 13 H4
Rousham Oxon 57 J3
Rous Lench Worcs 71 H4
Routenburn N Ayrs 173 L6
Routh E R Yk 126 D3
Row Cumb 129 K2
Rowanburn D & G 156 D6
Rowardennan Stirlg 183 L7
Rowarth Derbys 114 A4
Rowberrow Somset 38 C8
Rowde Wilts 39 L7
Rowen Conwy 109 L6
Rowfoot Nthumb 149 H3
Rowhedge Essex 62 B4
Rowington Warwks 72 B2
Rowland Derbys 114 E6
Rowland's Castle Hants 17 K1
Rowlands Gill Gatesd 150 E4
Rowledge Surrey 30 D3
Rowley Dur 150 D5
Rowley Regis Sandw 85 H6
Rowley Regis Crematorium Sandw 85 G6
Rowlstone Herefs 54 A3
Rowly Surrey 31 H4
Rowner Hants 17 H3
Rowney Green Worcs 71 J1
Rownhams Hants 29 G7
Rownhams Services Hants 29 H7
Rowrah Cumb 136 E4
Rowsham Bucks 58 D4
Rowsley Derbys 114 E7
Rowston Lincs 103 H2
Rowton Ches W 112 C8
Rowton Wrekin 98 E8
Roxburgh Border 167 L4
Roxby N Linc 125 L6
Roxton Bed 75 G4
Roxwell Essex 61 G6
Royal Leamington Spa Warwks 72 D2
Royal Sutton Coldfield Birm 85 K4
Royal Tunbridge Wells Kent 33 G5
Royal Wootton Bassett Wilts 40 B4
Royal Yacht Britannia C Edin 177 H3
Roy Bridge Highld 192 D1
Roydon Essex 60 C6
Roydon Norfk 92 D7
Roydon Norfk 105 H7
Roydon Hamlet Essex 60 C6
Royston Barns 124 B7
Royston Herts 75 L6
Royton Oldham 122 D8
Rozel Jersey 236 e6
Ruabon Wrexhm 97 L4
Ruaig Ag & B 188 D6
Ruan Lanihorne Cnwll 4 D7
Ruan Major Cnwll 3 J7
Ruan Minor Cnwll 3 J7
Ruardean Gloucs 54 F4
Ruardean Hill Gloucs 54 F5
Ruardean Woodside Gloucs 54 F5
Rubery Birm 85 H7
Rubha Ban W Isls 233 c9
Ruckhall Herefs 69 J6
Ruckinge Kent 34 D7
Ruckley Shrops 83 K4
Rudby N York 141 L6
Rudchester Nthumb 150 E2
Ruddington Notts 101 L6
Rudge Somset 27 J2
Rudgeway S Glos 38 F3
Rudgwick W Susx 31 H5
Rudheath Ches W 112 F6
Rudley Green Essex 61 K7
Rudloe Wilts 39 J6
Rudry Caerph 37 J3
Rudston E R Yk 135 H6
Rudyard Staffs 99 L2
Ruecastle Border 167 J5
Rufford Lancs 120 F7
Rufford Abbey Notts 115 M8
Rufforth C York 124 D1
Rugby Warwks 87 G7
Rugeley Staffs 100 B8
Ruishton Somset 25 K6
Ruislip Gt Lon 43 H3
Rùm Highld 198 F5
Rumbach Moray 215 J4
Rumbling Bridge P & K 185 L7
Rumburgh Suffk 93 H7
Rumford Cnwll 4 D2
Rumford Falk 176 C3
Rumney Cardif 37 K5
Runcorn Halton 112 D5
Runcton W Susx 18 B5
Runcton Holme Norfk 90 E2
Runfold Surrey 30 E3
Runhall Norfk 92 C3
Runham Norfk 93 K2
Runnington Somset 25 H6
Runswick N York 143 G4
Runtaleave Angus 195 L3
Runway Visitor Park Manch 113 J5
Runwell Essex 46 C2
Ruscombe Wokham 42 D5
Rushall Herefs 70 B7
Rushall Norfk 92 E6
Rushall Wilts 28 C1
Rushall Wsall 85 H4
Rushbrooke Suffk 77 K3
Rushbury Shrops 83 K5
Rushden Herts 60 A2
Rushden Nhants 74 D2
Rushenden Kent 46 E5
Rushford Norfk 91 K7
Rush Green Essex 62 E5
Rush Green Gt Lon 45 K3
Rush Green Warrtn 113 G4
Rushlake Green E Susx 20 D3

Rushmere Suffk 93 K6
Rushmoor Surrey 30 E4
Rushock Worcs 70 F1
Rusholme Manch 113 J3
Rushton Nhants 88 B6
Rushton Spencer Staffs 113 L8
Rushwick Worcs 70 E4
Rushyford Dur 141 G2
Ruskie Stirlg 184 D7
Ruskington Lincs 103 H3
Rusland Cross Cumb 129 H2
Rusper W Susx 31 K4
Ruspidge Gloucs 54 F5
Russell's Water Oxon 42 B3
Russ Hill Surrey 31 L4
Rusthall Kent 32 F5
Rustington W Susx 18 E5
Ruston N York 134 E3
Ruston Parva E R Yk 135 G6
Ruswarp N York 143 H5
Rutherford Border 167 K4
Rutherglen S Lans 175 H6
Ruthernbridge Cnwll 4 F3
Ruthin Denbgs 97 H2
Ruthrieston C Aber 207 H4
Ruthven Abers 215 L5
Ruthven Angus 195 L6
Ruthven Highld 203 H5
Ruthvoes Cnwll 4 E4
Ruthwell D & G 147 J2
Ruyton-XI-Towns Shrops 98 B7
Ryal Nthumb 158 C7
Ryall Dorset 13 K4
Ryall Worcs 70 F6
Ryarsh Kent 33 H2
Rydal Cumb 137 K6
Ryde IoW 17 H4
Rye E Susx 21 H2
Rye Foreign E Susx 21 H2
Rye Street Worcs 70 D7
Ryhall Rutlnd 88 F2
Ryhill Wakefd 124 B7
Ryhope Sundld 151 K4
Ryland Lincs 117 G5
Rylands Notts 101 K5
Rylstone N York 131 H7
Ryme Intrinseca Dorset 14 B1
Ryther N York 124 E3
Ryton Gatesd 150 E3
Ryton Shrops 84 D3
Ryton-on-Dunsmore Warwks 86 E8

S

Sabden Lancs 122 B3
Sacombe Herts 60 B4
Sacriston Dur 151 G5
Sadberge Darltn 141 H4
Saddell Ag & B 161 K3
Saddington Leics 87 J5
Saddle Bow Norfk 90 E1
Saddlescombe W Susx 19 H4
Saffron Walden Essex 76 D6
Sageston Pembks 49 H6
Saham Hills Norfk 91 K3
Saham Toney Norfk 91 K3
Saighton Ches W 98 C1
St Abbs Border 179 J5
St Agnes Border 178 E5
St Agnes Cnwll 3 J2
St Agnes IoS 2 a2
St Agnes Mining District Cnwll 3 J2
St Albans Herts 59 J6
St Allen Cnwll 4 C5
St Andrew Guern 236 c3
St Andrews Fife 187 H4
St Andrews Botanic Garden Fife 187 H4
St Andrew's Major V Glam 37 H6
St Andrews Well Dorset 13 L4
St Anne's Lancs 120 D5
St Ann's D & G 155 J4
St Ann's Chapel Cnwll 6 B2
St Ann's Chapel Devon 6 F6
St Anthony Cnwll 3 K6
St Anthony's Hill E Susx 20 D5
St Arvans Mons 38 D2
St Asaph Denbgs 110 E6
St Athan V Glam 36 F6
St Aubin Jersey 236 b7
St Austell Cnwll 4 F5
St Bees Cumb 136 D5
St Blazey Cnwll 5 G5
St Boswells Border 167 J3
St Brelade Jersey 236 b7
St Brelade's Bay Jersey 236 b7
St Breock Cnwll 4 F2
St Breward Cnwll 5 H1
St Briavels Gloucs 54 E6
St Bride's Major V Glam 36 D5
St Brides-super-Ely V Glam 37 H5
St Brides Wentlooge Newpt 37 L4
St Budeaux C Plym 6 C4
Saintbury Gloucs 71 K6
St Buryan Cnwll 2 D6
St Catherines Ag & B 183 G6
St Chloe Gloucs 55 J7
St Clears Carmth 50 C3
St Cleer Cnwll 5 K3
St Clement Cnwll 4 D6
St Clement Jersey 236 e8
St Clether Cnwll 9 G7
St Colmac Ag & B 173 H5
St Columb Major Cnwll 4 E3
St Columb Minor Cnwll 4 D4
St Columb Road Cnwll 4 E4
St Combs Abers 217 K2
St Cross South Elmham Suffk 93 G6
St Cyrus Abers 197 J4
St David's P & K 185 K4
St Davids Pembks 48 C3
St Davids Cathedral Pembks 48 C3
St Day Cnwll 3 J3
St Dennis Cnwll 4 E4
St Dogmaels Pembks 65 G5
St Dominick Cnwll 6 B3
St Donats V Glam 36 E6
St Endellion Cnwll 4 F1
St Enoder Cnwll 4 D4
St Erme Cnwll 4 D6
St Erney Cnwll 6 B4
St Erth Cnwll 2 F4
St Erth Praze Cnwll 3 G4
St Ervan Cnwll 4 D2
St Eval Cnwll 4 D3
St Ewe Cnwll 4 F6
St Fagans Cardif 37 H5
St Fagans: National History Museum Cardif 37 H5
St Fergus Abers 217 K4
St Fillans P & K 184 F3
St Florence Pembks 49 J7
St Gennys Cnwll 8 F5
St George Conwy 110 D6
St Georges N Som 38 B7
St George's V Glam 37 H5
St Germans Cnwll 6 A4
St Giles in the Wood Devon 23 H7
St Giles-on-the-Heath Devon 9 K6
St Harmon Powys 81 L8
St Helen Auckland Dur 140 F2
St Helen's E Susx 21 G4
St Helens IoW 17 J5
St Helens St Hel 112 D3
St Helens Crematorium St Hel 112 C3
St Helier Gt Lon 44 E6
St Helier Jersey 236 d7
St Hilary Cnwll 2 F5
St Hilary V Glam 36 F5
St Ippollitts Herts 59 K3
St Ishmael's Pembks 48 E6
St Issey Cnwll 4 E2
St Ive Cnwll 5 L3
St Ives Cambs 75 K1
St Ives Cnwll 2 F3
St James's End Nhants 73 L3
St James South Elmham Suffk 93 G7
St Jidgey Cnwll 4 E3
St John Cnwll 6 B5
St John Jersey 236 c5
St John's IoM 237 b5
St Johns Kent 32 F3
St Johns Surrey 43 G8
St Johns Worcs 70 E4
St John's Chapel Devon 23 H5
St John's Chapel Dur 149 M7
St John's Fen End Norfk 90 D2
St John's Kirk S Lans 165 J3
St John's Town of Dalry D & G 154 B6
St John's Wood Gt Lon 44 F4
St Jude's IoM 237 d3
St Just Cnwll 2 C5
St Just-in-Roseland Cnwll 4 D8
St Just Mining District Cnwll 2 D5
St Katherines Abers 216 E7
St Keverne Cnwll 3 K6
St Kew Cnwll 5 G1
St Kew Highway Cnwll 5 G2
St Keyne Cnwll 5 K4
St Lawrence Essex 62 A6
St Lawrence IoW 17 G6
St Lawrence Jersey 236 c6
St Lawrence Kent 35 K2
St Leonards Bucks 58 E6
St Leonards Dorset 15 L2
St Leonards E Susx 20 F4
St Levan Cnwll 2 C6
St Lythans V Glam 37 H6
St Mabyn Cnwll 5 G2
St Madoes P & K 186 C3
St Margarets Herefs 69 G7
St Margarets Herts 60 B5
St Margaret's at Cliffe Kent 35 K5
St Margaret's Hope Ork 234 c7
St Margaret South Elmham Suffk 93 G6
St Marks IoM 237 c6
St Martin Cnwll 3 J6
St Martin Cnwll 5 K5
St Martin Guern 236 d3
St Martin Jersey 236 e6
St Martin's IoS 2 b1
St Martin's P & K 186 B2
St Martin's Shrops 97 L5
St Mary Jersey 236 b6
St Mary Bourne Hants 29 H2
St Marychurch Torbay 7 L3
St Mary Church V Glam 36 F6
St Mary Cray Gt Lon 45 J6
St Mary in the Marsh Kent 21 L1
St Marylebone Crematorium Gt Lon 44 E3
St Mary's IoS 2 b1
St Mary's Ork 234 c6
St Mary's Bay Kent 21 L1
St Mary's Hoo Medway 46 D5
St Maughans Green Mons 54 C5
St Mawes Cnwll 3 L5
St Mawgan Cnwll 4 D3
St Mellion Cnwll 6 B3
St Mellons Cardif 37 K4
St Merryn Cnwll 4 D2
St Michael Caerhays Cnwll 4 F7
St Michael Church Somset 25 L5
St Michael Penkevil Cnwll 4 D7
St Michaels Kent 34 B7
St Michaels Worcs 69 L2
St Michael's Mount Cnwll 2 F5
St Michael's on Wyre Lancs 120 F3
St Minver Cnwll 4 F1
St Monans Fife 187 H6
St Neot Cnwll 5 J3
St Neots Cambs 75 H3
St Newlyn East Cnwll 4 C5
St Nicholas Pembks 64 C7
St Nicholas V Glam 37 H5
St Nicholas at Wade Kent 47 L6
St Ninians Stirlg 185 G8
St Olaves Norfk 93 J4
St Osyth Essex 62 D5
St Ouen Jersey 236 b6
St Owens Cross Herefs 54 D3
St Paul's Cray Gt Lon 45 J6
St Paul's Walden Herts 59 K4
St Peter Jersey 236 b6
St Peter Port Guern 236 d3
St Peter's Guern 236 b3
St Peter's Kent 35 K2
St Peter's Hill Cambs 89 J8
St Pinnock Cnwll 5 J3
St Quivox S Ayrs 163 J5
St Sampson Guern 236 d2
St Saviour Guern 236 c3
St Saviour Jersey 236 d7
St Stephen Cnwll 4 E5
St Stephens Cnwll 6 B4
St Stephens Cnwll 9 J7
St Teath Cnwll 8 E8
St Tudy Cnwll 5 G1
St Twynnells Pembks 48 F7
St Veep Cnwll 5 J5
St Vigeans Angus 197 G7
St Wenn Cnwll 4 F3
St Weonards Herefs 54 D3
Salcey Forest Nhants 74 B4
Salcombe Devon 7 H7
Salcombe Regis Devon 12 F5
Salcott-cum-Virley Essex 61 M5
Sale Traffd 113 H3
Saleby Lincs 118 F5
Sale Green Worcs 71 G3
Salehurst E Susx 20 F2
Salem Cerdgn 80 F6
Salen Ag & B 190 C7
Salen Highld 190 D4
Salford C Beds 74 D6
Salford Oxon 56 F3
Salford Salfd 113 J2
Salford Priors Warwks 71 J4
Salfords Surrey 32 B4
Salhouse Norfk 93 G1
Saline Fife 185 L8
Salisbury Wilts 28 C5

Salisbury Crematorium Wilts 28 D5
Salisbury Plain Wilts 28 B3
Salkeld Dykes Cumb 148 F7
Salle Norfk 106 D7
Salmonby Lincs 118 D6
Salperton Gloucs 56 B4
Salsburgh N Lans 175 L5
Salt Staffs 99 L6
Saltaire C Brad 123 H3
Saltaire C Brad 123 H3
Saltash Cnwll 6 B4
Saltburn Highld 223 G7
Saltburn-by-the-Sea R & Cl 142 E3
Saltby Leics 102 D7
Saltcoats N Ayrs 163 G2
Saltdean Br & H 19 K5
Salterbeck Cumb 136 D3
Salterforth Lancs 122 D2
Salterton Wilts 28 C4
Saltfleet Lincs 118 F3
Saltfleetby All Saints Lincs 118 F4
Saltfleetby St Clement Lincs 118 F3
Saltfleetby St Peter Lincs 118 F4
Saltford BaNES 39 G6
Salthouse Norfk 106 C4
Saltley Birm 85 K6
Saltmarshe E R Yk 125 J5
Saltney Flints 111 L8
Salton N York 133 L4
Saltrens Devon 23 G6
Saltwell Crematorium Gatesd 151 G3
Saltwood Kent 34 F7
Salvington W Susx 18 F5
Salwarpe Worcs 70 F3
Salway Ash Dorset 13 L3
Sambourne Warwks 71 J3
Sambrook Wrekin 99 G7
Sampford Arundel Somset 25 H7
Sampford Brett Somset 25 G3
Sampford Courtenay Devon 10 F5
Sampford Moor Somset 25 H7
Sampford Peverell Devon 25 G8
Sampford Spiney Devon 6 D2
Samsonlane Ork 234 d5
Samuelston E Loth 178 B4
Sanaigmore Ag & B 170 E4
Sancreed Cnwll 2 D5
Sancton E R Yk 125 L3
Sandaig Highld 199 L5
Sandal Magna Wakefd 123 L6
Sandavore Highld 199 G7
Sanday Ork 234 d4
Sanday Airport Ork 234 d4
Sandbach Ches E 99 H1
Sandbach Services Ches E 99 H1
Sandbank Ag & B 173 K3
Sandbanks Poole 15 K5
Sandend Abers 216 B2
Sanderstead Gt Lon 45 G7
Sandford Cumb 139 G4
Sandford Devon 11 J4
Sandford Dorset 15 H5
Sandford Hants 15 M3
Sandford IoW 17 G6
Sandford N Som 38 B8
Sandford S Lans 164 E2
Sandford-on-Thames Oxon 57 K7
Sandford Orcas Dorset 26 F7
Sandford St Martin Oxon 57 H3
Sandgate Kent 35 G7
Sandhaven Abers 217 H2
Sandhead D & G 144 D5
Sand Hills Leeds 124 B3
Sandhills Oxon 57 K6
Sandhills Surrey 30 F4
Sandhoe Nthumb 150 B2
Sandhole Ag & B 182 E7
Sand Hole E R Yk 125 J3
Sandholme E R Yk 125 J4
Sandhurst Br For 42 D7
Sandhurst Gloucs 55 J4
Sandhurst Kent 33 K7
Sandhutton N York 132 F3
Sand Hutton N York 133 L7
Sandiacre Derbys 101 J5
Sandilands Lincs 119 G5
Sandleheath Hants 28 C7
Sandleigh Oxon 57 J7
Sandley Dorset 27 H6
Sandness Shet 235 b5
Sandon Essex 61 H6
Sandon Herts 75 K7
Sandon Staffs 99 L6
Sandon Bank Staffs 99 L6
Sandown IoW 17 H5
Sandplace Cnwll 5 K4
Sandridge Herts 59 K6
Sandringham Norfk 105 H6
Sandsend N York 143 H5
Sandtoft N Linc 125 H8
Sandway Kent 34 B5
Sandwell Valley Crematorium Sandw 85 H5
Sandwich Kent 35 J3
Sandwick Shet 235 c7
Sandwick W Isls 232 g2
Sandwith Cumb 136 D4
Sandy C Beds 75 H5
Sandyford D & G 155 L4
Sandygate Devon 7 K2
Sandygate IoM 237 d3
Sandyhills D & G 146 F4
Sandylands Lancs 129 J6
Sandy Lane Wilts 39 L6
Sandy Park Devon 11 G6
Sangobeg Highld 228 F3
Sangomore Highld 228 F3
Sankyn's Green Worcs 70 E2
Sanna Bay Highld 189 K3
Sanndabhaig W Isls 232 g2
Sannox N Ayrs 162 C1
Sanquhar D & G 164 F7
Santon Bridge Cumb 136 F6
Santon Downham Suffk 91 J6
Sapcote Leics 86 F5
Sapey Common Herefs 70 C2
Sapiston Suffk 91 K7
Sapperton Gloucs 55 L7
Sapperton Lincs 103 G5
Saracen's Head Lincs 104 B6
Sarclet Highld 231 L6
Sarisbury Hants 17 G2
Sarn Gwynd 94 D6
Sarn Powys 81 K4
Sarn Powys 82 E5
Sarnau Cerdgn 65 K4
Sarnau Powys 82 E1
Sarn Park Services Brdgnd 36 D4
Saron Carmth 51 H3
Saron Gwynd 109 G7
Sarratt Herts 59 H7
Sarre Kent 47 L6
Sarsden Oxon 56 F4
Satley Dur 150 E6
Satterleigh Devon 23 L6
Satterthwaite Cumb 129 H2
Sauchen Abers 206 D3
Saucher P & K 186 C2
Sauchieburn Abers 197 G3
Saul Gloucs 55 H6
Saundby Notts 116 C4
Saundersfoot Pembks 49 K6
Saunderton Bucks 58 C7
Saunton Devon 23 G4
Sausthorpe Lincs 118 E7
Savile Town Kirk 123 K6
Sawbridge Warwks 73 G2
Sawbridgeworth Herts 60 D5
Sawdon N York 134 E3
Sawley Lancs 122 B2
Sawley N York 132 C6
Sawston Cambs 76 C5
Sawtry Cambs 89 H6
Saxby Leics 102 D8
Saxby Lincs 117 G4
Saxby All Saints N Linc 126 B7
Saxelbye Leics 102 B7
Saxham Street Suffk 78 C3
Saxilby Lincs 116 E6
Saxlingham Norfk 106 B5
Saxlingham Green Norfk 92 F4
Saxlingham Nethergate Norfk 92 F4
Saxlingham Thorpe Norfk 92 E4
Saxmundham Suffk 79 H2
Saxondale Notts 102 B4
Saxon Street Cambs 76 F3
Saxtead Suffk 78 F2
Saxtead Green Suffk 78 F2
Saxtead Little Green Suffk 78 F2
Saxthorpe Norfk 106 D6
Saxton N York 124 D3
Sayers Common W Susx 19 H3
Scackleton N York 133 K5
Scafell Pike Cumb 137 H5
Scaftworth Notts 116 A3
Scagglethorpe N York 134 C5
Scalasaig Ag & B 180 E8
Scalby E R Yk 125 K5
Scalby N York 134 F2
Scaldwell Nhants 73 L1
Scaleby Cumb 148 D3
Scalebyhill Cumb 148 D3
Scales Cumb 129 G5
Scales Cumb 137 K2
Scalford Leics 102 C7
Scaling N York 142 F4
Scalloway Shet 235 c6
Scalpay Highld 209 J7
Scamblesby Lincs 118 C5
Scamodale Highld 191 G2
Scampston N York 134 D4
Scampton Lincs 116 F5
Scaniport Highld 212 F6
Scapegoat Hill Kirk 123 G7
Scarba Ag & B 181 K6
Scarborough N York 135 G2
Scarcewater Cnwll 4 E5
Scarcliffe Derbys 115 J7
Scarcroft Leeds 124 B3
Scarfskerry Highld 231 J2
Scarinish Ag & B 188 D7
Scarisbrick Lancs 120 E7
Scarning Norfk 91 L2
Scarrington Notts 102 B4
Scartho NE Lin 118 C1
Scatsta Airport Shet 235 c4
Scawby N Linc 116 F1
Scawsby Donc 115 K1
Scawthorpe Donc 115 K1
Scawton N York 133 H3
Scayne's Hill W Susx 19 K2
Scethrog Powys 53 H3
Scholar Green Ches E 99 J2
Scholemoor Crematorium C Brad 123 H4
Scholes Kirk 123 H8
Scholes Leeds 124 B3
Scholes Rothm 115 H3
Scholes Wigan 112 E1
Scissett Kirk 123 K7
Scleddau Pembks 64 C7
Scofton Notts 115 L5
Scole Norfk 92 D7
Scone P & K 186 B3
Sconser Highld 209 H7
Scoonie Fife 186 F6
Scopwick Lincs 103 H2
Scoraig Highld 220 C3
Scorborough E R Yk 126 C2
Scorrier Cnwll 3 J3
Scorton Lancs 121 G2
Scorton N York 141 G7
Scotby Cumb 148 D4
Scotch Corner N York 140 F6
Scotforth Lancs 129 K7
Scothern Lincs 117 G6
Scotlandwell P & K 186 C6
Scotscalder Station Highld 231 G4
Scot's Gap Nthumb 158 C5
Scotsmill Abers 206 B2
Scotstoun C Glas 174 F5
Scotswood N u Ty 150 F3
Scotter Lincs 116 E2
Scotterthorpe Lincs 116 E2
Scottish Seabird Centre E Loth 178 C2
Scottish Wool Centre Stirlg 184 C7
Scotton Lincs 116 E2
Scotton N York 132 E7
Scotton N York 140 F7
Scoulton Norfk 92 B4
Scourie Highld 228 B6
Scourie More Highld 228 B6
Scousburgh Shet 235 c7
Scrabster Highld 231 G2
Scraesburgh Border 167 K5
Scrane End Lincs 104 C4
Scraptoft Leics 87 J3
Scratby Norfk 93 K1
Scrayingham N York 133 L7
Scredington Lincs 103 H4
Scremby Lincs 118 F7
Scremerston Nthumb 179 L8
Screveton Notts 102 B4
Scriven N York 132 E7
Scrooby Notts 115 M4
Scropton Derbys 100 D6
Scrub Hill Lincs 103 L2
Scruton N York 132 D2
Scullomie Highld 229 J4
Sculthorpe Norfk 105 L6
Scunthorpe N Linc 125 K7
Seaborough Dorset 13 K2
Seabridge Staffs 99 J4
Seabrook Kent 35 G7
Seaburn Sundld 151 J3
Seacombe Wirral 111 K4
Seacroft Leeds 124 B4
Seafield Highld 209 G5
Seafield W Loth 176 D5
Seafield Crematorium C Edin 177 J4
Seaford E Susx 20 A6
Seaforth Sefton 111 K3
Seagrave Leics 101 L8
Seaham Dur 151 K5
Seahouses Nthumb 169 J3
Seal Kent 32 F2
Sealand Flints 111 K7
Seale Surrey 30 E2
Seamer N York 134 F3
Seamer N York 142 B5
Seamill N Ayrs 173 L8
Sea Palling Norfk 107 J6
Searby Lincs 117 H1
Seasalter Kent 47 H6
Seascale Cumb 136 E6
Seathwaite Cumb 137 H7
Seatoller Cumb 137 H4
Seaton Cnwll 5 L5
Seaton Cumb 136 E2

Seaton Devon 13 G4
Seaton E R Yk 126 E2
Seaton Kent 35 G3
Seaton Nthumb 159 H6
Seaton Rutlnd 88 C4
Seaton Carew Hartpl 142 B2
Seaton Delaval Nthumb 159 H6
Seaton Ross E R Yk 125 J3
Seaton Sluice Nthumb 159 H6
Seatown Dorset 13 K4
Seave Green N York 142 C7
Seaview IoW 17 J4
Seaville Cumb 147 K4
Seavington St Mary Somset 26 B7
Seavington St Michael Somset 26 B7
Sebergham Cumb 148 C6
Seckington Warwks 86 C3
Sedbergh Cumb 130 C2
Sedbury Gloucs 38 D2
Sedbusk N York 131 G2
Sedgeberrow Worcs 71 H6
Sedgebrook Lincs 102 D5
Sedgefield Dur 141 J2
Sedgeford Norfk 105 H5
Sedgehill Wilts 27 K5
Sedgemoor Crematorium Somset 25 L3
Sedgemoor Services Somset 26 A2
Sedgley Dudley 85 G5
Sedgley Park Bury 113 J2
Sedgwick Cumb 129 L3
Sedlescombe E Susx 20 F3
Sedrup Bucks 58 D5
Seend Wilts 39 L7
Seend Cleeve Wilts 39 L7
Seer Green Bucks 42 F3
Seething Norfk 93 G4
Sefton Sefton 111 K2
Seighford Staffs 99 K7
Seion Gwynd 109 H7
Seisdon Staffs 84 E4
Selattyn Shrops 97 K5
Selborne Hants 30 C5
Selby N York 124 F4
Selham W Susx 30 F7
Selhurst Gt Lon 45 G6
Selkirk Border 167 G4
Sellack Herefs 54 E3
Sellafield Station Cumb 136 E6
Sellafirth Shet 235 d2
Sellindge Kent 34 E6
Selling Kent 34 D4
Sells Green Wilts 39 L7
Selly Oak Birm 85 J6
Selmeston E Susx 20 B4
Selsdon Gt Lon 45 G7
Selsey Gloucs 55 J7
Selsey W Susx 18 B6
Selside N York 130 E4
Selsted Kent 35 G5
Selston Notts 101 J2
Selworthy Somset 24 E3
Semer Suffk 78 B5
Semington Wilts 39 K7
Semley Wilts 27 K6
Send Surrey 31 G1
Senghenydd Caerph 37 H3
Sennen Cnwll 2 C6
Sennen Cove Cnwll 2 C6
Sennybridge Powys 52 E3
Sessay N York 133 G4
Setchey Norfk 90 F2
Seton Mains E Loth 177 L4
Settle N York 130 F6
Settrington N York 134 C5
Sevenhampton Gloucs 56 B4
Sevenhampton Swindn 40 E3
Seven Hills Crematorium Suffk 78 F6
Seven Kings Gt Lon 45 J3
Sevenoaks Kent 32 F3
Sevenoaks Weald Kent 32 F3
Seven Sisters Neath 52 C6
Seven Star Green Essex 61 M3
Severn Beach S Glos 38 D4
Severn Stoke Worcs 70 F5
Severn View Services S Glos 38 E3
Sevington Kent 34 D6
Sewards End Essex 76 E6
Sewell C Beds 59 G4
Sewerby E R Yk 135 J5
Seworgan Cnwll 3 J5
Sewstern Leics 102 E7
Sgiogarstaigh W Isls 232 g1
Shabbington Bucks 58 A6
Shackerstone Leics 86 D3
Shackleford Surrey 30 F3
Shader W Isls 232 f1
Shadforth Dur 151 H6
Shadingfield Suffk 93 J6
Shadoxhurst Kent 34 C7
Shadwell Norfk 91 L6
Shaftenhoe End Herts 76 B6
Shaftesbury Dorset 27 K6
Shafton Barns 124 B7
Shakerley Wigan 113 G2
Shalbourne Wilts 40 F7
Shalden Hants 30 B3
Shaldon Devon 7 L2
Shalfleet IoW 16 E5
Shalford Essex 61 H3
Shalford Surrey 31 G3
Shalford Green Essex 61 H3
Shalmsford Street Kent 34 E4
Shalstone Bucks 73 J7
Shamley Green Surrey 31 G3
Shandford Angus 196 D4
Shandon Ag & B 174 B2
Shandwick Highld 223 J6
Shangton Leics 87 K4
Shanklin IoW 17 H6
Shap Cumb 138 E4
Shapinsay Ork 234 c5
Shapwick Dorset 15 H3
Shapwick Somset 26 B4
Shard End Birm 85 L5
Shardlow Derbys 101 H6
Shareshill Staffs 85 G3
Sharlston Wakefd 124 B6
Sharman's Cross Solhll 85 K7
Sharnbrook Bed 74 E3
Sharnford Leics 86 F5
Sharoe Green Lancs 121 G4
Sharow N York 132 E5
Sharpenhoe C Beds 59 H2
Sharperton Nthumb 158 B2
Sharpness Gloucs 54 F7
Sharrington Norfk 106 C5
Shatterford Worcs 84 E7
Shaugh Prior Devon 6 D3
Shavington Ches E 99 G3
Shaw Oldham 122 D8
Shaw Swindn 40 C4
Shaw W Berk 41 J6
Shaw Wilts 39 K7
Shawbirch Wrekin 84 B2
Shawbost W Isls 232 e2
Shawbury Shrops 98 E7
Shawell Leics 87 G7
Shawford Hants 29 J6
Shawhead D & G 154 F6
Shaw Mills N York 132 C6
Shawsburn S Lans 175 K7
Shearington D & G 147 H2
Shearsby Leics 87 J5
Shearston Somset 25 L5
Shebbear Devon 10 C3
Shebdon Staffs 99 H7
Shebster Highld 230 E3
Sheddens E Rens 175 G6
Shedfield Hants 29 K8
Sheen Staffs 100 C1
Sheepridge Kirk 123 H6
Sheepscar Leeds 123 L4
Sheepscombe Gloucs 55 K6
Sheepstor Devon 6 E3
Sheepwash Devon 10 C4
Sheepy Magna Leics 86 D3
Sheepy Parva Leics 86 D3
Sheering Essex 60 E5
Sheerness Kent 46 F5
Sheerwater Surrey 43 H7
Sheet Hants 30 C6
Sheffield Sheff 115 G4
Sheffield City Road Crematorium Sheff 115 G4
Sheffield Park E Susx 19 L2
Shefford C Beds 75 G6
Sheigra Highld 228 B4
Sheinton Shrops 83 L3
Shelderton Shrops 83 H7
Sheldon Birm 85 L6
Sheldon Derbys 114 D7
Sheldon Devon 12 E2
Sheldwich Kent 34 D4
Shelfanger Norfk 92 D6
Shelford Notts 102 A4
Shelley Kirk 123 J7
Shelley Suffk 78 B6
Shellingford Oxon 40 F2
Shellow Bowells Essex 60 F6
Shelsley Beauchamp Worcs 70 D2
Shelsley Walsh Worcs 70 C2
Shelton Bed 74 F2
Shelton Norfk 92 F5
Shelton Notts 102 C4
Shelton Lock C Derb 101 G6
Shelton Under Harley Staffs 99 J5
Shelve Shrops 83 G4
Shelwick Herefs 69 K6
Shenfield Essex 45 L2
Shenington Oxon 72 D6
Shenley Herts 59 K7
Shenley Brook End M Keyn 74 B7
Shenley Church End M Keyn 74 B7
Shenmore Herefs 69 H6
Shennanton D & G 145 H3
Shenstone Staffs 85 K3
Shenstone Worcs 84 F8
Shenton Leics 86 E4
Shenval Moray 214 F7
Shephall Herts 59 L4
Shepherd's Bush Gt Lon 44 E4
Shepherdswell Kent 35 H5
Shepley Kirk 123 J8
Shepperton Surrey 43 H6
Shepreth Cambs 76 B5
Shepshed Leics 101 J8
Shepton Beauchamp Somset 26 B7
Shepton Mallet Somset 26 F3
Shepton Montague Somset 27 G5
Shepway Kent 33 K3
Sheraton Dur 151 K7
Sherborne Dorset 26 F7
Sherborne Gloucs 56 D5
Sherborne Somset 26 E1
Sherborne St John Hants 29 L1
Sherbourne Warwks 72 C3
Sherburn Dur 151 H6
Sherburn N York 134 E4
Sherburn Hill Dur 151 H6
Sherburn in Elmet N York 124 D4
Shere Surrey 31 H2
Shereford Norfk 105 L6
Sherfield English Hants 28 F6
Sherfield on Loddon Hants 42 B8
Sherford Devon 7 H6
Sheriffhales Shrops 84 D2
Sheriff Hutton N York 133 K6
Sheringham Norfk 106 E4
Sherington M Keyn 74 C5
Shernborne Norfk 105 H6
Sherrington Wilts 27 L4
Sherston Wilts 39 J3
Sherwood C Nott 101 K4
Sherwood Forest Notts 101 L1
Sherwood Forest Crematorium Notts 116 A7
Shetland Islands Shet 235 c5
Shettleston C Glas 175 H5
Shevington Wigan 121 H8
Sheviock Cnwll 6 B5
Shibden Head C Brad 123 G5
Shide IoW 16 F5
Shidlaw Nthumb 168 B2
Shiel Bridge Highld 200 E2
Shieldaig Highld 210 C4
Shieldhill D & G 155 H5
Shieldhill Falk 176 B3
Shieldhill House Hotel S Lans 165 J2
Shields N Lans 175 K7
Shielfoot Highld 190 D3
Shielhill Angus 196 C5
Shielhill Inver 173 L4
Shifnal Shrops 84 D2
Shilbottle Nthumb 169 J7
Shildon Dur 141 G3
Shillford E Rens 174 E6
Shillingford Devon 24 F6
Shillingford Oxon 41 L2
Shillingford Abbot Devon 11 K6
Shillingford St George Devon 11 K7
Shillingstone Dorset 14 F1
Shillington C Beds 75 G7
Shilton Oxon 56 E6
Shilton Warwks 86 E6
Shimpling Norfk 92 D6
Shimpling Suffk 77 J4
Shimpling Street Suffk 77 K4
Shincliffe Dur 151 H6
Shiney Row Sundld 151 H4
Shinfield Wokham 42 B6
Shinness Highld 225 L5
Shipbourne Kent 33 G3
Shipdham Norfk 91 L3
Shipham Somset 38 C8
Shiphay Torbay 7 K3
Shiplake Oxon 42 C5
Shipley C Brad 123 H3
Shipley W Susx 31 J6
Shipley Bridge Surrey 32 B5
Shipmeadow Suffk 93 H5
Shippon Oxon 41 J2
Shipston-on-Stour Warwks 72 B6
Shipton Gloucs 56 B4
Shipton N York 133 H7
Shipton Shrops 83 L5
Shipton Bellinger Hants 28 E3
Shipton Gorge Dorset 13 L4
Shipton Green W Susx 17 L3
Shipton Moyne Gloucs 39 K3
Shipton-on-Cherwell Oxon 57 J5
Shiptonthorpe E R Yk 125 K2
Shipton-under-Wychwood Oxon 56 F4

Shirburn Oxon 42 B2
Shirdley Hill Lancs 120 E7
Shirebrook Derbys 115 K7
Shiregreen Sheff 115 G3
Shirehampton Bristl 38 D5
Shiremoor N Tyne 159 H7
Shirenewton Mons 38 C2
Shireoaks Notts 115 K5
Shirland Derbys 101 H2
Shirley C Sotn 29 H8
Shirley Derbys 100 E4
Shirley Gt Lon 45 G6
Shirley Solhll 85 K7
Shirrell Heath Hants 29 L8
Shirvan Ag & B 172 E2
Shirwell Devon 23 J4
Shiskine N Ayrs 162 B4
Shobdon Herefs 69 H3
Shobrooke Devon 11 K5
Shoby Leics 102 B7
Shocklach Ches W 98 C3
Shoeburyness Sthend 46 F3
Sholden Kent 35 K4
Sholing C Sotn 16 F1
Shop Cnwll 9 G2
Shoreditch Gt Lon 45 G4
Shoreditch Somset 25 K6
Shoreham Kent 45 K7
Shoreham Airport W Susx 19 G5
Shoreham-by-Sea W Susx 19 H5
Shorley Hants 29 L6
Shorne Kent 46 B6
Shortgate E Susx 20 A3
Short Heath Birm 85 K5
Short Heath Wsall 85 H4
Shortlanesend Cnwll 4 C6
Shortlees E Ayrs 163 K3
Shortstown Bed 74 F5
Shorwell IoW 16 F5
Shoscombe BaNES 27 G1
Shotesham Norfk 92 F4
Shotgate Essex 46 C2
Shotley Suffk 78 F7
Shotley Bridge Dur 150 D4
Shotley Gate Suffk 78 F7
Shotley Street Suffk 78 F7
Shottenden Kent 34 D4
Shottery Warwks 71 L4
Shotteswell Warwks 72 E5
Shottisham Suffk 79 G5
Shottlegate Derbys 100 F3
Shotton Dur 151 K6
Shotton Flints 111 J7
Shotton Colliery Dur 151 J6
Shotts N Lans 176 B6
Shotwick Ches W 111 K6
Shougle Moray 214 F4
Shouldham Norfk 90 F2
Shouldham Thorpe Norfk 90 F2
Shoulton Worcs 70 E3
Shrawardine Shrops 83 H1
Shrawley Worcs 70 E2
Shrewley Warwks 72 B2
Shrewsbury Shrops 83 J2
Shrewton Wilts 28 B3
Shripney W Susx 18 C5
Shrivenham Oxon 40 E3
Shropham Norfk 92 B5
Shucknall Herefs 69 L6
Shudy Camps Cambs 76 E5
Shuna Ag & B 181 M5
Shurdington Gloucs 55 L4
Shurlock Row W & M 42 D5
Shurrery Highld 230 F4
Shurrery Lodge Highld 230 F4
Shurton Somset 25 J3
Shustoke Warwks 86 B5
Shute Devon 11 K5
Shute Devon 13 G3
Shutford Oxon 72 E6
Shut Heath Staffs 99 K7
Shuthonger Gloucs 70 F7
Shutlanger Nhants 73 K4
Shuttington Warwks 86 B3
Shuttlewood Derbys 115 J6
Shuttleworth Bury 122 B6
Siabost W Isls 232 e2
Siadar W Isls 232 f1
Sibbertoft Nhants 87 K6
Sibford Ferris Oxon 72 D6
Sibford Gower Oxon 72 D6
Sible Hedingham Essex 77 H7
Sibley's Green Essex 60 F3
Sibsey Lincs 104 B3
Sibson Cambs 89 G4
Sibson Leics 86 D4
Sibster Highld 231 K5
Sibthorpe Notts 102 C4
Sibthorpe Notts 116 B6
Sibton Suffk 79 H1
Sicklesmere Suffk 77 K3
Sicklinghall N York 124 B2
Sidbury Devon 12 E4
Sidbury Shrops 84 C6
Sidcot N Som 38 B8
Sidcup Gt Lon 45 J5
Siddington Ches E 113 J7
Siddington Gloucs 56 B7
Sidestrand Norfk 106 F4
Sidford Devon 12 E4
Sidlesham W Susx 18 B6
Sidley E Susx 20 E4
Sidmouth Devon 12 E5
Sigglesthorne E R Yk 126 E2
Sigingstone V Glam 36 F6
Silchester Hants 41 L7
Sileby Leics 87 H1
Silecroft Cumb 128 D3
Silfield Norfk 92 D4
Silkstone Barns 114 F1
Silkstone Common Barns 114 F1
Silk Willoughby Lincs 103 H4
Silloth Cumb 147 K4
Silpho N York 134 E2
Silsden C Brad 122 F2
Silsoe C Beds 74 F7
Silton Dorset 27 H5
Silverburn Mdloth 177 G6
Silverdale Lancs 129 K4
Silverdale Staffs 99 J3
Silver End Essex 61 K4
Silverford Abers 216 E2
Silverstone Nhants 73 J5
Silverton Devon 12 B2
Silvington Shrops 84 B7
Simonburn Nthumb 157 L7
Simonsbath Somset 24 B4
Simonstone Lancs 122 B4
Simprim Border 168 C1
Simpson M Keyn 74 C7
Simpson Cross Pembks 48 F4
Sinclair's Hill Border 179 G7
Sinclairston E Ayrs 163 L6
Sinderby N York 132 E3
Sinderland Green Traffd 113 G4
Sindlesham Wokham 42 C6
Sinfin C Derb 101 G6
Singleton Kent 34 D6
Singleton Lancs 120 E3
Singleton W Susx 18 B3
Singlewell Kent 46 A6
Sinnarhard Abers 205 K3
Sinnington N York 134 B3
Sinton Worcs 70 E3
Sinton Worcs 70 F2
Sinton Green Worcs 70 E3
Sissinghurst Kent 33 K5
Siston S Glos 39 G5
Sithney Cnwll 3 H5
Sittingbourne Kent 34 B3
Six Ashes Shrops 84 E5
Sixhills Lincs 117 K4
Six Mile Bottom Cambs 76 E3
Sixpenny Handley Dorset 27 M7
Six Rues Jersey 236 c6
Skaill Ork 234 d6
Skara Brae Ork 234 b5
Skares E Ayrs 164 B6
Skateraw Abers 207 G6
Skateraw E Loth 178 F4
Skeabost Highld 208 F5
Skeeby N York 140 F6
Skeffington Leics 87 L3
Skeffling E R Yk 127 J6
Skegby Notts 101 J1
Skegby Notts 116 C7
Skegness Lincs 119 H8
Skelbo Highld 223 H3
Skelbo Street Highld 223 H3
Skelbrooke Donc 124 D7
Skeldyke Lincs 104 B5
Skellingthorpe Lincs 116 F6
Skellow Donc 124 E7
Skelmanthorpe Kirk 123 J7
Skelmersdale Lancs 112 C1
Skelmorlie N Ayrs 173 L5
Skelpick Highld 229 L4
Skelston D & G 154 E5
Skelton C York 133 J7
Skelton Cumb 148 D7
Skelton E R Yk 125 H5
Skelton N York 132 E5
Skelton R & Cl 142 E4
Skelwith Bridge Cumb 137 K6
Skendleby Lincs 118 F7
Skene House Abers 206 E4
Skenfrith Mons 54 C4
Skerne E R Yk 135 G7
Skerray Highld 229 K3
Skerricha Highld 228 C5
Skerries Airport Shet 235 e4
Skerton Lancs 129 K6
Sketchley Leics 86 E5
Sketty Swans 51 J6
Skewsby N York 133 K5
Skiall Highld 230 E3
Skidby E R Yk 126 C4
Skigersta W Isls 232 g1
Skilgate Somset 24 F6
Skillington Lincs 102 E7
Skinburness Cumb 147 K4
Skinflats Falk 176 B2
Skinidin Highld 208 C5
Skipness Ag & B 172 F6
Skipper's Bridge D & G 156 C5
Skipsea E R Yk 135 J8
Skipton N York 122 E1
Skipton-on-Swale N York 132 E4
Skipwith N York 125 G3
Skirlaugh E R Yk 126 E3
Skirling Border 165 L2
Skirmett Bucks 42 C3
Skirpenbeck E R Yk 134 B7
Skirwith Cumb 149 G7
Skirza Highld 231 L2
Skokholm Island Pembks 48 C6
Skomer Island Pembks 48 C5
Skulamus Highld 199 K2
Skye Green Essex 61 L4
Skye of Curr Highld 204 B1
Slack Calder 122 E5
Slacks of Cairnbanno Abers 216 F5
Slad Gloucs 55 K6
Slade Devon 23 H3
Slade Green Gt Lon 45 K5
Slade Hooton Rothm 115 K4
Slaggyford Nthumb 149 H4
Slaidburn Lancs 130 D8
Slaithwaite Kirk 123 G7
Slaley Nthumb 150 B4
Slamannan Falk 176 B4
Slapton Bucks 58 F4
Slapton Devon 7 J6
Slapton Nhants 73 J5
Slaugham W Susx 31 L5
Slaughterford Wilts 39 J5
Slawston Leics 87 L5
Sleaford Hants 30 D4
Sleaford Lincs 103 H4
Sleagill Cumb 138 E4
Sleapford Wrekin 84 B1
Sleasdairidh Highld 222 E3
Sledmere E R Yk 134 E6
Sleetbeck Cumb 156 E6
Sleights N York 143 H5
Slickly Highld 231 K3
Sliddery N Ayrs 162 B5
Sligachan Highld 209 G7
Sligrachan Ag & B 173 K1
Slimbridge Gloucs 55 H7
Slindon Staffs 99 J6
Slindon W Susx 18 C4
Slinfold W Susx 31 J5
Slingsby N York 133 L4
Slip End C Beds 59 H4
Slip End Herts 75 K6
Slipton Nhants 88 D7
Slitting Mill Staffs 100 B8
Slockavullin Ag & B 182 B7
Sloncombe Devon 11 H7
Sloothby Lincs 119 G7
Slough Slough 43 G4
Slough Crematorium Bucks 43 G4
Slough Green Somset 25 L7
Slumbay Highld 210 D6
Slyne Lancs 129 K6
Smailholm Border 167 K3
Smallburgh Norfk 107 G7
Small Dole W Susx 19 G3
Smalley Derbys 101 H4
Smallfield Surrey 32 B5
Small Heath Birm 85 K6
Small Hythe Kent 34 B8
Smallridge Devon 13 H3
Smallthorne C Stke 99 K3
Smallworth Norfk 92 B7
Smannell Hants 29 G2
Smarden Kent 34 B6
Smarden Bell Kent 34 B6
Smart's Hill Kent 32 F5
Smearisary Highld 190 D2
Smeatharpe Devon 12 F1
Smeeth Kent 34 E6
Smeeton Westerby Leics 87 K5
Smerral Highld 227 L2
Smestow Staffs 84 F5
Smethwick Sandw 85 H6
Smisby Derbys 101 G8
Smithfield Cumb 148 D2
Smith's Green Essex 76 F6
Smithstown Highld 219 J6
Smithton Highld 213 H5
Smoo Highld 228 F3
Smythe's Green Essex 61 L4
Snade D & G 154 E5
Snailbeach Shrops 83 G3
Snailwell Cambs 76 F2
Snainton N York 134 E3
Snaith E R Yk 124 F6
Snape N York 132 D3
Snape Suffk 79 H3
Snape Street Suffk 79 H3
Snaresbrook Gt Lon 45 H3
Snarestone Leics 86 D2
Snarford Lincs 117 H5
Snargate Kent 34 D8
Snave Kent 34 D8
Sneaton N York 143 J5
Snelland Lincs 117 H5
Snelston Derbys 100 D4
Snetterton Norfk 92 B5
Snettisham Norfk 105 G5
Snitter Nthumb 158 C2
Snitterby Lincs 117 G3
Snitterfield Warwks 72 B3
Snitton Shrops 83 L7
Snodland Kent 46 B7
Snowdon Gwynd 95 K2
Snowdonia National Park 96 C6

Snow End Herts 60 C2
Snowshill Gloucs 71 K7
Soake Hants 17 J1
Soay Highld 199 G3
Soberton Hants 29 L7
Soberton Heath Hants 29 L8
Sockburn Darltn 141 J5
Soham Cambs 90 E8
Solas W Isls 232 c5
Soldridge Hants 29 M4
Sole Street Kent 34 E5
Sole Street Kent 46 A6
Solihull Solhll 85 L7
Sollers Dilwyn Herefs 69 H4
Sollers Hope Herefs 54 E2
Solva Pembks 48 D3
Solwaybank D & G 156 B6
Somerby Leics 87 L2
Somerby Lincs 117 H1
Somercotes Derbys 101 H2
Somerford Dorset 15 M4
Somerford Keynes Gloucs 40 A2
Somerley W Susx 17 M3
Somerleyton Suffk 93 K4
Somersal Herbert Derbys 100 C5
Somersby Lincs 118 D6
Somersham Cambs 89 L7
Somersham Suffk 78 C5
Somerton Oxon 57 J3
Somerton Somset 26 C5
Somerton Suffk 77 J4
Sompting W Susx 19 G5
Sonning Wokham 42 C5
Sonning Common Oxon 42 B4
Sopley Hants 15 M3
Sopwell Herts 59 J6
Sopworth Wilts 39 J3
Sorbie D & G 145 J5
Sordale Highld 231 G3
Sorisdale Ag & B 189 H4
Sorn E Ayrs 164 B4
Sortat Highld 231 K3
Sotby Lincs 117 K5
Sotterley Suffk 93 J6
Soughton Flints 111 H7
Soulbury Bucks 58 E3
Soulby Cumb 139 H5
Souldern Oxon 57 K2
Souldrop Bed 74 E3
Sound Ches E 98 F3
Sound Muir Moray 215 H4
Soundwell S Glos 38 F5
Sourton Devon 10 D6
Soutergate Cumb 128 F3
South Acre Norfk 91 J2
South Alkham Kent 35 H6
Southall Gt Lon 43 J4
South Allington Devon 7 J7
South Alloa Falk 185 J8
Southam Gloucs 55 L3
Southam Warwks 72 E3
South Ambersham W Susx 30 E7
Southampton C Sotn 29 H8
Southampton Airport Hants 29 J7
Southampton Crematorium Hants 29 H7
South Anston Rothm 115 K5
South Ashford Kent 34 D6
South Baddesley Hants 16 D3
South Ballachulish Highld 191 K5
South Bank C York 124 F1
South Barrow Somset 26 E5
South Beddington Gt Lon 44 F7
South Benfleet Essex 46 C3
South Bersted W Susx 18 C5
Southborough Gt Lon 45 H6
Southborough Kent 33 G5
Southbourne Bmouth 15 L4
Southbourne W Susx 17 L2
South Bramwith Donc 124 F7
South Brent Devon 7 G4
South Brewham Somset 27 G4
South Bristol Crematorium Bristl 38 E6
South Broomhill Nthumb 159 G3
Southburgh Norfk 92 B3
South Burlingham Norfk 93 H3
Southburn E R Yk 134 F8
South Cadbury Somset 26 F6
South Carlton Lincs 116 F6
South Carlton Notts 115 L5
South Cave E R Yk 125 L4
South Cerney Gloucs 40 B2
South Chailey E Susx 19 K3
South Charlton Nthumb 169 H5
South Cheriton Somset 27 G6
South Church Dur 140 F2
Southchurch Sthend 46 E3
South Cliffe E R Yk 125 K4
South Clifton Notts 116 D7
South Cockerington Lincs 118 E4
South Cornelly Brdgnd 36 C4
Southcott Cnwll 9 G5
Southcott Devon 11 H8
Southcourt Bucks 58 D5
South Cove Suffk 93 K7
South Creake Norfk 105 K5
South Croxton Leics 87 K2
South Dalton E R Yk 126 B2
South Darenth Kent 45 K6
South Dell W Isls 232 g1
South Downs National Park 19 K4
South Duffield N York 125 G4
Southease E Susx 19 L5
South Elkington Lincs 118 D4
South Elmsall Wakefd 124 D7
Southend Ag & B 161 H7
Southend Airport Essex 46 E3
Southend Crematorium Sthend 46 E3
Southend-on-Sea Sthend 46 E3
Southerndown V Glam 36 D5
Southerness D & G 147 G4
South Erradale Highld 219 H7
Southerton Devon 12 D4
Southery Norfk 90 E5
South Essex Crematorium Gt Lon 45 L3
South Fambridge Essex 46 E2
South Ferriby N Linc 126 B6
South Field E R Yk 126 C5
Southfield Falk 175 L4
Southfleet Kent 45 L5
Southgate Gt Lon 44 F2
Southgate Swans 51 G7
South Gorley Hants 15 M1
South Gosforth N u Ty 151 G2
South Green Essex 46 B2
South Green Kent 33 L2
South Green Norfk 92 C2
South Gyle C Edin 177 G4
South Hanningfield Essex 61 H8
South Harting W Susx 30 C7
South Hayling Hants 17 K3
South Heath Bucks 58 E7
South Heighton E Susx 19 L5
South Hetton Dur 151 J6
South Hiendley Wakefd 124 B7
South Hill Cnwll 5 M2
South Hinksey Oxon 57 K7
South Holmwood Surrey 31 K3
South Hornchurch Gt Lon 45 K4
South Huish Devon 7 G7
South Hykeham Lincs 116 F8
South Hylton Sundld 151 J4
Southill C Beds 75 H6
Southington Hants 29 J2
South Kelsey Lincs 117 H2
South Kessock Highld 213 G5
South Killingholme N Linc 126 E7
South Kilvington N York 132 F3
South Kilworth Leics 87 H6
South Kirkby Wakefd 124 C7
South Kyme Lincs 103 K3
South Lanarkshire Crematorium S Lans 175 J7
South Leicestershire Crematorium Leics 87 H4
Southleigh Devon 12 F4
South Leigh Oxon 57 H6
South Leverton Notts 116 C5
South Lincolnshire Crematorium Lincs 103 L6
South Littleton Worcs 71 J5
South London Crematorium Gt Lon 44 F6
South Lopham Norfk 92 C7
South Luffenham Rutlnd 88 D3
South Malling E Susx 19 L4
South Marston Swindn 40 D3
South Merstham Surrey 32 B3
South Milford N York 124 D4
South Milton Devon 7 G7
South Mimms Herts 59 L7
South Mimms Services Herts 59 L7
Southminster Essex 62 A7
South Molton Devon 23 L6
South Moor Dur 150 F5
Southmoor Oxon 41 H2
South Moreton Oxon 41 K3
Southmuir Angus 196 C5
South Mundham W Susx 18 B5
South Newbald E R Yk 125 L4
South Newington Oxon 57 H2
South Newton Wilts 28 C4
South Normanton Derbys 101 H2
South Norwood Gt Lon 45 G6
South Ockendon Thurr 45 L4
Southoe Cambs 75 H2
Southolt Suffk 78 E2
South Ormsby Lincs 118 E6
Southorpe C Pete 88 F3
South Otterington N York 132 E3
Southover Dorset 14 C4
South Owersby Lincs 117 H3
Southowram Calder 123 G5
South Oxfordshire Crematorium Oxon 41 H2
South Park Surrey 31 L2
South Perrott Dorset 13 L2
South Petherton Somset 26 B7
South Petherwin Cnwll 9 J8
South Pickenham Norfk 91 J3
South Pill Cnwll 6 B4
South Pool Devon 7 H7
South Poorton Dorset 13 M3
Southport Sefton 120 D6
Southport Crematorium Lancs 120 E7
South Queensferry C Edin 176 F3
South Rauceby Lincs 103 G4
South Raynham Norfk 105 L7
South Reddish Stockp 113 K3
Southrepps Norfk 106 F5
South Reston Lincs 118 E5
Southrey Lincs 117 J7
South Ronaldsay Ork 234 c7
Southrop Gloucs 56 D7
Southrope Hants 30 A3
South Runcton Norfk 90 F2
South Scarle Notts 116 D8
Southsea C Port 17 J3
South Shian Ag & B 191 H7
South Shields S Tyne 151 J2
South Shields Crematorium S Tyne 151 J3
South Shore Bpool 120 D4
Southside Dur 140 E2
South Stainley N York 132 D6
South Stoke BaNES 39 H7
South Stoke Oxon 41 L4
South Stoke W Susx 18 D4
South Street Kent 34 E3
South Street Kent 47 J6
South Tarbrax S Lans 176 D7
South Tawton Devon 10 F6
South Tehidy Cnwll 3 H3
South Thoresby Lincs 118 E6
Southtown Norfk 93 L3
South Uist W Isls 233 c8
Southwaite Cumb 148 D6
Southwaite Services Cumb 148 D6
South Walsham Norfk 93 H2
Southwark Gt Lon 44 F4
South Warnborough Hants 30 B3
Southwater W Susx 31 J6
South Weald Essex 45 L2
Southwell Notts 102 B2
South West Middlesex Crematorium Gt Lon 43 J5
South Weston Oxon 42 B2
South Wheatley Notts 116 C4
Southwick Hants 17 J2
Southwick Nhants 88 E5
Southwick Sundld 151 J4
Southwick W Susx 19 H5
Southwick Wilts 27 J1
South Widcombe BaNES 38 E8
South Wigston Leics 87 H4
South Willesborough Kent 34 D6
South Willingham Lincs 117 K5
South Wingfield Derbys 101 G2
South Witham Lincs 102 F8
Southwold Suffk 93 K7
South Woodham Ferrers Essex 61 J7
South Wootton Norfk 105 G7
South Wraxall Wilts 39 J7

South Zeal Devon 10 F6
Sovereign Harbour E Susx 20 D5
Sowerby Calder 122 F6
Sowerby N York 132 F4
Sowerby Bridge Calder 122 F5
Sowood Calder 123 G6
Sowton Devon 6 D3
Sowton Devon 12 C4
Soyland Town Calder 122 F6
Spain's End Essex 76 F6
Spalding Lincs 103 L7
Spaldington E R Yk 125 H4
Spaldwick Cambs 89 G8
Spalford Notts 116 D7
Spanby Lincs 103 H5
Sparham Norfk 106 C8
Spark Bridge Cumb 129 G3
Sparkford Somset 26 E6
Sparkhill Birm 85 K6
Sparkwell Devon 6 E4
Sparrowpit Derbys 114 C5
Sparrows Green E Susx 33 H6
Sparsholt Hants 29 H5
Sparsholt Oxon 41 G3
Spaunton N York 133 L2
Spaxton Somset 25 K4
Spean Bridge Highld 201 K8
Spearywell Hants 28 F6
Speen Bucks 58 D7
Speen W Berk 41 J6
Speeton N York 135 J5
Speke Lpool 112 C5
Speldhurst Kent 32 F5
Spellbrook Herts 60 D4
Spencers Wood Wokham 42 B6
Spen Green Ches E 99 J1
Spennithorne N York 131 L2
Spennymoor Dur 151 G7
Spetchley Worcs 70 F4
Spetisbury Dorset 15 G3
Spexhall Suffk 93 H7
Spey Bay Moray 215 H2
Speybridge Highld 204 C1
Speyview Moray 215 G6
Spilsby Lincs 118 E7
Spinkhill Derbys 115 J5
Spinningdale Highld 222 F4
Spital Hill Donc 115 L3
Spittal E Loth 178 B3
Spittal Highld 231 H5
Spittal Nthumb 179 L7
Spittal Pembks 49 G3
Spittalfield P & K 195 H7
Spittal of Glenmuick Abers 205 G7
Spittal of Glenshee P & K 195 H3
Spittal-on-Rule Border 167 J5
Spixworth Norfk 92 F1
Splatt Devon 10 E4
Splayne's Green E Susx 19 L2
Splottlands Cardif 37 K5
Spofforth N York 124 B1
Spondon C Derb 101 H5
Spooner Row Norfk 92 D4
Sporle Norfk 91 J2
Spott E Loth 178 E4
Spottiswoode Border 178 D7
Spratton Nhants 73 K1
Spreakley Surrey 30 D3
Spreyton Devon 11 G5
Spriddlestone Devon 6 D5
Spridlington Lincs 117 G5
Springburn C Glas 175 G5
Springfield D & G 148 B2
Springfield Essex 61 H6
Springfield Fife 186 E5
Springholm D & G 154 E7
Springside N Ayrs 163 J2
Springthorpe Lincs 116 E4
Springwell Sundld 151 H4
Springwood Crematorium Lpool 112 B4
Sproatley E R Yk 126 F4
Sproston Green Ches W 113 G7
Sprotbrough Donc 115 K2
Sproughton Suffk 78 D5
Sprouston Border 168 A3
Sprowston Norfk 92 F2
Sproxton Leics 102 D7
Sproxton N York 133 J3
Spurstow Ches E 98 D2
Spyway Dorset 14 A4
Stableford Shrops 84 D4
Stacey Bank Sheff 114 F4
Stackhouse N York 130 F6
Stackpole Pembks 49 G7
Staddiscombe C Plym 6 D5
Stadhampton Oxon 57 L7
Stadhlaigearraidh W Isls 233 b7
Staffield Cumb 148 F6
Staffin Highld 218 D7
Stafford Staffs 99 L7
Stafford Crematorium Staffs 99 L7
Stafford Services (Northbound) Staffs 99 K6
Stafford Services (Southbound) Staffs 99 K6
Stagsden Bed 74 E5
Stainburn Cumb 136 E2
Stainby Lincs 102 E7
Staincross Barns 123 L7
Staindrop Dur 140 E3
Staines-upon-Thames Surrey 43 G6
Stainforth Donc 124 F7
Stainforth N York 130 F6
Staining Lancs 120 D4
Stainland Calder 123 G6
Stainsacre N York 143 J5
Stainton Cumb 129 L3
Stainton Cumb 138 C2
Stainton Donc 115 K3
Stainton Dur 140 D4
Stainton Middsb 141 L4
Stainton by Langworth Lincs 117 H6
Staintondale N York 143 K7
Stainton le Vale Lincs 117 K3
Stainton with Adgarley Cumb 128 F5
Stair E Ayrs 163 K5
Stairhaven D & G 144 E4
Staithes N York 143 G4
Stakes Hants 17 K2
Stalbridge Dorset 27 G7
Stalbridge Weston Dorset 27 G7
Stalham Norfk 107 H7
Stalisfield Green Kent 34 C4
Stallen Dorset 26 E7
Stallingborough NE Lin 126 F7
Stalmine Lancs 120 E2
Stalybridge Tamesd 113 L2
Stambourne Essex 77 G6
Stambourne Green Essex 77 G6
Stamford Lincs 88 E3
Stamford Nthumb 169 J5
Stamford Bridge Ches W 112 C7
Stamford Bridge E R Yk 133 L7
Stamfordham Nthumb 158 D7
Stamford Hill Gt Lon 45 G3
Stanbridge C Beds 58 F3
Stanbury C Brad 122 F3
Stand N Lans 175 K5
Standburn Falk 176 C4
Standeford Staffs 85 G3
Standen Kent 33 L5
Standerwick Somset 27 J2
Standford Hants 30 D4
Standingstone Cumb 147 J7
Standish Wigan 121 H7
Standlake Oxon 57 H7
Standon Hants 29 H6
Standon Herts 60 C4
Standon Staffs 99 J5
Stane N Lans 176 B6
Stanfield Norfk 105 M7
Stanford C Beds 75 H6
Stanford Kent 34 F6
Stanford Bishop Herefs 70 C4
Stanford Bridge Worcs 70 C2
Stanford Dingley W Berk 41 L6
Stanford in the Vale Oxon 41 G2
Stanford le Hope Thurr 46 B4
Stanford on Avon Nhants 87 H7
Stanford on Soar Notts 101 K7
Stanford on Teme Worcs 70 C2
Stanfree Derbys 115 J6
Stanghow R & Cl 142 E4
Stanground C Pete 89 H4
Stanhoe Norfk 105 J5
Stanhope Border 165 L4
Stanhope Dur 150 C6
Stanhope Kent 34 D6
Stanion Nhants 88 D6
Stanley Derbys 101 H4
Stanley Dur 150 F4
Stanley P & K 186 B2
Stanley Staffs 99 L3
Stanley Crook Dur 150 E7
Stanley Pontlarge Gloucs 55 M3
Stanmer Br & H 19 K4
Stanmore Gt Lon 44 D2
Stanmore Hants 29 J5
Stannersburn Nthumb 157 J5
Stanningfield Suffk 77 K3
Stannington Nthumb 158 F6
Stannington Sheff 114 F4
Stannington Station Nthumb 158 F5
Stansbatch Herefs 69 G3
Stansfield Suffk 77 H4
Stanstead Suffk 77 J5
Stanstead Abbotts Herts 60 C5
Stansted Kent 45 L7
Stansted Airport Essex 60 E4
Stansted Mountfitchet Essex 60 E3
Stanton Gloucs 71 J7
Stanton Nthumb 158 E4
Stanton Staffs 100 C4
Stanton Suffk 91 L8
Stanton by Bridge Derbys 101 G6
Stanton by Dale Derbys 101 J5
Stanton Drew BaNES 38 E7
Stanton Fitzwarren Swindn 40 D3
Stanton Harcourt Oxon 57 H6
Stanton in Peak Derbys 114 E8
Stanton Lacy Shrops 83 K7
Stanton Lees Derbys 114 E8
Stanton Long Shrops 83 L5
Stanton on the Wolds Notts 101 M6
Stanton Prior BaNES 39 G7
Stanton St Bernard Wilts 40 C7
Stanton St John Oxon 57 L6
Stanton St Quintin Wilts 39 K4
Stanton Street Suffk 77 L2
Stanton under Bardon Leics 86 F2
Stanton upon Hine Heath Shrops 98 E7
Stanton Wick BaNES 38 E7
Stanway Essex 61 M3
Stanway Gloucs 56 B2
Stanwell Surrey 43 H5
Stanwick Nhants 74 E1
Stanwix Cumb 148 D4
Staoinebrig W Isls 233 b8
Stape N York 143 G7
Stapeley Ches E 99 G3
Stapenhill Staffs 100 E7
Staple Kent 35 H4
Staple Cross Devon 25 G7
Staplecross E Susx 20 F2
Staplefield W Susx 32 B7
Staple Fitzpaine Somset 25 K7
Stapleford Cambs 76 C4
Stapleford Herts 60 A5
Stapleford Leics 102 D8
Stapleford Lincs 102 E2
Stapleford Notts 101 J5
Stapleford Wilts 28 B4
Stapleford Abbotts Essex 45 K2
Staplegrove Somset 25 K6
Staplehay Somset 25 K6
Staplehurst Kent 33 K5
Staplestreet Kent 34 E3
Stapleton Herefs 69 G2
Stapleton Leics 86 E4
Stapleton N York 141 G5
Stapleton Shrops 83 J3
Stapleton Somset 26 C7
Stapley Somset 25 J8
Staploe Bed 75 G3
Staplow Herefs 70 C6
Star Fife 186 E6
Star Pembks 65 H7
Star Somset 38 C8
Starbeck N York 132 E7
Starbotton N York 131 H5
Starcross Devon 12 C6
Stareton Warwks 72 D1
Starlings Green Essex 60 D2
Starston Norfk 92 F6
Startforth Dur 140 D4
Startley Wilts 39 L4
Statenborough Kent 35 J4
Statham Warrtn 112 F4
Stathe Somset 26 A5
Stathern Leics 102 C6
Staughton Green Cambs 75 G2
Staunton Gloucs 54 D5
Staunton Gloucs 55 H3
Staunton on Arrow Herefs 69 G3
Staunton on Wye Herefs 69 G5
Staveley Cumb 129 H3
Staveley Cumb 138 C7
Staveley Derbys 115 H6
Staveley N York 132 E6
Staverton Devon 7 J3
Staverton Gloucs 55 K4
Staverton Nhants 73 G3
Staverton Wilts 39 J7
Stawell Somset 26 A4
Stawley Somset 25 G6
Staxigoe Highld 231 L5
Staxton N York 134 F4
Staynall Lancs 120 E2
Stean N York 131 K5
Stearsby N York 133 J5
Steart Somset 25 L3
Stebbing Essex 61 G3
Stechford Birm 85 K6

Stedham W Susx 30 E6
Steelend Fife 185 L8
Steele Road Border 156 F4
Steen's Bridge Herefs 69 K3
Steep Hants 30 C6
Steep Lane Calder 122 F5
Steeple Essex 61 M7
Steeple Ashton Wilts 27 K1
Steeple Aston Oxon 57 J3
Steeple Bumpstead Essex 76 F6
Steeple Claydon Bucks 58 B3
Steeple Gidding Cambs 89 G7
Steeple Langford Wilts 28 B4
Steeple Morden Cambs 75 K6
Steeton C Brad 122 F2
Stein Highld 208 D3
Stelling Minnis Kent 34 F5
Stembridge Somset 26 B7
Stenalees Cnwll 4 F4
Stenhouse D & G 154 D4
Stenhousemuir Falk 176 B2
Stenscholl Highld 218 D7
Stenson Fields Derbys 101 G6
Stenton E Loth 178 D4
Steornabhagh W Isls 232 f2
Stepaside Pembks 49 K6
Stepford D & G 154 E5
Stepney Gt Lon 45 G4
Steppingley C Beds 74 E7
Stepps N Lans 175 H5
Sternfield Suffk 79 H3
Stert Wilts 40 B8
Stetchworth Cambs 76 F3
Stevenage Herts 59 L3
Stevenston N Ayrs 163 H2
Steventon Hants 29 K2
Steventon Oxon 41 J3
Steventon End Essex 76 E6
Stevington Bed 74 E4
Stewartby Bed 74 E6
Stewartfield S Lans 175 H7
Stewarton E Ayrs 163 K1
Stewkley Bucks 58 D3
Stewley Somset 25 L7
Steyning W Susx 19 G4
Steynton Pembks 48 F6
Stibb Cnwll 9 G3
Stibbard Norfk 106 B6
Stibb Cross Devon 10 C2
Stibb Green Wilts 40 E7
Stibbington Cambs 88 F4
Stichill Border 167 L2
Sticker Cnwll 4 F5
Stickford Lincs 104 B1
Sticklepath Devon 10 F6
Stickney Lincs 104 B2
Stiffkey Norfk 106 A4
Stilligarry W Isls 233 b7
Stillingfleet N York 124 F3
Stillington N York 133 J6
Stillington S on T 141 J3
Stilton Cambs 89 H5
Stinchcombe Gloucs 55 G7
Stinsford Dorset 14 D4
Stiperstones Shrops 83 G4
Stirchley Wrekin 84 C3
Stirling Abers 217 L6
Stirling Stirlg 185 G8
Stirling Castle Stirlg 185 G8
Stirling Services Stirlg 175 L2
Stirtloe Cambs 75 H2
Stirton N York 131 H8
Stisted Essex 61 J3
Stithians Cnwll 3 J4
Stivichall Covtry 86 D7
Stixwould Lincs 117 K7
Stoak Ches W 112 B6
Stobo Border 166 B2
Stoborough Dorset 15 H5
Stobs Castle Border 167 G7
Stobswood Nthumb 158 F3
Stock Essex 61 H7
Stock N Som 38 C7
Stockbridge Hants 29 G4
Stockbriggs S Lans 164 F3
Stockbury Kent 46 D7
Stockcross W Berk 41 H6
Stockerston Leics 88 B4
Stock Green Worcs 71 H3
Stocking Herefs 54 F2
Stockingford Warwks 86 D5
Stocking Pelham Herts 60 D3
Stockland Devon 13 G2
Stockland Bristol Somset 25 K3
Stockleigh English Devon 11 K4
Stockleigh Pomeroy Devon 11 K4
Stockley Wilts 39 M6
Stocklinch Somset 26 B7
Stockport Stockp 113 K4
Stockport Crematorium Stockp 113 K4
Stocksbridge Sheff 114 E2
Stocksfield Nthumb 150 D3
Stockton Herefs 69 K3
Stockton Norfk 93 H5
Stockton Shrops 84 C4
Stockton Warwks 72 E2
Stockton Wilts 27 M4
Stockton Wrekin 84 D1
Stockton Brook Staffs 99 K3
Stockton Heath Warrtn 112 E4
Stockton-on-Tees S on T 141 K4
Stockton on Teme Worcs 70 C2
Stockton on the Forest C York 133 K7
Stockwell End Wolves 84 F4
Stockwood Bristl 38 F6
Stockwood Dorset 14 B2
Stock Wood Worcs 71 H3
Stodmarsh Kent 35 G3
Stody Norfk 106 C5
Stoer Highld 224 C3
Stoford Somset 26 E8
Stoford Wilts 28 B4
Stogumber Somset 25 H4
Stogursey Somset 25 J3
Stoke Covtry 86 D7
Stoke Devon 22 C6
Stoke Hants 17 K3
Stoke Hants 29 H2
Stoke Medway 46 D5
Stoke Abbott Dorset 13 L3
Stoke Albany Nhants 88 B5
Stoke Ash Suffk 78 D1
Stoke Bardolph Notts 101 M4
Stoke Bliss Worcs 70 B2
Stoke Bruerne Nhants 73 L4
Stoke-by-Clare Suffk 77 G5
Stoke-by-Nayland Suffk 78 B7
Stoke Canon Devon 12 B3
Stoke Charity Hants 29 J4
Stoke Climsland Cnwll 6 A2
Stoke Cross Herefs 70 B4
Stoke D'Abernon Surrey 43 J8
Stoke Doyle Nhants 88 E6
Stoke Dry Rutlnd 88 C4
Stoke Edith Herefs 69 L6
Stoke Farthing Wilts 28 B6
Stoke Ferry Norfk 91 G4
Stoke Fleming Devon 7 K6
Stokeford Dorset 15 G5
Stoke Gabriel Devon 7 J4
Stoke Gifford S Glos 38 F4
Stoke Golding Leics 86 E4
Stoke Goldington M Keyn 74 B5
Stokeham Notts 116 C6
Stoke Hammond Bucks 58 E3
Stoke Holy Cross Norfk 92 F3
Stokeinteignhead Devon 7 L2
Stoke Lacy Herefs 70 B5
Stoke Lyne Oxon 57 K3
Stoke Mandeville Bucks 58 D6
Stokenchurch Bucks 42 C2
Stoke Newington Gt Lon 45 G3
Stokenham Devon 7 J7
Stoke-on-Trent C Stke 99 K3
Stoke Orchard Gloucs 55 K3
Stoke Poges Bucks 42 F4
Stoke Prior Herefs 69 K3
Stoke Prior Worcs 71 G2
Stoke Rivers Devon 23 K4
Stoke Rochford Lincs 102 F6
Stoke Row Oxon 42 B4
Stoke St Gregory Somset 25 M6
Stoke St Mary Somset 25 K6
Stoke St Michael Somset 26 F3
Stoke St Milborough Shrops 83 L6
Stokesby Norfk 93 J2
Stokesley N York 142 B5
Stoke sub Hamdon Somset 26 C7
Stoke Talmage Oxon 58 B7
Stoke Trister Somset 27 H5
Stoke upon Tern Shrops 98 F6
Stolford Somset 25 K3
Stondon Massey Essex 60 F7
Stone Bucks 58 C5
Stone Gloucs 39 G2
Stone Rothm 115 K4
Stone Staffs 99 K5
Stone Worcs 84 F7
Stone Allerton Somset 26 B2
Ston Easton Somset 26 F2
Stonebridge N Som 38 B7
Stonebridge Warwks 86 B6
Stonebroom Derbys 101 H2
Stone Cross Kent 35 J4
Stonecrouch Kent 33 J6
Stoneferry C KuH 126 D4
Stonefield Castle Hotel Ag & B 172 E4
Stonegate E Susx 33 H7
Stonegrave N York 133 K4
Stonehaven Abers 207 G7
Stonehenge Wilts 28 C3
Stonehouse C Plym 6 C5
Stonehouse Gloucs 55 J6
Stonehouse S Lans 175 K8
Stone in Oxney Kent 21 J1
Stoneleigh Warwks 86 D8
Stonesby Leics 102 D7
Stonesfield Oxon 57 H4
Stones Green Essex 62 E3
Stone Street Kent 33 G3
Stone Street Suffk 93 H6
Stonewells Moray 215 G2
Stoneybridge W Isls 233 b8
Stoneyburn W Loth 176 D5
Stoneygate C Leic 87 H3
Stoneykirk D & G 144 C4
Stoney Middleton Derbys 114 E6
Stoney Stanton Leics 86 F4
Stoney Stoke Somset 27 G5
Stoney Stratton Somset 26 F4
Stoneywood C Aber 207 G3
Stoneywood Falk 175 L2
Stonham Aspal Suffk 78 D3
Stonnall Staffs 85 J3
Stonor Oxon 42 B3
Stonton Wyville Leics 87 K4
Stony Houghton Derbys 115 J7
Stony Stratford M Keyn 73 L6
Stoodleigh Devon 23 K5
Stoodleigh Devon 24 E7
Stop 24 Services Kent 34 F7
Stopham W Susx 18 D2
Stopsley Luton 59 J3
Stornoway W Isls 232 f2
Stornoway Airport W Isls 232 g2
Storrington W Susx 18 E3
Storth Cumb 129 K4
Storwood E R Yk 125 H2
Stotfield Moray 214 F1
Stotfold C Beds 75 J7
Stottesdon Shrops 84 C6
Stoughton Leics 87 J3
Stoughton Surrey 31 G2
Stoughton W Susx 17 L1
Stoulton Worcs 70 F4
Stourbridge Dudley 84 F6
Stourbridge Crematorium Dudley 84 F6
Stourhead Wilts 27 H5
Stourpaine Dorset 15 G1
Stourport-on-Severn Worcs 70 E1
Stour Provost Dorset 27 H6
Stour Row Dorset 27 J7
Stourton Staffs 84 F6
Stourton Warwks 72 C6
Stourton Wilts 27 H5
Stourton Caundle Dorset 27 G7
Stove Shet 235 c7
Stoven Suffk 93 J6
Stow Border 167 G1
Stow Lincs 116 E5
Stow Bardolph Norfk 90 F3
Stow Bedon Norfk 91 L4
Stowbridge Norfk 90 E3
Stow-cum-Quy Cambs 76 D3
Stowe Shrops 82 F8
Stowe by Chartley Staffs 100 A6
Stowell Somset 27 G6
Stowey BaNES 38 E7
Stowford Devon 10 C7
Stowlangtoft Suffk 77 L2
Stow Longa Cambs 75 G1
Stow Maries Essex 61 K7
Stowmarket Suffk 78 C3
Stow-on-the-Wold Gloucs 56 D3
Stowting Kent 34 F6
Stowting Common Kent 34 F6
Stowupland Suffk 78 C3
Straanruie Highld 204 B3
Strachan Abers 206 D6
Strachur Ag & B 182 F6
Stradbroke Suffk 92 F8
Stradishall Suffk 77 H4
Stradsett Norfk 90 F3
Stragglethorpe Lincs 102 E3
Straiton Mdloth 177 H5
Straiton S Ayrs 153 H2
Straloch Abers 207 G2
Straloch P & K 195 G4
Stramshall Staffs 100 B5
Strang IoM 237 c5
Strangeways Salfd 113 J2
Strangford Herefs 54 E3
Stranraer D & G 144 C3
Stratfield Mortimer W Berk 42 A7
Stratfield Saye Hants 42 B7
Stratfield Turgis Hants 42 B7
Stratford Gt Lon 45 H3
Stratford St Andrew Suffk 79 H3

Stratford St Mary Suffk 78 C7
Stratford sub Castle Wilts 28 C5
Stratford Tony Wilts 28 C6
Stratford-upon-Avon Warwks 72 B4
Strath Highld 219 J5
Strathan Highld 224 D4
Strathan Highld 229 J3
Strathaven S Lans 164 D1
Strathblane Stirlg 175 G3
Strathcanaird Highld 220 F2
Strathcarron Highld 210 E6
Strathcoil Ag & B 181 K2
Strathdon Abers 205 H3
Strathkinness Fife 187 G4
Strathloanhead W Loth 176 C4
Strathmashie House Highld 202 F6
Strathmiglo Fife 186 C5
Strathpeffer Highld 212 D3
Strathtay P & K 194 E5
Strathwhillan N Ayrs 162 D3
Strathy Highld 230 B3
Strathy Inn Highld 230 B3
Strathyre Stirlg 184 C4
Stratton Cnwll 9 G4
Stratton Dorset 14 C4
Stratton Gloucs 56 A7
Stratton Audley Oxon 57 L3
Stratton-on-the-Fosse Somset 26 F2
Stratton St Margaret Swindn 40 D3
Stratton St Michael Norfk 92 E5
Stratton Strawless Norfk 106 F7
Streat E Susx 19 K3
Streatham Gt Lon 44 F5
Streatley C Beds 59 H3
Streatley W Berk 41 L4
Street Devon 12 F5
Street Somset 26 C4
Street Ashton Warwks 86 F6
Street Dinas Shrops 97 M5
Street End Kent 34 F4
Street End W Susx 18 A5
Streethay Staffs 85 K2
Streetlam N York 141 H7
Streetly Crematorium Wsall 85 J4
Streetly End Cambs 76 E5
Street on the Fosse Somset 26 F4
Strelitz P & K 186 C1
Strelley Notts 101 K4
Strensall C York 133 K7
Strensham Services (northbound) Worcs 70 F6
Strensham Services (southbound) Worcs 70 F6
Stretcholt Somset 25 L3
Strete Devon 7 J6
Stretford Traffd 113 H3
Strethall Essex 76 C6
Stretham Cambs 90 D8
Strettington W Susx 18 B4
Stretton Derbys 101 H1
Stretton RutInd 88 D1
Stretton Staffs 84 F2
Stretton Staffs 100 E7
Stretton Warrtn 112 F5
Stretton Grandison Herefs 70 B5
Stretton-on-Dunsmore Warwks 86 E8
Stretton on Fosse Warwks 72 B6
Stretton Sugwas Herefs 69 J6
Stretton under Fosse Warwks 86 F7
Stretton Westwood Shrops 83 L4
Strichen Abers 217 H4
Stringston Somset 25 J3
Strixton Nhants 74 C3
Stroat Gloucs 38 E2
Stroma Highld 231 L1
Stromeferry Highld 210 D7
Stromness Ork 234 b6
Stronachlachar Stirlg 183 L5
Stronafian Ag & B 173 H3
Stronchrubie Highld 224 F5
Strone Ag & B 173 L3
Strone Highld 192 B1
Strone Highld 212 E8
Stronenaba Highld 201 J8
Stronmilchan Ag & B 183 G2
Stronsay Ork 234 d5
Stronsay Airport Ork 234 d5
Strontian Highld 191 G4
Strood Medway 46 B6
Stroud Gloucs 55 J6
Stroud Hants 30 B6
Stroud Green Gloucs 55 J6
Stroxton Lincs 102 E6
Struan Highld 208 E6
Struan P & K 194 C4
Strumpshaw Norfk 93 H3
Strutherhill S Lans 175 K7
Struthers Fife 186 F5
Struy Highld 212 B6
Stuartfield Abers 217 H5
Stubbers Green Wsall 85 J3
Stubbington Hants 17 G2
Stubbins Lancs 122 B6
Stubton Lincs 102 E3
Stuckton Hants 28 D8
Studham C Beds 59 G5
Studland Dorset 15 J6
Studley Warwks 71 J2
Studley Wilts 39 L6
Studley Roger N York 132 D5
Studley Royal N York 132 D5
Studley Royal Park & Fountains Abbey N York 132 D5
Stuntney Cambs 90 D7
Sturmer Essex 77 G5
Sturminster Common Dorset 27 H8
Sturminster Marshall Dorset 15 H3
Sturminster Newton Dorset 27 H8
Sturry Kent 35 G3
Sturton N Linc 116 F2
Sturton by Stow Lincs 116 E5
Sturton le Steeple Notts 116 C5
Stuston Suffk 92 D7
Stutton N York 124 D3
Stutton Suffk 78 D7
Styal Ches E 113 J5
Stynie Moray 215 H3
Styrrup Notts 115 L4
Succoth Ag & B 183 K6
Suckley Worcs 70 C4
Sudborough Nhants 88 D6
Sudbourne Suffk 79 J4
Sudbrook Lincs 102 F4
Sudbrook Mons 38 D3
Sudbrooke Lincs 117 G6
Sudbury Derbys 100 D6
Sudbury Gt Lon 44 D3
Sudbury Suffk 77 K6
Suffield N York 134 F2
Suffield Norfk 106 F6
Sugnall Staffs 99 H6
Sugwas Pool Herefs 69 J6
Suisnish Highld 199 J3
Sulby IoM 237 d3
Sulgrave Nhants 73 G5
Sulham W Berk 41 M5
Sulhamstead W Berk 41 M6
Sullom Shet 235 c4
Sullom Voe Shet 235 c4
Sully V Glam 37 J6
Sumburgh Airport Shet 235 c8
Summerbridge N York 132 C6
Summercourt Cnwll 4 D5
Summerfield Norfk 105 J5
Summerhill Pembks 49 K6
Summerhouse Darltn 140 F4
Summersdale W Susx 18 B4
Summerseat Bury 122 B7
Summertown Oxon 57 K6
Sunbury-on-Thames Surrey 43 J6
Sundaywell D & G 154 E5
Sunderland Ag & B 170 E5
Sunderland Cumb 147 L7
Sunderland Lancs 129 J7
Sunderland Sundld 151 J4
Sunderland Bridge Dur 151 G7
Sunderland Crematorium Sundld 151 J4
Sundhope Border 166 E4
Sundon Park Luton 59 H3
Sundridge Kent 32 E3
Sunningdale W & M 42 F6
Sunninghill W & M 42 F6
Sunningwell Oxon 57 J7
Sunniside Dur 150 E7
Sunniside Gatesd 150 F3
Sunnyhill C Derb 101 G6
Sunnyhurst Bl w D 121 K6
Sunnylaw Stirlg 185 G7
Sunnymead Oxon 57 J6
Surbiton Gt Lon 44 D6
Surfleet Lincs 103 L6
Surlingham Norfk 93 G3
Surrex Essex 61 L4
Surrey & Sussex Crematorium W Susx 32 B5
Sustead Norfk 106 E5
Susworth Lincs 116 D2
Sutcombe Devon 9 J3
Sutcombemill Devon 9 J3
Sutterby Lincs 118 E6
Sutterton Lincs 103 M5
Sutton C Beds 75 J5
Sutton C Pete 89 G4
Sutton Cambs 90 C7
Sutton Devon 7 G7
Sutton E Susx 20 A5
Sutton Gt Lon 44 E7
Sutton Kent 35 J5
Sutton N York 124 D5
Sutton Norfk 107 H7
Sutton Notts 102 C5
Sutton Oxon 57 H6
Sutton Shrops 84 D6
Sutton Staffs 99 H7
Sutton Suffk 79 G5
Sutton W Susx 18 D3
Sutton-at-Hone Kent 45 K6
Sutton Bassett Nhants 87 L5
Sutton Benger Wilts 39 L5
Sutton Bonington Notts 101 K7
Sutton Bridge Lincs 104 D7
Sutton Cheney Leics 86 E4
Sutton Coldfield Birm 85 K4
Sutton Coldfield Crematorium Birm 85 K4
Sutton Courtenay Oxon 41 J2
Sutton cum Lound Notts 116 B5
Sutton Green Surrey 31 G1
Sutton Howgrave N York 132 D4
Sutton-in-Ashfield Notts 101 J2
Sutton-in-Craven N York 122 F2
Sutton Maddock Shrops 84 C3
Sutton Mallet Somset 26 A4
Sutton Mandeville Wilts 27 M5
Sutton Montis Somset 26 F6
Sutton-on-Hull C KuH 126 E4
Sutton on Sea Lincs 119 G5
Sutton-on-the-Forest N York 133 J6
Sutton on the Hill Derbys 100 E5
Sutton on Trent Notts 116 D7
Sutton St Edmund Lincs 89 L2
Sutton St James Lincs 104 C8
Sutton St Nicholas Herefs 69 K5
Sutton Scotney Hants 29 J4
Sutton-under-Brailes Warwks 72 C6
Sutton-under-Whitestonecliffe N York 133 G3
Sutton upon Derwent E R Yk 125 G2
Sutton Valence Kent 33 L4
Sutton Veny Wilts 27 K3
Sutton Waldron Dorset 27 K7
Sutton Weaver Ches W 112 D5
Sutton Wick BaNES 38 E8
Sutton Wick Oxon 41 J2
Swaby Lincs 118 E6
Swadlincote Derbys 100 F8
Swaffham Norfk 91 J2
Swaffham Bulbeck Cambs 76 D3
Swaffham Prior Cambs 76 E2
Swafield Norfk 107 G6
Swainby N York 141 L6
Swainsthorpe Norfk 92 F4
Swainswick BaNES 39 H6
Swalcliffe Oxon 72 E6
Swalecliffe Kent 47 J6
Swallow Lincs 117 K2
Swallow Beck Lincs 116 F7
Swallowcliffe Wilts 27 L6
Swallowfield Wokham 42 B7
Swanage Dorset 15 J6
Swanbourne Bucks 58 D3
Swan Green Ches W 113 G6
Swanland E R Yk 126 B5
Swanley Kent 45 K6
Swanley Village Kent 45 K6
Swanmore Hants 29 L7
Swannington Leics 86 E1
Swannington Norfk 106 D8
Swanpool Lincs 116 F7
Swanscombe Kent 45 L5
Swansea Swans 51 J6
Swansea Airport Swans 51 H7
Swansea Crematorium Swans 51 J5
Swansea West Services Swans 51 J5
Swanton Abbot Norfk 106 F7
Swanton Morley Norfk 92 B1
Swanton Novers Norfk 106 B6
Swan Village Sandw 85 H5
Swanwick Derbys 101 H2
Swanwick Hants 17 G1
Swarby Lincs 103 H4
Swardeston Norfk 92 E3
Swarkestone Derbys 101 G6

Swarland Nthumb 158 F2
Swarraton Hants 29 K4
Swarthmoor Cumb 129 G4
Swaton Lincs 103 J5
Swavesey Cambs 75 L2
Sway Hants 16 C3
Swayfield Lincs 103 G7
Swaythling C Sotn 29 H7
Sweetham Devon 11 K5
Sweethaws E Susx 32 E7
Sweets Cnwll 8 F5
Sweetshouse Cnwll 5 H4
Swefling Suffk 79 H2
Swepstone Leics 86 D2
Swerford Oxon 57 G2
Swettenham Ches E 113 J7
Swilland Suffk 78 E4
Swillington Leeds 124 B4
Swimbridge Devon 23 K5
Swimbridge Newland Devon 23 J5
Swinbrook Oxon 56 F5
Swincliffe N York 132 C7
Swinderby Lincs 116 E8
Swindon Gloucs 55 L3
Swindon Staffs 84 F5
Swindon Swindn 40 D4
Swine E R Yk 126 E4
Swinefleet E R Yk 125 H6
Swineshead Bed 74 F2
Swineshead Lincs 103 L4
Swiney Highld 227 M2
Swinford Leics 87 H7
Swingfield Minnis Kent 35 G6
Swingfield Street Kent 35 H6
Swingleton Green Suffk 77 L5
Swinhoe Nthumb 169 J4
Swinithwaite N York 131 K2
Swinside Cumb 137 H3
Swinstead Lincs 103 G7
Swinton Border 179 H8
Swinton N York 132 C4
Swinton N York 134 B5
Swinton Rothm 115 J2
Swinton Salfd 113 H2
Swithland Leics 87 G2
Swordale Highld 212 E2
Swordland Highld 200 B6
Swordly Highld 229 M3
Swynnerton Staffs 99 J5
Swyre Dorset 13 M5
Sychtyn Powys 81 L3
Syde Gloucs 55 L5
Sydenham Gt Lon 45 G5
Sydenham Oxon 58 B7
Sydenham Damerel Devon 6 B2
Syderstone Norfk 105 K6
Sydling St Nicholas Dorset 14 C3
Sydmonton Hants 41 J8
Syerston Notts 102 C3
Sykehouse Donc 124 F6
Symbister Shet 235 d4
Symington S Ayrs 163 J3
Symington S Lans 165 J3
Symondsbury Dorset 13 K4
Symonds Yat (West) Herefs 54 E5
Syre Highld 229 L6
Syreford Gloucs 56 B4
Syresham Nhants 73 J6
Syston Leics 87 J2
Syston Lincs 102 F4
Sytchampton Worcs 70 E2
Sywell Nhants 74 B2

T

Tackley Oxon 57 J4
Tacolneston Norfk 92 D4
Tadcaster N York 124 D2
Taddington Derbys 114 C7
Tadley Hants 41 L7
Tadlow Cambs 75 K5
Tadmarton Oxon 72 E6
Tadworth Surrey 44 E8
Taff's Well Rhondd 37 H4
Taibach Neath 36 B3
Tain Highld 223 G5
Tain Highld 231 J3
Tairbeart W Isls 232 e4
Takeley Essex 60 F4
Takeley Street Essex 60 E4
Talaton Devon 12 D3
Talbenny Pembks 48 E5
Taleford Devon 12 E3
Talerddig Powys 81 K4
Talgarreg Cerdgn 65 L4
Talgarth Powys 68 D7
Talisker Highld 208 E7
Talke Staffs 99 J2
Talke Pits Staffs 99 J3
Talkin Cumb 148 F4
Talladale Highld 219 L7
Talla Linnfoots Border 165 M5
Tallaminnock S Ayrs 153 J3
Tallarn Green Wrexhm 98 C4
Tallentire Cumb 147 K7
Talley Carmth 66 E7
Tallington Lincs 88 F2
Talmine Highld 229 J3
Talog Carmth 50 D1
Talsarn Cerdgn 66 D4
Talsarnau Gwynd 95 K5
Talskiddy Cnwll 4 E3
Talwrn IoA 109 G6
Tal-y-bont Cerdgn 80 E5
Tal-y-Bont Conwy 109 L7
Tal-y-bont Gwynd 95 K7
Tal-y-bont Gwynd 109 J7
Talybont-on-Usk Powys 53 H4
Tal-y-Cafn Conwy 109 M7
Tal-y-coed Mons 54 B5
Talysarn Gwynd 95 H2
Tamar Valley Mining District Devon 6 C3
Tamerton Foliot C Plym 6 C4
Tamworth Staffs 86 B3
Tamworth Services Warwks 86 B4
Tandridge Surrey 32 C3
Tanfield Dur 150 F4
Tanfield Lea Dur 150 F4
Tangley Hants 28 F2
Tangmere W Susx 18 B4
Tangusdale W Isls 233 b9
Tankerness Ork 234 c6
Tankersley Barns 115 G2
Tankerton Kent 47 J6
Tannach Highld 231 K6
Tannachie Abers 206 E8
Tannadice Angus 196 D5
Tanner's Green Worcs 85 J8
Tannington Suffk 78 F2
Tannochside N Lans 175 J6
Tansley Derbys 100 F1
Tansor Nhants 88 F5
Tantobie Dur 150 F4
Tanworth in Arden Warwks 71 K1
Tan-y-groes Cerdgn 65 J5
Taobh Tuath W Isls 232 d5
Taplow Bucks 42 E4
Tarbert Ag & B 172 B7
Tarbert Ag & B 172 E5
Tarbert W Isls 232 e4
Tarbet Ag & B 183 K6
Tarbet Highld 200 B6
Tarbet Highld 228 B5
Tarbolton S Ayrs 163 K4
Tarbrax S Lans 176 D7
Tardebigge Worcs 71 H2
Tarfside Angus 196 D1
Tarland Abers 205 K4
Tarleton Lancs 120 F6
Tarlton Gloucs 55 L7
Tarnock Somset 26 B2
Tarporley Ches W 112 D8
Tarrant Crawford Dorset 15 H2
Tarrant Gunville Dorset 27 L8
Tarrant Hinton Dorset 15 H1
Tarrant Keyneston Dorset 15 H2
Tarrant Launceston Dorset 15 H1
Tarrant Monkton Dorset 15 H2
Tarrant Rawston Dorset 15 H2
Tarrant Rushton Dorset 15 H2
Tarring Neville E Susx 19 L5
Tarrington Herefs 70 B6
Tarskavaig Highld 199 J4
Tarves Abers 217 G7
Tarvin Ches W 112 C7
Tasburgh Norfk 92 E4
Tatenhill Staffs 100 D7
Tathwell Lincs 118 D5
Tatsfield Surrey 32 D2
Tattenhall Ches W 98 C2
Tatterford Norfk 105 K6
Tattersett Norfk 105 K6
Tattershall Lincs 103 K2
Tattershall Thorpe Lincs 103 L1
Tattingstone Suffk 78 D6
Tattingstone White Horse Suffk 78 D6
Tatton Park Ches E 113 H5
Tatworth Somset 13 J2
Tauchers Moray 215 J4
Taunton Somset 25 K6
Taunton Deane Crematorium Somset 25 J6
Taunton Deane Services Somset 25 J7
Taverham Norfk 92 E2
Tavernspite Pembks 49 K5
Tavistock Devon 6 C2
Tavistock Devon 6 C2
Taw Green Devon 10 F5
Tawstock Devon 23 J5
Taxal Derbys 114 A5
Tay Bridge C Dund 187 G2
Taychreggan Hotel Ag & B 182 F3
Tay Forest Park P & K 194 C4
Tayinloan Ag & B 161 H1
Taynton Gloucs 55 G4
Taynton Oxon 56 E5
Taynuilt Ag & B 182 E2
Tayport Fife 187 G2
Tayvallich Ag & B 172 C2
Tealby Lincs 117 J4
Tealing Angus 196 C8
Team Valley Gatesd 151 G3
Teangue Highld 199 K4
Teanord Highld 212 F2
Tebay Cumb 138 E6
Tebay Services Cumb 138 E6
Tebworth C Beds 59 G3
Tedburn St Mary Devon 11 J6
Teddington Gloucs 55 L2
Teddington Gt Lon 44 D6
Tedstone Delamere Herefs 70 C3
Tedstone Wafer Herefs 70 C3
Teesside Crematorium Middsb 141 L4
Teeton Nhants 73 K1
Teffont Evias Wilts 27 M5
Teffont Magna Wilts 27 M5
Tegryn Pembks 65 H7
Teigh Rutlnd 88 C1
Teigngrace Devon 7 K2
Teignmouth Devon 12 B7
Teindside Border 166 F7
Telford Wrekin 84 C2
Telford Crematorium Wrekin 84 D2
Telford Services Shrops 84 D2
Tellisford Somset 27 J1
Telscombe E Susx 19 L5
Tempar P & K 193 L5
Templand D & G 155 J5
Temple Cnwll 5 J2
Temple Mdloth 177 J6
Temple Bar Cerdgn 66 C4
Temple Cloud BaNES 38 F8
Templecombe Somset 27 G6
Temple Grafton Warwks 71 K4
Temple Guiting Gloucs 56 C3
Temple Hirst N York 124 F5
Temple Normanton Derbys 115 H7
Temple of Fiddes Abers 197 K1
Temple Sowerby Cumb 138 E2
Templeton Devon 11 K3
Templeton Pembks 49 J5
Templetown Dur 150 E5
Tempsford C Beds 75 H4
Tenbury Wells Worcs 69 L2
Tenby Pembks 49 J7
Tendring Essex 62 D3
Tendring Green Essex 62 D3
Tendring Heath Essex 62 D3
Ten Mile Bank Norfk 90 E4
Tenterden Kent 34 B7
Terling Essex 61 J5
Ternhill Shrops 98 F6
Terregles D & G 155 G6
Terrington N York 133 K5
Terrington St Clement Norfk 104 E7
Terrington St John Norfk 90 D2
Teston Kent 33 J3
Testwood Hants 29 G8
Tetbury Gloucs 39 K2
Tetchill Shrops 98 B6
Tetcott Devon 9 J5
Tetford Lincs 118 D6
Tetney Lincs 118 D2
Tetsworth Oxon 58 B7
Tettenhall Wolves 84 F4
Tettenhall Wood Wolves 84 F4
Teversal Notts 101 J1
Teversham Cambs 76 C3
Teviothead Border 156 D2
Tewin Herts 59 L5
Tewkesbury Gloucs 55 K2
Teynham Kent 34 C3
Thackley C Brad 123 H3
Thainstone Abers 206 E2
Thakeham W Susx 18 F3
Thame Oxon 58 B6
Thames Ditton Surrey 44 D6
Thamesmead Gt Lon 45 J4
Thamesport Medway 46 E5
Thanet Crematorium Kent 35 K2
Thanington Kent 34 F4
Thankerton S Lans 165 J2
Tharston Norfk 92 E5
Thatcham W Berk 41 K6
Thaxted Essex 60 F2
Theakston N York 132 D3
Thealby N Linc 125 K6
Theale Somset 26 C3
Theale W Berk 41 M6
Thearne E R Yk 126 D3
The Beeches Gloucs 56 B7
Theberton Suffk 79 J2
The Braes Highld 209 H7

The Brunt E Loth 178 E4
The Bungalow IoM 237 d4
The Burf Worcs 70 E2
The Butts Gloucs 55 K5
The City Bucks 42 C2
The Common Wilts 28 E5
The Counties Crematorium Nhants 73 K3
Theddingworth Leics 87 J6
Theddlethorpe All Saints Lincs 118 F4
Theddlethorpe St Helen Lincs 119 G4
The Den N Ayrs 174 C7
The Forstal Kent 34 D6
The Garden of England Crematorium Kent 46 E6
The Green Cumb 128 E3
The Green Essex 61 J4
The Green N York 143 G6
The Green Wilts 27 K5
The Headland Hartpl 151 M7
The Hill Cumb 128 E3
The Lee Bucks 58 E6
The Lhen IoM 237 d2
Thelnetham Suffk 92 B7
The Lochs Moray 215 G2
Thelveton Norfk 92 E7
Thelwall Warrtn 112 F4
Themelthorpe Norfk 106 C7
The Middles Dur 150 F5
The Moor Kent 33 K7
The Mumbles Swans 51 J7
The Murray S Lans 175 H7
The Neuk Abers 206 D5
Thenford Nhants 73 G6
The Park Crematorium Hants 30 E2
The Reddings Gloucs 55 K4
Therfield Herts 75 L6
The Ross P & K 185 G3
The Stocks Kent 21 H1
The Strand Wilts 39 L8
Thetford Norfk 91 K6
Thetford Forest Park 91 J5
The Vale Crematorium Luton 59 J3
Theydon Bois Essex 60 D7
Thickwood Wilts 39 J5
Thimbleby Lincs 118 C7
Thimbleby N York 141 K7
Thingwall Wirral 111 J5
Thirkleby N York 133 G4
Thirlby N York 133 G3
Thirlestane Border 178 C8
Thirn N York 132 C3
Thirsk N York 132 F3
Thistleton Lancs 120 E3
Thistleton Rutlnd 102 E8
Thistley Green Suffk 90 F7
Thixendale N York 134 C7
Thockrington Nthumb 158 B6
Tholomas Drove Cambs 90 B3
Tholthorpe N York 133 G6
Thomastown Abers 216 B6
Thompson Norfk 91 K4
Thongsbridge Kirk 123 H8
Thoralby N York 131 J3
Thoresway Lincs 117 K3
Thorganby Lincs 117 K3
Thorganby N York 125 G3
Thorgill N York 142 E7
Thorington Suffk 93 J8
Thorington Street Suffk 78 B7
Thorlby N York 131 H8
Thorley Herts 60 D4
Thorley Street IoW 16 D5
Thormanby N York 133 G5
Thornaby-on-Tees S on T 141 K4
Thornage Norfk 106 C5
Thornborough Bucks 73 L7
Thornborough N York 132 D4
Thornbury C Brad 123 J4
Thornbury Devon 9 K3
Thornbury Herefs 70 B3
Thornbury S Glos 38 F3
Thornby Nhants 87 J7
Thorncliff Staffs 100 A2
Thorncliffe Crematorium Cumb 128 E5
Thorncombe Dorset 13 J2
Thorndon Suffk 78 D1
Thorndon Cross Devon 10 D6
Thorne Donc 125 G7
Thorner Leeds 124 B3
Thorne St Margaret Somset 25 H7
Thorney C Pete 89 K3
Thorney Notts 116 E6
Thorney Somset 26 B6
Thorney Hill Hants 16 A3
Thorney Island W Susx 17 L2
Thornfalcon Somset 25 L6
Thornford Dorset 26 E8
Thorngrafton Nthumb 149 K2
Thorngumbald E R Yk 126 F5
Thornham Norfk 105 H4
Thornham Magna Suffk 78 D1
Thornham Parva Suffk 92 D8
Thornhaugh C Pete 88 F4
Thornhill C Sotn 29 J8
Thornhill Cumb 136 D5
Thornhill D & G 154 F3
Thornhill Derbys 114 D5
Thornhill Kirk 123 K6
Thornhill Stirlg 184 E7
Thornholme E R Yk 135 H6
Thornicombe Dorset 15 G2
Thornington Nthumb 168 D3
Thornley Dur 150 E7
Thornley Dur 151 J6
Thornliebank E Rens 174 F6
Thorns Suffk 77 G4
Thornsett Derbys 114 A4
Thornthwaite Cumb 137 H3
Thornthwaite N York 132 B7
Thornton Angus 196 C6
Thornton Bucks 73 L7
Thornton C Brad 123 G4
Thornton E R Yk 125 H2
Thornton Fife 186 E7
Thornton Lancs 120 D3
Thornton Leics 86 F3
Thornton Middsb 141 L4
Thornton Nthumb 179 K8
Thornton Curtis N Linc 126 D6
Thornton Garden of Rest Crematorium Sefton 111 K2
Thorntonhall S Lans 175 G7
Thornton Heath Gt Lon 44 F6
Thornton Hough Wirral 111 J5
Thornton-in-Craven N York 122 D2
Thornton in Lonsdale N York 130 D5
Thornton-le-Beans N York 132 F2
Thornton-le-Clay N York 133 L6
Thornton-le-Dale N York 134 C3
Thornton le Moor Lincs 117 H3
Thornton-le-Moor N York 132 F2
Thornton-le-Moors Ches W 112 C6
Thornton-le-Street N York 132 F3
Thorntonloch E Loth 178 F4
Thornton Rust N York 131 H2
Thornton Steward N York 132 B3
Thornton Watlass N York 132 C3
Thornydykes Border 178 D8
Thornythwaite Cumb 137 L3
Thoroton Notts 102 C4
Thorp Arch Leeds 124 C2
Thorpe Derbys 100 D3
Thorpe E R Yk 126 B2
Thorpe N York 131 J6
Thorpe Notts 102 C3
Thorpe Surrey 43 G6
Thorpe Abbotts Norfk 92 E7
Thorpe Arnold Leics 102 C7
Thorpe Audlin Wakefd 124 D7
Thorpe Bassett N York 134 D5
Thorpe Bay Sthend 46 E3
Thorpe by Water Rutlnd 88 C4
Thorpe Constantine Staffs 86 C2
Thorpe End Norfk 93 G2
Thorpe Green Essex 62 E4
Thorpe Green Suffk 77 L4
Thorpe Hesley Rothm 115 G3
Thorpe in Balne Donc 124 F7
Thorpe Langton Leics 87 L5
Thorpe Lea Surrey 43 G6
Thorpe-le-Soken Essex 62 E4
Thorpe le Street E R Yk 125 K2
Thorpe Malsor Nhants 88 B7
Thorpe Mandeville Nhants 73 G5
Thorpe Market Norfk 106 F5
Thorpe Marriot Norfk 92 E1
Thorpe Morieux Suffk 77 L4
Thorpeness Suffk 79 K3
Thorpe on the Hill Lincs 116 E7
Thorpe Park Surrey 43 G6
Thorpe St Andrew Norfk 92 F2
Thorpe St Peter Lincs 104 D1
Thorpe Salvin Rothm 115 K5
Thorpe Satchville Leics 87 K2
Thorpe Thewles S on T 141 J3
Thorpe Tilney Lincs 103 J2
Thorpe Underwood N York 133 G7
Thorpe Waterville Nhants 88 E7
Thorpe Willoughby N York 124 E4
Thorrington Essex 62 C4
Thorverton Devon 11 L4
Thrandeston Suffk 92 D7
Thrapston Nhants 88 E7
Threapwood Ches W 98 C4
Threapwood Staffs 100 B4
Threave S Ayrs 163 J7
Three Bridges W Susx 32 B5
Three Chimneys Kent 33 L5
Three Cocks Powys 68 D6
Three Counties Crematorium Essex 61 J3
Three Crosses Swans 51 H6
Three Cups Corner E Susx 20 D2
Threekingham Lincs 103 H5
Three Leg Cross E Susx 33 H6
Three Legged Cross Dorset 15 K2
Three Mile Cross Wokham 42 B6
Threemilestone Cnwll 3 K3
Three Miletown W Loth 176 E3
Three Oaks E Susx 21 G3
Threlkeld Cumb 137 J3
Threshers Bush Essex 60 D6
Threshfield N York 131 J6
Thrigby Norfk 93 K2
Thrintoft N York 132 D2
Thriplow Cambs 76 B5
Throcking Herts 60 B3
Throckley N u Ty 150 E2
Throckmorton Worcs 71 H4
Throop Bmouth 15 L4
Thropton Nthumb 158 C2
Throsk Stirlg 176 B1
Throughgate D & G 154 F5
Throwleigh Devon 11 G6
Throwley Forstal Kent 34 C4
Thrumpton Notts 101 J6
Thrumster Highld 231 L6
Thrunscoe NE Lin 127 H8
Thrupp Gloucs 55 K7
Thrussington Leics 87 J1
Thruxton Hants 28 F3
Thruxton Herefs 69 J7
Thrybergh Rothm 115 J3
Thulston Derbys 101 H6
Thundersley Essex 46 C3
Thurcaston Leics 87 H2
Thurcroft Rothm 115 J4
Thurgarton Norfk 106 E5
Thurgarton Notts 102 B3
Thurgoland Barns 114 F2
Thurlaston Leics 87 G4
Thurlaston Warwks 72 F1
Thurlbear Somset 25 K7
Thurlby Lincs 89 G1
Thurlby Lincs 102 E1
Thurlby Lincs 119 G6
Thurleigh Bed 74 F3
Thurlestone Devon 7 G7
Thurloxton Somset 25 L5
Thurlstone Barns 114 E2
Thurlton Norfk 93 J4
Thurmaston Leics 87 H2
Thurnby Leics 87 J3
Thurne Norfk 93 J1
Thurnham Kent 33 K2
Thurning Nhants 88 F6
Thurning Norfk 106 C6
Thurnscoe Barns 115 J1
Thurrock Services Thurr 45 L4
Thursby Cumb 148 B5
Thursford Norfk 106 B5
Thursley Surrey 30 E4
Thurso Highld 231 G2
Thurstaston Wirral 111 H5
Thurston Suffk 77 L2
Thurstonfield Cumb 148 B4
Thurstonland Kirk 123 H7
Thurton Norfk 93 G4
Thurvaston Derbys 100 E5
Thuxton Norfk 92 B3
Thwaite N York 139 K7
Thwaite Suffk 78 D2
Thwaite Head Cumb 129 H2
Thwaite St Mary Norfk 93 G4
Thwing E R Yk 135 G5
Tibbermore P & K 185 L3
Tibbers D & G 154 E3
Tibberton Gloucs 55 H4
Tibberton Worcs 70 F3
Tibberton Wrekin 99 G7
Tibbie Shiels Inn Border 166 C5
Tibenham Norfk 92 D5
Tibshelf Derbys 101 H1

Tibshelf Services Derbys 101 H1
Tibthorpe E R Yk 134 E7
Ticehurst E Susx 33 H7
Tichborne Hants 29 L5
Tickencote Rutlnd 88 E2
Tickenham N Som 38 C6
Tickhill Donc 115 L3
Ticklerton Shrops 83 J5
Ticknall Derbys 101 G7
Tickton E R Yk 126 D3
Tidcombe Wilts 40 F8
Tiddington Oxon 57 M6
Tiddington Warwks 72 B4
Tidebrook E Susx 33 G7
Tideford Cnwll 6 A4
Tidenham Gloucs 38 E2
Tideswell Derbys 114 D6
Tidmarsh W Berk 41 M5
Tidmington Warwks 72 C6
Tidworth Wilts 28 E2
Tiers Cross Pembks 48 F5
Tiffield Nhants 73 K4
Tigerton Angus 196 E4
Tigh a Ghearraidh W Isls 233 b6
Tigharry W Isls 233 b6
Tighnabruaich Ag & B 173 G4
Tigley Devon 7 H4
Tilbrook Cambs 74 F2
Tilbury Thurr 45 M5
Tile Cross Birm 85 L6
Tile Hill Covtry 86 C7
Tilehurst Readg 42 A5
Tilford Surrey 30 E3
Tilgate W Susx 31 L4
Tilham Street Somset 26 E4
Tillicoultry Clacks 185 J7
Tillietudlem S Lans 164 F1
Tillingham Essex 62 B7
Tillington Herefs 69 J5
Tillington W Susx 30 F6
Tillington Common Herefs 69 J5
Tillybirloch Abers 206 D4
Tillyfourie Abers 206 C3
Tillygreig Abers 207 G2
Tillyrie P & K 186 B6
Tilmanstone Kent 35 J4
Tilney All Saints Norfk 104 F8
Tilney High End Norfk 104 E8
Tilney St Lawrence Norfk 90 D2
Tilshead Wilts 28 B2
Tilstock Shrops 98 D5
Tilston Ches W 98 C3
Tilstone Fearnall Ches W 98 E1
Tilsworth C Beds 59 G3
Tilton on the Hill Leics 87 L3
Tiltups End Gloucs 39 J2
Timberland Lincs 103 J2
Timbersbrook Ches E 113 K8
Timberscombe Somset 24 E3
Timble N York 132 B8
Timpanheck D & G 156 B7
Timperley Traffd 113 H4
Timsbury BaNES 38 F8
Timsbury Hants 29 G6
Timsgarry W Isls 232 d2
Timsgearraidh W Isls 232 d2
Timworth Suffk 77 J2
Timworth Green Suffk 77 J2
Tincleton Dorset 14 E4
Tindale Cumb 149 G3
Tingewick Bucks 58 A2
Tingrith C Beds 59 G2
Tingwall Airport Shet 235 c6
Tingwell Ork 234 c5
Tinhay Devon 9 K7
Tinsley Sheff 115 H4
Tinsley Green W Susx 32 B5
Tintagel Cnwll 8 E7
Tintern Parva Mons 54 D7
Tintinhull Somset 26 D7
Tintwistle Derbys 114 A3
Tinwald D & G 155 H5
Tinwell Rutlnd 88 E3
Tipton Sandw 85 G5
Tipton Green Sandw 85 G5
Tipton St John Devon 12 E4
Tiptree Essex 61 L5
Tiptree Heath Essex 61 L5
Tirabad Powys 67 J6
Tiree Ag & B 188 D7
Tiree Airport Ag & B 188 C7
Tiretigan Ag & B 172 C6
Tirley Gloucs 55 J3
Tiroran Ag & B 181 G2
Tirphil Caerph 53 H7
Tirril Cumb 138 D2
Tisbury Wilts 27 L5
Tissington Derbys 100 D3
Titchberry Devon 22 C6
Titchfield Hants 17 G2
Titchmarsh Nhants 88 E7
Titchwell Norfk 105 J4
Tithby Notts 102 B5
Titley Herefs 69 G3
Titsey Surrey 32 D3
Titson Cnwll 9 H5
Tittensor Staffs 99 K5
Tittleshall Norfk 105 L7
Titton Worcs 70 E1
Tiverton Ches W 98 D1
Tiverton Devon 24 E8
Tivetshall St Margaret Norfk 92 E6
Tivetshall St Mary Norfk 92 E6
Tixall Staffs 99 L7
Tixover Rutlnd 88 E4
Toab Shet 235 c8
Tobermory Ag & B 189 L5
Toberonochy Ag & B 181 L5
Tobha Mor W Isls 233 b7
Tocher Abers 216 D7
Tochieneal Moray 215 L2
Tockenham Wilts 40 B4
Tockholes Bl w D 121 K6
Tockington S Glos 38 E3
Tockwith N York 133 G8
Todber Dorset 27 J7
Toddington C Beds 59 G3
Toddington Gloucs 56 B2
Toddington Services C Beds 59 G3
Todenham Gloucs 72 B7
Todhills Angus 196 C8
Todhills Services Cumb 148 C3
Todmorden Calder 122 D5
Todwick Rothm 115 J5
Toft Cambs 75 L4
Toft Lincs 88 F1
Toft Shet 235 c3
Toft Hill Dur 140 E2
Toft Monks Norfk 93 J4
Toft next Newton Lincs 117 H4
Toftrees Norfk 105 L6
Togston Nthumb 159 G2
Tokavaig Highld 199 J3
Tokers Green Oxon 42 B5
Tolastadh W Isls 232 g2
Toll W Isls 232 g2
Tolland Somset 25 H5
Tollard Royal Wilts 27 L7
Toll Bar Donc 124 E8
Toller Fratrum Dorset 14 B3
Toller Porcorum Dorset 14 B3
Tollerton N York 133 H6
Tollerton Notts 101 L5
Tollesbury Essex 62 A6
Tolleshunt D'Arcy Essex 61 L5
Tolleshunt Knights Essex 61 L5
Tolleshunt Major Essex 61 L5
Tolpuddle Dorset 14 E4
Tolsta W Isls 232 g2
Tolworth Gt Lon 44 D6
Tomatin Highld 213 J8
Tomchrasky Highld 201 K3
Tomdoun Highld 201 H5
Tomich Highld 211 L8
Tomich Highld 212 E5
Tomich Highld 222 F7
Tomich Highld 226 A7
Tomintoul Moray 204 E2
Tomnacross Highld 212 D6
Tomnavoulin Moray 204 F1
Tonbridge Kent 33 G4
Tondu Brdgnd 36 D4
Tonedale Somset 25 H6
Tong C Brad 123 J4
Tong Kent 34 C4
Tong Shrops 84 E3
Tonga W Isls 232 g2
Tonge Leics 101 H7
Tongham Surrey 30 E2
Tongland D & G 146 C4
Tong Norton Shrops 84 E2
Tongue Highld 229 J4
Tongwynlais Cardif 37 H4
Tonmawr Neath 36 C2
Tonna Neath 52 B7
Tonwell Herts 60 B5
Tonypandy Rhondd 36 F3
Tonyrefail Rhondd 36 F3
Toot Baldon Oxon 57 K7
Toot Hill Essex 60 E7
Toothill Swindn 40 C4
Tooting Gt Lon 44 F5
Tooting Bec Gt Lon 44 F5
Topcliffe N York 132 F4
Topcroft Norfk 92 F5
Topcroft Street Norfk 92 F5
Toppesfield Essex 77 G6
Toprow Norfk 92 E4
Topsham Devon 12 C5
Torbeg N Ayrs 162 A4
Torboll Highld 223 G2
Torbreck Highld 213 G6
Torbryan Devon 7 J3
Torcastle Highld 192 B2
Torcross Devon 7 J7
Tore Highld 212 F4
Torinturk Ag & B 172 D5
Torksey Lincs 116 D5
Tormarton S Glos 39 H5
Tormore N Ayrs 161 M3
Tornagrain Highld 213 J4
Tornaveen Abers 206 C4
Torness Highld 212 E8
Toronto Dur 140 F2
Torpenhow Cumb 147 L6
Torphichen W Loth 176 C4
Torphins Abers 206 C5
Torpoint Cnwll 6 C5
Torquay Torbay 7 L3
Torquay Crematorium Torbay 7 K3
Torquhan Border 177 L8
Torran Highld 209 J5
Torrance E Duns 175 H4
Torranyard N Ayrs 163 J1
Torridon Highld 210 D3
Torridon House Highld 210 D3
Torrin Highld 199 J2
Torrisdale Ag & B 161 K3
Torrisdale Highld 229 K3
Torrish Highld 227 G5
Torrisholme Lancs 129 K6
Torrobull Highld 226 A7
Torry C Aber 207 H4
Torryburn Fife 176 D2
Torteval Guern 236 b4
Torthorwald D & G 155 H6
Tortington W Susx 18 D5
Torton Worcs 84 E8
Tortworth S Glos 39 G2
Torvaig Highld 209 H5
Torver Cumb 137 J7
Torwood Falk 175 L2
Torwoodlee Border 167 G2
Torworth Notts 116 A4
Toscaig Highld 209 L6
Toseland Cambs 75 J3
Tosside Lancs 130 E7
Tostock Suffk 77 L2
Totaig Highld 208 C4
Tote Highld 208 F5
Tote Highld 209 H3
Totland IoW 16 D5
Totley Sheff 114 F5
Totnes Devon 7 J4
Toton Notts 101 J5
Totronald Ag & B 188 F5
Totscore Highld 208 F2
Tottenham Gt Lon 45 G3
Tottenhill Norfk 90 F2
Totteridge Gt Lon 44 E2
Totternhoe C Beds 59 G4
Tottington Bury 122 B7
Totton Hants 29 G8
Toulton Somset 25 J5
Toulvaddie Highld 223 J5
Tovil Kent 33 K3
Toward Ag & B 173 K5
Toward Quay Ag & B 173 J5
Towcester Nhants 73 K5
Towednack Cnwll 2 E4
Tower of London Gt Lon 45 G4
Towersey Oxon 58 B6
Towie Abers 205 K3
Tow Law Dur 150 E6
Town End Cambs 90 B4
Townend W Duns 174 D3
Townhead Barns 114 D2
Townhead D & G 155 H4
Townhead of Greenlaw D & G 146 C3
Townhill Fife 176 F1
Town Littleworth E Susx 19 L3
Towns End Hants 41 K8
Townshend Cnwll 3 G5
Town Street Suffk 91 H6
Town Yetholm Border 168 B4
Towthorpe C York 133 K7
Towton N York 124 D3
Towyn Conwy 110 D5
Toxteth Lpool 111 K4
Toynton All Saints Lincs 118 E8
Toy's Hill Kent 32 E3
Trabboch E Ayrs 163 K5
Trabbochburn E Ayrs 163 L5
Tradespark Highld 213 K3
Trafford Park Traffd 113 H3
Trallong Powys 52 E3
Tranent E Loth 177 L4
Tranmere Wirral 111 J4
Trantelbeg Highld 230 C5
Trantlemore Highld 230 C5
Trapp Carmth 51 J2
Traprain E Loth 178 D4
Traquair Border 166 E3
Trawden Lancs 122 D3
Trawsfynydd Gwynd 96 A5
Trealaw Rhondd 36 F3
Treales Lancs 120 F4
Trearddur Bay IoA 108 C5
Treaslane Highld 208 F4
Trebetherick Cnwll 4 E1
Treborough Somset 24 F4
Trebullett Cnwll 5 M1
Treburley Cnwll 6 A1
Trecastle Powys 52 D3
Trecwn Pembks 64 D7
Trecynon Rhondd 52 F7
Tredegar Blae G 53 H6
Tredington Gloucs 55 K3
Tredington Warwks 72 C5
Tredunnock Mons 38 B2
Treen Cnwll 2 D6
Treeton Rothm 115 H4
Trefasser Pembks 64 C6
Trefecca Powys 53 H2
Trefeglwys Powys 81 L5

Treffgarne Pembks 49 G3
Treffgarne Owen Pembks 48 E3
Trefforest Rhondd 37 G3
Trefilan Cerdgn 66 D3
Trefin Pembks 64 B7
Trefnant Denbgs 110 E7
Trefonen Shrops 97 K6
Trefor Gwynd 94 F4
Trefriw Conwy 109 L8
Tregadillett Cnwll 9 H7
Tregare Mons 54 B6
Tregaron Cerdgn 66 F3
Tregarth Gwynd 109 H7
Tregeare Cnwll 9 H7
Tregeiriog Wrexhm 97 J5
Tregele IoA 108 D3
Treglemais Pembks 48 D2
Tregonetha Cnwll 4 E3
Tregonning & Gwinear Mining District Cnwll 3 G5
Tregony Cnwll 4 E6
Tregorrick Cnwll 4 F5
Tregoyd Powys 68 E6
Tre-groes Cerdgn 65 L5
Tregynon Powys 82 C4
Tre-gynwr Carmth 50 E2
Trehafod Rhondd 37 G3
Trehan Cnwll 6 B4
Treharris Myr Td 37 H2
Treherbert Rhondd 52 E7
Trekenner Cnwll 6 A1
Treknow Cnwll 8 D7
Trelawnyd Flints 110 F5
Trelech Carmth 65 J7
Treleddyd-fawr Pembks 48 C2
Trelewis Myr Td 37 H2
Trelights Cnwll 8 C8
Trelill Cnwll 5 G1
Trellech Mons 54 D6
Trelogan Flints 110 F5
Tremadog Gwynd 95 K4
Tremail Cnwll 8 F7
Tremain Cerdgn 65 H5
Tremaine Cnwll 9 G6
Tremar Cnwll 5 K3
Trematon Cnwll 6 B4
Tremeirchion Denbgs 110 F6
Trenance Cnwll 4 D3
Trenance Cnwll 4 E2
Trench Wrekin 84 C2
Trenear Cnwll 3 H5
Treneglos Cnwll 9 G7
Trent Dorset 26 E7
Trentham C Stke 99 K4
Trentishoe Devon 23 K2
Trent Vale C Stke 99 K4
Treoes V Glam 36 E5
Treorchy Rhondd 36 E2
Trequite Cnwll 5 G1
Trerhyngyll V Glam 36 F5
Trerulefoot Cnwll 5 M4
Tresaith Cerdgn 65 J4
Tresco IoS 2 a1
Trescowe Cnwll 3 G5
Tresean Cnwll 4 C4
Tresham Gloucs 39 H3
Treshnish Isles Ag & B 189 G7
Tresillian Cnwll 4 D6
Treskinnick Cross Cnwll 9 G5
Tresmeer Cnwll 9 G7
Tresparrett Cnwll 8 F6
Tressait P & K 194 C4
Tresta Shet 235 c5
Tresta Shet 235 e3
Treswell Notts 116 C5
Treswithian Downs Crematorium Cnwll 3 H3
Tre Taliesin Cerdgn 80 E5
Trethevey Cnwll 8 E6
Trethewey Cnwll 2 C6
Trethurgy Cnwll 5 G5
Tretire Herefs 54 D4
Tretower Powys 53 J4
Treuddyn Flints 97 K2
Trevalga Cnwll 8 E6
Trevalyn Wrexhm 98 B2
Trevarrian Cnwll 4 D3
Treveal Cnwll 4 C4
Treveighan Cnwll 8 E8
Trevellas Downs Cnwll 3 J2
Trevelmond Cnwll 5 K3
Treverva Cnwll 3 K5
Trevescan Cnwll 2 C6
Treviscoe Cnwll 4 E5
Trevone Cnwll 4 D2
Trevor Wrexhm 97 L4
Trewalder Cnwll 8 E7
Trewarmett Cnwll 8 E7
Trewavas Mining District Cnwll 3 G6
Trewen Cnwll 9 H7
Trewint Cnwll 9 G8
Trewithian Cnwll 4 D7
Trewoon Cnwll 4 F5
Treyford W Susx 30 D7
Trimdon Dur 151 J7
Trimdon Colliery Dur 151 J7
Trimdon Grange Dur 151 J7
Trimingham Norfk 107 G5
Trimley St Martin Suffk 78 F6
Trimley St Mary Suffk 79 G7
Trimsaran Carmth 50 F5
Trimstone Devon 23 H3
Trinafour P & K 194 B4
Tring Herts 58 F5
Trinity Angus 196 F4
Trinity Jersey 236 d6
Trinity Gask P & K 185 K4
Triscombe Somset 25 J4
Trislaig Highld 191 L2
Trispen Cnwll 4 D5
Tritlington Nthumb 158 F4
Trochry P & K 194 F7
Troedyraur Cerdgn 65 K5
Troedyrhiw Myr Td 53 G7
Trois Bois Jersey 236 c6
Troon Cnwll 3 H4
Troon S Ayrs 163 H3
Tropical World Roundhay Park Leeds 123 L3
Trossachs Stirlg 184 B5
Trossachs Pier Stirlg 184 B6
Troston Suffk 91 K8
Trotshill Worcs 70 F4
Trottiscliffe Kent 33 H2
Trotton W Susx 30 D6
Troutbeck Cumb 137 L6
Troutbeck Bridge Cumb 137 L7
Troway Derbys 115 H5
Trowbridge Wilts 39 J8
Trowell Notts 101 J4
Trowell Services Notts 101 J4
Trowse Newton Norfk 92 F3
Trudoxhill Somset 27 H3
Trull Somset 25 K6
Trumpan Highld 208 C3
Trumpet Herefs 70 B6
Trumpington Cambs 76 C4
Trunch Norfk 107 G5
Truro Cnwll 4 C6
Trusham Devon 11 K7
Trusley Derbys 100 E5
Trusthorpe Lincs 119 G5
Trysull Staffs 84 F5
Tubney Oxon 57 H7
Tuckenhay Devon 7 J5
Tuckhill Shrops 84 E6
Tuckingmill Cnwll 3 H3
Tuckingmill Wilts 27 L5
Tuckton Bmouth 15 L4
Tuddenham Suffk 77 G1
Tuddenham Suffk 78 E5
Tudeley Kent 33 G4
Tudhoe Dur 151 G7
Tudweiliog Gwynd 94 D5
Tuffley Gloucs 55 J5
Tufton Hants 29 J3
Tufton Pembks 49 H2
Tugby Leics 87 L4
Tugford Shrops 83 L6
Tughall Nthumb 169 J4
Tullibody Clacks 185 H7
Tullich Highld 212 F8
Tullich Highld 223 J6
Tulliemet P & K 194 F5
Tulloch Abers 216 F7
Tullochgorm Ag & B 182 D7
Tulloch Station Highld 192 F1
Tullymurdoch P & K 195 J5
Tullynessle Abers 206 B2
Tulse Hill Gt Lon 44 F5
Tumble Carmth 51 G3
Tumby Lincs 103 L1
Tumby Woodside Lincs 103 L2
Tummel Bridge P & K 194 B5
Tunbridge Wells Kent 33 G5
Tundergarth D & G 155 L6
Tunley BaNES 39 G8
Tunstall E R Yk 127 H4
Tunstall Kent 34 B3
Tunstall Lancs 130 B5
Tunstall N York 140 F7
Tunstall Norfk 93 J2
Tunstall Staffs 99 H6
Tunstall Suffk 79 H4
Tunstall Sundld 151 J4
Tunstead Derbys 114 C6
Tunstead Norfk 107 G7
Tunstead Milton Derbys 114 B5
Turgis Green Hants 42 B8
Turkdean Gloucs 56 C4
Tur Langton Leics 87 K5
Turleigh Wilts 39 J7
Turnastone Herefs 69 G7
Turnberry S Ayrs 152 E2
Turnditch Derbys 100 F3
Turner's Hill W Susx 32 C6
Turnhouse C Edin 177 G4
Turnworth Dorset 14 F2
Turriff Abers 216 D4
Turton Bottoms Bl w D 121 L7
Turves Cambs 89 L4
Turvey Bed 74 D4
Turville Bucks 42 C3
Turweston Bucks 73 H6
Tushielaw Inn Border 166 D5
Tutbury Staffs 100 E6
Tutshill Gloucs 38 D2
Tuttington Norfk 106 F6
Tuxford Notts 116 C7
Twatt Ork 234 b5
Twatt Shet 235 c5
Twechar E Duns 175 J3
Tweedbank Border 167 H3
Tweedmouth Nthumb 179 K7
Tweedsmuir Border 165 L4
Twelveheads Cnwll 3 K3
Twemlow Green Ches E 113 H7
Twenty Lincs 103 J7
Twerton BaNES 39 G7
Twickenham Gt Lon 44 D5
Twigworth Gloucs 55 J4
Twineham W Susx 19 H2
Twinstead Essex 77 J6
Twitchen Devon 24 C5
Two Dales Derbys 114 F8
Two Gates Staffs 86 B4
Twycross Leics 86 D3
Twycross Zoo Leics 86 C3
Twyford Bucks 58 A3
Twyford Hants 29 J6
Twyford Leics 87 K2
Twyford Norfk 106 B7
Twyford Wokham 42 C5
Twynholm D & G 146 B4
Twyning Green Gloucs 70 F6
Twynllanan Carmth 51 L2
Twywell Nhants 88 D7
Tyberton Herefs 69 H6
Tyburn Birm 85 K5
Tycroes Carmth 51 H4
Tycrwyn Powys 97 H8
Tydd Gote Lincs 104 D8
Tydd St Giles Cambs 90 B1
Tydd St Mary Lincs 104 C8
Tye Green Essex 76 E7
Tyldesley Wigan 113 G2
Tyler Hill Kent 34 F3
Tylorstown Rhondd 36 F2
Ty-nant Conwy 96 F4
Tyndrum Stirlg 183 K2
Ty'n-dwr Denbgs 97 K4
Tynemouth N Tyne 151 J2
Tynemouth Crematorium N Tyne 151 J2
Tyne Tunnel S Tyne 151 H2
Tyninghame E Loth 178 D3
Tynron D & G 154 E4
Tynygraig Cerdgn 66 F1
Ty'n-y-Groes Conwy 109 L7
Tyn-y-nant Rhondd 37 G4
Tyringham M Keyn 74 C5
Tyseley Birm 85 K6
Tythegston Brdgnd 36 D5
Tytherington Ches E 113 K6
Tytherington S Glos 38 F3
Tytherington Wilts 27 K3
Tytherleigh Devon 13 H2
Tytherton Lucas Wilts 39 L5
Tywardreath Cnwll 5 H5
Tywyn Gwynd 80 D4

U

Ubbeston Green Suffk 79 G1
Ubley BaNES 38 D8
Uckfield E Susx 19 M2
Uckinghall Worcs 70 F6
Uckington Gloucs 55 K3
Uddingston S Lans 175 J6
Uddington S Lans 165 G3
Udimore E Susx 21 H2
Udny Green Abers 207 G1
Udny Station Abers 207 G1
Uffculme Devon 25 G8
Uffington Lincs 88 F3
Uffington Oxon 40 F3
Uffington Shrops 83 K2
Ufford C Pete 89 G3
Ufford Suffk 79 G4
Ufton Warwks 72 E3
Ufton Nervet W Berk 41 M6
Ugadale Ag & B 161 K4
Ugborough Devon 7 G5
Uggeshall Suffk 93 J7
Ugglebarnby N York 143 H5
Ughill Sheff 114 E4
Ugley Essex 60 E3
Ugley Green Essex 60 E3
Ugthorpe N York 143 G5
Uibhist A Deas W Isls 233 c8
Uibhist A Tuath W Isls 233 b6
Uig Ag & B 188 F5
Uig Highld 208 C4
Uig Highld 208 F2
Uig W Isls 232 d2
Uigshader Highld 209 G5
Uisken Ag & B 180 E4
Ulbster Highld 231 K7
Ulceby Lincs 118 F6
Ulceby N Linc 126 D7
Ulceby Skitter N Linc 126 E7
Ulcombe Kent 33 L4
Uldale Cumb 147 M7
Uley Gloucs 55 H7
Ulgham Nthumb 159 G4

Ullapool Highld 220 E3
Ullenhall Warwks 71 K2
Ulleskelf N York 124 D3
Ullesthorpe Leics 87 G6
Ulley Rothm 115 J4
Ullingswick Herefs 69 L4
Ullinish Lodge Hotel Highld 208 E6
Ullock Cumb 136 E3
Ullswater Cumb 138 B3
Ullswater Steamers Cumb 137 L4
Ulpha Cumb 128 E2
Ulrome E R Yk 135 J7
Ulsta Shet 235 d3
Ulva Ag & B 189 K7
Ulverley Green Solhll 85 K6
Ulverston Cumb 129 G4
Ulwell Dorset 15 J6
Ulzieside D & G 164 F7
Umberleigh Devon 23 J6
Unapool Highld 224 F2
Underbarrow Cumb 129 K2
Under Burnmouth Border 156 E5
Undercliffe C Brad 123 J4
Underdale Shrops 83 K2
Under River Kent 32 F3
Underwood Notts 101 J3
Undy Mons 38 C3
Union Mills IoM 237 c5
Unst Shet 235 d1
Unstone Derbys 115 G6
Upavon Wilts 28 C1
Upchurch Kent 46 D6
Upcott Devon 24 B5
Up Exe Devon 12 B2
Upgate Norfk 106 D8
Uphall Dorset 14 B2
Uphall W Loth 176 E4
Upham Devon 11 K3
Upham Hants 29 K7
Uphampton Herefs 69 H2
Uphampton Worcs 70 E2
Uphill N Som 37 L8
Up Holland Lancs 112 D1
Uplawmoor E Rens 174 E7
Upleadon Gloucs 55 H3
Upleatham R & Cl 142 D4
Uploders Dorset 13 L4
Uplowman Devon 24 F7
Uplyme Devon 13 H4
Up Marden W Susx 30 D8
Upminster Gt Lon 45 K3
Up Mudford Somset 26 E7
Up Nately Hants 30 B2
Upottery Devon 12 F2
Upper Affcot Shrops 83 J6
Upper Ardchronie Highld 222 E4
Upper Arley Worcs 84 D7
Upper Basildon W Berk 41 L5
Upper Beeding W Susx 19 G4
Upper Benefield Nhants 88 E5
Upper Bentley Worcs 71 H2
Upper Bighouse Highld 230 C4
Upper Boddington Nhants 72 F4
Upper Brailes Warwks 72 C6
Upper Breakish Highld 199 L2
Upper Broadheath Worcs 70 E4
Upper Broughton Notts 102 B7
Upper Bucklebury W Berk 41 K6
Upper Burgate Hants 28 D7
Upperby Cumb 148 D4
Upper Caldecote C Beds 75 H5
Upper Chapel Powys 67 L6
Upper Chicksgrove Wilts 27 L5
Upper Chute Wilts 28 F2
Upper Clapton Gt Lon 45 G3
Upper Clatford Hants 29 G3
Upper Cound Shrops 83 K3
Upper Cumberworth Kirk 123 J8
Upper Dallachy Moray 215 H2
Upper Deal Kent 35 K4
Upper Dean Bed 74 F2
Upper Denby Kirk 114 E1
Upper Dicker E Susx 20 B4
Upper Dounreay Highld 230 E3
Upper Dovercourt Essex 62 F2
Upper Drumbane Stirlg 184 E6
Upper Dunsforth N York 133 G6
Upper Eashing Surrey 30 F3
Upper Eathie Highld 213 J2
Upper Egleton Herefs 70 B5
Upper Elkstone Staffs 100 B2
Upper Ellastone Staffs 100 C4
Upper Farringdon Hants 30 B4
Upper Framilode Gloucs 55 H6
Upper Froyle Hants 30 C3
Upperglen Highld 208 E4
Upper Godney Somset 26 C3
Upper Gravenhurst C Beds 75 G7
Upper Green W Berk 41 G7
Upper Grove Common Herefs 54 E3
Upper Hale Surrey 30 D2
Upper Halliford Surrey 43 H6
Upper Hambleton Rutlnd 88 C3
Upper Harbledown Kent 34 F3
Upper Hartfield E Susx 32 E6
Upper Hatherley Gloucs 55 L4
Upper Heaton Kirk 123 H6
Upper Helmsley N York 133 L7
Upper Hergest Herefs 68 F4
Upper Heyford Nhants 73 J3
Upper Heyford Oxon 57 J3
Upper Hill Herefs 69 J4
Upper Hopton Kirk 123 J6
Upper Hulme Staffs 100 A1
Upper Inglesham Swindn 40 D2
Upper Killay Swans 51 H6
Upper Kinchrackine Ag & B 183 G2
Upper Lambourn W Berk 40 F4
Upper Landywood Staffs 85 H3
Upper Langford N Som 38 C7
Upper Langwith Derbys 115 K7
Upper Largo Fife 187 G6
Upper Leigh Staffs 100 A5
Upper Lochton Abers 206 D6
Upper Longdon Staffs 85 J2
Upper & Lower Stondon C Beds 75 H7
Upper Lybster Highld 231 J7
Upper Lydbrook Gloucs 54 E5
Upper Lye Herefs 69 H2
Uppermill Oldham 113 M1
Upper Milton Worcs 84 E8
Upper Minety Wilts 40 A3
Upper Mulben Moray 215 H4
Upper Netchwood Shrops 83 L5
Upper Nobut Staffs 100 B5
Upper Norwood W Susx 18 C3
Upper Poppleton C York 133 H8
Upper Ratley Hants 28 F6
Upper Rissington Gloucs 56 D4
Upper Rochford Worcs 70 B2
Upper Ruscoe D & G 145 L3
Upper Sapey Herefs 70 C2
Upper Seagry Wilts 39 L4
Upper Shelton C Beds 74 E5
Upper Sheringham Norfk 106 D4
Upper Skelmorlie N Ayrs 173 L5
Upper Slaughter Gloucs 56 D4
Upper Soudley Gloucs 54 F6
Upper Standen Kent 35 H6
Upper Stoke Norfk 92 F3
Upper Stowe Nhants 73 J3
Upper Street Hants 28 D7
Upper Street Norfk 93 H1
Upper Street Norfk 107 G8
Upper Street Suffk 77 H4
Upper Street Suffk 78 D4
Upper Sundon C Beds 59 H3
Upper Swell Gloucs 56 D3
Upper Tasburgh Norfk 92 E4
Upper Tean Staffs 100 A5
Upperthong Kirk 123 H8
Upperton W Susx 30 F6
Upper Town Herefs 69 L5
Uppertown Highld 231 L1
Upper Town N Som 38 D7
Upper Town Suffk 77 K2
Upper Tumble Carmth 51 G3
Upper Tysoe Warwks 72 D5
Upper Victoria Angus 187 J1
Upper Wardington Oxon 72 F5
Upper Welland Worcs 70 D6
Upper Wellingham E Susx 19 L3
Upper Weybread Suffk 92 F7
Upper Wield Hants 29 L4
Upper Winchendon Bucks 58 C5
Upper Woodford Wilts 28 C4
Upper Wraxall Wilts 39 J5
Uppingham Rutlnd 88 C4
Uppington Shrops 83 L2
Upsall N York 133 G3
Upsettlington Border 168 C1
Upshire Essex 60 C7
Up Somborne Hants 29 H5
Upstreet Kent 35 G3
Upton Bucks 58 C5
Upton C Pete 89 G4
Upton Cambs 89 H7
Upton Ches W 112 B7
Upton Cnwll 5 L2
Upton Devon 7 G7
Upton Devon 12 E2
Upton Dorset 14 E5
Upton Dorset 15 J4
Upton Halton 112 C4
Upton Hants 29 G1
Upton Hants 29 G7
Upton Leics 86 D4
Upton Lincs 116 E4
Upton Norfk 93 H2
Upton Notts 102 B2
Upton Notts 116 C6
Upton Oxon 41 K3
Upton Slough 43 G5
Upton Somset 24 F5
Upton Somset 26 C6
Upton Wakefd 124 D7
Upton Wirral 111 J4
Upton Bishop Herefs 54 F3
Upton Cheyney S Glos 39 G6
Upton Cressett Shrops 84 B5
Upton Grey Hants 30 B2
Upton Hellions Devon 11 J4
Upton Lovell Wilts 27 L4
Upton Magna Shrops 83 K2
Upton Noble Somset 27 G4
Upton Pyne Devon 11 L5
Upton St Leonards Gloucs 55 K5
Upton Scudamore Wilts 27 K2
Upton Snodsbury Worcs 71 G4
Upton-upon-Severn Worcs 70 F6
Upton Warren Worcs 71 G2
Upwaltham W Susx 18 C3
Upwell Norfk 90 C3
Upwood Cambs 89 J6
Urchfont Wilts 40 B8
Urmston Traffd 113 H3
Urquhart Moray 215 G2
Urquhart Castle Highld 212 E8
Urra N York 142 C6
Urray Highld 212 D4
Usan Angus 197 H5
Ushaw Moor Dur 151 G6
Usk Mons 54 B7
Usselby Lincs 117 H3
Usworth Sundld 151 H4
Utkinton Ches W 112 D7
Utley C Brad 122 F3
Uton Devon 11 J5
Utterby Lincs 118 D3
Uttoxeter Staffs 100 C5
Uxbridge Gt Lon 43 H4
Uyeasound Shet 235 d2
Uzmaston Pembks 49 G5

V

Vale Guern 236 d2
Vale of Glamorgan Crematorium V Glam 37 H6
Valley IoA 108 C5
Valtos Highld 209 H2
Valtos W Isls 232 d2
Vange Essex 46 B3
Vatsetter Shet 235 d3
Vatten Highld 208 D5
Vaynor Myr Td 53 G6
Veensgarth Shet 235 c6
Velindre Powys 68 D7
Venngreen Devon 9 K3
Venn Ottery Devon 12 D4
Ventnor IoW 17 G6
Venton Devon 6 E4
Vernham Dean Hants 29 G1
Vernham Street Hants 41 G8
Verwood Dorset 15 K2
Veryan Cnwll 4 E7
Vickerstown Cumb 128 E5
Victoria Cnwll 4 F4
Vidlin Shet 235 d4
Viewfield Moray 215 G2
Viewpark N Lans 175 J6
Vigo Kent 45 M7
Village de Putron Guern 236 d3
Ville la Bas Jersey 236 a5
Villiaze Guern 236 c3
Vines Cross E Susx 20 C3
Vinters Park Crematorium Kent 33 K2

Virginia Water Surrey 43 G6
Virginstow Devon 9 K6
Vobster Somset 27 G2
Voe Shet 235 c4
Vowchurch Herefs 69 G7

W

Waberthwaite Cumb 128 D2
Wackerfield Dur 140 E3
Wacton Norfk 92 E5
Wadborough Worcs 70 F5
Waddesdon Bucks 58 C5
Waddesdon Manor Bucks 58 B5
Waddeton Devon 7 K4
Waddingham Lincs 117 G3
Waddington Lancs 121 L2
Waddington Lincs 116 F8
Wadebridge Cnwll 4 F2
Wadeford Somset 13 H1
Wadenhoe Nhants 88 E6
Wadesmill Herts 60 B4
Wadhurst E Susx 33 H6
Wadshelf Derbys 114 F7
Wadworth Donc 115 K3
Wainfleet All Saints Lincs 104 D2
Wainfleet St Mary Lincs 104 D2
Wainhouse Corner Cnwll 9 G5
Wainscott Medway 46 C6
Wainstalls Calder 122 F5
Waitby Cumb 139 H5
Waithe Lincs 118 C2
Wakefield Wakefd 123 L6
Wakefield Crematorium Wakefd 123 L7
Wake Green Birm 85 K6
Wakehurst Place W Susx 32 C6
Wakerley Nhants 88 D4
Wakes Colne Essex 61 L3
Walberswick Suffk 93 K8
Walberton W Susx 18 C4
Walbutt D & G 146 D2
Walcombe Somset 26 D3
Walcot Lincs 103 H5
Walcot Shrops 83 L2
Walcot Swindn 40 D4
Walcote Leics 87 H6
Walcot Green Norfk 92 D7
Walcott Lincs 103 J2
Walcott Norfk 107 H6
Walden Stubbs N York 124 E6
Walderslade Medway 46 C7
Walderton W Susx 17 L1
Walditch Dorset 13 L4
Waldridge Dur 151 G5
Waldringfield Suffk 79 G5
Waldron E Susx 20 B2
Wales Rothm 115 J5
Wales Somset 26 E6
Walesby Lincs 117 J3
Walesby Notts 116 B7
Wales Millennium Centre Cardif 37 J5
Walford Herefs 54 E4
Walford Herefs 83 H8
Walford Heath Shrops 98 C8
Walgherton Ches E 99 G3
Walgrave Nhants 74 B1
Walkden Salfd 113 G2
Walker N u Ty 151 H3
Walkerburn Border 166 E3
Walkeringham Notts 116 C3
Walkerith Lincs 116 C3
Walkern Herts 59 M3
Walker's Heath Birm 85 J7
Walkerton Fife 186 D6
Walkford Dorset 16 B4
Walkhampton Devon 6 D2
Walkington E R Yk 126 B3
Walkley Sheff 115 G4
Walk Mill Lancs 122 C5
Walkwood Worcs 71 J2
Wall Nthumb 150 A2
Wall Staffs 85 K3
Wallacetown S Ayrs 153 G2
Wallacetown S Ayrs 163 J5
Wallands Park E Susx 19 L4
Wallasey Wirral 111 J3
Wall Heath Dudley 84 F5
Wallingford Oxon 41 L3
Wallington Gt Lon 44 F6
Wallington Hants 17 H2
Wallington Herts 75 K7
Wallisdown Poole 15 K4
Walls Shet 235 b5
Wallsend N Tyne 151 H2
Wallyford E Loth 177 K4
Walmer Kent 35 K5
Walmer Bridge Lancs 121 G5
Walmley Birm 85 K5
Walmley Ash Birm 85 K5
Walpole Suffk 93 H8
Walpole Cross Keys Norfk 104 E8
Walpole Highway Norfk 90 D2
Walpole St Andrew Norfk 104 D8
Walpole St Peter Norfk 90 C1
Walsall Wsall 85 H4
Walsden Calder 122 D6
Walsgrave on Sowe Covtry 86 E7
Walsham le Willows Suffk 78 B1
Walshford N York 132 F8
Walsoken Norfk 90 C2
Walston S Lans 165 K1
Walsworth Herts 59 K3
Walter's Ash Bucks 42 D2
Waltham Kent 34 E5
Waltham NE Lin 118 C2
Waltham Abbey Essex 60 C7
Waltham Chase Hants 29 K7
Waltham Cross Herts 60 B7
Waltham on the Wolds Leics 102 D7
Waltham St Lawrence W & M 42 D5
Walthamstow Gt Lon 45 G3
Walton Cumb 148 F3
Walton Derbys 115 G7
Walton Leeds 124 C2
Walton Leics 87 H6
Walton M Keyn 74 C7
Walton Powys 68 F3
Walton Somset 26 C4
Walton Suffk 79 G7
Walton W Susx 17 M2
Walton Wakefd 123 L6
Walton Wrekin 98 E8
Walton Cardiff Gloucs 55 K2
Walton East Pembks 49 H3
Walton-in-Gordano N Som 38 B5
Walton Lea Crematorium Warrtn 112 E4
Walton-le-Dale Lancs 121 H5
Walton-on-Thames Surrey 43 J6
Walton-on-the-Hill Staffs 99 L7
Walton on the Hill Surrey 31 L1
Walton-on-the-Naze Essex 62 F4
Walton on the Wolds Leics 101 L8
Walton-on-Trent Derbys 100 E8
Walton Park N Som 38 B6
Walton West Pembks 48 E5
Waltonwrays Crematorium N York 122 E1
Walworth Darltn 141 G4
Walworth Gt Lon 45 G4
Walwyn's Castle Pembks 48 E5
Wambrook Somset 13 H2
Wanborough Surrey 30 F2
Wanborough Swindn 40 E4
Wandsworth Gt Lon 44 E5
Wangford Suffk 93 K7
Wanlip Leics 87 H2
Wanlockhead D & G 165 G6
Wannock E Susx 20 C5
Wansford C Pete 88 F4
Wansford E R Yk 135 G7
Wanshurst Green Kent 33 K4
Wanstead Gt Lon 45 H3
Wanstrow Somset 27 G3
Wanswell Gloucs 55 G7
Wantage Oxon 41 H3
Wappenbury Warwks 72 E2
Wappenham Nhants 73 J5
Warbleton E Susx 20 C3
Warborough Oxon 41 L2
Warboys Cambs 89 K7
Warbreck Bpool 120 D3
Warbstow Cnwll 9 G6
Warburton Traffd 113 G4
Warcop Cumb 139 H4
Warden Nthumb 150 A2
Ward End Birm 85 K5
Wardington Oxon 72 F5
Wardle Ches E 98 E2
Wardle Rochdl 122 D6
Wardley Gatesd 151 H3
Wardley Rutlnd 88 B4
Wardlow Derbys 114 D6
Wardy Hill Cambs 90 C6
Ware Herts 60 B5
Wareham Dorset 15 H5
Warehorne Kent 34 D7
Warenford Nthumb 169 H4
Wareside Herts 60 C5
Waresley Cambs 75 J4
Warfield Br For 42 E6
Warfleet Devon 7 K6
Wargrave Wokham 42 C5
Warham All Saints Norfk 105 M4
Warham St Mary Norfk 105 M4
Wark Nthumb 157 L6
Wark Nthumb 168 C2
Warkleigh Devon 23 K6
Warkton Nhants 88 C7
Warkworth Nhants 72 F6
Warkworth Nthumb 159 G2
Warlaby N York 132 E2
Warleggan Cnwll 5 J3
Warley Town Calder 122 F5
Warlingham Surrey 32 C2
Warmfield Wakefd 124 B6
Warmingham Ches E 99 G1
Warmington Nhants 88 F5
Warmington Warwks 72 E5
Warminster Wilts 27 K3
Warmley S Glos 38 F5
Warmsworth Donc 115 K2
Warmwell Dorset 14 E5
Warner Bros Studio Tour Herts 59 H7
Warnford Hants 29 L6
Warnham W Susx 31 J5
Warningcamp W Susx 18 D4
Warninglid W Susx 31 L6
Warren Ches E 113 K7
Warren Pembks 48 F7
Warrenhill S Lans 165 J2
Warren Row W & M 42 D4
Warren Street Kent 34 C4
Warrington M Keyn 74 C4
Warrington Warrtn 112 E4
Warriston C Edin 177 H4
Warriston Crematorium C Edin 177 H3
Warsash Hants 16 F2
Warslow Staffs 100 C2
Warter E R Yk 125 K1
Warthermaske N York 132 C4
Warthill N York 133 K7
Wartling E Susx 20 D4
Wartnaby Leics 102 B7
Warton Lancs 120 E5
Warton Lancs 129 K5
Warton Warwks 86 C3
Warwick Warwks 72 C2
Warwick Bridge Cumb 148 E4
Warwick Castle Warwks 72 C2
Warwick Services Warwks 72 D3
Wasbister Ork 234 c4
Wasdale Head Cumb 137 G5
Washaway Cnwll 5 G2
Washbourne Devon 7 J5
Washbrook Suffk 78 D6
Washfield Devon 11 L2
Washford Somset 25 G3
Washford Pyne Devon 11 J3
Washingborough Lincs 117 G7
Washington Sundld 151 H4
Washington W Susx 18 F3
Washington Services Gatesd 151 G4
Washwood Heath Birm 85 K5
Wasperton Warwks 72 C3
Wass N York 133 H4
Wast Water Cumb 137 G6
Watchet Somset 25 G3
Watchfield Oxon 40 E3
Watchgate Cumb 138 D7
Water Devon 11 H8
Waterbeach Cambs 76 C2
Waterbeach W Susx 18 B4
Waterbeck D & G 155 M6
Water End E R Yk 125 J3
Waterfall Staffs 100 B3
Waterfoot E Rens 175 G7
Waterford Herts 60 A5
Waterheads Border 177 H7
Waterhouses Staffs 100 B3
Wateringbury Kent 33 H3
Waterloo Highld 199 K2
Waterloo N Lans 175 L7
Waterloo P & K 195 G8
Waterloo Pembks 49 G6
Waterloo Sefton 111 K2
Waterlooville Hants 17 J1
Watermillock Cumb 138 C3
Water Newton Cambs 89 G4
Water Orton Warwks 85 L5
Waterperry Oxon 57 L6
Waterrow Somset 25 G6
Watersfield W Susx 18 D3
Waterside Bl w D 121 K5
Waterside E Ayrs 163 K7
Waterside E Ayrs 163 L2
Waterside E Duns 175 J4
Waterstein Highld 208 B5
Waterstock Oxon 57 M6
Waterston Pembks 48 F6
Water Stratford Bucks 73 J7
Waters Upton Wrekin 98 F8
Watford Herts 43 J2
Watford Nhants 73 H2
Watford Gap Services Nhants 73 H2
Wath N York 132 B6
Wath N York 132 E4
Wath upon Dearne Rothm 115 H2
Watlington Norfk 90 E2
Watlington Oxon 42 B2

Watten Highld 231 J5
Wattisfield Suffk 92 B8
Wattisham Suffk 78 B4
Watton Dorset 13 L4
Watton E R Yk 126 C1
Watton Norfk 91 K4
Watton-at-Stone Herts 60 A4
Wattston N Lans 175 K4
Wattsville Caerph 37 J3
Waulkmill Abers 206 C6
Waunarlwydd Swans 51 H6
Waunfawr Cerdgn 80 E6
Waunfawr Gwynd 95 J2
Wavendon M Keyn 74 C6
Waveney Crematorium Suffk 93 J6
Waverbridge Cumb 147 L5
Waverton Ches W 112 C8
Waverton Cumb 147 L5
Wawne E R Yk 126 D3
Waxham Norfk 107 J7
Wayford Somset 13 K2
Waytown Dorset 13 L3
Way Village Devon 11 K3
Weacombe Somset 25 H4
Weald Oxon 56 F7
Wealdstone Gt Lon 44 D3
Weardley Leeds 123 K2
Weare Somset 26 B2
Weare Giffard Devon 23 G6
Wearhead Dur 149 L6
Wearne Somset 26 B5
Wear Valley Crematorium Dur 141 G2
Weasenham All Saints Norfk 105 K7
Weasenham St Peter Norfk 105 K7
Weaste Salfd 113 J2
Weaverham Ches W 112 E6
Weaverthorpe N York 134 E5
Webheath Worcs 71 H2
Wedderlairs Abers 216 F7
Weddington Warwks 86 D5
Wedhampton Wilts 40 B8
Wedmore Somset 26 C2
Wednesbury Sandw 85 H4
Wednesfield Wolves 85 G4
Weedon Bucks 58 D4
Weedon Nhants 73 J3
Weedon Lois Nhants 73 H5
Weeford Staffs 85 K3
Weeke Hants 29 J5
Weekley Nhants 88 C7
Week St Mary Cnwll 9 H5
Weel E R Yk 126 D3
Weeley Essex 62 D4
Weeley Crematorium Essex 62 D4
Weeley Heath Essex 62 D4
Weem P & K 194 D6
Weethley Warwks 71 J4
Weeting Norfk 91 H5
Weeton E R Yk 127 H6
Weeton Lancs 120 E4
Weeton N York 123 K2
Weetwood Leeds 123 K3
Weir Lancs 122 C5
Weir Quay Devon 6 C3
Weisdale Shet 235 c5
Welborne Norfk 92 C2
Welbourn Lincs 102 F2
Welburn N York 133 L6
Welbury N York 141 J6
Welby Lincs 102 F5
Welcombe Devon 22 C7
Weldon Nhants 88 D5
Welford Nhants 87 J7
Welford W Berk 41 H5
Welford-on-Avon Warwks 71 K4
Welham Leics 87 L5
Welham Notts 116 B5
Welham Green Herts 59 L6
Well Hants 30 C3
Well Lincs 118 F6
Well N York 132 D3
Welland Worcs 70 E6
Wellbank Angus 196 D8
Wellesbourne Warwks 72 C4
Well Head Herts 59 K3
Welling Gt Lon 45 J5
Wellingborough Nhants 74 C2
Wellingham Norfk 105 L7
Wellingore Lincs 103 G2
Wellington Cumb 136 F6
Wellington Herefs 69 K5
Wellington Somset 25 H7
Wellington Wrekin 84 B2
Wellington Heath Herefs 70 C6
Wellow BaNES 39 H8
Wellow IoW 16 E5
Wellow Notts 116 A7
Wells Somset 26 D3
Wells-next-the-Sea Norfk 105 L4
Wellstye Green Essex 61 G4
Welltree P & K 185 K3
Wellwood Fife 176 E2
Welney Norfk 90 D5
Welshampton Shrops 98 C5
Welsh Frankton Shrops 98 A6
Welsh Newton Herefs 54 D4
Welshpool Powys 82 E3
Welsh St Donats V Glam 36 F5
Welton Cumb 148 C6
Welton E R Yk 126 B5
Welton Lincs 117 G5
Welton Nhants 73 H2
Welton le Marsh Lincs 119 G7
Welton le Wold Lincs 118 C4
Welwick E R Yk 127 H6
Welwyn Herts 59 L5
Welwyn Garden City Herts 59 L5
Wem Shrops 98 D6
Wembdon Somset 25 L4
Wembley Gt Lon 44 D3
Wembury Devon 6 D6
Wembworthy Devon 10 F3
Wemyss Bay Inver 173 L4
Wendens Ambo Essex 76 D7
Wendlebury Oxon 57 K4
Wendling Norfk 91 L2
Wendover Bucks 58 E6
Wendron Cnwll 3 H5
Wendron Mining District Cnwll 3 J5
Wendy Cambs 75 K5
Wenhaston Suffk 93 J7
Wennington Cambs 89 J7
Wennington Gt Lon 45 K4
Wennington Lancs 130 C5
Wensley Derbys 100 E1
Wensley N York 131 K2
Wentbridge Wakefd 124 D6
Wentnor Shrops 83 H5
Wentworth Cambs 90 C7
Wentworth Rothm 115 G2
Wenvoe V Glam 37 H6
Weobley Herefs 69 H4
Wepham W Susx 18 E4
Wereham Norfk 90 F3
Werrington C Pete 89 H3
Werrington Cnwll 9 J7
Wervin Ches W 112 B6
Wesham Lancs 120 F4
Wessex Vale Crematorium Hants 29 J7
Wessington Derbys 101 G2
West Acre Norfk 91 H1
West Alvington Devon 7 G6
West Anstey Devon 24 D6
West Ashby Lincs 118 C6
West Ashling W Susx 17 M2
West Ashton Wilts 27 K1
West Auckland Dur 140 F3
West Ayton N York 134 F3
West Bagborough Somset 25 J5
West Bank Halton 112 D5
West Barkwith Lincs 117 K5
West Barnby N York 143 G5
West Barns E Loth 178 E3
West Barsham Norfk 105 L5
West Bay Dorset 13 L4
West Beckham Norfk 106 D5
West Bedfont Surrey 43 H5
Westbere Kent 35 G3
West Bergholt Essex 62 A3
West Berkshire Crematorium W Berk 41 K6
West Bexington Dorset 14 A5
West Bilney Norfk 91 G1
West Blatchington Br & H 19 J4
West Boldon S Tyne 151 J3
Westborough Lincs 102 D4
Westbourne Bmouth 15 K4
Westbourne W Susx 17 L2
West Bowling C Brad 123 H4
West Bradenham Norfk 91 K2
West Bradford Lancs 121 L2
West Bradley Somset 26 E4
West Bretton Wakefd 123 K7
West Bridgford Notts 101 L5
West Bromwich Sandw 85 H5
Westbrook Kent 35 J2
Westbrook W Berk 41 H6
West Buckland Devon 23 K5
West Buckland Somset 25 J7
West Burrafirth Shet 235 b5
West Burton N York 131 J3
Westbury Bucks 73 J7
Westbury Shrops 83 G2
Westbury Wilts 27 K2
Westbury Leigh Wilts 27 K2
Westbury on Severn Gloucs 55 G5
Westbury-on-Trym Bristl 38 E5
Westbury-sub-Mendip Somset 26 D2
West Butterwick N Linc 116 D1
Westby Lancs 120 E4
West Byfleet Surrey 43 H7
West Cairngaan D & G 144 D8
West Caister Norfk 93 K2
West Calder W Loth 176 D5
West Camel Somset 26 E6
West Chaldon Dorset 14 E5
West Challow Oxon 41 G3
West Charleton Devon 7 H7
West Chiltington W Susx 18 E3
West Chinnock Somset 26 C8
West Clandon Surrey 31 H2
West Cliffe Kent 35 J5
Westcliff-on-Sea Sthend 46 E3
West Coker Somset 26 D8
Westcombe Somset 27 G4
West Compton Somset 26 E3
West Compton Abbas Dorset 14 B4
Westcote Gloucs 56 E4
Westcote Barton Oxon 57 H3
Westcott Bucks 58 B5
Westcott Devon 12 C2
Westcott Surrey 31 J2
West Cottingwith N York 125 G3
Westcourt Wilts 40 E7
West Cowick E R Yk 124 F6
West Cross Swans 51 H7
West Curthwaite Cumb 148 B5
Westdean E Susx 20 B5
West Dean W Susx 18 B3
West Dean Wilts 28 E6
West Deeping Lincs 89 G2
West Derby Lpool 111 L3
West Dereham Norfk 90 F4
West Down Devon 23 H3
Westdowns Cnwll 8 E7
West Drayton Gt Lon 43 H4
West Drayton Notts 116 B6
West Dunnet Highld 231 J2
West Ella E R Yk 126 C5
West End Bed 74 E4
West End Hants 29 J8
West End N Som 38 C6
West End Norfk 93 K2
West End Surrey 42 F7
West End Wilts 27 M6
West End Green Hants 42 A7
Wester Aberchalder Highld 202 E2
Westerdale Highld 231 G5
Westerdale N York 142 E6
Westerfield Suffk 78 E5
Westergate W Susx 18 C5
Westerham Kent 32 D3
Westerhope N u Ty 150 F2
Westerland Devon 7 K4
Westerleigh S Glos 39 G4
Westerleigh Crematorium S Glos 39 G5
Western Isles W Isls 232 d5
Wester Ochiltree W Loth 176 D4
Wester Pitkierie Fife 187 J6
Wester Ross Highld 220 C5
Westerton of Rossie Angus 197 G5
Westerwick Shet 235 c6
West Farleigh Kent 33 J3
West Farndon Nhants 73 G4
West Felton Shrops 97 M7
Westfield BaNES 26 F2
Westfield Cumb 136 D2
Westfield E Susx 21 G3
Westfield Highld 230 F3
Westfield N Lans 175 J4
Westfield Norfk 92 B2
Westfield W Loth 176 C4
Westfields of Rattray P & K 195 J6
Westgate Dur 150 A7
Westgate N Linc 125 J8
Westgate on Sea Kent 35 J2
West Grafton Wilts 40 E7
West Green Hants 30 C1
West Grimstead Wilts 28 E6
West Grinstead W Susx 31 K6
West Haddlesey N York 124 E5
West Haddon Nhants 73 J1
West Hagbourne Oxon 41 K3
West Hagley Worcs 84 F7
Westhall Suffk 93 J7
West Hallam Derbys 101 H4
West Halton N Linc 125 L6
Westham Dorset 14 C6
Westham E Susx 20 D5
West Ham Gt Lon 45 H4
Westham Somset 26 B3
Westhampnett W Susx 18 B4
West Handley Derbys 115 H6
West Hanney Oxon 41 H2
West Hanningfield Essex 61 H7
West Harnham Wilts 28 C5
West Harptree BaNES 38 E8

West Harting W Susx 30 C7
West Hatch Somset 25 L7
West Hatch Wilts 27 L5
West Haven Angus 187 J1
Westhay Somset 26 C3
West Heath Birm 85 J7
West Helmsdale Highld 227 H5
West Hendred Oxon 41 H3
West Hertfordshire Crematorium Herts 59 J7
West Heslerton N York 134 E4
West Hewish N Som 38 B7
Westhide Herefs 69 L5
Westhill Abers 206 F4
West Hill Devon 12 D4
West Hoathly W Susx 32 C6
West Holme Dorset 15 G5
Westhope Herefs 69 J4
Westhope Shrops 83 J6
West Horndon Essex 45 M3
Westhorpe Lincs 103 L6
Westhorpe Suffk 78 C2
West Horrington Somset 26 E3
West Horsley Surrey 31 H2
West Hougham Kent 35 H6
Westhoughton Bolton 112 F1
Westhouse N York 130 D5
Westhouses Derbys 101 H2
West Howe Bmouth 15 K4
Westhumble Surrey 31 K2
West Huntingtower P & K 185 M3
West Huntspill Somset 25 L3
West Hythe Kent 34 F7
West Ilsley W Berk 41 J4
West Itchenor W Susx 17 L3
West Kennett Wilts 40 C6
West Kilbride N Ayrs 173 L8
West Kingsdown Kent 45 L7
West Kington Wilts 39 J5
West Kirby Wirral 111 H4
West Knapton N York 134 D4
West Knighton Dorset 14 D5
West Knoyle Wilts 27 K5
Westlake Devon 6 F5
West Lambrook Somset 26 B7
West Langdon Kent 35 J5
West Lavington W Susx 30 E7
West Lavington Wilts 28 A2
West Layton N York 140 E5
West Leake Notts 101 K7
Westleigh Devon 23 G5
Westleigh Devon 25 G7
West Leigh Somset 25 H5
Westleton Suffk 79 J2
West Lexham Norfk 91 J1
Westley Suffk 77 J2
Westley Waterless Cambs 76 E3
West Lilling N York 133 K6
Westlington Bucks 58 C6
West Linton Border 176 F7
Westlinton Cumb 148 D3
West Littleton S Glos 39 H5
West Lockinge Oxon 41 H3
West London Crematorium Gt Lon 44 E4
West Lothian Crematorium W Loth 176 D5
West Lulworth Dorset 14 F6
West Lutton N York 134 E5
West Lydford Somset 26 E5
West Lyng Somset 25 L5
West Lynn Norfk 104 F7
West Malling Kent 33 H2
West Malvern Worcs 70 D5
West Marden W Susx 30 C8
West Markham Notts 116 B6
Westmarsh Kent 35 H3
West Marsh NE Lin 127 G8
West Marton N York 122 D1
West Melbury Dorset 27 K7
West Meon Hants 29 M6
West Mersea Essex 62 B5
Westmeston E Susx 19 K3
West Midland Safari Park Worcs 84 E7
Westmill Herts 60 B3
West Milton Dorset 13 L3
Westminster Gt Lon 44 F4
West Minster Kent 46 E5
Westminster Abbey & Palace Gt Lon 44 F4
West Molesey Surrey 43 J6
West Monkton Somset 25 K5
West Moors Dorset 15 K2
West Morden Dorset 15 G4
West Morriston Border 167 J2
West Mudford Somset 26 E7
Westmuir Angus 196 B5
West Ness N York 133 L4
Westnewton Cumb 147 K6
West Newton E R Yk 126 F3
West Newton Norfk 105 H6
West Newton Somset 25 L5
West Norwood Gt Lon 44 F5
West Norwood Crematorium Gt Lon 44 F5
Westoe S Tyne 151 J2
West Ogwell Devon 7 J2
Weston BaNES 39 G6
Weston Ches E 99 G3
Weston Devon 12 E3
Weston Devon 12 F5
Weston Hants 30 B6
Weston Herts 59 L3
Weston Lincs 103 M7
Weston N York 123 H2
Weston Nhants 73 H5
Weston Notts 116 C7
Weston Shrops 83 L5
Weston Shrops 97 L6
Weston Staffs 99 L6
Weston W Berk 41 H5
Weston Beggard Herefs 69 L6
Westonbirt Gloucs 39 J3
Weston by Welland Nhants 87 L5
Weston Colville Cambs 76 E4
Weston Corbett Hants 30 B3
Weston Coyney C Stke 99 L4
Weston Favell Nhants 73 L3
Weston Green Cambs 76 F4
Weston Heath Shrops 84 D2
Westoning C Beds 59 G2
Weston-in-Gordano N Som 38 C5
Weston Jones Staffs 99 H7
Weston Longville Norfk 92 D1
Weston Lullingfields Shrops 98 B7
Weston Mill Crematorium C Plym 6 C4
Weston-on-the-Green Oxon 57 K4
Weston Park Staffs 84 E2
Weston Patrick Hants 30 B3
Weston Rhyn Shrops 97 L5
Weston-sub-Edge Gloucs 71 K6
Weston-super-Mare N Som 37 L7
Weston-super-Mare Crematorium N Som 38 A7
Weston Turville Bucks 58 D6
Weston-under-Lizard Staffs 84 E2
Weston under Penyard Herefs 54 F4
Weston-under-Redcastle Shrops 98 E6
Weston under Wetherley Warwks 72 D1
Weston Underwood Derbys 100 F4
Weston Underwood M Keyn 74 C4
Weston-upon-Trent Derbys 101 H6
Westonzoyland Somset 25 M4
West Orchard Dorset 27 J7
West Overton Wilts 40 C6
Westow N York 134 B6
West Park Abers 206 E5
West Parley Dorset 15 K3
West Peckham Kent 33 H3
West Pelton Dur 151 G4
West Pennard Somset 26 D4
West Pentire Cnwll 4 B4
West Perry Cambs 75 G2
West Porlock Somset 24 D3
Westport Somset 26 B7
West Putford Devon 9 K2
West Quantoxhead Somset 25 H3
Westquarter Falk 176 B3
West Rainton Dur 151 H5
West Rasen Lincs 117 H4
Westray Ork 234 c3
Westray Airport Ork 234 c3
West Raynham Norfk 105 L7
Westrigg W Loth 176 B5
West Road Crematorium N u Ty 150 F2
Westrop Swindn 40 D2
West Rounton N York 141 K6
West Row Suffk 90 F7
West Rudham Norfk 105 K6
West Runton Norfk 106 E4
Westruther Border 178 D7
Westry Cambs 90 B4
West Saltoun E Loth 178 B5
West Sandford Devon 11 J4
West Sandwick Shet 235 d3
West Scrafton N York 131 K3
West Stafford Dorset 14 D4
West Stockwith Notts 116 C3
West Stoke W Susx 17 M2
West Stour Dorset 27 H6
West Stourmouth Kent 35 H3
West Stow Suffk 77 J1
West Stowell Wilts 40 C7
West Street Suffk 78 B1
West Suffolk Crematorium Suffk 77 J2
West Tanfield N York 132 D4
West Taphouse Cnwll 5 J3
West Tarbert Ag & B 172 E5
West Tarring W Susx 18 F5
West Thirston Nthumb 158 F3
West Thorney W Susx 17 L3
West Thorpe Notts 101 L7
West Thurrock Thurr 45 L4
West Tilbury Thurr 46 A4
West Tisted Hants 29 M5
West Torrington Lincs 117 J5
West Town Hants 17 K3
West Town N Som 38 C6
West Tytherley Hants 28 F5
West Walton Norfk 90 C2
West Walton Highway Norfk 90 C2
Westward Cumb 148 B6
Westward Ho! Devon 23 G5
Westwell Kent 34 D5
Westwell Oxon 56 E6
Westwell Leacon Kent 34 C5
West Wellow Hants 28 F7
West Wembury Devon 6 D6
West Wemyss Fife 186 E7
Westwick Cambs 76 B2
West Wickham Cambs 76 E5
West Wickham Gt Lon 45 G6
West Williamston Pembks 49 H6
West Wiltshire Crematorium Wilts 39 K7
West Winch Norfk 90 F1
West Winterslow Wilts 28 E5
West Wittering W Susx 17 L3
West Witton N York 131 K2
Westwood Devon 12 C3
Westwood Kent 35 K2
Westwood Wilts 39 J8
West Woodburn Nthumb 157 M5
West Woodhay W Berk 41 H7
Westwoodside N Linc 116 C2
West Worldham Hants 30 C4
West Worthing W Susx 18 F5
West Wratting Cambs 76 E4
Wetheral Cumb 148 E4
Wetherby Leeds 124 B2
Wetherby Services N York 124 C1
Wetherden Suffk 78 B3
Wetheringsett Suffk 78 D2
Wethersfield Essex 61 H2
Wetherup Street Suffk 78 D2
Wetley Rocks Staffs 99 L3
Wettenhall Ches E 98 F1
Wetton Staffs 100 C2
Wetwang E R Yk 134 E7
Wetwood Staffs 99 H5
Wexcombe Wilts 40 F8
Weybourne Norfk 106 D4
Weybourne Surrey 30 D2
Weybread Suffk 92 F7
Weybread Street Suffk 92 F7
Weybridge Surrey 43 H7
Weycroft Devon 13 H3
Weydale Highld 231 H3
Weyhill Hants 28 F3
Weymouth Dorset 14 D6
Weymouth Crematorium Dorset 14 C6
Whaddon Bucks 74 B7
Whaddon Cambs 75 L5
Whaddon Gloucs 55 J5
Whaddon Gt Lon 44 F7
Whaddon Wilts 28 D6
Whaddon Wilts 39 K7
Whaley Derbys 115 K7
Whaley Bridge Derbys 114 A5
Whaley Thorns Derbys 115 K7
Whaligoe Highld 231 K7
Whalley Lancs 121 L4
Whalsay Shet 235 d4
Whalton Nthumb 158 E6
Whaplode Lincs 104 A7
Whaplode Drove Lincs 89 K2

Wharf Warwks....72 E4
Wharfe N York....130 E5
Wharles Lancs....120 F4
Wharley End C Beds....74 D5
Wharncliffe Side Sheff....114 F3
Wharram-le-Street N York....134 D6
Wharton Herefs....69 K4
Whashton N York....140 E6
Whasset Cumb....129 L4
Whatcote Warwks....72 C5
Whateley Warwks....86 B4
Whatfield Suffk....78 B5
Whatley Somset....13 J2
Whatley Somset....27 G3
Whatlington E Susx....20 F3
Whatton Notts....102 C5
Whauphill D & G....145 J5
Wheal Peevor Cnwll....3 J3
Wheatacre Norfk....93 K5
Wheathampstead Herts....59 K5
Wheatley Hants....30 C4
Wheatley Oxon....57 L6
Wheatley Hill Dur....151 J6
Wheatley Hills Donc....115 L1
Wheaton Aston Staffs....84 F2
Wheddon Cross Somset....24 E4
Wheelock Ches E....99 H2
Wheelton Lancs....121 J6
Wheldrake C York....125 G2
Whelford Gloucs....56 D7
Whelpley Hill Bucks....59 G6
Whempstead Herts....60 A4
Whenby N York....133 K5
Whepstead Suffk....77 J3
Wherstead Suffk....78 E6
Wherwell Hants....29 H3
Wheston Derbys....114 C6
Whetsted Kent....33 H4
Whetstone Leics....87 G4
Whicham Cumb....128 D3
Whichford Warwks....72 C7
Whickham Gatesd....150 F3
Whiddon Down Devon....11 G6
Whigstreet Angus....196 D7
Whilton Nhants....73 J2
Whimple Devon....12 D3
Whimpwell Green Norfk....107 H6
Whinburgh Norfk....92 B2
Whinnie Liggate D & G....146 C4
Whinnyfold Abers....217 K7
Whippingham IoW....17 G4
Whipsnade C Beds....59 G4
Whipsnade Zoo ZSL C Beds....59 G4
Whipton Devon....12 B4
Whisby Lincs....116 E7
Whissendine Rutlnd....88 B2
Whissonsett Norfk....105 L7
Whistlefield Ag & B....183 J8
Whistlefield Inn Ag & B....183 G8
Whistley Green Wokham....42 C5
Whiston Knows....112 C3
Whiston Nhants....74 B3
Whiston Rothm....115 H4
Whiston Staffs....84 F2
Whiston Staffs....100 B3
Whitbeck Cumb....128 D3
Whitbourne Herefs....70 D3
Whitburn S Tyne....151 J3
Whitburn W Loth....176 C5
Whitby N York....143 J5
Whitchester Border....178 F6
Whitchurch BaNES....38 F6
Whitchurch Bucks....58 D4
Whitchurch Cardif....37 J4
Whitchurch Devon....6 D2
Whitchurch Hants....29 J2
Whitchurch Herefs....54 D4
Whitchurch Oxon....41 M5
Whitchurch Pembks....48 D3
Whitchurch Shrops....98 D4
Whitchurch Canonicorum Dorset....13 K4
Whitchurch Hill Oxon....41 M5
Whitcombe Dorset....14 D5
Whitcot Shrops....83 H5
Whitcott Keysett Shrops....82 F6
Whiteacre Heath Warwks....86 B5
White Ball Somset....25 H7
Whitebridge Highld....202 D3
Whitebrook Mons....54 D6
Whitecairns Abers....207 H2
Whitechapel Gt Lon....45 G4
White Chapel Lancs....121 H3
Whitecliffe Gloucs....54 E6
White Colne Essex....61 L3
Whitecraig E Loth....177 K4
Whitecrook D & G....144 E4
White Cross Cnwll....3 H6
Whitecross Falk....176 C3
Whiteface Highld....222 F4
Whitefarland N Ayrs....161 L2
Whitefaulds S Ayrs....163 H7
Whitefield Bury....113 J1
Whitefield Somset....25 G5
Whiteford Abers....206 D1
Whitegate Ches W....112 F7
Whitehall Ork....234 d5
Whitehaven Cumb....136 D4
Whitehill and Bordon Hants....30 C5
Whitehills Abers....216 C2
Whitehouse Abers....206 C3
Whitehouse Ag & B....172 D6
Whitehouse Common Birm....85 K4
Whitekirk E Loth....178 D3
White Lackington Dorset....14 D3
Whitelackington Somset....26 B7
White Ladies Aston Worcs....71 G4
Whiteleaf Bucks....58 D6
Whiteley Hants....17 G1
Whiteley Bank IoW....17 G6
Whitemire Moray....214 B4
Whitemoor C Nott....101 K4
Whitemoor Cnwll....4 F4
Whiteness Shet....235 c6
White Notley Essex....61 J4
Whiteparish Wilts....28 E6
White Pit Lincs....118 E6
Whiterashes Abers....206 F2
White Roding Essex....60 E5
Whiterow Highld....231 L5
Whiterow Moray....214 C3
Whiteshill Gloucs....55 J6
Whitesmith E Susx....20 B3
Whitestaunton Somset....13 H1
Whitestone Cross Devon....11 K6
White Waltham W & M....42 D5
Whitewell Lancs....121 K2
Whitfield C Dund....187 G2
Whitfield Kent....35 J5
Whitfield Nhants....73 H6
Whitfield Nthumb....149 K4
Whitfield S Glos....38 F3
Whitford Devon....13 G4
Whitford Flints....111 G5
Whitgift E R Yk....125 J6
Whitgreave Staffs....99 K6
Whithorn D & G....145 J6
Whiting Bay N Ayrs....162 D4
Whitkirk Leeds....124 B4
Whitland Carmth....49 L4
Whitlaw Border....167 G6
Whitletts S Ayrs....163 J5
Whitley N York....124 E6
Whitley Readg....42 B6
Whitley Sheff....115 G3
Whitley Wilts....39 K6
Whitley Bay N Tyne....159 J7
Whitley Bay Crematorium N Tyne....159 H7
Whitley Chapel Nthumb....150 B4
Whitley Lower Kirk....123 J6
Whitminster Gloucs....55 H6
Whitmore Staffs....99 J4
Whitnage Devon....25 G7
Whitnash Warwks....72 D2
Whitney-on-Wye Herefs....68 F5
Whitsbury Hants....28 C7
Whitsome Border....179 H7
Whitson Newpt....38 B4
Whitstable Kent....47 J6
Whitstone Cnwll....9 H5
Whittingham Nthumb....168 F6
Whittingslow Shrops....83 H5
Whittington Derbys....115 G6
Whittington Gloucs....56 A4
Whittington Lancs....130 B4
Whittington Norfk....91 G4
Whittington Shrops....97 L6
Whittington Staffs....84 F6
Whittington Staffs....85 L2
Whittington Warwks....86 C4
Whittington Worcs....70 F4
Whittlebury Nhants....73 K5
Whittle-le-Woods Lancs....121 H6
Whittlesey Cambs....89 J4
Whittlesford Cambs....76 C5
Whitton N Linc....125 L5
Whitton Nthumb....158 D3
Whitton Powys....68 F2
Whitton S on T....141 J3
Whitton Shrops....83 L8
Whittonstall Nthumb....150 D4
Whitway Hants....41 J8
Whitwell Derbys....115 K6
Whitwell Herts....59 K4
Whitwell IoW....17 G6
Whitwell N York....141 G7
Whitwell Rutlnd....88 D2
Whitwell-on-the-Hill N York....133 L6
Whitwell Street Norfk....106 D7
Whitwick Leics....86 E1
Whitworth Lancs....122 D6
Whixall Shrops....98 D5
Whixley N York....133 G7
Whorlton Dur....140 E4
Whyle Herefs....69 L3
Whyteleafe Surrey....32 C2
Wibsey C Brad....123 H4
Wibtoft Warwks....86 F6
Wichenford Worcs....70 D3
Wichling Kent....34 B4
Wick Bmouth....15 L4
Wick Highld....231 L5
Wick S Glos....39 G5
Wick V Glam....36 E6
Wick W Susx....18 D5
Wick Worcs....71 G5
Wicken Cambs....76 E1
Wicken Nhants....73 L6
Wicken Bonhunt Essex....60 D2
Wickenby Lincs....117 H5
Wicken Green Village Norfk....105 K6
Wickersley Rothm....115 J3
Wicker Street Green Suffk....77 L6
Wickford Essex....46 C2
Wickham Hants....17 H1
Wickham W Berk....41 H6
Wickham Bishops Essex....61 K5
Wickhambreaux Kent....35 G3
Wickhambrook Suffk....77 H4
Wickhamford Worcs....71 J6
Wickham Green Suffk....78 D2
Wickham Market Suffk....79 G4
Wickhampton Norfk....93 J3
Wickham St Paul Essex....77 J7
Wickham Skeith Suffk....78 C2
Wickham Street Suffk....78 C1
Wick John o' Groats Airport Highld....231 L5
Wicklewood Norfk....92 C3
Wickmere Norfk....106 E5
Wick St Lawrence N Som....38 A7
Wicksteed Park Nhants....88 C7
Wickwar S Glos....39 G3
Widdington Essex....60 E2
Widdrington Nthumb....159 G3
Widdrington Station Nthumb....159 G4
Widecombe in the Moor Devon....7 G1
Widegates Cnwll....5 L4
Widemouth Bay Cnwll....9 G4
Wide Open N Tyne....159 G7
Widford Essex....61 H6
Widford Herts....60 C5
Widmer End Bucks....42 E2
Widmerpool Notts....101 M6
Widmore Gt Lon....45 H6
Widnes Halton....112 D5
Widnes Crematorium Halton....112 D4
Widworthy Devon....13 G3
Wigan Wigan....112 E1
Wigan Crematorium Wigan....112 E2
Wigborough Somset....26 C7
Wiggaton Devon....12 E4
Wiggenhall St Germans Norfk....90 E2
Wiggenhall St Mary Magdalen Norfk....90 E2
Wiggenhall St Mary the Virgin Norfk....90 E2
Wigginton C York....133 J7
Wigginton Herts....58 F6
Wigginton Oxon....57 H2
Wigginton Staffs....86 B3
Wigglesworth N York....130 F7
Wiggonby Cumb....148 B4
Wighill N York....124 D2
Wighton Norfk....105 M4
Wightwick Wolves....84 F4
Wigley Hants....29 G7
Wigmore Herefs....69 H2
Wigmore Medway....46 D6
Wigsley Notts....116 E7
Wigsthorpe Nhants....88 F6
Wigston Leics....87 H4
Wigston Parva Leics....86 F5
Wigthorpe Notts....115 L5
Wigtoft Lincs....103 L5
Wigton Cumb....148 A5
Wigtown D & G....145 J4
Wike Leeds....123 L3
Wilbarston Nhants....88 B5
Wilberfoss E R Yk....125 H1
Wilburton Cambs....90 C7
Wilby Nhants....74 C2
Wilby Norfk....92 B5
Wilby Suffk....78 F1
Wilcot Wilts....40 C7
Wilcott Shrops....98 B8
Wildboarclough Ches E....113 M7
Wilden Bed....75 G4
Wilden Worcs....84 E8
Wildmanbridge S Lans....175 L7
Wildmoor Worcs....85 G7
Wildsworth Lincs....116 D3
Wilford C Nott....101 K5

Wilford Hill Crematorium Notts 101 L5
Wilkesley Ches E 98 F4
Wilkhaven Highld 223 K4
Wilkieston W Loth 176 F5
Willand Devon 12 D1
Willaston Ches E 99 G3
Willaston Ches W 111 K6
Willen M Keyn 74 C6
Willenhall Covtry 86 D7
Willenhall Wsall 85 H4
Willerby E R Yk 126 C4
Willerby N York 134 F4
Willersey Gloucs 71 K6
Willersley Herefs 68 F5
Willesborough Kent 34 D6
Willesborough Lees Kent 34 D6
Willesden Gt Lon 44 E3
Willesley Wilts 39 J3
Willett Somset 25 H5
Willey Shrops 84 C4
Willey Warwks 86 F6
Willey Green Surrey 30 F2
Williamscot Oxon 72 F5
Willian Herts 59 L2
Willingale Essex 60 F6
Willingdon E Susx 20 C5
Willingham Cambs 76 B1
Willingham by Stow Lincs 116 E5
Willington Bed 75 G4
Willington Derbys 100 F6
Willington Dur 150 F7
Willington Kent 33 K3
Willington N Tyne 151 H2
Willington Warwks 72 C6
Willitoft E R Yk 125 H4
Williton Somset 25 H4
Willoughby Lincs 119 G6
Willoughby Warwks 73 G2
Willoughby-on-the-Wolds Notts 101 M7
Willoughby Waterleys Leics 87 H5
Willoughton Lincs 116 F3
Willows Green Essex 61 H4
Willtown Somset 26 B6
Wilmcote Warwks 71 L3
Wilmington Devon 13 G3
Wilmington E Susx 20 B5
Wilmington Kent 45 K5
Wilmslow Ches E 113 J5
Wilpshire Lancs 121 K4
Wilsden C Brad 123 G3
Wilsford Lincs 103 G4
Wilsford Wilts 28 C4
Wilsford Wilts 40 C8
Wilshaw Kirk 123 G8
Wilsill N York 132 B6
Wilson Leics 101 H7
Wilsontown S Lans 176 C7
Wilstead Bed 74 F5
Wilsthorpe Lincs 88 F2
Wilstone Herts 58 E5
Wilton Herefs 54 E3
Wilton N York 134 D3
Wilton R & Cl 142 C4
Wilton Wilts 28 C5
Wilton Wilts 40 E7
Wilton Dean Border 167 G6
Wimbish Green Essex 76 E7
Wimbledon Gt Lon 44 E6
Wimblington Cambs 90 B5
Wimboldsley Ches W 113 G8
Wimborne Minster Dorset 15 J3
Wimborne St Giles Dorset 28 B8
Wimbotsham Norfk 90 E3
Wimpole Cambs 75 L4
Wimpstone Warwks 72 B5
Wincanton Somset 27 G5
Winchburgh W Loth 176 E4
Winchcombe Gloucs 56 A3
Winchelsea E Susx 21 H3
Winchester Hants 29 J5
Winchester Services Hants 29 K4
Winchet Hill Kent 33 J5
Winchfield Hants 30 C1
Winchmore Hill Bucks 42 F2
Winchmore Hill Gt Lon 44 F2
Wincle Ches E 113 L7
Wincobank Sheff 115 G3
Windermere Cumb 137 L7
Windermere Steamboats & Museum Cumb 137 L7
Winderton Warwks 72 D6
Windhill Highld 212 E5
Windlesham Surrey 42 F7
Windmill Cnwll 4 D2
Windmill Hill E Susx 20 D4
Windmill Hill Somset 25 L7
Windrush Gloucs 56 D5
Windsole Abers 216 B3
Windsor W & M 42 F5
Windsor Castle W & M 42 F5
Windsoredge Gloucs 55 J7
Windsor Green Suffk 77 K4
Windy Arbour Warwks 72 C1
Windygates Fife 186 E7
Wineham W Susx 31 L7
Winestead E R Yk 127 G5
Winfarthing Norfk 92 D6
Winford IoW 17 G5
Winford N Som 38 D7
Winforton Herefs 68 F5
Winfrith Newburgh Dorset 14 F5
Wing Bucks 58 E4
Wing Rutlnd 88 C3
Wingate Dur 151 J7
Wingerworth Derbys 115 G7
Wingfield C Beds 59 G3
Wingfield Suffk 92 F7
Wingfield Wilts 27 J1
Wingham Kent 35 H3
Wingrave Bucks 58 E4
Winkburn Notts 102 B2
Winkfield Br For 42 E6
Winkfield Row Br For 42 E6
Winkhill Staffs 100 B3
Winkleigh Devon 10 F4
Winksley N York 132 C5
Winlaton Gatesd 150 F3
Winless Highld 231 K5
Winmarleigh Lancs 120 F2
Winnall Hants 29 J5
Winnersh Wokham 42 C6
Winnington Ches W 112 F6
Winscombe N Som 38 B8
Winsford Ches W 112 F7
Winsford Somset 24 E4
Winsham Somset 13 J2
Winshill Staffs 100 F7
Winshwen Swans 51 K6
Winskill Cumb 149 G7
Winsley Wilts 39 J7
Winslow Bucks 58 C3
Winson Gloucs 56 C6
Winsor Hants 28 F8
Winster Cumb 129 J2
Winster Derbys 100 E1
Winston Dur 140 E4
Winston Suffk 78 E3
Winstone Gloucs 55 L6
Winswell Devon 10 D3
Winterborne Came Dorset 14 D5
Winterborne Clenston Dorset 14 F2
Winterborne Houghton Dorset 14 F2
Winterborne Kingston Dorset 15 G3
Winterborne Monkton Dorset 14 D5
Winterborne Stickland Dorset 14 F2
Winterborne Whitechurch Dorset 14 F3
Winterborne Zelston Dorset 15 G3
Winterbourne S Glos 38 F4
Winterbourne W Berk 41 J6
Winterbourne Abbas Dorset 14 C4
Winterbourne Bassett Wilts 40 C5
Winterbourne Dauntsey Wilts 28 D4
Winterbourne Earls Wilts 28 D5
Winterbourne Gunner Wilts 28 D4
Winterbourne Monkton Wilts 40 C6
Winterbourne Steepleton Dorset 14 C4
Winterbourne Stoke Wilts 28 B3
Winterburn N York 131 H7
Winteringham N Linc 125 L6
Winterley Ches E 99 H2
Winterslow Wilts 28 E5
Winterton N Linc 125 L6
Winterton-on-Sea Norfk 107 K8
Winthorpe Notts 102 D2
Winton Bmouth 15 K4
Winton Cumb 139 H5
Wintringham N York 134 D5
Winwick Cambs 89 G7
Winwick Nhants 87 J8
Winwick Warrtn 112 E3
Wirksworth Derbys 100 F2
Wirral 111 J4
Wirswall Ches E 98 D4
Wisbech Cambs 90 C2
Wisbech St Mary Cambs 90 B2
Wisborough Green W Susx 31 H6
Wiseman's Bridge Pembks 49 K6
Wiseton Notts 116 B4
Wishaw N Lans 175 L7
Wishaw Warwks 85 L5
Wisley Garden RHS Surrey 43 H8
Wispington Lincs 117 K6
Wissett Suffk 93 H7
Wissington Suffk 62 A2
Wistanstow Shrops 83 H6
Wistanswick Shrops 98 F6
Wistaston Ches E 99 G2
Wiston Pembks 49 H4
Wiston S Lans 165 J3
Wiston W Susx 18 F3
Wistow Cambs 89 K7
Wistow N York 124 F4
Wiswell Lancs 121 L3
Witcham Cambs 90 C7
Witchampton Dorset 15 J2
Witchford Cambs 90 C7
Witcombe Somset 26 C6
Witham Essex 61 K5
Witham Friary Somset 27 H3
Witham on the Hill Lincs 88 F1
Withcall Lincs 118 C5
Withdean Br & H 19 J4
Witherenden Hill E Susx 33 H7
Witheridge Devon 11 J3
Witherley Leics 86 D4
Withern Lincs 118 F5
Withernsea E R Yk 127 H5
Withernwick E R Yk 126 F3
Withersdale Street Suffk 92 F7
Withersfield Suffk 76 F5
Witherslack Cumb 129 J3
Withiel Cnwll 4 F3
Withiel Florey Somset 24 F5
Withington Gloucs 56 B5
Withington Herefs 69 L5
Withington Manch 113 J3
Withington Shrops 83 L2
Withington Staffs 100 B5
Withleigh Devon 11 K3
Withnell Lancs 121 J6
Withybed Green Worcs 85 H8
Withybrook Warwks 86 E6
Withycombe Somset 24 F3
Withyham E Susx 32 E6
Withypool Somset 24 D4
Withywood Bristl 38 E6
Witley Surrey 30 F4
Witnesham Suffk 78 E4
Witney Oxon 57 G6
Wittering C Pete 88 F3
Wittersham Kent 21 H1
Witton Birm 85 J5
Witton Norfk 93 G2
Witton Norfk 107 H6
Witton Gilbert Dur 151 G5
Witton le Wear Dur 140 E2
Witton Park Dur 140 F2
Wiveliscombe Somset 25 G5
Wivelrod Hants 30 A4
Wivelsfield E Susx 19 K2
Wivelsfield Green E Susx 19 K2
Wivenhoe Essex 62 C4
Wiveton Norfk 106 C4
Wix Essex 62 E3
Wixford Warwks 71 K4
Wixoe Suffk 77 G6
Woburn C Beds 58 F2
Woburn Safari Park C Beds 74 D7
Woburn Sands M Keyn 74 D7
Woking Surrey 43 G8
Woking Crematorium Surrey 42 F8
Wokingham Wokham 42 D6
Woldingham Surrey 32 C3
Wold Newton E R Yk 135 G5
Wold Newton NE Lin 118 C3
Wolfclyde S Lans 165 K3
Wolferton Norfk 105 G6
Wolfhill P & K 186 B2
Wolf's Castle Pembks 49 G3
Wolfsdale Pembks 48 F3
Wollaston Dudley 84 F6
Wollaston Nhants 74 C2
Wollaston Shrops 83 G2
Wollaton C Nott 101 K4
Wollaton Hall & Park C Nott 101 K5
Wollerton Shrops 98 F6
Wollescote Dudley 85 G6
Wolseley Bridge Staffs 100 A7
Wolsingham Dur 150 D7
Wolstanton Staffs 99 J3
Wolston Warwks 86 E7
Wolvercote Oxon 57 J6
Wolverhampton Wolves 85 G4
Wolverhampton Halfpenny Green Airport Staffs 84 E5
Wolverley Worcs 84 E7
Wolverton Hants 41 K8
Wolverton M Keyn 74 B6
Wolverton Warwks 72 B3
Wolverton Wilts 27 H5
Wolvesnewton Mons 54 C7
Wolvey Warwks 86 E6
Wolvey Heath Warwks 86 E5
Wolviston S on T 141 K3
Wombleton N York 133 K3
Wombourne Staffs 84 F5
Wombwell Barns 115 H2
Womenswold Kent 35 G5

Womersley N York 124 E6
Wonersh Surrey 31 G3
Wonford Devon 12 B4
Wonston Dorset 14 E2
Wonston Hants 29 J4
Wooburn Bucks 42 E3
Wooburn Green Bucks 42 E3
Woodacott Devon 9 K4
Woodall Rothm 115 J5
Woodall Services Rothm 115 J5
Woodbastwick Norfk 93 G1
Wood Bevington Warwks 71 J4
Woodborough Notts 101 M3
Woodborough Wilts 40 C7
Woodbridge Suffk 78 F5
Woodbury Devon 12 C5
Woodbury Salterton Devon 12 C5
Woodchester Gloucs 55 J7
Woodchurch Kent 34 C7
Woodcombe Somset 24 E3
Woodcote Gt Lon 44 F7
Woodcote Oxon 41 M4
Woodcote Wrekin 84 D1
Woodcroft Gloucs 38 D2
Wood Dalling Norfk 106 C6
Woodditton Cambs 76 F3
Woodeaton Oxon 57 K5
Wood End Gt Lon 43 J4
Wood End Herts 60 B3
Woodend Highld 190 F4
Woodend Nhants 73 H5
Woodend W Loth 176 C4
Woodend W Susx 17 M2
Wood End Warwks 71 K1
Wood End Wolves 85 G4
Wood Enderby Lincs 118 C8
Woodfalls Wilts 28 D7
Woodford Cnwll 9 G3
Woodford Gloucs 39 G2
Woodford Gt Lon 45 H2
Woodford Nhants 88 D7
Woodford Stockp 113 K5
Woodford Bridge Gt Lon 45 H2
Woodford Halse Nhants 73 G4
Woodford Wells Gt Lon 45 H2
Woodgate Birm 85 H6
Woodgate Devon 25 H7
Woodgate W Susx 18 C5
Woodgate Worcs 71 H2
Wood Green Gt Lon 44 F2
Woodgreen Hants 28 D7
Woodhall N York 131 J2
Woodhall Spa Lincs 117 K8
Woodham Bucks 58 B4
Woodham Surrey 43 H7
Woodham Ferrers Essex 61 J7
Woodham Mortimer Essex 61 K6
Woodham Walter Essex 61 K6
Wood Hayes Wolves 85 G3
Woodhead Abers 216 E6
Woodhill Shrops 84 D6
Woodhill Somset 26 A6
Woodhorn Nthumb 159 H4
Woodhouse Leeds 123 K4
Woodhouse Leics 87 G1
Woodhouse Sheff 115 H4
Woodhouse Wakefd 124 B6
Woodhouse Eaves Leics 87 G2
Woodhouselee Mdloth 177 H5
Woodhouselees D & G 156 D6
Woodhouses Oldham 113 K2
Woodhouses Staffs 100 D8
Woodhurst Cambs 89 K7
Woodingdean Br & H 19 K5
Woodkirk Leeds 123 K5
Woodland Abers 207 G2
Woodland Devon 6 F5
Woodland Devon 7 J3
Woodland Dur 140 D2
Woodland S Ayrs 152 E3
Woodlands Abers 206 E6
Woodlands Donc 124 E8
Woodlands Dorset 15 K2
Woodlands Hants 16 C1
Woodlands N York 132 E8
Woodlands (Coleshill) Crematorium Warwks 85 L5
Woodlands Park W & M 42 E5
Woodlands (Scarborough) Crematorium N York 134 F3
Woodlands (Scunthorpe) Crematorium N Linc 125 K7
Woodleigh Devon 7 H6
Woodley Wokham 42 C5
Woodmancote Gloucs 39 H2
Woodmancote Gloucs 55 L3
Woodmancote Gloucs 56 A6
Woodmancote W Susx 17 L2
Woodmancote W Susx 19 H3
Woodmancott Hants 29 K3
Woodmansey E R Yk 126 C3
Woodmansgreen W Susx 30 E6
Woodmansterne Surrey 32 B2
Woodmanton Devon 12 C5
Woodnesborough Kent 35 J4
Woodnewton Nhants 88 F5
Wood Norton Norfk 106 B6
Woodplumpton Lancs 121 G4
Woodrising Norfk 92 B3
Wood's Corner E Susx 20 D2
Woodseaves Staffs 99 H7
Woodsetts Rothm 115 K5
Woodsford Dorset 14 E4
Wood's Green E Susx 33 H6
Woodside Br For 42 F6
Woodside Fife 187 G5
Woodside Gt Lon 45 G6
Woodside P & K 195 K8
Woodside Crematorium Inver 174 B3
Woodstock Oxon 57 H5
Woodston C Pete 89 H4
Wood Street Norfk 107 H7
Wood Street Village Surrey 30 F2
Woodton Norfk 93 G5
Woodtown Devon 22 F6
Woodvale Crematorium Br & H 19 J4
Wood Walton Cambs 89 J7
Woofferton Shrops 69 K2
Wookey Somset 26 D3
Wookey Hole Somset 26 D2
Wool Dorset 14 F5
Woolacombe Devon 23 G3
Woolage Green Kent 35 H5
Woolaston Gloucs 54 E7
Woolaston Common Gloucs 54 E7
Woolavington Somset 25 M3
Woolbeding W Susx 30 E6
Woolbrook Devon 12 E5
Wooler Nthumb 168 E4
Woolfardisworthy Devon 11 J3
Woolfardisworthy Devon 22 E7
Woolfords S Lans 176 D6
Woolhampton W Berk 41 L6
Woolhope Herefs 69 L7
Woolland Dorset 14 E2
Woolley BaNES 39 H6
Woolley Cambs 89 G8
Woolley Wakefd 123 L7
Woolley Edge Services Wakefd 123 K7
Woolmere Green Worcs 71 G2
Woolmer Green Herts 59 L4
Woolminstone Somset 13 K2
Woolpit Suffk 77 L3
Woolstaston Shrops 83 J4
Woolsthorpe Lincs 102 D5
Woolsthorpe-by-Colsterworth Lincs 102 F7
Woolston C Sotn 16 E1
Woolston Shrops 97 L7
Woolston Somset 25 H4
Woolston Somset 26 F5
Woolston Warrtn 112 F4
Woolstone Gloucs 55 L3
Woolstone M Keyn 74 C6
Woolstone Oxon 40 F3
Woolston Green Devon 7 H3
Woolton Lpool 112 B4
Woolton Hill Hants 41 H7
Woolverstone Suffk 78 E6
Woolverton Somset 27 H2
Woolwich Gt Lon 45 H4
Woonton Herefs 69 G4
Woore Shrops 99 G4
Wootten Green Suffk 92 F8
Wootton Bed 74 E5
Wootton Kent 35 G5
Wootton N Linc 126 D7
Wootton Nhants 73 L3
Wootton Oxon 57 H4
Wootton Oxon 57 J7
Wootton Staffs 100 C4
Wootton Bassett Wilts 40 B4
Wootton Bridge IoW 17 G4
Wootton Courtenay Somset 24 E3
Wootton Fitzpaine Dorset 13 J4
Wootton Rivers Wilts 40 D7
Wootton St Lawrence Hants 29 L2
Wootton Wawen Warwks 71 L2
Worcester Worcs 70 F4
Worcester Crematorium Worcs 70 F3
Worcester Park Gt Lon 44 E6
Wordsley Dudley 84 F6
Worfield Shrops 84 D4
Workington Cumb 136 D2
Worksop Notts 115 L5
Worlaby N Linc 126 C7
Worlds End Hants 29 M8
Worlds End W Susx 19 J2
Worle N Som 38 A7
Worleston Ches E 98 F2
Worlingham Suffk 93 J5
Worlington Devon 11 H3
Worlington Suffk 91 G8
Worlingworth Suffk 78 F2
Wormbridge Herefs 54 B2
Wormegay Norfk 90 F2
Wormelow Tump Herefs 54 C3
Wormhill Derbys 114 C6
Wormingford Essex 61 M2
Worminghall Bucks 57 M6
Wormington Gloucs 71 J7
Wormit Fife 186 F3
Wormleighton Warwks 72 F4
Wormley Herts 60 B6
Wormley Surrey 30 F4
Wormshill Kent 34 B3
Wormsley Herefs 69 H5
Worplesdon Surrey 30 F2
Worrall Sheff 114 F3
Worsbrough Barns 115 G2
Worsbrough Bridge Barns 115 G2
Worsbrough Dale Barns 115 G2
Worsley Salfd 113 H2
Worstead Norfk 107 G7
Worsthorne Lancs 122 C4
Worston Devon 6 E5
Worston Lancs 122 B3
Worth Kent 35 J4
Wortham Suffk 92 C7
Worthen Shrops 83 G3
Worthenbury Wrexhm 98 B4
Worthing Norfk 106 B8
Worthing W Susx 18 F5
Worthing Crematorium W Susx 18 F4
Worthington Leics 101 H7
Worth Matravers Dorset 15 H6
Wortley Barns 114 F2
Wortley Leeds 123 K4
Worton N York 131 H2
Worton Wilts 39 L8
Wortwell Norfk 92 F6
Wotton-under-Edge Gloucs 39 H2
Wotton Underwood Bucks 58 B5
Woughton on the Green M Keyn 74 C6
Wouldham Kent 46 B7
Wrabness Essex 62 E2
Wrafton Devon 23 H4
Wragby Lincs 117 J6
Wragby Wakefd 124 C6
Wrangaton Devon 7 G4
Wrangle Lincs 104 C3
Wrangway Somset 25 H7
Wrantage Somset 25 L6
Wrawby N Linc 126 C8
Wraxall N Som 38 C6
Wraxall Somset 26 E4
Wray Lancs 130 B6
Wraysbury W & M 43 G5
Wrayton Lancs 130 C5
Wrea Green Lancs 120 E4
Wreay Cumb 148 D5
Wrecclesham Surrey 30 D3
Wrekenton Gatesd 151 G3
Wrelton N York 134 B3
Wrenbury Ches E 98 E3
Wreningham Norfk 92 E4
Wrentham Suffk 93 K6
Wrentnall Shrops 83 H3
Wressle E R Yk 125 G4
Wressle N Linc 126 B8
Wrestlingworth C Beds 75 J5
Wretton Norfk 91 G4
Wrexham Wrexhm 97 M3
Wrexham Industrial Estate Wrexhm 98 B3
Wribbenhall Worcs 84 E7
Wrinehill Staffs 99 H3
Wrington N Som 38 C7
Writhlington BaNES 27 G1
Writtle Essex 61 G6
Wrockwardine Wrekin 84 B2
Wroot N Linc 116 B2
Wrose C Brad 123 H3
Wrotham Kent 33 G2

Wroughton Swindn 40 C4
Wroxall IoW 17 G6
Wroxall Warwks 72 B1
Wroxeter Shrops 83 L2
Wroxham Norfk 107 G8
Wroxham Barns Norfk 107 G7
Wroxton Oxon 72 E6
Wyaston Derbys 100 D4
Wyberton East Lincs 104 B4
Wyboston Bed 75 H3
Wybunbury Ches E 99 G3
Wychbold Worcs 71 G2
Wychnor Staffs 85 L1
Wyck Rissington Gloucs 56 D4
Wycliffe Dur 140 E4
Wycoller Lancs 122 D3
Wycomb Leics 102 C7
Wycombe Marsh Bucks 42 E3
Wyddial Herts 60 B2
Wye Kent 34 E5
Wyke C Brad 123 H5
Wyke Dorset 27 H6
Wyke Champflower Somset 26 F4
Wykeham N York 134 E3
Wyken Covtry 86 D7
Wyken Shrops 84 D4
Wyke Regis Dorset 14 C6
Wykey Shrops 98 B7
Wylam Nthumb 150 E3
Wylde Green Birm 85 K5
Wylye Wilts 28 A4
Wymeswold Leics 101 L7
Wymington Bed 74 D2
Wymondham Leics 102 D8
Wymondham Norfk 92 D3
Wynford Eagle Dorset 14 B3
Wyre Forest Crematorium Worcs 84 E8
Wyre Piddle Worcs 71 G5
Wysall Notts 101 L6
Wythall Worcs 85 J7
Wytham Oxon 57 J6
Wythenshawe Manch 113 J4
Wyton Cambs 89 K8
Wyton E R Yk 126 E4
Wyverstone Suffk 78 C2
Wyverstone Street Suffk 78 B2

Y

Yaddlethorpe N Linc 116 E1
Yafforth N York 141 H7
Yalberton Torbay 7 K4
Yalding Kent 33 J3
Yanwath Cumb 138 D2
Yanworth Gloucs 56 B5
Yapham E R Yk 125 J1
Yapton W Susx 18 D5
Yarborough N Som 38 B8
Yarburgh Lincs 118 E3
Yarcombe Devon 13 G2
Yard Devon 24 B6
Yardley Birm 85 K6
Yardley Crematorium Birm 85 K6
Yardley Gobion Nhants 73 L5
Yardley Hastings Nhants 74 C3
Yardley Wood Birm 85 K7
Yarkhill Herefs 69 L6
Yarley Somset 26 D3
Yarlington Somset 26 F5
Yarm S on T 141 K5
Yarmouth IoW 16 D4
Yarnbrook Wilts 27 K1
Yarnfield Staffs 99 K6
Yarnscombe Devon 23 J6
Yarnton Oxon 57 J5
Yarpole Herefs 69 J2
Yarrow Border 166 E4
Yarrow Feus Border 166 E4
Yarrowford Border 166 F4
Yarwell Nhants 88 F4
Yate S Glos 39 G4
Yateley Hants 42 D7
Yatesbury Wilts 40 B6
Yattendon W Berk 41 K5
Yatton Herefs 69 H2
Yatton N Som 38 B7
Yatton Keynell Wilts 39 K5
Yaverland IoW 17 H5
Yaxham Norfk 92 B2
Yaxley Cambs 89 H5
Yaxley Suffk 92 D8
Yazor Herefs 69 H5
Yeading Gt Lon 43 J4
Yeadon Leeds 123 J3
Yealand Conyers Lancs 129 K5
Yealand Redmayne Lancs 129 K4
Yealmpton Devon 6 E5
Yearsley N York 133 J5
Yeaton Shrops 98 B8
Yeaveley Derbys 100 D4
Yeavering Nthumb 168 D4
Yedingham N York 134 D4
Yelford Oxon 57 G6
Yell Shet 235 d3
Yelling Cambs 75 J3
Yelvertoft Nhants 87 H7
Yelverton Devon 6 D3
Yelverton Norfk 93 G3
Yenston Somset 27 G7
Yeoford Devon 11 H5
Yeolmbridge Cnwll 9 J7
Yeovil Somset 26 D7
Yeovil Crematorium Somset 26 D7
Yeovil Marsh Somset 26 D7
Yeovilton Somset 26 D6
Yesnaby Ork 234 b5
Yetminster Dorset 14 B1
Yettington Devon 12 D5
Yetts o'Muckhart Clacks 185 L6
Yew Tree Sandw 85 H4
Y Felinheli Gwynd 109 G7
Y Ferwig Cerdgn 65 G5
Y Ffor Gwynd 95 G5
Y Gyffylliog Denbgs 97 G2
Yielden Bed 74 E2
Yieldshields S Lans 176 B7
Yiewsley Gt Lon 43 H4
Y Maerdy Conwy 96 F4
Ynysboeth Rhondd 37 G2
Ynysddu Caerph 37 J2
Ynyshir Rhondd 36 F3
Ynystawe Swans 51 K5
Ynysybwl Rhondd 37 G2
Yockleton Shrops 83 H2
Yokefleet E R Yk 125 J5
Yoker C Glas 174 F5
York C York 124 F1
York City Crematorium C York 124 F2
Yorkletts Kent 34 E3
Yorkley Gloucs 54 F6
York Minster C York 124 F1
Yorkshire Dales National Park 131 G4
York Town Surrey 42 E7
Youlgreave Derbys 114 E8
Youlthorpe E R Yk 134 B7
Youlton N York 133 G6
Yoxall Staffs 100 C8
Yoxford Suffk 79 H2
Y Rhiw Gwynd 94 D6
Ysbyty Ifan Conwy 96 C3
Ysbyty Ystwyth Cerdgn 67 G1
Ysceifiog Flints 111 G7
Ystalyfera Neath 52 B6
Ystrad Rhondd 36 F2
Ystrad Aeron Cerdgn 66 C4
Ystradfellte Powys 52 E5
Ystradgynlais Powys 52 C6
Ystrad Meurig Cerdgn 66 F2
Ystrad Mynach Caerph 37 H2
Ystradowen V Glam 36 F5
Ythanbank Abers 217 G7
Ythanwells Abers 216 C6
Ythsie Abers 217 G7

Z

Zeal Monachorum Devon 11 G4
Zeals Wilts 27 H5
Zelah Cnwll 4 C5
Zennor Cnwll 2 E4
Zouch Notts 101 J7
ZSL London Zoo Gt Lon 44 F4
ZSL Whipsnade Zoo C Beds 59 G4

Ireland

Troon (Mar–Oct)
Rathlin Island
Malin Head
Portrush
Ballycastle
Cairnryan
Toraigh
Tory Island
Coleraine
Douglas (Apr–Sept) Cairnryan
CITY OF DERRY
Limavady
Árainn Mhór
Arranmore
(Aran Island)
DONEGAL
LONDONDERRY
DERRY
Letterkenny
Ballymena
Larne
An Clochán Liath
Dunglow/Dungloe
Strabane
Maghera
Liverpool (Birkenhead)
Ballybofey
SPERRIN MTS
Antrim
Bangor
NORTHERN
BELFAST INTERNATIONAL
BELFAST
GEORGE BEST BELFAST CITY
Newtownards
Cookstown
Omagh
Donegal
Dungannon
NORTH ATLANTIC OCEAN
IRELAND
Portaferry
Ballyshannon
Portadown
Bundoran
Armagh
Downpatrick
Donegal Bay
Enniskillen
Newcastle
Monaghan
Newry
MOURNE MTS
Béal an Mhuirthead
Belmullet
Sligo
Castleblayney
IRISH SEA
Bangor
Ballina
OX MTS
Carrickmacross
Dundalk
Charlestown
Cavan
Achill Island
Oileán Acla
Boyle
Ardee
Foxford
Carrick-on-Shannon
Douglas (June–Sept) Holyhead
IRELAND WEST AIRPORT KNOCK
Virginia
Castlebar
Drogheda
Knock
Slane
Clare Island
Castlerea
Kells
Westport
Longford
Navan
Claremorris
Inishturk
REPUBLIC
Balbriggan
Roscommon
DUBLIN
Inishbofin
Mullingar
Kinnegad
Lambay
Tuam
Cherbourg Liverpool Holyhead
Clifden
Athlone
OF
DUBLIN
Oughterard
Tullamore
Dún Laoghaire
GALWAY
Garumna
Gorumna Island
GALWAY
Kildare
Naas
Bray
Oranmore
Loughrea
IRELAND
Blessington
Galway Bay
Oileáin Árann
Aran Islands
Portumna
Birr
SLIEVE BLOOM MTS
Wicklow
Gort
Portlaoise
Roscrea
WICKLOW MTS
Nenagh
Carlow
Ennistimon/
Ennistymon
Ennis
Newmarket-on-Fergus
Tullow
Arklow
Gorey
SHANNON
LIMERICK
Thurles
Kilkenny
Kilkee
Kilrush
Loop Head
Adare
Cashel
Enniscorthy
Tipperary
Clonmel
Wexford
Abbeyfeale
GALTY MTS
Cahir
New Ross
Rosslare
Charleville
KNOCKMEALDOWN MTS
Rosslare Harbour
WATERFORD
Tralee
Castleisland
Mitchelstown
WATERFORD
Carnsore Point
Fishguard Pembroke
An Daingean
Dingle
KERRY
Mallow
Lismore
An Blascaod Mór
Great Blasket Island
Killorglin
Fermoy
Dungarvan
Killarney
BOGGERAGH MTS
Dingle Bay
Youghal
Celtic Sea
Cahersiveen
CORK
Macroom
Parknasilla
Kenmare
CORK
Ringaskiddy
An Coireán
Waterville
Cherbourg Roscoff (Apr–Oct)
Glengarriff
Kinsale
Bantry
Clonakilty
Dursey Island
Bantry Bay
Skibbereen
Roscoff (Apr–Oct)
Mizen Head
Oileán Chléire
Cape Clear Island
0 20 40 miles
0 20 40 60 kilometres

Map pages north

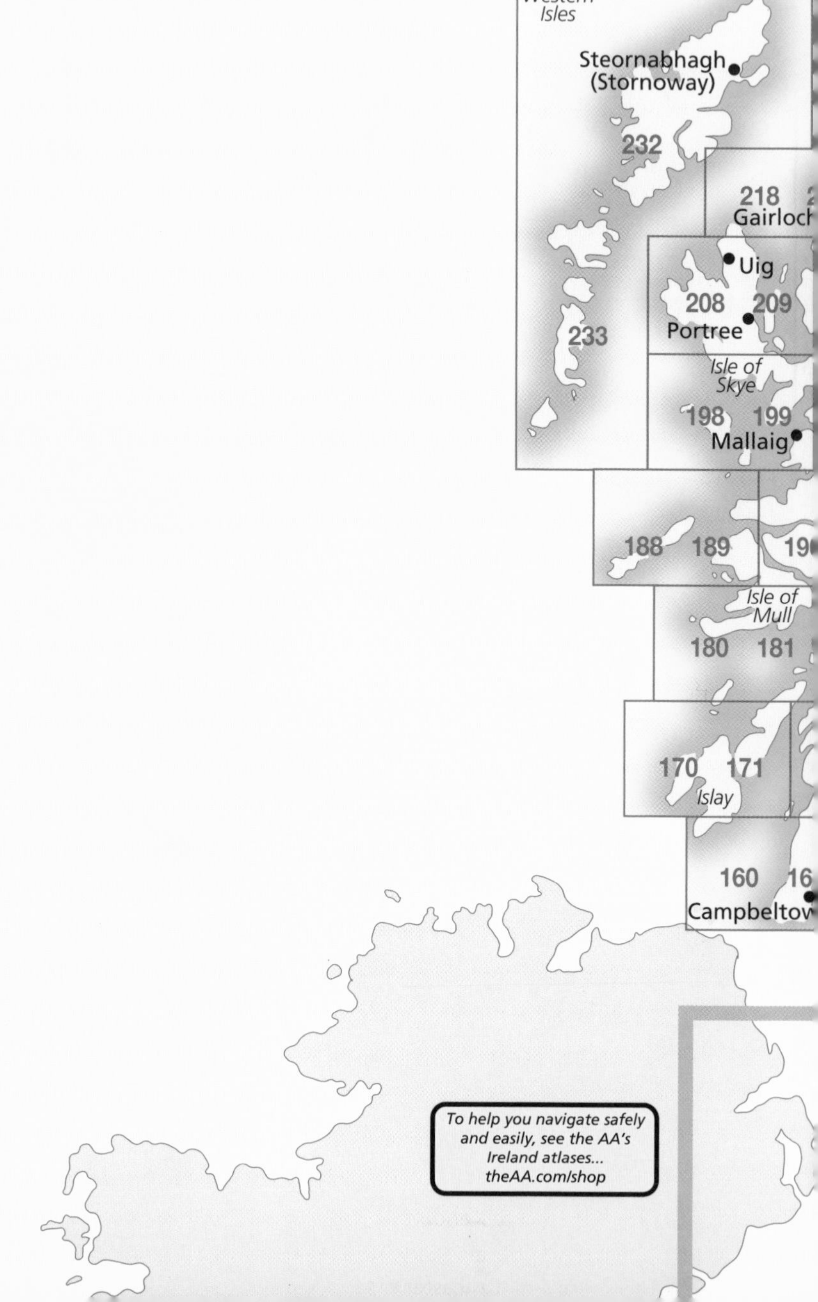